Question Help

MyLab Accounting homework and practice questions are correlated to the textbook, and many generate algorithmically to give students unlimited opportunity for mastery of concepts. If students get stuck, Learning Aids including Help Me Solve This, Demo Docs, videos and eText Pages walk them through the problem and identify helpful info in the text, giving them assistance when they need it most.

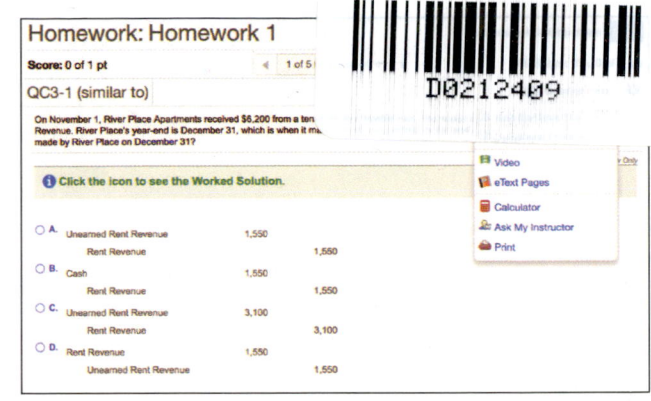

"Learning online can be a challenge. The Help Me Solve This option is incredibly helpful. It helped me see each step explained the way I needed it to be."

— Lauren Miller, Southern New Hampshire University

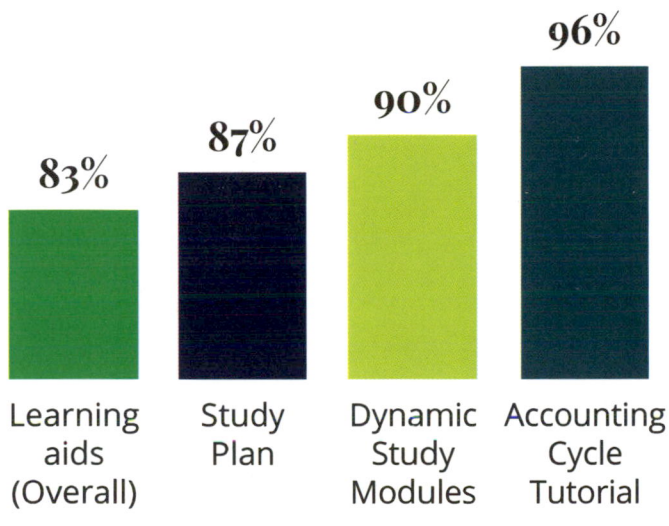

% of students who found learning tool helpful

Dynamic Study Modules help students study chapter topics effectively on their own by continuously assessing their **knowledge application** and performance in real time. These are available as graded assignments prior to class, and accessible on smartphones, tablets, and computers.

Pearson eText enhances student learning—both in and outside the classroom. Worked examples and videos bring learning to life, while algorithmic practice and self-assessment opportunities test students' understanding of the material. Accessible anytime, anywhere via MyLab or the app.

The **MyLab Gradebook** offers an easy way for students and instructors to view course performance. Item Analysis allows instructors to quickly see trends by analyzing details like the number of students who answered correctly/incorrectly, time on task, and median time spend on a question by question basis. And because it's correlated with the AACSB Standards, instructors can track students' progress toward outcomes that the organization has deemed important in preparing students to be **leaders.**

of students would tell their instructor to keep using MyLab Accounting

For additional details visit: www.pearson.com/mylab/accounting

College Accounting

A Practical Approach

College Accounting

A Practical Approach

Fourteenth Edition

Chapters 1–25

Jeffrey Slater

North Shore Community College
Danvers, Massachusetts

Mike Deschamps

MiraCosta Community College
Oceanside, California

330 Hudson Street, NY NY 10013

Vice President, Business, Economics, and UK Courseware: Donna Battista
Director of Portfolio Management: Adrienne D'Ambrosio
Senior Portfolio Manager: Ellen Geary
Editorial Assistant: Elisa Marks
Vice President, Product Marketing: Roxanne McCarley
Product Marketing Assistant: Marianela Silvestri
Manager of Field Marketing, Business Publishing: Adam Goldstein
Field Marketing Manager: Nayke Popovich
Vice President, Production and Digital Studio, Arts and Business: Etain O'Dea
Director of Production, Business: Jeff Holcomb
Managing Producer, Business: Melissa Feimer
Content Producer: Daniel Edward Petrino and Emily Throne
Operations Specialist: Carol Melville

Design Lead: Kathryn Foot
Manager, Learning Tools: Brian Surette
Content Developer, Learning Tools: Michael Trinchetto
Managing Producer, Digital Studio and GLP, Media Production and Development: Ashley Santora
Managing Producer, Digital Studio: Diane Lombardo
Digital Studio Producer: Mary Kate Murray
Digital Studio Producer: Alana Coles
Digital Content Team Lead: Noel Lotz
Digital Content Project Lead: Martha LaChance
Editorial Project Manager: Clara Bartunek, SPi Global
Production Project Manager: Nathaniel J. Jones, SPi Global
Interior Design: Laurie Entringer
Cover Design: Kay Lieberherr
Printer/Binder: LSC Communications, Inc.
Cover Printer: LSC Communications, Inc.

Library of Congress Cataloging-in-Publication Data. Data is on file at the Library of Congress.

Names: Slater, Jeffrey, author. | Deschamps, Michael, author.
Title: College accounting : a practical approach / Jeffrey Slater, Mike Deschamps.
Description: Fourteenth edition. | New York : Pearson, [2018]
Identifiers: LCCN 2018011267| ISBN 0134729315 | ISBN 9780134729312
Subjects: LCSH: Accounting–Textbooks.
Classification: LCC HF5635 .S6315 2018 | DDC 657/.044--dc23
LC record available at https://lccn.loc.gov/2018011267

12 2022

ISBN 10:   0-13-472931-5
ISBN 13: 978-0-13-472931-2

To my best friends: Bernie and Fejjie

Brief Contents

Contents

15 Accounting for Merchandise Inventory   523

16 Accounting for Property, Plant, Equipment, and Intangible Assets   557

Preface

NEW TO THIS EDITION

- Inventory coverage has been changed to the perpetual method to reflect the current business practice most students will encounter in the workplace. However, the text does offer a comprehensive discussion of the periodic method in a chapter appendix.
- Updated discussion of the revenue recognition principle for the newly released standard.
- New Computer Workshops for QuickBooks and Sage 50 (formerly Peachtree) give students an opportunity to practice in real-world applications.
- New American Institute of Professional Bookkeeping (AIPB) boxes: Students can get a glimpse into what it takes to be a successful certified bookkeeper with this feature found throughout the text. The Instructor Resource page will also include information on how to expand your bookkeeping program, including sample course offerings, to prepare students for both career readiness and the AIPB certifying exam.
- New discussions of modern accounting techniques and tools bring accounting practice into the 21st century while still focusing on building basic skills and background knowledge so students can critically understand their practice.
- Updated Chapter Introductions as well as updated end-of-chapter exercise and problem material.
- Updated formatting for the chapter Try Its to give students real-time feedback on their attempts.
- New Success Tip format in every chapter to assist with student learning and retention.
- Revised Chapter Learning Objectives to more easily tie to individual course student learning objectives.

SAMPLE OF CHAPTER-SPECIFIC CHANGES

- **Chapter 1:** Accounting Concepts and Procedures
  - New chapter scenarios for a better illustration of accounting in action.
  - Updated chapterwide continuing demonstration problems.
- **Chapter 4:** The Accounting Cycle Continued
  - New appendix on depreciation to help beginning accounting students in mastering the concept.
- **Chapter 6:** Banking Procedures and Control of Cash
  - A fresh update on how technology is changing the banking and finance functions including a look at some fast-developing innovations like Bitcoin.
- **Chapter 7:** Calculating Pay and Recording Payroll Taxes
  - Revisions that provide a more concise and effective explanation of the payroll process. The tables, figures, and rates have been updated to the 2017 rates. New examples provide an easier path for student learning.
- **Chapter 8:** Paying the Payroll, Depositing Payroll Taxes, and Filing the Required Quarterly and Annual Tax Forms
  - New forms that reflect the current procedures and rates as well as a more efficient approach in the presentation of material, with the goal of enhancing student understanding by easier access to the concepts.
- **Chapters 9–12:** Sales, Purchases, Merchandise Transactions, and Completion of the Accounting Cycle for a Merchandise Company

- All of these chapters have been extensively revised to reflect the Perpetual Method of Inventory Valuation. As this is the method that is most commonly in place in today's business environment, it is important that students be introduced to this concept as early as possible in their accounting education.
- To help instructors and students maintain currency with the periodic method of inventory evaluation, there is a brand new appendix to Chapter 12 that provides coverage of this topic as well as assignable exercises and problems in MyLab Accounting.

Visual Walkthrough

SOLVING TEACHING AND LEARNING CHALLENGES

Many students who take a college accounting course have difficulty understanding how they can use what they learn in the future. We use the following resources to engage students with the content and to highlight how college accounting is relevant and important for their employability and careers:

Inventory and revenue recognition accounting methods have been updated to follow current business trends so students are familiar with the rules and practices when they enter the workforce.

Accounting Cycle Tutorial – accessed by computer, smartphone, or tablet, the ACT provides students with brief explanations of each concept in the accounting cycle through engaging interactive activities.

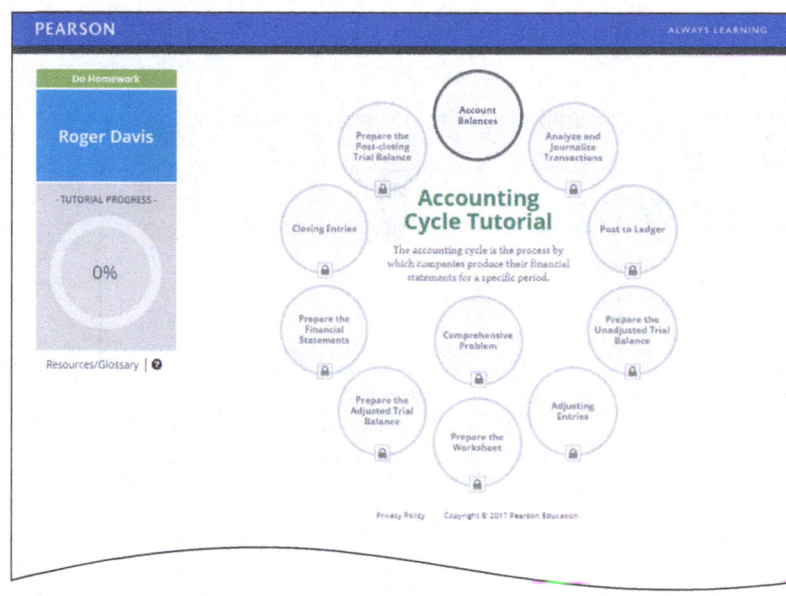

Discussion Questions, Critical Thinking, Ethical Cases, and Concept Checks afford an opportunity for students to think critically about what they've just learned. This content can be used to generate discussion in class or assigned as homework.

Discussion Questions and Critical Thinking/Ethical Case

1. What are the functions of accounting?
2. Define, compare, and contrast sole proprietorships, partnerships, and corporations.
3. How are businesses classified?
4. How has technology affected the role of the bookkeeper?
5. List the three elements of the basic accounting equation.
6. Define *capital*.
7. The total of the left-hand side of the accounting equation must equal the total of the right-hand side. True or false? Please explain.
8. A balance sheet tells a company where it is going and how well it performs. True or false? Please explain.
9. Revenue is an asset. True or false? Please explain.
10. Owner's equity is subdivided into what categories?
11. A withdrawal is a business expense. True or false? Please explain.
12. As expenses increase they cause owner's equity to increase. Defend or reject.
13. What does an income statement show?
14. The statement of owner's equity only calculates ending withdrawals. True or false? Please explain.
15. Paul Kloss, accountant for Lowe & Co., traveled to New York on company business. His total expenses came to $350. Paul felt that because the trip extended over the weekend he would "pad" his expense account with an additional $100 of expenses. After all, weekends represent his own time, not the company's. What would you do? Write your specific recommendations to Paul.

Concept Checks

Classifying Accounts

1. Classify each of the following items as an Asset (A), Liability (L), or part of Owner's Equity (OE).   **L01** *(5 min)*

   a. iPad

Designed to help students achieve success in their course, Success Tips have been placed strategically throughout the text where students are known to need a hint or reminder.

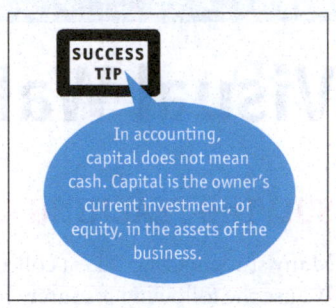

The Exercises and Problems (Sets A and B) have been updated for the new edition. Short exercises can be assigned or used in class to focus on building skills. The longer problems give students a chance to do one learning unit at a time or combine many units in one problem. These problems help put the pieces together. They're a great reinforcement of the accounting principles.

Each Learning Unit of the chapter is summarized in the Success Coach section as a "Do It Right Tip" for students to review before taking the "Do It Right Now Checkup." These true/false questions, created by the authors, challenge the student to apply what's learned in each section and help students focus on the key topics in each chapter.

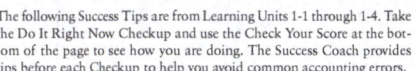

SUCCESS COACH

The following Success Tips are from Learning Units 1-1 through 1-4. Take the Do It Right Now Checkup and use the Check Your Score at the bottom of the page to see how you are doing. The Success Coach provides tips before each Checkup to help you avoid common accounting errors.

LU 1-1 Accounting, Business, and the Accounting Equation

Do It Right Tips: After a transaction is recorded in the accounting equation, the sum of all the assets must equal the total of all the liabilities and owner's equity.

Do It Right Now Checkup: Answer true or false to the following statements.

1. Capital is cash.
2. Accounts Payable is a liability.
3. A shift in assets means liabilities will increase.
4. Assets − Liabilities = Owner's Equity.
5. Assets represent what is owned by the business.

LU 1-2 The Balance Sheet

Do It Right Tips: The Balance Sheet is a formal report listing assets, liabilities, and owner's equity as of a particular date.

LU 1-3 The Accounting Equation Expanded: Revenue, Expenses, and Withdrawals

Do It Right Tips: Revenue is recorded when earned even if cash is not received. Expenses are recorded when they happen (incurred) whether they are paid or to be paid later.

Do It Right Now Checkup: Answer true or false to the following statements.

1. Revenue is an asset.
2. Withdrawals increase owner's equity.
3. As expenses go down, owner's equity goes down.
4. An advertising bill incurred but unpaid is recorded as an increase in Advertising Expense and a decrease in a liability.
5. Revenue inflows can only be in the form of cash.

LU 1-4 The Three Financial Statements

Do It Right Tips: Net income from the income statement is

MYLAB ACCOUNTING

Reach every student with MyLab Accounting

MyLab is the teaching and learning platform that empowers you to reach *every* student. By combining trusted author content with digital tools and a flexible platform, MyLab personalizes the learning experience and improves results for each student. Learn more about MyLab Accounting at www.pearsonmylabs.com/accounting.

   Students get the benefit of immediate feedback, on-demand help, and continuous practice to achieve success.

Deliver trusted content

You deserve teaching materials that meet your own high standards for your course. That's why we partner with highly respected authors to develop interactive content and course-specific resources that you can trust—and that keep your students engaged.

Empower each learner

Each student learns at a different pace. Personalized learning pinpoints the precise areas where each student needs practice, giving all students the support they need—when and where they need it—to be successful.

Teach your course your way

Your course is unique. So whether you'd like to build your own assignments, teach multiple sections, or set prerequisites, MyLab gives you the flexibility to easily create *your* course to fit *your* needs.

Improve student results

When you teach with MyLab, student performance improves. That's why instructors have chosen MyLab for over 15 years, touching the lives of over 50 million students.

Developing Employability Skills

For students to succeed in a rapidly changing job market, they should be aware of their career options and how to go about developing a variety of skills. In this book and MyLab, we focus on developing these skills in the following ways:

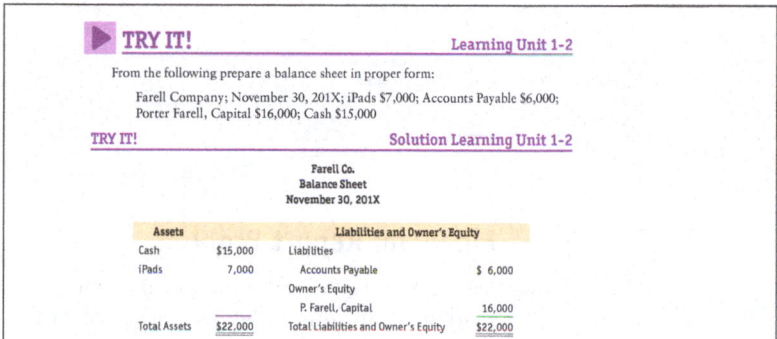

Try It! Interactive Questions

Found at the end of each Learning Unit, these questions provide students a chance to check their understanding of key concepts in the unit. Linking in the eText will allow students to practice in MyLab Accounting without interrupting their interaction with the eText. Students' performance on the questions creates a precise adaptive study plan for additional practice.

American Institute of Professional Bookkeepers (AIPB) Boxes

American Institute of Professional Bookkeepers (AIPB) boxes have been added throughout the text so students are introduced to a future employability path as a bookkeeper.

> **American Institute of Professional Bookkeepers (AIPB) –**
> The AIPB is the bookkeeping profession's national association. AIPB's mission is to achieve recognition of bookkeepers as accounting profession and to certify bookkeepers who meet high, national standards. More on the AIPB can found at **https://www.aipb.org**

Sage50 and Quickbooks Software Simulations

Computer workshops allow students to experience software companies use in the real world, like Quickbooks and Sage 50.

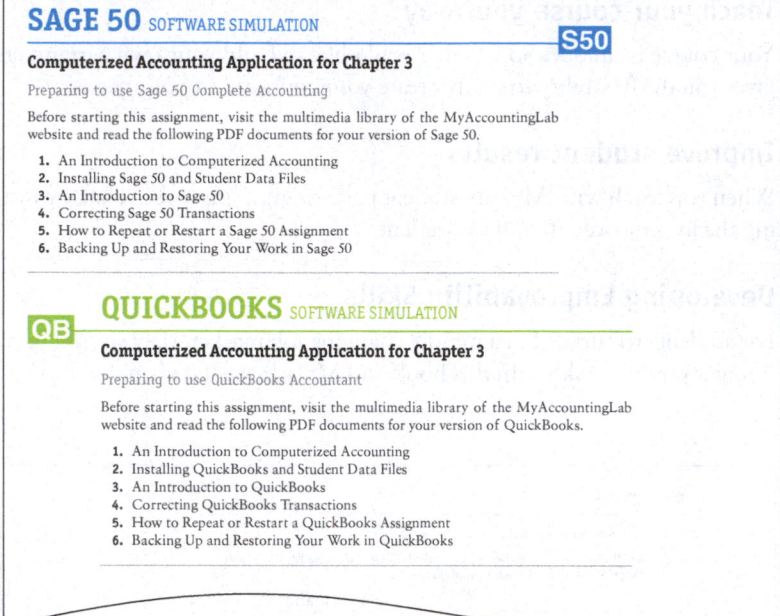

SAGE 50 SOFTWARE SIMULATION **S50**

Computerized Accounting Application for Chapter 3

Preparing to use Sage 50 Complete Accounting

Before starting this assignment, visit the multimedia library of the MyAccountingLab website and read the following PDF documents for your version of Sage 50.

1. An Introduction to Computerized Accounting
2. Installing Sage 50 and Student Data Files
3. An Introduction to Sage 50
4. Correcting Sage 50 Transactions
5. How to Repeat or Restart a Sage 50 Assignment
6. Backing Up and Restoring Your Work in Sage 50

QUICKBOOKS SOFTWARE SIMULATION

Computerized Accounting Application for Chapter 3

Preparing to use QuickBooks Accountant

Before starting this assignment, visit the multimedia library of the MyAccountingLab website and read the following PDF documents for your version of QuickBooks.

1. An Introduction to Computerized Accounting
2. Installing QuickBooks and Student Data Files
3. An Introduction to QuickBooks
4. Correcting QuickBooks Transactions
5. How to Repeat or Restart a QuickBooks Assignment
6. Backing Up and Restoring Your Work in QuickBooks

Financial Report Problem

Reading Amazon's Annual Report

Go to **https://tinyurl.com/slaterca14e** to access Amazon's 2016 Annual Report. Find the Consolidated Statement of Operations. How much did Amazon's net product sales increase or decrease from 2015 to 2016?

◀ **L03** *(5 min)*

Financial Report Problem

Using Amazon's 2016 annual financial report, students can apply theory and applications learned throughout the chapter to a real company.

Keeping It Real Continuing Problem

Students follow the activities of a fictional company, *Suarez Computer Center*, and then are asked to apply concepts to solve specific accounting problems for the company. Problems can be found in Chapters 1–15 and can be solved manually or by using Sage50 or Quickbooks.

KEEPING IT REAL SUAREZ COMPUTER CENTER

MyLabAccounting

L01,2,3 *(45 min)*

The computer center's business is picking up, so Troy Falco, the owner, has decided to expand his bookkeeping system to a general journal/ledger system. The balances from August have been forwarded to the ledger accounts.

Assignment

1. Use the chart of accounts in Chapter 2 to record the following transactions in Figures 3.37 through 3.47.

Mini Practice Set

Sherman Realty

Reviewing the Accounting Cycle Twice

Est. Time: 5 hours

This comprehensive review problem requires you to complete the accounting cycle for Sherman Realty twice. This practice set allows you to review Chapters 1–5 while reinforcing the relationships between all parts of the accounting cycle. By completing two cycles, you will see how the ending April balances in the ledger are used to accumulate data in May.

First, look at the chart of accounts for Sherman Realty.

Sherman Realty
Chart of Accounts

Assets	Revenue
111 Cash	411 Commissions Earned
112 Accounts Receivable	**Expenses**
114 Prepaid Rent	511 Rent Expense
115 Office Supplies	512 Salaries Expense
121 Office Equipment	513 Gas Expense
122 Accumulated Depreciation, Office Equipment	514 Repairs Expense
123 Automobile	515 Telephone Expense
124 Accumulated Depreciation, Automobile	516 Advertising Expense

Mini Practice Sets

The in-text Sherman Reality Practice Set (Chapter 5) includes actual source documents for each transaction and The Fantastic Dress Shop Practice Set (Chapter 12) enable students to complete two cycles of transactions (either manually or with Sage50 or Quickbooks).

Table of Contents Overview

Chapter 1: Accounting Concepts and Procedures	Introduces the recording of business transactions into the basic and expanded accounting equation. The three financial statements are introduced.
Chapter 2: Debits and Credits: Analyzing and Recording Business Transactions	The T accounts and chart of accounts are introduced. Focus is on using debits and credits to prepare financial statements and the trial balance.
Chapter 3: Beginning the Accounting Cycle	Business transactions are journalized and posted to the ledger. A trial balance is prepared from the ledger.
Chapter 4: The Accounting Cycle Continued	Explanation of adjustments are done step by step and placed one at a time on a worksheet. The worksheet is completed and financial statements are prepared from the worksheet. The Appendix provides an introduction to different methods of depreciation.
Chapter 5: The Accounting Cycle Completed	From a worksheet, the adjusting and closing entries are journalized. Focus is on preparing a post-closing trial balance. The mini practice set shows a two-cycle problem including source documents.
Chapter 6: Banking Procedures and Control of Cash	The latest trends in banking are covered. Time is spent illustrating the completion of a bank reconciliation. Petty cash establishment and replenishment are covered.
Chapter 7: Calculating Pay and Recording Payroll Taxes: The Beginning of the Payroll Process	New circular E is included for income tax calculations. New rates for Social Security and Medicare have been updated. Payroll register is completed. Discussion of FUTA and SUTA are included.
Chapter 8: Paying the Payroll, Depositing Payroll Taxes, and Filing the Required Quarterly and Annual Tax Forms: The Conclusion of the Payroll Process	New streamlined chapter that simplifies the payroll responsibilities of the employer. Form for 941 is illustrated along with W-2 and W-3. Discussion of when deposits are made is visually illustrated.
Chapter 9: Sales and Cash Receipts in a Perpetual Inventory System	**New:** Perpetual approach is now used to explain sales and cash receipts. A periodic approach can be found in the appendix after Chapter 12.
Chapter 10: Purchases and Cash Payments in a Perpetual Inventory System	**New:** Continued from Chapter 9, the perpetual approach is used to illustrate and explain the purchase and cash payments journal. A periodic approach can be found in the Appendix after Chapter 12.
Chapter 11: Preparing a Worksheet for a Merchandise Company Using the Perpetual Method	**New:** Perpetual approach is now used to complete a worksheet for a merchandise company. Emphasis is placed on cost of goods sold and merchandise inventory.
Chapter 12: Completion of the Accounting Cycle for a Merchandise Company Using the Perpetual Inventory Method	**New:** Using the perpetual approach, the completion of the merchandise cycle is illustrated. Financial statements are prepared from a worksheet and a post-closing trial balance is prepared. Following the chapter is an appendix covering the periodic method. Problem material is included.
Chapter 13: Corporations: Organizations and Stock	Accrual accounting is explained. The allowance method as well as the direct method are illustrated. Estimating bad debts is covered.
Chapter 14: Notes Receivable and Notes Payable	Introduction presents interest calculations and determining maturity dates. Focus on chapter is to illustrate journal entries to record notes as well as the discounting process.
Chapter 15: Accounting for Merchandise Inventory	Both the periodic as well as perpetual methods are used to calculate cost of goods sold and ending inventory. Discussion also includes the retail and gross profit methods.
Chapter 16: Accounting for Property, Plant, Equipment, and Intangible Assets	Introduces how to calculate cost of Property, Plant, and Equipment. Depreciation methods are illustrated along with journal entries involving capital and revenue expenditures. Intangible assets are discussed.
Chapter 17: Partnership	Journal entries are illustrated to record forming a partnership. Calculations are illustrated to record division of net income and loss among partners. Discussion includes journal entries for admission and withdrawal of a partner. Liquidation of a partnership is illustrated.
Chapter 18: Organizations and Stock	Completion of stockholders' equity is illustrated. Calculations of dividends is shown along with journal entries. A subscription plan is journalized.
Chapter 19: Corporations: Stock Values, Dividends, Treasury Stocks, and Retained Earnings	Redemption, market, and book values are calculated. Journal entries are shown to record dividends. Treasury stock transactions are journalized. A statement of retained earnings is prepared.

Chapter 20: Corporations and Bonds Payable	The straight-line method and the interest method are compared and contrasted. All calculations and tables are illustrated. Transactions for sinking funds are journalized.
Chapter 21: Statement of Cash Flows	Statements of cash flow are prepared by the indirect as well as direct method.
Chapter 22: Analyzing Financial Statements	Horizontal and vertical analyses are competed for the income statement as well as balance sheet. Financial ratio explanations and calculations are provided.
Chapter 23: The Voucher System	Using a perpetual system, transactions are journalized in a voucher system.
Chapter 24: Departmental Accounting	Various income statements illustrated how gross profit can be shown by departments. A discussion of operating expenses is illustrated. Contribution margin is calculated and illustrated on income statement.
Chapter 25: Manufacturing Accounting	Cost of goods manufactured is calculated. The flow of manufacturing costs are journalized. A worksheet is prepared for a merchandise company.

INSTRUCTOR TEACHING RESOURCES

This program comes with the following teaching resources.

Supplements available to instructors www.pearsonhighered.com/slater	Features of the Supplement
Instructor's Manual authored by Carolyn Strauch from Crowder College accuracy checked by Ron Premuroso	• Chapter-by-chapter summaries • Examples and activities not in the main book • Teaching outlines • Teaching tips
Solutions Manual authored by Robert Chamberlain from MiraCosta College and Connie Belden from Butler Community College accuracy checked by Carolyn Streuly	Solutions to the end-of-chapter content
Test Bank authored by William Jefferson from Metropolitan Community College accuracy checked by Ron Premuroso	Over 3,000 multiple-choice, true/false, and computational questions with these annotations: • Difficulty level (1 for straight recall, 2 for some analysis, 3 for complex analysis) • Learning Objective to which the question correlates • Learning outcome • AACSB learning standard (Written and Oral Communication; Ethical Understanding and Reasoning; Analytical Thinking; Information Technology; Interpersonal Relations and Teamwork; Diverse and Multicultural Work; Reflective Thinking; Application of Knowledge)
Computerized TestGen	TestGen allows instructors to: • Customize, save, and generate classroom tests • Edit, add, or delete questions from the test item files • Analyze test results • Organize a database of tests and student results
PowerPoints authored by Kim Potts from North Arkansas College	Slides include tables and equations from the textbook PowerPoints meet accessibility standards for students with disabilities. Features include but are not limited to: • Keyboard and Screen Reader access • Alternative text for images • High color contrast between background and foreground colors

Acknowledgments

The guidance and recommendations of the following instructors helped us revise the content and features of this text. We are grateful for their reviews and truly believe that their feedback was indispensable.

Mark Sutton – Hawkeye Community College
Michelle Randall – Schoolcraft College
Anna Boulware – St. Charles Community College
Robert Gronstal – Metropolitan Community College
Roger McMillian – Mineral Area College
Vaun Day – Central Arizona College
Dawn Diskin – Mira Costa College
Kerry Dolan – Great Falls College – MSU
Marina Grau – Houston Area Community College
Christine Lebar – Allan Hancock College
Bryan Monson – Chemeketa Community College
David Juriga – St. Louis Community College
Lydia Tisdale – Horry Georgetown Technical College
Delyse Totten – Portland Community College – Sylvania
Marc Lafond – Arizona Western College
Bill Jefferson – Metropolitan Community College

We would like to thank the following individuals who contributed in the review, accuracy check, and creation of the supplemental material:

Carolyn Strauch
Robert Chamberlain
Kim Potts
William Jefferson
Marc Lafond
Deniz Appelbaum
Michael Griffin
Erin Dischler
Connie Belden

Our great appreciation is also extended to Carolyn Streuly for her revision and review of the book content and supplemental material. Her expertise and knowledge were crucial to the publication of this text.

About the Authors

Jeff Slater has taught at North Shore Community College for 48 years. He has published 12 different texts selling over 2 million copies. Jeff has also worked as a consultant for the federal government. Jeff's teaching philosophy is to keep it simple. Over the years he has been known for his innovative ideas. Jeff received the Nisod Excellence Award for his teaching. He resides in Lexington, Massachusetts, with his wife Shelley and their two golden doodles Bernie and Fejjie. Jeff loves what he does and understands that students are his customers that need to be served in a professional manner. Jeff is available at jeffslater@aol.com, and promises to get back to any student queries within 24 hours or less.

Mike Deschamps received a Bachelor of Science degree in accounting, graduating from the University of San Diego, where he served as the chapter president for Beta Alpha Psi, the national accounting honor society. Mike transferred to USD after completing several years at San Diego City Community College, where he really found his direction as a student, which was a significant factor in his desire to become a community college instructor.

After working in public accounting and obtaining his CPA license, Mike returned to San Diego State University, where he earned a master's degree in Accounting and a Certificate in Financial Planning. In addition, he earned his Enrolled Agent certification in 2004. He is currently pursuing a Master's degree in Online Teaching and Learning in the School of Education at California State University-East Bay. He believes that the delivery of meaningful accounting instruction for students must keep up with the changing technology environment in which accounting operates.

He is currently in his tenth year at MiraCosta Community College and previously was a tenured professor of accounting and financial services at Chaffey Community College, where he also served as the program coordinator for 6 years. He is an active member of Teachers of Accounting at Two-Year Colleges (TACTYC) and has presented at the National Convention a number of times, including the 2017 convention, where he presented on developing tax curriculum for community colleges. He is also a member of the American Institute of Professional Bookkeepers and was instrumental in redesigning the bookkeeping curriculum at MiraCosta to better reflect the skills needed in today's bookkeeping environment. Having a curriculum that not only prepares students for the workplace but also assists them in preparing for a professional bookkeeping certification exam, such as the AIPB's Certified Bookkeeper Designation, was a key goal of that effort.

Accounting Concepts and Procedures

1

CHAPTER PREVIEW: ACCOUNTING IN ACTION

Gabriella Sandoval, a devout techie, has been yearning for an Apple watch and has finally decided to take the plunge on a Series 2 sport watch in her favorite color pink. She decided the best deal for her was online at the Apple Store for $369.00, which included free shipping and, as a budget-conscious student, that was important for her. Payment could be via a major credit card or debit card. Gabriella wondered how the Apple Store could keep track of all of the millions of sales transactions that Apple proccessed each day. Her accounting professor told her that Apple tracks the sale in its accounting software program account called a Revenue account. In this chapter, we see how a company records transactions and communicates its sales to the business world. How important is it for Apple to know just how much revenue has been generated by sales on the Apple watch on any given day?

Learning Objectives – Relating Accounting Theory By Unit

LO1 Explain Accounting, Business, and the Accounting Equation

LO2 Prepare a Balance Sheet

LO3 Record Transactions into the Expanded Accounting Equation

LO4 Prepare the Three Financial Statements

L01

Accounting, Business, and the Accounting Equation

Public companies like Apple have to comply with many federal statutes as well as with accounting standards. These accounting standards are the rules that companies have to follow in the preparation of their financial information. These standards are called *GAAP*, or *Generally Accepted Accounting Principles.*

Accounting is the language of business; it provides information to managers, owners, investors, government agencies, and others inside and outside the organization. Accounting provides answers and insights to questions like:

- Which computer software will best fit our company?
- Should I invest in Amazon or Tesla stock?
- How will increasing fuel costs affect Southwest Airlines?
- Can Boeing pay its debt obligations?
- What percentage of the Target marketing budget is allocated to electronic commerce? How does that percentage compare with that of the competition? What is the overall financial condition of Target?

Smaller businesses also need answers to their financial questions:

- At a local Coffee Bean, did business increase enough over the last year to warrant hiring a new barrista?
- Should a local real estate agency spend more money to design, produce, and send out new brochures in an effort to generate more home listings and sales?
- What role should social media play in the future of business spending?

Accounting is as important to individuals as it is to businesses; it answers questions like:

- Should I take out a loan to buy a new computer or wait until I can afford to pay cash for it?
- With interest rates fluctuating, would my money work better in a money market or in the stock market?

The accounting process analyzes, records, classifies, summarizes, reports, and interprets financial information for decision makers—whether individuals, small businesses, large corporations, or governmental agencies—in a timely fashion. It is important that students understand the "whys" of this accounting process. Just knowing the mechanics is not enough.

Types of Business Organizations

The four main categories of business organizations are (1) sole proprietorships, (2) partnerships, (3) corporations, and (4) limited liability companies. Let's define each of them and look at their advantages and disadvantages. This information also appears in Table 1.1, page 3.

Sole Proprietorship. A sole proprietorship, such as Susan's Web Design, is a business that has one owner. That person is both the owner and the manager of the business. An advantage of a sole proprietorship is that the owner makes all the decisions for the business. A disadvantage is that if the business cannot pay its obligations, the business owner must pay them, which means that the owner could lose some or all of his or her personal assets (e.g., house or savings).

Sole proprietorships are easy to form. They end if the business closes or when the owner dies.

Partnership. A partnership, such as Gail and Reggie, is a form of business ownership that has at least two owners (partners). Each partner acts as an owner of the company, which is an advantage because the partners can share the decision making and the risks of the business usually outlined in a partnership agreement. A disadvantage is that, as in

Accounting System that measures the business's activities in financial terms, provides written reports and financial statements about those activities, and communicates these reports to decision-makers and others.

American Institute of Professional Bookkeepers (AIPB) – The AIPB is the bookkeeping profession's national association. AIPB's mission is to achieve the recognition of bookkeepers as accounting professionals and to certify bookkeepers who meet high, national standards. More on the AIPB can found at **https://www.aipb.org**

Sole proprietorship Type of business organization that has one owner. The owner is personally liable for paying the business's debts.

Partnership Form of business organization that has at least two owners. The partners usually are personally liable for the partnership's debts.

TABLE 1.1 Types of Business Organizations

	Sole Proprietorship (Susan's Web Design)	Partnerships (Gail and Reggie)	Corporation (Apple vs Facebook)	Limited Liability Companies (LLC) (Stolle, Watson, and Ramirez, LLC)
Ownership	Business owned by one person.	Business owned by more than one person.	Business owned by stockholders.	Business owned by a limited number of members.
Formation	No formal filing or agreement necessary to form.	Requires a partnership agreement to define the terms of partnership.	Requires filing with the state to be recognized.	Requires filing with the state a document called articles of organization.
Liability	Owner could lose personal assets to meet obligations of business.	Partners could lose personal assets to meet obligations of partnership.	Limited personal risk. Stockholders' loss is limited to their investment in the company.	Limited personal risk. Members' loss is limited to their investment.
Closing	Ends with death of owner or closing of business.	Ends with death of partner or closing of business.	Can continue indefinitely.	May end with death of member.

a sole proprietorship, the partners' personal assets could be lost if the partnership cannot meet its obligations.

Partnerships are easy to form. They end when a partner dies or leaves the partnership, or when the partners decide to close the business.

Corporation. A corporation, such as Apple, is a business owned by stockholders. The corporation may have only a few stockholders, or it may have many. The stockholders are not personally liable for the corporation's debts, and they usually do not have input into the business's decisions.

Corporations are more difficult to form than sole proprietorships or partnerships, as the corporation must file with the state in order to gain the protections provided by this form of business. Corporations can exist indefinitely.

Limited Liability Company (LLC). A limited liability company, such as the law firm of Stolle, Watson, and Ramirez LLC, is a business owned by a few members. The members are liable only to the extent of their investment in the firm and, unlike a corporation, have input into the business's decisions. Like corporations, the LLC must file with the state in which it does business in order to gain the liability protection of this form of business.

Classifying Business Organizations

Whether we are looking at a sole proprietorship, a partnership, or a corporation, the business can be classified by what it does to earn money. Companies are categorized as service, merchandise, or manufacturing businesses.

A limo service is a good example of a service company because it provides a service. The first part of this book focuses on service businesses.

Old Navy and Crate and Barrel sell products. They are called merchandise companies. Merchandise companies can either make their own products or sell products that are made by another supplier. Companies such as Nike and Tesla that make their own products are called manufacturers. (See Table 1.2, page 4.)

Definition of Accounting

Accounting (also called the *accounting process*) is a system that measures the activities of a business in financial terms. It provides reports and financial statements that show how the various transactions the business undertook (e.g., buying and selling goods) affected the business. This accounting process performs the following functions:

- **Analyzing:** Looking at what happened and how the business was affected.
- **Recording:** Putting the information into the accounting system.
- **Classifying:** Grouping all the same activities (e.g., all purchases) together.
- **Summarizing:** Totaling the results.

Corporation Type of business organization that is owned by stockholders. Stockholders are usually not personally liable for the corporation's debts.

Limited liability company Type of business organization that is owned by a few members. Members are only liable to the extent of their investment.

Service company Business that provides a service.

Merchandise company Business that makes its own products or buys a product from a manufacturing company to sell to its customers.

Manufacturer Business that makes a product and sells it to its customers.

TABLE 1.2 Examples of Service, Merchandise, and Manufacturing Businesses

Service Businesses	Merchandise Businesses	Manufacturing Businesses
Susan's Web Design	Crate and Barrel	General Mills
Twitter	Costco	Tesla
Samuel Agarwal L.Ac.	Wayfair.com	Caterpillar Inc.
Kelly Services	Lowes	Nike
Deshaun Plumbing	Old Navy	Apple

- **Reporting:** Issuing the statements that tell the results of the previous functions.
- **Interpreting:** Examining the statements to determine how the various pieces of information they contain relate to each other.
- **Communication:** Providing the reports and financial statements to people who are interested in the information, such as the business's decision makers, investors, creditors, and government agencies (e.g., the Internal Revenue Service).

As you can see, a lot of people use these reports. A set of procedures and guidelines was developed to make sure that everyone prepares and interprets them the same way. As mentioned earlier, these guidelines are known as generally accepted accounting principles (GAAP). While GAAP is an United States accounting standard, the International Financial Reporting Standards (IFRS) are a group of guidelines developed by the International Accounting Standards Board that are becoming the international standard for the preparation of public companies' financial statements.

Now let's look at the difference between bookkeeping and accounting. Keep in mind that we use the terms *accounting* and the *accounting process* interchangeably.

Computer Software and the Bookkeeper

Bookkeeping is the recording (record keeping) function of the accounting process. Today, computers are used for routine bookkeeping operations that formerly took weeks or months to complete. This book explains the processes and logical steps behind those operations, giving the reader the hands-on knowledge that a bookkeeper needs even though computers perform many tasks. Bookkeepers today need to be trained to use the latest computer software that is available, including QuickBooks, Excel, and Sage 50.

An accountant takes the bookkeeping records and prepares the financial statements that are used to analyze the company's financial position. Accounting involves many complex activities. Often, it includes the preparation of tax and financial reports, budgeting, and analyses of financial information.

The Accounting Equation: Assets, Liabilities, and Equities

Let's begin our study of accounting concepts and procedures by looking at a small business: Jess Bora's computer consulting firm. Jess decided to open his firm at the end of August. He consulted his accountant before he made his decision, and she gave him some important information. First, she told him the new business would be considered a separate business entity whose finances had to be kept separate and distinct from Jess's personal finances. The accountant went on to say that all transactions can be analyzed using the basic accounting equation: Assets = Liabilities + Owner's Equity.

Jess had never heard of the basic accounting equation. He listened carefully as the accountant explained the terms used in the equation and how the equation works.

Assets. Cash, land, supplies, office equipment, buildings, and other properties of value *owned* by a firm are called assets.

Equities. The rights or financial claims to the assets are called equities. Equities belong to those who supply the assets. If you are the only person to supply assets to the firm, you have the sole rights or financial claims to them. For example, if you supply the consulting firm with $6,000 in cash and $8,000 in office equipment, your equity in the firm is $14,000.

Generally accepted accounting principles (GAAP) Procedures and guidelines that must be followed during the accounting process.

International Financial Reporting Standards (IFRS) Group of accounting standards and procedures that if adopted by the United States, could replace GAAP.

Bookkeeping Recording function of the accounting process.

Assets Properties (resources) of value owned by a business (cash, supplies, equipment, land).

Equities Rights or financial claims of creditors (liabilities) and owners (owner's equity) who supply the assets to a firm.

Relationship between Assets and Equities. The relationship between assets and equities is

$$\text{Assets} = \text{Equities}$$
(Total value of items *owned* by business)   (Total claims against the assets)

The total dollar value of the assets of your consulting firm will be equal to the total dollar value of the financial claims to those assets, that is, equal to the total dollar value of the equities.

The total dollar value is broken down on the left-hand side of the equation to show the specific items of value owned by the business and on the right-hand side to show the types of claims against the assets owned.

Liabilities. A firm may have to borrow money to buy more assets; when it does, it *buys assets on account* (buy now, pay later). Suppose the consulting firm purchases some new computer equipment for $3,000 on account from Dell, and the company is willing to wait 10 days for payment. The consulting firm has created a liability: an obligation to pay that comes due in the future. Dell is called the creditor. This liability—the amount owed to Dell—gives the company the right, or the financial claim, to $3,000 of the consulting firm's assets. When Dell is paid, the company's rights to the assets of the consulting firm will end because the obligation has been paid off.

Liabilities Obligations that come due in the future; financial rights or claims of creditors to assets.

Creditor Someone who has a claim to assets.

Basic Accounting Equation. To best understand the various claims to a business's assets, accountants divide equities into two parts. The claims of creditors—outside persons or businesses—are labeled *liabilities*. The claim of the business's owner is labeled owner's equity. Let's see how the accounting equation looks now.

Owner's equity Rights or financial claims to the assets of a business by the owner (in the accounting equation, assets minus liabilities).

$$\text{Assets} = \qquad \text{Equities}$$

1. Liabilities: rights of creditors
2. Owner's equity: rights of owner

Assets = Liabilities + Owner's Equity

The total value of all the assets of a firm equals the combined total value of the financial claims of the creditors (liabilities) and the claim of the owner (owner's equity). This calculation is known as the basic accounting equation. The basic accounting equation provides a basis for understanding the conventional accounting system of a business. The equation records business transactions in a logical and orderly way that shows their impact on the company's assets, liabilities, and owner's equity.

Basic accounting equation Assets = Liabilities + Owner's Equity.

Importance of Creditors. Another way of presenting the basic accounting equation is

$$\text{Assets} - \text{Liabilities} = \text{Owner's Equity}$$

This form of the equation stresses the importance of creditors. The owner's rights to the business's assets are determined after the rights of the creditors are subtracted. In other words, creditors have first claim to assets. If a firm has no liabilities—therefore no creditors—the owner has the total rights to assets. Another term for the owner's current investment, or equity, in the business's assets is capital.

As Jess Bora's consulting firm engages in business transactions (paying bills, serving customers, and so on), changes will take place in the assets, liabilities, and owner's equity (capital). Let's analyze some of these transactions.

Capital The owner's investment of equity in the company.

Transaction A Aug. 28: Jess invests $6,000 in cash and $200 of computer equipment into the business.

On August 28, Jess withdraws $6,000 from his personal bank account and deposits the money in the consulting firm's newly opened bank account. He also invests $200 of computer equipment in the business. He plans to be open for business on September 1. With

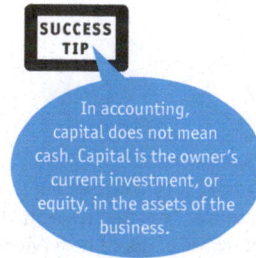

SUCCESS TIP

In accounting, capital does not mean cash. Capital is the owner's current investment, or equity, in the assets of the business.

the help of his accountant, Jess begins to prepare the accounting records for the business. We put this information into the basic accounting equation as follows:

Assets			= Liabilities + Owner's Equity	
Cash	+	Computer Equipment	=	Jess Bora, Capital
Transaction +$6,000	+	+$200	=	+$6,200

$$\$6,200 = \$6,200$$

Note that the total value of the assets, cash, and computer equipment—$6,200—is equal to the combined total value of liabilities (none, so far) and owner's equity ($6,200). Remember, Jess has supplied all the cash and computer equipment, so he has the sole financial claim to the assets. Note how the heading "Jess Bora, Capital" is written under the owner's equity heading. The $6,200 is Jess's investment, or equity, in the firm's assets.

Transaction B Aug. 29: Consulting practice buys computer equipment for cash, $500.

Supplies One type of asset acquired by a firm; it has a much shorter life than equipment.

From the initial investment of $6,000 cash, the consulting firm buys $500 worth of computer equipment (such as a tablet), which lasts a long time, whereas supplies (such as pens) tend to be used up relatively quickly.

	Assets			= Liabilities + Owner's Equity	
	Cash	+	Computer Equipment	=	Jess Bora, Capital
Beginning Balance	$6,000	+	$200	=	$6,200
Transaction	−500		+500		
Ending Balance	$5,500	+	$700	=	$6,200

$$\$6,200 = \$6,200$$

Shift in assets Shift that occurs when the composition of the assets has changed but the total of the assets remains the same.

Shift in Assets. As a result of the last transaction, the consulting firm has less cash but has increased its amount of computer equipment. This shift in assets indicates that the makeup of the assets has changed, but the total of the assets remains the same.

Suppose you go food shopping at Walmart with $100 and spend $60. Now you have two assets, food and money. The composition of your assets has *shifted*—you have more food and less money than you did—but the *total* of the assets has not increased or decreased. The total value of the food, $60, plus the cash, $40, is still $100. When you borrow money from the bank, on the other hand, you increase cash (an asset) and increase liabilities at the same time. This action results in an increase in assets, not just a shift.

An accounting equation can remain in balance even if only one side is updated. The key point to remember is that the left-hand-side total of assets must always equal the right-hand-side total of liabilities and owner's equity.

Transaction C Aug. 30: Consulting firm buys additional computer equipment on account, $300.

The consulting firm purchases an additional $300 worth of computer equipment from Wilmington Company. Instead of demanding cash right away, Wilmington agrees to deliver the equipment and to allow up to 60 days for the consulting practice to pay the invoice (bill).

Accounts payable Amounts owed to creditors that result from the purchase of goods or services on account—a liability.

This liability, or obligation to pay in the future, has some interesting effects on the basic accounting equation. Wilmington Company accepts as payment a partial claim against the assets of the consulting practice. This claim exists until the consulting firm pays off the bill. This unwritten promise to pay the creditor is a liability called accounts payable.

Assets			=	Liabilities	+	Owner's Equity	
Cash	+	Computer Equipment	=	Accounts Payable	+	Jess Bora, Capital	
$5,500	+	$ 700	=			$6,200	Beginning Balance
		+ 300		+ $300			Transaction
$5,500	+	$1,000	=	$300	+	$6,200	Ending Balance
		$6,500 = $6,500					

When this information is analyzed, we can see that the consulting practice increased what it owes (accounts payable) as well as what it owns (office equipment) by $300. The consulting practice gains $300 in an asset but also takes on an obligation to pay Wilmington Company at a future date.

The owner's equity remains unchanged. This transaction results in an increase of total assets from $6,200 to $6,500.

Finally, note that after each transaction the basic accounting equation remains in balance. Now it's your turn to see if you understood what we have covered. This TRY IT! feature will be found after each learning unit. The solutions are right after the TRY IT! feature, but first give it an attempt to see how you do and then check your answer. If you are still having some difficulty with the concept, review the Success Tips at the end of the chapter.

 **TRY IT!**   **Learning Unit 1-1**

Record the following transactions into the basic accounting equation:

Cash + Salon Equipment = Accounts Payable + B. Reynold, Capital

1. Benson Reynold invests $27,000 to open a hair salon company.
2. The hair salon company buys new salon equipment for $15,000, paying $3,000 down and charging the balance.

Calculate the ending balances.

TRY IT!   **Solution Learning Unit 1-1**

	Assets			=	Liabilities	+	Owner's Equity	
	Cash	+	Salon Equip.	=	Accounts Pay.	+	B. Reynold, Capital	
1.	+$27,000			=		+	$27,000	
2.	−$ 3,000	+	$15,000	=	+$12,000			
	$24,000	+	$15,000	=	$12,000	+	$27,000	

The Balance Sheet

 L02

In the first learning unit, the transactions for Jess Bora's computer consulting firm were recorded in the accounting equation. The transactions we recorded occurred before the consulting firm opened for business. A statement called a balance sheet or statement of financial position can show the financial position of a company before it opened. The balance sheet is a formal statement that presents the information from the ending balances of both sides of the accounting equation. Think of the balance sheet as a snapshot of the business's financial position as of a particular date.

Balance sheet Statement, as of a particular date, that shows the amount of assets owned by a business as well as the amount of claims (liabilities and owner's equity) against these assets; also known as **statement of financial position**.

Let's look at the balance sheet of Jess Bora's consulting practice for August 31, 201X, shown in Figure 1.1. The figures in the balance sheet come from the ending balances of the accounting equation for the consulting practice as shown in Learning Unit 1-1.

Note in Figure 1.1 that the assets owned by the consulting practice appear on the left-hand side and that the liabilities and owner's equity appear on the right-hand side. Both sides equal $6,500. This *balance* between left and right gives the balance sheet its name. In later chapters we look at other ways to set up a balance sheet.

Figure 1.1
The Balance Sheet

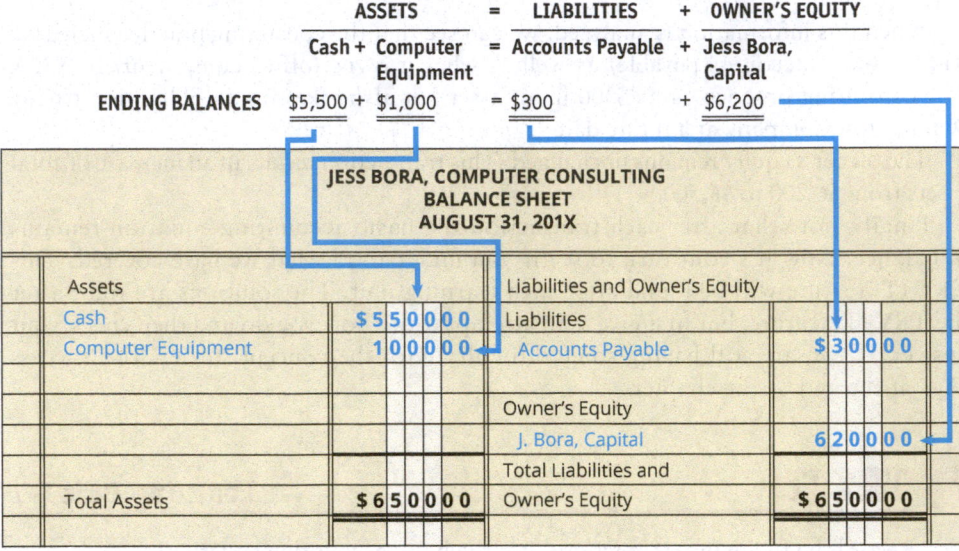

Points to Remember in Preparing a Balance Sheet

The Heading. The heading of the balance sheet provides the following information:

- The company name: Jess Bora, Computer Consulting
- The name of the statement: Balance Sheet
- The date for which the report is prepared: August 31, 201X

Use of the Dollar Sign. Note that the dollar sign is not repeated each time a figure appears. As shown in Figure 1.2, the partial balance sheet for Jess Bora's consulting practice, it is usually placed to the left of each column's top figure and to the left of the column's total.

> **SUCCESS TIP**
>
> The balance sheet shows the company's financial position as of a particular date. (In our example, that date is at the end of August.)

Figure 1.2 Partial Balance Sheet

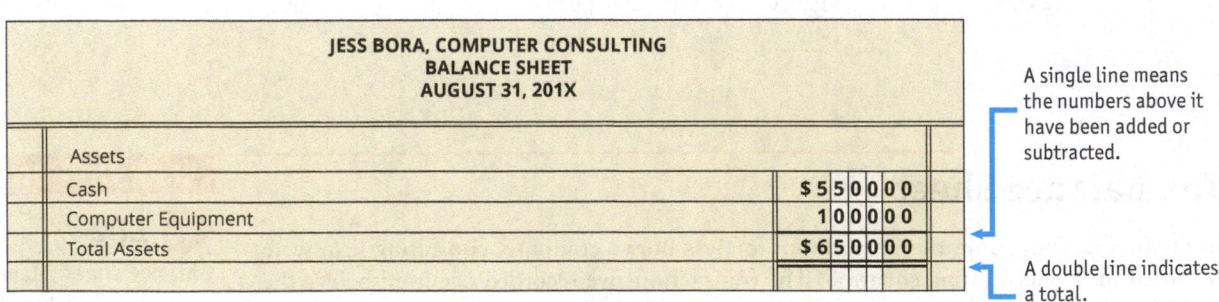

Distinguishing the Total. If you are using a paper ledger, when adding numbers down a column, use a single line above the total and a double line beneath it. A single line means that the numbers above it have been added or subtracted. A double line indicates a total.

These rules are the same for all accounting reports. With computer software today, the dollar sign and total are just a click away as the balance sheet's layout is preprogrammed.

The balance sheet gives Jess the information he needs to see the consulting firm's financial position before it opens for business. This information does not tell him, however, whether the firm made a profit.

 **TRY IT!**   **Learning Unit 1-2**

From the following prepare a balance sheet in proper form:

> Farell Company; November 30, 201X; iPads $7,000; Accounts Payable $6,000; Porter Farell, Capital $16,000; Cash $15,000

TRY IT!   **Solution Learning Unit 1-2**

Farell Co.
Balance Sheet
November 30, 201X

Assets		Liabilities and Owner's Equity	
Cash	$15,000	Liabilities	
iPads	7,000	Accounts Payable	$ 6,000
		Owner's Equity	
		P. Farell, Capital	16,000
Total Assets	$22,000	Total Liabilities and Owner's Equity	$22,000

The Accounting Equation Expanded: Revenue, Expenses, and Withdrawals

 L03

As soon as Jess Bora's office opened on September 1, he began performing computer consulting services for his clients and earning revenue, by generating consulting fees, for the business. At the same time, as a part of doing business, he incurred various expenses such as rent. Jess's accountant explained there are two types of accounting systems to record business transactions: the cash basis system and the accrual basis system. In the cash basis system, revenues are recorded when cash is received, and expenses are recorded when cash is paid. Some small businesses use this method, and individuals use the cash basis to do their personal income taxes. In the accrual basis system, revenue transactions are generally recorded when the earning process is completed (not when money is received), and expenses are recorded when they are incurred (or happen) whether paid in cash or not. The accountant told Jess that she would be using the accrual basis system of accounting because this system matches revenues and expenses in the same time period (not just when cash is paid). Now let's look at how the revenue transaction is recorded for Jess's business.

Revenue

A service company earns revenue when it provides services to its clients. Jess's consulting firm earned revenue when he provided consulting services to his clients for consulting fees. When revenue is earned, owner's equity is increased. In effect, revenue is a subdivision of owner's equity.

Assets are increased. The increase is in the form of cash if the client pays right away. If the client promises to pay in the future, the increase is called accounts receivable. When revenue is earned, the transaction is recorded as an increase in revenue and an increase in assets (either as cash or as accounts receivable, depending on whether it was paid right away or will be paid in the future).

Cash basis Accounting system that records revenue when cash is received and expenses when paid. This system does not match revenues and expenses like in the accrual basis of accounting.

Accrual basis Accounting system that matches revenues when earned with expenses that are incurred.

Revenue Amount earned by performing services for customers or selling goods to customers; can be in the form of cash or accounts receivable. Subdivision of owner's equity: As revenue increases, owner's equity increases.

Accounts receivable Asset that indicates amounts owed by customers.

Expense Cost incurred in running a business by consuming goods or services in producing revenue. Subdivision of owner's equity.

Net income When revenue totals more than expenses, the result is net income.

Net loss When expenses total more than revenue, the result is net loss.

Withdrawals Subdivision of owner's equity that records money or other assets an owner withdraws from a business for personal use.

Figure 1.3
Owner's Equity

Expanded accounting equation Assets = Liabilities + Capital − Withdrawals + Revenue − Expenses.

Expenses

A business's expenses are the costs the company incurs in carrying on operations in its effort to create revenue. Expenses are also a subdivision of owner's equity; when expenses are incurred, they *decrease* owner's equity. Expenses can be paid for in cash or they can be charged.

Net Income/Net Loss

When revenue totals more than expenses, net income is the result; when expenses total more than revenue, net loss is the result.

Withdrawals

At some point Jess Bora may need to withdraw cash or other assets from the business to pay living or other personal expenses that do not relate to the business. We will record these transactions in an account called withdrawals. Sometimes this account is called the *owner's drawing account*. Withdrawals is a subdivision of owner's equity that records personal expenses not related to the business. Withdrawals decrease owner's equity (see Figure 1.3).

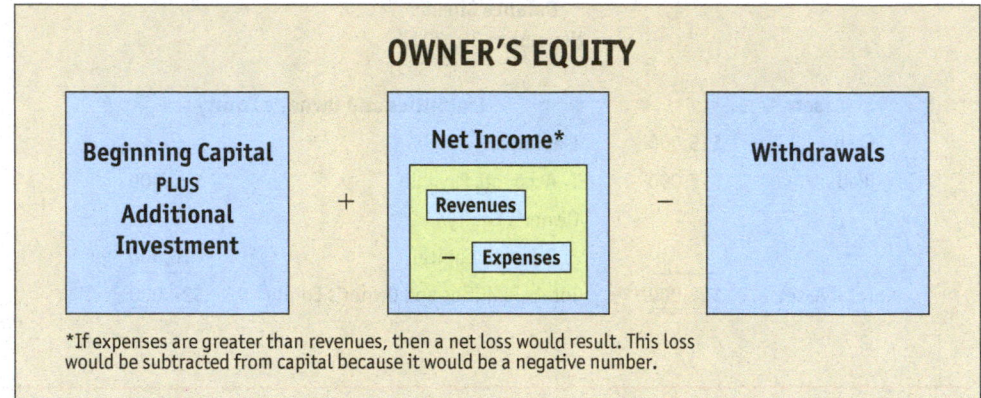

OWNER'S EQUITY

Beginning Capital PLUS Additional Investment + Net Income* (Revenues − Expenses) − Withdrawals

*If expenses are greater than revenues, then a net loss would result. This loss would be subtracted from capital because it would be a negative number.

It is important to remember the difference between expenses and withdrawals. Expenses relate to business operations; withdrawals are the result of personal needs outside the normal operations of the business.

Now let's analyze the September transactions for Jess Bora's computer consulting firm using an expanded accounting equation that includes withdrawals, revenues, and expenses.

Expanded Accounting Equation

Transaction D Sept. 1–30: Provided consulting services for cash, $2,000.

Transactions A, B, and C were discussed earlier, when the consulting firm was being formed in August. See Learning Unit 1-1.

	Assets			=	Liabilities	+			Owner's Equity				
	Cash	+ Accts. Rec.	+ Computer Equip.	= Accts. Pay.		+	Jess Bora, Capital	− Jess Bora, Withdr.	+	Revenue	−	Expenses
Balance Forward	$5,500		+ $1,000	=	$ 300	+	$6,200					
Transaction	+ 2,000									+ $2,000		
Ending Balance	$7,500		+ $1,000	=	$ 300	+	$6,200		+	$2,000		
				$8,500	=	$8,500						

In the consulting firm's first month of operation, a total of $2,000 in cash was received for consulting services performed. In the accounting equation, the asset Cash is increased by $2,000. Revenue is also increased by $2,000, resulting in an increase in total owner's equity.

A revenue column was added to the basic accounting equation. Amounts are recorded in the revenue column when they are earned. They are also recorded in the assets column under Cash and/or Accounts Receivable (see also Transaction E below). Do not think of revenue as an asset. It is part of owner's equity. It is the revenue that creates an inward flow of cash and accounts receivable.

> **SUCCESS TIP**
>
> *Remember:* Accounts Receivables result from earning revenue even when cash is not yet received. Record an expense when it is incurred, whether it is paid immediately or is to be paid later.

Transaction E Sept. 1–30: Provided consulting services on account, $3,000.

Jess's consulting firm performed consulting work on account for $3,000. The firm did not receive the cash for these earned consulting fees; it accepted an unwritten promise from these clients that payment would be received in the future.

Assets			=	Liabilities	+			Owner's Equity			
Cash	+ Accts. Rec.	+ Computer Equip.	=	Accts. Pay.	+	J. Bora, Capital	− J.Bora, Withdr.	+ Revenue	− Expenses		
$7,500		+ $ 1,000	=	$ 300	+	$6,200		+$2,000			Bal. Forward
	+ $3,000							+ $3,000			Transaction
$7,500	+ $3,000	+ $ 1,000	=	$ 300	+	$6,200		+$5,000			End. Bal.
		$11,500	=	$11,500							

Transaction F Sept. 1–30: Received $900 cash as partial payment from previous consulting services performed on account.

During September some of Jess's clients who had received services and promised to pay in the future decided to reduce what they owed the firm by making a payment of $900. This decision is shown as follows on the expanded accounting equation:

Assets			=	Liabilities	+			Owner's Equity			
Cash	+ Accts. Rec.	+ Computer Equip.	=	Accts. Pay.	+	J. Bora, Capital	− J. Bora, Withdr.	+ Revenue	− Expenses		
$7,500	+ $3,000	+ $ 1,000	=	$ 300	+	$6,200		+ $5,000			Bal. Forward
+900	−900										Transaction
$8,400	+ $2,100	+ $ 1,000	=	$ 300	+	$6,200		+ $5,000			End. Bal.
		$11,500	=	$11,500							

The consulting firm increased the asset Cash by $900 and reduced another asset, Accounts Receivable, by $900. The *total* of assets does not change. The right-hand side of the expanded accounting equation has not been touched because the total on the left-hand side of the equation has not changed. The revenue was recorded when it was earned (see Transaction E), and the *same revenue cannot be recorded twice*. This transaction analyzes the situation *after* the revenue has been previously earned and recorded. Transaction F shows a shift in assets resulting in more cash and less accounts receivable.

Transaction G Sept. 1–30: Paid salaries expense, $700.

	Assets			=	Liabilities	+		Owner's Equity				
	Cash	+ Accts. Rec.	+ Computer Equip.	=	Accts. Pay.	+	J. Bora, Capital	− J. Bora, Withdr.	+	Revenue	−	Expenses
Bal. Forward	$8,400	+ $2,100	+ $ 1,000	=	$ 300	+	$6,200		+	$5,000		
Transaction	− 700											+ $700
End. Bal.	$7,700	+ $2,100	+ $ 1,000	=	$ 300	+	$6,200		+	$5,000	−	$700
			$10,800	=	$10,800							

As expenses increase, they decrease owner's equity. This incurred expense of $700 reduces the cash by $700. Although the expense was paid, the total of the expenses to date has *increased* by $700. Keep in mind that owner's equity decreases as expenses increase, so the accounting equation remains in balance because expenses are deducted from owner's equity.

Transaction H Sept. 1–30: Paid rent expense, $400.

	Assets			=	Liabilities	+		Owner's Equity				
	Cash	+ Accts. Rec.	+ Computer Equip.	=	Accts. Pay.	+	J. Bora, Capital	− J. Bora, Withdr.	+	Revenue	−	Expenses
Bal. Forward	$7,700	+ $2,100	+ $ 1,000	=	$ 300	+	$6,200		+	$5,000	−	$ 700
Transaction	− 400											+ 400
End. Bal.	$7,300	+ $2,100	+ $ 1,000	=	$ 300	+	$6,200		+	$5,000	−	$1,100
			$10,400	=	$10,400							

During September, the practice incurred rent expenses of $400. This rent was not paid in advance; it was paid when it came due. The payment of rent reduces the asset Cash by $400 as well as increases the expenses of the firm, resulting in a decrease in owner's equity. The firm's expenses are now $1,100.

Transaction I Sept. 1–30: Incurred advertising expenses of $200, to be paid next month.

	Assets			=	Liabilities	+		Owner's Equity				
	Cash	+ Accts. Rec.	+ Computer Equip.	=	Accts. Pay.	+	J. Bora, Capital	− J. Bora, Withdr.	+	Revenue	−	Expenses
Bal. Forward	$7,300	+ $2,100	+ $ 1,000	=	$ 300	+	$6,200		+	$5,000	−	$1,100
Transaction					+ 200							+ 200
End. Bal.	$7,300	+ $2,100	+ $ 1,000	=	$ 500	+	$6,200		+	$5,000	−	$1,300
			$10,400	=	$10,400							

Jess ran an ad in the local newspaper and incurred an expense of $200. This increase in expenses caused a corresponding decrease in owner's equity. Because Jess has not paid the newspaper for the advertising yet, he owes $200. Thus his liabilities (Accounts Payable) increase by $200. Eventually, when the bill comes in and is paid, both Cash and Accounts Payable will be decreased.

Transaction J Sept. 1–30: Jess withdrew $100 for personal use.

	Assets			=	Liabilities	+		Owner's Equity				
Cash	+ Accts. Rec.	+	Computer Equip.	=	Accts. Pay.	+	J. Bora, Capital	− J. Bora, Withdr.	+	Revenue	− Expenses	
$7,300	+ $2,100	+	$ 1,000	=	$ 500	+	$6,200		+	$5,000	− $1,300	Bal. Forward
− 100								+ $100				Transaction
$7,200	+ $2,100	+	$ 1,000	=	$ 500	+	$6,200	− $100	+	$5,000	− $1,300	End. Bal.
			$10,300	=	$10,300							

By taking $100 for personal use, Jess *increased* his withdrawals from the business by $100 and decreased the asset Cash by $100. Note that as withdrawals increase, the owner's equity *decreases*. Keep in mind that a withdrawal is *not* a business expense. It is a subdivision of owner's equity that records money or other assets an owner withdraws from the business for *personal* use.

Subdivision of Owner's Equity Take a moment to review the subdivisions of owner's equity:

- As capital increases, owner's equity increases (see Transaction A).
- As withdrawals increase, owner's equity decreases (see Transaction J).
- As revenue increases, owner's equity increases (see Transactions D and E).
- As expenses increase, owner's equity decreases (see Transactions G through I).

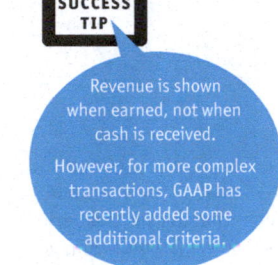

Revenue is shown when earned, not when cash is received.

However, for more complex transactions, GAAP has recently added some additional criteria.

Jess Bora's Expanded Accounting Equation The following is a summary of the expanded accounting equation for Jess Bora's computer consulting firm.

Jess Bora,
Computer Consultant
Expanded Accounting Equation: A Summary

	Assets			=	Liabilities	+		Owner's Equity				
Cash	+ Accts. Rec.	+	Computer Equip.	=	Accts. Pay.	+	J. Bora, Capital	− J. Bora, Withdr.	+	Revenue	− Expenses	
+ $6,000			+ $200	=			+ $6,200					A.
6,000		+	200	=			6,200					Balance
− 500			+ 500									B.
5,500		+	700	=			6,200					Balance
			+ 300	=	+ $300							C.
5,500	+		1,000	=	300	+	6,200					Balance
+ 2,000										+ $2,000		D.
7,500		+	1,000	=	300	+	6,200		+	2,000		Balance
	+ $3,000									+ 3,000		E.
7,500	+ 3,000	+	1,000	=	300	+	6,200		+	5,000		Balance
+ 900	− 900											F.
8,400	+ 2,100	+	1,000	=	300	+	6,200		+	5,000		Balance
− 700											+ $700	G.
7,700	+ 2,100	+	1,000	=	300	+	6,200		+	5,000	− 700	Balance
− 400											+ 400	H.
7,300	+ 2,100	+	1,000	=	300	+	6,200		+	5,000	− 1,100	Balance
					+ 200						+ 200	I.
7,300	+ 2,100	+	1,000	=	500	+	6,200		+	5,000	− 1,300	Balance
− 100								+ $100				J.
$7,200	+ $2,100	+	$ 1,000	=	$ 500	+	$6,200	− $100	+	$5,000	− $1,300	End. Balance
			$10,300	=	$10,300							

 **TRY IT!**   Learning Unit 1-3

Use the expanded accounting equation to solve for the missing amount.

Assets $37,000; Liabilities ?; Owner's Capital, Beginning Balance $19,000; Revenues $13,000; Expenses $6,000; Withdrawals $4,000

TRY IT!   Solution Learning Unit 1-3

Total Assets $37,000 Less Owner's Equity $22,000 = Liabilities $15,000

The calculation of $22,000 was Owner's Capital, Beginning Balance $19,000 + Revenue of $13,000 Less Expenses and Withdrawals of $10,000

LEARNING UNIT 1-4

 LO4

Income statement Accounting statement that details the performance of a firm (revenue minus expenses) for a specific period of time.

Figure 1.4
The Income Statement

The Three Financial Statements

Jess Bora would like to be able to find out if his firm is making a profit, so he asks his accountant if she can measure the firm's financial performance on a monthly basis. His accountant replies that a number of financial statements that she can prepare, such as the income statement, will show Jess how well the consulting practice has performed over a specific period of time. The accountant can use the information in the income statement to prepare other reports.

The Income Statement

An income statement is an accounting statement that shows business results in terms of revenue and expenses. If revenues are greater than expenses, the report shows net income. If expenses are greater than revenues, the report shows net loss. An income statement typically covers 1, 3, 6, or 12 months. It cannot cover more than 1 year. The statement shows the result of all revenues and expenses throughout the entire period and not just as of a specific date. The income statement for Jess Bora's consulting firm is shown in Figure 1.4.

JESS BORA, COMPUTER CONSULTING
INCOME STATEMENT
FOR MONTH ENDED SEPTEMBER 30, 201X

Revenue:		
Consulting Fees		$5 000 00
Operating Expenses:		
Salaries Expense	$7 000 0	
Rent Expense	4 000 0	
Advertising Expense	2 000 0	
Total Operating Expenses		1 300 00
Net Income		$3 700 00

Points to Remember in Preparing an Income Statement

Heading. The heading of an income statement tells the company's name, the name of the statement, and the period of time the statement covers.

The Setup. As you can see on the income statement, the inside column of numbers ($700, $400, and $200) is used to subtotal all expenses ($1,300) before subtracting them from revenue ($5,000 − $1,300 = $3,700).

Operating expenses may be listed in alphabetical order, in order of largest amount to smallest, or in a set order established by the accountant.

SUCCESS TIP

The income statement is prepared from data found in the revenue and expense columns of the expanded accounting equation. The inside column of numbers ($700, $400, $200) is used to subtotal all expenses ($1,300) before subtracting from revenue.

The Statement of Owner's Equity

As we said, the income statement is a business statement that shows business results in terms of revenue and expenses, but how does net income or net loss affect owner's equity? To find out, we have to look at a second type of statement, the statement of owner's equity.

The statement of owner's equity shows for a certain period of time what changes occurred in Jess Bora, Capital. The statement of owner's equity is shown in Figure 1.5.

Statement of owner's equity Financial statement that reveals the change in capital. The ending figure for capital is then placed on the balance sheet.

JESS BORA, COMPUTER CONSULTING STATEMENT OF OWNER'S EQUITY FOR MONTH ENDED SEPTEMBER 30, 201X		
Jess Bora, Capital, September 1, 201X		$ 6 2 0 0 0 0
Net Income for September	$ 3 7 0 0 0 0	
Less: Withdrawals for September	− 1 0 0 0 0	
Increase in Capital		3 6 0 0 0 0
Jess Bora, Capital, September 30, 201X		$ 9 8 0 0 0 0

Figure 1.5
Statement of Owner's Equity—Net Income

Comes from Income Statement

The capital of Jess Bora can be:

Increased by: Owner Investment (in this case there is no additional investment by the owner)

Net Income (Revenue − Expenses) and Revenue Greater Than Expenses

Decreased by: Owner Withdrawals

Net Loss (Revenue − Expenses) and Expenses Greater Than Revenue

SUCCESS TIP

If this statement of owner's equity is omitted, the information will be included in the owner's equity section of the balance sheet.

Remember, a withdrawal is *not* a business expense and thus is not involved in the calculation of net income or net loss on the income statement. It appears on the statement of owner's equity. The statement of owner's equity summarizes the effects of all the subdivisions of owner's equity (revenue, expenses, and withdrawals) on beginning capital. The ending capital figure ($9,800) will be the beginning figure in the next statement of owner's equity.

Suppose Jess's consulting firm had operated at a loss in the month of September. Suppose that instead of net income, a $400 net loss occurred and an additional investment of $700 was made on September 15. Figure 1.6 shows how the statement would look with this net loss and additional investment.

JESS BORA, COMPUTER CONSULTING STATEMENT OF OWNER'S EQUITY FOR MONTH ENDED SEPTEMBER 30, 201X		
Jess Bora, Capital, September 1, 201X		$ 6 2 0 0 0 0
Additional Investment, September 15, 201X		7 0 0 0 0
Total Investment for September*		$ 6 9 0 0 0 0
Less: Net Loss for September	$ 4 0 0 0 0	
Withdrawals for September	1 0 0 0 0	
Decrease in Capital		− 5 0 0 0 0
Jess Bora, Capital, September 30, 201X		$ 6 4 0 0 0 0

*Beginning capital and additional investments.

Figure 1.6
Statement of Owner's Equity—Net Loss

The Balance Sheet

Now let's look at how to prepare a balance sheet from the expanded accounting equation (see Figure 1.7). As you can see, the asset accounts (cash, accounts receivable, and office equipment) appear on the left side of the balance sheet.

Accounts payable and Jess Bora, Capital appear on the right side. Notice that the $9,800 of capital can be calculated within the accounting equation or can be read from the statement of owner's equity.

Main Elements of the Income Statement, the Statement of Owner's Equity, and the Balance Sheet

In this chapter we have discussed three financial statements: the income statement, the statement of owner's equity, and the balance sheet. A fourth statement, called the *statement of cash flows*, is not covered at this time. Let us review what elements of the expanded accounting equation go into each statement and the usual order in which the statements are prepared. Figure 1.7 presents a diagram of the accounting equation and the balance sheet. Table 1.3, page 17 summarizes the following points:

Figure 1.7
The Accounting Equation and the Balance Sheet

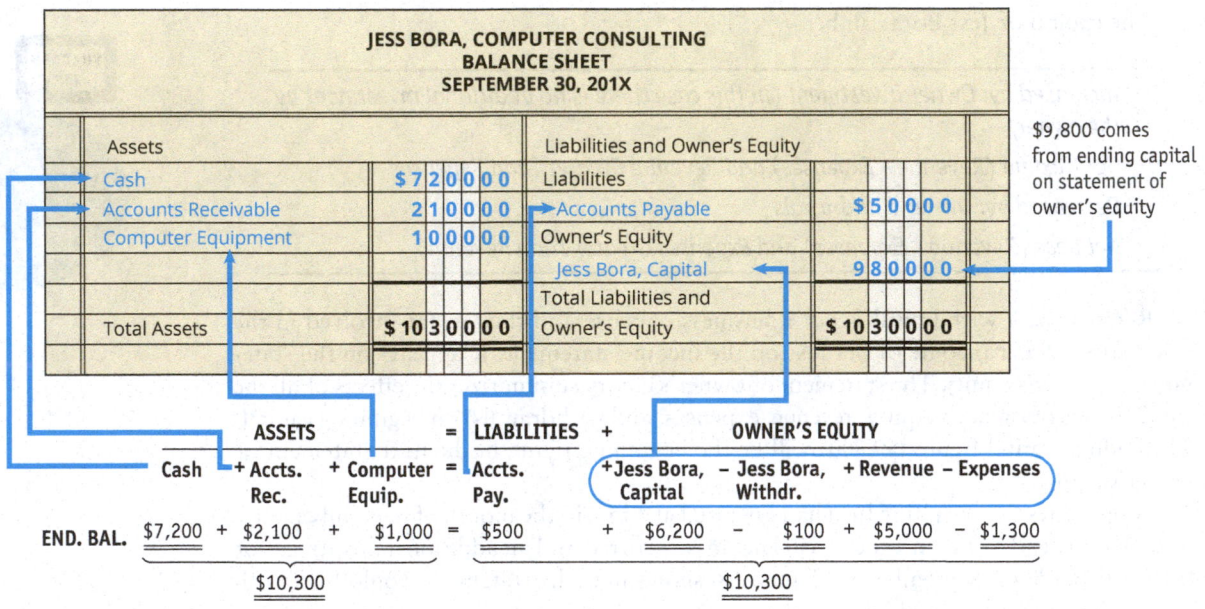

- The income statement is prepared first; it includes revenues and expenses and shows net income or net loss. This net income or net loss is used to update the next statement, the statement of owner's equity.
- The statement of owner's equity is prepared second; it includes beginning capital and any additional investments, the net income or net loss shown on the income statement, withdrawals, and the total, which is the ending capital.
- The balance sheet is prepared last; it includes the final balances of each of the elements listed in the accounting equation under Assets and Liabilities. The balance in Capital comes from the statement of owner's equity.

Ending capital
Beginning Capital + Additional Investments + Net Income − Withdrawals = Ending Capital; or Beginning Capital + Additional Investments − Net Loss − Withdrawals = Ending Capital.

TABLE 1.3 What Goes on Each Financial Statement

	Income Statement	Statement of Owner's Equity	Balance Sheet
Assets			X
Liabilities			X
Capital* (beg.)		X	
Capital (end.)		X	X
Withdrawals		X	
Revenues	X		
Expenses	X		

* Additional investments go on the statement of owner's equity.

SUCCESS TIP

Net income is reported separately from capital on the balance sheet in the equity section in both QuickBooks and Sage 50.

▶ **TRY IT!**   **Learning Unit 1-4**

From the following titles identify which financial statement(s) they would be placed on (Income Statement [IS], Statement of Owner's Equity [SOE], Balance Sheet [BS]).

1. Accounts Payable
2. John Ryan, Capital (ending)
3. Accounts Receivable
4. Computer Equipment
5. Legal Fees (Revenue)
6. Office Expense
7. Advertising Expense
8. John Ryan, Withdrawals
9. Salaries Payable
10. Cash

TRY IT!   **Solution Learning Unit 1-4**

1. BS
2. SOE, BS
3. BS
4. BS
5. IS
6. IS
7. IS
8. SOE
9. BS
10. BS

DEMONSTRATION SUMMARY PROBLEM

 **LO3,4**

Michael Brown opened his law office on June 1, 201X. During the first month of operation, Michael conducted the following transactions:

A. Invested $6,000 in cash into the law practice.
B. Paid $600 for office equipment.
C. Purchased additional office equipment on account, $1,000.
D. Received cash for performing legal services for clients, $2,000.
E. Paid salaries, $800.
F. Performed legal services for clients on account, $1,000.
G. Paid rent, $1,200.
H. Withdrew $500 from his law practice for personal use.
I. Received $500 from customers in partial payment for legal services performed, transaction f.

Requirements

1. Record these transactions in the expanded accounting equation. Keep a running balance.
2. Prepare the financial statements at June 30 for Michael Brown, Attorney-at-Law.

Solutions

Requirement 1

Record these transactions in the expanded accounting equation.

Tips to Expanded Accounting Equation

- **Transaction A:** The business increased its Cash by $6,000. Owner's Equity (capital) increased when Michael supplied the cash to the business. Note how the equation is now in balance.
- **Transaction B:** A shift in assets occurred when the equipment was purchased. The business lowered its Cash by $600, and a new column—Office Equipment—was increased for the $600 of equipment that was bought. The amount of capital is not touched because the owner did not supply any new funds. You do not have to touch both sides of the equation to make it balance.
- **Transaction C:** When creditors supply $1,000 of additional equipment, the business shows an increase in its debt. The business had increased what it *owes* the creditors. The end result is an increase in an asset and an increase in a liability.

Solution to Recording Transactions into Expanded Accounting Equation

		Assets			=	Liabilities	+			Owner's Equity			
	Cash	+ Accts. Rec.	+	Office Equip.	=	Accounts Payable	+	M. Brown, Capital	−	M. Brown, Withdr.	+ Legal Fees	−	Expenses
A.	+$6,000							+$6,000					
Bal.	6,000				=			6,000					
B.	−600			+$ 600									
Bal.	5,400		+	600	=			6,000					
C.				+1,000		+$1,000							
Bal.	5,400		+	1,600	=	1,000	+	6,000					
D.	+2,000										+$2,000		
Bal.	7,400		+	1,600	=	1,000	+	6,000			+ 2,000		
E.	−800												+$ 800
Bal.	6,600		+	1,600	=	1,000	+	6,000			+ 2,000	−	800
F.		+$1,000									+1,000		
Bal.	6,600	+ 1,000	+	1,600	=	1,000	+	6,000			+ 3,000	−	800
G.	−1,200												+1,200
Bal.	5,400	+ 1,000	+	1,600	=	1,000	+	6,000			+ 3,000	−	2,000
H.	−500									+$500			
Bal.	4,900	+ 1,000	+	1,600	=	1,000	+	6,000	−	500	+ 3,000	−	2,000
I.	+500	−500											
End. Bal.	$5,400	+ $ 500	+	$1,600	=	$1,000	+	$ 6,000	−	$500	+ $3,000	−	$2,000
				$7,500	=	$7,500							

- **Transaction D:** Legal Fees, a subdivision of Owner's Equity, is increased when the law firm provides a service even if no money is received. The service provides an inward flow of $2,000 to Cash, an asset. Remember that Legal Fees is *not* an asset. As Legal Fees revenue increases, Owner's Equity increases. Keep in mind that revenue can provide an inflow of cash and/or accounts receivable. Cash and accounts receivable are assets. The revenue is part of Owner's Equity.

- **Transaction E:** The salary paid by Michael creates an $800 increase in Expenses and a corresponding decrease in Owner's Equity as well as a decrease in Cash. Keep in mind that as the expenses increase they do in fact lower Owner's Equity.

- **Transaction F:** Michael did the work and earned the $1,000. That $1,000 is recorded as revenue. This time the legal fees create an inward flow of assets called Accounts Receivable for $1,000. Remember that Legal Fees is *not* an asset. It is a subdivision of Owner's Equity.

- **Transaction G:** The $1,200 rent expense reduces Owner's Equity as well as Cash. Remember to think of expenses as increasing. This increase in expenses then causes Owner's Equity to decrease.

- **Transaction H:** Withdrawals are for personal use. Here the business decreases Cash by $500 while Michael's withdrawals increase by $500. Withdrawals decrease the Owner's Equity. Remember to think of withdrawals as increasing. This is the amount withdrawn by the owner for personal use, decreasing Owner's Equity.

- **Transaction I:** This transaction does not reflect new revenue in the form of Legal Fees. It is only a shift in assets: more Cash and less Accounts Receivable.

Requirement 2

Prepare the financial statements at June 30 for Michael Brown, Attorney-at-Law. Figures 1.8 and 1.9 show the completed statements for Michael.

Solutions to Preparing Financial Statements

A	MICHAEL BROWN, ATTORNEY-AT-LAW INCOME STATEMENT FOR MONTH ENDED JUNE 30, 201X		
Revenue:			
Legal Fees			$3,000
Operating Expenses:			
Salaries Expense		$ 800	
Rent Expense		1,200	
Total Operating Expenses			2,000
Net Income			$1,000

Figure 1.8
Michael Brown's Income Statement and Statement of Owner's Equity

B	MICHAEL BROWN, ATTORNEY-AT-LAW STATEMENT OF OWNER'S EQUITY FOR MONTH ENDED JUNE 30, 201X		
Michael Brown, Capital, June 1, 201X			$6,000*
Net income for June		$1,000	
Less: Withdrawls for June		− 500	
Increase in Capital			500
Michael Brown, Capital, June 30, 201X			$6,500

*No additional investments were made after the $6,000. The capital balance before the investment was 0.

Figure 1.9
Michael Brown's Balance Sheet

C	MICHAEL BROWN, ATTORNEY-AT-LAW BALANCE SHEET JUNE 30, 201X		
Assets		**Liabilities and Owner's Equity**	
Cash	$5,400	Liabilities	
Accounts Receivable	500	Accounts Payable	$ 1,000
Office Equipment	1,600	Owner's Equity	
		M. Brown, Capital	$6,500
Total Assets	$7,500	Total Liabilities and Owner's Equity	$7,500

Tips to Preparing Financial Statements

A. The income statement lists only revenues and expenses for a period of time. The inside column is for subtotaling. Withdrawals are not listed here.

B. The statement of owner's equity takes the net income figure of $1,000 and adds it to beginning capital less any withdrawals. This new capital figure of $6,500 will go on the balance sheet. This statement shows changes in capital for a period of time.

C. The $5,400, $500, $1,600 (Assets), and $1,000 (Liabilities) came from the totals of the expanded accounting equation. The capital figure of $6,500 came from the statement of owner's equity. This balance sheet reports assets, liabilities, and a new figure for capital at a specific date.

SUCCESS COACH

The following Success Tips are from Learning Units 1-1 through 1-4. Take the Do It Right Now Checkup and use the Check Your Score at the bottom of the page to see how you are doing. The Success Coach provides tips before each Checkup to help you avoid common accounting errors.

LU 1-1 Accounting, Business, and the Accounting Equation

Do It Right Tips: After a transaction is recorded in the accounting equation, the sum of all the assets must equal the total of all the liabilities and owner's equity.

Do It Right Now Checkup: Answer true or false to the following statements.

1. Capital is cash.
2. Accounts Payable is a liability.
3. A shift in assets means liabilities will increase.
4. Assets − Liabilities = Owner's Equity.
5. Assets represent what is owned by the business.

LU 1-2 The Balance Sheet

Do It Right Tips: The Balance Sheet is a formal report listing assets, liabilities, and owner's equity as of a particular date.

Do It Right Now Checkup: Answer true or false to the following statements.

1. Cash is a liability.
2. Office Equipment is an asset.
3. Accounts Payable is listed under assets.
4. Capital is listed under liabilities.
5. A heading of a financial report has no particular date.

LU 1-3 The Accounting Equation Expanded: Revenue, Expenses, and Withdrawals

Do It Right Tips: Revenue is recorded when earned even if cash is not received. Expenses are recorded when they happen (incurred) whether they are paid or to be paid later.

Do It Right Now Checkup: Answer true or false to the following statements.

1. Revenue is an asset.
2. Withdrawals increase owner's equity.
3. As expenses go down, owner's equity goes down.
4. An advertising bill incurred but unpaid is recorded as an increase in Advertising Expense and a decrease in a liability.
5. Revenue inflows can only be in the form of cash.

LU 1-4 The Three Financial Statements

Do It Right Tips: Net income from the income statement is used to update the statement of owner's equity. The ending figure for capital on the statement of owner's equity is the one used to update the balance sheet.

Do It Right Now Checkup: Answer true or false to the following statements.

1. Net income occurs when expenses are greater than revenue.
2. Withdrawals will reduce owner's capital on the income statement.
3. The balance sheet lists assets, liabilities, and expenses.
4. Withdrawals are listed on the income statement.
5. Assets are listed on the income statement.

CHECK YOUR SCORE: Answers to the Do It Right Now Checkup

LU 1-1
1. False—Capital represents the owner's claim to the assets.
2. True.
3. False—A shift in assets means liabilities will stay the same.
4. True.
5. True.

LU 1-2
1. False—Cash is an asset.
2. True.
3. False—Accounts Payable is listed under liabilities.
4. False—Capital is listed under owner's equity.
5. False—A heading of a financial report does have a particular date.

LU 1-3
1. False—Revenue is part of owner's equity.
2. False—Withdrawals decrease owner's equity.
3. False—As expenses go down, owner's equity goes up.
4. False—An advertising bill incurred but unpaid is recorded as an increase in Advertising Expense and an increase in liability.
5. False—Revenue inflows can be in the form of cash and/or accounts receivable.

LU 1-4
1. False—Net income occurs when expenses are less than revenue.
2. False—Withdrawals will reduce owner's capital on the statement of owner's equity.
3. False—Expenses are listed on the income statement.
4. False—Withdrawals are listed on the statement of owner's equity.
5. False—Assets are listed on the balance sheet.

BLUEPRINT: FINANCIAL STATEMENTS

❶ Income Statement

Measuring performance

Revenue:		XXX	
Operating Expenses	XX		
Other Expenses	XX	XXX	
Net Income		XXX	

❷ Statement of Owner's Equity

Calculating new figure for capital

Beginning Capital		XXX	
Additional Investments		XXX	
Total Investments		XXX	
Net Income (or loss)	XXX		
Less: Withdrawals	XXX		
Increase in Capital (or decrease)		XXX	
Ending Capital		XXX	

❸ Balance Sheet

Where do we now stand?

Assets			Liabilities and Owner's Equity	
		XXX	Liabilities	XXX
		XXX	Owner's Equity	
		XXX	Ending Capital	XXX
Total Assets		XXX	Total Liab. + OE	XXX

Discussion Questions and Critical Thinking/Ethical Case

1. What are the functions of accounting?

2. Define, compare, and contrast sole proprietorships, partnerships, and corporations.

3. How are businesses classified?

4. How has technology affected the role of the bookkeeper?

5. List the three elements of the basic accounting equation.

6. Define *capital*.

7. The total of the left-hand side of the accounting equation must equal the total of the right-hand side. True or false? Please explain.

8. A balance sheet tells a company where it is going and how well it performs. True or false? Please explain.

9. Revenue is an asset. True or false? Please explain.

10. Owner's equity is subdivided into what categories?

11. A withdrawal is a business expense. True or false? Please explain.

12. As expenses increase they cause owner's equity to increase. Defend or reject.

13. What does an income statement show?

14. The statement of owner's equity only calculates ending withdrawals. True or false? Please explain.

15. Paul Kloss, accountant for Lowe & Co., traveled to New York on company business. His total expenses came to $350. Paul felt that because the trip extended over the weekend he would "pad" his expense account with an additional $100 of expenses. After all, weekends represent his own time, not the company's. What would you do? Write your specific recommendations to Paul.

Concept Checks

MyLabAccounting

Classifying Accounts

1. Classify each of the following items as an Asset (A), Liability (L), or part of Owner's Equity (OE).

L01 *(5 min)*

    a. iPad   _____

    b. Accounts Receivable   _____

    c. Accounts Payable   _____

    d. Smartphone   _____

    e. B. Long, Capital   _____

    f. Cash   _____

The Accounting Equation

2. Complete the following statements.

L01 *(5 min)*

    a. _____: rights of the creditors

    b. _____ are total value of items owned by a business.

    c. _____ _____ is an unwritten promise to pay the creditor.

Shift versus Increase in Assets

(5 min) **LO1**

3. Identify which transaction results in a shift in assets (S) and which transaction causes an increase in assets (I).

    a. Target bought computer equipment on account.

    b. Macy's bought office equipment for cash.

The Balance Sheet

(5 min) **LO2**

4. From the following, calculate what would be the total of assets on the balance sheet.

B. Fleese, Capital	$40,000
Computer Equipment	20,000
Accounts Payable	6,000
Cash	26,000

The Accounting Equation Expanded

(5 min) **LO3**

5. From the following, which are subdivisions of owner's equity?

    a. Smartphone   _____

    b. J. Penny, Capital   _____

    c. Accounts Payable   _____

    d. J. Penny, Withdrawals   _____

    e. Accounts Receivable   _____

    f. Advertising Expense   _____

    g. Taxi Fees Earned   _____

    h. Microsoft Tablet   _____

Identifying Assets

(5 min) **LO2**

6. Identify which of the following are *not* assets.

    a. Sony DVD Player   _____

    b. Accounts Receivable   _____

    c. Accounts Payable   _____

    d. Grooming Fees Earned   _____

The Accounting Equation Expanded

(5 min) **LO3**

7. Which of the following statements are false?

    a. _____ Revenue provides only outward flows of cash.

    b. _____ Revenue is a subdivision of Assets.

    c. _____ Revenue provides an inward flow of cash or accounts receivable.

    d. _____ Expenses are part of Total Assets.

Preparing Financial Statements

8. Indicate whether the following items would appear on the income statement (IS), statement of owner's equity (OE), or balance sheet (BS).

 **L04** *(5 min)*

a. _____ Tutoring Fees Earned

b. _____ Office Equipment

c. _____ Accounts Receivable

d. _____ Office Supplies

e. _____ Legal Fees Earned

f. _____ Advertising Expenses

g. _____ J. Earl, Capital (Beg.)

h. _____ Accounts Payable

Preparing Financial Statements

9. Indicate next to each statement whether it refers to the income statement (IS), statement of owner's equity (OE), or balance sheet (BS).

 **L04** *(5 min)*

a. _____ Withdrawals found on it

b. _____ List total of all assets

c. _____ Statement that is prepared last

d. _____ Statement listing net income

Exercises

MyLabAccounting

Set A

1A-1. Complete the following table:

 **L01** *(5 min)*

	Assets	=	Liabilities	+	Owner's Equity
a.	$17,500	=	?	+	$11,500
b.	?	=	$5,000	+	$60,000
c.	$15,000	=	$12,000	+	?

1A-2. Record the following transactions in the basic accounting equation. Treat each one separately.

 **L01** *(5 min)*

$$\text{Assets} = \text{Liabilities} + \text{Owner's Equity}$$

a. Morgan invests $124,000 in company.
b. Bought equipment for cash, $1,300.
c. Bought equipment on account, $900.

1A-3. From the following, prepare a balance sheet for Rabbitt Co. Cleaners at the end of September 201X: Cash, $67,000; Equipment, $7,000; Accounts Payable, $13,000; B. Rabbitt, Capital.

L02 *(10 min)*

1A-4. Record the following transactions in the expanded accounting equation. Do not calculate a running balance.

L03 *(15 min)*

Assets			=	Liabilities	+		Owner's Equity			
Cash	+ Accounts Receivable	+ Computer Equipment	=	Accounts Payable	+	B. Baker, Capital	− B. Baker, Withdrawals	+ Revenues	− Expenses

a. Baker invested $80,000 in a computer company.
b. Bought computer equipment on account, $4,000.
c. Baker paid personal telephone bill from company checkbook, $125.
d. Received cash for services rendered, $13,600.
e. Billed customers for services rendered for month, $30,000.
f. Paid current rent expense, $4,100.
g. Paid supplies expense, $1,490.

(20 min) **LO4** ▶ **1A-5.** From the following account balances, prepare in proper form for June (a) an income statement, (b) a statement of owner's equity, and (c) a balance sheet for Freeman Realty.

Cash	$5,200	S. Freeman, Withdrawals	$ 225
Accounts Receivable	1,370	Professional Fees	3,100
Office Equipment	11,500	Salaries Expense	450
Accounts Payable	6,000	Utilities Expense	150
S. Freeman, Capital, June 1, 201X	10,245	Rent Expense	450

Set B

(5 min) **LO1** ▶ **1B-1.** Complete the following table:

	Assets	=	Liabilities	+	Owner's Equity
a.	$19,000	=	?	+	$13,000
b.	?	=	$ 4,000	+	$96,000
c.	$45,000	=	$10,000	+	?

(5 min) **LO1** ▶ **1B-2.** Record the following transactions in the basic accounting equation. Treat each one separately.

$$\text{Assets} = \text{Liabilities} + \text{Owner's Equity}$$

a. Melody invests $128,000 in company.
b. Bought equipment for cash, $1,650.
c. Bought equipment on account, $1,200.

(10 min) **LO2** ▶ **1B-3.** From the following, prepare a balance sheet for Rauscher Co. Cleaners at the end of November 201X: Cash, $65,000; Equipment, $10,000; Accounts Payable, $29,000; B. Rauscher, Capital.

(15 min) **LO3** ▶ **1B-4.** Record the following transactions in the expanded accounting equation. Do not calculate a running balance.

Assets			=	Liabilities	+		Owner's Equity			
Cash	+ Accounts Receivable	+ Computer Equipment	=	Accounts Payable	+	B. Beadell, Capital	− B. Beadell, Withdrawals	+ Revenues	− Expenses

a. Beadell invested $65,000 in a computer company.
b. Bought computer equipment on account, $7,500.
c. Beadell paid personal telephone bill from company checkbook, $225.
d. Received cash for services rendered, $13,500.
e. Billed customers for services rendered for month, $29,600.
f. Paid current rent expense, $3,800
g. Paid supplies expense, $1,530.

1B-5. From the following account balances, prepare in proper form for November (a) an income statement, (b) a statement of owner's equity, and (c) a balance sheet for Fairmont Realty.

 **L04** *(20 min)*

Cash	$4,500	S. Fairmont, Withdrawals	$ 175
Accounts Receivable	1,490	Professional Fees	4,000
Office Equipment	13,000	Salaries Expense	300
Accounts Payable	6,000	Utilities Expense	250
S. Fairmont, Capital, Nov. 1, 201X	10,015	Rent Expense	300

Problems

MyLab**Accounting**

Set A

1A-1. Melody Abington decided to open Melody's Nail Spa. Melody completed the following transactions:

L01 *(15 min)*

a. Invested $19,000 cash from her personal bank account into the business.
b. Bought store equipment for cash, $3,400.
c. Bought additional store equipment on account, $6,100.
d. Paid $1,200 cash to partially reduce what was owed from Transaction C.

Based on this information, record these transactions into the basic accounting equation.

Check Figure:
Cash $14,400

1A-2. Bob Simon is the accountant for Simon's Internet Service. From the following information, his task is to construct a balance sheet as of November 30, 201X, in proper form. Could you help him?

L02 *(15 min)*

Building	$30,000	Cash	$45,000
Accounts Payable	16,500	Equipment	24,000
B. Simon, Capital	82,500		

Check Figure:
Total Assets $99,000

1A-3. At the end of June, Rob Falco decided to open his own computer service. Analyze the following transactions he completed by recording their effects in the expanded accounting equation.

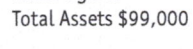 **L03** *(20 min)*

a. Invested $40,000 in his computer service.
b. Bought new computer equipment on account, $6,500.
c. Received cash for computer services rendered, $1,300.
d. Performed computer services on account, $2,200.
e. Paid secretary's salary, $325.
f. Paid office supplies expense for the month, $220.
g. Rent expenses for office due but unpaid, $800.
h. Withdrew cash for personal use, $300.

Check Figure:
Total Assets $49,155

(30 min) **L04**

1A-4. Jackie Wengler, owner of Wengler Home Decorating Service, has requested that you prepare from the following balances (a) an income statement for June 201X, (b) a statement of owner's equity for June, and (c) a balance sheet as of June 30, 201X.

Cash	$2,300	Home Decorating Fees	$2,400
Accounts Receivable	1,200	Advertising Expense	145
Decorating Equipment	1,155	Repair Expense	55
Accounts Payable	250	Travel Expense	250
J. Wengler, Capital, June 1, 201X	3,885	Supplies Expense	55
J. Wengler, Withdrawals	1,000	Rent Expense	375

Check Figure:
Total Liabilities and Owner's Equity
$4,655

(45 min) **L03,4**

1A-5. Joe Truman, a retired army officer, opened Truman's Catering Service. As his accountant, analyze the transactions listed next and present them in proper form.

a. The analysis of the transactions by using the expanded accounting equation.
b. A balance sheet showing the position of the firm before opening for business on May 31, 201X.
c. An income statement for the month of June.
d. A statement of owner's equity for June.
e. A balance sheet as of June 30, 201X.

201X	
May 25	Joe Truman invested $33,000 in the catering business from his personal savings account.
27	Bought equipment for cash from Connelley Co., $1,600.
28	Bought additional equipment on account from Keegan Co., $2,100.
29	Paid $200 to Keegan Co. as partial payment of the May 28 transaction.

Check Figure:
Total Assets, June 30 $38,785

(You should now prepare your balance sheet as of May 31, 201X.)

June 1	Catered a graduation and immediately collected cash, $2,400.
5	Paid salaries of employees, $690.
8	Prepared desserts for customers on account, $175.
10	Received $120 cash as partial payment of June 8 transaction.
15	Paid telephone bill, $60.
17	Paid his home electric bill from the company's checkbook, $90.
20	Catered a wedding and received cash, $1,900.
25	Bought additional equipment on account, $800.
28	Rent expense due but unpaid, $500.
30	Paid supplies expense, $550.

Set B

(15 min) **L01**

1B-1. Madeline Abdul decided to open Madeline's Nail Spa. Madeline completed the following transactions:

a. Invested $17,000 cash from her personal bank account into the business.
b. Bought store equipment for cash, $3,900.
c. Bought additional store equipment on account, $6,200.
d. Paid $800 cash to partially reduce what was owed from Transaction c.

Check Figure:
Ending Balance Cash $12,300

Based on this information, record these transactions into the basic accounting equation.

1B-2. Breck Sam is the accountant for Sam's Internet Service. From the following information, his task is to construct a balance sheet as of September 30, 201X, in proper form. Can you help him?

 **L02** *(15 min)*

Building	$45,000	Cash	5,000
Accounts Payable	15,500	Equipment	34,000
B. Sam, Capital	68,500		

Check Figure:
Total Assets $84,000

1B-3. At the end of April, Rich Fannier decided to open his own computer service. Analyze the following transactions he completed by recording their effects into the expanded accounting equation. Keep a running balance.

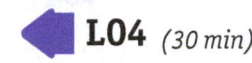 **L03** *(20 min)*

a. Invested $17,000 in his computer service business.
b. Bought new computer equipment on account, $5,000.
c. Received cash for computer services rendered, $700.
d. Performed computer services on account, $1,200.
e. Paid secretary's salary, $300.
f. Paid office supplies expense for the month, $180.
g. Rent expenses for office due but unpaid, $1,000.
h. Withdrew cash for personal use, $800.

Check Figure:
Total Assets $22,620

1B-4. Jenn Wadden, owner of Wadden Home Decorating Service, has requested that you prepare from the following balances (a) an income statement for September 201X, (b) a statement of owner's equity for September, and (c) a balance sheet as of September 30, 201X.

 **L04** *(30 min)*

Cash	$2,500	Home Decorating Fees	$2,400
Accounts Receivable	550	Advertising Expense	250
Decorating Equipment	725	Repair Expense	40
Accounts Payable	935	Travel Expense	750
J. Wadden, Capital, Sept. 1, 201X	2,675	Supplies Expense	95
J. Wadden, Withdrawals	800	Rent Expense	300

Check Figure:
J. Wadden, Capital, $2,840
September 30, 201X

1B-5. Jim Trickett, a retired army officer, opened Trickett's Catering Service. As his accountant, analyze the transactions listed and present them in proper form.

 **L03,4**

a. The analysis of the transactions by using the expanded accounting equation.
b. A balance sheet showing the financial position of the firm before opening on October 31, 201X.
c. An income statement for the month of November.
d. A statement of owner's equity for November.
e. A balance sheet as of November 30, 201X.

201X	
Oct. 25	Jim Trickett invested $22,000 in the catering business from his personal savings account.
27	Bought equipment for cash from Codair Co., $700.
28	Bought additional equipment on account from Keegan Co., $2,100.
29	Paid $800 to Keegan Co. as partial payment of the October 28 transaction.

(You should now prepare your balance sheet as of October 31, 201X.)

Nov. 1	Catered a graduation and collected cash, $2,000.
5	Paid salaries of employees, $1,500.
8	Prepared desserts for customers on account, $150.
10	Received $100 cash as partial payment of November 8 transaction.
15	Paid telephone bill, $50.

17	Paid his home electric bill from the company's checkbook, $400.
20	Catered a wedding and received cash, $1,000.
25	Bought additional equipment on account, $400.
28	Rent expense due but unpaid, $550.
30	Paid supplies expense, $250.

Check Figure:
Total Liabilities and Owner's Equity
November 30 $24,650

(5 min) **L02**

Financial Report Problem

Reading Amazon's Annual Report

Go to https://tinyurl.com/slaterca14e to access Amazon's 2016 Annual Report.
   Find the balance sheet and calculate the following:
   How much did cash increase or decrease in 2016 from 2015?

MyLabAccounting

(45 min) **L03,4**

KEEPING IT REAL SUAREZ COMPUTER CENTER

The following problem continues from one chapter to the next, carrying the balances of each month forward. Each chapter focuses on the learning experience of the chapter, adds information as the business grows, and shows how critical the knowledge of accounting is to the performance of a business decision-maker.

Assignment

1. Set up an expanded accounting equation spreadsheet using the following accounts:

Assets	Liabilities	Owner's Equity
Cash	Accounts Payable	Falco, Capital
Supplies		Falco, Withdrawal
Computer Shop Equipment		Service Revenue
Office Equipment		Expenses (notate type)

2. Analyze and record each transaction in the expanded accounting equation. Keep a running balance.

3. Prepare the financial statements ending July 31 for Suarez Computer Center.

   On July 1, 201X, Troy Falco decided to start his own computer service business. He named the business the Suarez Computer Center. During the first month, Troy conducted the following business transactions:

a. Invested $12,500 of his savings into the business.

b. Paid $1,260 (check #8095) for a computer from Hardware Haven, Inc.

c. Paid $1,500 (check #8096) for office equipment from In Office Furniture, Inc.

d. Set up a new account with Nuts and Bolts and purchased $500 in office supplies on credit.

e. Paid July rent, $800 (check #8097).

f. Repaired a system for a customer and collected $1,000.

g. Collected $700 for system upgrade labor charge from a customer.

h. Electric bill due but unpaid, $100.

i. Collected $1,400 for services performed on Viral Video computers.

j. Withdrew $1,500 (check #8098) to take his wife, Carol, out in celebration of opening the new business.

Debits and Credits: Analyzing and Recording Business Transactions

2

CHAPTER PREVIEW: ACCOUNTING IN ACTION

Bobby Tran was ordering pizza on his phone by using the new Domino's ordering app. As an accounting student, Bobby wondered how he could apply the accounting equation and the rules of debits and credits he had just learned to better explain how Domino's is accurately reporting its financial activities, even in this age of rapid technological change. In this chapter, we learn how businesses—both small and large—like Domino's are required to use the accounting equation to ensure it balances. By following the rules associated with the accounting equation, investors and creditors, when reviewing financial statements, can have confidence that businesses like Domino's are accurately reporting their financial activities.

Learning Objectives – Relating Accounting Theory By Unit

LO1 Explain T Accounts and How to Foot and Balance

LO2 Use a Chart of Accounts to Record Transactions in T Accounts According to the Rules of Debits and Credits

LO3 Prepare a Trial Balance and the Financial Statements

In Chapter 1 we used the expanded accounting equation to document the financial transactions performed by Jess Bora's computer consulting firm. Remember how long it was? The cash column has a long list of pluses and minuses, with no quick system of recording and summarizing the increases and decreases of cash or other items. Can you imagine the problem Domino's would have if it used the expanded accounting equation to track the thousands of business transactions it makes each day?

LEARNING UNIT 2-1

L01

Account Accounting device used in bookkeeping to record increases and decreases of business transactions relating to individual assets, liabilities, capital, withdrawals, revenue, expenses, and so on.

Standard account Formal account that includes columns for date, explanation, posting reference, debit, and credit.

Ledger Group of accounts that records data from business transactions.

T account Skeleton version of a standard account, used for demonstration purposes.

The T Account and How to Foot and Balance

Let's look at the problem a little more closely. Each business transaction is recorded in the accounting equation under a specific account. Different accounts are used for each of the subdivisions of the accounting equation: asset accounts, liability accounts, expense accounts, revenue accounts, and so on. What is needed is a way to record the increases and decreases in specific account *categories* and yet keep them together in one place. The answer is the standard account form (see Figure 2.1). A standard account is a formal account that includes columns for date, explanation, posting reference (PR), debit, and credit. Each account has a separate form, and all transactions affecting that account are recorded on the form. All the business's account forms (which often are referred to as *ledger accounts*) are then placed in a ledger. Each page of the ledger, or tab of the electronic file, contains one account. If computers are used, the ledger may be part of a computer file. For simplicity's sake, we use the T account form. This form got its name because it looks like the letter *T*. Generally, T accounts are used for demonstration purposes. Each T account contains three basic parts:

1

Title of Account

2 Left side | Right side **3**

All T accounts have this structure.

In accounting, the left side of any T account is called the debit side.

Left side

Dr. (debit)

Just as the word *left* has many meanings, the word *debit* for now in accounting means a position, the left side of an account. Do not think of it as good (+) or bad (−).

Amounts entered on the left side of any account are said to be *debited* to an account. The abbreviation for debit, *Dr.*, is from the Latin *debere*.

The right side of any T account is called the credit side.

Debit Left-hand side of any account. A number entered on the left side of any account is said to be debited to an account.

Credit Right-hand side of any account. A number entered on the right side of any account is said to be credited to an account.

Right side

Cr. (credit)

Amounts entered on the right side of an account are said to be *credited* to an account. The abbreviation for credit, *Cr.*, is from the Latin *credere*.

At this point do not associate the definition of debit and credit with the words *increase* or *decrease*. Think of debit or credit as only indicating a *position* (left or right side) of a T account.

Balancing an Account

No matter which individual account is being balanced, the procedure used to balance it is the same.

Account Title								Account No.
Date	Item	PR	Debit	Date	Item	PR	Credit	

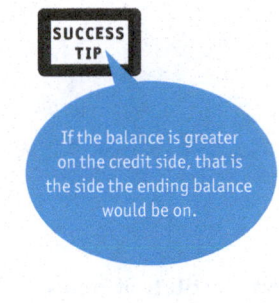

Figure 2.1
The Standard Account Form Is the Source of the T Account's Shape

SUCCESS TIP

If the balance is greater on the credit side, that is the side the ending balance would be on.

		Dr.	Cr.
Entries	→	5,000	400
		600	500
Footings	→	5,600	900
Balance		4,700	

In the "real" world, the T account would also include the date of the transaction.

		Dr.	Cr.	
4/2		5,000	400	4/3
4/20		600	500	4/25
		5,600	900	
Bal		4,700		

Note that on the debit (left) side the numbers add up to $5,600. On the credit (right) side the numbers add up to $900. The $5,600 and the $900 written in small type are called footings. Footings help in calculating the new (or ending) balance. The ending balance $4,700 is placed on the debit or left side because the balance of the debit side is greater than that of the credit side.

Remember that the ending balance does not tell us anything about increase or decrease. It only tells us that we have an ending balance of $4,700 on the debit side.

Footings Totals of each side of a T account.

Ending balance Difference between footings in a T account.

 **TRY IT!**   **Learning Unit 2-1**

From the following cash T account, prepare footings and calculate the ending balance:

		Cash		
		Dr.	Cr.	
4/4		16,000	400	4/6
4/24		12,000	700	4/18

TRY IT!   **Solution Learning Unit 2-1**

		Cash		
		Dr.	Cr.	
4/4		16,000	400	4/6
4/24		12,000	700	4/18
		28,000	1,100	
BAL		26,900		

LEARNING UNIT 2-2

LO2

The Chart of Accounts: Recording Transactions In T Accounts According to Rules of Debits and Credits

Can you get a checkmate in poker? In a soccer game, can a player pick up the ball and throw it into the opponent's net? No. Most of us don't do such things because we follow the rules of the game. Usually we learn the rules first and reflect on the reasons for them afterward. Today people write emails instead of letters, but the rules of grammar still apply; thus, formats may change, but certain rules still need to be followed. The same is true in accounting.

Instead of first trying to understand all the rules of debit and credit and how they were developed in accounting, it is easier to learn the rules by "playing the game."

T Account Entries for Accounting in the Accounting Equation

Have patience. Learning the rules of debit and credit is like learning to play any game: The more you play, the easier it becomes. Table 2.1 shows the rules for the side on which you enter an increase or a decrease for each of the separate account categories in the accounting equation. For example, an increase is entered on the debit side in the asset account but on the credit side for a liability account.

American Institute of Professional Bookkeepers (AIPB) – AIPB, established in 1987, has created a high-level certification for bookkeepers, and provides job opportunities on its free Jobs Site, which is devoted exclusively to the bookkeeping profession. More on the AIPB can found at **https://www.aipb.org**

TABLE 2.1 Rules of Debit and Credit

Account Category	Increase (Normal Balance)	Decrease
Assets	Debit	Credit
Liabilities	Credit	Debit
Owner's Equity		
Capital	Credit	Debit
Withdrawals	Debit	Credit
Revenue	Credit	Debit
Expenses	Debit	Credit

It might be easier to visualize these rules of debit and credit if we look at them in the T account form, using + to show increase and − to show decrease.

Assets	=	Liabilities	+	Owner's Equity				
				Capital −	**Withdrawals** +	**Revenue** −	**Expenses**	
Dr. | Cr.		Dr. | Cr.	+	Dr. | Cr.	Dr. | Cr.	Dr. | Cr.	Dr. | Cr.	
+ | −		− | +		− | +	+ | −	− | +	+ | −	

In a computerized accounting system, like QuickBooks, the computer will record the debits and credits based on the account type.

Rules for Assets Work in the Opposite Direction to Those for Liabilities. When you look at the equation you can see that the rules for assets work in the opposite direction than those for liabilities. That is, for assets the increases appear on the debit side and the decreases are shown on the credit side; the opposite is true for liabilities. As for the owner's equity, the rules for withdrawals and expenses, which *decrease* owner's equity, work in the opposite direction than the rules for capital and revenue, which *increase* owner's equity.

Normal Balance

Dr.	Cr.
Assets	Liabilities
Withdrawals	Capital
Expenses	Revenue

Assets +	**Withdrawals** +	**Expenses** =	**Liabilities** +	**Capital** +	**Revenue**
Dr. | Cr.	Dr. | Cr.	Dr. | Cr.	Dr. | Cr.	Dr. | Cr.	Dr. | Cr.
+ | −	+ | −	+ | −	− | +	− | +	− | +

This setup may help you visualize how the rules for withdrawals and expenses are just the opposite of those for capital and revenue.

A normal balance of an account is the side that increases by the rules of debit and credit. For example, the normal balance of cash is a debit balance because an asset is increased by a debit. We discuss normal balances further in Chapter 3.

Normal balance of an account Side of an account that increases by the rules of debit and credit.

Balancing the Equation. It is important to remember that any amount(s) entered on the debit side of a T account or accounts also must appear on the credit side of another T account or accounts. This approach ensures that the total amount added to the debit side will equal the total amount added to the credit side, thereby keeping the accounting equation in balance.

Chart of Accounts. Our job is to analyze Jess Bora's business transactions—the transactions we looked at in Chapter 1—using a system of accounts guided by the rules of debit and credit that will summarize increases and decreases of individual accounts in the ledger. The goal is to prepare an income statement, statement of owner's equity, and balance sheet for Jess Bora's business. Sound familiar? If this system works, the rules of debit and credit and the use of accounts will give us the same answers as in Chapter 1, but with greater ease.

Jess's accountant developed what is called a chart of accounts. The chart of accounts is a numbered list of all of the business's accounts. It allows accounts to be located quickly. In Jess's business, for example, 100s are assets, 200s are liabilities, and so on. As you see in Table 2.2, each separate asset and liability account has its own number. Note that the chart may be expanded as the business grows.

Chart of accounts Numbering system of accounts that lists the account titles and account numbers to be used by a company.

TABLE 2.2 Chart of Accounts for Jess Bora's Consulting Firm

Balance Sheet Accounts	
Assets	**Liabilities**
111 Cash	211 Accounts Payable
112 Accounts Receivable	**Owner's Equity**
121 Computer Equipment	311 Jess Bora, Capital
	312 Jess Bora, Withdrawals
Income Statement Accounts	
Revenue	**Expenses**
411 Consulting Fees	511 Salaries Expense
	512 Rent Expense
	513 Advertising Expense

The Transaction Analysis: Five Steps

We analyze the transactions in Jess Bora's consulting firm using a teaching device called a *transaction analysis chart* to record these five steps. (Keep in mind that the transaction analysis chart is not a part of any formal accounting system.) The five steps to analyzing each business transaction include:

STEP 1: Determine which accounts are affected. Example: Cash, Accounts Payable, Rent Expense. A transaction always affects at least two accounts.

STEP 2: Determine which categories the accounts belong to: assets, liabilities, capital, withdrawals, revenue, or expenses. Example: Cash is an asset.

STEP 3: Determine whether the accounts increase or decrease. Example: If you receive cash, that account increases.

STEP 4: What do the rules of debit and credit say (Table 2.1)?

STEP 5: What does the T account look like? Place amounts into accounts either on the left or right side depending on the rules in Table 2.1.

SUCCESS TIP

Remember that the rules of debit and credit only tell us on which side to place information. Whether the debit or credit represents increases or decreases depends on the account category.

The following chart shows the five-step analysis from another perspective.

1	2	3	4	5
		↓ ↑		**Appearance of**
Accounts Affected	**Category**	**(decrease) (increase)**	**Rules of Dr. and Cr.**	**T Accounts**

Let us emphasize a major point: *Do not try to debit or credit an account until you go through the first three steps of the transaction analysis.*

Applying the Transaction Analysis to Jess Bora's Consulting Firm

Transaction A Aug. 28: Jess Bora invests $6,000 cash and $200 of computer equipment in the business.

SUCCESS TIP

Note that in column 3 of the chart it doesn't matter if all three arrows are going up, as long as the sum of the debits equals the sum of the credits in the T accounts in column 5.

1	2	3	4	5
Accounts Affected	**Category**	↓ ↑	**Rules of Dr. and Cr.**	**Appearance of T Accounts**
Cash	Asset	↑	Dr.	Cash 111
				(A) 6,000 |
Computer Equipment	Asset	↑	Dr.	Computer Equipment 121
				(A) 200 |
Jess Bora , Capital	Capital	↑	Cr.	Jess Bora, Capital 311
				| 6,200 (A)

Note again that every transaction affects at least two T accounts and that the total amount added to the debit side(s) must equal the total amount added to the credit side(s) of the T accounts of each transaction.

Analysis of Transaction A

STEP 1: Which accounts are affected? The computer consulting firm receives its cash and computer equipment, so three accounts are involved: Cash, Computer Equipment, and Jess Bora, Capital. These account titles come from the chart of accounts.

STEP 2: Which categories do these accounts belong to? Cash and Computer Equipment are assets. Jess Bora, Capital is capital.

STEP 3: Are the accounts increasing or decreasing? Cash and Computer Equipment, both assets, are increasing in the business. The rights or claims of Jess Bora, Capital are also increasing because he invested money and computer equipment in the business.

STEP 4: What do the rules say? According to the rules of debit and credit, an increase in assets (Cash and Computer Equipment) is a debit. An increase in Capital is a credit. Note that the total dollar amount of debits will equal the total dollar amount of credits when the T accounts are updated in column 5.

STEP 5: What does the T account look like? The amount for Cash and Computer Equipment is entered on the debit side. The amount for Jess Bora, Capital goes on the credit side.

Compound entry Transaction involving more than one debit or credit.

A transaction that involves more than one debit or more than one credit is called a compound entry. This first transaction of Jess Bora's consulting firm is a compound entry; it involves a debit of $6,000 to Cash and a debit of $200 to Computer Equipment (as well as a credit of $6,200 to Jess Bora, Capital).

The name for this double-entry analysis of transactions, where two or more accounts are affected and the total of debits and credits is equal, is double-entry bookkeeping. This double-entry system helps in checking the recording of business transactions.

As we continue, the explanations will be brief, but do not forget to apply the five steps in analyzing and recording each business transaction.

Double-entry bookkeeping
Accounting system in which the recording of each transaction affects two or more accounts and the total of the debits is equal to the total of the credits.

Transaction B Aug. 29: Computer consulting firm bought computer equipment for cash, $500.

1 Accounts Affected	2 Category	3 ↓↑	4 Rules of Dr. and Cr.	5 T Account Update
Computer Equipment	Asset	↑	Dr.	Computer Equipment 121
				(A) 200
				(B) 500
Cash	Asset	↓	Cr.	Cash 111
				(A) 6,000 │ 500 (B)

Analysis of Transaction B

STEP 1: The computer consulting firm paid $500 cash for the computer equipment it purchased. The accounts involved in the transaction are Cash and Computer Equipment.

STEP 2: The accounts belong to these categories: Computer Equipment is an asset; Cash is an asset.

STEP 3: The asset Computer Equipment is increasing. The asset Cash is decreasing; it is being reduced to buy the computer equipment.

STEP 4: An increase in the asset Computer Equipment is a debit; a decrease in the asset Cash is a credit.

STEP 5: When the amounts are placed in the T accounts, the amount for Computer Equipment is entered on the debit side and the amount for Cash on the credit side.

Transaction C Aug. 30: Bought more computer equipment on account, $300.

1 Accounts Affected	2 Category	3 ↓↑	4 Rules of Dr. and Cr.	5 T Account Update
Computer Equipment	Asset	↑	Dr.	Computer Equipment 121
				(A) 200
				(B) 500
				(C) 300
Accounts Payable	Liability	↑	Cr.	Accounts Payable 211
				│ 300 (C)

Analysis of Transaction C

STEP 1: The computer consulting firm receives computer equipment totaling $300 by promising to pay in the future. An obligation or liability, Accounts Payable, is created. The accounts affected are Computer Equipment and Accounts Payable.

STEP 2: Computer Equipment is an asset. Accounts Payable is a liability.

STEP 3: The asset Computer Equipment is increasing; the liability Accounts Payable is increasing because the consulting firm is increasing what it owes.

STEP 4: An increase in the asset Computer Equipment is a debit. An increase in the liability Accounts Payable is a credit.

STEP 5: Enter the amount for Computer Equipment on the debit side of the T account. The amount for Accounts Payable goes on the credit side.

Transaction D Sept. 1–30: Provided consulting services for cash, $2,000.

1 Accounts Affected	2 Category	3 ↓↑	4 Rules of Dr. and Cr.	5 T Account Update			
Cash	Asset	↑	Dr.	Cash 111			
				(A)	6,000	500	(B)
				(D)	2,000		
Consulting Fees	Revenue	↑	Cr.	Consulting Fees 411			
						2,000	(D)

Analysis of Transaction D

STEP 1: The firm earned revenue from consulting services and received $2,000 in cash. The accounts affected are Consulting Fees and Cash.

STEP 2: Cash is an asset. Consulting Fees is revenue.

STEP 3: Cash, an asset, is increasing. Consulting Fees, or revenue, is also increasing.

STEP 4: An increase in Cash, an asset, is debited. An increase in Consulting Fees, or revenue, is credited.

STEP 5: Enter the amount for Cash on the debit side of the T account. Enter the amount for Consulting Fees on the credit side.

Transaction E Sept. 1–30: Provided consulting services on account, $3,000.

1 Accounts Affected	2 Category	3 ↓↑	4 Rules of Dr. and Cr.	5 T Account Update			
Accounts Receivable	Asset	↑	Dr.	Accounts Receivable 112			
				(E)	3,000		
Consulting Fees	Revenue	↑	Cr.	Consulting Fees 411			
						2,000	(D)
						3,000	(E)

Analysis of Transaction E

STEP 1: The computer consulting firm has earned revenue of $3,000 but has not yet received payment (cash). The amounts owed by these clients are called Accounts Receivable. Revenue is earned at the time the consulting services are provided, regardless of whether payment is received then or will be received some time in the future. The accounts affected are Accounts Receivable and Consulting Fees.

STEP 2: Accounts Receivable is an asset. Consulting Fees are revenue.

STEP 3: Accounts Receivable is increasing because the computer consulting firm increased the amount owed to it for consulting fees earned but not yet received. Consulting Fees, or revenue, is increasing.

STEP 4: An increase in the asset Accounts Receivable is a debit. An increase in Consulting Fees is a credit.

STEP 5: Enter the amount for Accounts Receivable on the debit side of the T account. The amount for Consulting Fees goes on the credit side.

Transaction F Sept. 1–30: Received $900 cash from clients for services rendered previously on account.

---

1 Accounts Affected	2 Category	3 ↓↑	4 Rules of Dr. and Cr.	5 T Account Update
Cash	Asset	↑	Dr.	Cash 111
				(A) 6,000 | 500 (B) (D) 2,000 | (F) 900 |
Accounts Receivable	Asset	↓	Cr.	Accounts Receivable 112
				(E) 3,000 | 900 (F)

Analysis of Transaction F

STEP 1: The consulting firm collects $900 in cash from previous revenue earned. Because the revenue is recorded at the time it is earned, and not when the collection is received, in this transaction we are concerned only with the collection, which affects the Cash and Accounts Receivable accounts.

STEP 2: Cash is an asset. Accounts Receivable is an asset.

STEP 3: Because clients are paying what is owed, Cash (asset) is increasing and the amount owed (Accounts Receivable) is decreasing (the total amount owed by clients to Bora is going down). This transaction results in a shift in assets, more Cash for less Accounts Receivable.

STEP 4: An increase in Cash, an asset, is a debit. A decrease in Accounts Receivable, an asset, is a credit.

STEP 5: Enter the amount for Cash on the debit side of the T account. The amount for Accounts Receivable goes on the credit side.

Transaction G Sept. 1–30: Paid salaries expense, $700.

1	2	3	4	5
Accounts Affected	**Category**	**↓↑**	**Rules of Dr. and Cr.**	**T Account Update**
Salaries Expense	Expense	↑	Dr.	Salaries Expense 511
				(G) 700	
Cash	Asset	↓	Cr.	Cash 111
				(A) 6,000	500 (B)
				(D) 2,000	700 (G)
				(F) 900	

Analysis of Transaction G

STEP 1: The consulting firm pays $700 of salaries expense by cash. The accounts affected are Salaries Expense and Cash.

STEP 2: Salaries Expense is an expense. Cash is an asset.

STEP 3: The Salaries Expense of the consulting firm is increasing, which results in a decrease in Cash.

STEP 4: An increase in Salaries Expense, an expense, is a debit. A decrease in Cash, an asset, is a credit.

STEP 5: Enter the amount for Salaries Expense on the debit side of the T account. The amount for Cash goes on the credit side.

Transaction H Sept. 1–30: Paid rent expense, $400.

1	2	3	4	5
Accounts Affected	**Category**	**↓↑**	**Rules of Dr. and Cr.**	**T Account Update**
Rent Expense	Expense	↑	Dr.	Rent Expense 512
				(H) 400	
Cash	Asset	↓	Cr.	Cash 111
				(A) 6,000	500 (B)
				(D) 2,000	700 (G)
				(F) 900	400 (H)

Analysis of Transaction H

STEP 1: The consulting firm's rent expense of $400 is paid in cash. The accounts affected are Rent Expense and Cash.

STEP 2: Rent is an expense. Cash is an asset.

STEP 3: The Rent Expense increases the expenses, and the payment for the Rent Expense decreases the cash.

STEP 4: An increase in Rent Expense, an expense, is a debit. A decrease in Cash, an asset, is a credit.

STEP 5: Enter the amount for Rent Expense on the debit side of the T account. Place the amount for Cash on the credit side.

Transaction I Sept. 1–30: Received a bill for Advertising Expense (to be paid next month), $200.

1	2	3	4	5
Accounts Affected	Category	↓↑	Rules of Dr. and Cr.	T Account Update
Advertising Expense	Expense	↑	Dr.	Advertising Expense 513
				(I) 200	
Accounts Payable	Liability	↑	Cr.	Accounts Payable 211
					300 (C)
					200 (I)

Analysis of Transaction I

STEP 1: The advertising bill in the amount of $200 has come in and payment is due but has not yet been made. Therefore, the accounts involved here are Advertising Expense and Accounts Payable; the expense has created a liability.

STEP 2: Advertising Expense is an expense. Accounts Payable is a liability.

STEP 3: Both the expense and the liability are increasing.

STEP 4: An increase in an expense is a debit. An increase in a liability is a credit.

STEP 5: Enter the amount for Advertising Expense on the debit side of the T account. Enter the amount for Accounts Payable on the credit side.

Transaction J Sept. 1-30: Bora withdrew cash for personal use, $100.

1	2	3	4	5
Accounts Affected	Category	↓↑	Rules of Dr. and Cr.	T Account Update
Jess Bora, Withdrawals	Withdrawals	↑	Dr.	Jess Bora, Withdrawals 312
				(J) 100	
Cash	Asset	↓	Cr.	Cash 111
				(A) 6,000	500 (B)
				(D) 2,000	700 (G)
				(F) 900	400 (H)
					100 (J)

Analysis of Transaction J

STEP 1: Jess Bora withdraws $100 cash from business for *personal* use. This withdrawal is not a business expense. The accounts affected are Jess Bora, Withdrawals and Cash.

STEP 2: This transaction affects Jess Bora, Withdrawals and Cash accounts.

STEP 3: Jess has increased what he has withdrawn from the business for personal use. The business cash decreased.

STEP 4: An increase in Withdrawals is a debit. A decrease in Cash is a credit. (*Remember:* Withdrawals go on the statement of owner's equity; expenses go on the income statement.)

STEP 5: Enter the amount for Jess Bora, Withdrawals, on the debit side of the T account. The amount for Cash goes on the credit side.

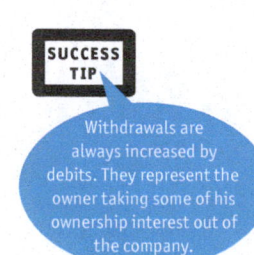

SUCCESS TIP

Withdrawals are always increased by debits. They represent the owner taking some of his ownership interest out of the company.

Summary of Transactions for Jess Bora

Assets	=	Liabilities	+	Owner's Equity					
				Capital −	**Withdrawals** +	**Revenue** −	**Expenses**		

Assets = **Liabilities** + **Owner's Equity**

Cash 111		=	Accounts Payable 211	+
(A) 6,000	500 (B)			
(D) 2,000	700 (G)		300 (C)	
(F) 900	400 (H)		200 (I)	
	100 (J)			

Capital −	Withdrawals +	Revenue −	Expenses
Jess Bora, Capital 311	Jess Bora, Withdrawals 312	Consulting Fees 411	Salaries Expense 511
6,200 (A)	(J) 100	2,000 (D)	(G) 700
		3,000 (E)	

Accounts Receivable 112	
(E) 3,000	900 (F)

Computer Equipment 121
(A) 200
(B) 500
(C) 300

− Rent Expense 512

(H) 400	

− Advertising Expense 513

(I) 200	

TRY IT!   Learning Unit 2-2

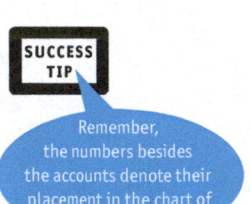

> **SUCCESS TIP**
> Remember, the numbers besides the accounts denote their placement in the chart of accounts.

Given the following partial chart of accounts for Eddie Mayer's law office, complete a transaction analysis box for Eddie's transactions below:

Cash 111

Accounts Receivable 112

Accounts Payable 211

Legal Fees 411

Legal Expenses 511

Transaction: Eddie completed legal work for $14,000. The client paid Eddie $1,000 in cash and promised to pay the balance next month.

TRY IT!   **Solution Learning Unit 2-2**

Acct. Affected	Cat.	Inc./Dec.	Rules	T Account
				Cash 111
Cash	Asset	Inc.	Dr.	1,000 Dr.
				Acc. Rec. 112
Acc. Receivable	Asset	Inc.	Dr.	13,000 Dr.
				Leg. Fees 411
Legal Fees	Revenue	Inc.	Cr.	14,000 Cr.

The Trial Balance and Preparation of Financial Statements

 **L03**

Let us look at all the transactions we have discussed, arranged by T accounts and recorded using the rules of debit and credit. This grouping of accounts is much easier to use than the expanded accounting equation because all the transactions that affect a particular account are in one place.

Summary of Transactions of Jess Bora's Computer Consulting Firm

Assets = Liabilities + Owner's Equity

Cash 111 = **Accounts Payable 211** + **Capital** − **Withdrawals** + **Revenue** − **Expenses**

Cash 111
(A) 6,000	500 (B)
(D) 2,000	700 (G)
(F) 900	400 (H)
	100 (J)
8,900	**1,700**
7,200	

Footings
New Balance

Accounts Payable 211
	300 (C)
	200 (I)
	500

Jess Bora, Capital 311
| | 6,200 (A) |

Jess Bora, Withdrawals 312
| (J) 100 | |

Consulting Fees 411
	2,000 (D)
	3,000 (E)
	5,000

Salaries Expenses 511
| (G) 700 | |

Rent Expense 512
| (H) 400 | |

Advertising Expense 513
| (I) 200 | |

Accounts Receivable 112
| (E) 3,000 | 900 (F) |
| **2,100** | |

Computer Equipment 121
(A) 200	
(B) 500	
(C) 300	
1,000	

As we saw in Learning Unit 2-2, when all the transactions are recorded in the accounts, the total of all the debits should be equal to the total of all the credits. (If they are not, the accountant must go back and find the error by checking the numbers and adding every column again.)

The Trial Balance

Trial balance List of the ending balances of all the accounts in a ledger. The total of the debits should equal the total of the credits.

Footings are used to obtain the totals of each side of every T account that has more than one entry. The footings are used to find the ending balance. The ending balances are used to prepare a trial balance. The trial balance is not a financial statement, although it is used to prepare financial statements. The trial balance lists all the accounts with their balances in the same order as they appear in the chart of accounts. It proves the accuracy of the ledger. For example, look at the preceding Cash account. The footing for the debit side is $8,900, and the footing for the credit side is $1,700. Because the debit side is larger, we subtract $1,700 from $8,900 to arrive at an *ending debit balance* of $7,200. Remember that the normal balance of an account is represented by that which increases it. Since debits represent an increase to an asset account, a debit would be the normal or expected balance of the cash account. Now look at the Rent Expense account. It doesn't need a footing because it has only one entry. The amount itself is the ending balance. When the ending balance has been found for every account, we should be able to show that the total of all debits equals the total of all credits.

In the ideal situation, businesses would take a trial balance every day. The large number of transactions most businesses conduct each day makes this impractical. Instead, trial balances are prepared periodically.

Keep in mind that the figure for Capital might not be the beginning figure if any additional investment has taken place during the period. You can tell by looking at the Capital account in the ledger.

A more detailed discussion of the trial balance is provided in the next chapter. For now, notice the heading, how the accounts are listed, the debits in the left column, the credits in the right, and that the total of debits is equal to the total of credits.

A trial balance of Jess Bora's accounts is shown in Figure 2.2.

Figure 2.2
Trial Balance for Jess Bora's Computer Consulting Firm.

JESS BORA, COMPUTER CONSULTING TRIAL BALANCE SEPTEMBER 30, 201X	Dr.	Cr.
Cash	7 2 0 0 0 0	
Accounts Receivable	2 1 0 0 0 0	
Computer Equipment	1 0 0 0 0 0	
Accounts Payable		5 0 0 0 0
Jess Bora, Capital		6 2 0 0 0 0
Jess Bora, Withdrawals	1 0 0 0 0	
Consulting Fees		5 0 0 0 0 0
Salaries Expense	7 0 0 0 0	
Rent Expense	4 0 0 0 0	
Advertising Expense	2 0 0 0 0	
Totals	11 7 0 0 0 0	11 7 0 0 0 0

Preparing Financial Statements

The trial balance is used to prepare the financial statements. The diagram in Figure 2.3 on page 45 shows how financial statements can be prepared from a trial balance. Statements do not have debit or credit columns. The left column is used only to subtotal numbers.

Figure 2.3 Steps in Preparing Financial Statements from a Trial Balance

JESS BORA, COMPUTER CONSULTING
INCOME STATEMENT
FOR MONTH ENDED SEPTEMBER 30, 201X

Revenue:		
Consulting Fees		$5 000 00
Operating Expenses:		
Salaries Expense	$7 000 00	
Rent Expense	4 000 00	
Advertising Expense	2 000 00	
Total Operating Expenses		1 300 00
Net Income		$3 700 00

JESS BORA, COMPUTER CONSULTING
TRIAL BALANCE
SEPTEMBER 30, 201X

	Dr.	Cr.
Cash	7 200 00	
Accounts Receivable	2 100 00	
Office Equipment	1 000 00	
Accounts Payable		500 00
Jess Bora, Capital		6 200 00
Jess Bora, Withdrawals	100 00	
Consulting Fees		5 000 00
Salaries Expense	700 00	
Rent Expense	400 00	
Advertising Expense	200 00	
Totals	11 700 00	11 700 00

JESS BORA, COMPUTER CONSULTING
STATEMENT OF OWNER'S EQUITY
FOR MONTH ENDED SEPTEMBER 30, 201X

Jess Bora, Capital		
September 1, 201X		$6 200 00
Net Income for September	$3 700 00	
Less: Withdrawals		
for September	–1 000 0	
Increase in Capital		3 600 00
Jess Bora, Capital		
September 30, 201X		$9 800 00

JESS BORA, COMPUTER CONSULTING
BALANCE SHEET
SEPTEMBER 30, 201X

Assets		Liabilities and Owner's Equity	
Cash	$7 200 00	Liabilities	
Accts. Receivable	2 100 00	Accounts Payable	$500 00
Computer Equipm.	1 000 00	Owner's Equity	
		Jess Bora, Capital	9 800 00
		Total Liab. and	
Total Assets	$10 300 00	Owner's Eq.	$10 300 00

▶ **TRY IT!** **Learning Unit 2-3**

From the following trial balance, prepare the three financial statements.

Hall's Gym
Trial Balance
Sept. 30, 201X

	Dr.	Cr.
Cash	1,250	
Accounts Receivable	450	
Gym Equipment	5,500	
Accounts Payable		1,200
Paul Hall, Capital		5,725
Paul Hall, Withdrawals	550	
Gym Fees		3,300
Rent Expense	1,100	
Advertising Expense	75	
Salaries Expense	1,300	
Totals	10,225	10,225

TRY IT! **Solution Learning Unit 2-3**

Hall's Gym
Income Statement for Month Ended
Sept. 30, 201X

Revenue:		
Gym Fees		$3,300
Operating Expenses:		
Rent Expense	$1,100	
Advertising Expense	75	
Salaries Expense	1,300	
Total Operating Expenses		2,475
Net Income		$ 825

Hall's Gym
Statement of Owner's Equity for Month Ended
Sept. 30, 201X

Paul Hall, Capital Sept. 1, 201X		$5,725
Net Income for Sept.	$825	
Less: Withdrawals for Sept.	−550	
Increase in Capital		275
Paul Hall, Capital Sept. 30, 201X		$6,000

Hall's Gym
Balance Sheet
Sept. 30, 201X

Assets		Liabilities and Owner's Equity	
Cash	$1,250	Liabilities	
Accts. Rec.	450	Accts. Payable	$1,200
Gym Equip.	5,500	Owner's Equity	
		P. Hall, Capital	6,000
Total Assets	$7,200	Total Liab. and Owner's Equity	$7,200

DEMONSTRATION SUMMARY PROBLEM

 **LO1,2,3**

The chart of accounts of Mel's Delivery Service includes the following: Cash, 111; Accounts Receivable, 112; Office Equipment, 121; Delivery Trucks, 122; Accounts Payable, 211; Mel Free, Capital, 311; Mel Free, Withdrawals, 312; Delivery Fees Earned, 411; Advertising Expense, 511; Gas Expense, 512; Salaries Expense, 513; and Telephone Expense, 514. The following transactions resulted for Mel's Delivery Service during the month of July:

Transaction A: Mel invested $10,000 in the business from his personal savings account.

Transaction B: Bought delivery trucks on account, $17,000.

Transaction C: Advertising bill received but unpaid, $700.

Transaction D: Bought office equipment for cash, $1,200.

Transaction E: Received cash for delivery services rendered, $15,000.

Transaction F: Paid salaries expense, $3,000.

Transaction G: Paid gas expense for company trucks, $1,250.

Transaction H: Billed customers for delivery services rendered, $4,000.

Transaction I: Paid telephone bill, $300.

Transaction J: Received $3,000 as partial payment of Transaction H.

Transaction K: Mel paid home telephone bill from company checkbook, $150.

Requirements

As Mel's newly employed accountant, you must do the following:

1. Set up T accounts in a ledger.
2. Record transactions in the T accounts. (Place the letter of the transaction next to the entry.)
3. Foot and take the balance of each account where appropriate.
4. Prepare a trial balance at the end of July.
5. Prepare from the trial balance, in proper form, (a) an income statement for the month of July, (b) a statement of owner's equity, and (c) a balance sheet as of July 31, 201X.

Solutions

Requirements 1, 2

Set up T accounts, record transactions, foot each account, and prepare a trial balance.

General Ledger

Cash 111			
(A)	10,000	1,200	(D)
(E)	15,000	3,000	(F)
(J)	3,000	1,250	(G)
		300	(I)
		150	(K)
	28,000	**5,900**	
	22,100		

Accts. Receivable 112			
(H)	4,000	3,000	(J)
	1,000		

Office Equipment 121		
(D)	1,200	

Delivery Trucks 122		
(B)	17,000	

Accts. Payable 211		
	17,000	(B)
	700	(C)
	17,700	

Mel Free, Capital 311		
	10,000	(A)

Mel Free, Withdrawals 312		
(K)	150	

Delivery Fees Earned 411		
	15,000	(E)
	4,000	(H)
	19,000	

Advertising Expense 511		
(C)	700	

Gas Expense 512		
(G)	1,250	

Salaries Expense 513		
(F)	3,000	

Telephone Expense 514		
(I)	300	

Tips to Recording Transactions

A. Cash	Asset	↑	Dr.
Mel Free, Capital	Capital	↑	Cr.
B. Delivery Trucks	Asset	↑	Dr.
Accts. Payable	Liability	↑	Cr.
C. Advertising Expense	Expense	↑	Dr.
Accts. Payable	Liability	↑	Cr.
D. Office Equipment	Asset	↑	Dr.
Cash	Asset	↓	Cr.
E. Cash	Asset	↑	Dr.
Del. Fees Earned	Revenue	↑	Cr.
F. Salaries Expense	Expense	↑	Dr.
Cash	Asset	↓	Cr.
G. Gas Expense	Expense	↑	Dr.
Cash	Asset	↓	Cr.
H. Accts. Receivable	Asset	↑	Dr.
Del. Fees Earned	Revenue	↑	Cr.
I. Tel. Expense	Expense	↑	Dr.
Cash	Asset	↓	Cr.
J. Cash	Asset	↑	Dr.
Accts. Receivable	Asset	↓	Cr.
K. Mel Free, Withdrawals	Withdrawals	↑	Dr.
Cash	Asset	↓	Cr.

Mel's Delivery Service
Trial Balance
July 31, 201X

	Dr.	Cr.
Cash	22,100	
Accounts Receivable	1,000	
Office Equipment	1,200	
Delivery Trucks	17,000	
Accounts Payable		17,700
Mel Free, Capital		10,000
Mel Free, Withdrawals	150	
Delivery Fees Earned		19,000
Advertising Expense	700	
Gas Expense	1,250	
Salaries Expense	3,000	
Telephone Expense	300	
Totals	46,700	46,700

Tips to Taking the Balance of an Account and Preparation of a Trial Balance

3. Footings:	Cash	Add left side, $28,000.
		Add right side, $5,900.
		Take difference, $22,100, and stay on side that is larger.
	Accounts Payable	Add $17,000 + $700 and stay on same side.
		Total is $17,700.

4. Trial balance is a list of the ledger's ending balances. The list is in the same order as the chart of accounts. Each account has only one number listed as either a debit or a credit balance.

Requirement 5

Prepare an Income Statement, Statement of Owner's Equity, and a Balance Sheet from the Trial Balance (see Figure 2.4). When the Statement of Owner's Equity is prepared, assume the initial investment represents the beginning figure for capital and that no additional investments were made.

4a.

MEL'S DELIVERY SERVICE
INCOME STATEMENT
FOR MONTH ENDED JULY 31, 201X

Revenue:		
Delivery Fees Earned		$ 19 0 0 0 00
Operating Expenses:		
Advertising Expense	$ 7 0 0 00	
Gas Expense	1 2 5 0 00	
Salaries Expense	3 0 0 0 00	
Telephone Expense	3 0 0 00	
Total Operating Expenses		5 2 5 0 00
Net Income		$ 13 7 5 0 00

b.

MEL'S DELIVERY SERVICE
STATEMENT OF OWNER'S EQUITY
FOR MONTH ENDED JULY 31, 201X

Mel Free, Capital		
July 1, 201X		$ 10 0 0 0 00
Net Income for July	$13 7 5 0 00	
Less: Withdrawals for July	– 1 5 0 00	
Increase in Capital		$ 13 6 0 0 00
Mel Free, Capital		
July 31, 201X		$ 23 6 0 0 00

c.

MEL'S DELIVERY SERVICE
BALANCE SHEET
JULY 31, 201X

Assets			Liabilities and Owner's Equity		
Cash	$22 1 0 0 00		Liabilities		
Accounts Receivable	1 0 0 0 00		Accounts Payable	$17 7 0 0 00	
Office Equipment	1 2 0 0 00				
Delivery Trucks	17 0 0 0 00				
			Owner's Equity		
			Mel Free, Capital	23 6 0 0 00	
			Total Liab. and		
Total Assets	$41 3 0 0 00		Owner's Equity	$41 3 0 0 00	

Figure 2.4
Financial Statements

Tips to Prepare Financial Statements from a Trial Balance

Trial Balance

		Dr.	Cr.
Balance Sheet	Assets	X	
	Liabilities		X
Statement of Owner's Equity	Capital		X
	Withdrawals	X	
Income Statement	Revenues		X
	Expenses	X	
		XX	XX

Net income of $13,750 on the income statement goes on the statement of owner's equity.

Ending capital of $23,600 on the statement of owner's equity goes on the balance sheet as the new figure for capital.

Note: Financial statements do not show debits or credits. The inside column is used for subtotaling.

SUCCESS COACH

The following Success Tips are from Learning Units 2-1 to 2-3. Take the Do It Right Now Checkup and use the Check Your Score at the bottom of the page to see how you are doing. The Success Coach provides tips before each Checkup to help you avoid common accounting errors.

LU 2-1 The T Account and How to Foot and Balance

Do It Right Tips: Think of "debit" or "credit" as only indicating a position (left or right). To balance an account, total the left (debit) side and the right (credit) side and take the difference between the two totals. This ending balance is placed on the side that is greater. Do not think at this point of "debit" or "credit" as being good or bad. They simply indicate a position, left or right.

Do It Right Now Checkup: Answer true or false to the following statements.

1. A number entered on the left side of an account is said to be credited to the account.
2. Debits are always positive.
3. Footings are always a credit balance.
4. "Credit" always means the number should be put on the right side.
5. A ledger does not use debits or credits.

LU 2-2 The Chart of Accounts: Recording Transactions in T Accounts According to Rules of Debits and Credits

Do It Right Tips: Assets, withdrawals, and expenses will increase on the debit side, while liabilities, capital, and revenues will increase on the credit side. The normal balance of an account is on the side that increases it. The goal of each transaction is for the sum of the left side of the accounting equation to equal the sum of the right side. Compound entries result when three or more accounts affect a transaction.

Do It Right Now Checkup: Answer true or false to the following statements.

1. Rules for debit and credit work in the opposite direction for capital and revenue.
2. An increase in an asset is always a debit.
3. Withdrawals increase with a credit.
4. After a transaction is recorded it can have only one debit and one credit.
5. An unpaid bill results in a debit to a liability and a credit to an expense.

LU 2-3 The Trial Balance and Preparation of Financial Statements

Do It Right Tips: A trial balance is a list of the accounts in the ledger with their ending balances. Each account can only have either a debit or a credit balance. A trial balance will list assets, liabilities, capital, withdrawals, revenue, and expenses. When the financial statements are prepared there are no debits or credits on the financial reports. It is the ending balance of each account that is listed. The inside columns of financial reports are used for subtotaling.

Do It Right Now Checkup: Answer true or false to the following statements.

1. Withdrawals are usually a credit balance on the trial balance.
2. A balance sheet will list only debit accounts.
3. The balance sheet is always prepared before the income statement.
4. Subtotaling is only used on the trial balance.
5. The beginning balance of capital is shown on the balance sheet.

CHECK YOUR SCORE: Answers to the Do It Right Now Checkup

LU 2-1
1. False—A number entered on the left side of an account is said to be debited to the account.
2. False—Debits are on the left-hand side of the account.
3. False—Whether or not footings are a credit balance depends on which side is larger after balancing.
4. True.
5. False—A ledger does use debits and credits.

LU 2-2
1. False—Rules for debit and credit work in the same direction for capital and revenue.
2. True.
3. False—Withdrawals increase with a debit.
4. False—After a transaction is recorded it can have more than one debit or credit as long as the total of debits equals the total of credits.
5. False—An unpaid bill results in a debit to expense and a credit to liability.

LU 2-3

1. False—Withdrawals are usually a debit balance on the trial balance.
2. False—The balance sheet can list accounts with either a debit or credit balance, but the balance sheet does not show debits or credits.
3. False—The balance sheet is prepared after the income statement.
4. False—Subtotaling is used in preparing financial reports; the trial balance is not a financial report.
5. False—The ending figure for capital is shown on the balance sheet.

BLUEPRINT: PREPARING FINANCIAL STATEMENTS FROM A TRIAL BALANCE

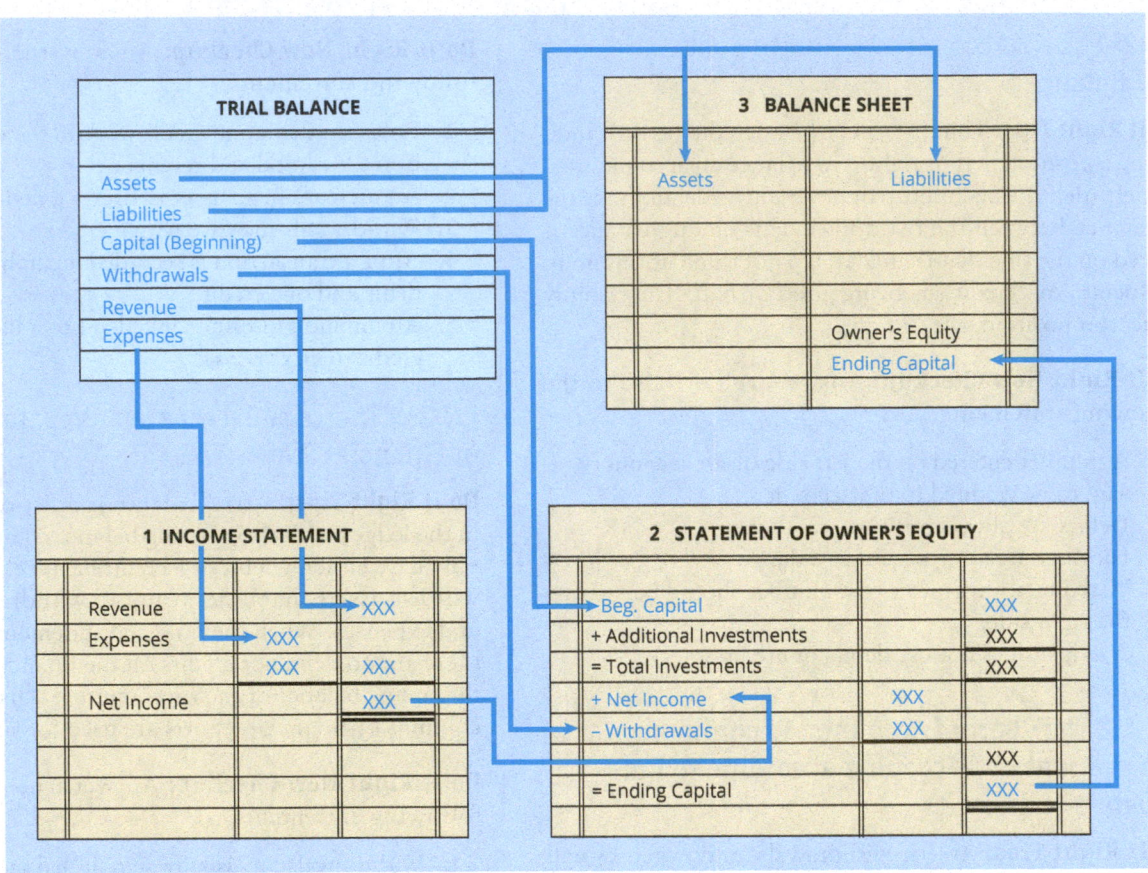

Discussion Questions and Critical Thinking/Ethical Case

1. Define *ledger*.

2. Why is the left-hand side of an account called a debit?

3. Footings are used in balancing all accounts. True or false? Please explain.

4. What is the end product of the accounting process?

5. What do we mean when we say that a transaction analysis chart is a teaching device?

6. What are the five steps of the transaction analysis chart?

7. Computers cannot do debits and credits—agree or disagree and explain why.

8. A trial balance is a formal statement. True or false? Please explain.

9. Why are there no debit or credit columns on financial statements?

10. Compare the financial statements prepared from the expanded accounting equation with those prepared from a trial balance.

11. Joshua Rangel, the bookkeeper of Logan Co., was scheduled to leave on a 3-week vacation at 5:00 on Friday. He couldn't get the company's trial balance to balance. At 4:30, he decided to put in fictitious figures in his computer to make it balance. Joshua told himself he would fix it when he got back from his vacation. Was Joshua right or wrong to do this? Why?

Concept Checks

MyLabAccounting

The T Account

 (5 min)

1. From the following, foot and balance each account.

Cash 110			
6/24	8,000	500	6/26
6/28	12,000		

C. Rice, Capital 311	
11,000	6/1
6,000	6/8
1,000	6/22

Transaction Analysis

 (5 min)

2. Complete the following:

Account	Category	↑	↓	Normal Balance
A. Salaries Payable				
B. Taxable Fees Earned				
C. Accounts Receivable				
D. Sam Slater, Capital				
E. Sam Slater, Withdrawals				
F. Prepaid Advertising				
G. Rent Expense				

(5 min) **LO2**

Transaction Analysis

3. Record the following transaction in the transaction analysis chart: Provided design fees for $3,500, receiving $600 cash with the remainder to be paid next month.

Accounts Affected	Category	↓	↑	Rules of Dr. and Cr.	T Accounts

(5 min) **LO3**

Trial Balance

4. Rearrange the following titles in the order they would appear on a trial balance:

B. O'Mally, Withdrawals	Hair Salon Fees Earned
Accounts Receivable	Selling Expense
Cash	Salary Expense
B. O'Mally, Capital	Advertising Expense
Office Equipment	Accounts Payable

(10 min) **LO3**

Trial Balance/Financial Statements

5. From the following trial balance, identify on which statement each title will appear:

   a. Income statement (IS)

   b. Statement of owner's equity (OE)

   c. Balance sheet (BS)

Bradford Co.
Trial Balance
Nov. 30, 201X

		Dr.	Cr.
A. _____	Cash	600	
B. _____	Computer	100	
C. _____	Computer Equipment	1,000	
D. _____	Accounts Payable		800
E. _____	L. Bradford, Capital		200
F. _____	L. Bradford, Withdrawals	500	
G. _____	Legal Fees Earned		1,500
H. _____	Consulting Fees Earned		300
I. _____	Wage Expense	200	
J. _____	Supplies Expense	250	
K. _____	Internet Advertising Expense	150	
	Totals	2,800	2,800

Exercises

Set A

2A-1. From the following, prepare a chart of accounts.

Microsoft Surface Tablet	Legal Fees
Salary Expense	L. Janas, Capital
Accounts Payable	Cash
Accounts Receivable	Advertising Expense
Repair Expense	L. Janas, Withdrawals

L02 *(10 min)*

2A-2. Record the following transaction in the transaction analysis chart: Shaylin Princeton bought a new piece of computer equipment for $26,000, paying $9,000 down and charging the rest.

L02 *(5 min)*

2A-3. Complete the following table. For each account listed on the left, fill in what category it belongs to, whether increases and decreases in the account are marked on the debit or credit sides, and on which financial statement the account appears. A sample is provided.

L02 *(5 min)*

Accounts Affected	Category	↑	↓	Appears on Which Financial Statements
Computer Supplies	Asset	Dr.	Cr.	Balance Sheet
Legal Fees Earned				
P. Roy, Withdrawals				
Accounts Payable				
Salaries Expense				
Auto				

2A-4. Given the following accounts, complete the table by inserting appropriate numbers next to the individual transaction to indicate which account is debited and which account is credited.

L02 *(20 min)*

1. Cash
2. Accounts Receivable
3. Equipment
4. Accounts Payable
5. B. Barker, Capital
6. B. Barker, Withdrawals
7. Plumbing Fees Earned
8. Salaries Expense
9. Advertising Expense
10. Supplies Expenses

		Transaction	Rules Dr.	Cr.
Example:	A.	Paid salaries expense.	8	1
	B.	Bob paid personal utilities bill from the company checkbook.		
	C.	Advertising bill received but unpaid.		
	D.	Received cash from plumbing fees.		
	E.	Paid supplies expense.		
	F.	Bob invested in additional equipment for the business.		
	G.	Billed customers for plumbing services rendered.		
	H.	Received one-half the balance from Transaction G.		
	I.	Bought equipment on account.		

(20 min) **LO3** ▶ **2A-5.** From the trial balance of Helm's Cleaners in Figure 2.5, prepare the following for March:

- Income statement
- Statement of owner's equity
- Balance sheet

Figure 2.5

HELM'S CLEANERS TRIAL BALANCE MARCH 31, 201X		
	Dr.	Cr.
Cash	7 5 0 0 0	
Equipment	5 0 0 0 0	
Accounts Payable		4 0 0 0 0
J. Helm, Capital		7 2 6 0 0
J. Helm, Withdrawals	5 5 0 0	
Cleaning Fees		4 6 6 0 0
Salaries Expense	1 2 5 0 0	
Utilities Expense	1 6 2 0 0	
Totals	1 5 9 2 0 0	1 5 9 2 0 0

Set B

(10 min) **LO2** ▶ **2B-1.** From the following, prepare a chart of accounts.

Apple iPad	Legal Fees Earned
Salary Expense	L. Jones, Capital
Accounts Payable	Cash
Accounts Receivable	Advertising Expense
Rent Expense	L. Jones, Withdrawals

(5 min) **LO2** ▶ **2B-2.** Record the following transaction in the transaction analysis chart: Selma Pallermo bought a new piece of computer equipment for $28,000, paying $8,000 down and charging the rest.

(5 min) **LO 2** ▶ **2B-3.** Complete the following table. For each account listed on the left, fill in what category it belongs to, whether increases and decreases in the account are marked on the debit or credit sides, and on which financial statement the account appears. A sample is provided.

Accounts Affected	Category	↑	↓	Appears on Which Financial Statements
Office Supplies	Asset	Dr.	Cr.	Balance Sheet
Rental Fees Earned				
A. Troy, Withdrawals				
Accounts Payable				
Wage Expense				
Computer				

2B-4. Given the following accounts, complete the table by inserting appropriate numbers next to the individual transactions to indicate which account is debited and which account is credited.

L02 *(20 min)*

1. Cash
2. Accounts Receivable
3. Furniture
4. Accounts Payable
5. B. Martin, Capital
6. B. Martin, Withdrawals
7. Photography Fees Earned
8. Salaries Expense
9. Advertising Expense
10. Supplies Expense

	Transaction	Rules Dr.	Cr.
Example: A.	Paid salaries expense.	8	1
B.	Bill paid personal utilities bill from the company checkbook.		
C.	Advertising bill received but unpaid.		
D.	Received cash from photography fees.		
E.	Paid supplies expense.		
F.	Bill invested in additional furniture for the business.		
G.	Billed customers for photography services rendered.		
H.	Received one-half the balance from transaction G.		
I.	Bought furniture on account.		

2B-5. From the following trial balance of Hilton's Cleaners in Figure 2.6, prepare the following for January:

L03 *(20 min)*

- Income statement
- Statement of owner's equity
- Balance sheet

Figure 2.6

HILTON'S CLEANERS
TRIAL BALANCE
JANUARY 31, 201X

	Dr.	Cr.
Cash	7 5 0 0 0	
Equipment	5 0 0 0 0	
Accounts Payable		4 5 5 0 0
J. Hilton, Capital		8 6 6 0 0
J. Hilton, Withdrawals	2 5 0 0 0	
Cleaning Fees		4 6 0 0 0
Salaries Expense	1 1 0 0 0	
Utilities Expense	1 7 1 0 0	
Totals	1 7 8 1 0 0	1 7 8 1 0 0

Problems

MyLabAccounting

Set A

2A-1. The following transactions occurred in the opening and operation of Brent's Delivery Service.

L02 *(20 min)*

A. Brent Omara opened the delivery service by investing $45,000 from his personal savings account.
B. Purchased used delivery trucks on account, $5,000.
C. Rent expense due but unpaid, $1,000.
D. Received cash for delivery, $1,200.
E. Billed a client on account, $1,010.
F. Brent withdrew cash for personal use, $1,000.

Complete a transaction analysis chart for each of the transactions.

The chart of accounts includes Cash; Accounts Receivable; Delivery Trucks; Accounts Payable; Brent Omara, Capital; Brent Omara, Withdrawals; Delivery Fees Earned; and Rent Expense.

(20 min) **LO2**

2A-2. Bud Peters opened a consulting company, and the following transactions resulted:

A. Bud invested $34,000 in the consulting agency.
B. Bought office equipment on account, $1,000.
C. Agency received cash for consulting work that it completed for a client, $3,100.
D. Bud paid a personal bill from the company checkbook, $80.
E. Paid advertising expense for the month, $650.
F. Rent expense for the month due but unpaid, $900.
G. Paid $600 as partial payment of what was owed from Transaction B.

As Bud's accountant, analyze and record the transactions in T account form. Set up the T accounts and label each entry with the letter of the transaction.

Chart of Accounts

Assets	Revenue
Cash 111	Consulting Fees Earned 411
Office Equipment 121	**Expenses**
Liabilities	Advertising Expense 511
Accounts Payable 211	Rent Expense 512
Owner's Equity	
Bud Peters, Capital 311	
Bud Peters, Withdrawals 312	

(20 min) **LO1,3**

2A-3. From the following T accounts of Brian's Cleaning Service, (a) foot and determine ending balances, and (b) prepare a trial balance in proper form for October 201X.

Cash 111				Accounts Payable 211				Cleaning Fees Earned 411			
(A)	17,000	(D)	600	(D)	600	(C)	1,400			(B)	11,000
(G)	5,500	(E)	100								
		(F)	100								
		(H)	340								
		(I)	320								

Accounts Receivable 112				Brian Jett, Capital 311				Rent Expense 511		
(B)	11,000	(G)	5,500			(A)	17,000	(F)	100	

Office Equipment 121				Brian Jett, Withdrawals 312			Utilities Expense 512		
(C)	1,400			(I)	320		(E)	100	
(H)	340								

2A-4. From the trial balance of Gabriella Leitz, Attorney-at-Law, given in Figure 2.7, prepare (a) an income statement for the month of January, (b) a statement of owner's equity for the month ended January 31, and (c) a balance sheet at January 31, 201X.

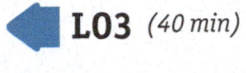

GABRIELLA LEITZ, ATTORNEY-AT-LAW TRIAL BALANCE JANUARY 31, 201X		
Account	Debit	Credit
Cash	7 0 0 0 0 0	
Accounts Receivable	8 0 0 0 0	
Office Equipment	5 0 0 0 0	
Accounts Payable		2 2 0 0 0 0
Salaries Payable		9 5 0 0 0
G. Leitz, Capital		4 6 0 0 0 0
G. Leitz, Withdrawals	4 0 0 0 0	
Revenue from Legal Fees		1 6 0 0 0 0
Utilities Expense	1 5 0 0 0	
Rent Expense	3 5 0 0 0	
Salaries Expense	1 5 0 0 0	
Totals	9 3 5 0 0 0	9 3 5 0 0 0

Figure 2.7

Check Figure:
Total Assets $8,300

2A-5. The chart of accounts for Alto's Delivery Service is as follows:

Chart of Accounts	
Assets	**Revenue**
Cash 111	Delivery Fees Earned 411
Accounts Receivable 112	**Expenses**
Office Equipment 121	Advertising Expense 511
Delivery Trucks 122	Gas Expense 512
Liabilities	Salaries Expense 513
Accounts Payable 211	Telephone Expense 514
Owner's Equity	
Amy Alto, Capital 311	
Amy Alto, Withdrawals 312	

Alto's Delivery Service completed the following transactions during the month of October:

a. Amy Alto invested $20,000 in the delivery service from her personal savings account.

b. Bought used delivery trucks on account, $6,000.

c. Bought office equipment for cash, $1,300.

d. Paid advertising expense, $250.

e. Collected cash for delivery services rendered, $2,600.

f. Paid drivers' salaries, $650.

g. Paid gas expense for trucks, $1,600.

h. Performed delivery services for a customer on account, $1,500.

i. Telephone expense due but unpaid, $700.

j. Received $100 as partial payment of Transaction H.

k. Amy withdrew cash for personal use, $700.

Check Figure:
Total Trial Balance $30,800

As Amy's newly hired accountant, you must perform the following:

1. Set up T accounts using the chart of accounts. Record transactions in the T accounts. (Place the letter of the transaction next to the entry.)

2. Foot the T accounts where appropriate and determine the ending balances.

3. Prepare a trial balance at the end of October.

4. Prepare from the trial balance, in proper form, (a) an income statement for the month of October, (b) a statement of owner's equity, and (c) a balance sheet as of October 31, 201X.

Set B

(20 min) **LO2**

Check Figure:
After F:

Cash	
(A) 50,000	400 (F)
(D) 2,500	

2B-1. The following transactions occurred in the opening and operation of Blaine Delivery Service.

A. Blaine Orwell opened the delivery service by investing $50,000 from his personal savings account.

B. Purchased used delivery trucks on account, $13,000.

C. Rent expense due but unpaid, $1,100.

D. Received cash for delivery, $2,500.

E. Billed a client on account, $1,200.

F. Blaine withdrew cash for personal use, $400.

Complete a transaction analysis chart for each of the transactions.

The chart of accounts for the shop includes Cash; Accounts Receivable; Delivery Trucks; Accounts Payable; B. Orwell, Capital; B. Orwell, Withdrawals; Delivery Fees Earned; and Rent Expense.

(20 min) **LO2**

Check Figure:
After G:

Cash	
(A) 33,000	150(D)
(C) 2,000	250 (E)
	600(G)

2B-2. Brad Piascik opened a consulting company, and the following transactions resulted.

A. Brad invested $33,000 in the consulting agency.

B. Bought office equipment on account, $2,500.

C. Agency received cash for consulting work that it completed for a client, $2,000.

D. Brad paid a personal bill from the company checkbook, $150.

E. Paid advertising expense for the month, $250.

F. Rent expense for the month due but unpaid, $500.

G. Paid $600 as partial payment of what was owed from Transaction B.

As Brad's accountant, analyze and record the transactions in T account form. Set up the T accounts and label each entry with the letter of the transaction.

Chart of Accounts	
Assets	**Revenue**
Cash 111	Consulting Fees Earned 411
Office Equipment 121	**Expenses**
Liabilities	Advertising Expense 511
Accounts Payable 211	Rent Expense 512
Owner's Equity	
Brad Piascik, Capital 311	
Brad Piascik, Withdrawals 312	

(20 min) **LO1,3**

Check Figure:
Trial Balance Total $19,700

2B-3. From the following T accounts of Brent's Cleaning Service, (a) foot and determine the ending balances, and (b) prepare a trial balance in proper form for July 31, 201X.

Cash 111		
(A)	7,000	(D) 400
(G)	2,000	(E) 500
		(F) 550
		(H) 550
		(I) 320

Accounts Receivable 112	
(B) 11,000	(G) 2,000

Office Equipment 121	
(C) 2,100	
(H) 550	

Accounts Payable 211	
(D) 400	(C) 2,100

Brent Jane, Capital 311
(A) 7,000

Brent Jane, Withdrawals 312
(I) 320

Cleaning Fees Earned 411
(B) 11,000

Rent Expense 511
(F) 550

Utilities Expense 512
(E) 500

2B-4. From the trial balance of Gail Lantz, Attorney-at-Law, given in Figure 2.8, prepare (a) an income statement for the month of July, (b) a statement of owner's equity for the month ended July 31, and (c) a balance sheet at July 31, 201X.

 **L03** *(40 min)*

Figure 2.8

GAIL LANTZ, ATTORNEY-AT-LAW
TRIAL BALANCE
JULY 31, 201X

Account	Dr.	Cr.
Cash	5 0 0 0 0	
Accounts Receivable	7 5 0 0 0	
Office Equipment	2 7 0 0 0 0	
Accounts Payable		3 0 0 0 0 0
Salaries Payable		1 0 0 0 0 0
G. Lantz, Capital		4 7 0 0 0 0
G. Lantz, Withdrawals	1 1 0 0 0 0	
Revenue from Legal Fees		1 6 0 0 0 0
Utilities Expense	1 0 0 0 0	
Rent Expense	4 5 0 0 0	
Salaries Expense	2 0 0 0 0	
Totals	10 3 0 0 0 0	10 3 0 0 0 0

Check Figure:
Total Assets $8,450

2B-5. The chart of accounts of Avery's Delivery Service is as follows:

L02,3 *(60 min)*

Chart of Accounts

Assets	Revenue
Cash 111	Delivery Fees Earned 411
Accounts Receivable 112	**Expenses**
Office Equipment 121	Advertising Expense 511
Delivery Trucks 122	Gas Expense 512
Liabilities	Salaries Expense 513
Accounts Payable 211	Telephone Expense 514
Owner's Equity	
Audrey Avery, Capital 311	
Audrey Avery, Withdrawals 312	

Check Figure:
Trial Balance Total $50,350

Avery's Delivery Service completed the following transactions during the month of October:

a. Audrey Avery invested $33,000 in the delivery service from her personal savings account.
b. Bought used delivery trucks on account, $13,000.
c. Bought office equipment for cash, $1,100.
d. Paid advertising expense, $250.
e. Collected cash for delivery services rendered, $3,500.
f. Paid drivers' salaries, $750.
g. Paid gas expense for trucks, $1,000.
h. Performed delivery services for a customer on account, $800.
i. Telephone expense due but unpaid, $50.
j. Received $100 as partial payment of transaction H.
k. Audrey withdrew cash for personal use, $700.

As Audrey's newly hired accountant, you must perform the following:

1. Set up T accounts using the chart of accounts. Record transactions in the T accounts. (Place the letter of the transaction next to the entry.)
2. Foot the T accounts where appropriate and determine the ending balances.
3. Prepare a trial balance at the end of October.
4. Prepare from the trial balance, in proper form, (a) an income statement for the month of October, (b) a statement of owner's equity, and (c) a balance sheet as of October 31, 201X.

Financial Report Problem

(5 min) **LO2**

Reading Amazon's Annual Report

Go to https://tinyurl.com/slaterca14e to access Amazon 2016 Annual Report. Did Amazon's Accounts Payable go up or down from 2015 to 2016? What does change mean?

MyLabAccounting

KEEPING IT REAL SUAREZ COMPUTER CENTER

(60 min) **LO1,2,3**

The Suarez Computer Center created its chart of accounts as follows:

Chart of Accounts as of July 1, 201X

Assets		Revenue	
1000	Cash	4000	Service Revenue
1020	Accounts Receivable	**Expenses**	
1030	Supplies	5010	Advertising Expense
1080	Computer Shop Equipment	5020	Rent Expense
1090	Office Equipment	5030	Utilities Expense
Liabilities		5040	Phone Expense
2000	Accounts Payable	5050	Supplies Expense
Owner's Equity		5060	Insurance Expense
3000	Falco, Capital	5070	Postage Expense
3010	Falco, Withdrawals		

You will use this chart of accounts to complete the Continuing Problem.
The following problem continues from Chapter 1.

Assignment

1. Set up T accounts in a ledger and post the ending balances from Chapter 1.

2. Record Transactions K through S in the appropriate T accounts.

3. Foot and take the balances of the T accounts where appropriate.

4. Prepare a trial balance at the end of August.

5. From the trial balance, prepare an income statement, statement of owner's equity, and a balance sheet for the 2 months ending with August 31, 201X.

k. Received the phone bill for the month of July, $200.

l. Paid $300 (check #8099) for insurance for the month.

m. Paid $50 (check #8100) of the amount due from Transaction D in Chapter 1.

n. Paid advertising expense for the month, $500 (check #8101).

o. Billed a client (Kristen Tarsia) for services rendered, $1,100.

p. Collected $1,400 for services rendered. (Assume cash collection occurred at the same time services were rendered.)

q. Paid the electric bill in full for the month of July (check #8102, Transaction H, Chapter 1).

r. Paid cash (check #8103) for $20 in stamps.

s. Purchased $500 worth of supplies from The Computer Store on credit.

Beginning the Accounting Cycle

3

CHAPTER PREVIEW: ACCOUNTING IN ACTION

Cynthia Rice is majoring in Hospitality at a local community college. Her freshman year program requires her to take an accounting class. Cynthia is curious whether large hotel chains like Marriot effectively use accounting to maintain their records. The reality is that Marriott Hotels must follow specific steps in accounting to properly maintain its accounting records over a period of time. These procedures or steps are referred to as the accounting cycle. Once one cycle is completed (usually called a fiscal year), another cycle is begun. Learning the accounting procedures necessary during an accounting cycle will help you understand how businesses like Marriott Hotels maintain consistent accounting records.

Learning Objectives – Relating Accounting Theory By Unit

LO1   Analyze and Record Business Transactions into a Journal

LO2   Posting to the Ledger

LO3   Preparing the Trial Balance

Accounting cycle For each accounting period, the process that begins with the recording of business transactions or procedures into a journal and ends with the completion of a post-closing trial balance.

Accounting period Period of time for which an income statement is prepared.

Calendar year Calendar year January 1 through December 31. Alternatively known as **fiscal year** and **natural business year**. A fiscal year can be something other than a calendar year.

Interim reports Financial statements that are prepared for a month, quarter, or some other portion of the fiscal year.

Companies like Marriott Hotels have to perform certain accounting procedures. The normal accounting procedures that are performed over a period of time are called the accounting cycle. The accounting cycle takes place in a period of time called an accounting period. An accounting period is the period of time covered by the income statement. Although it can be any time period up to 1 year (e.g., 1 month or 3 months), most businesses use a 1-year accounting period. The year can be either a calendar year (January 1 through December 31) or a fiscal year.

A fiscal year is an accounting period that runs for any 12 consecutive months, so it can be the same as a calendar year. Big Dollar Stores and Aeropostale, Inc., end their accounting periods on January 31. A business can choose any fiscal year that is convenient. For example, some retailers may decide to end their fiscal year when inventories and business activity are at a low point, such as after the Christmas season. This period is called a natural business year. Using a natural business year allows the business to count its year-end inventory when it is easiest to do so.

Businesses would not be able to operate successfully if they only prepared financial reports at the end of their calendar or fiscal year. For more timely information, most businesses prepare interim reports on a monthly, quarterly, or semiannual basis.

In this chapter, as well as in Chapters 4 and 5, we follow Rob Sinclair's new business, Hilight Graphic Services. We follow the normal accounting procedures that the business performs over a period of time. Sinclair has chosen to use a fiscal period of January 1 to December 31, which also is the calendar year.

LEARNING UNIT 3-1

LO1

Analyzing and Recording Business Transactions into a Journal (Steps 1 and 2 of the Accounting Cycle)

The General Journal

Journal Listing of business transactions in chronological order. The journal links on one page the debit and credit parts of transactions. Alternatively known as **general journal**.

Journal entry Transaction (debits and credits) that is recorded into a journal once it is analyzed.

Journalizing Process of recording a transaction into the journal.

Book of original entry Book that records the first formal information about business transactions (e.g., a journal).

Book of final entry Book that records information about business transactions from a book of original entry (a journal) (e.g., a ledger).

Chapter 2 taught us how to analyze and record business transactions into T accounts, or ledger accounts. Recording a debit in an account on one page of the ledger and recording the corresponding credit on a different page of the ledger, however, can make it difficult to find errors. It would be much easier if all the business's transactions were located in the same place. That is the function of the journal or general journal. Transactions are entered in the journal in chronological order (January 1, 8, 15, etc.), and then this recorded information is used to update the ledger accounts. In computerized accounting, a journal may be stored on a desktop computer or on the Cloud. Think of the general journal as the diary of the business and there is an entry by date every time an accounting event occurs.

We use a general journal, the simplest form of a journal, to record the transactions of Hilight Graphic Services. A transaction [debit(s) + credit(s)] that has been analyzed and recorded in a journal is called a journal entry. The process of recording the journal entry into the journal is called journalizing.

The journal is called the book of original entry because it contains the first formal information about business transactions. The ledger is known as the book of final entry because the information the journal contains will be transferred to the ledger. With today's technology, much has changed how entries are recorded in journals and ledgers. For now, we need to focus on the manual aspects; however, at the end of this chapter, there are software simulations that show how the manual system is computerized. Each of the journal pages looks like or is similar to the one in Figure 3.1. The pages of the journal are numbered consecutively from page 1. Keep in mind that the journal and the ledger are separate books in a manual accounting system.

Relationship between the Journal and the Chart of Accounts. The accountant must refer to the business's chart of accounts for the account names that are to be used in the journal. Every company has its own "unique" chart of accounts.

ROB SINCLAIR'S HILIGHT GRAPHIC SERVICES GENERAL JOURNAL					
					Page 1
Date	Account Titles and Description	PR	Dr.	Cr.	

Figure 3.1
The General Journal

The following chart of accounts for Rob Sinclair's Hilight Graphic Services lists the accounts used in the business. By the end of Chapter 5, we will have discussed each of these accounts.

Rob Sinclair's Hilight Graphic Services
Chart of Accounts

Assets (100–199)	**Owner's Equity (300–399)**
111 Cash	311 Rob Sinclair, Capital
112 Accounts Receivable	312 Rob Sinclair, Withdrawals
114 Computer Supplies	313 Income Summary
115 Prepaid Rent	**Revenue (400–499)**
121 Computer Equipment	411 Graphic Design Fees
122 Accumulated Depreciation,	**Expenses (500–599)**
Computer Equipment	511 Office Salaries Expense
Liabilities (200–299)	512 Advertising Expense
211 Accounts Payable	513 Telephone Expense
212 Salaries Payable	514 Computer Supplies Expense
	515 Depreciation Expense, Computer Equipment

Journalizing the Transactions of Rob Sinclair's Hilight Graphic Services. Certain formalities must be followed in making journal entries:

- The debit portion of the transaction is always recorded first.
- The credit portion of a transaction is indented ½ inch and placed below the debit portion.
- The explanation of the journal entry follows immediately after the credit and is indented 1 inch from the date column.
- One line space follows each transaction and explanation. This makes the journal easier to read, and there is less chance of mixing transactions.
- Each transaction must affect at least two different accounts.
- Finally, as always, the total amount of debits must equal the total amount of credits. The same format is used for each of the entries in the journal.

Note that we continue to use transaction analysis charts as a teaching aid in the journalizing process.

May 1, 201X: Rob Sinclair Began the Business by Investing $10,000 in Cash			
1	**2**	**3**	**4**
Accounts Affected	**Category**	**↓↑**	**Rules of Dr. and Cr.**
Cash	Asset	↑	Dr.
Rob Sinclair, Capital	Capital	↑	Cr.

Figure 3.2
Owner Investment

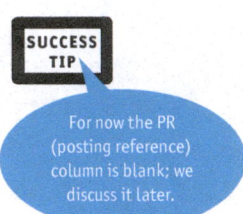

For now the PR (posting reference) column is blank; we discuss it later.

	ROB SINCLAIR'S HILIGHT GRAPHIC SERVICES GENERAL JOURNAL				
					Page 1
Date	Account Titles and Description	PR	Dr.	Cr.	
201X May 1	Cash		10 000 00		
	Rob Sinclair, Capital			10 000 00	
	Initial investment of cash by owner				

American Institute of Professional Bookkeepers (AIPB) – The AIPB is the bookkeeping profession's national association. AIPB's mission is to achieve recognition of bookkeepers as accounting profession and to certify bookkeepers who meet high, national standards. More on the AIPB can found at **https://www.aipb.org**

Let's now look at the structure of this journal entry (Figure 3.2). The entry contains the following information:

1. Year of the journal entry   201X
2. Month of the journal entry   May
3. Day of the journal entry   1
4. Name(s) of accounts debited   Cash
5. Name(s) of accounts credited   Rob Sinclair, Capital
6. Explanation of transaction   Initial investment by owner
7. Amount of debit(s) $10,000
8. Amount of credit(s) $10,000

May 1: Purchased Computer Equipment from Giga Co. for $6,000, Paying $1,000 and Promising to Pay the Balance Within 30 Days			
1	2	3	4
Accounts Affected	**Category**	**↓↑**	**Rules of Dr. and Cr.**
Computer Equipment	Asset	↑	Dr.
Cash	Asset	↓	Cr.
Accounts Payable	Liability	↑	Cr.

Compound journal entry Journal entry that affects more than two accounts.

This transaction affects three accounts. When a journal entry has more than two accounts, it is called a compound journal entry.

In this entry (Figure 3.3), only the day is entered in the date column because the year and month were entered at the top of the page from the first transaction. This information doesn't need to be repeated until a new page is needed or a change of months occurs.

Figure 3.3
Purchase of Equipment

1	Computer Equipment	6 000 00		
	Cash		1 000 00	
	Accounts Payable		5 000 00	
	Purchase of computer equipment from Giga Co.			

May 1: Rented Office Space, Paying $1,200 in Advance for the First Three Months			
1	**2**	**3**	**4**
Accounts Affected	**Category**	↓↑	**Rules of Dr. and Cr.**
Prepaid Rent	Asset	↑	Dr.
Cash	Asset	↓	Cr.

In this transaction (Figure 3.4), Sinclair gains an asset called prepaid rent and gives up an asset, cash. The prepaid rent does not become an expense until it expires.

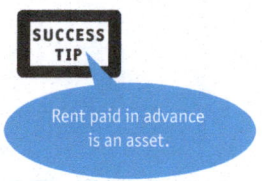

SUCCESS TIP

Rent paid in advance is an asset.

	1	Prepaid Rent		1 2 0 0 00	
		Cash			1 2 0 0 00
		Rent paid in advance—(3 months)			

Figure 3.4
Paid Rent in Advance

May 3: Purchased Computer Supplies from Vision Co. on Account, $600			
1	**2**	**3**	**4**
Accounts Affected	**Category**	↓↑	**Rules of Dr. and Cr.**
Computer Supplies	Asset	↑	Dr.
Accounts Payable	Liability	↑	Cr.

Remember, computer supplies are an asset when they are purchased. Once they are used up or consumed in the operation of business, they become an expense (Figure 3.5).

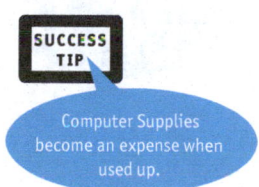

SUCCESS TIP

Computer Supplies become an expense when used up.

	3	Computer Supplies		6 0 0 00	
		Accounts Payable			6 0 0 00
		Purchase of computer supplies on account			
		from Vision			

Figure 3.5
Purchased Supplies on Account

May 7: Completed a Graphic Design Project for a Client and Immediately Collected $3,000			
1	**2**	**3**	**4**
Accounts Affected	**Category**	↓↑	**Rules of Dr. and Cr.**
Cash	Asset	↑	Dr.
Graphic Design Fees	Revenue	↑	Cr.

Revenue is earned and cash is received (Figure 3.6).

	7	Cash		3 0 0 0 00	
		Graphic Design Fees			3 0 0 0 00
		Cash received for services rendered			

Figure 3.6
Services Rendered

May 13: Paid Office Salaries, $650			
1	**2**	**3**	**4**
Accounts Affected	**Category**	↓↑	**Rules of Dr. and Cr.**
Office Salaries Expense	Expense	↑	Dr.
Cash	Asset	↓	Cr.

Salaries expenses are increasing and cash is going down (see Figure 3.7).

Figure 3.7
Paid Salaries

	13	Office Salaries Expense			6 5 0 00		
		Cash				6 5 0 00	
		Payment of office salaries					

May 18: Advertising Bill from Digital Insert Co. Comes in But Is Not Paid, $250			
1	**2**	**3**	**4**
Accounts Affected	**Category**	↓↑	**Rules of Dr. and Cr.**
Advertising Expense	Expense	↑	Dr.
Accounts Payable	Liability	↑	Cr.

Here an expense increases although no cash was yet paid (see Figure 3.8).

Figure 3.8
Received Advertising Bill

	18	Advertising Expense			2 5 0 00		
		Accounts Payable				2 5 0 00	
		Bill in but not paid from Digital Insert					

May 20: Rob Sinclair Wrote a Check on the Bank Account of the Business to Pay His Home Mortgage Payment of $625			
1	**2**	**3**	**4**
Accounts Affected	**Category**	↓↑	**Rules of Dr. and Cr.**
Rob Sinclair, Withdrawals	Withdrawals	↑	Dr.
Cash	Asset	↓	Cr.

Rob is gaining a withdrawal while the business is losing cash (see Figure 3.9).

Figure 3.9
Personal Withdrawal

	20	Rob Sinclair, Withdrawals			6 2 5 00		
		Cash				6 2 5 00	
		Personal withdrawal of cash					

May 22: Billed Merlin Company for a Large Graphic Design Project, $5,000

1	2	3	4
Accounts Affected	**Category**	↓↑	**Rules of Dr. and Cr.**
Accounts Receivable	Asset	↑	Dr.
Graphic Design Fees	Revenue	↑	Cr.

Note the revenue is earned, although cash was not received (see Figure 3.10).

	22	Accounts Receivable		5 0 0 0 00	
		Graphic Design Fees			5 0 0 0 00
		Billed Merlin Co. for fees earned			

Figure 3.10
Fees Earned

May 27: Paid Office Salaries, $650

1	2	3	4
Accounts Affected	**Category**	↓↑	**Rules of Dr. and Cr.**
Office Salaries Expense	Expense	↑	Dr.
Cash	Asset	↓	Cr.

Salaries expense is increasing while the cash in the business is decreasing (see Figure 3.11).

ROB SINCLAIR'S HILIGHT GRAPHIC SERVICES GENERAL JOURNAL					
					Page 2
Date		Account Titles and Description	PR	Dr.	Cr.
201X May	27*	Office Salaries Expense		6 5 0 00	
		Cash			6 5 0 00
		Payment of office salaries			

Figure 3.11
Paid Salaries

*Note that this is a new page, so the year and month are repeated.

May 28: Paid Half the Amount Owed for Computer Equipment Purchased May 1 from Giga Co., $2,500

1	2	3	4
Accounts Affected	**Category**	↓↑	**Rules of Dr. and Cr.**
Accounts Payable	Liability	↓	Dr.
Cash	Asset	↓	Cr.

A liability is being reduced by the payment of cash (see Figure 3.12).

	28	Accounts Payable		2 5 0 0 00	
		Cash			2 5 0 0 00
		Paid half the amount owed Giga Co.			

Figure 3.12
Partial Payment

SUCCESS TIP

Reminder: Computer repair fees, a revenue, is generally recorded when earned and not necessarily when the cash is received.

May 29: Received and Paid Telephone Bill, $220			
1	**2**	**3**	**4**
Accounts Affected	**Category**	**↓↑**	**Rules of Dr. and Cr.**
Telephone Expense	Expense	↑	Dr.
Cash	Asset	↓	Cr.

The company expense for telephone use is increasing and is being paid with cash (see Figure 3.13).

Figure 3.13
Paid Telephone Bill

	29	Telephone Expense			2 2 0 00		
		Cash				2 2 0 00	
		Paid telephone bill					

This concludes the journal transactions of Rob Sinclair's Hilight Graphic Services for the month of May.

 ## TRY IT!   Learning Unit 3-1

Given the following partial chart of accounts:

> Cash (110), Accounts Receivable (111), Supplies (112), and Accounts Payable (210)

Complete a transaction analysis chart and journal entry from the following transaction:

> June 30, 201X Lawson Co. purchased supplies for $800, paying $200 down and the balance due next month.

TRY IT!   Solution Learning Unit 3-1

Accounts Affected	**Category**	**↓↑**	**Rule**
Supplies	Asset	↑	Dr. $800
Accounts Payable	Liability	↑	Cr. $600
Cash	Asset	↓	Cr. $200

Date	**Account Title and Description**	**PR**	**Dr.**	**Cr.**
201X June 30				
	Supplies		800	
	Accounts Payable			600
	Cash			200
	Bought supplies			

Posting to the Ledger (Step 3 of the Accounting Cycle)

The general journal serves a particular purpose: It puts every transaction the business does in one place. It cannot do certain things, though. For example, if you were asked to find the balance of the Cash account from the general journal, you would have to go through the entire journal and look for only the cash entries. Then you would have to add up the debits and credits for the Cash account and determine the difference between the two.

What we really need to do to find the balances of accounts is to transfer the information from the journal to the ledger. This process is called posting. In the ledger, we accumulate an ending balance for each account so that we can prepare financial statements.

In Chapter 2 we used the T account form to make our ledger entries. T accounts are simple, but are not used in the real business world; they are only used for demonstration purposes, but are a great tool in visualizing the elements of a transaction. In practice, accountants often use a four-column account form that includes a column for the business's running balance. Figure 3.14 shows a standard four-column account. We use this format in the text from now on.

Posting Transferring, copying, or recording of information from a journal to a ledger.

Four-column account Running balance account that records debits and credits and has a column for an ending balance (debit or credit). It replaces the standard two-column account we used earlier.

Accounts Payable								Account No. 211	
Date	Explanation	Post. Ref.	Dr.	Cr.	Balance Dr.	Cr.
201X May 1		GJ1		5 000 00		5 000 00
3		GJ1		6 00 00		5 600 00
18		GJ1		2 50 00		5 850 00
28		GJ2	2 500 00			3 350 00

Figure 3.14
Four-Column Account

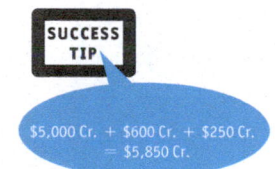

$5,000 Cr. + $600 Cr. + $250 Cr. = $5,850 Cr.

Posting

Now let's look at how to post the journal entries of Rob Sinclair's Hilight Graphic Services from its journal. The diagram in Figure 3.15 (page 74) shows how to post the cash line from the journal to the ledger. The steps in the posting process are numbered and illustrated in the figure.

STEP 1: In the Cash account in the ledger, record the date (May 1, 201X).

STEP 2: Record the page number of the journal "GJ1" in the posting reference (PR) column of the Cash account.

STEP 3: Transfer the dollar amount of the debit portion of the entry to the ledger. Calculate the new balance of the account. To keep a running balance in each account, as you would in your personal checkbook, take the present balance in the account on the previous line and add or subtract the transaction as necessary to arrive at your new balance.

STEP 4: Record the account number of Cash (111) in the posting reference (PR) column of the journal. This listing is known as cross-referencing.

The same sequence of steps occurs for each line in the journal. In a manual system like Sinclair's, the debits and credits in the journal may be posted in the order they were recorded, or all the debits may be posted first and then all the credits. If Sinclair used a computerized accounting system, the program menu would post at the press of a button.

Cross-referencing Adding to the PR column of the journal the account number of the ledger account that was updated from the journal.

Figure 3.15
How to Post from Journal
to Ledger

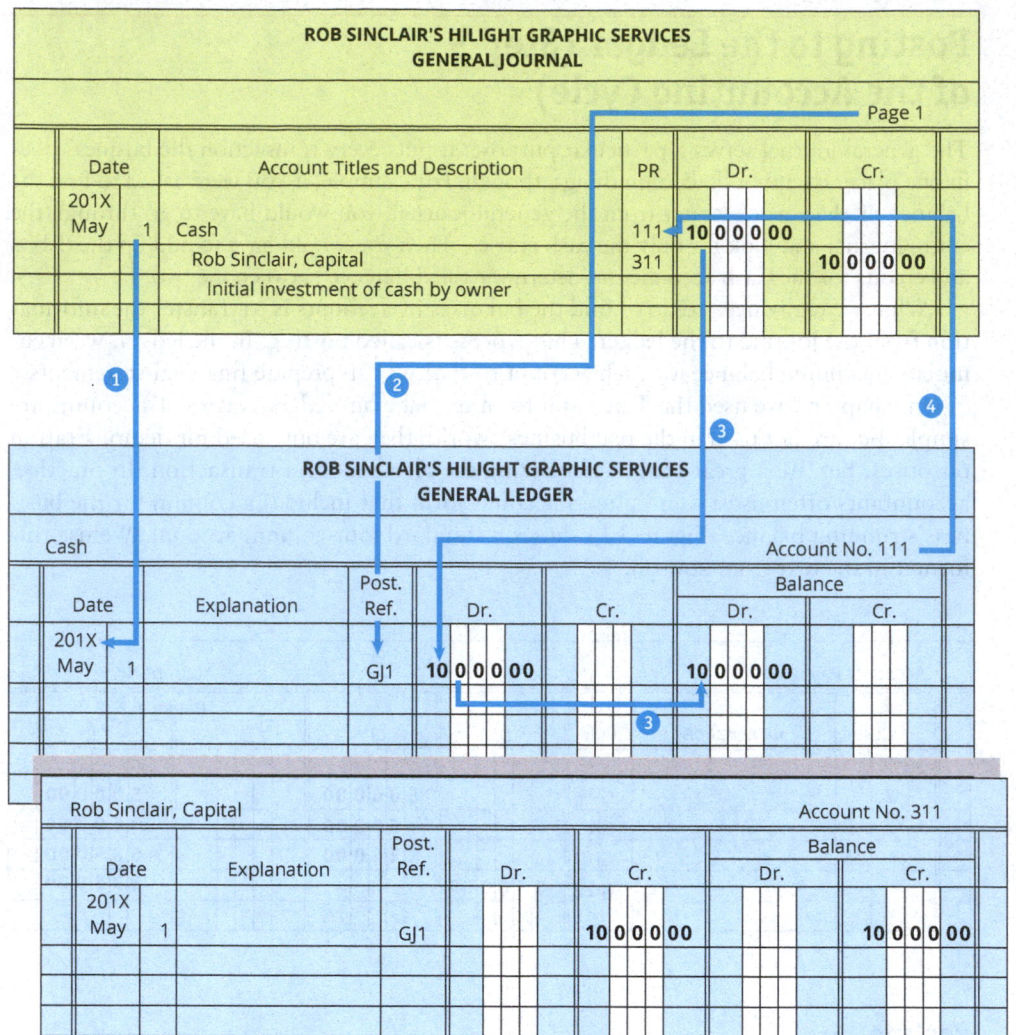

Using Posting References. The posting references are helpful. In the journal, the PR column tells us which journal entries have or have not been posted and also to which accounts they were posted. In the ledger, the posting reference leads us back to the original journal entry in its entirety, so we can see why the debit or credit was recorded and what other accounts were affected. (It leads us back to the original journal entry by identifying the journal and the page in the journal from which the information came.) Figure 3.16 shows the completed journal and ledger for Rob Sinclair's Hilight Graphic Services after postings:

ROB SINCLAIR'S HILIGHT GRAPHIC SERVICES
GENERAL JOURNAL

Page 1

Date		Account Titles and Description	PR	Dr.	Cr.
201X May	1	Cash	111	10 000 00	
		Rob Sinclair, Capital	311		10 000 00
		Initial investment of cash by owner			
	1	Computer Equipment	121	6 000 00	
		Cash	111		1 000 00
		Accounts Payable	211		5 000 00
		Purchase of equip. from Giga Co.			
	1	Prepaid Rent	115	1 200 00	
		Cash	111		1 200 00
		Rent paid in advance (3 months)			
	3	Computer Supplies	114	600 00	
		Accounts Payable	211		600 00
		Purchase of supplies on acct. from Vision			
	7	Cash	111	3 000 00	
		Graphic Design Fees	411		3 000 00
		Cash received from services rendered			
	13	Office Salaries Expense	511	650 00	
		Cash	111		650 00
		Payment of office salaries			
	18	Advertising Expense	512	250 00	
		Accounts Payable	211		250 00
		Bill received but not paid from Digital Insert			
	20	Rob Sinclair, Withdrawals	312	625 00	
		Cash	111		625 00
		Personal withdrawal of cash			
	22	Accounts Receivable	112	5 000 00	
		Graphic Design Fees	411		5 000 00
		Billed Digital Insert Co. for fees earned			

Figure 3.16
Posting from Journal to Ledger
Using PR Columns

(continued on page 76)

Figure 3.16
(*continued*)

ROB SINCLAIR'S HILIGHT GRAPHIC SERVICES
GENERAL JOURNAL

Page 2

Date		Account Titles and Description	PR	Dr.	Cr.
201X May	27	Office Salaries Expense	511	6 5 0 00	
		Cash	111		6 5 0 00
		Payment of office salaries			
	28	Accounts Payable	211	2 5 0 0 00	
		Cash	111		2 5 0 0 00
		Paid half the amount owed Giga Co.			
	29	Telephone Expense	513	2 2 0 00	
		Cash	111		2 2 0 00
		Paid telephone bill			

ROB SINCLAIR'S HILIGHT GRAPHIC SERVICES
PARTIAL GENERAL LEDGER

Cash   Account No. 111

Date		Explanation	Post. Ref.	Dr.	Cr.	Balance Dr.	Balance Cr.
201X May	1		GJ1	10 0 0 0 00		10 0 0 0 00	
	1		GJ1		1 0 0 0 00	9 0 0 0 00	
	1		GJ1		1 2 0 0 00	7 8 0 0 00	
	7		GJ1	3 0 0 0 00		10 8 0 0 00	
	13		GJ1		6 5 0 00	10 1 5 0 00	
	20		GJ1		6 2 5 00	9 5 2 5 00	
	27		GJ2		6 5 0 00	8 8 7 5 00	
	28		GJ2		2 5 0 0 00	6 3 7 5 00	
	29		GJ2		2 2 0 00	6 1 5 5 00	

Accounts Receivable   Account No. 112

Date		Explanation	Post. Ref.	Dr.	Cr.	Balance Dr.	Balance Cr.
201X May	22		GJ1	5 0 0 0 00		5 0 0 0 00	

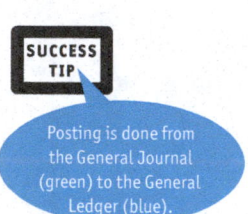

SUCCESS TIP

Posting is done from the General Journal (green) to the General Ledger (blue).

(*continued on page 77*)

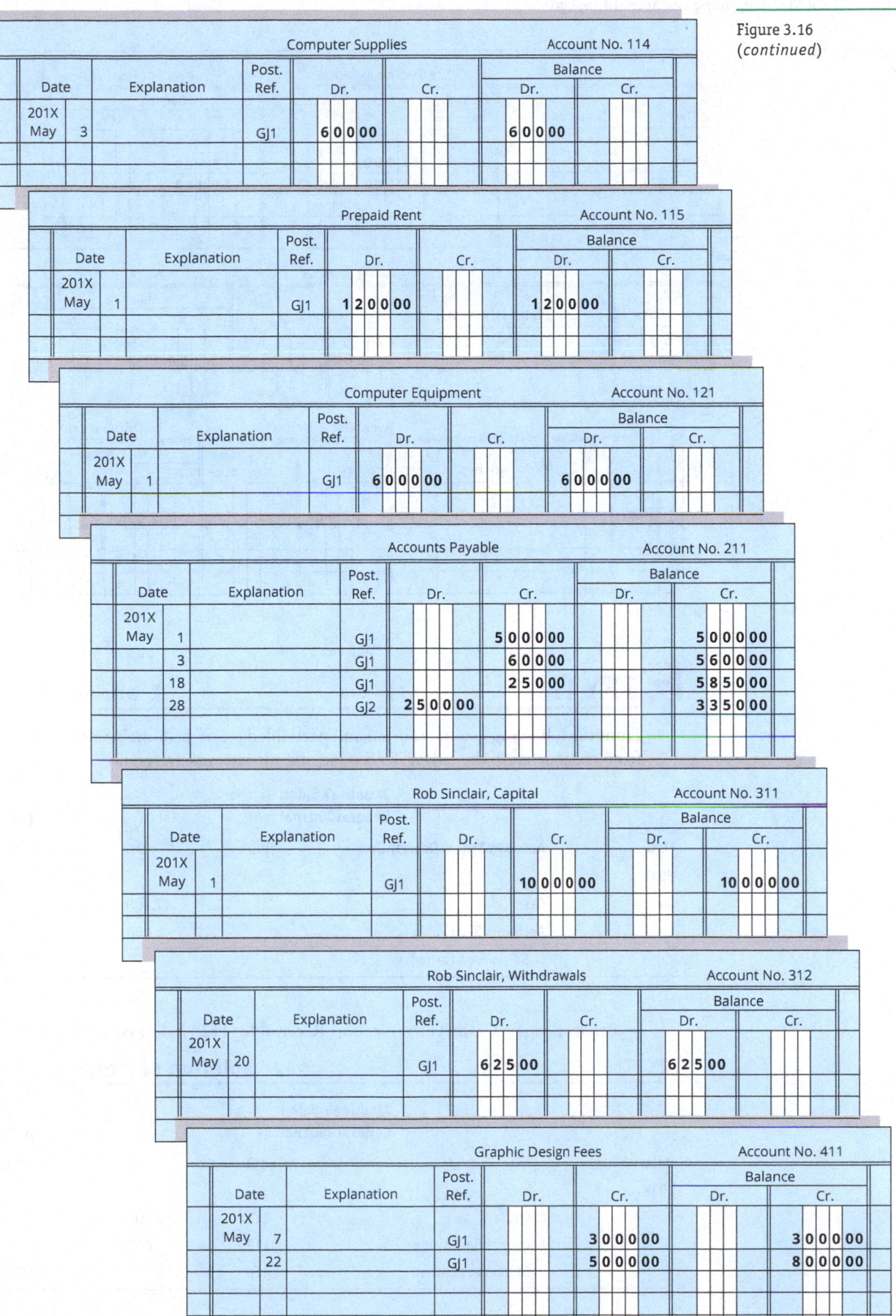

Figure 3.16
(*continued*)

Computer Supplies   Account No. 114

Date		Explanation	Post. Ref.	Dr.	Cr.	Balance Dr.	Balance Cr.
201X May	3		GJ1	600 00		600 00	

Prepaid Rent   Account No. 115

Date		Explanation	Post. Ref.	Dr.	Cr.	Balance Dr.	Balance Cr.
201X May	1		GJ1	1200 00		1200 00	

Computer Equipment   Account No. 121

Date		Explanation	Post. Ref.	Dr.	Cr.	Balance Dr.	Balance Cr.
201X May	1		GJ1	6000 00		6000 00	

Accounts Payable   Account No. 211

Date		Explanation	Post. Ref.	Dr.	Cr.	Balance Dr.	Balance Cr.
201X May	1		GJ1		5000 00		5000 00
	3		GJ1		600 00		5600 00
	18		GJ1		250 00		5850 00
	28		GJ2	2500 00			3350 00

Rob Sinclair, Capital   Account No. 311

Date		Explanation	Post. Ref.	Dr.	Cr.	Balance Dr.	Balance Cr.
201X May	1		GJ1		10000 00		10000 00

Rob Sinclair, Withdrawals   Account No. 312

Date		Explanation	Post. Ref.	Dr.	Cr.	Balance Dr.	Balance Cr.
201X May	20		GJ1	625 00		625 00	

Graphic Design Fees   Account No. 411

Date		Explanation	Post. Ref.	Dr.	Cr.	Balance Dr.	Balance Cr.
201X May	7		GJ1		3000 00		3000 00
	22		GJ1		5000 00		8000 00

(*continued on page 78*)   77

Figure 3.16
(*continued*)

Office Salaries Expense					Account No. 511	
Date	Explanation	Post. Ref.	Dr.	Cr.	Balance Dr.	Balance Cr.
201X May 13		GJ1	6 5 0 00		6 5 0 00	
27		GJ2	6 5 0 00		1 3 0 0 00	

Advertising Expense					Account No. 512	
Date	Explanation	Post. Ref.	Dr.	Cr.	Balance Dr.	Balance Cr.
201X May 18		GJ1	2 5 0 00		2 5 0 00	

Telephone Expense					Account No. 513	
Date	Explanation	Post. Ref.	Dr.	Cr.	Balance Dr.	Balance Cr.
201X May 29		GJ2	2 2 0 00		2 2 0 00	

▶ **TRY IT!**   **Learning Unit 3-2**

From the following general journal and partial ledger of Jasmine's Salon, post
from the journal to the ledger T accounts. Be sure to cross-reference.

Jasmine's Salon
General Journal   **p. 3**

Date	Account Titles/Description	PR	Dr.	Cr.
201X				
June 4	Cash		1,100	
	Accounts Receivable		600	
	Salon Fees Earned			1,700

Partial Ledger: Cash (111); Accounts Receivable (112); Salon Fees Earned (410)

TRY IT!   **Solution Learning Unit 3-2**

Jasmine's Salon
General Journal   **p. 3**

Date	Account Titles/Description	PR	Dr.	Cr.
201X				
June 4	Cash	111	1,100	
	Accounts Receivable	112	600	
	Salon Fees Earned	410		1,700

	Cash	111
Dr.		Cr.
6/4/1X GJ3 1,100		

	Accounts Receivable	112
Dr.		Cr.
6/4/1X GJ3 600		

	Salon Fees Earned	410
Dr.		Cr.
		6/4/1X GJ3 1,700

Preparing the Trial Balance (Step 4 of the Accounting Cycle)

LEARNING UNIT 3-3

 **L03**

The list of the individual accounts with their balances taken from the ledger is called a trial balance. The trial balance shown in Figure 3.17 was developed from the ledger accounts of Rob Sinclair's Hilight Graphic Services that were posted and balanced in Figure 3.16. If the information is journalized or posted incorrectly, the trial balance will not be correct.

Trial balance Informal listing of the ledger accounts and their balances in the ledger to aid in proving the equality of debits and credits.

A trial balance has two separate columns for accounts with debit or credit balances. When preparing a trial balance, the following chart is helpful:

TRIAL BALANCE

Debits	Credits
Assets	*Liabilities*
Expenses	*Revenue*
Withdrawals	*Capital*

The trial balance will not show everything:

- The capital figure on the trial balance may not be the beginning capital figure. For instance, if Rob Sinclair had made additional investments during the period, the additional investment would have been journalized and posted to the Capital account. The only way to tell if the capital balance on the trial balance is the original balance is to check the ledger Capital account to see whether any additional investments were made. This confirmation of beginning capital will be important when we make financial reports.
- Even careful cross-referencing does not guarantee that transactions have been properly recorded. For example, the following errors would remain undetected: (1) a transaction that may have been omitted in the journalizing process, (2) a transaction incorrectly analyzed and recorded in the journal, and (3) a journal entry journalized or posted twice.

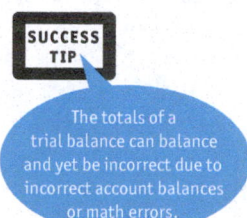

SUCCESS TIP

The totals of a trial balance can balance and yet be incorrect due to incorrect account balances or math errors.

What to Do if a Trial Balance Doesn't Balance

The trial balance of Rob Sinclair's Hilight Graphic Services shows that the total of debits is equal to the total of credits. What happens, however, if the trial balance is in balance but the correct amount is not recorded in each ledger account? Accuracy in the journalizing and posting process will help ensure that no errors are made.

Figure 3.17
Trial Balance

ROB SINCLAIR'S HILIGHT GRAPHIC SERVICES TRIAL BALANCE MAY 31, 201X	Dr.	Cr.
Cash	6 1 5 5 00	
Accounts Receivable	5 0 0 0 00	
Computer Supplies	6 0 0 00	
Prepaid Rent	1 2 0 0 00	
Computer Equipment	6 0 0 0 00	
Accounts Payable		3 3 5 0 00
Rob Sinclair, Capital		10 0 0 0 00
Rob Sinclair, Withdrawals	6 2 5 00	
Graphic Design Fees		8 0 0 0 00
Office Salaries Expense	1 3 0 0 00	
Advertising Expense	2 5 0 00	
Telephone Expense	2 2 0 00	
Totals	21 3 5 0 00	21 3 5 0 00

The trial balance lists the accounts in the same order as in the ledger. The $6,155 figure of cash came from the ledger.

Even if you find an error, the first rule is "don't panic." Everyone makes mistakes, and accepted ways of correcting them are available. Once an entry has been made in ink, correcting an error in it must always show that the entry has been changed and who changed it. Sometimes the change should be explained.

Some Common Mistakes

If the trial balance does not balance, the cause could be something relatively simple. Here are some common errors and how they can be fixed:

- If the difference (the amount you are off) is 10, 100, 1,000, and so forth, it is probably a mathematical error in addition.
- If the difference is equal to an individual account balance in the ledger, the amount could have been omitted. It is also possible the figure was not posted from the general journal.
- Divide the difference by two, then check to see whether a debit should have been a credit, or vice versa, in the ledger or trial balance. Example: $150 difference ÷ 2 = $75 means you may have placed $75 as a debit to an account instead of a credit, or vice versa.
- If the difference is evenly divisible by nine, a slide or transposition may have occurred. A slide is an error resulting from adding or deleting zeros in writing numbers. For example, $4,175.00 may have been copied as $41.75. A transposition is the accidental rearrangement of digits of a number. For example, $4,175 might have been accidentally written as $4,157.
- Compare the balances in the trial balance with the ledger accounts to check for copying errors.
- Recompute balances in each ledger account.
- Trace all postings from journal to ledger.

If you cannot find the error after taking all these steps, take an espresso break. Then start all over again.

Slide Error that results in adding or deleting zeros in the writing of a number (e.g., 79,200 → 7,920).

Transposition Accidental rearrangement of digits of a number (e.g., 152 → 125).

Making a Correction Before Posting

Before posting, manual error correction is straightforward. Simply draw a line through the incorrect entry, write the correct information above the line, and write your initials near the change. It is important to remember we are looking at a manual system. When a company is using a computerized accounting system it is quite easy to make corrections that the software has built in. Understanding a manual system gives you an appreciation of what computerized accounting systems can do today.

Correcting an Error in an Account Title. Figure 3.18 shows an error and its correction in an account title.

1	Computer Equipment		6 0 0 0 00				
	Cash ~~Accounts Payable~~ *amp*				1 0 0 0 00		
	~~Accounts Receivable~~				5 0 0 0 00		
	Purchase of equipment from Giga Co.						

Figure 3.18
Account Error

Correcting a Numerical Error. Numbers are handled the same way as account titles, as the next change from 520 to 250 in Figure 3.19 shows.

18	Advertising Expense		2 5 0 00		
	Accounts Payable			*amp* 2 5 0 00 ~~5 2 0 00~~	
	Bill from Digital Insert				

Figure 3.19
Number Error

Correcting an Entry Error. If a number has been entered in the wrong column, a straight line is drawn through it. The number is then written in the correct column, as shown in Figure 3.20.

1	Computer Equipment		6 0 0 0 00		
	Cash			1 0 0 0 00	
	Accounts Payable		*amp* ~~5 0 0 0 00~~	5 0 0 0 00	
	Purchase of equip. from Giga Co.				

Figure 3.20
Correcting Entry

Making a Correction After Posting

It is also possible to manually correct an amount that is correctly entered in the journal but posted incorrectly to the ledger of the proper account. The first step is to draw a line through the error and write the correct figure above it. The next step is changing the running balance to reflect the corrected posting. Here, too, a line is drawn through the balance and the corrected balance is written above it. Both changes must be initialed, as shown in Figure 3.21.

				Graphic Design Fees			Account No. 411	
			Post.			Balance		
Date		Explanation	Ref.	Dr.	Cr.	Dr.	Cr.	
201X May	7		GJ1		2 5 0 0 00		2 5 0 0 00	
	22		GJ1		4 1 0 0 00 ~~1 0 0 0 00~~ *amp*		6 6 0 0 00 ~~2 6 0 0 00~~ *amp*	

Figure 3.21
Correction After Posting

Correcting an Entry Posted to the Wrong Account

Drawing a line through an error and writing the correction above it is possible when a mistake has occurred within the proper account, but when an error involves a posting to the wrong account, the journal must include a correction accompanied by an explanation. In addition, the correct information must be posted to the appropriate accounts in the ledger.

Suppose, for example, that as a result of tracing postings from journal entries to ledgers you find that a $180 telephone bill was incorrectly debited as an advertising expense. The following illustration shows how this correction is done.

STEP 1:   The journal entry is corrected and the correction is explained (Figure 3.22).

Figure 3.22
Corrected Entry for Telephone

	Date		Account Titles and Description	PR	Dr.	Cr.
	201X May	29	Telephone Expense	513	1 8 0 00	
			Advertising Expense	512		1 8 0 00
			To correct error in which			
			Advertising Exp. was debited			
			for charges to Telephone Exp.			

GENERAL JOURNAL — Page 3

STEP 2:   The Advertising Expense ledger account is corrected (Figure 3.23).

Figure 3.23
Ledger Update for Advertising

Advertising Expense — Account No. 512

	Date		Explanation	Post. Ref.	Dr.	Cr.	Balance Dr.	Balance Cr.
	201X May	18		GJ1	1 7 5 00		1 7 5 00	
		23		GJ1	1 8 0 00		3 5 5 00	
		29	Correcting entry	GJ3		1 8 0 00	1 7 5 00	

STEP 3:   The Telephone Expense ledger is corrected (Figure 3.24).

Figure 3.24
Ledger Update for Telephone

Telephone Expense — Account No. 513

	Date		Explanation	Post. Ref.	Dr.	Cr.	Balance Dr.	Balance Cr.
	201X May	29		GJ3	1 8 0 00		1 8 0 00	

 **TRY IT!**   **Learning Unit 3-3**

Given the following ledger accounts for Mitchell Cleaners, prepare a trial balance as of January 31, 201X.

Cash	110			Prepaid Rent	111		Detailing Equipment	112
Dr.	Cr.			Dr.	Cr.		Dr.	Cr.
1/1/1X 5,200 GJ1	200 1/3/1X GJ1			1/3/1X 200 GJ1			1/5/1X 800 GJ1	
1/1/1X 1,300 GJ2	800 1/5/1X GJ1						1/10/1X 400 GJ2	
	500 1/15/1X GJ2							
	750 1/18/1X GJ2							
	900 1/18/1X GJ2							

Accounts Payable	210
Dr.	Cr.
	400 1/10/1X GJ2

J. Mitchell, Capital	310
Dr.	Cr.
	5,200 1/1/1X GJ1

J. Mitchell, Withdrawals	311
Dr.	Cr.
1/15/1X 500 GJ2	

Cleaning Fees	410
Dr.	Cr.
	1,300 1/1/1X GJ2

Advertising Expense	510
Dr.	Cr.
1/18/1X 750 GJ2	

Salaries Expense	520
Dr.	Cr.
1/18/1X 900 GJ2	

TRY IT!   **Solution Learning Unit 3-3**

MITCHELL CLEANERS
TRIAL BALANCE
JANUARY 31, 201X

Account	Dr.	Cr.
Cash	3 3 5 0 00	
Prepaid Rent	2 0 0 00	
Cleaning Equipment	1 2 0 0 00	
Accounts Payable		4 0 0 00
J. Mitchell, Capital		5 2 0 0 00
J. Mitchell, Withdrawals	5 0 0 00	
Cleaning Fees		1 3 0 0 00
Advertising Expense	7 5 0 00	
Salaries Expense	9 0 0 00	
Totals	6 9 0 0 00	6 9 0 0 00

DEMONSTRATION SUMMARY PROBLEM

LO1,2,3

In March, Riki's Advertising Agency had the following transactions:

201X		
Mar.	1	Riki Sims invested $5,000 cash in her new advertising agency.
	4	Bought equipment for cash, $200.
	5	Earned advertising fee, $200, but payment from Azul Co. will not be received once June.
	6	Paid wages expense, $300.
	7	Riki paid her home utility bill from the company checkbook, $75.
	9	Completed an ad campaign for VCR Corporation, receiving $1,200 cash.
	15	Paid cash for supplies, $200.
	28	Telephone bill received but not paid, $180.
	29	Digital media bill received but not paid, $400.

The chart of accounts includes Cash, 111; Accounts Receivable, 112; Supplies, 131; Equipment, 141; Accounts Payable, 211; R. Sims, Capital, 311; R. Sims, Withdrawals, 321; Advertising Fees Earned, 411; Wage Expense, 511; Telephone Expense, 521; and Digital Media Expense, 531.

Requirements

Your tasks are to do the following:

1. Journalize business transactions in the General Journal (all page 1).
2. Set up a ledger based on the chart of accounts.
3. Post journal entries.
4. Prepare a trial balance for March 31.

Solutions

Requirements 1, 2, 3

Set up ledger based on chart of accounts. Journalize (all page 1) and post journal entries. (See Figures 3.25 and 3.26 on page 85.)

Figure 3.25
Journal Entries and Posting
References

Date			Account Titles and Description	PR	Dr.	Cr.
201X Mar.	1		Cash	111	5 0 0 0 00	
			Riki Sims, Capital	311		5 0 0 0 00
			Owner investment			
		4	Equipment	141	2 0 0 00	
			Cash	111		2 0 0 00
			Bought equipment for cash			
		5	Accounts Receivable	112	2 0 0 00	
			Advertising Fees Earned	411		2 0 0 00
			Fees on account from Azul Co.			
		6	Wage Expense	511	3 0 0 00	
			Cash	111		3 0 0 00
			Paid wages			
		7	R. Sims, Withdrawals	321	7 5 00	
			Cash	111		7 5 00
			Personal withdrawals			
		9	Cash	111	1 2 0 0 00	
			Advertising Fees Earned	411		1 2 0 0 00
			Cash fees			
		15	Supplies	131	2 0 0 00	
			Cash	111		2 0 0 00
			Bought supplies for cash			
		28	Telephone Expense	521	1 8 0 00	
			Accounts Payable	211		1 8 0 00
			Telephone bill owed			
		29	Digital Media Expense	531	4 0 0 00	
			Accounts Payable	211		4 0 0 00
			Digital Media bill received			

RIKI SIMMS ADVERTISING AGENCY — Page 1

Cash 111

Date		PR	Dr.	Cr.	Balance Dr.	Balance Cr.
201X Mar.	1	GJ1	5,000		5,000	
	4	GJ1		200	4,800	
	6	GJ1		300	4,500	
	7	GJ1		75	4,425	
	9	GJ1	1,200		5,625	
	15	GJ1		200	5,425	

Accounts Receivable 112

Date		PR	Dr.	Cr.	Balance Dr.	Balance Cr.
201X Mar.	5	GJ1	200		200	

Supplies 131

Date		PR	Dr.	Cr.	Balance Dr.	Balance Cr.
201X Mar.	15	GJ1	200		200	

Equipment 141

Date		PR	Dr.	Cr.	Balance Dr.	Balance Cr.
201X Mar.	4	GJ1	200		200	

Accounts Payable 211

Date		PR	Dr.	Cr.	Balance Dr.	Balance Cr.
201X Mar.	28	GJ1		180		180
	29	GJ1		400		580

R. Sims, Capital 311

Date		PR	Dr.	Cr.	Balance Dr.	Balance Cr.
201X Mar.	1	GJ1		5,000		5,000

R. Sims, Withdrawals 321

Date		PR	Dr.	Cr.	Balance Dr.	Balance Cr.
201X Mar.	7	GJ1	75		75	

Advertising Fees Earned 411

Date		PR	Dr.	Cr.	Balance Dr.	Balance Cr.
201X Mar.	5	GJ1		200		200
	9	GJ1		1,200		1,400

Wage Expense 511

Date		PR	Dr.	Cr.	Balance Dr.	Balance Cr.
201X Mar.	6	GJ1	300		300	

Telephone Expense 521

Date		PR	Dr.	Cr.	Balance Dr.	Balance Cr.
201X Mar.	28	GJ1	180		180	

Digital Media Expense 531

Date		PR	Dr.	Cr.	Balance Dr.	Balance Cr.
201X Mar.	29	GJ1	400		400	

Figure 3.26
General Ledger

Tips to Journalizing

1. When journalizing, the PR column is not filled in.
2. Write the name of the debit against the date column. Indent credits and list them below debits. Be sure total debits for each transaction equal total credits.
3. Skip a line between each transaction.

The Analysis of the Journal Entries

Mar.	1	Cash	Asset	↑	Dr.	$5,000
		R. Sims, Capital	Capital	↑	Cr.	$5,000
	4	Equipment	Asset	↑	Dr.	$ 200
		Cash	Asset	↓	Cr.	$ 200
	5	Accts. Receivable	Asset	↑	Dr.	$ 200
		Adv. Fees Earned	Revenue	↑	Cr.	$ 200
	6	Wage Expense	Expense	↑	Dr.	$ 300
		Cash	Asset	↓	Cr.	$ 300
	7	R. Sims, Withdrawals	Withdrawal	↑	Dr.	$ 75
		Cash	Asset	↓	Cr.	$ 75
	9	Cash	Asset	↑	Dr.	$1,200
		Adv. Fees Earned	Revenue	↑	Cr.	$1,200
	15	Supplies	Asset	↑	Dr.	$ 200
		Cash	Asset	↓	Cr.	$ 200
	28	Telephone Expense	Expense	↑	Dr.	$ 180
		Accounts Payable	Liability	↑	Cr.	$ 180
	29	Digital Media Expense	Expense	↑	Dr.	$ 400
		Accounts Payable	Liability	↑	Cr.	$ 400

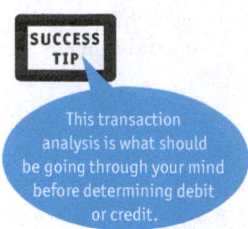

SUCCESS TIP

This transaction analysis is what should be going through your mind before determining debit or credit.

Tips for the General Ledger

The PR column in the ledger Cash account tells you from which page journal information came. After the ledger Cash account is posted, account number 111 is put in the PR column of the journal for cross-referencing.

Note how we keep a running balance in the cash account. A $5,000 debit balance and a $200 credit entry result in a new debit balance of $4,800.

Requirement 4

Preparing a Trial Balance from the Ledger. See Figure 3.27.

Figure 3.27

RIKI'S ADVERTISING AGENCY
TRIAL BALANCE
MARCH 31, 201X

	Dr.	Cr.
Cash	5 4 2 5 00	
Accounts Receivable	2 0 0 00	
Supplies	2 0 0 00	
Equipment	2 0 0 00	
Accounts Payable		5 8 0 00
R. Sims, Capital		5 0 0 0 00
R. Sims, Withdrawals	7 5 00	
Advertising Fees Earned		1 4 0 0 00
Wage Expense	3 0 0 00	
Telephone Expense	1 8 0 00	
Advertising Expense	4 0 0 00	
Totals	6 9 8 0 00	6 9 8 0 00

Solution to Preparing a Trial Balance

The trial balance lists the ending balances of the accounts in the order in which they appear in the ledger. The total of 6,980 on the left equals 6,980 on the right in Figure 3.27.

SUCCESS COACH

The following Success Tips are from Learning Units 3-1 to 3-3. Take the Do It Right Now Checkup and use the Check Your Score at the bottom of the page to see how you are doing. The Success Coach provides tips before each Checkup to help you avoid common accounting errors.

LU 3-1 Analyzing and Recording Business Transactions into a Journal (Steps 1 and 2 of the Accounting Cycle)

Do It Right Tips: When journalizing transactions be sure to use the Chart of Accounts. It provides the specific titles you will use for either debit(s) or credit(s). You will not use the Chart of Accounts for the explanations in the journal. In the journal, the debit portion of the transaction is listed first, followed by the credit portion. Remember that these titles come from the Chart of Accounts. The total of all debits must equal the total of all credits for each individual transaction.

Do It Right Now Checkup: Answer true or false to the following statements.

1. The ledger is the book of original entry.
2. Compound journal entries must have no more than three credits.
3. Billing a company for services on account would result in a debit to cash.
4. When you journalize, the PR column must be completed.
5. Rent paid in advance is an expense.

LU 3-2 Posting to the Ledger (Step 3 of the Accounting Cycle)

Do It Right Tips: Posting is transferring information from the journal to the ledger. The ledger accounts keep a running balance of each account, while the journal does not. Cross-referencing helps to fill in the PR column of the journal to show the account number that was posted from that line. With computer software, today's posting could be just a click away.

Do It Right Now Checkup: Answer true or false to the following statements.

1. Posting can only be done manually.
2. Posting means transferring information from the ledger to the journal.
3. Cross-referencing means the PR column in the ledger is up to date.
4. Posting can only be done once a month.
5. Posting results in information being accumulated in the journal.

LU 3-3 Preparing the Trial Balance (Step 4 of the Accounting Cycle)

Do It Right Tips: The trial balance is listed in the same order as the general ledger. Only one balance is shown for each account in the trial balance. Keep in mind that the trial balance could be in balance and still be incorrect due to posting twice, missing transactions, or analyzing them incorrectly.

Do It Right Now Checkup: Answer true or false to the following statements.

1. The trial balance is in the same order as the journal.
2. A trial balance can have two balances for some accounts.
3. Slides and transpositions can help locate errors in the trial balance.
4. If a journal entry is posted, no corrections can be made.
5. In the trial balance, account titles that have credit balances are indented.

CHECK YOUR SCORE: Answers to the Do It Right Now Checkup

LU 3-1

1. False—The ledger is the book of final entry.
2. False—Compound journal entries must have more than two accounts.
3. False—Billing a company for services on account would result in a debit to accounts receivable.
4. False—When you post, the PR column is completed.
5. False—Rent paid in advance is an asset.

LU 3-2

1. False—Posting can be done by computer.
2. False—Posting means transferring information from the journal to the ledger.

3. False—Cross-referencing means the PR column is updated in the journal.
4. False—Posting can be done at various times.
5. False—Posting results in information being accumulated in the ledger.

LU 3-3

1. False—The trial balance is in the same order as the ledger.
2. False—A trial balance can have only one balance per title.
3. True
4. False—If a journal entry is posted, corrections can still be made.
5. False—All account titles are listed with no indentations.

BLUEPRINT OF FIRST FOUR STEPS OF ACCOUNTING CYCLE

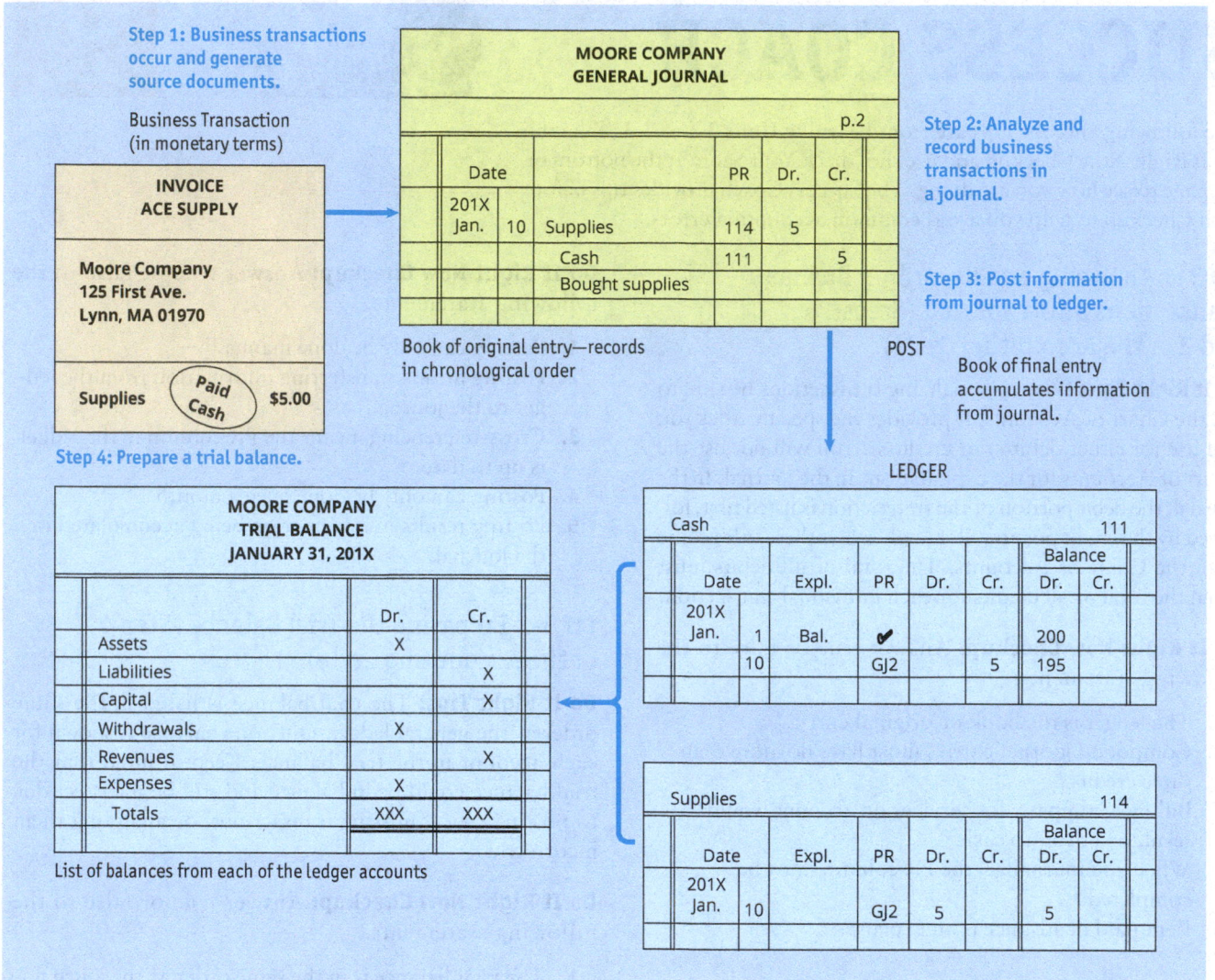

Step 1: Business transactions occur and generate source documents.

Business Transaction (in monetary terms)

INVOICE ACE SUPPLY
Moore Company 125 First Ave. Lynn, MA 01970
Supplies   Paid Cash $5.00

Step 4: Prepare a trial balance.

MOORE COMPANY GENERAL JOURNAL					
					p.2
Date			PR	Dr.	Cr.
201X Jan.	10	Supplies	114	5	
		Cash	111		5
		Bought supplies			

Book of original entry—records in chronological order

Step 2: Analyze and record business transactions in a journal.

Step 3: Post information from journal to ledger.

POST

Book of final entry accumulates information from journal.

LEDGER

MOORE COMPANY TRIAL BALANCE JANUARY 31, 201X		
	Dr.	Cr.
Assets	X	
Liabilities		X
Capital		X
Withdrawals	X	
Revenues		X
Expenses	X	
Totals	XXX	XXX

List of balances from each of the ledger accounts

Cash   111

Date		Expl.	PR	Dr.	Cr.	Balance Dr.	Balance Cr.
201X Jan.	1	Bal.	✔			200	
	10		GJ2		5	195	

Supplies   114

Date		Expl.	PR	Dr.	Cr.	Balance Dr.	Balance Cr.
201X Jan.	10		GJ2	5		5	

Discussion Questions and Critical Thinking/Ethical Case

1. Not all businesses have or need an accounting cycle. Agree or disagree and defend your position.

2. An accounting period is based on the balance sheet. Agree or disagree and defend your position.

3. Compare and contrast a calendar year versus a fiscal year.

4. What are interim statements?

5. With computers today, ledgers are not needed in today's accounting system. Agree or disagree and defend your position.

6. How do transactions get "linked" in a general journal?

7. What is the relationship of the chart of accounts to the general journal?

8. What is a compound journal entry?

9. Posting means updating the journal. Agree or disagree? Please comment.

10. The side that decreases an account is the normal balance. True or false?

11. The PR column of a general journal is the last item to be filled in during the manual posting process. Agree or disagree?

12. Discuss the concept of cross-referencing.

13. What is the difference between a transposition and a slide?

14. Mandy Peters, the lead accountant of Ross Co., would like to buy a new general ledger software program. She couldn't do it because all funds were frozen for the rest of the fiscal period. Mandy called her friend at Flick Industries and asked whether she could copy its software. Comment on why it is or is not okay for Mandy to make such a request.

Concept Checks

MyLab**Accounting**

General Journal

1. Complete the following from the general journal of Munro Co. (see Figure 3.28):

    L01 *(5 min)*

    a. Year of journal entry   _____

    b. Month of journal entry   _____

    c. Day of journal entry   _____

    d. Name(s) of accounts debited   _____

    e. Name(s) of accounts credited   _____

    f. Explanation of transaction   _____

    g. Amount of debit(s)   _____

    h. Amount of credit(s)   _____

    i. Page of journal   _____

Figure 3.28
General Journal

		MUNRO COMPANY GENERAL JOURNAL					
							Page 1
Date		Account Titles and Description	PR	Dr.		Cr.	
201X Mar.	2	Cash		4 0 0 00			
		Equipment		19 0 0 0 00			
		B. Munro, Capital				19 4 0 0 00	
		Initial Investment by Owner					

General Journal

(5 min)   **LO2**

2.   Provide the explanation for each of the general journal entries in Figure 3.29.

Figure 3.29
Journal Entries

		GENERAL JOURNAL				Page 4	
Date		Account Titles and Descriptions	PR	Dr.		Cr.	
201X Nov.	10	Cash		30 0 0 0 00			
		Office Equipment		7 0 0 00			
		J. Walsh, Capital				30 7 0 0 00	
		(A)					
	16	Cash		1 2 5 00			
		Accounts Receivable		1 5 0 00			
		Consulting Fees Earned				2 7 5 00	
		(B)					
	18	Salaries Expense		2 0 0 00			
		Salaries Payable				2 0 0 00	
		(C)					

Posting and Balancing

(5 min)   **LO2**

3.   Balance this four-column account. What function does the PR column serve? When will Account 111 be used in the journalizing and posting process?

				Cash		Acct. 111	
						Balance	
Date		Explanation	PR	Dr.	Cr.	Dr.	Cr.
201X							
Jan.	6		GJ 1	22			
	16		GJ 1	31			
	20		GJ 2		20		
	22		GJ 3	40			

The Trial Balance

4. The following trial balance (Figure 3.30) was prepared *incorrectly*.

    a. Rearrange the accounts in proper order.

Figure 3.30

ERICKSON CO. TRIAL BALANCE JULY 31, 201X		
Account	Dr.	Cr.
D. Erickson, Capital	1 6 00	
Equipment	1 2 00	
Rent Expense		5 00
Advertising Expense		6 00
Accounts Payable		1 2 00
Taxi Fees	1 9 00	
Cash	1 6 00	
D. Erickson, Withdrawals		8 00
Totals	6 3 00	3 1 00

b. Calculate the total of the trial balance. (Small numbers are used intentionally so that you can do the calculations in your head.) Assume each account has a normal balance.

Correcting Entry

5. On June 1, 201X, a telephone expense for $175 was debited to Repair Expense. On June 10, 201X, this error was found. Prepare the corrected journal entry. When would a correcting entry *not* be needed?

Exercises

MyLabAccounting

Set A

3A-1. Prepare journal entries for the following transactions that occurred during May:

201X		
May	1	Joan Doxbury invested $170,000 cash and $20,000 of equipment into her new business.
	3	Purchased building for $50,000 on account.
	12	Purchased a truck from Lexington Co. for $9,000 cash.
	18	Bought supplies from May Co. for $300 on account.

3A-2. Record the following into the general journal of Reggie's Auto Shop.

201X		
May	1	Reggie Stathos invested $90,000 cash in the auto shop.
	5	Paid $7,000 for auto equipment.
	8	Bought auto equipment from Lancaster Co. for $10,000 on account.
	14	Received $900 for repair fees earned.
	18	Billed McNeil Co. $750 for services rendered.
	20	Reggie withdrew $400 for personal use.

(10 min) **LO2**

3A-3. Post the journal entries in Figure 3.31 to the ledger of Kilmer Company. The partial ledger of Kilmer Company is Cash, 111; Equipment, 121; Accounts Payable, 211; and A. Kilmer, Capital, 311. Please use four-column accounts in the posting process.

Figure 3.31
Journal Entries

Date				PR	Dr.	Cr.
201X Feb.	6	Cash			8 0 0 0 00	
		A. Kilmer, Capital				8 0 0 0 00
		Cash investment				
	14	Equipment			4 2 0 0 00	
		Cash				3 5 0 0 00
		Accounts Payable				7 0 0 00
		Purchase of equipment				

Page 4

(20 min) **LO1,2,3**

3A-4. From the following transactions for Leslie Company for the month of July, (a) prepare journal entries (assume that it is page 1 of the journal), (b) post journal entries to the ledger (use a four-column account), and (c) prepare a trial balance.

	201X	
July	1	Jasmine Leslie invested $9,000 in the business.
	4	Bought equipment from Brasa Co. for $800 on account.
	15	Billed Cuz Co. for services rendered, $7,000.
	18	Received $5,000 cash for services rendered.
	24	Paid salaries expense, $1,200.
	28	Jasmine withdrew $700 for personal use.

A partial chart of accounts includes Cash, 111; Accounts Receivable, 112; Equipment, 121; Accounts Payable, 211; J. Leslie, Capital, 311; J. Leslie, Withdrawals, 312; Fees Earned, 411; and Salaries Expense, 511.

(15 min) **LO3**

3A-5. You have been hired to correct the trial balance in Figure 3.32 that has been recorded improperly from the ledger to the trial balance.

Figure 3.32
Incorrect Trial Balance

SCARSDALE CO. TRIAL BALANCE OCTOBER 31, 201X		
Account	**Dr.**	**Cr.**
Accounts Payable	3 5 0 0 00	
A. Scarsdale, Capital		3 8 0 0 00
A. Scarsdale, Withdrawals		8 0 0 00
Services Earned		9 2 0 0 00
Concessions Earned	3 2 0 0 00	
Rent Expense	5 0 0 00	
Salaries Expense	2 7 0 0 00	
Miscellaneous Expense		1 2 0 0 00
Cash	13 0 0 0 00	
Accounts Receivable		1 5 0 0 00
Totals	22 9 0 0 00	16 5 0 0 00

3A-6. On February 6, 201X, Mark Sullivan made the journal entry in Figure 3.33 to record the purchase on account of office equipment priced at $1,200. This journal entry had not yet been posted when the error was discovered. Make the appropriate correction.

 **L03** *(10 min)*

		GENERAL JOURNAL						
Date		Account Titles and Description	PR	Dr.		Cr.		
201X Feb.	6	Office Equipment		8 0 0 00				
		Accounts Payable				8 0 0 00		
		Purchase of office equip. on account						

Figure 3.33
Recording Error

Set B

3B-1. Prepare journal entries for the following transactions that occurred during March:

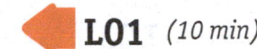 **L01** *(10 min)*

201X

March 1 Jill Spinali invested $50,000 cash and $9,000 of equipment into her new business.

3 Purchased building for $90,000 on account.

12 Purchased a truck from Lynfield Co. for $13,000 cash.

18 Bought supplies from Lumb Co. for $400 on account.

3B-2. Record the following into the general journal of Raymond's Auto Shop.

 **L01** *(10 min)*

201X

May 1 Raymond Tacks invested $100,000 cash in the auto shop.

5 Paid $7,000 for auto equipment.

8 Bought auto equipment from Lawrence Co. for $6,000 on account.

14 Received $1,800 for repair fees earned.

18 Billed Lumb Co. $800 for services rendered.

20 Raymond withdrew $450 for personal use.

3B-3. Post the journal entries in Figure 3.34 to the ledger of Kilian Company. The partial ledger of Kilian Company is Cash, 111; Equipment, 121; Accounts Payable, 211; and A. Kilian, Capital, 311. Please use four-column accounts in the posting process.

 **L02** *(10 min)*

Figure 3.34

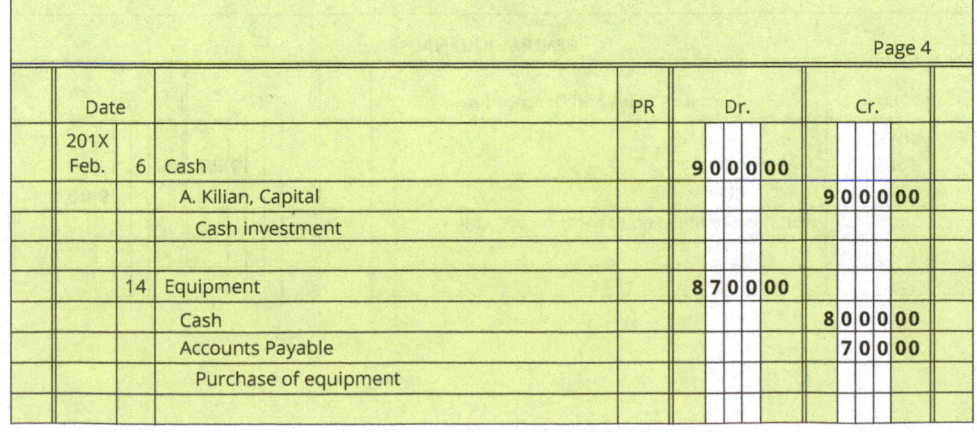

							Page 4	
Date			PR	Dr.		Cr.		
201X Feb.	6	Cash		9 0 0 0 00				
		A. Kilian, Capital				9 0 0 0 00		
		Cash investment						
	14	Equipment		8 7 0 0 00				
		Cash				8 0 0 0 00		
		Accounts Payable				7 0 0 00		
		Purchase of equipment						

(20 min) **L01,2,3**

3B-4. From the following transactions for Leslie Company for the month of July, (a) prepare journal entries (assume that it is page 1 of the journal), (b) post journal entries to the ledger (use a four-column account), and (c) prepare a trial balance.

	201X	
Nov	1	Jasmine Leslie invested $22,0000 in the business.
	6	Bought equipment from Brasa Co. for $18,000 on account.
	15	Billed Cuz Co. for services rendered, $7,000.
	18	Received $5,000 cash for services rendered.
	24	Paid salary expense, $1,200.
	28	Jasmine withdrew $700 for personal use.

A partial chart of accounts includes Cash, 111; Accounts Receivable, 112; Equipment, 121; Accounts Payable, 211; J. Leslie, Capital, 311; J. Leslie, Withdrawals, 312; Fees Earned, 411; and Salaries Expense, 511.

(15 min) **L03**

3B-5. You have been hired to correct the trial balance in Figure 3.35 that has been recorded improperly from the ledger to the trial balance.

Figure 3.35

SIMONE CO. TRIAL BALANCE AUGUST 31, 201X		
Account	Dr.	Cr.
Accounts Payable	6 0 0 0 00	
A. Simone, Capital		5 0 00
A. Simone, Withdrawals		1 1 5 0 00
Services Earned		4 7 0 0 00
Concessions Earned	2 9 0 0 00	
Rent Expense	1 3 0 0 00	
Salaries Expense	2 6 0 0 00	
Miscellaneous Expense		1 8 0 0 00
Cash	5 0 0 0 00	
Accounts Receivable		1 8 0 0 00
Totals	17 8 0 0 00	9 5 0 0 00

(10 min) **L03**

3B-6. On February 6, 201X, Morris Sanford made the journal entry in Figure 3.36 to record the purchase on account of office equipment priced at $1,000. This journal entry had not yet been posted when the error was discovered. Make the appropriate correction.

Figure 3.36

GENERAL JOURNAL					
Date	Account Titles and Description	PR	Dr.	Cr.	
201X Feb. 6	Office Equipment		9 00		
	Accounts Payable			9 00	
	Purchase of office equipment on account				

Problems

MyLabAccounting

Set A

3A-1. John Murley operates John's Cleaning Service. As the bookkeeper, you have been requested to journalize the following transactions:

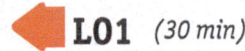

L01 *(30 min)*

201X		
Aug. 1	Paid 2 months' rent in advance, $10,000.	
6	Purchased cleaning equipment on account from Houton's Supply House, $15,000.	
12	Purchased cleaning supplies from Lancaster's Wholesale for $800 cash.	
14	Received $1,300 cash from cleaning fees earned.	
20	John withdrew $150 for personal use.	
21	Advertising bill received from *Sullivan News* but unpaid, $250.	
25	Paid electrical expense, $120.	
28	Paid salaries expense, $500.	
29	Performed cleaning work for $2,600, but payment will not be received until October.	
30	Paid Houton's Supply House half the amount owed from August 6 transaction.	

Check Figure:
August 21
Dr. Advertising Expense $250
Cr. Accounts Payable $250

The chart of accounts for John's Cleaning Service is as follows:

Chart of Accounts

Assets		Owner's Equity		
111	Cash	311	John Murley, Capital
112	Accounts Receivable	312	John Murley, Withdrawals
114	Prepaid Rent	**Revenue**	
116	Cleaning Supplies	411	Cleaning Fees Earned
120	Cleaning Equipment	**Expenses**	
121	Office Equipment	511	Advertising Expense
Liabilities		512	Electrical Expense
211	Accounts Payable	514	Salaries Expense

3A-2. On September 1, 201X, Brittney Slater opened Brittney's Art Studio. The following transactions occurred in September:

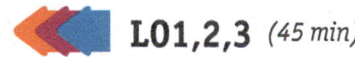

L01,2,3 *(45 min)*

201X	
Sept. 1	Brittney Slater invested $20,000 in the art studio.
1	Paid 10 months' rent in advance, $2,100.
3	Purchased $2,100 of equipment from Ushem Co. on account.
5	Received $7,000 cash for art-training workshop for teachers.
8	Purchased art supplies for $250 cash.
9	Billed Simon Co. $2,000 for group art lesson for its employees.
10	Paid salaries of assistants, $700.
15	Brittney withdrew $700 for personal use.
28	Paid electric bill, $100.
29	Paid telephone bill for September, $200.

Check Figure:
Trial Balance Total $31,100

Your tasks are to do the following:

a. Set up the ledger based on the following chart of accounts using four-column accounts.
b. Journalize (journal is page 1) and post the September journal entries.
c. Prepare a trial balance as of September 30, 201X.

The chart of accounts for Brittney's Art Studio is as follows:

Chart of Accounts

Assets			Owner's Equity		
111	Cash		311	B. Slater, Capital	
112	Accounts Receivable		312	B. Slater, Withdrawals	
114	Prepaid Rent		**Revenue**		
121	Art Supplies		411	Art Fees Earned	
131	Equipment		**Expenses**		
Liabilities			511	Electrical Expense	
211	Accounts Payable		521	Salaries Expense	
			531	Telephone Expense	

(45 min) **L01,2,3**    **3A-3.**   The following transactions occurred in September 201X for A. Freeman's Placement Agency:

201X		
Sept.	1	A. Freeman invested $6,000 cash in the placement agency.
	1	Bought equipment from Tiger Co. for $1,800 on account.
	3	Earned placement fees of $2,100, but payment will not be received until October.
	5	A. Freeman withdrew $500 for personal use.
	7	Paid wages expense, $600.
	9	Placed a client on a local TV show, receiving $1,300 cash.
	15	Bought supplies from Howdi Co. for $250 on account.
	28	Paid telephone bill for September, $210.
	29	Advertising bill from Shaker Co. received but not paid, $110.

Check Figure:
Trial Balance Total $11,560

The chart of accounts for A. Freeman Placement Agency is as follows:

Chart of Accounts

Assets			Owner's Equity		
111	Cash		311	A. Freeman, Capital	
112	Accounts Receivable		312	A. Freeman, Withdrawals	
131	Supplies		**Revenue**		
141	Equipment		411	Placement Fees Earned	
Liabilities			**Expenses**		
211	Accounts Payable		511	Wage Expense	
			521	Telephone Expense	
			531	Advertising Expense	

Your tasks are to do the following:

a. Set up the ledger based on the chart of accounts using four-column accounts.
b. Journalize (page 1) and post the September journal entries.
c. Prepare a trial balance as of September 30, 201X.

Set B

3B-1   Jarad Stone operates Jarad's Cleaning Service. As the bookkeeper, you have been requested to journalize the following transactions:

 **LO1** *(30 min)*

201X		
May 1	Paid 2 months' rent in advance, $12,000.
6	Purchased cleaning equipment from Emery's Supply House for $6,000 on account.
12	Purchased cleaning supplies from Littleton's Wholesale for $1,000 cash.
14	Received $1,900 cash from cleaning fees earned.
20	Jarad withdrew $450 for personal use.
21	Advertising bill received from Morning News but unpaid, $300.
25	Paid electrical expense, $80.
28	Paid salaries expense, $1,100.
29	Performed cleaning work for $1,800, but payment will not be received until July.
30	Paid Emery's Supply House half the amount owed from the May 6 transaction.

Check Figure:
May 21
Dr. Advertising expense $300
Cr. Accounts payable $300

The chart of accounts for Jarad's Cleaning Service is as follows:

Chart of Accounts

Assets		Owner's Equity	
111	Cash	311	Jarad Stone, Capital
112	Accounts Receivable	312	Jarad Stone, Withdrawals
114	Prepaid Rent	**Revenue**	
116	Cleaning Supplies	411	Cleaning Fees Earned
120	Cleaning Equipment	**Expenses**	
121	Office Equipment	511	Advertising Expense
Liabilities		512	Electrical Expense
211	Accounts Payable	514	Salaries Expense

3B-2.   On November 1, 201X, Bette Sirota opened Bette's Art Studio. The following transactions occurred in November.

 **LO1,2,3** *(45 min)*

201X		
Nov. 1	Bette Sirota invested $25,000 in the art studio.
1	Paid 2 months' rent in advance, $4,200.
3	Purchased equipment from Mesa Co. for $2,500 on account.
5	Received $2,000 cash for art-training workshop for teachers.
8	Purchased art supplies for $150 cash.
9	Billed Joseph Co. $3,900 for group art lessons for its employees.
10	Paid salaries of assistants, $1,400.
15	Bette withdrew $1,100 for personal use.
28	Paid electric bill, $130.
29	Paid telephone bill for November, $140.

Check Figure:
Total Trial Balance $33,400

Your tasks are to do the following:

a. Set up a ledger based on the following chart of accounts using four-column accounts.

b. Journalize (journal is page 1) and post the November journal entries.

c. Prepare a trial balance as of November 30, 201X.

The chart of accounts for Bette's Art Studio is as follows:

Chart of Accounts

Assets			Owner's Equity		
111	Cash		311	B. Sirota, Capital	
112	Accounts Receivable		312	B. Sirota, Withdrawals	
114	Prepaid Rent		**Revenue**		
121	Art Supplies		411	Art Fees Earned	
131	Equipment		**Expenses**		
Liabilities			511	Electrical Expense	
211	Accounts Payable		521	Salaries Expense	
			531	Telephone Expense	

(45 min) **L01,2,3**

3B-3. The following transactions occurred in November 201X for A. Hopper's Placement Agency:

201X		
Nov.	1	A. Hopper invested $15,000 cash in the placement agency.
	1	Bought equipment from Tiger Co. for $2,100 on account.
	3	Earned placement fees of $3,300, but payment will not be received until December.
	5	A. Hopper withdrew $1,000 for personal use.
	7	Paid wages expense, $400.
	9	Placed a client on a local TV show, receiving $14,000 cash.
	15	Bought supplies from Holly Co. for $300 on account.
	28	Paid telephone bill for November, $200.
	29	Advertising bill from Sheet Co. received but not paid, $900.

Check Figure:
Total Trial Balance $35,600

The chart of accounts for A. Hopper Placement Agency is as follows:

Chart of Accounts

Assets			Owner's Equity		
111	Cash		311	A. Hopper, Capital	
112	Accounts Receivable		312	A. Hopper, Withdrawals	
131	Supplies		**Revenue**		
141	Equipment		411	Placement Fees Earned	
Liabilities			**Expenses**		
211	Accounts Payable		511	Wage Expense	
			521	Telephone Expense	
			531	Advertising Expense	

Your task is to do the following:

a. Set up a ledger based on the chart of accounts using four-column accounts.
b. Journalize (page 1) and post the November journal entries.
c. Prepare a trial balance at November 30, 201X.

Financial Report Problem

Reading Amazon's Annual Report

L03 *(5 min)*

Go to **https://tinyurl.com/slaterca14e** to access Amazon's 2016 Annual Report. Find the Consolidated Statement of Operations. How much did Amazon's net product sales increase or decrease from 2015 to 2016?

KEEPING IT REAL SUAREZ COMPUTER CENTER

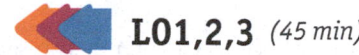
MyLabAccounting

L01,2,3 *(45 min)*

The computer center's business is picking up, so Troy Falco, the owner, has decided to expand his bookkeeping system to a general journal/ledger system. The balances from August have been forwarded to the ledger accounts.

Assignment

1. Use the chart of accounts in Chapter 2 to record the following transactions in Figures 3.37 through 3.47.

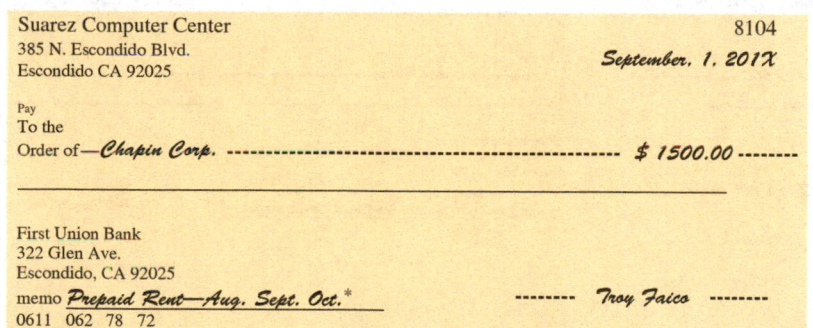

Figure 3.37
Prepaid Rent

*One check is written for 3 months' rent on September 1. That included August rent. For this problem, consider it all prepaid.

Figure 3.38
Service Revenue

Figure 3.39
Service Revenue

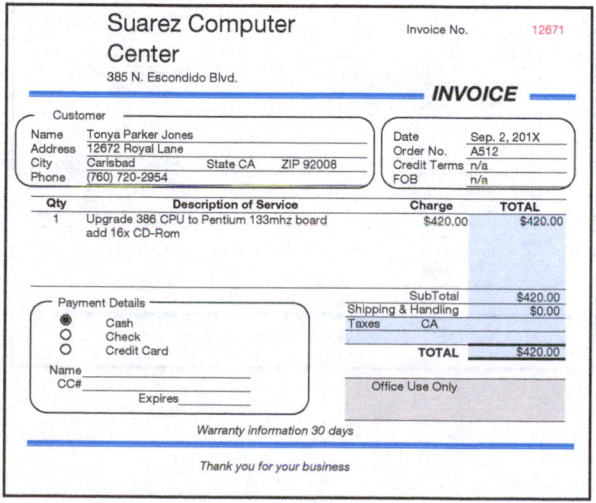

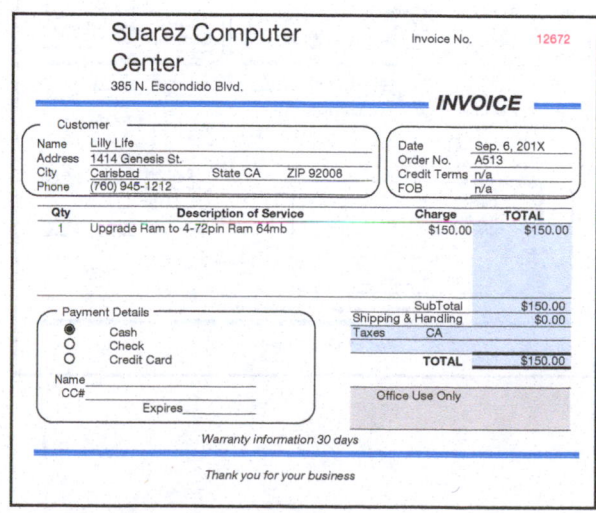

Figure 3.40
Telephone Bill

Suarez Computer Center	8105
385 N. Escondido Blvd.	September, 8, 201X
Escondido CA 92025	

Pay
To the
Order of —*Pacific Bell* -------------------------- $ 200.00 ---------

First Union Bank
322 Glen Ave.
Escondido, CA 92025
memo *August phone bill transaction (6)*   ------ *Troy Falco* -------
0611 062 78 72

Refer back to Chapter 2, Transaction K.

Figure 3.41
Tarsia Collection

Kristen Tarsia	251
1919 Sierra St.	September, 12, 201X
Escondido CA 92025	

Pay
To the
Order of —*Suarez Computer Center*---------------------- $ 1,100.00 -----

Bank First
322 Cardiff Ave.
Escondido, CA 92025
memo *Computer Fixed, Transaction (o)*   ------ *Kristen Tarsia* -------
0611 062 78 72

Refer back to Chapter 2, Transaction O.

Figure 3.42
Paid The Computer Store

Suarez Computer Center	8106
385 N. Escondido Blvd.	September, 15, 201X
Escondido CA 92025	

Pay
To the
Order of —*The Computer Store* ---------------------- $ 500.00 --------

First Union Bank
322 Glen Ave.
Escondido, CA 92025
memo *Account due from transaction (s)*   ------ *Troy Falco* -------
0611 062 78 72

Refer back to Chapter 2, Transaction S.

Figure 3.43
Purchased Computer Equipment

Suarez Computer Center	8107
385 N. Escondido Blvd.	September, 17, 201X
Escondido CA 92025	

Pay
To the
Order of —*Hardware Haven* ----------------------- $ 2,100.00 -------

First Union Bank
322 Glen Ave.
Escondido, CA 92025
   Purchase order 200
memo *Computer Equipment-Bench Workstations*   ------ *Troy Falco* -------
0611 062 78 72

Figure 3.44
Received Telephone Bill

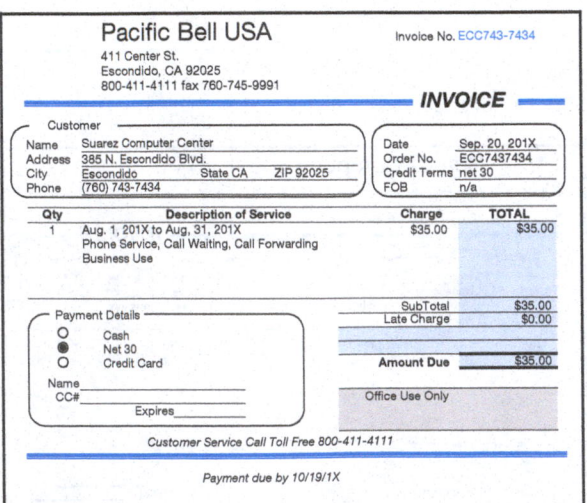

Figure 3.45
Received Electric Bill

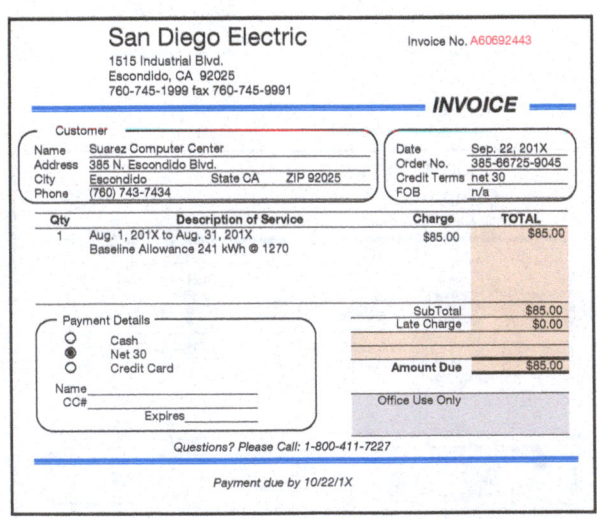

Figure 3.46
Service Revenue

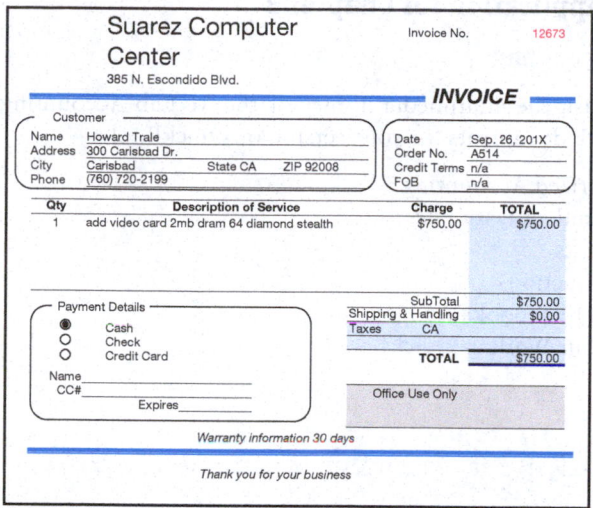

Figure 3.47
Service Revenue

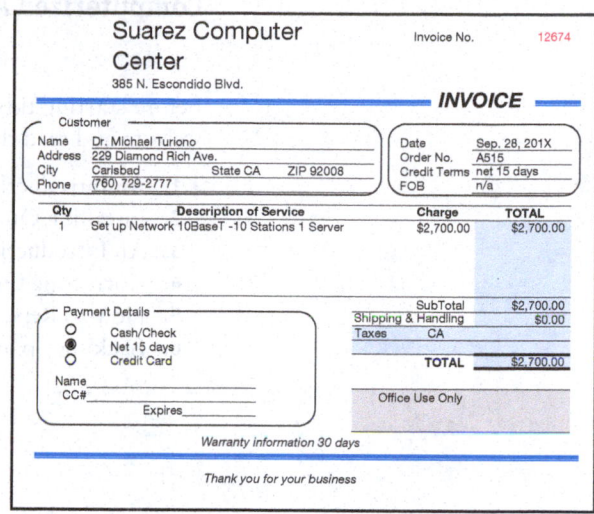

2. Post all journal entries to the general ledger accounts (the Prepaid Rent Account #1025 has been added to the chart of accounts).

3. Prepare a trial balance for September 30, 201X.

4. Prepare the financial statements for the 3 months ended September 30, 201X.

SAGE 50 SOFTWARE SIMULATION

S50

Computerized Accounting Application for Chapter 3

Preparing to use Sage 50 Complete Accounting

Before starting this assignment, visit the multimedia library of the MyLab Accounting website and read the following PDF documents for your version of Sage 50.

1. An Introduction to Computerized Accounting
2. Installing Sage 50 and Student Data Files
3. An Introduction to Sage 50
4. Correcting Sage 50 Transactions
5. How to Repeat or Restart a Sage 50 Assignment
6. Backing Up and Restoring Your Work in Sage 50

Workshop 1:

Journalizing, Posting, General Ledger, Trial Balance, and Chart of Accounts

In this workshop, you will enter, post, and edit journal entries for the Atlas Company using Sage 50. You will also print the general journal report, trial balance, and chart of accounts.

Instructions and data files for completing this assignment are in the multimedia library of the MyLab Accounting website. Open the *Workshop 1 Atlas Company* PDF document for your version of Sage 50 and download the *Atlas Company* data file for your version of Sage 50.

QB   # QUICKBOOKS SOFTWARE SIMULATION

Computerized Accounting Application for Chapter 3

Preparing to use QuickBooks Accountant

Before starting this assignment, visit the multimedia library of the MyLab Accounting website and read the following PDF documents for your version of QuickBooks.

1. An Introduction to Computerized Accounting
2. Installing QuickBooks and Student Data Files
3. An Introduction to QuickBooks
4. Correcting QuickBooks Transactions
5. How to Repeat or Restart a QuickBooks Assignment
6. Backing Up and Restoring Your Work in QuickBooks

Workshop 1:

Journalizing, Posting, General Ledger, Trial Balance, and Chart of Accounts

In this workshop, you will enter, post, and edit journal entries for the Atlas Company using QuickBooks. You will also print the general journal report, trial balance, and chart of accounts.

Instructions and data files for completing this assignment are in the multimedia library of the MyLab Accounting website. Open the *Workshop 1 Atlas Company* PDF document for your version of QuickBooks and download the *Atlas Company* data file for your version of QuickBooks.

The Accounting Cycle Continued

4

CHAPTER PREVIEW: ACCOUNTING IN ACTION

New cars have more advanced technology than ever before. Isaiah Rashad loves his new Tesla Model X, which can park itself. Designers at Tesla Motors first sketched the concept of parallel parking using software and then considered how this new feature could be manufactured. While accountants do not design cars, they do use a sketch pad called a worksheet to make changes and adjustments to the trial balance and financial statements. Today, whether in the accounting department at Tesla Motors or a small business, these "design sheets" or worksheets are "sketched" by accounting software. Laying out a worksheet will provide you with a tool to aid you in understanding the "design"—the financial statements generated by your accounting software.

Learning Objectives – Relating Accounting Theory By Unit

LO1   Explain Adjustments and How to Record Them on a Worksheet

LO2   Complete the Worksheet

LO3   Prepare Financial Statements from the Worksheet

Each year, Tesla Motors completes an accounting cycle. Figure 4.1 shows the first four steps of the manual accounting cycle that were completed for Rob Sinclair's Hilight Graphic Services in the previous chapter. This chapter continues the cycle with Steps 5–6: the preparation of a worksheet and three financial statements.

LO1

Worksheet Columnar device used by accountants to aid them in completing the accounting cycle—often just referred to as "spreadsheet." It is not a formal report.

Explaining Adjustments and How to Record them on a Worksheet

An accountant uses a worksheet to organize and check data before preparing the financial statements necessary to complete the accounting cycle. When an accounting software package is used, a worksheet is not needed. Most worksheets are completed using Microsoft Excel. The most important function of the worksheet is to allow the accountant to find and correct errors before financial statements are prepared. In a way, the worksheet acts as the accountant's scratch pad. No one sees the worksheet once the financial statements are prepared. A sample partial worksheet is shown in Figure 4.2.

The accounts listed on the far left of the worksheet are taken from the ledger. The rest of the worksheet has five sections: the trial balance, adjustments, adjusted trial balance, income statement, and balance sheet. Each of these sections is divided into debit and credit columns.

The Trial Balance Section

We discussed how to prepare a trial balance in Chapter 2. Some companies prepare a separate trial balance; others, such as Rob Sinclair's Hilight Graphic Services, prepare the trial balance directly on the worksheet. A trial balance is taken on every account listed in the ledger that has a balance. Additional titles from the ledger are added as they are needed. (We show how to add account titles later.)

The Adjustments Section

Chapters 1–3 discussed transactions that occurred with outside suppliers and companies. In a business, inside transactions also occur during the accounting cycle.

Figure 4.1

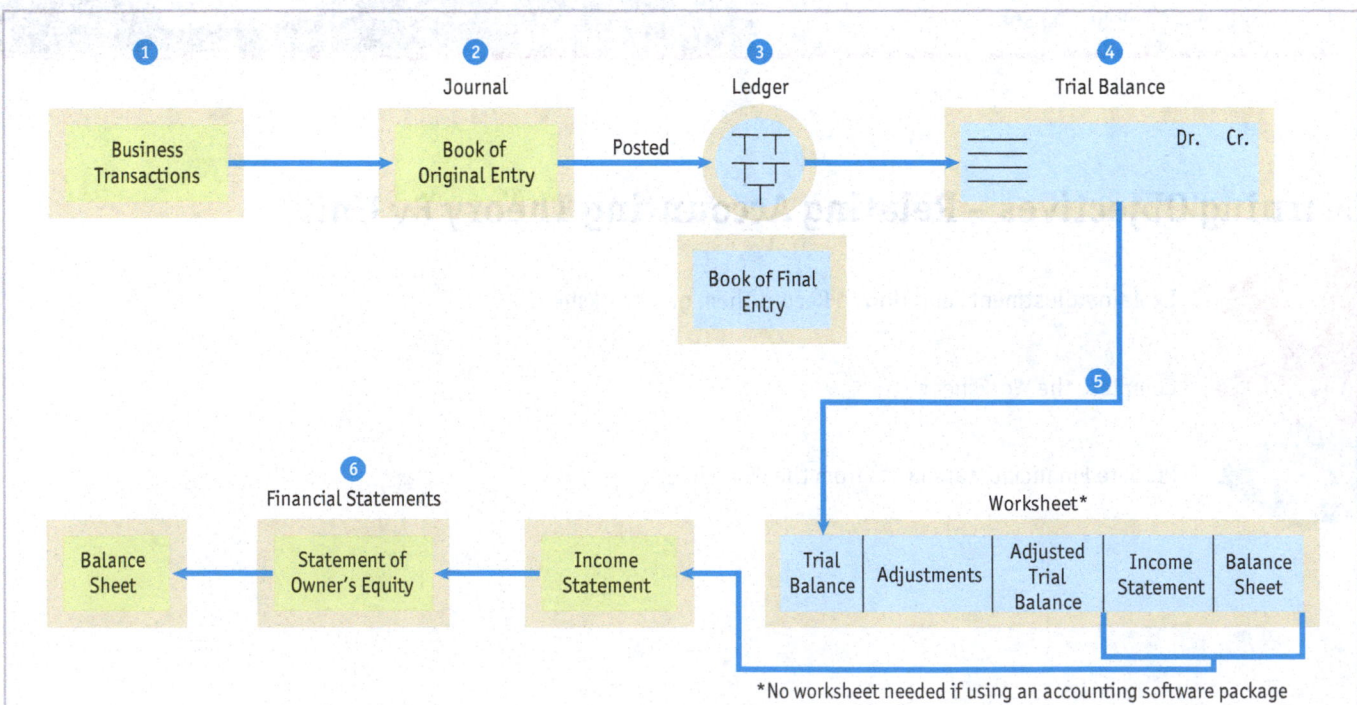

*No worksheet needed if using an accounting software package

Figure 4.2 Sample Worksheet

	ROB SINCLAIR'S HILIGHT GRAPHIC SERVICES WORKSHEET FOR MONTH ENDING MAY 31, 201X									
	Trial Balance		Adjustments		Adjusted Trial Balance		Income Statement			
Account Titles	Dr.	Cr.	Dr.	Cr.	Dr.	Cr.	Dr.	Cr.		
Cash	6 1 5 5 00									
Accounts Receivable	5 0 0 0 00									
Computer Supplies	6 0 0 00									
Prepaid Rent	1 2 0 0 00									
Computer Equipment	6 0 0 0 00									
Accounts Payable		3 3 5 0 00								
Rob Sinclair, Capital		10 0 0 0 00								
Rob Sinclair, Withdrawals	6 2 5 00									
Graphic Design Fees		8 0 0 0 00								
Office Salaries Expense	1 3 0 0 00									
Advertising Expense	2 5 0 00									
Telephone Expense	2 2 0 00									
Totals	21 3 5 0 00	21 3 5 0 00								

These transactions must be recorded, too. At the end of the worksheet process, the accountant will have all of the business's accounts up-to-date and ready to be used to prepare the formal financial statements. Accounting rules specifically state the need to have accurate financial statements. By analyzing each of Sinclair's accounts on the worksheet, the accountant will be able to identify specific accounts that must be adjusted to bring them up-to-date. The accountant for Rob Sinclair's Hilight Graphic Services needs to adjust the following accounts:

a. Computer Supplies
b. Prepaid Rent
c. Computer Equipment
d. Office Salaries Expense

Let's look at how to analyze and adjust each of these accounts.

A. Adjusting the Computer Supplies Account. On May 31, the accountant found out that the company had only $100 worth of computer supplies on hand. When the company had originally purchased $600 of computer supplies, they were considered an asset. As the supplies were used up, they became an expense.

- Computer supplies available: $600 on trial balance.
- Computer supplies left or on hand as of May 31: $100 will end up on adjusted trial balance.
- Computer supplies used up in the operation of the business for the month of May: $500 is shown in the adjustments column.

As a result, the asset Computer Supplies is too high on the trial balance (it should be $100, not $600). At the same time, if we don't show the additional expense of supplies used, the company's *net income* will be too high.

If Sinclair's accountant does not adjust the trial balance to reflect the change, the company's net income will be too high on the income statement and both sides (Assets and Owner's Equity) of the balance sheet will be too high.

Worksheets can be completed on Excel spreadsheets. Knowing Excel is a must for today's accountant.

Adjusting Process of calculating the latest up-to-date balance of each account at the end of an accounting period.

American Institute of Professional Bookkeepers (AIPB) –"Demand for full-charge bookkeepers is expected to increase as they are called upon to do much of the work of accountants. Those with several years of accounting or bookkeeper certification will have the best job prospects." *Occupational Outlook Handbook U.S. Department of Labor Bureau of Labor Statistics*. More on the AIPB can found at **www.aipb .org**

Now let's look at the adjustment for computer supplies in terms of the transaction analysis chart.

Will go on income statement

Accounts Affected	Category	↓↑	Rules
Computer Supplies Expense	Expense	↑	Dr.
Computer Supplies	Asset	↓	Cr.

Will go on balance sheet

Computer Supplies Exp. 514	Computer Supplies 114
500	600 | 500
This amount is supplies used up.	100 |

↑
This amount is supplies on hand.

SUCCESS TIP

The adjustment for supplies deals with the amount of supplies *used up*.

The Computer Supplies Expense account comes from the chart of accounts in Chapter 3. Because it is not listed in the account titles, it must be listed below the trial balance. Let's see how we enter this adjustment in the worksheet in Figure 4.3.

Place $500 in the debit column of the adjustments section on the same line as Computer Supplies Expense. Place $500 in the credit column of the adjustments section on the same line as Computer Supplies. The numbers in the adjustment column show what is used, *not* what is on hand.

B. Adjusting the Prepaid Rent Account. Back on May 1, Rob Sinclair's Hilight Graphic Services paid 3 months' rent in advance. The accountant realized that the rent expense would be $400 per month ($1,200 ÷ 3 months = $400).

Figure 4.3

ROB SINCLAIR'S HILIGHT GRAPHIC SERVICES
WORKSHEET
FOR MONTH ENDED MAY 31, 201X

Account Titles	Trial Balance Dr.	Trial Balance Cr.	Adjustments Dr.	Adjustments Cr.
Cash	6 1 5 5 00			
Accounts Receivable	5 0 0 0 00			
Computer Supplies	6 0 0 00			(A) 5 0 0 00
Prepaid Rent	1 2 0 0 00			
Computer Equipment	6 0 0 0 00			
Accounts Payable		3 3 5 0 00		
Rob Sinclair, Capital		10 0 0 0 00		
Rob Sinclair, Withdrawals	6 2 5 00			
Graphic Design Fees		8 0 0 0 00		
Office Salaries Expense	1 3 0 0 00			
Advertising Expense	2 5 0 00			
Telephone Expense	2 2 0 00			
Totals	21 3 5 0 00	21 3 5 0 00		
Computer Supplies Expense			(A) 5 0 0 00	

A decrease in Computer Supplies, $500

An increase in Computer Supplies Expense, $500

"Used up"

Note: Amount "used up" for computer supplies, $500, goes in adjustments section.

Remember, when rent is paid in advance, it is considered an asset called *prepaid rent*. When the asset, prepaid rent, begins to expire or be used up, it becomes an expense. Now it is May 31, and 1 month's prepaid rent has become an expense.

How is this type of rent handled? Should the account be $1,200, or is only $800 of prepaid rent left as of May 31? What do we need to do to bring Prepaid Rent to the "true" balance? The answer is that we must increase Rent Expense by $400 and decrease Prepaid Rent by $400 (so that there is only $800 left; see Figure 4.4).

Without this adjustment, the expenses for Rob Sinclair's Hilight Graphic Services for May will be too low, and the asset prepaid rent will be too high. If unadjusted amounts were used in the formal reports, the net income shown on the income statement would be too high, and both sides (Assets and Owner's Equity) would be too high on the balance sheet. In terms of our transaction analysis chart, the adjustment would look like this:

Will go on income statement

Accounts Affected	Category	↓↑	Rules
Rent Expense	Expense	↑	Dr.
Prepaid Rent	Asset	↓	Cr.

Will go on balance sheet

Rent Expense 515		Prepaid Rent 115	
400		1200	400
		800	

SUCCESS TIP

Rent Expense is listed below other trial balance accounts because it was not on the original trial balance.

Like the Computer Supplies Expense account, the Rent Expense account comes from the chart of accounts in Chapter 3.

Figure 4.4 shows how to enter an adjustment to Prepaid Rent.

Figure 4.4

ROB SINCLAIR'S HILIGHT GRAPHIC SERVICES
WORKSHEET
FOR MONTH ENDED MAY 31, 201X

Account Titles	Trial Balance		Adjustments	
	Dr.	Cr.	Dr.	Cr.
Cash	6 1 5 5 00			
Accounts Receivable	5 0 0 0 00			
Computer Supplies	6 0 0 00			(A) 5 0 0 00
Prepaid Rent	1 2 0 0 00			(B) 4 0 0 00
Computer Equipment	6 0 0 0 00			
Accounts Payable		3 3 5 0 00		
Rob Sinclair, Capital		10 0 0 0 00		
Rob Sinclair, Withdrawals	6 2 5 00			
Graphic Design Fees		8 0 0 0 00		
Office Salaries Expense	1 3 0 0 00			
Advertising Expense	2 5 0 00			
Telephone Expense	2 2 0 00			
Totals	21 3 5 0 00	21 3 5 0 00		
Computer Supplies Expense			(A) 5 0 0 00	
Rent Expense			(B) 4 0 0 00	

A decrease in Prepaid Rent, $400

An increase in Rent Expense, $400

C. Adjusting the Computer Equipment Account for Depreciation. The life of the asset affects how it is adjusted. The two accounts we just discussed, Computer Supplies and Prepaid Rent, involve things that are used up relatively quickly. Computer Equipment is expected to last much longer. Computer Equipment is expected to help produce revenue over a longer period. For that reason accountants treat it differently. The balance sheet reports the historical cost, or original cost, of the equipment. The original cost is also reflected in the ledger. The adjustment shows how the cost of the equipment is allocated (spread) over its expected useful life. This spreading is called depreciation, which is supported by the Matching Principle. The Matching Principle states that expenses will be matched to revenues in the period in which they are incurred. To depreciate the equipment, we have to figure out how much its cost goes down each month. Then we have to keep a running total of how that depreciation mounts up over time. The Internal Revenue Service (IRS) issues guidelines, tables, and formulas to estimate the amount of depreciation. The IRS tax guidelines are used for tax purposes and do not have to be used in financial reporting. Different methods can be used to calculate depreciation. We will use the simplest method—straight-line depreciation—to calculate the depreciation of Rob Sinclair's Hilight Graphic Services. Under the straight-line method, equal amounts are taken over successive periods of time. Table 4.1 shows how some companies estimate the lives of equipment using the straight-line method.

The calculation of depreciation for the year for Sinclair's Hilight Graphic Services is:

$$\frac{\text{Cost of Equipment} - \text{Residual Value}}{\text{Estimated Years of Usefulness}} = \text{Depreciation per Year}$$

According to the IRS, computer equipment has an expected life of 5 years. At the end of that time, the property's value is called its "residual value." Think of residual value as the estimated value of the equipment at the end of the fifth year. For Sinclair, the equipment has an estimated residual value of $1,200.

$$\frac{\$6,000 - \$1,200}{5 \text{ Years}} = \frac{\$4,800}{5} = \$960 \text{ Depreciation per Year}$$

Our trial balance is for 1 month, so we must determine the adjustment for that month:

$$\frac{\$960}{12 \text{ Months}} = \$80 \text{ Depreciation per Month}$$

This $80 is known as depreciation expense, which will be shown on the income statement.

Next, we create a new account to keep a running total of the depreciation amount separate from the original cost of the equipment. The "running total" account is called Accumulated Depreciation.

Accumulated Depreciation	
Dr.	Cr.

Historical cost Actual cost of an asset at time of purchase.

Depreciation Allocation (spreading) of the cost of an asset (such as an auto or equipment) over its expected useful life.

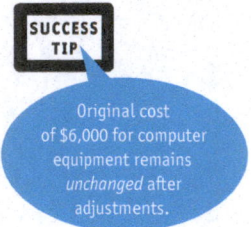

Original cost of $6,000 for computer equipment remains *unchanged* after adjustments.

Residual value Estimated value of an asset after all the allowable depreciation has been taken.

Accumulated Depreciation Contra-asset account that summarizes or accumulates the amount of depreciation that has been taken on an asset.

TABLE 4.1 How Companies Estimate Useful Life

Company	Method of Depreciation	Estimated Life of Equipment
Claire's Stores	Straight-line	Furniture: 3–25 years
Merck	Straight-line	Building: 10–50 years
		Office Equip.: 3–15 years
Big Lots	Straight-line	Building: 40 years
		Equipment: 3–15 years
Dollar General	Straight-line	Building: 39–40 years
		Furniture: 3–10 years

Accumulated Depreciation is a contra-asset account found on the balance sheet. A credit will increase it.

The Accumulated Depreciation account shows the relationship between the original cost of the equipment and the amount of depreciation that has been taken or accumulated over a period of time. This *contra-asset* account has the opposite balance of an asset such as equipment. Accumulated Depreciation will summarize, accumulate, or build up the amount of depreciation that is taken on the computer equipment over its estimated useful life.

Figure 4.5 shows how this calculation of depreciation would look on a partial balance sheet of Rob Sinclair's Hilight Graphic Services.

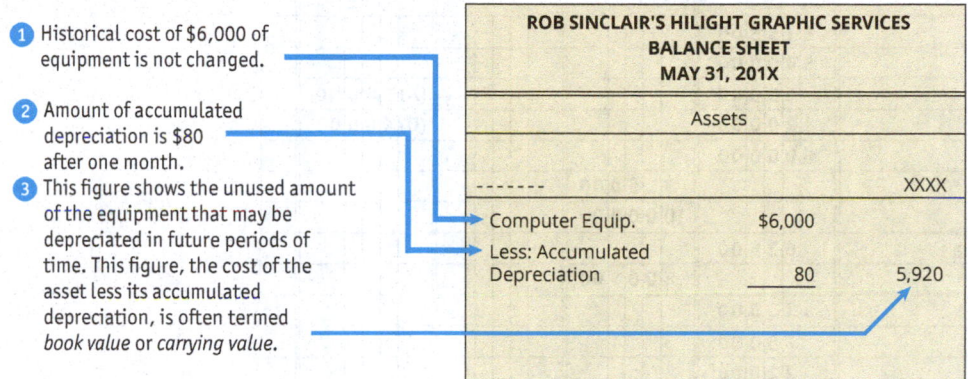

Figure 4.5

Let's summarize the key points before going on to mark the adjustment on the worksheet:

1. Depreciation Expense goes on the income statement, which results in:
   - an increase in total expenses,
   - a decrease in net income, and, therefore,
   - less to be paid in taxes.
2. Accumulated Depreciation is a contra-asset account found on the balance sheet next to its related equipment account. Accumulated depreciation increases with a credit.
3. The original cost of equipment is not reduced; it stays the same until the equipment is sold or removed.
4. Each month the amount in the Accumulated Depreciation account grows larger while the cost of the equipment remains the same.

Now, let's analyze the adjustment on the transaction analysis chart:

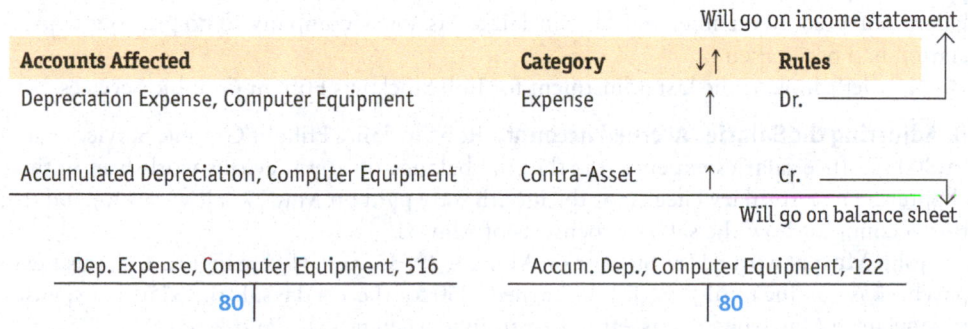

Remember, the original cost of the equipment never changes. The Equipment account is not included among the affected accounts because the original cost of equipment remains the same. As the accumulated depreciation increases (as a credit), the equipment's book value decreases. Book value is the original cost of the asset minus the accumulated depreciation at any given point in time.

Book value Cost of equipment less accumulated depreciation.

Figure 4.6 shows how we enter the adjustment for depreciation of computer equipment.

Figure 4.6

ROB SINCLAIR'S HILIGHT GRAPHIC SERVICES WORKSHEET FOR MONTH ENDED MAY 31, 201X				
Account Titles	Trial Balance		Adjustments	
	Dr.	Cr.	Dr.	Cr.
Cash	6 1 5 5 00			
Accounts Receivable	5 0 0 0 00			
Computer Supplies	6 0 0 00			(A) 5 0 0 00
Prepaid Rent	1 2 0 0 00			(B) 4 0 0 00
Computer Equipment	6 0 0 0 00			
Accounts Payable		3 3 5 0 00		
Rob Sinclair, Capital		10 0 0 0 00		
Rob Sinclair, Withdrawals	6 2 5 00			
Graphic Design Fees		8 0 0 0 00		
Office Salaries Expense	1 3 0 0 00			
Advertising Expense	2 5 0 00			
Telephone Expense	2 2 0 00			
Totals	21 3 5 0 00	21 3 5 0 00		
Computer Supplies Expense			(A) 5 0 0 00	
Rent Expense			(B) 4 0 0 00	
Depreciation Exp., Computer Equip.			(C) 8 0 00	
Accum. Deprec., Computer Equip.				(C) 8 0 00

An increase in Depreciation Expense, Computer Equipment

An increase in Accumulated Depreciation, Computer Equipment

Because it is a new business, neither account had a previous balance. Therefore, neither is listed in the account titles of the trial balance. We need to list both accounts below Rent Expense in the account titles section. On the worksheet, put $80 in the debit column of the adjustments section on the same line as Depreciation Expense, Computer Equipment, and put $80 in the credit column of the adjustments section on the same line as Accumulated Depreciation, Computer Equipment.

Next month, on June 30, $80 would be entered under Depreciation Expense, Computer Equipment, and Accumulated Depreciation, Computer Equipment would show a balance of $160. Remember, in May, Sinclair's was a new company so no previous depreciation had been taken.

Now let's look at the last adjustment for Rob Sinclair's Hilight Graphic Services.

D. Adjusting the Salaries Accrued Account. Rob Sinclair's Hilight Graphic Services paid $1,300 in office salaries expense (see the trial balance of any previous worksheet in this chapter). The last salary checks for the month were paid on May 27. How can we update this account to show the salary expense as of May 31?

John Murray worked for Sinclair on May 28, 29, 30, and 31 (see Figure 4.7). His next paycheck is not due until June 3. John earned $350 for these 4 days. Is the $350 an expense to Sinclair in May when it was earned, or in June when it is due and is paid?

Think back to Chapter 1, in which we first discussed revenue and expenses. We noted then that revenue is recorded when it is earned and expenses are recorded when they are incurred, not when they are actually paid. This principle is discussed further in a later chapter. For now, it is enough to remember that we record revenue and expenses when they occur because we want to match earned revenue with the expenses that resulted in earning those revenues. In this case, by working those 4 days, John Murray created some revenue

May						
Sunday	**Monday**	**Tuesday**	**Wednesday**	**Thursday**	**Friday**	**Saturday**
						1
2	3	4	5	6	7	8
9	10	11	12	13	14	15
16	17	18	19	20	21	22
23	24	25	26	27	28	29
30	31					

Figure 4.7

for Sinclair in May. Therefore, the office salaries expense must be shown in May—the month the revenue was earned.

The results are as follows:

- Office Salaries Expense is increased by $350. This unpaid and unrecorded expense for salaries for which payment is not yet due is called accrued salaries payable. In effect, we now show the true expense for salaries ($1,650 instead of $1,300):

Office Salaries Expense	
1,300	
350	
1,650	

- Salaries Payable is also increased by $350. Sinclair created a liability called salaries payable, which means that the firm owes money for salaries. When the firm pays John Murray, it will reduce its liability salaries payable as well as decrease its cash.

In terms of the transaction analysis chart, the following would be done:

Accrued salaries payable
Salaries that are earned by employees but unpaid and unrecorded during the period (and thus need to be recorded by an adjustment) and will not come due for payment until the next accounting period.

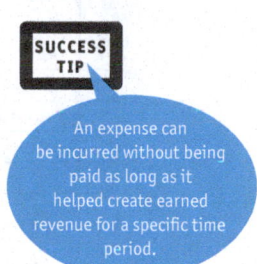

An expense can be incurred without being paid as long as it helped create earned revenue for a specific time period.

Will go on income statement

Accounts Affected	Category	↓↑	Rules
Office Salaries Expense	Expense	↑	Dr.
Salaries Payable	Liability	↑	Cr.

Will go on balance sheet

Office Salaries Exp. 511		Salaries Payable 212	
1,300			350
350			

How the adjustment for accrued salaries is entered in the worksheet is shown in Figure 4.8, page 112.

The account Office Salaries Expense is already listed in the account titles, so $350 is placed in the debit column of the adjustments section on the same line as Office Salaries Expense. However, because Salaries Payable is not listed in the account titles, it is added below the trial balance after Accumulated Depreciation, Computer Equipment. The amount of $350 is also placed in the credit column of the adjustments section on the same line as Salaries Payable.

Now that we have finished all the adjustments that we intended to make, we total the adjustments section, as shown in Figure 4.9, page 112.

Now let's check your progress.

Figure 4.8

Account Titles	Trial Balance Dr.	Trial Balance Cr.	Adjustments Dr.	Adjustments Cr.
ROB SINCLAIR'S HILIGHT GRAPHIC SERVICES WORKSHEET FOR MONTH ENDED MAY 31, 201X				
Cash	6155 00			
Accounts Receivable	5000 00			
Computer Supplies	600 00			(A) 500 00
Prepaid Rent	1200 00			(B) 400 00
Computer Equipment	6000 00			
Accounts Payable		3350 00		
Rob Sinclair, Capital		10000 00		
Rob Sinclair, Withdrawals	625 00			
Graphic Design Fees		8000 00		
Office Salaries Expense	1300 00		(D) 350 00	
Advertising Expense	250 00			
Telephone Expense	220 00			
Totals	21350 00	21350 00		
Computer Supplies Expense			(A) 500 00	
Rent Expense			(B) 400 00	
Depreciation Exp., Computer Equip.			(C) 80 00	
Accum. Deprec., Computer Equip.				(C) 80 00
Salaries Payable				(D) 350 00

An increase in Office Salaries Expense, $350

An increase in Salaries Payable, $350

Figure 4.9
The Adjustments Section of a Worksheet

Account Titles	Trial Balance Dr.	Trial Balance Cr.	Adjustments Dr.	Adjustments Cr.
ROB SINCLAIR'S HILIGHT GRAPHIC SERVICES WORKSHEET FOR MONTH ENDED MAY 31, 201X				
Cash	6155 00			
Accounts Receivable	5000 00			
Computer Supplies	600 00			(A) 500 00
Prepaid Rent	1200 00			(B) 400 00
Computer Equipment	6000 00			
Accounts Payable		3350 00		
Rob Sinclair, Capital		10000 00		
Rob Sinclair, Withdrawals	625 00			
Graphic Design Fees		8000 00		
Office Salaries Expense	1300 00		(D) 350 00	
Advertising Expense	250 00			
Telephone Expense	220 00			
Totals	21350 00	21350 00		
Computer Supplies Expense			(A) 500 00	
Rent Expense			(B) 400 00	
Depreciation Exp., Computer Equip.			(C) 80 00	
Accum. Deprec., Computer Equip.				(C) 80 00
Salaries Payable				(D) 350 00
Totals			1330 00	1330 00

 **TRY IT!**   Learning Unit 4-1

Given the following, prepare transaction analysis boxes to record the adjustments for computer supplies and computer equipment:

Beginning Computer Supplies $8,500

Computer Supplies on hand at end of period $6,000

Cost of Computer Equipment $22,000

Beginning balance in Accumulated Depreciation, Computer Equipment $800

Depreciation to be taken for this period $225

TRY IT!   **Solution Learning Unit 4-1**

Account	Category	Rule	
$8,500 − $6,000 on hand = $2,500 used up			
Computer Supplies Expense	Expense	Increased by Debit	$2,500
Computer Supplies	Asset	Decreased by Credit	$2,500
Depreciation Expense, Computer Equipment	Expense	Increased by Debit	$ 225
Accumulated Depreciation, Computer Equipment	Contra-asset	Increased by Credit	$ 225

The Worksheet (Step 5 of the Accounting Cycle)

LEARNING UNIT 4-2

 **L02**

The Adjusted Trial Balance

The adjusted trial balance is the next section on the worksheet. To fill it out we must summarize the information in the trial balance and adjustments sections, as shown in Figure 4.10 on page 114.

Note that when the numbers are brought across from the trial balance to the adjusted trial balance, two debits will be added together and two credits will be added together. If the numbers include a debit and a credit, take the difference between the two and place it on the side that is larger.

Now that we have completed the adjustments and adjusted trial balance sections of the worksheet, it is time to move on to the income statement and the balance sheet sections. Before we tackle the statements, look at the chart shown in Table 4.2, page 114. This table should be used as a reference to help you in filling out the next two sections of the worksheet.

Keep in mind that the numbers from the adjusted trial balance are carried over to one of the last four columns of the worksheet before the bottom section is completed.

The Income Statement Section

As shown in Figure 4.11 on page 115, the income statement section lists only revenue and expenses from the adjusted trial balance. Note that Accumulated Depreciation and Salaries Payable do not go on the income statement. Accumulated Depreciation is a contra-asset found on the balance sheet. Salaries Payable is a liability found on the balance sheet.

The revenue $8,000 and all the individual expenses are listed in the income statement section. The revenue is placed in the credit column of the income statement section because it has a credit balance. The expenses have debit balances so they are placed in the debit column of the income statement section. The following steps must be taken after the debits and credits are placed in the correct columns:

STEP 1: Total the debits and credits.

STEP 2: Calculate the difference between the debit and credit columns and place the difference on the smaller side.

STEP 3: Total the columns.

Figure 4.10 The Adjusted Trial Balance Section of the Worksheet

ROB SINCLAIR'S HILIGHT GRAPHIC SERVICES
WORKSHEET
FOR MONTH ENDED MAY 31, 201X

Account Titles	Trial Balance Dr.	Cr.	Adjustments Dr.	Cr.	Adjusted Trial Balance Dr.	Cr.
Cash	6 1 5 5 00				6 1 5 5 00	
Accounts Receivable	5 0 0 0 00				5 0 0 0 00	
Computer Supplies	6 0 0 00			(A) 5 0 0 00	1 0 0 00	
Prepaid Rent	1 2 0 0 00			(B) 4 0 0 00	8 0 0 00	
Computer Equipment	6 0 0 0 00				6 0 0 0 00	
Accounts Payable		3 3 5 0 00				3 3 5 0 00
Rob Sinclair, Capital		1 0 0 0 0 00				1 0 0 0 0 00
Rob Sinclair, Withdrawals	6 2 5 00				6 2 5 00	
Graphic Design Fees		8 0 0 0 00				8 0 0 0 00
Office Salaries Expense	1 3 0 0 00		(D) 3 5 0 00		1 6 5 0 00	
Advertising Expense	2 5 0 00				2 5 0 00	
Telephone Expense	2 2 0 00				2 2 0 00	
Totals	2 1 3 5 0 00	2 1 3 5 0 00				
Computer Supplies Expense			(A) 5 0 0 00		5 0 0 00	
Rent Expense			(B) 4 0 0 00		4 0 0 00	
Depreciation Exp., Computer Equip.			(C) 8 0 00		8 0 00	
Accum. Deprec., Computer Equip.				(C) 8 0 00		8 0 00
Salaries Payable				(D) 3 5 0 00		3 5 0 00
Totals			1 3 3 0 00	1 3 3 0 00	2 1 7 8 0 00	2 1 7 8 0 00

Annotations (right margin):

If no adjustment is made, just carry over amount from trial balance on same side.

Supplies were $600, but we used up $500, leaving us with a $100 balance (on hand) in Supplies. *Note:* If the account lists both a debit and a credit, take the *difference* between the two and place it on the side that is larger.

Note: Equipment is *not* adjusted here.

Two debits are added together. If there were two credits, they also would be added together.

Carry these amounts over to adjusted trial balance in the same positions.

Note: The total of the left (debit) must equal the total of the right (credit) ($21,780).

114

TABLE 4.2 Normal Balances and Account Categories

Account Titles	Category	Normal Balance on Adjusted Trial Balance	Income Statement		Balance Sheet	
			Dr.	Cr.	Dr.	Cr.
Cash	Asset	Dr.			X	
Accounts Receivable	Asset	Dr.			X	
Computer Supplies	Asset	Dr.			X	
Prepaid Rent	Asset	Dr.			X	
Computer Equipment	Asset	Dr.			X	
Accounts Payable	Liability	Cr.				X
Rob Sinclair, Capital	Capital	Cr.				X
Rob Sinclair, Withdrawals	Withdrawal	Dr.			X	
Graphic Design Fees	Revenue	Cr.		X		
Office Salaries Exp.	Expense	Dr.	X			
Advertising Expense	Expense	Dr.	X			
Telephone Expense	Expense	Dr.	X			
Computer Supplies Exp.	Expense	Dr.	X			
Rent Expense	Expense	Dr.	X			
Dep. Exp., Computer Equip.	Expense	Dr.	X			
Acc. Dep., Computer Equip.	Contra-Asset	Cr.				X
Salaries Payable	Liability	Cr.				X

Figure 4.11 The Income Statement Section of the Worksheet

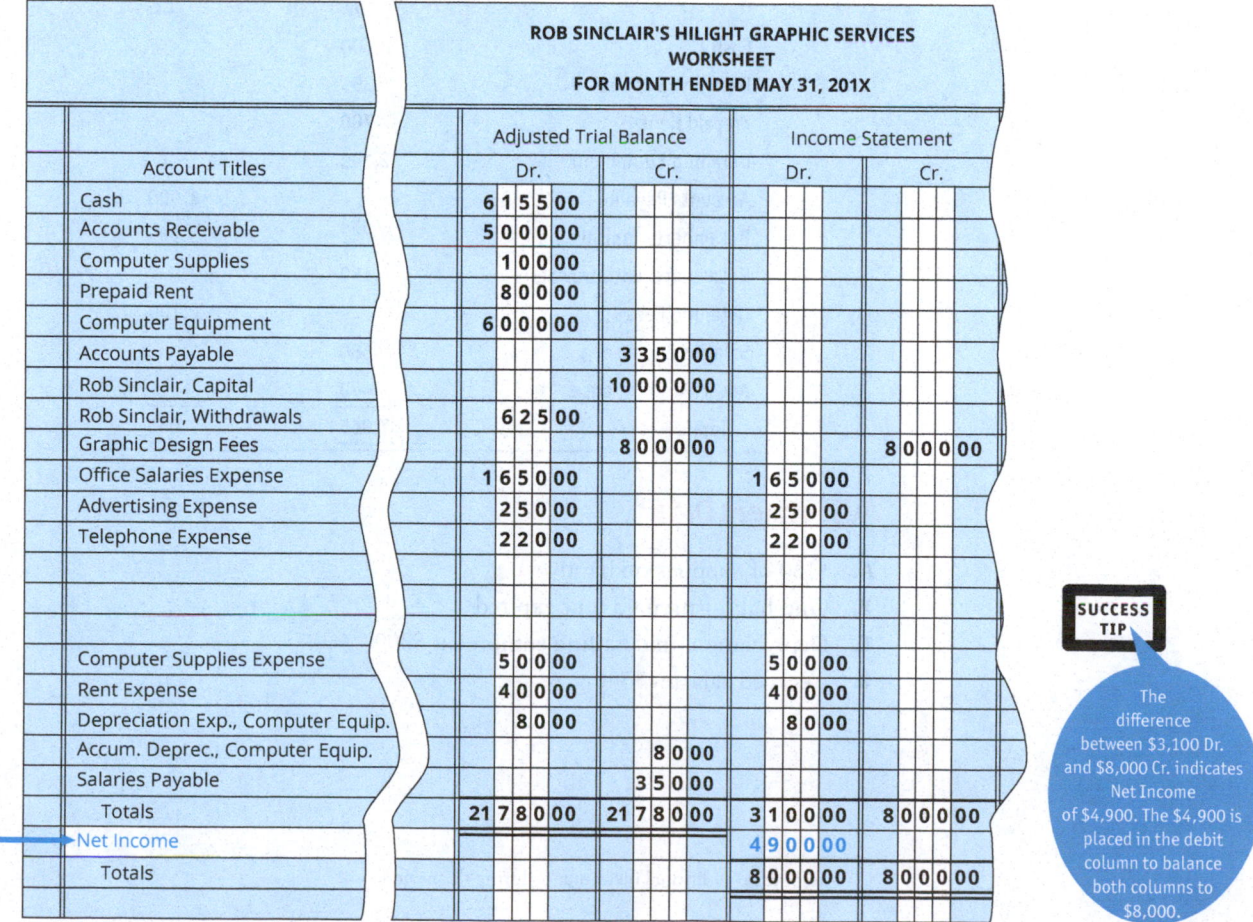

ROB SINCLAIR'S HILIGHT GRAPHIC SERVICES
WORKSHEET
FOR MONTH ENDED MAY 31, 201X

Account Titles	Adjusted Trial Balance Dr.	Adjusted Trial Balance Cr.	Income Statement Dr.	Income Statement Cr.
Cash	6 1 5 5 00			
Accounts Receivable	5 0 0 0 00			
Computer Supplies	1 0 0 00			
Prepaid Rent	8 0 0 00			
Computer Equipment	6 0 0 0 00			
Accounts Payable		3 3 5 0 00		
Rob Sinclair, Capital		10 0 0 0 00		
Rob Sinclair, Withdrawals	6 2 5 00			
Graphic Design Fees		8 0 0 0 00		8 0 0 0 00
Office Salaries Expense	1 6 5 0 00		1 6 5 0 00	
Advertising Expense	2 5 0 00		2 5 0 00	
Telephone Expense	2 2 0 00		2 2 0 00	
Computer Supplies Expense	5 0 0 00		5 0 0 00	
Rent Expense	4 0 0 00		4 0 0 00	
Depreciation Exp., Computer Equip.	8 0 00		8 0 00	
Accum. Deprec., Computer Equip.		8 0 00		
Salaries Payable		3 5 0 00		
Totals	21 7 8 0 00	21 7 8 0 00	3 1 0 0 00	8 0 0 0 00
Net Income			4 9 0 0 00	
Totals			8 0 0 0 00	8 0 0 0 00

$8,000
−3,100
$4,900

SUCCESS TIP

The difference between $3,100 Dr. and $8,000 Cr. indicates Net Income of $4,900. The $4,900 is placed in the debit column to balance both columns to $8,000.

The worksheet in Figure 4.11 shows that the label Net Income is added in the account titles column on the same line as $4,900. When the figures result in a net income, it will be placed in the debit column of the income statement section of the worksheet. A net loss is placed in the credit column. The $8,000 total indicates that the two columns are in balance.

The Balance Sheet Section

To fill out the balance sheet section of the worksheet, the following are carried over from the adjusted trial balance section: assets, contra-assets, liabilities, capital, and withdrawals. Because the beginning figure for Capital* is used on the worksheet, Net Income is brought over to the credit column of the balance sheet so both columns balance.

Let's now look at the completed worksheet in Figure 4.12 page 118 to see how the balance sheet section is completed. Note how the Net Income of $4,900 is brought over to the credit column of the balance sheet section. The figure for Capital is also in the credit column while the figure for Withdrawals is in the debit column. By placing Net Income in the credit column, both sides total $18,680. If a net loss were to occur, it would be placed in the debit column of the balance sheet section.

Now that we have completed the worksheet, it's time to check your progress.

TRY IT!   Learning Unit 4-2

Given the following trial balance and adjustment data, complete a partial worksheet up to the adjusted trial balance:

Lambert's Car Detailing
Trial Balance
June 30, 201X

	Dr.	Cr.
Cash	2,600	
Detailing Supplies	355	
Prepaid Rent	700	
Detailing Equipment	2,100	
Accounts Payable		1,000
B. Lambert, Capital		3,965
B. Lambert, Withdrawals	150	
Detailing Fees		2,100
Salaries Expense	680	
Advertising Expense	480	
Totals	7,065	7,065

Adjustment Data

A. $180 of supplies on hand
B. One-half of prepaid rent expired
C. Depreciation on detailing equipment $300
D. Accrued Salaries $340

---

* We assume no additional investments during the period.

Lambert's Car
Detailing Worksheet
For Month Ended June 30, 201X

Acct Titles	Trial Balance		Adjustments		Adj. TB	
	Dr.	Cr.	Dr.	Cr.	Dr.	Cr.
Cash	2,600				2,600	
Detailing Supplies	355			(a) 175	180	
Prepaid Rent	700			(b) 350	350	
Detailing Equipment	2,100				2,100	
Accounts Payable		1,000				1,000
B. Lambert, Capital		3,965				3,965
B. Lambert, Withdrawals	150				150	
Detailing Fees		2,100				2,100
Salaries Expense	680		(d) 340		1,020	
Advertising Expense	480				480	
Totals	7,065	7,065				
Detailing Supplies Expense			(a) 175		175	
Rent Expense			(b) 350		350	
Depreciation Expense, Detailing Equipment			(c) 300		300	
Accumulated Depreciation, Detailing Equipment				(c) 300		300
Salaries Payable				(d) 340		340
Totals			1,165	1,165	7,705	7,705

The Financial Statements from the Worksheet (Step 6 of the Accounting Cycle)

LEARNING UNIT 4-3

LO3

The formal financial statements can be prepared from the worksheet completed in Learning Unit 4-2. Before beginning, we must check that the entries on the worksheet are correct and in balance. To ensure the accuracy of the figures, we double-check that (1) all entries are recorded in the appropriate column, (2) the correct amounts are entered in the proper places, (3) the addition is correct across the columns (i.e., from the trial balance to the adjusted trial balance to the financial statements), and (4) the columns are added correctly.

Preparing the Income Statement

The first statement to be prepared for Rob Sinclair's Hilight Graphic Services is the income statement. When preparing the income statement it is important to remember the following:

1. Every figure on the formal statement is on the worksheet. Figure 4.13 on page 119 shows where each of these figures goes on the income statement.
2. No debit or credit columns appear on the formal statement.
3. The inside column on financial statements is used for subtotaling.
4. Withdrawals do not go on the income statement; they go on the statement of owner's equity.

Take a moment to look at the income statement in Figure 4.13. Note where items go from the income statement section of the worksheet onto the formal statement.

Figure 4.12

"Used up" "On hand"

Original cost of $6,000 is *not* adjusted

ROB SINCLAIR'S HILIGHT GRAPHIC SERVICES
WORKSHEET
FOR MONTH ENDED MAY 31, 201X

Account Titles	Trial Balance Dr.	Trial Balance Cr.	Adjustments Dr.	Adjustments Cr.	Adjusted Trial Balance Dr.	Adjusted Trial Balance Cr.	Income Statement Dr.	Income Statement Cr.	Balance Sheet Dr.	Balance Sheet Cr.
Cash	6 1 5 5 00				6 1 5 5 00				6 1 5 5 00	
Accounts Receivable	5 0 0 0 00				5 0 0 0 00				5 0 0 0 00	
Computer Supplies	6 0 0 00			(A) 5 0 0 00	1 0 0 00				1 0 0 00	
Prepaid Rent	1 2 0 0 00			(B) 4 0 0 00	8 0 0 00				8 0 0 00	
Computer Equipment	6 0 0 0 00				6 0 0 0 00				6 0 0 0 00	
Accounts Payable		3 3 5 0 00				3 3 5 0 00				3 3 5 0 00
Rob Sinclair, Capital		1 0 0 0 0 00				1 0 0 0 0 00				1 0 0 0 0 00
Rob Sinclair, Withdrawals	6 2 5 00				6 2 5 00				6 2 5 00	
Graphic Design Fees		8 0 0 0 00				8 0 0 0 00		8 0 0 0 00		
Office Salaries Expense	1 3 0 0 00		(D) 3 5 0 00		1 6 5 0 00		1 6 5 0 00			
Advertising Expense	2 5 0 00				2 5 0 00		2 5 0 00			
Telephone Expense	2 2 0 00				2 2 0 00		2 2 0 00			
Totals	21 3 5 0 00	21 3 5 0 00								
Computer Supplies Expense			(A) 5 0 0 00		5 0 0 00		5 0 0 00			
Rent Expense			(B) 4 0 0 00		4 0 0 00		4 0 0 00			
Depreciation Exp., Computer Equip.			(C) 8 0 00		8 0 00		8 0 00			
Accum. Deprec., Computer Equip.				(C) 8 0 00		8 0 00				8 0 00
Salaries Payable				(D) 3 5 0 00		3 5 0 00				3 5 0 00
Totals			1 3 3 0 00	1 3 3 0 00	21 7 8 0 00	21 7 8 0 00	3 1 0 0 00	8 0 0 0 00	18 6 8 0 00	13 7 8 0 00
Net Income							4 9 0 0 00			4 9 0 0 00
							8 0 0 0 00	8 0 0 0 00	18 6 8 0 00	18 6 8 0 00

contra-asset

118

Figure 4.13 From Worksheet to Income Statement

Account Titles	Income Statement	
	Dr.	Cr.
Cash		
Accounts Receivable		
Computer Supplies		
Prepaid Rent		
Computer Equipment		
Accounts Payable		
Rob Sinclair, Capital		
Rob Sinclair, Withdrawals		
Graphic Design Fees		8 0 0 0 00
Office Salaries Expense	1 6 5 0 00	
Advertising Expense	2 5 0 00	
Telephone Expense	2 2 0 00	
Computer Supplies Expense	5 0 0 00	
Rent Expense	4 0 0 00	
Depreciation Expense, Computer Equip.	8 0 00	
Accum. Deprec., Computer Equip.		
Salaries Payable		
Totals	3 1 0 0 00	8 0 0 0 00
Net Income	4 9 0 0 00	
Totals	8 0 0 0 00	8 0 0 0 00

ROB SINCLAIR'S HILIGHT GRAPHIC SERVICES
INCOME STATEMENT
FOR MONTH ENDED MAY 31, 201X

Revenue:			
Graphic Design Fees			$ 8 0 0 0 00
Operating Expenses:			
Office Salaries Expense	$ 1 6 5 0 00		
Advertising Expense	2 5 0 00		
Telephone Expense	2 2 0 00		
Computer Supplies Expense	5 0 0 00		
Rent Expense	4 0 0 00		
Depreciation Expense, Computer Equipment	8 0 00		
Total Operating Expenses			3 1 0 0 00
Net Income			$ 4 9 0 0 00

Figure 4.14 Completing a Statement of Owner's Equity

ROB SINCLAIR'S HILIGHT GRAPHIC SERVICES
STATEMENT OF OWNER'S EQUITY
FOR MONTH ENDED MAY 31, 201X

Rob Sinclair, Capital, May 1, 201X		$ 1 0 0 0 0 00
Net Income for May	$ 4 9 0 0 00	
Less Withdrawals for May	– 6 2 5 00	
Increase in Capital		4 2 7 5 00
Rob Sinclair, Capital, May 31, 201X		$ 1 4 2 7 5 00

Balance Sheet Cr. column on worksheet

From income statement, Net Income on worksheet (or from formal report just prepared)

Balance Sheet Dr. column on worksheet

This figure is not on the worksheet. It is calculated here and used to prepare the balance sheet. Note that no additional investments were made during May.

Preparing the Statement of Owner's Equity

Figure 4.14 is the statement of owner's equity for Sinclair. The figure shows where the information comes from on the worksheet. It is important to remember that if additional investments were made, the figure on the worksheet for Capital would not be the beginning figure for Capital in the Statement of Owner's Equity. Checking the ledger account for Capital will tell you whether the amount is correct. Note how Net Income and Withdrawals aid in calculating the new figure for Capital.

Preparing the Balance Sheet

In preparing the balance sheet (Figure 4.15, page 122), remember that the balance sheet section totals on the worksheet ($18,680) do *not* match the totals on the formal balance sheet ($17,975). This information is grouped differently on the formal statement. First, in the formal report Accumulated Depreciation, Computer Equipment ($80) is subtracted from Computer Equipment, reducing the balance. Second, Withdrawals ($625) are subtracted from Owner's Equity, reducing the balance further. These two reductions (−$80 − $625 = −$705) represent the difference between the worksheet total and the total on the formal report of the balance sheet ($17,975 − $18,680 = −$705). Figure 4.15 shows how to prepare the balance sheet from the worksheet.

 **TRY IT!**   **Learning Unit 4-3**

From the last four columns of this partial worksheet for Lawson's Nails, complete the three financial statements:

Lawson's Nails
Partial Worksheet
For Month Ended September 30, 201X

	Income Statement		Balance Sheet	
	Dr.	Cr.	Dr.	Cr.
Cash			5,600	
Accounts Receivable			1,700	
Nail Supplies			410	
Salon Equipment			1,200	
Accounts Payable				1,000
P. Lawson, Capital				7,320
P. Lawson, Withdrawals			150	
Nail Fees		2,100		
Advertising Expense	240			
Rent Expense	500			
Salaries Expense	660			
Nail Supplies Expense	135			
Depreciation Expense, Salon Equip.	240			
Accumulated Depreciation, Salon Equip.				240
Salaries Payable				175
Totals	1,775	2,100	9,060	8,735
Net Income	325			325
Totals	2,100	2,100	9,060	9,060

Solution Learning Unit 4-3

Lawson's Nails
Income Statement
For Month Ended September 30, 201X

Revenue:		
Nail Fees		$2,100
Operating Expenses:		
Advertising Expense	$240	
Rent Expense	500	
Salaries Expense	660	
Nail Supplies Expense	135	
Depreciation Expense, Salon Equip.	240	
Total Operating Expenses		1,775
Net Income		$ 325

Lawson's Nails
Statement of Owner's Equity
For Month Ended September 30, 201X

P. Lawson, Capital, September 1, 201X		$7,320
Net Income for September	$325	
Less: Withdrawals for September	−150	
Increase in Capital		175
P. Lawson, Capital, September 30, 201X		$7,495

Lawson's Nails
Balance Sheet
September 30, 201X

Assets			Liabilities and Owner's Equity		
Cash		$5,600	Liabilities		
Acc. Rec.		1,700	Accounts Payable	$1,000	
Nail Supplies		410	Salaries Payable	175	
Salon Equip.	$1,200		Total Liabilities		$1,175
Less: Acc. Dep.	240	960	Owner's Equity		7,495
			P. Lawson, Capital		
Total Assets		$8,670	Total Liabilities and Owner's Equity		$8,670

Figure 4.15 From Worksheet to Balance Sheet

Account Titles		Balance Sheet	
		Dr.	Cr.
Cash		6 1 5 5 00	
Accounts Receivable		5 0 0 0 00	
Computer Supplies		1 0 0 00	
Prepaid Rent		8 0 0 00	
Computer Equip.		6 0 0 0 00	
Accounts Payable			3 3 5 0 00
Rob Sinclair, Capital			10 0 0 0 00
Rob Sinclair, Withdrawals		6 2 5 00	
Accum. Depr., Computer Equip.			8 0 00
Salaries Payable			3 5 0 00
		18 6 8 0 00	13 7 8 0 00
			4 9 0 0 00
		18 6 8 0 00	18 6 8 0 00

From Worksheet

From statement of owner's equity or from worksheet:

$10,000	Beg. Capital
+4,900	Net Income
− 625	Withdrawals
$14,275	

ROB SINCLAIR'S HILIGHT GRAPHIC SERVICES
BALANCE SHEET
MAY 31, 201X

Assets			Liabilities and Owner's Equity		
Cash		$6 1 5 5 00	Liabilities		
Accounts Receivable		5 0 0 0 00	Accounts Payable	$3 3 5 0 00	
Computer Supplies		1 0 0 00	Salaries Payable	3 5 0 00	
Prepaid Rent		8 0 0 00	Total Liabilities		$3 7 0 0 00
Computer Equip.	$6 0 0 0 00				
Less Acc. Dep., Computer Equip.	8 0 00	5 9 2 0 00	Owner's Equity		
			Rob Sinclair, Capital		14 2 7 5 00
Total Assets		$17 9 7 5 00	Total Liabilities and Owner's Equity		$17 9 7 5 00

DEMONSTRATION SUMMARY PROBLEM

LO1,2,3

From the following trial balance and adjustment data, complete (1) a worksheet and (2) three financial statements (numbers are intentionally small so you may concentrate on the theory).

Frost Company
Trial Balance
December 31, 201X

	Dr.	Cr.
Cash	14	
Accounts Receivable	4	
Prepaid Insurance	5	
Plumbing Supplies	3	
Plumbing Equipment	7	
Accumulated Depreciation, Plumbing Equipment		5
Accounts Payable		1
J. Frost, Capital		12
J. Frost, Withdrawals	3	
Plumbing Fees		27
Rent Expense	4	
Salaries Expense	5	
Totals	45	45

Adjustment Data

a. Insurance Expired, $3.
b. Plumbing Supplies on hand, $1.
c. Depreciation Expense, Plumbing Equipment, $1.
d. Salaries owed but not paid to employees, $2.

Requirements

1. Prepare a worksheet
2. Prepare financial statements for month of December

Solutions

Requirement 1

Preparing a worksheet

Tips for Adjustments

a.

Insurance Expense	Expense	↑	Dr.	$3
Prepaid Insurance	Asset	↓	Cr.	$3
			Expired means used up.	

b.

Plumbing Supplies Expense	Expense	↑	Dr.	$2
Plumbing Supplies	Asset	↓	Cr.	$2
			$3 − 1 = $2 *used up*	

Figure 4.16 Solution to Worksheet

"Original cost not adjusted"

"Used up"   "On hand"

FROST COMPANY
WORKSHEET
FOR MONTH ENDED DECEMBER 31, 201X

Account Titles	Trial Balance Dr.	Trial Balance Cr.	Adjustments Dr.	Adjustments Cr.	Adjusted Trial Balance Dr.	Adjusted Trial Balance Cr.	Income Statement Dr.	Income Statement Cr.	Balance Sheet Dr.	Balance Sheet Cr.
Cash	14 00				14 00				14 00	
Accounts Receivable	4 00				4 00				4 00	
Prepaid Insurance	5 00			(A) 3 00	2 00				2 00	
Plumbing Supplies	3 00			(B) 2 00	1 00				1 00	
Plumbing Equipment	7 00				7 00				7 00	
Accum. Depr., Plumb. Equip.		5 00		(C) 1 00		6 00				6 00
Accounts Payable		1 00				1 00				1 00
J. Frost, Capital		12 00				12 00				12 00
J. Frost, Withdrawals	3 00				3 00				3 00	
Plumbing Fees		27 00				27 00		27 00		
Rent Expense	4 00				4 00		4 00			
Salaries Expense	5 00		(D) 2 00		7 00		7 00			
Totals	45 00	45 00								
Insurance Expense			(A) 3 00		3 00		3 00			
Plumbing Supplies Expense			(B) 2 00		2 00		2 00			
Depr. Exp. Plumb. Equip.			(C) 1 00		1 00		1 00			
Salaries Payable				(D) 2 00		2 00				2 00
Totals			8 00	8 00	48 00	48 00	17 00	27 00	31 00	21 00
Net Income							10 00			10 00
Totals							27 00	27 00	31 00	31 00

124

c.

Depreciation Expense, Plumbing Equipment	Expense	↑	Dr.	$1
Accumulated Depreciation, Plumbing Equipment	Contra-Asset	↑	Cr.	$1

The original cost of equipment of $7 is not "touched."

d.

Salaries Expense	Expense	↑	Dr.	$2
Salaries Payable	Liability	↑	Cr.	$2

The last four columns of the worksheet (Figure 4.16, page124) are prepared from the Adjusted Trial Balance.

Capital of $12 is the old figure. Net income of $10 (revenue – expenses) is brought over to the same side as Capital on the balance sheet Cr. column to balance columns. This is done because the worksheet contains the old figure for Capital.

Requirement 2

Preparing financial statements

Tips for Preparing Financial Statements from a Worksheet

The inside columns of the three financial statements are used for subtotaling. No debits or credits appear on the formal statements.

	Statements
Income Statement	From Income Statement columns of worksheet for revenue and expenses.
Statement of Owner's Equity	Beginning figure for Capital from Balance Sheet worksheet Cr. column. Net Income from income statement. Withdrawals figure from Balance Sheet worksheet Dr. column.
Balance Sheet	Assets from Balance Sheet worksheet Dr. column. Liabilities and Accumulated Depreciation from Balance Sheet worksheet Cr. Column. New figure for Capital from statement of owner's equity.

Note how Plumbing Equipment $7 and Accumulated Depreciation $6 are rearranged on the formal balance sheet. The Total Assets of $22 is not on the worksheet. Remember, no debits or credits appear on formal statements (see Figure 4.17, page 126).

Figure 4.17

FROST COMPANY
INCOME STATEMENT
FOR MONTH ENDED DECEMBER 31, 201X

Revenue:		
Plumbing Fees		$27
Operating Expenses:		
Rent Expense	$4	
Salaries Expense	7	
Insurance Expense	3	
Plumbing Supplies Expense	2	
Depreciation Expense, Plumbing Equipment	1	
Total Operating Expenses		17
Net Income		$10

FROST COMPANY
STATEMENT OF OWNER'S EQUITY
FOR MONTH ENDED DECEMBER 31, 201X

J. Frost, Capital, Dec. 1, 201X	$12
Net Income for December	$10
Less: Withdrawals for December	−3
Increase in Capital	7
J. Frost, Capital, Dec. 31, 201X	$19

FROST COMPANY
BALANCE SHEET
DECEMBER 31, 201X

Assets			**Liabilities and Owner's Equity**		
Cash		$14	Liabilities		
Accounts Receivable		4	Accounts Payable	$1	
Prepaid Insurance		2	Salaries Payable	2	
Plumbing Supplies		1	Total Liabilities		$3
Plumbing Equipment	$7				
Less: Accumulated Dep.	6	1	Owner's Equity		
			J. Frost, Capital		19
			Total Liabilities and Owner's Equity		
Total Assets		$22			$22

SUCCESS COACH

The following Success Tips are from Learning Units 4-1, 4-2, and 4-3. Take the Do It Right Now Checkup and use the Check Your Score at the bottom of the page to see how you are doing. The Success Coach provides tips before each Checkup to help you avoid common accounting errors.

LU 4-1 Explaining Adjustments and How to Record Them on a Worksheet

Do It Right Tips: When preparing adjustments on a worksheet, the accounts listed below the trial balance will always be increasing. In the adjustment for supplies, the adjustment is the amount of supplies used, not what is on hand. Keep in mind that for the adjustment for depreciation the original cost of the asset is not touched. The adjustment is an increase in Depreciation Expense and an increase in Accumulated Depreciation. Depreciation Expense goes on the income statement as an expense, and accumulated depreciation goes on the balance sheet as a contra-asset account. Keep in mind that the original cost of the asset and accumulated depreciation are both listed on the balance sheet.

Do It Right Now Checkup: Answer true or false to the following statements.
1. Prepaid Rent is a liability.
2. Accumulated Depreciation is a contra-liability.
3. The adjustment for supplies is the amount of supplies on hand.
4. The normal balance of Accumulated Depreciation is a debit.
5. The historical cost of equipment is not adjusted.

LU 4-2 The Worksheet (Step 5 of the Accounting Cycle)

Do It Right Tips: The income statement columns record revenues and expenses. Net income will be recorded at the bottom of the balance sheet section on the same side as capital since old capital is on the worksheet. Withdrawals go in the debit column of the balance sheet section of the worksheet. Accumulated depreciation is a contra-asset in the credit column of the balance sheet. Depreciation Expense goes in the debit column of the income statement.

Do It Right Now Checkup: Answer true or false to the following statements.
1. Net loss is the result of revenues greater than expenses.
2. Accumulated Depreciation is never adjusted.
3. Assets do not go in the income statement column on a worksheet.
4. A net loss would go in the debit column of the balance sheet on a worksheet.
5. Withdrawals go in the credit column of the balance sheet on a worksheet.

LU 4-3 The Financial Statements from the Worksheet (Step 6 of the Accounting Cycle)

Do It Right Tips: The worksheet uses debits and credits; however, when the three formal financial statements are prepared they do not use debits and credits. The worksheet uses the beginning figure for Capital (no additional investment during the month), but when the financial statements are complete the formal balance sheet will list the figure for ending Capital from the statement of owner's equity.

Do It Right Now Checkup: Answer true or false to the following statements.
1. Subtotaling is not used in preparing the formal financial statements from a worksheet.
2. Withdrawals are listed on the income statement.
3. Accumulated Depreciation is added to the cost of the asset on the balance sheet.
4. Debits are the inside column on the formal reports.
5. Totals on the formal balance sheet will match totals on the worksheet.

CHECK YOUR SCORE: Answers to the Do It Right Now Checkup

LU 4-1
1. False—Prepaid Rent is an asset.
2. False—Accumulated Depreciation is a contra-asset.
3. False—The adjustment for Supplies is the amount of supplies used up.
4. False—The normal balance of Accumulated Depreciation is a credit.
5. True.

LU 4-2
1. False—Revenues are less than expenses.
2. False—Accumulated Depreciation is usually adjusted by an increase to the Accumulated Account.
3. True
4. True
5. False—Withdrawals go in the debit column.

LU 4-3

1. False—Subtotaling *is* used in preparing the formal financial statements from a worksheet.
2. False—Withdrawals are listed on the statement of owner's equity.
3. False—Accumulated depreciation is subtracted from the cost of the asset on the balance sheet.

4. False—There are no debits or credits on financial statements.
5. False—Totals on formal reports do not match totals on the worksheet since there are no debits and credits on financial reports and subtotaling is used.

BLUEPRINT OF STEPS 5 AND 6 OF THE ACCOUNTING CYCLE

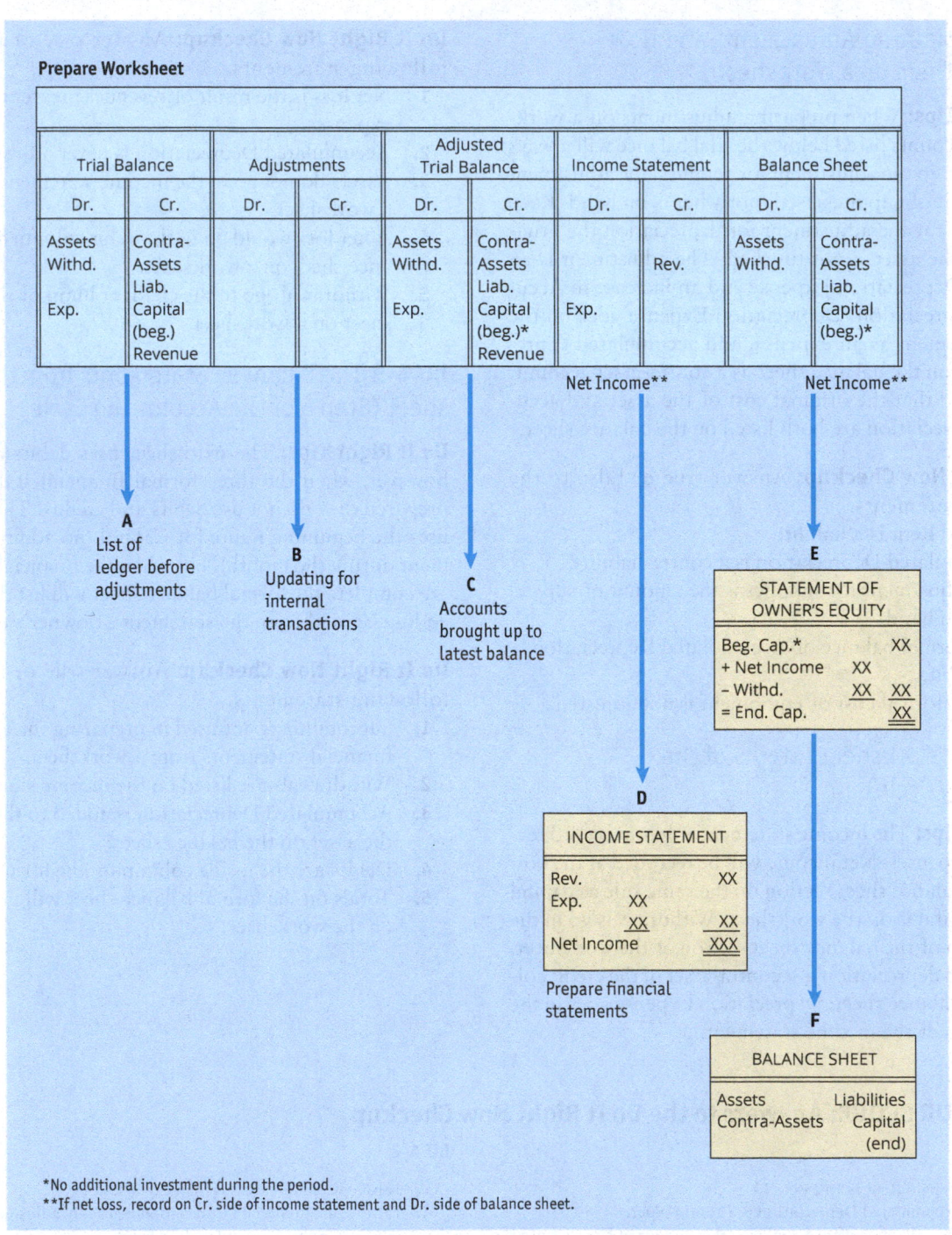

*No additional investment during the period.
**If net loss, record on Cr. side of income statement and Dr. side of balance sheet.

Discussion Questions and Critical Thinking/Ethical Case

1. With computer software, the need for worksheets has been completely eliminated. Agree or disagree and explain your answer.

2. What is the purpose of adjusting accounts?

3. What is the relationship of internal transactions to the adjusting process?

4. Explain how an adjustment can affect both the income statement and balance sheet. Please give an example.

5. Why do we need the Accumulated Depreciation account?

6. Depreciation expense goes on the balance sheet. True or false. Why?

7. Each month Accumulated Depreciation grows while Equipment goes up. Agree or disagree? Defend your position.

8. Define the term *accrued salaries*.

9. Why don't the formal financial statements contain debit or credit columns?

10. Explain how the financial statements are prepared from the worksheet.

11. Alice Hawkins, president of Realon Co., went to a conference on tax planning. One of the speakers at the seminar advised the audience to put off showing expenses until next year because doing so would allow them to take advantage of a new tax law. When Alice returned to the office, she called in her accountant, Lynn O'Riley. She told Lynn to forget about making any adjustments for salaries in the old year so more expenses could be shown in the new year. Lynn told her that putting off these expenses would not follow generally accepted accounting procedures. Alice said she should do it anyway. You make the call. Write your specific recommendations to Lynn.

Concept Check

MyLabAccounting

Adjustment for Supplies

1. *Before Adjustment*

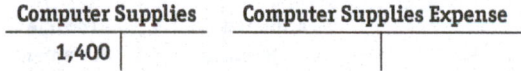

L01 *(5 min)*

Computer Supplies	Computer Supplies Expense
1,400	

Given: At year end, an inventory of Computer Supplies showed $800.

   a. How much is the adjustment for Computer Supplies?
   b. Complete a transaction analysis box for this adjustment.
   c. What will the balance of Computer Supplies be on the adjusted trial balance?

Adjustment for Prepaid Rent

2. *Before Adjustment*

L01 *(10 min)*

Prepaid Rent	Rent Expense
700	

Given: At year end, rent expired is $125.

   a. How much is the adjustment for Prepaid Rent?
   b. Complete a transaction analysis box for this adjustment.
   c. What will be the balance of Prepaid Rent on the adjusted trial balance?

Adjustment for Depreciation

(10 min) **LO1** ▶

3.　*Before Adjustment*

Equip.	Acc. Dep., Equip.	Dep. Exp., Equip.
10,600	500	

Given: At year end, depreciation on Equipment is $1,300.

　a. Which of these three T accounts is not affected?
　b. Which account is a contra-asset?
　c. Complete a transaction analysis box for this adjustment.
　d. What will be the balance of these three accounts on the adjusted trial balance?

Adjustment for Accrued Salaries

(10 min) **LO1** ▶

4.　*Before Adjustment*

Salaries Expense	Salaries Payable
1,800	

Given: Accrued Salaries, $175.

　a. Complete a transaction analysis box for this adjustment.
　b. What will be the balance of these two accounts on the adjusted trial balance?

Worksheet

(15 min) **LO2** ▶

5.　From the following adjusted trial balance titles of a worksheet, identify in which column each account will be listed on the last four columns of the worksheet:

　　(ID) Income Statement Dr. Column
　　(IC) Income Statement Cr. Column
　　(BD) Balance Sheet Dr. Column
　　(BC) Balance Sheet Cr. Column

	Adjusted Trial Balance		Income Statement	Balance Sheet
A. Ex: Legal Fees Earned	~~~	~~~	IC	____
B. Accts. Payable	~~~	~~~	____	____
C. Cash	~~~	~~~	____	____
D. Prepaid Advertising	~~~	~~~	____	____
E. Salaries Payable	~~~	~~~	____	____
F. Dep. Expense	~~~	~~~	____	____
G. V., Capital	~~~	~~~	____	____
H. V., Withdrawals	~~~	~~~	____	____
I. Computer Supplies	~~~	~~~	____	____
J. Rent Expense	~~~	~~~	____	____
K. Supplies Payable	~~~	~~~	____	____
L. Advertising Expense	~~~	~~~	____	____
M. Accum. Depreciation	~~~	~~~	____	____
N. Wages Payable	~~~	~~~	____	____

6. From the following balance sheet (Figure 4.18, which was made from the worksheet and other financial statements), explain why the lettered numbers were not found on the worksheet. *Hint:* No debits or credits appear on the formal financial statements.

LO2,3 *(15 min)*

NGUYEN CO. BALANCE SHEET DECEMBER 31, 201X				
Assets			**Liabilities and Owner's Equity**	
Cash	$6		Liabilities	
Acc. Receivable	2		Accounts Payable	$2
Supplies	2		Salaries Payable	1
Equipment	$10		Total Liabilities	$3 (B)
Less: Acc. Dep.	4	6 (A)	Owner's Equity	
			T. Nguyen, Capital	13
Total Assets		$16	**Total Liabilities and Owner's Equity**	$16

Figure 4.18

Exercises

MyLab Accounting

Set A

4A-1. Complete the following table.

LO3 *(5 min)*

Account	Category	Normal Balance	Which Financial Statement(s) Found
Accumulated Depreciation, Office Equipment			
Prepaid Rent			
Office Equipment			
Depreciation Expense, Office Equipment			
T. Nguyen, Capital			
T. Nguyen, Withdrawals			
Wages Payable			

4A-2. Use transaction analysis charts to analyze the following adjustments:
  a. Depreciation on equipment, $1,400.
  b. Rent expired, $900.

LO1 *(10 min)*

4A-3. From the following adjustment data, calculate the adjustment amount and record appropriate debits or credits:
  a. Supplies purchased, $1,100.
     Supplies on hand, $550.
  b. Store equipment, $12,500.
     Accumulated depreciation, store equipment, before adjustment, $500.
     Depreciation expense, store equipment, $100.

LO1 *(10 min)*

4A-4. From the following trial balance (Figure 4.19, page 132) and adjustment data, complete a worksheet for J. Trent as of July 31, 201X:
  a. Depreciation expense, store equipment, $2.
  b. Insurance expired, $1.
  c. Store supplies on hand, $8.
  d. Wages owed, but not paid for (they are an expense in the old year), $2.

LO1,2 *(20 min)*

Figure 4.19

J. TRENT TRIAL BALANCE JULY 31, 201X		
Account Titles	Dr.	Cr.
Cash	5 00	
Accounts Receivable	10 00	
Prepaid Insurance	7 00	
Store Supplies	9 00	
Store Equipment	10 00	
Accumulated Depreciation, Store Equipment		4 00
Accounts Payable		7 00
J. Trent, Capital		19 00
J. Trent, Withdrawals	2 00	
Revenue from Clients		28 00
Rent Expense	5 00	
Wage Expense	10 00	
Totals	58 00	58 00

(20 min) **L03** **4A-5.** From the completed worksheet in Exercise 4A-4, prepare:
   a. An income statement for July
   b. A statement of owner's equity for July
   c. A balance sheet as of July 31, 201X

Set B

(5 min) **L03** **4B-1.** Complete the following table.

Account	Category	Normal Balance	Which Financial Statement(s) Found
Accounts Payable			
Prepaid Insurance			
Computer Equipment			
Depreciation Expense, Computer Equipment			
B. Free, Capital			
B. Free, Withdrawals			
Salaries Payable			
Accumulated Depreciation, Computer Equipment			

(5 min) **L01** **4B-2.** Use transaction analysis charts to analyze the following adjustments:
   a. Depreciation on equipment, $1,000.
   b. Rent expired, $600.

(10 min) **L01** **4B-3.** From the following adjustment data, calculate the adjustment amount and record appropriate debits or credits:
   a. Supplies purchased, $600.
      Supplies on hand, $100.
   b. Store equipment, $14,500.
      Accumulated depreciation, store equipment, before adjustment, $800.
      Depreciation expense, store equipment, $600.

4B-4. From the following trial balance (Figure 4.20) and adjustment data, complete a worksheet for J. Tren as of May 31, 201X:

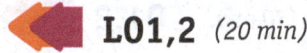 **LO1,2** *(20 min)*

   a. Depreciation expense, store equipment, $4.
   b. Insurance expired, $9.
   c. Store supplies on hand, $1.
   d. Wages owed but not paid for (they are an expense in the old year), $6.

Figure 4.20

J. TREN TRIAL BALANCE MAY 31, 201X		
Account Titles	Dr.	Cr.
Cash	13 00	
Accounts Receivable	8 00	
Prepaid Insurance	12 00	
Store Supplies	3 00	
Store Equipment	15 00	
Accumulated Depreciation, Store Equipment		5 00
Accounts Payable		9 00
J. Tren, Capital		20 00
J. Tren, Withdrawals	5 00	
Revenue from Clients		32 00
Rent Expense	2 00	
Wage Expense	8 00	
Totals	66 00	66 00

4B-5. From the completed worksheet in Exercise 4B-4, prepare:

 **LO3** *(20 min)*

   a. An income statement for May
   b. A statement of owner's equity for May
   c. A balance sheet as of May 31, 201X

Problems

MyLabAccounting

Set A

4A-1. Use the following adjustment data on July 31 to complete a partial worksheet up to the adjusted trial balance (see Figure 4.21).

 **LO1** *(15 min)*

   a. Fitness supplies on hand, $1,700.
   b. Depreciation taken on fitness equipment, $1,000.

Figure 4.21

JAMES'S FITNESS CENTER TRIAL BALANCE JULY 31, 201X		
Account Titles	Dr.	Cr.
Cash in Bank	7 500 00	
Accounts Receivable	5 400 00	
Fitness Supplies	5 100 00	
Fitness Equipment	9 700 00	
Accumulated Depreciation, Fitness Equipment		6 300 00
J. Wickers, Capital		9 750 00
J. Wickers, Withdrawals	2 750 00	
Fitness Fees		15 300 00
Rent Expense	750 00	
Advertising Expense	150 00	
Totals	31 350 00	31 350 00

Check Figure:
Total of Adjusted Trial Balance $32,350

(30 min) **LO1,2**

4A-2.   Update the trial balance for Leah's Landscaping Service (Figure 4.22) for December 31, 201X.

Adjustment Data to Update the Trial Balance

  a. Rent expired, $750.
  b. Landscaping supplies on hand (remaining), $225.
  c. Depreciation expense, landscaping equipment, $150.
  d. Wages earned by workers but not paid or due until January, $300.

Figure 4.22

Check Figure:
Total of Adjusted Trial Balance
$13,485

Account Titles	Dr.	Cr.
LEAH'S LANDSCAPING SERVICE **TRIAL BALANCE** **DECEMBER 31, 201X**		
Cash in Bank	4 0 0 0 00	
Accounts Receivable	2 0 0 00	
Prepaid Rent	2 4 0 0 00	
Landscaping Supplies	8 9 5 00	
Landscaping Equipment	3 6 0 0 00	
Accumulated Depreciation, Landscaping Equipment		1 0 2 0 00
Accounts Payable		6 3 2 00
A. Leah, Capital		5 0 2 1 00
Landscaping Revenue		6 3 6 2 00
Heat Expense	4 0 0 00	
Advertising Expense	1 8 0 00	
Wage Expense	1 3 6 0 00	
Totals	13 0 3 5 00	13 0 3 5 00

Your task is to prepare a worksheet for Leah's Landscaping Service for the month of December.

(60 min) **LO1,2,3**

4A-3.   Update the trial balance for Kole's Moving Co. (Figure 4.23 on page 135) for July 31, 201X.

Adjustment Data to Update Trial Balance

  a. Insurance expired, $800.
  b. Moving supplies on hand, $1,200.
  c. Depreciation on moving truck, $400.
  d. Wages earned but unpaid, $220.

Your task is to:

1. Complete a worksheet for Kole's Moving Co. for the month of July.
2. Prepare an income statement for July, a statement of owner's equity for July, and a balance sheet as of July 31, 201X.

KOLE'S MOVING CO. TRIAL BALANCE JULY 31, 201X		
Account Titles	Dr.	Cr.
Cash	2 0 0 0 00	
Prepaid Insurance	2 1 0 0 00	
Moving Supplies	1 5 0 0 00	
Moving Truck	8 0 0 0 00	
Accumulated Depreciation, Moving Truck		7 5 0 0 00
Accounts Payable		2 3 0 0 00
K. Hues, Capital		7 2 0 00
K. Hues, Withdrawals	1 2 0 0 00	
Revenue from Moving		8 6 0 0 00
Wage Expense	3 3 8 0 00	
Rent Expense	7 0 0 00	
Advertising Expense	2 4 0 00	
Totals	19 1 2 0 00	19 1 2 0 00

Figure 4.23

Check Figure:
Net Income $2,560

4A-4. The trial balance for Dick's Repair Service appears in Figure 4.24.

L01,2,3 *(60 min)*

S50 / QB

Adjustment Data to Update Trial Balance

a. Insurance expired, $450.
b. Repair supplies on hand, $2,800.
c. Depreciation on repair equipment, $300.
d. Wages earned but unpaid, $240.

Your task is to:

1. Complete a worksheet for Dick's Repair Service for the month of June.
2. Prepare an income statement for June, a statement of owner's equity for June, and a balance sheet as of June 30, 201X.

DICK'S REPAIR SERVICE TRIAL BALANCE JUNE 30, 201X		
Account Titles	Dr.	Cr.
Cash	4 2 0 0 00	
Prepaid Insurance	5 3 0 0 00	
Repair Supplies	4 4 0 0 00	
Repair Equipment	3 5 0 0 00	
Accumulated Depreciation, Repair Equipment		8 0 0 00
Accounts Payable		5 4 6 0 00
D. Homer, Capital		4 1 6 0 00
Revenue from Repairs		10 0 0 0 00
Wages Expense	2 4 0 0 00	
Rent Expense	5 5 0 00	
Advertising Expense	7 0 00	
Totals	20 4 2 0 00	20 4 2 0 00

Figure 4.24

Check Figure:
Net Income $4,390

Set B

4B-1. Use the following adjustment data on March 31 to complete a partial worksheet up to the adjusted trial balance (see Figure 4.25) p. 136.

L01 *(15 min)*

a. Fitness supplies on hand, $1,400.
b. Depreciation taken on fitness equipment, $700.

Figure 4.25

JAMES'S FITNESS CENTER TRIAL BALANCE MARCH 31, 201X		
Account Titles	Dr.	Cr.
Cash in Bank	10 5 0 0 00	
Accounts Receivable	6 1 0 0 00	
Fitness Supplies	5 3 0 0 00	
Fitness Equipment	11 2 0 0 00	
Accumulated Depreciation, Fitness Equipment		4 8 0 0 00
J. Winston, Capital		18 1 2 5 00
J. Winston, Withdrawals	1 5 0 0 00	
Fitness Fees		12 3 0 0 00
Rent Expense	3 5 0 00	
Advertising Expense	2 7 5 00	
Totals	35 2 2 5 00	35 2 2 5 00

Check Figure:
Total of Adjusted Trial Balance
$35,925

(30 min) **L01,2**

4B-2. Update the trial balance for Ling's Landscaping Service (Figure 4.26) for January 31, 201X.

Adjustment Data to Update the Trial Balance

a. Rent expired, $500.
b. Landscaping supplies on hand (remaining), $150.
c. Depreciation expense, landscaping equipment, $250.
d. Wages earned by workers but not paid or due until February, $725.

Your task is to prepare a worksheet for Ling's Landscaping Service for the month of January.

Figure 4.26

LING'S LANDSCAPING SERVICE TRIAL BALANCE JANUARY 31, 201X		
Account Titles	Dr.	Cr.
Cash in Bank	3 7 0 0 00	
Accounts Receivable	1 0 0 0 00	
Prepaid Rent	2 0 0 0 00	
Landscaping Supplies	1 2 7 5 00	
Landscaping Equipment	2 2 0 0 00	
Accumulated Depreciation, Landscaping Equipment		8 8 0 00
Accounts Payable		8 0 0 00
A. Ling, Capital		4 9 4 0 00
Landscaping Revenue		5 2 0 0 00
Heat Expense	3 2 5 00	
Advertising Expense	6 0 00	
Wage Expense	1 2 6 0 00	
Totals	11 8 2 0 00	11 8 2 0 00

Check Figure:
Total of Adjusted Trial Balance
$12,795

(60 min) **L01,2,3**

4B-3. Update the trial balance for Kreg's Moving Co. (Figure 4.27 on page 137) for October 31, 201X.

Adjustment Data to Update Trial Balance

a. Insurance expired, $550.
b. Moving supplies on hand, $800.
c. Depreciation on moving truck, $550.
d. Wages earned but unpaid, $300.

Your task is to:

1. Complete a worksheet for Kreg's Moving Co. for the month of October.
2. Prepare an income statement for October, a statement of owner's equity for October, and a balance sheet as of October 31, 201X.

Figure 4.27

KREG'S MOVING CO.
TRIAL BALANCE
OCTOBER 31, 201X

Account Titles	Dr.	Cr.
Cash	6 0 0 0 00	
Prepaid Insurance	2 4 0 0 00	
Moving Supplies	1 0 0 0 00	
Moving Truck	18 0 0 0 00	
Accumulated Depreciation, Moving Truck		6 0 0 0 00
Accounts Payable		2 7 6 8 00
K. Hill, Capital		16 3 9 3 00
K. Hill, Withdrawals	1 5 0 0 00	
Revenue from Moving		8 8 0 0 00
Wages Expense	3 7 1 2 00	
Rent Expense	7 2 0 00	
Advertising Expense	6 2 9 00	
Totals	33 9 6 1 00	33 9 6 1 00

Check Figure:
Net Income $2,139

4B-4. The trial balance for Dennis's Repair Service appears in Figure 4.28.

L01,2,3 *(60 min)*

S50 / QB

Adjustment Data to Update Trial Balance

a. Insurance expired, $200.
b. Repair supplies on hand, $2,300.
c. Depreciation on repair equipment, $700.
d. Wages earned but unpaid, $220.

Your task is to:

1. Complete a worksheet for Dennis's Repair Service for the month of November.
2. Prepare an income statement for November, a statement of owner's equity for November, and a balance sheet as of November 30, 201X.

Figure 4.28

DENNIS' REPAIR SERVICE
TRIAL BALANCE
NOVEMBER 30, 201X

Account Titles	Dr.	Cr.
Cash	3 2 0 0 00	
Prepaid Insurance	4 9 0 0 00	
Repair Supplies	5 1 0 0 00	
Repair Equipment	5 5 0 0 00	
Accumulated Depreciation, Repair Equipment		9 0 0 00
Accounts Payable		4 6 7 0 00
D. Horn, Capital		6 7 9 0 00
Revenue from Repairs		8 4 0 0 00
Wages Expense	1 4 0 0 00	
Rent Expense	5 5 0 00	
Advertising Expense	1 1 0 00	
Totals	20 7 6 0 00	20 7 6 0 00

Check Figure:
Net Income $2,420

(20 min) **L01**

Financial Report Problem

Reading Amazon's Annual Report

Go to **https://tinyurl.com/slaterca14e** to access Amazon's 2016 Annual Report. How does Amazon depreciate its equipment?

MyLabAccounting

KEEPING IT REAL SUAREZ COMPUTER CENTER

(45 min) **L01,2,3**

At the end of September, Troy, the owner, took a complete inventory of his supplies and found the following:

> 3 dozen ¼-inch screws at a cost of $5.00 a dozen
> 6 dozen ½-inch screws at a cost of $10.00 a dozen
> 5 cartons of computer inventory paper at a cost of $8 a carton
> 7 feet of coaxial cable at a cost of $11.00 per foot

After speaking to his accountant, Troy found that a reasonable depreciation amount for each of his long-term assets is as follows:

Computer purchased July 5, 201X	Depreciation $35 a month
Office equipment purchased July 17, 201X	Depreciation $25 a month
Computer workstations purchased Sept. 17, 201X	Depreciation $35 a month

Troy uses the straight-line method of depreciation and declares no salvage value for any of the assets. If any long-term asset is purchased in the first 15 days of the month, he will charge depreciation for the full month. If an asset is purchased on the 16th of the month, or later, he will not charge depreciation in the month it was purchased.

August and September's rent has now expired.

Assignment

Use your trial balance from the completed problem in Chapter 3 and the adjusting information given here to complete the worksheet for the 3 months ended September 30, 201X. From the worksheets, prepare the financial statements.

S50 | SAGE 50 SOFTWARE SIMULATION

Computerized Accounting Application for Chapter 4

Refresher on using Sage 50 Complete Accounting

Before starting this assignment, you may want to refresh your memory by reading the following PDF documents found in the multimedia library on the MyLab Accounting website. Remember to choose the PDF document for your version of Sage 50.

1. An Introduction to Sage 50
2. Correcting Sage 50 Transactions
3. How to Repeat or Restart a Sage 50 Assignment
4. Backing Up and Restoring Your Work in Sage 50

    You also should have completed Workshop 1 for the Atlas Company in Chapter 3.

Workshop 2

Compound Journal Entries, Adjusting Entries, and Financial Reports

In this workshop, you will post compound journal entries and adjusting journal entries for Zell Company using Sage 50. You will also print the general journal report, trial balance, income statement, and balance sheet.

Instructions and the data file for completing this assignment are in the multimedia library of the MyAccountingLab website. Open the *Workshop 2 Zell Company* PDF document for your version of Sage 50 and download the *Zell Company* data file for your version of Sage 50.

QUICKBOOKS SOFTWARE SIMULATION

QB

Computerized Accounting Application for Chapter 4

Refresher on using QuickBooks Accountant

Before starting this assignment, you may want to refresh your memory by reading the following PDF documents found in the multimedia library on the MyAccountingLab website. Remember to choose the PDF document for your version of QuickBooks.

1. An Introduction to Computerized Accounting
2. Installing QuickBooks Pro and Student Data Files
3. An Introduction to QuickBooks
4. Correcting QuickBooks Transactions
5. How to Repeat or Restart a QuickBooks Assignment
6. Backing Up and Restoring Your Work in QuickBooks

You also should have completed Workshop 1 for the Atlas Company in Chapter 3.

Workshop 2

Compound Journal Entries, Adjusting Entries, and Financial Reports

In this workshop you will post compound journal entries and adjusting journal entries for Zell Company using Quickbooks. You will also print the general journal report, trial balance, income statement, and balance sheet.

Instructions and the data file for completing this assignment are in the multimedia library of the MyAccountingLab Web site. Open the *Workshop 2 Zell Company* PDF document for your version of Quickbooks and download the *Zell Company* data file for your version of Quickbooks.

Appendix for Chapter 4

DEPRECIATION

Assets such as computer equipment are examples of assets that will benefit a company for more than one year or one accounting cycle. To account for these assets, we must recognize a portion of the cost of these assets that is being used up during the account period, be it a month, a quarter, or year. For purposes of illustration, we will focus on a year.

The calculation and accounting for depreciation requires that we use two accounts: Depreciation Expense, which is an Income Statement account, and Accumulated Depreciation, which is a Balance Sheet account. It is important to note from the discussion that occurred in Chapter 4 concerning Adjusting Journal Entries that every adjusting journal entry will affect at least one Income Statement account and at least one Balance Sheet account. Since the recording of depreciation at the end of a period is an Adjusting Journal Entry, we know that both of these accounts will be involved.

The portion of the asset cost that is used up in a period is reported as Depreciation Expense on the income statement. In effect, Depreciation Expense is the transfer of a portion of the asset's cost from the balance sheet to the income statement during each year of the asset's life; while Accumulated Depreciation is the recognition of the reduction of the cost of the asset on the Balance Sheet resulting in the current Book Value of the asset.

The calculation and reporting of depreciation is based upon two key accounting principles: one is the Cost Principle which requires that the Depreciation Expense reported on the income statement, and the asset amount that is recorded on the balance sheet, should be based on the original cost of the asset. The other is the Matching principle which requires that the asset's cost be allocated to Depreciation Expense over the life of the asset. In essence, the original cost of the asset is divided up and allocated on each of the income statements issued during the life of the asset. This then accomplishes the matching a portion of the asset's cost with each period in which the asset is used.

There are two general depreciation methods used for the recording of financial statement depreciation and these methods can be grouped into two categories: **Straight-line Depreciation** and **Accelerated Depreciation**. The most common method of depreciating assets for financial statement purposes is the straight-line method. Under this depreciation method, the depreciation expense determined for each full year is the same amount, assuming that in the first year the asset was placed in service in the beginning of the year.

The formula for **Straight-line Depreciation** is as follows:

$$\frac{\text{Cost of the asset minus Residual or Salvage Value}}{\text{Useful Life of Asset}} \text{ (expressed as function of time)}$$

In this formula, the Cost of the Asset is the original cost of the asset, plus any cost to get it ready for use; Residual, or Salvage Value, is any remaining value of the asset at the end of its useful life; and the Useful Life of the asset is the amount of time over which the cost will be recovered.

To illustrate:
On January 1, 20X0 Ellen Company purchases equipment having an original cost of $13,000.

The company estimates that the equipment will have a useful life of 4 years and, at the end of its useful life, the company expects to sell the equipment for $1,000. Ellen Company will use Straight Line Depreciation for its financial reporting purposes at the end of each year.

$$\frac{\$13,000 - 1,000}{4 \text{ years}} = \$3,000 \text{ of depreciation expense for each year.}$$

12/31/X0	Dr. Depreciation Expense $3,000
	Cr. Accumulated Depreciation $3,000
	Record depreciation expense for the year

Since we are using Straight-line Depreciation for the asset, the journal entry will be the same for each year of the asset's useful life.

Accelerated depreciation is the other major method of computing depreciation for financial reporting purposes. In comparison to the straight-line method, the accelerated depreciation methods provide for more depreciation expense in the early years of an asset's life but less depreciation in the later years, which means that amount of depreciation expense will decrease over the useful life of the asset. But it is important to remember that the total depreciation expense recorded over the life of an asset is limited to the original depreciable cost of the asset.

The formula for the **Accelerated Method of Double Declining Balance** is as follows:

Cost of Asset − Accumulated Depreciation = Book Value X Depreciation Rate (%)
= Depreciation Expense

In this formula, we start with the Cost of the Asset, then subtract any Accumulated Depreciation that has been recorded to date (*in the first year the answer is always 0*), which gives you the Book Value of the asset, which is the amount of the cost of the asset still to be depreciated. We then multiply this by the Depreciation Rate, which is a % that is applied to the Book Value to give you the depreciation expense for that year.

The % rate is determined by taking the Straight-line Rate and multiplying it by 2, thus doubling the rate of depreciation; that is how you get the Double in Double Declining Balance. So, in our example since the asset has a useful like of 4 years, you are depreciating on a straight line basis ¼ or 25% of the asset's cost each year. If you multiply 25% by 2, the rate for DDB is going to be 50%.

To illustrate:

Asset Cost	− Accum. Depreciation	= Book Value	X Deprec. Rate (%)	= Depreciation Expense
1. $13,000 −	$ 0	= $13,000 X	.50	= $6,500
2. $13,000 −	$6,500	= $ 6,500 X	.50	= $3,250

12/31/X0	Dr. Depreciation Expense $6,500
	Cr. Accumulated Depreciation $6,500
	Record depreciation expense for year one

12/31/X1	Dr. Depreciation Expense $3,250
	Cr. Accumulated Depreciation $3,250
	Record depreciation expense for the year two

Unlike the Straight-line method, we can see that the amount of depreciation expense will be different each year, with most of the depreciation expense being recorded in the early years of the asset's life and less in the later years of its life. Also, it is important to note that while in both cases Residual or Salvage Value comes into play, as we saw for Straight Line it is a factor in the very beginning of our calculations; for DDB is not a factor till the completion of our calculations; in essence it is the amount that you are left with at the end.

The Accounting Cycle Completed

5

CHAPTER PREVIEW: ACCOUNTING IN ACTION

On April 15, Keshawn Barber e-filed his federal income tax forms; he had complied with a reporting requirement that most people have. The same concept holds true in accounting for companies as well. For example, SeaWorld must report to investors and government regulators how operations performed during its accounting cycle. When one accounting cycle is closed, the next one begins. This period of time is called the *fiscal year*. Many companies end their fiscal years in March, July, or October. Other companies, like retailers, end on December 31 so holiday sales can be included in the final results. No matter when companies end their fiscal years, the accounting cycle must be completed and financial reports prepared so that companies can report to the appropriate governmental authorities, such as the Securities and Exchange Commission and the Internal Revenue Service, investors, and creditors.

Learning Objectives – Relating Accounting Theory By Unit

LO1   Journalize and Post Adjusting Entries

LO2   Journalize and Post Closing Entries

LO3   Prepare a Post-Closing Trial Balance

Each accounting cycle completed by SeaWorld will end with the preparation of a post-closing trial balance. In Chapters 3 and 4 we completed these steps of the manual accounting cycle for Rob Sinclair's Hilight Graphic Services:

STEP 1: Business transactions occurred and generated source documents.

STEP 2: Business transactions were analyzed and recorded in a journal.

STEP 3: Information was posted or transferred from journal to ledger.

STEP 4: A trial balance was prepared.

STEP 5: A worksheet was completed.

STEP 6: Financial statements were prepared.

This chapter covers the following steps to complete Hilight's accounting cycle for the month of May:

STEP 7: Journalizing and posting adjusting entries.

STEP 8: Journalizing and posting closing entries.

STEP 9: Preparing a post-closing trial balance.

LEARNING UNIT 5-1

L01 ➤

Adjusting Entries (Step 7 of the Accounting Cycle)

Recording Journal Entries from the Worksheet

The information in the worksheet is up-to-date. The financial reports prepared from that information can give the business's management and other interested parties a good idea of where the business stands as of a particular date. However, the worksheet is only an informal report. The information concerning the adjustments has not been placed into the journal or posted to the ledger accounts yet, which means that the books are not up-to-date and ready for the next accounting cycle to begin. For example, the ledger shows $1,200 of Prepaid Rent, but the balance sheet we prepared in Chapter 4 shows an $800 balance. Essentially, the work-sheet is a tool for preparing financial statements. Now we must use the adjustment columns of the worksheet as a basis for bringing the ledger up-to-date. To update the ledger, we use adjusting journal entries (see Figures 5.1 and 5.2 on page 145). Again, the updating must be done before the next accounting period starts. For Rob Sinclair's Hilight Graphic Services, the next period begins on June 1.

Figure 5.2 shows the adjusting journal entries for Hilight Graphic Services taken from the adjustments section of the worksheet. Once the adjusting journal entries are posted to the ledger, the accounts making up the financial statements that were prepared from the worksheet will equal the updated ledger. (Keep in mind that we are using the same journal and ledger as in the previous chapters.) Let's look at some simplified T accounts to show how Hilight's ledger looked before and after the adjustments (A–D) were posted.

Adjusting journal entries Journal entries that are needed in order to update specific ledger accounts to reflect correct balances at the end of an accounting period.

American Institute of Professional Bookkeepers (AIPB) – A Certified Bookkeeper (CB) has the training required to keep the books for a company of up to 100 employees. This includes preparing the trial balance and computing and recording the year-end adjustments to prepare the adjusted trial balance so that preparation of the financial state-ments and tax return can begin. These steps are crucial because the financial statements and tax returns can only be as good as the company's books given to the CPA. More on the AIPB can be found **https://www.aipb.org**

Adjustment (A)

Before Posting:	Computer Supplies 114		Computer Supplies Expense 514	
	600			
After Posting:	Computer Supplies 114		Computer Supplies Expense 514	
	600	500	500	

Adjustment (B)

Before Posting:	Prepaid Rent 115		Rent Expense 515	
	1,200			
After Posting:	Prepaid Rent 115		Rent Expense 515	
	1,200	400	400	

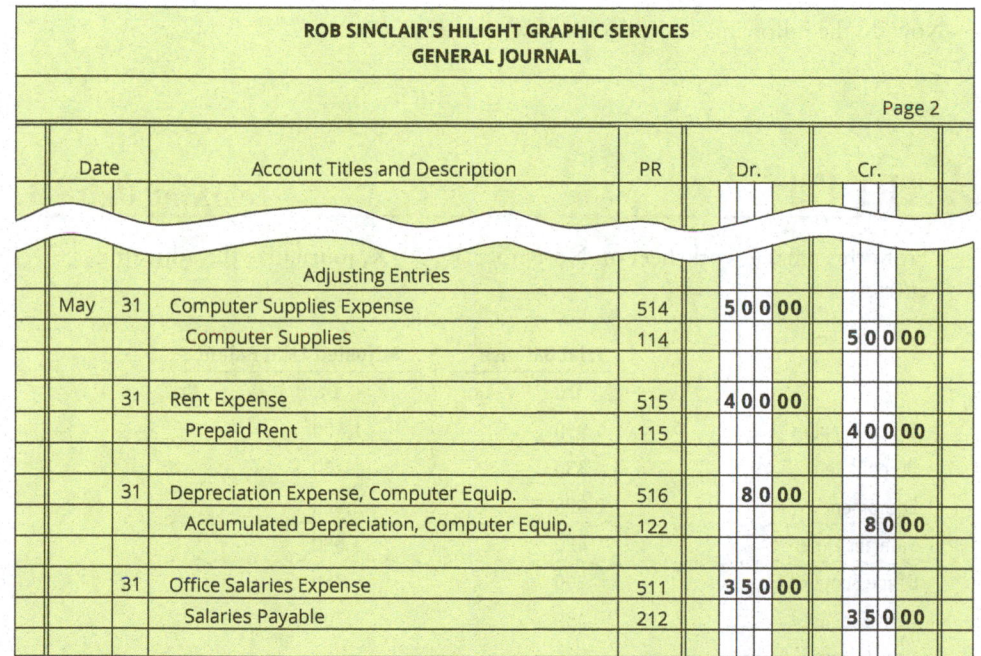

Account Titles	Trial Balance		Adjustments	
	Dr.	Cr.	Dr.	Cr.
Cash	6 1 5 5 00			
Accounts Receivable	5 0 0 0 00			
Computer Supplies	6 0 0 00			(A) 5 0 0 00
Prepaid Rent	1 2 0 0 00			(B) 4 0 0 00
Computer Equipment	6 0 0 0 00			
Accounts Payable		3 3 5 0 00		
Rob Sinclair, Capital		10 0 0 0 00		
Rob Sinclair, Withdrawals	6 2 5 00			
Graphic Design Fees		8 0 0 0 00		
Office Salaries Expense	1 3 0 0 00		(D) 3 5 0 00	
Advertising Expense	2 5 0 00			
Telephone Expense	2 2 0 00			
Totals	21 3 5 0 00	21 3 5 0 00		
Computer Supplies Expense			(A) 5 0 0 00	
Rent Expense			(B) 4 0 0 00	
Depreciation Exp., Computer Equip.			(C) 8 0 00	
Accum. Deprec., Computer Equip.				(C) 8 0 00
Salaries Payable				(D) 3 5 0 00
Totals			1 3 3 0 00	1 3 3 0 00

Figure 5.1
Adjustments A–D in the Adjustments Section of the Worksheet Must Be Recorded in the Journal and Posted to the Ledger

ROB SINCLAIR'S HILIGHT GRAPHIC SERVICES
GENERAL JOURNAL

Page 2

Date		Account Titles and Description	PR	Dr.	Cr.
		Adjusting Entries			
May	31	Computer Supplies Expense	514	5 0 0 00	
		Computer Supplies	114		5 0 0 00
	31	Rent Expense	515	4 0 0 00	
		Prepaid Rent	115		4 0 0 00
	31	Depreciation Expense, Computer Equip.	516	8 0 00	
		Accumulated Depreciation, Computer Equip.	122		8 0 00
	31	Office Salaries Expense	511	3 5 0 00	
		Salaries Payable	212		3 5 0 00

Figure 5.2
Journalizing and Posting Adjustments from the Adjustments Section of the Worksheet

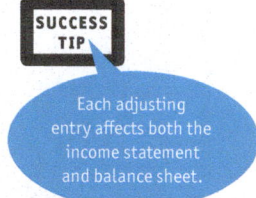

SUCCESS TIP

Each adjusting entry affects both the income statement and balance sheet.

Adjustment (C)

Before Posting:

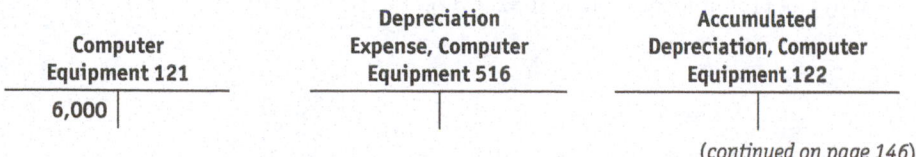

Computer Equipment 121	Depreciation Expense, Computer Equipment 516	Accumulated Depreciation, Computer Equipment 122
6,000		

(continued on page 146)

After Posting:

Computer Equipment 121	Depreciation Expense, Computer Equipment 516	Accumulated Depreciation, Computer Equipment 122
6,000	80	80

The first adjustment in (C) shows the same balances for Depreciation Expense, Computer Equipment and Accumulated Depreciation, Computer Equipment. However, in subsequent adjustments the Accumulated Depreciation balance will keep getting larger, but the debit to Depreciation Expense and the credit to Accumulated Depreciation will stay the same. We will see why in a moment.

Adjustment (D)

Before Posting:

Office Salaries Expense 511	Salaries Payable 212
650	
650	

After Posting:

Office Salaries Expense 511	Salaries Payable 212
650	350
650	
350	

Now do the following Try It! to see how you are doing.

 ## TRY IT!   Learning Unit 5-1

From this partial worksheet on November 30, 201X, journalize the adjusting entries:

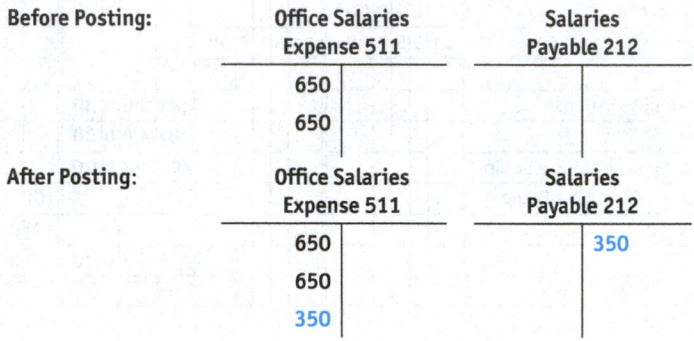

	Trial Balance		Adjusted Trial Balance	
	Dr.	Cr.	Dr.	Cr.
Office Supplies	1,950		1,400	
Prepaid Rent	330		80	
Equipment	2,925		2,925	
Salaries Expense	420		680	
Office Supplies Expense	200		750	
Rent Expense	450		700	
Dep. Expense, Equip.	75		400	
Acc. Depreciation, Equip.		75		400
Salaries Payable				260

Why does Equipment remain at $2,925 on the adjusted trial balance?

TRY IT!   **Solution Learning Unit 5-1**

Date		Account Title	Dr.	Cr.
201X				
Nov.	30	Office Supplies Expense	550	
		Office Supplies		550
	30	Rent Expense	250	
		Prepaid Rent		250
	30	Depreciation Expense, Equipment	325	
		Accumulated Depreciation, Equipment		325
	30	Salaries Expense	260	
		Salaries Payable		260

The original cost of equipment is not adjusted. It is the historical cost. The adjustment data is reflected in Depreciation Expense, Equipment and Accumulated Depreciation, Equipment.

Closing Entries (Step 8 of the Accounting Cycle)

To make recording of the next period's transactions easier, a mechanical step, called *closing*, is performed by Hilight's accountant. Closing is intended to end—or close off—the revenue, expense, and withdrawal accounts at the end of the accounting period. The information needed to complete closing entries will be found in the income statement and balance sheet sections of the worksheet.

To make it easier to understand this process, we first look at the difference between temporary (nominal) accounts and permanent (real) accounts.

Here is the expanded accounting equation we used in an earlier chapter:

$$\text{Assets} = \text{Liabilities} + \text{Capital} - \text{Withdrawals} + \text{Revenues} - \text{Expenses}$$

Three of the items in that equation—Assets, Liabilities, and Capital—are known as real or permanent accounts because their balances are carried over from one accounting period to another. The other three items—Withdrawals, Revenues, and Expenses—are called nominal or temporary accounts because their balances are not carried over from one accounting period to another. Instead, their "balances" are reset at zero at the beginning of each accounting period by closing their balances at the end of the previous period. This process allows us to accumulate new data about revenue, expenses, and withdrawals in the new accounting period. Think of these accounts as representing the "scoreboard" for the business for this period. You would not take last week's score from a sporting event to determine this week's result; the same principle applies here. The process of closing summarizes the effects of the temporary accounts on Capital for that period using closing journal entries. When the closing process is complete, the accounting equation will be reduced to

$$\text{Assets} = \text{Liabilities} + \text{Ending Capital}$$

If you look back to Chapter 4, you will see that we already calculated the new capital on the balance sheet to be $14,275 for Rob Sinclair's Hilight Graphic Services. Before the mechanical closing procedures are journalized and posted, Sinclair's Capital account in the ledger is only $10,000 (see Chapter 3). Let's now look at how to journalize and post closing entries.

Permanent (real) accounts Accounts whose balances are carried over to the next accounting period (e.g., Assets, Liabilities, Capital).

Temporary (nominal) accounts Accounts whose balances at the end of an accounting period are not carried over to the next accounting period.

Closing journal entries Journal entries that are prepared to (a) reset all temporary accounts to a zero balance and (b) update Capital to a new balance.

Think of the goals of closing like sweeping a room. First, you sweep or clear all revenue and expenses into a dustpan (Income Summary), and then you place the balance into a barrel (like Capital).

How to Journalize Closing Entries

Four steps are needed in journalizing closing entries:

STEP 1: Clear to zero the revenue balance and transfer it to Income Summary. Income Summary is a temporary account in the ledger needed for closing. At the end of the closing process, Income Summary will no longer hold a balance.

Revenue → Income Summary

STEP 2: Clear to zero the individual expense balances and transfer them to Income Summary.

Expenses → Income Summary

STEP 3: Clear to zero the balance in Income Summary and transfer it to Capital.

Income Summary → Capital

STEP 4: Clear to zero the balance in Withdrawals and transfer it to Capital.

Withdrawals → Capital

Figure 5.3 is a visual representation of these four steps. Keep in mind that this information must first be journalized and then posted to the appropriate ledger accounts. The worksheet presented in Figure 5.4 contains all the figures we will need for the closing process.

Step 1: Clear Revenue Balance and Transfer to Income Summary Here is what is in the ledger before closing entries are journalized and posted:

Graphic Design Fees 411	Income Summary 313
8,000	

The income statement section on the worksheet in Figure 5.4 on page 149 shows that Graphic Design Fees has a credit balance of $8,000. To close or clear this balance to zero, a debit of $8,000 is needed. But if we add an amount to the debit side, we must also add a credit—so we add $8,000 on the credit side of the Income Summary.

Income Summary Temporary account in the ledger that summarizes revenue and expenses and transfers the balance (net income or net loss) to Capital. This account does not have a normal balance (i.e., it could have a debit or a credit balance).

After all closing entries are journalized and posted to the ledger, all temporary accounts have a zero balance in the ledger. Closing is a step-by-step process.

Figure 5.3
Four Steps in Journalizing Closing Entries (All numbers can be found on the worksheet in Figure 5.4.)

Don't forget two goals of closing:
1. Clear all temporary accounts in ledger.
2. Update Capital to a new balance that reflects a summary of all the temporary accounts.

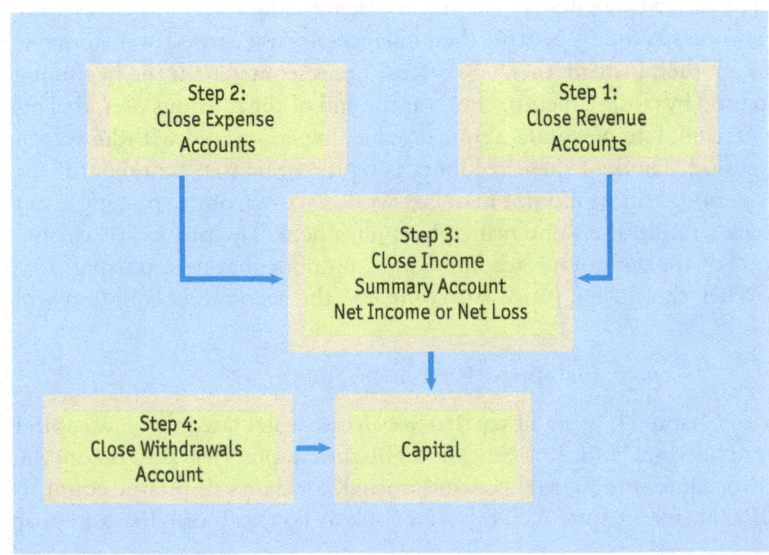

Figure 5.4
Closing Figures on the Worksheet

Account Titles	Income Statement		Balance Sheet	
	Dr.	Cr.	Dr.	Cr.
Cash			6 1 5 5 00	
Accounts Receivable			5 0 0 0 00	
Computer Supplies			1 0 0 00	
Prepaid Rent			8 0 0 00	
Computer Equipment			6 0 0 0 00	
Accounts Payable				3 3 5 0 00
Rob Sinclair, Capital		For Step 1		10 0 0 0 00
Rob Sinclair, Withdrawals	For Step 2		6 2 5 00	
Graphic Design Fees		8 0 0 0 00		
Office Salaries Expense	1 6 5 0 00		For Step 4	
Advertising Expense	2 5 0 00			
Telephone Expense	2 2 0 00			
Computer Supplies Expense	5 0 0 00			
Rent Expense	4 0 0 00			
Depreciation Exp., Computer Equip.	8 0 00			
Acc. Depreciation, Computer Equip.		For Step 3		8 0 00
Salaries Payable				3 5 0 00
Totals	3 1 0 0 00	8 0 0 0 00	18 6 8 0 00	13 7 8 0 00
Net Income	4 9 0 0 00			4 9 0 0 00
Totals	8 0 0 0 00	8 0 0 0 00	18 6 8 0 00	18 6 8 0 00

All numbers used in the closing process can be found on the worksheet.

Figure 5.5 is the journalized closing entry for Step 1.

May	31	Graphic Design Fees	411	8 0 0 0 00		
		Income Summary	313		8 0 0 0 00	

Figure 5.5
Closing Revenue to Income Summary

After the first step of closing entries is journalized and posted, the Graphic Design Fees and Income Summary ledger accounts should look like the following:

Graphic Design Fees 411		Income Summary 313	
8,000	8,000		8,000
Closing	Revenue		Revenue

Note that the revenue balance is cleared to zero and transferred to Income Summary, a temporary account also located in the ledger.

Step 2: Clear Individual Expense Balances and Transfer the Total to Income Summary The ledger for each expense account is shown here before closing entries are journalized and posted. Each expense is listed on the worksheet in the debit column of the income statement section in Figure 5.4.

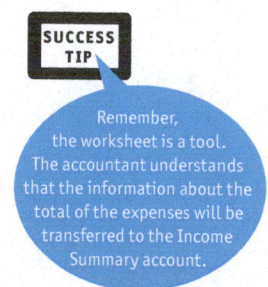

Remember, the worksheet is a tool. The accountant understands that the information about the total of the expenses will be transferred to the Income Summary account.

Office Salaries Expense 511	
650	
650	
350	

Advertising Expense 512	
250	

Telephone Expense 513	
220	

Computer Supplies Expense 514	
500	

Rent Expense 515	
400	

Depreciation Expense, Computer Equipment 516	
80	

The income statement section of the worksheet lists all the expenses as debits. If we want to reduce each expense to zero, each one must be credited.

Figure 5.6 is the journalized closing entry for Step 2.

Figure 5.6
Closing Each Expense Account Balance to Income Summary

				Debit	Credit
	31	Income Summary	313	3 1 0 0 00	
		Office Salaries Expense	511		1 6 5 0 00
		Advertising Expense	512		2 5 0 00
		Telephone Expense	513		2 2 0 00
		Computer Supplies Expense	514		5 0 0 00
		Rent Expense	515		4 0 0 00
		Depreciation Expense, Computer Equip.	516		8 0 00

Individual expenses and Income Summary accounts should look like the following after closing entries are journalized and posted:

Office Salaries Expense 511			
650	Closing		1,650
650			
350			

Advertising Expense 512			
250	Closing		250

Telephone Expense 513			
220	Closing		220

Computer Supplies Expense 514			
500	Closing		500

Rent Expense 515			
400	Closing		400

Depreciation Expense, Computer Equipment 516			
80	Closing		80

Income Summary 313		
	Expenses	Revenue
Step 2	3,100	8,000　Step 1

Step 3: Clear Balance in Income Summary (Net Income) and Transfer It to Capital　The Income Summary and Rob Sinclair, Capital accounts look this way before Step 3:

Income Summary 313	
3,100	8,000
	4,900

Rob Sinclair, Capital 311	
	10,000

Note that the ending balance of Income Summary is $4,900. (Revenues minus Expenses, or $8,000 Cr. − $3,100 Dr. = $4,900 Cr.) We must clear that amount from the Income Summary account and transfer it to the Rob Sinclair, Capital account.

In order to transfer the Credit Balance of $4,900 from Income Summary to Capital, it will be necessary to debit Income Summary for $4,900 and credit or increase Capital of Rob Sinclair for $4,900.

Figure 5.7 is the journalized closing entry for Step 3:

| | | 31 | Income Summary | 313 | 4 9 0 0 00 | |
| | | | Rob Sinclair, Capital | 311 | | 4 9 0 0 00 |

Figure 5.7
Closing Net Income for Rob Sinclair, Capital

The Income Summary and Rob Sinclair, Capital accounts will look like the following in the ledger after the closing entries of Step 3 are journalized and posted:

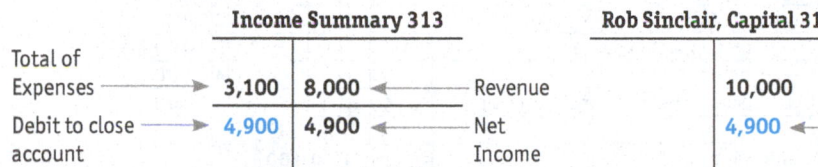

Step 4: Clear the Withdrawals Balance and Transfer It to Capital Next, we must close the Withdrawals account. The Rob Sinclair, Withdrawals and Rob Sinclair, Capital accounts currently look like this:

Rob Sinclair, Withdrawals 312		**Rob Sinclair, Capital 311**	
625			10,000
			4,900

To bring the Withdrawals account to a zero balance and summarize its effect on Capital, we must credit Withdrawals and debit Capital.

Remember, withdrawals are a nonbusiness expense and thus are not transferred to Income Summary. The closing entry is journalized, as shown in Figure 5.8.

| | | 31 | Rob Sinclair, Capital | 311 | 6 2 5 00 | |
| | | | Rob Sinclair, Withdrawals | 312 | | 6 2 5 00 |

Figure 5.8
Closing Withdrawal to Rob Sinclair, Capital

At this point the Rob Sinclair, Withdrawals and Rob Sinclair, Capital accounts would look this way in the ledger:

Rob Sinclair, Withdrawals 312		**Rob Sinclair, Capital 311**	
625	Closing 625	625 Withdrawals	10,000 Beg. Balance
			4,900 Net Income

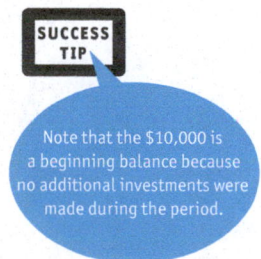

Now let's look at a summary of the closing entries in Figure 5.9.

Figure 5.9
Four Closing Entries

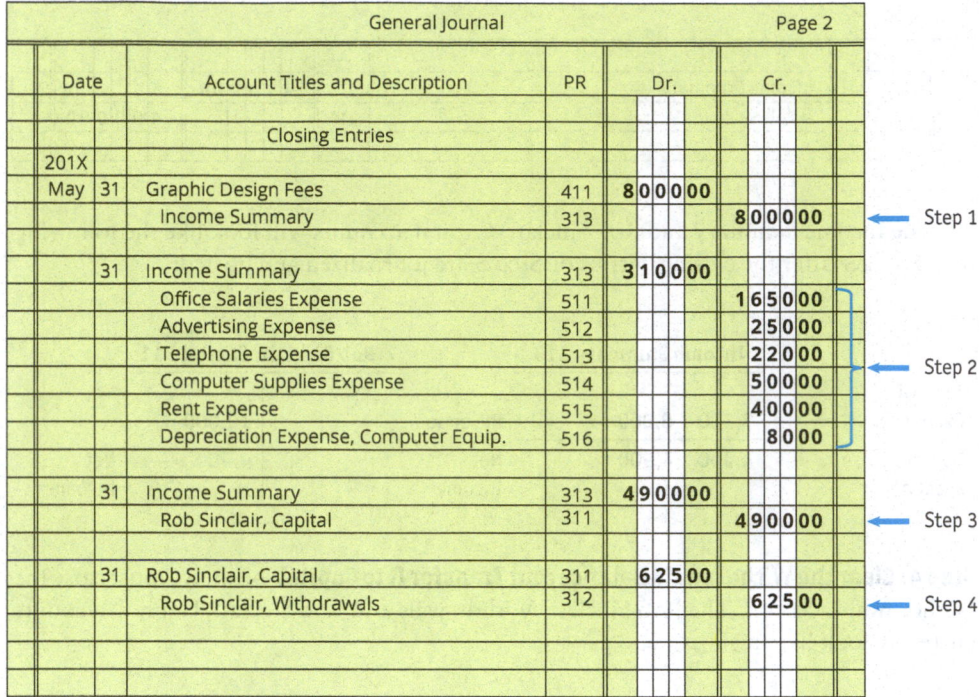

	Date		Account Titles and Description	PR	Dr.	Cr.	
			General Journal			Page 2	
			Closing Entries				
201X							
	May	31	Graphic Design Fees	411	8 0 0 0 00		
			Income Summary	313		8 0 0 0 00	← Step 1
		31	Income Summary	313	3 1 0 0 00		
			Office Salaries Expense	511		1 6 5 0 00	
			Advertising Expense	512		2 5 0 00	
			Telephone Expense	513		2 2 0 00	
			Computer Supplies Expense	514		5 0 0 00	← Step 2
			Rent Expense	515		4 0 0 00	
			Depreciation Expense, Computer Equip.	516		8 0 00	
		31	Income Summary	313	4 9 0 0 00		
			Rob Sinclair, Capital	311		4 9 0 0 00	← Step 3
		31	Rob Sinclair, Capital	311	6 2 5 00		
			Rob Sinclair, Withdrawals	312		6 2 5 00	← Step 4

Figure 5.10 shows the complete ledger for Rob Sinclair's Hilight Graphic Services after posting adjusting and closing entries.

Figure 5.10
Complete Ledger

ROB SINCLAIR'S HILIGHT GRAPHIC SERVICES
GENERAL LEDGER

Cash   Account No. 111

			Post.			Balance	
Date		Explanation	Ref.	Dr.	Cr.	Dr.	Cr.
201X							
May	1		GJ1	10 0 0 0 00		10 0 0 0 00	
	1		GJ1		1 0 0 0 00	9 0 0 0 00	
	1		GJ1		1 2 0 0 00	7 8 0 0 00	
	7		GJ1	3 0 0 0 00		10 8 0 0 00	
	13		GJ1		6 5 0 00	10 1 5 0 00	
	20		GJ1		6 2 5 00	9 5 2 5 00	
	27		GJ2		6 5 0 00	8 8 7 5 00	
	28		GJ2		2 5 0 0 00	6 3 7 5 00	
	29		GJ2		2 2 0 00	6 1 5 5 00	

Accounts Receivable   Account No. 112

			Post.			Balance	
Date		Explanation	Ref.	Dr.	Cr.	Dr.	Cr.
201X							
May	22		GJ1	5 0 0 0 00		5 0 0 0 00	

Computer Supplies   Account No. 114

			Post.			Balance	
Date		Explanation	Ref.	Dr.	Cr.	Dr.	Cr.
201X							
May	3		GJ1	6 0 0 00		6 0 0 00	
	31	Adjusting	GJ2		5 0 0 00	1 0 0 00	

Figure 5.10 (*continued*)

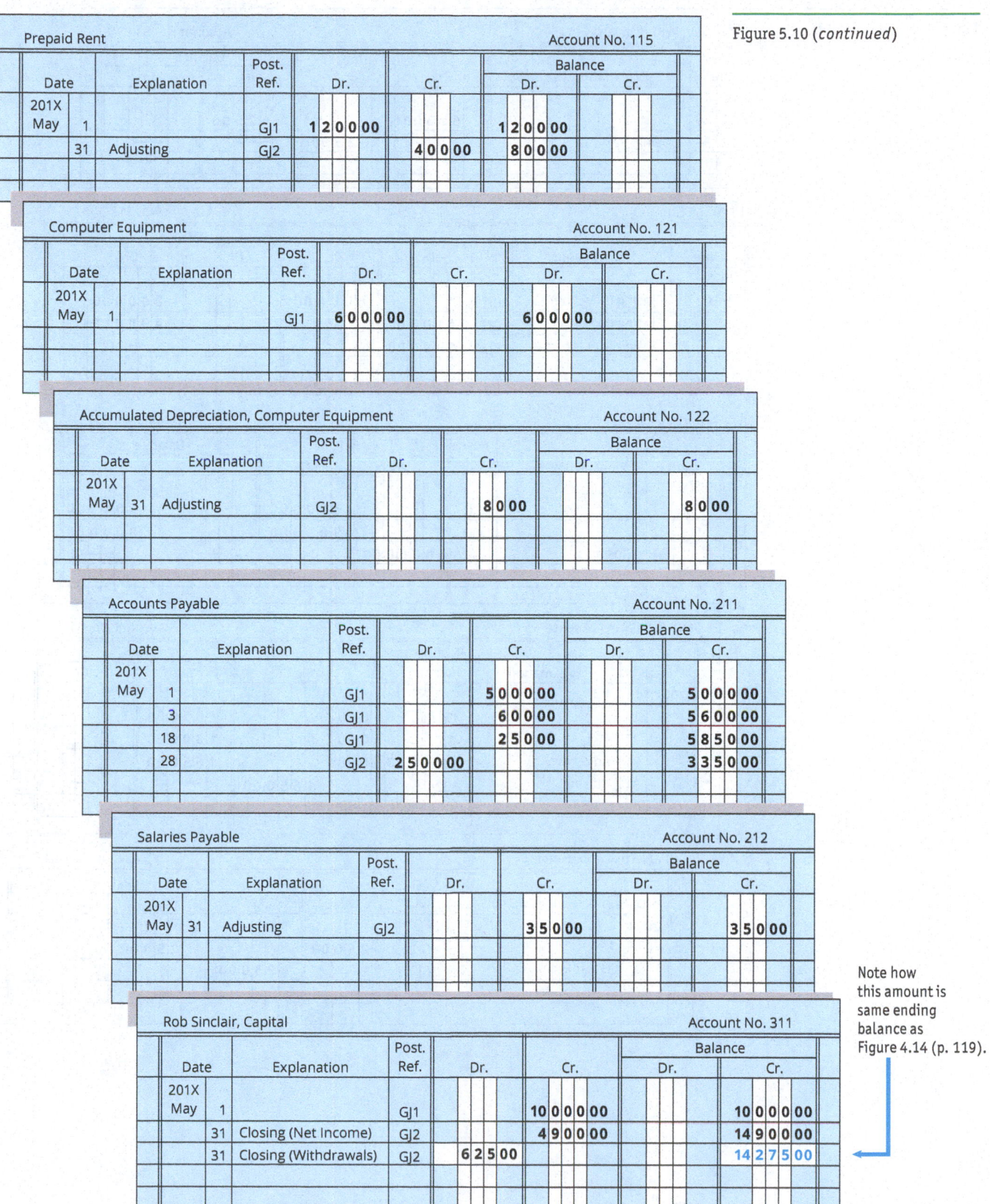

Prepaid Rent   Account No. 115

Date		Explanation	Post. Ref.	Dr.	Cr.	Balance Dr.	Balance Cr.
201X May	1		GJ1	1 2 0 0 00		1 2 0 0 00	
	31	Adjusting	GJ2		4 0 0 00	8 0 0 00	

Computer Equipment   Account No. 121

Date		Explanation	Post. Ref.	Dr.	Cr.	Balance Dr.	Balance Cr.
201X May	1		GJ1	6 0 0 0 00		6 0 0 0 00	

Accumulated Depreciation, Computer Equipment   Account No. 122

Date		Explanation	Post. Ref.	Dr.	Cr.	Balance Dr.	Balance Cr.
201X May	31	Adjusting	GJ2		8 0 00		8 0 00

Accounts Payable   Account No. 211

Date		Explanation	Post. Ref.	Dr.	Cr.	Balance Dr.	Balance Cr.
201X May	1		GJ1		5 0 0 0 00		5 0 0 0 00
	3		GJ1		6 0 0 00		5 6 0 0 00
	18		GJ1		2 5 0 00		5 8 5 0 00
	28		GJ2	2 5 0 0 00			3 3 5 0 00

Salaries Payable   Account No. 212

Date		Explanation	Post. Ref.	Dr.	Cr.	Balance Dr.	Balance Cr.
201X May	31	Adjusting	GJ2		3 5 0 00		3 5 0 00

Rob Sinclair, Capital   Account No. 311

Date		Explanation	Post. Ref.	Dr.	Cr.	Balance Dr.	Balance Cr.
201X May	1		GJ1		10 0 0 0 00		10 0 0 0 00
	31	Closing (Net Income)	GJ2		4 9 0 0 00		14 9 0 0 00
	31	Closing (Withdrawals)	GJ2	6 2 5 00			14 2 7 5 00

Note how this amount is same ending balance as Figure 4.14 (p. 119).

(*continued on next page*)

Figure 5.10 (*continued*)

Rob Sinclair, Withdrawals   Account No. 312

Date		Explanation	Post. Ref.	Dr.	Cr.	Balance Dr.	Balance Cr.
201X May	20		GJ1	6 2 5 00		6 2 5 00	
	31	Closing	GJ2		6 2 5 00	—	—

Income Summary   Account No. 313

Date		Explanation	Post. Ref.	Dr.	Cr.	Balance Dr.	Balance Cr.
201X May	31	Closing (Revenue)	GJ2		8 0 0 0 00		8 0 0 0 00
	31	Closing (Expenses)	GJ2	3 1 0 0 00			4 9 0 0 00
	31	Closing (Net Income)	GJ2	4 9 0 0 00		—	—

Graphic Design Fees   Account No. 411

Date		Explanation	Post. Ref.	Dr.	Cr.	Balance Dr.	Balance Cr.
201X May	7		GJ1		3 0 0 0 00		3 0 0 0 00
	22		GJ1		5 0 0 0 00		8 0 0 0 00
	31	Closing	GJ2	8 0 0 0 00		—	—

Office Salaries Expense   Account No. 511

Date		Explanation	Post. Ref.	Dr.	Cr.	Balance Dr.	Balance Cr.
201X May	13		GJ1	6 5 0 00		6 5 0 00	
	27		GJ2	6 5 0 00		1 3 0 0 00	
	31	Adjusting	GJ2	3 5 0 00		1 6 5 0 00	
	31	Closing	GJ2		1 6 5 0 00	—	—

Advertising Expense   Account No. 512

Date		Explanation	Post. Ref.	Dr.	Cr.	Balance Dr.	Balance Cr.
201X May	18		GJ1	2 5 0 00		2 5 0 00	
	31	Closing	GJ2		2 5 0 00	—	

Figure 5.10 (continued)

Telephone Expense — Account No. 513

Date		Explanation	Post. Ref.	Dr.	Cr.	Balance Dr.	Balance Cr.
201X May	29		GJ2	2 2 0 00		2 2 0 00	
	31	Closing	GJ2		2 2 0 00	—	—

Computer Supplies Expense — Account No. 514

Date		Explanation	Post. Ref.	Dr.	Cr.	Balance Dr.	Balance Cr.
201X May	31	Adjusting	GJ2	5 0 0 00		5 0 0 00	
	31	Closing	GJ2		5 0 0 00	—	—

Note: Accounts 312 to 516 are temporary and are closed to zero.

Rent Expense — Account No. 515

Date		Explanation	Post. Ref.	Dr.	Cr.	Balance Dr.	Balance Cr.
201X May	31	Adjusting	GJ2	4 0 0 00		4 0 0 00	
	31	Closing	GJ2		4 0 0 00	—	—

Depreciation Expense, Computer Equipment — Account No. 516

Date		Explanation	Post. Ref.	Dr.	Cr.	Balance Dr.	Balance Cr.
201X May	31	Adjusting	GJ2	8 0 00		8 0 00	
	31	Closing	GJ2		8 0 00	—	—

Note how "adjusting" or "closing" is written in the explanation column of individual accounts, as, for example, in the one for Computer Supplies. If the goals of closing have been achieved, only permanent accounts will have balances carried to the next accounting period. All temporary accounts should have zero balances.

Insight into Closing in a Computerized System

In a computerized accounting system, the closing entries are done in seconds because the software automatically closes the books. The end results are permanent accounts that have balances. At the end of this chapter is a Mini Practice Set for a fictional company called Sherman Realty that allows you to use Sage 50 or QuickBooks to see how fast a computer can journal and post. (Check with your instructor to see if this Mini Practice Set will be covered in your course.)

Now you can check your progress with a Try It!

TRY IT!   Learning Unit 5-2

Given the following accounts, journalize the closing entries for September 30, 201X, and calculate the new ending balance for B. Burnett, Capital.

Account	Acct. No.	Ending Balance
Cash	110	2,400 Dr.
B. Burnett, Capital	310	600 Cr.
B. Burnett, Withdrawals	311	240 Dr.
Income Summary	312	—
Consulting Fees	410	1,100 Cr.
Supplies Expense	510	20 Dr.
Salaries Expense	520	350 Dr.
Rent Expense	530	275 Dr.

TRY IT!   **Solution Learning Unit 5-2**

Date			Account Title	Dr.	Cr.
201X					
Sept.	30		Consulting Fees	1,100	
			Income Summary		1,100
	30		Income Summary	645	
			Supplies Expense		20
			Salaries Expense		350
			Rent Expense		275
	30		Income Summary	455	
			B. Burnett, Capital		455
	30		B. Burnett, Capital	240	
			B. Burnett, Withdrawals		240
			B. Burnett, Capital, Beg.		$600
			Plus Net Income	$455	
			Less Withdrawals	$240	215
			B. Burnett, Capital, End.		$815

LEARNING UNIT 5-3

L03

The Post-Closing Trial Balance (Step 9 of the Accounting Cycle)

Preparing a Post-Closing Trial Balance

Post-closing trial balance Final step in the accounting cycle that lists only permanent accounts in the ledger and their balances after adjusting and closing entries have been posted.

The last step in the accounting cycle is the preparation of a post-closing trial balance, which lists only permanent accounts in the ledger and their balances after adjusting and closing entries have been posted. This post-closing trial balance aids in checking whether the ledger is in balance. This checking is important because so many new postings go to the ledger from the adjusting and closing process.

The procedure for taking a post-closing trial balance is the same as for a trial balance, except that, because closing entries have closed all temporary accounts, the post-closing trial balances will contain only permanent accounts (balance sheet). See Figure 5.10 which shows the complete ledger for Rob Sinclair's Hilight Graphic Services.

Figure 5.11 shows a completed post-closing trial balance that reflects the permanent accounts. Now let's review the accounting cycle.

ROB SINCLAIR'S HILIGHT GRAPHIC SERVICES POST-CLOSING TRIAL BALANCE MAY 31, 201X		
	Dr.	Cr.
Cash	6 1 5 5 00	
Accounts Receivable	5 0 0 0 00	
Computer Supplies	1 0 0 00	
Prepaid Rent	8 0 0 00	
Computer Equipment	6 0 0 0 00	
Accumulated Depreciation, Computer Equip.		8 0 00
Accounts Payable		3 3 5 0 00
Salaries Payable		3 5 0 00
Rob Sinclair, Capital		14 2 7 5 00
Totals	18 0 5 5 00	18 0 5 5 00

Figure 5.11
Post-Closing Trial Balance for Rob Sinclair's Hilight Graphic Services

The Accounting Cycle Reviewed

Table 5.1 lists the steps we completed in the manual accounting cycle for Rob Sinclair's Hilight Graphic Services for the month of May.

TABLE 5.1 Steps of the Manual Accounting Cycle

Steps	Explanation
1. Collect source documents from business transactions as they occur.	Cash register tape, sales tickets, bills, checks, payroll cards
2. Analyze and record business transactions in a journal.	Called *journalizing*
3. Post or transfer information from journal to ledger.	Copying the debits and credits of the journal entries into the ledger accounts
4. Prepare a trial balance.	Summarizing each individual ledger account and listing those accounts to test for mathematical accuracy in recording transactions
5. Prepare a worksheet.	A multicolumn form that summarizes accounting information to complete the accounting cycle
6. Prepare financial statements.	Income statement, statement of owner's equity, and balance sheet
7. Journalize and post adjusting entries.	Using figures in the adjustment columns of the worksheet
8. Journalize and post closing entries.	Using figures in the income statement and balance sheet sections of the worksheet
9. Prepare a post-closing trial balance.	Proving the mathematical accuracy of the adjusting and closing process of the accounting cycle

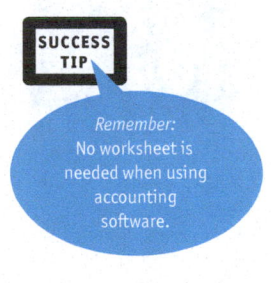

Remember: No worksheet is needed when using accounting software.

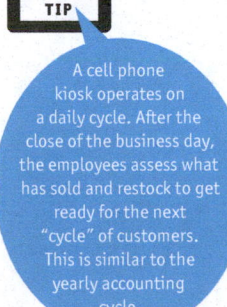

A cell phone kiosk operates on a daily cycle. After the close of the business day, the employees assess what has sold and restock to get ready for the next "cycle" of customers. This is similar to the yearly accounting cycle.

Trending. Most companies journalize and post adjusting and closing entries only at the end of their fiscal year. A company that prepares interim statements may complete only the first six steps of the cycle. Worksheets allow the preparation of interim reports without the formal adjusting and closing of the books. In this case, footnotes on the interim report will indicate the extent to which adjusting and closing entries were completed.

Now do the following Try It! to check your progress.

TRY IT!   Learning Unit 5-3

From the following accounts, list those that will not be found on the Post-Closing Trial Balance. Please explain your answers.

Cash; Accounts Receivable; Office Supplies; Prepaid Rent; iPad Equipment; Accumulated Depreciation, iPad Equipment; Accounts Payable; Salaries Payable; B. Boy, Capital; B. Boy, Withdrawals; Income Summary; Computer Fees; Software Fees; Rent Expense; Salaries Expense; Office Supplies Expense; and Depreciation Expense, iPad Equipment

TRY IT!   Solution Learning Unit 5-3

Boy, Withdrawals; Income Summary; Computer Fees; Software Fees; Rent Expense; Salaries Expense; Office Supplies Expense; Depreciation Expense, iPad Equipment

All temporary accounts are closed to a zero balance when closing entries are journalized and posted.

L01,2,3

DEMONSTRATION SUMMARY PROBLEM

Requirements

1. Journalize transactions and post to ledger.
2. Prepare a worksheet.
3. Prepare financial statements.
4. Journalize adjusting and closing entries and prepare a post-closing trial balance.

Note: Accounts 312 to 515 are temporary accounts. That means they will be zeroed out at the end of the period.

Assets	Owner's Equity
111 Cash	311 R. Kern, Capital
112 Accounts Receivable	312 R. Kern, Withdrawals
114 Prepaid Rent	313 Income Summary
115 Office Supplies	**Revenue**
121 Office Equipment	411 Fees Earned
122 Accumulated Depreciation, Office Equipment	**Expenses**
Liabilities	511 Salaries Expense
211 Accounts Payable	512 Advertising Expense
212 Salaries Payable	513 Rent Expense
	514 Office Supplies Expense
	515 Depreciation Expense, Office Equipment

We will use unusually small numbers to simplify calculation and emphasize the theory.

201X

Jan.	1	Rolo Kern invested $1,200 cash and $100 of office equipment to open Rolo Co.
	1	Paid rent for 3 months in advance, $300.
	4	Purchased office equipment on account, $50.
	6	Bought office supplies for cash, $40.
	8	Collected $400 for services rendered.
	12	Rolo paid his home electric bill from the company checkbook, $20.
	14	Provided $100 worth of services to clients who will not pay until next month.
	16	Paid salaries, $60.
	18	Advertising bill received for $70 but will not be paid until next month.

Adjustment Data on January 31

A. Supplies on hand, $6.
B. Rent expired, $100.
C. Depreciation, Office Equipment, $20.
D. Salaries accrued, $50.

Solutions

Requirement 1

Journalize transactions and post to ledger (see Figure 5.12).

General Journal					PR	Dr.			Cr.				
Date			Account Titles and Description		PR	Dr.			Cr.			Page 1	
201X Jan	1		Cash		111	1 2 0 0	00						
			Office Equipment		121	1 0 0	00						
			R. Kern, Capital		311				1 3 0 0	00			
			Initial Investment										
		1	Prepaid Rent		114	3 0 0	00						
			Cash		111				3 0 0	00			
			Rent Paid in Advance—3 months										
		4	Office Equipment		121	5 0	00						
			Accounts Payable		211				5 0	00			
			Purchased Equipment on Account										
		6	Office Supplies		115	4 0	00						
			Cash		111				4 0	00			
			Supplies purchased for cash										
		8	Cash		111	4 0 0	00						
			Fees Earned		411				4 0 0	00			
			Services rendered										
		12	R. Kern, Withdrawals		312	2 0	00						
			Cash		111				2 0	00			
			Personal payment of a bill										
		14	Accounts Receivable		112	1 0 0	00						
			Fees Earned		411				1 0 0	00			
			Services rendered on account										
		16	Salaries Expense		511	6 0	00						
			Cash		111				6 0	00			
			Paid salaries										
		18	Advertising Expense		512	7 0	00						
			Accounts Payable		211				7 0	00			
			Advertising bill, but not paid										

Figure 5.12
Journal Entries for Rolo Company

Tips to Journalizing and Posting Transactions

Jan.	1	Cash	Asset	↑	Dr.	$1,200
		Office Equipment	Asset	↑	Dr.	$ 100
		R. Kern, Capital	Capital	↑	Cr.	$1,300
	1	Prepaid Rent	Asset	↑	Dr.	$ 300
		Cash	Asset	↓	Cr.	$ 300
	4	Office Equipment	Asset	↑	Dr.	$ 50
		Accounts Payable	Liability	↑	Cr.	$ 50
	6	Office Supplies	Asset	↑	Dr.	$ 40
		Cash	Asset	↓	Cr.	$ 40
	8	Cash	Asset	↑	Dr.	$ 400
		Fees Earned	Revenue	↑	Cr.	$ 400
	12	R. Kern, Withdrawals	Withdrawals	↑	Dr.	$ 20
		Cash	Asset	↓	Cr.	$ 20
	14	Accounts Receivable	Asset	↑	Dr.	$ 100
		Fees Earned	Revenue	↑	Cr.	$ 100
	16	Salaries Expense	Expense	↑	Dr.	$ 60
		Cash	Asset	↓	Cr.	$ 60
	18	Advertising Expense	Expense	↑	Dr.	$ 70
		Accounts Payable	Liability	↑	Cr.	$ 70

Note: All account titles come from the chart of accounts. When journalizing, the PR column of the general journal is blank. It is in the posting process that we update the ledger. The PR column in the ledger accounts tells us from what journal page the information came. After the title in the ledger is posted to, we fill in the PR column of the journal, telling us to what account number the information was transferred.

Requirement 2

Prepare a worksheet (Figure 5.13 p. 161).

Tips to the Trial Balance and Completion of the Worksheet

After the posting process is complete from the journal to the ledger, we take the ending balance in each account and prepare a trial balance on the worksheet (see Figure 5.13). If a title has no balance, it is not listed on the trial balance. New titles on the worksheet will be added as needed.

Adjustments

Office Supplies Expense	Expense	↑	Dr.	$ 34	($40 – $6)
Office Supplies	Asset	↓	Cr.	$ 34	
Rent Expense	Expense	↑	Dr.	$100	
Prepaid Rent	Asset	↓	Cr.	$100	
Depr. Exp., Office Equip.	Expense	↑	Dr.	$ 20	
Accum. Dep., Office Equip.	Contra-Asset	↑	Cr.	$ 20	
Salaries Expense	Expense	↑	Dr.	$ 50	
Salaries Payable	Liability	↑	Cr.	$ 50	

Figure 5.13
Completed Worksheet for Rolo Company

Supplies used up   Supplies on hand

ROLO CO.
WORKSHEET
FOR MONTH ENDED JANUARY 31, 201X

Account Titles	Trial Balance Dr.	Cr.	Adjustments Dr.	Cr.	Adjusted Trial Balance Dr.	Cr.	Income Statement Dr.	Cr.	Balance Sheet Dr.	Cr.
Cash	1 18000				1 18000				1 18000	
Accounts Receivable	1 00000				1 00000				1 00000	
Prepaid Rent	3 00000			(B) 1 00 00	2 00000				2 00000	
Office Supplies	4000			(A) 3 4 00	600				600	
Office Equipment	1 5000				1 5000				1 5000	
Accounts Payable		1 20000				1 20000				1 20000
R. Kern, Capital		1 30000				1 30000				1 30000
R. Kern, Withdrawals	2000				2000				2000	
Fees Earned		5 00000				5 00000		5 00000		
Salaries Expense	6000		(D) 5000		1 1000		1 1000			
Advertising Expense	7000				7000		7000			
Totals	1 92000	1 92000								
Office Supplies Expense			(A) 3400		3400		3400			
Rent Expense			(B) 1 0000		1 0000		1 0000			
Depr. Exp., Office Equip.			(C) 2000		2000		2000			
Acc. Dep., Office Equip.				(C) 2000		2000				2000
Salaries Payable				(D) 5000		5000				5000
Totals			20400	20400	1 99000	1 99000	3 3400	5 00000	1 65600	1 49000
Net Income							1 66600			1 66600
Totals							5 00000	5 00000	1 65600	1 65600

Note: This information on the worksheet has *not* been updated in the ledger. (Updating happens when we journalize and post adjustments at the end of the cycle.)

Note that the last four columns of the worksheet come from numbers on the adjusted trial balance.

On the worksheet, we copy the Net Income of $166 to the Balance Sheet credit column in order to make it balance because the Capital figure there is the old one, hence the net income has not yet been included.

Requirement 3

Prepare the financial statements (see Figures 5.14, 5.15, and 5.16).

Figure 5.14
Income Statement for Rolo Company

ROLO CO. INCOME STATEMENT FOR MONTH ENDED JANUARY 31, 201X			
Revenue:			
Fees Earned			$5 0 0 00
Operating Expenses			
Salaries Expense	$1 1 0 00		
Advertising Expense	7 0 00		
Office Supplies Expense	3 4 00		
Rent Expense	1 0 0 00		
Depreciation Expense, Office Equipment	2 0 00		
Total Operating Expenses			3 3 4 00
Net Income			$1 6 6 00

Figure 5.15
Statement of Owner's Equity for Rolo Company

ROLO CO. STATEMENT OF OWNER'S EQUITY FOR MONTH ENDED JANUARY 31, 201X			
R. Kern, Capital, January 1, 201X			$1 3 0 0 00*
Net Income for January	$1 6 6 00		
Less: Withdrawals for January	− 2 0 00		
Increase in Capital			1 4 6 00
R. Kern, Capital, January 31, 201X			$1 4 4 6 00

*This capital is made up of zero beginning investment plus investment of Kern on January 1.

Tips for Preparing the Financial Statements

The statements are prepared from the worksheet. (Many of the ledger accounts are not up-to-date.) The income statement (Figure 5.14) lists revenue and expenses. The Net Income figure of $166 is used to update the statement of owner's equity. The statement of owner's equity (Figure 5.15) calculates a new figure for Capital, $1,446 (Beginning Capital + Investments + Net Income − Withdrawals). This new figure is then listed on the balance sheet (Figure 5.16) (Assets, Liabilities, and a new figure for Capital).

Requirement 4

Journalize and post adjusting and closing entries and prepare a post-closing trial balance (Figure 5.17).

ROLO CO. BALANCE SHEET JANUARY 31, 201X						
Assets				Liabilities & Owner's Equity		
Cash			$1 18 000	Liabilities		
Accounts Receivable			1 0 0 00	Accounts Payable	$1 2 000	
Prepaid Rent			2 0 0 00	Salaries Payable	5 0 00	
Office Supplies			6 00	Total Liabilities		$1 7 0 00
Office Equipment	$ 1 5 0 00			Owner's Equity		
Less: Accum. Depr.	2 0 00		1 3 0 00	R. Kern, Capital		1 4 4 6 00
				Total Liabilities &		
Total Assets			$1 6 1 6 00	Owner's Equity		$1 6 1 6 00

Figure 5.16
Balance Sheet for Rolo Company

Figure 5.17
Adjusting and Closing Entries Journalized and Posted

General Journal					Page 2	
Date		Account Titles and Description	PR	Dr.	Cr.	
		ADJUSTING ENTRIES				
Jan.	31	Office Supplies Expense	514	3 4 00		
		Office Supplies	115		3 4 00	
	31	Rent Expense	513	1 0 0 00		
		Prepaid Rent	114		1 0 0 00	
	31	Depr. Expense, Office Equipment	515	2 0 00		
		Accum. Depr., Office Equip.	122		2 0 00	
	31	Salaries Expense	511	5 0 00		
		Salaries Payable	212		5 0 00	
		CLOSING ENTRIES				
	31	Fees Earned	411	5 0 0 00		
		Income Summary	313		5 0 0 00	
	31	Income Summary	313	3 3 4 00		
		Salaries Expense	511		1 1 0 00	
		Advertising Expense	512		7 0 00	
		Office Supplies Expense	514		3 4 00	
		Rent Expense	513		1 0 0 00	
		Depr. Expense, Office Equip.	515		2 0 00	
	31	Income Summary	313	1 6 6 00		
		R. Kern, Capital	311		1 6 6 00	
	31	R. Kern, Capital	311	2 0 00		
		R. Kern, Withdrawals	312		2 0 00	

Step 1 →
Step 2 →
Closing
Step 3 →
Step 4 →

Tips to Journalizing and Posting Adjusting and Closing Entries

Adjustments

The adjustments from the worksheet are journalized (same journal as transactions) and posted to the ledger. Now ledger accounts will be brought up-to-date. Remember, we have already prepared the financial statements from the worksheet. Our goal now is to get the ledger up-to-date.

Closing

Note that Income Summary is a temporary account located in the ledger.

Goals

1. Wipe out all temporary accounts in the ledger to zero balances.
2. Get a new figure for Capital in the ledger.

Steps in the Closing Process

STEP 1: Close revenue accounts to Income Summary.

STEP 2: Close expense accounts to Income Summary.

STEP 3: Close balance of Income Summary to Capital. (This amount really is the Net Income and is equal to the figure on the worksheet.)

STEP 4: Close balance of Withdrawals to Capital.

All the journal closing entries are posted. (No new calculations are needed because all figures are on the worksheet.) The result in the ledger is that all temporary accounts have a zero balance (Figure 5.18).

Figure 5.18
General Ledger for Rolo Company

GENERAL LEDGER

Cash					111
				Balance	
Date	PR	Dr.	Cr.	Dr.	Cr.
1/1	GJ1	1,200		1,200	
1/1	GJ1		300	900	
1/6	GJ1		40	860	
1/8	GJ1	400		1,260	
1/12	GJ1		20	1,240	
1/16	GJ1		60	1,180	

Accounts Receivable					112
				Balance	
Date	PR	Dr.	Cr.	Dr.	Cr.
1/14	GJ1	100		100	

Accumulated Depreciation, Office Equipment 122					
				Balance	
Date	PR	Dr.	Cr.	Dr.	Cr.
1/31 Adj.	GJ2		20		20

Accounts Payable					211
				Balance	
Date	PR	Dr.	Cr.	Dr.	Cr.
1/4	GJ1		50		50
1/18	GJ1		70		120

Salaries Payable					212
				Balance	
Date	PR	Dr.	Cr.	Dr.	Cr.
1/31 Adj.	GJ2		50		50

Figure 5.18 (*continued*)

Prepaid Rent 114

Date	PR	Dr.	Cr.	Balance Dr.	Balance Cr.
1/1	GJ1	300		300	
1/31 Adj.	GJ2		100	200	

Office Supplies 115

Date	PR	Dr.	Cr.	Balance Dr.	Balance Cr.
1/6	GJ1	40		40	
1/31 Adj	GJ2		34	6	

Office Equipment 121

Date	PR	Dr.	Cr.	Balance Dr.	Balance Cr.
1/1	GJ1	100		100	
1/4	GJ1	50		150	

Fees Earned 411

Date	PR	Dr.	Cr.	Balance Dr.	Balance Cr.
1/8	GJ1		400		400
1/14	GJ1		100		500
1/31 Clos.	GJ2	500			—

Salaries Expense 511

Date	PR	Dr.	Cr.	Balance Dr.	Balance Cr.
1/16	GJ1	60		60	
1/31 Adj.	GJ2	50		110	
1/31 Clos.	GJ2		110	—	

Advertising Expense 512

Date	PR	Dr.	Cr.	Balance Dr.	Balance Cr.
1/18	GJ1	70		70	
1/31 Clos.	GJ2		70	—	

R. Kern, Capital 311

Date	PR	Dr.	Cr.	Balance Dr.	Balance Cr.
1/1	GJ1		1,300		1,300
1/31 Clos.	GJ2		166		1,466
1/31 Clos.	GJ2	20			1,446

R. Kern, Withdrawals 312

Date	PR	Dr.	Cr.	Balance Dr.	Balance Cr.
1/12	GJ1	20		20	
1/31 Clos.	GJ2		20	—	

Income Summary 313

Date	PR	Dr.	Cr.	Balance Dr.	Balance Cr.
1/31 Clos.	GJ2		500		500
1/31 Clos.	GJ2	334			166
1/31 Clos.	GJ2	166			—

Rent Expense 513

Date	PR	Dr.	Cr.	Balance Dr.	Balance Cr.
1/31 Adj.	GJ2	100		100	
1/31 Clos.	GJ2		100	—	

Office Supplies Expense 514

Date	PR	Dr.	Cr.	Balance Dr.	Balance Cr.
1/31 Adj.	GJ2	34		34	
1/31 Clos.	GJ2		34	—	

Depreciation Expense, Office Equipment 515

Date	PR	Dr.	Cr.	Balance Dr.	Balance Cr.
1/31 Adj.	GJ2	20		20	
1/31 Clos.	GJ2		20	—	

Tips for the Post-Closing Trial Balance

The post-closing trial balance is a list of the ledger *after* adjusting and closing entries have been completed. Note that the figure for Capital, $1,446, is the new figure (see Figure 5.19).

Figure 5.19
Post-Closing Trial Balance for Rolo Company

	Dr.	Cr.
ROLO CO. POST-CLOSING TRIAL BALANCE JANUARY 31, 201X		
Cash	1 1 8 0 00	
Accounts Receivable	1 0 0 00	
Prepaid Rent	2 0 0 00	
Office Supplies	6 00	
Office Equipment	1 5 0 00	
Accum. Dep., Office Equipment		2 0 00
Accounts Payable		1 2 0 00
Salaries Payable		5 0 00
R. Kern, Capital		1 4 4 6 00
Totals	1 6 3 6 00	1 6 3 6 00

SUCCESS TIP

The post-closing trial balance contains all permanent accounts. This brings us back to the basic accounting equation:
A = L+OE

Beginning Capital	$1,300*
+ Net Income	166
– Withdrawals	20
= Ending Capital	$1,446

* Beginning capital zero plus $1,300 investment

The post-closing trial balance is made up of permanent accounts only. Next In the next accounting period we will enter new amounts in the Revenues, Expenses, and Withdrawal accounts.

SUCCESS COACH

The following Success Tips are from Learning Units 5-1 to 5-3. Take the Do It Right Now Checkup and use the Check Your Score at the bottom of the page to see how you are doing. The Success Coach provides tips before each Checkup to help you avoid common accounting errors.

LU 5-1 Adjusting Entries (Step 7 of the Accounting Cycle)

Do It Right Tips: All adjustments can be journalized and posted from the adjustments section of the worksheet. Remember that all accounts listed below the original trial balance are increasing. The adjustment for supplies is the amount used up. The adjustment for rent is the amount of rent that has expired. The adjustment for depreciation does not affect the original cost of the asset. The adjustment for salaries shows a new expense creating a liability because it is not yet paid.

Do It Right Now Checkup: Answer true or false to the following statements.

1. After the adjustment is posted, the Supplies ledger account shows the amount on hand.
2. After posting, Accumulated Depreciation has a debit balance.
3. Adjustments on a worksheet do not have to be journalized and posted.
4. After the adjustment is posted, Prepaid Rent shows the amount expired.
5. Depreciation Expense is a contra-asset.

LU 5-2 Closing Entries (Step 8 of the Accounting Cycle)

Do It Right Tips: The goal of closing is to update the ledger for the next accounting cycle. All temporary accounts need to be cleared, and a new figure for capital results. In the process, Income Summary is a temporary account that is used to close revenues and expenses to Capital. Withdrawals will be closed directly to Capital since it is not a business expense. When the closing process is complete, all temporary accounts will be closed. All information needed to do the closing can be found in the income statement and balance sheet sections of the worksheet.

Do It Right Now Checkup: Answer true or false to the following statements.

1. Income Summary is a permanent account.
2. Income Summary is found on the worksheet.
3. Expenses are permanent accounts.
4. The balance in Income Summary is closed to the Cash account.
5. Income Summary has a normal debit balance.

LU 5-3 The Post-Closing Trial Balance (Step 9 of the Accounting Cycle)

Do It Right Tips: The post-closing trial balance lists the accounts of the ledger after all closing entries have been posted. Only permanent accounts remain, and all temporary accounts now have a zero balance. The account "Income Summary" is used only in the closing process and thus never ends up on the post-closing trial balance.

Do It Right Now Checkup: Answer true or false to the following statements.

1. Income Summary is listed on the post-closing trial balance.
2. Interim reports are always prepared each month.
3. Capital on the post-closing trial balance is the beginning balance for the next accounting cycle.
4. Accumulated Depreciation is a temporary account.
5. Supplies on the post-closing trial balance represent the amount of supplies used up.

CHECK YOUR SCORE: Answers to the Do It Right Now Checkup

LU 5-1

1. True
2. False—After posting, Accumulated Depreciation has a credit balance.
3. False—Adjustments on a worksheet must be journalized and posted.
4. False—After the adjustment is posted, Prepaid Rent shows the amount that has not expired yet.
5. False—Depreciation Expense is an expense.

LU 5-2

1. False—Income Summary is a temporary account.
2. False—Income Summary is not found on the worksheet.
3. False—Expenses are temporary accounts.
4. False—The balance in Income Summary is closed to Capital.
5. False—Income Summary has no normal balance.

LU 5-3

1. False—Income Summary is a temporary account and thus not listed on the post-closing trial balance since it is closed.
2. False—Interim reports are only optional and there is no set requirement for when or how often they are prepared.

3. True
4. False—Accumulated Depreciation is a permanent account.
5. False—Supplies on the post-closing trial balance represent the amount of supplies on hand.

BLUEPRINT: CLOSING PROCESS
BLUEPRINT OF CLOSING PROCESS FROM THE WORKSHEET

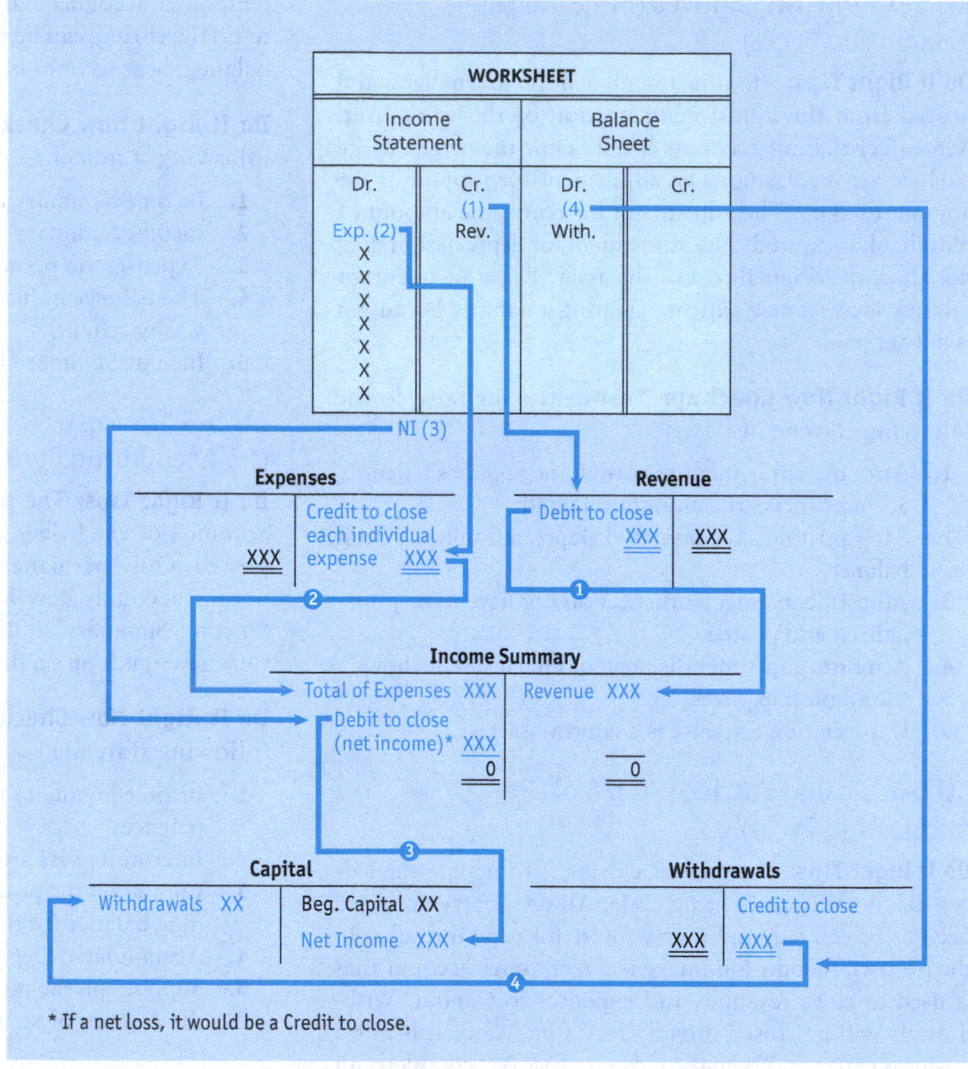

* If a net loss, it would be a Credit to close.

The Closing Steps

1. Close revenue ($) balance to Income Summary.
2. Close each *individual* expense and transfer *total* of all expenses to Income Summary.
3. Transfer balance in Income Summary (net income or net loss) to Capital.
4. Close Withdrawals to Capital.

Discussion Questions and Critical Thinking/Ethical Case

1. When a worksheet is completed, what balances are found in the general ledger?

2. Why must adjusting entries be journalized even though the formal statements have already been prepared?

3. "Closing slows down the recording of next year's transactions." Defend or reject this statement with supporting evidence.

4. What is the difference between temporary and permanent accounts?

5. How has computer software affected the use of closing entries?

6. List the four steps of closing.

7. What is the purpose of Income Summary and where is it located?

8. How can a worksheet aid in the closing process?

9. What accounts are usually listed on a post-closing trial balance?

10. Closing entries are always prepared once a month. Agree or disagree? Why?

11. Burton Fish is the purchasing agent for Lyle Co. One of his suppliers, Grant Co., offers Burton a free vacation to Spain if he buys at least 50% of Lyle's supplies from Grant Co. Burton, who is upset because Lyle Co. has not given him a raise in over a year, is considering the offer. Write your recommendation to Burton.

Concept Checks

L01 *(5 min)*

Journalizing and Posting Adjusting Entries

1. Post the following adjusting entries that came from the adjustments section of the following worksheet to the T accounts and be sure to cross-reference back to the journal. (See Figure 5.20.)

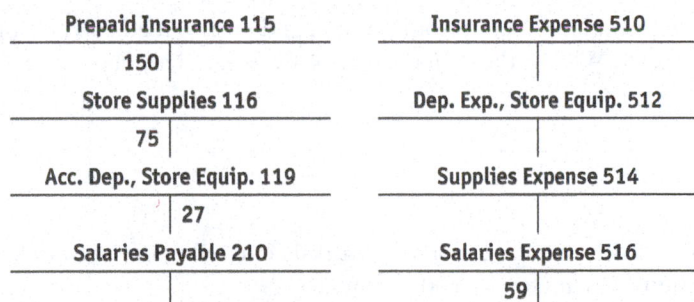

LEDGER ACCOUNTS BEFORE ADJUSTING ENTRIES POSTED

Prepaid Insurance 115		Insurance Expense 510	
150			

Store Supplies 116		Dep. Exp., Store Equip. 512	
75			

Acc. Dep., Store Equip. 119		Supplies Expense 514	
	27		

Salaries Payable 210		Salaries Expense 516	
		59	

Figure 5.20
Journalized Adjusting Entries

	General Journal			Dr.	Page 3 Cr.	
Date		Account Titles and Description	PR			
Aug. 31		Insurance Expense		15 00		
		Prepaid Insurance			15 00	
31		Supplies Expense		12 00		
		Store Supplies			12 00	
31		Depr. Exp., Store Equipment		9 00		
		Accum. Depr., Store Equipment			9 00	
31		Salaries Expense		27 00		
		Salaries Payable			27 00	

(10 min) **L02** ▶   **Steps of Closing and Journalizing Closing Entries**

2.   Explain the four steps of the closing process given the following:

May 31 ending balance, before closing	
Fees Earned	$ 800
Rent Expense	1000
Advertising Expense	70
G. Remy, Capital	5,000
G. Remy, Withdrawals	60

(15 min) **L02** ▶   **Journalizing Closing Entries**

3.   From the following accounts, journalize the closing entries (assume March 31).

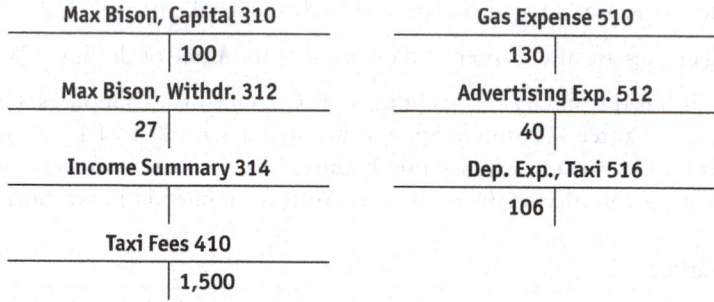

Max Bison, Capital 310	**Gas Expense 510**
	100	130	
Max Bison, Withdr. 312	**Advertising Exp. 512**
27		40	
Income Summary 314	**Dep. Exp., Taxi 516**
		106	
Taxi Fees 410	
	1,500	

(10 min) **L02** ▶   **Posting to Income Summary**

4.   Draw a T account of Income Summary and post to it all entries from Question 3 that affect it. Is Income Summary a temporary or permanent account?

(10 min) **L02** ▶   **Posting to Capital**

5.   Draw a T account for Max Bison, Capital, and post to it all entries from Question 3 that affect it. What is the final balance of the Capital account?

MyLabAccounting   **Exercises**

Set A

(15 min) **L01**   5A-1.   From the adjustments section of a worksheet (see Figure 5.21), prepare adjusting journal entries for the end of January.

Figure 5.21
Adjustments on Worksheet

		Adjustments		
		Dr.	Cr.	
Prepaid Rent			(A) 1 5 0 0 00	
Office Supplies			(B) 6 5 0 00	
Accumulated Depreciation, Equipment			(C) 3 2 5 00	
Salaries Payable			(D) 8 0 0 00	
Rent Expense	(A) 1 5 0 0 00			
Office Supplies Expense	(B) 6 5 0 00			
Depreciation Expense, Equipment	(C) 3 2 5 00			
Salaries Expense	(D) 8 0 0 00			
Totals	3 2 7 5 00		3 2 7 5 00	

5A-2.   Complete the following table by placing an X in the correct column.    **LO1,2** *(10 min)*

		Temporary	Permanent	Will Be Closed
Ex.	Accounts Receivable		X	
1.	Income Summary			
2.	Jan Ralls, Capital			
3.	Rent Expense			
4.	Jan Ralls, Withdrawals			
5.	Fees Earned			
6.	Accounts Payable			
7.	Cash			

5A-3.   From the following T accounts, journalize the four closing entries on May 31, 201X.   **LO2** *(15 min)*

J. Kody, Capital		Rent Expense	
	27,000	8,000	

J. Kody, Withdrawals		Wage Expense	
1,000		7,300	

Income Summary		Insurance Expense	
		900	

Fees Earned		Depr. Expense, Office Equipment	
	61,000	900	

5A-4.   From the following posted T accounts, reconstruct the closing journal entries for May 31, 201X.   **LO2** *(20 min)*

M. Fernendez, Capital		Insurance Expense	
Withdrawals 700	6,000 (May 1)	75	Closing 75
	2,025 Net Income		

M. Fernendez, Withdrawals		Wage Expense	
700	Closing 700	1,100	Closing 1,100

Income Summary		Rent Expense	
Expenses 2,775	Revenue 4,800	1,000	Closing 1,000
Closing 2,025	Balance 2,025		

Salon Fees		Depreciation Expense, Equipment	
Closing 4,800	4,800	600	Closing 600

5A-5.   From the following accounts (not in order), prepare a post-closing trial balance for Wey Co. on August 31, 201X. *Note:* These balances are *before* closing.   **LO3** *(20 min)*

Accounts Receivable	$18,875	P. Wey, Capital	$40,825
Legal Supplies	14,250	P. Wey, Withdrawals	5,500
Office Equipment	30,000	Legal Fees Earned	18,000
Repair Expense	2,000	Accounts Payable	40,000
Salaries Expense	2,200	Cash	26,000

Set B

(15 min) **L01**

5B-1. From the adjustments section of a worksheet presented in Figure 5.22, prepare adjusting journal entries for the end of March.

Figure 5.22
Adjustments on Worksheet

		Adjustments			
		Dr.		Cr.	
Prepaid Rent				(A)	9 0 0 00
Office Supplies				(B)	3 0 0 00
Accumulated Depreciation, Equipment				(C)	3 2 5 00
Salaries Payable				(D)	2 0 0 00
Rent Expense	(A)	9 0 0 00			
Office Supplies Expense	(B)	3 0 0 00			
Depreciation Expense, Equipment	(C)	3 2 5 00			
Salaries Expense	(D)	2 0 0 00			
Totals		1 7 2 5 00		1 7 2 5 00	

(10 min) **L01,2**

5B-2. Complete the following table by placing an X in the correct column.

		Temporary	Permanent	Will Be Closed
Ex.	Accounts Receivable		X	
1.	Income Summary			
2.	Jen Rich, Capital			
3.	Salary Expense			
4.	Jen Rich, Withdrawals			
5.	Fees Earned			
6.	Accounts Payable			
7.	Cash			

(15 min) **L02**

5B-3. From the following T accounts, journalize the four closing entries on August 31, 201X.

J. Kohl, Capital			Rent Expense	
	18,800		10,000	

J. Kohl, Withdrawals			Wage Expense	
4,000			8,300	

Income Summary			Insurance Expense	
			1,200	

Fees Earned			Depr. Expense, Office Equipment	
	33,000		1,500	

5B-4. From the following posted T accounts, reconstruct the closing journal entries for October 31, 201X.

L02 *(20 min)*

M. Figg, Capital	
Withdrawals 1,900	3,000 (Oct. 1)
	750 Net Income

M. Figg, Withdrawals	
1,900	Closing 1,900

Income Summary	
Expenses 1,550	Revenue 2,300
Closing 750	Balance 750

Salon Fees	
Closing 2,300	2,300

Insurance Expense	
150	Closing 150

Wage Expense	
800	Closing 800

Rent Expense	
400	Closing 400

Depreciation Expense, Equipment	
200	Closing 200

5B-5. From the following accounts (not in order), prepare a post-closing trial balance for Winter Company on July 31, 201X. *Note:* These balances are *before* closing.

L03 *(20 min)*

Accounts Receivable	$25,050	P. Winter, Capital	$29,910
Legal Supplies	9,700	P. Winter, Withdrawals	3,500
Office Equipment	47,000	Legal Fees Earned	30,000
Repair Expense	1,740	Accounts Payable	46,000
Salaries Expense	1,920	Cash	17,000

Problems

MyLab**Accounting**

Set A

5A-1. Consider the data in Figure 5.23 for Daffy's Dance Studio:

L01,2 *(40 min)*

Figure 5.23
Trial Balance for Daffy's Dance Studio

Check Figure:
Net Income $15,300

DAFFY'S DANCE STUDIO TRIAL BALANCE NOVEMBER 30, 201X		
Account Titles	Dr.	Cr.
Cash	42 5 0 0 00	
Accounts Receivable	4 0 0 0 00	
Prepaid Insurance	1 1 0 0 00	
Dance Supplies	2 0 0 0 00	
Dance Equipment	23 0 0 0 00	
Accumulated Depreciation, Dance Equipment		8 6 0 0 00
Accounts Payable		30 0 0 0 00
D. Dominico, Capital		14 7 0 0 00
D. Dominico, Withdrawals	9 0 0 00	
Dance Fees Earned		22 4 0 0 00
Salaries Expense	1 4 0 0 00	
Telephone Expense	6 0 0 00	
Advertising Expense	2 0 0 00	
Totals	75 7 0 0 00	75 7 0 0 00

Adjustment Data

a. Insurance expired, $100.
b. Dance supplies on hand, $200.
c. Depreciation on dance equipment, $2,500.
d. Salaries earned by employees but not to be paid until December, $500.

Your task is to do the following:

1. Prepare a worksheet.
2. Journalize adjusting and closing entries.

(35 min) **L01,2,3**

Check Figure:
Post-Closing Trial Balance $5,386

5A-2. Enter the beginning balance in each account in your working papers from the Trial Balance columns of the worksheet (Figure 5.24 on page 173). From that worksheet, (1) journalize and post adjusting and closing entries and (2) prepare from the ledger a post-closing trial balance for the month of December.

(150 min) **L01,2,3**

5A-3. As the bookkeeper of Panji's Plowing, you have been asked to complete the entire accounting cycle for Panji from the following information.

201X			
Nov.	1	Panji invested $11,000 cash and $9,600 worth of snow equipment into the plowing company.	
	1	Paid rent 3 months in advance for garage space, $1,500.	
	4	Purchased office equipment from Lally Corp. for $6,000 on account.	
	6	Purchased snow supplies for $700 cash.	
	8	Collected $7,000 from plowing local shopping centers.	
	12	Panji Maki withdrew $6,000 from the business for personal use.	
	20	Plowed Middleton parking lots, payment not to be received until January, $2,500.	
	26	Paid salaries to employees, $1,800.	
	28	Paid Lally Corp. one-half amount owed for office equipment.	
	29	Advertising bill received from Garfield Co. but will not be paid until January, $900.	
	30	Paid telephone bill, $160.	

(40 min) **L01,2**

Use the following chart of accounts.

Chart of Accounts

Assets	Owner's Equity
111 Cash	311 P. Maki, Capital
112 Accounts Receivable	312 P. Maki, Withdrawals
114 Prepaid Rent	313 Income Summary
115 Snow Supplies	**Revenue**
121 Office Equipment	411 Plowing Fees
122 Accumulated Depreciation, Office Equipment	**Expenses**
123 Snow Equipment	511 Salaries Expense
124 Accumulated Depreciation, Snow Equipment	512 Advertising Expense
Liabilities	513 Telephone Expense
211 Accounts Payable	514 Rent Expense
212 Salaries Payable	515 Snow Supplies Expense
	516 Depreciation Expense, Office Equipment
	517 Depreciation Expense, Snow Equipment

Figure 5.24
Worksheet for Pennington's Cleaning Service

PENNINGTON'S CLEANING SERVICE
WORKSHEET
FOR MONTH ENDED DECEMBER 31, 201X

Account Titles	Trial Balance Dr.	Trial Balance Cr.	Adjustments Dr.	Adjustments Cr.	Adjusted Trial Balance Dr.	Adjusted Trial Balance Cr.	Income Statement Dr.	Income Statement Cr.	Balance Sheet Dr.	Balance Sheet Cr.
Cash	130000				130000				130000	
Prepaid Insurance	74000			(A)38000	36000				36000	
Cleaning Supplies	38000			(B)22400	15600				15600	
Auto	357000				357000				357000	
Accum. Depr., Auto		84000		(C)15000		99000				99000
Accounts Payable		22400				22400				22400
B. Pennington, Capital		238600				238600				238600
B. Pennington, Withdrawals	55000				55000				55000	
Cleaning Fees		468000				468000		468000		
Salaries Expense	99000		(D)32000		131000		131000			
Telephone Expense	21000				21000		21000			
Advertising Expense	31000				31000		31000			
Gas Expense	8000				8000		8000			
Totals	813000	813000								
Insurance Expense			(A)38000		38000		38000			
Cleaning Supplies Expense			(B)22400		22400		22400			
Depr. Expense, Auto			(C)15000		15000		15000			
Salaries Payable				(D)32000		32000				32000
Totals			107400	107400	860000	860000	266400	468000	593600	392000
Net Income							201600			201600
Totals							468000	468000	593600	593600

Adjustment Data

a. Snow supplies on hand, $300.
b. Rent expired, $500.
c. Depreciation on office equipment, $100:
   ($6,000/5 yr. = $1,200/12 mo. = $100).
d. Depreciation on snow equipment, $160:
   ($9,600/5 yr. = $1,920/12 mo. = $160).
e. Accrued salaries, $190.

Set B

(40 min) **LO1,2** ▶

5B-1. Consider the data in Figure 5.25 for Deb's Dance Studio:

Figure 5.25
Trial Balance for Deb's Dance
Studio

DEB'S DANCE STUDIO TRIAL BALANCE NOVEMBER 30, 201X		
Account Titles	Dr.	Cr.
Cash	47 4 0 0 00	
Accounts Receivable	9 0 0 0 00	
Prepaid Insurance	1 3 0 0 00	
Dance Supplies	1 6 0 0 00	
Dance Equipment	18 0 0 0 00	
Accumulated Depreciation, Dance Equipment		8 2 0 0 00
Accounts Payable		20 0 0 0 00
D. Dee, Capital		34 4 0 0 00
D. Dee, Withdrawals	6 0 0 00	
Dance Fees Earned		18 7 0 0 00
Salaries Expense	1 8 0 0 00	
Telephone Expense	1 0 0 0 00	
Advertising Expense	6 0 0 00	
Totals	81 3 0 0 00	81 3 0 0 00

Adjustment Data

a. Insurance expired, $1,000.
b. Dance supplies on hand, $1,100.
c. Depreciation on dance equipment, $2,500.
d. Salaries earned by employees but not due to be paid until December, $800.

Your task is to do the following:

1. Prepare a worksheet.
2. Journalize adjusting and closing entries.

(35 min) **LO1,2** ▶

5B-2. Enter the beginning balance in each account in your working papers from the Trial Balance columns of the worksheet (Figure 5.26 on page 177). From the worksheet, (1) journalize and post adjusting and closing entries and (2) prepare from the ledger a post-closing trial balance at the end of December.

Figure 5.26
Worksheet for Perking's Cleaning Service

PERKING'S CLEANING SERVICE
WORKSHEET
FOR MONTH ENDED DECEMBER 31, 201X

Account Titles	Trial Balance Dr.	Trial Balance Cr.	Adjustments Dr.	Adjustments Cr.	Adjusted Trial Balance Dr.	Adjusted Trial Balance Cr.	Income Statement Dr.	Income Statement Cr.	Balance Sheet Dr.	Balance Sheet Cr.
Cash	120000				120000				120000	
Prepaid Insurance	101000			(A) 15000	86000				86000	
Cleaning Supplies	22200			(B) 12600	9600				9600	
Auto	348000				348000				348000	
Accumulated Depreciation, Auto		78000		(C) 25000		103000				103000
Accounts Payable		44400				44400				44400
B. Perking, Capital		102300				102300				102300
B. Perking, Withdrawals	116000				116000				116000	
Cleaning Fees		650000				650000		650000		
Salaries Expense	99000		(D) 5000		104000		104000			
Telephone Expense	21000				21000		21000			
Advertising Expense	22500				22500		22500			
Gas Expense	25000				25000		25000			
Totals	874700	874700								
Insurance Expense			(A) 15000		15000		15000			
Cleaning Supplies Expense			(B) 12600		12600		12600			
Depreciation Expense, Auto			(C) 25000		25000		25000			
Salaries Payable				(D) 5000		5000				5000
Totals			57600	57600	904700	904700	225100	650000	679600	254700
Net Income							424900			424900
Totals							650000	650000	679600	679600

177

(150 min) **L01,2,3**

Check Figure:
Net Income $6,420

5B-3. As the bookkeeper of Phil's Plowing, you have been asked to complete the entire accounting cycle for Phil from the following information.

201X		
Mar.	1	Phil invested $11,000 cash and $6,000 worth of snow equipment into the plowing company.
	1	Paid 3 months' rent in advance for garage space, $1,200.
	4	Purchased office equipment from Lite Corp. for $10,800 on account.
	6	Purchased snow supplies for $1,100 cash.
	8	Collected $10,000 from plowing local shopping centers.
	12	Phil Mack withdrew $6,000 from the business for personal use.
	20	Plowed Holiday parking lots, payment not to be received until May, $1,000.
	26	Paid salaries to employees, $2,100.
	28	Paid Lite Corp. one-half amount owed for office equipment.
	29	Advertising bill received from Washington Co. but will not be paid until May, $600.
	30	Paid telephone bill, $130.

Use the following chart of accounts.

Chart of Accounts

Assets	Owner's Equity
111 Cash	311 P. Mack, Capital
112 Accounts Receivable	312 P. Mack, Withdrawals
114 Prepaid Rent	313 Income Summary
115 Snow Supplies	**Revenue**
121 Office Equipment	411 Plowing Fees
122 Accumulated Depreciation, Office Equipment	**Expenses**
123 Snow Equipment	511 Salaries Expense
124 Accumulated Depreciation, Snow Equipment	512 Advertising Expense
Liabilities	513 Telephone Expense
211 Accounts Payable	514 Rent Expense
212 Salaries Payable	515 Snow Supplies Expense
	516 Depreciation Expense, Office Equipment
	517 Depreciation Expense, Snow Equipment

Adjustment Data

    a. Snow supplies on hand, $300.
    b. Rent expired, $400.
    c. Depreciation on office equipment, $180:
        ($10,800/5 yr. = $2,160/12 mo. = $180).
    d. Depreciation on snow equipment, $100:
        ($6,000/5 yr. = $1,200/12 mo. = $100).
    e. Accrued salaries, $270.

(15 min) **L03**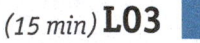

Financial Report Problem

Reading Amazon's Annual Report

Go to **https://tinyurl.com/slaterca14e** to access Amazon's 2016 Annual Report and find out what is the fiscal year for Amazon.

KEEPING IT REAL SUAREZ COMPUTER CENTER

L01,2,3 *(60 min)*

Troy decided to end the Suarez Computer Center's first year as of September 30, 201X. Following is an updated chart of accounts.

Assets	Revenue
1000 Cash	4000 Service Revenue
1020 Accounts Receivable	**Expenses**
1025 Prepaid Rent	5010 Advertising Expense
1030 Supplies	5020 Rent Expense
1080 Computer Shop Equip.	5030 Utilities Expense
1081 Accum. Depr., C.S. Equip.	5040 Telephone Expense
1090 Office Equipment	5050 Supplies Expense
1091 Accum. Depr., Office Equip.	5060 Insurance Expense
Liabilities	5070 Postage Expense
2000 Accounts Payable	5080 Depr. Exp., C.S. Equip.
Owner's Equity	5090 Depr. Exp., Office Equip.
3000, T. Falco, Capital	
3010, T. Falco, Withdrawals	
3020 Income Summary	

Assignment

1. Journalize the adjusting entries from Chapter 4.
2. Post the adjusting entries to the ledger.
3. Journalize the closing entries.
4. Post the closing entries to the ledger.
5. Prepare a post-closing trial balance.

Mini Practice Set

Sherman Realty

Reviewing the Accounting Cycle Twice

Est. Time: 5 hours

This comprehensive review problem requires you to complete the accounting cycle for Sherman Realty twice. This practice set allows you to review Chapters 1–5 while reinforcing the relationships between all parts of the accounting cycle. By completing two cycles, you will see how the ending April balances in the ledger are used to accumulate data in May.

First, look at the chart of accounts for Sherman Realty.

Sherman Realty
Chart of Accounts

Assets	Revenue
111 Cash	411 Commissions Earned
112 Accounts Receivable	**Expenses**
114 Prepaid Rent	511 Rent Expense
115 Office Supplies	512 Salaries Expense
121 Office Equipment	513 Gas Expense
122 Accumulated Depreciation, Office Equipment	514 Repairs Expense
123 Automobile	515 Telephone Expense
124 Accumulated Depreciation, Automobile	516 Advertising Expense

(continued on next page)

Liabilities	517 Office Supplies Expense
211 Accounts Payable	518 Depreciation Expense, Office Equipment
212 Salaries Payable	519 Depreciation Expense, Automobile
Owner's Equity	524 Miscellaneous Expense
311 Jacob Sherman, Capital	
312 Jacob Sherman, Withdrawals	
313 Income Summary	

On April 1, 201X, Jacob Sherman opened a real estate office called Sherman Realty. The following transactions were completed for the month of April:

201X

April 1   Jacob Sherman invested $14,000 cash in the real estate agency along with $9,000 of office equipment.

⊣ **DEPOSIT TICKET** ⊢

SHERMAN REALTY (213) 478-3584
8200 SUNSET BOULEVARD
Los Angeles, CA 90028

DATE _April 1_   201X

SIGN HERE IN PRESENCE OF TELLER FOR CASH RET'D FROM DEP. →

BAY BANK
Box 1739 Terminal Annex
Los Angeles, CA 90052

⑈⑆⑈ 122000⑈66 ⑈⑆⑈ 1400⑈03857⑈0136 2⑈

CASH	CURRENCY	14,000	00
	COIN		
LIST CHECKS SINGLY			
TOTAL FROM OTHER SIDE			
TOTAL		14,000	00
LESS CASH RECEIVED			
NET DEPOSIT		14,000	00

16-66/1220

A hold for uncollected funds may be placed on funds deposited by check or similar instruments. This could delay your ability to withdraw such funds. The delay if any would not exceed the period of time permitted by law.

April 1   Rented and paid 4 months' rent in advance to McLay Property Management, $3,600.

SHERMAN REALTY (213) 478-3584   0001

8200 SUNSET BOULEVARD
LOS ANGELES, CA 90028   _April 1_   201X

PAY TO THE
ORDER OF _McLay Property Mgmt Co._ $ | 3,600 XX/100 |

_____ _Three Thousand six Hundred_ XX/100 ~~~~ DOLLARS

BAY BANK
Box 1739 Terminal Annex
Los Angeles, CA 90052

MEMO _Rent April-July 201X_   _Jacob Sherman_

April 1   Bought an automobile on account from Jeep East, $14,000.

INVOICE

Jeep East

1 Salem St.
Los Angeles, CA 90052
(213) 639-1917

INVOICE NO. 1113

DATE: April 1/1X

TERMS: Net 90

To: SHERMAN REALTY
      8200 Sunset Blvd.
      Los Angeles, CA 90028

QUANTITY		DESCRIPTION	UNIT PRICE	AMOUNT
1	ONLY	4-Door Automatic	$14,000.00	$14,000.00

Make all checks payable to Jeep East		
	SUBTOTAL	14,000.00
	FREIGHT	
	TAX	
	TOTAL DUE	$14,000.00

THANK YOU FOR YOUR BUSINESS!

April 4   Purchased office supplies from The Office Store, for cash, $900.

The Office Store

INVOICE

1 Ferncroft Rd.
Los Angeles, CA 90052
Phone (213) 631-0288

DATE: April 4/1X
NUMBER: D198795
TERMS: Cash

SOLD TO:
      Sherman Realty
      8200 Sunset Blvd.
      Los Angeles, CA 90028

SHIPPED TO:
      Sherman Realty
      8200 Sunset Blvd.
      Los Angeles, CA 90028

DATE	DESCRIPTION	UNIT PRICE	AMOUNT
April. 4/1X	Office supplies PAYMENT RECEIVED - - CHK #0002 - THANK YOU		$900.00
		Subtotal	900.00
		Total	$900.00

Business Number: 115555559

THANK YOU FOR YOUR BUSINESS

PLEASE PAY
THE ABOVE

SHERMAN REALTY (213) 478-3584   0002

8200 SUNSET BOULEVARD
LOS ANGELES, CA 90028   *April 4*   *201X*

PAY TO THE
ORDER OF *The office Store* $ *900 XX/100*

Nine Hundred and XX/100 ———————————————— DOLLARS

BAY BANK
Box 1739 Terminal Annex
Los Angeles, CA 90052

MEMO *Office supplies*   *Jacob Sherman*

April 5   Purchased additional office supplies from The Office Store, on account, $450.

The Office Store   INVOICE

1 Ferncroft Rd.   **DATE:**   April 5/1X
Los Angeles, CA 90052   **NUMBER:** D198825
Phone (213) 631-0288   **TERMS:**   net 60

SOLD TO:	SHIPPED TO:
Sherman Realty 8200 Sunset Blvd. Los Angeles, CA 90028	Sherman Realty 8200 Sunset Blvd. Los Angeles, CA 90028

DATE	DESCRIPTION	UNIT PRICE	AMOUNT
April. 5/1X	Office supplies		$450.00
		Subtotal	450.00
		Total	$450.00

Business Number: 115555559

THANK YOU FOR YOUR BUSINESS

PLEASE PAY
THE ABOVE

April 6   Sold a house to Bryce Lyman and collected a $6,500 commission.

—| DEPOSIT TICKET |—

SHERMAN REALTY (213) 478-3584
8200 SUNSET BOULEVARD
Los Angeles, CA 90028

CASH	CURRENCY		
	COIN		
LIST CHECKS SINGLY *250-99*		6,500	00

16-66/1220

DATE _April 6_   _201X_

SIGN HERE IN PRESENCE OF TELLER FOR CASH RET'D FROM DEP.

TOTAL FROM OTHER SIDE		
TOTAL		
LESS CASH RECEIVED		
NET DEPOSIT	6,500	00

A hold for uncollected funds may be placed on funds deposited by check or similar instruments. This could delay your ability to withdraw such funds. The delay if any would not exceed the period of time permitted by law.

BAY BANK
Box 1739 Terminal Annex
Los Angeles, CA 90052

⑆122000661⑈1400⑉03857⑊0136 2⑈

SHERMAN REALTY COMMISSION REPORT				**Date:** April 6, 201X
Name:	Bryce Lyman			
Date:	**Sales Description**	**Sales No.**	**Commission Amount**	
April. 6/1X	Home at 66 Sullivan St.	A1001	$6,500.00	Paid in full.
C001		**Remarks:**		

April 8   Paid gas bill to Harvey Petroleum Gas Co., $25.

SHERMAN REALTY (213) 478-3584	0003

SHERMAN REALTY (213) 478-3584   0003

8200 SUNSET BOULEVARD   *April 8*   *201X*
LOS ANGELES, CA 90028

PAY TO THE
ORDER OF   *Harvey Petroleum Gas Co.* $ *25 $\frac{XX}{100}$*

Twenty-Five and $\frac{XX}{100}$ ——————————————— DOLLARS

BAY BANK
Box 1739 Terminal Annex
Los Angeles, CA 90052

MEMO   *Gas Bill – April. 6*   *Jacob Sherman*

April 15   Paid Tessa Hardy, office secretary, $550.

SHERMAN REALTY (213) 478-3584   0004

8200 SUNSET BOULEVARD   *April 15*   *201X*
LOS ANGELES, CA 90028

PAY TO THE
ORDER OF   *Tessa Hardy* $ *550 $\frac{XX}{100}$*

Five Hundred Fifty and $\frac{XX}{100}$ ———————————— DOLLARS

BAY BANK
Box 1739 Terminal Annex
Los Angeles, CA 90052

MEMO   *Salary – April 1–15*   *Jacob Sherman*

April 17   Sold a building lot to Wet Land Developers and earned a commission, $7,500; payment to be
received on May 8.

SHERMAN REALTY **COMMISSION REPORT**				**Date:** April 17, 201X
Name:	Wet Land Developers			
Date:	**Sales Description**	**Sales No.**	**Commission Amount**	
April 17/1X	Lot at 8 Ridge Rd.	A1002	$7,500.00	
C002		**Remarks:** Payment due May 8, 201X		

April 20   Jacob Sherman withdrew $3,000 from the business to pay personal expenses.

SHERMAN REALTY (213) 478-3584	0005
8200 SUNSET BOULEVARD LOS ANGELES, CA 90028	April 20 201X

PAY TO THE ORDER OF _Jacob Sherman_ $ | 3,000 XX/100

Three Thousand and XX/100 ———————————————————— DOLLARS

BAY BANK
Box 1739 Terminal Annex
Los Angeles, CA 90052

MEMO _Withdrawal_   _Jacob sherman_

April 21   Sold a house to Mary Dappler and collected a $8,000 commission.

———| DEPOSIT TICKET |———

SHERMAN REALTY (213) 478-3584
8200 SUNSET BOULEVARD
Los Angeles, CA 90028

DATE _April 21_   201X

SIGN HERE IN PRESENCE OF TELLER FOR CASH RET'D FROM DEP.

BAY BANK
Box 1739 Terminal Annex
Los Angeles, CA 90052

⑊12200066⑊1⑊1400⫸03857⫸0136 2⑊

CASH	CURRENCY		
	COIN		
LIST CHECKS SINGLY 270-88		8,000	00
TOTAL FROM OTHER SIDE			
TOTAL			
LESS CASH RECEIVED			
NET DEPOSIT		8,000	00

16-66/1220

A hold for uncollected funds may be placed on funds deposited by check or similar instruments. This could delay your ability to withdraw such funds. The delay if any would not exceed the period of time permitted by law.

SHERMAN REALTY COMMISSION REPORT				**Date:** April 21, 201X
Name: Mary Dappler				
Date:	**Sales Description**	**Sales No.**	**Commission Amount**	
April. 21/1X	Home at 666 Jersey St.	A1003	$8,000.00	Paid in full.
C003		**Remarks:**		

April 22   Paid gas bill, $90, to Harvey Petroleum Gas Co.

SHERMAN REALTY (213) 478-3584   0006

8200 SUNSET BOULEVARD   April 22   201X
LOS ANGELES, CA 90028

PAY TO THE
ORDER OF   Harvey Petroleum Gas Co. $ 90 XX/100

Ninety and XX/100 _____ DOLLARS

BAY BANK
Box 1739 Terminal Annex
Los Angeles, CA 90052

MEMO Gas Bill–April 22   *Jacob Sherman*

April 24   Paid Jeep East $450 to repair automobile.

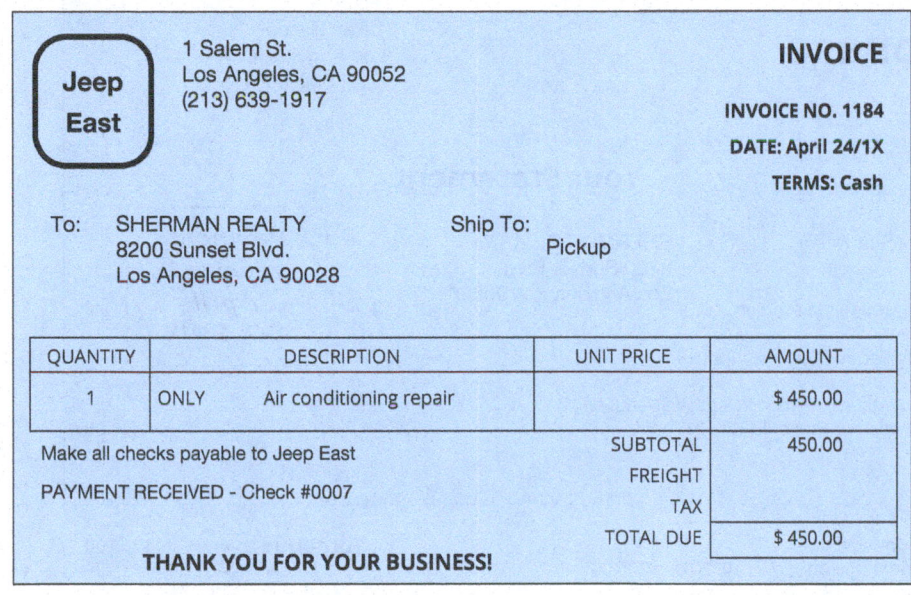

| Jeep East | 1 Salem St.
Los Angeles, CA 90052
(213) 639-1917 | | **INVOICE** |

INVOICE NO. 1184
DATE: April 24/1X
TERMS: Cash

To: SHERMAN REALTY   Ship To:
      8200 Sunset Blvd.   Pickup
      Los Angeles, CA 90028

QUANTITY	DESCRIPTION	UNIT PRICE	AMOUNT
1	ONLY Air conditioning repair		$ 450.00
Make all checks payable to Jeep East		SUBTOTAL	450.00
PAYMENT RECEIVED - Check #0007		FREIGHT	
		TAX	
		TOTAL DUE	$ 450.00

THANK YOU FOR YOUR BUSINESS!

SHERMAN REALTY (213) 478-3584   0007

8200 SUNSET BOULEVARD   April 24   201X
LOS ANGELES, CA 90028

PAY TO THE
ORDER OF   Jeep East $ 450 XX/100

Four Hundred Fifty and XX/100 _____ DOLLARS

BAY BANK
Box 1739 Terminal Annex
Los Angeles, CA 90052

MEMO Auto Repairs – Inv. 1184   *Jacob Sherman*

April 30   Paid Tessa Hardy, office secretary, $550.

SHERMAN REALTY (213) 478-3584   0008

8200 SUNSET BOULEVARD
LOS ANGELES, CA 90028   April 30   201X

PAY TO THE
ORDER OF   Tessa Hardy $ 550 XX/100

Five Hundred Fifty and XX/100 ————————————————— DOLLARS

BAY BANK
Box 1739 Terminal Annex
Los Angeles, CA 90052

MEMO Salary – April 16–30   Jacob Sherman

April 30   Paid Vonage April telephone bill, $200.

Vonage

1 Park Place
Los Angeles, CA 90052
(213) 862-8061

Your Statement

In Account with   SHERMAN REALTY   Payment
                             8200 Sunset Blvd.   received
                             Los Angeles, CA 90028   April
Account #09444 710-190   30, 201X

Billing Period: April 1 to April 28

Payments/Adjustments/Deposits Details
Opened account April 1, 201X. Thank you. $0.00

                             Monthly rental and changes to service   200.00

Amount now due   **Total Due** $200.00
Payment due after May 10, 201X $200.00

SHERMAN REALTY (213) 478-3584   0009

8200 SUNSET BOULEVARD
LOS ANGELES, CA 90028   April 30   201X

PAY TO THE
ORDER OF Vonage $ 200 XX/100

Two Hundred and XX/100 ————————————————— DOLLARS

BAY BANK
Box 1739 Terminal Annex
Los Angeles, CA 90052

MEMO April Phone Bill   Jacob Sherman

April 30   Received advertising bill for April, $700, from *Tampa Herald*. The bill is to be paid on May 2.

Tampa Herald
1 Long Rd., Tampa Florida, IL 60527
(352) 744-1000

I N V O I C E

SOLD TO: Sherman Realty
8200 Sunset Blvd.
Los Angeles, CA 90028

Invoice No.: 4879
Date: April 30, 201X
Due Date: May 2, 201X

DATE	DESCRIPTION	AMOUNT
April 26/1X	Advertising in Tampa Herald during September 201X	$700.00
	SUBTOTAL	700.00
Business Number 944122338	TOTAL	$700.00

MAKE ALL CHECKS PAYABLE TO TAMPA HERALD

Required Work for April

1. Journalize transactions and post to ledger accounts.
2. Prepare a trial balance in the first two columns of the worksheet and complete the worksheet using the following adjustment data:

   a. One month's rent had expired.
   b. An inventory shows $150 of office supplies remaining.
   c. Depreciation on office equipment, $170.
   d. Depreciation on automobile, $300.

5. Prepare an April income statement, statement of owner's equity, and balance sheet.
6. From the worksheet, journalize and post adjusting and closing entries (p. 3 of journal).

Prepare a post-closing trial balance. During May, Sherman Realty completed these transactions:

Check Figure:
April Post-Closing Trial Balance
$52,485

May 1   Purchased additional office supplies on account from The Office Store, $900.

The Office Store

INVOICE

1 Ferncroft Rd.
Los Angeles, CA 90052
Phone (213) 631-0288

DATE: May 1/1X
NUMBER: D1996035
TERMS: Net 60

SOLD TO:
Sherman Realty
8200 Sunset Blvd.
Los Angeles, CA 90028

SHIPPED TO:
Sherman Realty
8200 Sunset Blvd.
Los Angeles, CA 90028

DATE	DESCRIPTION	UNIT PRICE	AMOUNT
May 1/1X	Office supplies		$900.00
	Subtotal		900.00
	Total		$900.00

Business Number: 115555559

PLEASE PAY
THE ABOVE

THANK YOU FOR YOUR BUSINESS

May 2   Paid *Tampa Herald* advertising bill for April, $700.

SHERMAN REALTY (213) 478-3584	0010

SHERMAN REALTY (213) 478-3584   0010

8200 SUNSET BOULEVARD
LOS ANGELES, CA 90028   *May 2   201X*

PAY TO THE
ORDER OF   *Tampa Herald* $ 700 XX/100

Seven Hundred and XX/100 _____ DOLLARS

BAY BANK
Box 1739 Terminal Annex
Los Angeles, CA 90052

MEMO   *Invoice # 4879*   *Jacob Sherman*

⑆12200066⑆ 1⑈1400⑉03857⑉0136 2⑈0010

May 3   Sold a house to Carol Turner and collected a commission of $5,900.

SHERMAN REALTY				
COMMISSION REPORT			*Date:*	May 3, 201X
Name:	Carol Turner			
Date:	*Sales Description*	*Sales No.*	*Commission Amount*	
May 3/1X	Home at 800 Rose Ave.	A1004	$5,900.00	*Paid in full.*
C004		*Remarks:*		

⊣ **DEPOSIT TICKET** ⊢

SHERMAN REALTY (213)478-3584
8200 SUNSET BOULEVARD
Los Angeles, CA 90028

DATE   *May 3   201X*

_____
SIGN HERE IN PRESENCE OF TELLER FOR CASH RET'D FROM DEP.

BAY BANK
Box 1739 Terminal Annex
Los Angeles, CA 90052

⑆12200066⑆ 1⑈1400⑉03857⑉0136 2⑈

CASH	CURRENCY		
	COIN		
LIST CHECKS SINGLY 278-92		5,900	00
TOTAL FROM OTHER SIDE			
TOTAL			
LESS CASH RECEIVED			
NET DEPOSIT		5,900	00

16-66/1220

A hold for uncollected funds may be placed on funds deposited by check or similar instruments. This could delay your ability to withdraw such funds. The delay if any would not exceed the period of time permitted by law.

May 6   Paid gas bill to Harvey Petroleum Gas Co., $42.

SHERMAN REALTY (213) 478-3584   0011

8200 SUNSET BOULEVARD
LOS ANGELES, CA 90028   May 6   201X

PAY TO THE
ORDER OF   Harvey Petroleum Gas Co. $ 42 $\frac{XX}{100}$

Forty-Two and $\frac{XX}{100}$ ————————————————— DOLLARS

BAY BANK
Box 1739 Terminal Annex
Los Angeles, CA 90052

MEMO   Gas Bill – May 6   Jacob Sherman

May 8   Collected commission from Wet Land Developers for sale of building lot on April 17, $7,500.

—| DEPOSIT TICKET |—

SHERMAN REALTY (213) 478-3584
8200 SUNSET BOULEVARD
Los Angeles, CA 90028

DATE   May 8   201X

SIGN HERE IN PRESENCE OF TELLER FOR CASH RET'D FROM DEP.

BAY BANK
Box 1739 Terminal Annex
Los Angeles, CA 90052

⑈12200066⑈:1400⋯03857⋯0136 2⑈

CASH	CURRENCY		
	COIN		
LIST CHECKS SINGLY 228-114		7,500	00
TOTAL FROM OTHER SIDE			
TOTAL			
LESS CASH RECEIVED			
NET DEPOSIT		7,500	00

16-66/1220

A hold for uncollected funds may be placed on funds deposited by check or similar instruments. This could delay your ability to withdraw such funds. The delay if any would not exceed the period of time permitted by law.

May 12   Paid $450 to Foster Realtors Assoc. to send employees to realtors' workshop.

SHERMAN REALTY (213) 478-3584   0012

8200 SUNSET BOULEVARD
LOS ANGELES, CA 90028   May 12   201X

PAY TO THE
ORDER OF   Foster Realtors $ 450 $\frac{XX}{100}$

Four Hundred Fifty and $\frac{XX}{100}$ ——————————— DOLLARS

BAY BANK
Box 1739 Terminal Annex
Los Angeles, CA 90052

MEMO   Workshop Registration   Jacob Sherman

May 15   Paid Tessa Hardy, office secretary, $550.

SHERMAN REALTY (213) 478-3584   0013

8200 SUNSET BOULEVARD   May 15   201X
LOS ANGELES, CA 90028

PAY TO THE
ORDER OF   Tessa Hardy $ 550 XX/100

Five Hundred Fifty and XX/100 ━━━━━━━━━━━━━ DOLLARS

BAY BANK
Box 1739 Terminal Annex
Los Angeles, CA 90052

MEMO   Salary – May 1–15   Jacob Sherman

May 17   Sold a house to Eric Harmon and earned a commission of $3,700. Commission to be
              received on June 10.

SHERMAN REALTY COMMISSION REPORT				**Date:** May 17, 201X	
Name:	Eric Harmon				
Date:	**Sales Description**	**Sales No.**	**Commission Amount**		
May 17/1X	Home at RR2, Site 3	A1010	$3,700.00		
C005		**Remarks:** Payment due June 10, 201X			

May 18   Sold a building lot to Argento Builders and collected a commission of $5,000.

┤ **DEPOSIT TICKET** ├

SHERMAN REALTY (213) 478-3584
8200 SUNSET BOULEVARD
Los Angeles, CA 90028

DATE   May 18   201X

SIGN HERE IN PRESENCE OF TELLER FOR CASH RET'D FROM DEP. →

BAY BANK
Box 1739 Terminal Annex
Los Angeles, CA 90052

⑆122000066⑈1400⑈03857⑈0136 2⑆

CASH	CURRENCY		
	COIN		
LIST CHECKS SINGLY 269-10		5,000	00
TOTAL FROM OTHER SIDE			
TOTAL		5,000	00
LESS CASH RECEIVED			
NET DEPOSIT		5,000	00

16-66/1220

A hold for uncollected funds may be placed on funds deposited by check or similar instruments. This could delay your ability to withdraw such funds. The delay if any would not exceed the period of time permitted by law.

SHERMAN REALTY COMMISSION REPORT			**Date:**	May 18, 201X	
Name:	Argento Builders				
Date:	**Sales Description**	**Sales No.**	**Commission Amount**		
May 18/1X	Building lot at 5004 King St. E	A1005	$5,000.00	Paid in full.	
C006			**Remarks:**		

May 22   Sent a check to Samaritan Charities for $50 to help sponsor a local road race to aid the poor. (This amount is not to be considered an advertising expense; it is a business expense and is posted to Miscellaneous Expense.)

SHERMAN REALTY (213) 478-3584   0014

8200 SUNSET BOULEVARD
LOS ANGELES, CA 90028   May 22   201X

PAY TO THE
ORDER OF _Samaritan Charities_ $ 50 $\frac{XX}{100}$

Fifty and $\frac{XX}{100}$ _____ DOLLARS

BAY BANK
Box 1739 Terminal Annex
Los Angeles, CA 90052

MEMO _Aid to Poor_   _Jacob Sherman_

⑈ ⑈2 200066 ⑈⑈⑈ ⑈400 ⁗03857 ⁗0 ⑈36 2⑈⁗00⑈4

May 24   Paid Jeep East $690 for repairs to automobile due to accident.

Jeep East   1 Salem St.
Los Angeles, CA 90052
(213) 639-1917

INVOICE

INVOICE NO. 2119

DATE: May 24/1X

TERMS: Cash

To: SHERMAN REALTY
8200 Sunset Blvd.
Los Angeles, CA 90028

QUANTITY	DESCRIPTION	UNIT PRICE	AMOUNT
	Accident Repairs		$ 690.00

Make all checks payable to Jeep East

PAYMENT RECEIVED - Check #0015

SUBTOTAL	690.00
FREIGHT	
TAX	
TOTAL DUE	$ 690.00

SHERMAN REALTY (213) 478-3584   0015

8200 SUNSET BOULEVARD
LOS ANGELES, CA 90028   May 24   201X

PAY TO THE
ORDER OF   *Jeep East* $ 690 XX/100

Six Hundred Ninety and XX/100 _____ DOLLARS

BAY BANK
Box 1739 Terminal Annex
Los Angeles, CA 90052

MEMO   *Auto Repairs – Inv. 2119*   **Jacob Sherman**

May 28   Jacob Sherman withdrew $1,600 from the business to pay personal expenses.

SHERMAN REALTY (213) 478-3584   0016

8200 SUNSET BOULEVARD
LOS ANGELES, CA 90028   May 28   201X

PAY TO THE
ORDER OF   *Jacob Sherman* $ 1,600 XX/100

One Thousand Six Hundred and XX/100 _____ DOLLARS

BAY BANK
Box 1739 Terminal Annex
Los Angeles, CA 90052

MEMO   *Withdrawal*   **Jacob Sherman**

May 30   Paid Tessa Hardy, office secretary, $550.

SHERMAN REALTY (213) 478-3584   0017

8200 SUNSET BOULEVARD
LOS ANGELES, CA 90028   May 30   201X

PAY TO THE
ORDER OF   *Tessa Hardy* $ 550 XX/100

Five Hundred Fifty and XX/100 _____ DOLLARS

BAY BANK
Box 1739 Terminal Annex
Los Angeles, CA 90052

MEMO   *Salary – May 16–31*   **Jacob Sherman**

May 30   Paid Vonage telephone bill, $530.

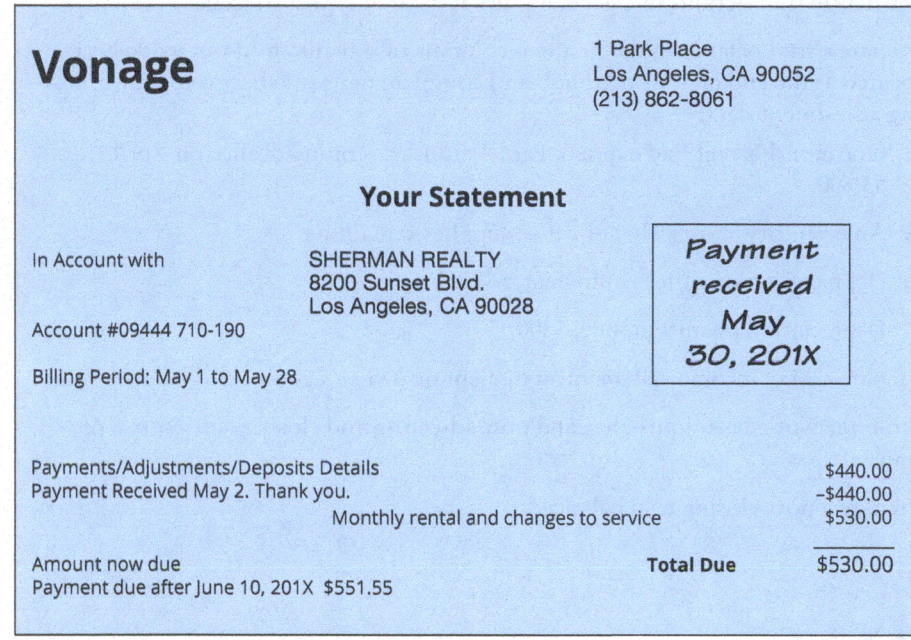

Vonage   1 Park Place
                                  Los Angeles, CA 90052
                                  (213) 862-8061

Your Statement

In Account with   SHERMAN REALTY   *Payment*
                         8200 Sunset Blvd.   *received*
                         Los Angeles, CA 90028   *May*
Account #09444 710-190   *30, 201X*

Billing Period: May 1 to May 28

Payments/Adjustments/Deposits Details	$440.00
Payment Received May 2. Thank you.	–$440.00
Monthly rental and changes to service	$530.00

Amount now due   **Total Due** $530.00
Payment due after June 10, 201X $551.55

SHERMAN REALTY (213) 478-3584   0018

8200 SUNSET BOULEVARD
LOS ANGELES, CA 90028   *May 30   201X*

PAY TO THE
ORDER OF   *Vonage* $ *530 XX/100*

Five Hundred Thirty and XX/100 ————————— DOLLARS

BAY BANK
Box 1739 Terminal Annex
Los Angeles, CA 90052

MEMO *May Phone Bill*   *Jacob Sherman*

May 30   Advertising bill from *Tampa Herald* for May, $1,700. The bill is to be paid on June 2.

Tampa Herald
1 Long Rd. Tampa Florida, IL 60527
(352) 744-1000
I N V O I C E

SOLD TO: Sherman Realty   **Invoice No.:** 5400
             8200 Sunset Blvd.   **Date:** May 30, 201X
             Los Angeles, CA 90028   **Due Date:** June 2, 201X

DATE	DESCRIPTION		AMOUNT
May 30/1X	Advertising in Tampa Herald during May 201X		$1,700.00
		SUBTOTAL	1,700.00
Business Number 944122338		TOTAL	$1,700.00
MAKE ALL CHECKS PAYABLE TO TAMPA HERALD			

Check Figure:
Post-Closing Trial Balance end of May
$60,973

Required Work for May

1. Journalize transactions in a general journal (p. 4) and post to ledger accounts.

2. Prepare a trial balance in the first two columns of a blank, fold-out worksheet located at the end of your textbook and complete the worksheet using the following adjustment data:

   a. One month's rent had expired. Paid 4 months' rent in advance on April 1, $3,600

   b. An inventory shows $100 of office supplies remaining.

   c. Depreciation on office equipment, $170.

   d. Depreciation on automobile, $300.

3. Prepare a May income statement, statement of owner's equity, and balance sheet.

4. From the worksheet, journalize and post adjusting and closing entries (p. 6 of journal).

5. Prepare a post-closing trial balance.

S50	# SAGE 50 SOFTWARE SIMULATION

Computerized Accounting Application for Chapter 5

Refresher on using Sage 50 Complete Accounting

Before starting this assignment, you may want to refresh your memory by reading the following PDF documents in the multimedia library of the My Lab Accounting website. Remember to choose the PDF document for your version of Sage 50.

1. An Introduction to Sage 50
2. Correcting Sage 50 Transactions
3. How to Repeat or Restart a Sage 50 Assignment
4. Backing Up and Restoring Your Work in Sage 50

You also should have completed the following workshops:

1. Workshop 1 Atlas Company from Chapter 3
2. Workshop 2 Zell Company from Chapter 4

Workshop 3

Accounting Cycle Mini Practice Set

In this workshop, you will complete the April and May accounting cycles for Sherman Realty using Sage 50. Tasks include posting journal entries and adjusting journal entries, printing reports and financial statements, and closing the accounting period.

Instructions and the data file for completing this assignment are in the multimedia library of the My Lab Accounting website. Open the *Workshop 3 Sherman Realty* PDF document for your version of Sage 50 and download the *Sherman Realty* data file for your version of Sage 50.

QUICKBOOKS SOFTWARE SIMULATION

Computerized Accounting Application for Chapter 5

Refresher on using QuickBooks Accountant

Before starting this assignment, you may want to refresh your memory by reading the following PDF documents in the multimedia library of the My Lab Accounting website. Remember to choose the PDF document for your version of QuickBooks.

1. An Introduction to QuickBooks
2. Correcting QuickBooks Transactions
3. How to Repeat or Restart a QuickBooks Assignment
4. Backing Up and Restoring Your Work in QuickBooks

You also should have completed the following workshops:

1. Workshop 1 Atlas Company from Chapter 3
2. Workshop 2 Zell Company from Chapter 4

Workshop 3

Accounting Cycle Mini Practice Set

In this workshop, you will complete the April and May accounting cycles for Sherman Realty using QuickBooks. Tasks include posting journal entries and adjusting journal entries, printing reports and financial statements, and closing the accounting period.

Instructions and the data file for completing this assignment are in the multimedia library of the My Lab Accounting website. Open the **Workshop 3 Sherman Realty** PDF document for your version of QuickBooks and download the **Sherman Realty** data file for your version of QuickBooks.

Banking Procedures and Control of Cash

6

CHAPTER PREVIEW: ACCOUNTING IN ACTION

Miriam Eagle does all her banking with her mobile device. She believes mobile banking is the best way to bank. With her downloaded app, she can send money, check her balance before a large purchase, and make a deposit. In this chapter, we look at banking procedures, the reconciliation of bank statements with company accounting records, and the control of cash. Maintaining accurate records of transactions, rather than just relying on bank-prepared statements, is important to the control of cash and shows the importance of accounting in business.

Learning Objectives – Relating Accounting Theory By Unit

LO1 Explain Banking Procedures and Checking Accounts

LO2 Explain Bank Reconciliation

LO3 Explain Petty Cash and Change Funds

L01

Banking Procedures And Checking Accounts

Today, your mobile device, a tool that can be used for both personal and business banking, is part of a growing trend in banking. Before we look at specific trends in banking it is important to understand the manual system of banking. First, we turn our attention to Becca's Bling Emporium, a merchandising company that earns revenue by selling goods (or merchandise) to customers. When Becca's business began to increase, she became concerned that she was not monitoring the business's cash closely. She understood that a business with good internal control systems safeguards cash. Cash is the asset that is most easily stolen, lost, or mishandled. Therefore, it is important to protect all cash receipts and to control cash payments so that payments are made only for authorized business purposes.

Internal control system
Procedures and methods to control a firm's assets as well as monitor its operations.

After studying the situation carefully, Becca began a series of procedures that were to be followed by all company employees. The new company policies that Becca's Bling Emporium put into place are:

1. Responsibilities and duties of employees will be divided. For example, the person receiving the cash, whether at the register or by opening the mail, will not record this information into the accounting records. The accountant will not be handling the cash receipts.

2. All cash receipts of Becca's Bling Emporium will be deposited into the bank the same day they arrive.

3. All cash payments will be made by check (except petty cash, which is discussed later in this chapter).

4. Employees will be rotated. This change allows workers to become acquainted with the work of others as well as to prepare for a possible changeover of jobs.

5. Becca Baker will sign all checks after receiving authorization to pay from the departments concerned.

6. At time of payment, all supporting invoices or documents will be stamped "paid." The stamp will show when the invoice or document is paid as well as the number of the check used.

7. All checks will be prenumbered. Periodically, the number of the checks that were issued and the numbers of the blank check forms remaining will be verified to make sure that all check numbers are accounted for. This change will control the use of checks and make it difficult to use a check fraudulently without it being revealed at some point.

8. Monthly bank statements will be sent to and reconciled by someone other than the employees who handle, record, or deposit the cash.

Becca knew that a checking account is one of the most useful and common banking services available, but she had many questions and decisions to make. She wanted to know about account options, monthly service charges, check-printing charges, minimum balance requirements, interest paid on the account, availability of automatic teller machines (ATMs), line of credit, and debit cards. Before Becca's Bling Emporium opened on April 1, 201X, she met with the manager of Oceanic Bank to discuss opening and using a checking account for the company.

Opening a Checking Account

Signature card Form signed by a bank customer that the bank uses to verify signature authenticity on all checks.

A signature card is another internal control safeguard.

The bank manager gave Becca a signature card to fill out. The bank uses the signature card to verify the authenticity of the signature on company checks. Because Becca would be signing all the checks for her company, she was the only person who needed to sign the card.

The bank account enabled Becca to implement two basic internal control procedures. First, all revenue sources (cash and checks from cash sales and accounts receivable collections as well as credit card and debit card proceeds) were deposited in the bank account. Second, all withdrawals were to be made by check.

After Becca completed the initial paperwork, she received deposit slips and a set of checks. A deposit slip is a form that is used when making deposits of currency, coins, or checks in a bank or other financial institution. When filling out a deposit slip, you list the total amount of currency, coins, and checks that you are depositing (see Figure 6.1, page 200).

You list each check that you are depositing individually. Also, alongside each check you list its American Bankers Association (ABA) code. The ABA code is found in the upper-right corner of each check, below the check number. In Figure 6.1, the *16* identifies the large city or state in which the bank is located, and the *21* identifies the bank. The *112* is split into two parts: *1* represents the First Federal Reserve District, and *12* is a routing number used by the Federal Reserve Bank. When completing a deposit slip, only the first two numbers are required.

When a deposit is completed, the depositor receives a copy of the deposit slip as a receipt or proof of the transaction. The deposit should also be recorded on the current check stub. The bank manager told Becca that she could give the deposits to a bank teller or she could use an ATM. Often, Becca makes her deposits after business hours when the bank is closed. (Keep in mind that today many people use their smartphones to make deposits. We discuss trends in banking later in this chapter.) At those times, the bank will credit Becca's account when the deposit is processed. Becca plans to make all business payments by written check (except petty cash) and deposit all money received (cash and checks) in the bank account.

Check Endorsement

Checks have to be *endorsed* (signed) by the person to whom the check is made out before they can be deposited or cashed. Endorsement is the signing or stamping of one's name on the back left-hand side of the check. This signature means that the payee has transferred the right to deposit or cash the check to someone else (the bank). The bank can then collect the money from the person or company that issued the check.

Three different types of endorsement can be used (see Figure 6.2, page 201). The first is a *blank endorsement*. A blank endorsement does not specify that a particular person or firm must endorse it. It can be further endorsed by someone else. The bank will pay the last person who signs the check. This type of endorsement is not very safe. If the check is lost, the person who finds it can sign it and get the money.

The second type of endorsement is a *full endorsement*. The person or company signing (or stamping) the back of the check indicates the name of the company or the person to whom the check is to be paid. Only the person or company named in the endorsement can transfer the check to someone else.

Restrictive endorsements, the third type of endorsement, are the safest for businesses. Becca's Bling Emporium stamps the back of the check so that it must be deposited in the firm's account. This stamp limits any further use of the check.

Deposit slip Form provided by a bank for use in depositing money or checks into a checking account.

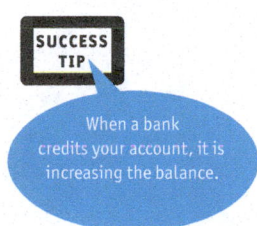

When a bank credits your account, it is increasing the balance.

Endorsement Blank: Could be further endorsed. Full: Restricts further endorsement to only the person or company named. Restrictive: Restricts any further endorsement.

Endorsements can be made by using a rubber stamp instead of a handwritten signature.

The regulations require the endorsement to be within the top 1½ inches to speed up the check-clearing process.

Figure 6.1
Deposit Slip

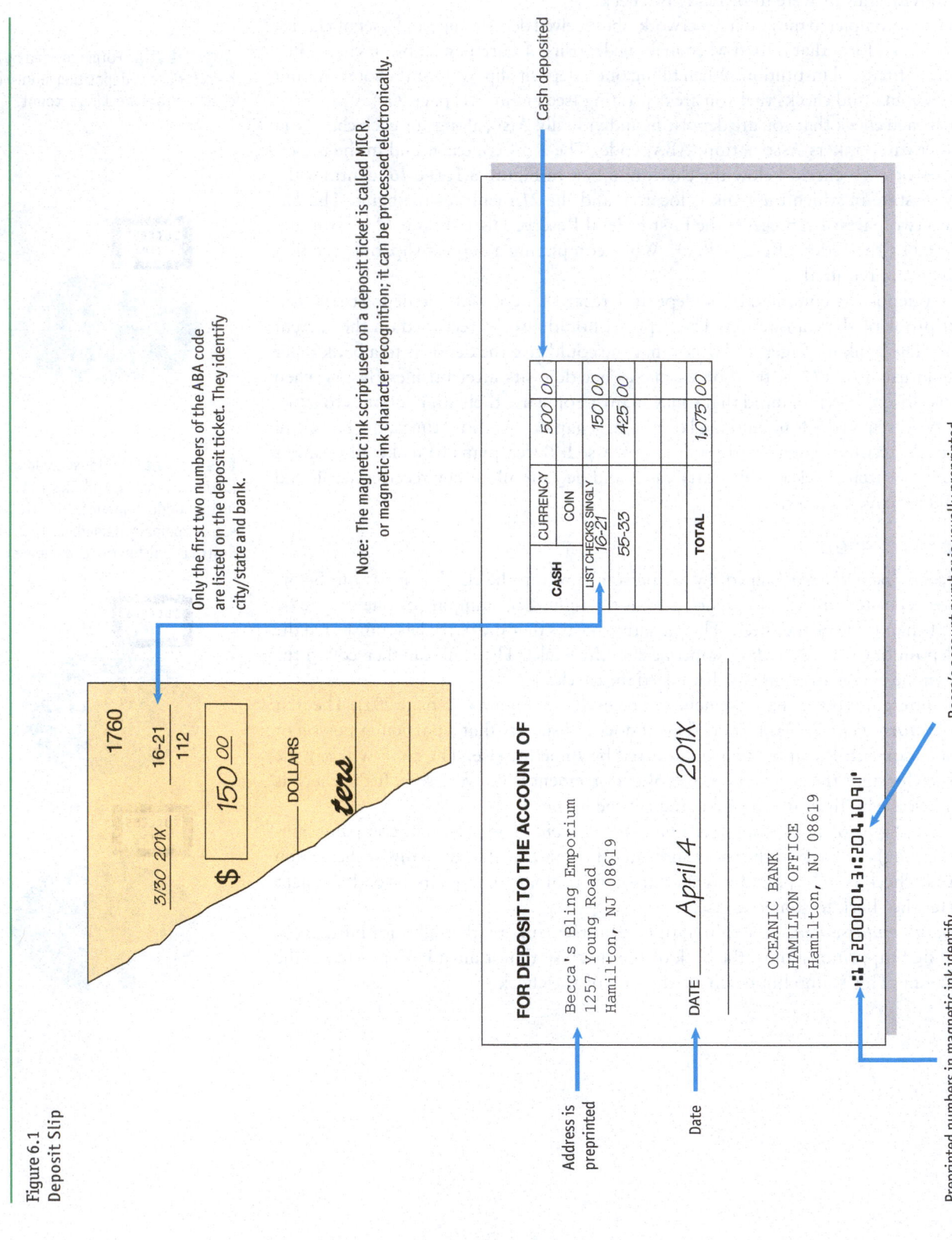

Only the first two numbers of the ABA code are listed on the deposit ticket. They identify city/state and bank.

Note: The magnetic ink script used on a deposit ticket is called MICR, or magnetic ink character recognition; it can be processed electronically.

Cash deposited

CASH	CURRENCY	500	00
	COIN		
	LIST CHECKS SINGLY 16-21	150	00
	55-33	425	00
	TOTAL	1,075	00

1760
16-21
112

3/30 201X

$ 150 00

DOLLARS

tens

FOR DEPOSIT TO THE ACCOUNT OF

Becca's Bling Emporium
1257 Young Road
Hamilton, NJ 08619

DATE _____ April 4 _____ 201X

OCEANIC BANK
HAMILTON OFFICE
Hamilton, NJ 08619

⑆ 200004 ⑈ 204 109 ⑈

Address is preprinted

Date

Preprinted numbers in magnetic ink identify bank number and routing and sorting of check.

Becca's account number is usually preprinted.

200

Types of Check Endorsement

Blank Endorsement

Becca Baker

204109

A signature on the back left side of a check of the person or firm the check is payable to. This check can be *further* endorsed by someone else; the bank will give the money to the last person who signs the check. This type of endorsement is not very safe. If the check is lost, anyone who picks it up can sign it and get the money.

Full Endorsement

Pay to the order of
Oceanic Bank
Becca's Bling Emporium
204109

This type of endorsement is safer than a simple signature, because the person or company signing (or stamping) the back of the check indicates the name of the company or person to whom the check is to be paid. Only the person or company named in the endorsement can transfer the check to someone else.

Restrictive Endorsement

Payable to the order of
Oceanic Bank
for deposit only.
Becca's Bling Emporium
204109

This endorsement is the safest for businesses. Becca's Bling Emporium stamps the back of the check so that it must be deposited in the firm's account. This endorsement limits any further use of the check (it can only be deposited in the specified account).

Figure 6.2
Types of Check Endorsement

In the past and to a lesser extent in the present, the primary sources of cash were cash sales and the collection of company accounts receivable. The journal entries to record the collection and deposit of cash in a bank vary only by the source. If the deposit is composed of the proceeds of cash sales, the journal entry appears as in Figure 6.3.

Date	Accounts	PR	Dr.	Cr.
	Cash		5 0 0 00	
	Sales			5 0 0 00

Figure 6.3
Journal Entry to Record the Deposit of the Proceeds of a Cash Sale

If the deposit is composed of collections of company accounts receivable, the journal entry would be as in Figure 6.3A.

Date	Accounts	PR	Dr.	Cr.
	Cash		7 5 0 00	
	Accounts Receivable			7 5 0 00

Figure 6.3A
Journal Entry to Record the Collection of a Company's Accounts Receivable

There are two other sources of revenue that have taken on greater importance to businessmen and businesswomen: the credit card and the debit card. There are two categories of credit cards: those issued by financial institutions and those issued by credit card companies. Many of those issued by financial institutions, such as MasterCard, VISA, and Discover, are co-branded by other institutions such as airlines, NFL teams, and colleges and universities. These credit cards offer revolving credit facilities. Other credit cards, such as American Express, are issued by credit card companies. These companies generally extend credit for 30 days at a time.

There are several good reasons for a merchant to accept credit cards in payment for its goods or services. The seller does not have to make a decision as to whether it should grant credit or the amount of the credit to be granted. The seller also avoids the risk that the purchaser cannot or will not pay. Additionally, the seller does not have to maintain an accounts receivable system. Credit cards offer a greater number of repayment plans than do merchants, and this may actually increase sales. The increase in mobile banking means that many transactions can be processed instantly. A drawback of accepting credit cards is that merchants typically must pay a service fee associated with the cost of processing the credit card transaction. The example in Figure 6.4 reflects a 1.5% service charge.

Figure 6.4
Journal Entry to Record the Deposit of the Proceeds of Credit Card Sales

Date	Account	PR	Dr.	Cr.
	Cash		9 8 5 00	
	Service Charge Expense		1 5 00	
	Sales			1 0 0 0 00

A debit card is an instrument very similar to the credit card that is used by the buyer to purchase goods and services. Debit cards are issued by banks, savings and loan institutions, and credit unions on behalf of depositors having an account with the institution. In addition, a debit card is not an extension of credit, as the debit card holder cannot spend more than the balance currently in his or her institutional account. As far as the merchant accepting the card is concerned, a debit card, with minor exceptions, is the same as a credit card. Both eliminate the need for the buyer to carry cash or checks to complete a purchase. Within 24 hours the merchant usually receives payment that is reduced by the amount of the service charge fee associated with the debit card transaction. The journal entry to record a debit card transaction is the same as the one shown in Figure 6.4.

The Checkbook

When Becca opened her business's checking account, she received checks. These checks can be used to buy items for the business or to pay bills or salaries.

A check is a written order signed by a drawer (the person who writes the check) instructing a drawee (the person who pays the check) to pay a specific sum of money to the payee (the person to whom the check is payable). Figure 6.5 on page 203 shows a check issued by Becca's Bling Emporium. Becca Baker is the drawer, Oceanic Bank is the drawee, and Millenial Distributers is the payee.

Look at the check in Figure 6.5. Notice that certain features, such as the company's name and address and the check number, are preprinted. Also notice (1) the line drawn after xx/100, which is to fill up the empty space and ensure that the amount cannot be changed, and (2) the word *and*, which should be used only to differentiate between dollars and cents.

Figure 6.5 includes a check stub. The check stub is used to record transactions, and it is kept for future reference. The information found on the stub includes the beginning

Check Form used to indicate a specific amount of money that is to be paid by the bank to a named person or company.

Drawer Person who writes a check.

Drawee Bank that drawer has an account with.

Payee Person or company to whom the check is payable.

Figure 6.5
A Company Check

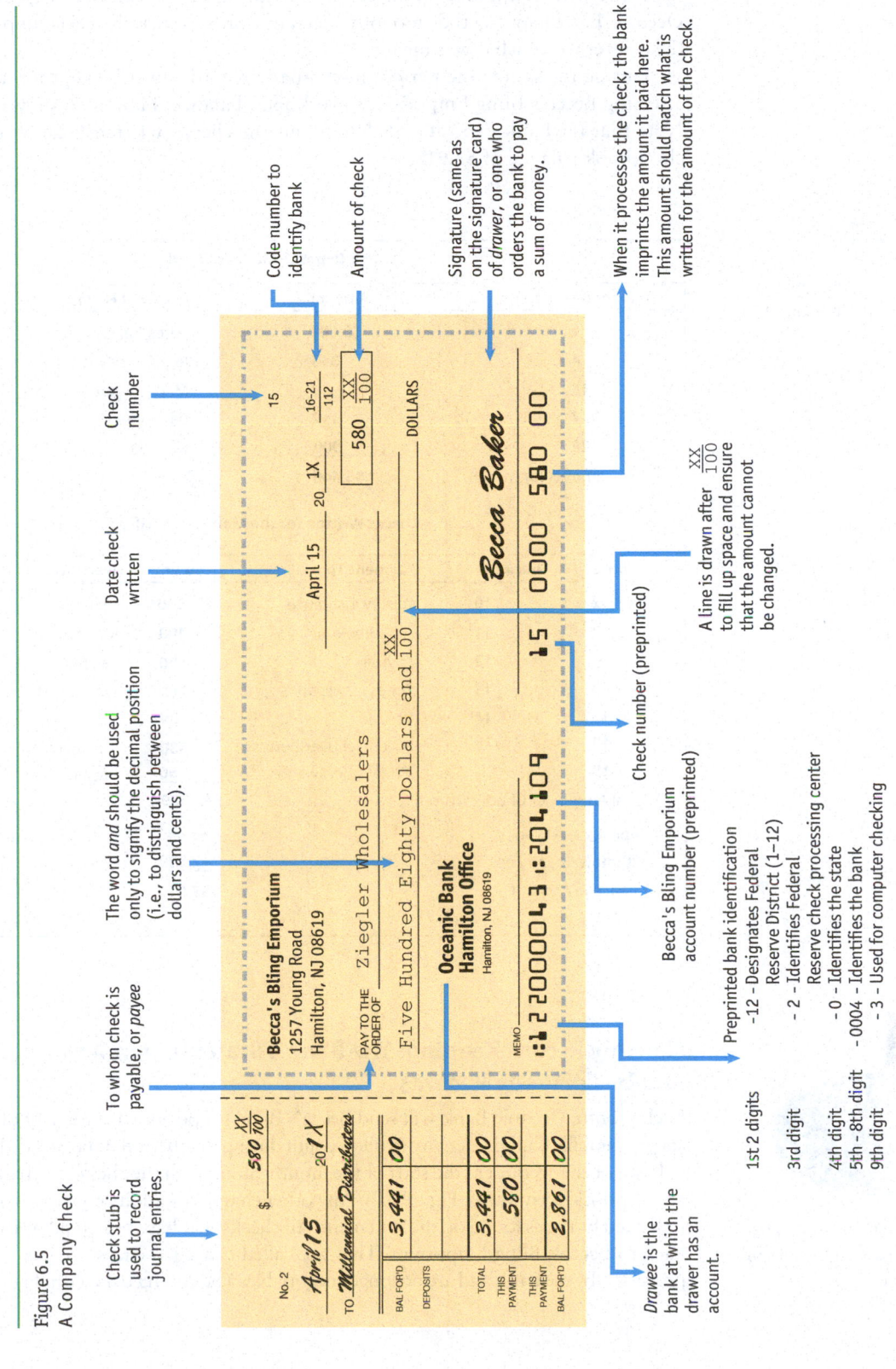

Check stub is used to record journal entries.

To whom check is payable, or *payee*

The word *and* should be used only to signify the decimal position (i.e., to distinguish between dollars and cents).

Code number to identify bank

Amount of check

Check number

Date check written

Signature (same as on the signature card) of *drawer*, or one who orders the bank to pay a sum of money.

When it processes the check, the bank imprints the amount it paid here. This amount should match what is written for the amount of the check.

A line is drawn after $\frac{XX}{100}$ to fill up space and ensure that the amount cannot be changed.

Check number (preprinted)

Becca's Bling Emporium account number (preprinted)

Preprinted bank identification

1st 2 digits — -12 – Designates Federal Reserve District (1–12)

3rd digit — - 2 – Identifies Federal Reserve check processing center

4th digit — - 0 – Identifies the state

5th – 8th digit — -0004 – Identifies the bank

9th digit — - 3 – Used for computer checking

Drawee is the bank at which the drawer has an account.

203

balance of the checkbook ($3,441), the amount of any deposits ($0), the total amount in the account ($3,441), the amount of the check being written ($580), and the ending balance ($2,861). The check stub should be filled out before the check is written.

If the written amount on the check does not match the amount expressed in figures, Oceanic Bank may pay the amount written in words, return the check unpaid, or contact the drawer to see what was meant.

During the same time period, in-company records must be kept for all transactions affecting Becca's Bling Emporium's checkbook balance. Figure 6.6 shows these records. Note that the bank deposits ($6,446) minus the checks written ($2,529) give an ending checkbook balance of $3,917.

Figure 6.6
Transactions (In-Company Records) Affecting Checkbook Balance

Bank Deposits Made for April		
Date of Deposit	**Amount**	**Received From**
Apr. 1	$5,000	Becca Baker, Capital
4	340	Jennifer Leung
15	89	Mary Figueroa
27	117	Carl Jones
28	900	Cash Sales
Total deposits for month:	$6,446	

Checks Written for the Month of April				
Date	**Check No.**	**Payment To**	**Amount**	**Description**
Apr. 2	10	Quality Insurance	$ 500	Insurance paid in advance
7	11	ABC Wholesalers	400	Merchandise
9	12	Payroll	800	Salaries
10	13	Times Newspaper	100	Advertising
12	14	Verizon	99	Telephone
15	15	Millennial Distributers	580	Merchandise
15		ATM Withdrawal	50	Postage
Total Amount of Checks Written:			$2,529	
Deposits and Credits			$6,446	
Withdrawals and Fees			−2,529	
Balance in Account			$3,917	

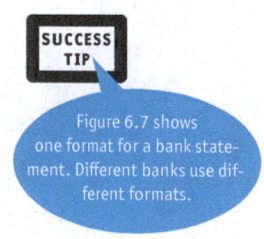

Figure 6.7 shows one format for a bank statement. Different banks use different formats.

Cancelled check Check that has been processed by a bank and is no longer negotiable.

Monthly Record Keeping: The Bank's Statement of Account and In-Company Records

Each month, Oceanic Bank will send Becca's Bling Emporium a statement of account. This statement reflects all the activity in the account during that period. It begins with the beginning balance of the account at the start of the month, along with the checks the bank has paid and any deposits received (see Figure 6.7). Any other charges or additions to the bank balance are indicated by codes found on the statement. All checks that have been paid by the bank are sent back to Becca's Bling Emporium. They are called cancelled checks because they have been processed by the bank and are no longer negotiable. The ending balance in Figure 6.7 is $3,592.

Figure 6.7
A Bank Statement

Oceanic Bank

Becca's Bling Emporium
1257 Young Road
Hamilton, NJ 08619

ACCOUNT
NUMBER   20   410   9

CLOSING
PERIOD   4/30/1X

AMOUNT
ENCLOSED $ _____

RETURN THIS PORTION WITH YOUR PAYMENT IF YOU ARE NOT USING OUR AUTOMATIC PAYMENT PLAN   Address Correction on Reverse Side ☐

	CHECKING ACCOUNT					
ON	YOUR BALANCE WAS	NO.	WE SUBTRACTED CHECKS TOTALING	LESS SERVICE CHARGE	NO.	WE ADDED DEPOSITS OF	MAKING YOUR PRESENT BALANCE
	0	5	1,949.00	5.00	4	5,546.00	3,592.00

DATE	CHECKS • WITHDRAWALS • PAYMENTS	DEPOSITS • INTEREST • ADVANCES	BALANCE
4/1		5,000.00	5,000.00
4/2	500.00		4,500.00
4/4		340.00	4,840.00
4/7	400.00		4,440.00
4/9	800.00		3,640.00
4/10	100.00		3,540.00
4/12	99.00		3,441.00
4/15		89.00	3,530.00
4/15	50.00 ATM		3,480.00
4/27		117.00	3,597.00
4/30	5.00 SC		3,592.00

Now let's check your progress.

 **TRY IT!**   **Learning Unit 6-1**

Answer true or false to the following statements.

1. The payee is the person or organization to whom a check is made payable.
2. A check stub is used to record journal entries.
3. Computers today require more internal controls in banking than ever.
4. Restrictive endorsement is the safest for a business.
5. Mobile devices have no place in banking.

TRY IT!   **Solution Learning Unit 6-1**

Only number 5 is false. Mobile devices are used heavily in banking today.

The Bank Reconciliation Process

The problem is that the ending bank balance of $3,592 does not agree with the amount in Becca's checkbook, $3,917, or the balance in the Cash account in the ledger, $3,917. Such differences are caused partly by the time a bank takes to process a company's transactions. A company records a transaction when it occurs, but a bank cannot record a deposit until it receives that deposit, and it cannot pay a check until the check is presented by the payee. In addition, the bank statement will report fees and transactions that the company did not know about.

SUCCESS TIP

Online banking and computer software have made the reconciliation process even easier.

Bank reconciliation Process of reconciling the checkbook balance with the bank balance given on the bank statement.

Bank statement Report sent by a bank to a customer indicating the previous balance, ATM transactions, nonsufficient funds, individual checks processed, individual deposits received, service charges, and ending bank balance.

Becca's accountant has to find out why there is a $325 difference between the balances and how the records can be brought into balance. The process of reconciling the bank balance on the bank statement versus the company's checkbook balance is called a bank reconciliation. Bank reconciliations involve several steps, including calculating the deposits in transit and the outstanding checks. The bank reconciliation is usually done on the back of the bank statement (see Figure 6.8). However, it can also be done by accounting software.

Figure 6.8
Bank Reconciliation Using Back of the Bank Statement

Keep in mind that both the bank and the depositor can make mistakes that will not be discovered until the reconciliation process.

CHECKS OUTSTANDING					
NUMBER	AMOUNT		1. Enter balance shown on this statement	3,592	00
15	580	00	2. If you have made deposits since the date of this statement add them to the above balance.	900	00
			3. SUBTOTAL	4,492	00
			4. Deduct total of checks outstanding	580	00
			5. ADJUSTED BALANCE This should agree with your checkbook.		
TOTAL OF CHECKS OUTSTANDING	580	00		3,912	00 *

TO VERIFY YOUR CHECKING BALANCE
1. Sort checks by number or by date issued and compare with your check stubs and prior outstanding list. Make certain all checks paid have been recorded in your checkbook. If any of your checks were not included with this statement, list the numbers and amounts under "CHECKS OUTSTANDING."
2. Deduct the Service Charge as shown on the statement from your checkbook balance.
3. Review copies of charge advices included with this statement and check for proper entry in your checkbook.

IF THE ADJUSTED BALANCE DOES NOT AGREE WITH YOUR CHECKBOOK BALANCE, THE FOLLOWING SUGGESTIONS ARE OFFERED FOR YOUR ASSISTANCE.

- Recheck additions and subtractions in your checkbook and figures to the left.
- Make certain checkbook balances have been carried forward properly.
- Verify deposits recorded on statement against deposits entered in checkbook.
- Compare amount on each checkbook stub.

*Note that the $5 service charge is included

Deposits in Transit In comparing the list of deposits received by the bank with the checkbook, the accountant notices that a deposit made on April 28 for $900 was not on the bank's statement. The accountant realizes that to prepare this statement, the bank only included deposit information about Becca's Bling Emporium up to April 27. This deposit made by Becca was not shown on the monthly bank statement because it arrived at the bank after the cutoff date of April 27. Thus, timing becomes a consideration in the reconciliation process. Deposits not yet added to the bank balance are called deposits in transit. This deposit needs to be added to the bank balance shown on the bank statement. Becca's checkbook is not affected because the deposit has already been added to its balance. The bank has no way of knowing that the deposit is coming until it receives it.

Deposits in transit Deposits that were made by customers of a bank but did not reach, or were not processed by, the bank before the preparation of the bank statement.

Outstanding Checks The first thing the accountant does when the bank statement is received is put the checks in numerical order (1, 2, 3, etc.). In doing so, the accountant notices that one payment was not made by the bank and check no. 15 was not returned by the bank.

Becca's books showed that this check had been deducted from the checkbook balance. The outstanding check, however, had not yet been presented to the bank for payment or deducted from the bank balance. When this check does reach the bank, the bank will reduce the amount of Becca's bank balance.

Service Charges Becca's accountant also notices a bank service charge of $5. Becca's book balance will be lowered by $5.

A journal entry is also needed to bring the ledger accounts of Cash and Service Charge expense up-to-date. Any adjustment to the checkbook balance results in a journal entry. The entry in Figure 6.9 was made to accomplish this step.

Apr.	30	Service Charge Expense		5 00	
		Cash			5 00
		Bank service charge for April			

Nonsufficient Funds While Becca's Bling Emporium did not experience either of the following two transactions, both may occur in the normal course of business. An NSF (non-sufficient funds) check is a check that has been returned because the drawer did not have enough money in its account to pay the check. Accountants are continually on the lookout for NSF checks. An NSF check means that there is less money in the checking account than was thought. Becca will have to (1) lower the checkbook balance and (2) try to collect the amount from the customer. The bank will notify Becca of an NSF check (or other deductions) by a debit memorandum. Think of a *debit* memorandum as a *deduction* from the account holder's balance.

If the bank acts as a collecting agent for Becca's Bling Emporium, say in collecting notes, it will charge Becca a small fee, and the net amount collected will be added to Becca's bank balance. The bank will send to Becca a credit memorandum verifying the increase in the depositor's balance.

It is important for Becca to prepare a bank reconciliation when she receives her bank statement every month as part of the cash control procedure. It verifies the amount of cash in her checking account. Another important reason to do a bank reconciliation is that it may uncover irregularities such as employee theft of funds.

Here are step-by-step instructions for preparing a bank reconciliation:

1. **Prepare a list of deposits in transit.** Compare the deposits listed on your bank statement with the bank deposits shown in your checkbook. On your bank reconciliation, list any deposits that have not yet cleared the bank statement. Also, take a look at the bank reconciliation you prepared last month. Did all of last month's deposits in transit clear on this month's bank statement? If not, you should find out what happened. Today, many customers are checking their bank balances online with their tablets or smartphones.

2. **Prepare a list of outstanding checks.** In your checkbook, mark each check that cleared the bank statement this month. On your bank reconciliation, list all the checks in your checkbook that did not clear. Also, take a look at the bank reconciliation you prepared last month. Did any checks outstanding from last month still not clear the bank? If so, be sure they are on your list of outstanding checks this month. If a check is several months old and still has not cleared the bank, you may want to investigate further.

3. **Record any bank charges or credits.** Take a close look at your bank statement. Are all special charges made by the bank recorded in your books? If not, journalize them now as if you had just written a check for that amount. By the same token, any credits made to your account by the bank should be journalized as well. Post the entries to your general ledger.

Outstanding checks Checks written by a company or person that were not received or not processed by the bank before the preparation of the bank statement.

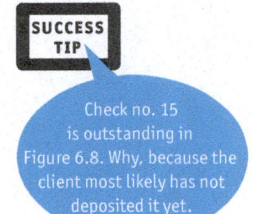

Check no. 15 is outstanding in Figure 6.8. Why, because the client most likely has not deposited it yet.

Figure 6.9
Service Charge Journalized

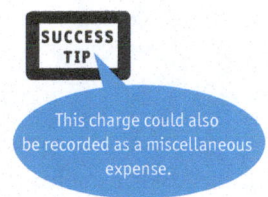

This charge could also be recorded as a miscellaneous expense.

NSF (non-sufficient funds) Notation indicating that a check has been written on an account that lacks sufficient funds to back it up.

Debit memorandum Decrease in depositor's balance.

Credit memorandum Increase in depositor's balance.

Adjustments to the checkbook balance must be journalized and posted. These steps keep the depositor's ledger accounts (especially Cash) up-to-date.

4. **Compute the cash balance per your books.**

5. **Enter the bank balance on the reconciliation.** At the top of the bank reconciliation statement, enter the ending balance from the bank statement.

6. **Total the deposits in transit.** Add up the deposits in transit and enter the total on the reconciliation. Add the total deposits in transit to the bank balance to arrive at a subtotal.

7. **Total the outstanding checks.** Add up the outstanding checks, and enter the total on the reconciliation.

8. **Compute the balance per the reconciliation.** Subtract the total outstanding checks (see Step 7) from the subtotal in Step 6. The result should equal the balance shown in your general ledger.

Before we look at a more comprehensive bank statement, let's look at trends in banking.

Trends in Banking

Have you ever heard of mobile remote deposit capture (RDC)? By 2015 it is projected that more than 40 million bank customers will take a picture of a check with their mobile device and transfer it to a financial institution for posting and clearing. Customers can download apps to check balances, pay bills, or make deposits.

Today, financial institutions have developed ways to transfer funds electronically, without the use of paper checks. Such systems are called electronic funds transfers (EFTs). Most EFTs are established to save money and avoid theft.

Electronic funds transfer (EFT) Electronic system that transfers funds without the use of paper checks.

Financial institutions use powerful computer networks to automate millions of daily transactions. Today, banks are able to use computer technology to give you the option of bypassing the time-consuming, paper-based aspects of traditional banking so that you can manage your finances more quickly and efficiently.

The first step toward online banking, automatic teller machines (ATMs), were first installed in banks about 40 years ago. For the first time, customers could make deposits, withdraw money, and obtain account balances without having to stand in line during the times that the bank was open. Today, customers are able to use an ATM in banks, supermarkets, malls, on college campuses, etc., or on their mobile device to complete banking transactions.

ATM (automatic teller machine) Machine that allows for depositing, withdrawal, and advanced banking transactions.

The latest development in banking is Internet or online banking. Most of the large banks offer fully secure, fully functional online banking for free or for a small fee. Some smaller banks offer limited access; for instance, you may be able to view your account balance and history but may not be able to initiate transactions online. As more banks are succeeding online and more customers are using their sites, fully functional online banking is becoming as common as ATMs.

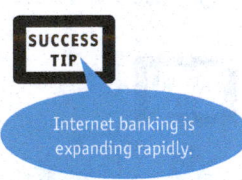

Internet banking is expanding rapidly.

With a debit card and personal identification number (PIN), you can use an ATM to withdraw cash, make deposits, or transfer funds between accounts. Some ATMs charge a fee if you are not a member of their ATM network or are making a transaction at a remote location.

Immediately call the card issuer when you suspect a debit card may be lost or stolen. Most companies have toll-free numbers and 24-hour service to deal with such emergencies. Although federal law limits your liability for a stolen credit card to $50, your liability for unauthorized use of your ATM or debit card can be much greater—depending on how quickly you report the loss. Also, it is important to remember that when you use a debit card, federal law does not give you the right to stop payment. You must resolve the problem with the seller.

If you don't mind foregoing the teller window and the lobby cookie, a virtual bank or e-bank, such as Virtual Bank or Giant Bank, may save you real money. Virtual banks are banks without bricks. They exist entirely online and offer much of the same range of services and adhere to the same regulations as your corner bank. Virtual banks pass the money that they save on overhead, such as buildings and tellers, along to you in the form of higher yields and lower fees. Banking is available everywhere, all the time.

Advantages of Online Banking Customers who use online banking services enjoy many advantages. They can do almost everything from the comfort of their own homes at convenient times and without standing in long lines.

- *Convenience:* Unlike your corner bank, online banks never close. They are available 24 hours a day, 7 days a week.
- *Availability:* If you are out of state or even out of the country when a money problem arises, you can log on instantly to your online bank and take care of business, 24/7.
- *Transaction speed:* Online bank sites generally execute and confirm transactions as quickly or even faster than ATM processing speeds.
- *Efficiency:* You can access and manage all of your bank accounts, including IRAs and CDs, from one secure site.
- *Effectiveness:* Many online banking sites now offer sophisticated tools to help you manage all of your assets more effectively. Most of these tools are compatible with money managing programs such as Quicken and Microsoft Money.

Disadvantages of Online Banking Although online banking has many advantages, it also has some disadvantages.

- *Start-up may take time:* In order to register for your bank's online program, you will probably have to provide some personal identification and sign a form at a branch bank.
- *Learning curve:* Banking sites can be difficult to navigate at first. Plan to invest time to read the tutorials in order to become comfortable in your virtual lobby.
- *Bank site changes:* Even the largest banks periodically upgrade their online programs, adding new features in unfamiliar places. In some cases, you may need to reenter account information.
- *Trust:* For many people, the biggest hurdle to online banking is learning to trust it. Did my transaction go through? Did I push the transfer button once or twice? Best bet: Always print the transaction receipt and keep it with your bank records until it shows up on your personal site or your bank statement.

Perhaps the biggest problem with online banking is security. It is important to keep passwords safe and to be aware of fake e-mails that may arrive in your inbox. These e-mails pretend to be from your bank and attempt to obtain log-in information from you. This kind of fraud is called phishing.

Fraudulent practices can happen at cash registers when you make a purchase or at restaurants when you pay with a credit card and the waiter is out of your sight. *Skimming* is the theft of credit card information used in an otherwise legitimate debit card or credit card transaction. Skimming at ATMs can be much more damaging because of the number of accounts and the amount of money that can be quickly accessed. Card-based purchases—online, debit, and credit—are convenient for consumers. For example, tens of thousands of ATMs are swipe-based. The large number of ATMs contributes to the skimming problem. In a way, we've become victims of the convenience we demand.

Here are some tips to help you avoid becoming a skimming victim.

- Keep your PIN safe. Don't give it to anyone.
- Watch out for people who try to "help" you at an ATM.
- Look at the ATM before using it. If it doesn't look right, don't use it.

Phishing Fake e-mails that attempt to obtain information about online banking customers.

- If an ATM has any unusual signage, don't use it. No bank would hang a sign that says, "Swipe your ATM here before inserting it in the card reader" or something to that effect.
- If your card is not returned after the transaction or after pressing cancel, immediately contact the institution that issued the card.
- Check your statement to be sure that no unusual withdrawals appear on it.

Check Truncation (Safekeeping) Some banks do not return cancelled checks to the depositor but instead use a procedure called check truncation or safekeeping. This practice is increasing rapidly. The bank holds a cancelled check for a specific period of time (usually 90 days) and then keeps a microfilm copy handy and destroys the original check. In Texas, for example, some credit unions and savings and loan institutions do not send back checks. Instead, the check date, number, and amount are listed on the bank statement. If the customer needs a copy of a check, the bank will provide the check or a photocopy for a small fee. (Photocopies are accepted as evidence in Internal Revenue Service tax returns and audits.)

Truncation cuts down on the amount of "paper" that is returned to customers and thus provides substantial cost savings. It is estimated that about 28 million checks are written each day in the United States.

Example of a More Comprehensive Bank Statement The bank reconciliation of Becca's Bling Emporium was not as complicated as it is for many companies, even using today's computer technology. Let's look at a reconciliation for Matty's Supermarket (Figures 6.10 and 6.11, on pages 210-211), which is based on the following business transactions:

Matty's checkbook balance		$13,176.84
Bank balance		23,726.04
Leased space to Subway		8,456.00
Leased space to Starbucks		3,616.12
Both lease payments are deposited by electronic transfer.		
Matty pays a health insurance payment each month by electronic transfer		1,444.00
Deposits in transit 6/30		6,766.52
Checks outstanding		
Ck #738	$1,144.00	
739	1,277.88	
740	332.00	
741	812.56	
742	1,834.12	
Check #734 was overstated by $1,440 in the company's books.		

Note that in Figure 6.11, each adjustment to Matty's checkbook in the reconciliation process would result in general journal entries in the company's accounting records.

Check truncation (safekeeping) Procedure whereby checks are not returned to the drawer with the bank statement but are instead kept at the bank for a certain amount of time before being first transferred to microfilm and then destroyed.

Figure 6.10
Bank Statement for Matty's
Supermarket

Ranger Bank
1 Left St.
Marblehead, MA 01945

ACCOUNT STATEMENT

Matty's Supermarket
20 Sullivan St.
Lynn, MA 01917

Checking Account: 775800061

Checking Account Summary as of 6/30/1X

Beginning Balance	Total Deposits	Total Withdrawals	Service Charge	Ending Balance
$26,224.48	$17,410.56	$19,852.00	$57.00	$23,726.04

Checking Account Transactions

Deposits	Date	Amount
Deposit	6/05	4,000.00
Deposit	6/05	448.00
Deposit	6/09	778.40
EFT leasing: Dunkin' Donuts	6/18	3,616.12
EFT leasing: Subway	6/27	8,456.00
Interest	6/30	112.04

Charges	Date	Amount
EFT: Blue Cross/Blue Shield	6/21	1,444.00
NSF	6/21	208.00
Service charge: Check printing	6/30	57.00

Checks

Number	Date	Amount
401	6/07	400.00
733	6/13	12,000.00
734	6/13	600.00
735	6/11	400.00
736	6/18	400.00
737	6/30	4,400.00

Daily Balance

Date	Balance	Date	Balance
5/31	26,224.48	6/18	21,267.00
6/05	30,672.48	6/21	19,615.00
6/07	30,272.48	6/27	28,071.00
6/09	31,050.88	6/30	23,726.04
6/11	30,650.88		
6/13	18,050.88		

Figure 6.11
Bank Reconciliation for Matty's
Supermarket

MATTY'S SUPERMARKET Bank Reconciliation as of June 30, 201X					
Checkbook balance			**Bank balance**		
Matty's checkbook balance		$13,176.84	Bank balance		$23,726.04
Add:			Add:		
EFT leasing: Dunkin' Donuts			Deposits in transit, 6/30		6,766.52
	$ 3,616.12				$30,492.56
EFT leasing: Subway					
	8,456.00				
Interest	112.04				
Error: Overstated					
check no. 734	1,440.00	13,624.16			
		$26,801.00			
Deduct:			Deduct:		
Service charge	$ 57.00		Outstanding checks:		
NSF check	208.00		No. 738	$1,144.00	
EFT health insurance			No. 739	1,277.88	
payment	1,444.00	1,709.00	No. 740	332.00	
			No. 741	812.56	
			No. 742	1,834.12	5,400.56
Reconciled balance		$25,092.00	Reconciled balance		$25,092.00

Now let's check your understanding with a Try It!

 **TRY IT!**   **Learning Unit 6-2**

From the following information, construct a bank reconciliation for R.T. Co. as of
July 31, 201X:

Checkbook balance	$3,235
Bank statement balance	2,200
Deposits (in transit)	900
Outstanding checks	35
Bank service charge	75
NSF check	95

(Jenny Bennett's check in payment of an account was returned for insufficient
funds.)

TRY IT!   **Solution Learning Unit 6-2**

R.T. Co. Bank Reconciliation as of July 31, 201X

Checkbook Balance		$3,235	Bank Balance		$2,200
Deduct:			Add:		
NSF Check	95		Deposits in Transit		900
Bank Service Charge	75	170			$3,100
			Deduct:		
			Outstanding Checks		35
Reconciled Balance		$3,065	Reconciled Balance		$3,065

The Establishment of Petty Cash and Change Funds

 L03

Becca realized how time-consuming and expensive it would be to write checks for small amounts to pay for postage, small supplies, and so forth, so she set up a petty cash fund. Similarly, she established a *change fund* to make cash transactions more convenient. This unit explains how to manage petty cash and change funds.

Petty cash fund Fund (source) that allows payment of small amounts without the writing of checks.

Setting Up the Petty Cash Fund

The petty cash fund is an account dedicated to paying small day-to-day expenses. These petty cash expenses are recorded in an auxiliary record and later summarized, journalized, and posted. Becca estimated that the company would need a fund of $60 to cover small expenditures during the month of May. This petty cash was not expected to last longer than 1 month. She gave one of her employees the responsibility for overseeing the fund, called a *custodian*.

Becca named her office manager, John Sullivan, as custodian. In other companies, the cashier or secretary may be in charge of petty cash. Check no. 6 was drawn to the order of the custodian and cashed to establish the fund. John keeps the petty cash fund in a small tin box in the office safe.

Shown here is the transaction analysis chart for the establishment of a $60 petty cash fund, which would be journalized on May 1, 201X, as shown in Figure 6.12.

SUCCESS TIP

Petty Cash is an asset on the balance sheet that is established by writing a new check. The Petty Cash account is debited only once unless a greater or lesser amount of petty cash is needed on a regular basis.

Accounts Affected	Category	↓↑	Rules
Petty Cash	Asset	↑	Dr.
Cash (checks)	Asset	↓	Cr.

Note that the new asset called Petty Cash, which was created by writing check no. 6, reduced the asset Cash. In reality, the total assets stay the same; what has occurred is a shift from the asset Cash (check no. 6) to a new asset account called Petty Cash.

	GENERAL JOURNAL				Page 1
Date	Account Title and Description	PR	Dr.	Cr.	
201X May 1	Petty Cash		60 00		
	Cash			60 00	
	Establishment of petty cash.				

Figure 6.12
Establishing Petty Cash

The Petty Cash account is not debited or credited again if the size of the fund is not changed. If the $60 fund is used up quickly, the fund should be increased. If the fund is too large, the Petty Cash account should be reduced. We take a closer look at this issue when we discuss the replenishment of petty cash.

Making Payments from the Petty Cash Fund

John Sullivan has the responsibility for filling out a petty cash voucher for each cash payment made from the petty cash fund. The petty cash vouchers are numbered in sequence.

Note that when the voucher (shown in Figure 6.13, page 213) is completed, it will include:

Petty cash voucher Petty cash form to be completed when money is taken out of petty cash.

- The voucher number (which will be in sequence)
- The date
- The person or organization to whom the payment was made
- The amount of payment
- The reason for payment (in this case, cleaning)
- The signature of the person who approved the payment
- The signature of the person who received the payment from petty cash
- The account to which the expense will be charged

Figure 6.13
Petty Cash Voucher

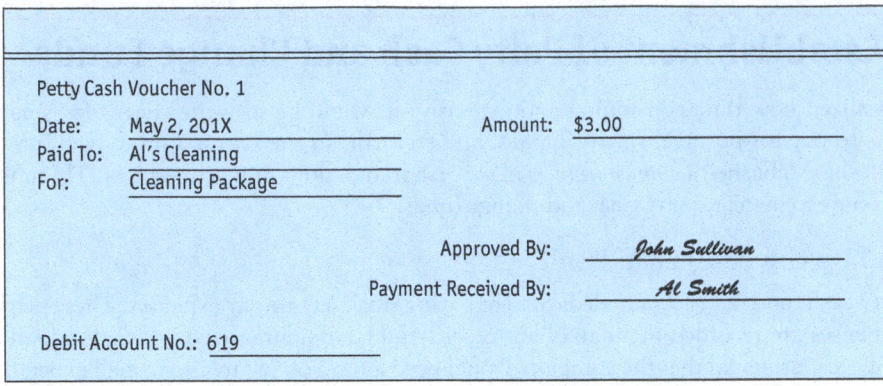

Petty Cash Voucher No. 1

Date: May 2, 201X   Amount: $3.00
Paid To: Al's Cleaning
For: Cleaning Package

Approved By: _John Sullivan_

Payment Received By: _Al Smith_

Debit Account No.: 619

SUCCESS TIP

The check for $60 is usually drawn to the order of the custodian and is cashed, and the proceeds are turned over to John Sullivan, the custodian.

The completed vouchers are placed in the petty cash box. No matter how many vouchers John Sullivan fills out, the total of the vouchers in the box and the cash on hand should equal the original amount of petty cash with which the fund was established ($60).

Assume that at the end of May the following items are documented by petty cash vouchers in the petty cash box as having been paid by John Sullivan:

201X May	2	Cleaning package,	$ 3.00
	5	Postage stamps,	$ 9.00
	8	First-aid supplies,	$15.00
	9	Delivery expense,	$ 6.00
	14	Delivery expense,	$15.00
	27	Postage stamps,	$ 6.00

Auxiliary petty cash record Supplementary record for summarizing petty cash information.

John records this information in the auxiliary petty cash record shown in Figure 6.14. It is not a required record but it is an aid to John. In other words, it is an auxiliary record that is not essential but that is quite helpful as part of the petty cash system. You may want to think of the auxiliary petty cash record as an optional worksheet. Let's look at how to replenish the petty cash fund.

Figure 6.14 Auxiliary Petty Cash Record

| | | | | | | Category of Payments | | | |
| | | | | | | | | Sundry | |
Date	Voucher No.	Description	Receipts	Payments	Postage Expense	Delivery Expense	Account	Amount	
201X May	1	Establishment	60 00						
2	1	Cleaning		3 00			Cleaning	3 00	
5	2	Postage		9 00	9 00				
8	3	First Aid		15 00			Misc.	15 00	
9	4	Delivery		6 00		6 00			
14	5	Delivery		15 00		15 00			
27	6	Postage		6 00	6 00				
		Total	60 00	54 00	15 00	21 00		18 00	

AUXILIARY PETTY CASH RECORD

How to Replenish the Petty Cash Fund

No postings are done from the auxiliary record because it is not a journal. At some point the summarized information found in the auxiliary petty cash record is used as a basis for a journal entry in the general journal and eventually posted to appropriate ledger accounts to reflect up-to-date balances.

The $54 of expenses (see Figure 6.14) is recorded in the general journal (Figure 6.15) and a new check, no. 17, for $54 is cashed and returned to John Sullivan. In replenishment, old expenses are updated in the journal and ledger to show where money has gone. The petty cash box now once again reflects $60 cash. The old vouchers that were used are stamped to indicate that they have been processed and the fund replenished.

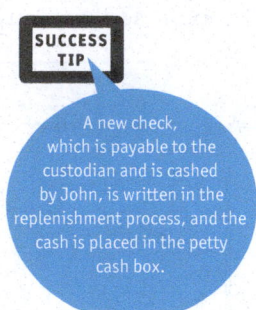

SUCCESS TIP

A new check, which is payable to the custodian and is cashed by John, is written in the replenishment process, and the cash is placed in the petty cash box.

Figure 6.15 Establishment and Replenishment of Petty Cash Fund

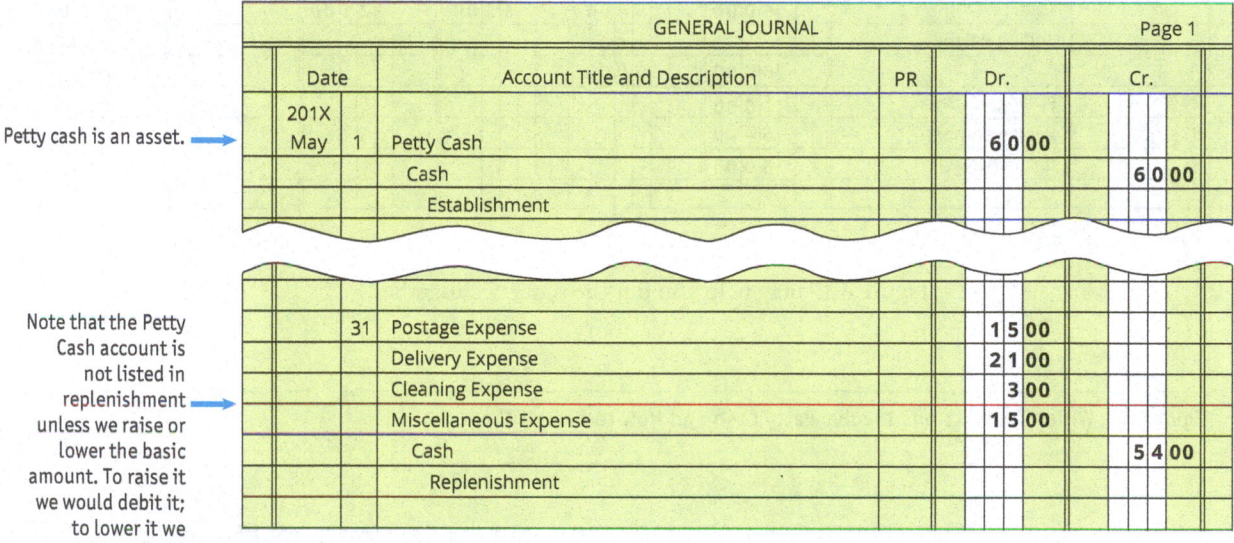

	Date		Account Title and Description	PR	Dr.	Cr.
	201X					
	May	1	Petty Cash		60 00	
			Cash			60 00
			Establishment			
		31	Postage Expense		15 00	
			Delivery Expense		21 00	
			Cleaning Expense		3 00	
			Miscellaneous Expense		15 00	
			Cash			54 00
			Replenishment			

GENERAL JOURNAL — Page 1

Petty cash is an asset. ➡️

Note that the Petty Cash account is not listed in replenishment ➡️ unless we raise or lower the basic amount. To raise it we would debit it; to lower it we would credit it.

Note that in the replenishment process the debits are a summary of the totals (except sundry because individual items are different) of expenses or other items from the auxiliary petty cash record. Posting these specific expenses will ensure that the expenses will not be understated on the income statement. The credit to Cash allows us to draw a check for $54 to put money back in the petty cash box. The $60 in the box now agrees with the Petty Cash account balance. The end result is that our petty cash box is filled, and we have justified for which accounts the petty cash money was spent. Think of replenishment as a single, summarizing entry.

Remember that if at some point the petty cash fund is to be greater than $60, a check can be written that will increase Petty Cash and decrease Cash. If the Petty Cash account balance is to be reduced, we can credit or reduce Petty Cash. For our present purpose, however, Petty Cash will remain at $60.

The auxiliary petty cash record after replenishment would look as shown in Figure 6.16 on page 216 (keep in mind that no postings are made from the auxiliary).

Figure 6.16 Auxiliary Petty Cash Record with Replenishment

						Category of Payments			
								Sundry	
Date	Voucher No.	Description	Receipts	Payments	Postage Expense	Delivery Expense	Account	Amount
201X May 1		Establishment	60 00					
2	1	Cleaning		3 00			Cleaning	3 00
5	2	Postage		9 00	9 00			
8	3	First Aid		15 00			Misc.	15 00
9	4	Delivery		6 00		6 00		
14	5	Delivery		15 00		15 00		
27	6	Postage		6 00	6 00			
		Total	60 00	54 00	15 00	21 00		18 00
		Ending Balance		6 00				
			60 00	60 00				
		Ending Balance	6 00					
31		Replenishment	54 00					
31		Balance (New)	60 00					

Figure 6.17 may help you put the sequence together.

Figure 6.17 Which Transactions Involve Petty Cash and How to Record Them

Date	Description	New Check Written	Petty Cash Voucher Prepared	Recorded in Auxiliary Petty Cash Record	
201X May 1	Establishment of petty cash for $60	X		X	Dr. Petty Cash Cr. Cash
2	Paid salaries, $2,000	X			
10	Paid $10 from petty cash for Band-Aids		X	X	No journal entries
19	Paid $8 from petty cash for postage		X	X	
24	Paid light bill, $200	X			
29	Replenishment of petty cash to $60	X		X	Dr. individual expenses Cr. Cash

Has nothing to do with petty cash (amounts too great)

In this step the old expenses are listed in the general journal and a new check is written to replenish. All old vouchers are removed from the petty cash box.

Before concluding this unit, let's look at how Becca will handle setting up a change fund and problems with cash shortages and overages.

Setting Up a Change Fund

If a company such as Becca's Bling Emporium expects to have many cash transactions occurring, it may be a good idea to establish a change fund. This fund is placed in the cash register drawer and used to make change for customers who pay cash. Becca decides to put $120 in the change fund, made up of various denominations of bills and coins. Let's look at a transaction analysis chart and the journal entry (Figure 6.18) for this sort of transaction.

Change fund Fund made up of various denominations that are used to make change for customers.

Accounts Affected	Category	↓↑	Rules
Change Fund	Asset	↑	Dr.
Cash	Asset	↓	Cr.

Apr.	1	Change Fund		1 2 0 00	
		Cash			1 2 0 00
		Establish change fund			

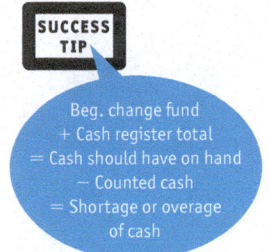

Beg. change fund
+ Cash register total
= Cash should have on hand
− Counted cash
= Shortage or overage of cash

Figure 6.18
Change Fund Established

At the close of the business day, Becca will place the amount of the change fund back in the safe in the office. She will prepare the change fund (the same $120) in the appropriate denominations for the next business day. She will deposit in the bank the *remainder* of the cash taken in for the day.

In the next section, we look at how to record errors that are made in making change, called cash short and over.

Cash Short and Over

Cash Short and Over Account that records cash shortages and overages. If the ending balance is a debit, it is recorded on the income statement as a miscellaneous expense; if it is a credit, it is recorded as miscellaneous income.

In a local pizza shop the total cash sales for the day did not match the amount of cash on hand. Errors often happen in making change. To record and summarize the differences in cash, an account called *Cash Short and Over* is used. This account records both overages (too much money) and shortages (not enough money). Let's first look at the account (in T account form).

Cash Short and Over

Dr.	Cr.
shortage	overage

All shortages will be recorded as debits and all overages will be recorded as credits. This account is temporary. If the ending balance of the account is a debit (a shortage), it is considered a miscellaneous expense that would be reported on the income statement. If the balance of the account is a credit (an overage), it is considered as miscellaneous income reported on the income statement. Let's look at how the Cash Short and Over account could be used to record shortages or overages in sales as well as in the petty cash process.

Example 1: Shortages and Overages in Sales On December 5 a pizza shop rang up cash sales of $560 for the day but only had $530 in cash.

Accounts Affected	Category	↓↑	Rules
Cash	Asset	↑	Debit $530
Cash Short and Over	Misc. Exp.	↑	Debit $ 30
Sales	Revenue	↑	Credit $560

The journal entry would be as shown in Figure 6.19.

Figure 6.19
Cash Shortage

Dec.	5	Cash		5 3 0 00		
		Cash Short and Over		3 0 00		
		Sales			5 6 0 00	
		Cash shortage				

Note that the shortage of $30 is a debit and would be recorded on the income statement as a miscellaneous expense.

What would the entry look like if the pizza shop showed a $50 overage (i.e., if the cash at the end of the day was $610)?

Accounts Affected	Category	↓↑	Rules
Cash	Asset	↑	Debit $610
Cash Short and Over	Miscellaneous Income	↑	Credit $50
Sales	Revenue	↑	Credit $560

The journal entry would be as shown in Figure 6.20.

Figure 6.20
Cash Overage

Dec.	5	Cash		6 1 0 00		
		Cash Short and Over			5 0 00	
		Sales			5 6 0 00	
		Cash overage				

Note that the Cash Short and Over account would be reported as miscellaneous income on the income statement. Now let's look at how to use this Cash Short and Over account to record petty cash transactions.

Example 2: Cash Short and Over in Petty Cash A local computer company established petty cash for $200. On November 30, the petty cash box had $160 in vouchers as well as $32 in coin and currency. What would be the journal entry to replenish petty cash? Assume the vouchers were made up of $90 for postage and $70 for supplies expense.

If you add up the vouchers and cash in the box, cash is short by $8.

SUCCESS TIP

The account Petty Cash is not used since the level in petty cash is not raised or lowered.

Accounts Affected	Category	↓↑	Rules
Postage Expense	Expense	↑	Debit $ 90
Supplies Expense	Expense	↑	Debit $ 70
Cash Short and Over	Misc. Expense	↑	Debit $ 8
Cash	Asset	↓	Credit $168

The journal entry is shown in Figure 6.21.

Figure 6.21
Petty Cash Replenished with Shortage

Nov.	30	Postage Expense		9 0 00		
		Supplies Expense		7 0 00		
		Cash Short and Over		8 00		
		Cash			1 6 8 00	

In the case of an overage, the Cash Short and Over would be a credit as miscellaneous income.

Now it's time to check your progress.

TRY IT! Learning Unit 6-3

Prepare a general journal entry to establish, replenish, and raise the petty cash level from the following:

On September 1, 201X, a $300 Petty Cash Fund was established. At the end of the month, Petty Cash had a balance of $131 plus the following paid vouchers:

Donations Expense $32; Postage Expense $46; Office Supplies Expense $36; and Miscellaneous Expenses $55

On September 30 replenishment of Petty Cash was complete.

On October 2 it was decided that the Petty Cash level was too low, and thus it was raised to a new level of $330.

TRY IT! Solution Learning Unit 6-3

Date		Account Title	Dr.	Cr.
201X				
September	1	Petty Cash	300	
		Cash		300
		Established Petty Cash		
	30	Donations Expense	32	
		Postage Expense	46	
		Office Supplies Expense	36	
		Miscellaneous Expense	55	
		Cash		169
		Replenished Petty Cash		
October	2	Petty Cash	30	
		Cash		30
		Increased Petty Cash Level		

DEMONSTRATION SUMMARY PROBLEM

Janet Fong, the bookkeeper for Lee Co., received the bank statement for March 31, 201X, from Ryan Federal Bank. She noted the following:

Bank Balance $1,525.60

Checkbook Balance 1,599.60

Checks not clearing bank:

No. 160 $261.10

No. 169 133.60

No. 171 205.80

Janet made a deposit of $1,640.30 that did not show up on the bank statement. A mortgage payment paid by the bank was $1,234.60. An IRS refund check was mailed directly to the bank for $2,200.40.

Also, Janet received a memo indicating the following transactions regarding Petty Cash that needed to be journalized:

201X		
March	1	Petty Cash established for $400.
	12	Needed to replenish Petty Cash; Petty Cash had a balance of $50 with vouchers for donations of $60, vouchers for Supplies Expense for $70, and Miscellaneous Expenses for $220.

On March 18 the Petty Cash level was raised to $500.

Requirements

Please do the following:

1. Prepare a bank reconciliation for Janet.
2. Prepare three journal entries to record Petty Cash transactions.

Solutions

Requirement 1

Prepare a bank reconciliation for Janet.

Tips for Preparing a Bank Reconciliation

IRS Refund Check to bank—add to checkbook

Automatic Mortgage Withdrawal—subtract from checkbook

Deposits in Transit—add to bank balance

Outstanding Checks—subtract from bank balance

Lee Co. Bank Reconciliation as of March 31, 201X				
Checkbook Bal.	$1,599.60	Bank Bal.		$1,525.60
Add:		Add:		
IRS Refund Check	2,200.40	Dep. in Transit		1,640.30
	$3,800.00			$3,165.90
Deduct:		Deduct:		
Mortg. Withdrawals	1,234.60	Outstanding checks:		
		No. 160	$261.10	
		No. 169	133.60	
		No. 171	205.80	600.50
Reconciled Balance	$2,565.40	Reconciled Balance		$2,565.40

Requirement 2

Prepare three journal entries to record Petty Cash transactions.

Date		Account Title	Dr.	Cr.
201X				
March	1	Petty Cash	400	
		Cash		400
	12	Donation Expense	60	
		Supplies Expense	70	
		Miscellaneous Expense	220	
		Cash		350
	18	Petty Cash	100	
		Cash		100

Tips for Journaling Petty Cash Transactions

Petty Cash is an asset. It is only debited to establish it or raise or lower its level. Note in Replenishment all old expenses are shown, and a new check is written to bring Petty Cash back to its original level ($400).

When Petty Cash is increased to a new level of $500, $100 is added to the Petty Cash account and a check is cashed for that amount.

SUCCESS COACH

The following Success Tips are from Learning Units 6-1 through 6-3. Take the Do It Right Now Checkup and use the Check Your Score at the bottom of the page to see how you are doing. The Success Coach provides tips before each Checkup to help you avoid common accounting errors.

LU 6-1 Banking Procedures and Checking Accounts

Do It Right Tips: With mobile banking today checks can be processed or deposited via your mobile device. Banks will vary on policies about deposit requirements and minimum balances required to receive free checking or interest. It is still important to know the manual structure of checks, deposits, and endorsements as they still are tools used in mobile banking.

Do It Right Now Checkup: Answer true or false to the following statements.

1. A credit memo from the bank means that it is decreasing your balance.
2. Restrictive endorsements are not very safe.
3. Blank endorsements are the safest type of endorsement.
4. The drawer is the one receiving a check.
5. The drawee is the bank at which the drawer has an account.

LU 6-2 The Bank Reconciliation Process

Do It Right Tips: When reconciling a bank statement, timing is a key consideration. Deposits in transit would be added to the bank balance while checks outstanding would be subtracted. Sometimes on the bank statement, interest is shown and must be updated on the checkbook side. If you forget to record a withdrawal from an ATM, you must update your book balance. Keep in mind that any adjustments to the checkbook will require journal entries so the cash ledger account will be correct. Today, online banking is taking over many of the manual tasks, but the accounting theory remains the same.

Do It Right Now Checkup: Answer true or false to the following statements.

1. All reconciliations must be done on paper and not on computers.
2. Automatic payment of a mortgage by a bank will increase the checkbook balance.
3. A note collected by a bank will lower the checkbook balance.
4. An IRS refund collected by the bank will decrease your checkbook balance.
5. Reconciliations can only be done once a year.

LU 6-3 The Establishment of Petty Cash and Change Funds

Do It Right Tips: Petty cash is an asset. When petty cash is replenished to the same level, all of the old expenses are shown and a new check is written. The account Petty Cash is not touched. When a new level of petty cash is desired, the account Petty Cash will be debited to increase it or credited to decrease it. Keep in mind that the account Cash Short and Over is a miscellaneous account found on the income statement. A debit balance on Cash Short and Over means that you have a shortage, and a credit balance means you have an overage.

Do It Right Now Checkup: Answer true or false to the following statements.

1. Petty cash is an expense.
2. Increasing the Petty Cash account means that you have to credit it.
3. In the replenishment process, cash is not involved.
4. When petty cash is established, the Petty Cash account is debited.
5. A shortage in the Cash Short and Over account results in a credit balance.

CHECK YOUR SCORE: Answers to the Do It Right Now Checkup

LU 6-1

1. False—A credit memo from the bank means that it is increasing your balance.
2. False—Restrictive endorsements are the safest type of endorsement.
3. False—Restrictive endorsements are the safest type of endorsement.
4. False—The payee is to whom a check is payable.
5. True

LU 6-2

1. False—Many reconciliations today are done by computer.
2. False—Automatic payment of a mortgage will decrease the checkbook balance.
3. False—A note will increase the checkbook balance.
4. False—An IRS refund will increase the checkbook balance.
5. False—Reconciliations are usually done monthly.

LU 6-3

1. False—Petty cash is an asset.
2. False—Increasing the Petty Cash account means that you have to debit it.
3. False—In the replenishment process, a new check (cash) needs to be written.
4. True
5. False—A shortage in the Cash Short and Over account results in a debit balance.

BLUEPRINT: A BANK RECONCILIATION

Checkbook Balance	Bank Balance
+/− EFT (electronic funds transfer)	+ Deposits in transit
+ Interest earned	− Outstanding checks
+ Notes collected	± Bank errors
+ Direct deposits	
− ATM withdrawals	
− Check redeposits	
− NSF check	
− Online fees	
− Automatic withdrawals	
− Overdrafts	
− Service charges	
− Stop payments	
± Book errors*	
+ Credit Memo—adds to balance	
− Debit Memo—deducts from balance	

*If a $60 check is recorded as $50, we must decrease the checkbook balance by $10.

Discussion Questions and Critical Thinking/Ethical Case

1. Discuss how mobile device apps are making banking more accessible.

2. What is the advantage of having preprinted deposit slips?

3. Explain the difference between a blank endorsement and a restrictive endorsement.

4. Explain the difference between payee, drawer, and drawee.

5. Why should check stubs be filled out first, before the check itself is written?

6. A bank statement is sent twice a month. True or false? Please explain.

7. Explain the end product of a bank reconciliation.

8. Why are outstanding checks subtracted from the bank balance?

9. An NSF check results in a bank issuing the depositor a credit memorandum. Agree or disagree? Please explain your response.

10. Why do adjustments to the checkbook balance in the reconciliation process need to be journalized?

11. What is EFT?

12. What are the major advantages and disadvantages of online banking?

13. What is meant by check truncation or safekeeping?

14. Petty cash is a liability. Agree or disagree? Explain.

15. Explain the relationship of the auxiliary petty cash record to the recording of the cash payment.

16. At the time of replenishment, why are the totals of individual expenses debited?

17. Explain the purpose of a change fund.

18. Explain how Cash Short and Over can be a miscellaneous expense.

19. Sean Nah, the bookkeeper for Revell Co., received a bank statement from Lone Bank. Sean noticed a $250 mistake made by the bank in the company's favor. Sean called his supervisor, who said that as long as it benefits the company, he should not tell the bank about the error. You make the call. Write your specific recommendations to Sean.

Concept Checks

MyLabAccounting

Bank Reconciliation

◀ **L02** *(10 min)*

1. Indicate what effect (#1–4) each situation (#a–f) will have on the bank reconciliation process.

   1. Add to bank balance.

   2. Deduct from bank balance.

   3. Add to checkbook balance.

   4. Deduct from checkbook balance.

   _____ a. Check no. 140 was outstanding for $200.

   _____ b. $300 deposit in transit.

   _____ c. $190 NSF check.

   _____ d. A check written for $15 was recorded in the company's books as $25.

   _____ e. Bank collected a $1,000 note less a $50 collection fee.

   _____ f. $12 bank service charge.

(5 min) **LO2**   **Journal Entries in Reconciliation Process**

2.   Which of the transactions in Exercise 1 would require a journal entry?

(10 min) **LO2**   **Bank Reconciliation**

3.   From the following, construct a bank reconciliation for Dab Co. as of September 30, 201X.

Checkbook balance	$1,900.60
Bank statement balance	1,938.20
Deposits in transit	283.70
Outstanding checks	394.10
Bank service charge	13.90
NSF check	58.90

(10 min) **LO3**   **Petty Cash**

4.   Indicate what effects (#1–4) each situation (#a–f) will have. (*Note:* There might be more than one effect applicable for a situation.)

  1.   New check written.
  2.   Recorded in general journal.
  3.   Petty cash voucher prepared.
  4.   Recorded in auxiliary petty cash record.

  _____ a. Established petty cash.

  _____ b. Paid $1,400 bill.

  _____ c. Paid $3 for Band-Aids from petty cash.

  _____ d. Paid $4 for stamps from petty cash.

  _____ e. Paid electric bill, $270.

  _____ f. Replenished petty cash.

(15 min) **LO3**   **Replenishment of Petty Cash**

5.   Petty cash was originally established for $21.00. During the month, $4.70 was paid out for pencils and $5.70 for straws. During replenishment, the custodian discovered that the balance in petty cash was $7.70. Record, using a general journal entry, the replenishment of petty cash back to $21.00.

(10 min) **LO3**   **Increasing Petty Cash**

6.   In Exercise 5, if the custodian decided to raise the level of petty cash to $29.75, what would be the journal entry to replenish? (Use a general journal entry.)

MyLab**Accounting**   ## Exercises

Set A

(15 min) **LO2**   **6A-1.**   From the following information, construct a bank reconciliation for Boom Co. as of February 28, 201X. Then prepare journal entries if needed.

Checkbook balance	$1,493	Outstanding checks	$738
Bank statement balance	1,450	Bank service charge	60
Deposits (in transit)	700	NSF: Elizabeth Klecan's check in payment of account was returned for insufficient funds	21

6A-2. In general journal form, prepare journal entries to establish a petty cash fund on October 1 and replenish it on October 31.

LO3 *(15 min)*

201X		
October	1	A $101 petty cash fund is established.
	31	At the end of the month, $14 cash plus the following paid vouchers exist: donations expense, $15; postage expense, $18; office supplies expense, $30; miscellaneous expense, $24.

6A-3. If in Exercise 6A-2 cash on hand is $12, prepare the entry to replenish the petty cash on October 31.

LO3 *(15 min)*

6A-4. If in Exercise 6A-2 cash on hand is $19, prepare the entry to replenish the petty cash on October 31.

LO3 *(15 min)*

6A-5. At the end of the day the clerk for Aaron's Variety Shop noticed an error in the amount of cash he should have. Total cash sales from the sales tape were $1,206, whereas the total cash in the register was $1,158. Ken keeps a $24 change fund in his shop. Prepare an appropriate general journal entry to record the cash sales as well as reveal the cash shortage.

LO3 *(15 min)*

Set B

6B-1. From the following information, construct a bank reconciliation for Blast Co. as of February 28, 201X. Then prepare journal entries if needed.

LO2 *(15 min)*

Checkbook balance	$1,971	Outstanding checks	$642
Bank statement balance	1,500	Bank service charge	55
Deposits (in transit)	1,000	NSF: Elizabeth Klecan's check in payment of account was returned for insufficient funds	58

6B-2. In general journal form, prepare journal entries to establish a petty cash fund on December 1 and replenish it on December 31.

LO3 *(15 min)*

201X		
December	1	A $108 petty cash fund is established.
	31	At the end of the month, $35 cash plus the following paid vouchers exist: donations expense, $15; postage expense, $13; office supplies expense, $26; miscellaneous expense, $19.

6B-3. If in Exercise 6B-2 cash on hand is $20, prepare the entry to replenish the petty cash on December 31.

LO3 *(15 min)*

6B-4. If in Exercise 6B-2 cash on hand is $45, prepare the entry to replenish the petty cash on December 31.

LO3 *(15 min)*

6B-5. At the end of the day the clerk for Wale's Variety Shop noticed an error in the amount of cash he should have. Total cash sales from the sales tape were $1,204, whereas the total cash in the register was $1,154. Wale keeps a $26 change fund in his shop. Prepare an appropriate general journal entry to record the cash sales as well as reveal the cash shortage.

LO3 *(15 min)*

Problems

Set A

6A-1. Canvas.com received a bank statement from Buttermilk Bank indicating a bank balance of $7,600. Based on Canvas.com's check stubs, the ending checkbook balance was $8,231. Your task is to prepare a bank reconciliation for

LO2 *(20 min)*

Canvas.com as of July 31, 201X, from the following information (journalize entries as needed):

a. Checks outstanding: no. 122, $810; no. 130, $720.

b. Deposits in transit, $1,800.

c. Canvas.com forgot to record a $1,240 equipment purchase made with a debit card.

d. Bank service charges, $60.

e. Buttermilk Bank collected a note for Canvas.com, $950, less an $11 collection fee.

Check Figure:
Reconciled Balance $7,870

(20 min) **L02**

Check Figure:
Reconciled Balance $5,630

6A-2. From the following bank statement, please (1) complete the bank reconciliation for Tony's Deli found on the reverse of the following bank statement and (2) journalize the appropriate entries as needed.

a. A deposit of $2,000 is in transit.

b. Tony's Deli has an ending checkbook balance of $5,760.

c. Checks outstanding: no. 111, $950; no. 119, $1,250; no. 121, $330.

d. Bob Ryan's check for $100 bounced due to lack of sufficient funds.

e. Bank service charge $30.

Millbury National Bank
Rio Mean Branch
Bugna, Texas
Tony's Deli
8811 2nd St.
Bugna, Texas

Old Balance	Checks and Other Withdrawals in Order of Payment		Deposits	Date	New Balance
6,500				2/2	6,500
	90.00	200.00		2/3	6,210
	160.00		240.00	2/10	6,290
	530.00		570.00	2/15	6,330
	100.00	NSF	350.00	2/20	6,580
	1,100.00		1,210.00	2/24	6,690
	660.00	30.00 SC	160.00	2/28	6,160

(30 min) **L03**

Check Figure:
Cash Replenishment $86

6A-3. The following transactions occurred in April for Jubilant Co.:

201X Apr.		
	1	Issued check no. 14 for $140 to establish a petty cash fund.
	5	Paid $19 from petty cash for postage, voucher no. 1.
	8	Paid $17 from petty cash for office supplies, voucher no. 2.
	15	Issued check no. 15 to Reliable Corp. for $150 from past purchases on account.
	17	Paid $16 from petty cash for office supplies, voucher no. 3.
	20	Issued check no. 16 to Rabbit Corp., $700 for past purchases on account.
	24	Paid $19 from petty cash for postage, voucher no. 4.
	26	Paid $15 from petty cash for local church donation, voucher no. 5 (a miscellaneous payment).
	28	Issued check no. 17 to Jay Moon to pay for office equipment, $800.
	30	Replenished petty cash, check no. 18. Assume no shortage or overage.

Your tasks are to do the following:

a. Record the appropriate entries in the general journal as well as the auxiliary petty cash record as needed.

b. Replenish the petty cash fund on April 30 (check no. 18).

6A-4. From the following, record the transactions in Burbank's auxiliary petty cash record and general journal as needed:

L03 *(40 min)*

201X			
Oct.	1	A check was drawn (no. 444) payable to Matt Couch, petty cashier, to establish a $220 petty cash fund.	
	5	Paid $29 for postage stamps, voucher no. 1.	
	9	Paid $16 for delivery charges on goods for resale, voucher no. 2.	
	12	Paid $10 for donation to a church (miscellaneous expense), voucher no. 3.	
	14	Paid $13 for postage stamps, voucher no. 4.	
	17	Paid $23 for delivery charges on goods for resale, voucher no. 5.	
	27	Purchased computer supplies from petty cash for $21, voucher no. 6.	
	28	Paid $12 for postage, voucher no. 7.	
	29	Drew check no. 611 to replenish petty cash and a $10 shortage.	

Check Figure:
Cash Replenishment $134

Set B

6B-1. Slacks.com received a bank statement from Cobb Bank indicating a bank balance of $7,700. Based on Slacks.com's check stubs, the ending checkbook balance was $8,136. Your task is to prepare a bank reconciliation for Slacks.com as of July 31, 201X, from the following information (journalize as needed):

L02 *(20 min)*

a. Checks outstanding: no. 122, $760; no. 130, $670.

b. Deposits in transit, $1,700.

c. Slacks.com forgot to record a $1,210 equipment purchase made with a debit card.

d. Bank service charges, $40.

e. Cobb Bank collected a note for Slacks.com, $1,090, less a $6 collection fee.

Check Figure:
Reconciled Balance $7,970

6B-2. From the following statement, please (1) complete the bank reconciliation for Roger's Deli found on the reverse of the following bank statement and (2) journalize the appropriate entries as needed.

L02 *(20 min)*

S50 / **QB**

a. A deposit of $1,900 is in transit.

b. Roger's Deli has an ending checkbook balance of $6,000.

c. Checks outstanding: no. 111, $850; no. 119, $1,200; no. 121, $310.

d. Carl Bennett's check for $1,300 bounced due to lack of sufficient funds.

e. Bank service charges, $55.

Check Figure:
Reconciled Balance $4,645

Nantucket National Bank
Rio Mean Branch
Bugna, Texas
Roger's Deli
8811 2nd St.
Bugna, Texas

Old Balance	Checks and Other Withdrawals in Order of Payment		Deposits	Date	New Balance
6,400				2/2	6,400
	70.00	180.00		2/3	6,150
	200.00		250.00	2/10	6,200
	620.00		640.00	2/15	6,220
	1,300.00	NSF	330.00	2/20	5,250
	1,050.00		1,260.00	2/24	5,460
	540.00	55.00 SC	240.00	2/28	5,105

(30 min) **L03**

S50 / **QB**

Check Figure:
Cash Replenishment $82

6B-3.   The following transactions occurred in April for Pleasant Co.:

201X			
Apr.	1	Issued check no. 14 for $130 to establish a petty cash fund.
	5	Paid $16 from petty cash for postage, voucher no. 1.
	8	Paid $17 from petty cash for office supplies, voucher no. 2.
	15	Issued check no. 15 to Deceptive Corp. for $140 for past purchases on account.
	17	Paid $22 from petty cash for office supplies, voucher no. 3.
	20	Issued check no. 16 to Danish Corp. for $750 for past purchases on account.
	24	Paid $20 from petty cash for postage, voucher no. 4.
	26	Paid $7 from petty cash for local church donation, voucher no. 5 (a miscellaneous payment).
	28	Issued check no. 17 to Jim Ploon to pay for office equipment, $700.
	30	Replenished petty cash, check no. 18. Assume no shortage or overage.

Your tasks are to do the following:

a.   Record the appropriate entries in the general journal as well as the auxiliary petty cash record as needed.

b.   Replenish the petty cash fund on April 30 (check no. 18).

(40 min) **L03**

6B-4.   From the following, record the transactions in O'Hare's auxiliary petty cash record and general journal as needed:

Check Figure:
Cash Replenishment $112

201X		
Oct.	1	A check was drawn (no. 444) payable to Cylinda Scruggs, petty cashier, to establish a $130 petty cash fund.
	5	Paid $21 for postage stamps, voucher no. 1.
	9	Paid $10 for delivery charges on goods for resale, voucher no. 2.
	12	Paid $15 for donation to a church (miscellaneous expense), voucher no. 3.
	14	Paid $10 for postage stamps, voucher no. 4.
	17	Paid $16 for delivery charges on goods for resale, voucher no. 5.
	27	Purchased computer supplies from petty cash for $11, voucher no. 6.
	28	Paid $22 for postage, voucher no. 7.
	29	Drew check no. 611 to replenish petty cash and a $7 shortage.

Financial Report Problem

Reading Amazon's Annual Report

LO2 *(15 min)*

Go to https://tinyurl.com/slaterca14e to access Amazon's 2016 Annual Report on pages 43–45. How much did Amazon spend in 2014–2015 and 2016 for Internet-use software and website development?

KEEPING IT REAL SUAREZ COMPUTER CENTER

MyLabAccounting

LO2, 3 *(60 min)*

The books have been closed for the first year of business for Suarez Computer Center. The company ended up with a marginal profit for the first 3 months in operation. Troy expects faster growth as he enters a busy season.

Following is a list of transactions for the month of October. Petty Cash account #1010 and Miscellaneous Expense account #5100 have been added to the chart of accounts.

Oct.	1	Paid rent for November, December, and January, $1,500 (check no. 8108).
	2	Established a petty cash fund for $300.
	4	Collected $4,600 from a cash customer for building five systems.
	5	Collected $2,700, the amount due from Dr. Michael Turiono's invoice no. 12674, customer on account.
	6	Purchased $40 worth of stamps using petty cash voucher no. 101.
	7	Withdrew $900 (check no. 8109) for personal use.
	8	Purchased $25 worth of supplies using petty cash voucher no. 102.
	12	Paid the newspaper carrier $15 using petty cash voucher no. 103.
	16	Paid the amount due on the August phone bill, $35 (check no. 8110). (Recorded on Sept. 20)
	17	Paid the amount due on the August electric bill, $85 (check no. 8111). (Recorded on Sept. 22)
	22	Performed computer services for Viral Video; billed the client $5,400 (invoice no. 12675).
	23	Paid $20 for computer paper using petty cash voucher no. 104.
	30	Took $15 out of petty cash for lunch, voucher no. 105.
	31	Replenished the petty cash. Coin and currency in drawer total $185.

Because Troy was so busy trying to close his books, he forgot to reconcile his last 3 months of bank statements. A list of all deposits and checks written for the past 3 months (each entry is identified by chapter, transaction date, or transaction letter) and the bank statements for July through September are provided. The statement for October won't arrive until the first week of November.

Assignment

1. Record the transactions in general journal and auxiliary petty cash record.

2. Post the transactions to the general ledger accounts.

3. Prepare a trial balance.

4. Compare the Suarez Computer Center's deposits and checks with the bank statements and complete a bank reconciliation as of September 30, 201X.

Suarez Computer Center Summary of Deposits and Checks

Chapter	Transaction	Deposits Payor/Payee	Amount
1	a	Troy Falco	$12,500
1	f	Cash customer	1,000
1	i	Viral Video	1,400
1	g	Cash customer	700
2	p	Cash customer	1,400
3	Sept. 2	Tonya Parker Jones	420
3	Sept. 6	Lilly Life	150
3	Sept. 12	Erin Caffrey	1,100
3	Sept. 26	Howard Trale	750

Chapter	Transaction	Check #	Checks Payor/Payee	Amount
1	b	8095	Hardware Haven, Inc.	$1,260
1	c	8096	In Office Furniture, Inc.	1,500
1	e	8097	Chapin Corp.	800
1	j	8098	Troy Falco	1,500
2	l	8099	Insurance Protection, Inc.	300
2	m	8100	Nuts and Bolts	50
2	n	8101	Computer Edge Magazine	500
2	q	8102	San Diego Electric	100
2	r	8103	U.S. Postmaster	20
3	Sept. 1	8104	Chapin Corp.	1,500
3	Sept. 8	8105	Pacific Bell USA	200
3	Sept. 15	8106	The Computer Store	500
3	Sept. 17	8107	Hardware Haven, Inc.	2,100

Bank Statement

First Union Bank 322 Glen Ave. Escondido, CA 92025

Suarez Computer Center			Statement Date: July 22, 201X	
Checks Paid:			Deposits and Credits:	
Date paid	Number	Amount	Date received	Amount
7-4	8095	1,260.00	7-1	12,500.00
7-7	8096	1,500.00	7-10	1,000.00
7-15	8097	800.00	7-20	1,400.00
			7-21	700.00
Total 3 checks paid for $3,560.00			Total Deposits	$15,600.00
Ending balance on July 22—$12,040.00				

Received statement July 29, 201X.

Bank Statement

First Union Bank 322 Glen Ave. Escondido, CA 92025

Suarez Computer Center			Statement Date: August 21, 201X	
Checks Paid:			Deposits and Credits:	
Date paid	Number	Amount	Date received	Amount
8-2	8098	1,500.00	8-12	1,400.00
8-3	8099	300.00		
8-10	8100	50.00		
8-15	8101	500.00		
8-20	8102	100.00		
Total 5 checks paid for $2,450.00			Total Deposits	$1,400.00
Beginning balance on July 22—$12,040.00			Ending balance on August 21—$10,990.00	

Received statement August 27, 201X.

Bank Statement

First Union Bank 322 Glen Ave. Escondido, CA 92025

Suarez Computer Center			Statement Date: September 20, 201X	
Checks Paid:			Deposits and Credits:	
Date paid	Number	Amount	Date received	Amount
9-2	8103	20.00	9-4	420.00
9-6	8104	1,500.00	9-7	150.00
9-12	8105	200.00	9-14	1,100.00
Total 3 checks paid for $1,720.00			Total Deposits	$1,670.00
Beginning balance on August 21			Ending balance on September 20	
$10,990.00			$10,940.00	

Received statement September 20, 201X.

Calculating Pay and Recording Payroll Taxes: The Beginning of the Payroll Process

7

CHAPTER PREVIEW: ACCOUNTING IN ACTION

Congratulations! You just landed your first job as a professional and you just received your first paycheck from your new job at Google. You expected a check for $1,000 but are disappointed when you realize the check is for much less. Although your friends warned you about taxes taken out of your pay, you forgot. Where did all of the "missing" money go?

Google, like many other companies, has a payroll department that prepares its payroll. Clerks within the payroll department calculate employee earnings and all deductions to be withheld. These deductions include federal and state income tax as well as Social Security and Medicare taxes. You realize the company is probably correct, but you want to understand where all the deducted money went. Your new mission is to understand the payroll process. In this chapter, you learn how to compute gross pay and all of the taxes and other deductions that lead to the net pay.

Learning Objectives – Relating Accounting Theory By Unit

LO1 Calculate Gross Pay, Employee Payroll Tax Deductions for Federal Income Tax Withholding, State Income Tax Withholding, FICA (OASDI, Medicare), and Net Pay

LO2 Prepare a Payroll Register and Maintain an Employee Earnings Record

LO3 Calculate Employer Taxes for FICA (OASDI, Medicare), FUTA, SUTA, and Workers' Compensation Insurance

LO4 Journalize the Payroll Register, Employer Tax Liability, and Workers' Compensation Insurance

American Institute of Professional Bookkeepers (AIPB) – A Certified Bookkeeper (CB) assists with payroll by:

- completing and filing key federal forms;
- avoiding misclassifying workers who are employees as "independent contractors";
- saving on overtime pay by knowing what paid time to include— or not to include — in overtime calculations. More on the AIPB can be found at **www.aipb.org**

Most businesses can't run without employees, so hiring and paying employees are pretty typical business events. The accounting for payroll transactions is really the same whether a business is a small, family-owned gardening business in your town or a nationwide retail department store. Either way, it's important to know how to calculate, pay, record, and report payroll and payroll taxes in this payroll process.

Federal, state, and maybe even local laws regulate the payroll process. A business may be fined substantial penalties and interest for failing to follow these laws properly. Because of this, there are many companies—such as ADP, Paychex, and Ceridian—that will handle payroll processing and tax reporting for a fee. However, it is often less costly for the business to complete the payroll functions in-house.

In this chapter, we take a close look at the employees of Travelwithus.com to see how a payroll is computed and recorded. Travelwithus.com is a new Internet-based company specializing in cruises and business travel. The company was formed as a corporation. We look at how its payroll is affected by federal, state, and local taxes and how the accountant at Travelwithus.com handles payroll transactions for the company.

LEARNING UNIT 7-1

L01

Gross Pay, Employee Payroll Tax Deductions for Federal Income Tax Withholding, State Income Tax Withholding, FICA (OASDI, Medicare), and Net Pay

Katherine Kurtz is the owner and accountant for Travelwithus.com who calculates and records each payroll for the company. Several parts of Katherine's job are especially important. First, Katherine must be accurate in everything she does because any mistake she makes in working with the payroll may affect both the employee and the company. Second, Katherine needs to be on time when working on the company's payroll so that employees get their paychecks as expected and governments receive payroll taxes when due. Third, Katherine must at all times obey the appropriate federal, state, and local laws governing payroll matters. Fourth, because processing payroll involves personal employee information such as pay rates and marital status, Katherine always needs to keep payroll data confidential.

Gross Earnings

Fair Labor Standards Act (Federal Wage and Hour Law) Law the majority of employers must follow that contains rules stating the minimum hourly rate of pay and the maximum number of hours a worker will work before being paid time and a half for overtime hours worked. This law also has other rules and regulations that employers must follow for payroll purposes.

Interstate commerce Test applied to determine whether an employer must follow the rules of the Fair Labor Standards Act. If an employer communicates or does business with another business in some other state, it is usually considered to be involved in interstate commerce.

Pay or payroll period Length of time used by an employer to calculate the amount of an employee's earnings. Pay periods can be daily, weekly, biweekly (once every 2 weeks), semimonthly (twice each month), monthly, quarterly, or annually.

It is important to understand that there is a federal law governing most employers as to how employee payroll is handled. This law is the Fair Labor Standards Act (FLSA), sometimes referred to as the Federal Wage and Hour Law. A company must follow the Fair Labor Standards Act if it is involved in interstate commerce; in other words, if it is doing business in more than one state. Most businesses follow this Act because interstate commerce involves the sale or receipt of anything outside of the state border. Child labor laws, the federal minimum wage, and overtime requirements are included within the FLSA.

To begin the payroll process, Katherine must first calculate the earnings for Travelwithus.com's employees. To make the correct calculations, Katherine must know how each employee has been classified for payroll purposes. As a rule, a company will classify every employee either as "hourly" or "salaried." If an employee is an hourly employee, that employee is paid only for the hours he or she worked. Employees classified as salaried exempt employees receive a fixed dollar amount for the time period worked. The FLSA identifies the correct treatment of hourly and salaried exempt employees. This means you cannot classify an employee as salaried exempt solely to avoid overtime pay. A salaried exempt employee is exempt from overtime per the guidelines of the FLSA (*https://www .dol.gov/whd/overtime/final2016/*).

Travelwithus.com classified three of its five employees as hourly. For these three employees, Katherine must compute the hours they worked during a specific time period known as a pay period; the number of hours determines how much each has earned. For payroll purposes, pay periods are defined as daily, weekly, biweekly (every 2 weeks), semimonthly (twice each month), monthly, quarterly, or annually. A pay period can start on any day of the week and must end after the specified period of time has passed. Most companies use weekly, biweekly, semimonthly, or monthly pay periods when calculating their payrolls.

Companies can use different pay periods for different groups of employees. However, Travelwithus.com chose a biweekly pay period for its employees, both salaried and hourly. The biweekly pay period starts on Monday and ends 2 weeks later on a Sunday. All employees actually receive their paychecks on the following Wednesday because it takes Katherine a few days to calculate the payroll.

After determining the pay period, Katherine will calculate the gross earnings for each employee. Gross earnings includes all earnings before any deductions. This includes salaries, regular and overtime hours, bonuses, and commissions. Katherine first completes the hourly employees. She knows that overtime earnings must be computed according to the FLSA. For most employers, this law says that an hourly employee must be paid at least one and a half times his or her regular pay rate for any hours worked in excess of 40 in a workweek. A workweek, according to the law, is a 7-day (or 168-hour) period that can start at any time, but once the starting time for the week is determined, it must stay the same for each week.

> **Gross earnings (gross pay)** All earnings before any deductions.

It is important to know that some states also have payroll laws that need to be followed in determining pay. For example, California requires employers to pay overtime pay to hourly employees who have worked more than 8 hours in any day, even if they work less than 40 hours total for that week. (**http://www.blr.com/HR-Employment/Compensation/Fair-Labor-Standards-Act-FLSA-in-California#**). Employers must follow both sets of laws Travelwithus.com is located in Massachusetts so they do not have to follow California law.

> **Workweek** Seven-day (168-hour) period used to determine overtime hours for employees. A workweek can begin on any given day, but must end 7 days later.

Hourly employees of Travelwithus.com have two workweeks in each biweekly pay period. Travelwithus.com's hourly workweek starts on Monday morning at 12:01 A.M. each week and ends 7 days later on Sunday evening at 12:00 midnight. Thus, Katherine must calculate overtime pay for any employee who worked more than 40 hours in each week of this 2-week period.

Stephanie Higuera is one of the three hourly employees working for Travelwithus.com. Travelwithus.com's most recent biweekly pay period began on Monday, October 13, at 12:01 A.M. and ended on Sunday, October 26, at 12:00 midnight. The first week of this period ended on Sunday, October 19, and during this week Stephanie worked 44 hours. During the second week that ended on October 26, Stephanie worked 38 hours.

How much should she be paid? Katherine will answer this question by first calculating both Stephanie's regular hours and her overtime hours. According to federal law, Katherine must look at each week separately. Stephanie worked 44 hours during the first week, which means that she worked 40 regular hours and 4 overtime hours. Because she worked fewer than 40 hours in the second week, all of these hours are regular hours.

Week No.	Week Ending	Regular Hours	Overtime Hours	Total Hours
1	October 19	40	4	44
2	October 26	38	0	38
Total		78	4	82

Stephanie earns $11.40 for each hour she works, so Katherine computes Stephanie's pay as follows:

$11.40 *regular rate* × 1.5 = $17.10 *overtime rate*

78 *regular hours* × $11.40 *regular rate* = $889.20 *regular earnings*

4 *overtime hours* × $17.10 *overtime rate* =   68.40 *overtime earnings*

$889.20 *regular earnings* + $68.40 *overtime earnings* = $957.60 *gross earnings*

After computing all hourly employees, Katherine starts the process with the salaried employees. Julia Regan also works for Travelwithus.com. She qualifies as a salaried employee and earns $4,875 per month. To convert her monthly pay into biweekly pay, first annualize the monthly pay, then divide by 26 pay periods ($4,875 × 12 = $58,500/26 = $2,250).

Federal Income Tax Withholding

After Katherine determines Stephanie's and Julia's gross earnings, she figures out how much each of them will actually receive in their paychecks after several different taxes have been withheld. These taxes are called payroll taxes and must be paid by the employees. Employees pay these amounts by having them withheld from their paychecks. Their employer then sends them to the Internal Revenue Service (IRS), state governments, and maybe even local governments so they count against the amount of federal, state, and possible local income taxes that the employees will owe for the year.

In this way, Stephanie and Julia pay their taxes on a "pay as you go basis." In other words, when Stephanie and Julia complete their federal income tax returns at the end of the year, they will deduct the amount of income tax withheld during the year from the total amount owed for the year. How and when Travelwithus.com turns these amounts over to the federal, state, and local governments is discussed in Chapter 8. Katherine computes the amount of taxes to be withheld based on each employee's gross earnings for the pay period.

Katherine starts figuring out how much to withhold from each employee's pay by looking at the W-4 that he or she completed. The IRS Form W-4, Employee's Withholding Allowance Certificate, is completed by every employee and provides information that will be used to determine the amount of federal income tax (FIT) withholdings. Figure 7.1 is Stephanie's W-4 form. Notice that it shows Stephanie's marital status and total number of allowances she claims for federal income tax purposes. Usually, an employee may claim one allowance for him- or herself, one for his or her spouse, and one for each of his or her dependents, such as a child. Employees who want more withheld from their paychecks can claim fewer allowances than they really have.

Form W-4 (Employee's Withholding Allowance Certificate) Form filled out by employees and used by employers to supply needed information about the number of allowances claimed, marital status, and so forth. The form is used for payroll purposes to determine federal income tax withholding from an employee's paycheck.

Allowances (also called exemptions) Certain dollar amounts of a person's income tax that will be considered nontaxable for income tax withholding purposes.

Federal income tax (FIT) withholding Amount of federal income tax withheld by the employer from the employee's gross pay; the amount withheld is determined by the employee's gross pay, the pay period, the number of allowances claimed by the employee on the W-4 form, and the marital status indicated on the W-4 form.

Figure 7.1 Completed W-4 Form

To look up the amount of federal income tax that needs to be withheld from Stephanie's paycheck, Katherine uses Stephanie's marital status and the number of claimed allowances listed on her Form W-4. She also uses Stephanie's gross earnings for the pay period and the length of the pay period. The amount of federal income tax that needs to be withheld is listed in a wage bracket table that can be found in IRS Publication 15 *Employer's Tax Guide*, also called Circular E. Check out one of the tables from the Circular that's shown in Figure 7.2. Notice from the heading "SINGLE Persons—BIWEEKLY Payroll Period" that this table applies to single persons who are paid biweekly. Wage bracket tables are prepared according to marital status and pay period; Circular E has a similar table for married persons who are paid biweekly, as well as tables for single and married persons who are paid daily, weekly, semimonthly, or monthly. Also notice that the table has rows for different ranges of gross pay, starting from lower amounts of pay in the top rows of the table to higher amounts in the bottom rows.

Katherine determines the amount of federal income tax that needs to be withheld from Stephanie's paycheck by first locating the correct table in Publication 15. She finds the table for single persons who are paid biweekly. Then, she locates the row that says "At least $940 but less than $960." Stephanie's gross pay for this pay period is $957.60, so this row applies to her. Katherine traces this row to the column for one withholding allowance and finds that the amount of withholding tax is $88. Based on Stephanie's gross earnings of $957.60 and her one claimed allowance, Katherine will withhold $88 in federal income taxes from Stephanie's pay.

State Income Tax Withholding

Most states also charge their residents an income tax based on the amount of money they earn from their employers. In 2017, only Alaska, Florida, Nevada, South Dakota, Texas, Washington, and Wyoming do not. (Technically, New Hampshire and Tennessee also do not have a state income tax; it is only imposed on interest and dividends.) So, in addition to withholding federal income taxes, Katherine may also have to determine amounts for state income tax (SIT) withholding. Fortunately for Katherine, the process for withholding state income tax is much the same as it is for withholding federal income tax. In many states, withholding amounts are based on the same information that is listed in the employee's W-4, although some states do have their own versions of this form that are used instead. Employers use state publications similar to the federal Publication 15 to figure the amount to be withheld for state income taxes. However, because the 43 states can differ significantly in the way they calculate income tax, we keep our discussion simple by assuming that state income tax is a fixed percentage of employee earnings. For our example we use an 8% tax rate. Therefore, Katherine calculates Stephanie's SIT withholding at (8% of $957.60)

Other Income Tax Withholding

We pointed out previously that employees would have state income taxes withheld from their paychecks if they live in one of the 43 states collecting such a tax. In addition, many cities and counties tax employee earnings. Sometimes the tax will be a percentage of gross earnings much like federal income tax, or it may be a fixed dollar amount that the employer will withhold for every pay period. These cities and counties have their own rules regarding payroll tax deposits and tax reports for this type of withholding tax.

Employee Withholding for FICA Taxes

In addition to withholding federal and, probably, state income tax, Katherine must also compute and withhold Social Security and Medicare taxes from Travelwithus.com employees. A brief history shows that Social Security taxes came about with the signing of the Social Security Act in 1935. When this taxes was incorporated into the Internal Revenue Code in 1939, it was renamed the Federal Insurance Contributions Act (FICA). Later, in 1965, Medicare was signed into law as an amendment to the Social Security Act of 1935. Today, the term *FICA* includes both Social Security taxes (OASDI, or The Old Age, Survivors and Disability Insurance) and Medicare taxes.

Wage bracket table One of various charts in IRS Circular E that provide information about deductions for federal income tax based on earnings and data supplied on the W-4 form.

Circular E IRS tax publication of payroll procedures, including tax tables.

State income tax (SIT) withholding Amount of state income tax withheld by the employer from the employee's gross pay.

FICA (Federal Insurance Contributions Act) Part of the Social Security Act of 1935, this law taxes both the employer and employee up to a certain maximum rate and wage base for OASDI tax purposes. It also taxes both the employer and employee for Medicare purposes, but this tax has no wage base maximum.

Figure 7.2 Wage Bracket Tables

SINGLE Persons—BIWEEKLY Payroll Period
(For Wages Paid through December 31, 201X)

And the wages are—		And the number of withholding allowances claimed is—										
At least	But less than	0	1	2	3	4	5	6	7	8	9	10
		The amount of income tax to be withheld is—										
$800	$820	$90	$67	$44	$25	$10	$0	$0	$0	$0	$0	$0
820	840	93	70	47	27	12	0	0	0	0	0	0
840	860	96	73	50	29	14	0	0	0	0	0	0
860	880	99	76	53	31	16	0	0	0	0	0	0
880	900	102	79	56	33	18	2	0	0	0	0	0
900	920	105	82	59	35	20	4	0	0	0	0	0
920	940	108	85	62	38	22	6	0	0	0	0	0
940	960	111	88	65	41	24	8	0	0	0	0	0
960	980	114	91	68	44	26	10	0	0	0	0	0
980	1,000	117	94	71	47	28	12	0	0	0	0	0
1,000	1,020	120	97	74	50	30	14	0	0	0	0	0
1,020	1,040	123	100	77	53	32	16	1	0	0	0	0
1,040	1,060	126	103	80	56	34	18	3	0	0	0	0
1,060	1,080	129	106	83	59	36	20	5	0	0	0	0
1,080	1,100	132	109	86	62	39	22	7	0	0	0	0
1,100	1,120	135	112	89	65	42	24	9	0	0	0	0
1,120	1,140	138	115	92	68	45	26	11	0	0	0	0
1,140	1,160	141	118	95	71	48	28	13	0	0	0	0
1,160	1,180	145	121	98	74	51	30	15	0	0	0	0
1,180	1,200	147	124	101	77	54	32	17	1	0	0	0
1,200	1,220	150	127	104	80	57	34	19	3	0	0	0
1,220	1,240	153	130	107	83	60	36	21	5	0	0	0
1,240	1,260	156	133	110	86	63	39	23	7	0	0	0
1,260	1,280	159	136	113	89	66	42	25	9	0	0	0
1,280	1,300	162	139	116	92	69	45	27	11	0	0	0
1,300	1,320	165	142	119	95	72	48	29	13	0	0	0
1,320	1,340	168	145	122	98	75	51	31	15	0	0	0
1,340	1,360	171	148	125	101	78	54	33	17	2	0	0
1,360	1,380	174	151	128	104	81	57	35	19	4	0	0
1,380	1,400	177	154	131	107	84	60	37	21	6	0	0
1,400	1,420	180	157	134	110	87	63	40	23	8	0	0
1,420	1,440	183	160	137	113	90	66	43	25	10	0	0
1,440	1,460	186	163	140	116	93	69	46	27	12	0	0
1,460	1,480	189	166	143	119	96	72	49	29	14	0	0
1,480	1,500	192	169	146	122	99	75	52	31	16	0	0
1,500	1,520	195	172	149	125	102	78	55	33	18	2	0
1,520	1,540	198	175	152	128	105	81	58	35	20	4	0
1,540	1,560	201	178	155	131	108	84	61	38	22	6	0
1,560	1,580	206	181	158	134	111	87	64	41	24	8	0
1,580	1,600	211	184	161	137	114	90	67	44	26	10	0
1,600	1,620	216	187	164	140	117	93	70	47	28	12	0
1,620	1,640	221	190	167	143	120	96	73	50	30	14	0
1,640	1,660	226	193	170	146	123	99	76	53	32	16	0
1,660	1,680	231	196	173	149	126	102	79	56	34	18	2
1,680	1,700	236	199	176	152	129	105	82	59	36	20	4
1,700	1,720	241	203	179	155	132	108	85	62	38	22	6
1,720	1,740	246	208	182	158	135	111	88	65	41	24	8
1,740	1,760	251	213	185	161	138	114	91	68	44	26	10
1,760	1,780	256	218	188	164	141	117	94	71	47	28	12
1,780	1,800	261	223	191	167	144	120	97	74	50	30	14
1,800	1,820	266	228	194	170	147	123	100	77	53	32	16
1,820	1,840	271	233	197	173	150	126	103	80	56	34	18
1,840	1,860	276	238	200	176	153	129	106	83	59	36	20
1,860	1,880	281	243	204	179	156	132	109	86	62	39	22
1,880	1,900	286	248	209	182	159	135	112	89	65	42	24
1,900	1,920	291	253	214	185	162	138	115	92	68	45	26
1,920	1,940	296	258	219	188	165	141	118	95	71	48	28
1,940	1,960	301	263	224	191	168	144	121	98	74	51	30
1,960	1,980	306	268	229	194	171	147	124	101	77	54	32
1,980	2,000	311	273	234	197	174	150	127	104	80	57	34
2,000	2,020	316	278	239	200	177	153	130	107	83	60	37
2,020	2,040	321	283	244	205	180	156	133	110	86	63	40
2,040	2,060	326	288	249	210	183	159	136	113	89	66	43
2,060	2,080	331	293	254	215	186	162	139	116	92	69	46
2,080	2,100	336	298	259	220	189	165	142	119	95	72	49

$2,100 and over   Use Table 2(a) for a **SINGLE person** on page 45. Also see the instructions on page 43.

The government uses the taxes collected to make the following payments:

- Monthly retirement benefits for persons over 62 years old
- Medical benefits for persons over 65 years old
- Benefits for persons who have become disabled
- Benefits for families of deceased workers who were covered by this law

Because each tax is calculated differently, it is important you understand that OASDI and Medicare are separate taxes. OASDI puts a limit on the amount of tax that an employee must pay by setting a maximum annual dollar amount of earnings that can be taxed. This amount is called the wage base. The same is not true of Medicare; all wages earned are subject to the Medicare taxes.[1] The OASDI and Medicare tax rates and the OASDI wage base amount are all set by Congress; the OASDI wage base increases annually based on cost-of-living adjustments. The amounts for 2017 are:

Tax	2017 Tax Rate	2017 Wage Base
OASDI	6.2%	$127,200
Medicare	1.45%	None

Katherine begins to calculate the amount of Social Security taxes that needs to be withheld from Stephanie's pay by looking at Stephanie's current and year-to-date (YTD) gross earnings. She needs to know the amount of earnings from the current pay period so that she can calculate the current amount of taxes. However, she also needs to know the YTD earnings so that she can see whether Stephanie had previously reached the maximum amount of OASDI taxable earnings or if Stephanie will reach it in this pay period. YTD earnings include all gross pay earned and paid to an employee from January 1 to December 31 of any year, also known as a calendar year. Employers must use a calendar year for payroll purposes, even if the employer uses a fiscal year for financial statements or for any other reason. So far in this calendar year, Stephanie has earned a total of $19,471.20. This amount includes the $957.60 that she has earned for the most recent biweekly pay period.

Katherine calculates Stephanie's OASDI and Medicare taxes as follows:

$957.60 gross earnings × 6.2 %   OASDI tax rate = $59.37 OASDI taxes
$957.60 gross earnings × 1.45% Medicare tax rate = $13.89 Medicare taxes

Because Stephanie has earned less than the wage base limit of $127,200, all of her earnings for the current pay period are taxable.

Other Withholdings (Voluntary Deductions)

Sometimes employees have additional amounts withheld from their paychecks for various reasons. For example, they may choose to buy medical insurance for themselves and maybe even for their spouse and dependents through an insurance plan offered by their employer. Sometimes the employer pays the premium for this insurance coverage, or at least pays for the part of the premium that covers the employee. Even if the employer pays some of the premium, however, it is common for the employee to pay the rest. The employee pays this premium by having it withheld from his or her pay, just as the employee pays income and Social Security taxes by having these amounts withheld by the employer. Travelwithus.com currently offers this opportunity to its employees, and the cost to the hourly and salaried employee is $33 for each pay period. Other companies may allow their employees to have funds withheld from their paychecks for union dues, retirement plan contributions, or life insurance premiums.

Net Pay

Katherine's next step in the payroll accounting process is to calculate the amount of pay that Stephanie will actually receive in her paycheck; this amount is called net pay. At this point,

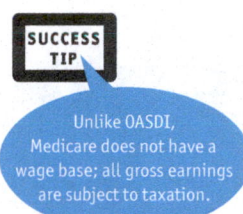

SUCCESS TIP

Unlike OASDI, Medicare does not have a wage base; all gross earnings are subject to taxation.

Taxable earnings Shows amount of earnings subject to a tax. The tax itself is not shown.

Calendar year One-year period beginning on January 1 and ending on December 31. Employers must use a calendar year for payroll purposes, even if the employer uses a fiscal year for financial statements and for any other reason.

Medical insurance Health care insurance for which premiums may be paid through a deduction from an employee's paycheck.

Net pay Gross earnings, less deductions. Net pay, or take-home pay, is what the worker actually takes home.

---

[1]*Note to Student:* Any employee who earns more than $200,000 in a calendar year is subject to a 0.9% (0.009) additional Medicare withholding tax.

Katherine has computed all of the amounts necessary to determine Stephanie's net pay. Now she simply needs to combine them as follows:

Gross earnings for the current biweekly pay period:		$957.60
Deductions for employee withholding taxes:		
Federal income tax	$88.00	
State income tax	76.61	
OASDI tax	59.37	
Medicare taxes	13.89	
Medical insurance	33.00	
Total deductions		270.87
Net pay		$686.73

 # TRY IT!   **Learning Unit 7-1**

1. Jason Jackman is a salaried employee earning $9,100.00 per month. What is Jason's weekly salary?
2. Megan Sherman is a bookkeeper who is paid $14 per hour on a biweekly basis. Please compute her gross pay if she worked 34 hours in week 1 and 44 hours in week 2. Assume her company falls under the FLSA.
3. Assume Jim Campbell earns gross pay of $1,800.00 during the current biweekly pay period ending January 26. Calculate Jim's net pay based on the following assumptions:
   - Jim claims S-1 on his Form W-4. Use Figure 7.2 to compute federal income tax withholding.
   - The state income tax rate is 3%, with no wage base limit.
   - FICA tax rates are: OASDI = 6.2% on a wage base limit of $127,200; Medicare = 1.45%.

TRY IT! Solution   **Learning Unit 7-1**

1. Weekly pay = $2,100.00: [$9,100.00 × 12 months/52 weeks]
2. Biweekly pay = $1,120.00: [Regular pay (74 hours × $14.00 = $1,036) + OT pay (4 hours × $21.00 = 84)]
3. Net pay = $1,380.30: [$1,800.00 − $228.00 (FIT) − $54.00 (SIT) − $111.60 (OASDI) − $26.10 (Medicare)]

LEARNING UNIT 7-2

L02

Preparing a Payroll Register and Maintaining an Employee Earnings Record

At this point, Katherine Kurtz, the accountant for Travelwithus.com, knows how much each of the three hourly employees earned for the most recent biweekly pay period and how many dollars of taxes need to be withheld from their paychecks. She now needs to enter this information into the accounting records for the company. Two primary records are used in accounting systems to keep track of payroll information for a company. The first of these records is a worksheet, known as a payroll register, which shows all information related to an entire pay period. The second record is called the employee earnings record and is used to keep track of an individual employee's payroll history for an entire calendar year.

The Payroll Register

Payroll register Multicolumn form that is used to record payroll data.

Katherine enters information about the current payroll period for all employees in a payroll register. The register includes each employee's gross earnings, employee withholding taxes, net pay, taxable earnings, cumulative earnings, and the accounts to be charged (Travel Scheduling or Administrative) for the salary and wage expense for that pay period. Figure 7.3 shows the

Figure 7.3 Payroll Register

TRAVELWITHUS.COM INC
PAYROLL REGISTER

PAY PERIOD: OCTOBER 13–26, 201X   **PAY DATE: OCTOBER 29, 201X**

Employee Name	W-4 Allow	Prior Earnings (YTD)	Salary	Regular Hours	Regular Rate	Regular Amount	Overtime Hours	Overtime Rate	Overtime Amount	Gross Pay	Current Earnings (YTD)
Higuera, Stephanie	S-1	18513 60		78	1140	889 20	400	1710	68 40	957 60	19471 20
Kurtz, Katherine	S-3	40000 00	2000 00							2000 00	42000 00
Regan, Julia	M-2	45000 00	2250 00							2250 00	47250 00
Sui, Annie	S-0	2121 00		80	1515	1212 00	400	2273	90 92	1302 92	3423 92
Taylor, Harold	S-2	19043 70		78	1210	943 80	400	1815	72 60	1016 40	20060 10
Totals		124678 30	4250 00	236 00	3865	3045 00	1200	5798	231 92	7526 92	132205 22

TRAVELWITHUS.COM INC
PAYROLL REGISTER

PAY PERIOD: OCTOBER 13–26, 201X   **PAY DATE: OCTOBER 29, 201X**

Employee Name	Taxable Earnings FUTA/SUTA	Taxable Earnings OASDI	FIT	SIT	FICA OASDI	FICA Medicare	Medical Insurance	Net Pay	Check #	Travel Scheduling	Admin.
Higuera, Stephanie		957 60	88 00	76 61	59 37	13 89	33 00	686 73	820	957 60	
Kurtz, Katherine		2000 00	200 00	160 00	124 00	29 00	33 00	1454 00	821		2000 00
Regan, Julia		2250 00	205 00	180 00	139 50	32 62	33 00	1659 88	822	2250 00	
Sui, Annie	1302 92	1302 92	165 00	104 23	80 78	18 89	33 00	901 02	823	1302 92	
Taylor, Harold		1016 40	74 00	81 31	63 02	14 74	33 00	750 33	824	1016 40	
Totals	1302 92	7526 92	732 00	602 15	466 67	109 14	165 00	5451 96		5526 92	2000 00

Individual employee earnings record Accounting document that summarizes the total amount of wages paid and the deductions for the calendar year. It aids in preparing governmental reports. A new record is prepared for each employee each year.

completed payroll register for the payroll covering the biweekly pay period from October 13 through October 26. Remember, however, that the biweekly payroll takes additional processing time. This means that the actual biweekly paychecks will be distributed the Wednesday after the pay period ends, so in this case, the checks are dated and distributed October 29.

The Employee Earnings Record

After Katherine prepares the payroll register for the period, and in order to comply with all applicable employment laws and regulations, she also completes a payroll record known as the individual employee earnings record. This record provides a summary of each employee's earnings, withholding taxes, net pay, and cumulative earnings during each calendar year, as shown in Figure 7.4. Katherine uses the information summarized in this record to prepare quarterly and annual payroll tax reports. Thus, the employee earnings record is split into calendar quarters, with each quarter being 13 weeks long. It is important to understand that the wages are listed in the quarter based on the date of pay, not the pay period covered.

TRY IT!   Learning Unit 7-2

Answer true or false to the following statements.

1. The payroll register is used to compute and total all employees' earnings, tax deductions, other authorized deductions, and net pay for a single pay period.
2. The payroll register does not show current YTD earnings.
3. The individual employee earnings record is updated each pay period after the completion of the payroll register.

TRY IT! Solution   Learning Unit 7-2

1. True
2. False—The payroll register shows both prior and current YTD earnings. This information is needed to keep track of wages subject to the FICA-OASDI wage base limit and SUTA/FUTA wage base limits.
3. True

LEARNING UNIT 7-3

L03

Employer Taxes for FICA (OASDI, Medicare), FUTA, SUTA, and Workers' Compensation Insurance

Employer Payment for FICA Taxes

As we discussed, employees pay payroll taxes including federal income tax, FICA taxes, probably state income tax, and maybe even a city or county income tax. It surprises some employees to find that their employers pay payroll taxes, too. As a matter of fact, employers pay exactly the same amount of FICA taxes (OASDI and Medicare) for each employee as the employee pays. In addition to paying OASDI and Medicare taxes for each employee, employers also pay unemployment taxes that are used to provide unemployed workers with benefits while they are looking for work.

As Travelwithus.com's accountant, Katherine calculates the amount of FICA taxes that the company must pay as an employer much the same way that she calculated them for each employee. She first determines the amount of current gross earnings for all employees that fall below the wage base limit of $127,200. She looks at the OASDI Taxable Earnings total in the payroll register for the current period. She then multiplies this total by the OASDI tax rate of 6.2% to determine the OASDI tax that Travelwithus.com must pay:

$7,526.92 gross earnings × 6.2% OASDI tax rate = $466.67 OASDI tax

Katherine then calculates Travelwithus.com's Medicare taxes by taking the current gross earnings for all employees and multiplying this total by the Medicare tax rate of 1.45%.

Figure 7.4 Employee Earnings Record

TRAVELWITHUS.COM INC.
EMPLOYEE EARNINGS RECORD
Stephanie Higuera   Social Security No. 123-45-6789

Pay Period	Pay Date	Hours Regular	Hours Overtime	Earnings Regular	Earnings Overtime	Earnings Gross	FIT	SIT	Deductions FICA OASDI	Deductions FICA Medicare	Medical Insurance	Net Pay	Check No.	YTD Earnings
09/15–09/28	10/1/201X	80	0	912 00	0 00	912 00	82 00	72 96	56 54	13 22	33 00	654 28	790	17601 60
09/29–10/12	10/15/201X	80	0	912 00	0 00	912 00	82 00	72 96	56 54	13 22	33 00	654 28	806	18513 60
10/13–10/26	10/29/201X	78	4	889 20	68 40	957 60	88 00	76 61	59 37	13 89	33 00	686 73	820	19471 20
10/27–11/09	11/12/201X	76	0	866 40	0 00	866 40	76 00	69 31	53 72	12 56	33 00	621 81	825	20337 60
11/10–11/23	11/26/201X	80	2	912 00	34 20	946 20	88 00	75 70	58 66	13 72	33 00	677 12	839	21283 80
11/24–12/07	12/10/201X	80	4	912 00	68 40	980 40	94 00	78 43	60 78	14 22	33 00	699 97	844	22264 20
12/08–12/21	12/24/201X	80	0	912 00	0 00	912 00	82 00	72 96	56 54	13 22	33 00	654 28	858	23176 20
4th Quarter Totals		554	10	6315 60	171 00	6486 60	592 00	518 93	402 15	94 05	231 00	4648 47		
YTD Totals				22594 80	581 40	23176 20	2241 86	1854 10	1436 92	336 05	858 00	16449 27		

Remember that the amount of Medicare taxes for each employee is not subject to any limit; every dollar that an employee earns is taxed at the Medicare tax rate of 1.45%.

$7,526.92 gross earnings × 1.45% Medicare tax rate = $109.14 Medicare taxes

The way Katherine computes these taxes differs in only one way compared to how she computed them for each employee. Because Katherine is now calculating Travelwithus.com's share of these taxes, Katherine uses current gross earnings for the company in total instead of using each employee's current gross earnings as she did when she was determining the amount to withhold from each employee's paycheck. Please note: The employer share of OASDI and Medicare should match, or be within a few cents of, the payroll register totals for the same taxes (see Figure 7.3). Many employers just record matching amounts found on the payroll register, without going through any additional computations.

FUTA and SUTA

In addition to paying its employer share of FICA taxes, Travelwithus.com must also pay unemployment taxes. Unemployment tax, or unemployment insurance as it is sometimes called, was created by the same 1935 law that created Social Security. This federal law requires all 50 states, the District of Columbia, and U.S. territories to run unemployment compensation programs that are approved and monitored by the federal government. Unemployment taxes are paid by employers based on wages paid to employees. Federal Unemployment Tax Act (FUTA) taxes pay the costs of administering the federal and state programs but do not pay benefits to employees. State Unemployment Tax Act (SUTA) taxes pay the benefits to unemployed persons.

Currently, employers pay FUTA tax at a rate of 6.0% on wages earned by each employee up to a wage base limit of $7,000. However, the federal government allows employers to take a tax credit for SUTA tax against this tax, up to a maximum credit of 5.4%.

FUTA tax rate	6.0%
Less: Normal FUTA tax credit	5.4%
Net FUTA tax rate	0.6%

Employers are allowed to take this credit as long as they have paid all amounts that they owe for SUTA taxes and have paid them on time. In other words, the federal law essentially says to employers, "Comply with your state's unemployment tax laws and your total FUTA tax rate will not exceed a maximum of 0.6% to the federal government." Remember that employers alone are responsible for paying FUTA tax; it is never withheld from the earnings of employees.

Katherine calculates FUTA tax by referring to the FUTA Taxable Earnings total in the current payroll register. This column tells her how much, in total, Travelwithus.com's employees have earned this period that falls below the FUTA wage base limit of $7,000. She uses this amount to calculate the FUTA tax by multiplying it by the net FUTA tax rate as follows:

$1,302.92 FUTA taxable earnings × 0.6% FUTA tax rate = $7.82 FUTA tax

Because states run their own unemployment programs, each state may use a different SUTA wage base limit. These amounts are based on the needs of the unemployment funds in each state. In 2017 the wage base limits for states ranged from $7,000 to $41,300. Different states have different SUTA tax rates for the same reason that the wage base limits vary; they are based on the needs of the unemployment funds in each state. Some states require the employees to pay a portion of the unemployment taxes.

Additionally, the SUTA tax rate can vary from employer to employer within a state. In any state, an employer's SUTA tax rate will be based on how many dollars it contributes to the state unemployment fund and the dollar amount of claims that its employees make against that fund. The rate is tied to the employer's employment history. In other

SUCCESS TIP

Only employers, not employees, must calculate and pay both FUTA and SUTA taxes.

Federal Unemployment Tax Act (FUTA) Tax paid by employers to the federal government. The current rate is 0.6% on the first $7,000 of earnings of each employee after the normal FUTA tax credit is applied.

State Unemployment Tax Act (SUTA) Tax usually paid only by employers to the state for employee unemployment insurance. However several states require the employee to also pay a portion.

words, employers who rarely lay off their workers will be charged a lower SUTA rate than employers who lay off workers often. In this way, the SUTA tax rate motivates employers to stabilize their workforce.

Travelwithus.com's current SUTA rate is 5.4% and the wage base limit for the state in which it is located is $7,000. Katherine calculates Travelwithus.com's SUTA tax similar to the way she calculated its FUTA tax. She first looks at the SUTA Taxable Earnings total in the current payroll register to see how much, in total, Travelwithus.com's employees earned this period below the SUTA wage base limit of $7,000. She then calculates the SUTA tax by multiplying this amount by the SUTA tax rate as follows:

$1,302.92 SUTA taxable earnings × 5.4% SUTA tax rate = $70.36 SUTA tax

Workers' Compensation Insurance

Workers' compensation insurance insures employees against losses they may incur due to work-caused injury or death while on the job. Most employers purchase this insurance through an insurance broker or state agency. In most states, this cost is paid completely by the employer, not the employee.

Travelwithus.com's premium for this insurance is based on its total estimated gross payroll, and the rate is calculated for each $100 of weekly payroll. By estimating payroll before the beginning of the year, the insurance company can determine the amount of the premium to charge Travelwithus.com. If actual payroll for the year turns out to differ from estimated payroll, then the insurance company will either credit Travelwithus.com for any overpayment or bill it for any underpayment. The experience or merit rating for Travelwithus.com is based on the type of work that its employees perform as well as the amount and extent of any on-the-job injuries that its employees experience. The rate is based on physical difficulty of jobs within various industries and the history/cost of prior employee accident claims submitted. Dangerous jobs and large numbers of claims filed result in a higher rate.

Travelwithus.com has two groups of employees: travel schedulers and administrative. It estimated that it would have $50,000 of gross payroll for its schedulers in the next year, and its rate is $1.80 for every $100 of this payroll. The company also estimated that it will incur $190,000 of payroll for managers, and its rate for this group is $0.22 for every $100 of payroll. Travelwithus.com then calculated its premium as follows:

Workers' compensation insurance   Insurance purchased by most employers to protect their employees against losses due to injury or death while on the job.

Experience or merit rating   Rate assigned by an insurance company to determine the cost of insurance coverage. This rate is based on the physical difficulty of jobs within various industries and the history/cost of prior employee accident claims submitted.

Workers' compensation premium for schedulers:	$50,000/$100 = 500	500 × $1.80 =	$ 900.00
Workers' compensation premium for managers:	$190,000/$100 = 1,900	1,900 × $0.22 =	418.00
Total workers' compensation premium =			**$1,318.00**

▶ **TRY IT!**   **Learning Unit 7-3**

Compute the employer's payroll tax expense based on the following totals found on a completed payroll register dated November 15.

- Gross pay = $41,000.00
- Taxable earnings for FUTA/SUTA = $1,250.00
- Taxable earnings for OASDI = $33,000.00
- Deductions: FIT = $6,400.00; SIT = $2,870.00; FICA OASDI = $2,046.00; FICA Medicare = $594.50
- Other information: FUTA rate = 0.6%; SUTA rate = 2.7%

Payroll Tax Expense = $2,681.75, computed as follows:

- FICA OASDI = $2,046.00 match employee total deduction, ($33,000.00 × 6.2%)
- FICA Medicare = $594.50 match employee total deduction, ($41,000.00 × 1.45%)
- FUTA = $7.50 ($1,250.00 × 0.6%)
- SUTA = $33.75 ($1,250.00 × 2.7%)

LEARNING UNIT 7-4

L04

The Payroll Register, Employer Tax Liability, and Workers' Compensation Insurance

At this point in the payroll process, Katherine Kurtz, the accountant for Travelwithus.com, has calculated gross earnings, deductions for employee withholding taxes, and net pay for each of Travelwithus.com's employees. She entered these amounts into two accounting records for Travelwithus.com called the payroll register and the employee earnings record. She also computed the amount of payroll taxes that Travelwithus.com must pay as an employer. Now Katherine must record these payroll amounts in the accounts of Travelwithus.com by making journal entries and posting these entries to accounts in the general ledger. By entering these amounts into Travelwithus.com's accounting system, Travelwithus.com's financial statements will include these payroll transactions.

Recording Payroll

Before we discuss how payroll transactions are recorded, let's first review the accounts that we will be using and the rules for increasing and decreasing these account types:

Accounts Affected	Category	↑↓	Rules	Financial Statement
Travel Scheduling Expense	Expense	↑	Dr.	Income Statement
Administrative Expense	Expense	↑	Dr.	Income Statement
Payroll Tax Expense	Expense	↑	Dr.	Income Statement
Workers' Compensation Expense	Expense	↑	Dr.	Income Statement
Insurance Expense	Expense	↑	Dr.	Income Statement
Payroll Cash	Asset	↑	Dr.	Balance Sheet
Prepaid Workers' Compensation Insurance	Asset	↑	Dr.	Balance Sheet
FICA OASDI Payable	Liability	↑	Cr.	Balance Sheet
FICA Medicare Payable	Liability	↑	Cr.	Balance Sheet
FIT Payable	Liability	↑	Cr.	Balance Sheet
SIT Payable	Liability	↑	Cr.	Balance Sheet
FUTA Payable	Liability	↑	Cr.	Balance Sheet
SUTA Payable	Liability	↑	Cr.	Balance Sheet
Medical Insurance Payable	Liability	↑	Cr.	Balance Sheet
Wages and Salaries Payable	Liability	↑	Cr.	Balance Sheet

Katherine needs to record the expense of wages and salaries. The information needed to make these journal entries comes from the payroll register. Figure 7.3 shows the payroll register for the current payroll period. Katherine locates this register and uses totals from it to make the following journal entry:

	GENERAL JOURNAL				
Date		PR	Dr.	Cr.	
201X					
Oct. 26	Travel Scheduling Expense		5 5 2 6 92		
	Administrative Expense		2 0 0 0 00		
	FIT Payable			7 3 2 00	
	SIT Payable			6 0 2 15	
	FICA OASDI Payable			4 6 6 67	
	FICA Medicare Payable			1 0 9 14	
	Medical Insurance Payable			1 6 5 00	
	Wages and Salaries Payable			5 4 5 1 46	
	To record payroll for the pay period				
	ending October 26, 201X				

A couple of things may be surprising about the journal entry. First, notice that the gross earnings, not the net pay, are recorded as expenses for the two different departments in which the employees worked. This total amount of earnings is the real expense to Travelwithus.com. Employees will actually only receive the lower, net pay; the difference relates to deductions that are made for FICA, FIT, and state income taxes, and one other deduction authorized by the employee.

Also notice that the amounts of taxes withheld are recorded in "Payable" accounts, which means that they are liabilities of Travelwithus.com. How can Travelwithus.com be liable for these taxes if the taxes are paid by employees? The answer is that Travelwithus.com collects these amounts by withholding them from the paychecks of its employees and then turns them over to the federal and, in this case, state government. In other words, Travelwithus.com is the intermediary in this process. Until it does pay these amounts to the governments, Travelwithus.com owes these taxes. The same is true of the medical insurance premiums that the employees pay; the company collects them and then pays them to the insurance company.

Recording Payroll Tax Expense

Katherine's next task is to record the employer payroll taxes for Travelwithus.com. The entry to record the taxes for the current payroll follows:

	GENERAL JOURNAL				
Date		PR	Dr.	Cr.	
201X					
Oct. 26	Payroll Tax Expense		6 5 3 99		
	FICA OASDI Payable			4 6 6 67	
	FICA Medicare Payable			1 0 9 14	
	FUTA Payable			7 82	
	SUTA Payable			7 0 36	
	To record payroll tax expense				
	for pay period ending October 26, 201X				

Notice that FICA OASDI, FICA Medicare, FUTA, and SUTA were recorded in separate liability accounts because they are different taxes and, except for the FICA taxes, are paid to different government agencies. Also note that the amount of all of these taxes are added together and recorded as one amount for Travelwithus.com's payroll tax expense. These amounts are an expense to Travelwithus.com because they represent the cost of the payroll taxes that it must pay as an employer.

Payroll tax expense Cost to employers that includes the total of the employer's FICA OASDI, FICA Medicare, FUTA, and SUTA taxes. Remember, the employer matches the employee contributions for OASDI and Medicare.

▶ # TRY IT!   **Learning Unit 7-4**

Complete the following journal entries:

1. Journalize the information from a completed payroll register dated November 15.
   - Gross pay = $41,100.00
   - Taxable earnings for FUTA/SUTA = $1,500.00
   - Taxable earnings for OASDI = $32,000.00
   - Deductions: FIT = $6,550; SIT = $1,644.00; FICA OASDI = $1,984.00; FICA Medicare = $595.95

2. Journalize the employer's payroll tax expense based on the above information as well as FUTA rate = 0.6%; SUTA rate = 2.7%

TRY IT! Solution   **Learning Unit 7-4**

Date	Account Name	PR	Dr.	Cr.
Nov. 15	Wages and Salaries Expense		41,100.00	
	FIT Payable			6,550.00
	SIT Payable			1,644.00
	FICA OASDI Payable			1,984.00
	FICA Medicare Payable			595.95
	Wages and Salaries Payable			30,326.05
	To record payroll register			

Date	Account Name	PR	Dr.	Cr.
Nov. 15	Payroll Tax Expense		2,629.45	
	FICA OASDI Payable			1,984.00
	FICA Medicare Payable			595.95
	FUTA Payable			9.00
	SUTA Payable			40.50
	To record employer's payroll tax expense			

LO1,3,4 ▶▶

DEMONSTRATION SUMMARY PROBLEM

Davidson Company pays their employees biweekly and is required to follow the FLSA. The FICA-OASDI rate is 6.2% on earnings up to $127,200 per year; the FICA-Medicare rate is 1.45% on all earnings; the SIT rate = 4%; medical insurance = $35.00 per employee; FUTA rate is 0.6%; and SUTA rate is 3.2%. Both unemployment taxes are computed on earnings up to $7,000.00 per year. The salaried employee is charged to Administrative Expense, and hourly employees are charged to Sales Expense. The following information is available for Davidson Company's three employees:

		Pay Period: February 17–March 2, 201X;		Pay Date: March 5, 20XX		
Employee Name	**W-4 Allow**	**Prior YTD Earnings**	**Salary or Rate of Pay**		**Hours Week 1**	**Hours Week 2**
Jennie Davis	S-1	$6,000.00	$3,250.00 per month			
Michelle Foy	S-3	$3,966.00	$15.00 per hour		41	39
Charles Leon	S-2	$4,900.00	$17.00 per hour		45	43

Requirements

Use the above information to:

1. Complete the 2-week payroll register (the first check number is 141).
2. Journalize the payroll register.
3. Journalize the employer's payroll tax expense.

Solutions

Requirement 1

Complete the payroll register.

Jennie's biweekly salary is computed as follows: $3,250 × 12/26 = $1,500

Michelle earned 40 regular hours in week 1 and 39 regular hours in week 2. Michelle receives 1 hour of overtime for week 1 because she worked more than 40 hours that week. The overtime rate is computed at her regular rate of $15.00 × 1.5 = $22.50.

Charles worked more than 40 hours each week. Therefore, Charles earned 80 regular hours with the remaining 8 hours at his overtime rate of $17 × 1.5 = $25.50.

Gross Pay = the sum of the Salary + Regular Pay + Overtime Pay

Current Earnings YTD = Prior Earnings YTD + Gross Pay

FUTA/SUTA Taxable: Jennie is the only employee who went over the $7,000 wage base. Her FUTA/SUTA taxable income is $1,500 salary − $500 in excess of wage base = $1,000.

OASDI wages: No employee has earned more than the wage base of $127,200. Therefore, OASDI wages = Gross Pay.

FIT: Use the biweekly tax chart (Figure 7.2)

SIT = Gross Pay × 4.0%

Net pay = Gross Pay less deductions for FIT, SIT, FICA-OASDI, FICA-Medicare, and insurance.

Total Admin. Expense + Total Sales Expense = Total Gross Pay

Verify totals: Foot and crossfoot each column and row.

Additional accuracy checks recommended: Total Gross Pay × 4.0% should equal or be within pennies of the column total for SIT deductions; Total OASDI wages × 6.2% should equal or be within pennies of the column total for OASDI deductions; Total Gross Pay × 1.45% should equal or be within pennies of the column total for Medicare deductions.

Davidson Company Payroll Register

Pay Period: February 17–March 2, 201X   Pay Date: March 5, 201X

Employee Name	W-4 Allow	Prior Earnings YTD	Salary	Regular			Overtime			Gross Pay	Current Earnings YTD
				Hours	Rate	Amount	Hours	Rate	Amount		
Jennie Davis	S-1	6,000.00	1,500.00							1,500.00	7,500.00
Michelle Foy	S-3	3,966.00		79.00	15.00	1,185.00	1.00	22.50	22.50	1,207.50	5,173.50
Charles Leon	S-2	4,900.00		80.00	17.00	1,360.00	8.00	25.50	204.00	1,564.00	6,464.00
		14,866.00	1,500.00	159.00		2,545.00	9.00		226.50	4,271.50	19,137.50

Davidson Company Payroll Register

Pay Period: February 17–March 2, 201X   Pay Date: March 5, 201X

| Employee Name | Taxable Earnings | | | | Deductions | | | | Net Pay | Check # | Expense Account | |
	FUTA/SUTA	OASDI	FIT	SIT	FICA OASDI	FICA Medicare	Medical Insurance				Admin.	Sales
Jennie Davis	1,000.00	1,500.00	172.00	60.00	93.00	21.75	35.00	1,118.25	141	1,500.00	
Michelle Foy	1,207.50	1,207.50	80.00	48.30	74.87	17.51	35.00	951.82	142		1207.50
Charles Leon	1,564.00	1,564.00	158.00	62.56	96.97	22.68	35.00	1,188.79	143		1564.00
	3,771.50	4,271.50	410.00	170.86	264.84	61.94	105.00	3,258.86		1,500.00	2,771.50

Requirement 2

Journalize the payroll register.

Use the payroll register second-page totals to journalize the payroll. Remember to list the debits (expenses) first when journalizing.

GENERAL JOURNAL						
Date		Account	PR	Dr.	Cr.
20XX					
Mar.	2	Administrative Expense		1 5 0 0 00	
		Sales Expense		2 7 7 1 50	
		FIT Payable			4 1 0 00
		SIT Payable			1 7 0 86
		FICA OASDI Payable			2 6 4 84
		FICA Medicare Payable			6 1 94
		Medical Insurance Payable			1 0 5 00
		Wages and Salaries Payable			3 2 5 8 86
		To record payroll for the pay period ending March 2, 20XX			

Requirement 3

Journalize the employer's payroll tax expense.

GENERAL JOURNAL						
Date		Account	PR	Dr.	Cr.
20XX					
Mar.	2	Payroll Tax Expense		4 7 0 10	
		FICA OASDI Payable			2 6 4 84
		FICA Medicare Payable			6 1 94
		FUTA Payable			2 2 63
		SUTA Payable			1 2 0 69
		To record payroll tax expense for pay period ending March 2, 20XX			

SUCCESS COACH

7

The following Success Tips are from Learning Units 7-1 through 7-4. Take the Do It Right Checkup and use the Check Your Score to see how you are doing. The Success Coach provides tips before each Checkup to help you avoid common accounting errors.

LU 7-1 Gross Pay, Employee Payroll Tax Deductions for Federal Income Tax Withholding, State Income Tax Withholding, FICA (OASDI, Medicare), and Net Pay

Do It Right Tips: The maximum amount of FICA (OASDI) tax is capped by a wage base of $127,200, while the FICA (Medicare) tax has no limit on the amount that may be collected.

Do It Right Now Checkup: Answer true or false to the following statements.

1. A pay period is always defined as a 2-week period.
2. The Fair Labor Standards Act states that an employee must be paid overtime pay if he or she works over 40 hours in a workweek.
3. An employee may claim fewer allowances on his or her IRS Form-W4, Employee's Withholding Allowance Certificate than he or she really has.
4. Withholding of FICA taxes (OASDI and Medicare) are limited to the amount due on all earnings below $127,200 (the wage base) in 2017.
5. Gross pay is the amount the employee receives in his or her paycheck.

LU 7-2 Preparing a Payroll Register and Maintaining an Employee Earnings Record

Do It Right Tips: Following the calculation of gross and net pay, records must be maintained on both a pay period and individual employee basis to ensure that appropriate reports are prepared timely and accurately.

Do It Right Now Checkup: Answer true or false to the following statements.

1. The employee earnings record shows gross earnings, deductions, net pay, and taxable earnings for only a single payroll period.
2. The individual employee earnings record is used to update the payroll register.
3. The taxable earnings columns of the payroll register do not show the amount of tax owed.
4. Only the employee earnings record indicates the employee's marital status and the number of allowances claimed.

5. The payroll register shows gross earnings, deductions, net pay, and taxable earnings for a payroll period.

LU 7-3 Employer Taxes for FICA (OASDI, Medicare), FUTA, SUTA, and Workers' Compensation Insurance

Do It Right Tips: Not only must employees pay a variety of payroll taxes, but their employers must also pay a number of payroll taxes.

Do It Right Now Checkup: Answer true or false to the following statements.

1. Employers must pay FICA (OASDI and Medicare) equal to $1\frac{1}{2}$ times the employee payment.
2. Only employers, not employees, must calculate and pay both FUTA and SUTA taxes.
3. FUTA and SUTA taxes are calculated on a wage base of $127,200.
4. Workers' compensation insurance is paid by the employer to insure that each employee is fairly compensated.
5. Workers' compensation insurance has a single rate for each employee of a firm, much like FICA.

LU 7-4 The Payroll Register, Employer Tax Liability, and Workers' Compensation Insurance

Do It Right Tips: The FICA (OASDI and Medicare) payable accounts contain both the employee deductions and the matching amount from the employer.

Do It Right Now Checkup: Answer true or false to the following statements.

1. The payroll register is the source of the data used to journalize the payroll in the general journal.
2. The FICA (OASDI and Medicare) payable accounts reflect the tax liability of only the employer.
3. Deductions for payroll withholding taxes represent a liability of the employees until the taxes are paid by the employer.
4. Workers' compensation insurance is paid by the employer to ensure that employees are compensated if they lose their job.

CHECK YOUR SCORE: Answers to the Do It Right Now Checkup

LU 7-1

1. False—Pay periods are defined as daily, weekly, biweekly, semi-monthly, monthly, quarterly, or annually.
2. True
3. True
4. False—(OASDI) tax is limited by a wage base of $127,200. (Medicare) tax does not have a wage base limit; therefore, all wages earned are subject to the Medicare taxes.
5. False—Gross pay is the amount calculated as earned by the employee before employee withholdings such as FIT, SIT, and FICA (OASDI and Medicare). After these deductions from gross pay, the employee receives his or her net pay.

LU 7-2

1. False—The employee earnings record shows gross earnings, deductions, and net pay for the employee for each calendar quarter and the entire calendar year.
2. False—The payroll register is used to update the employee earnings record.
3. True—They show the amount of earnings to be taxed for unemployment taxes and Social Security (OASDI).
4. False—The employee's marital status and the number of allowances are found on the payroll register.
5. True

LU 7-3

1. False—The employer pays exactly the same amount of FICA taxes (OASDI and Medicare) as do its employees.
2. True
3. False—In this text, both FUTA and SUTA are calculated on a wage base of $7,000 for each employee.
4. False—Workers' compensation insurance is paid by the employer to insure employees against work-related death or injury.
5. False—The rate paid by the employer is based on the type of work each employee performs (more hazardous jobs have higher rates) and the extent of any previous on-the-job injuries or deaths.

LU 7-4

1. True
2. False—The FICA (OASDI and Medicare) payable accounts accumulate FICA taxes from both the employees and the employer.
3. False—The employee's liability for FICA (OASDI and Medicare) cease the moment the employer deducts the taxes from the employee's gross pay. Those taxes then become the responsibility of the employer.
4. False—Workers' compensation insurance premiums are paid by the employer to insure the employee against work-related injury or death.

BLUEPRINT FOR RECORDING TRANSACTIONS IN A PAYROLL REGISTER

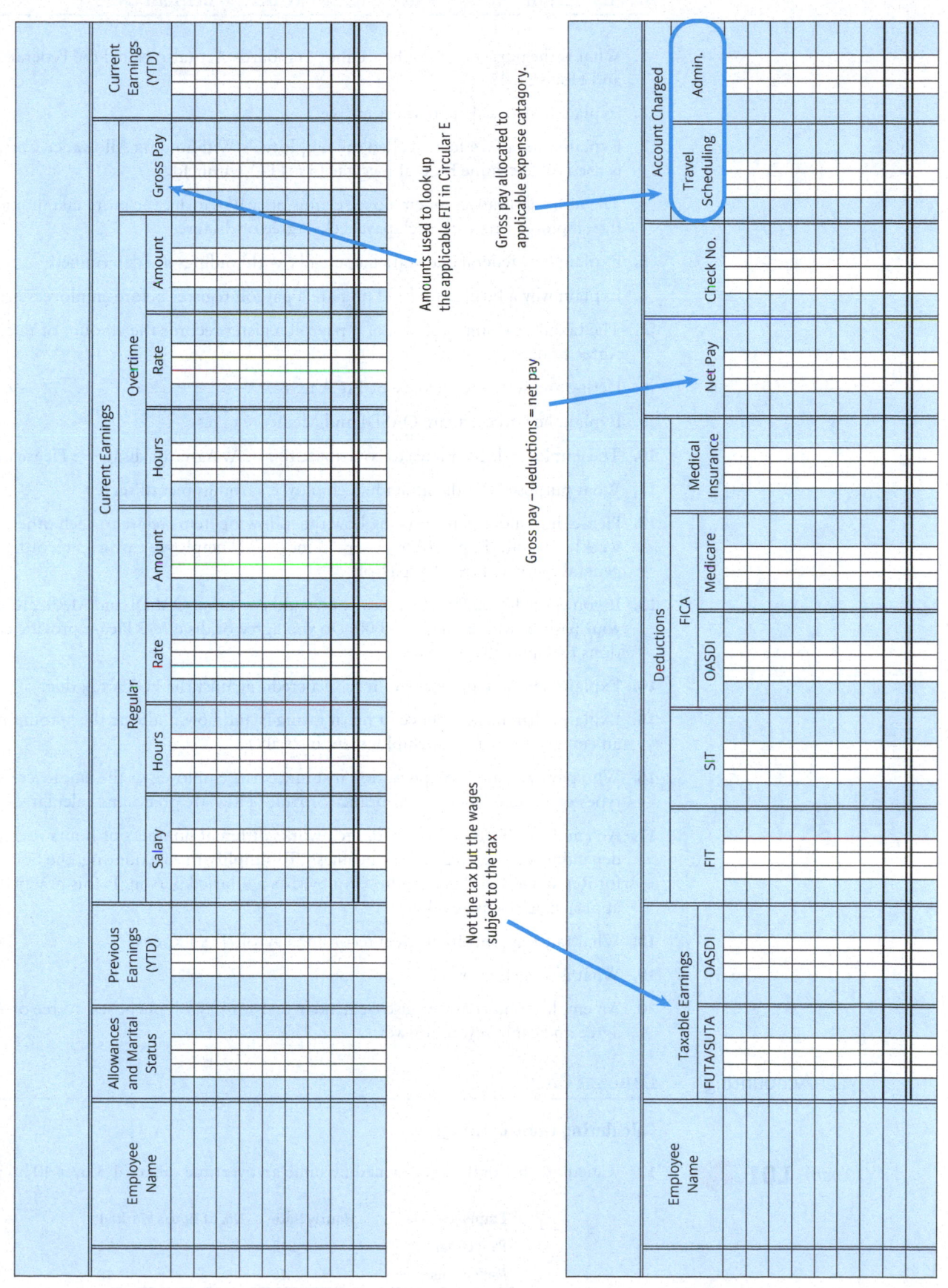

Amounts used to look up the applicable FIT in Circular E

Gross pay allocated to applicable expense catagory.

Gross pay – deductions = net pay

Not the tax but the wages subject to the tax

Discussion Questions and Critical Thinking/Ethical Case

1. What is the purpose of the Fair Labor Standards Act (also called the Federal Wage and Hour Law)?

2. Explain how to calculate overtime pay.

3. Explain how a W-4 form, called the Employee's Withholding Allowance Certificate, is used to determine Federal Income Tax (FIT) withheld.

4. The more allowances an employee claims on a W-4 form, the more take-home pay the employee gets with each paycheck. Agree or disagree?

5. Explain how federal and state income tax withholdings are determined.

6. Explain why a business should prepare a payroll register before employees are paid.

7. The taxable earnings column of a payroll register records the amount of tax due. Agree or disagree?

8. Define and state the purpose of FICA taxes.

9. Explain how to calculate OASDI and Medicare taxes.

10. The employer doesn't have to contribute to FICA. Agree or disagree? Please explain.

11. What purpose does the individual employee earnings record serve?

12. Please draw a diagram showing how the following items relate to each other: (a) weekly payroll, (b) payroll register, (c) individual employee earnings record, and (d) general journal entries for payroll.

13. If you earned $130,000 this year, you would pay more OASDI and Medicare than your partner who earned $75,000. Do you agree or disagree? Please provide calculations to support your answer.

14. Explain how an employer can receive a credit against the FUTA tax due.

15. Explain what an experience or merit rating is and how it affects the amount paid by an employer for state unemployment insurance.

16. Who pays workers' compensation insurance, the employee or the employer? What types of benefits does this insurance provide? How are premiums calculated?

17. An employee for Repairs to Go, Inc., works different numbers of hours each week depending on the needs of the business. To simplify the accounting, the bookkeeper for Repairs to Go classifies this employee as a salaried person. Is this practice appropriate? Please explain.

18. What taxes are recorded when recording Payroll Tax Expense?

19. What is a calendar year?

20. An employer must always use a calendar year for payroll purposes. Agree or disagree and explain your answer.

MyLabAccounting

Concept Check

Calculating Gross Earnings

(10 min) **LO1**

1. Calculate the total wages earned (assume an overtime rate of 1.5 over 40 hours).

Employee	Hourly Rate	No. of Hours Worked
Paul Leman	$13	31
Mark Hamel	16	52

FIT and FICA

2. Tom Hanson, single, claiming one exemption, has cumulative earnings before this biweekly pay period of $126,000. If he is paid $1,930 this period, what will his deductions be for FIT and FICA (OASDI and Medicare)? The FICA tax rate for Social Security is 6.2% on $127,200, and Medicare is 1.45% on all earnings. Round to nearest cent as needed.

 **L01** *(15 min)*

Net Pay

3. From Exercise 2, calculate Tom's net pay. The state income tax rate is 5%, and health insurance is $35.

L01 *(15 min)*

Payroll Register

4. Match the following:

    1. Total gross pay
    2. A deduction
    3. Net pay

    a. _____ Office Salary Expense
    b. _____ FICA OASDI
    c. _____ FICA Medicare
    d. _____ Federal Income Tax
    e. _____ Medical Insurance
    f. _____ Wages and Salaries Payable

L02 *(10 min)*

Employer and Employee Taxes

5. Identify which of the following taxes are paid by the employee (EE) and which are paid by the employer (ER):

    a. _____ FICA Medicare
    b. _____ FIT
    c. _____ FUTA
    d. _____ SUTA

L02,3 *(10 min)*

Account Classifications

6. Complete the following table. Indicate whether a debit or credit results in an increase or decrease to the account balance.

L04 *(10 min)*

Accounts Affected	Category	↑↓	Rules
a. Payroll Tax Expense			
b. FICA OASDI Payable			
c. SIT Payable			
d. SUTA Payable			

Exercises

MyLabAccounting

Set A

7A-1.   **a.** Calculate the total wages earned for each hourly employee assuming an overtime rate of 1.5 over 40 hours.

 **L01** *(15 min)*

Employee	Hourly Rate	No. of Hours Worked
Lindsay Lane	$ 8.00	36
Freda Walker	$14.00	42
Louis Jones	$19.00	52

b. Calculate the total biweekly earnings of these newly hired salaried employees.

	Monthly Salary
John Smith	$3,575
Jane Doe	$7,475

(20 min) **L01**

7A-2. Compute the net pay for each employee using the federal income tax withholding table in Figure 7.2. Assume that FICA OASDI tax is 6.2% on a wage base limit of $127,200, Medicare is 1.45% on all earnings, the payroll is paid biweekly, and no state income tax applies.

Employee	Status	Allowances	Cumulative Pay	Biweekly Pay
Han Gan	Single	2	$57,500	$1,710
James Pilcher	Single	1	61,000	1,580

(20 min) **L03**

7A-3. From the following information, calculate the payroll tax expense for Bowling Company for the payroll of April 9:

Employee	Cumulative Earnings Before Weekly Payroll	Gross Pay for the Week
H. Adams	$3,900	$825
L. Karson	6,700	675
F. Mason	7,600	260

The FICA tax rate for OASDI is 6.2% on the first $127,200 earned, and Medicare is 1.45% on all earnings. Federal unemployment tax is 0.6% on the first $7,000 earned by each employee. The SUTA tax rate for Bowling Company is 5.4% on the first $7,000 of employee earnings for state unemployment purposes.

(15 min) **L03**

7A-4. Refer to Exercise 7A-3 and assume that the state changed Bowling Company's SUTA tax rate to 4.6%. What effect would this change have on the total payroll tax expense?

(15 min) **L03**

7A-5. Refer to Exercise 7A-3. If F. Mason earned $2,100 for the week instead of $260, what effect would this change have on the total payroll tax expense?

(20 min) **L03,4**

7A-6. The total wage expense for Grande Co. was $156,000. Of this total, $32,000 was above the OASDI wage base limit and not subject to this tax. All earnings are subject to Medicare taxes, and $58,000 was above the federal and state unemployment wage base limits and not subject to unemployment taxes. Please calculate and journalize the total payroll tax expense for Grande Co. given the following rates and wage base limits:

a. FICA tax rate: OASDI, 6.2% with a wage base limit of $127,200; Medicare, 1.45% with no wage base limit

b. State unemployment tax rate: 5.5% with a wage base limit of $7,000

c. Federal unemployment tax rate (after credit): 0.6% with a wage base limit of $7,000

7A-7. At the end of the first quarter of 201X, you are asked to determine the FUTA tax liability for Old Company. The FUTA tax rate is 0.6% on the first $7,000 each employee earns during the year (assuming 13 weeks for the first quarter and each employee earned the same gross weekly pay for all 13 weeks).

LO3,4 *(20 min)*

Employee	Gross Pay Per Week
Y. Connor	$750
C. Hart	740
J. Mathison	600
Y. Ralph	390

7A-8. From the following data, estimate the annual premium for workers' compensation insurance:

Type of Work	Estimated Payroll	Rate per $100
Office	$32,000	$0.22
Repairs	77,000	1.78

Set B

7B-1. **a.** Calculate the total wages earned for each employee assuming an overtime rate of 1.5 over 40 hours.

LO1 *(15 min)*

Employee	Hourly Rate	No. of Hours Worked
Penny Cooper	$18.00	36
Samantha York	$16.00	47
Tim Larson	$10.00	50

b. Calculate the total biweekly earnings of these newly hired salaried employees.

	Monthly Salary
Patrick Garcia	$4,875
Erin Caux	$5,525

7B-2. Compute the net pay for each employee using the federal income tax withholding table in Figure 7.2. Assume that FICA OASDI tax is 6.2% on a wage base limit of $127,200; Medicare is 1.45% on all earnings, the payroll is paid biweekly, and no state income tax applies.

LO1 *(20 min)*

Employee	Status	Allowances	Cumulative Pay	Biweekly Pay
Li Kan	Single	1	$57,500	$1,720
David Parker	Single	0	63,700	1,570

7B-3. From the following information, calculate the payroll tax expense for Gray Company for the payroll of April 9:

LO3 *(20 min)*

Employee	Cumulative Earnings Before Weekly Payroll	Gross Pay for the Week
R. Frank	$3,500	$950
G. Jill	6,300	725
L. Peter	7,800	290

The FICA tax rate for OASDI is 6.2% on the first $127,200 earned, and Medicare is 1.45% on all earnings. Federal unemployment tax is 0.6% on the first $7,000 earned by each employee. The SUTA tax rate for Gray Company is 5.1% on the first $7,000 of earnings for state unemployment purposes.

(15 min) **L03**   **7B-4.**   Refer to Exercise 7B-3 and assume that the state changed Gray's SUTA tax rate to 4.6%. What effect would this change have on the total payroll tax expense?

(15 min) **L03**   **7B-5.**   Refer to Exercise 7B-3. If L. Peter earned $2,100 for the week instead of $290, what effect would this change have on the total payroll tax expense?

(20 min) **L03,4**   **7B-6.**   The total wage expense for Bell Co. was $168,000. Of this total, $31,000 was above the OASDI wage base limit and not subject to this tax. All earnings are subject to Medicare taxes, and $54,000 was above the federal and state unemployment wage base limits and not subject to unemployment taxes. Please calculate and journalize the total payroll tax expense for Bell Co. given the following rates and wage base limits:

    a. FICA tax rate: OASDI, 6.2% with a wage base limit of $127,200; Medicare, 1.45% with no wage base limit.

    b. State unemployment tax rate 5.8% with a wage base limit of $7,000.

    c. Federal unemployment tax rate (after credit): 0.6% with a wage base limit of $7,000.

(20 min) **L03,4**   **7B-7.**   At the end of the first quarter of 201X, you are asked to determine the FUTA tax liability for Franklin Company. The FUTA tax rate is 0.6% on the first $7,000 each employee earns during the year (assuming 13 weeks for the first quarter and each employee earned the same gross weekly pay for all 13 weeks).

Employee	Gross Pay Per Week
P. Franklin	$740
O. Hienze	840
Q. Roberts	620
R. Waters	390

(10 min) **L03**   **7B-8.**   From the following data, estimate the annual premium for worker's compensation insurance:

Type of Work	Estimated Payroll	Rate per $100
Office	$29,000	$0.23
Repairs	78,000	1.62

MyLabAccounting   ## Problems

Set A

(20 min) **L01**   **7A-1.**   From the following information, please complete the chart for gross earnings for the week. (Assume an overtime rate of time and a half over 40 hours.)

Check Figure:
Danny Geary: $976.00 Gross Earnings

Employee	Hourly Rate	No. of Hours Worked	Gross Earnings
Jacques Bergeron	$ 7.00	45	
Leena Haffner	$13.00	43	
Nicola Richard	$17.00	39	
Danny Geary	$16.00	54	

7A-2. September Company has five salaried employees. Your task is to use the following information to prepare a payroll register to calculate net pay for each employee:

 **L01** *(30 min)*

Employee	Allowance and Marital Status	Cumulative Earnings Before This Payroll	Biweekly Salary	Department
Dunn, Holly	S-0	$ 39,000	$1,250	Customer Service
Herman, Kacey	S-1	35,000	1,400	Office
Roberts, Hazel	S-1	53,800	1,000	Office
Bothwell, Brodie	S-3	125,950	2,040	Customer Service
Ackerman, Lee	S-3	29,000	1,110	Customer Service

Assume the following:

1. FICA OASDI is 6.2% on $127,200; FICA Medicare is 1.45% on all earnings.
2. Each employee contributes $35 biweekly for medical insurance.
3. State income tax is 2% of gross pay.
4. FIT is calculated from Figure 7.2.

Check Figure:
Total Net Pay $5,332.77

7A-3. The bookkeeper of Jungle Co. gathered the following data from individual employee earnings records and daily time cards. Your task is to complete a payroll register on October 13.

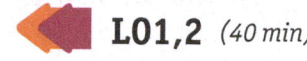 **L01,2** *(40 min)*

Employee	Allowance and Marital Status	Cumulative Earnings Before This Payroll	M	T	W	T	F	Hourly Rate of Pay	FIT
Fine, Paul	M-1	$65,400	5	5	7	7	10	$17	$34
Rock, Danika	S-0	15,500	7	6	6	7	8	9	43
Ford, Randy	M-3	68,000	11	12	8	7	7	14	27
Judd, Jay	S-1	16,000	6	11	9	10	11	21	157

Assume the following:

1. FICA OASDI is 6.2% on $127,200; FICA Medicare is 1.45% on all earnings.
2. Federal income tax has been calculated from a weekly table for you.
3. Each employee contributes $27 weekly for health insurance.
4. Overtime is paid at a rate of 1.5 over 40 hours.
5. Fine and Ford work in the office; the other employees work in sales.

Check Figure:
Total Net Pay $2,040.87

7A-4. You gathered the following data from time cards and individual employee earnings records. Your tasks are as follows:

 **L01,2,3,4** *(40 min)*

1. On December 5, 201X, prepare a payroll register for this biweekly payroll.
2. Calculate the employer taxes of FICA OASDI, FICA Medicare, FUTA, and SUTA.
3. Journalize the Payroll Register and the employer's tax liability.

Employee	Allowance and Marital Status	Cumulative Earnings Before This Payroll	Biweekly Salary	Check No.	Department
Akin, Joan	S-3	$37,400	$1,560	30	Production
Gus, Napp	S-1	47,500	2,000	31	Office
Mayo, Jules	S-2	64,300	2,070	32	Production
Sams, Phil	S-1	4,200	800	33	Office

Check Figure:
Total Net Pay $4,582.40

Assume the following:

1. FICA OASDI is 6.2% on $127,200; FICA Medicare is 1.45% on all earnings.
2. Federal income tax is calculated from Figure 7.2.
3. State income tax is 9% of gross pay.
4. Union dues are $11 biweekly.
5. The SUTA rate is 5.0% and the FUTA rate is 0.6% on earnings up to $7,000.

(20 min) **LO1**   **Set B**

7B-1. From the following information, please complete the chart for gross earnings for the week. (Assume an overtime rate of 1.5 over 40 hours.)

Employee	Hourly Rate	No. of Hours Worked	Gross Earnings
Jacoby Bothwell	$8.00	41	
Laina Moore	12	37	
Nicolette Wittman	15	38	
Danyl Klecan	16	55	

Check Figure:
Danyl Klecan Gross Pay $1,000

(30 min) **LO1**   **7B-2.** Fall Company has five salaried employees. Your task is to use the following information to prepare a payoll register to calculate net pay for each employee:

Employee	Allowance and Marital Status	Cumulative Earnings Before This Payroll	Biweekly Salary	Department
Dunn, Heidi	S-1	$ 40,000	$1,350	Customer Service
Howell, Kaitlynn	S-1	35,000	1,300	Office
Sheldon, Heidi	S-1	58,300	1,500	Office
Conway, Bryce	S-2	126,300	2,020	Customer Service
Clinton, Larry	S-3	27,000	1,110	Customer Service

Assume the following:

1. FICA OASDI is 6.2% on $127,200; FICA Medicare is 1.45% on all earnings.
2. Each employee contributes $50 biweekly for medical insurance.
3. State income tax is 6% of gross pay.
4. FIT is calculated from Figure 7.2

Check Figure:
Total Net Pay $5,334.71

(40 min) **LO1,2**   **7B-3.** The bookkeeper of Butterfly Co. gathered the following data from individual employee earnings records and daily time cards. Your task is to complete a payroll register on August 8.

Employee	Allowance and Marital Status	Cumulative Earnings Before This Payroll	Daily Time					Hourly Rate of Pay	FIT
			M	T	W	T	F		
Keys, Payton	M-1	$68,100	3	10	5	9	10	$19	$53
Bale, Donna	S-0	14,500	9	7	9	8	4	14	62
Chen, Rian	M-3	59,000	9	6	12	8	10	16	39
Judd, Jason	S-1	22,000	6	8	9	11	7	25	149

Assume the following:

1. FICA OASDI is 6.2% on $127,200; FICA Medicare is 1.45% on all earnings.
2. Federal income tax has been calculated from a weekly table for you.
3. Each employee contributes $34 weekly for health insurance.
4. Overtime is paid at a rate of 1.5 over 40 hours.
5. Keys and Chen work in the office; the other employees work in sales.

Check Figure:
Total Net Pay $2,348.58

7B-4. You gathered the following data from time cards and individual employee earnings records. Your tasks are as follows:

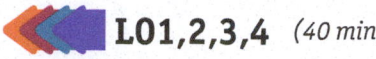
L01,2,3,4 *(40 min)*

1. On December 5, 201X, prepare a payroll register for this biweekly payroll.
2. Calculate the employer taxes of FICA OASDI, FICA Medicare, FUTA, and SUTA.
3. Journalize the Payroll Register and employer's tax liability.

S50 / **QB**

Employee	Allowance and Marital Status	Cumulative Earnings Before This Payroll	Biweekly Salary	Check No.	Department
Atha, Jan	S-3	$37,500	$1,520	30	Production
Gary, Nab	S-1	47,600	1,980	31	Office
Mas, Jess	S-2	65,200	2,040	32	Production
Sass, Paul	S-1	5,100	810	33	Office

Assume the following:

1. FICA OASDI is 6.2% on $127,200; FICA Medicare is 1.45% on all earnings.
2. Federal income tax is calculated from Figure 7.2.
3. State income tax is 9% of gross pay.
4. Union dues are $13 biweekly.
5. The SUTA rate is 5.4%, and the FUTA rate is 0.6% on earnings up to $7,000.

Check Figure:
Total Net Pay $4,523.72

Financial Report Problem

Reading Amazon's Annual Report
Go to **https://tinyurl.com/slaterca14e** to access Amazon 2016 Annual Report on page 4 and find out the total number of full and part-time employees Amazon has.

KEEPING IT REAL SUAREZ COMPUTER CENTER

MyLabAccounting

During the month of November, the following transactions occurred.

Assignment

1. Record the following transactions in the general journal and post them to the general ledger.
2. Prepare a trial balance as of November 30, 201X.

L01 *(60 min)*

Nov.	1	Billed Vital Tax Services $6,600, invoice no. 12676, for services rendered.
	3	Billed Value Pac, Inc. $4,300, invoice no. 12677, for services rendered.
	5	Purchased new shop benches for $1,500 on account from System Design Furniture.
	9	Received the phone bill, $155.
	12	Collected $625 of the amount due from Viral Video.
	18	Collected $825 of the amount due from Viral Video.
	20	Purchased a fax machine for the office from Hardware Haven, on credit, $675.00.

Paying the Payroll, Depositing Payroll Taxes, and Filing the Required Quarterly and Annual Tax Forms: The Conclusion of the Payroll Process

8

CHAPTER PREVIEW:
ACCOUNTING IN ACTION

When reviewing all the deductions on your paycheck, did you ever wonder what they were for? Your employer must report these deductions in order to meet its state and federal reporting requirements. For example, Google must take federal and state taxes out of its employees' paychecks and report the amounts to the federal and state authorities. By law, Google will have to make periodic payroll deposits of these taxes along with some matching requirements like Social Security. Google and other companies are also required by law to contribute to unemployment programs. This chapter focuses on the payroll reporting responsibilities of employers. For both small and large businesses the payroll process is an inseparable part of the accounting process.

Learning Objectives – Relating Accounting Theory By Unit

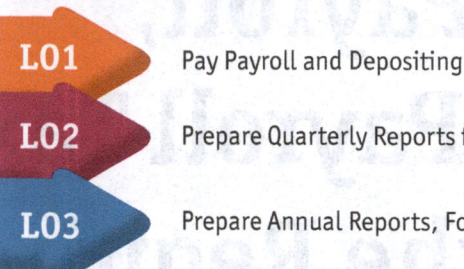

L01   Pay Payroll and Depositing Taxes

L02   Prepare Quarterly Reports for Federal and State Governments

L03   Prepare Annual Reports, Forms W-2 and W-3

Google has many thousands of employees. With the aid of computers, the accounting department of Google must monitor as well as complete in a timely manner its employer tax responsibilities. In Chapter 7 we learned how to calculate gross earnings, employee withholding taxes, net pay, and employer payroll taxes. We now look at how businesses pay, record, and report these amounts. The journal entries necessary to record all of the payroll transactions for Travelwithus.com appear in the next section.

LEARNING UNIT 8-1

Payroll and Depositing Taxes

L01

Transferring Funds to the Payroll Account and Distributing the Paychecks

Katherine must write and distribute paychecks to the employees of Travelwithus.com. Like most companies, Travelwithus.com uses a special checking account for paying its payroll. This account is called Cash – Payroll Checking and only paychecks are written from this account. A company with a substantial number of employees might want to use an extra account just for payroll for a number of reasons. First, having a separate account just for paychecks provides much better internal control over the funds deposited to pay employees. Also, because only payroll checks are written from this account, it is easier to reconcile it to the bank statement each month and determine whether someone has not cashed his or her paycheck for some reason. Finally, the business can still manage its cash effectively even with this extra bank account; the business simply deposits the total net pay amount in this account and thus has enough money to pay every paycheck without leaving extra in the account that could be used for other purposes. The following journal entry illustrates the transfer of funds from the general bank account to the payroll bank account. This transfer is made sometime between the completion of the payroll register and the date the checks are distributed.

	GENERAL JOURNAL				
Date		PR	Dr.	Cr.
201X				
Oct. 26	Cash – Payroll Checking		5 4 5 1 94	
	Cash – Regular Checking			5 4 5 1 94
	To record transfer between two accounts			

The following journal entry illustrates the distribution of the payroll dated October 29.

	GENERAL JOURNAL				
Date		PR	Dr.	Cr.
201X				
Oct. 29	Wages & Salaries Payable		5 4 5 1 94	
	Cash – Payroll Checking			5 4 5 1 94
	To record distribution of paychecks			

American Institute of Professional Bookkeepers (AIPB) – A Certified Bookkeeper (CB) helps with payroll by:

- keeping an eye on your outside payroll service (if your company uses one).

- helping to avoid IRS penalties—or even worse, endless IRS correspondence.

- reducing the chance of a costly wage-and-hour audit.

- Avoiding late-filing penalties and interest. More on the AIPB can be found at **www.aipb.org**

SUCCESS TIP

Many companies now pay their employees electronically. The pay stub information is available for each employee through their confidential, online payroll records.

The paychecks that Travelwithus.com gives to its employees are, like the paychecks of most companies, attached to pay stubs that show the employee's gross earnings, deductions for employee withholding taxes, and net pay. Figure 8.1 illustrates Stephanie Higuera's current paycheck and stub.

Figure 8.1
Stephanie Higuera's
Paycheck and Stub

Travelwithus.com Inc.

Employee	Social Security	Check	Net Pay	Pay Date	Marital Status	Allowances
Stephanie Higuera	123-45-6789	820	$686.73	October 29, 201X	S	1

Earnings	Current			Deductions		
	Pay Rate	Hours	Earnings	Item	Current	YTD
Regular Earnings	11.40	78	889.20	FIT	$88.00	2,067.00
Overtime Earnings	17.10	4	68.40	SIT	76.61	1,557.70
Current Gross Earnings			957.60	OASDI	59.37	1,207.21
				Medicare	13.89	282.33
				Medical insurance	33.00	693.00
				Total	$270.87	5,807.24

Travelwithus.com Inc.
10 Lovett Road
Salem, MA 01970

11-325/1210

No. 820

October 29, 201X

PAY TO THE ORDER OF Stephanie Higuera

$686.73

Six hundred eighty-six and 73/100 _____ DOLLARS

BC | Bank of Commerce

MEMO Oct 13–26 payroll

Julia Regan

Depositing Payroll Taxes

As we discussed in Chapter 7, both employers and employees pay payroll taxes. Employers continue recording the various tax liabilities until it is time to remit to the tax authorities. Any payment obligations for state or local taxes are specific to that taxing unit. Because these tax authorities have various rules, we omit discussion of the topic in this text. Therefore, we focus only on the federal requirements for depositing and reporting payroll taxes. Let's now discuss how Travelwithus.com carries out these responsibilities.

For Travelwithus.com, the process began when the business opened. When opening a business, every employer must get a federal identification number. This number is also called an employer identification number (EIN) and is like a Social Security number for businesses in the sense that it identifies businesses to the government. To get an EIN, an employer fills out Form SS-4, much like individuals fill out Form SS-5 to get a Social Security number. Travelwithus.com will use its EIN, 58-1213479, when remitting or reporting any business tax.

Employer identification number (EIN) Number assigned by the IRS that is used by an employer when recording and paying payroll and income taxes.

Form SS-4 Form filled out by an employer to get an EIN. The form is sent to the IRS, which assigns the number to the business.

Form 941 taxes Another term used to describe FIT, OASDI, and Medicare. This name comes from the form used to report these taxes.

Remember, payrolls are entered on the register based on the date the check is actually given to the employee.

After the paychecks have been released, the company needs to evaluate the need of remitting to the IRS the federal taxes owed. The rules on how and when to remit the tax payments are lengthy and are covered in more detail later. However, because Travelwithus. com is a new employer this year, the company is allowed to deposit the taxes monthly. As a monthly depositor, all FIT and FICA taxes withheld and matched during the month (also referred to as **Form 941 taxes**) will be electronically transferred to the IRS on or before the 15th day of the following month.

The Worksheet Summary of Payroll Registers (see Figure 8.4 on page 269) contains all payroll detail for the fourth quarter. This worksheet helps Katherine compute the 941 tax deposit needed for each month within that quarter. For now, let's focus on the month of October.

To compute the tax deposit, Katherine will add the total October federal income tax and twice the FICA taxes. Why do we pay twice the total FICA? Remember, in the previous chapter, the employer had to match the employee FICA deductions. To illustrate her computation, look at the October totals for each federal tax category found on the worksheet summary:

FIT	FICA × 2	Total Deposit
$2,098.00	($1,377.07 + $322.06) × 2	$5,496.26

Because Travelwithus.com is a monthly depositor, the total deposit for the three October pay dates must be paid to the IRS on or before November 15. If that date is a Saturday, Sunday, or bank holiday, the due date is extended to the next banking day. Additionally, the IRS requires that businesses submit all tax payments electronically if they owe more than $2,500.00 in a calendar quarter.

Let's also view the general ledger accounts for the October Form 941 taxes. You can see the postings to the individual accounts for FIT, FICA-OASDI, and FICA-Medicare. This will also clarify how to journalize the deposit needed.

FIT Payable			FICA OASDI Payable			FICA Medicare Payable	
10/1	683.00		10/1	455.20		10/1	106.46
10/15	683.00		10/1	455.20		10/1	106.46
10/29	732.00		10/15	455.20		10/15	106.46
	2,098.00		10/15	455.20		10/15	106.46
			10/29	466.67		10/29	109.14
			10/29	466.67		10/29	109.14
				2,754.14			644.12

GENERAL JOURNAL					
Date			PR	Dr.	Cr.
201X					
Oct.	29	FIT Payable		2 0 9 8 00	
		FICA OASDI Payable		2 7 5 4 14	
		FICA Medicare Payable		6 4 4 12	
		Cash-Regular Checking			5 4 9 6 26

Look-back period Period of time used to determine whether a business should make its Form 941 tax deposits on a monthly or semiweekly basis. The IRS defines this period as July 1 through June 30 of the year prior to the year in which Form 941 tax deposits will be made.

General Rules for Determining a Depositor Classification

As mentioned earlier, the rules for depositing payroll taxes are lengthy. Let's start by discussing the look-back period. The IRS determines a company's tax depositor classification by reviewing the taxes paid during the **look-back period**. This period of time is a 12-month period that starts July 1 two years earlier. If a company's payroll tax liability was less than $50,000 in that

12-month period, the company is considered a monthly depositor. However, if the company owes more than $50,000 during that time frame, the company is considered a semiweekly depositor.

As a new company this year, Travelwithus.com does not have a 12-month tax-paying history. Therefore, they are considered a monthly depositor. You should read all of the exact rules and exceptions that are found in Publication 15 online at **www.IRS.gov**. Figure 8.2 provides general information about the look-back period.

Monthly depositor   Business classified as a monthly depositor will make its payroll tax deposits only once each month for the amount of Form 941 taxes due from the prior month.

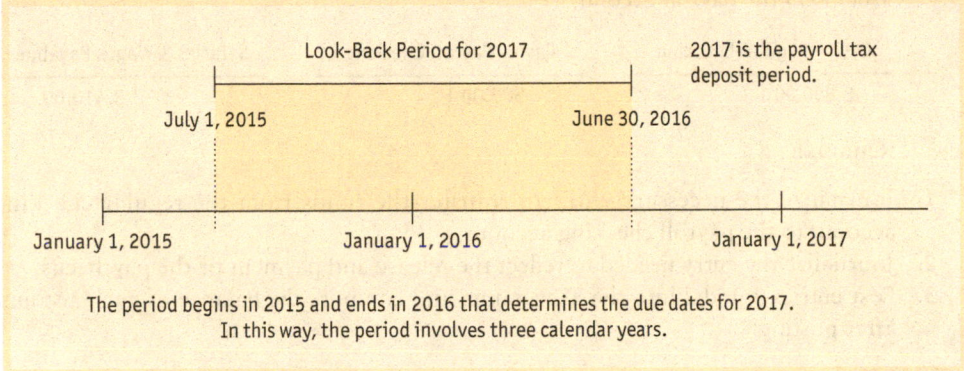

Figure 8.2
Look-Back Illustration

General Rules for Depositing Payroll Taxes

Once the classification is determined, Katherine knows when she must deposit the 941 taxes collected. In addition to the two primary classifications (see 1 and 2 below), there are two other rules that may apply (see 3 and 4 below).

1. **Monthly Depositor Classification:** Deposit payroll taxes collected by the 15th day of the month following the payroll month. Example: Any pay date that falls in January must have taxes deposited by February 15.

2. **Semiweekly Depositor Classification:** If your pay date falls on Saturday, Sunday, Monday, or Tuesday, the company must deposit taxes on the third banking day after Tuesday (usually Friday). If your pay date falls on Wednesday, Thursday, or Friday, the company must deposit taxes on the third banking day after Friday (usually the following Wednesday). See Figure 8.3.

3. **One-Day Rule:** If the payroll tax liability for either classification above exceeds $100,000 at any time during the quarter, the company must deposit all taxes by the close of the next business day (also known as the 24-hour rule). Normally, this rule applies to very large employers such as Google, ExxonMobil, or Walmart.

4. **Deposits Not Required:** If the company is very small, and the tax liability is less than $2,500 for the quarter, the taxes can be sent with the 941 quarterly report.

Semiweekly depositor   Business classified as a semiweekly depositor may have to make its payroll tax deposits up to twice in one week, depending on when payroll is paid.

Banking day   Any day that a bank is open to the public for business. Generally, a banking day will end at 2:00 or 3:00 p.m. local time. Banking business transacted after this time is usually considered to be the next day's business. Saturdays, Sundays, and federal holidays are usually not considered banking days.

	Sat	Sun	Mon	Tues	Wed	Thurs	Fri	Sat	Sun	Mon	Tues	Wed
If payday is												
Then deposit is due												

Figure 8.3
Semiweekly Deposit Rules Illustration

Tax Deposit Exceptions

1. Monthly depositors only: If the deposit date falls on a Saturday, Sunday, or legal holiday, the deposit date is extended to the next business day.

2. Semiweekly depositors only: If a legal holiday falls on any of the three banking days referenced, the company gets one additional day to deposit. Example: The pay date is on a Thursday. The following Monday is a federal holiday. The deposit, which is normally due on Wednesday, can be made on Thursday.

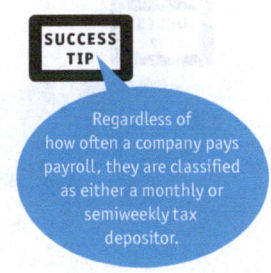

SUCCESS TIP

Regardless of how often a company pays payroll, they are classified as either a monthly or semiweekly tax depositor.

▶ TRY IT!   Learning Unit 8-1

The following T accounts reflect a partial list of general ledger account balances for N & L Company after recording the payroll register for the pay period ending March 3, 201X. It is now March 5, 201X, and Mr. Nelson, the company owner, needs to transfer money from the regular account to the payroll account so that the paychecks can be released. Mr. Nelson wants to maintain a minimum of $500.00 in the payroll account.

Cash – Regular Checking	Cash – Payroll Checking	Salaries & Wages Payable
8,890.00	500.00	3,410.00

Required:

1. Journalize the necessary entry to transfer the funds from the regular checking account to the payroll checking account.
2. Journalize the entry needed to reflect the release and payment of the paychecks.
3. Post entries 1 and 2 into the T accounts and compute the balance of each account after posting.

TRY IT!   Solution Learning Unit 8-1

1.

GENERAL JOURNAL			PR	Dr.	Cr.
Cash – Payroll Checking				3 4 1 0 00	
Cash – Regular Checking					3 4 1 0 00
To transfer money to the payroll account					

2.

GENERAL JOURNAL			PR	Dr.	Cr.
Salaries & Wages Payable				3 4 1 0 00	
Cash – Payroll Checking					3 4 1 0 00
To record release of paychecks dated Mar. 5					

3.

Cash – Regular Checking		Cash – Payroll Checking		Salaries & Wages Payable	
8,890.00		500.00			3,410.00
	3,410.00 (1)	(1) 3,410.00	3,410.00 (2)	(2) 3,410.00	
5,480.00		500.00			0.00

Form 941, Employer's Quarterly Federal Tax Return Tax report that a business will complete after the end of each calendar quarter indicating the total FICA (OASDI and Medicare) taxes owed plus the amount of FIT withheld from employees' pay for the quarter. If federal tax deposits have been made correctly and on time, the total amount deposited should equal the amount due on Form 941. Any difference results in a payment due or a refund.

Calendar quarter Three-month, 13-week time period. Four calendar quarters occur during a calendar year that runs from January 1 through December 31. The first quarter is January through March, the second is April through June, the third is July through September, and the fourth is October through December.

LEARNING UNIT 8-2

LO2 ▶

Quarterly Reports for Federal and State Governments

Form 941

The IRS requires all employers to periodically report all tax liability incurred for FIT and FICA as well as all deposits made toward payment of those taxes. This is done by filing a quarterly tax report on **Form 941, Employer's Quarterly Federal Tax Return**. The reporting periods are calendar quarters ending on March 31, June 30, September 30, and December 31. The filing date for any of the reports is the last day of the month following the quarter. This gives the company time to gather and verify the information before needing to file Form 941. In order to find Form 941 and see the instructions for reporting and filing, go to **www.irs.gov** and click on Forms and Publications.

Katherine Kurtz, the accountant for Travelwithus.com, used the worksheet in Figure 8.4 to prepare Form 941 for the last quarter of the year. See the completed

SUCCESS TIP

Remember, 941 taxes include FIT and FICA (both employee and employer).

Figure 8.4 Worksheet Summary of Payroll Register

TRAVELWITHUS.COM, INC.
Worksheet Summary of Payroll Registers
4th Quarter, 201X

Pay Period Ending	Pay Date	Total Gross Earnings	OASDI Taxable Earnings	FIT	SIT	FICA OASDI	FICA Medicare	Medical Insurance	Net Pay
9/28	10/1	7 342 00	7 342 00	683 00	587 36	455 20	106 46	165 00	5 344 98
10/12	10/15	7 342 00	7 342 00	683 00	587 36	455 20	106 46	165 00	5 344 98
10/26	10/29	7 526 92	7 526 92	732 00	602 15	466 67	109 14	165 00	5 451 96
October Total		22 210 92	22 210 92	2 098 00	1 776 87	1 377 07	322 06	495 00	16 141 92
11/9	11/12	12 450 00	12 450 00	1 520 00	996 00	771 90	180 53	198 00	8 783 57
11/23	11/26	12 683 00	12 683 00	1 580 00	1 014 64	786 35	183 90	198 00	8 920 11
November Total		25 133 00	25 133 00	3 100 00	2 010 64	1 558 25	364 43	396 00	17 703 68
12/7	12/10	12 450 00	12 450 00	1 520 00	996 00	771 90	180 53	198 00	8 783 57
12/21	12/24	12 342 00	12 342 00	1 495 00	987 36	765 20	178 96	198 00	8 717 48
December Total		24 792 00	24 792 00	3 015 00	1 983 36	1 537 10	359 48	396 00	17 501 05
4th Qtr Total		72 135 92	72 135 92	8 213 00	5 770 87	4 472 42	1 045 97	1 287 00	51 346 63
YTD Total		308 647 68	308 647 68	37 155 00	24 691 81	19 136 16	4 475 39	5 049 00	218 140 32

Form 941 in Figure 8.5 on pages 270–271. The top section of Travelwithus.com's fourth quarter Form 941 in Figure 8.5 identifies the taxpayer, Travelwithus.com, and lists its address, the date that the quarter ended, and its EIN. For Part 1, compare the data found on Form 941 to the Worksheet (Figure 8.4).

Part 1:

- Line 1 asks for the number of employees on one specific date during the quarter.
- Line 2 requires the total gross pay for the quarter.
- Line 3 lists the total quarterly Federal Income Tax (FIT) withheld from all employees.
- Line 5 – Please notice that line 5 is divided into two columns and several sections.
  - Line 5a, column 1 records the total Social Security (FICA-OASDI) wages paid. This total is multiplied by 0.124, and that result is recorded in column 2.
  - Line 5c records the FICA-Medicare tax. Again, the employee portion is 0.0145 (1.45%), but, when matched by the employer, the total is 0.029 (2.9%).
  - Line 5e adds all line 5, column 2 amounts.
- Line 6 adds lines 3, 5e, and 5f.

Part 2:

- You should now skip to Part 2 (page 2) of the form. Complete and total the monthly tax liabilities found on line 16. The total of Part 2 is rewritten on line 12 of Part 1 (page 1).
- Line 10 equals Line 12 plus Line 11. Compare lines 6 and 10. The amounts should be equal or within a few cents. Please add/subtract the small adjustment needed for Line 7, which is the difference between lines 6 and 10. This kind of adjustment is due to rounding and happens often.
- Line 13 records the total of all deposits made for the quarter, and this line should equal line 12 if each monthly liability was deposited as required.

SUCCESS TIP

Can you figure out where the 0.124 comes from? Remember that the Social Security rate withheld from each employee is 0.062 (6.2%). In addition, the employer matches the amount withheld from the employee. Therefore, 0.062 x 0.062 = 0.124 (12.4%).

SUCCESS TIP

If a line is not needed, it should remain blank.

Figure 8.5 Completed Form 941

Form **941 for 201X:** **Employer's QUARTERLY Federal Tax Return**
Department of the Treasury — Internal Revenue Service

950117

OMB No. 1545-0029

Employer identification number (EIN) `5` `8` – `1` `2` `1` `3` `4` `7` `9`

Name *(not your trade name)* Katherine Kurtz

Trade name *(if any)* Travelwithus.com, Inc.

Address 10 Lovett Road
Number   Street   Suite or room number

Salem   MA   01970
City   State   ZIP code

Foreign country name   Foreign province/county   Foreign postal code

Report for this Quarter of 201X
(Check one.)

☐ 1: January, February, March

☐ 2: April, May, June

☐ 3: July, August, September

☒ 4: October, November, December

Instructions and prior year forms are available at *www.irs.gov/form941*.

Read the separate instructions before you complete Form 941. Type or print within the boxes.

Part 1: **Answer these questions for this quarter.**

1	Number of employees who received wages, tips, or other compensation for the pay period including: *Mar. 12* (Quarter 1), *June 12* (Quarter 2), *Sept. 12* (Quarter 3), or *Dec. 12* (Quarter 4)	1	5
2	Wages, tips, and other compensation	2	72135 . 90
3	Federal income tax withheld from wages, tips, and other compensation	3	8213 . 00

4   If no wages, tips, and other compensation are subject to social security or Medicare tax   ☐ Check and go to line 6.

		Column 1		Column 2	
5a	Taxable social security wages . .	72135 . 90	× 0.124 =	8944 . 85	
5b	Taxable social security tips . . .	.	× 0.124 =	.	
5c	Taxable Medicare wages & tips. .	72135 . 90	× 0.029 =	2091 . 94	
5d	Taxable wages & tips subject to Additional Medicare Tax withholding	.	× 0.009 =	.	

5e	Add Column 2 from lines 5a, 5b, 5c, and 5d	5e	11036 . 79
5f	Section 3121(q) Notice and Demand—Tax due on unreported tips (see instructions) . .	5f	.
6	Total taxes before adjustments. Add lines 3, 5e, and 5f	6	19249 . 79
7	Current quarter's adjustment for fractions of cents	7	- . 01
8	Current quarter's adjustment for sick pay	8	.
9	Current quarter's adjustments for tips and group-term life insurance	9	.
10	Total taxes after adjustments. Combine lines 6 through 9	10	19249 . 78
11	Qualified small business payroll tax credit for increasing research activities. Attach Form 8974	11	.
12	Total taxes after adjustments and credits. Subtract line 11 from line 10	12	19249 . 78
13	Total deposits for this quarter, including overpayment applied from a prior quarter and overpayments applied from Form 941-X, 941-X (PR), 944-X, or 944-X (SP) filed in the current quarter	13	19249 . 78
14	Balance due. If line 12 is more than line 13, enter the difference and see instructions . . .	14	.

15   Overpayment. If line 13 is more than line 12, enter the difference   `.`   Check one: ☐ Apply to next return.   ☐ Send a refund.

▶ **You MUST complete both pages of Form 941 and SIGN it.**

Next ▶

For Privacy Act and Paperwork Reduction Act Notice, see the back of the Payment Voucher.   Cat. No. 17001Z   Form **941**

Figure 8.5 (continued)

950217

Name *(not your trade name)*	Employer identification number (EIN)
Katherine Kurtz	58-1213479

Part 2: **Tell us about your deposit schedule and tax liability for this quarter.**

If you are unsure about whether you are a monthly schedule depositor or a semiweekly schedule depositor, see section 11 of Pub. 15.

16   Check one: ☐   Line 12 on this return is less than $2,500 or line 12 (line 10 if the prior quarter was the fourth quarter of 2016) on the return for the prior quarter was less than $2,500, and you didn't incur a $100,000 next-day deposit obligation during the current quarter. If line 12 (line 10 if the prior quarter was the fourth quarter of 2016) for the prior quarter was less than $2,500 but line 12 on this return is $100,000 or more, you must provide a record of your federal tax liability. If you are a monthly schedule depositor, complete the deposit schedule below; if you are a semiweekly schedule depositor, attach Schedule B (Form 941). Go to Part 3.

☒   **You were a monthly schedule depositor for the entire quarter.** Enter your tax liability for each month and total liability for the quarter, then go to Part 3.

Tax liability:	Month 1	5496.26
	Month 2	6945.36
	Month 3	6808.16
Total liability for quarter		19249.78	**Total must equal line 12.**

☐   **You were a semiweekly schedule depositor for any part of this quarter.** Complete Schedule B (Form 941), Report of Tax Liability for Semiweekly Schedule Depositors, and attach it to Form 941.

Part 3: **Tell us about your business. If a question does NOT apply to your business, leave it blank.**

17   If your business has closed or you stopped paying wages . . . . ☐ Check here, and

enter the final date you paid wages   [/   /]   .

18   If you are a seasonal employer and you don't have to file a return for every quarter of the year   . . ☐ Check here.

Part 4: **May we speak with your third-party designee?**

Do you want to allow an employee, a paid tax preparer, or another person to discuss this return with the IRS? See the instructions for details.

☐ Yes. Designee's name and phone number [   ] [   ]

Select a 5-digit Personal Identification Number (PIN) to use when talking to the IRS. ☐ ☐ ☐ ☐ ☐

☑ No.

Part 5: **Sign here. You MUST complete both pages of Form 941 and SIGN it.**

Under penalties of perjury, I declare that I have examined this return, including accompanying schedules and statements, and to the best of my knowledge and belief, it is true, correct, and complete. Declaration of preparer (other than taxpayer) is based on all information of which preparer has any knowledge.

X   **Sign your name here**   *Katherine Kurtz*

Print your name here   Katherine Kurtz

Print your title here   Controller

Date   01/31/1Y

Best daytime phone   (978)555-4040

Paid Preparer Use Only   Check if you are self-employed   . . . ☐

Preparer's name		PTIN	
Preparer's signature		Date	/ /
Firm's name (or yours if self-employed)		EIN	
Address		Phone	
City		State	ZIP code	

For your information, although Travelwithus.com is a monthly depositor now, it's probable the company will change to a semiweekly depositor in the future based on the YTD information.

When a change in classification occurs, the company will need to check the semiweekly depositor box in Part 2, line 16 of Form 941. Semiweekly depositors are required to submit an additional form named Schedule B, which details individual pay date liability for the quarter. This form is not covered in this chapter.

Additional Quarterly Requirements

State Unemployment Tax (SUTA). Although we do not demonstrate a state form, this is a reminder that, in most cases, the SUTA form and payment will be due by the last day of the month following the quarter. Please note that in Chapter 7 we computed and journalized the employer's payroll tax expense at the same time as we recorded the payroll. Remember that this entry recorded the cost of the SUTA. Similar journal entries are completed for each payroll within the quarter. The payment of the accumulated fourth-quarter SUTA liability is made in the following month, in this situation usually no later than January 31 of the next year. The following journal entry illustrates the accounts debited and credited when paying the SUTA liability.

GENERAL JOURNAL					
Date		PR	Dr.		Cr.
201Y					
Jan.	31	SUTA Payable		X X X	
		Cash			X X X

Federal Unemployment Tax (FUTA). FUTA tax returns (Form 940) are completed annually. However, the employer is responsible for computing the FUTA liability quarterly. If the federal unemployment tax liability exceeds $500 by the end of any calendar quarter, the employer must electronically remit a quarterly tax deposit. This deposit should be made by the last day of the month following the quarter. However, any amount due at the end of a calendar year must be paid by January 31 of the next year. As with SUTA, the FUTA tax expense is journalized when recording the employer's payroll tax liability for each payroll. The following journal entry shows how to record the payment of FUTA tax:

GENERAL JOURNAL					
Date		PR	Dr.		Cr.
201Y					
Jan.	31	FUTA Payable		X X X	
		Cash			X X X

 **TRY IT!**   **Learning Unit 8-2**

Answer the following questions.

1. True or false: Payroll quarters are based on pay date, not pay period ending.
2. On Form 941, line 5a, why are Social Security wages multiplied by 0.124?
3. What creates an adjustment on line 7 of Form 941?
4. Yes or no: On Part 2 of Form 941, are monthly depositors required to submit Schedule B?

1. True
2. The rate of 0.124 is twice the employee rate of 6.2% because the employer must match the employee FICA OASDI tax withheld.
3. This adjustment comes from rounding differences when computing individual payroll register tax to the total tax for the quarter.
4. No. Only semiweekly depositors are required to submit Form 941, Schedule B.

Annual Reports, Forms W-2 and W-3

Preparing Form 940 and Remitting Unpaid Liability

Form 940, Employer's Annual Federal Unemployment Tax Return, the federal unemployment tax report, is completed annually and filed by the last day of the month following the year. Currently, the tax report requires payment of 0.6% of the first $7,000 earned by each employee per calendar year, provided that all state unemployment taxes were filed and paid in a timely manner. Based on the payroll register (see Figure 7.3), it looks like all five employees of Travelwithus.com will exceed $7,000 by year end. This means that the employer will pay $42 per employee, for a total amount of $210.00 ($7000 × .6% × 5). Any unpaid current-year FUTA taxes should be electronically remitted by the last day of the month following the year. Based on the previous assumptions, please view Figure 8.6 (pages 274–275) to see a completed Form 940. As we learned earlier, all IRS forms and complete instructions can be found at **www.irs .gov**. To view this form, click on Current Forms and Publications and then type in "940."

Based on Form 940, you can see the balance due is $210.00. The journal entry to record the payment is illustrated below. Remember, you must make this payment no later than the last day of the month following the report year.

Form 940, Employer's Annual Federal Unemployment Tax Return Form used by employers at the end of the calendar year to report the amount of unemployment tax due for the year. If more than $500 is cumulatively owed at the end of a quarter, it should be paid 1 month after the end of that quarter. Normally, the report is due January 31 after the calendar year, or February 10 if an employer has already made all deposits.

		GENERAL JOURNAL					
	Date		PR	Dr.		Cr.	
201Y							
Jan.	31	FUTA Payable		2 1 0 00			
		Cash-General Checking				2 1 0 00	
		To pay FUTA liability for year 201X					

Preparing Form W-2: Wage and Tax Statement

The Internal Revenue Service requires that all employers complete Form W-2, Wage and Tax Statement, in a multipart format. The IRS requires Travelwithus.com to give or mail parts B, C, and copies 1 and 2 of Form W-2 to each person who worked for the company in the past year. These forms must be distributed by January 31 of the following year. Employees will use the amounts on Form W-2 to prepare their federal and state income tax returns. They must attach Copy B of the form to their federal income tax return (Form 1040), and attach other copies to any state or local income tax returns that they may be required to file. Taxpayers who file electronically do not attach a copy of their W-2 but must furnish a copy if requested by the IRS.

Figure 8.7 shows the W-2 that Stephanie Higuera received. Travelwithus.com prepares the W-2s by using information from Stephanie's employee earnings record (see Figure 7.4 on page 243). Note that OASDI and Medicare wages and taxes are shown on separate lines of the form because of the wage base limit for the OASDI tax that does not apply to the Medicare tax.

In addition to giving each employee a Form W-2, Travelwithus.com must also submit copies of all W-2s to the Social Security Administration and state and local governments. It will also keep a copy for its own records.

Form W-2, Wage and Tax Statement Form completed by the employer at the end of the calendar year to provide a summary of gross earnings and deductions to each employee. At least three copies go to the employee, one copy to the IRS, one copy to any state where employee income taxes have been withheld, one copy to the Social Security Administration, and one copy into the records of the business.

Figure 8.6 Completed Form 940

Form **940 for 201X:** **Employer's Annual Federal Unemployment (FUTA) Tax Return**

Department of the Treasury — Internal Revenue Service

850113

OMB No. 1545-0028

Employer identification number (EIN)   5 8 – 1 2 1 3 4 7 9

Name (not your trade name)   Katherine Kurtz

Trade name (if any)   Travelwithus.com, Inc.

Address   10 Lovett Road
Number   Street   Suite or room number

Salem   MA   01970
City   State   ZIP code

Foreign country name   Foreign province/county   Foreign postal code

Type of Return
(Check all that apply.)

☐ **a.** Amended
☐ **b.** Successor employer
☐ **c.** No payments to employees in 2016
☐ **d.** Final: Business closed or stopped paying wages

Instructions and prior-year forms are available at *www.irs.gov/form940.*

Read the separate instructions before you complete this form. Please type or print within the boxes.

Part 1:   Tell us about your return. If any line does NOT apply, leave it blank. See instructions before completing Part 1.

1a   If you had to pay state unemployment tax in one state only, enter the state abbreviation .   **1a**   M   A

1b   If you had to pay state unemployment tax in more than one state, you are a multi-state employer .   **1b** ☐ Check here. Complete Schedule A (Form 940).

2   If you paid wages in a state that is subject to CREDIT REDUCTION .   **2** ☐ Check here. Complete Schedule A (Form 940).

Part 2:   Determine your FUTA tax before adjustments. If any line does NOT apply, leave it blank.

3   Total payments to all employees .   **3**   308647 . 68

4   Payments exempt from FUTA tax .   **4**   .

Check all that apply: **4a** ☐ Fringe benefits   **4c** ☐ Retirement/Pension   **4e** ☐ Other
4b ☐ Group-term life insurance   **4d** ☐ Dependent care

5   Total of payments made to each employee in excess of $7,000 .   **5**   273647 . 68

6   Subtotal (line 4 + line 5 = line 6) .   **6**   273647 . 68

7   Total taxable FUTA wages (line 3 – line 6 = line 7). See instructions .   **7**   35000 . 00

8   FUTA tax before adjustments (line 7 x 0.006 = line 8) .   **8**   210 . 00

Part 3:   Determine your adjustments. If any line does NOT apply, leave it blank.

9   If ALL of the taxable FUTA wages you paid were excluded from state unemployment tax, multiply line 7 by 0.054 (line 7 x 0.054 = line 9). Go to line 12 .   **9**   .

10   If SOME of the taxable FUTA wages you paid were excluded from state unemployment tax, OR you paid ANY state unemployment tax late (after the due date for filing Form 940), complete the worksheet in the instructions. Enter the amount from line 7 of the worksheet .   **10**   .

11   If credit reduction applies, enter the total from Schedule A (Form 940) .   **11**   .

Part 4:   Determine your FUTA tax and balance due or overpayment. If any line does NOT apply, leave it blank.

12   Total FUTA tax after adjustments (lines 8 + 9 + 10 + 11 = line 12) .   **12**   210 . 00

13   FUTA tax deposited for the year, including any overpayment applied from a prior year .   **13**   .

14   Balance due. If line 12 is more than line 13, enter the excess on line 14.
• If line 14 is more than $500, you must deposit your tax.
• If line 14 is $500 or less, you may pay with this return. See instructions .   **14**   210 . 00

15   Overpayment. If line 13 is more than line 12, enter the excess on line 15 and check a box below   **15**   .

▶ You **MUST** complete both pages of this form and **SIGN** it.

Check one: ☐ Apply to next return.   ☐ Send a refund.

Next ▶

For Privacy Act and Paperwork Reduction Act Notice, see the back of Form 940-V, Payment Voucher.   Cat. No. 11234O   Form **940**

Figure 8.6 (continued)

850212

Name *(not your trade name)*	**Employer identification number (EIN)**
Katherine Kurtz	58-1213479

Part 5: Report your FUTA tax liability by quarter only if line 12 is more than $500. If not, go to Part 6.

16 Report the amount of your FUTA tax liability for each quarter; do NOT enter the amount you deposited. If you had no liability for a quarter, leave the line blank.

16a **1st quarter** (January 1 – March 31) . . . . 16a [.]

16b **2nd quarter** (April 1 – June 30) . . . . 16b [.]

16c **3rd quarter** (July 1 – September 30) . . . . 16c [.]

16d **4th quarter** (October 1 – December 31) . . . . 16d [.]

17 Total tax liability for the year (lines 16a + 16b + 16c + 16d = line 17) **17** [.] Total must equal line 12.

Part 6: May we speak with your third-party designee?

Do you want to allow an employee, a paid tax preparer, or another person to discuss this return with the IRS? See the instructions for details.

[ ] **Yes.** Designee's name and phone number

Select a 5-digit Personal Identification Number (PIN) to use when talking to IRS

[✓] **No.**

Part 7: Sign here. You MUST complete both pages of this form and SIGN it.

Under penalties of perjury, I declare that I have examined this return, including accompanying schedules and statements, and to the best of my knowledge and belief, it is true, correct, and complete, and that no part of any payment made to a state unemployment fund claimed as a credit was, or is to be, deducted from the payments made to employees. Declaration of preparer (other than taxpayer) is based on all information of which preparer has any knowledge.

X **Sign your name here** *Katherine Kurtz*

Print your name here Katherine Kurtz
Print your title here Controller

Date 01/31/1Y

Best daytime phone (978)555-4040

Paid Preparer Use Only   Check if you are self-employed [ ]

Preparer's name		PTIN	
Preparer's signature		Date	/ /
Firm's name (or yours if self-employed)		EIN	
Address		Phone	
City		State	ZIP code	

Figure 8.7 Stephanie Higuera's W-2 Form

22222	Void ☐	**a** Employee's social security number 123-45-6789	For Official Use Only ▶ OMB No. 1545-0008	

b Employer identification number (EIN) 58-1213479		**1** Wages, tips, other compensation 23,176.20	**2** Federal income tax withheld 2,241.86

c Employer's name, address, and ZIP code **Travelwithus.com, Inc.** **10 Lovett Road** **Salem, MA 01970**	**3** Social security wages 23,176.20	**4** Social security tax withheld 1,436.92
	5 Medicare wages and tips 23,176.20	**6** Medicare tax withheld 336.05
	7 Social security tips	**8** Allocated tips

d Control number	**9**	**10** Dependent care benefits

e Employee's first name and initial	Last name	Suff.	**11** Nonqualified plans	**12a** See instructions for box 12
Stephanie A.	**Higuera**			

13 Statutory employee ☐ Retirement plan ☐ Third-party sick pay ☐	**12b**
14 Other	**12c**
	12d

1014 Inverness Way
Southside, MA   01945

f Employee's address and ZIP code

15 State	Employer's state ID number	**16** State wages, tips, etc.	**17** State income tax	**18** Local wages, tips, etc.	**19** Local income tax	**20** Locality name
MA	621-8966-4	23,176.20	1,854.10			

Form **W-2**   Wage and Tax Statement   **201X**

Copy A For Social Security Administration — Send this entire page with
Form W-3 to the Social Security Administration; photocopies are **not** acceptable.

Department of the Treasury—Internal Revenue Service
**For Privacy Act and Paperwork Reduction
Act Notice, see the separate instructions.**

Cat. No. 10134D

Do Not Cut, Fold, or Staple Forms on This Page

Form W-3, Transmittal of Wage and Tax Statements Form completed by the employer to verify the number of W-2s and amounts withheld as shown on them. This form is sent to the Social Security Administration data processing center along with copies of each employee's W-2 forms.

Preparing Form W-3: Transmittal of Income and Tax Statements

The IRS also requires Travelwithus.com to prepare its Form W-3, Transmittal of Wage and Tax Statements. Employers such as Travelwithus.com send this form to the Social Security Administration along with Copy A of the W-2s for all employees. Form W-3 (see Figure 8.8) reports the total amounts of wages, tips, and compensation paid to employees, the total OASDI and Medicare taxes withheld, and some other information. Figure 8.9 provides the information for Figure 8.8.

The Social Security Administration, under a special agreement with the IRS, makes all information found on individual W-2 forms electronically available to the IRS so that it can check the accuracy of the employer's 941 forms and individual employees' federal income tax returns.

Employers not using tax software or a tax preparation service can create forms W-2 and W-3 electronically by using Business Services Online found at **www.socialsecurity.gov**. This is a free service and easy to use.

Other Annual Reporting Requirements

If an employer hires independent contractors, the company is required to prepare and distribute Form 1099 to each contractor that was paid $600 or more during the calendar year. These forms are submitted to the IRS with a recap Form 1096. Travelwithus.com did not use independent contractors during the year. Therefore, there are no forms to file or exhibit.

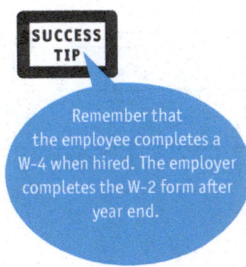

SUCCESS TIP

Remember that the employee completes a W-4 when hired. The employer completes the W-2 form after year end.

Figure 8.8 Travelwithus.com's W-3 Form

DO NOT STAPLE

a Control number	For Official Use Only ▶ OMB No. 1545-0008		
33333			

b Kind of Payer (Check one)	941 [X] Military [ ] 943 [ ] 944 [ ] CT-1 [ ] Hshld. emp. [ ] Medicare govt. emp. [ ]	Kind of Employer (Check one)	None apply [ ] 501c non-govt. [ ] State/local non-501c [ ] State/local 501c [ ] Federal govt. [ ]	Third-party sick pay (Check if applicable) [ ]

c Total number of Forms W-2 **5**	d Establishment number	1 Wages, tips, other compensation 308,647.68	2 Federal income tax withheld 37,155.00

e Employer identification number (EIN) 58-1213479	3 Social security wages 308,647.68	4 Social security tax withheld 19,136.16

f Employer's name Travelwithus.com, Inc.	5 Medicare wages and tips 308,647.68	6 Medicare tax withheld 4,475.39

10 Lovett Road
Salem, MA   01970

	7 Social security tips	8 Allocated tips
	9	10 Dependent care benefits
	11 Nonqualified plans	12a Deferred compensation

g Employer's address and ZIP code

h Other EIN used this year	13 For third-party sick pay use only	12b

15 State MA Employer's state ID number 621-8966-4	14 Income tax withheld by payer of third-party sick pay

16 State wages, tips, etc. 308,647.68	17 State income tax 24,691.81	18 Local wages, tips, etc.	19 Local income tax

Employer's contact person Katherine Kurtz	Employer's telephone number 978-555-4040	For Official Use Only

Employer's fax number	Employer's email address kkurtz@travelwithus.com

Under penalties of perjury, I declare that I have examined this return and accompanying documents and, to the best of my knowledge and belief, they are true, correct, and complete.

Signature ▶   Title ▶ Controller   Date ▶ 2/28/201Y

Form **W-3** **Transmittal of Wage and Tax Statements**   **201X**   Department of the Treasury Internal Revenue Service

Send this entire page with the entire Copy A page of Form(s) W-2 to the Social Security Administration (SSA). Photocopies are not acceptable. Do not send Form W-3 if you filed electronically with the SSA. Do not send any payment (cash, checks, money orders, etc.) with Forms W-2 and W-3.

Figure 8.9 Travelwithus.com's Employee YTD Earnings Summary

TRAVELWITHUS.COM INC.
Employee YTD Earnings Summary
201X

Employee Name		Gross Earnings YTD	OASDI Taxable Earnings	FIT	SIT	FICA OASDI	FICA Medicare	FUTA Taxable	FUTA Rate 0.60%
Higuera, Stephanie		23,176 20	23,176 20	2,241 86	1,854 10	1,436 92	336 05	7,000 00	42 00
Kurtz, Katherine		124,999 98	124,999 98	6,406 00	10,000 00	7,750 00	1,812 50	7,000 00	42 00
Regan, Julia		1,262 50	1,262 50	135 10 21	101 00 00	78 27 50	18 30 63	7,000 00	42 00
Sui, Annie		10,095 80	10,095 80	807 66	807 66	625 94	146 39	7,000 00	42 00
Taylor, Harold		24,125 70	24,125 70	2,052 14	1,930 05	1,495 80	349 82	7,000 00	42 00
Total YTD	per W-3	308,647 68	308,647 68	37,155 00	24,691 81	19,136 16	4,475 39	35,000 00	210 00

 **TRY IT!** **Learning Unit 8-3**

Answer true or false to the following statements.

1. A Form W-2 is sent annually to each employee on or before December 31 of the pay year.
2. Form W-3 is a recap of all W-2s and is submitted to the Social Security Administration.
3. FUTA tax Form 940 is submitted and paid annually.

TRY IT! **Solution Learning Unit 8-3**

1. False. Form W-2 is distributed to each employee no later than January 31.
2. True
3. False. If the FUTA tax liability is equal to or greater than $500.00 at the end of any quarter, the FUTA tax must be electronically submitted to the IRS by the last day of the month following the quarter. However, Form 940 is an annual report filed by the last day of the month following the year.

LO1,2,3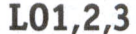

DEMONSTRATION SUMMARY PROBLEM

House of Colors, owned by Jordan Lewis, is a growing company providing interior design services. The company is located at 123 Pine Street, Concord, MA 01742. House of Colors is classified as a monthly tax depositor, and their EIN # is 22-2222222. They currently have four employees who are paid monthly on the last day of the month. In the current year, all employees earned in excess of the FUTA wage limit; however, only one earned in excess of the OASDI wage limit. The following is a Worksheet Summary of the fourth-quarter payroll activity for House of Colors.

House of Colors
Worksheet Summary of Monthly Payroll Registers
4th Quarter, 201X

Pay Period Ending and Pay Date	Total Gross Earnings	OASDI Taxable Earnings	FIT	SIT	FICA OASDI	FICA Medicare	Medical Insurance	Net Pay
YTD @ September 30	147,600.00	147,600.00	18,980.00	7,380.00	9,151.20	2,140.20	2,700.00	107,248.60
10/31/1X	17,517.40	17,517.40	2,180.00	875.87	1,086.08	254.00	300.00	12,821.45
11/30/1X	17,229.17	17,229.17	2,010.00	861.46	1,068.21	249.82	300.00	12,739.68
12/31/1X	18,686.00	18,686.00	2,416.00	934.30	1,158.53	270.95	300.00	13,606.22
4th Qtr. Total	53,432.57	53,432.57	6,606.00	2,671.63	3,312.82	774.77	900.00	39,167.35
YTD Total	201,032.57	201,032.57	25,586.00	10,051.63	12,464.02	2,914.97	3,600.00	146,415.95

Requirements

1. Compute the payroll tax deposit for each month. When is the general due date for each deposit?
2. Prepare a Form 941 for the fourth quarter.
3. Prepare a Form 940.
4. Find the general due date for filing Forms 941 and 940.

Solutions

Requirement 1

Compute the payroll tax deposit for each month.

Using the Worksheet Summary above, compute each month's tax deposit by adding the total FIT + twice the OASDI + twice the Medicare. Why twice? Remember, the employer is required to match the employee deduction for OASDI and Medicare. See the computation schedule below. Because the company is a monthly depositor, the general deposit due date is the 15th day of the following month.

Computations

Month of Pay	FIT + 2(OASDI + Medicare)
October 201X	$2,180.00 + 2($1,086.08 + $254.00)
November 201X	$2,010.00 + 2($1,068.21 + $249.82)
December 201X	$2,416.00 + 2($1,158.53 + $270.95)

Solution

Month of Pay	Amount of Deposit	Deposit Due Date
October 201X	$4,860.16	November 15, 201X
November 201X	$4,646.06	December 15, 201X
December 201X	$5,274.96	January 15, 201Y

Requirement 2

Prepare a Form 941 for the fourth quarter.

Tips for Computing a Basic Form 941

STEP 1: Complete the employer information at the top of page 1. This includes the company name, address, EIN, and quarter.

STEP 2: Complete necessary lines 1–6 of Part 1 using the information given. If a line is not used, leave it blank. Lines 2, 3, 5a (column 1), and 5c (column 1) are found on the 4th Qtr. Total line of the Worksheet Summary of Monthly Payroll Registers.

STEP 3: Complete page 2 of the form. In Part 2, House of Colors marks the monthly depositor box, then lists the liability per individual month. Use the amounts computed in Requirement 1. The total liability for the quarter is recorded here and on page 1, line 12.

STEP 4: On page 1, Line 12 plus Line 11 equals Line 10. Compare page 1, lines 6 and 10. If these amounts differ by only a few cents, record the pennies on line 7, so that line 6 plus/minus line 7 will equal line 10. Record all deposits made on line 13. Lines 12 and 13 should equal, if all deposits were accurately made.

STEP 5: The owner will sign and date page 2, Part 5. Mail by due date.

Solution of completed Form 941 for House of Colors (see pages 281–282).

Requirement 3

Prepare a Form 940.

Tips for Computing a Basic Form 940

STEP 1: Complete the employer information at the top of page 1. This includes the company name, address, EIN, and quarter.

STEP 2: Complete Part 1.

STEP 3: Complete Part 2 by recording the total YTD earnings for all employees on line 3. The problem stated that all four employees earned in excess of the FUTA wage limit of $7,000.00. Therefore, line 7 = $28,000.00 (4 × $7,000). The difference between lines 3 and 7 is the amount of compensation in excess of the FUTA limit and is recorded on lines 5

SUCCESS TIP

When operating as a sole proprietorship, the owner's name is listed as NAME, with company name listed as TRADE NAME.

and 6. Line 8 records the FUTA owed, the result of line 7 ($28,000.00 × .6% = $168.00). Because this amount is less than $500.00, a check can be sent with the report.

STEP 4:   Complete Parts 3 and 4.

STEP 5:   Complete page 2. The owner will sign and date page 2, Part 7. Mail by due date.

Completed solution Form 940 for House of Colors (see pages 283–284).

Requirement 4

Find the general due date for filing Forms 941 and 940.

The general due date for filing Form 941 (Quarterly Report) is the last day of the month following the calendar quarter. The general due date for filing Form 940 (Annual Report) is the last day of the month following the calendar year. In this specific case, both reports should be filed by January 31, 201Y.

Form **941 for 201X:** **Employer's QUARTERLY Federal Tax Return**

950117

Department of the Treasury — Internal Revenue Service

OMB No. 1545-0029

Employer identification number (EIN) `2` `2` – `2` `2` `2` `2` `2` `2` `2`

Name *(not your trade name)* Jordan Lewis

Trade name *(if any)* House of Colors

Address 123 Pine Street
Number   Street   Suite or room number

Concord   MA   01742
City   State   ZIP code

Foreign country name   Foreign province/county   Foreign postal code

Report for this Quarter of 201X
(Check one.)

☐ **1:** January, February, March

☐ **2:** April, May, June

☐ **3:** July, August, September

☒ **4:** October, November, December

Instructions and prior year forms are available at *www.irs.gov/form941.*

Read the separate instructions before you complete Form 941. Type or print within the boxes.

Part 1: **Answer these questions for this quarter.**

1	Number of employees who received wages, tips, or other compensation for the pay period including: *Mar. 12* (Quarter 1), *June 12* (Quarter 2), *Sept. 12* (Quarter 3), or *Dec. 12* (Quarter 4)	1	4
2	Wages, tips, and other compensation	2	53432 . 57
3	Federal income tax withheld from wages, tips, and other compensation	3	6606 . 00
4	If no wages, tips, and other compensation are subject to social security or Medicare tax	☐ Check and go to line 6.	

		Column 1		Column 2
5a	Taxable social security wages	53432 . 57	× 0.124 =	6625 . 64
5b	Taxable social security tips	.	× 0.124 =	.
5c	Taxable Medicare wages & tips	53432 . 57	× 0.029 =	1549 . 54
5d	Taxable wages & tips subject to Additional Medicare Tax withholding	.	× 0.009 =	.

5e	Add Column 2 from lines 5a, 5b, 5c, and 5d	5e	8175 . 18
5f	Section 3121(q) Notice and Demand—Tax due on unreported tips (see instructions)	5f	.
6	Total taxes before adjustments. Add lines 3, 5e, and 5f	6	14781 . 18
7	Current quarter's adjustment for fractions of cents	7	.
8	Current quarter's adjustment for sick pay	8	.
9	Current quarter's adjustments for tips and group-term life insurance	9	.
10	Total taxes after adjustments. Combine lines 6 through 9	10	14781 . 18
11	Qualified small business payroll tax credit for increasing research activities. Attach Form 8974	11	.
12	Total taxes after adjustments and credits. Subtract line 11 from line 10	12	14781 . 18
13	Total deposits for this quarter, including overpayment applied from a prior quarter and overpayments applied from Form 941-X, 941-X (PR), 944-X, or 944-X (SP) filed in the current quarter	13	14781 . 18
14	Balance due. If line 12 is more than line 13, enter the difference and see instructions	14	.
15	Overpayment. If line 13 is more than line 12, enter the difference	.	Check one: ☐ Apply to next return. ☐ Send a refund.

▶ **You MUST complete both pages of Form 941 and SIGN it.**

Next ▶

For Privacy Act and Paperwork Reduction Act Notice, see the back of the Payment Voucher.   Cat. No. 17001Z   Form **941**

950217

Name *(not your trade name)*	Employer identification number (EIN)
Jordan Lewis	22-2222222

Part 2:   Tell us about your deposit schedule and tax liability for this quarter.

If you are unsure about whether you are a monthly schedule depositor or a semiweekly schedule depositor, see section 11 of Pub. 15.

16   Check one: ☐   Line 12 on this return is less than $2,500 or line 12 (line 10 if the prior quarter was the fourth quarter of 2016) on the return for the prior quarter was less than $2,500, and you didn't incur a $100,000 next-day deposit obligation during the current quarter. If line 12 (line 10 if the prior quarter was the fourth quarter of 2016) for the prior quarter was less than $2,500 but line 12 on this return is $100,000 or more, you must provide a record of your federal tax liability. If you are a monthly schedule depositor, complete the deposit schedule below; if you are a semiweekly schedule depositor, attach Schedule B (Form 941). Go to Part 3.

☒   **You were a monthly schedule depositor for the entire quarter.** Enter your tax liability for each month and total liability for the quarter, then go to Part 3.

	Tax liability:	Month 1	4860 . 16
		Month 2	4646 . 06
		Month 3	5274 . 96
	Total liability for quarter		14781 . 18 **Total must equal line 12.**

☐   **You were a semiweekly schedule depositor for any part of this quarter.** Complete Schedule B (Form 941), Report of Tax Liability for Semiweekly Schedule Depositors, and attach it to Form 941.

Part 3:   Tell us about your business. If a question does NOT apply to your business, leave it blank.

17   If your business has closed or you stopped paying wages . . . .   ☐ Check here, and

enter the final date you paid wages   [/   /   ] .

18   If you are a seasonal employer and you don't have to file a return for every quarter of the year   . .   ☐ Check here.

Part 4:   May we speak with your third-party designee?

Do you want to allow an employee, a paid tax preparer, or another person to discuss this return with the IRS? See the instructions for details.

☐ Yes.   Designee's name and phone number   [   ]   [   ]

Select a 5-digit Personal Identification Number (PIN) to use when talking to the IRS.   ☐ ☐ ☐ ☐ ☐

☒ No.

Part 5:   Sign here. You MUST complete both pages of Form 941 and SIGN it.

Under penalties of perjury, I declare that I have examined this return, including accompanying schedules and statements, and to the best of my knowledge and belief, it is true, correct, and complete. Declaration of preparer (other than taxpayer) is based on all information of which preparer has any knowledge.

X	Sign your name here	*Jordan Lewis*	Print your name here	Jordan Lewis
			Print your title here	Owner
	Date	01/31/1Y	Best daytime phone	

Paid Preparer Use Only   Check if you are self-employed . . . ☐

Preparer's name		PTIN	
Preparer's signature		Date	/ /
Firm's name (or yours if self-employed)		EIN	
Address		Phone	
City		State		ZIP code	

Form **940 for 201X:**   **Employer's Annual Federal Unemployment (FUTA) Tax Return**

Department of the Treasury — Internal Revenue Service

850113

OMB No. 1545-0028

Employer identification number (EIN)   2 2 – 2 2 2 2 2 2 2

Name *(not your trade name)*   Jordan Lewis

Trade name *(if any)*   House of Colors

Address   123 Pine Street
Number   Street   Suite or room number

Concord   MA   01742
City   State   ZIP code

Foreign country name   Foreign province/county   Foreign postal code

Type of Return
(Check all that apply.)

☐ a. Amended
☐ b. Successor employer
☐ c. No payments to employees in 2013
☐ d. Final: Business closed or stopped paying wages

Instructions and prior-year forms are available at *www.irs.gov/form940.*

Read the separate instructions before you complete this form. Please type or print within the boxes.

Part 1:   Tell us about your return. If any line does NOT apply, leave it blank.

1a   If you had to pay state unemployment tax in one state only, enter the state abbreviation .   1a   M   A

1b   If you had to pay state unemployment tax in more than one state, you are a multi-state employer . . . .   1b ☐   Check here. Complete Schedule A (Form 940).

2   If you paid wages in a state that is subject to CREDIT REDUCTION . . . .   2 ☐   Check here. Complete Schedule A (Form 940).

Part 2:   Determine your FUTA tax before adjustments for 2013. If any line does NOT apply, leave it blank.

3   Total payments to all employees   3   201032 . 57

4   Payments exempt from FUTA tax   4   .

Check all that apply: **4a** ☐ Fringe benefits   **4c** ☐ Retirement/Pension   **4e** ☐ Other
4b ☐ Group-term life insurance   **4d** ☐ Dependent care

5   Total of payments made to each employee in excess of $7,000   5   173032 . 57

6   Subtotal (line 4 + line 5 = line 6)   6   173032 . 57

7   Total taxable FUTA wages (line 3 – line 6 = line 7) (see instructions)   7   28000 . 00

8   FUTA tax before adjustments (line 7 x .006 = line 8)   8   168 . 00

Part 3:   Determine your adjustments. If any line does NOT apply, leave it blank.

9   If ALL of the taxable FUTA wages you paid were excluded from state unemployment tax, multiply line 7 by .054 (line 7 × .054 = line 9). Go to line 12   9   .

10   If SOME of the taxable FUTA wages you paid were excluded from state unemployment tax, OR you paid ANY state unemployment tax late (after the due date for filing Form 940), complete the worksheet in the instructions. Enter the amount from line 7 of the worksheet . .   10   .

11   If credit reduction applies, enter the total from Schedule A (Form 940)   11   .

Part 4:   Determine your FUTA tax and balance due or overpayment for 2013. If any line does NOT apply, leave it blank.

12   Total FUTA tax after adjustments (lines 8 + 9 + 10 + 11 = line 12)   12   168 . 00

13   FUTA tax deposited for the year, including any overpayment applied from a prior year .   13   .

14   Balance due (If line 12 is more than line 13, enter the excess on line 14.)
• If line 14 is more than $500, you must deposit your tax.
• If line 14 is $500 or less, you may pay with this return. (see instructions)   14   168 . 00

15   Overpayment (If line 13 is more than line 12, enter the excess on line 15 and check a box below.)   15   .

▶ You **MUST** complete both pages of this form and **SIGN** it.   Check one: ☐ Apply to next return.   ☐ Send a refund.

Next ▶

For Privacy Act and Paperwork Reduction Act Notice, see the back of Form 940-V, Payment Voucher.   Cat. No. 11234O   Form **940**

850212

Name *(not your trade name)*	Employer identification number (EIN)
Jordan Lewis	22-2222222

Part 5: Report your FUTA tax liability by quarter only if line 12 is more than $500. If not, go to Part 6.

16 Report the amount of your FUTA tax liability for each quarter; do NOT enter the amount you deposited. If you had no liability for a quarter, leave the line blank.

16a **1st quarter** (January 1 – March 31) . . . . 16a [.]

16b **2nd quarter** (April 1 – June 30) . . . . 16b [.]

16c **3rd quarter** (July 1 – September 30) . . . . 16c [.]

16d **4th quarter** (October 1 – December 31) . . . . . . 16d [.]

17 **Total tax liability for the year** (lines 16a + 16b + 16c + 16d = line 17) 17 [.] Total must equal line 12.

Part 6: May we speak with your third-party designee?

Do you want to allow an employee, a paid tax preparer, or another person to discuss this return with the IRS? See the instructions for details.

☐ **Yes.**   Designee's name and phone number

Select a 5-digit Personal Identification Number (PIN) to use when talking to IRS

☒ **No.**

Part 7: Sign here. You MUST complete both pages of this form and SIGN it.

Under penalties of perjury, I declare that I have examined this return, including accompanying schedules and statements, and to the best of my knowledge and belief, it is true, correct, and complete, and that no part of any payment made to a state unemployment fund claimed as a credit was, or is to be, deducted from the payments made to employees. Declaration of preparer (other than taxpayer) is based on all information of which preparer has any knowledge.

✗ **Sign your name here** *Jordan Lewis*

Print your name here Jordan Lewis

Print your title here owner

Date 01/31/1Y

Best daytime phone

Paid Preparer Use Only

Check if you are self-employed ☐

Preparer's name		PTIN
Preparer's signature		Date / /
Firm's name (or yours if self-employed)		EIN
Address		Phone
City	State	ZIP code

SUCCESS COACH

The following Success Tips are from Learning Units 8-1 through 8-3. Take the Do It Right Now Checkup and use the Check Your Score at the bottom of the page to see how you are doing. The Success Coach provides tips before each Checkup to help you avoid common accounting errors.

LU 8-1 Payroll and Depositing Taxes

Do It Right Tips: Federal Form 941 reports the FIT, OASDI, and Medicare taxes withheld from employees, as well as reports the OASDI and Medicare taxes due from the employer.

Do It Right Now Checkup: Answer true or false to the following statements.

1. If an employer owed less than $50,000 in total taxes during the look-back period, it would be classified as a quarterly depositor.
2. The majority of businesses normally make their payroll tax deposits to pay their Form 941 taxes either monthly or semiweekly.
3. FIT, OASDI, Medicare, and FUTA taxes are known as Form 941 taxes.
4. Regardless of the amount of taxes owed, an employer must pay its Form 941 taxes using the Electronic Federal Tax Payment System (EFTPS).
5. Very few companies use a special checking account for paying their payroll.

LU 8-2 Quarterly Reports for Federal and State Governments

Do It Right Tips: Form 941 is filed quarterly. This form is used by the IRS to reconcile payroll tax liability to the tax deposits made.

Do It Right Now Checkup: Answer true or false to the following statements.

1. If the amount of FUTA tax is less than $500 during a given quarter, no deposit is required until the FUTA tax liability reaches $500 or until the year ends.
2. Form 941 is prepared monthly.
3. Form 941 reports OASDI taxable earnings.
4. Line 7 of Form 941 is used to adjust for small differences between line 6 and line 10.
5. Line 6 of Form 941 is the total of lines 1–5f.

LU 8-3 Annual Reports, Forms W-2 and W-3

Do It Right Tips: At the end of a calendar year, a company prepares a form W-2 for each employee. This form records the gross earnings of and taxes withheld by the employee during the year.

Do It Right Now Checkup: Answer true or false to the following statements.

1. Generally, the Employer's Annual Federal Unemployment (FUTA) Tax Return, Form 940 is not due until January 31.
2. Form W-2s must be distributed to employees no later than February 10.
3. Small employers can electronically file W-2s and W-3s using the Business Services Office found on the Social Security website.
4. Employers send Form W-2s and Form W-3s to the Social Security Administration so employees' individual federal income tax returns may be checked.
5. FUTA taxes owed at the end of the year are always paid electronically.

CHECK YOUR SCORE: Answers to the Do It Right Now Checkup

LU 8-1
1. False—If an employer owed less than $50,000 in total taxes during the look-back period, it would be classified as a monthly depositor.
2. True
3. False—FIT, OASDI, and Medicare taxes are known as Form 941 taxes. FUTA is not a Form 941 tax; it is paid using a Form 940, FUTA Tax Return.
4. False—An employer is required to use EFTPS only if the employer owes more than $2,500 in a quarter.
5. False—Almost all large companies establish a special account for paying their payroll. It strengthens cash control, simplifies check reconciliation, and reduces the likelihood of an overdraft.

LU 8-2
1. True
2. False—Form 941 is prepared quarterly.

3. True—OASDI taxable earnings are reported on line 5a, column 1.
4. True
5. False—Line 6 is the total of lines 3, 5e, and 5f.

LU 8-3
1. True
2. False—Form W-2s must be distributed to employees by January 31.
3. True
4. True
5. False—FUTA taxes owed at the end of the year are usually paid electronically, but can be paid by check if the amount owed is less than $500.00.

BLUEPRINT: FORM 941 TAX DEPOSIT RULES

Ten Frequently Asked Questions and Answers About Depositing OASDI, Medicare, and FIT to the Government

Here is a summary of questions and answers to help you understand the payroll tax deposit rules for Form 941 taxes:

1. **What are Form 941 taxes?** The term *Form 941 taxes* is used to describe the amount of FIT, OASDI, and Medicare paid by employees and the amount of OASDI and Medicare taxes that are matched and paid by an employer. The total of these taxes is known as Form 941 taxes because it is reported on Form 941 each quarter.

2. **When does an employer deposit Form 941 taxes?** How often an employer deposits Form 941 taxes depends on how the employer is classified for this purpose. The IRS usually classifies an employer as either a monthly or semiweekly depositor based on the amount of Form 941 taxes paid during a time period known as a look-back period.

3. **When is a look-back period?** A look-back period is a fiscal year that begins on July 1, 2 years earlier, and ends on June 30 of the year before the calendar year when the deposits will be made. For example, for the 2017 calendar year, an employer's look-back period will begin on July 1, 2015, and end on June 30, 2016.

4. **What is the dollar amount used to classify an employer for Form 941 tax deposits?** The key dollar amount used to determine whether an employer is a monthly or semiweekly depositor is $50,000 in Form 941 taxes. Two rules apply here:

    a. If the total amount deposited in Form 941 taxes is less than $50,000 during the look-back period, the employer is considered a monthly tax depositor.

    b. If the total amount deposited in Form 941 taxes is $50,000 or more during the look-back period, the employer is considered a semiweekly tax depositor.

5. **How do employers deposit Form 941 taxes?** Unless an employer pays Form 941 taxes of less than $2,500 per quarter the employer must utilize the Electronic Federal Tax Payment System (EFTPS) to deposit Form 941 taxes. If the amount of Form 941 taxes owed is less than $2,500 per quarter, payment may be made by check at the time of the submission of Form 941.

6. **When do monthly depositors make their deposits?** A monthly depositor will figure the total amount of Form 941 taxes owed in a calendar month and then pay this amount by the 15th of the next month. If an employer owes $3,125 in Form 941 taxes for the month of June, it will deposit this same amount no later than July 15 of the same year.

7. **When do semiweekly depositors make their deposits?** The rules for making deposits are a little more complicated for a semiweekly depositor. When a tax deposit is due depends on when the employees are paid. To keep the rules consistent, the IRS has taken a calendar week and divided it into two payday time periods.

    Two deposit rules apply to these two time periods. We can call these rules the Wednesday and Friday rules.

    a. Wednesday rule: If employees are paid during the Wednesday through Friday of week 1 period, the tax deposit will be due on Wednesday of week 2.

    b. Friday rule: If employees are paid anytime from Saturday of week 1 through Tuesday of week 2, the tax deposit will be due on Friday of week 2.

    c. Exception to the rules: If an employer owes more than $100,000 Form 941 tax at any time during the pay period, the money must be deposited within 24 hours. If an employer owes less than $2,500 in a calendar quarter, the money can be submitted with Form 941.

8. **What is a banking day?** The term *banking day* refers to any day that banks are open to the public for business. Saturdays, Sundays, and legal holidays are not banking days.

9. **How do legal holidays affect payroll tax deposits?** If a legal holiday occurs after the last day of a payday time period, the employer will get one extra day to make its Form 941 tax deposit as follows:

    a. For monthly depositors: If the 15th of the month is a Saturday, Sunday, or legal holiday, the deposit will be due and payable on the next banking day.

    b. For semiweekly depositors: A deposit due on Wednesday will be due on Thursday of the same week, and a Friday deposit will be due on Monday of the following week. Remember that the employer will always have three banking days after the last day of either payday time period to make its payroll tax deposit.

10. **What happens if an employer is late with its Form 941 tax deposit?** If a Form 941 tax deposit is not made the day it should be deposited, the employer may be assessed a fine for lateness and may even be charged interest, depending on how late the deposit is.

Discussion Questions and Critical Thinking/Ethical Case

1. Why might a company have a separate cash account for payroll?

2. How do you transfer money into the payroll cash account?

3. What account is debited when recording the distribution of the payroll checks to the employees?

4. What is a look-back period?

5. How is an employer classified as a monthly or semiweekly depositor for Form 941 tax purposes?

6. How are Form 941 taxes paid to the Treasury Department?

7. How often is Form 941 completed?

8. Under what circumstance(s) does the amount on line 14 of Form 941 match the amount found on line 12?

9. Bill Smith leaves his job on July 9. He requests a copy of his W-2 form when he leaves. His boss tells him to wait until January of next year. Please discuss whether Bill's boss is correct in making this statement.

10. Why would one employer prepare a Form 940 completing Part 1, line 1a, but another would prepare a Form 940 Part 1, line 1b?

11. Employer A has a FUTA tax liability of $67.49 on March 31 of the current year. When does the employer have to make the deposit for this liability?

12. Employer B has a FUTA tax liability of $553.24 on January 31 of the current year. When does the employer have to make the deposit for this liability?

13. Who completes Form W-2? Form W-3? When is each form completed?

14. Discuss ways an employer can prepare and submit forms W-2 and W-3 online.

15. Happy Carpet Cleaning, Inc., collects FIT, OASDI, and Medicare from its employees by withholding these taxes from its employees' pay. However, Happy does not pay these amounts to the federal government until the end of the calendar year so that it can maximize its cash during the year. Because it will be paying these amounts to the government, it believes that this practice does not affect its employees. Please comment on this practice.

Concept Check

Look-Back Periods

L01 *(10 min)*

1. Label the following look-back periods for 20XC by months.

A	B	C	D
20XA		20XB	

Monthly versus Semiweekly Depositor

L01 *(15 min)*

2. In December 200B, Becky tries to find out whether she is a monthly or semiweekly depositor for FICA (OASDI and Medicare) and federal income tax for 20XC. Please advise based on the following taxes owed:

20XA	Quarter 3	$44,000
	Quarter 4	10,000
20XB	Quarter 1	3,100
	Quarter 2	10,700

(15 min) **LO1**

Monthly versus Semiweekly Depositor

3. In December 200B, Becky is trying to find out whether she is a monthly or semi-weekly depositor for FICA (OASDI and Medicare) and federal income tax for 20XC. Please advise based on the following taxes owed:

20XA	Quarter 3	$38,000
	Quarter 4	10,000
20XB	Quarter 1	3,100
	Quarter 2	10,700

(15 min) **LO1**

Paying the Tax

4. Complete the following table:

Depositor	4-Quarter Look-Back Period Tax Liability	Payroll Paid	Tax Paid by
Monthly	$28,000	November	a.
Semiweekly	$66,000	On Wednesday	b.
		On Thursday	c.
		On Friday	d.
		On Saturday	e.
		On Sunday	f.
		On Monday	g.

(15 min) **LO1,2,3**

Payroll Account

5. Indicate which of the following items apply to the following account titles.

    1. An asset
    2. A liability
    3. An expense
    4. Appears on the income statement
    5. Appears on the balance sheet

    _____ a. FICA OASDI Payable

    _____ b. Office Salaries Expense

    _____ c. Federal Income Tax Payable

    _____ d. FICA Medicare Payable

    _____ e. Wages and Salaries Payable

MyLabAccounting

Exercises

Set A

(10 min) **LO1**

8A-1. Lopez Company uses a special payroll account to pay employees. The gross amount of the payroll this week is $5,320; the net amount is $4,545. Journalize the transfer of funds to the payroll account and the distribution of paychecks to the employees.

8A-2. Based on the following payroll tax depositor classifications, determine the 941 tax deposit due date for each taxpayer:

L01 *(15 min)*

   a. Monthly depositor, owing $1,500 tax for the first quarter. _____

   b. Monthly depositor, owing $5,000 tax for the month of July. _____

   c. Monthly depositor, owing $110,000 tax as of Tuesday. _____

   d. Semiweekly depositor, owing $110,000 tax as of Tuesday. _____

   e. Semiweekly depositor, owing $20,000 tax as of Friday. _____

8A-3. Using a blank form 941, complete Part 1, lines 1–6, using the following information:

L02 *(20 min)*

Total employees during the first quarter	3
Total wages during the first quarter, none came from tips	$26,980.39
Federal income tax withheld	$ 2,125.00

8A-4. At the end of November 201X, the total amount of OASDI, $480, and Medicare, $250, was withheld as tax deductions from the employees of Calm Waters, Inc. Federal income tax of $2,980 was also deducted from their paychecks. Calm Waters is classified as a monthly depositor of Form 941 taxes. Indicate when this payroll tax deposit is due and provide a general journal entry to record the payment.

L01 *(20 min)*

8A-5. Magenta Company has four employees, and each employee earned $56,000 for the calendar year. Using a blank Form 940, complete Part 2, lines 3–8, to answer the following questions:

L03 *(20 min)*

Total annual payroll for the year	?
Payments made in excess of $7,000 FUTA limit	?
Total FUTA liability before any adjustments	?

8A-6. Louise's Grocery Store made the following Form 941 payroll tax deposits during the look-back period of July 1, 201A, through June 30, 201B:

L01 *(10 min)*

Quarter Ended	Amount Paid in 941 Taxes
September 30, 201A	$15,780.98
December 31, 201A	13,891.89
March 31, 201B	13,600.02
June 30, 201B	14,021.69

Should Louise's Grocery Store make Form 941 tax deposits monthly or semiweekly for 201C?

8A-7. If Lauren's Grocery Store downsized its operation during the second quarter of 201B and, as a result, paid only $6,121.54 in Form 941 taxes for the quarter that ended on June 30, 201B, should Louise's Grocery Store make its Form 941 payroll tax deposits monthly or semiweekly for 201C?

8A-8. Assuming a semiweekly depositor, from the following T accounts, record: (a) the July 3 payment for FICA (OASDI and Medicare) and federal income taxes, (b) the July 31 payment of SUTA tax, and (c) the July 31 deposit of any FUTA tax that may be required.

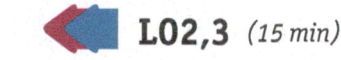

FICA OASDI Payable 203		FICA Medicare Payable 204	
	June 30 390 (EE)		June 30 110 (EE)
	390 (ER)		110 (ER)

FIT Payable 205		FUTA Payable 206	
	June 30 3,007		June 30 142

SUTA Payable 207	
	June 30 607

Set B

(10 min) **LO1**   **8B-1.**   Amador Company uses a special payroll account to pay employees. The gross amount of the payroll this week is $5,900; the net amount is $5,000. Journalize the transfer of funds to the payroll account and the distribution of paychecks to the employees.

(15 min) **LO1**   **8B-2.**   Based on the following payroll tax depositor classifications, determine the 941 tax deposit due date for each taxpayer:

    a.   Monthly depositor, owing $1,850 tax for the third quarter.   _____

    b.   Monthly depositor, owing $4,100 tax for the month of May.   _____

    c.   Monthly depositor, owing $121,000 tax as of Thursday.   _____

    d.   Semiweekly depositor, owing $121,000 tax as of Friday.   _____

    e.   Semiweekly depositor, owing $32,000 tax as of Friday.   _____

(20 min) **LO2**   **8B-3.**   Using a blank Form 941, complete Part 1, lines 1–6, using the following information:

Total employees during the first quarter	3
Total wages during the first quarter, none came from tips	$26,800.15
Federal income tax withheld	$ 2,025.00

(20 min) **LO1**   **8B-4.**   At the end of April 201X, the total amount of OASDI, $550, and Medicare, $220, was withheld as tax deductions from the employees of Lucky, Inc. Federal income tax of $2,950 was also deducted from their paychecks. Lucky is classified as a monthly depositor of Form 941 taxes. Indicate when this payroll tax deposit is due and provide a general journal entry to record the payment.

(20 min) **LO3**   **8B-5.**   Copper Company has four employees, and each employee earned $40,000 for the calendar year. Using a blank Form 940, complete Part 2, lines 3–8, to answer the following questions:

Total annual payroll for the year	?
Payments made in excess of $7,000 FUTA limit	?
Total FUTA liability before any adjustments	?

(10 min) **LO1**   **8B-6.**   Rachel's Grocery Store made the following Form 941 payroll tax deposits during the look-back period of July 1, 201A, through June 30, 201B:

Quarter Ended	Amount Paid in 941 Taxes
September 30, 201A	$15,783.81
December 31, 201A	13,893.81
March 31, 201B	13,601.04
June 30, 201B	14,021.29

Should Rachel's Grocery Store make Form 941 tax deposits monthly or semiweekly for 201C?

8B-7. If Rachel's Grocery Store downsized its operation during the second quarter of 20XB and, as a result, paid only $6,121.54 in Form 941 taxes for the quarter that ended on June 30, 20XB, should Rachel's Grocery Store make Form 941 tax deposits monthly or semiweekly for 20XC?

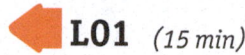 **L01** *(15 min)*

8B-8. Assuming a semiweekly depositor, from the following T accounts, record: (a) the July 3 payment for FICA (OASDI and Medicare) and federal income taxes, (b) the July 31 payment of SUTA tax, and (c) the July 31 deposit of any FUTA tax that may be required.

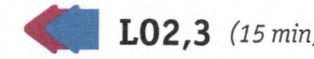 **L02,3** *(15 min)*

FICA OASDI Payable 203		
	June 30	450 (EE)
		450 (ER)

FICA Medicare Payable 204		
	June 30	140 (EE)
		140 (ER)

FIT Payable 205		
	June 30	3,004

FUTA Payable 206		
	June 30	139

SUTA Payable 207		
	June 30	613

Problems

MyLabAccounting

Set A

8A-1. The following is the monthly payroll of Andersen Company, owned by Donald Andersen. Employees are paid on the last day of each month.

 **L01,2** *(50 min)*

JANUARY

Employee	Monthly Earnings	YTD Earnings	FICA OASDI	Medicare	Federal Income Tax
Sam Fish	$1,900	$1,900	$117.80	$ 27.55	$ 264.00
Joy Bryant	3,150	3,150	195.30	45.68	351.00
Ariana Hess	3,760	3,760	233.12	54.52	498.00
	$8,810	$8,810	$546.22	$127.75	$1,113.00

FEBRUARY

Employee	Monthly Earnings	YTD Earnings	FICA OASDI	Medicare	Federal Income Tax
Sam Fish	$2,220	$ 4,120	$137.64	$ 32.19	$ 308.00
Joy Bryant	3,500	6,650	217.00	50.75	321.00
Ariana Hess	3,780	7,540	234.36	54.81	430.00
	$9,500	$18,310	$589.00	$137.75	$1,059.00

MARCH

Employee	Monthly Earnings	YTD Earnings	FICA OASDI	Medicare	Federal Income Tax
Sam Fish	$2,175	$ 6,295	$134.85	$ 31.54	$ 590.00
Joy Bryant	2,425	9,075	150.35	35.16	568.00
Ariana Hess	4,060	11,600	251.72	58.87	537.00
	$8,660	$26,970	$536.92	$125.57	$1,695.00

Check Figure:
Deposit of SUTA Tax $1,156.82

Andersen Company is located at 2 Square Street, Marblehead, MA 01945. Its EIN is 29-3458822. The FICA tax rate for Social Security is 6.2% on up to $127,200 in earnings during the year, and Medicare is 1.45% on all earnings. The SUTA tax rate is 5.7% on the first $7,000. The FUTA tax rate is 0.6% on the first $7,000 of earnings. Andersen Company is classified as a monthly depositor for Form 941 taxes.

Your tasks are to do the following:

1. Journalize the entries to record the employer's payroll tax expense for each pay period in the general journal.

2. Journalize entries for the payment of each tax liability in the general journal.

(50 min) **LO1,2**

Check Figure:
Total Liability for Quarter $7,993.42

8A-2. Ted James, the accountant for Andersen Company, must complete Form 941 for the first quarter of the current year. Ted gathered the needed data as presented in Problem 8A-1. Suddenly called away to an urgent budget meeting, Ted requested that you assist him by preparing Form 941 for the first quarter. Please note that the difference in the tax liability, a few cents, should be adjusted on line 7; this difference is due to the rounding of FICA tax amounts.

(60 min) **LO1,2**

8A-3. The following is the monthly payroll for the last 3 months of the year for Smith's Sporting Goods Shop, 2 Boat Road, Lynn, MA 01945. The shop is a sole proprietorship owned and operated by Bill Smith. The EIN for Smith's Sporting Goods Shop is 28-9311893.

The employees at Smith's are paid once each month on the last day of the month. Paula Bush is the only employee who has contributed the maximum into Social Security. None of the other employees will reach the Social Security wage base limit by the end of the year. Assume the rate for Social Security to be 6.2% with a wage base maximum of $127,200 and the rate for Medicare to be 1.45% on all earnings. Smith's is classified as a monthly depositor for Form 941 payroll tax deposit purposes.

Check Figure:
Dec. 31 Payroll Tax Expense $895.90

Your tasks are to do the following:

1. Compute the December OASDI tax for Paula Bush.

2. Journalize the entries to record the employer's payroll tax expense for each period in the general journal. SUTA rate: 5.7%; FUTA rate: 0.6%.

3. Journalize the payment of each tax liability in the general journal.

4. Complete Form 941 for the fourth quarter of the current year.

OCTOBER

Employee	Monthly Earnings	YTD Earnings	FICA OASDI	Medicare	Federal Income Tax
Paula Bush	$ 2,900	$120,750	$179.80	$ 42.05	$ 527.00
Joe Lapine	3,580	39,450	221.96	51.91	431.00
Harley Shaw	3,740	44,200	231.88	54.23	537.00
	$10,220	$204,400	$633.64	$148.19	$1,495.00

NOVEMBER

Employee	Monthly Earnings	YTD Earnings	FICA OASDI	Medicare	Federal Income Tax
Paula Bush	$ 3,060	$123,810	$189.72	$ 44.37	$ 595.00
Joe Lapine	3,780	43,230	234.36	54.81	470.00
Harley Shaw	3,840	48,040	238.08	55.68	562.00
	$10,680	$215,080	$662.16	$154.86	$1,627.00

DECEMBER

Employee	Monthly Earnings	YTD Earnings	FICA OASDI	FICA Medicare	Federal Income Tax
Paula Bush	$ 4,240	$128,050	$210.18	$ 61.48	$ 870.00
Joe Lapine	3,720	46,950	230.64	53.94	474.00
Harley Shaw	4,440	52,480	275.28	64.38	700.00
	$12,400	$227,480	$716.10	$179.80	$2,044.00

8A-4. Using the information from Problem 8A-3, please complete Form 940 for Smith's Sporting Goods for the current year. Additional information needed to complete the form is as follows:

L03 *(20 min)*

a. State reporting number: 025-319-2

b. No FUTA tax deposits were made for this year.

c. Smith's three employees for the year all earned over $7,000.

Check Figure:
Total Exempt Payments Line 5 $206,480

Set B

8B-1. The following is the monthly payroll of White Company, owned by Dale White. Employees are paid on the last day of each month.

L01,2 *(50 min)*

Check Figure:
Deposit of SUTA Tax $1,151.40

JANUARY

Employee	Monthly Earnings	YTD Earnings	FICA OASDI	FICA Medicare	Federal Income Tax
Fred Hill	$1,980	$1,980	$122.76	$ 28.71	$ 250.00
Daniel Boy	3,180	3,180	197.16	46.11	359.00
Holla Vogt	3,840	3,840	238.08	55.68	506.00
	$9,000	$9,000	$558.00	$130.50	$1,115.00

FEBRUARY

Employee	Monthly Earnings	YTD Earnings	FICA OASDI	FICA Medicare	Federal Income Tax
Fred Hill	$2,140	$ 4,120	$132.68	$ 31.03	$ 296.00
Daniel Boy	3,320	6,500	205.84	48.14	332.00
Holla Vogt	3,840	7,680	238.08	55.68	424.00
	$9,300	$18,300	$576.60	$134.85	$1,052.00

MARCH

Employee	Monthly Earnings	YTD Earnings	FICA OASDI	FICA Medicare	Federal Income Tax
Fred Hill	$2,080	$ 6,200	$128.96	$ 30.16	$ 584.00
Daniel Boy	2,550	9,050	158.10	36.98	564.00
Holla Vogt	4,060	11,740	251.72	58.87	543.00
	$8,690	$26,990	$538.78	$126.01	$1,691.00

White Company is located at 2 Square Street, Marblehead, MA 01945. Its EIN is 29-3458822. The FICA tax rate for Social Security is 6.2% on up to $127,200 in earnings during the year, and Medicare is 1.45% on all earnings. The SUTA tax rate is 5.7% on the first $7,000 of earnings. The FUTA tax rate is 0.6% on the first $7,000 of earnings. White Company is classified as a monthly depositor for Form 941 taxes.

Your tasks are to do the following:

1. Journalize the entries to record the employer's payroll tax expense for each pay period in the general journal.

2. Journalize entries for the payment of each tax liability in the general journal.

(50 min) **LO1,2**

Check Figure:
Liability for Quarter $7,987.48

8B-2. Henry House, the accountant for White Company, must complete Form 941 for the first quarter of the current year. Henry gathered the needed data as presented in Problem 8B-1. Suddenly called away to an urgent budget meeting, Henry requested that you assist him by preparing Form 941 for the first quarter. Please note that the difference in the tax liability, a few cents, should be adjusted on line 7; this difference is due to the rounding of FICA tax amounts.

(60 min) **LO1,2**

8B-3. The following is the monthly payroll for the last 3 months of the year for Dell's Sporting Goods Shop, 2 Boat Road, Lynn, MA 01945. The shop is a sole proprietorship owned and operated by Bill Dell. The EIN for Dell's Sporting Goods Shop is 28-9311893.

The employees at Dell's are paid once each month on the last day of the month. Pete Clinton is the only employee who has contributed the maximum into Social Security. None of the other employees will reach the Social Security wage base limit by the end of the year. Assume the rate for Social Security to be 6.2% with a wage base maximum of $127,200 and the rate for Medicare to be 1.45% on all earnings. Dell's is classified as a monthly depositor for Form 941 payroll tax deposit purposes.

Your tasks are to do the following:

1. Compute the December OASDI tax for Pete Clinton.

Check Figure:
Dec. 31 Payroll Tax Expense $902.06

2. Journalize the entries to record the employer's payroll tax expense for each period in the general journal. SUTA rate: 5.7%; FUTA rate: 0.6%.

3. Journalize the payment of each tax liability in the general journal.

4. Complete Form 941 for the fourth quarter of the current year.

OCTOBER

Employee	Monthly Earnings	YTD Earnings	FICA OASDI	FICA Medicare	Federal Income Tax
Pete Clinton	$ 2,780	$120,800	$172.36	$ 40.31	$ 530.00
Susan Lincoln	3,600	39,350	223.20	52.20	424.00
Samantha Sweet	3,780	44,100	234.36	54.81	531.00
	$10,160	$204,250	$629.92	$147.32	$1,485.00

NOVEMBER

Employee	Monthly Earnings	YTD Earnings	FICA OASDI	FICA Medicare	Federal Income Tax
Pete Clinton	$ 2,980	$123,780	$184.76	$ 43.21	$ 596.00
Susan Lincoln	3,840	43,190	238.08	55.68	463.00
Samantha Sweet	3,700	47,800	229.40	53.65	564.00
	$10,520	$214,770	$652.24	$152.54	$1,623.00

DECEMBER

Employee	Monthly Earnings	YTD Earnings	FICA OASDI	FICA Medicare	Federal Income Tax
Pete Clinton	$ 4,220	$128,000	$212.04	$ 61.19	$ 868.00
Susan Lincoln	3,800	46,990	235.60	55.10	478.00
Samantha Sweet	4,420	52,220	274.04	64.09	704.00
	$12,440	$227,210	$721.68	$180.38	$2,050.00

8B-4. Using the information from Problem 8B-3, please complete Form 940 for Dell's Sporting Goods for the current year. Additional information needed to complete the form is as follows:

L03 *(20 min)*

    a. State reporting number: 025-319-2

    b. No FUTA tax deposits were made for this year.

    c. Dell's three employees for the year all earned over $7,000.

Check Figure:
Line 5 Total Exempt Payments
$206,210

Financial Report Problem

Reading Amazon's Annual Report

https://tinyurl.com/slaterca14e to access Amazon's 2016 Annual Report. The 2016 Amazon Annual report was issued way before the new tax act of 2018. How do you expect the income statement to change in 2018 since the new tax rates are much lower than in 2016?

KEEPING IT REAL SUAREZ COMPUTER CENTER

MyLabAccounting

L01,2,3 *(00 min)*

In preparing for next year, on December 1, Troy Falco hired two hourly employees to assist with some troubleshooting and repair work.
    More information:

    Dec. 7 Paid employee wages: Ken Joe, 36 hours, and Arto Landry, 44 hours

    Dec. 14 Paid employee wages: Ken Joe, 28 hours, and Arto Landry, 32 hours

    Dec. 21 Paid employee wages: Ken Joe, 20 hours, and Arto Landry, 32 hours

a. The following accounts have been added to the chart of accounts: Wages Payable #2010, FICA OASDI Payable #2020, FICA Medicare Payable #2030, FIT Payable #2040, State Income Tax Payable #2050, FUTA Tax Payable #2060, SUTA Tax Payable #2070, Wages Expense #5110, and Payroll Tax Expense #5120.

b. Assume FICA OASDI is taxed at 6.2% up to $127,200 in earnings, and Medicare is taxed at 1.45% on all earnings.

c. State income tax is 4% of gross pay.

d. None of the employees has federal income tax taken out of his or her pay.

e. Each employee earns $12.50 an hour and is paid $1\frac{1}{2}$ times salary for hours worked in excess of 40 weekly.

As December comes to an end, Troy Falco wants to take care of his payroll obligations. He will complete Form 941 for the fourth quarter of the current year and Form 940 for federal unemployment taxes. Troy will make the necessary deposits and payments associated with his payroll.

Assignment

1. Prepare the payroll register for the three pay periods.

2. Using the payroll registers, record the December payrolls and the payment of the payrolls in the general journal and post them to the general ledger.

3. Using the payroll registers, record payroll tax expense for the fourth quarter in the general journal. Use December 31 as the date of the journal entry to record the payroll tax expense for the entire quarter. The FUTA tax ceiling is $7,000, and the SUTA tax ceiling is $7,000 in cumulative wages for each employee. The Suarez Computer Center's FUTA rate is 0.6% and the SUTA rate is 2.5%. Post the entry to the general ledger.

4. Record the payment of each tax liability in the general journal and post each entry to the general ledger. Suarez Computer Center is classified as a monthly depositor. The company wishes to pay all payroll taxes on December 31 even if no deposits are required.

5. Prepare Form 941 for the fourth quarter. Suarez Computer Center's employer identification number is 35-4132588.

6. Complete Form 940 for Suarez Computer Center. The state reporting number is 025-025-2.

Hint: Sometimes the amount of Social Security taxes paid by the employee for the quarter will not equal the employee's tax liability because of rounding. Any difference should be reported on line 7 of Form 941.

SAGE 50 SOFTWARE SIMULATION

Computerized Accounting Application for Chapter 8

Refresher on using Sage 50 Complete Accounting

Before starting this assignment, you may want to refresh your memory by reading the following PDF documents in the multimedia library of the MyAccountingLab website. Remember to choose the PDF document for your version of Sage 50.

1. An Introduction to Sage 50
2. Correcting Sage 50 Transactions
3. How to Repeat or Restart a Sage 50 Assignment
4. Backing Up and Restoring Your Work in Sage 50

You also should have completed the following workshops:

1. Workshop 1 Atlas Company from Chapter 3
2. Workshop 2 Zell Company from Chapter 4
3. Workshop 3 Sherman Realty from Chapter 5

Workshop 4

Payroll Mini Practice Set

In this workshop, you will prepare January, February, and March payroll for Pete's Market using Sage 50. Tasks include entering payroll data, producing paychecks, and remitting payroll taxes. You will also print payroll reports.

Instructions and the data file for completing this assignment are in the multimedia library of the MyAccountingLab website. Open the *Workshop 4 Pete's Market* PDF document for your version of Sage 50 and download the *Pete's Market* data file for your version of Sage 50.

QUICKBOOKS SOFTWARE SIMULATION

QB

Computerized Accounting Application for Chapter 8

Refresher on using QuickBooks Accountant

Before starting this assignment, you may want to refresh your memory by reading the following PDF documents in the multimedia library of the MyLab Accounting website. Remember to choose the PDF document for your version of QuickBooks.

1. An Introduction to QuickBooks
2. Correcting QuickBooks Transactions
3. How to Repeat or Restart a QuickBooks Assignment
4. Backing Up and Restoring Your Work in QuickBooks

You also should have completed the following workshops:

1. Workshop 1 Atlas Company from Chapter 3
2. Workshop 2 Zell Company from Chapter 4
3. Workshop 3 Sherman Realty from Chapter 5

Workshop 4

Payroll Mini Practice Set

In this workshop, you will prepare January, February, and March payroll for Pete's Market using QuickBooks. Tasks include entering payroll data, producing paychecks, and remitting payroll taxes. You will also print payroll reports.

Instructions and the data file for completing this assignment are in the multimedia library of the MyAccountingLab website. Open the *Workshop 4 Pete's Market* PDF document for your version of QuickBooks and download the *Pete's Market* data file for your version of QuickBooks.

Sales and Cash Receipts in a Perpetual Inventory System

9

Learning Objectives – Relating Accounting Theory By Unit

LO1 Explain and Journalize Entries for Sales, Sales Discounts, and Sales Returns and Allowances for Transactions for a Perpetual Inventory System

LO2 Record to Subsidiary Ledgers and Post to General Ledger Sales Transactions and Returns

LO3 Record and Post Cash Receipt Transactions and Prepare a Schedule of Accounts Receivable

LEARNING UNIT 9-1

LO1 ➡

Journalizing Transactions for a Perpetual Inventory System

Introduction to the Merchandise Cycle

In this learning unit we focus on recording transactions using a perpetual inventory system. This is an inventory system that continually monitors its levels of inventory. Advances in technology, and the need for real time information regarding inventory levels, and the related Cost of Goods Sold, has spurred the use of this system by businesses both large and small.

Let's use Walmart as an example as both the buyer and seller. We know that Walmart must buy inventory from suppliers to sell to you, the customer. This inventory is called Merchandise Inventory. It is an asset sold to you for cash or accounts receivable and represents *sales revenue* or sales for Walmart.

What did it cost Walmart to bring the inventory into the store? The Cost of Goods Sold is the total cost of Merchandise Inventory brought into the store and sold. These costs do not include any operating expenses such as heat, advertising, and salaries. To find Walmart's profit before operating expenses, we take the sales revenue less Cost of Goods Sold. Figure 9.1 is called *gross profit on sales*.

Perpetual inventory system
An inventory system that keeps *continual track* of each type of inventory by recording units on hand at the beginning of each accounting period, units sold, and the current balance after each sale or purchase.

Merchandise Inventory
Goods brought into a store for resale to customers.

Cost of Goods Sold
In a perpetual inventory system, an account that records the cost of Merchandise Inventory used to make the sale.

Figure 9.1
Calculating Gross Profit on Sales

| Walmart Sales Revenue | − | Cost of Goods Sold | = | Gross Profit on Sales |

For example, if Walmart sells a TV for $500 that cost $300 to bring into the store, its gross profit is $200. To find its net income or net loss, Walmart would subtract its operating expenses. Figure 9.2 shows how a merchandiser calculates its net income or net loss.

Figure 9.2
Introduction to Perpetual Inventory for a Merchandise Company

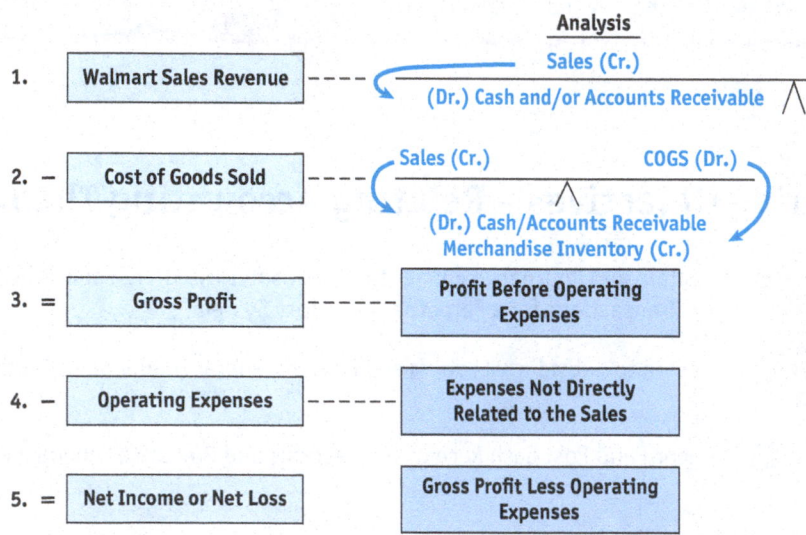

Note: In step 1 the sales provide an inflow of cash or accounts receivable. Step 2 shows that when the inventory is sold, it is recognized as a cost (Cost of Goods Sold). By subtracting Cost of Goods Sold from sales, we arrive at the gross profit in step 3. Step 4 shows that operating expenses subtracted from gross profit result in a net income or net loss in step 5.

The Inventory System Walmart Uses

When you pay at Walmart you see the use of barcodes and optical scanners. Walmart keeps detailed records of the inventory it brings into the store and what inventory is sold. With this method, Walmart keeps track of what it costs to make the sale (Cost of Goods Sold) by matching revenues and costs (see Figure 9.3).

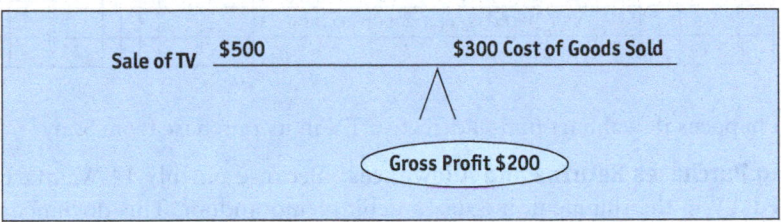

Figure 9.3
Matching Revenues and Costs

More and more companies, large or small, are using the perpetual inventory system due to increasing computerization. Walmart knows that using the perpetual inventory system will help control stocks of inventory as well as lost or stolen goods.

Recording Merchandise Transactions

Now let's look at Walmart as both a buyer and a seller. Let's first focus on Walmart the buyer.

Walmart: The Buyer. When Walmart brings Merchandise Inventory into the stores from suppliers it is recorded in the *Merchandise Inventory account*. Think of this account as purchases of merchandise—for cash or on account—that is for resale to customers. Each order is documented by an invoice for Walmart. Keep in mind that Merchandise Inventory is the cost of bringing the merchandise into the store, not the price at which the merchandise will be sold to customers. Let's assume that on July 9 , Walmart bought flatscreen TVs from Sony Corporation for $7,000 on account with terms 2/10, n/30. Walmart would record the purchase as shown in Figure 9.4. Suppliers often offer discount terms to their customers as an incentive to pay their bill in cash within a certain period of time. An example of this is Sony offering Walmart the terms of 2/10, n30, which means that Walmart would get a 2% discount if they pay within 10 days of the date of the invoice; otherwise, the balance is due in full in 30 days. However, at the time of the purchase Walmart does not know if they will take advantage of the discount, so the purchase is recorded at the gross or total amount.

Analysis:	Merchandise Inventory	A	↑	Dr.	$7,000
	Accounts Payable	L	↑	Cr.	$7,000

Figure 9.4
Purchase of Inventory on Account

Journal Entry:		Jul.	9	Merchandise Inventory		7 0 0 0 00	
				Accounts Payable/Sony			7 0 0 0 00
				Purchased inventory on account			
				from Sony 2/10, n/30			

Keep in mind that not all purchases will go to Merchandise Inventory. Walmart will buy supplies, equipment, and so forth that are not for resale to customers. These amounts will be debited to the specific account such as Equipment and not Merchandise Inventory. For example, if Walmart bought $5,000 of shelving equipment on account for its store on November 9, the transaction would be recorded as in Figure 9.5 which can be found on the following page.

Figure 9.5
Purchase of Equipment
on Account

Analysis:	Shelving Equipment	A	↑	Dr.	$5,000
	Accounts Payable	L	↑	Cr.	$5,000

Journal Entry:		Nov.	9	Shelving Equipment		5 0 0 0 00	
				Accounts Payable/Moore Co.			5 0 0 0 00
				Purchased equipment on account			

What happens if Walmart finds a defective TV in its purchase from Sony?

Recording Purchases Returns and Allowances. Because on July 14 Walmart noticed a damaged TV in the shipment, it issues a debit memorandum. This document notifies Sony, the supplier, that Walmart is reducing what is owed Sony by $600, the cost of the TV (to bring it into the store) and that the TV is being returned. On Walmart's books, the analysis and journal entry in Figure 9.6 results.

Figure 9.6
Recording a Debit Memorandum

Analysis:	Accounts Payable	L	↓	Dr.	$600
	Merchandise Inventory	A	↓	Cr.	$600

Journal Entry:		Jul.	14	Accounts Payable/Sony		6 0 0 00	
				Merchandise Inventory			6 0 0 00
				To record debit memo no. 10			

Note that the cost of Merchandise Inventory has been reduced by $600 due to the return. In the perpetual inventory system there is no Purchases Returns and Allowances account. The reduction in cost from the return is recorded *directly* into the Merchandise Inventory account. Let's now look at how Walmart would record any cash discounts it receives due to payment of the Sony bill within the discount period.

Recording Purchase Discounts. As stated earlier, suppliers often offer discount terms to their customers if they pay their bill in cash within a certain period of time. Let's assume that Walmart pays Sony within the first 10 days. Keep in mind that we take no discounts on returned goods (the $600 return). The amount of purchase discount will be recorded as a reduction to the cost of Merchandise Inventory. Figure 9.7 shows the analysis and journal entry on July 16. A discount lowers the cost of inventory.

Figure 9.7
Recording a Purchase Discount

Analysis:	Accounts Payable	L	↓	Dr.	$6,400
	Cash	A	↓	Cr.	$6,272
	Merchandise Inventory	A	↓	Cr.	$ 128

($7,000 – $600 Return)

Journal Entry:		Jul.	16	Accounts Payable/Sony		6 4 0 0 00	
				Cash			6 2 7 2 00
				Merchandise Inventory			1 2 8 00

2% × $6,400

Keep in mind that had Walmart missed the discount period, it would have debited $6,400 to Accounts Payable and credited Cash for $6,400. Merchandise Inventory would not be reduced.

Recording Cost of Freight. The cost of freight ($300) is to be paid by Walmart. When the purchaser is responsible for cost of freight, it is added to the cost of Merchandise Inventory. If the cost of freight is paid by the seller, it could be recorded in an operating expense account called Freight-Out. Figure 9.8 is the analysis and journal entry for freight on July 10.

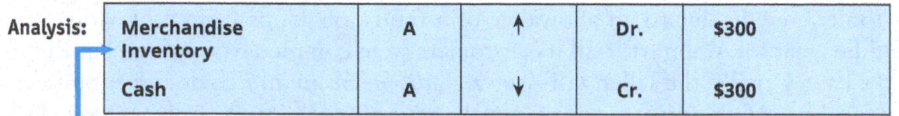

Analysis:

Merchandise Inventory	A	↑	Dr.	$300
Cash	A	↓	Cr.	$300

Freight Cost added to Merchandise Inventory

Journal Entry:

Jul.	10	Merchandise Inventory		3 0 0 00		
		Cash			3 0 0 00	
		Payment of freight				

Figure 9.8
Recording Cost of Freight

Notice then when the buyer pays for the freight cost, it is added to the cost of Merchandise Inventory. Under the perpetual method of inventory valuation, the Merchandise Inventory account is adjusted every time there is a transaction that affects the cost of the inventory; whether it is an increase, as in this case, or a decrease, as occurred when Walmart took advantage of the offered discount.

Walmart: The Seller. Now let's look at Walmart as the *seller* of merchandise.

Recording Sales at Walmart. Sales revenues are earned at Walmart when the goods are transferred to the buyer. The earned revenue can be for cash and/or credit. Let's look at the following example of the sale of a TV at Walmart for $950 on credit to customer Jones on August 10, which cost Walmart $600. Keep in mind when using the perpetual inventory system that at the time of the earned sale Walmart will do the following:

At selling price ⟶	1. Record the sales (cash and/or credit).
At cost ⟶	2. Record the cost of the inventory sold and the reduction in inventory.

First, let's analyze the transaction in Figure 9.9. Note that we will have two entries, one to record the sale and one to show the cost of the merchandise sold and the reduction of the inventory on hand.

Selling Price <	Accounts Receivable	Asset	↑	Dr.	$950
	Sales	Revenue	↑	Cr.	$950
Cost to < Make Sale	Cost of Goods Sold	Cost	↑	Dr.	$600
	Merchandise Inventory	Asset	↓	Cr.	$600

Figure 9.9
Recording Sales and Cost of Goods Sold

Journal Entries:

Aug.	10	Account Receivable/Jones		9 5 0 00		
		Sales			9 5 0 00	
		Charge Sales				
	10	Cost of Goods Sold		6 0 0 00		
		Merchandise Inventory			6 0 0 00	
		To record cost of				
		merchandise sold on account				

Be sure to go back to steps 1 and 2 in Figure 9.2 on pg. 300. These two steps reinforce the preceding journal entries. Remember that if the sale were a cash sale, we would have debited Cash instead of Accounts Receivable. Note also that the Sales account only records sales of goods held for resale.

How Walmart Records Sales Returns Allowances and Sales Discounts. Keep in mind that we are now looking at how the *seller* of merchandise records a transaction giving the customer a credit due to an allowance or a return of goods from a previous sale. It would be great for Walmart if all its customers were completely satisfied, but that is rarely the case. Usually, the seller will issue a *credit memorandum*, a document informing the customer of the adjustment due to the return or allowance. For example, let's look at a customer, Smith Co., who returned a $950 TV on August 15 that had been purchased on account at Walmart. On Walmart's books, the analysis and journal entry in Figure 9.10 resulted.

The first entry records the return at the original selling price using the contra-revenue account Sales Returns and Allowances. This account is a contra-revenue account with a debit balance, meaning it will go against or opposite that of Sales. It will be reported on the income statement.

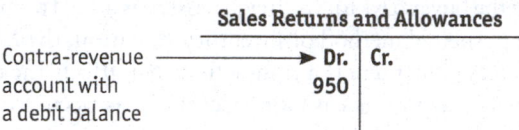

The second entry records putting the inventory back in Walmart's books at cost and reducing its Cost of Goods Sold because the inventory was not sold. Remember that we only record the Cost of Goods Sold when the sale has been earned. Keep in mind that if the customer kept the TV but at a reduced price, no entry affecting Merchandise Inventory and Cost of Goods Sold would be needed.

Figure 9.10
Return of Goods

The Analysis:
at Selling Price

Sales Returns and Allowances	Contra-Revenue	↑	Dr.	$950
Accounts Receivable	Asset	↓	Cr.	$950

At Cost

Merchandise Inventory	Asset	↑	Dr.	$600
Cost of Goods Sold	Cost	↓	Cr.	$600

Journal Entries:

Aug.	15	Sales Returns and Allowances	9 5 0 00	
		Accounts Receivable/Smith Co.*		9 5 0 00
		Returned goods		
	15	Merchandise Inventory	6 0 0 00	
		Cost of Goods Sold		6 0 0 00
		Cost of returned goods		

*If it were a *cash* customer, cash would be credited.

Let's assume a customer, Smith Co., on August 25 gets a 2% discount for paying for a $950 TV early. Previously we discussed the purchase discount from Walmart's perspective as a buyer and now we look at the sales discounts from their perspective as the seller, the one offering the discount.

Sales Discount Policies.

2/10, n/30	*2% discount is allowed off price of bill if paid within the first 10 days or full amount is due within 30 days.*
n/10, EOM	*No discount. Full amount of bill is due within 10 days after the end of the month.*

Note that the discount period is the time when a discount is granted. The discount period is less time than the credit period, which is the length of time allowed to pay the amount owed on the invoice.

If Smith Co. pays the $950 bill early, they will get a $19.00 discount. This is recorded in the Sales Discount account, which is a contra-revenue account, just as Sales Returns and Allowances is. This information is recorded in the Sales Discount account as follows:

Sales Discount

	Dr.	Cr.
Contra-revenue account with a debit balance →	19.00	

Smith Co.'s discount is calculated as follows:

$$2\% \times \$950 = \$19.00$$

The analysis and entry in Figure 9.11 would result on the seller's books.

The Analysis:

		↑↓	Dr./Cr.	
Cash	Asset	↑	Dr.	$931
Sales Discount	Contra-Revenue	↑	Dr.	$ 19
Accounts Receivable	Asset	↓	Cr.	$950

Journal Entry:

Aug.	25	Cash		931 00	
		Sales Discount		19 00	
		Accounts Receivable/Smith Co.			950 00

Figure 9.11
Recording Sales Discount

Sales Tax Payable

None of the preceding examples shows state sales tax. As some states do have a sales tax, Walmart must collect that tax from their customers and send it to the state. Sales tax represents a liability to Walmart. The amount Walmart must pay to the state is recorded in the Sales Tax Payable account, which is a liability account.

Assume the state this Walmart store is located in charges a 5% sales tax. Remember that Walmart's sale to Smith Co. on August 14 was for $950. Walmart must figure out the sales tax on the purchase. For this purpose, let's assume in this case the sale was a cash sale.

The sales tax on the cash purchase is calculated as follows:

$$\$950.00 \times 0.05 = \$ 47.50$$
$$\$950.00 + 47.50 = \$997.50 \text{ Cash}$$

Let's look at a transaction analysis chart of this transaction.

Sales Tax Payable account An account in the general ledger that accumulates the amount of sales tax owed. It has a credit balance.

Accounts Affected	Category	↑↓	Rules	T Account Update	
Cash	Asset	↑	Dr.	**Cash**	
				Dr. | Cr.	
				997.50	
Sales Tax Payable	Liability	↑	Cr.	**Sales Tax Payable**	
				Dr. | Cr.	
				| 47.50	
Sales	Revenue	↑	Cr.	**Sales**	
				Dr. | Cr.	
				| 950	

SUCCESS TIP

Gross Sales
− Sales Discounts
− Sales Returns

= Net Sales

Now let's summarize (Figure 9.12) all the entries for both the buyer and the seller (in this case, Walmart) as it relates to the perpetual method of inventory valuation.

Figure 9.12 Entries for Both the Buyer and the Seller

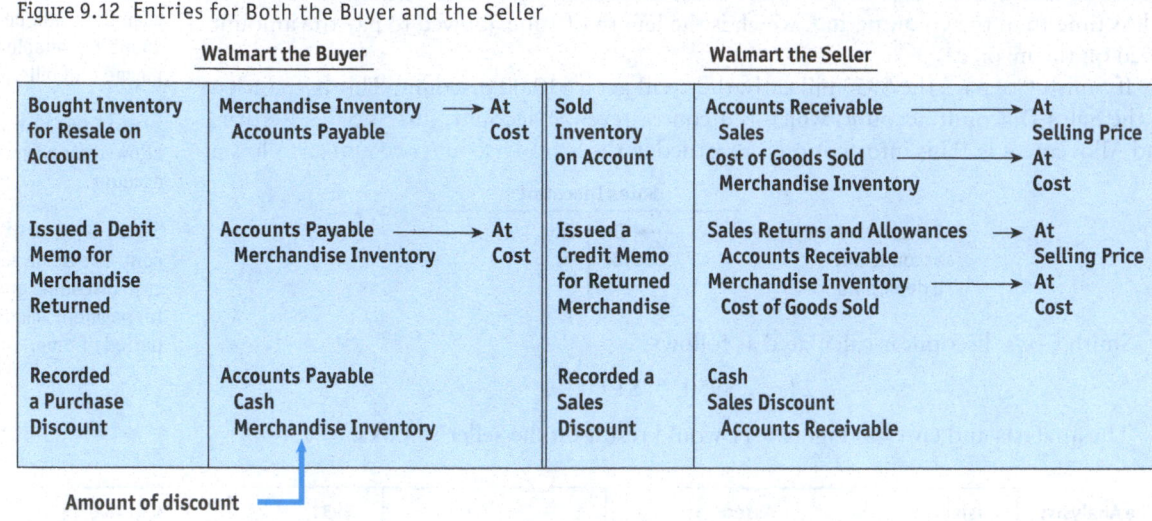

Figure 9.13 shows a comparison of both the perpetual inventory system, which we have covered here and is our focus in the text, and the alternative periodic inventory system.

Figure 9.13 Comparison of Perpetual and Periodic Systems

Transaction	Perpetual System		Periodic System**	
(A) Sold merchandise that cost $8,000 on account for $20,000.	Accts. Receivable	20 00 0 00	Accts. Receivable	20 00 0 00
	Sales	20 00 0 00	Sales	20 00 0 00
	Cost of Goods Sold	8 00 0 00		
	Merch. Inventory	8 00 0 00		
(B) Purchased $900 of merchandise on account.	Merch. Inventory	9 00 00	Purchases	9 00 00
	Accts. Payable	9 00 00	Accts. Payable	9 00 00
(C) Paid $50 freight charges.	Merch. Inventory	5 0 00	Freight-In	5 0 00
	Cash	5 0 00	Cash	5 0 00
(D) Cash customer returned $200 of merchandise. Cost of merchandise was $100.	Sales Ret. & Allow.	2 0 0 00	Sales Ret. & Allow.	2 0 0 00
	Cash*	2 0 0 00	Cash*	2 0 0 00
	Merch. Inventory	1 0 0 00		
	Cost of Goods Sold	1 0 0 00		
(E) Returned $400 of merchandise previously bought on account because of defects.	Accts. Payable	4 0 0 00	Accts. Payable	4 0 0 00
	Merch. Inventory	4 0 0 00	Pur. Ret. & Allow.	4 0 0 00

*or Accounts Receivable if made to charge customers
**See the Appendix at the end of the Chapter 12 for further illustration of this method.

In Learning Unit 9.2, we look in detail at Art's Wholesale Company. Now it's time to check your progress.

 **TRY IT!**   **Learning Unit 9-1**

Journalize the following transactions in July 201X for Elgin Co. using a perpetual inventory system. Partial charts of accounts include Cash 110; Accounts Receivable 112; Merchandise Inventory 120; Accounts Payable 210; A. Elgin, Capital 310; Sales 410; Sales Returns and Allowances 411; Sales Discounts 412; Cost of Goods Sold 510. Omit explanations.

July 8	Sold merchandise costing $5,000 on account for $9,000.
14	Purchased $1,200 of merchandise on account.
18	Paid freight charges of $100.
22	A charge customer returned $300 of merchandise. Cost of merchandise was $100.
30	Returned $500 of merchandise previously bought on account because of defects.

TRY IT!   **Solution Learning Unit 9-1**

Date	Accounts	PR	Dr.	Cr.
201X				
July 8	Accounts Receivable		9,000	
	Sales			9,000
	Cost of Goods Sold		5,000	
	Merchandise Inventory			5,000
14	Merchandise Inventory		1,200	
	Accounts Payable			1,200
18	Merchandise Inventory		100	
	Cash			100
22	Sales Returns and Allowances		300	
	Accounts Receivable			300
	Merchandise Inventory		100	
	Cost of Goods Sold			100
30	Accounts Payable		500	
	Merchandise Inventory			500

Subsidiary Ledgers and General Ledger Sales Transactions and Returns

Art's Wholesale Clothing Company, as a wholesaler, buys merchandise from suppliers and sells the items to retailers, who in turn sell it to individual consumers.

The following transactions occurred in April for Art's Wholesale Clothing Company:

Wholesalers Merchants who buy goods from suppliers and manufacturers for sale to retailers.

201X		
Apr.	3	Sold on account merchandise to Hal's Clothing, $800; invoice no. 1; terms 2/10, n/30. The cost of the merchandise to Art's was $600.
	6	Sold on account merchandise to Bevans Company, $1,600; invoice no. 2; terms 2/10, n/30. The cost of the merchandise to Art's was $1,200.
	12	Credit memo #1 to Bevans Company for returned merchandise, $600. The cost of the merchandise to Art's was $450.
	18	Sold on account merchandise to Roe Company, $2,000; invoice no. 3; terms 2/10, n/30. The cost of the merchandise to Art's was $1,500.

(continued on page 308)

201X		
Apr.	24	Sold on account merchandise to Roe Company, $500; invoice no. 4; terms 2/10, n/30. The cost of the merchandise to Art's was $400.
	28	Sold on account merchandise to Mel's Department Store, $900; invoice no. 5; terms 2/10, n/30. The cost of the merchandise to Art's was $700.
	29	Sold on account merchandise to Mel's Department Store, $700; invoice no. 6; terms 2/10, n/30. The cost of the merchandise to Art's was $550.

Sales invoice A bill sent to customer(s) reflecting a credit sale.

Figure 9.14
Sales Invoice

Let's look closer at the April 3 transaction of Art selling to Hal's Clothing. Figure 9.14 shows the actual bill or the sales invoice for this sale:

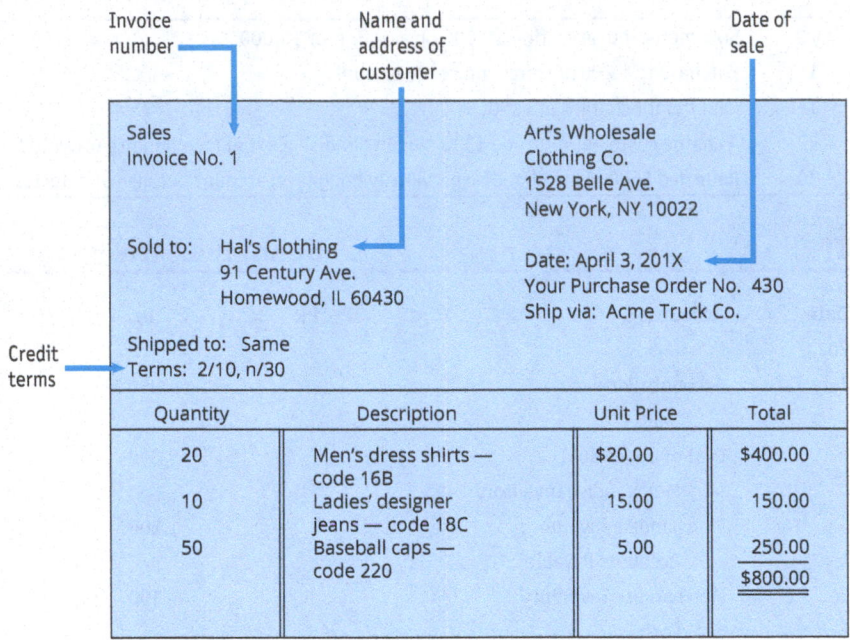

April 3   Sold on account merchandise to Hal's Clothing, $800; terms 2/10, n/30. The cost of the merchandise to Art's was $600.

Here is an analysis of the transaction by the transaction analysis chart.

Accounts Affected	Category	↑↓	Rules	Amount
Accounts Receivable, Hal's Clothing	Asset	↑	Dr.	$800
Sales	Revenue	↑	Cr.	$800
Cost of Goods Sold	Expense	↑	Dr.	$600
Merchandise Inventory	Asset	↓	Cr.	$600

The general journal is shown in Figure 9.15.

Figure 9.15
Merchandise Sold and Accounts Receivable

	ART'S WHOLESALE CLOTHING COMPANY GENERAL JOURNAL				Page 2
Date	Account Titles and Description	PR	Dr.	Cr.	
201X					
Apr. 3	Accounts Receivable, Hal's Clothing		800 00		
	Sales			800 00	
	Sale on account to Hal's				
	Cost of Goods Sold		600 00		
	Merchandise Inventory			600 00	
	Record cost of the sale to Hal's				

Accounts Receivable Subsidiary Ledgers

So far in this text, the only title we have used for recording amounts owed to the seller has been Accounts Receivable. Art could have replaced the Accounts Receivable title in the general ledger with the following list of customers who owe him money:

- Accounts Receivable, Bevans Company
- Accounts Receivable, Hal's Clothing
- Accounts Receivable, Mel's Department Store
- Accounts Receivable, Roe Company

As you can see, this system would not be manageable if Art had 1,000 credit customers. To solve this problem, Art sets up a separate accounts receivable subsidiary ledger. Such a special ledger, often simply called a subsidiary ledger, contains a single type of account, such as credit customers. An account is opened for each customer, and the accounts are arranged alphabetically. Keep in mind that with computer software available today, the accounts can be stored on the computer's hard drive or on the Cloud and continually updated.

The diagram in Figure 9.16 shows how the accounts receivable subsidiary ledger fits in with the general ledger. To clarify the difference in updating the general ledger versus the subsidiary ledger, we will *post* to the general ledger and *record* to the subsidiary ledger. The word *post* refers to information that is moved from the journal to the general ledger; the word *record* refers to information that is transferred from the journal into the individual customer's account in the subsidiary ledger.

Accounts receivable subsidiary ledger A book or file that contains the individual records, in alphabetical order, of amounts owed by various credit customers.

Subsidiary ledger A ledger that contains accounts of a single type. Example: The accounts receivable subsidiary ledger records all credit customers.

Figure 9.16
Partial General Ledger of Art's Wholesale Clothing Company and Accounts Receivable Subsidiary Ledger

The accounts receivable subsidiary ledger, or any other subsidiary ledger in a manual system, can be in the form of a hardcopy book or file setup. The accounts receivable subsidiary ledger is organized alphabetically based on customers' names and addresses; new customers can be added and inactive customers deleted. Keep in mind that with the use of computers, many companies now use accounting software such as QuickBooks and Sage 50 that updates customer accounts stored on either the computer's hard drive or on the Cloud. With the click of a key, the subsidiary ledger can be updated and easily printed out. At the end of Chapter 10, the computer workshops show you how a computerized system works to record transactions and update customer and vendor accounts for a merchandise company.

When using an accounts receivable subsidiary ledger, the account title Accounts Receivable in the general ledger is called the controlling account—Accounts Receivable because it summarizes or controls the accounts receivable subsidiary ledger. At the end of the month the total of the individual accounts in the accounts receivable ledger will equal the ending balance in Accounts Receivable in the general ledger.

Figure 9.17 shows how the general journal looks for Art before posting to the general ledger and recording to the subsidiary ledger this month's sales transactions on account.

Controlling account—Accounts Receivable The Accounts Receivable account in the general ledger, after postings are complete, shows a firm the total amount of money owed to it by credit customers. This figure is broken down in the accounts receivable subsidiary ledger, where it indicates specifically who owes the money.

Figure 9.17
Before Posting and Recording
Sales Transactions

		ART'S WHOLESALE CLOTHING COMPANY GENERAL JOURNAL				Page 2
Date		Account Titles and Description	PR	Dr.	Cr.	
201X						
Apr.	3	Accounts Receivable, Hal's Clothing		8 0 0 00		
		Sales			8 0 0 00	
		Sale on account to Hal's				
	3	Cost of Goods Sold		6 0 0 00		
		Merchandise Inventory			6 0 0 00	
		Record cost of the sale to Hal's				
	6	Accounts Receivable, Bevans Company		1 6 0 0 00		
		Sales			1 6 0 0 00	
		Sale on account to Bevans				
	6	Cost of Goods Sold		1 2 0 0 00		
		Merchandise Inventory			1 2 0 0 00	
		Record cost of the sale to Bevans				
	12	Sales Returns and Allowances		6 0 0 00		
		Accounts Receivable, Bevans Company			6 0 0 00	
		Issued credit memo no. 1				
	12	Merchandise Inventory		4 5 0 00		
		Cost of Goods Sold			4 5 0 00	
		Returned goods to inventory				
	18	Accounts Receivable, Roe Company		2 0 0 0 00		
		Sales			2 0 0 0 00	
		Sale on account to Roe				
	18	Cost of Goods Sold		1 5 0 0 00		
		Merchandise Inventory			1 5 0 0 00	
		Record cost of the sale to Roe				
	24	Accounts Receivable, Roe Company		5 0 0 00		
		Sales			5 0 0 00	
		Sale on account to Roe				
	24	Cost of Goods Sold		4 0 0 00		
		Merchandise Inventory			4 0 0 00	
		Record cost of the sale to Roe				
	28	Accounts Receivable, Mel's Dept. Store		9 0 0 00		
		Sales			9 0 0 00	
		Sale on account to Mel's				
	28	Cost of Goods Sold		7 0 0 00		
		Merchandise Inventory			7 0 0 00	
		Record cost of the sale to Mel's				
	29	Accounts Receivable, Mel's Dept. Store		7 0 0 00		
		Sales			7 0 0 00	
		Sale on account to Mel's				
	29	Cost of Goods Sold		5 5 0 00		
		Merchandise Inventory			5 5 0 00	
		Record cost of the sale to Mel's				

Posting and Recording Sales Transactions.   Before we post to the general ledger and record to the subsidiary ledger, consider the following T accounts, which show what each title would look like.

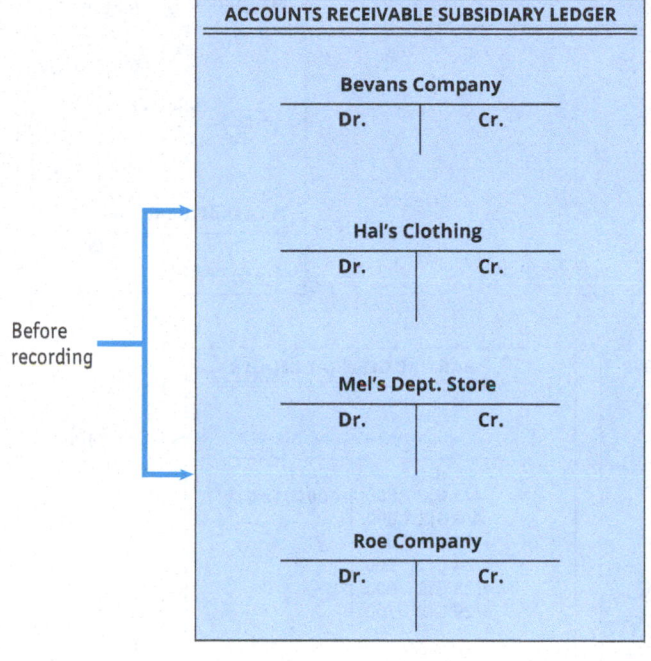

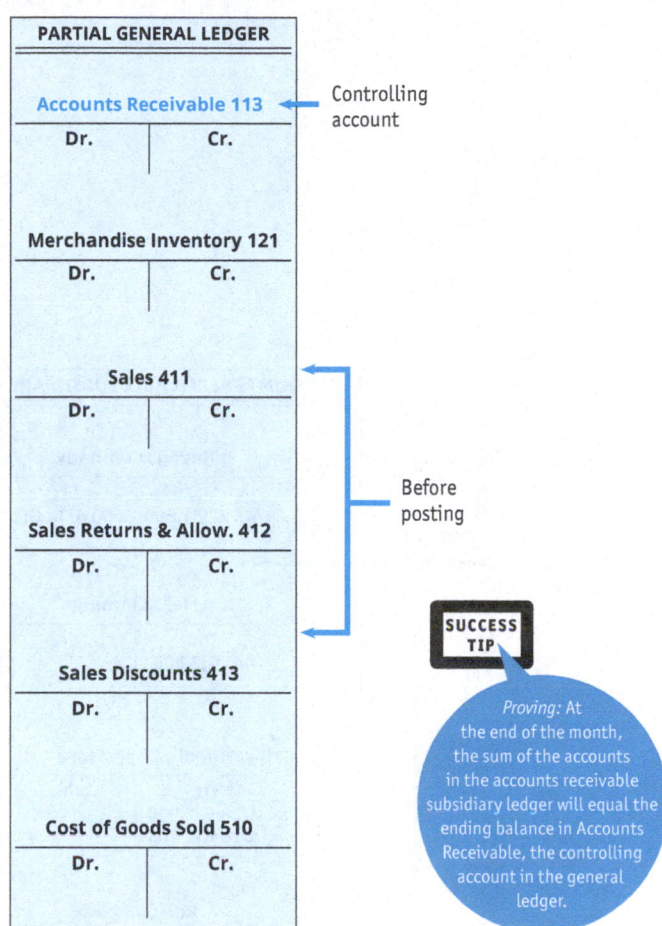

Proving: At the end of the month, the sum of the accounts in the accounts receivable subsidiary ledger will equal the ending balance in Accounts Receivable, the controlling account in the general ledger.

Figure 9.18 shows how the April 3 transaction is posted and recorded.

For this transaction we *post* to the general ledger Accounts Receivable and Sales accounts as well as the Merchandise Inventory and Cost of Goods Sold accounts. Note how the account numbers of 113, 411, 121, and 510 are entered into the PR column of the general journal. We must also *record* to Hal's Clothing in the accounts receivable subsidiary ledger. The amount is placed on the debit side because Hal owed Art the money. When the subsidiary ledger is updated, a checkmark (✔) is placed in the PR column of the general journal. The continuation of Figure 9.18 on the following page shows how the accounts receivable subsidiary ledger and partial general ledger would look after postings.

	GENERAL JOURNAL				**Page 2**
Date	Account Titles and Description	PR	Dr.	Cr.	
201X					
Apr. 3	Accounts Receivable, Hal's Clothing	113 ✔	8 0 0 00		
	Sales	411		8 0 0 00	
	Sale on account to Hal's				
3	Cost of Goods Sold	510	6 0 0 00		
	Merchandise Inventory	121		6 0 0 00	
	Record cost of the sale to Hal's				

Figure 9.18
Transaction for April 3 Posted and Recorded

(continued on page 312)

Figure 9.18
Continued

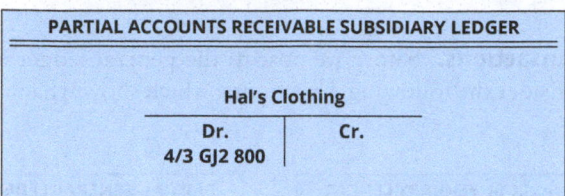

PARTIAL ACCOUNTS RECEIVABLE SUBSIDIARY LEDGER

Hal's Clothing

Dr.	Cr.
4/3 GJ2 800	

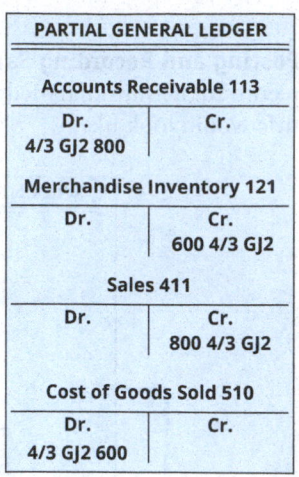

PARTIAL GENERAL LEDGER

Accounts Receivable 113

Dr.	Cr.
4/3 GJ2 800	

Merchandise Inventory 121

Dr.	Cr.
	600 4/3 GJ2

Sales 411

Dr.	Cr.
	800 4/3 GJ2

Cost of Goods Sold 510

Dr.	Cr.
4/3 GJ2 600	

Tells us what page of the general journal information comes from

After recording

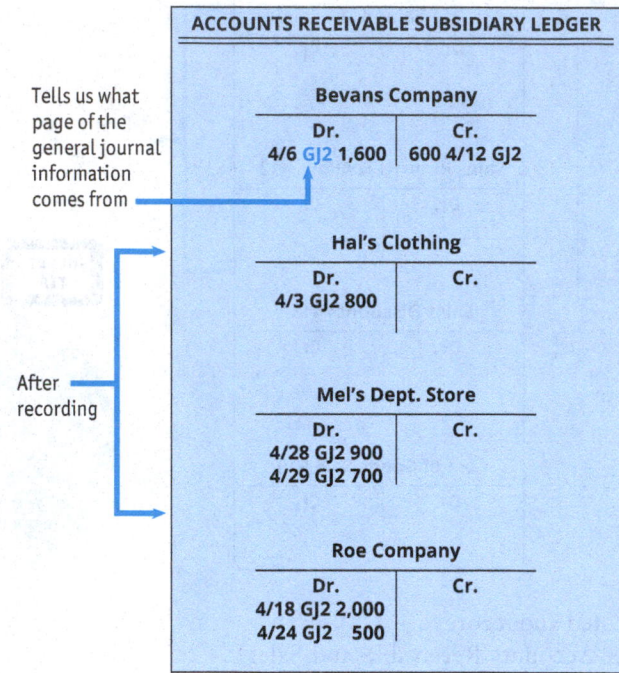

ACCOUNTS RECEIVABLE SUBSIDIARY LEDGER

Bevans Company

Dr.	Cr.
4/6 GJ2 1,600	600 4/12 GJ2

Hal's Clothing

Dr.	Cr.
4/3 GJ2 800	

Mel's Dept. Store

Dr.	Cr.
4/28 GJ2 900	
4/29 GJ2 700	

Roe Company

Dr.	Cr.
4/18 GJ2 2,000	
4/24 GJ2 500	

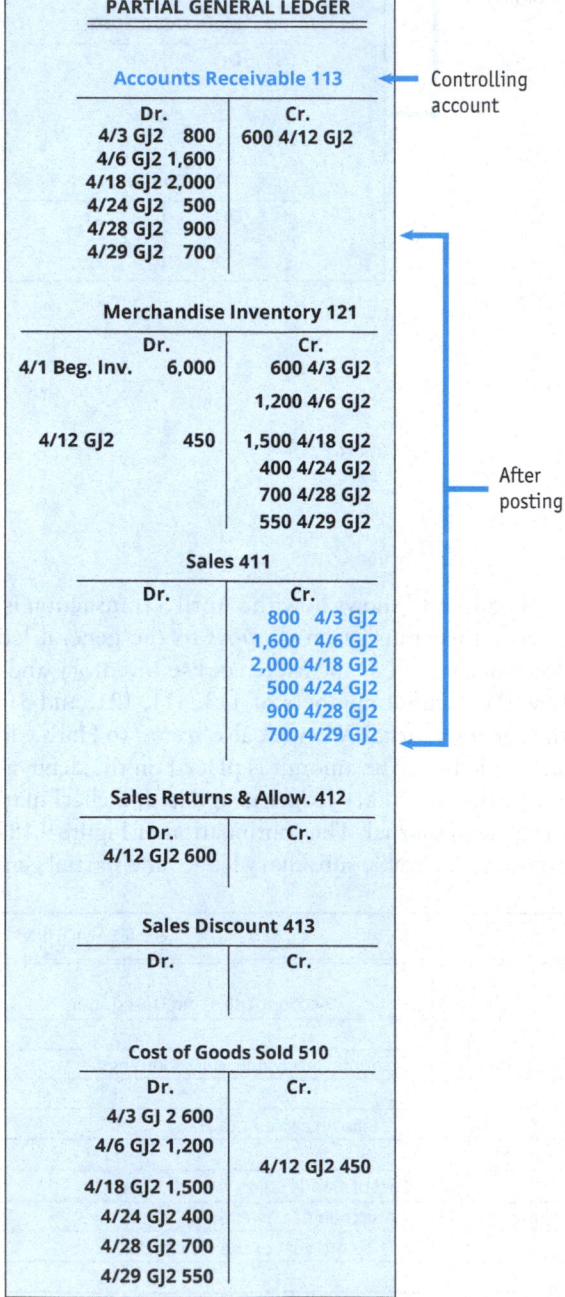

PARTIAL GENERAL LEDGER

Accounts Receivable 113

Dr.	Cr.
4/3 GJ2 800	600 4/12 GJ2
4/6 GJ2 1,600	
4/18 GJ2 2,000	
4/24 GJ2 500	
4/28 GJ2 900	
4/29 GJ2 700	

Controlling account

Merchandise Inventory 121

Dr.	Cr.
4/1 Beg. Inv. 6,000	600 4/3 GJ2
	1,200 4/6 GJ2
4/12 GJ2 450	1,500 4/18 GJ2
	400 4/24 GJ2
	700 4/28 GJ2
	550 4/29 GJ2

Sales 411

Dr.	Cr.
	800 4/3 GJ2
	1,600 4/6 GJ2
	2,000 4/18 GJ2
	500 4/24 GJ2
	900 4/28 GJ2
	700 4/29 GJ2

After posting

Sales Returns & Allow. 412

Dr.	Cr.
4/12 GJ2 600	

Sales Discount 413

Dr.	Cr.

Cost of Goods Sold 510

Dr.	Cr.
4/3 GJ 2 600	
4/6 GJ2 1,200	
4/18 GJ2 1,500	4/12 GJ2 450
4/24 GJ2 400	
4/28 GJ2 700	
4/29 GJ2 550	

The Credit Memorandum

Companies usually handle sales returns and allowances by means of a credit memorandum. Credit memoranda inform customers that the amount of the goods returned or the amount allowed for damaged goods has been subtracted (credited) from the customer's ongoing account with the company.

A sample credit memorandum from Art's Wholesale Clothing Company appears in Figure 9.19. It shows that on April 12, Credit Memorandum No. 1 was issued to Bevans Company for defective merchandise that had been returned.

Credit memorandum A piece of paper sent by the seller to a customer who has returned merchandise previously purchased on credit. The credit memorandum indicates to the customer that the seller is reducing the amount owed by the customer.

Art's Wholesale
Clothing Co.
1528 Belle Ave.
New York, NY 10022

Credit
Memorandum No. 1
Date: April 12, 201X
Credit to Bevans Company
    110 Aster Rd.
    Cincinnati, Ohio 45227
We credit your account as follows:
Merchandise returned 60 model 8 B men's dress gloves—$600

Figure 9.19
Sample Credit Memorandum from Art's Wholesale Clothing Company

Let's look at a transaction analysis chart before we journalize, record, and post this transaction.

Accounts Affected	Category	↑↓	Rules
Sales Returns and Allowances	Contra-revenue account	↑	Dr.
Accounts Receivable, Bevans Co.	Asset	↓	Cr.
Merchandise Inventory	Asset	↑	Dr.
Cost of Goods Sold	Expense	↓	Cr.

Journalizing, Recording, and Posting the Credit Memorandum

The credit memorandum results in two postings to the general ledger and one recording to the accounts receivable subsidiary ledger (see Figure 9.20).

SUCCESS TIP

Remember: Sales discounts are not taken on returns.

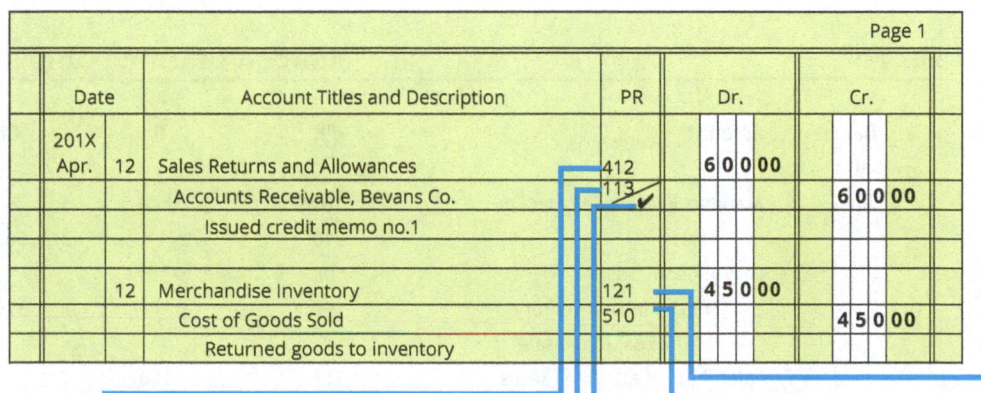

Figure 9.20
Postings and Recording for the Credit Memorandum into the Subsidiary and General Ledgers

412 – A debit of $600 is posted to Sales Returns and Allowances, account no. 412 in the general ledger. When the amount is posted, the account number is placed in the PR column of the journal.

113 – The credit of $600 is also posted to Accounts Receivable in the controlling account in the general ledger. Then, the account number (113) is placed in the PR column of the journal.

✔ The check indicates that $600 has been recorded as a credit to the account of Bevans Company in the accounts receivable subsidiary ledger.

510 – a credit of $450 is posted to Cost of Goods sold, account no. 510 in the general ledger. When the account is posted, the account number is posted in the PR column of the journal.

121 – a debit of $450 is posted to Merchandise Inventory, account no. 121 in the general ledger. When the account is posted, the account number is posted in the PR column of the journal.

Note that in the PR column next to Accounts Receivable, Bevans Co., a diagonal line separates account number 113 above and a ✓ below. This notation shows that the amount of $600 has been credited to Accounts Receivable in the controlling account in the general ledger *and* credited to the account of Bevans Co. in the accounts receivable subsidiary ledger. Keep in mind that with accounting software available today, information about returns, for example, is easily updated in the accounting system, and customer accounts are immediately updated in the appropriate ledgers. Now it's time to check your progress.

 ## TRY IT!   Learning Unit 9-2

Given the following, journalize and post these two transactions (it is on pg. 6 in the General Journal):

201X	
June 5	Sold merchandise on account to Leser Co., $500; terms 2/10, n/30. The cost of these goods was $375.
7	Issued Credit Memorandum No. 1 to Leser Co. for $100 of returned goods. The cost of the returned goods was $75.

Partial General Ledger

Accounts Receivable 151			Sales 310	
Dr.	Cr.		Dr.	Cr.
Bal. 900				

Merchandise Inventory 160			Sales Returns and Allowances 312	
Dr.	Cr.		Dr.	Cr.
Bal. 1,000			**Cost of Goods Sold 502**	
			Dr.	Cr.
			Bal. 700	

Accounts Receivable Subsidiary Ledger

Bloom Co.			Leser Co.	
Dr.	Cr.		Dr.	Cr.
Bal. 900				

TRY IT!   Solution Learning Unit 9-2

Date	Account	PR	Dr.	Cr.
201X				
June 5	Accounts Receivable Leser Co.	151/✓	500	
	Sales	310		500
	Cost of Goods Sold	502	375	
	Merchandise Inventory	160		375
	Record cost of the sale			
7	Sales Returns and Allowances	312	100	
	Accounts Receivable, Leser Co.	151/✓		100
	Issued Credit to Leser Co.			
7	Merchandise Inventory	160	75	
	Cost of Goods Sold	502		75
	Returned goods to inventory			

Partial General Ledger

Accounts Receivable 151

Dr.	Cr.
Bal. 900	100 6/7 GJ6
6/5 GJ6 500	

Merchandise Inventory 160

Dr.	Cr.
Bal. 1,000	375 6/5 GJ6
6/7 GJ6 75	

Sales 310

Dr.	Cr.
	500 6/5 GJ6

Sales Returns and Allowances 312

Dr.	Cr.
6/7 GJ6 100	

Cost of Goods Sold 502

Dr.	Cr.
Bal. 700	
6/5 GJ6 375	
	75 6/7 GJ6

Accounts Receivable Subsidiary Ledger

Bloom Co.

Dr.	Cr.
Bal. 900	

Leser Co.

Dr.	Cr.
6/5 GJ6 500	100 6/7 GJ6

LEARNING UNIT 9-3

Cash Receipt Transactions and Preparation of Schedule of Accounts Receivable

 LO3

The following cash receipt transactions occurred for Art's Wholesale Clothing in April:

201X

Apr.	1	Art Newner invested $8,000 in the business.
	4	Received check from Hal's Clothing for payment of invoice no. 1, less 2% discount.
	15	Cash sales for first half of April, $900. The cost of the sales was $675.
	16	Received check from Bevans Company in settlement of invoice no. 2, less returns and 2% discount.
	22	Received check from Roe Company for payment of invoice no. 3, less 2% discount.
	27	Sold store equipment, $500.
	30	Cash sales for second half of April, $1,200. The cost of the sales was $900.

Figure 9.21 provides a closer look at how the April 4 transaction would be journalized. Let's first look at the transaction analysis chart before showing the journalized transaction.

Apr.	4	Cash		7 8 4 00	
		Sales Discount		1 6 00	
		Accounts Receivable, Hal's Clothing			8 0 0 00

Figure 9.21
Recording Sales Discount in General Journal

SUCCESS TIP

Hal's Clothing is located in the accounts receivable subsidiary ledger.

Accounts Affected	Category	↑↓	Rules	T Account Update
Cash	Asset	↑	Dr.	**Cash**
				Dr. 784 | Cr.
Sales Discount	Contra-revenue	↑	Dr.	**Sales Discount**
				Dr. 16 | Cr.
Accounts Receivable, Hal's Clothing	Asset	↓	Cr.	**Acc. Rec.** Dr. 800 | Cr. 800 **Hal's Clothing** Dr. 800 | Cr. 800

Figure 9.22 shows the complete set of April cash receipts transactions for Art's Wholesale journalized for the month, followed by a complete posting to the general ledger and recordings to the accounts receivable subsidiary ledger. (Remember from the past unit that we posted all the sales on account information.)

Figure 9.22
Journalized Cash Receipts Transactions

		GENERAL JOURNAL			Page 2	
Date		Account Titles and Description	PR	Dr.	Cr.	
201X						
Apr.	1	Cash	111	8 0 0 0 00		
		Art Newner, Capital	311		8 0 0 0 00	
		Owner Investment				
	4	Cash	111	7 8 4 00		
		Sales Discount	413	1 6 00		
		Accounts Receivable, Hal's Clothing	113 ✔		8 0 0 00	
		Hal's paid invoice no. 1				
	15	Cash	111	9 0 0 00		
		Sales	411		9 0 0 00	
		Cash sales for first half of April				
	15	Cost of Goods Sold	510	6 7 5 00		
		Merchandise Inventory	121		6 7 5 00	
		Cost of cash sales for first half of April				
	16	Cash	111	9 8 0 00		
		Sales Discount	413	2 0 00		
		Accounts Receivable, Bevan's Company	113 ✔		1 0 0 0 00	
		Bevans paid invoice no. 2				
	22	Cash	111	1 9 6 0 00		
		Sales Discount	413	4 0 00		
		Accounts Receivable, Roe Co.	113 ✔		2 0 0 0 00	
		Roe paid invoice no. 3				
	27	Cash	111	5 0 0 00		
		Store Equipment	125		5 0 0 00	
		Sold store equipment				
	30	Cash	111	1 2 0 0 00		
		Sales	411		1 2 0 0 00	
		Cash sales for second half of April				
	30	Cost of Goods Sold	510	9 0 0 00		
		Merchandise Inventory	121		9 0 0 00	
		Cost of cash sales for second half of April				

Figure 9.22
Continued

ACCOUNTS RECEIVABLE SUBSIDIARY LEDGER

Bevans Company

Dr.	Cr.
4/6 GJ2 1,600	600 4/12 GJ2
	1,000 4/16 GJ2
0	

Hal's Clothing

Dr.	Cr.
4/3 GJ2 800	800 4/4 GJ2
0	

Mel's Dept. Store

Dr.	Cr.
4/28 GJ2 900	
4/29 GJ2 700	
1,600	

Roe Company

Dr.	Cr.
4/18 GJ2 2,000	2,000 4/22 GJ2
4/24 GJ2 500	
2,500	2,000
500	

PARTIAL GENERAL LEDGER

Cash 111

Dr.	Cr.
4/1 GJ2 8,000	
4/4 GJ2 784	
4/15 GJ2 900	
4/16 GJ2 980	
4/22 GJ2 1,960	
4/27 GJ2 500	
4/30 GJ2 1,200	
14,324	

Accounts Receivable 113 ← Controlling account

Dr.	Cr.
4/3 GJ2 800	800 4/4 GJ2
4/6 GJ2 1,600	600 4/12 GJ2
4/18 GJ2 2,000	1,000 4/16 GJ2
4/24 GJ2 500	2,000 4/22 GJ2
4/28 GJ2 900	4,400
4/29 GJ2 700	
6,500	
Bal. 2,100	

Inventory 121

Dr.	Cr.
4/1 Beg. Inv. 6,000	600 4/3 GJ2
	1,200 4/6 GJ2
4/12 GJ2 450	675 4/15 GJ2
	1,500 4/18 GJ2
	400 4/24 GJ2
	700 4/28 GJ2
	550 4/29 GJ2
	900 4/30 GJ2

Store Equipment 125

Dr.	Cr.
4/1 Bal. 24,000	500 4/27 GJ2
23,500	

Art Newner, Capital 311

Dr.	Cr.
	8,000 4/1 GJ2
	8,000

Sales 411

Dr.	Cr.
	800 4/3 GJ2
	1,600 4/6 GJ2
	900 4/15 GJ2
	2,000 4/18 GJ2
	500 4/24 GJ2
	900 4/28 GJ2
	700 4/29 GJ2
	1,200 4/30 GJ2
	8,600

Sales Returns & Allow. 412

Dr.	Cr.
4/12 GJ2 600	
600	

Sales Discount 413

Dr.	Cr.
4/4 GJ2 16	
4/16 GJ2 20	
4/22 GJ2 40	
76	

Cost of Goods Sold 510

Dr.	Cr.
4/3 GJ2 600	
4/6 GJ2 1,200	
4/15 GJ2 675	4/12 GJ2 450
4/18 GJ2 1,500	
4/24 GJ2 400	
4/28 GJ2 700	
4/29 GJ2 550	
4/30 GJ2 900	

Schedule of accounts receivable A list of the customers, in alphabetical order, that have an outstanding balance in the accounts receivable subsidiary ledger. This total should be equal to the balance of the Accounts Receivable controlling account in the general ledger at the end of the month.

Figure 9.23
Schedule of Accounts Receivable

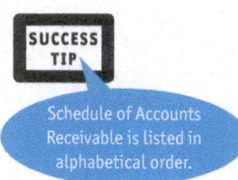

Schedule of Accounts Receivable is listed in alphabetical order.

Schedule of Accounts Receivable

The schedule of accounts receivable is an alphabetical list of the companies that have an outstanding balance in the accounts receivable subsidiary ledger. This total should be equal to the balance of the Accounts Receivable controlling account in the general ledger at the end of the month.

Let's examine the schedule of accounts receivable for Art's Wholesale Clothing Company in Figure 9.23.

ART'S WHOLESALE CLOTHING COMPANY SCHEDULE OF ACCOUNTS RECEIVABLE APRIL 30, 201X	
Mel's Dept. Store	$1 6 0 0 00
Roe Company	5 0 0 00
Total Accounts Receivable	$2 1 0 0 00

The balance of the controlling account, Accounts Receivable ($2,100), in the general ledger does indeed equal the sum of the individual customer balances in the accounts receivable ledger ($2,100) as shown in the schedule of accounts receivable. The schedule of accounts receivable can help forecast potential cash inflows as well as possible credit and collection decisions. Remember, if computer software is used, you would just click from a menu to prepare a new schedule and all information is stored on the computer's hard drive or on the Cloud. Now it's time to check your progress.

 **TRY IT!**   **Learning Unit 9-3**

Given the following, journalize, record, post, and prepare a schedule of accounts receivable at the end of April for King Co. (it is on pg. 8 in the General Journal).

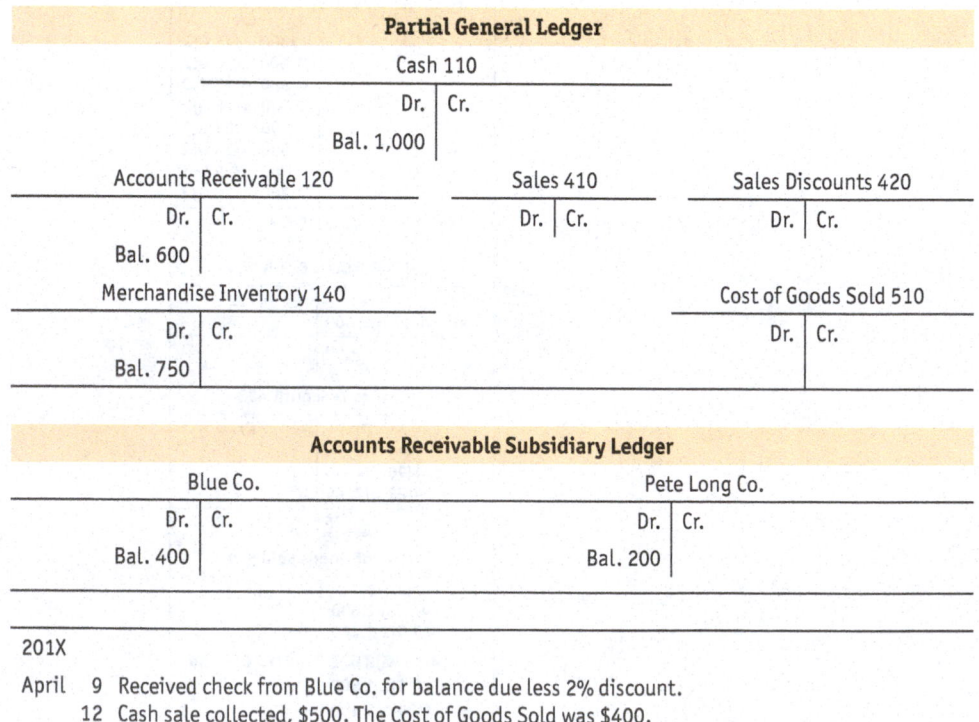

Partial General Ledger

Cash 110
Dr. | Cr.
Bal. 1,000 |

Accounts Receivable 120
Dr. | Cr.
Bal. 600 |

Sales 410
Dr. | Cr.

Sales Discounts 420
Dr. | Cr.

Merchandise Inventory 140
Dr. | Cr.
Bal. 750 |

Cost of Goods Sold 510
Dr. | Cr.

Accounts Receivable Subsidiary Ledger

Blue Co.
Dr. | Cr.
Bal. 400 |

Pete Long Co.
Dr. | Cr.
Bal. 200 |

201X
April 9 Received check from Blue Co. for balance due less 2% discount.
       12 Cash sale collected, $500. The Cost of Goods Sold was $400.

TRY IT! **Solution Learning Unit 9-3**

King Co.
General Journal p. 8

Date		Account	PR	Dr.	Cr.
201X					
April	9	Cash	110	392	
		Sales Discount	420	8	
		Accounts Receivable, Blue Co.	120/✓		400
		Received Cash from Blue Co.			
	12	Cash	110	500	
		Sales	410		500
		Cash Sale			
	12	Cost of Goods Sold	510	400	
		Merchandise Inventory	140		400
		Record cost of the cash sale			

King Co.

Partial General Ledger		

Cash 110

Dr.	Cr.
Bal. 1,000	
4/9 GJ8 392	
4/12 GJ8 500	

Accounts Receivable 120

Dr.	Cr.
Bal. 600	400 4/9 GJ8

Merchandise Inventory 140

Dr.	Cr.
Bal. 750	
	400 4/12 GJ8

Sales 410

Dr.	Cr.
	500 4/12 GJ8

Sales Discount 420

Dr.	Cr.
4/9 GJ8 8	

Cost of Goods Sold 510

Dr.	Cr.
4/12 GJ8 400	

(continued on page 320)

Accounts Receivable Subsidiary Ledger

Blue Co.

Dr.	Cr.
Bal. 400	400 GJ8 4/9
Bal. 0	

Pete Long Co.

Dr.	Cr.
Bal. 200	

Schedule of Accounts Receivable April 30, 201X

Pete Long Co.	$200
Total Accounts Receivable	$200

L01,2,3

DEMONSTRATION SUMMARY PROBLEM

Mia Kim owns Kim's Running Shop.

Requirements

From the following information:
1. Journalize the transactions (page 6 of journal). Do not provide explanations
2. Record to accounts receivable subsidiary ledger and post to general ledger as needed. Also, determine the ending balance in each account on June 30.
3. Prepare a schedule of accounts receivable for June 30, 201X.

Partial General Ledger

Cash 110

Dr.	Cr.
Bal. 4,000	

Accounts Receivable 120

Dr.	Cr.
Bal. 1,400	

Merchandise Inventory 140

Dr.	Cr.
Bal. 2,500	

Display Equipment 150

Dr.	Cr.
Bal. 900	

M. Kim, Capital 310

Dr.	Cr.
	Bal. 8,000

Sales 410

Dr.	Cr.
	Bal. 2,000

Sales Discounts 420

Dr.	Cr.

Sales Returns and Allowances 440

Dr.	Cr.

Cost of Goods Sold 510

Dr.	Cr.
Bal. 550	

Accounts Receivable Subsidiary Ledger

Roger Flynn

Dr.	Cr.
Bal. 200	

Bob Jey

Dr.	Cr.
Bal. 400	

Joe Lantz

Dr.	Cr.
Bal. 800	

Valerie Tog

Dr.	Cr.

201X

June	1	Mia Kim invested an additional $3,000 into the running shop.
	3	Sold $200 of merchandise on account to Bob Jey, sales ticket no. 60; terms 2/10, n/30. The cost of the merchandise was $110.
	4	Sold $100 of merchandise on account to Roger Flynn, sales ticket no. 61; terms 2/10, n/30. The cost of the merchandise was $65.
	9	Sold $150 of merchandise on account to Joe Lantz, sales ticket no. 62; terms 2/10, n/30. The cost of the merchandise was $95.
	10	Received cash from Bob Jey in payment of June 3 transaction, sales ticket no. 60, less discount.
	20	Sold $90 of merchandise on account to Valerie Tog, sales ticket no. 63; terms 2/10, n/30. The cost of the merchandise was $60.
	22	Received cash payment from Roger Flynn in payment of June 4 transaction, sales ticket no. 61.
	23	Collected cash sales, $900. The cost of the merchandise was $550.
	24	Issued credit memorandum no. 1 to Valerie Tog, $50. The cost of the merchandise was $28. The merchandise was returned to inventory.
	30	Sold display equipment for $400. (Beware, the cost is $400.)

Solutions

Requirements 1, 2, 3

Kim's Running Shop
General Journal Page 6

Date		Accounts	PR	Dr.	Cr.
201X					
June	1	Cash	110	3,000	
		Mia Kim, Capital	310		3,000
	3	Accounts Receivable, Bob Jey	120/✓	200	
		Sales	410		200
	3	Cost of Goods Sold	510	110	
		Merchandise Inventory	140		110
	4	Accounts Receivable, Roger Flynn	120/✓	100	
		Sales	410		100
	4	Cost of Goods Sold	510	65	
		Merchandise Inventory	140		65
		Record cost of the sale to Roger Flynn			
	9	Accounts Receivable, Joe Lantz	120/✓	150	
		Sales	410		150
	9	Cost of Goods Sold	510	95	
		Merchandise Inventory	140		95
	10	Cash	110	196	
		Sales Discount	420	4	
	20	Accounts Receivable, Valerie Tog	120/✓	90	
		Sales	410		90
	20	Cost of Goods Sold	510	60	
		Merchandise Inventory	140		60
	22	Cash	110	100	
		Accounts Receivable, Roger Flynn	120/✓		100
	23	Cash	110	900	
		Sales	410		900
	23	Cost of Goods Sold	510	550	
		Merchandise Inventory	140		550

(continued on page 322)

Date	Accounts	PR	Dr.	Cr.
24	Sales Returns and Allowances	440	50	
	Accounts Receivable, Valerie Tog	120/✓		50
	Merchandise Inventory	140	28	
	Cost of Goods Sold	510		28
30	Cash	110	400	
	Display Equipment	150		400

Tips for Journalizing Transactions and Posting to the Accounts Receivable Subsidiary Ledger and General Ledger

Account	Category	Normal Balance
Cash	Asset	Debit
Accounts Receivable	Asset	Debit
Merchandise Inventory	Asset	Debit
Sales	Revenue	Credit
Sales Discount	Contra-Revenue	Debit
Sales Returns and Allowances	Contra-Revenue	Debit
Cost of Goods Sold	Expense	Debit

Partial General Ledger

Cash 110

	Dr.	Cr.
Bal.	4,000	
6/1 GJ6	3,000	
6/10 GJ6	196	
6/22 GJ6	100	
6/23 GJ6	900	
6/30 GJ6	400	
Balance	8,596	

Accounts Receivable 120

	Dr.	Cr.	
Bal.	1,400	200	6/10 GJ6
6/3 GJ6	200	100	6/22 GJ6
6/4 GJ6	100	50	6/24 GJ6
6/9 GJ6	150		
6/20 GJ6	90		
Balance	1,590		

Merchandise Inventory 140

	Dr.	Cr.	
Bal.	2,500	110	6/3 GJ6
6/24 G16	28	65	6/4 GJ6
		95	6/9 GJ6
		60	6/20 GJ6
		550	6/23 GJ6
Balance	1,648		

Display Equipment 150

	Dr.	Cr.	
Bal.	900	400	6/30 GJ6
Balance	500		

Mia Kim, Capital 310

Dr.	Cr.
	8,000 Bal.
	3,000 6/1 GJ6
	Balance 11,000

Sales 410

Dr.	Cr.
	2,000 Bal.
	200 6/3 GJ6
	100 6/4 GJ6
	150 6/9 GJ6
	90 6/20 GJ6
	900 6/23 GJ6
	Balance 3,440

Sales Discount 420

Dr.	Cr.
6/10 GJ6 4	
Balance 4	

Sales Returns and Allowances 440

Dr.	Cr.
6/24 GJ6 50	
Balance 50	

Cost of Goods Sold 510

Dr.	Cr.
Bal. 550	
6/3 GJ6 110	
6/4 GJ6 65	
6/9 GJ6 95	
6/20 GJ6 60	
6/23 GJ6 550	
	28 6/24 GJ6
Balance 1,402	

Accounts Receivable Subsidiary Ledger

Roger Flynn

Dr.	Cr.
Bal. 200	100 6/22 GJ6
6/4 GJ6 100	
Balance 200	

Bob Jey

Dr.	Cr.
Bal. 400	200 6/10 GJ6
6/3 GJ6 200	
Balance 400	

Joe Lantz

Dr.	Cr.
Bal 800	
6/9 GJ6 150	
Balance 950	

Valerie Tog

Dr.	Cr.
6/20 GJ6 90	50 6/24 GJ6
Balance 40	

Tips for Preparing a Schedule of Accounts Receivable

The normal balance of the account receivable subsidiary ledger accounts is a debit. After posting to the general ledger and recording in the subsidiary ledger, the balance in Accounts Receivable in the general ledger should equal the total of all ending balances in the subsidiary ledger.

Kim's Running Shop
Schedule of Accounts Receivable
June 30, 201X

Roger Flynn	$ 200
Bob Jey	400
Joe Lantz	950
Valerie Tog	40
Total Accounts Receivable	$1,590

These amounts for Flynn, Jey, Lantz, and Tog came from the ending balances in the subsidiary ledger. Note this is the ending balance in Accounts Receivable in the general ledger.

SUCCESS COACH

The following Success Tips are from Learning Units 9-1 to 9-3. Take the Do It Right Now Checkup and use the Check Your Score to see how you are doing. The Success Coach provides tips before each Checkup to help you avoid common accounting errors.

LU 9-1 Explaining and Journalizing Entries for Sales, Sales Discounts, and Sales Returns and Allowances for Transactions for a Perpetual Inventory System

Do It Right Tips: Sales is a revenue account, while Sales Returns and Allowances and Sales Discounts are contra-revenue accounts. Sales Returns and Allowances and Sales Discounts have their normal balances on the debit side. Gross sales less sales returns and allowances, less sales discounts will equal net sales.

In a perpetual inventory system, all purchases of inventory are recorded in an asset account called Merchandise Inventory. The cost of selling inventory is recorded in the Cost of Goods Sold account. When a sale is made, the company gets cash and/or accounts receivable and a sale is shown. At the same time, the company records the Cost of Goods Sold along with a reduction in Merchandise Inventory since it is sold. Returns to the seller will increase the Merchandise Inventory account. If a seller pays for the cost of freight, it is a selling expense for the seller.

Do It Right Now Checkup: Answer true or false to the following statements.

1. Net sales and gross sales are the same.
2. Sales Tax Payable is an asset.
3. Sales Discounts is a revenue account with a debit balance.
4. Sales Returns and Allowances increase with a debit.
5. Sales Discounts increase with a credit.
6. In the perpetual system there are no Purchases, Purchases Discounts, or Purchases Returns and Allowances accounts.
7. Cost of freight results in a decrease to Merchandise Inventory.
8. Perpetual systems do not record cash sales.

LU 9-2 Subsidiary Ledgers and General Ledger Sales Transactions and Returns

Do It Right Tips: The controlling account, Accounts Receivable, in the general ledger will equal the sum of Accounts Receivable in the subsidiary ledger at the end of the month. If a credit memorandum is issued, Sales Returns and Allowances will increase with a debit, and an Accounts Receivable controlling account, as well as the specific subsidiary ledger, will be reduced. The normal balance of each account in the subsidiary ledger is a debit balance.

Do It Right Now Checkup: Answer true or false to the following statements.

1. The controlling account is located in the subsidiary ledger.
2. A checkmark in the posting reference column means the controlling account has been updated.
3. A credit memorandum only affects the controlling account.
4. Sales discounts are always taken on returns.
5. Subsidiary ledgers can be listed alphabetically.

LU 9-3 Cash Receipt Transactions and Preparation of a Schedule of Accounts Receivable

Do It Right Tips: When all postings are done, the sum of the accounts in the subsidiary ledger should equal the ending balance in the controlling account. It is the schedule of accounts receivable that lists each customer with its ending balance. This total in the schedule of accounts receivable is the one that matches the ending balance in the controlling account. There are no debits or credits on the schedule of accounts receivable.

Do It Right Now Checkup: Answer true or false to the following statements.

1. The schedule of accounts receivable lists debits first.
2. The normal balance of an Accounts Receivable account is a credit.
3. The controlling account does not match the total of the schedule of accounts receivable at the end of the month.
4. Sales Discounts is a contra-asset.
5. The schedule of accounts receivable shows what we owe vendors.

CHECK YOUR SCORE: Answers to the Do It Right Now Checkup

LU 9-1

1. False—Net sales is gross sales less returns and allowances and any discounts.
2. False—Sales Tax Payable is a liability.
3. False—Sales Discounts is a contra-revenue account with a debit balance.
4. True
5. False—Sales Discounts increase with a debit.
6. True—Changes go directly to the Merchandise Inventory and Cost of Goods Sold accounts.
7. False—Shipping charges are an increase to the Merchandise Inventory Account.
8. False—The perpetual method does record Cash sales.

LU 9-2

1. False—The controlling account is located in the general ledger.
2. False—A checkmark in the posting reference column means the subsidiary ledger has been updated.

3. False—Credit memorandum affects both the controlling account and the subsidiary ledger.
4. False—Sales discounts are never taken on returns.
5. True

LU 9-3

1. False—There are no debits on the schedule of accounts receivable.
2. False—The normal balance of an Accounts Receivable account is a debit.
3. False—The controlling account does match the total of the schedule of accounts receivable at the end of the month.
4. False—Sales Discounts is a contra-revenue account.
5. False—The schedule of accounts receivable shows the amount customers owe the seller.

BLUEPRINT: TRANSFERRING INFORMATION FROM THE GENERAL JOURNAL

Post → General Ledger (account)
Record → Subsidiary Ledger(✓)

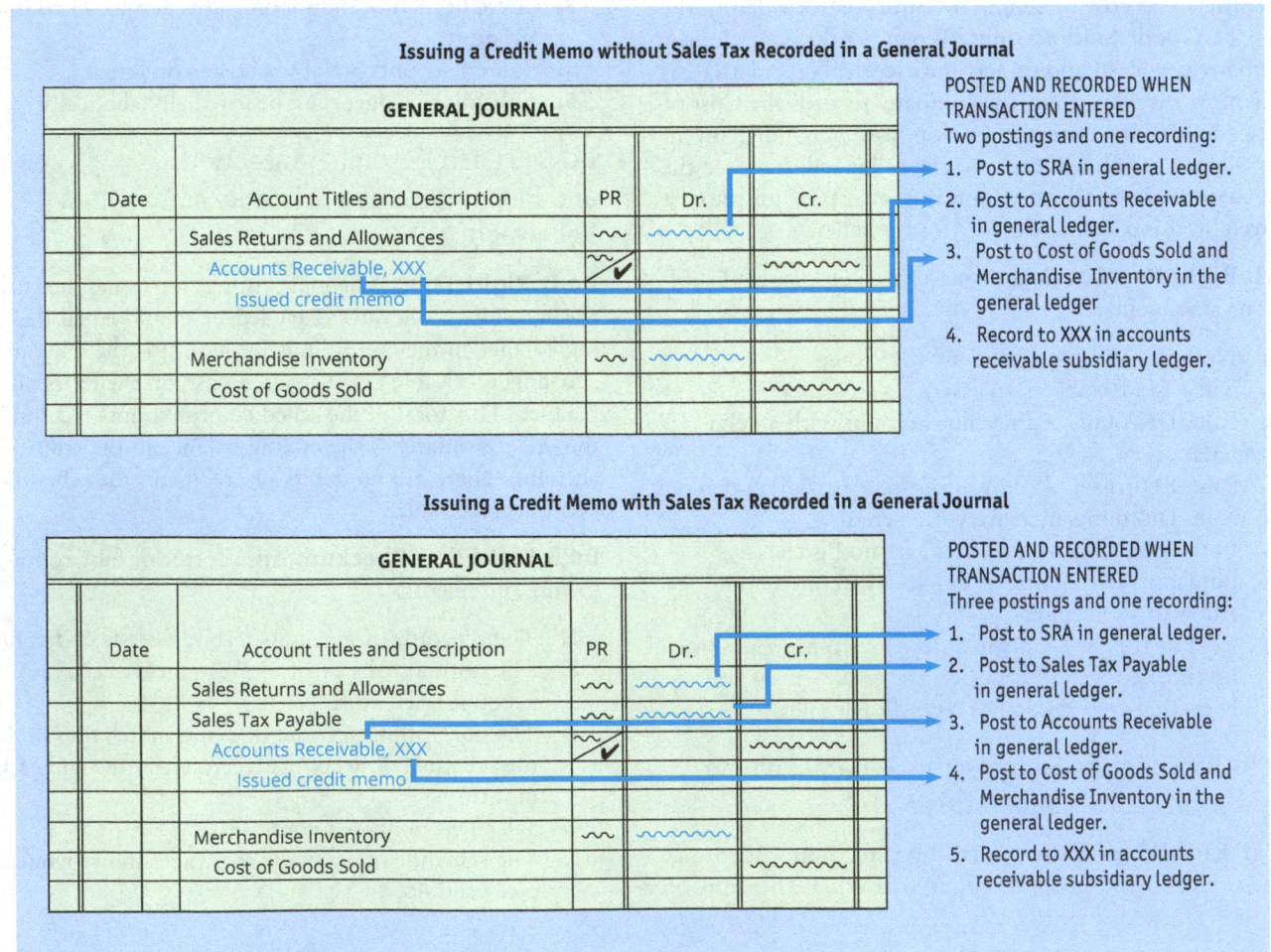

Discussion Questions and Critical Thinking/Ethical Case

1. Explain the purpose of a contra-revenue account.
2. What is the normal balance of Sales Discount?
3. Give two examples of contra-revenue accounts.
4. What is the difference between a discount period and a credit period?
5. Explain the terms:
   a. 2/10, n/30
   b. n/10, EOM
6. What category is Sales Discount in?
7. What is the normal balance of Cost of Goods Sold?
8. How are discounts recorded in a perpetual system?
9. Spring Co. bought merchandise from All Co. with terms 2/10, n/30. Joanne Ring, the bookkeeper, forgot to pay the bill within the first 10 days. She went to Mel Ryan, the head accountant, who told her to backdate the check so that it looked like the bill was paid within the discount period. Joanne told Mel that she thought they could get away with it. Should Joanne and Mel backdate the check to take advantage of the discount? You make the call. Write down your specific recommendations to Joanne.
10. Compare and contrast the Controlling Account—Accounts Receivable to the accounts receivable subsidiary ledger.
11. Why is the accounts receivable subsidiary ledger organized in alphabetical order?
12. When is a (✓) used?
13. What is an invoice? What purpose does it serve?
14. Why is sales tax a liability to the business?
15. Sales discounts are taken on sales tax. Agree or disagree? Explain why.
16. When a seller issues a credit memorandum (assume no sales tax), what accounts will be affected?
17. Amy Jak is the National Sales Manager of Land.com. To get sales up to the projection for the old year, Amy asked the accountant to put the first 2 weeks' sales in January back into December. Amy told the accountant that this secret would only be between them. Should Amy move the new sales into the old sales year? You make the call. Write down your specific recommendations to Amy.

Concept Checks

MyLabAccounting

Perpetual Inventory

LO1 *(15 min)*

1. Draw a seesaw similar to the one shown in Figure 9.3 and show a sale of $1,000 that cost the store $450. Be sure to label all the accounts.

Perpetual Inventory Discount

LO1 *(10 min)*

2. Balder Co. paid $200 to Pedro Co. and received a $20 purchases discount. Journalize the entry for Balder Co.

Perpetual Inventory Return

LO1 *(10 min)*

3. Porter Morse returned $275 (selling price) of merchandise purchased on account to Labrie Co. The cost of the merchandise to Labrie Co. is $100. What would be the journal entries on the books of both the buyer and seller?

Perpetual Inventory Freight

LO1 *(10 min)*

4. Capris Co. paid the cost of freight, $70. Journalize the transaction. Assume that Capris Co. is the buyer.

(10 min) **LO1,2,3** ▶▶▶

General Journal

5. Match the following activities to the three business transactions (more than one number can be used).

   1. Record to the accounts receivable subsidiary ledger.
   2. Journalize the transaction.
   3. Post to the general ledger.

      a. _____ Sold merchandise on account to Clo Co., invoice no. 1, $90. Cost of the merchandise was $55.
      b. _____ Sold merchandise on account to Flynn Co., invoice no. 2, $1,500. Cost of the merchandise was $925.
      c. _____ Issued credit memorandum no. 1 to Flynn Co. for defective merchandise, $50. Cost of the merchandise was $28.

(10 min) **LO2** ▶

Credit Memorandum

6. Complete the transactional analysis box for the following transaction: Issued credit memorandum to Pike.com for defective merchandise, $190. The cost of the merchandise was $114. It was a credit sale.

(15 min) **LO1,2** ▶▶

Journalize Transactions

7. Journalize the following transactions:

   a. Sold merchandise on account to Troy Co., invoice no. 10, $50. The cost of the merchandise was $28.
   b. Received check from Brown Co., $300, less 3% discount.
   c. Cash sales, $104. The cost of merchandise was $59.
   d. Issued credit memorandum no. 2 to Troy Co. for defective merchandise, $18. The cost of the merchandise was $11.

(15 min) **LO3** ▶

8. From the following, prepare a schedule of accounts receivable for Lucky Co. for May 31, 201X.

Accounts Receivable Subsidiary Ledger				General Ledger			
Jarad Co.				**Accounts Receivable**			
	Dr.	Cr.			Dr.	Cr.	
5/6 GJ1	104			5/31 GJ1	147	12	5/31 GJ1
Katz Co.							
	Dr.	Cr.					
5/20 GJ1	33	12 5/27 GJ1					
Turtle Co.							
	Dr.	Cr.					
5/9 GJ1	10						

MyLabAccounting   ## Exercises

Set A

(15 min) **LO1** ▶

9A-1. Journalize the following transactions. Assume the perpetual inventory system.

201X		
Dec.	4	Sold merchandise for $450 cash. The cost of merchandise was $350.
	9	Purchased merchandise from Ree Co. on account, $3,300, F.O.B. shipping point (buyer pays freight); terms 2/10, n/30. Freight to be paid on December 20.
	20	Paid freight on December 9 purchase, $110.

9A-2. From the general journal in fig. 9.24 record to the accounts receivable subsidiary ledger and post to the general ledger as appropriate.

General Journal						Page 1	
Date		Account Titles and Explanations	PR	Dr.		Cr.	
201X							
Sept.	18	Accounts Receivable, Twilight Co.		6 4 0 00			
		Sales				6 4 0 00	
		Sold merchandise to Twilight Co.					
	18	Cost of Goods Sold		3 0 0 00			
		Merchandise Inventory				3 0 0 00	
		Cost of merchandise inventory sold					
	19	Accounts Receivable, Falcon Co.		8 5 0 00			
		Sales				8 5 0 00	
		Sold merchandise to Falcon Co.					
	19	Cost of Goods Sold		4 7 0 00			
		Merchandise Inventory				4 7 0 00	
		Cost of merchandise inventory sold					

Figure 9.24
General Journal for September 18 and 19 and Blank Accounts Receivable Subsidiary Ledger

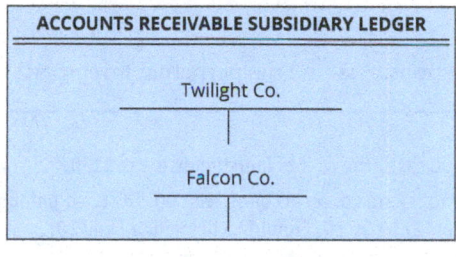

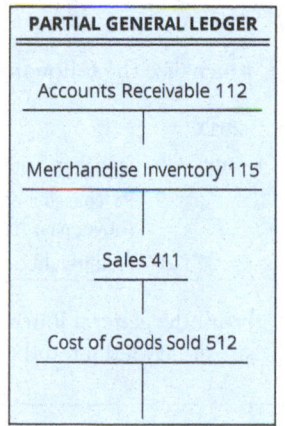

9A-3. Journalize the following transactions. Assume the perpetual inventory system.

 **L01** *(15 min)*

201X		
Apr.	5	Sold merchandise for $1,350 cash. The cost of the merchandise was $725.
	16	Made refunds to cash customers for defective merchandise, $50. The cost of defective merchandise was $10.

9A-4. Journalize the following transactions. Assume a perpetual inventory system.

 **L01** *(15 min)*

201X		
Jul.	8	Sold merchandise on account, $630, to Ring Co.; terms 3/10, n/30. Cost of merchandise was $390.
	12	Purchased office equipment on account from MEC Co., $1,600.
	13	Made refunds to cash customers, $200, for defective merchandise. The cost of defective merchandise was $25.

9A-5. From the following transactions for Ava Co., journalize, record, post, and prepare a schedule of accounts receivable when appropriate. You will have to set up your own accounts receivable subsidiary ledger and partial general ledger as needed. All sales terms are 1/10, n/30. The balance in merchandise inventory on October 1 is $2,000.

 **L02** *(20 min)*

201X		
Oct.	1	Ava Roberts invested $3,300 in the business.
	1	Sold merchandise on account to Charleston Co., invoice no. 1, $950. The cost of the merchandise was $455.
	2	Sold merchandise on account to William Co., invoice no. 2, $960. The cost of the merchandise was $625.
	3	Cash sale, $220. The cost of the merchandise was $140.
	8	Issued credit memorandum no. 1 to Charleston Co. for defective merchandise, $350. The cost of the merchandise was $225.
	10	Received check from Charleston Co. for invoice no. 1, less returns and discount.
	15	Cash sale, $440. The cost of the merchandise was $285.
	18	Sold merchandise on account to Charleston Co., invoice no. 3, $850. The cost of the merchandise was $550.

(10 min) **L01** ▶ **9A-6.** From the following facts calculate what Mike Hall paid Lakeville Co. for the purchase of a dining room set. Sale terms are 5/10, n/30.

a. Sales ticket price before tax, $11,000, dated April 5.
b. Sales tax, 10%.
c. Returned one defective chair for credit of $1,400 on April 8.
d. Paid bill on April 13.

Set B

(15 min) **L01** ▶ **9B-1.** Journalize the following transactions. Assume the perpetual inventory system.

201X		
July	9	Sold merchandise for $500 cash. The cost of merchandise was $150.
	9	Purchased merchandise from Rare Co. on account, $2,500, F.O.B. shipping point (buyer pays freight); terms 3/10, n/30. Freight to be paid on July 20.
	20	Paid freight on July 9 purchase, $100.

(10 min) **L02** ▶ **9B-2.** From the general journal in Figure 9.25, record to the accounts receivable subsidiary ledger and post to the general ledger accounts as appropriate.

Figure 9.25
General Journal for May 18 and 19 and Blank Accounts Receivable Subsidiary Ledger

General Journal					Page 1	
Date		Account Titles and Explanations	PR	Dr.	Cr.	
201X						
May	18	Accounts Receivable, Henry Co.		5 9 0 00		
		Sales			5 9 0 00	
		Sold merchandise to Henry Co.				
	18	Cost of Goods Sold		3 8 5 00		
		Merchandise Inventory			3 8 5 00	
		Record cost of the sale to Henry Co.				
	19	Accounts Receivable, Lincoln Co.		8 9 0 00		
		Sales			8 9 0 00	
		Sold merchandise to Lincoln Co.				
	19	Cost of Goods Sold		5 8 0 00		
		Merchandise Inventory			5 8 0 00	
		Record cost of the sale to Lincoln Co.				

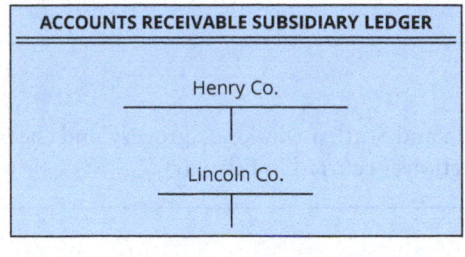

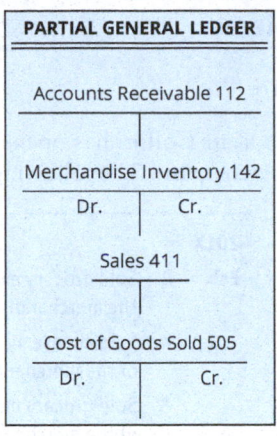

Figure 9.25
Continued

9B-3. Journalize the following transactions. Assume the perpetual inventory system.

201X

Apr. 5 Sold merchandise for $1,250 cash. The cost of the merchandise was $850.

16 Made refunds to cash customers for defective merchandise, $70. The cost of defective merchandise was $25.

9B-4. Journalize the following transactions. Assume a perpetual inventory system.

201X

Jul. 8 Sold merchandise on account, $620, to Ring Co.; terms 2/10, n/30. Cost of merchandise was $350.

12 Purchased office equipment on account from TRE Co., $1,900.

13 Made refunds to cash customers, $250, for defective merchandise. The cost of defective merchandise was $40.

9B-5. From the following transactions for Autumn Co., journalize, record, post, and prepare a schedule of accounts receivable when appropriate. You will have to set up your own accounts receivable subsidiary ledger and partial general ledger as needed. All sales terms are 3/10, n/30. The balance in merchandise inventory on August 1 is $3,000.

201X

Aug. 1 Andrew Rodgers invested $3,200 in the business.

1 Sold merchandise on account to Clearview Co., invoice no. 1, $650. The cost of merchandise was $420.

2 Sold merchandise on account to Nathan Co., invoice no. 2, $950. The cost of merchandise was $615.

3 Cash sale, $200. The cost of merchandise was $130.

8 Issued credit memorandum no. 1 to Clearview Co. for defective merchandise, $250. The cost of merchandise was $155.

10 Received check from Clearview Co. for invoice no. 1, less returns and discount.

15 Cash sale, $400. The cost of merchandise was $250.

18 Sold merchandise on account to Clearview Co., invoice no. 3, $550. The cost of merchandise was $340.

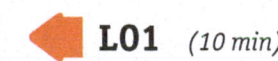

9B-6. From the following facts calculate what Becky Blain paid Rice Co. for the purchase of a dining room set. Sales terms are 1/10, n/30

a. Sales ticket price before tax, $10,000, dated April 5.

b. Sales tax, 5%.

c. Returned one defective chair for credit of $800 on April 8.

d. Paid bill on April 13.

Problems

Set A

(40 min) **LO1,2**

Check Figure:
Schedule of accounts receivable $4,490

9A-1.   Kate Collins has opened Fontina and Stuff, a wholesale grocery and cheese company. The following transactions occurred in February:

201X		
Feb.	1	Sold grocery merchandise to Fran Co. on account, $850, invoice no. 1. The cost of the merchandise was $640.
	4	Sold cheese merchandise to Groom Co. on account, $1,100, invoice no. 2. The cost of the merchandise was $825.
	8	Sold grocery merchandise to Dutch Co. on account, $1,100, invoice no. 3. The cost of the merchandise was $750.
	10	Issued credit memorandum no. 1 to Fran Co. for $160 of grocery merchandise returned due to spoilage. The cost of the merchandise was $90.
	15	Sold cheese merchandise to Groom Co. on account, $250, invoice no. 4. The cost of the merchandise was $180.
	19	Sold grocery merchandise to Dutch Co. on account, $650, invoice no. 5. The cost of the merchandise was $475.
	25	Sold cheese merchandise to Fran Co. on account, $700, invoice no. 6. The cost of the merchandise was $550.

Required

1. Journalize the transactions. Beginning balances of Merchandise Inventory is $5,000 for grocery merchandise and $7,000 for cheese.
2. Record to the accounts receivable subsidiary ledger and post to the general ledger as appropriate.
3. Prepare a schedule of accounts receivable for the end of February.

(50 min) **LO1,2**

Check Figure:
Schedule of accounts receivable $9,430

9A-2.   The following transactions of Jeff's Auto Supply occurred in February (Balances as of February 1 are given for general ledger and accounts receivable ledger accounts: Dick, $1,100 Dr.; Metcalf, $200 Dr.; Black, $100 Dr.; Accounts Receivable, $1,400 Dr.; Sales Tax Payable, $1,100 Cr. The balance of Merchandise Inventory is $8,000. Be sure to enter these balances in your working papers before beginning.):

201X		
Feb.	1	Sold auto parts merchandise to R. Dick on account, $800, invoice no. 10, plus 10% sales tax. The cost of the merchandise was $520.
	5	Sold auto parts merchandise to J. Metcalf on account, $800, invoice no. 11, plus 10% sales tax. The cost of the merchandise was $545.
	8	Sold auto parts merchandise to Lance Black on account, $6,000, invoice no. 12, plus 10% sales tax. The cost of the merchandise was $3,900.
	10	Issued credit memorandum no. 12 to R. Dick for $700 for defective auto parts merchandise returned from Feb. 1 transaction. (Be careful to record the reduction in Sales Tax Payable as well.) The cost of the merchandise was $500.
	12	Sold auto parts merchandise to J. Metcalf on account, $400, invoice no. 13, plus 10% sales tax. The cost of the merchandise was $260.

Required

1. Journalize the transactions.
2. Record to the accounts receivable subsidiary ledger and post to the general ledger as appropriate.
3. Prepare a schedule of accounts receivable for the end of February.

9A-3. Jared Payne owns Payne's Sneaker Shop. (Balances as of March 1 are provided for the accounts receivable and general ledger accounts as follows: Durant, $250 Dr.; Lanham, $550 Dr.; Pry, $800 Dr.; Zamara, $550 Dr.; Cash, $15,500 Dr.; Accounts Receivable, $2,150 Dr.; Sneaker Rack Equipment, $1,150 Dr.; J. Payne, Capital, $35,000 Cr.; Sales, $2,100 Cr. The balance of Merchandise Inventory is $12,000. Be sure to put beginning balances in your working papers.) The following transactions occurred in March:

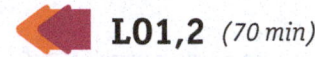

LO1,2 *(70 min)*

Check Figure:
Schedule of accounts receivable $5,155

201X		
March	1	Jared Payne invested an additional $10,500 in the store.
	3	Sold $700 of merchandise on account to B. Durant, sales ticket no. 50; terms 4/10, n/30. The cost of the merchandise was $385.
	4	Sold $500 of merchandise on account to Ron Lanham, sales ticket no. 51; terms 4/10, n/30. The cost of the merchandise was $375.
	9	Sold $200 of merchandise on account to Jim Zamara, sales ticket no. 52; terms 4/10, n/30. The cost of the merchandise was $85.
	10	Received cash from B. Durant in payment of March 3 transaction, sales ticket no. 50, less discount.
	20	Sold $3,000 of merchandise on account to Penny Pry, sales ticket no. 53; terms 4/10, n/30. The cost of the merchandise was $2,100.
	22	Received cash payment from Ron Lanham in payment of March 4 transaction, sales ticket no. 51.
	23	Collected cash sales, $3,400. The cost of the merchandise was $2,210.
	24	Issued credit memorandum no. 1 to Penny Pry for $2,000 of merchandise returned from March 20 sales on account. The cost of the merchandise was $1,250.
	26	Received cash from Penny Pry in payment of March 20, sales ticket no. 53. (Don't forget about the credit memo and discount.)
	28	Collected cash sales, $6,200. The cost of the merchandise was $4,030.
	30	Sold sneaker rack equipment for $150 cash. (Beware, sold at cost.)
	30	Sold merchandise priced at $3,400, on account to Ron Lanham, sales ticket no. 54; terms 4/10, n/30. The cost of the merchandise was $2,550.
	31	Issued credit memorandum no. 2 to Ron Lanham for $595 of merchandise returned from March 30 transaction, sales ticket no. 54. The cost of the merchandise was $390.

Required

1. Journalize the transactions.
2. Record to the accounts receivable subsidiary ledger and post to the general ledger as needed.
3. Prepare a schedule of accounts receivable for the end of March.

9A-4. Chevy Canton opened Chevy's Cosmetic Market on May 1. A 16% sales tax is calculated and added to all cosmetic sales. Chevy offers no sales discounts. The following transactions occurred in May:

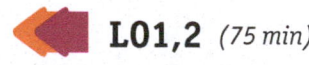

LO1,2 *(75 min)*

201X		
May	1	Chevy Canton invested $9,500 in the Cosmetic Market from his personal savings account.
	5	From the cash register tapes, lipstick cash sales were $4,600, plus sales tax. The cost of the merchandise was $3,000.
	5	From the cash register tapes, eye shadow cash sales were $1,900, plus sales tax. The cost of the merchandise was $890.
	8	Sold lipstick on account to Lois Kozak Co., $550, sales ticket no. 1, plus sales tax. The cost of the merchandise was $325.

(continued on page 334)

Check Figure:
Schedule of accounts receivable $2,146

201X		
May	9	Sold eye shadow on account to Ann Marie Maxwell Co., $1,600, sales ticket no. 2, plus sales tax. The cost of the merchandise was $950.
	15	Issued credit memorandum no. 1 to Lois Kozak Co. for $250 for lipstick returned. (Be sure to reduce Sales Tax Payable for Chevy.) The cost of the merchandise was $150.
	19	Ann Marie Maxwell Co. paid half the amount owed from sales ticket no. 2, dated May 9.
	21	Sold lipstick on account to David Parnell Co., $400, sales ticket no. 3, plus sales tax. The cost of the merchandise was $290.
	24	Sold eye shadow on account to Everette Tennis Co., $550, sales ticket no. 4, plus sales tax. The cost of the merchandise was $365.
	25	Issued credit memorandum no. 2 to David Parnell Co. for $200 for lipstick returned from sales ticket no. 3, dated May 21. The cost of the merchandise was $110.
	29	Cash sales taken from the cash register tape showed the following: 1. Lipstick: $1,200 + $192 sales tax collected. The cost of the merchandise was $550. 2. Eye shadow: $2,400 + $384 sales tax collected. The cost of the merchandise was $1,500.
	29	Sold lipstick on account to Ann Marie Maxwell Co., $550, sales ticket no. 5, plus sales tax. The cost of the merchandise was $170.
	31	Received payment from Ann Marie Maxwell Co. of sales ticket no. 5, dated May 29.

Required

1. Journalize, record, and post as appropriate. Beginning balances of Merchandise Inventory is $11,000 for lipstick $10,000 for eyeshadow.
2. Prepare a schedule of accounts receivable for the end of May.

Set B

(40 min) **LO1,2**

9B-1.   Sandra Hills has opened Macchiato and More, a wholesale grocery and coffee company. The following transactions occurred in June:

Check Figure:
Schedule of accounts receivable $3,730

201X		
June	1	Sold grocery merchandise to Fran Co. on account, $700, invoice no. 1. The cost of the merchandise was $500.
	4	Sold coffee merchandise to Groom Co. on account, $650, invoice no. 2. The cost of the merchandise was $475.
	8	Sold grocery merchandise to Dutch Co. on account, $750, invoice no 3. The cost of the merchandise was $600.
	10	Issued credit memorandum no. 1 to Fran Co. for $170 of grocery merchandise returned due to spoilage. The cost of the merchandise was $90.
	15	Sold coffee merchandise to Groom Co. on account, $700, invoice no. 4. The cost of the merchandise was $590.
	19	Sold grocery merchandise to Dutch Co. on account, $700, invoice no. 5. The cost of the merchandise was $610.
	25	Sold coffee merchandise to Fran Co. on account, $400, invoice no. 6. The cost of the merchandise was $280.

Required

1. Journalize the transactions. Beginning balances of merchandise inventory is $5,000 for grocery merchandise and $7,000 for coffee.
2. Record to the accounts receivable subsidiary ledger and post to the general ledger as appropriate.
3. Prepare a schedule of accounts receivable for the end of June.

(50 min) **LO1,2**

9B-2.   The following transactions of Jack's Auto Supply occurred in January (Balances as of January 1 are given for general ledger and accounts receivable ledger accounts: Nonack, $1,400 Dr.; Seth, $50 Dr.; Corner, $200 Dr.; Accounts Receivable, $1,650 Dr.; Merchandise Inventory, $14,000 Dr.; Sales Tax Payable, $1,000 Cr. Be sure to enter these balances in your working papers before beginning.

Check Figure:
Schedule of accounts receivable $14,593.80

201X		
January	1	Sold auto parts merchandise to R. Nonack on account, $700, invoice no. 70, plus 2% sales tax. The cost of the merchandise was $485.
	5	Sold auto parts merchandise to J. Seth on account, $600, invoice no. 71, plus 2% sales tax. The cost of the merchandise was $390.
	8	Sold auto parts merchandise to Lance Corner on account, $11,000, invoice no. 72, plus 2% sales tax. The cost of the merchandise was $7,150.
	10	Issued credit memorandum no. 12 to R. Nonack for $210 for defective auto parts merchandise returned from January 1 transaction. (Be careful to record the reduction in Sales Tax Payable as well.) The cost of the merchandise was $145.
	12	Sold auto parts merchandise to J. Seth on account, $600, invoice no. 73, plus 2% sales tax. The cost of the merchandise was $445.

Required

1. Journalize the transactions using the perpetual method of accounting for inventory.
2. Record to the accounts receivable subsidiary ledger and post to the general ledger as appropriate.
3. Prepare a schedule of accounts receivable for the end of January.

9B-3. Max Peney owns Peney's Sneaker Shop. (Balances as of Aug. 1 are provided for the accounts receivable and general ledger accounts as follows: Donavan, $375 Dr.; Littler, $900 Dr.; Pry $750 Dr.; Zamora $350 Dr.; Cash $16,500 Dr.; Accounts Receivable $2,375 Dr.; Sneaker Rack Equipment $1,000 Dr.; Max Peney, Capital, $42,000 Cr.; Sales $2,400 Cr. Begining balance in Merchandise Inventory is $18,000.)

 **L04** *(40 min)*

 **L01,2** *(70 min)*

Check Figure:
Schedule of accounts $6,105

201X		
August	1	Max Peney invested an additional $13,500 in the sneaker store.
	3	Sold $600 of merchandise on account to B. Donovan, sales ticket no. 70; terms 4/10, n/30. The cost of the merchandise was $410.
	4	Sold $400 of merchandise on account to Ron Littler, sales ticket no. 71; terms 4/10, n/30. The cost of the merchandise was $265.
	9	Sold $100 of merchandise on account to Jim Zamora, sales ticket no. 72; terms 4/10, n/30. The cost of the merchandise was $50.
	10	Received cash from B. Donovan in payment of August 3 transaction, sales ticket no. 70, less discount.
	20	Sold $4,000 of merchandise on account to Page Pry, sales ticket no. 73; terms 4/10, n/30. The cost of the merchandise was $2,750.
	22	Received cash payment from Ron Littler in payment of August 4 transaction, sales ticket no. 71.
	23	Collected cash sales, $3,000. The cost of the merchandise was $1,950.
	24	Issued credit memorandum no. 1 to Page Pry for $2,100 of merchandise returned from August 20 sales on account. The cost of the merchandise was $1,300.
	26	Received cash from Page Pry in payment of August 20 sales ticket no. 73. (Don't forget about the credit memo and discount.)
	28	Collected cash sales, $6,600. The cost of the merchandise was $5,200.
	30	Sold sneaker rack equipment for $650 cash. (Beware, sold at cost.)
	30	Sold merchandise priced at $4,400 on account to Ron Littler, sales ticket no. 74, terms 4/10, n/30. The cost of the merchandise was $3,500.
	31	Issued credit memorandum no. 2 to Ron Littler for $770 of merchandise returned from August 30 transaction, sales ticket no. 74. The cost of the merchandise was $375.

Required

1. Journalize the transactions using the perpetual method of inventory valuation.
2. Record to the accounts receivable subsidiary ledger and post to the general ledger as needed.
3. Prepare a schedule of accounts receivable for the end of August.

(75 min) **LO1,2**

S50 / QB

Check Figure:
Schedule of accounts receivable $1,728

9B-4. Al Franklin opened Al's Cosmetic Market on December 1. An 8% sales tax is calculated and added to all cosmetic sales. Al's offers no sales discounts. The following transactions occurred in December:

201X		
Dec.	1	Al Franklin invested $6,000 in the Cosmetic Market from his personal savings account.
	5	From the cash register tapes, lipstick cash sales were $5,100, plus sales tax. The cost of the merchandise was $4,025.
	5	From the cash register tapes, eye shadow cash sales were $1,700, plus sales tax. The cost of the merchandise was $975.
	8	Sold lipstick on account to Alexander Kozlosky Co., $200, sales ticket no. 1, plus sales tax. The cost of the merchandise was $110.
	9	Sold eye shadow on account to Douglas Sabin Co., $800, sales ticket no. 2, plus sales tax. The cost of the merchandise was $520.
	15	Issued credit memorandum no. 1 to Alexander Kozlosky Co. for $100 for lipstick returned. (Be sure to reduce Sales Tax Payable for Al's.) The cost of the merchandise was $55.
	19	Douglas Sabin Co. paid half the amount owed from sales ticket no. 2, dated December 9.
	21	Sold lipstick on account to John Tobin Co., $350, sales ticket no. 3, plus sales tax. The cost of the merchandise was $190.
	24	Sold eye shadow on account to Edward Wease Co., $1,000, sales ticket no. 4, plus sales tax. The cost of the merchandise was $625.
	25	Issued credit memorandum no. 2 to John Tobin Co. for $250 for lipstick returned from sales ticket no. 3, dated December 21. The cost of the merchandise was $105.
	29	Cash sales taken from the cash register tape showed the following: 1. Lipstick: $900 + $72 sales tax collected. The cost of the merchandise was $600. 2. Eye shadow: $2,900 + $232 sales tax collected. The cost of the merchandise was $1,800.
	29	Sold lipstick on account to Douglas Sabin Co., $300, sales ticket no. 5, plus sales tax. The cost of the merchandise was $175.
	31	Received payment from Douglas Sabin Co. of sales ticket no. 5, dated December 29.

Required

1. Journalize, record, and post as appropriate using the perpetual method of accounting for inventory. Beginning balances of Merchandise Inventory is $18,000 for eyeshadow and $11,000 for lipstick.
2. Prepare a schedule of accounts receivable for the end of December.

Financial Report Problem

(15 min) **LO1**

Reading Amazon's Annual Report

Access Amazon's Annual Report and see how Amazon records revenue at **https://tinyurl.com/slaterca14e**.

KEEPING IT REAL SUAREZ COMPUTER CENTER

MyLabAccounting

To assist you in recording these transactions for the month of January, at the end of this problem is the schedule of accounts receivable as of December 31 and an updated chart of accounts with the current balance listed for each account.

Assignment

1. Journalize the transactions.
2. Record in the accounts receivable subsidiary ledger and post to the general ledger as appropriate. A partial subsidiary ledger is included in the working papers that accompany this text.

   The following accounts have been added to the chart of accounts: Merchandise Inventory #1021, Sales #4010, Sales Returns and Allowances #4020, Sales Discounts #4030, and COGS #5000.

3. Prepare a schedule of accounts receivable as of January 31 201X.

   The January transactions are as follows:

Jan.	1	Purchased $12,000 worth of inventory for cash.
	5	Sold $780 worth of merchandise to Viral Video on credit, sales invoice no. 5000; terms 3/10, n/30. The cost of the merchandise was $510.
	10	Sold $3,600 worth of merchandise on account to Dr. Michael Turiono, sales invoice no. 5001; terms 3/10, n/30. The cost of the merchandise was $2,340.
	11	Received $2,800 from Vital Tax Services, toward payment of its balance; no discount allowed.
	12	Collected $2,800 cash sales. The cost of the merchandise was $1,775.
	19	Sold $4,500 worth of merchandise on account to Viral Video, sales invoice no. 5002; terms 3/10, n/30. The cost of the merchandise was $2,900.
	20	Collected balance in full from Dr. Michael Turiono, invoice no. 5001.
	29	Issued credit memorandum to Value Pac Inc. for $460 worth of merchandise returned, invoice no. 5000. The cost of the merchandise was $300.
	29	Collected full payment from Viral Video, invoice no. 5002.

Schedule of Accounts Receivable
Suarez Computer Center
December 31, 201X

Value Pac Inc.	$ 4,300.00
Viral Video	$ 3,950.00
Vital Tax Services	6,600.00
Total Amount Due	$14,850.00

(continued on page 338)

Chart of Accounts and Current Balances as of 12/31/1X

Account #	Account Name	Debit Balance	Credit Balance
1000	Cash	$ 12,219.29	
1010	Petty Cash	300.00	
1020	Accounts Receivable	14,850.00	
1021	Merchandise Inventory	0.00	
1025	Prepaid Rent	2,000.00	
1030	Supplies	192.00	
1080	Computer Shop Equipment	4,860.00	
1081	Accumulated Dep., C.S. Equip.		$ 105.00
1090	Office Equipment	2,175.00	
1091	Accumulated Dep., Office Equip.		50.00
2000	Accounts Payable		2,780.00
2010	Wages Payable		0.00
2020	FICA—OASDI Payable		0.00
2030	FICA—Medicare Payable		0.00
2040	FIT Payable		0.00
2050	SIT Payable		0.00
2060	FUTA Payable		0.00
2070	SUTA Payable		0.00
3000	Falco, Capital		16,617.00
3010	Falco, Withdrawals	915.00	
3020	Income Summary		0.00
4000	Service Revenue		20,900.00
4010	Sales		0.00
4020	Sales Returns and Allowances	0.00	
4030	Sales Discounts	0.00	
5000	Cost of Goods Sold	0.00	
5010	Advertising Expense	0.00	
5020	Rent Expense	0.00	
5030	Utilities Expense	0.00	
5040	Phone Expense	155.00	
5050	Supplies Expense	45.00	
5060	Insurance Expense	0.00	
5070	Postage Expense	40.00	
5080	Dep. Exp., C.S. Equipment	0.00	
5090	Dep. Exp., Office Equipment	0.00	
5100	Miscellaneous Expense	15.00	
5110	Wage Expense	2,425.00	
5120	Payroll Tax Expense	260.71	
5130	Interest Expense	0.00	
5140	Bad Debt Expense	0.00	

Purchases and Cash Payments in a Perpetual Inventory System

10

CHAPTER PREVIEW: ACCOUNTING IN ACTION

Mary Abingo heads to the Apple Store to purchase the new Apple iPhone. The advertisement says there are limited quantities so she asks the salesperson if the model is in stock. The salesperson goes to the computer and searches the inventory. Yes, there is one left in stock. Mary buys it, and now that item is reported temporarily out of stock in the accounting program, which will trigger an alert to the purchasing department. In this chapter, you learn how inventory is accounted for under the perpetual method by the accounting software when purchased by a company and sold to a buyer.

Learning Objectives

LO1 Journalize and Record Transactions to the Accounts Payable Subsidiary Ledger and Post to the General Ledger Along with a Debit Memorandum Using the Perpetual Inventory Method

LO2 Journalize, Record, and Post Cash Payments Transactions and Prepare a Schedule of Accounts Payable

L01

Journalizing and Recording Transactions to the Accounts Payable Subsidiary Ledger and Posting to the General Ledger Along with a Debit Memorandum Using the Perpetual Inventory Method

As we begin this chapter, we need to examine the issue of freight charges as it relates to the purchase of inventory. Under the perpetual method, if the buyer is responsible for paying for the freight, then those costs become a part of the cost of the inventory. This is in alignment with the concept, under the perpetual method, that the true cost of inventory is all the costs necessary to get it ready for sale.

If the seller is responsible for paying the shipping costs until the goods reach their destination, the freight charges are F.O.B. destination. (F.O.B. stands for "free on board" the carrier.) For example, if a seller located in Boston sold goods F.O.B. destination to a buyer in New York, the seller would have to pay the cost of shipping the goods to the buyer. These costs are an expense to the seller.

If the buyer is responsible for paying the shipping costs, the freight charges are F.O.B. shipping point. In this situation, the seller will sometimes prepay the freight charges as a matter of convenience and will add it to the invoice of the purchaser, as in the following example:

Bill amount ($800 + $80 prepaid freight)	$880
Less: 5% cash discount (0.05 × $800)	40
Amount to be paid by buyer	$840

Purchases discounts are not taken on freight. The discount is based on the purchase price.

If the seller ships goods F.O.B. shipping point, legal ownership (title) passes to the buyer *when the goods are shipped*. If goods are shipped by the seller F.O.B. destination, title will change *when goods have reached their destination*.

When the buyer is responsible for the costs of shipping, F.O.B. shipping point, those costs will flow through the Merchandise Inventory account as an addition, or debit, to the Merchandise Inventory account. (See Figure 10.1).

F.O.B. destination *Seller* pays or is responsible for the cost of freight to purchaser's location or destination.

F.O.B. shipping point *Buyer* pays or is responsible for the shipping costs from seller's shipping point to purchaser's location.

American Institute of Professional Bookkeepers (AIPB) - AIPB, founded in 1987, has the following mission:

- To recognize bookkeeping as a profession—and bookkeepers as professionals.
- To make sure that each member has the latest bookkeeping, accounting and tax information to be effective on the job.
- To answer members' everyday bookkeeping and accounting questions on the telephone at no charge.
- To provide bookkeepers with low-cost continuing professional education.

More on the AIPB can be found at **https://www.aipb.org**

Figure 10.1

Buyer						
Date	Merchandise Inventory			80 00		
	Cash				80 00	
	To pay transportation costs incurred by the buyer					

201X

Apr. 2 Purchased merchandise on account, $5,000, and paid freight charges of $50, from Abby Blake Co.; terms 2/10, n/60.

5 Purchased equipment on account, $4,000, from Joe Francis Co. No discount.

8 Purchased merchandise on account, $800, from Thorpe Co.; terms 1/10, n/30.

9 Purchased merchandise on account, $980, from John Sullivan Co.; terms n/10, EOM.

12 Art's issued debit memo #1, $200, to Thorpe Co. for defective merchandise.

15 Purchased merchandise on account, $600, from Abby Blake Co.; terms 1/10, n/30.

26 Purchased $500 of supplies on account from John Sullivan Co.

Let's look at the steps Art's Wholesale Clothing Company took when it ordered goods from Abby Blake Company on April 1.

Step 1: **Prepare a Purchase Requisition at Art's Wholesale Clothing Company.** The inventory clerk notes a low inventory level of ladies' jackets for resale, so the clerk sends a purchase requisition to the purchasing department. A duplicate copy is sent to the accounting department. A third copy remains with the department that initiated the request to be used as a check on the purchasing department.

Step 2: **Purchasing Department of Art's Wholesale Clothing Company Prepares a Purchase Order.** After checking various price lists and suppliers' catalogs, the purchasing department fills out a form called a purchase order. This form gives Abby Blake Company the authority to ship the ladies' jackets ordered by Art's Wholesale Clothing Company (see Figure 10.2).

Purchase requisition A form used within a business by the requesting department asking the purchasing department of the business to buy specific goods.

Purchase order A form used in business to place an order for the buying of goods from a seller.

PURCHASE ORDER NO. 1
ART'S WHOLESALE CLOTHING COMPANY
1528 BELLE AVE.
NEW YORK, NY 10022

Purchased From:	Abby Blake Company 12 Foster Road Englewood Cliffs, NJ 07632	Date: April 1, 201X Shipped VIA: Freight Truck Terms: 2/10, n/60 FOB: Englewood Cliffs

Quantity	Description	Unit Price	Total
100	Ladies' Jackets Code 14–0	$50	$5,000

Art's Wholesale
By: Bill Joy

Purchase order number must appear on all invoices.

SUCCESS TIP
Authorized personnel initiate purchase requisitions. No example is shown here because this is strictly an internal form.

Figure 10.2
Purchase Order

Step 3: **Sales Invoice Prepared by Abby Blake Company.** Abby Blake Company receives the purchase order and prepares a sales invoice. The sales invoice for the seller is the purchase invoice for the buyer. A sales invoice is shown in Figure 10.3.

Purchase invoice The seller's sales invoice, which is sent to the purchaser.

SALES INVOICE NO. 228
ABBY BLAKE COMPANY
12 FOSTER ROAD
ENGLEWOOD, CLIFFS, NJ 07632

Sold To:	Art's Wholesale Clothing Co. 1528 Belle Ave. New York, NY 10022	Date: April 2, 201X Shipped VIA: Freight Truck Terms: 2/10, n/60 Your Order No: 1 FOB: Englewood Cliffs

Quantity	Description	Unit Price	Total
100	Ladies' Jackets Code 14–0 Freight	$50	$5,000 50 $5,050

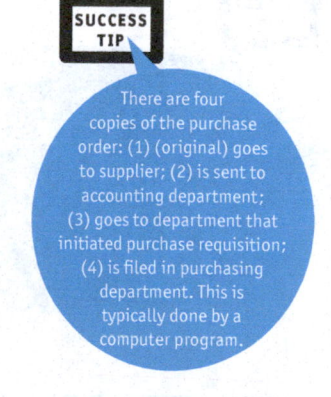

SUCCESS TIP
There are four copies of the purchase order: (1) (original) goes to supplier; (2) is sent to accounting department; (3) goes to department that initiated purchase requisition; (4) is filed in purchasing department. This is typically done by a computer program.

Figure 10.3
Sales Invoice

The invoice shows that the goods will be shipped F.O.B. Englewood Cliffs. This is an example of F.O.B. shipping point. Thus, Art's Wholesale Clothing Company, as the buyer, is responsible for paying the shipping costs.

The sales invoice also shows a freight charge. Thus, Abby Blake prepaid the shipping costs as a matter of convenience. Art's will repay the freight charges when it pays the invoice and add those charges as a cost of the Merchandise Inventory account.

Receiving report A business form used to notify the appropriate people of the ordered goods received along with the quantities and specific condition of the goods.

Step 4: **Receiving the Goods.** When goods are received, Art's Wholesale inspects the shipment and completes a receiving report. The receiving report verifies that the exact merchandise that was ordered was received in good condition.

Step 5: **Verifying the Numbers.** Before the invoice is approved for recording and payment, the accounting department must check the purchase order, invoice, and receiving report to make sure that all are in agreement and that no steps have been omitted. The form used for checking and approval is an invoice approval form (see Figure 10.4).

Invoice approval form Used by the accounting department in checking the invoice and finally approving it for recording and payment.

Figure 10.4 Invoice Approval Form

INVOICE APPROVAL FORM
Art's Wholesale Clothing Co.

Purchase Order #	_____
Requisition check	_____
Purchase Order check	_____
Receiving Report check	_____
Invoice check	_____
Approved for Payment	_____

Keep in mind that Art's Wholesale Clothing Company does not record this purchase until the *invoice is approved for recording and payment.* Abby Blake Company records this transaction in its records when the sales invoice is prepared, however.

Let's look closer at the April 2 transaction.

201X		
Apr.	2	Purchased Merchandise Inventory on account, $5,000, plus freight charges of $50, from Abby Blake Co.; terms 2/10, n/60

SUCCESS TIP

	Buyer		Seller
Purchases	Dr. Merchandise Inventory	Sale Cr.	Revenue
PRA	Cr. Merchandise Inventory	SRA Dr.	Contra-revenue
PD	Cr. Merchandise Inventory	SD Dr.	Contra-revenue

TRANSACTION ANALYSIS

Accounts Affected	Category	↑↓	Rules of Dr. and Cr.
Merchandise Inventory	Asset	↑	Dr. $5,000
Merchandise Inventory	Asset	↑	Dr. $ 50
Accounts Payable, Abby Blake Co.	Liability	↑	Cr. $5,050

Figure 10.5 shows how the general journal would look.

Figure 10.5
Inventory purchase and accounting for freight costs

Apr.	2	Merchandise Inventory		5 0 0 0 00					
		Merchandise Inventory, freight charges		5 0 00					
		Accounts Payable, Abby Blake					5 0 5 0 00		
		Purchased Merchandise Inventory on							
		account from Abby Blake							

Accounts Payable Subsidiary Ledger

In the last chapter we saw the accounts receivable subsidiary ledger. It listed customers owing Art's money from sales on account. Now we look at Art's, the buyer, and an accounts payable subsidiary ledger. See Figure 10.6.

Note that the normal balance is a credit for Accounts Payable and its subsidiary ledger, whereas in the last chapter Accounts Receivable had a debit normal balance.

Accounts payable subsidiary ledger A book or file that contains, in alphabetical order, the name of the creditor and amount owed from purchases on account.

Figure 10.6 Partial General Ledger of Art's Wholesale Clothing Company and Accounts Payable Subsidiary Ledger

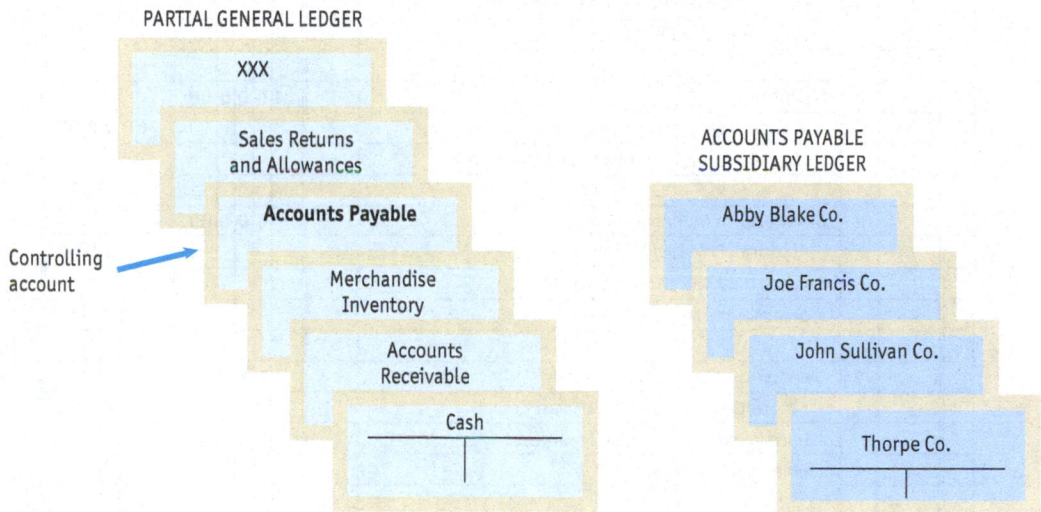

Accounts Payable is the controlling account in the ledger, and at the end of the month the sum of the individual amounts owed to the creditors should equal the balance in Accounts Payable at the end of the month.

Figure 10.7 shows how the general journal looks for Art's before posting to the General Ledger and recording to the Subsidiary Ledger this month's purchases on account.

Posting and Recording Purchases Transactions. Before we post to the general ledger and record to the subsidiary ledger, let's first examine the T accounts and what each one would look like.

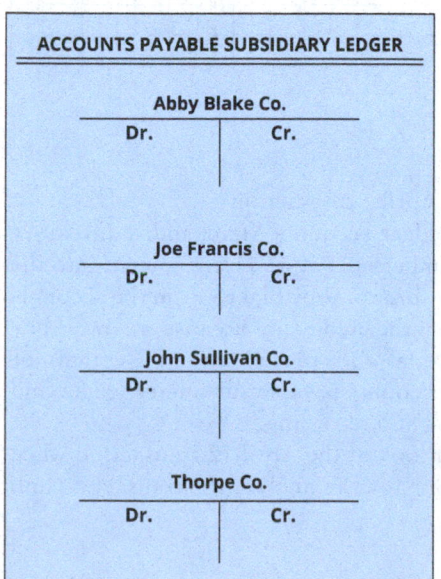

Figure 10.7 General Journal Before Posting to General Ledger and Recording to Subsidiary Ledger

Date		Account Titles and Description	PR	Dr.	Cr.
201X					
Apr.	2	Merchandise Inventory		5 0 0 0 00	
		Merchandise Inventory, freight charges		5 0 00	
		Accounts Payable, Abby Blake Co.			5 0 5 0 00
		Purchased Merchandise Inventory on			
		account from Abby Blake			
	5	Equipment		4 0 0 0 00	
		Accounts Payable, Joe Francis Co.			4 0 0 0 00
		Purchased equipment on account, Francis			
	8	Merchandise Inventory		8 0 0 00	
		Accounts Payable, Thorpe Co.			8 0 0 00
		Purchased Merchandise Inventory			
		on account, Thorpe			
	9	Merchandise Inventory		9 8 0 00	
		Accounts Payable, John Sullivan Co.			9 8 0 00
		Purchased Merchandise Inventory			
		on account, Sullivan			
	12	Accounts Payable, Thorpe Co.		2 0 0 00	
		Merchandise Inventory			2 0 0 00
		Debit memo no. 1			
	15	Merchandise Inventory		6 0 0 00	
		Accounts Payable, Abby Blake Co.			6 0 0 00
		Purchased Merchandise Inventory on			
		account, Blake			
	26	Supplies		5 0 0 00	
		Accounts Payable, John Sullivan Co.			5 0 0 00
		Purchased supplies on account, Sullivan			

Now let's look at how to post and record the April 2 transaction.

For this transaction, we post to the general ledger accounts Merchandise Inventory and Accounts Payable. Note how the account numbers 121 and 211 are entered into the PR column of the general journal. We must also *record* to Abby Blake Co. in the accounts payable subsidiary ledger. Note that it is placed on the credit side because we owe Abby the money. When the subsidiary ledger is updated, a (✔) is placed in the PR column of the general journal. Figure 10.8 shows how the accounts payable subsidiary ledger and the partial general ledger would look after posting and recording.

Before concluding this unit, let's take a closer look at the April 12 transaction when Art's issues a debit memorandum to Thorpe Company. We analyze the transaction and show how to post and record it on pages 345–346.

GENERAL JOURNAL					Page 2	
Date	Account Titles and Description	PR	Dr.		Cr.	
201X						
Apr. 2	Merchandise Inventory - purchase	121	5 0 0 0 00			
	Merchandise Inventory - freight charges	121	5 0 00			
	Accounts Payable - Abby Blake Co.	211 ✓			5 0 5 0 00	
	Purchased merchandise on account, Blake					

Figure 10.8
Posting and Recording the April 2
Transaction

PARTIAL ACCOUNTS PAYABLE SUBSIDIARY LEDGER

Abby Blake Co.

Dr.	Cr.
	5,050 GJ2 4/2

PARTIAL GENERAL LEDGER

Merchandise Inventory 121

Dr.	Cr.
4/2 GJ2 5,000	
4/2 GJ2 50	

Accounts Payable 211

Dr.	Cr.
	5,050 GJ2 4/2

Debit Memorandum

In Chapter 9, Art's Wholesale Clothing Company had to handle returned goods as a seller. It did so by issuing credit memoranda to customers who returned or received an allowance on the price. In this chapter, Art's must handle returns as a buyer. It does so by using debit memoranda. A debit memorandum is a piece of paper issued by a customer to a seller. It indicates that a return or allowance has occurred.

On April 8, Art's Wholesale had purchased men's hats for $800 from Thorpe Company. On April 12, 20 hats valued at $200 were found to have defective brims. Art's issued a debit memorandum to Thorpe Company, as shown in Figure 10.9. At some point in the future, Thorpe will issue Art's a credit memorandum. Let's look at how Art's Wholesale Clothing Company handles such a transaction in its accounting records.

Debit memorandum A memo issued by a purchaser to a seller, indicating that some return or allowance has occurred and therefore the purchaser now owes less money on account.

DEBIT MEMORANDUM		No. 1
Art's Wholesale Clothing Company 1528 Belle Ave. New York, NY 10022		
TO: Thorpe Comany 3 Access Road Beverly, MA 01915		April 8, 201X
WE DEBIT your account as follows:		
Quantity	Unit Cost	Total
20 Men's Hats Code 827 – defective brims	$10	$200

Figure 10.9
Debit Memorandum

Journalizing and Posting the Debit Memo. First, let's look at a transactional analysis chart.

Accounts Affected	Category	↑↓	Rules
Accounts Payable	Liability	↓	Dr.
Merchandise Inventory	Asset	↓	Cr.

SUCCESS TIP

Result of debit memo: debits or reduces Accounts Payable. On seller's books, accounts affected would include Sales Returns and Allowances, Cost of Goods Sold, Merchandise Inventory, and Accounts Receivable.

Next, let's examine the journal entry for the debit memorandum (Figure 10.10). The two postings and one recording are the following:

Figure 10.10
Debit Memorandum Journalized and Posted

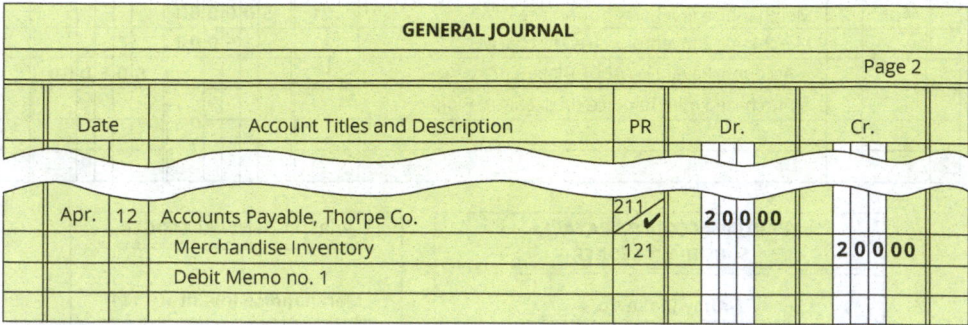

	GENERAL JOURNAL					Page 2
Date	Account Titles and Description	PR	Dr.		Cr.	
Apr. 12	Accounts Payable, Thorpe Co.	211 ✓	2 0 0 00			
	Merchandise Inventory	121			2 0 0 00	
	Debit Memo no. 1					

1. **211:** Post to Accounts Payable as a debit in the general ledger (account no. 211). When done, place in the PR column the account number, 211, above the diagonal line on the same line as Accounts Payable in the journal.

2. **✓:** Record to Thorpe Co. in the accounts payable subsidiary ledger to show that Art's doesn't owe Thorpe as much money. When done, place a ✓ in the journal in the PR column below the diagonal line on the same line as Accounts Payable in the journal. Remember, this check is for a manual system only. In a computerized system, both the general ledger and the subsidiary ledger are updated automatically when you click on "post."

3. **121:** Post to Merchandise Inventory as a credit in the general ledger (account no. 121). When done, place the account number, 121, in the PR column of the journal on the same line as Merchandise Inventory. (If equipment was returned that was not merchandise for resale, we would credit Equipment and not Merchandise Inventory.)

The following are the completed accounts payable subsidiary ledger and general ledger for Art's:

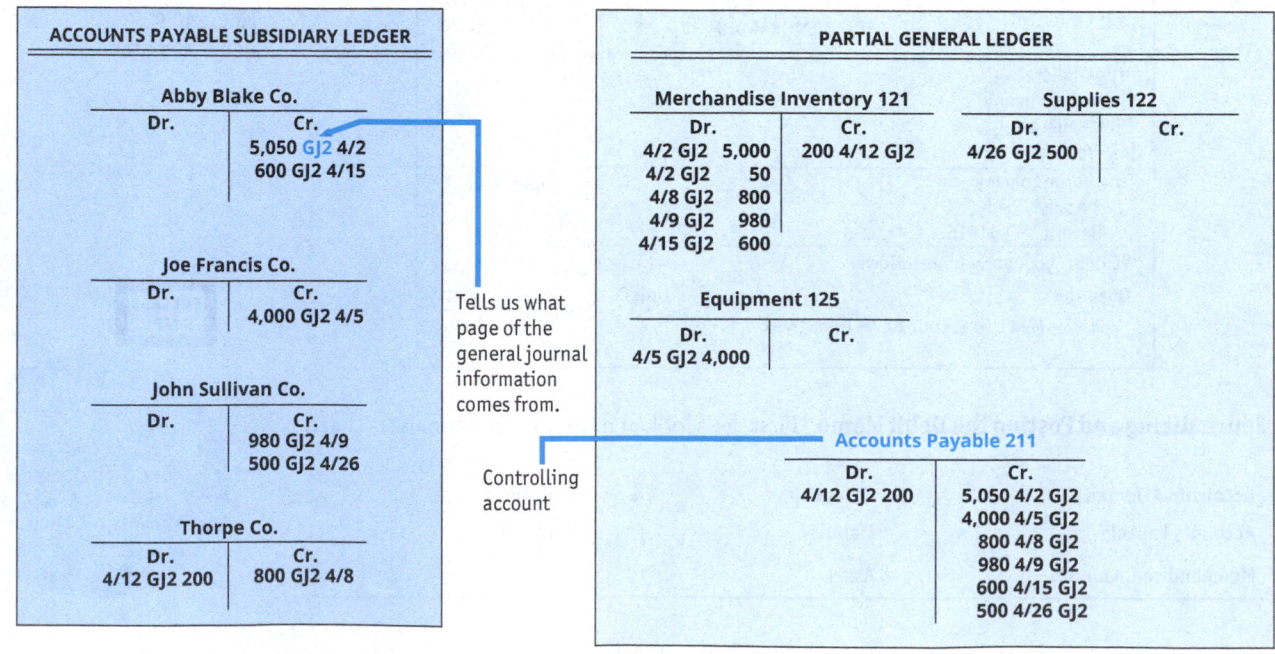

Now let's check your progress.

TRY IT! Learning Unit 10-1

Journalize, record, and post the following transactions for Moore Co. for July 201X (journal record is page 2). The partial ledger should include: Cash 110 balance of $8,000; Merchandise Inventory 115; Equipment 140; Accounts Payable 210.

Beam Co. is located in the Accounts Payable Subsidiary Ledger.

July 5	Purchased merchandise on account, $400, and freight charges F.O.B. shipping point, $25, from Beam Co.; invoice no. 1; terms 1/10, n/30.	
7	Purchased equipment on account, $700, from Beam Co., invoice no. 2, no discount.	
22	Issued debit memorandum no. 1, $100, to Beam Co. for merchandise returned from invoice no. 1.	

TRY IT! Solution Learning Unit 10-1

Moore Co. p. 2

Date	Account Titles and Description	PR	Dr.	Cr.
201X				
July 5	Merchandise Inventory	115	400	
	Merchandise Inventory – Freight Charges	115	25	
	Accounts Payable, Beam Co.	210/✓		425
	Bought merchandise on account from Beam			
7	Equipment	140	700	
	Accounts Payable, Beam Co.	210/✓		700
	Purchase of equipment on account			
22	Accounts Payable, Beam Co.	210/✓	100	
	Merchandise Inventory	115		100
	Debit memorandum no. 1			

Partial General Ledger

Cash 110		Merchandise Inventory 115	
Dr.	Cr.	Dr.	Cr.
Bal. 8,000		7/5 GJ2 400	100 7/22 GJ2
		7/5 GJ2 25	

Equipment 140	
Dr.	Cr.
7/7 GJ2 700	

Accounts Payable 210	
Dr.	Cr.
7/22 GJ2 100	425 7/5 GJ2
	700 7/7 GJ2

Partial Accounts Payable Subsidiary Ledger

Beam Co.	
Dr.	Cr.
7/22 GJ2 100	425 7/5 GJ2
	700 7/7 GJ2

LEARNING UNIT 10-2

LO2 ▶

Cash Payments Transactions and Schedules of Accounts Payable

The following cash payment transactions occurred for Art's Wholesale Clothing Company in April.

201X		
Apr.	2	Issued check no. 1 to Pete Blum for insurance paid in advance, $900.
	7	Issued check no. 2 to Joe Francis Company in payment of its April 5 invoice no. 388.
	9	Issued check no. 3 to Rick Flo Co. for merchandise purchased for cash, $800.
	14	Issued check no. 4 to Thorpe Company in payment of its April 8 invoice no. 414, less the return and 1% discount.
	26	Issued check no. 5, $700, for salaries paid.

Figure 10.11 provides a closer look at how the April 14 transaction would be journalized.

Accounts Affected	Category	↑↓	Rules	T Account Update
Cash	Asset	↓	Cr.	**Cash**
				Dr. | Cr.
				| 594
Merchandise Inventory	Asset	↓	Cr.	**Merchandise Inventory**
				Dr. | Cr.
				| 6
Account Payable, Thorpe Co.	Liability	↓	Dr.	**Accounts Payable**
				Dr. | Cr.
				600 | 600
				Thorpe Co.
				Dr. | Cr.
				600 | 600

Figure 10.11
Journalizing the April 14 Transaction

	Apr.	14	Accounts Payable, Thorpe Co.		6 0 0 00		
			Merchandise Inventory				6 00
			Cash				5 9 4 00
			Paid invoice no. 414				

Figure 10.12 on page 349 shows the complete set of cash payments transactions journalized for the month, followed by a complete posting to the general ledger and recordings to the accounts payable subsidiary ledger (remember from the past unit that we posted all the inventory purchases on account).

Now let's prove that the sum of the accounts payable subsidiary ledger at the end of the month is equal to the controlling account, Accounts Payable, at the end of April for Art's Wholesale Clothing Company.

To do so, creditors with an ending balance in Art's accounts payable subsidiary ledger must be listed in the schedule of accounts payable (see Figure 10.13 on page 350). At the end of the month, the total owed ($7,130) in Accounts Payable, the controlling account in the general ledger, should equal the sum owed the individual creditors that are listed on the schedule of accounts payable. If it doesn't, the journalizing, posting, and recording must be checked to ensure that they are complete. Also, the balances of each title should be checked.

Controlling account The account in the general ledger that summarizes or controls a subsidiary ledger. Example: The Accounts Payable account in the general ledger is the controlling account for the accounts payable subsidiary ledger. After postings are complete, it shows the total amount owed from purchases made on account.

Figure 10.12 Cash Payments Transactions Journalized for the Month and Posting to the General Journal

		GENERAL JOURNAL			Page 2	
Date		Account Titles and Description	PR	Dr.	Cr.	
201X						
Apr.	2	Prepaid Insurance	123	9 0 0 00		
		Cash	111		9 0 0 00	
		Paid for insurance in advance				
	7	Accounts Payable, Joe Francis Co.	211 ✔	4 0 0 0 00		
		Cash	111		4 0 0 0 00	
		Paid invoice no. 388				
	9	Merchandise Inventory	121	8 0 0 00		
		Cash	111		8 0 0 00	
		Cash Purchases				
	14	Accounts Payable, Thorpe Co.	211 ✔	6 0 0 00		
		Merchandise Inventory	121		6 00	
		Cash	111		5 9 4 00	
		Paid invoice no. 414				
	26	Salaries Expense	611	7 0 0 00		
		Cash	111		7 0 0 00	
		Paid salaries				

(continued on page 350)

Figure 10.12 *(continued)*

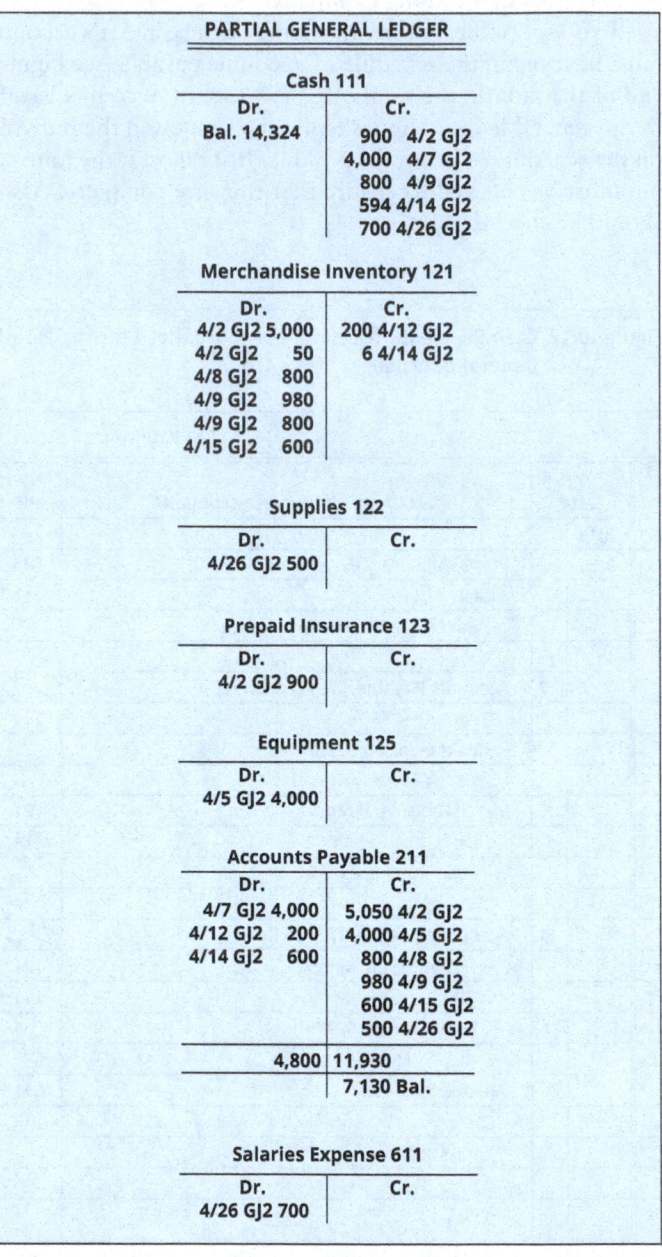

| ACCOUNTS PAYABLE SUBSIDIARY LEDGER | | | PARTIAL GENERAL LEDGER | |

ACCOUNTS PAYABLE SUBSIDIARY LEDGER

Abby Blake Co.

Dr.	Cr.
	5,050 4/2 GJ2
	600 4/15 GJ2
	5,650 Bal.

Joe Francis Co.

Dr.	Cr.
4/7 GJ2 4,000	4,000 4/5 GJ2
	0 Bal.

John Sullivan Co.

Dr.	Cr.
	980 4/9 GJ2
	500 4/26 GJ2
	1,480 Bal.

Thorpe Co.

Dr.	Cr.
4/12 GJ2 200	800 4/8 GJ2
4/14 GJ2 600	
	0 Bal.

PARTIAL GENERAL LEDGER

Cash 111

Dr.	Cr.
Bal. 14,324	900 4/2 GJ2
	4,000 4/7 GJ2
	800 4/9 GJ2
	594 4/14 GJ2
	700 4/26 GJ2

Merchandise Inventory 121

Dr.	Cr.
4/2 GJ2 5,000	200 4/12 GJ2
4/2 GJ2 50	6 4/14 GJ2
4/8 GJ2 800	
4/9 GJ2 980	
4/9 GJ2 800	
4/15 GJ2 600	

Supplies 122

Dr.	Cr.
4/26 GJ2 500	

Prepaid Insurance 123

Dr.	Cr.
4/2 GJ2 900	

Equipment 125

Dr.	Cr.
4/5 GJ2 4,000	

Accounts Payable 211

Dr.	Cr.
4/7 GJ2 4,000	5,050 4/2 GJ2
4/12 GJ2 200	4,000 4/5 GJ2
4/14 GJ2 600	800 4/8 GJ2
	980 4/9 GJ2
	600 4/15 GJ2
	500 4/26 GJ2
4,800	11,930
	7,130 Bal.

Salaries Expense 611

Dr.	Cr.
4/26 GJ2 700	

Figure 10.13 Schedule of Accounts Payable

ART'S WHOLESALE CLOTHING COMPANY SCHEDULE OF ACCOUNTS PAYABLE APRIL 30, 201X		
Abby Blake Co.		$ 5 6 5 0 00
John Sullivan Co.		1 4 8 0 00
Total Accounts Payable		$ 7 1 3 0 00

Now let's check your progress.

 **TRY IT!**   **Learning Unit 10-2**

From the following, prepare a Schedule of Accounts Payable for Digital Co. for September 30, 201X:

Accounts Payable 210			L. Von Co.	
Dr.	Cr.		Dr.	Cr.
	100 9/5 GJ4			100 9/5 GJ4
	200 9/7 GJ5		**Xon Co.**	
	300 9/15 GJ6		Dr.	Cr.
	800 9/18 GJ6			300 9/15 GJ6

J. Bee Co.			Zero Co.	
Dr.	Cr.		Dr.	Cr.
	800 9/18 GJ6			200 9/7 GJ5

TRY IT!   **Solution Learning Unit 10-2**

Digital Co. Schedule of Accounts Payable September 30, 201X	
J. Bee Co.	$ 800
L. Von Co.	100
Xon Co.	300
Zero Co.	200
Total Accounts Payable	$1,400

DEMONSTRATION SUMMARY PROBLEM

The following transactions occurred in November 201X for Dale's Electronics Shop. It uses the perpetual inventory system.

Nov. 9   Purchased $700 of Merchandise Inventory on account from Matty Co., invoice no. 398, dated Nov. 10; terms 2/10, n/60.

10   Purchased $1,200 of Merchandise Inventory on account from Mia Co., invoice no. 399, dated Nov. 11; terms 2/10, n/60.

15   Purchased $600 of electronic supplies on account from Hope Co., invoice no. 410, dated Nov. 16; terms 2/10, n/60.

17   Issued debit memorandum no. 7 to Matty Co. for merchandise returned, $200, from invoice no. 398.

18   Purchased $600 of electronic equipment on account from Sam Co., invoice no. 411, dated Nov. 19; terms 2/10, n/60.

Selected accounts are listed below:

Partial General Ledger
Electronic Supplies 112
Merchandise Inventory 115
Electronic Equipment 120
Accounts Payable 210

Accounts Payable Subsidiary Ledger
Hope Co.; Matty Co.; Mia Co.; Sam Co.

Requirements

1. Journalize (p. 2), post, and record the transactions for a perpetual system.
2. Prepare a Schedule of Accounts Payable.

Solutions

Requirement 1

Dale's Electronic Shop
General Journal   Page 2

Date	Account Titles and Description	PR	Dr.	Cr.
201X				
Nov. 9	Merchandise Inventory	115	700	
	Accounts Payable, Matty Co.	210/✓		700
	Invoice no. 398			
10	Merchandise Inventory	115	1,200	
	Accounts Payable, Mia Co.	210/✓		1,200
	Invoice no. 399			
15	Electronic Supplies	112	600	
	Accounts Payable, Hope Co.	210/✓		600
	Invoice no. 410			
17	Accounts Payable, Matty Co.	210/✓	200	
	Merchandise Inventory	115		200
	Debit Memorandum no. 7			
18	Electronic Equipment	120	600	
	Accounts Payable, Sam Co.	210/✓		600
	Invoice no. 411			

Tips for Journalizing, Posting, and Recording the Transactions for a Perpetual System

Merchandise Inventory has a normal balance of a debit. Note in the Nov. 17 transaction, Dale's Electronics owes less and its amount of Merchandise Inventory has decreased as a result. As Accounts Payable is affected, the accounts payable subsidiary ledger is updated.

Partial General Ledger

Electronic Supplies 112

Dr.	Cr.
11/15 GJ2 600	

Merchandise Inventory 115

Dr.	Cr.
11/9 GJ2 700	200 11/17 GJ2
11/10 GJ2 1,200	

Electronic Equipment 120

Dr.	Cr.
11/18 GJ2 600	

Accounts Payable 210

Dr.	Cr.
11/17 GJ2 200	700 11/9 GJ2
	1,200 11/10 GJ2
	600 11/15 GJ2
	600 11/18 GJ2
	Balance 2,900

Accounts Payable Subsidiary Ledger

Hope Co.

Dr.	Cr.
	600 11/15 GJ2

Matty Co.

Dr.	Cr.
11/17 GJ2 200	700 11/9 GJ2
	Balance 500

Mia Co.

Dr.	Cr.
	1,200 11/10 GJ2

Sam Co.

Dr.	Cr.
	600 11/18 GJ2

Requirement 2

Dale's Electronic Shop
Schedule of Accounts Payable
November 30, 201X

Hope Co.	$ 600
Matty Co.	500
Mia Co.	1,200
Sam Co.	600
Total Accounts Payable	$2,900

Tip for Preparing a Schedule of Accounts Payable

Note that the sum of the accounts payable subsidiary ledger of $2,900 is the ending balance in Accounts Payable in the general ledger.

Tips for Journalizing the Same Transactions Using the Perpetual System

In a perpetual system, purchases are recorded as Merchandise Inventory. Note in transactions dated Nov. 15 and Nov. 18 that the debit was not to Merchandise Inventory because they were not for resale. Note in a transaction dated Nov. 17 that the return lowers the amount in Merchandise Inventory. If Dale had sold some goods, then accounts receivable would increase as well as sales. At the same time, Dale's cost of goods sold account would increase and the Merchandise Inventory account would decrease.

SUCCESS COACH

10

The following Success Tips are from Learning Units 10-1 to 10-2. Take the Do It Right Now Checkup and use the Check Your Score to see how you are doing. The Success Coach provides tips before each Checkup to help you avoid common accounting errors.

LU 10-1 Journalizing and Recording Transactions to the Accounts Payable Subsidiary Ledger and Posting to the General Ledger Along with a Debit Memorandum Using the Perpetual Inventory Method

Do It Right Tips:

1. The normal balance of Accounts Payable, which indicates an increase in the account, is a credit.
2. The normal balance of the Merchandise Inventory account, which indicates an increase in the account, is a debit.
3. Who pays for shipping is determined by the designations of F.O.B. Shipping Point and F.O.B. Destination.
4. A debit memorandum will result in a decrease in Accounts Payable.

Do It Right Now Checkup: Answer true or false to the following statements.

1. F.O.B. shipping point means that the seller of the goods is responsible for covering the shipping costs.
2. A purchase return is a credit to Merchandise Inventory.
3. The controlling account, Accounts Payable, is located in the subsidiary ledger.
4. The normal balance of each vendor in the accounts payable subsidiary ledger is a credit.
5. Debit memorandums are issued by the seller.

Merchandise for resale to customers is called Merchandise Inventory. If shipping terms are F.O.B. shipping point, the buyer will pay the cost of freight. The cost of those freight charges will be added to the Merchandise Inventory account with a debit. As the freight charges are an element of getting the inventory ready for sale, this represents an increase to the cost of the inventory.

The accounts payable subsidiary ledger lists the amounts owed to each vendor. It is just the opposite of the accounts receivable subsidiary ledger. The normal balance of the accounts payable subsidiary ledger is a credit. The controlling account, Accounts Payable, is located in the general ledger. A debit memorandum means the buyer does not owe as much and thus Accounts Payable is reduced and a decrease in Merchandise Inventory results. The debit memorandum also reduces what is owed to the vendor in the subsidiary ledger.

LU 10-2 Cash Payments Transactions and Schedules of Accounts Payable

Do It Right Now Checkup: Answer true or false to the following statements.

1. Merchandise Inventory is a contra-revenue account.
2. The schedule of accounts payable is listed by debits and credits.
3. An increase in Merchandise Inventory is made by debiting the account.
4. Merchandise Inventory is shown on the income statement.
5. The normal balance of each vendor in the accounts payable subsidiary ledger is a debit.

When a cash payment is made within the discount period from a charge purchase, the result is a debit to Accounts Payable and the Subsidiary account and a credit to Merchandise Inventory and Cash. Remember that Merchandise Inventory is an asset account with a normal debit balance. At the end of the month the total from the schedule of accounts payable should equal the ending balance in Accounts Payable, the controlling account.

CHECK YOUR SCORE: Answers to the Do It Right Now Checkup

LU 10-1

1. False— F.O.B shipping point means that the buyer will pay the shipping costs.
2. True
3. False—The controlling account, Accounts Payable, is located in the general ledger.
4. True
5. False—Debit memorandums are issued by the buyer.

LU 10-2

1. False—Merchandise Inventory is an asset account.
2. False—The schedule of accounts payable contains no debits or credits.
3. True
4. False—Merchandise Inventory is shown on the balance sheet.
5. False—The normal balance of each vendor in the accounts payable subsidiary ledger is a credit.

BLUEPRINT: PERIODIC VERSUS PERPETUAL ACCOUNTS USED FOR JOURNAL ENTRIES

Periodic*		Perpetual
Purchases	←	Merchandise Inventory
Purchase Discounts	←	Merchandise Inventory
Sales/Accounts Receivable or Cash	←	Sales/Accounts Receivable or Cash Cost of Goods Sold/Merchandise Inventory
Freight-In	←	Merchandise Inventory
Sales Discounts	←	Sales Discounts
Sales Returns and Allowances	←	Sales Returns and Allowances

*Periodic Method is covered in the Chapter 12 Appendix on page 429.

Discussion Questions and Critical Thinking/Ethical Case

1. What does F.O.B. shipping point represent?
2. What is the normal balance of Merchandise Inventory?
3. What kind of account is cost of goods sold?
4. Explain the difference between F.O.B. shipping point and F.O.B. destination.
5. F.O.B. destination means that title to the goods will switch to the buyer when goods are shipped. Do you agree or disagree? Why?
6. What is the normal balance of each creditor in the accounts payable subsidiary ledger?
7. Why could the balance of the controlling account, Accounts Payable, equal the sum of the accounts payable subsidiary ledger during the month?
8. What is the relationship between a purchase requisition and a purchase order?
9. What purpose could a typical invoice approval form serve?
10. Explain the difference between merchandise and equipment.
11. Why would the purchaser issue a debit memorandum?
12. Explain why a trade discount is not a cash discount.
13. What is the normal balance of cost of goods sold?
14. How are discounts recorded in a perpetual system?
15. Spring Co. bought merchandise from All Co. with terms 2/10, n/30. Joanne Ring, the bookkeeper, forgot to pay the bill within the first 10 days. She went to Mel Ryan, the head accountant, who told her to backdate the check so that it looked like the bill was paid within the discount period. Joanne told Mel that she thought they could get away with it. Should Joanne and Mel backdate the check to take advantage of the discount? You make the call. Write down your specific recommendations to Joanne.

Concept Checks

MyLabAccounting

L01,2 *(10 min)*

Journalizing Transactions

1. Journalize the following transactions for a perpetual company:
    a. Issued credit memo no. 2, $43, to Lenny Co. An allowance was granted and the customer kept the merchandise. The sale was on account.
    b. Cash sales, $183, with a cost of $50.
    c. Received check from Dolly Co., $45, less 2% discount.
    d. Bought merchandise on account from Joseph Co., $31, invoice no. 20; terms 3/10, n/30.
    e. Cash purchase of merchandise, $16.
    f. Issued debit memo to Joseph Co., $9, for merchandise returned from invoice no. 20.

L02 *(10 min)*

Schedule of Accounts Payable

2. From the following prepare a schedule of Accounts Payable for Ronson.com for May 31, 201X:

Accounts Payable Subsidiary Ledger				General Ledger			
Beland Co.				**Accounts Payable**			
	Dr.	Cr.			Dr.	Cr.	
5/25 GJ1	12	53	5/20 GJ1	5/31 GJ1	12	118	5/31 GJ1
Roy Co.							
	Dr.	Cr.					
		65	5/7 GJ1				

(10 min) **LO1** ▶ **Perpetual Inventory Discount**

3.   Balder Co. paid $200 to Pedro Co. and received a $20 purchases discount. Journalize the entry.

(10 min) **LO2** ▶ **Perpetual Inventory Return**

4.   Porter Morse returned $275 (selling price) of merchandise to Labrie Co. The merchandise was purchased on credit. The cost of the merchandise to Labrie Co. is $100. What would be the journal entries on the books of both the buyer and seller?

(10 min) **LO2** ▶ **Perpetual Inventory Freight**

5.   Capris Co. paid the cost of freight, $70. Journalize the transaction. Assume that Capris Co. is the buyer.

MyLabAccounting   ## Exercises

Set A

(15 min) **LO1** ▶   **10A-1.** From the general journal in Figure 10.14, record to the accounts payable subsidiary ledger and post to general ledger accounts as appropriate.

Figure 10.14
General Journal Showing Purchases from Cortland.com, Harold.com, and Nickel.com

GENERAL JOURNAL						Page 2
Date	Account Titles and Description	PR	Dr.		Cr.	
201X						
Jun. 3	Merchandise Inventory		9 4 0 00			
	Accounts Payable, Cortland.com				9 4 0 00	
	Purchased merchandise on account					
4	Merchandise Inventory		6 2 0 00			
	Accounts Payable, Harold.com				6 2 0 00	
	Purchased merchandise on account					
8	Equipment		1 9 0 00			
	Accounts Payable, Nickel.com				1 9 0 00	
	Bought equipment on account					

Partial Accounts Payable Subsidiary Ledger

Cortland.com

Dr.	Cr.

Harold.com

Dr.	Cr.

Nickel.com

Dr.	Cr.

Partial General Ledger

Merchandise Inventory 105

Dr.	Cr.

Equipment 120

Dr.	Cr.

Accounts Payable 210

Dr.	Cr.

(15 min) **LO1** ▶   **10A-2.** On October 10, 201X, Carrol Co. issued debit memorandum no. 1 for $440 to Roger Co. for merchandise returned from invoice no. 312. The merchandise was purchased on account. Your task is to journalize, record, and post this transaction as appropriate. Use the perpetual inventory system.

10A-3. Journalize, record, and post when appropriate, the following transactions into the general journal (p. 2) for Jacob's Clothing. All purchases offer credit terms of 7/10, n/30. Assume the perpetual inventory system. If using working papers, be sure to put in beginning balances.

LO2 *(20 min)*

201X		
Apr.	1	Issued check no. 20 to A. Jordan Company in payment of its March 28 invoice no. 522.
	8	Issued check no. 21 to Farrow Advertising in payment of its advertising bill, $101, no discount.
	15	Issued check no. 22 to B. Thomas in payment of his March 25 invoice no. 488.

Accounts Payable Subsidiary Ledger

Name	Balance	Invoice No.
B. Campbell	100	821
A. Jordan	$500	522
B. Thomas	200	488
J. Wright	400	562

Partial General Ledger

Account	Balance
Cash 110	$3,100
Merchandise Inventory 115	
Accounts Payable 210	1,200
Advertising Expense 610	

10A-4. From Exercise 10A-3, prepare a schedule of accounts payable and verify that the total of the schedule equals the amount in the controlling account.

LO2 *(10 min)*

10A-5. Record the following transaction in a transaction analysis chart for the buyer: Bought merchandise for $9,400 on account. Shipping terms were F.O.B. destination. The cost of shipping was $470. Assume the perpetual inventory system.

LO2 *(10 min)*

Set B

10B-1. From the general journal in Figure 10.15, record to the accounts payable subsidiary ledger and post to the general ledger accounts as appropriate.

LO2 *(15 min)*

GENERAL JOURNAL				Page 2	
Date		Account Titles and Description	PR	Dr.	Cr.
201X					
Jun.	3	Merchandise Inventory		930 00	
		Accounts Payable, Eve.com			930 00
		Purchased merchandise on account			
	4	Merchandise Inventory		610 00	
		Accounts Payable, Jack.com			610 00
		Purchased merchandise on account			
	8	Equipment		220 00	
		Accounts Payable, Noel.com			220 00
		Bought equipment on account			

Figure 10.15
General Journal Showing Purchases from Eve.com, Jack.com, and Noel.com

Partial Accounts Payable Subsidiary Ledger	Partial General Ledger
Eve.com	Merchandise Inventory 105
Dr. | Cr.	Dr. | Cr.
Jack.com	Equipment 120
Dr. | Cr.	Dr. | Cr.
Noel.com	Accounts Payable 210
Dr. | Cr.	Dr. | Cr.

(15 min) **LO1** ➤ **10B-2.** On December 10, 201X, Brown Co. issued debit memorandum no. 1 for $430 to Line Co. for merchandise returned from invoice no. 312. The merchandise was purchased on account. Your task is to journalize, record, and post this transaction as appropriate. Use the perpetual inventory system.

(20 min) **LO2** ➤ **10B-3.** Journalize, record, and post when appropriate, the following transactions into the general journal (p. 2) for Cody's Clothing. All purchases offer credit terms of Merchandise 1/10, n/30. Assume the perpetual inventory system. If using working papers, be sure to put in beginning balances.

201X

Apr.	1	Issued check no. 20 to A. Jae Company in payment of its March 28 invoice no. 522.
	8	Issued check no. 21 to Flanders Advertising in payment of its advertising bill, $96, no discount.
	15	Issued check no. 22 to B. Miller in payment of its March 25 invoice no. 488.

Accounts Payable Subsidiary Ledger

Name	Balance	Invoice No.
J. Hall	1,100	562
A. Jae	$1,400	522
B. Miller	800	488
B. Parker	250	821

Partial General Ledger

Account	Balance
Cash 110	$3,600
Merchandise Inventory 115	
Accounts Payable 210	3,550
Advertising Expense 610	

(10 min) **LO2** ➤ **10B-4.** From Exercise 10B-3, prepare a schedule of accounts payable and verify that the total of the schedule equals the amount in the controlling account.

(10 min) **LO1** ➤ **10B-5.** Record the following transaction in a transaction analysis chart for the buyer: Bought merchandise for $8,900 on account. Shipping terms were F.O.B. destination. The cost of shipping was $510. Assume the perpetual inventory system.

MyLabAccounting   ## Problems

Set A

(30 min) **LO1,2** ➤ **10A-1.** Robert Chase recently opened Robert's Skate Shop. As the bookkeeper of the company, use the perpetual method to journalize, record, and post when appropriate the following transactions (account numbers are Store Supplies 115; Merchandise Inventory 120; Store Equipment 130; Accounts Payable 210).

201X		
May	4	Bought $600 of merchandise on account from Wales Co., invoice no. 442, dated May 5; terms 3/10, n/30.
	5	Bought $4,600 of store equipment on account from Kingston Co., invoice no. 502, dated May 6.
	8	Bought $1,700 of merchandise on account from Rolo Co., invoice no. 401, dated May 9; terms 3/10, n/30.
	14	Bought $1,000 of store supplies on account from Wales Co., invoice no. 419, dated May 14.

Check Figure:
Accounts payable ending balance
$7,900

10A-2. As the accountant for Riley's Natural Food Store, (1) journalize the following transactions into the general journal (p. 2), (2) record and post as appropriate, and (3) prepare a schedule of accounts payable. If using working papers, be sure to put in the following balances: Aris Co., $350; Brown Co., $800; Moose Co., $1,350; Ready Co., $700; Merchandise Inventory, $19,000; Accounts Payable, $3,200. Use the perpetual method.

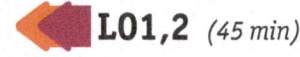 **L01,2** *(45 min)*

201X		
April	8	Purchased $750 of merchandise on account from Aris Co., invoice no. 400, dated April 9; terms 5/10, n/60.
	10	Purchased $1,350 of merchandise on account from Brown Co., invoice no. 420, dated April 11; terms 5/10, n/60.
	12	Purchased $400 of store supplies on account from Moose Co., invoice no. 510, dated April 13.
	14	Issued debit memo no. 8 to Aris Co. for merchandise returned, $300, from invoice no. 400.
	17	Purchased $640 of office equipment on account from Ready Co., invoice no. 810, dated April 18.
	24	Purchased $850 of additional store supplies on account from Moose Co., invoice no. 516, dated April 25; terms 5/10, n/30.

Check Figure:
Total schedule of accounts payable
$6,890

10A-3. Wendy Drew operates a wholesale computer center and has hired you as her bookkeeper to record the following transactions. She would like you to (1) journalize the following transactions, (2) record to the accounts payable subsidiary ledger and post to the general ledger as appropriate, and (3) prepare a schedule of accounts payable. If using working papers, be sure to put in the following beginning balances: Andersen Co., $1,200; Henderson Co., $400; Squash Co., $900; Xhosa Co., $1,300; Cash, $22,000; Accounts Payable, $3,800; Merchandise inventory $4,000. Use the perpetual method.

 **L01,2** *(45 min)*

201X		
March	1	Paid half the amount owed Henderson Co. from previous purchases of computers on account, less a 7% purchases discount, check no. 21.
	3	Bought a delivery truck for $8,000 cash, check no. 22, payable to Bill Singer Co.
	6	Bought computer merchandise from Lossless Co., check no. 23, $2,500.
	18	Bought additional computer merchandise from Paced Co., check no. 24, $750.
	24	Paid Xhosa Co. the amount owed for computer merchandise, less a 7% purchases discount, check no. 25.
	28	Paid rent expense to Viscount's Realty Trust, check no. 26, $2,200.
	29	Paid utilities expense to Granite Utility Co., check no. 27, $280.
	30	Paid half the amount owed Squash Co., no discount, check no. 28.

Check Figure:
Total of schedule of accounts payble
$1,850

(40 min) **LO1,2**

10A-4. Jackie's Toy Shop completed the following merchandise transactions in the month of April:

201X

Apr.	2	Purchased merchandise on account from Irwin Suppliers, $2,500; terms 3/10, n/30.
	4	Sold merchandise on account, $500; terms 3/10, n/30. The cost of the merchandise sold was $330.
	4	Received credit from Irwin Suppliers for merchandise returned, $230.
	10	Received collection in full, less discounts, from April 4 sales.
	11	Paid Irwin Suppliers in full, less discount.
	14	Purchased store equipment for cash, $250.
	15	Purchased $1,000 of merchandise from Foley Distribution for cash.
	16	Received a refund due to defective merchandise from supplier on cash purchase of $90.
	17	Purchased merchandise on account from Thompson Corp., $3,600, F.O.B. shipping point (buyer pays freight); terms 3/10, n/30. Freight to be paid on April 21.
	18	Sold merchandise for $3,300 cash; the cost of merchandise sold was $1,550.
	21	Paid freight on April 17 purchase, $120.
	25	Purchased merchandise on account from Boute Co., $1,240, F.O.B. destination (seller pays freight); terms 3/10, n/30.
	26	Paid Thompson Corp. in full, less discount.
	27	Made refunds to cash customers for defective toys, $250. The cost of the defective toys was $110.

Jackie's Toy Shop accounts included the following: Cash 101; Accounts Receivable 112; Merchandise Inventory 120; Store Equipment 124; Accounts Payable 201; J. Jackie, Capital 301; Sales 401; Sales Discounts 412; Sales Returns and Allowances 414; Cost of Goods Sold 501.

Assignment

Journalize the transactions using a perpetual inventory system.

Set B

(30 min) **LO1,2**

10B-1. Rasheed Chase recently opened Rasheed's Surf Shop. As the bookkeeper of the company, use the perpetual method to journalize, record, and post when appropriate the following transactions (account numbers are Store Supplies 115; Merchandise Inventory 120; Store Equipment 130; Accounts Payable 210):

201X

Mar	4	Bought $1,200 of merchandise on account from Newbury Co., invoice no. 442, dated March 5; terms 2/10, n/30.
	5	Bought $5,400 of store equipment on account from Andover Co., invoice no. 502, dated March 6.
	8	Bought $1,200 of merchandise on account from Lakeville Co., invoice no. 401, dated March 9, terms 2/10, n/30.
	14	Bought $1,300 of store supplies on account from Newbury Co., invoice no. 419, dated March 14.

(45 min) **LO1,2**

10B-2. As the accountant of Trina's Natural Food Store, (1) journalize the following transactions into the general journal (p. 2), (2) record and post as appropriate, and (3) prepare a schedule of accounts payable. If using working papers, be sure to put in the following balances: Antion Co., $450; Block Co., $500; Midden Co., $1,150; Rex Co., $250; Merchandise Inventory, $18,000; Accounts Payable, $2,350. Use the perpetual inventory method.

201X

Oct	8	Purchased $650 of merchandise on account from Antion Co., invoice no. 400, dated October 9; terms 9/10, n/60.
	10	Purchased $1,250 of merchandise on account from Block Co., invoice no. 420, dated October 11; terms 9/10, n/60.
	12	Purchased $700 of store supplies on account from Midden Co., invoice no. 510, dated October 13.
	14	Issued debit memo no. 8 to Antion Co. for merchandise returned, $500, from invoice no. 400.
	17	Purchased $620 of office equipment on account from Rex Co., invoice no. 810, dated October 18.
	24	Purchased $400 of additional store supplies on account from Midden Co., invoice no. 516, dated October 25; terms 9/10, n/30.

Check Figure:
Total schedule of accounts payable $5,470

10B-3. Wendy Johnson operates a wholesale computer center and has hired you as her bookkeeper to record the following transactions. She would like you to (1) journalize the following transactions, (2) record to the accounts payable subsidiary ledger and post to the general ledger as appropriate, and (3) prepare a schedule of accounts payable. If using working papers, be sure to put in the following beginning balances: Andersen Co., $1,050; Hack Co., $1,400; Soil Co., $850; Xydias Co., $1,000; Cash, $20,000; Merchandise inventory $5,000; Accounts Payable, $4,300. Use the perpetual method.

LO1,2 *(45 min)*

201X

May	1	Paid half the amount owed Hack Co. from previous purchases of computers on account, less a 7% purchases discount, check no. 21.
	3	Bought a delivery truck for $7,500 cash, check no. 22, payable to Bill Brown Co.
	6	Bought computer merchandise from Lectro Co., check no. 23, $2,700.
	18	Bought additional computer merchandise from Pink Co., check no. 24, $600.
	24	Paid Xydias Co. the amount owed for computer merchandise, less a 7% purchases discount, check no. 25.
	28	Paid rent expense to Queen's Realty Trust, check no. 26, $1,600.
	29	Paid utilities expense to Stone Utility Co., check no. 27, $360.
	30	Paid half the amount owed to Soil Co., no discount, check no. 28.

Check Figure:
Total schedule of accounts payable $2,175

10B-4. Jeanne's Toy Shop completed the following merchandise transactions in the month of April:

LO1,2 *(40 min)*

201X

Apr.	2	Purchased merchandise on account from Beech Suppliers, $3,500; terms 2/10, n/30.
	4	Sold merchandise on account $520; terms 2/10, n/30. The cost of the merchandise sold was $260.
	4	Received credit from Beech Suppliers for merchandise returned, $160.
	10	Received collection in full, less discounts, from April 4 sales.
	11	Paid Beech Suppliers in full, less discount.
	14	Purchased store equipment for cash, $290.
	15	Purchased $1,700 of merchandise from Soucy Distribution for cash.
	16	Received a refund due for defective merchandise from supplier on cash purchase of $80.
	17	Purchased merchandise on account from Tustin Corp., $3,700, F.O.B. shipping point (buyer pays freight); terms 2/10, n/30. Freight to be paid on April 21.
	18	Sold merchandise for $2,700 cash; the cost of the merchandise sold was $1,650.
	21	Paid freight on April 17 purchase, $130.
	25	Purchased merchandise on account from Oak Co., $1,040, F.O.B. destination (seller pays freight); terms 2/10, n/30.
	26	Paid Tustin Corp. in full, less discount.
	27	Made refunds to cash customers for defective toys, $190. The cost of the defective toys was $100.

Check Figure:
April 21
Dr. Merchandise Inventory $130
Cr. Cash $130

Jeanne's Toy Shop accounts included the following: Cash 101; Accounts Receivable 112; Merchandise Inventory 120; Office Equipment 124; Accounts Payable 201; B. Jeanne, Capital 301; Sales 401; Sales Discounts 412; Sales Returns and Allowances 414; Cost of Goods Sold 501.

Assignment

Journalize the transactions using the perpetual inventory system.

Financial Report Problem

(15 min) **LO1** ▶

Reading Amazon's Annual Report

Go to **https://tinyurl.com/slaterca14e**. How much has Merchandise Inventory increased or decreased from 2015 to 2016.

MyLabAccounting

(60 min) **LO1,2** ▶

KEEPING IT REAL SUAREZ COMPUTER CENTER

The following is an updated schedule of accounts payable as of January 31, 201X.

Schedule of Accounts Payable	
Hardware Haven	$675
Nuts and Bolts	450
Pacific Bell	155
System Design Furniture	1,500
Total Accounts Payable	$2,780

Assignment

1. Journalize the transactions. Use the perpetual method.
2. Record in the accounts payable subsidiary ledger and post to the general ledger as appropriate. A partial general ledger is included in the working papers that accompany this text.
   The following account has been added to the chart of accounts: Merchandise Inventory 1021.
3. Prepare a schedule of accounts payable as of February 28, 201X.

The transactions for the month of February are as follows:

201X		
Feb.	1	Prepaid the rent for the months of February, March, and April, $1,500, check #2585.
	4	Bought merchandise on account from A-Tech, Inc., purchase order no. 4010, $480; terms 3/10, n/30.
	8	Bought office supplies on account from The Staple Store, purchase order no. 4011, $300; terms n/30.
	9	Purchased merchandise on account from Computers R Us, purchase order no. 4012, $450; terms 2/10, n/60.
	15	Paid purchase order no. 4010 in full to A-Tech, Inc., check #2586.
	21	Issued debit memorandum no. 10 to Computers R Us for merchandise returned from purchase order no. 4012, $150.
	27	Paid for office supplies, $120, check #2587.

SAGE 50 COMPUTER WORKSHOP

Computerized Accounting Application for Chapter 10

Refresher on using Sage 50 Complete Accounting

Before starting this assignment, you may want to refresh your memory by reading the following PDF documents in the multimedia library of the MyAccountingLab website. Remember to choose the PDF document for your version of Sage 50.

1. An Introduction to Sage 50
2. Correcting Sage 50 Transactions
3. How to Repeat or Restart a Sage 50 Assignment
4. Backing Up and Restoring Your Work in Sage 50

   You also should have completed the following workshops:

1. Workshop 1 Atlas Company from Chapter 3
2. Workshop 2 Zell Company from Chapter 4
3. Workshop 3 Sherman Realty from Chapter 5
4. Workshop 4 Pete's Market from Chapter 8

Workshop 5:

Part A: Recording Transactions in the Sales, Receipts, and Payments Journals
Part B: Accounting Cycle Mini Practice Set with Sales and Purchasing

Part A: In this part of the workshop, you will learn to record customer sales on account, customer credit memos, customer cash receipts, inventory purchases from vendors on account, and payments to vendors for Mars Company using Sage 50. You will also print the aged receivables and aged payables reports and the sales journal, cash receipts journal, and cash disbursement journals.

Instructions and the data file for completing Part A of the assignment are in the multimedia library of the MyAccountingLab website. Open the *Workshop 5 Part A Mars Company* PDF document for your version of Sage 50 and download the *Mars Company* data file for your version of Sage 50.

Part B: In this part of the workshop, you will complete a mini practice set of March accounting transactions for Jeanne's Toy Shop using Sage 50. Transactions include customer sales on account, customer credit memos, customer cash receipts, purchases from vendors on account, payments to vendors, and general journal entries in Sage 50. You will also print the aged receivables and aged payables reports and the general journal and general ledger reports.

Instructions and the data file for completing Part B of the assignment are in the multimedia library of the MyAccountingLab website. Open the *Workshop 5 Part B Jeanne's Toy Shop* PDF document for your version of Sage 50 and download the *Jeanne's Toy Shop* data file for your version of Sage 50.

QUICKBOOKS SOFTWARE SIMULATIONS

Computerized Accounting Application for Chapter 10

Refresher on using QuickBooks Accountant

Before starting this assignment, you may want to refresh your memory by reading the following PDF documents in the multimedia library of the MyAccountingLab website. Remember to choose the PDF document for your version of QuickBooks.

1. An Introduction to QuickBooks
2. Correcting QuickBooks Transactions
3. How to Repeat or Restart a QuickBooks Assignment
4. Backing Up and Restoring Your Work in QuickBooks

You also should have completed the following workshops:

1. Workshop 1 Atlas Company from Chapter 3
2. Workshop 2 Zell Company from Chapter 4
3. Workshop 3 Sherman Realty from Chapter 5
4. Workshop 4 Pete's Market from Chapter 8

Workshop 5:

Part A: Recording Transactions in the Sales, Receipts, Purchases, and Payments Journals
Part B: Accounting Cycle Mini Practice Set with Sales and Purchasing

Part A: In this part of the workshop, you will learn to record customer sales on account, customer credit memos, customer cash receipts, inventory purchases from vendors on account, and payments to vendors for Mars Company using QuickBooks. You will also print the aged receivables and aged payables reports and the sales journal, cash receipts journal, and cash disbursement journals.

Instructions and the data file for completing Part A of the assignment are in the multimedia library of the MyAccountingLab website. Open the *Workshop 5 Part A Mars Company* PDF document for your version of QuickBooks and download the *Mars Company* data file for your version of QuickBooks.

Part B: In this part of the workshop, you will complete a mini practice set of March accounting transactions for Jeanne's Toy Shop using QuickBooks. Transactions include customer sales on account, customer credit memos, customer cash receipts, purchases from vendors on account, payments to vendors, and general journal entries in QuickBooks. You will also print the aged receivables and aged payables reports and the general journal and general ledger reports.

Instructions and the data file for completing Part B of the assignment are in the multimedia library of the MyAccountingLab website. ***Open the Workshop 5 Part B Jeanne's Toy Shop*** PDF document for your version of QuickBooks and download the *Jeanne's Toy Shop* data file for your version of QuickBooks.

Preparing a Worksheet for a Merchandise Company Using the Perpetual Method

CHAPTER PREVIEW: ACCOUNTING IN ACTION

Robert Arroyo is planning to go to the Microsoft Store to buy the latest version of the Surface Pro. He wonders if they may be out of stock. Microsoft Stores and its suppliers make adjustments to the inventory so customer demand can be met. In addition, Microsoft makes other adjustments that customers may not be aware of. These adjustments include supplies, rent, the wages of employees, and depreciation. Like the preparation of worksheets of nonmerchandising companies that you learned about in Chapter 4, to make these adjustments, many merchandise companies will also use a worksheet with some differences. In this chapter, you learn how a merchandising company prepares a worksheet and how it flows to the financial statements.

Learning Objectives

LO1 Figuring Adjustments for Merchandise Inventory using the Perpetual Method, Unearned Rent, Supplies Used, Insurance Expired, Depreciation Expense, and Salaries Accrued

LO2 Preparing a Worksheet for a Merchandise Company

When you shop at the Microsoft Store, do you ever wonder how Microsoft controls its inventory? In Chapters 9 and 10 we discussed the subsidiary ledgers as well as entries for a merchandise company. Additional material provided an introduction to perpetual inventory. Now we shift our attention to recording adjustments and completing a worksheet for a merchandise company. Note that the appendix at the end of the chapter shows worksheets for a periodic system.

LEARNING UNIT 11-1

L01

Adjustments for Merchandise Inventory Using the Perpetual Method, Unearned Rent, Supplies Used, Insurance Expired, Depreciation Expense, and Salaries Accrued

Cost of goods sold Total cost of the goods that were sold to customers.

Perpetual inventory system An inventory system that keeps *continual track* of each type of inventory by recording units on hand at the beginning, units sold, and the current balance after each sale or purchase.

Beginning Merchandise Inventory (Beginning Inventory) The cost of goods on hand in a company to *begin* an accounting period.

Note that Merchandise Inventory has a normal balance of debit or credit.

The Merchandise Inventory account shows the goods that a merchandise company has available to sell to customers. Companies have several ways to keep track of the cost of goods sold (the total cost of the goods sold to customers, which is an expense) and the quantity of inventory on hand. In this chapter we discuss the perpetual inventory system, in which the balance in inventory is continually, or *perpetually*, updated every time that there is a transaction that affects the Merchandise Inventory account. This system is used by a wide variety of companies, such as Art's Wholesale Clothing Company, that sell a variety of merchandise and want to keep track of both their Cost of Goods Sold and their inventory levels in real time. The proliferation of scanning technology has made this possible for many companies both large and small.

Assume that Art's Wholesale Clothing Company started the year with $19,000 worth of merchandise. This merchandise is called Beginning Merchandise Inventory or simply Beginning Inventory. The balance of inventory in the Merchandise Inventory account constantly changes during the accounting period as items are bought for resale to customers and then sold, as well as accounting for discounts applied to inventory purchases and the return of inventory by customers. All purchases of merchandise therefore are recorded in the Merchandise Inventory account. During the accounting period $52,000 worth of such purchases were made and recorded in the Merchandise Inventory account by Art's Wholesale.

Adjustment A: Merchandise Inventory, $19,000. Adjusting the Merchandise Inventory account is simply a one-step process that involves either adding to (Dr.) or subtracting from (Cr.) the inventory account, depending on the circumstances.

When using a perpetual inventory system, inventory is immediately updated after each purchase and sale transaction. However, the value of inventory on the balance sheet may not accurately represent the value of inventory actually on hand. To verify the accuracy of the accounting records, a physical inventory should be performed at the end of the reporting period. This is usually done near year end. If the count does not match the records, an adjustment must be made to bring the inventory to its correct balance. This difference is often referred to as inventory "shrinkage," resulting either from error in recording transactions, theft, or breakage. If the amount is considered immaterial, the following entry would be made if the balance in the Merchandise Inventory account was more than the physical count. Using the Merchandise Inventory of Art's Clothing Company as an example, assume Art's Wholesale Clothing Company shows a balance $19,000 worth of inventory. A physical count was taken and revealed a balance of $18,500. Art's Wholesale Clothing Company had an inventory shrinkage of $500. Figure 11.1 shows the journal entry that would reflect this adjustment.

Figure 11.1
Journal Entry for Inventory Shrinkage

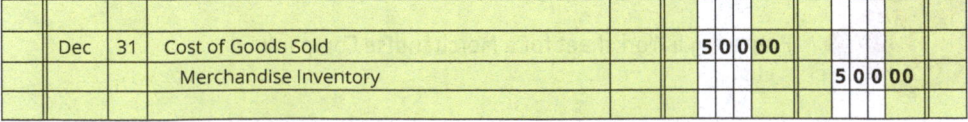

Dec	31	Cost of Goods Sold		50000	
		Merchandise Inventory			50000

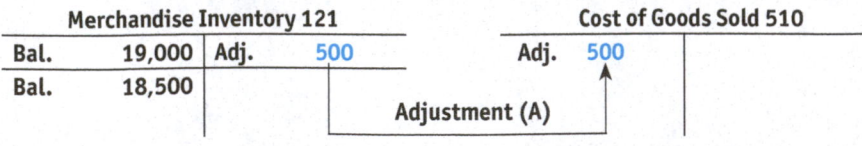

Merchandise Inventory 121

Bal.	19,000	Adj.	500
Bal.	18,500		

Cost of Goods Sold 510

Adj.	500

Adjustment (A)

Once this entry is posted, the Merchandise Inventory balance will match the physical count taken. Although rare, there may be a situation where the count shows more inventory than the Inventory account on the balance sheet.

Assume Art's Wholesale Clothing Company shows a balance of $19,000 worth of inventory. A physical count was taken and revealed a balance of $19,500, a difference of $500. This could be due to errors in recording or shipping. Research should be done into the cause of this error and Figure 11.2 shows the journal entry for this transaction.

Dec	31	Merchandise Inventory		5 0 0 00	
		Cost of Goods Sold			5 0 0 00

Figure 11.2
Journal Entry for COGS from Excel Spreadsheet

Once this entry is posted, the Merchandise Inventory balance will match the physical count taken.

Merchandise Inventory 121			Cost of Goods Sold 510	
Bal.	19,000		Adj.	500
Adj.	500			
Bal.	19,500		**Adjustment (B)**	

Adjustment B: Unearned Rent. Another new account we have not seen before is a liability called Unearned Rent or Rent Received in Advance. This account records the amount collected for rent before the service (renting the space) has been provided.

Suppose Art's Wholesale Clothing Company is subletting a portion of its space to Jesse Company for $200 per month. Jesse Company sends Art's cash for $600 for 3 months' rent paid in advance. This unearned rent ($600) is a liability on the balance sheet because Art's Wholesale owes Jesse Company 3 months' worth of occupancy.

When Art's Wholesale fulfills a portion of the rental agreement—when Jesse Company has been in the space for a period of time—this liability account will be reduced and the Rental Income account will be increased. Rental Income is another type of revenue for Art's Wholesale.

Remember that under accrual accounting, revenue is recognized when it is earned, whether payment is received then or not. Here, Art's Wholesale collected cash in advance for a service that it has not yet performed. A liability called Unearned Rent is the result. Art's Wholesale may have the cash, but the rental income is not recorded until it is earned. Examples of other types of unearned revenue besides unearned rent include prepaid subscriptions for magazines, legal fees collected before the work is performed, and prepaid insurance.

Now let's check your progress.

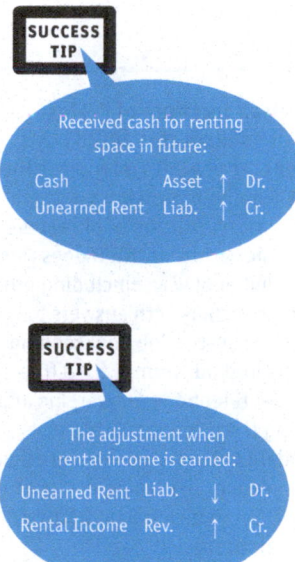

SUCCESS TIP

Received cash for renting space in future:

| Cash | Asset | ↑ | Dr. |
| Unearned Rent | Liab. | ↑ | Cr. |

SUCCESS TIP

The adjustment when rental income is earned:

| Unearned Rent | Liab. | ↓ | Dr. |
| Rental Income | Rev. | ↑ | Cr. |

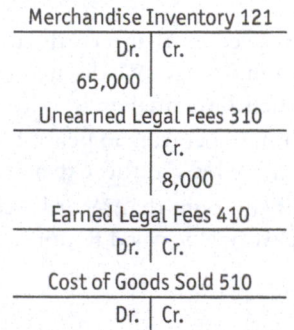

▶ TRY IT!   Learning Unit 11-1

Jones Co. has determined that under the perpetual method that Merchandise Inventory has a $30,000 balance at the end of the month. Jones also stated that the amount of unearned legal fees has been reduced by $4,000

Please update the following accounts to reflect the adjustment data for Merchandise Inventory and Unearned Legal Fees.

SUCCESS TIP

Cost of Goods Sold is an expense account that reflects the cost to the seller of the merchandise that was sold.

Merchandise Inventory 121	
Dr.	Cr.
65,000	

Unearned Legal Fees 310	
	Cr.
	8,000

Earned Legal Fees 410	
Dr.	Cr.

Cost of Goods Sold 510	
Dr.	Cr.

Merchandise Inventory 121		Unearned Legal Fees 310		Earned Legal Fees 410		Cost of Goods Sold 510	
Dr.	Cr.	Dr.	Cr.	Dr.	Cr.	Dr.	Cr.
65,000	35,000	4,000	8,000		4,000	35,000	

LEARNING UNIT 11-2

LO2

Worksheet for Merchandise Companies Using the Perpetual Inventory Method

In this unit, we prepare a worksheet for Art's Wholesale Clothing Company. For convenience, we reproduce the company's chart of accounts in Figure 11.3.

Figure 11.3
Art's Wholesale Clothing Company Chart of Accounts

CHART OF ACCOUNTS

Assets 100–199
- 111   Cash
- 112   Petty Cash
- 113   Accounts Receivable
- 121   Merchandise Inventory
- 122   Supplies
- 123   Prepaid Insurance
- 125   Store Equipment
- 126   Accum. Depreciation, Store Equipment

Liabilities 200–299
- 211   Accounts Payable
- 212   Salaries Payable
- 213   Federal Income Tax Payable
- 214   FICA—Social Security Payable
- 215   FICA—Medicare Payable
- 216   State Income Tax Payable
- 217   SUTA Tax Payable
- 218   FUTA Tax Payable
- 219   Unearned Rent*
- 220   Mortgage Payable

Owner's Equity 300–399
- 311   Art Newner, Capital
- 312   Art Newner, Withdrawals
- 313   Income Summary

Revenue 400–499
- 411   Sales
- 412   Sales Returns and Allowances
- 413   Sales Discount
- 414   Rental Income

Cost of Goods Sold 500–599
- 510   Cost of Goods Sold

Expenses 600–699
- 611   Salaries Expense
- 612   Payroll Tax Expense
- 613   Depreciation Expense, Store Equipment
- 614   Supplies Expense
- 615   Insurance Expense
- 616   Postage Expense
- 617   Miscellaneous Expense
- 618   Interest Expense
- 619   Cleaning Expense
- 620   Delivery Expense

*Although Unearned Rent is the only term under Liabilities not using payable, it is a liability and Cost of Goods Sold is an expense account.

Figure 11.4 shows the trial balance that was prepared on December 31 from Art's Wholesale ledger. (Note that it is placed directly in the first two columns of the worksheet.)

In looking at the trial balance, we see many new titles that did not appear in the trial balance that we completed for a service company in Chapter 5. Let's look specifically at these new titles, shown in Table 11.1.

Note the following:

- **Mortgage Payable** is a liability account that records the increases and decreases in the amount of debt owed on a mortgage. We discuss this account more in the next chapter, when financial statements are prepared.
- **Interest Expense** represents a nonoperating expense for Art's Wholesale and thus is categorized as Other Expense. We look at this expense in the next chapter.
- **Unearned Revenue** is a liability account that records receipt of payment for goods and services in advance of delivery. Unearned Rent is a particular example of this general type of account.

Mortgage Payable   A liability account showing amount owed on a mortgage.

Interest Expense   The cost of borrowing money.

Unearned Revenue   A liability account that records amount owed for goods or services in advance of delivery. The Cash account would record the receipt of cash.

			Trial Balance	
			Dr.	**Cr.**
Cash			12 9 2 0 00	
Petty Cash			1 0 0 00	
Accounts Receivable			14 5 0 0 00	
Merchandise Inventory			19 0 0 0 00	
Supplies			8 0 0 00	
Prepaid Insurance			9 0 0 00	
Store Equipment			4 0 0 0 00	
Acc. Dep., Store Equipment				4 0 0 00
Accounts Payable				17 9 0 0 00
Federal Income Tax Payable				8 0 0 00
FICA—Soc. Sec. Payable				4 5 4 00
FICA—Medicare Payable				1 0 6 00
State Income Tax Payable				2 0 0 00
SUTA Tax Payable				1 0 8 00
FUTA Tax Payable				3 2 00
Unearned Rent				6 0 0 00
Mortgage Payable				2 3 2 0 00
Art Newner, Capital				7 9 0 5 00
Art Newner, Withdrawals			8 6 0 0 00	
Sales				95 0 0 0 00
Sales Returns and Allowances			9 5 0 00	
Sales Discount			6 7 0 00	
Cost of Goods Sold			50 9 1 0 00	
Salaries Expense			11 7 0 0 00	
Payroll Tax Expense			4 2 0 00	
Postage Expense			2 5 00	
Miscellaneous Expense			3 0 00	
Interest Expense			3 0 0 00	
Totals			125 8 2 5 00	125 8 2 5 00

Figure 11.4
Trial Balance Section
of the Worksheet

TABLE 11.1 Summary of New Account Titles

Title	Category	Account Reported on	Normal Balance	Temporary or Permanent
Petty Cash	Asset	Balance Sheet	Dr.	Permanent
Merchandise Inventory	Asset	Balance Sheet	Dr.	Permanent
Cost of Goods Sold	Expense	Income Statement	Dr.	Temporary
Federal Income Tax Payable	Liability	Balance Sheet	Cr.	Permanent
FICA—Social Security Payable	Liability	Balance Sheet	Cr.	Permanent
FICA—Medicare Payable	Liability	Balance Sheet	Cr.	Permanent
State Income Tax Payable	Liability	Balance Sheet	Cr.	Permanent
SUTA Tax Payable	Liability	Balance Sheet	Cr.	Permanent
FUTA Tax Payable	Liability	Balance Sheet	Cr.	Permanent
Unearned Rent	Liability	Balance Sheet	Cr.	Permanent
Mortgage Payable	Liability	Balance Sheet	Cr.	Permanent
Sales	Revenue	Income Statement	Cr.	Temporary
Sales Returns and Allowances	Contra-Revenue	Income Statement	Dr.	Temporary
Sales Discount	Contra-Revenue	Income Statement	Dr.	Temporary
Payroll Tax Expense	Expense	Income Statement	Dr.	Temporary
Postage Expense	Expense	Income Statement	Dr.	Temporary
Interest Expense	Other Expense	Income Statement	Dr.	Temporary

We already discussed the process involved in adjusting Merchandise Inventory by the use of the perpetual method. Now we show T accounts and transaction analysis charts for other adjustments that need to be made at this point for a merchandise firm, just as they must be made for a service company.

Adjustment B: Rental Income Earned by Art's Wholesale, $200. A month ago, Cash was increased by $600, as was a liability, Unearned Rent. Art's Wholesale received payment in advance but had not earned the rental income. Now, because $200 has been earned, the liability is reduced and Rental Income can be recorded for the $200. This step is shown as follows:

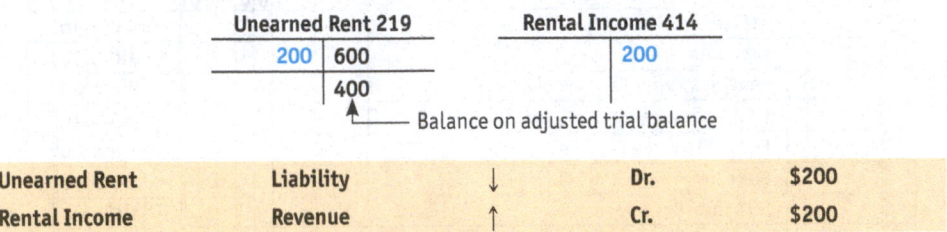

| Unearned Rent | Liability | ↓ | Dr. | $200 |
| Rental Income | Revenue | ↑ | Cr. | $200 |

Adjustment C: Supplies on Hand, $300. Because $500 worth of supplies were used up, Supplies Expense is increased and the asset Supplies is decreased.

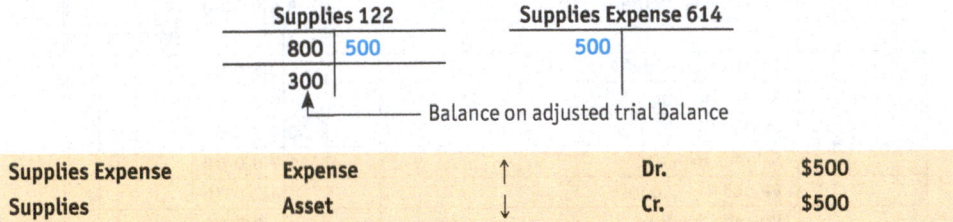

| Supplies Expense | Expense | ↑ | Dr. | $500 |
| Supplies | Asset | ↓ | Cr. | $500 |

Adjustment D: Insurance Expired, $300. Because insurance has expired by $300, Insurance Expense is increased by $300 and the asset Prepaid Insurance is decreased by $300.

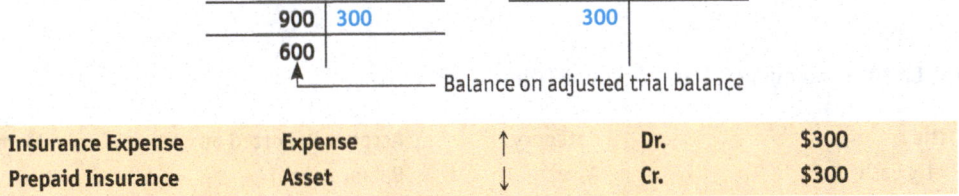

| Insurance Expense | Expense | ↑ | Dr. | $300 |
| Prepaid Insurance | Asset | ↓ | Cr. | $300 |

Adjustment E: Depreciation Expense, $50. When depreciation is taken, Depreciation Expense and Accumulated Depreciation are both increased by $50. Note that the cost of the store equipment remains the same.

Store Equipment 125	Accumulated Depreciation, Store Equipment 126	Depreciation Expense, Store Equipment 613
4,000 (remains unchanged)	400 / 50 / 450	50

Balance on adjusted trial balance

| Dep. Exp., Store Equip. | Expense | ↑ | Dr. | $50 |
| Acc. Dep., Store Equip. | Contra-Asset | ↑ | Cr. | $50 |

Adjustment F: Salaries Accrued, $600. The $600 in accrued salaries causes an increase in Salaries Expense and Salaries Payable.

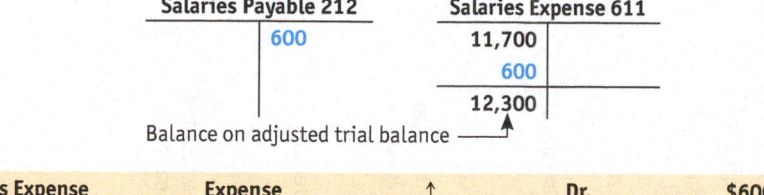

Salaries Payable 212		Salaries Expense 611	
	600	11,700	
		600	
		12,300	

Balance on adjusted trial balance ⟶

Salaries Expense	Expense	↑	Dr.	$600
Salaries Payable	Liability	↑	Cr.	$600

Figure 11.5 shows the worksheet with the adjustments and adjusted trial balance columns filled out.

The next step in completing the worksheet is to fill out the income statement columns from the adjusted trial balance, as shown in Figure 11.6 on page 374.

Figure 11.5 Worksheet with Six Columns

	Trial Balance Dr.	Trial Balance Cr.	Adjustments Dr.	Adjustments Cr.	Adjusted Trial Balance Dr.	Adjusted Trial Balance Cr.
Cash	12 9 2 0 00				12 9 2 0 00	
Petty Cash	1 0 0 00				1 0 0 00	
Accounts Receivable	14 5 0 0 00				14 5 0 0 00	
Merchandise Inventory	19 0 0 0 00			(A) 5 0 0 00	18 5 0 0 00	
Supplies	8 0 0 00			(C) 5 0 0 00	3 0 0 00	
Prepaid Insurance	9 0 0 00			(D) 3 0 0 00	6 0 0 00	
Store Equipment	4 0 0 0 00				4 0 0 0 00	
Acc. Dep., Store Equipment		4 0 0 00		(E) 5 0 00		4 5 0 00
Accounts Payable		17 9 0 0 00				17 9 0 0 00
Federal Income Tax Payable		8 0 0 00				8 0 0 00
FICA—Soc. Sec. Payable		4 5 4 00				4 5 4 00
FICA—Medicare Payable		1 0 6 00				1 0 6 00
State Income Tax Payable		2 0 0 00				2 0 0 00
SUTA Tax Payable		1 0 8 00				1 0 8 00
FUTA Tax Payable		3 2 00				3 2 00
Unearned Rent		6 0 0 00	(B) 2 0 0 00			4 0 0 00
Mortgage Payable		2 3 2 0 00				2 3 2 0 00
Art Newner, Capital		7 9 0 5 00				7 9 0 5 00
Art Newner, Withdrawals	8 6 0 0 00				8 6 0 0 00	
Sales		95 0 0 0 00				95 0 0 0 00
Sales Returns and Allowances	9 5 0 00				9 5 0 00	
Sales Discount	6 7 0 00				6 7 0 00	
Cost of Goods Sold	50 9 1 0 00		(A) 5 0 0 00		51 4 1 0 00	
Salaries Expense	11 7 0 0 00		(F) 6 0 0 00		12 3 0 0 00	
Payroll Tax Expense	4 2 0 00				4 2 0 00	
Postage Expense	2 5 00				2 5 00	
Miscellaneous Expense	3 0 00				3 0 00	
Interest Expense	3 0 0 00				3 0 0 00	
Totals	125 8 2 5 00	125 8 2 5 00				
Rental Income				(B) 2 0 0 00		2 0 0 00
Supplies Expense			(C) 5 0 0 00		5 0 0 00	
Insurance Expense			(D) 3 0 0 00		3 0 0 00	
Depreciation Expense, Store Equip.			(E) 5 0 00		5 0 00	
Salaries Payable				(F) 6 0 0 00		6 0 0 00
Totals			2 1 5 0 00	2 1 5 0 00	126 4 7 5 00	126 4 7 5 00

Figure 11.6 Income Statement Section of the Worksheet

Account Titles	Income Statement Dr.	Income Statement Cr.
Sales		95 000 00
Sales Returns and Allowances	9 50 00	
Sales Discounts	6 70 00	
Cost of Goods Sold	51 41 0 00	
Salaries Expense	12 30 0 00	
Payroll Tax Expense	4 2 0 00	
Postage Expense	2 5 00	
Miscellaneous Expense	3 0 00	
Interest Expense	3 0 0 00	
Rental Income		2 0 0 00
Supplies Expense	5 0 0 00	
Insurance Expense	3 0 0 00	
Depreciation Expense, Store Equipment	5 0 00	
Salaries Payable		
	66 9 5 5 00	95 2 0 0 00
Net Income	28 2 4 5 00	
	95 2 0 0 00	95 2 0 0 00

$95,000 is the credit balance of Sales. The Sales Returns and Allowances, $950, and Sales Discounts, $670, are placed on the debit side, which represents a reduction to total sales:

(Cr.) Sales
(Dr.) Less: Sales Returns and Allowances
(Dr.) Less: Sales Discounts

The Cost of Goods Sold account has been updated to reflect the actual physical count numbers.

Rental Income, which falls under the category "other income" for Art's Wholesale (other income is used as this is not his day-to-day revenue source), is increased by $200 because the first month's rental agreement has been fulfilled.

The next step in completing the worksheet is to fill out the balance sheet columns (Figure 11.7). Note how ending inventory is carried over to the balance sheet from the adjusted trial balance column. Take time also to look at the placement of the payroll tax liabilities as well as Unearned Rent on the worksheet.

Figure 11.8 is the completed worksheet.

Figure 11.7 Balance Sheet Section of the Worksheet

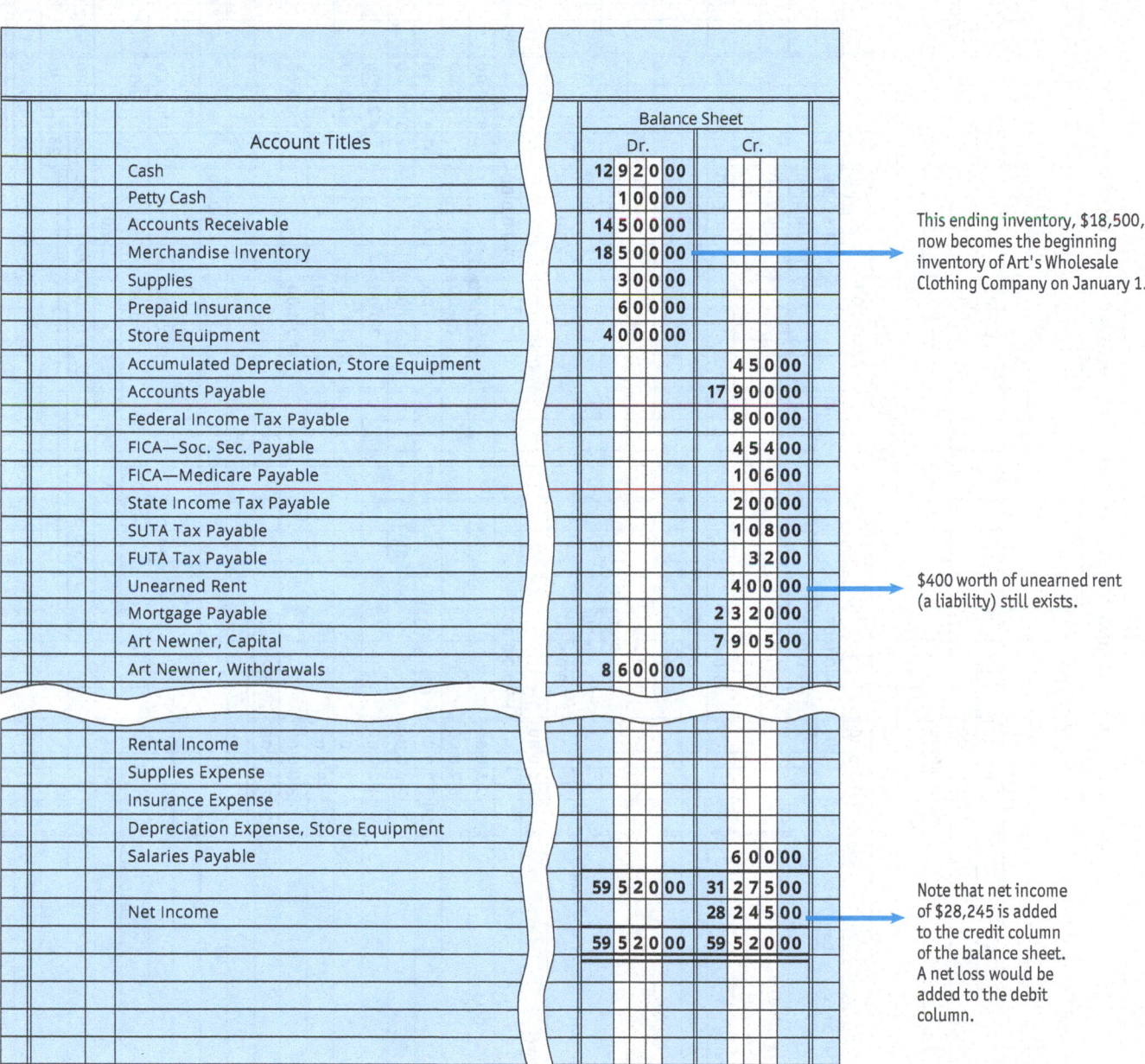

Account Titles	Balance Sheet Dr.	Balance Sheet Cr.	
Cash	12 9 2 0 00		This ending inventory, $18,500, now becomes the beginning inventory of Art's Wholesale Clothing Company on January 1.
Petty Cash	1 0 0 00		
Accounts Receivable	14 5 0 0 00		
Merchandise Inventory	18 5 0 0 00		
Supplies	3 0 0 00		
Prepaid Insurance	6 0 0 00		
Store Equipment	4 0 0 0 00		
Accumulated Depreciation, Store Equipment		4 5 0 00	
Accounts Payable		17 9 0 0 00	
Federal Income Tax Payable		8 0 0 00	
FICA—Soc. Sec. Payable		4 5 4 00	
FICA—Medicare Payable		1 0 6 00	
State Income Tax Payable		2 0 0 00	
SUTA Tax Payable		1 0 8 00	
FUTA Tax Payable		3 2 00	
Unearned Rent		4 0 0 00	$400 worth of unearned rent (a liability) still exists.
Mortgage Payable		2 3 2 0 00	
Art Newner, Capital		7 9 0 5 00	
Art Newner, Withdrawals	8 6 0 0 00		
Rental Income			
Supplies Expense			
Insurance Expense			
Depreciation Expense, Store Equipment			
Salaries Payable		6 0 0 00	
	59 5 2 0 00	31 2 7 5 00	Note that net income of $28,245 is added to the credit column of the balance sheet. A net loss would be added to the debit column.
Net Income		28 2 4 5 00	
	59 5 2 0 00	59 5 2 0 00	

Figure 11.8 Completed Worksheet

ART'S WHOLESALE CLOTHING COMPANY WORKSHEET FOR THE YEAR ENDED DECEMBER 31, 2019

Account Titles	Trial Balance Dr.	Trial Balance Cr.	Adjustments Dr.	Adjustments Cr.	Adjusted Trial Balance Dr.	Adjusted Trial Balance Cr.	Income Statement Dr.	Income Statement Cr.	Balance Sheet Dr.	Balance Sheet Cr.
Cash	12920 00				12920 00				12920 00	
Petty Cash	100 00				100 00				100 00	
Accounts Receivable	14500 00				14500 00				14500 00	
Merchandise Inventory	19000 00			(A) 500 00	18500 00				18500 00	
Supplies	800 00			(C) 500 00	300 00				300 00	
Prepaid Insurance	900 00			(D) 300 00	600 00				600 00	
Store Equipment	4000 00				4000 00				4000 00	
Accumulated Depreciation, Store Equipment		400 00		(E) 50 00		450 00				450 00
Accounts Payable		17900 00				17900 00				17900 00
Federal Income Tax Payable		800 00				800 00				800 00
FICA—Soc. Sec. Payable		454 00				454 00				454 00
FICA—Medicare Payable		106 00				106 00				106 00
State Income Tax Payable		200 00				200 00				200 00
SUTA Tax Payable		108 00				108 00				108 00
FUTA Tax Payable		32 00				32 00				32 00
Unearned Rent		600 00	(B) 200 00			400 00				400 00
Mortgage Payable		2320 00				2320 00				2320 00
Art Newner, Capital		7905 00				7905 00				7905 00
Art Newner, Withdrawals	8600 00				8600 00				8600 00	
Sales		95000 00				95000 00		95000 00		
Sales Returns and Allowances	950 00				950 00		950 00			
Sales Discounts	670 00				670 00		670 00			
Cost of Goods Sold	50910 00		(A) 500 00		51410 00		51410 00			
Salaries Expense	11700 00		(F) 600 00		12300 00		12300 00			
Payroll Tax Expense	420 00				420 00		420 00			
Postage Expense	25 00				25 00		25 00			
Miscellaneous Expense	30 00				30 00		30 00			
Interest Expense	300 00				300 00		300 00			
	125825 00	125825 00								
Rental Income				(B) 200 00		200 00		200 00		
Supplies Expense			(C) 500 00		500 00		500 00			
Insurance Expense			(D) 300 00		300 00		300 00			
Depreciation Expense, Store Equipment			(E) 50 00		50 00		50 00			
Salaries Payable				(F) 600 00		600 00				600 00
			2150 00	2150 00	126475 00	126475 00	66955 00	95200 00	59520 00	31275 00
Net Income							28245 00			28245 00
							95200 00	95200 00	59520 00	59520 00

376

Now let's check your progress.

▶ TRY IT!   Learning Unit 11-2

The following is a partial trial balance along with adjustment data. Complete a partial worksheet for Blue Company.

Partial Worksheet

	Trial Balance		Adjustments		Adjusted Trial Balance		Income Statement		Balance Sheet	
	Dr.	Cr.	Dr.	Cr.	Dr.	Cr.	Dr.	Cr.	Dr.	Cr.
Cash	4,000									
Merchandise Inventory	2,000									
Prepaid Rent	600									
Prepaid Insurance	900									
Pet Equipment	3,000									
Accum. Dep., Pet Equipment		1,000								
Unearned Pet Training Fees		700								
Accounts Payable		4,800								
P. Blue, Capital		3,500								
Pet Training Fees Earned		2,000								
Cost of Goods Sold		1,500								
Totals	12,000	12,000								

Adjustment Data

Rent Expired	$100
Insurance Expired	200
Depreciation Expense	300
Earned Pet Training Fees	400
Ending Merchandise Inventory	500

TRY IT!   Solution Learning Unit 11-2

Accounts	Trial Balance		Adjustments		Adjusted Trial Balance		Income Statement		Balance Sheet	
	Dr.	Cr.	Dr.	Cr.	Dr.	Cr.	Dr.	Cr.	Dr.	Cr.
Cash	4,000				4,000				4,000	
Merchandise Inv.	2,000			1,500	500				500	
Prepaid Rent	600			100	500				500	
Prepaid Insurance	900			200	700				700	
Pet Equipment	3,000				3,000				3,000	
Acc. Dep., Pet Equip.		1,000		300		1,300				1,300
Unearned Pet Training Fees		700	400			300				300
Accounts Payable		4,800				4,800				4,800
P. Blue, Capital		3,500				3,500				3,500
Pet Training Fees Earned		2,000		400		2,400		2,400		
Cost of Goods Sold	1,500		1,500		3,000		3,000			
Totals	12,000	12,000								
Rent Expense			100		100		100			
Insurance Expense			200		200		200			
Dep. Expense, Pet Equip.			300		300		300			
Totals			2,500	2,500	12,300	12,300	3,600	2,400		
Net Loss								1,200	1,200	
Totals							3,600	3,600	9,900	9,900

L01, 2

DEMONSTRATION SUMMARY PROBLEM

Requirement

From the following trial balance of Ledger Sport Shop for March 31 and adjustment data, complete the worksheet:

Ledger Sport Shop
Trial Balance
March 31, 201X

	Dr.	Cr.
Cash	6,000	
Merchandise Inventory	800	
Prepaid Rent	600	
Prepaid Insurance	500	
Display Equipment	3,000	
Accumulated Depr., Display Equip.		2,000
Unearned Training Fees		3,000
Accounts Payable		7,000
J. Loy, Capital		7,000
Sales		9,600
Sales Returns and Allowances	500	
Sales Discount	300	
Cost of Goods Sold	15,000	
Salary Expense	1,400	
Plumbing Expense	200	
Utilities Expense	300	
Totals	28,600	28,600

Additional Data (March 31, 201X)

a. Ending Merchandise Inventory $400
b. Training Fees Earned $200
c. Insurance Expired $100
d. Prepaid Rent Expired $300
e. Depreciation Expense, Display Equip. $100
f. Salaries Payable $500

Tips for Adjustments

The adjustment for Merchandise Inventory lowers the inventory balance to its new level. The credit for Merchandise Inventory goes on credit side of the adjustments column and the cost of goods sold is entered on debit column of adjustments.

Solutions

The completed worksheet:

Ledger Sport Shop
Worksheet
For month ended March 31, 201X

	Trial Balance Dr.	Trial Balance Cr.		Adjustments Dr.	Adjustments Cr.	Adj TB Dr.	Adj TB Cr.	Income Statement Dr.	Income Statement Cr.	Balance Sheet Dr.	Balance Sheet Cr.
Cash	6,000					6,000				6,000	
Merchandise Inv.	800		a		400	400				400	
Prepaid Rent	600		d		300	300				300	
Prepaid Insurance	500		c		100	400				400	
Display Equip	3,000					3,000				3,000	
Accum Dep, Disp Equip		2,000	e		100		2,100				2,100
Unearned Training Fees		3,000	b	200			2,800				2,800
Accounts Payable		7,000					7,000				7,000
J. Loy, Capital		7,000					7,000				7,000
Sales		9,600					9,600		9,600		
Sales Returns & Allow	500					500		500			
Sales Discounts	300					300		300			
COGS	15,000		a	400		15,400		15,400			
Salary Expense	1,400		f	500		1,900		1,900			
Plumbing Expense	200					200		200			
Utilities Expense	300					300		300			
Totals	**28,600**	**28,600**									
Training Fees Earned			b		200		200		200		
Insurance Expense			c	100		100		100			
Rent Expense			d	300		300		300			
Depreciation Expense			e	100		100		100			
Accrued Salaries Payable			f		500		500				500
				1,600	**1,600**	**29,200**	**29,200**	**19,100**	**9,800**	**10,100**	**19,400**
Net Income (Loss)									**9,300**	**9,300**	
Totals								**19,100**	**19,100**	**19,400**	**19,400**

Tip to Complete a Worksheet

Note that we have a net loss. If we had a net income, the $9,300 would have been in the debit column of the income statement and the credit column of the balance sheet.

SUCCESS COACH

The following Success Tips are from Learning Units 11-1 and 11-2. Take the Do It Right Now Checkup and use the Check Your Score at the bottom of the page to see how you are doing. The Success Coach provides tips before each Checkup to help you avoid common accounting errors.

LU 11-1 Adjustments for Merchandise Inventory Using the Perpetual Method, Unearned Rent, Supplies Used, Insurance Expired, Depreciation Expense, and Salaries Accrued

Do It Right Tips: The purpose of the adjustment for Merchandise Inventory is to adjust the balance in the Merchandise Inventory account to reflect the amount from when you counted all your inventory. Unearned Rent is not a revenue account; it is a liability. Revenue will be recognized when it is earned, and that is when an entry is made reducing the Unearned Rent and crediting Rental Revenue.

Do It Right Now Checkup: Answer true or false to the following statements.

1. Merchandise Inventory is lowered when there is inventory shrinkage.
2. When unearned rent is earned, the liability will go up.
3. The ending merchandise inventory of one period can never be the new inventory of the next period.

LU 11-2 Worksheets for Merchandise Companies

Do It Right Tips: Before you complete the worksheet, make sure you review this table:

Account	Category	Normal Balance	Financial Statement Found
Sales	Revenue	Credit balance	Income statement
Sales Returns and Allowances	Revenue (contra)	Debit balance	Income statement
Unearned Rent/Unearned Revenue	Liability	Credit balance	Balance sheet
Cost of Goods Sold	Expense	Debit balance	Income statement

Do It Right Now Checkup: Answer true or false to the following statements.

1. If there is inventory shrinkage (i.e., the physical count is lower than what the Merchandise Inventory account shows), we credit the Merchandise Inventory account.
2. Unearned Rent Revenue goes in the debit column of the balance sheet section of the worksheet.
3. Accumulated Depreciation goes in the credit column of the balance sheet section of the worksheet.

CHECK YOUR SCORE: Answers to Do It Right Now Checkup

LU 11-1

1. True.
2. False—When unearned rent is earned, the liability will go down.
3. False—The ending inventory of one period always becomes the new inventory of the next period.

LU 11-2

1. True.
2. False—Unearned Rent Revenue goes in the credit column of the balance sheet section of the worksheet.
3. True.

BLUEPRINT: A WORKSHEET FOR A MERCHANDISE COMPANY

Account Titles	Adjustments Dr.	Adjustments Cr.	Adjusted Trial Balance Dr.	Adjusted Trial Balance Cr.	Income Statement Dr.	Income Statement Cr.	Balance Sheet Dr.	Balance Sheet Cr.
Cash			X				X	
Petty Cash			X				X	
Accounts Receivable			X				X	
Merchandise Inventory			X				X	
Supplies			X				X	
Equipment			X				X	
Acc. Dep., Store Equipment				X				X
Accounts Payable				X				X
Federal Income Tax Payable				X				X
FICA—Social Security Payable				X				X
FICA—Medicare Payable				X				X
State Income Tax Payable				X				X
SUTA Tax Payable				X				X
FUTA Tax Payable				X				X
Unearned Rent				X				X
Mortgage Payable				X				X
A. Flynn, Capital				X				X
A. Flynn, Withdrawals			X				X	
Sales				X		X		
Sales Returns and Allow.			X		X			
Sales Discount			X		X			
Cost of goods sold			X		X			
Salaries Expense			X		X			
Payroll Tax Expense			X		X			
Insurance Expense			X		X			
Depreciation Expense			X		X			
Salaries Payable				X				X
Rental Income				X		X		

Discussion Questions and Critical Thinking/Ethical Case

1. When would a company consider using a periodic inventory system?

2. When would a company consider using a perpetual inventory system?

3. A low-volume, high-unit-price inventory requires a company to use a periodic inventory system. Accept or reject this statement and support your answer.

4. Explain why unearned revenue is a liability account.

5. What is the purpose of an inventory physical count?

6. Why do many unearned revenue accounts have to be adjusted?

7. Jim Heary is the custodian of petty cash. Jim, who is short on personal cash, decided to pay his home electrical and phone bills from petty cash. He plans to pay it back next month. Do you feel Jim should do so? You make the call. Write down your specific recommendations to Jim.

MyLabAccounting

Concept Checks

(10 min) **LO1**

Adjustment for Merchandise Inventory

1. Given the following, journalize the adjusting entry for Merchandise Inventory. Note that physical count of inventory showed a balance of $59,500.

Merchandise Inventory 114	Cost of Goods Sold 513
60,000	

(15 min) **LO1**

Adjustment for Unearned Fees

2. a. Given the following, journalize the adjusting entry. By December 31, $200 of the unearned dog walking fees were earned.

Unearned Dog Walking Fees 225		Earned Dog Walking Fees 441	
940	12/1/1X	4,800	12/1/1X

   b. What is the account category of unearned dog walking fees?

(10 min) **LO2**

Worksheet

3. Match each of the five items listed below with one of the following locations:
   1. Located on the Income Statement debit column of the worksheet
   2. Located on the Income Statement credit column of the worksheet
   3. Located on the Balance Sheet debit column of the worksheet
   4. Located on the Balance Sheet credit column of the worksheet
      a. Sales Returns and Allowances
      b. Accrued Salaries Payable
      c. Sales
      d. Merchandise Inventory
      e. Accounts Receivable

(10 min) **LO1**

Merchandise Inventory Adjustment on Worksheet

4. Given Merchandise Inventory of $2,000 and a physical count of inventory that reflected a balance of $1,950, what would be the adjusting entry?

Exercises

Set A

11A-1. Indicate the normal balance and category of each of the following accounts:
  a. Cost of Goods Sold
  b. Merchandise Inventory
  c. Payroll Tax Expense
  d. Sales Discount
  e. Federal Income Tax Payable
  f. Unearned Revenue

 **LO1** *(10 min)*

11A-2. From the following, calculate (a) net sales, (b) gross profit, and (c) net income.
  Data Sales, $22,000; Sales Discount, $500; Sales Returns and Allowances, $250; Cost of Goods Sold, $13,200; Operating Expenses, $3,600.

LO1 *(15 min)*

11A-3. Little Co. had the following balances on December 31, 201X:

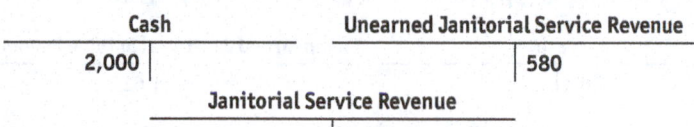

LO1 *(10 min)*

The accountant for Little has asked you to make an adjustment because $420 of janitorial services has just been performed for customers who had paid for 2 months. Construct a transaction analysis chart.

11A-4. Prepare a worksheet for Moore Co. from the following trial balance and additional data.

LO2 *(20 min)*

Additional Data

  a. Inventory physical count $13
  b. Store supplies on hand 4
  c. Depreciation on store equipment 4
  d. Accrued salaries 2

MOORE CO. TRIAL BALANCE DECEMBER 31, 2018	Dr.	Cr.
Cash	8 00	
Accounts Receivable	5 00	
Merchandise Inventory	1 1 00	
Store Supplies	1 0 00	
Store Equipment	2 0 00	
Accumulated Depreciation, Store Equipment		6 00
Accounts Payable		5 00
J. Moore, Capital		3 4 00
Sales		6 4 00
Sales Returns and Allowances	9 00	
Cost of Goods Sold	2 3 00	
Salaries Expense	1 0 00	
Advertising Expense	1 3 00	
Totals	1 0 9 00	1 0 9 00

Figure 11.9
Trial Balance for Moore Co.

Set B

(10 min) **LO1** ▶ **11B-1.** Indicate the normal balance and category of each of the following accounts:
  a. Sales Returns and Allowances
  b. Merchandise Inventory
  c. Miscellaneous Income
  d. Payroll Tax Expense
  e. Sales Discounts
  f. Cost of Goods Sold
  g. Income Tax Payable
  h. Prepaid Expenses

(15 min) **LO1** ▶ **11B-2.** From the following, calculate (a) net sales, (b) gross profit, and (c) net income. Data Sales, $35,000; Sales Discounts, $800; Sales Returns and Allowances, $5,000; Cost of Goods Sold, $13,700; Operating Expenses, $4,900.

(10 min) **LO1** ▶ **11B-3.** Bates Co. had the following balances on December 31, 201X:

Cash	Unearned Janitorial Service Revenue
1,700	610

Janitorial Service Revenue
7,400

The accountant for Bates has asked you to make an adjustment because $430 of janitorial services has just been performed for customers who had paid for 2 months. Construct a transaction analysis chart.

(20 min) **LO2** ▶ **11B-4.** Prepare a worksheet for Moore Co. from the following trial balance and additional data:
  a. Inventory physical count $11
  b. Store supplies on hand 5
  c. Depreciation on store equipment 7
  d. Accrued salaries payable 3

Figure 11.10
Trial Balance for Moore Co.

MOORE CO. TRIAL BALANCE DECEMBER 31, 2018	Dr.	Cr.
Cash	9 00	
Accounts Receivable	8 00	
Merchandise Inventory	12 00	
Store Supplies	9 00	
Store Equipment	24 00	
Accumulated Depreciation, Store Equipment		7 00
Accounts Payable		6 00
J. Moore, Capital		38 00
Sales		67 00
Sales Returns and Allowances	7 00	
Cost of Goods Sold	26 00	
Salaries Expense	12 00	
Advertising Expense	11 00	
Totals	118 00	118 00

Problems

MyLabAccounting

Set A

You can also use the foldout worksheets at the end of the working papers that accompany this text.

11A-1. On the basis of the accounts listed below, calculate
  a. Net sales
  b. Cost of goods sold (after adjustment)
  c. Gross profit
  d. Net income

 **L01** *(30 min)*

Accounts Payable	$ 6,000
Operating Expenses	2,000
J. Jensen, Capital	19,400
Cost of Goods Sold	4,137
Ending Inventory, December 31, 2019	1,250
Sales	10,210
Accounts Receivable	1,489
Cash	756
Sales Returns and Allowances	275
Physical Count of Inventory December 31, 2019	1,200
Sales Discount	394

Check Figure:
Net Income $3,354

11A-2. From the following trial balance and additional data, complete a worksheet for Jim's Hardware:

L01,2 *(60 min)*

Additional Data

  a. Physical count of inventory on December 31, $615
  b. Insurance expired, $150
  c. Depreciation expense on store equipment, $60
  d. Accrued wages, $90

Figure 11.11
Trial Balance for Jim's Hardware

Check Figure:
Net Income $2,289

JIM'S HARDWARE TRIAL BALANCE DECEMBER 31, 2018	Dr.	Cr.
Cash	7 8 6 00	
Accounts Receivable	1 1 5 2 00	
Merchandise Inventory	6 0 0 00	
Prepaid Insurance	6 8 4 00	
Store Equipment	2 1 6 0 00	
Accumulated Depreciation, Store Equipment		6 6 0 00
Accounts Payable		5 1 6 00
Jim Spool, Capital		1 6 3 2 00
Sales		11 0 4 0 00
Sales Returns and Allowances	5 4 6 00	
Sales Discounts	2 1 6 00	
Cost of Goods Sold	4 9 8 6 00	
Wages Expense	1 7 1 6 00	
Rent Expense	7 9 2 00	
Telephone Expense	1 1 4 00	
Miscellaneous Expense	9 6 00	
	13 8 4 8 00	13 8 4 8 00

(60 min) **LO1,2**

11A-3. The owner of Waltz Company has asked you to prepare a worksheet from the following trial balance and additional data:

Additional Data

a. Physical count of inventory on December 31, $4,805
b. Office supplies used up, $210
c. Rent expired, $195
d. Depreciation expense on office equipment, $550
e. Office salaries earned but not paid, $310

Figure 11.12
Trial Balance for Waltz Company

Check Figure:
Net Income $8,300

WALTZ COMPANY TRIAL BALANCE DECEMBER 31, 2020		
	Dr.	Cr.
Cash	5 4 0 8 00	
Petty Cash	2 4 0 00	
Accounts Receivable	2 5 1 2 00	
Merchandise Inventory	5 0 9 2 00	
Prepaid Rent	6 1 6 00	
Office Supplies	9 4 4 00	
Office Equipment	9 2 8 0 00	
Accumulated Depreciation, Office Equipment		7 6 0 0 00
Accounts Payable		5 9 6 4 00
K. Waltz, Capital		5 4 7 6 00
K. Waltz, Withdrawals	4 8 0 0 00	
Sales		52 4 8 4 00
Sales Returns and Allowances	9 6 00	
Sales Discounts	2 4 0 0 00	
Cost of Goods Sold	28 9 5 2 00	
Office Salaries Expense	7 4 0 8 00	
Insurance Expense	2 4 0 0 00	
Advertising Expense	8 0 0 00	
Utilities Expense	5 7 6 00	
	71 5 2 4 00	71 5 2 4 00

(60 min) **LO1,2**

11A-4. From the following trial balance and additional data, complete the worksheet for Ron's Wholesale Clothing Company.

Additional Data

a. Physical count of inventory on December 31, $8,500
b. Supplies on hand, $400
c. Insurance expired, $600
d. Depreciation expense on store equipment, $400
e. Storage fees earned, $176

RON'S WHOLESALE CLOTHING COMPANY TRIAL BALANCE DECEMBER 31, 2019	Dr.	Cr.
Cash	4 4 6 0 00	
Petty Cash	3 0 0 00	
Accounts Receivable	7 5 0 0 00	
Merchandise Inventory	9 0 0 0 00	
Supplies	1 0 0 0 00	
Prepaid Insurance	8 5 0 00	
Store Equipment	2 5 0 0 00	
Accumulated Depreciation, Store Equipment		1 5 0 0 00
Accounts Payable		10 6 3 5 00
Federal Income Tax Payable		1 0 6 0 00
FICA-Social Security Payable		1 0 8 00
FICA-Medicare		1 5 0 00
Unearned Storage Fees		3 5 7 00
Ron Win, Capital		12 5 0 0 00
Ron Win, Withdrawals	4 3 0 0 00	
Sales		45 0 0 0 00
Sales Returns and Allowances	1 4 7 5 00	
Sales Discount	1 3 3 5 00	
Cost of Goods Sold	25 2 7 5 00	
Salaries Expense	12 0 0 0 00	
Payroll Tax Expense	4 2 0 00	
Interest Expense	8 9 5 00	
	71 3 1 0 00	71 3 1 0 00

Figure 11.13
Trial Balance for Ron's Wholesale Clothing Company

Check Figure:
Net Income $1,676

Set B

11B-1. From the following accounts, calculate (a) net sales, (b) cost of goods sold (after adjustment), (c) gross profit, and (d) net income.

 **L01** *(30 min)*

Sales Discounts	$ 500
Physical Count of Inventory, December 31, 2019	79
Sales Returns and Allowances	$ 191
Cash	3,895
Accounts Receivable	441
Sales	3,950
Ending Inventory, December 31, 2019	75
Cost of Goods Sold	1,087
R. Roland, Capital	1,950
Operating Expenses	895
Accounts Payable	129

Check Figure:
Net Income $1,281

11B-2. As the accountant for Jim's Hardware, you have been asked to com-plete a worksheet from the following trial balance as well as additional data.

 **L01,2** *(60 min)*

Additional Data

a. Physical count of inventory on December 31, $836
b. Insurance expired, $112
c. Depreciation expense on store equipment, $90
d. Accrued wages, $150

Figure 11.14
Trial Balance for Jim's Hardware

JIM'S HARDWARE TRIAL BALANCE DECEMBER 31, 2018	Dr.	Cr.
Cash	9 6 0 00	
Accounts Receivable	1 6 0 0 00	
Merchandise Inventory	7 3 6 00	
Prepaid Insurance	1 1 1 2 00	
Store Equipment	3 2 0 0 00	
Accumulated Depreciation, Store Equipment		1 6 8 0 00
Accounts Payable		1 4 0 8 00
J. Spool, Capital		2 5 7 6 00
Sales		14 8 0 0 00
Sales Returns and Allowances	7 2 8 00	
Sales Discounts	6 8 8 00	
Cost of Goods Sold	6 6 0 0 00	
Wages Expense	2 3 0 4 00	
Rent Expense	1 8 4 0 00	
Telephone Expense	5 5 2 00	
Miscellaneous Expense	1 4 4 00	
	20 4 6 4 00	20 4 6 4 00

(60 min) **L01,2**

11B-3. From the following, complete a worksheet for Waltz Company from the following trial balance and additional data.

Additional Data

a. Physical count of inventory on December 31, $5,000
b. Office supplies on hand, $470
c. Rent expired, $600
d. Depreciation expense on office equipment, $250
e. Salaries accrued, $180

Figure 11.15
Trial Balance for Waltz Company

WALTZ COMPANY TRIAL BALANCE DECEMBER 31, 2020	Dr.	Cr.
Cash	3 8 0 0 00	
Petty Cash	1 0 0 00	
Accounts Receivable	3 4 0 0 00	
Merchandise Inventory	5 2 0 4 00	
Prepaid Rent	1 2 0 0 00	
Office Supplies	1 3 6 0 00	
Office Equipment	9 6 8 0 00	
Accumulated Depreciation, Office Equipment		4 0 4 0 00
Accounts Payable		7 9 6 4 00
K. Waltz, Capital		5 4 7 6 00
K. Waltz, Withdrawals	5 0 0 0 00	
Sales		52 4 6 2 00
Sales Returns and Allowances	1 1 6 00	
Sales Discounts	2 2 0 0 00	
Cost of Goods Sold	26 7 3 8 00	
Office Salaries Expense	7 4 0 8 00	
Insurance Expense	2 2 0 0 00	
Advertising Expense	8 0 0 00	
Utilities Expense	7 3 6 00	
	69 9 4 2 00	69 9 4 2 00

11B-4. From the following trial balance and additional data, complete the worksheet for Ron's Wholesale Clothing Company.

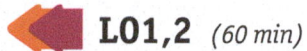
L01,2 *(60 min)*

Additional Data

a. Physical count of inventory on December 31, $3,950
b. Supplies on hand, $50
c. Insurance expired, $55
d. Depreciation expense on store equipment, $100
e. Storage fees earned, $115

Figure 11.16
Trial Balance for Ron's Wholesale
Clothing Company

Check Figure:
Net Income $3,636

RON'S WHOLESALE CLOTHING COMPANY TRIAL BALANCE DECEMBER 31, 2019	Dr.	Cr.
Cash	2 6 0 0 00	
Petty Cash	3 0 00	
Accounts Receivable	3 0 0 0 00	
Merchandise Inventory	3 6 0 0 00	
Supplies	2 7 0 00	
Prepaid Insurance	1 8 0 00	
Store Equipment	1 0 0 0 00	
Accumulated Depreciation, Store Equipment		4 9 6 00
Accounts Payable		4 5 9 0 00
Federal Income Tax Payable		5 9 0 00
FICA - Soc. Sec. Payable		7 4 00
FICA - Medicare Payable		1 0 0 00
Unearned Storage Fees		3 5 0 00
Ron Win, Capital		2 7 3 4 00
Ron Win, Withdrawals	1 8 0 0 00	
Sales		19 4 0 0 00
Sales Returns and Allowances	5 6 0 00	
Sales Discounts	4 8 0 00	
Cost of Goods Sold	8 3 0 0 00	
Salaries Expense	6 0 0 0 00	
Payroll Tax Expense	1 9 4 00	
Interest Expense	3 2 0 00	
	28 3 3 4 00	28 3 3 4 00

Financial Report Problem

Reading Amazon's Annual Report

L01 *(10 min)*

Go to **https://tinyurl.com/slaterca14e** and find the Consolidated Statement of Income. What is the cost of goods sold (cost of sales) in 2016?

KEEPING IT REAL SUAREZ COMPUTER CENTER

MyLabAccounting

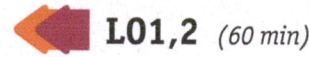
L01,2 *(60 min)*

The first 6 months of the year have concluded for Suarez Computer Center, and Falco wants to make the necessary adjustments to his accounts to prepare accurate financial statements.

Assignment

To prepare these adjustments, use the trial balance in Figure 11.17 and the following inventory that Falco took at the end of March:

Supplies

> 15 dozen ¼-inch screws at a cost of $15 a dozen
>
> 8 dozen ½-inch screws at a cost of $10 a dozen
>
> 4 feet of coaxial cable at a cost of $8 per foot

Figure 11.17
Trial Balance for Suarez
Computer Center

			SUAREZ COMPUTER CENTER TRIAL BALANCE MARCH 31, 201X				
					Trial Balance		
Account Titles				Dr.		Cr.	
Cash				11 5 7 6 29			
Petty Cash				3 0 0 00			
Accounts Receivable				12 3 7 0 00			
Merchandise Inventory				5 5 5 5 00			
Prepaid Rent				3 5 0 0 00			
Supplies				6 1 2 00			
Computer Shop Equipment				4 8 6 0 00			
Accumulated Depreciation, C. S. Equipment						1 0 5 00	
Office Equipment				2 1 7 5 00			
Accumulated Depreciation, Office Equipment						5 0 00	
Accounts Payable						3 3 8 0 00	
Falco, Capital						16 6 1 7 00	
Falco, Withdrawals				9 1 5 00			
Service Revenue						20 9 0 0 00	
Sales						11 6 8 0 00	
Sales Returns and Allowances				4 6 0 00			
Sales Discounts				2 4 3 00			
Cost of Goods Sold				7 2 2 5 00			
Advertising Expense							
Rent Expense							
Utilities Expense							
Phone Expense				1 5 5 00			
Supplies Expense				4 5 00			
Insurance Expense							
Postage Expense				4 0 00			
Miscellaneous Expense				1 5 00			
Wage Expense				2 4 2 5 00			
Payroll Tax Expense				2 6 0 71			
Totals				52 7 3 2 00		52 7 3 2 00	

Merchandise Inventory

A physical inventory taken on March 31 indicated that Merchandise Inventory remaining in stock was valued at $200.

Depreciation of Computer Equipment

> Computer depreciates at $35 a month; purchased July 5.
>
> Computer workstations depreciate at $35 per month; purchased September 17.
>
> Shop benches depreciate at $30 per month; purchased November 5.

Depreciation of Office Equipment

Office equipment depreciates at $25 per month; purchased July 17.
Fax machine depreciates at $15 per month; purchased November 20.
   Remember: If any long-term asset is purchased in the first 15 days of the month, Falco will charge depreciation for the full month. If an asset is purchased later than the 15th, he will not charge depreciation in the month it was purchased.

Expiration of Prepaid Rent

Six months' worth of rent at a rental rate of $500 per month has expired.
   Complete the 10-column worksheet for the 6 months ended March 31, 201X.

Completion of the Accounting Cycle for a Merchandise Company Using the Perpetual Inventory Method

12

CHAPTER PREVIEW: ACCOUNTING IN ACTION

Julie DeAngelo took her son to see a Pixar movie. After the show, Julie decided to go to the Disney Store to get a stuffed animal from the film. She knew the toy would be in stock. Stores like the Disney Store try to be competitive, but they have to make sure that they make a profit as well. Each year, companies prepare financial statements to see how their profit-making operations are performing. Two of the financial statements that they prepare are called the income statement and the balance sheet. In this chapter, you learn to prepare these two financial statements. The income statement will look at the company's revenues, amount of returns, cost of goods sold, and operating expenses. The balance sheet will provide a look at the company's assets, liabilities, and stockholders' equity on a certain date.

Learning Objectives

LO1 Prepare Financial Statements for a Merchandise Company Using the Perpetual Inventory Method

LO2 Complete Adjusting Entries, Closing Entries, and a Post-Closing Trial Balance for a Merchandise Company

LO3 Complete Reversing Entries

When you buy a toy at the Disney Store, just keep in mind all the steps the company must take to complete its accounting cycle. In this chapter, we discuss the steps involved in completing the accounting cycle for a merchandise company. These steps include preparing financial reports, journalizing and posting adjusting and closing entries, preparing a post-closing trial balance, and reversing entries.

LEARNING UNIT 12-1

L01

Financial Statements for Merchandise Companies Using the Perpetual Inventory Method

As we discussed in Chapter 5, when we were dealing with a service company rather than a merchandise company, the three financial statements can be prepared from the worksheet. Let's begin by looking at how Art's Wholesale Clothing Company prepares the income statement.

The Income Statement

Art is interested in knowing how well his business performed for the year ended December 31, 2019. What was its net sales? Were there many returns of goods from customers? What was the cost of the goods brought into the store versus the selling price received? What is the cost of the goods that have not been sold? The income statement in Figure 12.1 is prepared from the income statement columns of the worksheet. (Review it first, and then we will explain each section of the income statement and where the information came from on the worksheet.)

Note that there are no debit or credit columns on the formal income statement—the inside columns on financial reports are used for subtotaling, not for debit and credit.

Note also that the income statement is broken down into several sections. Remembering the sections can help you make sense of the statement and set it up correctly on your own. Basically what it presents is this:

	Net Sales
−	Cost of Goods Sold
=	Gross Profit
−	Operating Expenses
=	Net Income from Operations
+	Other Income
−	Other Expenses
=	Net Income

Let's take these sections one at a time and see where the figures come from on the worksheet.

Revenue Section: Net Sales. The first major category of the income statement shows net sales. The figure here of $93,380 is *not* found on the worksheet—the accountant must take the individual amounts for Gross Sales, Sales Returns and Allowances, and Sales Discounts found on the worksheet and *combine* them to arrive at a figure for net sales. Thus, although the worksheet has the individual components, it is not until the formal income statement that these individual amounts are summarized in one figure for net sales.

Cost of Goods Sold Section. As discussed in Chapter 11, the most important adjusting entry for a merchandising company compared to a service-industry company is to update the Merchandise Inventory account to reflect the numbers obtained in a physical count of inventory.

The entry would appear as follows if we had a shrinkage of $500:

SUCCESS TIP

Sales
− Sales Ret. & Allow.
− Sales Discount
= Net Sales

Dec.	31	Cost of Goods Sold	5 0 0 00	
		Merchandise Inventory		5 0 0 00

We will assume in Art's Wholesale Clothing Company that this is the first adjustment.

Figure 12.1 Partial Worksheet and Income Statement

ART'S WHOLESALE CLOTHING COMPANY
PARTIAL WORKSHEET FOR THE
YEAR ENDED DECEMBER 31, 2019

Account Titles	Income Statement	
	Dr.	Cr.
Sales		95 0 0 0 00
Sales Returns and Allowances	9 5 0 00	
Sales Discounts	6 7 0 00	
Cost of Goods Sold	51 4 1 0 00	
Salaries Expense	12 3 0 0 00	
Payroll Tax Expense	4 2 0 0 00	
Postage Expense	2 5 0 00	
Miscellaneous Expense	3 0 0 00	
Interest Expense	3 0 0 00	
Rental Income		2 0 0 00
Supplies Expense	5 0 0 00	
Insurance Expense	3 0 0 00	
Depreciation Expense, Store Equip.	5 0 00	
Accrued Salaries	66 9 5 5 00	95 2 0 0 00
Net Income	28 2 4 5 00	
	95 2 0 0 00	95 2 0 0 00

ART'S WHOLESALE CLOTHING COMPANY
INCOME STATEMENT
FOR THE YEAR ENDED DECEMBER 31, 2019

Revenue			
Gross Sales			$95 0 0 0 00
Less: Sales Ret. and Allow.	$9 5 0 00		
Sales Discounts	6 7 0 00	1 6 2 0 00	
Net Sales			93 3 8 0 00
Cost of Goods Sold			
Cost of Goods Sold			51 4 1 0 00
Gross Profit			41 9 7 0 00
Operating Expenses			
Salaries Expense	12 3 0 0 00		
Payroll Tax Expense	4 2 0 0 00		
Dep'n. Exp., Store Equip.	5 0 00		
Supplies Expense	5 0 0 00		
Insurance Expense	3 0 0 00		
Postage Expense	2 5 0 00		
Miscellaneous Expense	3 0 0 00		
Total Operating Expenses			13 6 2 5 00
Net Income from Operations			28 3 4 5 00
Other Income			
Rental Income		2 0 0 00	
Other Expenses			
Interest Expense		3 0 0 00	
Net Income			$28 2 4 5 00

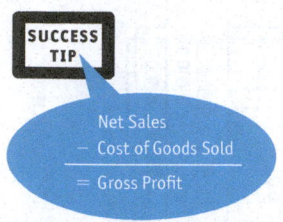

Net Sales
− Cost of Goods Sold
= Gross Profit

Selling expenses Operating expenses directly related to the sale of goods excluding Cost of Goods Sold.

Administrative expenses (general expenses) Operating expenses such as general office expenses that are incurred indirectly in the selling of goods.

Other income Any revenue other than revenue from sales and service revenue. It appears in a separate section on the income statement. Examples: Rental Income and Storage Fees.

Other expenses Nonoperating expenses that do not relate to the main operating activities of the business; they appear in a separate section on the income statement. One example given in the text is Interest Expense, interest owed on money borrowed by the company.

Classified balance sheet A balance sheet that categorizes assets as current assets or plant and equipment and groups liabilities as current or long-term liabilities.

Current assets Assets that can be converted into cash or used within 1 year or the normal operating cycle of the business, whichever is longer.

Operating cycle Average time it takes to buy and sell merchandise and then collect accounts receivable.

Gross Profit. The figure for gross profit ($41,970) is arrived at by subtracting Cost of Goods Sold from net sales ($93,380 − $51,410). The gross profit figure of $41,970 is not found by itself on the worksheet but, like others we have discussed, it is calculated by the accountant from separate figures on the worksheet.

Operating Expenses Section. The total of the operating expenses does not appear on its own on the worksheet; to get this figure of $13,625, the accountant adds up all the expenses on the worksheet that resulted from doing business.

Many companies break expenses down into those directly related to the selling activity of the company (selling expenses) and those related to administrative or office activity (administrative expenses or general expenses). Here's a sample list broken down into these two categories:

Operating Expenses

Selling Expenses	*Administrative Expenses*
Sales Salaries Expense	Rent Expense
Delivery Expense	Office Salaries Expense
Advertising Expense	Utilities Expense
Depreciation Expense, Store Equipment	Supplies Expense
Insurance Expense	Depreciation Expense, Office Equipment
Total Selling Expenses	Total Administrative Expenses

Other Income (or Other Revenue) Section. This section will record any Other Income or revenue besides revenue from sales not related to the main operating activities of the business. For example, Art's Wholesale Clothing Company makes a profit from subletting a portion of a building and earning monthly rental income of $200 and that income goes in this section.

Other Expenses Section. This section will record Other Expenses, nonoperating expenses—those not related to the main operating activities of the business. For example, Art's Wholesale Clothing Company has paid or owes $300 interest on money it has borrowed.

Statement of Owner's Equity

The information used to complete the statement of owner's equity comes from the balance sheet columns of the worksheet. Keep in mind that the capital account in the ledger should be checked to see if any additional investments have occurred during the period. Note in Figure 12.2 on page 397 that the worksheet aids in this. The ending figure of $27,550 for Art Newner, Capital, will be carried over to the balance sheet, which is the final report we will look at in this chapter.

The Balance Sheet

Figure 12.3 on page 398 shows how a worksheet is used to aid in the preparation of a Classified Balance sheet. A classified balance sheet breaks down the assets and liabilities into more detail. Classified balance sheets provide management, owners, creditors, and suppliers with more information about the company's ability to pay current and long-term debts. They also provide a more complete financial picture of the firm.

The categories on the classified balance sheet are as follows.

Current assets are defined as cash and assets that will be converted into cash or used up during the normal operating cycle of the company or 1 year, whichever is longer. (Think of the operating cycle as the time period it takes a company to buy and sell merchandise and then collect accounts receivable.)

Accountants list current assets in order of how easily they can be converted into cash (this is called *liquidity*). In most cases, Accounts Receivable can be turned into cash more

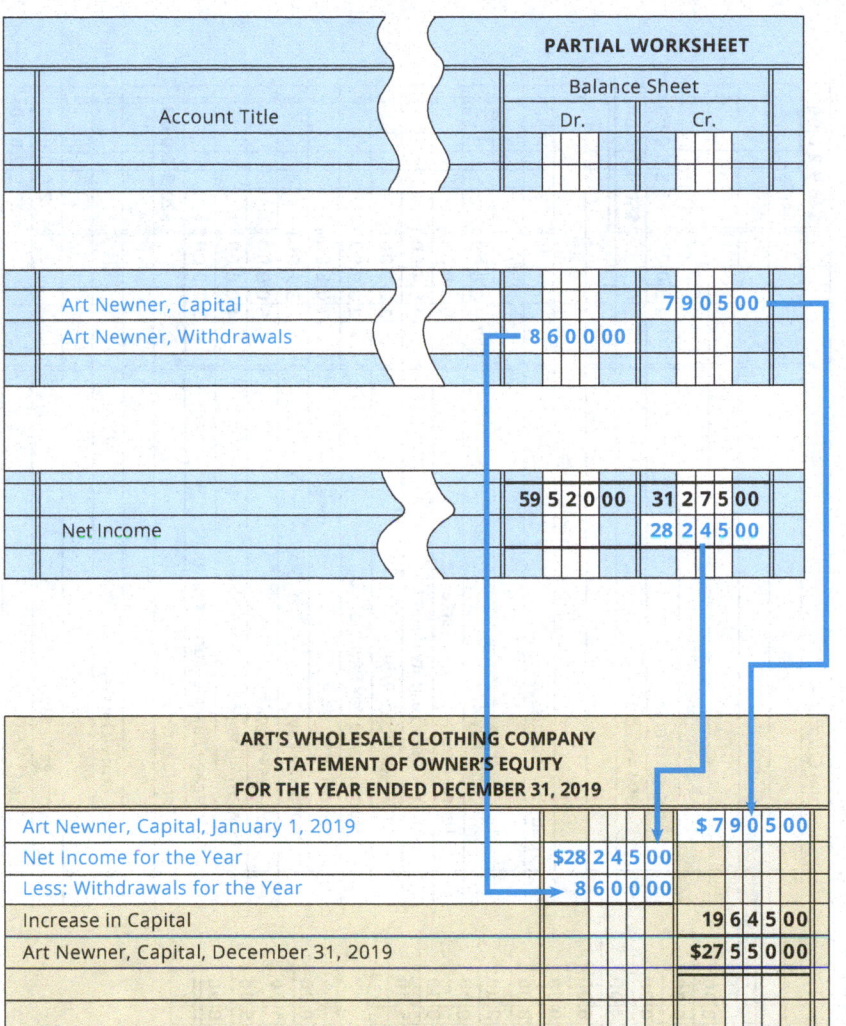

Figure 12.2
Preparing a Statement of Owner's Equity from the Worksheet

	PARTIAL WORKSHEET		
		Balance Sheet	
Account Title		Dr.	Cr.
Art Newner, Capital			7 9 0 5 00
Art Newner, Withdrawals		8 6 0 0 00	
Net Income		59 5 2 0 00	31 2 7 5 00
			28 2 4 5 00

ART'S WHOLESALE CLOTHING COMPANY STATEMENT OF OWNER'S EQUITY FOR THE YEAR ENDED DECEMBER 31, 2019		
Art Newner, Capital, January 1, 2019		$ 7 9 0 5 00
Net Income for the Year	$28 2 4 5 00	
Less: Withdrawals for the Year	8 6 0 0 00	
Increase in Capital		19 6 4 5 00
Art Newner, Capital, December 31, 2019		$27 5 5 0 00

SUCCESS TIP

Any additional investment by the owner would be added to his or her beginning capital amount.

SUCCESS TIP

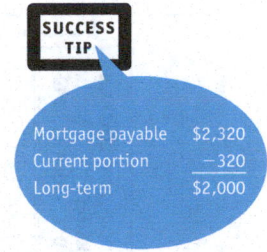

Mortgage payable	$2,320
Current portion	−320
Long-term	$2,000

quickly than Merchandise Inventory—for example, it can be quite difficult to sell an out-dated computer in a computer store or to sell last year's model car this year.

Capital assets are long-lived assets used in the production or sale of goods or services. Art's Wholesale Clothing Company has only one capital asset, store equipment; other capital assets could include buildings and land. The assets are usually listed in order of how long they will last; the longest-lived assets are listed first. Land would usually be the first asset listed (and land is never depreciated). Note that we still show the cost of the asset less its accumulated depreciation.

Current liabilities are the debts or obligations of Art's Wholesale Clothing Company that must be paid within 1 year or one operating cycle, whatever is longer. The order of listing accounts in this section is not always the same—many times companies will list their liabilities in the order in which they expect to pay them off. Note in Figure 12.3 on page 398 that the current portion of the mortgage, $320 (that portion due within 1 year), is listed toward the end of the list since that is paid off over the year.

Long-term liabilities are debts or obligations not due and payable for a comparatively long period, usually for more than 1 year. For Art's Wholesale Clothing Company there is only one long-term liability—Mortgage Payable. The long-term portion of the mortgage is listed here; the current portion, due within 1 year, is listed under Current Liabilities.

A classified balance sheet (when examined along with the income statement) can provide management, owners, creditors, and suppliers with more information about the company's ability to pay debts, both current and long-term. As well, it provides a more complete financial picture of the firm than a standard balance sheet would.

Capital assets Long-lived assets such as equipment, buildings, or land that are used in the production or sale of goods or services.

Current liabilities Obligations that will come due within 1 year or within the operating cycle, whichever is longer.

Long-term liabilities Obligations that are not due or payable for a long time, usually for more than a year.

Figure 12.3 Partial Worksheet and Classified Balance Sheet

ART'S WHOLESALE CLOTHING COMPANY
WORKSHEET
FOR YEAR ENDED DECEMBER 31, 2019

	Balance Sheet	
	Dr.	Cr.
Cash	12 9 2 0 00	
Petty Cash	1 0 0 00	
Accounts Receivable	14 5 0 0 00	
Merchandise Inventory	18 5 0 0 00	
Supplies	3 0 0 00	
Prepaid Insurance	6 0 0 00	
Store Equipment	4 0 0 0 00	
Acc. Dep., Store Equipment		4 5 0 00
Accounts Payable		17 9 0 0 00
Federal Income Tax Payable		8 0 0 00
FICA—Social Security Payable		4 5 4 00
FICA—Medicare Payable		1 0 6 00
State Income Tax Payable		2 0 0 00
SUTA Tax Payable		1 0 8 00
FUTA Tax Payable		3 2 00
Unearned Rent		4 0 0 00
Mortgage Payable		2 3 2 0 00
Art Newner, Capital		7 9 0 5 00
Salaries Payable		6 0 0 00
Totals	59 5 2 0 00	31 2 7 5 00
Net Income		28 2 4 5 00
Totals	59 5 2 0 00	59 5 2 0 00

ART'S WHOLESALE CLOTHING COMPANY
CLASSIFIED BALANCE SHEET
DECEMBER 31, 2019

Assets

Current Assets:			
Cash	$12 9 2 0 00		
Petty Cash	1 0 0 00		
Accounts Receivable	14 5 0 0 00		
Merchandise Inventory	18 5 0 0 00		
Supplies	3 0 0 00		
Prepaid Insurance	6 0 0 00		
Total Current Assets			$46 9 2 0 00
Plant and Equipment:			
Store Equipment	$ 4 0 0 0 00		
Less: Accum. Depreciation	4 5 0 00		3 5 5 0 00
Total Assets			$50 4 7 0 00

Liabilities

Current Liabilities:			
Accounts Payable	$17 9 0 0 00		
Federal Income Tax Payable	8 0 0 00		
FICA—Social Security Payable	4 5 4 00		
FICA—Medicare Payable	1 0 6 00		
State Income Tax Payable	2 0 0 00		
SUTA Tax Payable	1 0 8 00		
FUTA Tax Payable	3 2 00		
Salaries Payable	6 0 0 00		
Unearned Rent	4 0 0 00		
Mortgage Payable (current portion)	3 2 0 00		
Total Current Liabilities			$20 9 2 0 00
Long-Term Liabilities			
Mortgage Payable			2 0 0 0 00
Total Liabilities			$22 9 2 0 00

Owner's Equity

Art Newner, Capital, December 31, 201X			27 5 5 0 00
Total Liabilities and Owner's Equity			$50 4 7 0 00

 ## TRY IT!   Learning Unit 12-1

Complete the following chart by placing an (X) in the appropriate column(s).

Account Title	Income Statement	Statement of Owner's Equity	Balance Sheet	Current Assets	Current Liabilities	Property, Plant & Equipment
Merchandise Inventory						
Sales Discount						
Unearned Storage Fees						
Accum. Dep., Store Equip.						
Prepaid Insurance						
Ending Capital						
Sales Ret. and Allow.						
Store Equipment						
Sales						
Accounts Payable						

TRY IT!   Solution Learning Unit 12-1

Account Title	Income Statement	Statement of Owner's Equity	Balance Sheet	Current Assets	Current Liabilities	Property, Plant & Equipment
Merchandise Inventory			x	x		
Sales Discount	x					
Unearned Storage Fees			x		x	
Accum. Dep., Store Equip.			x			x
Prepaid Insurance			x	x		
Ending Capital		x	x			
Sales Ret. and Allow.	x					
Store Equipment			x			x
Sales	x					
Accounts Payable			x		x	

Journalizing and Posting Adjusting and Closing Entries; Preparing the Post-Closing Trial Balance

 LEARNING UNIT 12-2

L02

Journalizing and Posting Adjusting Entries

From the worksheet of Art's Wholesale Clothing Company, presented here as Figure 12.4 for your convenience, the adjusting entries can be journalized from the adjustments column and posted to the ledger. Keep in mind that the adjustments have been recorded only on the worksheet, not in the journal or in the ledger—at this point the journal does not reflect adjustments, and the ledger still contains only unadjusted amounts.

Figure 12.4
Completed Worksheet

ART'S WHOLESALE CLOTHING CO.
WORKSHEET
FOR YEAR ENDED DECEMBER 31, 2019

	Trial Balance Dr.	Trial Balance Cr.	Adjustments Dr.	Adjustments Cr.
Cash	12 9 2 0 00			
Petty Cash	1 0 0 00			
Accounts Receivable	14 5 0 0 00			
Merchandise Inventory	19 0 0 0 00			(F) 5 0 0 00
Supplies	8 0 0 00			(B) 5 0 0 00
Prepaid Insurance	9 0 0 00			(C) 3 0 0 00
Store Equipment	4 0 0 0 00			
Acc. Dep., Store Equipment		4 0 0 00		(D) 5 0 00
Accounts Payable		17 9 0 0 00		
Federal Income Tax Payable		8 0 0 00		
FICA—Social Security Payable		4 5 4 00		
FICA—Medicare Payable		1 0 6 00		
State Income Tax Payable		2 0 0 00		
SUTA Tax Payable		1 0 8 00		
FUTA Tax Payable		3 2 00		
Unearned Rent		6 0 0 00	(A) 2 0 0 00	
Mortgage Payable		2 3 2 0 00		
Art Newner, Capital		7 9 0 5 00		
Art Newner, Withdrawals	8 6 0 0 00			
Sales		95 0 0 0 00		
Sales Returns and Allowances	9 5 0 00			
Sales Discount	6 7 0 00			
Cost of Goods Sold	50 9 1 0 00		(F) 5 0 0 00	
Salaries Expense	11 7 0 0 00		(E) 6 0 0 00	
Payroll Tax Expense	4 2 0 00			
Postage Expense	2 5 00			
Miscellaneous Expense	3 0 00			
Interest Expense	3 0 0 00			
Totals	125 8 2 5 00	125 8 2 5 00		
Rental Income				(A) 2 0 0 00
Supplies Expense			(B) 5 0 0 00	
Insurance Expense			(C) 3 0 0 00	
Depreciation Expense, Store Equip.			(D) 5 0 00	
Salaries Payable				(E) 6 0 0 00
Totals			2 1 5 0 00	2 1 5 0 00
Net Income				
Totals				

Figure 12.4 Continued

	Adjusted Trial Bal. Dr.	Adjusted Trial Bal. Cr.	Income Statement Dr.	Income Statement Cr.	Balance Sheet Dr.	Balance Sheet Cr.
Cash	12 920 00				12 920 00	
Petty Cash	100 00				100 00	
Accounts Receivable	14 500 00				14 500 00	
Merchandise Inventory	18 500 00				18 500 00	
Supplies	300 00				300 00	
Prepaid Insurance	600 00				600 00	
Store Equipment	4 000 00				4 000 00	
Acc. Dep., Store Equipment		450 00				450 00
Accounts Payable		17 900 00				17 900 00
Federal Income Tax Payable		800 00				800 00
FICA—Social Security Payable		454 00				454 00
FICA—Medicare Payable		106 00				106 00
State Income Tax Payable		200 00				200 00
SUTA Tax Payable		108 00				108 00
FUTA Tax Payable		32 00				32 00
Unearned Rent		400 00				400 00
Mortgage Payable		2 320 00				2 320 00
Art Newner, Capital		79 055 00				79 055 00
Art Newner, Withdrawals	8 600 00				8 600 00	
Sales		95 000 00		95 000 00		
Sales Returns and Allowances	950 00		950 00			
Sales Discount	670 00		670 00			
Cost of Goods Sold	51 410 00		51 410 00			
Salaries Expense	12 300 00		12 300 00			
Payroll Tax Expense	420 00		420 00			
Postage Expense	25 00		25 00			
Miscellaneous Expense	30 00		30 00			
Interest Expense	300 00		300 00			
Rental Income		200 00		200 00		
Supplies Expense	500 00		500 00			
Insurance Expense	300 00		300 00			
Depreciation Expense, Store Equip.	50 00		50 00			
Salaries Payable		600 00				600 00
Totals	126 475 00	126 475 00	66 955 00	95 200 00	59 520 00	31 275 00
Net Income			28 245 00			28 245 00
Totals			95 200 00	95 200 00	59 520 00	59 520 00

The journalized and posted adjusting entries are shown below. Note that the liability Unearned Rent is reduced by $200 and Rental Income has increased by $200 to reflect a tenant living in the property for another month.

Figure 12.5
Journalized and Posted Adjusting Entries

ART'S WHOLESALE CLOTHING COMPANY
GENERAL JOURNAL

Page 2

Date			Account Titles and Description	PR	Dr.	Cr.
			Adjusting Entries			
2019 Dec.	31		Cost of Goods Sold	510	5 0 0 00	
			Merchandise Inventory	121		5 0 0 00
			Adjust for shrinkage			
	31		Unearned Rent	218	2 0 0 00	
			Rental Income	414		2 0 0 00
			Rental income earned			
	31		Supplies Expense	614	5 0 0 00	
			Supplies	122		5 0 0 00
			Supplies consumed			
	31		Insurance Expense	615	3 0 0 00	
			Prepaid Insurance	123		3 0 0 00
			Insurance expired			
	31		Depreciation Exp., Store Equipment	613	5 0 00	
			Acc. Depreciation, Store Equipment	126		5 0 00
			Depreciation on equipment			
	31		Salaries Expense	611	6 0 0 00	
			Salaries Payable	212		6 0 0 00
			Accrued salary			

Partial General Ledger

Merchandise Inventory 121		Accum. Dep'n., Store Equipment 126		Rental Income 414		Dep'n. Expense, Store Equipment 613	
19,000	500		400		200	50	
			50				

Supplies 122		Salaries Payable 212		Cost of Goods Sold 510		Supplies Expense 614	
800	500		600	51,410		500	
				500			

Prepaid Insurance 123		Unearned Rent 218		Salaries Expense 611		Insurance Exp. 615	
900	300	200	600	11,700		300	
				600			

Journalizing and Posting Closing Entries

In Chapter 5, we discussed the closing process for a service company. The goals of closing have not changed. They are to clear all temporary accounts in the ledger to zero and to update capital in the ledger to its latest balance. A merchandising company will also use the worksheet and the following steps to complete the closing process:

1. Close all balances in the income statement credit column of the worksheet by debits. Then credit the total to the Income Summary account.
2. Close all balances in the income statement debit column of the worksheet by credits. Then debit the total to the Income Summary account.
3. Transfer the balance of the Income Summary account to the Capital account.
4. Transfer the balance of the owner's Withdrawal account to the Capital account.

Let's look now at the journalized closing entries in Figure 12.6. When these entries are posted, all the temporary accounts will have zero balances in the ledger and the Capital account will be updated with a new balance.

ART'S WHOLESALE CLOTHING COMPANY
GENERAL JOURNAL

Page 2

Date		Account Titles and Description	PR	Dr.	Cr.
2019		Closing Entries			
Dec.	31	Sales	411	95 0 0 0 00	
		Rental Income	414	2 0 0 00	
		Income Summary	313		95 2 0 0 00
		To transfer credit account balances			
		on income statement column of			
		worksheet to Income Summary			
	31	Income Summary	313	66 9 5 5 00	
		Sales Returns and Allowances	412		9 5 0 00
		Sales Discounts	413		6 7 0 00
		Cost of Goods Sold	510		51 4 1 0 00
		Salaries Expense	611		12 3 0 0 00
		Payroll Tax Expense	612		4 2 0 00
		Postage Expense	616		2 5 00
		Miscellaneous Expense	617		3 0 00
		Interest Expense	618		3 0 0 00
		Supplies Expense	614		5 0 0 00
		Insurance Expense	615		3 0 0 00
		Depreciation Expense, Store Equip.	613		5 0 00
		To transfer all expenses and other			
		debit balances in the income			
		statement column of the worksheet			
		to Income Summary			
	31	Income Summary	313	28 2 4 5 00	
		A. Newner, Capital	311		28 2 4 5 00
		Transfer of net income to			
		Capital from Income Summary			
	31	A. Newner, Capital	311	8 6 0 0 00	
		A. Newner, Withdrawals	312		8 6 0 0 00
		Closes withdrawals to			
		Capital Account			

Figure 12.6
General Journal Closing Entries

Let's take a moment to look at the Income Summary account in T account form as it would exist after step 2 above:

	Income Summary 313		
Clos.	66,955	95,200	Clos.
Net income → Clos.	28,245	28,245	Bal.

The end result is that the net income of $28,245 is closed to the Capital account, and the Income Summary account has a zero balance.

The Post-Closing Trial Balance

The post-closing trial balance (often referred to as an opening trial balance), shown below, is prepared from the general ledger. Note first that all temporary accounts have been closed and thus are not shown on this post-closing trial balance.

Figure 12.7
Post-Closing Trial Balance for Art's Wholesale Clothing Company

ART'S WHOLESALE CLOTHING COMPANY POST-CLOSING TRIAL BALANCE DECEMBER 31, 201X		
	Dr.	Cr.
Cash	12 9 2 0 00	
Petty Cash	1 0 0 00	
Accounts Receivable	14 5 0 0 00	
Merchandise Inventory	18 5 0 0 00	
Supplies	3 0 0 00	
Prepaid Insurance	6 0 0 00	
Store Equipment	4 0 0 0 00	
Accum. Depreciation, Store Equipment		4 5 0 00
Accounts Payable		17 9 0 0 00
Federal Income Tax Payable		8 0 0 00
FICA—Social Security Payable		4 5 4 00
FICA—Medicare Payable		1 0 6 00
State Income Tax Payable		2 0 0 00
SUTA Tax Payable		1 0 8 00
FUTA Tax Payable		3 2 00
Salaries Payable		6 0 0 00
Unearned Rent		4 0 0 00
Mortgage Payable		2 3 2 0 00
Art Newner, Capital		27 5 5 0 00
Totals	50 9 2 0 00	50 9 2 0 00

 TRY IT!   Learning Unit 12-2

Complete the following table by placing an (X) in the appropriate column(s).

Accounts	Temp.	Perm.	Closed I/S	Included in Post - Closing Trial Balance
Cash				
Petty Cash				
Accounts Receivable				
Sales				
Sales Returns and Allowances				
Sales Discounts				
Accounts Payable				
Merchandise Inventory				
Depreciation Expense				
Accumulated Depreciation				
Capital				
Unearned Rent				

TRY IT!   **Solution Learning Unit 12-2**

Accounts	Temp.	Perm.	Closed I/S	Included in Post - Closing Trial Balance
Cash		x		x
Petty Cash		x		x
Accounts Receivable		x		x
Sales	x		x	
Sales Returns and Allowances	x		x	
Sales Discounts	x		x	
Accounts Payable		x		x
Merchandise Inventory		x		x
Depreciation Expense	x		x	
Accumulated Depreciation		x		x
Capital		x		x
Unearned Rent		x		x

LEARNING UNIT 12-3

LO3

Reversing entries Optional bookkeeping technique in which certain adjusting entries are reversed or switched on the first day of the new accounting period so that transactions in the new period can be recorded without referring back to prior adjusting entries.

Reversing Entries (Optional Section)

The accounting cycle for Art's Wholesale Clothing Company is completed. Now let's look at reversing entries, an optional way of handling some adjusting entries. Reversing entries are general journal entries that are the opposite of adjusting entries. Reversing entries help reduce potential errors and simplify the record-keeping process. If Art's accountant makes reversing entries, routine transactions can be made in the usual steps.

To help explain the concept of reversing entries, let's look at these two adjustments that could be reversed:

1. When an increase occurs in an asset account (no previous balance).
   Example: Dr. Interest Receivable
   Cr. Interest Income
   (Interest earned but not collected is covered in later chapters.)
2. When an increase occurs in a liability account (no previous balance).
   Example: Dr. Salaries Expense
   Cr. Salaries Payable

With the exception of businesses in their first year of operation, accounts such as Accumulated Depreciation or Inventory cannot be reduced because they have previous balances.

Art's bookkeeper handles an entry without reversing for salaries at the end of the year (see Figure 12.8). Note that the permanent account, Salaries Payable, carries over to the new accounting period a $600 balance. Remember that the $600 was an expense of the prior year.

Figure 12.8 Reversing Entries Not Used

① On December 31, an adjusting entry was journalized and posted for $600 of salaries incurred but not paid.

ADJUSTING JOURNAL ENTRY

Dec.	31	Salaries Expense	600 00	
		Salaries Payable		600 00

T ACCOUNT UPDATE

Salaries Exp.		Salaries Pay.	
11,700			600
600			
12,300			

② On January 1, after closing entries have been journalized and posted, Salaries Expense has a zero balance.

CLOSING JOURNAL ENTRY

Dec.	31	Income Summary	12 300 00	
		Salaries Expense		12 300 00

Salaries Exp.		Salaries Pay.	
11,700			600
600			
12,300	12,300 Closing		

On January 8 of the new year, the payroll to be paid is $2,000. If the optional reversing entry is *not* used, the bookkeeper must make the following compound journal entry as shown in Figure 12.9.

Figure 12.9 Entry When Optional Reversing Entry Is Not Used

Jan.	8	Salaries Payable	600 00	
		Salaries Expense	1 400 00	
		Cash		2 000 00

Salaries Exp.		Salaries Pay.		Cash	
1,400		600	600		2,000

To do so, the bookkeeper has to refer back to the adjustment on December 31 to determine how much of the salary of $2,000 is indeed a new salary expense and what portion was shown in the old year although not paid. It is easy to see how potential errors can result if the bookkeeper pays the payroll but forgets about the adjustment in the previous year. In this way, reversing entries can help avoid potential errors.

Figure 12.10 shows the four steps the bookkeeper would take if reversing entries were used. Note that steps 1 and 2 are the same whether the accountant uses reversing entries or not.

Figure 12.10 Reversing Entries Used

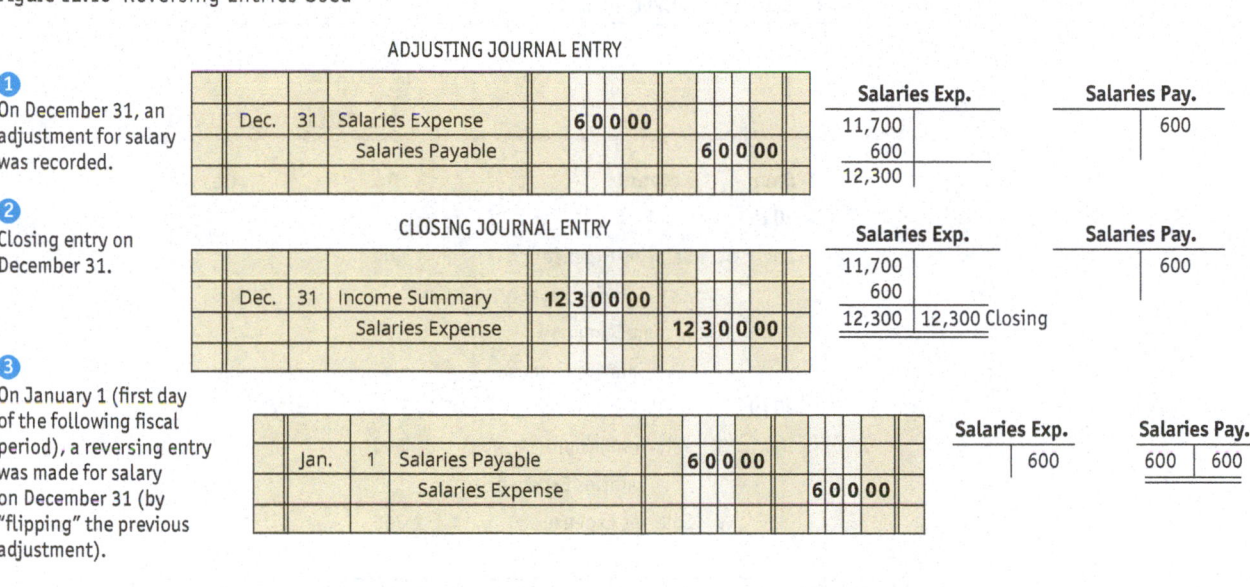

Note that the balance of Salaries Expense is indeed only $1,400, the *true* expense in the new year. Reversing results in switching the adjustment the first day of the new period. Also note that each of the accounts ends up with the same balance no matter which method is chosen. Using a reversing entry for salaries, however, allows the accountant to make the normal entry when it is time to pay salaries.

Now let's check your progress.

 ## TRY IT!   **Learning Unit 12-3**

Journalize the following transactions:

2018		
Dec.	31	Salaries were adjusted for $500 (beg. balance of salary expense was $400).
	31	Closing entry was prepared.
2019		
Jan.	1	A reversing entry for salaries was made.
	6	Salaries of $1,200 are paid.

TRY IT!   **Solution Learning Unit 12-3**

Date		Accounts	Dr.	Cr.
2018				
Dec.	31	Salaries Expense	500	
		Salaries Payable		500
	31	Income Summary	900	
		Salaries Expense		900
2019				
Jan.	1	Salaries Payable	500	
		Salaries Expense		500
	6	Salaries Expense	1,200	
		Cash		1,200

 *(40 min)* **LO1,2,3**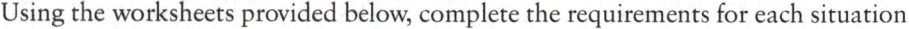

DEMONSTRATION SUMMARY PROBLEM

Requirements

Using the worksheets provided below, complete the requirements for each situation.

1. From the partial completed of Mikolaski Modern Design Company, shown on page 409, your task is to:
   a. Journalize the adjusting and closing entries.

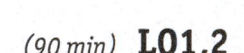 *(90 min)* **LO1,2**

Figure 12.11 Completed Worksheet for Mikolaski Modern Design Company

WORKSHEET FOR THE YEAR ENDED DECEMBER 31, 201X

Account Titles	Trial Balance Debit	Trial Balance Credit	Adjustments Debit	Adjustments Credit	Adjusted Trial Balance Debit	Adjusted Trial Balance Credit	Income Statement Debit	Income Statement Credit	Balance Sheet Debit	Balance Sheet Credit
Cash	3,465.78				3,465.78				3,465.78	
Petty Cash	50.00				50.00				50.00	
Accounts Receivable	11,575.20				11,575.20				11,575.20	
Merchandise Inventory	16,479.22			(A) 229.22	16,250.00				16,250.00	
Prepaid Insurance	765.85			(D) 257.75	508.10				508.00	
Equipment	21,575.00				21,575.00				21,575.00	
Accum. Dep., Equipment		14,762.40		(C) 1,357.60		16,120.00				16,120.00
Building	28,700.00				28,700.00				28,700.00	
Accum. Dep., Building		21,653.70		(C) 647.82		22,301.52				22,301.52
Accounts Payable		8,400.00				8,400.00				8,400.00
Mortgage Payable		11,446.00				11,446.52				11,446.52
Unearned Rent		2,400.00	(B) 800.00			1,600.00				1,600.00
Income Tax Payable		514.40				514.40				514.40
L. Mikolaski, Capital		32,420.22				32,420.22				32,420.22
L. Mikolaski, Withdrawals	16,450.00				16,450.00				16,450.00	
Sales		77,327.56				77,327.56		77,327.56		
Sales Discounts & Allow.	358.92				358.92		358.92			
Cost of Goods Sold	42,249.98		(A) 229.22		42,479.20		42,479.20			
Advertising Expense	1,245.00				1,245.00		1,245.00			
Cleaning Expense	2,605.60				2,605.60		2,605.60			
Repair Expense	876.20				876.20		876.20			
Salaries Expense	21,575.60				21,575.60		21,575.60			
Utilities Expense	952.45				952.45		952.45			
	168,924.80	168,924.80								
Rental Income Earned				(B) 800.00		800.00		800.00		
Dep. Exp., Eq. and Build.			(C) 2,005.42		2,005.42		2,005.42			
Insurance Expense			(D) 257.75		257.75		257.75			
			3,292.39	3,292.39	170,930.22		72,356.14	78,127.56	98,574.08	92,802.66
Net Income							5,771.42			5,771.42
							78,127.56	78,127.56	98,574.08	98,574.08

Solutions

Date	Account Titles and Description	PR	Dr.	Cr.
	Adjusting Entries			
Dec. 31	Cost of Goods Sold		229.22	
	Merchandise Inventory			229.22
31	Unearned Rent		800.00	
	Rental Income Earned			800.00
31	Depreciation Expense, Equipment & Build.		2,005.42	
	Accumulated Depreciation, Equipment			1,357.60
	Accumulated Depreciation, Building			647.82
31	Insurance Expense		257.75	
	Prepaid Insurance			257.75
	Closing Entries			
31	Sales		77,327.56	
	Rental Income		800.00	
	Income Summary			78,127.56
31	Income Summary		72,356.14	
	Sales Discounts and Allowances			358.92
	Repair Expense			876.20
	Cost of Goods Sold			42,479.20
	Advertising Expense			1,245.00
	Cleaning Expense			2,605.60
	Salaries Expense			21,575.60
	Depreciation Expense, Equipment & Build.			2,005.42
	Insurance Expense			257.75
	Utilities Expense			952.45
31	Income Summary		5,771.42	
	L. Mikolaski, Capital			5,771.42
31	L. Mikolaski, Capital		16,450.00	
	L. Mikolaski, Withdrawals			16,450.00

SUCCESS COACH

12

The following Success Tips are from Learning Units 12-1 to 12-3. Take the Do It Right Now Checkup and use the Check Your Score at the bottom of the page to see how you are doing. The Success Coach provides tips before each Checkup to help you avoid common accounting errors.

LU 12-1 Preparing Financial Statements

Do It Right Tips: The financial statements do not show debits or credits. The inside columns are for subtotalling. The totals on the financial statements will not always equal the same total amounts on the worksheet. Net Income will always be the same on the worksheet and income statement.

Revenue less Cost of Goods Sold equals Gross Profit. To get Net Income from Operations, we subtract from Gross Profit the Operating Expenses.

Do It Right Now Checkup: Answer true or false to the following statements.

1. Sales on the formal income statement has a credit balance.
2. Rental Income is shown on the balance sheet.
3. Accumulated Depreciation is a contra-asset on the balance sheet.
4. Unearned Rent is a revenue account on the income statement.

LU 12-2 Journalizing and Posting Adjusting and Closing Entries; Preparing the Post-Closing Trial Balance

Do It Right Tips: All adjustments are taken from the adjustments column on the worksheet. Income Summary is a temporary account and will not appear on the post-closing trial balance. The closing process transfers all temporary accounts through Income Summary except Withdrawals, which is closed directly to Owner's Equity (Capital).

Do It Right Now Checkup: Answer true or false to the following statements.

1. Some temporary accounts will go on the post-closing trial balance.
2. Inventory (ending) is listed as a debit on the post-closing trial balance.
3. Unearned Rent is a permanent account.
4. The Capital amount on the post-closing trial balance is listed before the closing process.
5. Purchases is listed on the post-closing trial balance.

LU 12-3 Reversing Entries (Optional Section)

Do It Right Tips: Reversing entries is a way of handling some adjusting entries. By making a reversing entry in the new period, the accountant does not have to worry about the past adjustment and will make the normal entry when a transaction occurs. Reversing entries can be done when an increase occurs in an asset (no previous balance) or when an increase occurs in a liability account (no previous balance).

Do It Right Now Checkup: Answer true or false to the following statements.

1. Reversing entries are required.
2. Interest Income and Interest Receivables may sometimes use a reversing entry.
3. Reversing entries are made in the old year, not the new.
4. Reversing entries for Salary will show true salary expense in the new year.
5. Regardless of whether reversing entries are used, the same balances will end up in each account.

CHECK YOUR SCORE: Answers to the Do It Right Now Checkup

LU 12-1

1. False—The Income Statement does not have debits or credits.
2. False—Rental Income is shown on the income statement with the Sales or Revenue.
3. True.
4. False—Unearned Rent is a liability on the balance sheet.

LU 12-2

1. False—No temporary accounts will go on the post-closing trial balance.
2. True.
3. True.

4. False—The Capital account on the post-closing trial balance is listed after the closing process.
5. False—Purchases is a temporary account and will not appear on the post-closing trial balance. Remember that under a perpetual inventory system, the purchase account is not used.

LU 12-3

1. False—Reversing entries are optional.
2. True.
3. False—Reversing entries are made in the new year.
4. True—the new entry after the reversing entry will show the true salary.
5. True.

BLUEPRINT: FINANCIAL STATEMENTS

(1) INCOME STATEMENT				
Revenue				
Sales			$ XXX	
Less: Sales Returns and Allowances		$ XXX		
Sales Discounts		XXX	XXX	
Net Sales			XXXX	
Cost of Goods Sold				
Cost of Goods Sold			XXXX	
Gross Profit			XXXX	
Operating Expenses				
~~		XXX		
~~		XXX		
~~		XXX		
Total Operating Expenses			XXX	
Net Income from Operations			XXX	
Other Income				
Rental Income		XXX		
Storage Fees Income		XXX		
Total Other Income			XXX	
Other Expenses				
Interest Expense		XXX	XXX	
Net Income			$ XXX	

(2) STATEMENT OF OWNER'S EQUITY				
Beginning Capital			$ XXX	
Additional Investments			XXX	
Total Investment			XXX	
Net Income*		$ XXX		
Less: Withdrawals		XXX		
Increase (Decrease) in Capital			XXX	
Ending Capital			$ XXX	

*From the income statement.

BLUEPRINT: FINANCIAL STATEMENTS (*continued*)

(3) BALANCE SHEET				
Assets				
Current Assets				
Cash		$ XXX		
Accounts Receivable		XXX		
Merchandise Inventory		XXX		
Prepaid Insurance		XXX		
Total Current Assets			$ XXX	
Plant and Equipment				
Store Equipment	$ XXX			
Less: Accumulated Depreciation	XXX	XXX		
Office Equipment	XXX			
Less: Accumulated Depreciation	XXX	XXX		
Total Plant and Equipment			XXX	
Total Assets			$ XXX	
Liabilities				
Current Liabilities				
Accounts Payable		$ XXX		
Accrued Salaries		XXX		
Income Taxes Payable		XXX		
Unearned Revenue		XXX		
Mortgage Payable (current portion)		XXX		
Total Current Liabilities			$ XXX	
Long-Term Liabilities				
Mortgage Payable			XXX	
Total Liabilities			XXX	
Owner's Equity				
Capital*			XXX	
Total Liabilities and Owner's Equity			$ XXX	

*From statement of owner's equity.

Discussion Questions and Critical Thinking/Ethical Case

1. Which columns of the worksheet aid in the preparation of the income statement?

2. Explain the components of Cost of Goods Sold.

3. Explain how operating expenses can be broken down into different categories.

4. What is the difference between Current Assets and Plant and Equipment?

5. What is an operating cycle?

6. Why journalize adjusting entries *after* the formal reports in a manual system have been prepared?

7. Explain the steps of closing for a merchandise company.

8. Temporary accounts could appear on a post-closing trial balance. Agree or disagree?

9. What is the purpose of using reversing entries? Are they mandatory? When should they be used?

10. Janet Flynn, owner of Reel Company, plans to apply for a bank loan at Petro National Bank. Because the company has a lot of debt on its balance sheet, Janet does not plan to show it to the loan officer. She plans only to bring the income statement. Do you feel that this move is a sound financial move by Janet? You make the call. Write down your specific recommendations to Janet.

Concept Checks

MyLab**Accounting**

(Excel templates for all questions are available in MyLab Accounting. Working papers for select questions are available in the print *Workbook*.)

Calculate Net Sales

1. From the following, calculate net sales:

Cost of Goods Sold	$100
Gross Sales	180
Sales Returns and Allowances	5
Sales Discounts	2
Operating Expenses	15

L01 *(5 min)*

Calculate Gross Profit and Net Income

2. Using Concept Check 1, calculate:
   a. Gross profit
   b. Net income or net loss

L01 *(10 min)*

Classification of Accounts

3. Match the following categories to each account listed.
   a. Current Assets
   b. Plant and Equipment
   c. Current Liabilities
   d. Long-Term Liabilities

L01 *(15 min)*

1. ____ Petty Cash		6. ____ Mortgage Payable (Current)
2. ____ Accounts Receivable		7. ____ SUTA Payable
3. ____ Prepaid Rent		8. ____ Accumulated Depreciation
4. ____ FICA Payable		9. ____ Computer Equipment
5. ____ Store Supplies		10. ____ Unearned Rent

Reversing Entries

(10 min) **LO3**

4. **a.** On January 1, prepare a reversing entry. On January 8, journalize the entry to record the paying of Salaries Expense, $760.

b. What will be the balance in Salaries Expense on January 8 (after posting)?

December 31:

Salaries Expense						Salaries Payable	
Dr.	Cr.					Dr.	Cr.
760							380 Adj.
Adj. 380							
1,140	1,140 closing						

MyLabAccounting   **Exercises**

Set A

(10 min) **LO1**

12A-1. Give the category, the classification, and the report(s) on which each of the following appears (e.g., Cash—asset, current asset, balance sheet):

a. Salaries Payable   **e.** Income Tax Payable

b. Accounts Payable   **f.** Office Equipment

c. Mortgage Payable   **g.** Land

d. Unearned Legal Fees

(10 min) **LO2**

12A-2. From the following partial worksheet, journalize the closing entries of December 31 for A. Slow Co.

Figure 12.12
Partial Worksheet
for A. Slow Co.

A. SLOW CO.
PARTIAL WORKSHEET
FOR THE YEAR ENDED DECEMBER 31, 2019

Account Titles	Income Statement		Balance Sheet	
	Dr.	Cr.	Dr.	Cr.
Cash			1 9 3 00	
Merchandise Inventory			3 6 2 00	
Prepaid Advertising			5 6 1 00	
Prepaid Insurance			3 0 00	
Office Equipment			1 0 8 0 00	
Accum. Dep'n., Office Equip.				2 1 0 00
Accounts Payable				2 5 8 00
A. Slow, Capital				9 6 6 00
Sales		5 5 2 0 00		
Sales Returns and Allowances	2 2 3 00			
Sales Discounts	1 0 8 00			
Cost of Goods Sold	2 5 4 3 00			
Salaries Expense	1 0 8 3 00			
Insurance Expense	6 9 6 00			
Utilities Expense	4 8 00			
Plumbing Expense	5 7 00			
Advertising Expense	1 5 00			
Dep'n. Expense, Office Equip.	3 0 00			
Salaries Payable				7 5 00
	4 8 0 3 00	5 5 2 0 00	2 2 2 6 00	1 5 0 9 00
Net Income	7 1 7 00			7 1 7 00
	5 5 2 0 00	5 5 2 0 00	2 2 2 6 00	2 2 2 6 00

12A-3. From the worksheet in Exercise 12A-2, prepare the assets section of a classified balance sheet.

 **LO1** (15 min)

12A-4. On December 31, 2019, $300 of salaries has been accrued. (Salary expense before the accrual adjustment totaled $26,000.) The next payroll to be paid will be on February 3, 2020, for $6,000. Do the following:

 **LO2,3** (30 min)

   a. Journalize and post the adjusting entry (use T accounts).
   b. Journalize and post the reversing entry on January 1.
   c. Journalize and post the payment of the payroll. Cash has a balance of $15,000 before the payment of payroll on February 3, 2020.

Set B

12B-1. Give the category, the classification, and the report(s) on which each of the following appears (e.g., Cash—asset, current asset, balance sheet):

 **LO1** (40 min)

   a. Mortgage Payable—current portion
   b. Accounts Receivable
   c. Rent Paid in Advance
   d. Unearned Accounting Fees
   e. Income Tax Payable
   f. Vehicles
   g. Accumulated Depreciation, Vehicles

12B-2. From the following partial worksheet, journalize the closing entries of December 31 for A. Slow Co.

LO2 (10 min)

Figure 12.13 Partial Worksheet for A. Slow Co.

A. SLOW CO.
PARTIAL WORKSHEET
FOR THE YEAR ENDED DECEMBER 31, 2019

Account Titles	Income Statement Dr.	Income Statement Cr.	Balance Sheet Dr.	Balance Sheet Cr.
Cash			2 0 3 00	
Merchandise Inventory			5 7 5 00	
Prepaid Advertising			6 8 0 00	
Prepaid Insurance			3 6 0 00	
Office Equipment			1 9 8 0 00	
Accum. Dep'n., Office Equip.				3 6 0 00
Accounts Payable				5 4 8 00
A. Slow, Capital				1 3 6 6 00
Sales		7 7 2 0 00		
Sales Returns and Allowances	3 6 4 00			
Sales Discounts	2 7 7 00			
Cost of Goods Sold	3 1 4 2 00			
Salaries Expense	1 5 7 6 00			
Insurance Expense	5 7 8 00			
Utilities Expense	1 3 5 00			
Plumbing Expense	8 8 00			
Advertising Expense	5 6 00			
Dep'n. Expense, Office Equip.	6 5 00			
Salaries Payable				8 5 00
	6 2 8 1 00	7 7 2 0 00	3 7 9 8 00	2 3 5 9 00
Net Income	1 4 3 9 00			1 4 3 9 00
	7 7 2 0 00	7 7 2 0 00	3 7 9 8 00	3 7 9 8 00

Check Figure:
Net Income from operations
$1,080

12B-3. From the worksheet in Exercise 12B-2, prepare the assets section of a classified balance sheet.

 **LO1** (15 min)

(30 min) **LO2,3**

12B-4. On December 31, 2019, $700 of salaries has been accrued. (Salaries before accrued amount totaled $29,000.) The next payroll to be paid will be on February 3, 2020, for $7,500. Do the following:
  a. Journalize and post the adjusting entry (use T accounts).
  b. Journalize and post the reversing entry on January 1.
  c. Journalize and post the payment of the payroll. Cash has a balance of $16,000 before the payment of payroll on February 3, 2020.

MyLabAccounting

Problems

Set A

(40 min) **LO1** ▶

S50 / **QB**

12A-1. Prepare a formal income statement from the following partial worksheet for Malorie's Dental Supply Co.

Figure 12.14 Partial Worksheet for Malorie's Dental Supply Co.

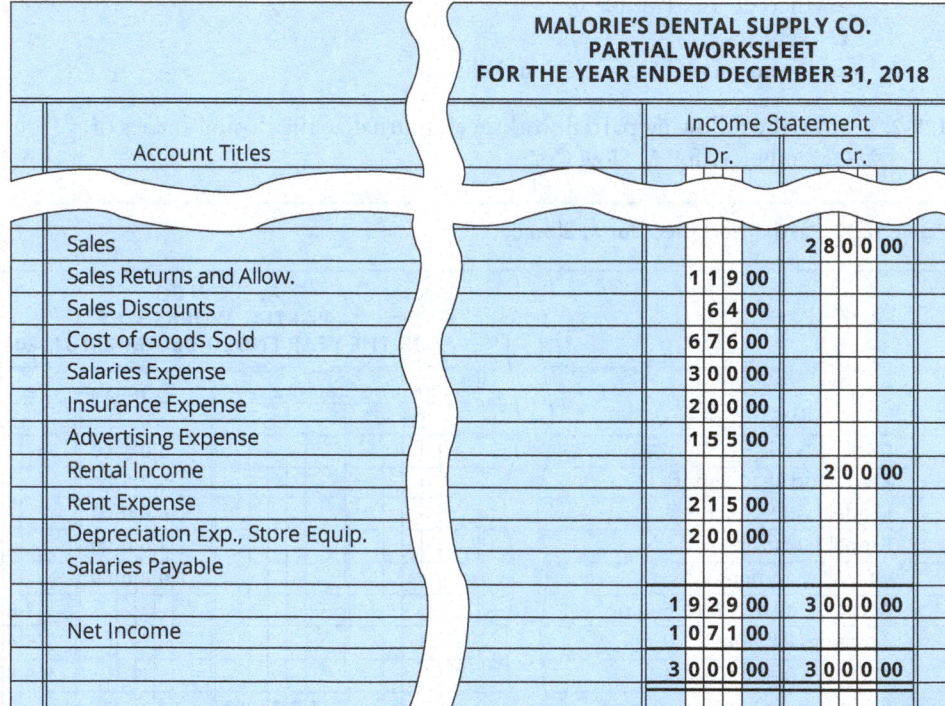

Check Figure:
Net Income from operations $871

	MALORIE'S DENTAL SUPPLY CO. PARTIAL WORKSHEET FOR THE YEAR ENDED DECEMBER 31, 2018	
	Income Statement	
Account Titles	Dr.	Cr.
Sales		2 8 0 0 00
Sales Returns and Allow.	1 1 9 00	
Sales Discounts	6 4 00	
Cost of Goods Sold	6 7 6 00	
Salaries Expense	3 0 0 00	
Insurance Expense	2 0 0 00	
Advertising Expense	1 5 5 00	
Rental Income		2 0 0 00
Rent Expense	2 1 5 00	
Depreciation Exp., Store Equip.	2 0 0 00	
Salaries Payable		
	1 9 2 9 00	3 0 0 0 00
Net Income	1 0 7 1 00	
	3 0 0 0 00	3 0 0 0 00

LO1 ▶

S50 / **QB**

12A-2. Prepare a statement of owner's equity and a classified balance sheet from the partial worksheet for Goods Company (page 417).
Note: Of the Mortgage Payable, $200 is due within one year.

Figure 12.15 Partial Worksheet for Goods Company

Account Titles	GOODS COMPANY PARTIAL WORKSHEET FOR THE YEAR ENDED DECEMBER 31, 2020	
	Balance Sheet	
	Dr.	Cr.
Cash	8 5 0 0 00	
Petty Cash	9 0 00	
Accounts Receivable	1 3 5 0 00	
Merchandise Inventory	4 0 0 0 00	
Supplies	3 2 5 00	
Prepaid Insurance	5 0 0 00	
Store Equipment	2 8 0 0 00	
Accum. Dep'n., Store Eq.		7 0 0 00
Automobile	1 7 0 0 00	
Accum. Dep'n., Auto		2 2 5 00
Accounts Payable		2 8 0 0 00
Taxes Payable		2 4 0 0 00
Unearned Rent		8 5 0 0 00
Mortgage Payable		4 5 0 0 00
Goods, Capital		7 4 0 0 00
Goods, Withdrawals	1 0 0 00	
Accrued Salaries Payable		6 0 0 00
	19 3 6 5 00	23 0 7 5 00
Net Loss	3 7 1 0 00	
	23 0 7 5 00	23 0 7 5 00

Check Figure:
Total Assets $18,340

12A-3.   **a.** Complete the partial worksheet for Jay's Supplies.
   b. Prepare an income statement, a statement of owner's equity, and a classified balance sheet. *Note:* The amount of the mortgage due the first year is $800.
   c. Journalize the adjusting and closing entries.

 **L01,2** *(90 min)*

Check Figure (for 12A-3):
Net Income $5,940

Figure 12.16 Worksheet for Jay's Supplies

JAY'S SUPPLIES WORKSHEET FOR THE YEAR ENDED DECEMBER 31, 2019						
	Trial Balance		Adjustments			
Account Titles	Dr.	Cr.	Dr.	Cr.		
Cash	2 0 0 0 00					
Accounts Receivable	3 0 0 0 00					
Merchandise Inventory	11 0 0 0 00		(A) 1 0 0 0 00			
Prepaid Insurance	1 8 8 0 00			5 0 0 00	(D)	
Equipment	3 4 0 0 00					
Accum. Dep'n., Equipment		1 0 8 0 00		4 0 0 00	(C)	
Accounts Payable		5 0 8 0 00				
Unearned Training Fees		2 1 2 0 00	(B) 3 2 0 00			
Mortgage Payable		1 2 0 0 00				
P. Jay, Capital		10 5 6 0 00				
P. Jay, Withdrawals	4 2 8 0 00					
Sales		95 8 0 0 00				
Sales Returns and Allowances	3 2 0 0 00					
Sales Discounts	2 6 0 0 00					
Cost of Goods Sold	49 4 8 0 00			1 0 0 0 00	(A)	
Advertising Expense	11 4 0 0 00					
Rent Expense	10 0 0 0 00					
Salaries Expense	13 6 0 0 00					
	115 8 4 0 00	115 8 4 0 00				
Training Fees Earned				3 2 0 00	(B)	
Dep'n. Exp., Equipment			(C) 4 0 0 00			
Insurance Expense			(D) 5 0 0 00			
			2 2 2 0 00	2 2 2 0 00		

(150 min) **L01,2,3**   12A-4.   Using the ledger balances and additional data shown on the next page, do the following for Meyer Lumber for the year ended December 31, 2019:

a. Prepare the worksheet.

b. Prepare the income statement, statement of owner's equity, and balance sheet.

c. Journalize and post adjusting and closing entries. (Be sure to put beginning balances in the ledger first.)

d. Prepare a post-closing trial balance.

e. Journalize the reversing entry for wages.

Check Figure:
Net Income $3,841

Account Balances for Meyer Lumber

Account No.

110	Cash	$ 1,680
111	Accounts Receivable	960
112	Merchandise Inventory	4,550
113	Lumber Supplies	269
114	Prepaid Insurance	218
121	Lumber Equipment	3,000
122	Accumulated Depreciation, Lumber Equipment	490
220	Accounts Payable	1,160

221	Wages Payable	—
330	L. Meyer, Capital	7,352
331	L. Meyer, Withdrawals	3,000
332	Income Summary	—
440	Sales	22,800
441	Sales Returns and Allowances	200
550	Cost of Goods Sold	14,215
660	Wages Expense	2,480
661	Advertising Expense	400
662	Rent Expense	830
663	Depreciation Expense, Lumber Equipment	—
664	Lumber Supplies Expense	—
665	Insurance Expense	—

Additional Data (for Problem 12A-4)

a. Physical count of inventory, December 31	4,420
b. Lumber supplies on hand, December 31	110
c. Insurance expired	120
d. Depreciation for the year	300
e. Accrued wages on December 31	125

Set B

12B-1. From the partial worksheet shown below, prepare a formal income statement.

L01 *(40 min)*

Figure 12.17 Partial Worksheet

S50 / **QB**

Check Figure:
Net Income from operations $850

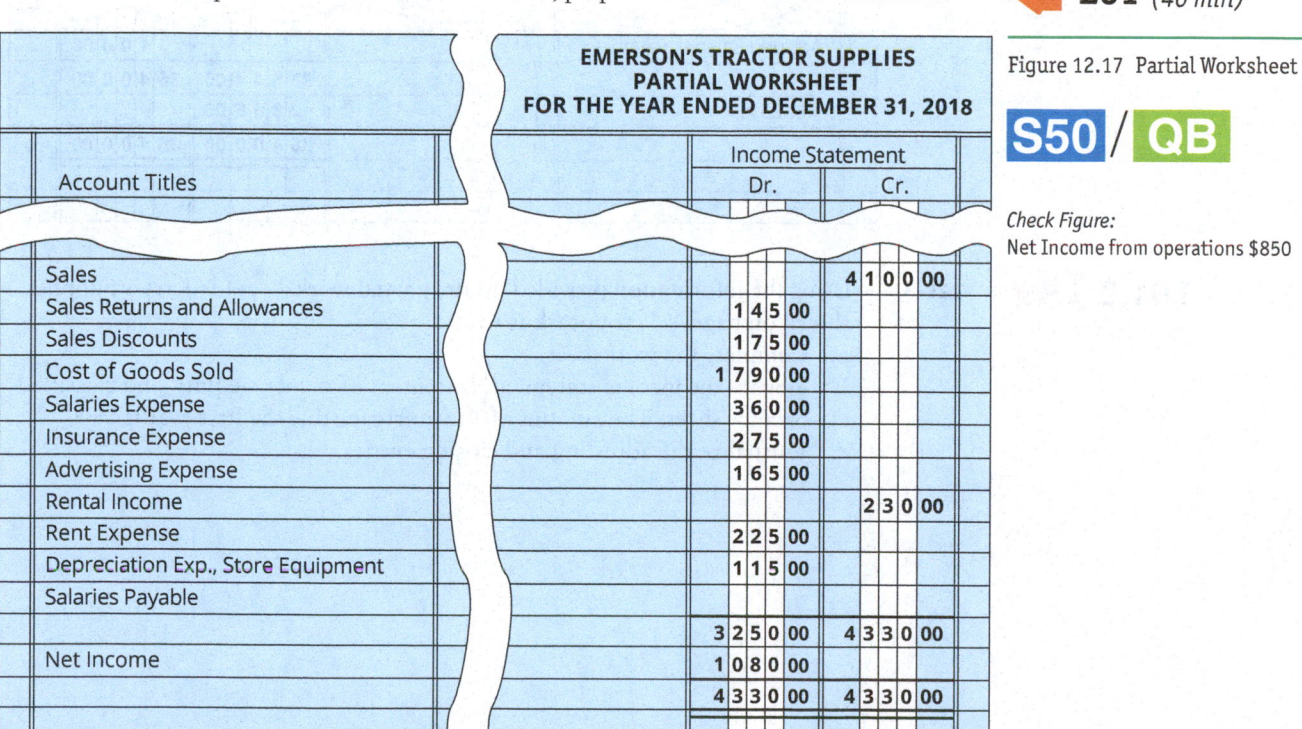

EMERSON'S TRACTOR SUPPLIES
PARTIAL WORKSHEET
FOR THE YEAR ENDED DECEMBER 31, 2018

	Income Statement	
Account Titles	Dr.	Cr.
Sales		4 1 0 0 00
Sales Returns and Allowances	1 4 5 00	
Sales Discounts	1 7 5 00	
Cost of Goods Sold	1 7 9 0 00	
Salaries Expense	3 6 0 00	
Insurance Expense	2 7 5 00	
Advertising Expense	1 6 5 00	
Rental Income		2 3 0 00
Rent Expense	2 2 5 00	
Depreciation Exp., Store Equipment	1 1 5 00	
Salaries Payable		
	3 2 5 0 00	4 3 3 0 00
Net Income	1 0 8 0 00	
	4 3 3 0 00	4 3 3 0 00

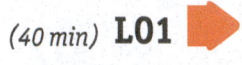

(40 min) **L01**

S50 / QB

12B-2. From the partial worksheet for Murray Company shown below, complete the following:
  a. Statement of owner's equity
  b. Classified balance sheet
     Note: Of the Mortgage Payable, $3,000 is due within one year.

Figure 12.18 Partial worksheet

Check Figure:
Total Assets $28,294

Account Titles	Balance Sheet Dr.	Balance Sheet Cr.
	MURRAY COMPANY WORKSHEET FOR THE YEAR ENDED DECEMBER 31, 2020	
Cash	2 5 0 0 00	
Petty Cash	5 0 00	
Accounts Receivable	1 3 0 0 00	
Merchandise Inventory	4 2 5 0 00	
Supplies	3 4 4 00	
Prepaid Insurance	6 0 0 00	
Store Equipment	18 0 0 0 00	
Accum. Dep'n., Store Eq.		7 5 0 00
Automobile	2 5 0 0 00	
Accum. Amort., Auto		5 0 0 00
Accounts Payable		3 4 5 0 00
Taxes Payable		2 1 0 0 00
Unearned Rent		11 0 0 0 00
Mortgage Payable		8 0 0 0 00
A. Murray, Capital		10 5 0 0 00
A. Murray, Withdrawals	4 0 0 0 00	
Accrued Salaries Payable		1 0 0 00
	33 5 4 4 00	36 4 0 0 00
Net Loss	2 8 5 6 00	
	36 4 0 0 00	36 4 0 0 00

(90 min) **L01,2**

12B-3. Using the information provided on the partial worksheet for Jerry's Supplies shown on page 421, your task is to
  a. Complete the worksheet.
  b. Prepare the income statement, statement of owner's equity, and classified balance sheet. The amount of the mortgage due the first year is $800.
  c. Journalize the adjusting and closing entries.

Figure 12.19

JERRY'S SUPPLIES WORKSHEET FOR THE YEAR ENDED DECEMBER 31, 2019							
Account Titles	Trial Balance		Adjustments				
	Dr.	Cr.	Dr.		Cr.		
Cash	3 0 0 0 00						
Accounts Receivable	3 0 0 0 00						
Merchandise Inventory	11 7 0 0 00				2 0 0 00	(A)	
Prepaid Insurance	1 0 0 0 00				3 5 0 00	(D)	
Equipment	5 0 0 0 00						
Accum. Dep'n., Equipment		1 9 0 0 00			5 0 0 00	(C)	
Accounts Payable		2 1 0 0 00					
Unearned Training Fees		1 4 5 0 00	(B) 4 0 0 00				
Mortgage Payable		2 4 0 0 00					
J. Vanwyk, Capital		27 7 5 0 00					
J. Vanwyk, Withdrawals	4 0 0 0 00						
Sales		100 8 0 0 00					
Sales Returns and Allowances	4 1 0 0 00						
Sales Discounts	2 8 0 0 00						
Cost of Goods Sold	69 3 0 0 00		(A) 2 0 0 00				
Advertising Expense	8 0 0 0 00						
Rent Expense	8 5 0 0 00						
Salaries Expense	16 0 0 0 00						
	136 4 0 0 00	136 4 0 0 00					
Training Fees Earned					4 0 0 00	(B)	
Depreciation Exp., Equipment			(C) 5 0 0 00				
Insurance Expense			(D) 3 5 0 00				
			1 4 5 0 00		1 4 5 0 00		

Check Figure:
Net Loss $8,550

12B-4. From the following ledger balances and additional data, do the following for Callahan Lumber for the year ended December 31, 2019:

 **L01,2,3** *(150 min)*

a. Prepare the worksheet.
b. Prepare the income statement, statement of owner's equity, and balance sheet.
c. Journalize and post adjusting and closing entries. (Be sure to put beginning balances in the ledger first.)
d. Prepare a post-closing trial balance.
e. Journalize the reversing entry for wages.

Check Figure:
Net Income $3,480

Account Balances for Callahan Lumber

110	Cash	$ 1,140
111	Accounts Receivable	1,270
112	Merchandise Inventory	5,600
113	Lumber Supplies	260
114	Prepaid Insurance	117
121	Lumber Equipment	2,600
122	Accumulated Depreciation, Lumber Equipment	340
220	Accounts Payable	1,330
221	Wages Payable	—

330	J. Callahan, Capital	7,562
331	J. Callahan, Withdrawals	3,500
332	Income Summary	—
440	Sales	23,000
441	Sales Returns and Allowances	400
550	Cost of Goods Sold	13,175
660	Wages Expense	2,390
661	Advertising Expense	940
662	Rent Expense	840
663	Depreciation Expense, Lumber Equipment	—
664	Lumber Supplies Expense	—
665	Insurance Expense	—

Additional Data

a. Physical count of inventory, December 31	$ 4,700
b. Lumber supplies on hand, December 31	80
c. Insurance expired	70
d. Depreciation for the year	460
e. Accrued wages on December 31	165

Financial Report Problem

Reading Amazon's Annual Report

Access Amazon's 2016 annual report at **https://tinyurl.com/slaterca14e** and locate the consolidated Statement of Income (Statement of Operations). How much has Selling, and General and Administrative Expenses increased from the previous year?

MyLabAccounting

KEEPING IT REAL SUAREZ COMPUTER CENTER

(60 min) **LO1,2**

Using the worksheet in Chapter 11 for Suarez Computer Center, journalize and post the adjusting entries and prepare the financial statements.

Mini Practice Set

The Fantastic Dress Shop
Reviewing the Accounting Cycle for a Merchandise Company
This practice set will help you review all the key concepts of a merchandise company, using the perpetual method of inventory valuation along with the integration of payroll, including the preparation of Form 941.

Because you are the professional bookkeeper for the Fantastic Dress Shop, we have gathered the following information for you. It will be your task to complete the accounting cycle for March using the knowledge and skills that you have acquired in this course. The company uses the perpetual inventory method.

THE FANTASTIC DRESS SHOP
POST-CLOSING TRIAL BALANCE
FEBRUARY 28, 201X

	1	2
Cash	2 3 5 0 80	
Petty Cash	5 5 00	
Accounts Receivable	1 8 0 0 00	
Merchandise Inventory	4 9 0 0 00	
Prepaid Rent	1 6 5 0 00	
Delivery Truck	12 0 0 0 00	
Accumulated Depreciation, Truck		3 0 0 0 00
Accounts Payable		2 0 0 0 00
FIT Payable		7 2 8 00
FICA—OASDI Payable		1 1 5 3 20
FICA—Medicare Payable		2 6 9 70
SIT Payable		6 5 1 00
SUTA Payable		8 5 4 40
FUTA Payable		1 0 6 80
Unearned Rent		1 0 0 0 00
B. Duval, Capital		12 9 9 2 70
Totals	22 7 5 5 80	22 7 5 5 80

Balances in subsidiary ledgers as of March 1 are as follows:

Accounts Receivable		Accounts Payable	
Bach Co.	$1,800	Danmark Co.	$2,000
Danmark Co.	—	Johnsons Co.	—
Young Co.	—	Manny's Garage	—
		Thomas Co.	—

Payroll is paid monthly:

FICA rate	OASDI 6.2% on $127,200
	Medicare 1.45% on all earnings
SUTA rate	4.8% on $7,000
FUTA rate	0.6% on $7,000
SIT rate	7%
FIT	Use the table provided at the end of this practice set.

The payroll register for January and February is provided. In March, salaries are as follows:

Jim Reed	$3,860
Emma Hyde	4,580
Sue Bolton	4,530

Your tasks are to do the following:

1. Set up a general ledger, accounts receivable subsidiary ledger, accounts payable subsidiary ledger, auxiliary petty cash record, and payroll register. (Be sure to update ledger accounts based on information given in the post-closing trial balance for February 28 before beginning.)

2. Journalize the transactions, prepare the payroll register, and prepare the auxiliary petty cash record.

3. Update the accounts payable and accounts receivable subsidiary ledgers.

4. Post to the general ledger.

5. Prepare a trial balance on a worksheet and complete the worksheet.

6. Prepare an income statement, statement of owner's equity, and classified balance sheet.

7. Journalize the adjusting and closing entries.

8. Post the adjusting and closing entries to the ledger.

9. Prepare a post-closing trial balance.

10. Complete Form 941 and sign it for the quarter ending March 31, 201X.

Chart of Accounts for the Fantastic Dress Shop

Assets
110 Cash
111 Petty Cash
112 Accounts Receivable
114 Merchandise Inventory
116 Prepaid Rent
120 Delivery Truck
121 Accumulated Depreciation, Truck

Liabilities
210 Accounts Payable
212 Salaries Payable
214 Federal Income Tax Payable
216 FICA—OASDI Payable
218 FICA—Medicare Payable
220 State Income Tax Payable
222 SUTA Tax Payable
224 FUTA Tax Payable
226 Unearned Rent

Owner's Equity
310 B. Duval, Capital
320 B. Duval, Withdrawals
330 Income Summary

Revenue
410 Sales
412 Sales Returns and Allowances
414 Sales Discount
416 Rental Income

Cost of Goods Sold
510 Cost of Goods Sold

Expenses
610 Sales Salaries Expense
611 Office Salaries Expense
612 Payroll Tax Expense
614 Cleaning Expense
616 Depreciation Expense, Truck
618 Rent Expense
620 Postage Expense
622 Delivery Expense
624 Miscellaneous Expense

THE FANTASTIC DRESS SHOP PAYROLL REGISTER JANUARY AND FEBRUARY 201X

Employees	Allow. and Marital Status	Cum. Earnings	Salary	Earnings Reg.	Earnings O/T	Earnings Gross	Cum. Earnings
Jim Reed	M – 2		2 1 0 0 00	2 1 0 0 00		2 1 0 0 00	2 1 0 0 00
Emma Hyde	M –1		3 3 0 0 00	3 3 0 0 00		3 3 0 0 00	3 3 0 0 00
Sue Bolton	M – 0		3 9 0 0 00	3 9 0 0 00		3 9 0 0 00	3 9 0 0 00
Totals for Jan.			9 3 0 0 00	9 3 0 0 00		9 3 0 0 00	9 3 0 0 00
Jim Reed	M – 2	2 1 0 0 00	2 1 0 0 00	2 1 0 0 00		2 1 0 0 00	4 2 0 0 00
Emma Hyde	M –1	3 3 0 0 00	3 3 0 0 00	3 3 0 0 00		3 3 0 0 00	6 6 0 0 00
Sue Bolton	M – 0	3 9 0 0 00	3 9 0 0 00	3 9 0 0 00		3 9 0 0 00	7 8 0 0 00
Totals for Feb.		9 3 0 0 00	9 3 0 0 00	9 3 0 0 00		9 3 0 0 00	18 6 0 0 00

PAYROLL REGISTER											
Taxable Earnings			Deductions						Distribution	
	FICA			FICA					Ck.	Office Salary Expense	Sales Salary Expense
Unemp.	OASDI	Medicare	OASDI	Medicare	FIT	SIT	Net Pay	No.		
2 1 0 0 00	2 1 0 0 00	2 1 0 0 00	1 3 0 20	3 0 45	7 0 00	1 4 7 00	1 7 2 2 35		2 1 0 0 00	
3 3 0 0 00	3 3 0 0 00	3 3 0 0 00	2 0 4 60	4 7 85	2 5 9 00	2 3 1 00	2 5 5 7 55			3 3 0 0 00
3 9 0 0 00	3 9 0 0 00	3 9 0 0 00	2 4 1 80	5 6 55	3 9 9 00	2 7 3 00	2 9 2 9 65			3 9 0 0 00
9 3 0 0 00	9 3 0 0 00	9 3 0 0 00	5 7 6 60	1 3 4 85	7 2 8 00	6 5 1 00	7 2 0 9 55		2 1 0 0 00	7 2 0 0 00
2 1 0 0 00	2 1 0 0 00	2 1 0 0 00	1 3 0 20	3 0 45	7 0 00	1 4 7 00	1 7 2 2 35		2 1 0 0 00	
3 3 0 0 00	3 3 0 0 00	3 3 0 0 00	2 0 4 60	4 7 85	2 5 9 00	2 3 1 00	2 5 5 7 55			3 3 0 0 00
3 1 0 0 00	3 9 0 0 00	3 9 0 0 00	2 4 1 80	5 6 55	3 9 9 00	2 7 3 00	2 9 2 9 65			3 9 0 0 00
8 5 0 0 00	9 3 0 0 00	9 3 0 0 00	5 7 6 60	1 3 4 85	7 2 8 00	6 5 1 00	7 2 0 9 55		2 1 0 0 00	7 2 0 0 00

201X

Mar. 1 Bach paid balance owed, no discount.

2 Purchased merchandise from Thomas Company on account, $8,000; terms 1/10, n/30.

2 Paid $10 from the petty cash fund for cleaning package, voucher no. 18 (consider it a cleaning expense).

3 Sold merchandise to Young Company on account, $8,000, invoice no. 51; terms 3/10, n/30. Cost of inventory, $2,510.

5 Paid $7 from the petty cash fund for postage, voucher no. 19.

6 Sold merchandise to Young Company on account, $8,000, invoice no. 52; terms 3/10, n/30. Cost of inventory, $2,240.

8 Paid $11 from the petty cash fund for first aid emergency, voucher no. 20.

9 Purchased merchandise from Thomas Company on account, $4,000; terms 1/10, n/30.

9 Paid $9 for delivery expense from petty cash fund, voucher no. 21. Relates to merchandise purchase.

9 Sold more merchandise to Young Company on account, $6,000, invoice no. 53; terms 3/10, n/30. Cost of inventory, $1,970.

9 Paid cleaning service, $100, check no. 110.

10 Young Company returned merchandise sold for $3,200 from invoice no. 52; the Fantastic Dress Shop issued credit memo no. 10 to Young Company for $3,200. Cost of inventory returned, $1,025.

11 Purchased merchandise from Johnsons Company on account, $14,000; terms 3/15, n/60.

12 Sold merchandise for $30,000 cash. Cost of inventory, $13,830.

12 Paid Thomas Company invoice dated March 2, check no. 111.

13 Sold $5,000 of merchandise for cash. Cost of inventory, $2,900.

14 Returned merchandise to Johnsons Company in the amount of $1,000; the Fantastic Dress Shop issued debit memo no. 4 to Johnsons Company.

14 Paid $2 from the petty cash fund for delivery expense, voucher no. 22. Relates to merchandise purchase.

15 Paid taxes due for FICA (OASDI and Medicare) and FIT for February payroll, check no. 112.

15 Bridget withdrew $250 for her own personal expenses, check no. 113.

15 Paid state income tax for February payroll, check no. 114.

16 Received payment from Young Company for invoice no. 52, less discount and return.

16 Young Company paid invoice no. 51, $8,000.

16 Sold merchandise to Bach Company on account, $4,600, invoice no. 54; terms 3/10, n/30. Cost of Inventory, $1,840.

21 Purchased delivery truck on account from Manny's Garage, $19,700.

22 Sold merchandise to Young Company on account, $5,000, invoice no. 55; terms 3/10, n/30. Cost of Inventory, $2,650.

23 Paid Johnsons Company the balance owed, check no. 115.

24 Sold merchandise to Bach Company on account, $1,400, invoice no. 56; terms 3/10, n/30. Cost of Inventory, $720.

25 Purchased merchandise for $1,800, check no. 116.

27 Purchased merchandise from Danmark Company on account, $5,000; terms 1/10, n/30.

27 Paid $3 postage from the petty cash fund, voucher no. 23.

28 Young Company paid invoice no. 55 dated March 22, less discount.

28 Bach Company paid invoice no. 54 dated March 16.

29 Purchased merchandise from Thomas Company on account, $13,000; terms 1/10, n/30.

30 Sold merchandise to Danmark Company on account, $9,000, invoice no. 57; terms 3/10, n/30. Cost of Inventory, $2,100.

30 Issued check no. 117 to replenish the petty cash fund to the same level. Assume no shortage or overage.

30 Recorded payroll in payroll register.

30 Journalized payroll entry (to be paid on 31st).

30 Journalized employer's payroll tax expense.

31 Paid payroll checks no. 118, no. 119, and no. 120.

Additional Data

a. During March, rent expired, $550.

b. Truck depreciated, $300.

c. Rental income earned, $250 (one month's rent from subletting).

d. Bridget Duval's dress shop is located at 1 Milgate Rd., Marblehead, MA 01945. Its identification number is 33-4158215.

MARRIED Persons-MONTHLY Payroll Period

(For Wages Paid through December 2017)

And the wages are—		And the number of withholding allowances claimed is—										
At least	But less than	0	1	2	3	4	5	6	7	8	9	10
		The amount of income tax to be withheld is—										
$3,400	$3,440	$327	$277	$226	$175	$135	$101	$67	$34	$0	$0	$0
3,440	3,480	333	283	232	181	139	105	71	38	4	0	0
3,480	3,520	339	289	238	187	143	109	75	42	8	0	0
3,520	3,560	345	295	244	193	147	113	79	46	12	0	0
3,560	3,600	351	301	250	199	151	117	83	50	16	0	0
3,600	3,640	357	307	256	205	155	121	87	54	20	0	0
3,640	3,680	363	313	262	211	161	125	91	58	24	0	0
3,680	3,720	369	319	268	217	167	129	95	62	28	0	0
3,720	3,760	375	325	274	223	173	133	99	66	32	0	0
3,760	3,800	381	331	280	229	179	137	103	70	36	2	0
3,800	3,840	387	337	286	235	185	141	107	74	40	6	0
3,840	3,880	393	343	292	241	191	145	111	78	44	10	0
3,880	3,920	399	349	298	247	197	149	115	82	48	14	0
3,920	3,960	405	355	304	253	203	153	119	86	52	18	0
3,960	4,000	411	361	310	259	209	158	123	90	56	22	0
4,000	4,040	417	367	316	265	215	164	127	94	60	26	0
4,040	4,080	423	373	322	271	221	170	131	98	64	30	0
4,080	4,120	429	379	328	277	227	176	135	102	68	34	0
4,120	4,160	435	385	334	283	233	182	139	106	72	38	4
4,160	4,200	441	391	340	289	239	188	143	110	76	42	8
4,200	4,240	447	397	346	295	245	194	147	114	80	46	12
4,240	4,280	453	403	352	301	251	200	151	118	84	50	16
4,280	4,320	459	409	358	307	257	206	155	122	88	54	20
4,320	4,360	465	415	364	313	263	212	161	126	92	58	24
4,360	4,400	471	421	370	319	269	218	167	130	96	62	28
4,400	4,440	477	427	376	325	275	224	173	134	100	66	32
4,440	4,480	483	433	382	331	281	230	179	138	104	70	36
4,480	4,520	489	439	388	337	287	236	185	142	108	74	40
4,520	4,560	495	445	394	343	293	242	191	146	112	78	44
4,560	4,600	501	451	400	349	299	248	197	150	116	82	48

4,600	4,640	507	457	406	355	305	254	203	154	120	86	52
4,640	4,680	513	463	412	361	311	260	209	159	124	90	56
4,680	4,720	519	469	418	367	317	266	215	165	128	94	60
4,720	4,760	525	475	424	373	323	272	221	171	132	98	64
4,760	4,800	531	481	430	379	329	278	227	177	136	102	68
4,800	4,840	537	487	436	385	335	284	233	183	140	106	72
4,840	4,880	543	493	442	391	341	290	239	189	144	110	76
4,880	4,920	549	499	448	397	347	296	245	195	148	114	80
4,920	4,960	555	505	454	403	353	302	251	201	152	118	84
4,960	5,000	561	511	460	409	359	308	257	207	156	122	88
5,000	5,040	567	517	466	415	365	314	263	213	162	126	92
5,040	5,080	573	523	472	421	371	320	269	219	168	130	96
5,080	5,120	579	529	478	427	377	326	275	225	174	134	100
5,120	5,160	585	535	484	433	383	332	281	231	180	138	104
5,160	5,200	591	541	490	439	389	338	287	237	186	142	108
5,200	5,240	597	547	496	445	395	344	293	243	192	146	112
5,240	5,280	603	553	502	451	401	350	299	249	198	150	116
5,280	5,320	609	559	508	457	407	356	305	255	204	154	120
5,320	5,360	615	565	514	463	413	362	311	261	210	160	124
5,360	5,400	621	571	520	469	419	368	317	267	216	166	128
5,400	5,440	627	577	526	475	425	374	323	273	222	172	132
5,440	5,480	633	583	532	481	431	380	329	279	228	178	136
5,480	5,520	639	589	538	487	437	386	335	285	234	184	140
5,520	5,560	645	595	544	493	443	392	341	291	240	190	144
5,560	5,600	651	601	550	499	449	398	347	297	246	196	148
5,600	5,640	657	607	556	505	455	404	353	303	252	202	152
5,640	5,680	663	613	562	511	461	410	359	309	258	208	157
5,680	5,720	669	619	568	517	467	416	365	315	264	214	163
5,720	5,760	675	625	574	523	473	422	371	321	270	220	169
5,760	5,800	681	631	580	529	479	428	377	327	276	226	175
5,800	5,840	687	637	586	535	485	434	383	333	282	232	181
5,840	5,880	693	643	592	541	491	440	389	339	288	238	187
5,880	5,920	699	649	598	547	497	446	395	345	294	244	193
5,920	5,960	705	655	604	553	503	452	401	351	300	250	199
5,960	6,000	711	661	610	559	509	458	407	357	306	256	205
6,000	6,040	717	667	616	565	515	464	413	363	312	262	211
6,040	6,080	723	673	622	571	521	470	419	369	318	268	217
6,080	6,120	729	679	628	577	527	476	425	375	324	274	223

SAGE 50 COMPUTER WORKSHOP

S50

Computerized Accounting Application for Chapter 12

Refresher on using Sage 50 Complete Accounting

Before starting this assignment, you may want to refresh your memory by reading the following PDF documents in the multimedia library of the MyAccountingLab website. Remember to choose the PDF document for your version of Sage 50.

1. An Introduction to Sage 50
2. Correcting Sage 50 Transactions
3. How to Repeat or Restart a Sage 50 Assignment
4. Backing Up and Restoring Your Work in Sage 50

You also should have completed the following workshops:

1. Workshop 1 Atlas Company from Chapter 3
2. Workshop 2 Zell Company from Chapter 4
3. Workshop 3 Sherman Realty from Chapter 5
4. Workshop 4 Pete's Market from Chapter 8
5. Workshop 5 Part A Mars Company from Chapter 10
6. Workshop 5 Part B Jeanne's Toy House from Chapter 10

Workshop 6:

Accounting Cycle for a Merchandising Company

In this workshop, you complete an accounting cycle for a merchandising business owned by the Fantastic Dress Shop using Sage 50. Tasks include maintaining inventory, recording sales on account, merchandise returns, merchandise purchases, vendor payments, and payroll. You will also prepare inventory reports, aged receivables and aged payable reports, general journal and general ledger reports, a trial balance, and financial statements. Finally, you will close the accounting period.

Instructions and the data file for completing this assignment are in the multimedia library of the MyAccountingLab website. Open the *Workshop 6 The Fantastic Dress Shop* PDF document for your version of Sage 50 and download *The Fantastic Dress Shop* data file for your version of Sage 50.

QUICKBOOKS COMPUTER WORKSHOP

QB

Computerized Accounting Application for Chapter 12

Refresher on using QuickBooks Accountant

Before starting this assignment, you may want to refresh your memory by reading the following PDF documents in the multimedia library of the MyAccountingLab website. Remember to choose the PDF document for your version of QuickBooks.

1. An Introduction to QuickBooks
2. Correcting QuickBooks Transactions
3. How to Repeat or Restart a QuickBooks Assignment
4. Backing Up and Restoring Your Work in QuickBooks

You also should have completed the following workshops:

1. Workshop 1 Atlas Company from Chapter 3
2. Workshop 2 Zell Company from Chapter 4
3. Workshop 3 Sherman Realty from Chapter 5
4. Workshop 4 Pete's Market from Chapter 8
5. Workshop 5 Part A Mars Company from Chapter 10
6. Workshop 5 Part B Jeanne's Toy House from Chapter 10

Workshop 6:

Accounting Cycle for a Merchandising Company

In this workshop, you complete an accounting cycle for a merchandising business owned by the Fantastic Dress Shop using QuickBooks. Tasks include maintaining inventory, recording sales on account, merchandise returns, merchandise purchases, vendor payments, and payroll. You will also prepare inventory reports, aged receivables and aged payable reports, general journal and general ledger reports, a trial balance, and financial statements. Finally, you will close the accounting period.

Instructions and the data file for completing this assignment are in the multimedia library of the MyAccountingLab website. Open the *Workshop 6 The Fantastic Dress Shop* PDF document for your version of Quickbooks and download the *The Fantastic Dress Shop* data file for your version of Quickbooks.

Appendix for Chapter 12

ACCOUNTING FOR MERCHANDISE INVENTORY USING THE PERIODIC METHOD OF INVENTORY VALUATION

Discounts, and Sales Returns and Allowances

Chou's Toy Shop, owned by Chou Li, is a retailer. It buys toys, games, bikes, and similar items from manufacturers and wholesalers and resells these goods (or merchandise) to its customers. The shelving, display cases, and so forth are called "fixtures" or "equipment." These items are not for resale.

LO1

Retailers Merchants who buy goods from wholesalers for resale to customers.

Merchandise Goods brought into a store for resale to customers.

Gross Sales

Each cash or charge sale made at Chou's Toy Shop is rung up at the register. Suppose the shop had $3,000 in sales on July 18. Of that amount, $1,800 was cash sales and $1,200 was charges. The account that recorded those sales would be

```
            Sales
       Dr.  |  Cr.
            |  3,000  ◄———— Revenue account with a credit balance
```

This account is a revenue account with a credit balance and will be found on the income statement. Figure 12A.1 shows the journal entry for the day. *Note:* We talk about sales tax later. Let's look at a transaction analysis chart of this transaction before we journalize.

Accounts Affected	Category	↑↓	Rules	T Account Update
Cash	Asset	↑	Dr.	**Cash**
				1,800	
Accounts Receivable	Asset	↑	Dr.	**Accounts Receivable**
				1,200	
Sales	Revenue	↑	Cr.	**Sales**
					3,000

July	18	Cash		1 8 0 0 00		
		Accounts Receivable		1 2 0 0 00		
		Sales				3 0 0 0 00
		Sales for July 18				

Figure 12A.1
Recording Cash and Charge Sales for the Day

Sales Returns and Allowances

It would be great for Chou if all the customers were completely satisfied, but that rarely is the case. On July 19, Michelle Reese brought back a doll she bought on account for $50. She told Chou that the doll was defective and that she wanted either a price reduction or a new doll. They agreed on a $10 price reduction. Michelle now owes Chou $40. The account called Sales Returns and Allowances (SRA) would record this information.

Sales Returns and Allowances (SRA) account A contra-revenue account that records price adjustments and allowances granted on merchandise that is defective and has been returned.

Sales Returns and Allowances

	Dr.	Cr.
Contra-revenue account with a debit balance	10	

This account is a contra-revenue account with a debit balance. It will be reported on the income statement. Figure 12A.2 shows how the journal entry would look. Let's first look at a transaction analysis chart of this transaction before we journalize.

Accounts Affected	Category	↑↓	Rules	T Account Update
Sales Returns and Allowances	Contra-revenue	↑	Dr.	**Sales Ret. & Allow.** Dr. 10 | Cr.
Accounts Receivable, Michelle Reese	Asset	↓	Cr.	**Accounts Receivable** Dr. 1,200 | Cr. 10

Figure 12A.2
Issuing a Credit Memorandum in the General Journal

July	19	Sales Returns and Allowances		10 00		
		Accounts Receivable, Michelle Reese			10 00	
		Issued credit memorandum				

Look at how the sales returns and allowances increase.

Sales Discount

Sales discount Amount a customer is allowed to deduct from the bill total for paying a bill during the discount period.

Chou gives a 2% sales discount to credit customers who pay their invoice early. He wants his customers to know about this policy, so he posted the following sign at the cash register:

Sales Discount Policies

2/10, n/30	*2% discount is allowed off price of bill if paid within the first 10 days or full amount is due within 30 days.*
n/10, EOM	*No discount. Full amount of bill is due within 10 days after the end of the month.*

Discount period A period shorter than the credit period when a discount is available to encourage early payment of bills.

Credit period Length of time allowed for payment of goods sold on account.

Sales Discount account A contra-revenue account that records cash discounts granted to customers for payments made within a specific period of time.

Note that the discount period is the time when a discount is granted. The discount period is less time than the credit period, which is the length of time allowed to pay the amount owed on the invoice.

If Michelle pays her $40 bill early, she will get an $0.80 discount. This information is recorded in the Sales Discount account as follows:

Sales Discount

	Dr.	Cr.
Contra-revenue account with a debit balance	0.80	

Michelle's discount is calculated as follows:

$$2\% \times \$40 = \$0.80$$

Michelle pays her bill on July 24. She is entitled to the discount because she paid her bill within 10 days. Figure 12A.3 shows how Chou would record this payment on his books. Let's first look at a transaction analysis chart before we journalize.

Accounts Affected	Category	↑↓	Rules	T Account Update
Cash	Asset	↑	Dr.	**Cash**
				Dr. 1,800 / 39.20　Cr.
Sales Discount	Contra-revenue	↑	Dr.	**Sales Discount**
				Dr. 0.80　Cr.
Accounts Receivable	Asset	↓	Cr.	**Accounts Receivable**
				Dr. 1,200　Cr. 10 / 40

SUCCESS TIP

Gross Sales
− Sales discount
− SRA
= Net sales

July	24	Cash		3 9 20		
		Sales Discount		80		
		Accounts Receivable, Michelle Reese			4 0 00	
		Payment from Sale on Account				

Figure 12A.3
Recording Sales Discount

Although Michelle pays $39.20, her Accounts Receivable is credited for the full amount, $40.

In the examples so far we have not shown any transactions with sales tax. Note that the actual or net sales for Chou would be gross sales less sales returns and allowances less any sales discounts. Let's look at how Chou would record his monthly sales if the sales tax were charged.

Sales Tax Payable

None of the preceding examples shows state sales tax. Still, like it or not, Chou must collect that tax from his customers and send it to the state. Sales tax represents a liability to Chou. The amount Chou must pay to the state is recorded in the Sales Tax Payable account.

Assume the state Chou's is located in charges a 5% sales tax. Remember that Chou's sales on July 18 were $3,000. Chou must figure out the sales tax on the purchases. For this purpose, let's assume only two sales were made on that date: the cash sale ($1,800) and the charge sale ($1,200).

The sales tax on the cash purchase is calculated as follows:

$$\$1,800 \times 0.05 = \$ \ 90 \text{ Tax}$$
$$\$1,800 + \$90 \text{ tax} = \$1,890 \text{ Cash}$$

Here is how the sales tax on the charge sale is computed:

$$\$1,200 \times 0.05 = \$60 \text{ Tax} + \$1,200 \text{ Charge} = \$1,260 \text{ Accounts Receivable}$$

It would be recorded as shown in Figure 12A.4. Let's first look at a transaction analysis chart of this transaction before we journalize.

Net sales Gross Sales less Sales Returns and Allowances less Sales Discounts.

Gross sales The revenue earned from sale of merchandise to customers.

Sales Tax Payable account A An account in the general ledger that accumulates the amount of sales tax owed. It has a credit balance.

Accounts Affected	Category	↑↓	Rules	T Account Update
Cash	Asset	↑	Dr.	**Cash**
				Dr.	Cr.
				1,890	
Accounts Receivable	Asset	↑	Dr.	**Accounts Receivable**
				Dr.	Cr.
				1,260	
Sales Tax Payable	Liability	↑	Cr.	**Sales Tax Payable**
				Dr.	Cr.
					90
					60
Sales	Revenue	↑	Cr.	**Sales**
				Dr.	Cr.
					3,000

Figure 12A.4
Sales with Sales Tax

July	18	Cash		1 8 9 0 00		
		Accounts Receivable		1 2 6 0 00		
		Sales Tax Payable				1 5 0 00
		Sales				3 0 0 0 00
		July 18 Sales				

L02 ▶

Purchases Transactions, Including Freight

Purchases

Purchases Merchandise for resale. It is a cost.

When you go into your local Target, do you ever wonder how a store records all of the merchandise it purchases from a company like Sony? First, let us look at Chou's Toy Shop. Chou brings merchandise into his toy store for resale to customers. The account that records the cost of this merchandise is called Purchases. Suppose Chou buys $4,000 worth of Barbie dolls on account from Mattel Manufacturing on July 6. The Purchases account records all merchandise bought for resale.

	Purchases	
Purchases is a cost.	Dr.	Cr.
The rules work the same as an expense.	4,000	

This account has a debit balance and is classified as a cost. Purchases represent costs that are directly related to bringing merchandise into the store for resale to customers. The July 6 entry would be analyzed and journalized as in Figure 12A.5 on the following page.

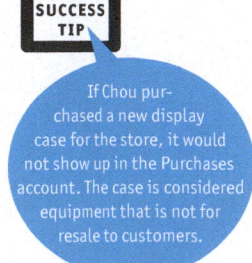

SUCCESS TIP

If Chou purchased a new display case for the store, it would not show up in the Purchases account. The case is considered equipment that is not for resale to customers.

Accounts Affected	Category	↑↓	Rules	T Account Update
Purchases	Cost	↑	Dr.	**Purchases**
				Dr.	Cr.
				4,000	
Accounts Payable, Mattel	Liability	↑	Cr.	**Acc. Payable**	**Mattel**
				Dr.	Cr.	Dr.	Cr.
					4,000		4,000

Jul.	6	Purchases		4 0 0 0 00		
		Accounts Payable, Mattel			4 0 0 0 00	
		Purchases on account				

Figure 12A.5
Purchased Merchandise
on Account

Keep in mind that we would have to record to Mattel in the accounts payable subsidiary ledger.

Purchases Returns and Allowances

Chou noticed that some of the dolls he received were defective, and he notified the manufacturer of the defects. On July 9, Mattel issued a credit memorandum indicating that Chou would get a $500 reduction from the original selling price. Chou then agreed to keep the dolls. The account that records a decrease to a buyer's cost is a contra-cost account called Purchases Returns and Allowances. The account lowers the cost of purchases.

Purchases Returns and Allow-ances A contra-cost account in the ledger that records the amount of defective or unacceptable merchandise returned to suppliers and/or price reductions given for defective items.

Purchases Returns and Allowances

Dr.	Cr.
	500 ← Normal balance is a credit.

Let's analyze this reduction to cost and prepare a general journal entry (Figure 12A.6).

Accounts Affected	Category	↑↓	Rules	T Account Update				
Accounts Payable, Mattel	Liability	↓	Dr.	**Acc. Payable**		**Mattel**		
				Dr.	Cr.	Dr.	Cr.	
				500	4,000	500	4,000	
Purchases Returns and Allowances	Contra-cost	↑	Cr.	**Purchases Ret. & Allow.**				
				Dr.	Cr.			
					500			

When posted to general ledger accounts as well as recorded to Mattel in the accounts payable subsidiary ledger, Chou owes $500 less.

Jul.	9	Accounts Payable, Mattel		5 0 0 00		
		Purchases Returns and Allowances			5 0 0 00	
		Received credit memorandum				

Figure 12A.6
Credit Memorandum Received

SUCCESS TIP

Remember: For Chou it is a purchases discount, whereas for Mattel it is a sales discount.

Purchases Discount

Now let's look at the analysis and journal entry when Chou pays Mattel. Mattel offers a 2% cash discount if the invoice is paid within 10 days. To take advantage of this cash discount, Chou sent a check to Mattel on July 15. The discount is taken after the allowance.

$4,000
− 500 allowance
$3,500 × 0.02 = $70 purchases discount

The account that records this discount is called Purchases Discount. It, too, is a contra-cost account because it lowers the cost of purchases.

Purchases Discount A contra-cost account in the general ledger that records discounts offered by vendors of merchandise for prompt payment of purchases by buyers.

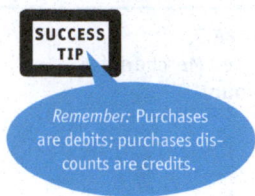

Purchases Discount

Dr.	Cr.
	70 ← **Normal balance is a credit.**

Let's analyze and prepare a general journal entry (Figure 12A.7).

Figure 12A.7
Purchase Discount Journalized

Jul.	15	Accounts Payable, Mattel		3 5 0 0 00		
		Purchases Discount			7 0 00	
		Cash			3 4 3 0 00	
		Paid Mattel balance owed				

Accounts Affected	Category	↑↓	Rules	T Account Update
Accounts Payable, Mattel	Liability	↓	Dr.	**Acc. Payable** Dr. 500 | Cr. 4,000 3,500 **Mattel** Dr. 500 | Cr. 4,000 3,500
Purchases Discount	Contra-cost	↑	Cr.	**Purchases Discount** Dr. | Cr. 70
Cash	Asset	↓	Cr.	**Cash** Dr. | Cr. 3,430

After the journal entry is posted and recorded to Mattel, the result will show that Chou saved $70 and reduced what he owed to Mattel. The actual—or net—cost of his purchase is $3,430, calculated as follows:

Purchases	$4,000
− Purchases Returns and Allowances	500
− Purchases Discounts	70
= Net Purchases	$3,430

Freight charges are not taken into consideration in calculating net purchases. Still, they are important. If the seller is responsible for paying the shipping cost until the goods reach their destination, the freight charges are F.O.B. destination. (F.O.B. stands for "free on board" the carrier.) For example, if a seller located in Boston sold goods F.O.B. destination to a buyer in New York, the seller would have to pay the cost of shipping the goods to the buyer.

If the buyer is responsible for paying the shipping costs, the freight charges are F.O.B. shipping point. In this situation, the seller will sometimes prepay the freight charges as a matter of convenience and will add it to the invoice of the purchaser, as in the following example:

F.O.B. destination *Seller* pays or is responsible for the cost of freight to purchaser's location or destination.

F.O.B. shipping point *Purchaser* pays or is responsible for the shipping costs from seller's shipping point to purchaser's location.

Bill amount ($800+$80 prepaid freight)	$880
Less: 5% cash discount (0.05 × $800)	40
Amount to be paid by buyer	$840

Purchase discounts are not taken on freight. The discount is based on the purchase price.

If the seller ships goods F.O.B. shipping point, legal ownership (title) passes to the buyer *when the goods are shipped*. If goods are shipped by the seller F.O.B. destination, title will change *when goods have reached their destination*. (See Exhibit 12A.1.)

SUCCESS TIP

Title changing hands means the ownership of the goods changes from seller to buyer.

Exhibit 12A.1

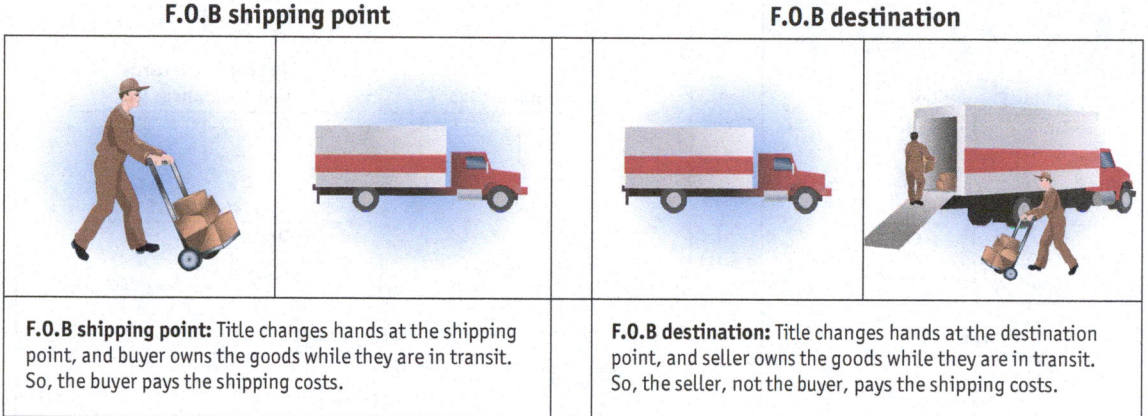

F.O.B shipping point

F.O.B destination

F.O.B shipping point: Title changes hands at the shipping point, and buyer owns the goods while they are in transit. So, the buyer pays the shipping costs.

F.O.B destination: Title changes hands at the destination point, and seller owns the goods while they are in transit. So, the seller, not the buyer, pays the shipping costs.

Journalizing and Recording Transactions and Posting to the General Ledger Along with a Debit Memorandum

 **L03**

On April 3 Art's Wholesale Clothing Company had the following transaction:

201X

Apr. 3   Purchased merchandise on account, $5,000, plus freight, $50, from Abby Blake Co.

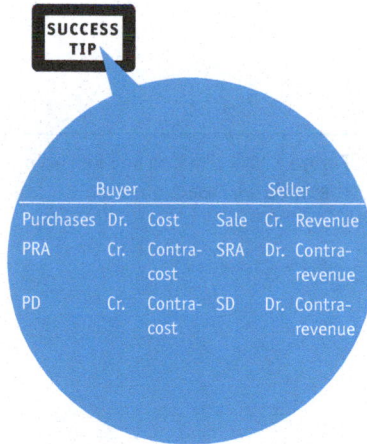

SUCCESS TIP

	Buyer			Seller	
Purchases	Dr.	Cost	Sale	Cr.	Revenue
PRA	Cr.	Contra-cost	SRA	Dr.	Contra-revenue
PD	Cr.	Contra-cost	SD	Dr.	Contra-revenue

	THE ANALYSIS		
Accounts Affected	**Category**	**↑↓**	**Rules of Dr. and Cr.**
Purchases	Cost	↑	Dr. $5,000
Freight-In	Cost	↑	Dr. $ 50
Accounts Payable, Abby Blake Co.	Liability	↑	Cr. $5,050

Figure 12A.8 shows how the general journal would look.

							Page 2	
Apr.	3	Purchases		5 0 0 0 00				
		Freight-In		5 0 00				
		Accounts Payable, Abby Blake Co.				5 0 5 0 00		
		Purchased merchandise on account						
		From Abby Blake						

Figure 12A.8
Merchandise Purchase, Plus Freight Cost

Posting and Recording Purchases Transactions

Before we post to the general ledger and record to the subsidiary ledger, let's first examine the T accounts and what each one would look like.

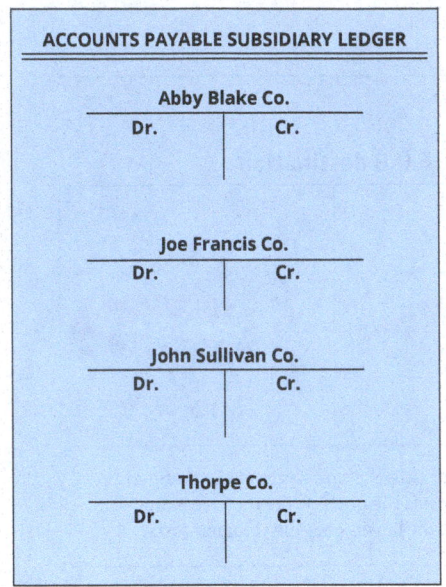

Now let's look at how to post and record the April 3 transaction.

For this transaction we post to the general ledger accounts Purchases, Freight-In, and Accounts Payable. Note how the account numbers 511, 514, and 211 are entered into the PR column of the general journal. We must also *record* to Abby Blake Co. in the accounts payable subsidiary ledger. Note that it is placed on the credit side because we owe Abby the money. When the subsidiary ledger is updated, a (✓) is placed in the PR column of the general journal. Figure 12A.9 shows how the accounts payable subsidiary ledger and the partial general ledger would look after posting and recording.

Figure 12A.9 Posting and Recording the April 3 Transaction

GENERAL JOURNAL					Page 2
Date	Account Titles and Description	PR	Dr.		Cr.
201X					
Apr. 3	Purchases	511	5 0 0 00		
	Freight-In	514	5 0 00		
	Accounts Payable, Abby Blake Co.	211 ✓			5 0 5 0 00
	Purchased merchandise on account, Blake				

PARTIAL ACCOUNTS PAYABLE SUBSIDIARY LEDGER

Abby Blake Co.

Dr.	Cr.
	5,050 GJ2 4/3

PARTIAL GENERAL LEDGER

Accounts Payable 211

Dr.	Cr.
	5,050 GJ2 4/3

Purchases 511

Dr.	Cr.
4/3 GJ2 5,000	

Freight-In 514

Dr.	Cr.
4/3 GJ2 50	

Before concluding this unit, let's take a closer look at the April 9 transaction when Art's issues a debit memorandum to Thorpe Company. We analyze the transaction and show how to post and record it.

Debit Memorandum

In Chapter 9, Art's Wholesale Clothing Company previously had to handle returned goods as a seller. It did so by issuing credit memoranda to customers who returned or received an allowance on the price. In this chapter, Art's must handle returns as a buyer. It does so by using debit memoranda. A debit memorandum is a piece of paper issued by a customer to a seller. It indicates that a return or allowance has occurred.

On April 6, Art's Wholesale purchased men's hats for $800 from Thorpe Company. On April 9, 20 hats valued at $200 were found to have defective brims. Art's issued a debit memorandum to Thorpe Company, as shown in Figure 12A.10. At some point in the future, Thorpe will issue Art's a credit memorandum. Let's look at how Art's Wholesale Clothing Company handles such a transaction in its accounting records.

Debit memorandum A memo issued by a purchaser to a seller, indicating that some Purchases Returns and Allowances have occurred and therefore the purchaser now owes less money on account.

DEBIT MEMORANDUM		No. 1
Art's Wholesale Clothing Company 1528 Belle Ave. New York, NY 10022		
TO: Thorpe Company 3 Access Road Beverly, MA 01915		April 9, 201X
WE DEBIT your account as follows:		
Quantity	Unit Cost	Total
20 Men's Hats Code 827 – defective brims	$10	$200

Figure 12A.10
Debit Memorandum

Journalizing and Posting the Debit Memo

First, let's look at a transaction analysis chart.

Accounts Affected	Category	↑↓	Rules
Accounts Payable	Liability	↓	Dr.
Purchases Returns and Allowances	Contra-cost	↑	Cr.

Next, let's examine the journal entry for the debit memorandum (Figure 12A.11).

SUCCESS TIP

Result of debit memo: debits or reduces Accounts Payable. On seller's books, accounts affected would include Sales Returns and Allowances, Cost of Goods Sold, Merchandise Inventory, and Accounts Receivable.

	GENERAL JOURNAL				
					Page 2
Date	Account Titles and Description	PR	Dr.		Cr.
Apr. 9	Accounts Payable, Thorpe Company	211 ✓	200 00		
	Purchases Returns and Allowances	513			200 00
	Debit memo no.1				

Figure 12A.11
Debit Memorandum Journalized and Posted

The two postings and one recording are the following:

1. **211:** Post to Accounts Payable as a debit in the general ledger (account no. 211). When done, place in the PR column the account number, 211, above the diagonal on the same line as Accounts Payable in the journal.

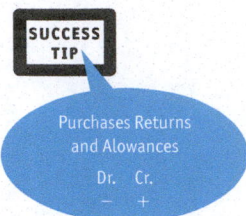

2. ✓: Record to Thorpe Co. in the accounts payable subsidiary ledger to show that Art's doesn't owe Thorpe as much money. When done, place a ✓ in the journal in the PR column below the diagonal line on the same line as Accounts Payable in the journal. Remember, this check is for a manual system only. In a computerized system, both the general ledger and the subsidiary ledger are updated automatically when you click on "post."

3. 513: Post to Purchases Returns and Allowances as a credit in the general ledger (account no. 513). When done, place the account number, 513, in the PR column of the journal on the same line as Purchases Returns and Allowances. (If equipment was returned that was not merchandise for resale, we would credit Equipment and not Purchases Returns and Allowances.)

The following are the completed accounts payable subsidiary ledger and general ledger for Art's:

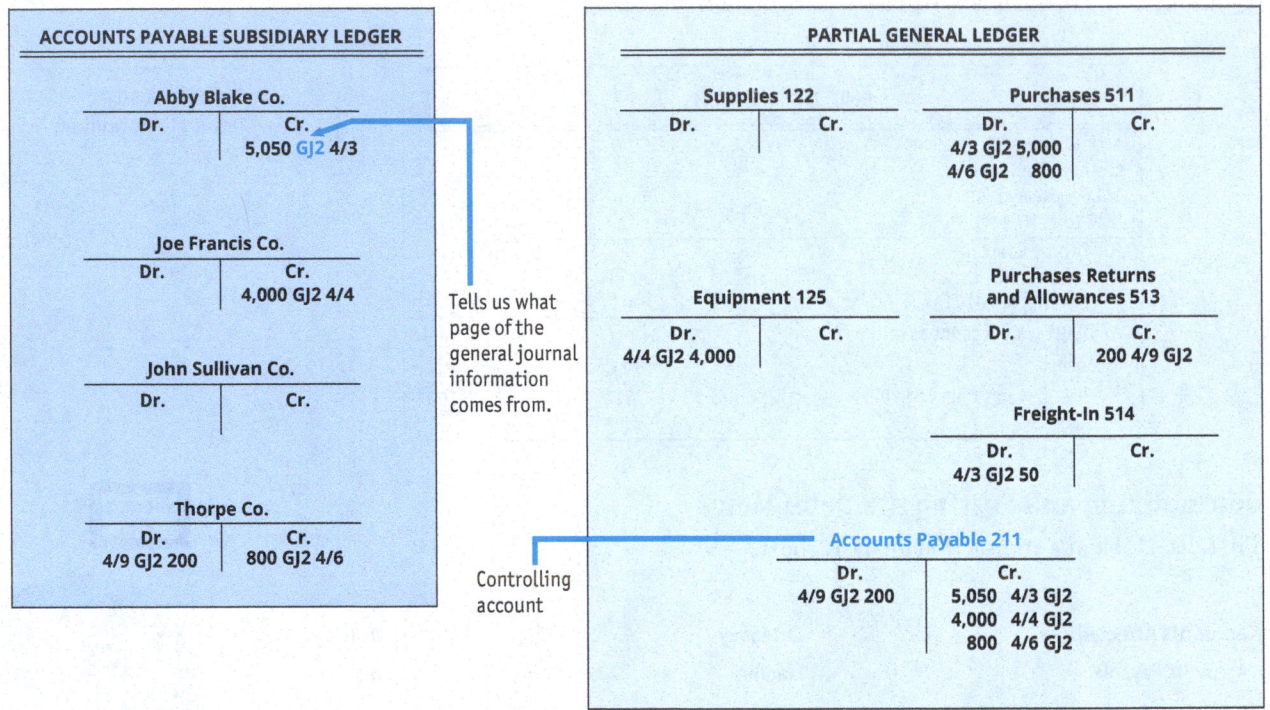

L04 ▶ Cash Payments Transactions and Schedules of Accounts Payable

The following cash payment transactions occurred for Art's Wholesale Clothing Company in April.

201X		
Apr.	2	Issued check no. 1 to Pete Blum for insurance paid in advance, $900.
	7	Issued check no. 2 to Joe Francis Company in payment of its April 4 invoice no. 388, $4,000.
	9	Issued check no. 3 to Rick Flo Co. for merchandise purchased for cash, $800.
	12	Issued check no. 4 to Thorpe Company in payment of its April 6 invoice no. 414, less the return and 1% discount.
	28	Issued check no. 5, $700, for salaries paid.

Figure 12A.12 on the following page provides a closer look at how the April 12 transaction would be journalized.

Accounts Affected	Category	↑↓	Rules	T Account Update
Cash	Asset	↓	Cr.	**Cash**

	Dr.	Cr.
		594

Accounts Affected	Category	↑↓	Rules	
Purchases Discount	Contra-cost	↑	Cr.	**Purchases Discount**

	Dr.	Cr.
		6

Accounts Affected	Category	↑↓	Rules	
Accounts Payable, Thorpe Co.	Liability	↓	Dr.	**Accounts Payable**

	Dr.	Cr.
	600	600

Thorpe Co.

	Dr.	Cr.
	600	600

Apr.	12	Accounts Payable, Thorpe Co.		6 0 0 00			
		Purchases Discount				6 00
		Cash			5 9 4 00
		Paid invoice no. 414			

Figure 12A.12
Journalizing the April 12
Transaction

Figure 12A.13 shows the complete set of cash payments transactions journalized for the month, followed by a complete posting to the general ledger and recordings to the accounts payable subsidiary ledger (remember from the past unit that we posted all the purchases on account).

GENERAL JOURNAL					Page 2		
Date		Account Titles and Description	PR	Dr.		Cr.	
201X							
Apr.	2	Prepaid Insurance	123	9 0 0 00			
		Cash	111			9 0 0 00
		Paid for insurance in advance				
	7	Accounts Payable, Joe Francis Co.	211 ✔	4 0 0 0 00		
		Cash	111			4 0 0 0 00
		Paid invoice no. 388				
	9	Purchases	511	8 0 0 00		
		Cash	111			8 0 0 00
		Cash Purchases				
	12	Accounts Payable, Thorpe Co.	211 ✔	6 0 0 00		
		Purchases Discount	512			6 00
		Cash	111			5 9 4 00
		Paid invoice no. 414				
	28	Salaries Expense	611	7 0 0 00		
		Cash	111			7 0 0 00
		Paid salaries				

Figure 12A.13
Cash Payments Transactions
Journalized for the Month
and Posting to the General
Journal

Figure 12A.13 (continued)

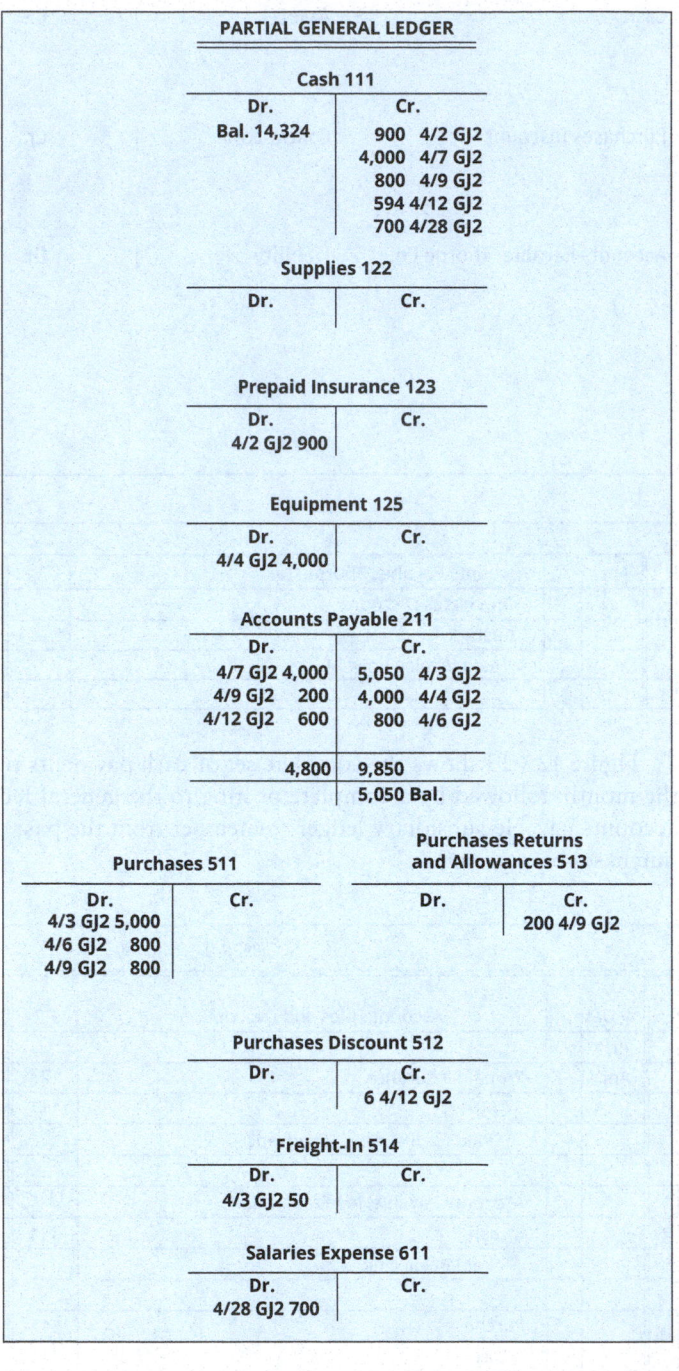

Now let's prove that the sum of the accounts payable subsidiary ledger at the end of the month is equal to the controlling account, Accounts Payable, at the end of April for Art's Wholesale Clothing Company.

To do so, creditors with an ending balance in Art's accounts payable subsidiary ledger must be listed in the schedule of accounts payable (see Figure 12A.14 on the following page). At the end of the month, the total owed ($5,050) in Accounts Payable, the controlling account in the general ledger, should equal the sum owed the individual creditors that are listed on the schedule of accounts payable. If it doesn't, the journalizing, posting, and recording must be checked to ensure that they are complete. Also, the balances of each title should be checked.

Controlling account The account in the general ledger that summarizes or controls a subsidiary ledger. Example: The Accounts Payable account in the general ledger is the controlling account for the accounts payable subsidiary ledger. After postings are complete, it shows the total amount owed from purchases made on account.

ART'S WHOLESALE CLOTHING COMPANY SCHEDULE OF ACCOUNTS PAYABLE APRIL 30, 201X	
Abby Blake Co.	$ 5 0 5 0 00
Total Accounts Payable	$ 5 0 5 0 00

Figure 12A.14
Schedule of Accounts Payable

Adjustments for Merchandise Inventory, Unearned Rent, Supplies Used, Insurance Expired, Depreciation Expense, and Accrued Salaries

 **L05**

The Merchandise Inventory account shows the goods that a merchandise company has available to sell to customers. Companies have several ways to keep track of the Cost of Goods Sold (the total cost of the goods sold to customers) and the quantity of inventory on hand. Here we discuss the periodic inventory system, in which the balance in inventory is updated only at the end of the accounting period. This system is used by companies, such as Art's Wholesale Clothing Company, that sell a variety of merchandise with low unit prices.

Assume that Art's Wholesale Clothing Company started the year with $19,000 worth of merchandise. This merchandise is called Beginning Merchandise Inventory or simply Beginning Inventory. The balance of beginning inventory in the Merchandise Inventory account never changes during the accounting period. Any purchases of merchandise are recorded in a separate account, the Purchases account. During the accounting period $52,000 worth of such purchases were made and recorded in the Purchases account by Art's Wholesale.

At the end of the period, the company takes a physical count of the merchandise in stock; this amount is called Ending Merchandise Inventory or simply Ending Inventory. It is calculated on an inventory sheet as shown in Figure 12A.15. This $4,000 is the ending inventory for this period and will become the beginning inventory for the next period.

Cost of Goods Sold Total cost of the goods which were sold to customers.

Periodic inventory system An inventory system that, at the *end* of each accounting period, calculates the cost of the unsold goods on hand by taking the cost of each unit times the number of units on hand of each product.

Beginning Merchandise Inventory (Beginning Inventory) The cost of goods on hand in a company to *begin* an accounting period.

Ending Merchandise Inventory (Ending Inventory) The cost of goods that remain unsold at the *end* of the accounting period. It is an asset on the new balance sheet.

Figure 12A.15
Ending Inventory Sheet

ART'S WHOLESALE CLOTHING COMPANY ENDING INVENTORY SHEET AS OF DECEMBER 31, 201X			
Amount	Explanation	Unit Cost	Total
20	Ladies' Jackets code 14-0	$50	$1,000
10	Men's Hats code 327	10	100
90	Men's Shirts code 423	10	900
100	Ladies' Blouses code 481	20	2,000
			$4,000
Counted by _____	Checked and priced by _____		

When the income statement is prepared, the cost of goods sold section requires two distinct numbers for inventory. The beginning inventory adds to the Cost of Goods Sold, and the ending inventory is subtracted from the cost of goods sold. Remember that the two figures for beginning and ending inventory were calculated months apart. Thus, combining these amounts to come up with one inventory figure would not be accurate.

Note that in the calculation of cost of goods sold, a title called **Freight-In** is shown.

Freight-In A Cost of Goods Sold account that records the shipping cost to the buyer.

	Cost of goods sold
	Beginning inventory
+	Net purchases
+	Freight-In
−	Ending inventory
=	Cost of goods sold

Freight-In is a Cost of Goods Sold account that records the shipping cost to the buyer. Note that net sales (Gross Sales less Sales Returns and Allowances and Sales Discounts) less Cost of Goods Sold equals **gross profit**. Subtracting operating expenses from gross profit equals net income.

Gross profit Net sales less cost of goods sold.

Adjustments A and B: Merchandise Inventory, $19,000

Adjusting the Merchandise Inventory account is a two-step process because we must record the beginning inventory and ending inventory amounts separately. The first step deals with beginning Merchandise Inventory.

Given: Beginning Inventory, $19,000

Our first adjustment removes the old outdated beginning inventory from the asset account (Merchandise Inventory) and transfers it to Income Summary. We do so by crediting Merchandise Inventory for $19,000 and debiting Income Summary for the same amount. This adjustment (A) is shown in the following T account form and on a transaction analysis chart.

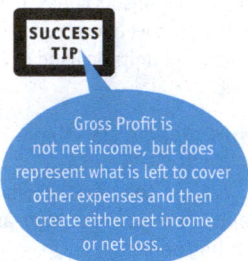

Gross Profit is not net income, but does represent what is left to cover other expenses and then create either net income or net loss.

Merchandise Inventory 114		Income Summary 313	
Bal. 19,000	Adj. 19,000	Adj. 19,000	

Adjustment (A)

Accounts Affected	Category	↑↓	Rules
Income Summary	—	—	Dr.
Merchandise Inventory	Asset	↓	Cr.

The second step adjustment updates the Merchandise Inventory account with a new figure for ending inventory.

(This, as well as the following adjusting entries, would be recorded first on the worksheet and then in the general journal.)

The second step is entering the amount of ending inventory ($4,000) in the Merchandise Inventory account. This step is done to record the up-to-date amount of goods on hand at the end of the period as an asset and to subtract this amount from the cost of goods sold (because we have not sold this inventory yet). To do so, we debit Merchandise Inventory for $4,000 and credit Income Summary for the same amount. This adjustment (B) is shown in the following T account form.

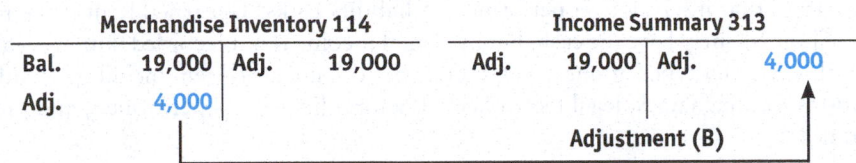

Merchandise Inventory 114				Income Summary 313			
Bal.	19,000	Adj.	19,000	Adj.	19,000	Adj.	4,000
Adj.	4,000						

Adjustment (B)

Let's look at how this process or method of recording merchandise inventory is reflected in the balance sheet and income statement (see Figure 12A.16). Note that the $19,000 of beginning inventory is assumed sold and is shown on the income statement as part of the cost of goods sold. The ending inventory of $4,000 is assumed not to be sold and is subtracted from the cost of goods sold on the income statement. The ending inventory becomes next month's beginning inventory on the balance sheet. When the income statement is prepared, we will need a figure for beginning inventory as well as a figure for ending inventory. The goal of this adjustment is to wipe out the old inventory (an expense) and show the new inventory (not yet an expense).

Beginning inventory	$19,000
+ Net cost of purchases*	50,910
= Cost of goods available for sale	$69,910
− Ending inventory	4,000
= Cost of goods sold	$65,910

*$52,000 Purchases − $860 PD − $680 PRA + $450 Freight-In

Figure 12A.16 Reporting Inventory on a Partial Balance Sheet and Income Statement

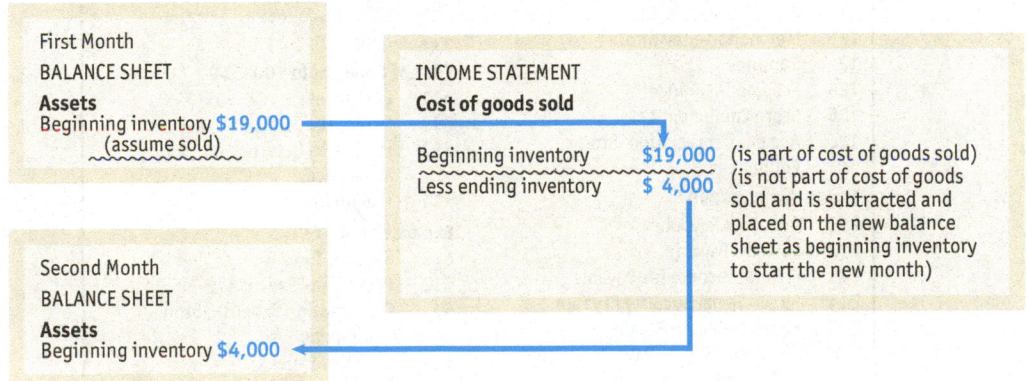

Adjustment C: Unearned Rent

Another new account we have not seen before is a liability called Unearned Rent or Rent Received in Advance. This account records the amount collected for rent before the service (renting the space) has been provided.

Suppose Art's Wholesale Clothing Company is subletting a portion of its space to Jesse Company for $200 per month. Jesse Company sends Art's cash for $600 for 3 months' rent paid in advance. This unearned rent ($600) is a liability on the balance sheet because Art's Wholesale owes Jesse Company 3 months' worth of occupancy.

When Art's Wholesale fulfills a portion of the rental agreement—when Jesse Company has been in the space for a period of time—this liability account will be reduced and

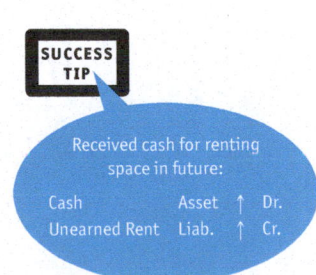

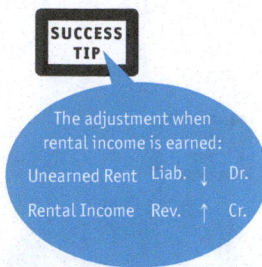

The adjustment when rental income is earned:

| Unearned Rent | Liab. | ↓ | Dr. |
| Rental Income | Rev. | ↑ | Cr. |

the Rental Income account will be increased. Rental income is another type of revenue for Art's Wholesale.

Remember that under accrual accounting, revenue is recognized when it is earned, whether payment is received then or not. Here, Art's Wholesale collected cash in advance for a service that it has not yet performed. A liability called Unearned Rent is the result. Art's Wholesale may have the cash, but the rental income is not recorded until it is earned. Examples of other types of unearned revenue besides unearned rent include prepaid subscriptions for magazines, legal fees collected before the work is performed, and prepaid insurance.

L06 ▶ Worksheets for Merchandise Companies Using the Periodic Inventory Method

Now let's look at how we would begin to prepare a worksheet for Art's Wholesale Clothing Company. For convenience, we reproduce the company's chart of accounts in Figure 12A.17.

Figure 12A.17
Art's Wholesale Clothing
Company Chart of Accounts

CHART OF ACCOUNTS	
Assets 100–199	**Revenue 400–499**
111 Cash	411 Sales
112 Petty Cash	412 Sales Returns and Allowances
113 Accounts Receivable	413 Sales Discount
121 Merchandise Inventory	414 Rental Income
122 Supplies	**Cost of Goods Sold 500–599**
123 Prepaid Insurance	511 Purchases
125 Store Equipment	512 Purchases Discount
126 Accum. Depreciation, Store Equipment	513 Purchases Returns and Allowances
Liabilities 200–299	514 Freight-In
211 Accounts Payable	**Expenses 600–699**
212 Salaries Payable	611 Salaries Expense
213 Federal Income Tax Payable	612 Payroll Tax Expense
214 FICA—Social Security Payable	613 Depreciation Expense, Store Equipment
215 FICA—Medicare Payable	614 Supplies Expense
216 State Income Tax Payable	615 Insurance Expense
217 SUTA Tax Payable	616 Postage Expense
218 FUTA Tax Payable	617 Miscellaneous Expense
219 Unearned Rent*	618 Interest Expense
220 Mortgage Payable	619 Cleaning Expense
Owner's Equity 300–399	620 Delivery Expense
311 Art Newner, Capital	
312 Art Newner, Withdrawals	
313 Income Summary	

*Although Unearned Rent is the only term under Liabilities not using payable, it is a liability.

Figure 12A.18 on the following page shows the trial balance that was prepared on December 31, 201X, from Art's Wholesale ledger. (Note that it is placed directly in the first two columns of the worksheet.)

	Trial Balance	
	Dr.	Cr.
Cash	12 920 00	
Petty Cash	100 00	
Accounts Receivable	14 500 00	
Merchandise Inventory	19 000 00	
Supplies	800 00	
Prepaid Insurance	900 00	
Store Equipment	4 000 00	
Acc. Dep., Store Equipment		400 00
Accounts Payable		17 900 00
Federal Income Tax Payable		800 00
FICA—Soc. Sec. Payable		454 00
FICA—Medicare Payable		106 00
State Income Tax Payable		200 00
SUTA Tax Payable		108 00
FUTA Tax Payable		32 00
Unearned Rent		600 00
Mortgage Payable		2 320 00
Art Newner, Capital		7 905 00
Art Newner, Withdrawals	8 600 00	
Income Summary		
Sales		95 000 00
Sales Returns and Allowances	950 00	
Sales Discount	670 00	
Purchases	52 000 00	
Purchases Discount		860 00
Purchases Returns and Allowances		680 00
Freight-In	450 00	
Salaries Expense	11 700 00	
Payroll Tax Expense	420 00	
Postage Expense	25 00	
Miscellaneous Expense	30 00	
Interest Expense	300 00	
Totals	127 365 00	127 365 00

Figure 12A.18
Trial Balance Section
of the Worksheet

In looking at the trial balance, we see many new titles that did not appear in the trial balance that we completed for a service company in Chapter 5. Let's look specifically at these new titles shown in Table 12A.1.

Note the following:

- Mortgage Payable is a liability account that records the increases and decreases in the amount of debt owed on a mortgage. We discuss this account more in the next chapter, when financial statements are prepared.

- Interest Expense represents a nonoperating expense for Art's Wholesale and thus is categorized as Other Expense. We look at this expense in the next chapter.

- Unearned Revenue is a liability account that records receipt of payment for goods and services in advance of delivery. Unearned Rent is a particular example of this general type of account.

We already discussed the adjustments that make up the two-step process involved in adjusting Merchandise Inventory at the end of the accounting period. Now we show T accounts and transaction analysis charts for other adjustments that need to be made at this point for a merchandise firm, just as they must be made for a service company.

Mortgage Payable A liability account showing amount owed on a mortgage.

Interest Expense The cost of borrowing money.

Unearned Revenue A liability account that records amount owed for goods or services in advance of delivery. The Cash account would record the receipt of cash.

TABLE 12A.1 Summary of New Account Titles

Title	Category	Account Reported on	Normal Balance	Temporary or Permanent
Petty Cash	Asset	Balance Sheet	Dr.	Permanent
Merchandise Inventory* (When sold)	Asset	Balance Sheet from prior period	Dr.	Permanent
Cost of Goods Sold	Expense	Income Statement of current period		
Federal Income Tax Payable	Liability	Balance Sheet	Cr.	Permanent
FICA—Social Security Payable	Liability	Balance Sheet	Cr.	Permanent
FICA—Medicare Payable	Liability	Balance Sheet	Cr.	Permanent
State Income Tax Payable	Liability	Balance Sheet	Cr.	Permanent
SUTA Tax Payable	Liability	Balance Sheet	Cr.	Permanent
FUTA Tax Payable	Liability	Balance Sheet	Cr.	Permanent
Unearned Rent†	Liability	Balance Sheet	Cr.	Permanent
Mortgage Payable	Liability	Balance Sheet	Cr.	Permanent
Sales	Revenue	Income Statement	Cr.	Temporary
Sales Returns and Allowances	Contra-Revenue	Income Statement	Dr.	Temporary
Sales Discount	Contra-Revenue	Income Statement	Dr.	Temporary
Purchases§	Cost of Goods Sold	Income Statement	Dr.	Temporary
Purchases Discount	Contra-Cost of Goods Sold	Income Statement	Cr.	Temporary
Purchases Returns and Allowances	Contra-Cost of Goods Sold	Income Statement	Cr.	Temporary
Freight-In	Cost of Goods Sold	Income Statement	Dr.	Temporary
Payroll Tax Expense	Expense	Income Statement	Dr.	Temporary
Postage Expense	Expense	Income Statement	Dr.	Temporary
Interest Expense	Other Expense	Income Statement	Dr.	Temporary

* The ending inventory of current period is a contra-cost of goods sold on the income statement and will be an asset on the balance sheet for the next period.

† Referred to as Unearned Revenue.

§ Note that the categories for Purchases and Freight-In are Cost of Goods Sold, whereas Purchases Discounts and Purchases Returns and Allowances are Contra-Cost of Goods Sold.

Adjustment C: Rental Income Earned by Art's Wholesale, $200

A month ago, Cash was increased by $600, as was a liability, Unearned Rent. Art's Wholesale received payment in advance but had not earned the rental income. Now, because $200 has been earned, the liability is reduced and Rental Income can be recorded for the $200. This step is shown as follows:

Unearned Rent 219		Rental Income 414
200	600	200
	400	

Balance on adjusted trial balance

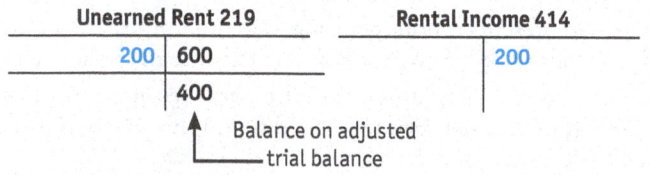

| Unearned Rent | Liability | ↓ | Dr. | $200 |
| Rental Income | Revenue | ↑ | Cr. | $200 |

Adjustment D: Supplies on Hand, $300

Because $500 worth of supplies were used up, Supplies Expense is increased, and the asset Supplies is decreased.

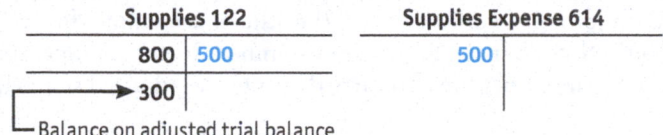

| Supplies Expense | Expense | ↑ | Dr. | $500 |
| Supplies | Asset | ↓ | Cr. | $500 |

Adjustment E: Insurance Expired, $300

Because insurance has expired by $300, Insurance Expense is increased by $300 and the asset Prepaid Insurance is decreased by $300.

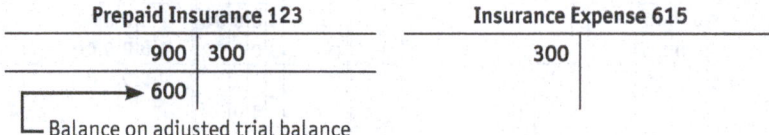

| Insurance Expense | Expense | ↑ | Dr. | $300 |
| Prepaid Insurance | Asset | ↓ | Cr. | $300 |

Adjustment F: Depreciation Expense, $50

When depreciation is taken, Depreciation Expense and Accumulated Depreciation are both increased by $50. Note that the cost of the store equipment remains the same.

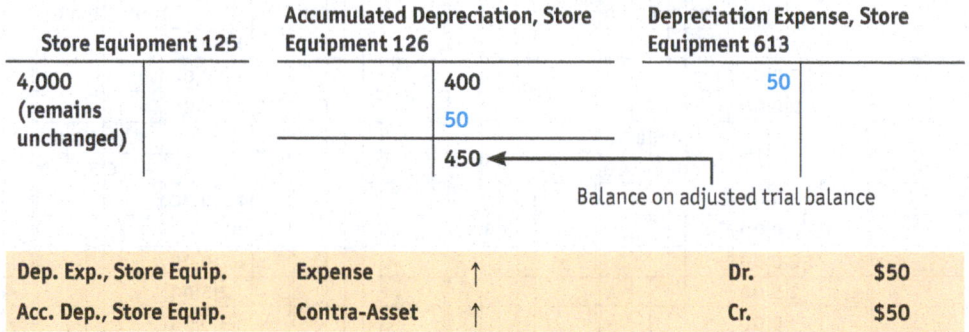

| Dep. Exp., Store Equip. | Expense | ↑ | Dr. | $50 |
| Acc. Dep., Store Equip. | Contra-Asset | ↑ | Cr. | $50 |

Adjustment G: Salaries Accrued, $600

The $600 in accrued salaries causes an increase in Salaries Expense and Salaries Payable.

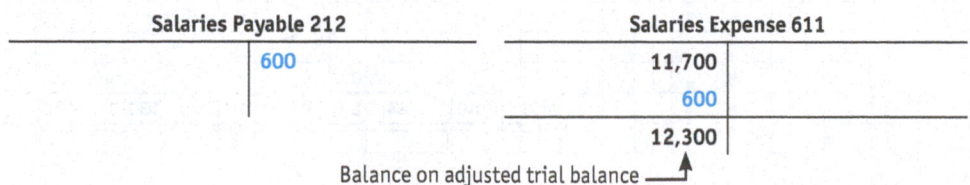

SUCCESS TIP

Remember: We do not combine the $19,000 and $4,000 in Income Summary. When we prepare the cost of goods sold section for the formal income statement, we will need both a beginning and an ending figure for inventory.

Salaries Expense	Expense	↑	Dr.	$600
Salaries Payable	Liability	↑	Cr.	$600

Figure 12A.19 shows the worksheet with the adjustments and adjusted trial balance columns filled out. Note that the adjustment numbers in the Income Summary from beginning and ending inventory are also carried over to the adjusted trial balance and are not combined.

Figure 12A.19 Worksheet with Six Columns

	Trial Balance		Adjustments		Adjusted Trial Balance	
	Dr.	Cr.	Dr.	Cr.	Dr.	Cr.
Cash	12 920 00				12 920 00	
Petty Cash	100 00				100 00	
Accounts Receivable	14 500 00				14 500 00	
Merchandise Inventory	19 000 00		(B) 4 000 00	(A) 19 000 00	4 000 00	
Supplies	800 00			(D) 500 00	300 00	
Prepaid Insurance	900 00			(E) 300 00	600 00	
Store Equipment	4 000 00				4 000 00	
Acc. Dep., Store Equipment		400 00		(F) 50 00		450 00
Accounts Payable		17 900 00				17 900 00
Federal Income Tax Payable		800 00				800 00
FICA—Soc. Sec. Payable		454 00				454 00
FICA—Medicare Payable		106 00				106 00
State Income Tax Payable		200 00				200 00
SUTA Tax Payable		108 00				108 00
FUTA Tax Payable		32 00				32 00
Unearned Rent		600 00	(C) 200 00			400 00
Mortgage Payable		2 320 00				2 320 00
Art Newner, Capital		7 905 00				7 905 00
Art Newner, Withdrawals	8 600 00				8 600 00	
Income Summary			(A) 19 000 00	(B) 4 000 00	19 000 00	4 000 00
Sales		95 000 00				95 000 00
Sales Returns and Allowances	950 00				950 00	
Sales Discount	670 00				670 00	
Purchases	52 000 00				52 000 00	
Purchases Discount		860 00				860 00
Purchases Returns and Allowances		680 00				680 00
Freight-In	450 00				450 00	
Salaries Expense	11 700 00		(G) 600 00		12 300 00	
Payroll Tax Expense	420 00				420 00	
Postage Expense	25 00				25 00	
Miscellaneous Expense	30 00				30 00	
Interest Expense	300 00				300 00	
Totals	127 365 00	127 365 00				
Rental Income				(C) 200 00		200 00
Supplies Expense			(D) 500 00		500 00	
Insurance Expense			(E) 300 00		300 00	
Depreciation Expense, Store Equip.			(F) 50 00		50 00	
Salaries Payable				(G) 600 00		600 00
Totals			24 650 00	24 650 00	132 015 00	132 015 00

Completion of the Accounting Cycle for a Merchandise Company Using the Periodic Method of Inventory Valuation

L07

As we discussed in Chapter 5, when we were dealing with a service company rather than a merchandise company, the three financial statements can be prepared from the worksheet showing the Unadjusted Trial Balance through the Adjustments to the Adjusted Trial Balance. Let's begin by looking at how Art's Wholesale Clothing Company prepares the income statement.

The Income Statement

Art is interested in knowing how well his shop performed for the year ended December 31, 201X. What were its net sales? What was the level of returns of goods from dissatisfied customers? What was the cost of the goods brought into the store versus the selling price received? How many goods were returned to suppliers? What is the cost of the goods that have not been sold? What was the cost of the Freight-In? The income statement in Figure 12A.20 is prepared from the income statement columns of the worksheet. Note that no debit or credit columns appear on the formal income statement; the inside columns in financial reports are used for subtotaling, not for debit and credit.

The income statement is broken down into several sections. Remembering the sections can help you set it up correctly on your own. The income statement shows the following:

	Net Sales
−	Cost of Goods Sold
=	Gross Profit
−	Operating Expenses
=	Net Income from Operations
+	Other Income
−	Other Expenses
=	Net Income

Let's take these sections one at a time and see where the figures come from on the worksheet.

Revenue Section: Net Sales. The first major category of the income statement shows net sales. The figure here—$93,380—is not on the worksheet. Instead, the accountant must combine the amounts for gross sales, sales returns and allowances, and sales discount found on the worksheet to arrive at a figure for net sales. Thus these individual amounts are not summarized in a single figure for net sales until the formal income statement is prepared.

Cost of Goods Sold Section. The figures for Merchandise Inventory are shown separately on the worksheet. The $19,000 represents the beginning inventory of the period, and the $4,000, calculated from an inventory sheet, is the ending inventory. Note that on the financial report the cost of goods sold section uses two separate figures for inventory.

Note that the following numbers are not found on the worksheet but are shown on the formal income statement (they are combined by the accountant in preparing the income statement):

- Net Purchases: $50,460 (Purchases − Purchases Discount − Purchases Returns and Allowances)
- Net Cost of Purchases: $50,910 (Net Purchases + Freight-In)
- Cost of Goods Available for Sale: $69,910 (Beginning Inventory + Net Cost of Purchases)
- Cost of Goods Sold: $65,910 (Cost of Goods Available for Sale − Ending Inventory)

SUCCESS TIP

Sales
− Sales Ret. & Allow.
− Sales Discount
= Net Sales

SUCCESS TIP

Beg. Inventory
+ Net Cost of Purchases
− Ending Inventory
= Cost of Goods

Figure 12A.20 Partial Worksheet and Income Statement

ART'S WHOLESALE CLOTHING COMPANY
PARTIAL WORKSHEET
FOR YEAR ENDED DECEMBER 31, 201X

Account	Income Statement Dr	Income Statement Cr
Income Summary	19 000 00	4 000 00
Sales		95 000 00
Sales Returns and Allowances	9 50 00	
Sales Discount	6 70 00	
Purchases	52 000 00	
Purchases Discount		8 60 00
Purchases Returns and Allowances		6 80 00
Freight-In	4 50 00	
Salaries Expense	12 30 00	
Payroll Tax Expense	4 20 00	
Postage Expense	2 50 00	
Miscellaneous Expense	3 00 00	
Interest Expense	3 00 00	
Rental Income		2 00 00
Supplies Expense	5 00 00	
Insurance Expense	3 00 00	
Depreciation Expense, Store Equip.	5 00 0	
Salaries Payable		
	86 99 5 00	100 74 0 00
Net Income	13 74 5 00	
Totals	100 74 0 00	100 74 0 00

ART'S WHOLESALE CLOTHING COMPANY
INCOME STATEMENT
FOR YEAR ENDED DECEMBER 31, 201X

Revenue:			
Gross Sales			$95 000 00
Less: Sales Ret. and Allow.		$ 9 50 00	
Sales Discount		6 70 00	16 20 00
Net Sales			$93 38 00
Cost of Goods Sold:			
Merchandise Inventory, 1/1/1X		$19 000 00	
Purchases	$52 000 00		
Less: Purch. Discount	$ 8 60 00		
Purch. Ret. and Allow.	6 80 00	15 40 00	
Net Purchases	$50 46 00		
Add: Freight-In	4 50 00		
Net Cost of Purchases		50 91 00	
Cost of Goods Available for Sale		$69 91 00	
Less: Merch. Inv., 12/31/1X		4 000 00	
Cost of Goods Sold			65 91 00
Gross Profit			$27 47 00
Operating Expenses:			
Salaries Expense		$12 30 00	
Payroll Tax Expense		4 20 00	
Dep. Exp., Store Equip.		5 00 0	
Supplies Expense		5 00 0	
Insurance Expense		3 00 0	
Postage Expense		2 50 0	
Miscellaneous Expense		3 00 0	
Total Operating Expenses			13 62 5 00
Net Income from Operations			$13 84 5 00
Other Income:			
Rental Income		$ 2 00 00	
Other Expenses:			
Interest Expense		3 00 00	1 00 00
Net Income			$13 74 5 00

Gross Profit. Gross profit ($27,470) is calculated by subtracting the Cost of Goods Sold from Net Sales ($93,380 − $65,910). This amount is not found on the worksheet.

Operating Expenses Section. Like the other figures we have discussed, the business's total operating expenses do not appear on the worksheet. To get this figure ($13,625), the accountant adds up all the operating expenses (excluding other expenses) from the worksheet.

Many operating companies break expenses down into those directly related to the selling activity of the company (selling expenses) and those related to administrative or office activity (administrative expenses or general expenses). Here's a sample list (not connected to the example for Art's Wholesale) broken down into these two categories:

Operating Expenses

- Selling Expenses:

    Sales Salaries Expense
    Delivery Expense
    Advertising Expense
    Depreciation Expense, Store Equipment
    Insurance Expense
        Total Selling Expenses

- Administrative Expenses:

    Rent Expense
    Office Salaries Expense
    Utilities Expense
    Office Supplies Expense
    Depreciation Expense, Office Equipment
        Total Administrative Expenses
            Total Operating Expenses

Other Income (or Other Revenue) Section. The other income, or other revenue, section is used to record any revenue other than revenue from sales and service revenue. For example, Art's Wholesale makes a profit from subletting a portion of a building. The $200 of rental income the company earns from this is reported in the other income section.

Other Expenses Section. The other expenses section is used to record nonoperating expenses, that is, expenses that are not related to the main operating activities of the business. For example, Art's Wholesale owes $300 interest on money it has borrowed. That expense is shown in the other expenses section.

Statement of Owner's Equity. The information used to prepare the statement of owner's equity comes from the balance sheet columns of the worksheet. Keep in mind that the capital account in the ledger should be checked to see whether any additional investments occurred during the period. Figure 12A.21 shows how the worksheet aids in this step. The ending figure of $13,050 for Art Newner, Capital is carried over to the balance sheet, which is the final report we look at in this appendix.

The Balance Sheet

Figure 12A.22 shows how a worksheet is used to aid in the preparation of a classified balance sheet. A classified balance sheet breaks down the assets and liabilities into more detail. Classified balance sheets provide management, owners, creditors, and suppliers with more information about the company's ability to pay current and long-term debts. They also provide a more complete financial picture of the firm.

Selling expenses Operating expenses directly related to the sale of goods excluding Cost of Goods Sold.

Administrative expenses (general expenses) Operating expenses such as general office expenses that are incurred indirectly in the selling of goods.

Other income Any revenue other than revenue from sales and service revenue. It appears in a separate section on the income statement. Examples: Rental Income and Storage Fees.

Other expenses Nonoperating expenses that do not relate to the main operating activities of the business; they appear in a separate section on the income statement. One example given in the text is Interest Expense, interest owed on money borrowed by the company.

Classified balance sheet A balance sheet that categorizes assets as current assets or plant and equipment and groups liabilities as current or long-term liabilities.

Figure 12A.21
Preparing a Statement of Owner's Equity from the Worksheet

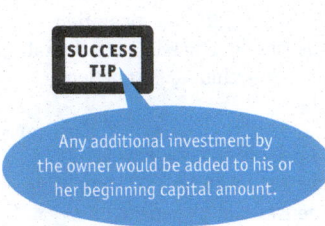

SUCCESS TIP

Any additional investment by the owner would be added to his or her beginning capital amount.

Account Name	PARTIAL WORKSHEET Balance Sheet	
	Dr.	Cr.
Art Newner, Capital		7 9 0 5 00
Art Newner, Withdrawals	8 6 0 0 00	
	45 0 2 0 00	31 2 7 5 00
Net Income		13 7 4 5 00

ART'S WHOLESALE CLOTHING COMPANY
STATEMENT OF OWNER'S EQUITY
FOR YEAR ENDED DECEMBER 31, 201X

Art Newner, Capital, January 1, 201X		$ 7 9 0 5 00
Net Income for the Year	$13 7 4 5 00	
Less: Withdrawals for the Year	− 8 6 0 0 00	
Increase in Capital		5 1 4 5 00
Art Newner, Capital, December 31, 201X		$13 0 5 0 00

Current assets Assets that can be converted into cash or used within 1 year or the normal operating cycle of the business, whichever is longer.

Operating cycle Average time it takes to buy and sell merchandise and then collect accounts receivable.

Plant and equipment Long-lived assets such as equipment, buildings, or land that are used in the production or sale of goods or services.

Current liabilities Obligations that will come due within 1 year or within the operating cycle, whichever is longer.

Long-term liabilities Obligations that are not due or payable for a long time, usually for more than a year.

The categories on the classified balance sheet are as follows:

- **Current assets** are defined as cash and assets that will be converted into cash or used up during the normal operating cycle of the company or 1 year, whichever is longer. (Think of the operating cycle as the time period it takes a company to buy and sell merchandise and then collect accounts receivable.)

- Accountants list current assets in order of how easily they can be converted into cash (called *liquidity*). In most cases, Accounts Receivable can be turned into cash more quickly than Merchandise Inventory. For example, it can be quite difficult to sell an outdated computer in a computer store or to sell last year's model car this year.

- **Plant and equipment** are long-lived assets that are used in the production or sale of goods or services. Art's Wholesale has only one plant asset, store equipment; other plant assets could include buildings and land. The assets are usually listed in order according to how long they will last; the shortest-lived assets are listed first. Land is always the last asset listed (and—keep in mind—land is never depreciated). Note that we still show the cost of the asset less its accumulated depreciation.

- **Current liabilities** are the debts or obligations of Art's Wholesale that must be paid within 1 year or one operating cycle. The order of listing accounts in this section is not always the same; many times companies will list their liabilities in the order they expect to pay them off. Note that the current portion of the mortgage, $320 (that portion due within 1 year), is listed at the end of Accounts Payable.

- **Long-term liabilities** are debts or obligations that are not due and payable for a comparatively long period, usually for more than 1 year. For Art's Wholesale the only long-term liability is Mortgage Payable. The long-term portion of the mortgage is listed here; the current portion, due within 1 year, is listed under current liabilities.

Figure 12A.22 Partial Worksheet and Classified Balance Sheet

ART'S WHOLESALE CLOTHING COMPANY
WORKSHEET
FOR YEAR ENDED DECEMBER 31, 200X

	Balance Sheet Dr.	Balance Sheet Cr.
Cash	12 9 2 0 00	
Petty Cash	1 0 0 00	
Accounts Receivable	14 5 0 0 00	
Merchandise Inventory	4 0 0 0 00	
Supplies	3 0 0 00	
Prepaid Insurance	6 0 0 00	
Store Equipment	4 0 0 0 00	
Acc. Dep., Store Equipment		4 5 0 00
Accounts Payable		17 9 0 0 00
Federal Income Tax Payable		8 0 0 00
FICA—Social Security Payable		4 5 4 00
FICA—Medicare Payable		1 0 6 00
State Income Tax Payable		2 0 0 00
SUTA Tax Payable		1 0 8 00
FUTA Tax Payable		3 2 00
Unearned Rent		4 0 0 00
Mortgage Payable		23 2 0 0 00
Art Newner, Capital		7 9 0 5 00
Salaries Payable		6 0 0 00
Totals	45 0 2 0 00	31 2 7 5 00
Net Income		13 7 4 5 00
Totals	45 0 2 0 00	45 0 2 0 00

ART'S WHOLESALE CLOTHING COMPANY
CLASSIFIED BALANCE SHEET
DECEMBER 31, 201X

Assets

Current Assets:		
Cash	$12 9 2 0 00	
Petty Cash	1 0 0 00	
Accounts Receivable	14 5 0 0 00	
Merchandise Inventory	4 0 0 0 00	
Supplies	3 0 0 00	
Prepaid Insurance	6 0 0 00	
Total Current Assets		$32 4 2 0 00
Plant and Equipment:		
Store Equipment	$ 4 0 0 0 00	
Less: Accum. Depreciation	4 5 0 00	3 5 5 0 00
Total Assets		$35 9 7 0 00

Liabilities

Current Liabilities:		
Accounts Payable	$17 9 0 0 00	
Federal Income Tax Payable	8 0 0 00	
FICA—Social Security Payable	4 5 4 00	
FICA—Medicare Payable	1 0 6 00	
State Income Tax Payable	2 0 0 00	
SUTA Tax Payable	1 0 8 00	
FUTA Tax Payable	3 2 00	
Salaries Payable	6 0 0 00	
Unearned Rent	4 0 0 00	
Mortgage Payable (current portion)	3 2 0 00	
Total Current Liabilities		$20 9 2 0 00
Long-Term Liabilities		
Mortgage Payable		2 0 0 0 00
Total Liabilities		$22 9 2 0 00

Owner's Equity

Art Newner, Capital, December 31, 201X		13 0 5 0 00
Total Liabilities and Owner's Equity		$35 9 7 0 00

Adjusting and Closing Entries and the Post-Closing Trial Balance for a Merchandise Company Using the Periodic Inventory Method

From the worksheet of Art's Wholesale (repeated in Figure 12A.23 for your convenience), the adjusting entries can be journalized from the adjustments column and posted to the ledger. Keep in mind that the adjustments have been placed only on the worksheet, not in the journal or in the ledger. At this point, the journal does not reflect adjustments and the ledger still contains only unadjusted amounts.

Figure 12A.23
Completed Worksheet

ART'S WHOLESALE CLOTHING CO.
WORKSHEET
FOR YEAR ENDED DECEMBER 31, 201X

	Trial Balance		Adjustments	
	Dr.	Cr.	Dr.	Cr.
Cash	12 9 2 0 00			
Petty Cash	1 0 0 00			
Accounts Receivable	14 5 0 0 00			
Merchandise Inventory	19 0 0 0 00		(B) 4 0 0 0 00	(A)19 0 0 0 00
Supplies	8 0 0 00			(D) 5 0 0 00
Prepaid Insurance	9 0 0 00			(E) 3 0 0 00
Store Equipment	4 0 0 0 00			
Acc. Dep., Store Equipment		4 0 0 00		(F) 5 0 00
Accounts Payable		17 9 0 0 00		
Federal Income Tax Payable		8 0 0 00		
FICA—Social Security Payable		4 5 4 00		
FICA—Medicare Payable		1 0 6 00		
State Income Tax Payable		2 0 0 00		
SUTA Tax Payable		1 0 8 00		
FUTA Tax Payable		3 2 00		
Unearned Rent		6 0 0 00	(C) 2 0 0 00	
Mortgage Payable		2 3 2 0 00		
Art Newner, Capital		7 9 0 5 00		
Art Newner, Withdrawals	8 6 0 0 00			
Income Summary			(A)19 0 0 0 00	(B) 4 0 0 0 00
Sales		95 0 0 0 00		
Sales Returns and Allowances	9 5 0 00			
Sales Discount	6 7 0 00			
Purchases	52 0 0 0 00			
Purchases Discount		8 6 0 00		
Purchases Returns and Allowances		6 8 0 00		
Freight-In	4 5 0 00			
Salaries Expense	11 7 0 0 00		(G) 6 0 0 00	
Payroll Tax Expense	4 2 0 00			
Postage Expense	2 5 00			
Miscellaneous Expense	3 0 00			
Interest Expense	3 0 0 00			
Totals	127 3 6 5 00	127 3 6 5 00		
Rental Income				(C) 2 0 0 00
Supplies Expense			(D) 5 0 0 00	
Insurance Expense			(E) 3 0 0 00	
Depreciation Expense, Store Equip.			(F) 5 0 00	
Salaries Payable				(G) 6 0 0 00
Totals			24 6 5 0 00	24 6 5 0 00
Net Income				
Totals				

Figure 12A.23 (continued)

	Adjusted Trial Bal.		Income Statement		Balance Sheet	
	Dr.	Cr.	Dr.	Cr.	Dr.	Cr.
Cash	12920 00				12920 00	
Petty Cash	100 00				100 00	
Accounts Receivable	1450 00				1450 00	
Merchandise Inventory	4000 00				4000 00	
Supplies	300 00				300 00	
Prepaid Insurance	600 00				600 00	
Store Equipment	4000 00				4000 00	
Acc. Dep., Store Equipment		450 00				450 00
Accounts Payable		17900 00				17900 00
Federal Income Tax Payable		800 00				800 00
FICA—Social Security Payable		454 00				454 00
FICA—Medicare Payable		106 00				106 00
State Income Tax Payable		200 00				200 00
SUTA Tax Payable		108 00				108 00
FUTA Tax Payable		32 00				32 00
Unearned Rent		400 00				400 00
Mortgage Payable		2320 00				2320 00
Art Newner, Capital		7905 00				7905 00
Art Newner, Withdrawals	860 00				860 00	
Income Summary	1900 00	400 00	1900 00	400 00		
Sales		9500 00		9500 00		
Sales Returns and Allowances	950 00		950 00			
Sales Discount	670 00		670 00			
Purchases	5200 00		5200 00			
Purchases Discount		860 00		860 00		
Purchases Returns and Allowances		680 00		680 00		
Freight-In	450 00		450 00			
Salaries Expense	12300 00		12300 00			
Payroll Tax Expense	420 00		420 00			
Postage Expense	25 00		25 00			
Miscellaneous Expense	30 00		30 00			
Interest Expense	300 00		300 00			
Rental Income		200 00		200 00		
Supplies Expense	500 00		500 00			
Insurance Expense	300 00		300 00			
Depreciation Expense, Store Equip.	50 00		50 00			
Salaries Payable		600 00				600 00
Totals	132015 00	132015 00	86995 00	100740 00	45020 00	31275 00
Net Income			13745 00			13745 00
Totals			100740 00	100740 00	45020 00	45020 00

Partial Ledger

Merchandise Inventory 121	
Dr.	Cr.
19,000	19,000 (A)
(B) 4,000	

Income Summary 313	
Dr.	Cr.
(A) 19,000	4,000 (B)

Unearned Rent 219	
Dr.	Cr.
(C) 200	600

Rental Income 414	
Dr.	Cr.
	200 (C)

Supplies 122	
Dr.	Cr.
800	500 (D)

Supplies Expense 614	
Dr.	Cr.
(D) 500	

Prepaid Insurance 123	
Dr.	Cr.
900	300 (E)

Insurance Expense 615	
Dr.	Cr.
(E) 300	

Accum. Dep., Store Equipment 126	
Dr.	Cr.
	400
	50 (F)

Dep. Expense, Store Equip. 613	
Dr.	Cr.
(F) 50	

Salaries Payable 212	
Dr.	Cr.
	600 (G)

Salaries Exp. 611	
Dr.	Cr.
11,700	
(G) 600	

The journalized and posted adjusting entries are shown in Figure 12A.24. Note that the liability Unearned Rent is reduced by $200 and Rental Income has increased by $200.

Figure 12A.24
Journalized and Posted Adjusting Entries

		ART'S WHOLESALE CLOTHING CO. GENERAL JOURNAL				
						Page 2
Date		Account Titles and Description	PR	Dr.	Cr.	
		Adjusting Entries				
	31	Income Summary	313	19 0 0 0 00		
		Merchandise Inventory	121		19 0 0 0 00	
		Transferred beginning inventory				
		to Income Summary				
	31	Merchandise Inventory	121	4 0 0 0 00		
		Income Summary	313		4 0 0 0 00	
		Records cost of ending inventory				
	31	Unearned Rent	219	2 0 0 00		
		Rental Income	414		2 0 0 00	
		Rental income earned				
	31	Supplies Expense	614	5 0 0 00		
		Supplies	122		5 0 0 00	
		Supplies consumed				
	31	Insurance Expense	615	3 0 0 00		
		Prepaid Insurance	123		3 0 0 00	
		Insurance expired				
	31	Dep. Exp., Store Equipment	613	5 0 00		
		Acc. Dep., Store Equipment	126		5 0 00	
		Depreciation on equipment				
	31	Salaries Expense	611	6 0 0 00		
		Salaries Payable	212		6 0 0 00	
		Accrued salaries				

Journalizing and Posting Closing Entries

In Chapter 5, we discussed the closing process for a service company. The goals of closing are the same for a merchandise company using the periodic method. These goals are (1) to clear all temporary accounts in the ledger to zero and (2) to update capital in the ledger to its latest balance. The company must use the worksheet and the steps listed here to complete the closing process.

STEP 1 Close all balances on the income statement credit column of the worksheet, except Income Summary, by debits.

Then credit the total to the Income Summary account.

STEP 2 Close all balances on the income statement debit column of the worksheet, except Income Summary, by credits.

Then debit the total to the Income Summary account.

STEP 3 Transfer the balance of the Income Summary account to the Capital account.

STEP 4 Transfer the balance of the owner's Withdrawals account to the Capital account.

Let's look now at the journalized closing entries in Figure 12A.25. When these entries are posted, all the temporary accounts will have zero balances in the ledger, and the Capital account will be updated with a new balance.

Let's take a moment to look at the Income Summary account in T account form.

Income Summary 313			
	Dr.	Cr.	
Adj.	19,000	4,000	Adj.
Clos.	67,995	96,740	Clos.
	86,995	100,740	
Closing	13,745	13,745	Net Income

Note that Income Summary before the closing process contains the adjustments for Merchandise Inventory. The end result is that the net income of $13,745 is closed to the Capital account.

The Post-Closing Trial Balance

The post-closing trial balance shown in Figure 12A.26 on page 459 is prepared from the general ledger. Note first that all temporary accounts have been closed and thus are not shown on this post-closing trial balance. Note also that the ending inventory figure of the last accounting period, $4,000, becomes the beginning inventory figure on January 1, 201X. In a computerized accounting system, the post-closing trial balance can be created by a click of a key in the main menu.

Figure 12A.25
General Journal Closing Entries

ART'S WHOLESALE CLOTHING CO.
GENERAL JOURNAL

Page 2

Date		Account Titles and Description	PR	Dr.	Cr.
		Closing Entries			
	31	Sales	411	95 0 0 0 00	
		Rental Income	414	2 0 0 00	
		Purchases Discount	512	8 6 0 00	
		Purchases Ret. and Allow.	513	6 8 0 00	
		Income Summary	313		96 7 4 0 00
		Transfers credit account balances			
		on income statement column of			
		worksheet to Income Summary			
	31	Income Summary	313	67 9 9 5 00	
		Sales Returns and Allowances	412		9 5 0 00
		Sales Discount	413		6 7 0 00
		Purchases	511		52 0 0 0 00
		Freight-In	514		4 5 0 00
		Salaries Expense	611		12 3 0 0 00
		Payroll Tax Expense	612		4 2 0 00
		Postage Expense	616		2 5 00
		Miscellaneous Expense	617		3 0 00
		Interest Expense	618		3 0 0 00
		Supplies Expense	614		5 0 0 00
		Insurance Expense	615		3 0 0 00
		Depreciation Expense, Store Equip.	613		5 0 00
		Transfers all expenses, and			
		deductions to Sales are			
		closed to Income Summary			
	31	Income Summary	313	13 7 4 5 00	
		A. Newner, Capital	311		13 7 4 5 00
		Transfer of net income to			
		Capital from Income Summary			
	31	A. Newner, Capital	311	8 6 0 0 00	
		A. Newner, Withdrawals	312		8 6 0 0 00
		Closes withdrawals to			
		Capital Account			

ART'S WHOLESALE CLOTHING COMPANY POST-CLOSING TRIAL BALANCE DECEMBER 31, 201X		
	Dr.	Cr.
Cash	12 9 2 0 00	
Petty Cash	1 0 0 00	
Accounts Receivable	14 5 0 0 00	
Merchandise Inventory	4 0 0 0 00	
Supplies	3 0 0 00	
Prepaid Insurance	6 0 0 00	
Store Equipment	4 0 0 0 00	
Accum. Depreciation, Store Equipment		4 5 0 00
Accounts Payable		17 9 0 0 00
Federal Income Tax Payable		8 0 0 00
FICA—Social Security Payable		4 5 4 00
FICA—Medicare Payable		1 0 6 00
State Income Tax Payable		2 0 0 00
SUTA Tax Payable		1 0 8 00
FUTA Tax Payable		3 2 00
Salary Payable		6 0 0 00
Unearned Rent		4 0 0 00
Mortgage Payable		2 3 2 0 00
Art Newner, Capital		13 0 5 0 00
Totals	36 4 2 0 00	36 4 2 0 00

Figure 12A.26
Post-Closing Trial Balance for Art's Wholesale Clothing Company

DEMONSTRATION SUMMARY PROBLEM

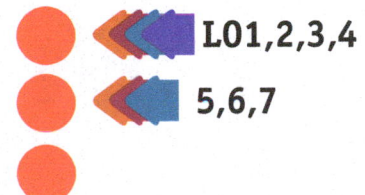

LO1,2,3,4
5,6,7

Journalizing Transactions to Special Journals*; Posting to Subsidiary and General Ledger Accounts from Special Journals: A Periodic Approach

All credit sales are 2/10, n/30. All merchandise purchased on account has 3/10, n/30 credit terms. Assume Periodic Inventory System. Ignore Sales Tax. The company uses Sales Journal, Purchases Journal, and Cash Receipt and Cash Payment Journals, as well as a General Journal.

Requirements

1. Identify journals to record transactions.
2. Record transactions in special journals or a general journal and post to subsidiary and general ledger accounts.

201X

Mar. 1 J. Ling invested $2,000 into the business.

1 Sold merchandise on account to Balder Co., $500, invoice no. 1.

2 Purchased merchandise on account from Case Co., $500.

4 Sold $2,000 of merchandise for cash.

6 Paid Case Co. from previous purchase on account, check no. 1.

8 Sold merchandise on account to Lewis Co., $1,000, invoice no. 2.

10 Received payment from Balder Co. for invoice no. 1.

12 Issued a credit memorandum to Lewis Co. for $200 for faulty merchandise.

14 Received payment from Lewis Co.

16 Purchased merchandise on account from Noone Co., $1,000.

17 Purchased equipment on account from Case Co., $300.

18 Issued a debit memorandum to Noone Co. for $500 for defective merchandise.

20 Paid salaries, $300, check no. 2.

24 Paid Noone balance owed, check no. 3.

Solutions

Requirement 1

Transaction	What to Do Step-by-Step
201X	
Mar. 1	*Money Received:* Record in cash receipts journal. Post immediately to J. Ling, Capital, because it is in sundry.
1	*Sale on Account:* Record in sales journal. Record immediately to Balder Co. in accounts receivable subsidiary ledger. Place a ✓ in Post. Ref. column of sales journal when subsidiary is updated.
2	*Buy Merchandise on Account:* Record in purchases journal. Record to Case Co. immediately in the accounts payable subsidiary ledger.
4	*Money In:* Record in cash receipts journal. No posting needed (put an ✕ in Post. Ref. column).
6	*Money Out:* Record in cash payments journal. Save $15, which is a Purchases Discount. Record immediately to Case Co. in accounts payable subsidiary ledger (the full amount of $500).
8	*Sales on Account:* Record in sales journal. Update immediately to Lewis Co. in accounts receivable subsidiary ledger.
10	*Money In:* Record in cash receipts journal. Because Balder pays within 10 days, it gets a $10 discount. Record the full amount immediately to Balder in the accounts receivable subsidiary ledger.
12	*Returns:* Record in general journal. Seller issues credit memo resulting in higher sales returns and customers owing less. All postings and recordings are done immediately.
14	*Money In:* Record in cash receipts journal:

$$\$1,000 - \$200 \text{ returns} = \$800.00$$
$$\times \quad 0.02$$
$$\$\ 16.00 \text{ discount}$$

Record immediately the $800 to Lewis Co. in the accounts receivable Subsidiary Ledger.

16	*Buy Now, Pay Later:* Record in purchases journal. Record immediately to Noone Co. in the accounts payable subsidiary ledger.
17	*Buy Now, Pay Later:* Record in purchases journal in Sundry. This item is not merchandise for resale. Record and post immediately.
18	*Returns:* Record in general ledger. Buyer issues a debit memo reducing the Accounts Payable due to Purchases Return and Allowances. Post and record immediately.
20	*Salaries:* Record in Cash Payments Journal, sundry column. Post immediately to Salaries Expense.
24	*Money Out:* Record in cash payments journal. Save 3% ($15), a purchases discount. Record immediately to Accounts Payable Subsidiary Ledger that you reduce Noone by $500.

Requirement 2

Record transactions in special journals or general journal and record to subsidiary and post to general ledger accounts.

Record accounts receivable subsidiary ledger immediately.

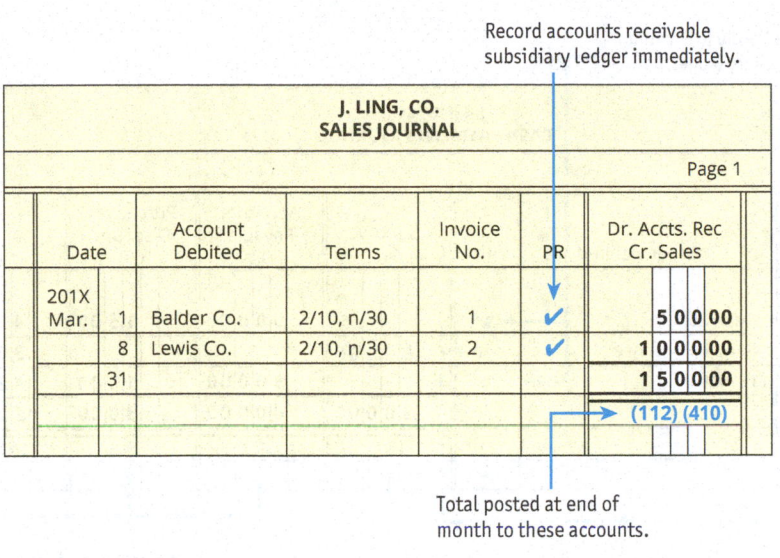

Figure 12A.27
Sales Journal

SUCCESS TIP

Remember, the sales journal only records sales on account.

Total posted at end of month to these accounts.

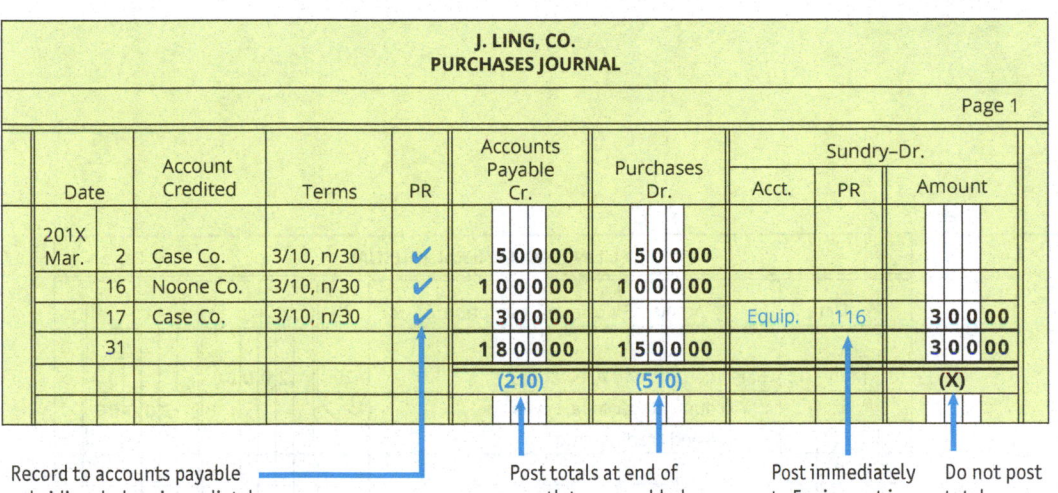

Figure 12A.28
Purchases Journal

SUCCESS TIP

Remember, the purchases journal records buy now, pay later transactions. Purchases are merchandise for resale, while equipment is not for resale.

Record to accounts payable subsidiary ledger immediately.

Post totals at end of month to general ledger.

Post immediately to Equipment in general ledger.

Do not post total.

Post to capital immediately.

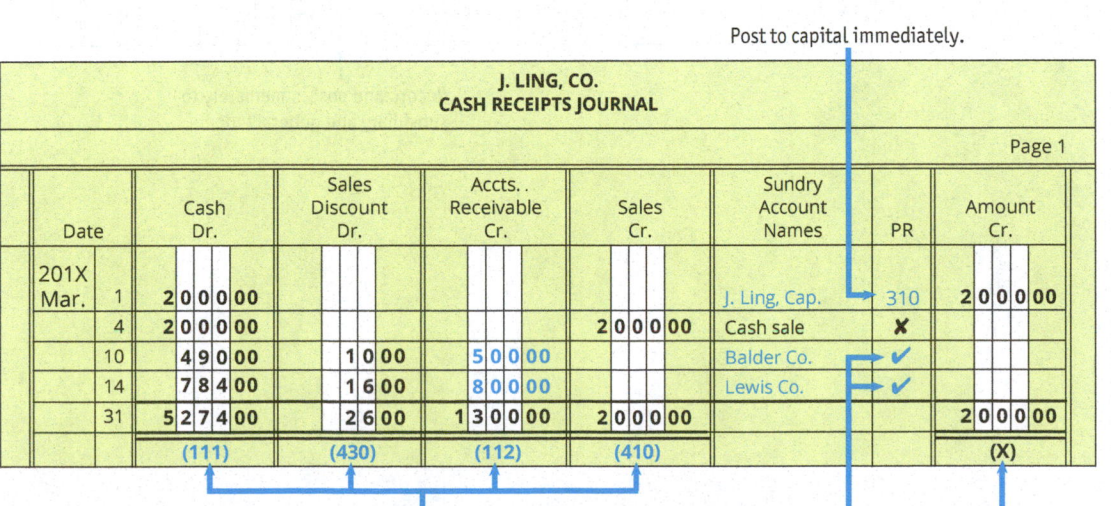

Figure 12A.29
Cash Receipts Journal

SUCCESS TIP

Remember, the cash receipts journal records any transaction that involves the receipt of cash.

Post totals at end of month to general ledger.

Record immediately to accounts receivable subsidiary ledger.

Don't post total.

Figure 12A.30
Cash Payments Journal

Record immediately to accounts payable subsidiary ledger.

J. LING, CO. CASH PAYMENTS JOURNAL

Page 1

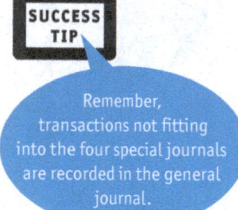

SUCCESS TIP

Remember, the cash payment journal records only transactions that result in the payment of cash.

Date		Ck. No.	Account Debited	PR	Sundry Dr.	Accounts Payable Dr.	Purchases Discount Cr.	Cash Cr.
201X Mar.	6	1	Case Co.	✔		5 0 0 00	1 5 00	4 8 5 00
	20	2	Salaries Expense	610	3 0 0 00			3 0 0 00
	24	3	Noone Co.	✔		5 0 0 00	1 5 00	4 8 5 00
	31				3 0 0 00	1 0 0 0 00	3 0 00	1 2 7 0 00
					(X)	(210)	(530)	(111)

Post immediately to Salaries Expense.

Do not post total.

Post totals at end of month to the general ledger.

Figure 12A.31
General Journal

J. LING, CO. GENERAL JOURNAL

Page 1

SUCCESS TIP

Remember, transactions not fitting into the four special journals are recorded in the general journal.

Date		Account Titles and Description	PR	Dr.	Cr.
201X Mar.	12	Sales Returns and Allowances	420	2 0 0 00	
		Accounts Receivable, Lewis Co.	112 ✔		2 0 0 00
		Issued credit memo			
	18	Accounts Payable, Noone Co.	210 ✔	5 0 0 00	
		Purchases Returns and Allowances	520		5 0 0 00
		Issued debit memo			

Record and post immediately to subsidiary and general ledgers.

Figure 12A.32
Subsidiary and General Ledgers

ACCOUNTS RECEIVABLE SUBSIDIARY LEDGER

Balder Company

Date	PR	Dr.	Cr.	Dr. Bal.
201X 3/1	SJ1	500		500
3/10	CRJ1		500	——

Lewis Company

Date	PR	Dr.	Cr.	Dr. Bal.
201X 3/8	SJ1	1,000		1,000
3/12	GJ1		200	800
3/14	CRJ1		800	——

ACCOUNTS PAYABLE SUBSIDIARY LEDGER

Case Company

Date	PR	Dr.	Cr.	Cr. Bal.
201X 3/2	PJ1		500	500
3/6	CPJ1	500		——
3/17	PJ1		300	300

Noone Company

Date	PR	Dr.	Cr.	Cr. Bal.
201X 3/16	PJ1		1,000	1,000
3/18	GJ1	500		500
3/24	CPJ1	500		——

SUCCESS TIP

Note that in the accounts receivable subsidiary ledger (Dr. balance) customers owe the seller, whereas in the accounts payable subsidiary ledger (Cr. balance) the seller owes the vendors it purchased items from.

GENERAL LEDGER

Cash 111

3/31 CRJ1 5,274		1,270	3/31 CPJ1
Bal. 4,004			

Accounts Receivable 112

3/31 SJ1 1,500		200	3/12 GJ1
		1,300	3/31 CRJ1
Bal. 0			

Equipment 116

3/17 PJ1 300		

Accounts Payable 210

3/18 GJ1 500		1,800	3/31 PJ1
3/31 CPJ1 1,000			
		300	Bal.

J. Ling, Capital 310

	2,000	3/1 CRJ1

Sales 410

		1,500	3/31 SJ1
		2,000	3/31 CRJ1
		3,500	Bal.

Sales Returns and Allowances 420

3/12 GJ1 200		

Sales Discount 430

3/31 CRJ1 26		

Purchases 510

3/31 PJ1 1,500		

Purchases Returns and Allowances 520

	500	3/18 GJ1

Purchases Discount 530

	30	3/31 CPJ1

Salaries Expense 610

3/20 CPJ1 300		

SUCCESS TIP

Remember, in the General Ledger Accounts Receivable and Accounts Payable are the controlling accounts.

Tips for Journalizing, Recording, and Posting from Special Journals

Seller	Buyer
Sales journal	Purchases journal
Cash receipts journal	Cash payments journal
Sales (Cr.)	Purchases (Dr.)
Sales Returns and Allowances (Dr.)	Purchase Returns and Allowances (Cr.)
Sales Discounts (Dr.)	Purchase Discounts (Cr.)
Accounts Receivable (Dr.)	Accounts Payable (Cr.)
Accounts receivable subsidiary ledger	Accounts payable subsidiary ledger
Schedule of accounts receivable	Schedule of accounts payable
Issue a credit memo or receive a debit memo	Receive a credit memo or issue a debit memo

End of Month Post totals (except sundry) of special journals to the general ledger.

Note: In this problem at the end of the month, (1) Accounts Receivable in the general ledger, the controlling account, has a zero balance, as does each title in the accounts receivable subsidiary ledger, and (2) the balance in Accounts Payable (the controlling account) is $300. In the accounts payable subsidiary ledger, J. Ling owes Case Co. $300. The sum of the accounts payable subsidiary ledger does equal the balance in the controlling account at the end of the month.

MyLabAccounting

Exercises

(10 min) **LO1**

12A-1. Journalize, record, and post when appropriate the following transactions in the general journal (page 2) (all sales carry terms of 2/10, n/30):

201X		
Aug.	16	Sold merchandise on account to Opal Co., invoice no. 1, $1,100.
	18	Sold merchandise on account to Glenda Co., invoice no. 2, $2,000.
	20	Issued credit memorandum no. 1 to Glenda Co. for defective merchandise, $740.

Use the following account numbers: Accounts Receivable, 112; Sales, 411; Sales Returns and Allowances, 412; Sales Discounts, 413. The company uses the periodic system.

(20 min) **LO2**

12A-2. Journalize, record, and post when appropriate the following transactions into the general journal (p. 2) for Joshua's Clothing. All purchases discounts are 2/10, n/30. Assume the periodic inventory system. If using working papers, be sure to put in beginning balances.

201X		
Apr.	1	Issued check no. 20 to A. Jackiewicz Company in payment of its March 28 invoice no. 522.
	8	Issued check no. 21 to Front Advertising in payment of its advertising bill, $95, no discount.
	15	Issued check no. 22 to B. Garcia in payment of its March 25 invoice no. 488.

Accounts Payable Subsidiary Ledger

Name	Balance	Invoice No.
A. Jackiewicz	$1,000	522
B. Garcia	400	488

Name	Balance	Invoice No.
J. Clark	800	562
B. Morris	200	821

Partial General Ledger

Account	Balance
Cash 110	$2,500
Accounts Payable 210	2,400
Purchases Discount 511	
Advertising Expense 610	

12A-3. Jacob Co. had the following balances on December 31, 201X:

Cash	Unearned Janitorial Service Revenue
1,800	550

Janitorial Service Revenue
7,100

L05 *(10 min)*

The accountant for Jacob has asked you to make an adjustment because $360 of janitorial services has just been performed for customers who had paid for 2 months. Construct a transaction analysis chart.

12A-4. From the partial worksheet in Figure 12A.33, journalize the closing entries for December 31 for A. Adams Co.

L06,7

Figure 12A.33

	A. ADAMS Co, WORKSHEET FOR YEAR ENDED DECEMBER 31, 201X				
	Income Statement		Balance Sheet		
Account	Dr.	Cr.	Dr.	Cr.	
Cash			1 8 8 00		
Merchandise Inventory			4 5 4 00		
Prepaid Advertising			5 6 5 00		
Prepaid Insurance			3 1 00		
Office Equipment			1 0 6 2 00		
Accum Dep. Office Equipment				2 1 1 00	
Accounts Payable				2 5 3 00	
A. Adams Capital				9 6 1 00	
Income Summary	3 5 9 00	4 5 4 00			
Sales		5 4 8 8 00			
Sales Returns and Allowances	2 2 7 00				
Sales Discount	1 0 5 00				
Purchases	2 6 2 1 00				
Purchases Returns and Allowances		3 5 00			
Purchases Discount		4 7 00			
Salaries Expense	1 0 7 8 00				
Insurance Expense	6 9 2 00				
Utilities Expense	4 0 00				
Plumbing Expense	5 7 00				
Advertising Expense	1 2 00				
Dep. Expenses Office Equip	2 8 00				
Salaries Payable				7 0 00	
Totals	5 2 1 9 00	6 0 2 4 00	2 3 0 0 00	1 4 9 5 00	
Net Income	8 0 5 00			8 0 5 00	

MyLabAccounting

Problems

(40 min) **L01**

12A-1. Liz Viera has opened Pizza and More, a wholesale grocery and pizza company. The following transactions occurred in March:

201X		
Mar.	1	Sold grocery merchandise to Felicity Co. on account, $950, invoice no. 1.
	4	Sold pizza merchandise to Vow Co. on account, $500, invoice no. 2.
	8	Sold grocery merchandise to Spanish Co. on account, $1,200, invoice no. 3.
	10	Issued credit memorandum no. 1 to Felicity Co. for $240 of grocery merchandise returned due to spoilage.
	15	Sold pizza merchandise to Vow Co. on account, $600, invoice no. 4.
	19	Sold grocery merchandise to Spanish Co. on account, $550, invoice no. 5.
	25	Sold pizza merchandise to Felicity Co. on account, $300, invoice no. 6.

Check Figure:
Schedule of accounts
receivable $3,860

Required

1. Journalize the transactions.

2. Record to the accounts receivable subsidiary ledger and post to the general ledger as appropriate.

3. Prepare a schedule of accounts receivable for the end of March.

(30 min) **L03**

12A-2. Reed Smith recently opened Reed's Skate Shop. The company uses the periodic system. As the bookkeeper of the company, use the periodic method to journalize, record, and post when appropriate the following transactions (account numbers are Store Supplies 115; Store Equipment 121; Accounts Payable 210; Purchases 510):

Check Figure:
Schedule of Accounts Payable $9,400

201X		
May	4	Bought $1,300 of merchandise on account from Waldo Co., invoice no. 442, dated May 5; terms 5/10, n/30.
	5	Bought $5,300 of store equipment on account from Kelowna Co., invoice no. 502, dated May 6.
	8	Bought $2,000 of merchandise on account from Redwood Co., invoice no. 401, dated May 9, terms 5/10, n/30.
	14	Bought $800 of store supplies on account from Waldo Co., invoice no. 419, dated May 14.

L06

12A-3. From the trial balance in Figure 11.16 and additional data, complete the worksheet for Sean's Wholesale Clothing Company.

Figure 12A.34

Account	Balance Debit		Balance Credit	

SEAN'S WHOLESALE CLOTHING COMPANY
TRIAL BALANCE
DECEMBER 31, 201X

Account	Debit	Credit
Cash	4 1 6 0 00	
Petty Cash	6 0 0 00	
Accounts Receivable	8 1 0 0 00	
Merchandise Inventory	8 5 0 0 00	
Supplies	9 0 0 00	
Prepaid Insurance	8 0 0 00	
Store Equipment	3 1 0 0 00	
Accumulated Depreciation, Store Equipment		2 0 0 0 00
Accounts Payable		11 3 0 0 00
Federal Income Tax Payable		1 2 0 0 00
FICA—Social Security Payable		4 6 2 00
FICA—Medicare Payable		1 1 8 00
State Income Tax Payable		1 0 0 00
SUTA Tax Payable		1 0 8 00
FUTA Tax Payable		2 8 00
Unearned Storage Fees		4 5 0 00
Sean Win, Capital		15 5 0 0 00
Sean Win, Withdrawals	4 3 0 0 00	
Income Summary	—	—
Sales		39 9 1 9 00
Sales Returns and Allowances	1 5 5 0 00	
Sales Discount	1 2 9 5 00	
Purchases	23 0 0 0 00	
Purchases Discount		4 5 0 00
Purchases Returns and Allowances		7 0 0 00
Freight-In	1 2 5 00	
Salaries Expense	14 5 0 0 00	
Payroll Tax Expense	4 7 0 00	
Interest Expense	9 3 5 00	
Totals	72 3 3 5 00	72 3 3 5 00

Additional Data

a./b. Ending merchandise inventory on December 31, $4,900.

c. Supplies on hand, $700.

d. Insurance expired, $750.

e. Depreciation on store equipment, $400.

f. Storage fees earned, $167.

Check Figure:
Net loss $5,589

12A-4. From the partial worksheet for Jamie's Supplies in Figure 12A.35, do the following:

 **L05,6,7** *(6 min)*

1. Complete the worksheet.

2. Prepare the income statement, statement of owner's equity, and classified balance sheet. (*Note:* The amount of the mortgage due the first year is $830.)

3. Journalize the adjusting and closing entries.

Check Figure:
Net income $4,520

Figure 12A.35

JAMIE'S SUPPLIES WORKSHEET FOR YEAR ENDED DECEMBER 31, 201X				
Account Titles	Trial Balance		Adjustments	
	Dr.	Cr.	Dr.	Cr.
Cash	2 40 0 00			
Accounts Receivable	3 40 0 00			
Merch. Inventory, 1/01/1X	11 30 0 00		(B) 10 40 0 00	(A) 11 30 0 00
Prepaid Insurance	1 88 0 00			(E) 5 60 00
Equipment	2 90 0 00			
Accum. Dep., Equipment		1 02 0 00		(D) 4 0 0 00
Accounts Payable		5 11 0 00		
Unearned Training Fees		2 09 0 00	(C) 2 70 00	
Mortgage Payable		1 23 0 00		
P. Jamie, Capital		10 60 0 00		
P. Jamie, Withdrawals	4 28 0 00			
Income Summary			(A) 11 30 0 00	(B) 10 40 0 00
Sales		96 37 0 00		
Sales Returns and Allowances	3 18 0 00			
Sales Discount	2 60 0 00			
Purchases	63 20 0 00			
Purchases Returns and Allow.		13 50 0 00		
Purchases Discounts		3 23 0 00		
Freight-In	2 71 0 00			
Advertising Expense	11 30 0 00			
Rent Expense	10 20 0 00			
Salaries Expense	13 80 0 00			
Totals	133 15 0 00	133 15 0 00		
Training Fees Earned				(C) 2 70 00
Dep. Exp., Equipment			(D) 4 0 0 00	
Insurance Expense			(E) 5 60 00	
Totals			22 93 0 00	22 93 0 00

(150 min) **L03,4** ▶

12A-5. Abby Ellen opened Abby's Toy House. As her newly hired accountant, your tasks are to do the following:

1. Journalize the transactions for the month of August. Abby uses special journals for sales on account, purchases on account, and cash receipts and cash payments, as well as a general journal. The company uses the periodic inventory system.

2. Record to subsidiary ledgers and post to the general ledger as appropriate.

3. Total and rule the journals.

4. Prepare a schedule of accounts receivable and a schedule of accounts payable.

5. Ignore Sales Tax.

Check Figures:
Total of schedule of accounts receivable
$7,000
Total of schedule of accounts payable
$8,600

The following is the partial chart of accounts for Abby's Toy House:

Abby's Toy House Chart of Accounts

Assets		Revenue	
110	Cash	410	Toy Sales
112	Accounts Receivable	412	Sales Returns and Allowances
114	Prepaid Rent	414	Sales Discounts
121	Delivery Truck	**Cost of Goods**	
Liabilities		510	Toy Purchases
210	Accounts Payable	512	Purchases Returns and Allowances
Owner's Equity		514	Purchases Discount
310	A. Ellen, Capital	**Expenses**	
		610	Salaries Expense
		612	Cleaning Expense

201X

Aug. 1 Abby Ellen invested $7,300 in the toy store.

1 Paid 3 months' rent in advance, check no. 1, $3,300.

1 Purchased merchandise from Rose Karpel Company on account, $3,400, invoice no. 410, dated August 2; terms 6/10, n/30.

3 Sold merchandise to Laura Capps on account, $1,600, invoice no. 1; terms 6/10, n/30.

6 Sold merchandise to Jim Rex on account, $1,100, invoice no. 2; terms 6/10, n/30.

8 Purchased merchandise from Rose Karpel Co. on account, $1,700, invoice no. 415, dated August 9; terms 6/10, n/30.

9 Sold merchandise to Laura Capps on account, $1,000, invoice no. 3; terms 6/10, n/30.

9 Paid cleaning service, check no. 2, $200.

10 Jim Rex returned merchandise with a selling price of $100 to Abby's Toy House. Abby issued credit memorandum no. 1 to Jim Rex for $100.

10 Purchased merchandise from Rose Kaufman on account, $3,300, invoice no. 311, dated August 11; terms 3/15, n/60.

12 Paid Rose Karpel Co. invoice no. 410, dated August 2, check no. 3.

13 Sold $1,800 of toy merchandise for cash.

13 Paid salaries, $400, check no. 4.

14 Returned merchandise to Rose Kaufman in the amount of $1,500. Abby's Toy House issued debit memorandum no. 1 to Rose Kaufman.

15 Sold merchandise for $4,200 cash.

16 Received payment from Jim Rex, invoice no. 2 (less returned merchandise), less discount.

16 Laura Capps paid invoice no. 1.

16 Sold toy merchandise to Amber Reade on account, $3,400, invoice no. 4; terms 6/10, n/30.

20 Purchased delivery truck on account from Sam Katz Garage, $2,900, invoice no. 111, dated August 21 (no discount).

22 Sold to Laura Capps merchandise on account, $300, invoice no. 5; terms 6/10, n/30.

23 Paid Rose Kaufman balance owed, check no. 5.

24 Sold toy merchandise on account to Amber Reade, $1,300, invoice no. 6; terms 6/10, n/30.

25	Purchased toy merchandise, $800, check no. 6.
26	Purchased toy merchandise from Sanya Burger on account, $4,000, invoice no. 211, dated August 27; terms 6/10, n/30.
28	Laura Capps paid invoice no. 5, dated August 22.
28	Amber Reade paid invoice no. 6, dated August 24.
28	Abby invested an additional $8,000 in the business.
28	Purchased merchandise from Rose Karpel Co. on account, $1,500, invoice no. 436, dated August 29; terms 6/10, n/30.
30	Paid Rose Karpel Co. invoice no. 436, check no. 7.
30	Sold merchandise to Berta Fick Company on account, $2,600, invoice no. 7; terms 6/10, n/30.

Accounting for Bad Debts

13

CHAPTER PREVIEW: ACCOUNTING IN ACTION

In the window of Freya's Cupcake Shop is a sign that reads, "No checks accepted. Cash is King!" Why do you think this business will not take checks? When a company makes sales, there is a certain portion of those sales that may not be collectible. Too often, checks are written, and they bounce because the bank accounts they are drawn from lack enough funds to cover them. The result is lost revenue. Many companies actually will increase their prices just to cover customers who do not pay their bills and are considered Bad Debts. In this chapter, we look at how companies estimate their accounts receivable that end up as Bad Debts Expense and how this may affect their financial statements.

Learning Objectives – Relating Accounting Theory By Unit

L01   Explain Accrual Accounting and Journalize Bad Debts Transactions

L02   Use the Allowance Method to Estimate Bad Debts and Prepare an Aging of Accounts Receivable

L03   Write Off and Recover Uncollectible Accounts by the Allowance and the Direct Methods

Today, even with the economy doing well, there are always some customers who will have trouble paying their bills. The question of these *Bad Debts* affects the company's credit policy. If a company extends credit too easily, it may end up with too many uncollectible accounts. On the other hand, if the credit policy is too strict, the company will end up losing customers to other firms with looser credit policies, which could also mean lost profit. For example, Walmart sells for cash and/or credit and therefore has low Bad Debts Expense.

This chapter looks at how Bad Debts are recorded in the accrual system of accounting. It also discusses when accounts receivable turn into Bad Debts (or uncollectible accounts), how and what account to charge them to, and how to write them off.

Accrual Accounting and Journalizing Bad Debts Transactions

As discussed in Chapter 1, the accrual system of accounting matches earned revenue with expenses that have been incurred in producing revenue during an accounting period. One expense incurred as a result of sales on credit or on account is Bad Debts Expense. The problem is that it may take as long as a year for the seller to realize that a debt is uncollectible. What happens in the meantime? How can a company be sure its accounting record keeping is up-to-date in matching revenues and expenses based on an accrual accounting system?

One way is to estimate at the end of the year what percentage of sales made during that year will turn out to be Bad Debts. Several approaches can be used to arrive at the percentage. At the moment, let's say Greg Roman Company estimates that 1.6% of its credit sales of $100,000 for the year 2018 will not be collectible; thus, the company expects not to collect $1,600 of the $100,000 owed to it from sales. (Other ways to estimate the amount are discussed in Learning Unit 13-2.)

Two accounts that we haven't discussed before, Bad Debts Expense and Allowance for Doubtful Accounts, are needed. Bad Debts Expense is an expense account whose normal balance is a debit; it is a temporary account that is closed to Income Summary at year's end. Allowance for Doubtful Accounts is a contra-asset account to the Accounts Receivable account that accumulates the expected amount of Bad Debts as of a given date; its normal balance is a credit. It is a permanent account that is *not* closed to Income Summary at the end of the year.

In the case of Greg Roman Company, which expects to be unable to collect $1,600 of the $100,000 owed to it from sales, at the end of the year (2018) an adjustment is made debiting Bad Debts Expense and crediting Allowance for Doubtful Accounts for $1,600. This transaction (Figure 13.1) is shown with a transaction analysis chart.

Bad Debts Expense Operating expense account that estimates the amount of credit sales that will probably not be collectible in a given accounting period when the Allowance method is used. For the direct write-off method, this account would be the actual amount written off.

Allowance for Doubtful Accounts Contra-asset account that is subtracted from Accounts Receivable. This account accumulates the *expected* amount of uncollectibles as of a given date.

1 **Accounts Affected**	2 **Category**	3 ↑↓	4 **Rules**
Bad Debts Expense	Expense	↑	Dr.
Allowance for Doubtful Accounts	Contra-Asset	↑	Cr.

Figure 13.1
Recording Estimated Bad Debts

	2018					
	Dec.	31	Bad Debts Expense	1 6 0 0 00	
			Allowance for Doubtful Accounts		1 6 0 0 00
			Record estimate of bad debts		

The allowance account is subtracted from Accounts Receivable, leaving a net-realizable value of $98,400. Net realizable value is the amount Greg Roman Company expects to collect. When an account is written off, the net realizable value doesn't change because both the Accounts Receivable and the Allowance for Doubtful Accounts are reduced (see Figure 13.2).

Net-realizable value Amount (Accounts Receivable – Allowance for Doubtful Accounts) that is expected to be collected.

GREG ROMAN COMPANY PARTIAL BALANCE SHEET DECEMBER 31, 2018		
Assets		
Current Assets:		
Cash		$ 51 4 0 0 00
Accounts Receivable	$100 0 0 0 00	
Less: Allowance for Doubtful Accounts	1 6 0 0 00	98 4 0 0 00
Merchandise Inventory		200 0 0 0 00
Total Current Assets		$349 8 0 0 00

Figure 13.2
Partial Balance Sheet

Think of the Allowance for Doubtful Accounts as a reservoir that is filled before Bad Debts occur. The reservoir is drained when a customer's bill is declared uncollectible. Greg Roman Company estimates that out of its $100,000 of credit sales, $1,600 will prove to be uncollectible, but it does not know which accounts those will be. The actual accounts will be determined down the road after the company has exhausted its efforts to collect on the outstanding debt.

Writing Off an Account Deemed Uncollectible

As mentioned, at some point a customer's bill must be written off as uncollectible. Let's look at how Greg Roman Company would write off the account of Petra Davis on June 5, 2019. (The $200 sale was made in 2018.)

Remember, at the end of 2018, Greg Roman made an adjusting entry increasing Bad Debts Expense (debit) and filling the Allowance for Doubtful Accounts (credit) with the estimate of accounts receivable that will not be collectible. The journal entry shown in Figure 13.3 is recorded to write off this account.

2019 June	5	Allowance for Doubtful Accounts	2 0 0 00	
		Accounts Receivable, P. Davis		2 0 0 00
		Writing off P. Davis account		

Figure 13.3
Bad Debts Written Off

Note that we did *not* debit the account Bad Debts Expense because the estimate for this account was made on December 31, 2018 (and applies to the sales made during that year, not to 2019). When that estimate was made, we did not know which debt would turn out to be uncollectible. Once the debt is identified as uncollectible, we reduce both the Allowance account and the controlling account, Accounts Receivable, and update the accounts receivable subsidiary ledger. The subsidiary ledger will be credited just as the controlling account is.

Now let's check your progress.

SUCCESS TIP

The Bad Debts Expense was recorded in the previous year when the credit sales were earned and recorded.

The Allowance account fills with a credit and drains with a debit.

 **TRY IT!** **Learning Unit 13-1**

1. Journalize the following transactions:

2017	
Dec. 31	Estimated Bad Debts of $3,000
2018	
Apr. 6	Wrote off B. Sherwood account for $300

2. What is the balance of the allowance account?

TRY IT! **Solution Learning Unit 13-1**

1.

Date		Accounts	Dr.	Cr.
2017				
Dec.	31	Bad Debts Expense	3,000	
		Allowance for Doubtful Accounts		3,000
		Estimate of Bad Debts		
2018				
Apr.	6	Allowance for Doubtful Accounts	300	
		Accounts Receivable, B. Sherwood		300
		Wrote off B. Sherwood Account		

2. $3,000 − $300 = $2,700 ending balance in the allowance account

LEARNING UNIT 13-2

L02

The Allowance Method

At the end of each year, companies must estimate what percentage of their sales for that year will turn out to be uncollectible accounts or Bad Debts. How is this estimate arrived at? In this unit we look at two of the most common ways of arriving at this amount: the income statement approach and the balance sheet approach. The diagram in Figure 13.4 outlines these methods.

The Income Statement Approach

Greg Roman Company uses the income statement approach to calculate how much Bad Debts Expense will be associated with this year's sales. Based on the past several years, the company has averaged Bad Debts Expense of 1% of *net* credit sales. Consider the following facts:

Bad Debts Expense can be based on a percentage of the dollar volume of net credit sales on the income statement.

Income statement approach A method that estimates the amount of Bad Debts Expense based on a percentage of net credit sales for the period. The amount of the expected Bad Debts is added to the existing balance of Allowance for Doubtful Accounts.

2018	Dr.	Cr.
Sales (all credit)		$95,000
Sales Returns and Allowances	$10,000	
Sales Discount	5,000	
Accounts Receivable	7,000	
Allowance for Doubtful Accounts		100

1 Accounts Affected	2 Category	3 ↑↓	4 Rules
Bad Debts Expense	Expense	↑	Dr.
Allowance for Doubtful Accounts	Contra-Asset	↑	Cr.

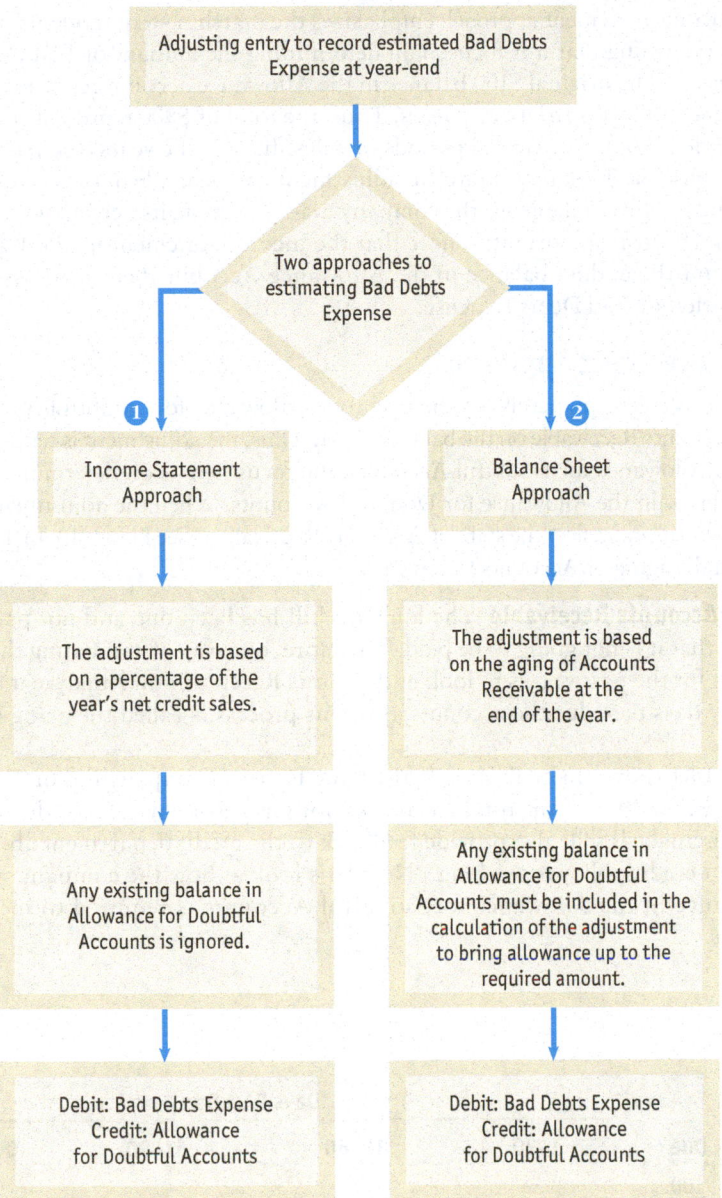

Figure 13.4
Two Approaches to Estimating
Amount of Bad Debts Expense

Let's prepare an adjusting entry to record the Bad Debts Expense that is based on a percentage of *net* credit sales (see Figure 13.5).

2018						
Dec.	31	Bad Debts Expense		8 0 0 00		
		Allowance for Doubtful Accounts			8 0 0 00	
		Record estimate of bad debts				
		(0.01 x $80,000)				

Figure 13.5
Estimating Bad Debts Based
on Percentage of Sales

When it is posted, the Allowance account looks like the following:

Allowance for Doubtful Accounts

Dr.	Cr.	
	100 ⟶	Balance *before* adjustment
	800 ⟶	Adjustment
	900 ⟶	New balance

The income statement approach emphasizes the matching requirements of the income statement; meaning that it is focused on determining the amount of Bad Debts Expense for the period. The original $100 balance in the Allowance account represents a carryover of potential Bad Debts from *prior* years. Thus, the total of $900 represents total potential uncollectible accounts of several periods of sales. If, over the years, the estimate for Bad Debts Expense has been inaccurate, an adjustment can be made in the current year's Bad Debts Expense. If that happens, the company may reevaluate its percentage and use $1\frac{1}{2}\%$ instead of 1%. It is important to note that the income statement method does not take into account the ending balance in the Allowance Account (before adjustment) in the determination of Bad Debts Expense.

The Balance Sheet Approach

The balance sheet approach bases the new total Allowance for Doubtful Accounts on the current Accounts Receivable on the balance sheet. Thus, the adjustment is reduced by the old balance in Allowance for Doubtful Accounts; the focus here is on determining the desired ending balance in the Allowance for Doubtful Accounts. When the adjustment is credited, the new balance will reflect the state of Accounts Receivable. (See Figure 13.4.) This approach focuses on the aging of Accounts Receivable.

Aging of Accounts Receivable   The longer a bill has been due and not paid, the more likely it is that it is not going to be paid. Therefore, one way of estimating the amount of Bad Debts for the past year is to look at Accounts Receivable and analyze it according to how many days past due the accounts are. This process is called the aging of Accounts Receivable.

Table 13.1 shows an analysis that the Greg Roman Company did on December 31, 2019. Note that 29% of the total receivables for Greg Roman are past due from 1 to 30 days. (This analysis will also provide feedback to the credit department about how well the current credit policy is working.) Now let's look at how the company will estimate what balance in the Allowance for Doubtful Accounts is required to meet probable Bad Debts.

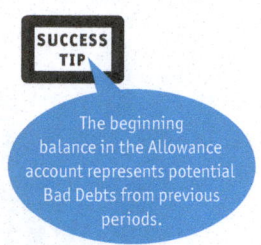

SUCCESS TIP

The beginning balance in the Allowance account represents potential Bad Debts from previous periods.

Balance sheet approach A method used to calculate the amount *required* in the Allowance for Doubtful Accounts to cover expected uncollectibles. This method is based on the Accounts Receivable amount and the aging process. The adjustment to the Allowance for Doubtful Accounts will bring the new balance of that account to the new required level.

Aging of Accounts Receivable The procedure of classifying accounts of individual customers by age group, where age is the number of days elapsed from due date.

TABLE 13.1 Aging of Accounts Receivable

Name of Customer	Total Balance	Not Yet Due	Days Past Due			
			1–30	31–60	61–90	Over 90
Petra Davis	$ 100	$ 100				
Joshua Harras	30			$30		
Alan Kedbury	160	160				
John Sullivan	180				$160	$ 20
Sheri Lissan	80	80				
Others	6,450	3,260	$2,000	840	40	310
Totals	$7,000	$3,600	$2,000	$870	$200	$330
Percent of total	100%	51%	29%	12%	3%	5%
(rounded to nearest whole percent)		$\left(\dfrac{\$3,600}{\$7,000}\right)$	$\left(\dfrac{\$2,000}{\$7,000}\right)$	$\left(\dfrac{\$870}{\$7,000}\right)$	$\left(\dfrac{\$200}{\$7,000}\right)$	$\left(\dfrac{\$330}{\$7,000}\right)$

The schedule shown in Table 13.2 was prepared to assist the company in calculating the needed balance. In this schedule, Abby Ellen Company applied a sliding scale of percentages (3, 4, 10, 20, 50), based on previous experience, to the total amount of receivables not due or past due in each time period. For example, of the $3,600 not yet due, 3%, or $108, will probably never be paid. Looking at this schedule reveals that Greg Roman Company needs $480 to cover estimated Bad Debts. *Currently*, the balance in the

Allowance account is $100. Thus, to reach a balance of $480, we must adjust the balance of the account by the adjusting journal entry shown in Figure 13.6.

Some companies that feel aging is too time-consuming may estimate Bad Debts based on a percentage of total Accounts Receivable.

Bad Debts Expense

	Dr.	Cr.
Adj.	380	

Allowance for Doubtful Accounts

	Dr.	Cr.	
		100	End. balance
		380	Adj.
		480	New balance in allowance

TABLE 13.2 Balance Required to Meet Probable Bad Debts

	Amount	Estimated Percentage Considered to Be Bad Debts Expense	Amount Needed in Allowance for Doubtful Accounts to Cover Estimated Bad Debts Expense
Not Yet Due	$3,600	3	$108*
Days Past Due			
1–30	2,000	4	80
31–60	870	10	87
61–90	200	20	40
Over 90	330	50	165
Total Accounts Receivable	$7,000	Total Balance Required in Allowance for Doubtful Accounts	$480
Less current balance			−100
Adjusting entry			$380

* ($3,600 × 0.03)

The desired balance of $480 is now reached. If the Allowance had a *debit* balance of $100 before the adjustment, the amount of the adjusting entry would be a $580 credit to the Allowance to arrive at the $480 balance. Once again, the adjustment *must* consider the existing balance in the Allowance account before the adjusting entry is prepared.

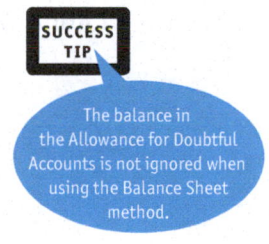

The balance in the Allowance for Doubtful Accounts is not ignored when using the Balance Sheet method.

	2019						
	Dec.	31	Bad Debts Expense		3 8 0 00	
			Allowance for Doubtful Accounts			3 8 0 00
			Estimate of bad debts			

Figure 13.6
Estimating Bad Debts based on Aging of Receivables

Let's check your progress.

▶ TRY IT!   Learning Unit 13-2

On December 31, 2018, Justice Company had a credit balance of $700 in the allowance for doubtful accounts. The accountant for Justice Co. estimated by the aging of accounts receivable approach (balance sheet approach) that Bad Debts would be $1,900. The accountant also estimated by the income statement approach that 4% of net credit sales should be Bad Debts. Net credit sales were $150,000. Journalize the adjusting entries for (1) the income statement approach and (2) the balance sheet approach.

1.

Date			Accounts	Dr.	Cr.
2018					
Dec.		31	Bad Debts Expense	6,000	
			Allowance for Doubtful Accounts		6,000
			Bad Debts Estimate		

2.

2018					
Dec.		31	Bad Debts Expense	1,200	
			Allowance for Doubtful Accounts		1,200
			Bad Debts Estimate		

LEARNING UNIT 13-3

Writing Off and Recovering Uncollectible Accounts

L03

Writing Off an Account Using the Allowance for Doubtful Accounts

Let's assume that on March 18, 2019, Greg Roman Company determines that the account of Jill Sullivan for $900 is uncollectible. (The sale to Jill Sullivan was back in 2018.) Thus, this Accounts Receivable amount should no longer be considered an asset and should be written off. The journal entry in Figure 13.7 reduces the Allowance for Doubtful Accounts and reduces the Accounts Receivable controlling account as well as the accounts receivable subsidiary ledger.

Figure 13.7
Jill Sullivan Account Written Off

2019 Mar.	18	Allowance for Doubtful Accounts	9 0 0 00	
		Accounts Receivable, Jill Sullivan		9 0 0 00
		Wrote off Sullivan account		

The following is a summary of the key points you should study:

- This journal entry does *not* affect any expenses. Remember that Bad Debts Expense is not affected when an account is finally written off. The estimate for Bad Debts Expense was recorded in the previous year before the bad debt actually occurred.
- If more than one customer's account is written off, a compound entry can be used, debiting Allowance for the total and crediting each individual account.
- The net realizable value of Accounts Receivable is unchanged. Let's prove it:

Balances Before the Write-Off		Balances After the Write-Off	
Accounts Receivable ⟶	$12,000	$900 write-off ⟶	$11,100
Less: Allowance for			
Doubtful Accounts ⟶	2,000	$900 drain ⟶	1,100
Estimated realizable value ⟶	$10,000	No change ⟶	$10,000
(what to expect to collect)			

Recording Recovered Debts Using Allowance for Doubtful Accounts What would happen if Jill Sullivan paid all or part of the debt after Greg Roman Company wrote it off? Consider this situation: Assume that Jill Sullivan is able to pay off half of her debt and sent a check to Greg Roman Company on February 1, 2020. (Keep in mind that her account was written off on March 18, 2019, and the original sale was made in 2018.) To record this payment, Greg Roman Company reverses in part the entry that was made to write off the account in the amount expected to be recovered and records the amount received from Jill.

Figure 13.8 shows the journal entries to record the recovery of $450 out of the original amount of $900.

Figure 13.8
Reinstatement of a Bad Debts

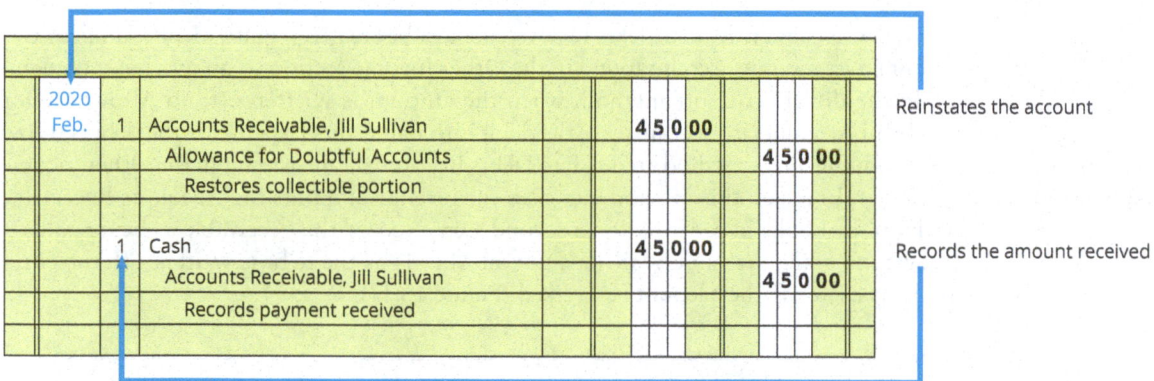

2020 Feb.	1	Accounts Receivable, Jill Sullivan	4 5 0 00			Reinstates the account
		Allowance for Doubtful Accounts		4 5 0 00		
		Restores collectible portion				
	1	Cash	4 5 0 00			Records the amount received
		Accounts Receivable, Jill Sullivan		4 5 0 00		
		Records payment received				

The reason we record both a debit and a credit to Accounts Receivable is that it provides a clear picture of the transactions involving Jill Sullivan. If the company is considering giving credit again to Jill Sullivan, these previous records could be of assistance in determining how much, if any, credit could be extended. Note how the first entry reinstates the account and the second entry records the cash received.

The Direct Write-Off Method

When a company cannot reasonably estimate its Bad Debts Expense, it may use the direct write-off method. Using this method, an account that is determined to be uncollectible would be directly written off to this year's Bad Debts Expense account without regard to when the original sale was made. In this method, the Allowance for Doubtful Accounts is not used because no adjustment is needed at the end of the year to estimate Bad Debts Expense. The journal entry would be a debit to Bad Debts Expense and a credit to Accounts Receivable. (See Figure 13.9.) The direct write-off method is not considered in alignment with generally accepted accounting principles (GAAP).

Direct write-off method Method of writing off uncollectibles when they occur and thus does *not* use the Allowance for Doubtful Accounts. This method does not fulfill the matching principle of accrual accounting.

2019 Mar.	18	Bad Debts Expense	9 0 0 00		
		Accounts Receivable, Jill Sullivan		9 0 0 00	
		Wrote off account			

Figure 13.9
Direct Write-Off Method to Record Bad Debts

Recording Recovered Debts Using the Direct Method Let's suppose that Jill Sullivan repays half of her outstanding debt after Greg Roman Company has written it off. The recovered debt would be accounted for using the direct write-off method as shown in Figure 13.10.

Figure 13.10
Direct Write-Off Method to
Record Recovery

Recovery of half
the amount owed by Jill
Sullivan on February 1, 2018.
Note that Bad Debts Recovered
is used instead of Allowance
for Doubtful Accounts.

2020 Feb.	1	Accounts Receivable, Jill Sullivan			4 5 0 00							
		Bad Debts Recovered						4 5 0 00			
		Restores collectible portion									
	1	Cash			4 5 0 00							
		Accounts Receivable, Jill Sullivan						4 5 0 00			
		Records payment received									

Bad Debts Recovered   When an
account receivable has been written
off and is recovered, this account,
which is in the Other Income category, is credited in the direct write-
off method if the recovery is in a year
following the write-off.

A new account title, Bad Debts Recovered, must be created (Figure 13.10). Think of this account as a revenue account found in the Other Income section of an income statement.

In the direct write-off method, when the amount is written off, no Allowance for Doubtful Accounts is used. Instead, the debit is to Bad Debts Expense. If the debt is recovered later, the direct method credits Bad Debts Recovered (an account in the Other Income category). In effect, this method increases the revenue and puts the Accounts Receivable back on the books in order to—in a second step—record this receivable as being paid. If recovery is made the same year (let's say on May 1) as the debt is written off, the entry made to write off the account is reversed (Figure 13.11).

Figure 13.11
Recovery Made in Same Year

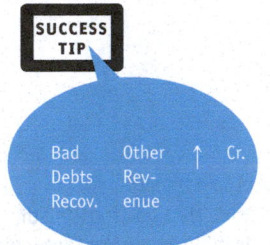

Bad Other ↑ Cr.
Debts Rev-
Recov. enue

2019 May	1	Accounts Receivable, Jill Sullivan			4 5 0 00							
		Bad Debts Expense						4 5 0 00			

Time to check your progress.

▶ **TRY IT!**   **Learning Unit 13-3**

Journalize the write-off of Mathew Baldwin's account for $650 on December 31, 2019, by (1) the allowance method and (2) the direct method.

TRY IT!   **Solution Learning Unit 13-3**

	Date		Accounts	Dr.	Cr.
1.	**2019**				
	Dec.	31	Allowance for Doubtful Accounts	650	
			Accounts Receivable, Mathew Baldwin		650
			Wrote off Baldwin account		
2.	**2019**				
	Dec.	31	Bad Debts Expense	650	
			Accounts Receivable, Mathew Baldwin		650
			Wrote off Baldwin account		

DEMONSTRATION SUMMARY PROBLEM

L01, 2, 3

Sing Co. uses the allowance method based on the income statement approach.

Requirements

1. Journalize the following transactions (the allowance for doubtful accounts has a credit balance of $300):

2018			
Dec.	31	Recorded Bad Debts Expense of $900.	
2019			
Jan.	5	Wrote off Kasha Sims account of $300 as uncollectible.	
	8	Wrote off Hugo Mendez account of $100 as uncollectible.	
	15	Recovered $200 from Kasha Sims.	

2. Journalize the December 31 entry if the balance sheet approach was used and the aging of accounts receivable shows Bad Debts at $800.
3. If the direct method was used, journalize the entry for January 5.

Solutions for Income Statement and Aging of Accounts Receivable Methods

Requirement 1

Date		Accounts	Dr.	Cr.
2018				
Dec.	31	Bad Debts Expense	900	
		Allowance for Doubtful Accounts		900
2019				
Jan.	5	Allowance for Doubtful Accounts	300	
		Accounts Receivable, Sims		300
	8	Allowance for Doubtful Accounts	100	
		Accounts Receivable, Mendez		100
	15	Accounts Receivable, Sims	200	
		Allowance for Doubtful Accounts		200
	15	Cash	200	
		Accounts Receivable, Sims		200

Requirement 2

When using the income statement approach, the balance in the allowance account is ignored.

Date		Accounts	Dr.	Cr.
2018				
Dec.	31	Bad Debts Expense	500	
		Allowance for Doubtful Accounts		500

Since the allowance account had a $300 beginning balance, it takes only another $500 to reach a balance of $800. In the balance sheet approach, the balance in the allowance account must be used (just the opposite of the income statement approach). The allowance for doubtful accounts is a contra-asset. It is increased by a credit and reduced by a debit.

Requirement 3

Date			Accounts	Dr.	Cr.
2019					
Jan.		5	Bad Debts Expense	300	
			Accounts Receivable, Sims		300

No allowance account in the direct method. This method, if used, may not match revenue to the period in which the bad debts actually occurred.

SUCCESS COACH

The following Success Tips are from Learning Units 13-1 to 13-3. Take the Do It Right Now Checkup and use the Check Your Score at the bottom of the page to see how you are doing. The Success Coach provides tips before each Checkup to help you avoid common accounting errors.

LU 13-1 Accrual Accounting and Journalizing Bad Debts Transactions

Do It Right Tips: Bad Debts Expense is an expense on the income statement. Allowance for Doubtful Accounts is a contra-asset found on the balance sheet. The normal balance of the Allowance account is a credit. Accounts Receivable less the Allowance account leave net realizable value, or what you would expect to collect from your Accounts Receivable. Think of the Allowance account as a reserve for Bad Debts. The Bad Debts Expense, when estimated, fills the bucket, and when a bad debts is finally recognized, we drain the bucket.

Do It Right Now Checkup: Answer true or false to the following statements.

1. The Allowance account is filled with a debit.
2. The Allowance account is a contra-revenue account.
3. A Bad Debts expense can be shown before it happens.
4. The Allowance account is drained with a debit.
5. When a Bad Debts is written off, net realizable value will change.

LU 13-2 The Allowance Method

Do It Right Tips: Estimating Bad Debts is an adjusting entry. In the income statement approach, any existing balance in the Allowance account is ignored. In the balance sheet approach, any balance remaining in the Allowance account must be used in determining the amount used for an adjusting entry. In both approaches there will be a debit to Bad Debts Expense and a credit to Allowance for Doubtful Accounts.

Do It Right Now Checkup: Answer true or false to the following statements.

1. Aging Accounts Receivable uses the balance sheet approach.

2. The balance in the Allowance account is not considered in the income statement approach.
3. Estimating Bad Debts is always very accurate.
4. The Allowance account is increased with a credit.
5. The Allowance account is reported on the income statement.

LU 13-3 Writing Off and Recovering Uncollectible Accounts

Do It Right Tips: The allowance method matches Bad Debts expense to sales made in an accounting period. It is the direct write-off method that does not try to match revenue and expenses. When the allowance method is used and a bad debts occurs, the journal entry is to lower the Allowance account and reduce Accounts Receivable. No Bad Debts Expense account is used since it was part of the adjusting entry last period.

In the direct write-off method, a bad debts (no matter when it happens) is a debit to Bad Debts Expense and a credit to Accounts Receivable.

Do It Right Now Checkup: Answer true or false to the following statements.

1. Reinstatement of a bad debt in the allowance method requires an entry to reinstate accounts receivable along with an entry to record the amount received.
2. The direct method uses the Allowance account.
3. The Allowance account accumulates the amount of estimated Bad Debts in the future.
4. The Allowance account is drained with a credit.
5. Bad Debts Expense is reported on the balance sheet.

CHECK YOUR SCORE: Answers to the Do It Right Now Checkup

LU 13-1
1. False—The Allowance account is filled with a credit.
2. False—The Allowance account is a contra-asset account.
3. True
4. True

5. False—When a bad debts is written off, there is no change to net realizable value.

LU 13-2
1. True
2. True

3. False—Estimating Bad Debts is just an estimate and may not be very accurate.
4. True
5. False—The Allowance account is reported on the balance sheet.

3. True
4. False—The Allowance account is drained with a debit.
5. False—Bad Debts Expense is reported on the income statement.

LU 13-3
1. True
2. False—The direct method does not use the Allowance account.

BLUEPRINT: ALLOWANCE METHOD BY INCOME AND BALANCE SHEET APPROACH

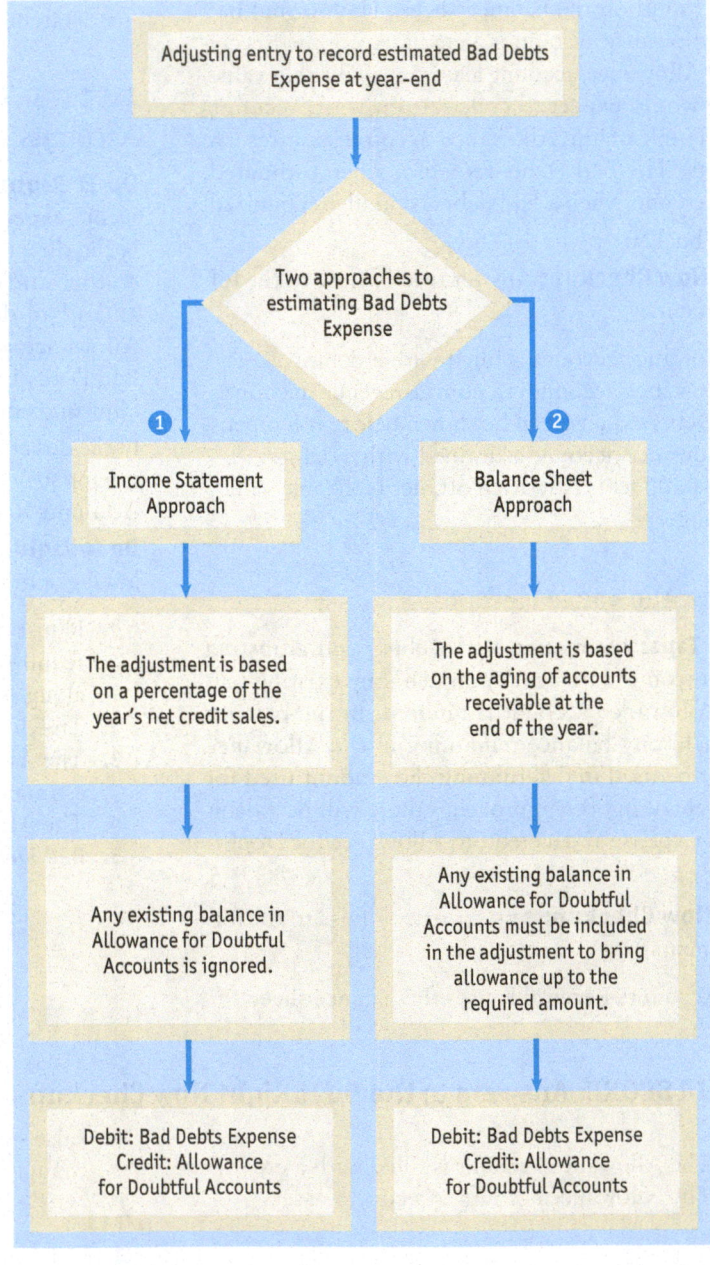

Discussion Questions and Critical Thinking/Ethical Case

1. Explain the matching principle in relation to recording Bad Debts Expense.

2. What is the purpose of the Allowance for Doubtful Accounts?

3. What is net realizable value?

4. When an account receivable is written off, Bad Debts Expense must be debited. True or false? Please discuss.

5. Explain why the Allowance for Doubtful Accounts is a contra-asset account.

6. Recording Bad Debts Expense is a closing entry. True or false? Defend your position.

7. The income statement approach used to estimate Bad Debts is based on Accounts Receivable on the balance sheet. Agree or disagree? Why?

8. In which approach is the balance of the Allowance for Doubtful Accounts considered when the estimate of Bad Debts Expense is made? Please explain.

9. Why would a company age its Accounts Receivable?

10. Using the Allowance for Doubtful Accounts method, what journal entries would be made to write off an account as well as later record the recovery of the accounts receivable?

11. Why doesn't net realizable value change when an account is written off in the use of the Allowance account?

12. What is the purpose of using a direct write-off method?

13. Explain the purpose of the Bad Debts Recovered account.

14. Pete Sazich, the accountant for Moore Company, feels that all Bad Debts will be eliminated if credit transactions are done by credit card. He also feels that the cost of the credit cards should be added to the price of the goods. Pete feels that in the future the allowance method will be totally eliminated. You make the call. Write a letter stating your opinion regarding this matter to Pete's boss.

Concept Checks

MyLabAccounting

Categorizing Accounts

 L03 *(5 min)*

1. **a.** Complete the following transaction analysis chart when employing the direct write-off method:

Accounts	Category	↑↓	Rules
Bad Debts Expense			
Accounts Receivable			

   b. On which financial statement will each title be reported?

Allowance Method

 L02 *(10 min)*

2. Explain under which method the balance in the Allowance account is ignored. Give an example.

Journalize Adjusting Entries for Income Statement and Balance Sheet Approaches

 L02 *(15 min)*

3. Given the balance in the Allowance for Doubtful Accounts of $240 credit, prepare adjusting entries for Bad Debts based on the following assumptions:

   a. Bad Debts to be 2.5% of net credit sales or $640.
   b. Based on aging of Accounts Receivable, Bad Debts should be $550.

(15 min) **LO3**

Writing Off Uncollectible Accounts and Reinstatement: Allowance Method

4. Journalize entries for the following situations (assume allowance method):
   Situation 1: Wrote off Mary Robert as a bad debts 2 years after the sale for $80.
   Situation 2: Reinstated Mary Robert, who sent in her past due amount.

(15 min) **LO3**

Writing Off Uncollectible Accounts and Reinstatement: Direct Write-Off Method

5. Journalize entries for the following situations (assume direct write-off method).
   Situation 1: Wrote off Mary Robert as a bad debts 2 years after the sale of $80.
   Situation 2: Reinstated Mary Robert, who sent in her past due amount 2 years after it had been written off.

MyLabAccounting

Exercises

Set A

(20 min) **LO1**

13A-1. **Kiln.com** has requested that you prepare a partial balance sheet on December 31, 2018, from the following: Cash, $110,000; Petty Cash, $71; Accounts Receivable, $72,000; Bad Debts Expense, $48,000; Allowance for Doubtful Accounts, $9,000; Merchandise Inventory, $14,000.

(20 min) **LO2**

13A-2. Journalize the adjusting entry on December 31, 2018, for Bad Debts Expense, which is estimated to be 5% of net credit sales. The income statement approach is used. The following information is given:

Accounts Receivable			Sales (credit)			Sales Returns and Allowances	
Dr.	Cr.		Dr.	Cr.		Dr.	Cr.
27,000				104,000		500	

	Sales Discount			Allowance for Doubtful Accounts	
	Dr.	Cr.		Dr.	Cr.
	9,600				5,800

(20 min) **LO2**

13A-3. Assuming that in Exercise 13A-2 the balance sheet approach is used, prepare a journalized adjusting entry for Bad Debts Expense. Based on an aging of Accounts Receivable, an $8,200 balance in the Allowance account will be needed to cover bad debts.

(20 min) **LO2, 3**

13A-4. Eagle Co., which uses an Allowance for Doubtful Accounts, had the following transactions in 2018, 2019, and 2020. (Use the income statement approach under the allowance method.)

2018		
Dec.	31	Recorded Bad Debts Expense of $12,500.
2019		
Apr.	3	Wrote off Adam Don account of $4,200 as uncollectible.
June	4	Wrote off Kim Nickles account of $3,100 as uncollectible.
2020		
Aug.	5	Recovered $440 from Kim Nickles.

a. Journalize the transactions. (The company uses the income statement approach in estimating Bad Debts.)

b. Journalize how Eagle Co. would record the Kim Nickles Bad Debts situation if the direct write-off method were used.

13A-5. Juniper Company had credit sales of $180,000 during 2018. The balance in Allowance for Doubtful Accounts is a $1,030 debit balance. Journalize the Bad Debts Expense for December 31 using each of the following methods:

 **LO2** *(20 min)*

a. Bad Debts Expense is estimated at 2% of credit sales.
b. The aging of Accounts Receivable indicates that $1,800 will be required in the Allowance account to cover Bad Debts Expense.

Set B

13B-1. Hamlet.com has requested that you prepare a partial balance sheet on December 31, 2018, from the following: Cash, $130,000; Petty Cash, $64; Accounts Receivable, $71,000; Bad Debts Expense, $50,000; Allowance for Doubtful Accounts, $19,000; Merchandise Inventory, $13,000.

LO1 *(20 min)*

13B-2. Journalize the adjusting entry on December 31, 2018, for Bad Debts Expense, which is estimated to be 4% of net credit sales. The income statement approach is used. The following information is given:

 **LO2** *(20 min)*

Accounts Receivable		Sales (credit)		Sales Returns and Allowances	
Dr.	Cr.	Dr.	Cr.	Dr.	Cr.
25,000			106,000	600	

		Sales Discount		Allowance for Doubtful Accounts	
		Dr.	Cr.	Dr.	Cr.
		9,400			6,000

13B-3. Assuming that in Exercise 13B-2 the balance sheet approach is used, prepare a journalized adjusting entry for Bad Debts Expense. Based on an aging of Accounts Receivable, an $8,000 balance in the Allowance account will be needed to cover Bad Debts.

 **LO2** *(20 min)*

13B-4. Carol Co., which uses an Allowance for Doubtful Accounts, had the following transactions in 2018, 2019, and 2020. (Use the income statement approach under the allowance method.)

LO2, 3 *(20 min)*

2018		
Dec.	31	Recorded Bad Debts Expense of $11,800.
2019		
Apr.	3	Wrote off Harry Longo account of $3,700 as uncollectible.
June	4	Wrote off John Mason account of $3,000 as uncollectible.
2020		
Aug.	5	Recovered $510 from John Mason.

a. Journalize the transactions. (The company uses the income statement approach in estimating Bad Debts.)
b. Journalize how Carol Co. would record the John Mason bad debts situation if the direct write-off method were used.

13B-5. Young Company had credit sales of $140,000 during 2018. The balance in Allowance for Doubtful Accounts is a $1,000 debit balance. Journalize the Bad Debts Expense for December 31 using each of the following methods:

LO2 *(20 min)*

a. Bad Debts Expense is estimated at 2.5% of credit sales.
b. The aging of Accounts Receivable indicates that $2,200 will be required in the Allowance account to cover Bad Debts Expense.

Problems

Set A

(25 min) **L01,2,3**

S50 / **QB**

Check Figure:
August 24:
Dr.: Allowance for Doubtful
Accounts $650
Cr.: Accounts Receivable,
Jill Neill $650

13A-1. Lars Co. has requested that you prepare journal entries from the following (this company uses the Allowance for Doubtful Accounts method based on the income statement approach):

2018		
Dec.	31	Recorded Bad Debts Expense of $16,000.
2019		
Jan.	7	Wrote off Gene Smore's account of $1,200 as uncollectible.
Mar.	5	Wrote off Paul Jurgen's account of $700 as uncollectible.
July	8	Recovered $250 from Paul Jurgen.
Aug.	19	Wrote off Bob Shakur's account of $1,200 as uncollectible.
Aug.	24	Wrote off Jill Neill's account of $650 as uncollectible.
Nov.	19	Recovered $550 from Bob Shakur.

(30 min) **L01,2**

Check Figure:
Net realizable value $155,770

13A-2. Given the information presented in Figure 13.12, do the following:

a. Prepare on December 31, 2018, the adjusting journal entry for Bad Debts Expense. Balances: Cash, $28,000; Accounts Receivable, $171,000; Allowance for Doubtful Accounts, $340; Merchandise Inventory, $18,000. The company uses the allowance method and the balance sheet approach.

b. Prepare a partial balance sheet on December 31, 2018, showing how net realizable value is calculated.

c. If the balance in the Allowance for Doubtful Accounts were a $340 debit balance, journalize the adjusting entry for Bad Debts Expense on December 31, 2018.

Figure 13.12
Aging of Accounts Receivable
for Masse Co.

MASSE CO. DECEMBER 31, 2018			
	Amount	Estimated Percent Considered to Be Bad Debts Expense	Estimated Amount Needed in Allowance for Doubtful Accounts
Not yet due	$140,000	7%	
0–60	11,000	9%	
61–180	13,000	18%	
Over 6 months	7,000	30%	
	$171,000		

(25 min) **L03**

Check Figure:
Dec. 7
Dr.: Bad Debts Expense $265
Cr.: Accts. Rec., J Maddox $265

13A-3. T. J. Rook Company uses the direct write-off method for recording Bad Debts Expense. At the beginning of 2018, Accounts Receivable has a $115,000 balance. Journalize the following transactions for T. J. Rook:

2018		
Mar.	13	Wrote off S. Rossel's account for $2,200.
Apr.	14	Wrote off P. Sower's account for $550.
2019		
Nov.	8	P. Sower paid bad debts of $550 that was written off April 14, 2018.
Dec.	7	Wrote off J. Maddox's account as uncollectible, $265.
Dec.	12	Wrote off D. Longfield's account for $450 due from sales made on account in 2018.

LO1,2,3 *(60 min)*

13A-4. Seay Company completed the following transactions:

2018		
Jan.	9	Sold merchandise on account to Roy's Supply, $1,700. Cost of merchandise sold, $1,000.
Jan.	15	Wrote off the account of Pete Ramos as uncollectible because of his death, $400.
Mar.	17	Received $450 from Rupe Co., whose account had been written off in 2017. The account was reinstated and the collection recorded.
Apr.	9	Received 14% of the $4,000 owed by Lane Daley. The remainder was written off as uncollectible.
June	15	The account for Mac's Garage was reinstated for $1,300. The account was written off 3 years ago and collected in full today.
Oct.	18	Prepared a compound entry to write the following accounts off as uncollectible: Jack's Diner, $140; Kail Auto, $440; Red's Hardware, $750.
Nov.	12	Sold merchandise on account to J. B. Rug, $1,500. Cost of merchandise sold, $900.
Dec.	31	Based on an aging of Accounts Receivable, it was estimated that $6,600 will be uncollectible out of a total of $175,000 in Accounts Receivable.
Dec.	31	Closed Bad Debts Expense to Income Summary.

From the preceding as well as the following additional data on January 1, 2018, complete a–c:

	Acct. No.	Balance
Allowance for Doubtful Accounts	114	$4,300
Income Summary	312	—
Bad Debts Expense	612	—

Check Figure:
Total current assets $286,590

a. Journalize the transactions. The company uses the perpetual and allowance methods.
b. Post to Allowance for Doubtful Accounts, Income Summary, and Bad Debts Expense accounts as needed. (Be sure to record the beginning balance in the Allowance account in the working papers that accompany this text.)
c. Prepare a current assets section of the balance sheet. Ending balances needed are as follows: Cash, $12,000; Accounts Receivable, $175,000; Office Supplies, $2,140; Merchandise Inventory, $103,000; Prepaid Rent, $1,050.

Set B

13B-1. Lee Co. has requested that you prepare journal entries from the following (this company uses the Allowance for Doubtful Accounts method based on the income statement approach):

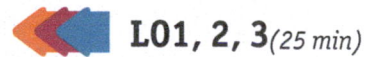
LO1, 2, 3 *(25 min)*

2018		
Dec.	31	Recorded Bad Debts Expense of $14,000.
2019		
Jan.	7	Wrote off Gene Sandler's account of $600 as uncollectible.
Mar.	5	Wrote off Paul Jackson's account of $1,000 as uncollectible.
July	8	Recovered $150 from Paul Jackson.
Aug.	19	Wrote off Bob Shaddix's account of $1,600 as uncollectible.
Aug.	24	Wrote off Jill Noonan's account of $800 as uncollectible.
Nov.	19	Recovered $500 from Bob Shaddix.

Check Figure:
Aug. 24:
Dr.: Allow. for D.A. $800
Cr.: Accts. Rec., Jill Noonan $800

(30 min) **LO1,2**

13B-2. Given the information presented in Figure 13.13, do the following:

a. Prepare on December 31, 2018, the adjusting journal entry for Bad Debts Expense. Balances: Cash, $32,000; Accounts Receivable, $152,000; Allowance for Doubtful Accounts, $260; Merchandise Inventory, $12,000. The company uses the allowance method and the balance sheet approach.

b. Prepare a partial balance sheet on December 31, 2018, showing how net realizable value is calculated.

c. If the balance in the Allowance for Doubtful Accounts were a $260 debit balance, journalize the adjusting entry for Bad Debts Expense on December 31, 2018.

Check Figure:
Net realizable value $143,850

Figure 13.13
Aging of Accounts Receivable for Masso Co.

		MASSO CO. DECEMBER 31, 2018		
	Amount	Estimated Percent Considered to Be Bad Debts Expense	Estimated Amount Needed in Allowance for Doubtful Accounts	
Not yet due	$120,000	2%		
0–60	11,000	4%		
61–180	11,000	21%		
Over 6 months	10,000	30%		
	$152,000			

(25 min) **LO3**

13B-3. T. J. Rack Company uses the direct write-off method for recording Bad Debts Expense. At the beginning of 2018, Accounts Receivable has a $117,000 balance. Journalize the following transactions for T. J. Rack:

2018		
Mar.	13	Wrote off S. Rosh's account for $1,400.
Apr.	14	Wrote off P. Spada's account for $600.
2019		
Nov.	8	P. Spada paid debt of $600 that was written off April 14, 2018.
Dec.	7	Wrote off J. Milton's account as uncollectible, $275.
Dec.	12	Wrote off D. Lovejoy's account for $400 from sales made on account in 2018.

Check Figure:
Dec. 7:
Dr.: Bad Debts Expense $275
Cr.: Accts. Rec., J. Milton $275

(60 min) **LO1,2,3**

13B-4. Simon Company completed the following transactions:

2018		
Jan.	9	Sold merchandise on account to Ryan's Supply, $1,600. Cost of merchandise sold, $1,000.
Jan.	15	Wrote off the account of Pete Runnels as uncollectible because of his death, $700.
Mar.	17	Received $350 from Romero Co., whose account had been written off in 2017. The account was reinstated and the collection recorded.
Apr.	9	Received 20% of the $4,600 owed by Lane Drug. The remainder was written off as uncollectible.
June	15	The account for Mel's Garage was reinstated for $1,600. The account was written off 3 years ago and collected in full today.
Oct.	18	Prepared a compound entry to write the following accounts off as uncollectible: Jane's Diner, $260; Kailey Auto, $440; Rod's Hardware, $600.
Nov.	12	Sold merchandise on account to J. B. Rug, $1,900. Cost of merchandise sold, $1,200.
Dec.	31	Based on an aging of Accounts Receivable, it was estimated that $6,800 will be uncollectible out of a total of $160,000 in Accounts Receivable.
Dec.	31	Closed Bad Debts Expense to Income Summary.

Check Figure:
Total current assets $269,270

From these transactions as well as the following additional data on January 1, 2018, complete a–c:

	Acct. No.	Balance
Allowance for Doubtful Accounts	114	$4,200
Income Summary	312	—
Bad Debts Expense	612	—

a. Journalize the transactions. The company uses the perpetual method.
b. Post to Allowance for Doubtful Accounts, Income Summary, and Bad Debts Expense accounts as needed. (Be sure to record the beginning balance in the Allowance account in the working papers that accompany this text.)
c. Prepare a current assets section of the balance sheet. Ending balances needed are as follows: Cash, $11,000; Accounts Receivable, $160,000; Office Supplies, $2,120; Merchandise Inventory, $102,000; Prepaid Rent, $950.

Financial Report Problem

 **LO2** *(10 min)*

Reading Amazon's Annual Report
Go to **https://tinyurl.com/slaterca14e** to access Amazon's 2016 Annual Report. Go to page 45 and find the balance in the Allowance for Doubtful Accounts in 2015 and 2016.

KEEPING IT REAL SUAREZ COMPUTER CENTER

 MyLabAccounting

 **LO1,2,3** *(15 min)*

Suarez Computer Center currently has a $12,370.00 balance in Accounts Receivable. Here is a current schedule of Accounts Receivable:

Suarez Computer Center
Schedule of Accounts Receivable
March 31, 201X

Phil's Photography	$ 320
Value Pac, Inc.	4,300
Viral Video	3,950
Vital Tax Service	3,800
Total	$12,370

Assignment

Although the Value Pac, Inc. account is not 90 days past due, Falco has determined that it is necessary to write off the entire balance because the business has been foreclosed. Make the necessary journal entry using the direct write-off method.

Bad Debts Expense is listed in the chart of accounts for this problem in Chapter 9 as #5140.

Notes Receivable and Notes Payable

14

CHAPTER PREVIEW: ACCOUNTING IN ACTION

Rick Green, a local organic farmer, was told by a sales agent at a John Deere showroom that he could finance the purchase of a tractor through John Deere. John Deere's finance arm would require Rick to sign a promissory note for the purchase. This note is a written promise to pay back a loan or debt. Notes are very common in business. Many companies like Rick's may finance a big purchase by signing a note. These promissory notes are known as notes receivable to the seller and notes payable to the buyer of the goods or services. In this chapter, we look at how notes, payments, and interest are calculated and journalized.

Learning Objectives – Relating Accounting Theory By Unit

LO1   Determine Interest Calculations and Maturity Dates on Notes

LO2   Journalize Entries to Record Notes

LO3   Journalize Entries to Discount a Note

LO4   Journalize Adjustments for Interest Expense and Interest Income

When you shop at Abercrombie & Fitch, do you ever wonder how much the inventory in the store is worth? Does Abercrombie & Fitch own the inventory, or did it borrow from banks to bring the goods in? So far the accounts receivable and accounts payable transactions we have been discussing have involved informal promises: Purchase orders and sales invoices are not formal written promises. In this chapter, we turn to transactions by buyers and sellers that require promissory notes (or notes), which are *formal written promises*. Notes receivable record amounts owed to a company by others. Notes payable record amounts the company itself owes.

Companies use notes instead of informal promises for many reasons, such as (1) recording sales of high-cost items such as farm machinery or construction equipment that have long-term credit periods (usually over 60 days), (2) giving additional time to settle past-due accounts, or (3) borrowing money from a bank for a fee. The fee that is charged for the use of one's money over a period of time is called interest. In addition, a note gives the seller or lender a stronger legal claim for collecting a past-due account because the note acts as formal proof of the transaction.

Interest Cost of using money for a period of time.

LEARNING UNIT 14-1

L01 ▶

Interest Calculations and Determining Maturity Dates on Notes

Before looking at recording notes receivable and notes payable, let's discuss the structure of a note and how to determine interest calculations and *maturity dates* (when the note comes due).

A promissory note (often called simply a *note*) is a written promise by a borrower to pay a certain sum of money to the lender at a fixed future date. Figure 14.1 is a promissory note that Able Company issued to Green Company. Take a moment to look at the structure of this note. The following explanation is key to the figure:

Promissory note Formal written promise by a borrower to pay a certain sum at a fixed future date.

Principal Face amount of a note.

A. Able Company is borrowing $20,000; this amount is called the principal.
B. Money is being borrowed for 60 days.
C. The note is issued on October 2, 201X.
D. The Green Company is the payee to whom the note is payable.
E. The note carries a 6% annual interest rate. (Even though the note is for 60 days, interest is stated as a yearly rate.)
F. The date the note will come due, December 1, 201X, is called the maturity date.
G. Able Company is the maker, or the one promising to pay the note plus interest when it comes due.

Payee One to whom a note is payable.

Maturity date Due date of the promissory note.

Maker One promising to pay a note.

Figure 14.1
A Promissory Note

$ 20,000 (A)	Bennington, Vermont	October 2 20 1X (C)
sixty days (B)	after date we promise to pay	
to the order of Green Company (D)		
Twenty Thousand and 00/100 ——————— Dollars		
Payable at National Bank		
Value received 6% (E)		
No. 115 Due. December 1, 201X (F)		
	Able Company (G)	
	Joe Mack	
	Treasurer	

The maker (Able Company) is the borrower. The borrower calls this obligation a note payable. The payee (Green Company) views this note as an asset called a note receivable. Able Company's interest expense is interest income for Green Company. Remember that interest expense is classified on the income statement as Other Expenses and interest income is Other Income.

Note payable Promissory note from the maker's point of view.

Note receivable Promissory note from the payee's point of view.

How to Calculate Interest

The formula for calculating the interest on a note is as follows:

Interest =	Principal	×	Rate	×	Time
	↑		↑		↑
	The face value or amount stated on note indicating amount borrowed		Percent per year		Years or fraction of year

Let's look at some illustrative situations to show specific interest calculations using the simple interest method.

Interest calculated for 1 year on a $20,000, 6% (0.06 or 6/100) note:

$$I = P \times R \times T$$
$$= \$20,000 \times 0.06 \times 1$$
$$= \$1,200$$

Interest calculated for 5 months on an $8,000, 10% note: Time is expressed in twelfths of a year; thus, 5 months is

$$I = P \times R \times T$$
$$= \$8,000 \times 0.10 \times \tfrac{5}{12}$$
$$= \$333.33$$

Interest calculated for exact number of days based on a 360-day year, 60 days at 6% on a $4,000 note: When the note is given in days, the fraction for time is

$$\frac{\text{Exact Number of Days}}{360}$$

So we have

$$I = P \times R \times T$$
$$= \$4,000 \times 0.06 \times \tfrac{60}{360}$$
$$= \$40$$

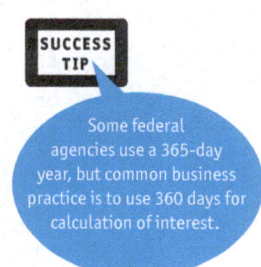

Some federal agencies use a 365-day year, but common business practice is to use 360 days for calculation of interest.

How to Determine Maturity Date

Maturity Date Determined by Exact Days To determine the maturity date of a 90-day note dated June 21, the following could be set up (or you could count on a calendar):

Number of days remaining in June (30–21)	9
Days in July	31
Days in August	31
Number of days at end of August	71
Days in September to reach 90	19
Term of note	90

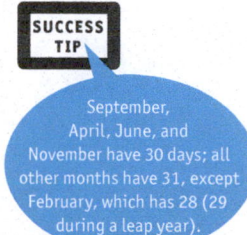

September, April, June, and November have 30 days; all other months have 31, except February, which has 28 (29 during a leap year).

Thus, the maturity date of the note is September 19. Another way to calculate the maturity date is to use a table of days in a year (see Table 14.1, page 496). Today, calendar software is available to automatically calculate maturity dates.

TABLE 14.1 Days in a Year

Day of Month	Jan.	Feb.*	Mar.	Apr.	May	June	July	Aug.	Sept.	Oct.	Nov.	Dec.	Day of Month
1	1	32	60	91	121	152	182	213	244	274	305	335	1
2	2	33	61	92	122	153	183	214	245	275	306	336	2
3	3	34	62	93	123	154	184	215	246	276	307	337	3
4	4	35	63	94	124	155	185	216	247	277	308	338	4
5	5	36	64	95	125	156	186	217	248	278	309	339	5
6	6	37	65	96	126	157	187	218	249	279	310	340	6
7	7	38	66	97	127	158	188	219	250	280	311	341	7
8	8	39	67	98	128	159	189	220	251	281	312	342	8
9	9	40	68	99	129	160	190	221	252	282	313	343	9
10	10	41	69	100	130	161	191	222	253	283	314	344	10
11	11	42	70	101	131	162	192	223	254	284	315	345	11
12	12	43	71	102	132	163	193	224	255	285	316	346	12
13	13	44	72	103	133	164	194	225	256	286	317	347	13
14	14	45	73	104	134	165	195	226	257	287	318	348	14
15	15	46	74	105	135	166	196	227	258	288	319	349	15
16	16	47	75	106	136	167	197	228	259	289	320	350	16
17	17	48	76	107	137	168	198	229	260	290	321	351	17
18	18	49	77	108	138	169	199	230	261	291	322	352	18
19	19	50	78	109	139	170	200	231	(262)	292	323	353	19
20	20	51	79	110	140	171	201	232	263	293	324	354	20
21	21	52	80	111	141	(172)	202	233	264	294	325	355	21
22	22	53	81	112	142	173	203	234	265	295	326	356	22
23	23	54	82	113	143	174	204	235	266	296	327	357	23
24	24	55	83	114	144	175	205	236	267	297	328	358	24
25	25	56	84	115	145	176	206	237	268	298	329	359	25
26	26	57	85	116	146	177	207	238	269	299	330	360	26
27	27	58	86	117	147	178	208	239	270	300	331	361	27
28	28	59	87	118	148	179	209	240	271	301	332	362	28
29	29		88	119	149	180	210	241	272	302	333	363	29
30	30		89	120	150	181	211	242	273	303	334	364	30
31	31		90		151		212	243		304		365	31

*For leap years, February has 29 days, and the number of each day after February 28 is one greater than the number given in the table.

The original note is dated June 21. Look at the top of the table for June and down the left column to day 21. The point of intersection reveals that June 21 is day 172 of the year. If we add 172 and 90 (length of note) we get 262. By searching in the table for 262, we see that the date of maturity is September 19.

Maturity Date Determined by Number of Months If the note were expressed in months rather than days, the table or calendar would not be needed. The maturity date could be found by counting the months from the date the note was issued, regardless of the number of days in each month. Here are some examples:

Date of Note	Length of Note	Maturity Date
March 31	Two months	May 31
April 30	Three months	July 30
July 31	Two months	September 30

Now let's check your progress.

 **TRY IT!**   **Learning Unit 14-1**

Calculate the interest and maturity date for the following:

$9,000 note at 11% for 100 days. Note is dated April 5.

TRY IT!   **Solution Learning Unit 14-1**

$9,000 × 0.11 × 100/360 = $275.00 interest
April 5 = 95th Day
  +100
    195 search in table; July 14 is date of maturity

Journalizing Entries to Record Notes

LEARNING UNIT 14-2

 **L02**

To understand how notes can be used to extend credit periods and to see how a note is paid off, let's look at some illustrative transactions involving Baez Company and Kim Company.

Sale of Merchandise on Account

On August 2, 201X, Baez Company sold $6,000 of merchandise on account that cost $4,000 to Kim Company (Figure 14.2), with credit terms of 2/10, net 30. Both companies use the perpetual inventory system.

		ON BOOKS OF SELLER—BAEZ COMPANY		
Aug.	2	Accounts Receivable, Kim Co.	6 0 0 0 00	
		Sales		6 0 0 0 00
		Sold merchandise on account		
		Cost of Goods Sold	4 0 0 0 00	
		Merchandise Inventory		4 0 0 0 00
		Cost of merchandise inventory sold		

		ON BOOKS OF BUYER—KIM COMPANY		
Aug.	2	Merchandise Inventory	6 0 0 0 00	
		Accounts Payable, Baez Co.		6 0 0 0 00
		Purchased merchandise on account		

Figure 14.2
Sale of Merchandise on Books of Seller and Buyer

Time Extension with a Note On September 1, the end of the credit period, Kim Company gave a $6,000, 60-day, 13% note to Baez Company to gain additional time to settle the past-due account. The entries in Figure 14.3 (page 498) would be made on the books of the buyer and seller.

Figure 14.3
Time Extension of a Note

Notes Receivable is a current asset on the balance sheet.

Notes Payable is a current liability on the balance sheet.

			SELLER—BAEZ COMPANY				
Sept.	1	Notes Receivable		6 0 0 0 00		
		Accounts Receivable, Kim Co.			6 0 0 0 00	
		Received 60-day, 13% note for				
		extension of past due account				

			BUYER—KIM COMPANY				
Sept.	1	Accounts Payable, Baez Co.		6 0 0 0 00		
		Notes Payable			6 0 0 0 00	
		Issued 60-day, 13% note for				
		extension of past due account				

When this transaction is journalized, both Accounts Receivable and Accounts Payable are reduced (i.e., replaced by Notes Receivable and Notes Payable, respectively). With *notes*, a subsidiary ledger is usually *not* needed because the file of the notes provides all the information.

Baez accepted this note as an extension because (1) if Kim Company doesn't pay, a formal written promise is in hand, and (2) interest is accumulating on the note.

Seller → *The end result of this transaction is a shift in current assets of Baez Company from Accounts Receivable to Notes Receivable.*

Buyer → *For Kim Company, the result is a shift in current liabilities from Accounts Payable to Notes Payable.*

Note Due and Paid at Maturity

Now let's look at the journal entries that will be made if Kim Company pays off the note on October 31 (Figure 14.4). It is important to emphasize that the interest is calculated and paid on the maturity date of the note.

Figure 14.4
Note Paid at Maturity

			SELLER—BAEZ COMPANY				
Oct.	31	Cash		6 1 3 0 00		
		Notes Receivable			6 0 0 0 00	
		Interest Income			1 3 0 00	
		Collected Kim Company note				

$$[\$6,000 \times 0.13 \times \frac{60}{360} = \$130 \text{ Interest Income}]$$

			BUYER—KIM COMPANY				
Oct.	31	Notes Payable		6 0 0 0 00		
		Interest Expense		1 3 0 00		
		Cash			6 1 3 0 00	
		Paid note to Baez Company				

$$[\$6,000 \times 0.13 \times \frac{60}{360} = \$130 \text{ Interest Expense}]$$

Note Renewed at Maturity

If Kim Company is unable to pay the $6,130 at maturity, it is possible for the company to renew all or part of the note. Let's assume that the company can pay the interest of $130 and give another note for 90 days at 13%. The transaction could be recorded as shown in Figure 14.5 on the books of the buyer and seller.

		SELLER—BAEZ COMPANY			
Oct.	31	Cash	1 3 0 00		
		Notes Receivable (new)	6 0 0 0 00		
		Notes Receivable (old)		6 0 0 0 00	
		Interest Income		1 3 0 00	
		Interest of old note collected and			
		renewal of note for 90 days			

		BUYER—KIM COMPANY			
Oct.	31	Notes Payable (old)	6 0 0 0 00		
		Interest Expense	1 3 0 00		
		Notes Payable (new)		6 0 0 0 00	
		Cash		1 3 0 00	
		Interest of old note paid and			
		renewal of note for 90 days			

Figure 14.5
Note Renewed at Maturity

Note from the seller's books how the interest is received, the old note is canceled, and the new note is put on the books.

Dishonored Note

Baez Company does not have to accept the renewed note if Kim Company fails to pay it at maturity. In this situation the note is said to be a dishonored note. Another way to describe this situation is to say that Kim Company has defaulted on its note.

On Baez's and Kim's books the amounts in Notes Receivable and Notes Payable will then be removed and transferred back to Accounts Receivable and Accounts Payable because the note has reached the maturity date. At the same time, whether the note is paid or not, the interest expense is due and payable and should be recorded (for Baez Company this is Interest Income, and for Kim Company it is Interest Expense).

Let's see what entries would look like if Kim Company first defaults and then finally pays the amount owed on December 1 (see Figure 14.6, page 500). To keep it simple, no additional charges will be calculated for the extra month Kim Company has taken to pay off the amount owed to Baez Company.

Dishonored note Note that was not paid at maturity by the maker.

Default Failure of maker to pay the maturity value of a note when due.

Note Given in Exchange for Equipment Purchased

A note may be given in exchange for an asset that is purchased. For instance, suppose Kim Company decided to buy from Ronald Company some display racks for $7,000. Because the price was high, Kim Company gave a note instead of buying the racks on account. The note issued by Kim Company was a 60-day, 9% interest-bearing note for $7,000. The cost of the display racks to the seller was $3,500. This transaction is recorded on the books of the buyer and seller as shown in Figure 14.7 (page 500).

When the note is paid at maturity, the same transactions discussed earlier would result.

Figure 14.6 Note Dishonored and Repaid on Books of Seller and Buyer

			SELLER—BAEZ COMPANY					
(A) Oct.	31	Accounts Receivable, Kim Co.		6 1 3 0 00			
		Interest Income				1 3 0 00	
		Notes Receivable				6 0 0 0 00	
		Recorded note receivable dishonored					

			BUYER—KIM COMPANY					
(A) Oct.	31	Notes Payable		6 0 0 0 00			
		Interest Expense		1 3 0 00			
		Accounts Payable, Baez Co.				6 1 3 0 00	
		Recorded note payable dishonored					

SUCCESS TIP

Only notes not yet matured are in the Notes Receivable account.

			SELLER—BAEZ COMPANY					
(B) Dec.	1	Cash		6 1 3 0 00			
		Accounts Receivable, Kim Co.				6 1 3 0 00	
		Recorded payment of note					
		receivable dishonored					

			BUYER—KIM COMPANY					
(B) Dec.	1	Accounts Payable, Baez Co.		6 1 3 0 00			
		Cash				6 1 3 0 00	
		Payment of note payable dishonored					

Figure 14.7
Note Exchanged for Equipment

			SELLER—RONALD COMPANY					
May	9	Notes Receivable		7 0 0 0 00			
		Sales				7 0 0 0 00	
		Sold merchandise (display racks) with a					
		60-day, 9% note					
		Cost of Goods Sold		3 5 0 0 00			
		Merchandise Inventory				3 5 0 0 00	
		Cost of merchandise sold					

			BUYER—KIM COMPANY					
May	9	Store Equipment		7 0 0 0 00			
		Notes Payable				7 0 0 0 00	
		Purchased display racks with a					
		60-day, 9% note					

Now let's check your progress.

TRY IT!   Learning Unit 14-2

Journalize the following transactions:

a. Bristol Co. recorded a 30-day, $17,000 note at 12% for a time extension of a past-due account of Anderman Co.

b. Collected the Anderman Co. note on maturity date.

c. Assuming Anderman Co. defaulted in transaction b, record the dishonored note.

TRY IT!   Solution Learning Unit 14-2

Accounts	Dr.	Cr.
a. Notes Receivable	17,000	
Accounts Receivable, Anderman Co.		17,000
Establish note		
b. Cash	17,170	
Interest Income		170
Notes Receivable		17,000
Collected note		
($17,000 × 0.12 × 30/360 = $170)		
c. Accounts Receivable, Anderman Co.	17,170	
Notes Receivable		17,000
Interest Income		170

Journalizing Entries to Discount a Note

LEARNING UNIT 14-3

 L03

Many times a company that accepts notes from customers will not (or cannot) wait to receive its cash until the maturity date. Instead, it goes to a bank and exchanges the note for cash. This process is called discounting a note. The company will endorse the note and receive the maturity value of the note (principal plus interest) less what the bank charges for holding the note from the date of discounting until the maturity date. The time period during which the bank holds the note (until maturity) is called the discount period.

The amount that the bank charges the company is called the bank discount. It is the difference between what the company receives from the bank and the maturity value of the note. The actual amount of money the company receives when a note is discounted is called the proceeds (maturity value of note less the bank discount).

Let's see how Marvin Company discounts an interest-bearing note receivable. The best way to understand the process is to take it step by step.

How to Discount an Interest-Bearing Note Receivable

Marvin Company received a $8,000, 90-day, 12% note from Gee Company dated October 1. On October 31 Marvin Company needed cash to finance its inventory, so it discounted the note to Blue Bank, which charges a bank discount rate of 14%. An overview of the process is shown in Figure 14.8.

Discounting a note Process or act of transferring the note to a bank before the maturity date.

Maturity value Amount of the note that is due on the date of maturity (Principal + Interest).

Discount period Amount of time the bank holds a note that was discounted until the maturity date.

Bank discount What the bank charges to hold a note until maturity (Maturity Value − Proceeds).

Proceeds Maturity value of note less bank discount.

Figure 14.8 Discounting a Note Receivable, $8,000 at 12% for 90 Days

Issue Date October 1	Date of Discount October 31	Maturity Date Dec. 30
Oct. 31 – Oct. 1 = 30 days	90 days – 30 days = 60 days = Discount Period	
Marvin Company holds note	Bank holds note	

Face
Value:
$8,000

Maturity
Value:
$8,240

90 days

STEP 1: Find the *maturity* value of the note:

a. $\$8{,}000 \times 0.12 \times \dfrac{90}{360} = \$240$ **Interest**

b. **Maturity Value = Principal + Interest**
= \$8,000 + \$240
= \$8,240

STEP 2: Calculate the *discount* period (number of days from the date of discounting until the maturity date):

90 Days	Note
− 30 Days	Expired before discounting (Oct. 1–Oct. 31)
= 60 Days	Days bank holds note until it comes due on Dec. 30

STEP 3: Calculate the bank discount (what the bank charges Marvin Company for holding the note until maturity). To do so, we use the following formula:

$$\frac{\textbf{Bank}}{\textbf{Discount}} = \frac{\textbf{Maturity}}{\textbf{Value}} \times \frac{\textbf{Bank Discount}}{\textbf{Rate}} \times \frac{\textbf{No. of Days Bank Holds Note Until Maturity}}{\textbf{360 Days}}$$

$$= \$8{,}240 \times 0.14 \times \frac{60}{360}$$

$$= \$192.27$$

Note that the bank discount is based on the maturity value because we are borrowing the maturity value for the number of days in the discount period.

STEP 4: Calculate the proceeds (what Marvin Company receives from the bank in the discounting process):

Proceeds = Maturity Value − Bank Discount
= \$8,240 − \$192.27
= \$8,047.73

If Marvin Company could have waited until the maturity date, it would have received $8,240. By discounting the note, the company lost interest of $192.27, or the cost charged by the bank to hold the note until maturity. Let's look at how Marvin Company would record this item on its accounting books (Figure 14.9).

Oct.	31	Cash	8 0 4 7 73			
		Notes Receivable			8 0 0 0 00	
		Interest Income				4 7 73
		Discounted Gee Company's				
		90-day, 12% note at 14%				

Figure 14.9
Discounting a Note with Interest Income

This transaction resulted in interest income because the proceeds Marvin Company received were more than the face value of the note ($8,000). In actuality, if the proceeds had been *less* than the $8,000, Marvin Company would have incurred an interest expense. For example, if Marvin Company held the note for only a short period of time and/or Blue Bank had a bank discount rate much higher than the original note interest rate, this could have resulted in an interest expense rather than interest income. Suppose the note was discounted after being held only 2 days and the bank's discount rate was 18%. The bank discount, or amount the bank charges, would be calculated as follows:

Maturity value   Discount period

$$\text{Bank Discount} = \$8,240 \times 0.18 \times \frac{88}{360} = \$362.56$$

Thus, the proceeds to Marvin Company would be

$$\text{Proceeds} = \$8,240 - \$362.56$$
$$= \$7,877.44$$

Note that here Marvin Company is receiving less than the $8,000 face value of the note. The general journal entry of Marvin Company would thus look as shown in Figure 14.10.

Oct.	3	Cash	7 8 7 7 44		
		Interest Expense	1 2 2 56		
		Notes Receivable		8 0 0 0 00	
		To record discount of note			

Figure 14.10
Discounting a Note with Interest Expense

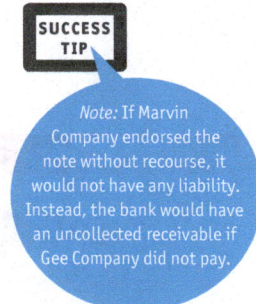

Note: If Marvin Company endorsed the note without recourse, it would not have any liability. Instead, the bank would have an uncollected receivable if Gee Company did not pay.

Contingent liability Liability on the part of one who discounts a note if the maker of the note defaults at maturity date.

Procedure When a Discounted Note Is Dishonored

Who is liable for the note if Gee Company fails to pay the note at maturity? The answer is Marvin Company.

When Marvin Company endorsed the note to Blue Bank, it agreed to pay the note at maturity if Gee Company defaulted. The potential liability is called a contingent liability. Until the note is paid, Marvin Company will state this contingent liability as a footnote on its online or printed balance sheet.

At some point before maturity, Gee Company is notified by Blue Bank that it is holding their note. Let's assume that the maturity date is reached and Gee Company defaults. Blue Bank notifies Marvin Company and charges Marvin Company the full amount of the note, including interest and a $5 protest fee, which is the charge made by Blue Bank for notifying Marvin Company that the note was presented to the maker for payment and was not received. Thus, the bank charges Marvin Company (and Marvin will in turn charge Gee Company) the following:

Note	$8,000
Interest	240
Protest Fee	5
	$8,245

The entry is recorded on Marvin Company's books as shown in Figure 14.11.

Figure 14.11
Default of a Discounted Note

Dec.	30	Accounts Receivable, Gee Co.	8 2 4 5 00	
		Cash		8 2 4 5 00
		To record default of discounted note		

You can be sure that Marvin Company will try to collect this $8,245 from Gee Company. Marvin Company may charge additional interest for this delay in paying the $8,245. For simplicity, we have left this step out. If the $8,245 becomes uncollectible, the account has to be written off as a bad debt, as discussed in Chapter 13.

Now it's time to check your progress.

 TRY IT!   **Learning Unit 14-3**

Cole Stone received a $25,000, 180-day, 4% note from Larry Co. dated May 3, 201X. On May 15, Cole Stone discounted the note to Lovely Bank, which charges a bank discount rate of 6%.

Calculate (a) maturity value, (b) amount of bank discount, and (c) proceeds.

TRY IT!   **Solution Learning Unit 14-3**

a. $25,000 × 0.04 × 180/360 = $500 interest at maturity
Maturity Value = Principal + Interest
            = $25,000 + $500
            = $25,500

b.   Discount period = 168 days
Amount of bank discount = $714.00
Maturity value − Bank discount = Proceeds
$25,500 − $714.00 = $24,786.00

LEARNING UNIT 14-4

Adjustments for Interest Expense and Interest Income

L04

Discounting One's Own Note

In the last unit we looked at how a note of a customer was discounted. Now our attention shifts to Jones Company, which is borrowing $10,000 by giving Alvin Bank its own 12%, 60-day note on December 16, 201X. In this case, Alvin Bank deducts the interest in advance. The following is the formula to calculate the bank discount (cost of borrowing) and the proceeds (what Jones Company gets):

SUCCESS TIP

Note that maturity value here is the same as the original principal because interest is deducted in advance.

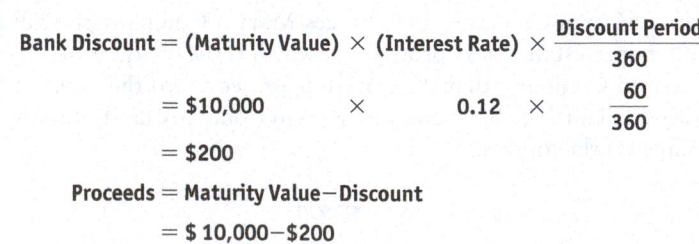

$$\text{Bank Discount} = (\text{Maturity Value}) \times (\text{Interest Rate}) \times \frac{\text{Discount Period}}{360}$$
$$= \$10,000 \times 0.12 \times \frac{60}{360}$$
$$= \$200$$
$$\text{Proceeds} = \text{Maturity Value} - \text{Discount}$$
$$= \$10,000 - \$200$$
$$= \$9,800$$

Thus, Jones Company receives $9,800 and at the time of maturity will pay back $10,000. The $200 of interest is recorded in a new account called Discount on Notes Payable. This account is a contra-liability account that is subtracted from Notes Payable on the balance sheet, where it looks like the following:

Current Liabilities	
Notes Payable	$10,000
Less: Discount on Notes Payable	200
	$ 9,800

Later in this unit, when we talk about adjustments, we will see that as the note matures, the discount will be reduced and then charged to Interest Expense. For now, however, let's record the journal entry for Jones Company as it discounts its own note with interest deducted in advance (Figure 14.12).

Dec.	16	Cash		9 80 0 00	
		Discount on Notes Payable		2 0 0 00	
		Notes Payable			10 0 0 0 00
		Discounted own note at 12% for 60 days			

Discount on Notes Payable Amount of interest deducted in advance by the lender. This account reduces Notes Payable.

Figure 14.12
Discounted Note with Interest Deducted in Advance

Accounts Affected	Category	↑↓		Rules
Cash	Asset	↑	Dr.	$ 9,800
Discount on Notes Payable	Contra-Liability	↑	Dr.	$ 200
Notes Payable	Liability	↑	Cr.	$10,000

When the note is paid, the accountant will debit Notes Payable for $10,000 and credit Cash for $10,000.

Note: Although the bank interest rate is stated at 12%, the truth is that Jones Company really has the use of only $9,800. To calculate the true interest rate, which is called the effective interest rate, the following formula applies:

$$\text{Effective Interest Rate} = \frac{\text{(Maturity Value of Note)} \times \text{(Bank Interest Rate)}}{\text{Amount of Cash Proceeds Received from Note}}$$

$$= \frac{\$10,000 \times 0.12}{\$9,800}$$

$$= 12.24\%$$

Effective interest rate True rate of simple interest.

Now let's look at how adjustments will be handled for some of the transactions presented in this chapter.

Interest: The Need for Adjustments

Because interest-bearing notes are often taken out and then paid off in different accounting periods, it is necessary to adjust or bring up-to-date Interest Income and Interest Expense. The following diagram shows why we need to adjust as well as who does the adjusting:

SUCCESS TIP

The payee is the seller and the maker is the buyer.

ACCRUED INTEREST INCOME	**ACCRUED INTEREST EXPENSE**
Must adjust for income that has been earned during the period but has not been received or recorded because payment is not yet due.	*Must adjust for interest that has been incurred during the period but has not been paid or recorded because payment is not yet due.*
↓	↓
Notes Receivable (*payee*)	(A) Note Payable (*maker*)
	(B) Company's own discounted note

Let's look at how to record adjustments for Interest Income and Interest Expense from the following: Bog Company receives a $24,000, 60-day, 10% note on December 16, 201X, from Jan Company (see Figure 14.13).

Figure 14.13
Adjusting for Interest Accrued

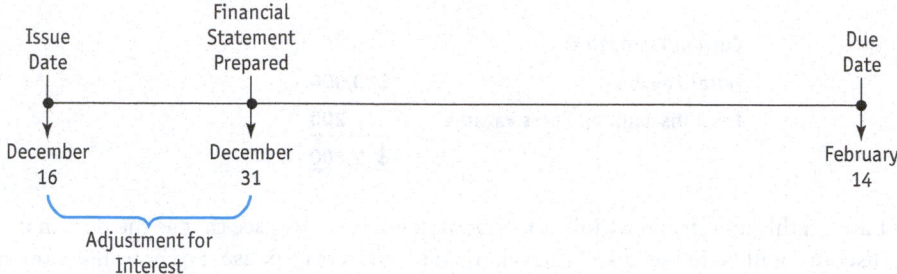

STEP 1: Calculate interest on the note:

$$\text{Interest} = \$24{,}000 \times 0.10 \times \frac{60}{360}$$
$$= \$400$$

STEP 2: Calculate the number of days the note has already run before the end of the current period (see Table 14.1):

Dec. 31	(end of period)
−Dec. 16	(starting date of note)
15	Days

STEP 3: Calculate interest incurred for this period:

$$\text{Length of note} \rightarrow \frac{\textbf{15 Days}}{\textbf{60 Days}} = \frac{1}{4} \times \$400 = \$100$$

Another way to calculate the interest is

$$\$24{,}000 \times 0.10 \times \frac{15}{360} = \$100$$

STEP 4: Prepare the adjusting journal entries (Figure 14.14).

Figure 14.14   Adjustment for Interest on Note

On Books of *Seller* (Holder of Note)

Dec.	31	Interest Receivable	1 0 0 00	
		Interest Income		1 0 0 00
		Adj. interest		
		for 15 days		

On Books of *Buyer* (Debtor)

Dec.	31	Interest Expense	1 0 0 00	
		Interest Payable		1 0 0 00
		Adj. interest		
		for 15 days		

Interest Receivable

Dr.	Cr.
100	
Current Asset on balance sheet	

Interest Expense

Dr.	Cr.
100	
Other Expense on income statement	

Interest Income

Dr.	Cr.
	100
	Other Income on income statement

Interest Payable

Dr.	Cr.
	100
	Current Liability on balance sheet

When the note is paid off on February 14, the following entries are made, assuming that no reversing entry is used, as shown in Figure 14.15.

Seller

	Feb.	14	Cash	24 4 0 0 00			
			Interest Receivable			1 0 0 00	
			Notes Receivable			24 0 0 0 00	
			Interest Income			3 0 0 00	
			Received payment of note				

Buyer

	Feb.	14	Notes Payable	24 0 0 0 00			
			Interest Expense	3 0 0 00			
			Interest Payable	1 0 0 00			
			Cash			24 4 0 0 00	
			Paid off note				

Figure 14.15
No Reversing Entry

Note that by not using reversing entries, the bookkeepers of the buyer and seller had to look up the amount of accrued interest that was recorded in the *old* year so that this year's interest expense or income would not be overstated.

If a reversing entry (which is optional) is used, the entries shown in Figure 14.16 are made.

Seller

	Feb.	14	Cash	24 4 0 0 00			
			Notes Receivable			24 0 0 0 00	
			Interest Income			4 0 0 00	
			Received payment of note				

Buyer

	Feb.	14	Notes Payable	24 0 0 0 00			
			Interest Expense	4 0 0 00			
			Cash			24 4 0 0 00	
			Paid off note				

Figure 14.16
Reversing Entry Made

The last adjustment deals with a firm discounting its own note. At the beginning of this unit, we saw Jones Company discounting its own note on December 16 for $10,000 for 60 days at 12% interest. Jones Company actually received $9,800 and recorded the $200 interest deducted in advance by the bank in a contra-liability account called *Discount on Notes Payable*.

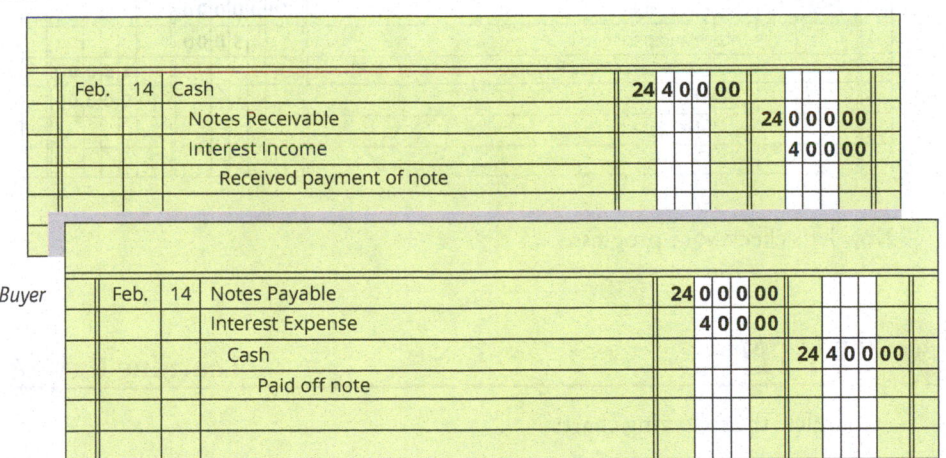

Discount on Notes Payable		Interest Expense	
Dr.	Cr.	Dr.	Cr.
200			

At the end of December, 15 out of the 60 days have passed. Thus, 15 days' worth of interest on this note should be recorded in the old year. To record this interest, we reduce the amount in the Discount on Notes Payable by $50 ($10,000 × 0.12 × 15/360). The journal entry shown in Figure 14.17 is made.

Figure 14.17
Recording Interest and Reducing Balance of Discount on Notes Payable

Dec.	31	Interest Expense		50 00	
		Discount on Notes Payable			50 00
		Recognition of expense incurred			

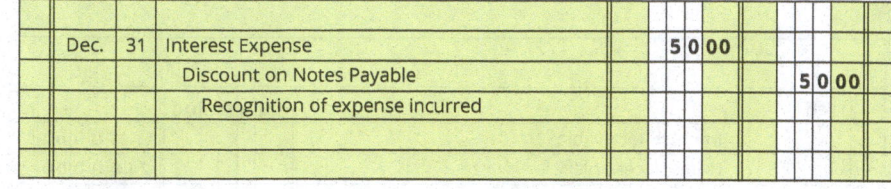

SUCCESS TIP

$10,000 × 12%

$\times \dfrac{45}{360} = \$150$

Accounts Affected	Category	↑↓	Rules	
Interest Expense	Other Expense	↑	Dr.	$50
Discount on Notes Payable	Contra-Liability	↓	Cr.	$50

The current liability on the balance sheet at December 31 will look as follows:

Current Liabilities	
Notes Payable	$10,000
Less: Discount on Notes Payable	150
	$ 9,850

When the note is paid in the following year, the journal entry shown in Figure 14.18 will result.

Figure 14.18
Note Paid Off

Feb.	14	Notes Payable	10 000 00		
		Interest Expense	150 00		
		Discount on Notes Payable		150 00	
		Cash		10 000 00	
		Note paid			

Now let's check your progress.

 **TRY IT!**   **Learning Unit 14-4**

Complete the following chart:

Account	Category	Normal Balance	Financial Statement
Notes Payable			
Cash			
Discount on Notes Payable			
Interest Receivable			
Interest Income			
Interest Expense			
Interest Payable			

Solution Learning Unit 14-4

Account	Category	Normal Bal.	Financial Statement
Notes Payable	Liability	Cr.	BS
Cash	Asset	Dr.	BS
Discount on Notes Payable	Contra-Liability	Dr.	BS
Interest Receivable	Asset	Dr.	BS
Interest Income	Revenue	Cr.	IS
Interest Expense	Expense	Dr.	IS
Interest Payable	Liability	Cr.	BS

DEMONSTRATION SUMMARY PROBLEM

 L01,2,3,4

Requirements

Journalize the following transactions for Baker Co.

201X

Mar. 10   Received $10,000, 90-day, 4% note from John Sullivan in payment of account due.

Apr. 8   Wrote off the Burton Bushman account as uncollectible for $500. (Baker uses the allowance method to record bad debts.)

June 8   John Sullivan paid Baker the note in full.

July 11   Gave Piston Co. an $8,000, 45-day, 5% note as a time extension of account now past due.

15   Burton Bushman paid Baker amount previously owed on April 8.

Aug. 3   Discounted its own $6,000, 120-day note at Beverly Bank at 4%.

5   Received $8,000, 60-day, 4% note dated Aug. 5 from Ellen Girad in payment of a past-due account.

25   Paid principal and interest due on the note issued to Piston Co. from July 11.

26   Received $15,000, 60-day, 3% note from Trio Co. in payment of account past due.

29   Discounted Ellen Girad note to Lawn Bank at 7%.

31   Recorded adjusting entries as appropriate.

Solutions

Date	Accounts	Dr.	Cr.
201X			
Mar. 10	Notes Receivable	10,000	
	Accounts Receivable, John Sullivan		10,000
	Transferred to a note		
Apr. 8	Allowance for Doubtful Accounts	500	
	Accounts Receivable, Burton Bushman		500
	Wrote off account		
June 8	Cash	10,100	
	Interest Income		100
	Notes Receivable		10,000
	Sullivan paid note		
	($10,000 × 0.04 × 90/360 = $100)		

Date	Accounts	Dr.	Cr.
July 11	Accounts Payable, Piston Co.	8,000	
	Notes Payable		8,000
	Transferred to a note		
15	Accounts Receivable, Burton Bushman	500	
	Allowance for Doubtful Accounts		500
	Reinstate account		
15	Cash	500	
	Accounts Receivable, Burton Bushman		500
	Collected from Bushman		
Aug. 3	Cash	5,920	
	Discount on Notes Payable	80	
	Notes Payable		6,000
	Borrowed at a discount		
	($6,000 × 0.04 × 120/360 = $80)		
5	Notes Receivable	8,000	
	Accounts Receivable, Ellen Girad		8,000
	Transferred to a note		
25	Notes Payable	8,000	
	Interest Expense	50	
	Cash		8,050
	Paid note		
	($8,000 × 0.05 × 45/360 = $50)		
26	Notes Receivable	15,000	
	Accounts Receivable, Trio Co.		15,000
	Transferred to a note		
29	Cash	7,996.96	
	Interest Expense	3.04	
	Notes Receivable		8,000
	Discounted note at bank		
	$\left(\begin{array}{l}\$8,053.33 \times 0.07 \times 36/360 = \$56.37\\ \$8,053.33 - \$56.37 = \$7,996.96\end{array}\right)$		
31	Interest Expense	18.67	
	Discount on Notes Payable		18.67
	Adjustment		
	(28/120 × $80 = $18.67)		
31	Interest Receivable	6.25	
	Interest Income		6.25
	Adjustment		
	$\left(\begin{array}{l}\$15,000 \times .03 \times 60/360 = \$75\\ \quad\ \ \$75 \times 5/60 = \$6.25\end{array}\right)$		

Tips for Journalizing Notes and Interest

Mar. 10   Converted the Accounts Receivable of John Sullivan into a note.

Apr. 8   To write off the Bushman account, the Allowance for Doubtful Accounts is reduced by a debit, and Accounts Receivable is reduced by a credit.

June 8	Receive $10,100 in cash since the note has built up interest of $100.
July 11	To transfer to a note, Accounts Payable is reduced, and Notes Payable is increased.
15	To reinstate an account, put it back on the books, put the $500 back into the allowance account, and show we have an accounts receivable. Following this, get the cash and reduce Accounts Receivable.
Aug. 3	By discounting, $5,920 is received, and the difference is shown in a contra-liability account called Discount on Notes Payable.
5	To change an accounts receivable to a note, the Notes Receivable is debited and Accounts Receivable is credited.
25	The note interest is $50. This results in paying the note of $8,000 and the cost of interest. The note payable is reduced by a debit, and Interest Expense is increased by a debit.
26	Transferred Accounts Receivable of Trio Company into Notes Receivable.
29	In discounting a note, the bank discount is $56.37. By taking the maturity value of $8,053.33, the difference results in interest expense of $3.04. Note the full amount of the note is not received; in this case, cash received is $7,996.96.
31	The discount on notes payable was $80. The $18.67 increases the interest expense for the year and lowers the discount on notes payable by a credit of $18.67. Remember, the $18.67 was calculated by $28/120 \times \$80$.
31	The note has built up interest of $6.25. This amount is the result of taking $5/60 \times \$75$. The $75 is the total interest amount. Interest Receivable is increased by a debit, and Interest Income is increased by a credit.

SUCCESS COACH

The following Success Tips are from Learning Units 14-1 to 14-4. Take the Do It Right Now Checkup and use the Check Your Score at the bottom of the page to see how you are doing. The Success Coach provides tips before each Checkup to help you avoid common accounting errors.

LU 14-1 Interest Calculations and Determining Maturity Dates on Notes

Do It Right Tips: Interest is found by this formula: principal $\times$ rate $\times$ time. The table of days in a year in this chapter helps you calculate the length of time. The denominator of time will be 360 for most calculations, but keep in mind that federal agencies like to use 365. The table then provides you with the exact number of days. If time is in months, you can use number of months divided by 12.

Do It Right Now Checkup: Answer true or false to the following statements.

1. A promissory note is not written.
2. A payee is to whom the note is payable.
3. Most promissory notes are interest free.
4. The maturity date is when the note begins.
5. The maker of the note is the borrower.

LU 14-2 Journalizing Entries to Record Notes

Do It Right Tips: A time extension of a past-due account for the seller results in an increase in Notes Receivable and a decrease in Accounts Receivable. Notes Receivable is a current asset on the balance sheet. For the buyer, the extension shifts Accounts Payable into Notes Payable. Keep in mind that Notes Payable is a current liability on the balance sheet.

Do It Right Now Checkup: Answer true or false to the following statements.

1. Notes Receivable is found on the income statement.
2. Failing to pay at maturity means that the note is dishonored or defaulted.
3. A note renewed means there is interest income recorded for the buyer.
4. Only matured notes are in the Notes Receivable account.
5. A note can never be given in exchange for equipment.

LU 14-3 Journalizing Entries to Discount a Note

Do It Right Tips: Discounting a note means exchanging the note for cash before the maturity date. The proceeds you get will result in the bank charging you a bank discount.

The longer the bank holds your note, the fewer proceeds you will receive. The discounting process involves calculating maturity value, calculating discount period, calculating bank discount, and calculating the proceeds.

Do It Right Now Checkup: Answer true or false to the following statements.

1. The first step of discounting a note receivable is to calculate the bank discount.
2. When discounting a note, interest income results if the amount of cash received is greater than the face value of the note.
3. Proceeds are never less than the face value of the note.
4. A contingent liability is a definite liability.
5. Interest Expense results if the amount of cash received is greater than the face value of the note.

LU 14-4 Adjustments for Interest Expense and Interest Income

Do It Right Tips: Discount on Notes Payable is a contra-liability account that is subtracted from Notes Payable on the balance sheet. An increase in Discount on Notes Payable is a debit. The interest in the Discount on Notes Payable account is adjusted by reducing the Discount on Notes Payable and recording it as an interest expense.

Do It Right Now Checkup: Answer true or false to the following statements.

1. Discounting a note never results in interest deducted in advance.
2. Discount on Notes Payable is a contra-asset account.
3. The effective interest rate is lower than the stated rate.
4. Adjustments can never be made for interest income.
5. Reversing entries may be used when a company received interest income.

CHECK YOUR SCORE: Answers to the Do It Right Now Checkup

LU14-1

1. False—A promissory note is written.
2. True
3. False—Most promissory notes are not interest free.
4. False—The maturity date is when the note ends.
5. True

LU14-2

1. False—Notes Receivable is found on the balance sheet.
2. True
3. False—A note renewed means there is interest income for the seller.
4. False—Only unmatured notes are in the Notes Receivable account.
5. False—A note can be given in exchange for equipment.

LU14-3

1. False—The first step of discounting is to calculate the maturity value.
2. True
3. False—Proceeds can be less than the face value of the note.
4. False—A contingent liability is a possible liability.
5. False—Interest income results if the amount of cash received is greater than the face value of the note.

LU14-4

1. False—Discounting a note results in interest deducted in advance.
2. False—Discount on Notes Payable is a contra-liability account.
3. False—Effective interest rate is higher than the stated rate.
4. False—Adjustments can be made for interest income.
5. True

BLUEPRINT: NOTES PAYABLE AND NOTES RECEIVABLE

Transaction	Seller (Payee)	Buyer (Maker)
Sales of merchandise on account	Accounts Receivable, XXX Sales Sold on account Cost of Goods Sold Merchandise Inventory Cost of merchandise sold	Merchandise Inventory Accounts Payable, XXX Bought on account
Time extension with a note	Notes Receivable Accounts Receivable, XXX Transferred to Note Rec.	Accounts Payable, XXX Notes Payable Transferred to Note Pay.
Note due and paid at maturity	Cash Interest Income Notes Receivable Received payment	Notes Payable Interest Expense Cash Paid off note
Note renewed at maturity (if maker paid interest)	Cash Notes Receivable (new) Notes Receivable (old) Interest Income Renewed note	Notes Payable (old) Interest Expense Notes Payable (new) Cash Renewed note
Note given in exchange for equipment purchased	Notes Receivable Sales Sold on Note Rec.	Store Equipment Notes Payable Bought equip. for note

BLUEPRINT: NOTES PAYABLE AND NOTES RECEIVABLE (*CONTINUED*)

Situations Affecting Seller Only

Discounting a note—
receiving more
than face value

Cash			
Interest Income			
Notes Receivable			
Discounted note at the bank			

Discounting a note—
receiving less
than face value

Cash			
Interest Expense			
Notes Receivable			
Discounted note at the bank			

Discounted note
dishonored

Accounts Receivable, XXX			
Cash			
Discounted customer note defaulted			

Situation Borrowing from Bank

Discounting one's
own note

Cash			
Discount on Notes Payable			
Notes Payable			
Borrowed with a discount			

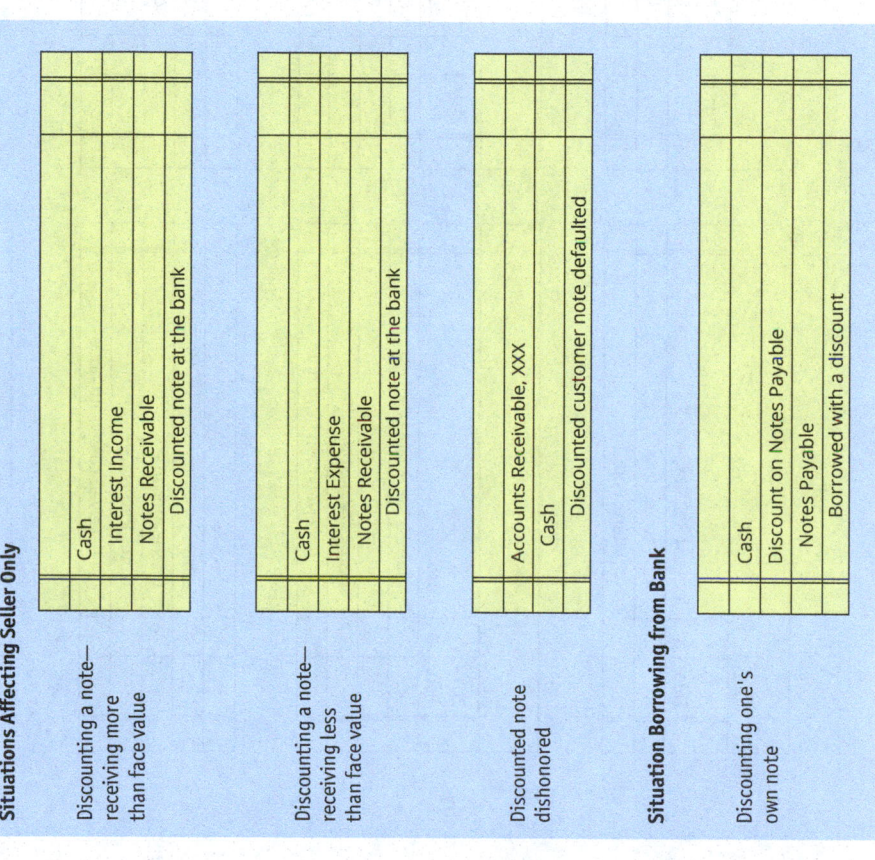

BLUEPRINT: NOTES PAYABLE AND NOTES RECEIVABLE (CONTINUED)

Adjustments	Seller	Buyer

Adjust interest	201X Dec. 31 Interest Receivable
	      Interest Income
	      Interest adj.
		201X Dec. 31 Interest Expense
		      Interest Payable
		      Interest adj.

Note paid (no reversing entry was made)	201X Feb. 1 Cash
	      Interest Receivable
	      Interest Income
	      Notes Receivable
	      Received cash from note
		201X Feb. 1 Interest Expense
		      Interest Payable
		      Notes Payable
		      Cash
		      Paid cash for note

Note paid (reversing entry was made)	Feb. 1 Cash
	      Interest Income
	      Notes Receivable
	      Received cash from note
		Feb. 1 Interest Expense
		      Notes Payable
		      Cash
		      Paid cash for note

Recognizing interest from Discount on Notes Payable	Dec. 31 Interest Expense
	      Discount on Notes Payable
	      Adjustment for interest	

Discussion Questions and Critical Thinking/Ethical Case

1. List three reasons why a company may use Notes Payable instead of Accounts Payable and whether the company is the maker or payee.

2. Explain the parts of a promissory note.

3. What is the difference between finding a maturity date by (a) days or (b) months?

4. Notes Receivable is a current liability on the balance sheet. Accept or reject. Why?

5. Why is a subsidiary ledger not needed for notes?

6. Only matured notes are listed in the Notes Receivable account. Agree or disagree? Please discuss.

7. Explain what will happen if a maker defaults on a note. (Assume that the note has not been discounted.)

8. List the four steps to arrive at proceeds in the process of discounting a note.

9. What is meant by a contingent liability?

10. When could interest be deducted in advance by a lender?

11. What is the normal balance of the Discount on Notes Payable account?

12. How is the effective interest rate calculated?

13. How could Discount on Notes Payable be adjusted?

14. Kevin Hoffaman works as a teller in Victory Bank. Yesterday, he looked up confidential information about promissory notes concerning several friends. Kevin told his girlfriend all about the confidential information. Do you think Kevin acted appropriately? You make the call. Write down your recommendations to Kevin.

Concept Checks

MyLabAccounting

Determining Maturity Date

1. Find the maturity date of the following:

    a. 120-day note dated May 14.
    b. 70-day note dated November 9.

L01 *(10 min)*

Calculate Maturity Value

2. Find the maturity value of the following:

    a. $4,000   3%   10 months
    b. $13,200   3%   90 days

L01 *(15 min)*

Journalizing Notes for Buyer and Seller

3. For each of the following transactions for Franklin Co. (the seller), journalize what the entry would be for the buyer (Oyster Co.). Franklin Company and Oyster Company use the perpetual method.

L02 *(15 min)*

a. Accounts Receivable, Oyster Co.	7,400	
Sales		7,400
Sold on account to Oyster Co.		
Cost of Goods Sold	5,000	
Merchandise Inventory		5,000
Cost of merchandise sold		

b. Notes Receivable   7,400

      Accounts Receivable, North Co.   7,400

        Transferred to Notes Receivable

c. Cash   7,500

      Notes Receivable   7,400

      Interest Income   100

        Note paid by North Co. on due date

(20 min) **LO3** ▶

Discounting a Note

4.   Jay Munson discounted a $9,600, 7%, 90-day note at Orchid Bank. He recorded the following entry:

Journal Entry

Accounts	PR	Debit	Credit
Cash		9,703	
Notes Receivable			9,600
Interest Income			103

How much interest did Jay Munson lose by discounting the note?

(20 min) **LO3** ▶

Four Steps in the Discounting Process

5.   Dove Co. received a $6,000, 8%, 90-day note from Pearl Co. dated June 6. On June 26, Dove discounted the note at Faithful Bank, which charged a discount rate of 10%. Calculate the following:

    a. Maturity value
    b. Discount period
    c. Bank discount
    d. Proceeds

(15 min) **LO3** ▶

Journal Entry for Discounting

6.   Journalize the discounted note for Dove Co. from Concept Check 5.

(15 min) **LO3** ▶

Defaulting

7.   If Pearl Co. defaults on the note from Concept Check 5, what would be the journal entry for Dove Co., assuming a $10 protest fee?

(10 min) **LO4** ▶

Discounting One's Own Note

8.   Nicole Co. discounts its own note at a bank. This $58,000 note results in the bank deducting $410 interest in advance. Draw a transaction analysis box for this situation.

(10 min) **LO4** ▶

Adjusting the Discount

9.   If in Concept Check 8 the discount needs to be adjusted at year-end by $50, what would be the journalized adjusting entry?

Exercises

Set A

14A-1. Calculate the interest for the following assume a 360-day year:

    a. $12,000   2%   2 years

    b. $19,000   9%   10 months

    c. $7,000   16%   90 days

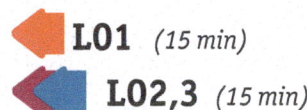

14A-2. Determine the maturity date for each of the following without the use of tables:

Note Issued	Length of Time
a. May 17, 201X	30 days
b. July 14, 201X	105 days
c. March 31, 201X	4 months
d. June 25, 201X	85 days

14A-3. Use the table in the text to check your answers for Exercise 14A-2.

14A-4. On May 15, 201X, Reed Co. gave Fuligin Co. a 180-day, $9,000, 8% note. On July 14, Fuligin Co. discounted the note at 10%. Assume a 360-day year.

    a. Journalize the entry for Fuligin to record the proceeds.

    b. Record the entry for Fuligin if Reed fails to pay at maturity.

14A-5. Jake Spady negotiated a bank loan for $36,000 for 150 days at a bank rate of 18%. Assuming the interest is deducted in advance, prepare the entry for Jake to record the bank loan. Assume a 360-day year.

Set B

14B-1. Calculate the interest for the following. Assume a 360-day year.

    a. $14,000   3%   2 years

    b. $20,000   11%   3 months

    c. $10,500   14%   120 days

14B-2. Determine the maturity date for each of the following without the use of tables:

Note Issued	Length of Time
a. January 17, 201X	30 days
b. July 14, 201X	85 days
c. May 31, 201X	4 months
d. June 25, 201X	90 days

14B-3. Use the table in the text to check your answers for Exercise 14B-2.

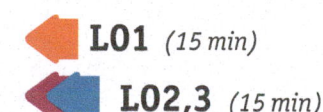

14B-4. On May 15, 201X, Ramon Co. gave Silver Co. a 180-day, $14,000, 10% note. On July 14, Silver Co. discounted the note at 12%.

    a. Journalize the entry for Silver to record the proceeds.

    b. Record the entry for Silver if Ramon fails to pay at maturity.

(15 min) **LO4**

14B-5. John Short negotiated a bank loan for $21,000 for 180 days at a bank rate of 10%. Assuming the interest is deducted in advance, prepare the entry for John to record the bank loan.

MyLab**Accounting**

Problems

Set A

(30 min) **LO2**

14A-1. Journalize the following entries for (1) the buyer and (2) the seller. Record all entries for the buyer first. Both companies use the perpetual inventory method.

201X		
June	11	Lincoln Company sold $7,500 of merchandise costing $6,000 on account to Rover Company.
July	11	Lincoln Company received a 90-day, $3,000, 8% note for a time extension of a past-due account of Rover Company.
Oct.	9	Collected the Rover Company note on the maturity date.
	9	Assume Rover Company defaulted on its July 11 note and record the dishonored note.
	15	Rover Company paid the note receivable that was dishonored on October 9 (no additional interest is charged).

Check Figure:
Oct. 9 Interest Income and Interest Expense $60

(35 min) **LO3**

S50 / **QB**

14A-2. On May 1, 201X, Jason Company received a $30,000, 90-day, 9% note from Quincy Company dated May 1. On June 20, 201X, Jason discounted the note at Pittsfield Bank at a discount rate of 12%.

1. Calculate the following:
   a. Maturity value of the note
   b. Number of days the bank will hold the note until maturity date
   c. Bank discount
   d. Proceeds
2. Journalize the entry to record the proceeds.

Check Figure:
Proceeds $30,266

(25 min) **LO4**

14A-3. Journalize the following transactions for Jackson Company:

201X		
June	18	Jackson Company discounted its own $43,000, 90-day note at Newport Bank at 12%.
Sept.	16	Paid the amount due on the note of June 18. (Be sure to record interest expense from Discount on Notes Payable.)
Nov.	2	Jackson Company discounted its own $40,000, 80-day note at Newport Bank at 9%.
Dec.	31	Record the adjusting entry for interest expense.

Check Figure:
Nov. 2 Discount on Notes Payable $800

(60 min) **LO1,2,3,4** ►►►

14A-4. Journalize the following transactions for Carney Company:

201X		
Apr.	18	Received a $14,000, 90-day, 10% note from Jake Crabill in payment of account past due.
May	9	Wrote off the Francis Dema account as uncollectible for $610. (Carney uses the Allowance method to record bad debts.)
July	17	Jake Crabill paid Carney the note in full.
Nov.	11	Gave Flower Company an $18,000, 30-day, 5% note as a time extension of account now past due.
Nov.	15	Francis Dema paid Carney the amount previously written off on May 9.
Dec.	3	Discounted its own $6,000, 60-day note at Chesterfield Bank at 9%.

Check Figure:
Dec. 31 Interest Expense $42

Dec.	5	Received a $2,000, 90-day, 5% note dated December 5 from Thomas Haden in payment of account past due.
Dec.	11	Paid principal and interest due on note issued to Flower Company from November 11 note.
Dec.	16	Received a $26,000, 180-day, 12% note from White Company in payment of account past due.
Dec.	23	Discounted the Thomas Haden note to Methuen Bank at 5%.
Dec.	31	Recorded adjusting entries as appropriate.

Set B

14B-1. Journalize the following entries for (1) the buyer and (2) the seller. Record all entries for the buyer first. Both companies use the perpetual inventory method. Assume a 360 day year.

 **L02** *(30 min)*

201X		
June	11	Lyons Company sold $8,000 of merchandise costing $7,000 on account to Ramsey Company.
July	11	Lyons Company received a 90-day, $3,500, 4% note for a time extension of past-due account of Ramsey Company.
Oct.	9	Collected the Ramsey Company note on the maturity date.
Oct.	9	Assume Ramsey Company defaulted on its July 11 note and record the dishonored note.
Oct.	15	Ramsey Company paid the note receivable that was dishonored on October 9 (no additional interest is charged).

Check Figure:
Oct. 15 Cash Cr. $3,535

14B-2. On May 1, 201X, Lake Company received a $26,000, 90-day, 5% note from Walker Company dated May 1. On June 20, 201X, Lake discounted the note at Reading Bank at a discount rate of 8%.

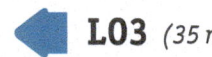 **L03** *(35 min)*

S50 / QB

   1. Calculate the following:
      a. Maturity value of the note
      b. Number of days the bank will hold the note until maturity date
      c. Bank discount
      d. Proceeds

Check Figure:
Proceeds $26,091

   2. Journalize the entry to record the proceeds.

14B-3. Journalize the following transactions for Jones Company:

L04 *(25 min)*

201X		
June	18	Jones Company discounted its own $49,000, 90-day note at International Bank at 16%.
Sept.	16	Paid the amount due on the note of June 18. (Be sure to record interest expense from Discount on Notes Payable.)
Nov.	2	Jones Company discounted its own $10,000, 210-day note at International Bank at 9%.
Dec.	31	Record the adjusting entry for Interest Expense.

Check Figure:
Dec. 31 Interest Expense $147.50

14B-4. Journalize the following transactions for Falcon Company:

L01,2,3,4 *(60 min)*

201X		
Apr.	18	Received an $11,000, 90-day, 4% note from Cathy Bora in payment of account past due.
May	9	Wrote off the April Deacy account as uncollectible for $640. (Falcon uses the Allowance method to record bad debts.)
July	17	Cathy Bora paid Falcon the note in full.

Check Figure:
Dec. 31 Interest Income $62.50

Nov.	11	Gave Quiet Company a $21,000, 30-day, 8% note as a time extension of account now past due.
Nov.	15	April Deacy paid Falcon the amount previously written off on May 9.
Dec.	3	Discounted its own $6,000, 60-day note at Dunstable Bank at 9%.
Dec.	5	Received a $5,000, 90-day, 10% note dated December 5 from Vickey Jacob in payment of account past due.
Dec.	11	Paid principal and interest due on the note issued to Quiet Company from November 11.
Dec.	16	Received a $15,000, 90-day, 10% note from Zoe Company in payment of account past due.
Dec.	23	Discounted the Vickey Jacob note to Swanson Bank at 10%.
Dec.	31	Recorded adjusting entries as appropriate.

Financial Report Problem

(15 min) **LO1**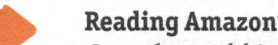

Reading Amazon's Annual Report

Go to **https://tinyurl.com/slaterca14e** to access Amazon's 2016 Annual Report. Go to page 37 and find the balance of interest income in 2016.

 MyLabAccounting

KEEPING IT REAL SUAREZ COMPUTER CENTER

(20 min) **LO1**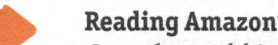

Several banks have offered loans to the Suarez Computer Center for its expansion. However, Falco wants to weigh each option to determine the best financial situation for the company. Currently, the Suarez Computer Center is trying to collect from its customers to strengthen the cash flow of the business.

Assignment

Using the information provided by each bank, determine the due date and interest amount for each.

Bank of America	A 90-day note dated April 15 for $25,000 at a 4% interest rate
Bank One	A 120-day note dated April 10 for $42,000 at an 8% interest rate
Capital One Bank	A 60-day note dated April 5 for $36,000 at a 6% interest rate

Accounting for Merchandise Inventory

15

CHAPTER PREVIEW: ACCOUNTING IN ACTION

Mary Cheung just tried to order a new tablet online at Best Buy. To her dismay, it is out of stock until next month. How could this happen? Was it Best Buy's fault for not ordering enough tablets for its warehouse, or was it the manufacturer who cannot fulfill its orders due to increased demand? Controlling inventory is a major task for most companies. Too much inventory on hand could lower profits, while not enough could result in lost sales. In this chapter, we look at the flow of inventory along with how to account for the cost of the inventory.

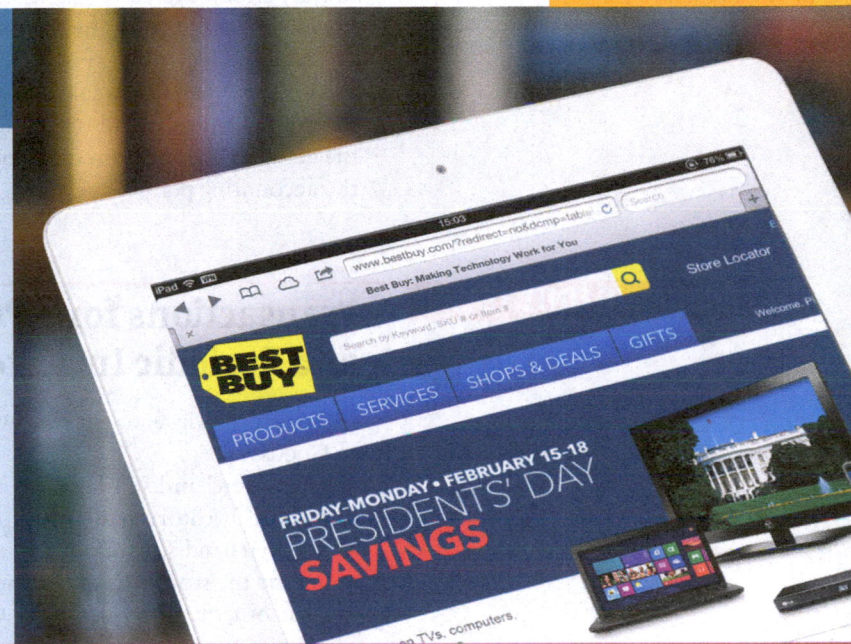

Learning Objectives – Relating Accounting Theory By Unit

LO1 Journalize Transactions for a Perpetual and Periodic Inventory System

LO2 Explain Using Subsidiary Ledgers in Calculating Cost of Ending Inventory in a Perpetual System

LO3 Explain Inventory Methods to Calculate Ending Inventory in a Periodic System

LO4 Estimate Ending Inventory by the Retail and Gross Profit Methods

For Best Buy to reach its projected profits, it must continually monitor its inventory to make sure that it does not run out or end up with excess inventory.

In Chapters 10 and 11, we discussed the perpetual inventory system. Today, with so many businesses using a digital inventory system, the trend is toward perpetual inventory. Managers need to have *current* information about how much of their capital is tied up in inventory and they need to have *current* information about the profitability of their sales of merchandise. The *perpetual* system of accounting for merchandise inventory provides this information on a transaction-by-transaction basis. Managers can know the balance of inventory and the profitability of sales as soon as each sale is completed. The perpetual system requires extra time and effort to gain these benefits, but, fortunately, computers can handle much of the detail. In this chapter, we look at how the perpetual inventory system can be used in a merchandising business. We also compare the perpetual system to the periodic system.

In the last part of the chapter, we discuss how to assign costs to inventory using the *periodic inventory system* because many businesses with small inventories still use this system. A major weakness of the periodic system is that inventory is checked and counted only at the end of the accounting period and therefore managers do not know the actual amount of inventory on hand or the actual cost of goods sold until the end of the accounting period.

<table>
<tr><td></td><td></td></tr>
</table>

LEARNING UNIT 15-1

LO1

Perpetual inventory system Inventory system of a company that keeps a continuous (perpetual) record of inventory on hand and of the cost of goods sold.

Transactions for a Perpetual and Periodic Inventory System

In the perpetual inventory system we have two key accounts: Merchandise Inventory and Cost of Goods Sold.

The Merchandise Inventory account is an asset account that will reveal the current balance of inventory at all times (perpetually). In the perpetual system, entries are recorded to the Merchandise Inventory account each time the store purchases new merchandise and each time the store sells merchandise to a customer.

The other key account is the Cost of Goods Sold account. As merchandise is sold to customers, an entry will be recorded that will remove the cost of the merchandise from the Merchandise Inventory account and transfer that cost to the Cost of Goods Sold account. Thus, the Merchandise Inventory account will show the correct cost for the inventory on hand, and the Cost of Goods Sold account will show the cumulative total cost of all merchandise that has been sold to customers during the accounting period. In the perpetual system, we are perpetually adjusting the inventory account, and the related expense account of Cost of Goods Sold, every time there is a transaction that affects inventory.

With the perpetual inventory system, the key accounts, Merchandise Inventory and Cost of Goods Sold, will always provide current information to managers about their investment in inventory and the cost of the merchandise sold to customers.

Accounts Affected	Category	↑↓	Rules
Merchandise Inventory	Asset	↑	Dr.
Cost of Goods Sold	Cost of Goods Sold	↑	Dr.

You have been hired to work for a software retail business called Big Bytes. A bestseller for Big Bytes is an accounting software package called A-I-B (<u>A</u>lways <u>I</u>n <u>B</u>alance). Let's record some transactions relating to buying and selling A-I-B software. Because most businesses buy their merchandise inventory on account, we use Accounts Payable in the transactions.

201X

June   2   Purchased 10 packages of A-I-B software at a cost of $25 per package for a total of $250 on account.

Note that the asset account, Merchandise Inventory, has been increased by the cost of the new merchandise we have purchased (Figure 15.1).

June	2	Merchandise Inventory		2 5 0 00		
		Accounts Payable			2 5 0 00	
		To record the purchase of inventory				

Figure 15.1
Purchase of Inventory in a Perpetual System

Now let's look at a sales transaction.

201X

June   3   Sold three software packages for cash to a customer at $50 each for a total of $150. The cost of each package was $25 each.

Note that in the perpetual inventory system we record both the retail value of the sale (three units at $50) in the Sales Revenue account and the cost of the sale (three units at $25) in the Cost of Goods Sold account with two related journal entries (Figure 15.2).

June	3	Cash		1 5 0 00		
		Sales Revenue			1 5 0 00	
		To record sale of three packages of A-I-B				
June	3	Cost of Goods Sold		7 5 00		
		Merchandise Inventory			7 5 00	
		To record the cost of goods sold				

Figure 15.2
Matching Sales to Cost of Goods Sold

What if the customer returns one of the packages? Assuming that the returned package is still in new condition, the journal entries are seen in Figure 15.3.

201X

June   5   Allowed the customer to return one package for a cash refund, $50. The cost of the package was $25.

In this transaction (Figure 15.3), we must record the reduction in revenue of $50, and we must also record that we now have returned one package of software to our inventory by adding the $25 cost of that unit back to the Merchandise Inventory account.

June	5	Sales Returns and Allowances		5 0 00		
		Cash			5 0 00	
		To record the return of one				
		package of A-I-B				

Figure 15.3
Sales Return from Customer

June	5	Merchandise Inventory		2 5 00		
		Cost of Goods Sold			2 5 00	
		To record return of one package of				
		A-I-B at cost				

201X			
June	6	Returned one damaged A-I-B software package from the June 2 purchase.	

Sometimes a business may have to return some inventory because it came in damaged or for some other reason. Big Bytes would prepare a debit memo. Let's see how this transaction is handled in a perpetual inventory system.

This transaction (Figure 15.4) reduced what is owed the vendor by $25, the cost of the package, and we reduced the asset account—Merchandise Inventory—because we returned the item to the vendor. *Note*: We do not use a Purchases Returns and Allowances account when we are recording in a perpetual inventory system. The asset account Merchandise Inventory is directly reduced by the amount we returned to our vendor.

Figure 15.4
Return by Buyer of Merchandise

June	6	Accounts Payable	25 00	
		Merchandise Inventory		25 00
		To record return of damaged A-I-B		
		package to vendor		

Now let's look at how these transactions relate to the accounts and to the financial statements. In the T accounts in Figure 15.5, you can see that the Merchandise Inventory account shows the correct balance for the seven software packages remaining in inventory and that the Cost of Goods Sold account shows the correct amount for the cost of the two software packages actually sold. Asset accounts such as Merchandise Inventory are shown on the balance sheet, and the Sales and Cost of Goods Sold accounts appear on the income statement. Remember that we calculate Gross Profit when we subtract Cost of Goods Sold from Sales. In fact, we know the gross profit on each sale just as soon as the sale is completed.

Figure 15.5
General Ledger Accounts

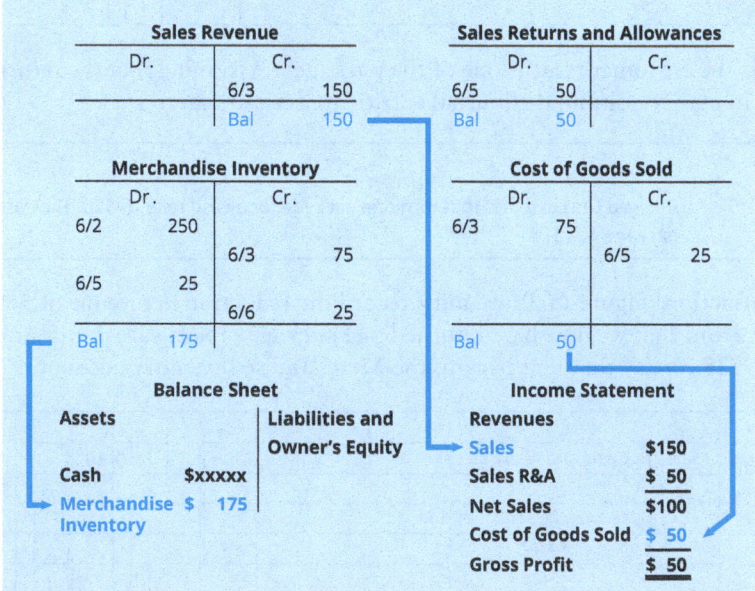

GENERAL LEDGER ACCOUNTS

Comparison of the Perpetual and Periodic Inventory Systems

In our discussion of the perpetual inventory system, the primary benefit from this system is that the value of merchandise inventory is known after every purchase and sale. The cost of goods sold is known after every sale. The Merchandise Inventory account becomes an active account. The cost of goods sold is now an account in the general ledger rather than just an item on the income statement. The *periodic inventory system* does not give accurate or up-to-date information about merchandise inventory or cost of goods sold until after an ending inventory is taken. This is considered a major weakness of the periodic system in that inventory is checked and counted only at the end of the accounting period and therefore managers do not know the actual amount of inventory on hand or the actual cost of goods sold until the end of the accounting period.

However, the taking of a physical inventory at least once a year is not eliminated by a business that uses the perpetual inventory system. An inventory must be taken at least once a year to detect any inventory recording errors, shoplifting, or damages to the merchandise inventory and then to reconcile those differences between the book's numbers and those reflected by the actual physical inventory.

The comparisons of the recording of transactions in the two systems are revealed in Figure 15.6. The chart shows that in a perpetual inventory system, Inventory and Cost of Goods Sold are updated immediately. With the periodic method, we use the Purchases, Purchases Returns and Allowances, and Freight-In accounts to account for inventory transactions.

Figure 15.6 Comparison of Perpetual and Periodic Systems

Transaction (A) Sold merchandise that cost $8,000 on account for $20,000.

Perpetual System:

Account	Debit	Credit
Accts. Receivable	20 0 0 0 00	
Sales		20 0 0 0 00
Cost of Goods Sold	8 0 0 0 00	
Merch. Inventory		8 0 0 0 00

Periodic System:

Account	Debit	Credit
Accts. Receivable	20 0 0 0 00	
Sales		20 0 0 0 00

Transaction (B) Purchased $900 of merchandise on account.

Perpetual System:

Account	Debit	Credit
Merch. Inventory	9 0 0 00	
Accts. Payable		9 0 0 00

Periodic System:

Account	Debit	Credit
Purchases	9 0 0 00	
Accts. Payable		9 0 0 00

Transaction (C) Paid $50 freight charges.

Perpetual System:

Account	Debit	Credit
Merch. Inventory	5 0 00	
Cash		5 0 00

Periodic System:

Account	Debit	Credit
Freight-In	5 0 00	
Cash		5 0 00

Transaction (D) Customer returned $200 of merchandise purchased on account. Cost of merchandise was $100.

Perpetual System:

Account	Debit	Credit
Sales Ret. & Allow.	2 0 0 00	
Accts. Receivable		2 0 0 00
Merch. Inventory	1 0 0 00	
Cost of Goods Sold		1 0 0 00

Periodic System:

Account	Debit	Credit
Sales Ret. & Allow.	2 0 0 00	
Accts. Receivable		2 0 0 00

Transaction (E) Returned $400 of merchandise previously bought on account due to defects.

Perpetual System:

Account	Debit	Credit
Accts. Payable	4 0 0 00	
Merch. Inventory		4 0 0 00

Periodic System:

Account	Debit	Credit
Accts. Payable	4 0 0 00	
Pur. Ret. & Allow.		4 0 0 00

Now let's check your progress.

 **TRY IT!**   **Learning Unit 15-1**

Journalize the following transactions for Black Co., which uses a perpetual system:

a. Sold merchandise costing $7,000 for $21,000 on account.
b. Purchased merchandise for $1,300 on account.
c. Paid $90 in freight.
d. Customer returned $450 of merchandise purchased on account. Cost of the merchandise was $150.

TRY IT!   **Solution Learning Unit 15-1**

Accounts	Dr.	Cr.
a. Accounts Receivable	21,000	
Sales		21,000
Cost of Goods Sold	7,000	
Merchandise Inventory		7,000
b. Merchandise Inventory	1,300	
Accounts Payable		1,300
c. Merchandise Inventory	90	
Cash		90
d. Sales Returns and Allowances	450	
Accounts Receivable		450
Merchandise Inventory	150	
Cost of Goods Sold		150

LEARNING UNIT 15-2

L02

Using a Subsidiary Ledger for Inventory; Calculating Cost of Ending Inventory Using a Perpetual System

Assume the business Big Bytes sells many different kinds of software packages. How can Big Bytes keep track of the cost and balances of a variety of inventory items? How do stores such as Best Buy keep track of the thousands of items that they keep in inventory? The answer is found in the use of a subsidiary ledger for inventory and the use of computers to maintain the subsidiary ledger.

Do you recall from Chapters 9 and 10 that when we had a large number of Accounts Receivable or Accounts Payable accounts, we used subsidiary ledgers to maintain the details for each customer or vendor? This same accounting procedure can be used to keep track of inventory. Our Merchandise Inventory account becomes a control account keeping track of the total balance of inventory, while the details are kept in separate inventory records in a subsidiary ledger for inventory. Let's first show our existing inventory account with a subsidiary ledger and with the transactions from Learning Unit 15-1. On the left is Big Bytes' inventory account in T form, and on the right is an inventory record form for their A-I-B product.

General Ledger Account

Merchandise Inventory

	Dr.	Cr.	
6/2	250		
		6/3	75
6/5	25		
		6/6	25
Bal	**175**		

Subsidiary Ledger Records

A-I-B Software

Date	Purchased	Sold	Balance
6/2	10 @ $25		$250
6/3		3 @ $25	$175
6/5		(1) @ $25	$200
6/6	(1) @ $25		$175

Notice that the inventory subsidiary ledger record form on the right contains the detail about the quantity and per-unit cost for the transactions posted to the general ledger account on the left. Notice too that the return of 6/5 is recorded in the inventory record as a negative sale and that the ending balances agree. The debit memo transaction of 6/6 is entered as a negative purchase, and again the ending balances agree. Try using your calculator to see whether you can also calculate the running balance shown in the inventory record.

In this next transaction Big Bytes adds R&C (Rows and Columns), a spreadsheet software package, to the line of software it sells.

June	6	Purchased 7 packages of R&C software on account at a cost of $225 per package and a total of $1,575.

Note in Figure 15.7 that the Merchandise Inventory account has again been increased by the cost of the new merchandise we have purchased. Because we now have two products in inventory, our inventory ledger will have a new inventory record form for the R&C product. Check out the way our inventory records relate to the Merchandise Inventory account.

June	6	Merchandise Inventory	1575 00	
		Accounts Payable		1575 00
		To record the purchase of inventory		

Figure 15.7
Purchase of Inventory in a Perpetual System

General Ledger Account

Merchandise Inventory

	Dr.	Cr.
6/2	250	
		6/3 75
6/5	25	
6/6	1,575	6/6 25
Bal	1,750	

Subsidiary Ledger Records

Product #1:   **A-I-B Software**

Date	Purchased	Sold	Balance
6/2	10@ $25		$250
6/3		3 @ $25	$175
6/5		(1) @ $25	$200
6/6	(1) @ $25		$175

Product #2:   **R&C Software**

Date	Purchased	Sold	Balance
6/6	7 @ $225		$1,575

Total $175 + $1,575 = $1,750

Does the total of the balances of the two inventory records agree with the Merchandise Inventory account?

Now let's try another sales transaction.

201X		
June	9	Sold two A-I-B packages at $50 each and three R&C packages at $295 each for a total of $985. This is a cash sale. The costs of the A-I-B and R&C packages are $25 and $225, respectively.

Again, we record both the total sales price of the transaction and the cost of the merchandise sold (Figure 15.8). Do you know how we arrived at the cost of goods sold figure of $725? A quick look at the inventory record forms will show us how we know the cost of goods sold.

June	9	Cash	985 00	
		Sales Revenue		985 00
		Sold 2 A-I-B and 3 R&C		
June	9	Cost of Goods Sold	725 00	
		Merchandise Inventory		725 00
		To record the cost of goods sold		

Figure 15.8
Matching Sales and Cost of Goods Sold

General Ledger Account

Merchandise Inventory

	Dr.		Cr.
6/2	250	6/3	75
6/5	25	6/6	25
6/6	1,575	6/9	725
Bal	1,025		

Subsidiary Ledger Records

Product #1:	A-I-B Software		
Date	Purchased	Sold	Balance
6/2	10 @ $25		$250
6/3		3 @ $25	$175
6/5		(1) @ $25	$200
6/6	(1) @ $25		$175
6/9		2 @ $25	$125

Product #2:	R&C Software		
Date	Purchased		Balance
6/6	7 @ $225		$1,575
6/9		3 @ $225	$ 900

Total $125 + $900 = $1,025

We obtained the cost of goods sold total when we posted the quantities sold to each of the inventory records. Two units of A-I-B at $25 each plus three units of R&C at $225 each equals a total cost of $725. Notice that the ending balances of the two products will total to the same amount as the balance shown in the Merchandise Inventory account.

In summary, a business with a variety of products in inventory will use an inventory subsidiary ledger with an individual record for each different product. These records will contain the details about the quantity and cost of inventory on hand and will allow calculation of the cost of goods sold on each sale.

Most modern computerized accounting systems can handle a perpetual inventory system with ease. You have no doubt seen such systems in operation when the clerk at your local store used a laser scanner or a bar code to enter your purchases into the cash register. The transaction put into the cash register will record the sale and update the cost of goods sold and inventory. Computerized systems keep track of inventory by many different methods. When figuring out the value of the inventory, they could use average cost, first-in, first-out (FIFO) or last-in, first-out (LIFO). The examples in Figure 15.9 and Figure 15.10 use the FIFO and LIFO methods to determine the cost of the merchandise for each sale of digital clocks. Keep in mind that in FIFO old inventory is sold first and in LIFO new inventory is sold first. This also means that under FIFO, the new inventory is what is left in the inventory account, and under LIFO, it is the old inventory that is remaining in the inventory account.

Note in Figure 15.9 that on January 25 the old inventory (12 at $50) is assumed sold in FIFO. On January 25, when 8 clocks are sold, they are taken from the 12 at $50 inventory, leaving 4 at $50 along with the 10 at $60. This gives a cost of ending inventory of $800. Note in Figure 15.10 under LIFO that when the 8 units are sold on January 25, they are taken from the 10 units at $60. This leaves 2 at $60 and the oldest inventory of 12 at $50. The cost of ending inventory is $720. Remember that under LIFO we assume that the newest inventory is sold first. Under FIFO, the oldest inventory is sold first.

SUCCESS TIP

Today, companies can employ two forms of automated data collection for inventory: barcodes and RFID systems.

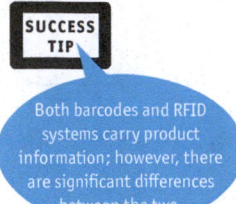

SUCCESS TIP

Both barcodes and RFID systems carry product information; however, there are significant differences between the two.

Figure 15.9
An Inventory Record Using FIFO

Inventory Control

Item VX113   Maximum 22
Description Digital Clock   Reorder Level 12
Location Storeroom 1   Reorder Quantity 10

	Received				Sold				Balance		
Date	Units	Cost per Unit	Total		Units	Cost per Unit	Total		Units	Cost per Unit	Total
201X Jan. 1	Balance		FWD						14	50	$ 700
12					2	50	100		12	50	600
19	10	60	600						12	50	
						Old Sold First			10	60	1,200
25					8	50	400		4	50	
									10	60	800

Figure 15.10
An Inventory Record Using LIFO

Inventory Control

Item VX113   Maximum 22
Description Digital Clock   Reorder Level 12
Location Storeroom 1   Reorder Quantity 10

	Received				Sold				Balance		
Date	Units	Cost per Unit	Total		Units	Cost per Unit	Total		Units	Cost per Unit	Total
201X Jan. 1	Balance		FWD						14	50	$ 700
12					2	50	100		12	50	600
19	10	60	600						12	50	
						New Sold First			10	60	1,200
25					8	60	480		12	50	
									2	60	720

Now let's check your progress.

TRY IT!   Learning Unit 15-2

From the following transactions, complete a subsidiary ledger for the milk and juice products. Also calculate the ending balance in the Merchandise Inventory account.

a. Bought 8 milks on account for $4 each.
b. Sold 5 milks for $6.
c. Bought 9 milks at $4 and 10 juices at $5 on account.
d. Sold for cash 9 milks at $6 and 7 juices at $6.

TRY IT!   Solution Learning Unit 15-2

MILK

Date	Purchases	Sold	Balance
a.	8@4		$32
b.		5@4	12
c.	9@4		48
d.		9@4	12

JUICE

Date	Purchases	Sold	Balance
c.	10@5		$50
d.		7@5	$15

Ending Merch. Inv. $27

<table>
<tr><td>LEARNING UNIT 15-3</td></tr>
</table>

Inventory Methods to Calculate Ending Inventory in a Periodic System

L03

Periodic inventory system
Inventory system that counts inventory only at the end of the accounting period.

For a small business or any business using the periodic inventory system, the method used to assign costs to ending inventory will have a direct effect on the company's cost of goods sold and gross profit.* Note in the following table how the ending inventory does in fact have an effect on the gross profit. Also note that we use a Purchases Returns and Allowances account when we are recording in a periodic inventory system.

	Situation A		Situation B		Situation C		Situation D	
Net Sales		$50,000		$50,000		$50,000		$50,000
Beginning Inventory	$ 4,000		$ 4,000		$ 4,000		$ 4,000	
Net Purchases	20,000		20,000		20,000		20,000	
Cost of Goods								
Available for Sale	24,000		24,000		24,000		24,000	
Ending Inventory	5,000		6,000		7,000		8,000	
Cost of Goods Sold		19,000		18,000		17,000		16,000
Gross Profit		$31,000		$32,000		$33,000		$34,000

If all inventory brought into a store had the same cost, it would be simple to calculate the ending inventory, and we would not have to have this discussion. Unfortunately, things are not that easy; often the same products are purchased and brought into the store at different costs during the same accounting period. Over the years, four generally accepted methods have been developed to assign a cost to ending inventory. The reason these methods are needed is that often inventory is made up of many past purchases at *different* prices. Think of the inventory methods as ways of tracing costs. These methods are (1) specific invoice (identification); (2) first-in, first-out; (3) last-in, first-out; and (4) weighted average. Both the perpetual and periodic inventory methods are based on an assumed flow of costs, not on the actual physical movement of goods sold in a store.

We now look at how the four inventory cost assumptions are applied within the periodic inventory system. The following situation occurred at Mason Hardware. Mason Hardware sells rakes. The job before us is to come up with the value of the ending inventory and cost of goods sold using the four methods we have listed. The following table provides us with all the information needed to accomplish our task.

Goods Available for Sale

		Units	Cost		Total
January 1	Beginning Inventory	10	@$10	=	$100
March 15	Purchases	9	@ 12	=	108
August 18	Purchases	20	@ 13	=	260
November 15	Purchases	5	@ 15	=	75
		44			$543

Actual inventory on December 31 revealed that 12 rakes remained in stock.

Specific Invoice Method

Specific invoice method
Valuing of inventory where each item is identified with a specific invoice.

In the specific invoice method, the cost of ending inventory is assigned by identifying each item in that inventory by a specific purchase price and invoice number and maybe even by serial number.

---

* This is true for a perpetual system as well.

For our example of this method, let's assume that Mason Hardware knew that six of the rakes not sold were from the March 15 invoice and the other six were from the August 18 purchase. Thus, $150 was assigned as the actual cost of ending inventory. If the total cost of goods available for sale is $543 and we subtract the actual cost of ending inventory ($150), this method provides a figure of $393 for cost of goods sold.

Specific Invoice Method

	Goods Available for Sale				Calculating Cost of Ending Inventory			
	Units	Cost		Total	Units		Cost	Total
January 1 Beg. Inventory	10 @	$10	=	$100				
March 15 Purchased	9 @	12	=	108	6 @		$12	$ 72
August 18 Purchased	20 @	13	=	260	6 @		13	78
November 15 Purchased	5 @	15	=	75				
	44			$543	12			$150

Cost of Goods Available for Sale → $543
Less: Cost of Ending Inventory = 150 ←
Cost of Goods Sold $393

Let's look at the pros and cons of this method.

Specific Invoice Method: A Reference Guide

Pros	Cons
1. Simple to use if company has small amount of high-cost goods, such as autos, jewels, boats, or antiques.	1. Difficult to use for goods with large unit volume and small unit prices, such as nails at a hardware store or packages of toothpaste at a drug store.
2. Flow of goods and flow of costs are the same.	2. Difficult to use for decision-making purposes; ordinarily an impractical approach because companies usually deal with high-cost unique items.
3. Costs are matched with the sales they helped to produce.	

First-In, First-Out Method (FIFO)

In the FIFO method, we assume that the oldest goods are sold first. Therefore, the items in the ending inventory will be valued at the costs shown on the most recent invoices.

FIFO (first-in, first-out) method Valuing of inventory assuming that the company sells the first goods received in the store.

FIFO Method

	Goods Available for Sale				Calculating Cost of Ending Inventory				
	Units	Cost		Total	Units		Cost		Total
January 1 Beg. Inventory	10 @	$10	=	$100					
March 15 Purchased	9 @	12	=	108					
August 18 Purchased	20 @	13	=	260	7 @		$13	=	$ 91
November 15 Purchased	5 @	15	=	75	5 @		15	=	75
	44			$543	12				$166

Cost of Goods Available for Sale → $543
Less: Cost of Ending Inventory = 166 ←
Cost of Goods Sold $377

In our Mason Hardware example the ending inventory of 12 rakes on hand is assigned a cost from the last two purchase invoices of rakes (purchases made on November 15 and part of the purchases made on August 18), totaling $166. Think of the inventory as being taken from the bottom layer first, then the next one up. If our ending inventory is valued at $166, our cost of goods sold must be $377.

The following are the pros and cons of this method.

FIFO Method: A Reference Guide

Pros	Cons
1. The cost flow tends to follow the physical flow; most businesses try to sell the old goods first (e.g., perishables such as fruits or vegetables).	1. During periods of inflation this method will produce higher income on the income statement and thus more taxes to be paid.
2. The figure for ending inventory is made up of current costs on the balance sheet (because inventory left over is assumed to be from goods last brought into the store).	2. Recent sales are not matched with recent costs because we assume *old* goods at old prices are sold first.

Last-In, First-Out Method (LIFO)

LIFO (last-in, first-out) method Valuing of inventory with the assumption the last goods received in the store are the first to be sold.

Under the LIFO method it is assumed that the goods *most recently acquired* are sold first. Therefore, the items in the ending inventory will be valued at the invoice costs shown from the top of the list down.

For Mason Hardware this assumption means that the 12 rakes not sold were assigned costs from the 10 listed in beginning inventory and 2 from the March 15 invoice. The ending inventory totals $124 and the cost of goods sold would be $419.

LIFO Method

	Goods Available for Sale				Calculating Cost of Ending Inventory				
	Units	Cost		Total	Units		Cost		Total
January 1 Beg. Inventory	10	@ $10	=	$100	10	@	$10	=	$100
March 15 Purchased	9	@ 12	=	108	2	@	12	=	24
August 18 Purchased	20	@ 13	=	260					
November 15 Purchased	5	@ 15	=	75					
	44			$543	12				$124

Cost of Goods Available for Sale   → $543

Less: Cost of Ending Inventory =   124 ←

Cost of Goods Sold $419

The pros and cons of this method are:

LIFO Method: A Reference Guide

Pros	Cons
1. Cost of goods sold is recorded at or near current costs because costs of *latest* goods acquired are used.	1. Ending inventory is valued at very old prices.
2. Matches current costs with current sales revenue.	2. Doesn't match physical flow of goods (but can still be used to calculate flow of costs).
3. During periods of inflation this method produces the lowest net income, which is a tax advantage. (The lower cost of ending inventory means a higher cost of goods sold; thus, gross profit and ultimately net income are smaller and thus taxes are lower.)	

SUCCESS TIP

The United Kingdom and Australia do not permit the use of LIFO In the US, there have been several attempts to eliminate LIFO, but the business community has pushed back against this.

Weighted-Average Method

Weighted-average method Valuing of inventory where each item is assigned the same unit cost. This unit cost is found by dividing the cost of goods available for sale by the total number of units for sale.

The weighted-average method calculates an average unit cost by dividing the *total cost* of goods available for sale by the *total units* of goods available for sale. In this example, the total cost of goods available for sale was $543, and the total units available for sale were 44. Taking the $543 and dividing that number by the 44 total units for the period gives a $12.34 weighted average cost per unit.

Weighted-Average Method

	Goods Available for Sale					
	Units		Cost		Total	
January 1 Beg. Inventory	10	@	$10	=	$100	
March 15 Purchased	9	@	12	=	108	
August 18 Purchased	20	@	13	=	260	
November 15 Purchased	5	@	15	=	75	
	44				$543	

$\dfrac{\$543}{44}$ = $12.34 weighted-average cost per unit

12 rakes × $12.34 = $148.08

Cost of Goods Available for Sale	$543.00
Less: Cost of Ending Inventory =	148.08
Cost of Goods Sold	$394.92

In this illustration, Mason Hardware assumes that the 12 units left on hand are *average* units and therefore assigns an *average* cost figure of $12.34 to each of the 12 rakes left in inventory. Thus, we have a fair approximation of the cost of the ending inventory at $148.08 and of the amount of cost of goods sold, $394.92.

The pros and cons of this method are:

Weighted-Average Method: A Reference Guide

Pros	Cons
1. Weighted average takes into account the number of units purchased at each amount, not a simple average cost. Good for products sold in large volume, such as grains and fuels. 2. Accountant assigns an equal unit cost to each unit of inventory; thus, when the income statement is prepared, net income will not fluctuate as much as with other methods.	1. Current prices have no more significance than prices of goods bought a month earlier. 2. Compared with other methods, the most recent costs are *not* matched with current sales. This does not provide an accurate picture of the company's profitability. 3. Cost of ending inventory is not as up-to-date as it could be using another method.

Remember that all four methods are acceptable accounting procedures. Management needs to select the method best suited to its business and be consistent in the application of that method.

When Can an Inventory Method Be Changed?

In accounting, the principle of consistency means that once a business selects a particular accounting method, it should follow it consistently from one year to the next without switching to another method. In the previous part of this chapter, we saw four methods of inventory valuations causing four different results for a business in terms of cost of goods sold and, ultimately, net income. Therefore, if a company kept switching from LIFO to FIFO each year, significant changes would result in the profit it reported. The financial reports would become undependable. Keeping with the same method allows readers of the financial reports to make meaningful comparisons of the cost of ending inventory, cost of goods sold, and so forth from year to year.

The principle of consistency doesn't mean that a company can *never* change from one method of inventory valuation to another. If a change is decided upon, however, the company should fully disclose the change, the effects of the change on profit and inventory valuation, and the justification for change in a footnote on the financial report. This principle is called the full disclosure principle in accounting.

Items That Should Be Included in the Cost of Inventory

Goods in Transit. On the date inventory is taken, goods in transit should be added to inventory if the ownership of the inventory has been transferred to the buyer. For example, if the merchandise was purchased *F.O.B. shipping point*, the buyer becomes

Consistency Accounting principle that requires companies to follow the same accounting methods or procedures from period to period.

Full disclosure principle Accounting principle that requires companies to fully disclose on their financial reports changes in accounting procedures and methods along with effects of the change as well as justification for change.

Consignment Sales of goods through an agent who has possession but not ownership.

Consignor One who consigns merchandise to the consignee.

Consignee Company or person to whom merchandise is consigned but who doesn't have ownership.

the owner of the merchandise when the merchandise is placed on the carrier at the shipping point. On the other hand, if the buyer purchases the merchandise *F.O.B. destination*, the seller has ownership of the merchandise until the merchandise reaches the destination, and it should not be included in the cost of the buyer's inventory.

Merchandise on Consignment. Consignment means that a business (the consignor) is selling its merchandise through an agent (the consignee) who doesn't own the merchandise but who has possession of it. Consigned merchandise belongs to the consignor and should not be included in the consignee's inventory cost.

Damaged or Obsolete Merchandise. If the merchandise is not saleable, it should *not* be added to the cost of the inventory. For merchandise that is saleable but at a lower cost, the value of that inventory should be estimated at a conservative figure and added to the cost of the inventory.

Now let's check your progress.

 ## TRY IT! Learning Unit 15-3

From the following, calculate the cost of goods sold using the LIFO method. Assume ending inventory shows 78 units.

	Number of iPads Purchased for Resale	Cost per Unit
January 1 Inventory	36	$390
March 1	52	210
April 1	24	490
November 1	69	650

TRY IT! **Solution Learning Unit 15-3**

Cost of Goods Available for Sale:

36 @ $390 =	$14,040
52 @ 210 =	10,920
24 @ 490 =	11,760
69 @ 650 =	44,850
Total	$81,570

36 units from Jan. @ $390 =	$14,040
42 units from Mar. 1 @ $210 =	8,820
Cost of Ending Inventory	$22,860

$81,570 − $22,860 = $58,710 Cost of Goods Sold

LEARNING UNIT 15-4

L04

Retail method Method used to determine the value of the ending inventory using a cost-to-retail ratio. Often used for interim financial reports.

Gross profit method Method used to determine the value of the ending inventory using a predetermined gross profit rate. This method can be used to determine the value of ending inventory if a loss from fire occurs.

Estimating Ending Inventory by the Retail and Gross Profit Methods

The actual taking of a physical inventory is time-consuming and expensive. Because of the time and expense involved, most businesses take a physical inventory only once a year. For the business using the periodic inventory system, the need to have an inventory cost figure more often may become necessary, especially when a business makes interim financial statements. This business may find that estimating the inventory rather than taking a physical inventory is accurate enough. Another reason to estimate the ending inventory is in case of a fire or other disaster when the inventory may be destroyed. The business would need an inventory cost figure when it submits a claim of loss to the insurance company.

Two common and recognized ways to estimate ending inventory are the retail method and the gross profit method.

Retail Method

To use the retail method, a business must have the following information available:

1. Beginning inventory at cost and at retail (selling price)
2. Cost of net purchases at both cost and at retail
3. The net sales at retail

Let's look at the diagram below to see how French Company estimates ending inventory at cost by the retail method.

French completed the following steps to arrive at an ending inventory cost of $3,600.

STEP 1: Calculate cost of merchandise available for sale at cost and retail.

STEP 2: Calculate the cost ratio (cost of goods available for sale at cost divided by cost of goods available for sale at retail). It costs French Company 0.60, or 60 cents, for each $1 of sales for the merchandise.

STEP 3: Deduct net sales from retail value of merchandise available for sale to arrive at an estimated ending inventory at retail.

STEP 4: Multiply cost ratio (0.60 in this case) by ending inventory at retail to arrive at ending inventory at cost of $3,600.

Keep in mind that at year-end French will take a physical inventory.

The Retail Inventory Method

			Cost	Retail
	Goods Available for Sale:			
	Beginning Inventory		$4,100	$6,900
	Net Purchases		7,900	13,100
Step 1 →	Cost of Goods Available for Sale		$12,000	$20,000
Step 2 →	Cost Ratio (relationship between cost and retail)	$\frac{\$12,000}{\$20,000} = 60\%$		
Step 3 →	Net Sales at Retail			−14,000
└→	Ending Inventory at Retail			$6,000
Step 4 →	Ending Inventory at Cost, $6,000 × 0.60		$3,600	

Gross Profit Method

Another method of estimating ending inventory without taking a physical count is the gross profit method. This method develops a relationship among sales, cost of goods sold, and gross profit in estimating the cost of ending inventory.

To use this method a company would have to keep track of the following:

1. Average gross profit rate (= gross profit/net sales)
2. Net sales, beginning inventory, and net purchases

The steps Moose Company takes to estimate its ending inventory are shown in the following diagram. We assume an average gross profit rate of 30% of net sales. If 30 cents of each dollar in net sales is profit, 70 cents on a dollar is cost.

SUCCESS TIP

Freight, if any, would be added to the cost of net purchases. Remember that the true cost of inventory is the total of all costs to get ready for sale.

The Gross Profit Method

	Cost of Goods Available for Sale:		
	Inventory, January 1, 201X		$10,000
	Net Purchases		+4,000
Step 1 →	Cost of Goods Available for Sale		$14,000
	Less: Estimated Cost of Goods Sold:		
	Net Sales at Retail	$6,000	
Step 2 →	Cost percentage (100% − 30%)	× 0.70	
	Estimated Cost of Goods Sold		−4,200
Step 3 →	Estimated Inventory, January 31, 201X		$9,800

STEP 1: Moose determines cost of goods available for sale (beginning inventory plus net purchases).

STEP 2: Moose estimates cost of goods sold by multiplying cost percentage (70%) times net sales.

STEP 3: Moose subtracts cost of goods sold from cost of goods available for sale to arrive at an estimated inventory of $9,800.

This method, besides helping prepare financial statements, can help determine the amount of inventory on hand at the time of a fire or can verify at year's end the accuracy of the physical inventory.

Before concluding this unit, let's look at how an error made in calculating ending inventory will affect the financial statements.

How Incorrect Calculation of Ending Inventory Affects Financial Statements As we stated before, assigning costs to ending inventory can have an effect on cost of goods sold, gross profit, net income, and current assets as well as owner's capital. Let's look at a diagram to see—if a mistake is in fact made—what items on the income statement will be affected and what the mistake's impact will be over time.

	Correct		Incorrect	
	2018	**2019**	**2018**	**2019**
Sales	$200	$300	$200	$300
Cost of Goods Sold:				
Beginning Inventory	$ 30	$ 70	$ 30	$ 60
Purchases	95	85	95	85
Cost of Goods Available for Sale	125	155	125	145
Ending Inventory	−70	−100	−60	−100
Cost of Goods Sold	55	55	65	45
Gross Profit	$145	$245	$135	$255

	Summary		
	Correct	**Incorrect**	**Difference**
Year 2018, Gross Profit	$145	$135	− $10
Year 2019, Gross Profit	245	255	+ 10
Total effect of mistake after two periods			0

Note that when the incorrect figure of $60 is used for ending inventory in 2018, it causes cost of goods sold to be $65 instead of $55 and profit to be $135 instead of $145. In other words, when ending inventory is understated ($60 instead of $70), cost of goods sold is overstated and profit is understated.

As we look next at 2019, we see that the incorrect ending inventory of 2018 is carried as the beginning inventory of 2019. The understatement of beginning inventory in 2019 of $60 (instead of $70) causes cost of goods sold to be understated and gross profit to be overstated. Thus, at the end of 2019, the error will be self-correcting.

To review, look at the following chart and prove it to yourself by going back over the previous explanation.

If the Item Is	Overstated	Understated
Beginning Inventory	Profit is understated	Profit is overstated
Ending Inventory	Profit is overstated	Profit is understated

SUCCESS TIP

Ending inventory works in the same direction as profit. Beginning inventory is inversely related, meaning moving in the opposite direction.

Keep in mind that, because ending inventory is recorded as a current asset on the balance sheet, any mistake will cause the assets to be under- or overstated. The statement of owner's equity will also be affected, with net income over- or understated.

Now let's check your progress.

 **TRY IT!**　　　　　　　　　　　　　Learning Unit 15-4

Fullerton Co. estimates its monthly ending inventory by the retail method. From the following, calculate the cost of ending inventory on November 30 using the retail method.

	Cost	Retail
Beginning Inventory	$11,000	$15,000
Net Purchases	9,000	10,000
Net Sales		16,000

TRY IT!　　　　　　　　　**Solution Learning Unit 15-4**

	Cost	Retail
Beginning Inventory	$ 11,000	$15,000
Net Purchases	9,000	10,000
Cost of Goods Available for Sale	$ 20,000	$25,000
Net Sales at Retail		16,000
End. Inventory at Retail		$ 9,000
Cost Ratio ($20,000/$25,000 = 80%)		
End. Inventory at Cost ($9,000 × 0.80)	$ 7,200	

DEMONSTRATION SUMMARY PROBLEM

 L01,2,3,4

Today, Allison Hasker, owner of Hasker Bookkeeping Service, will be working with two of her clients, Moore Co. and Linch Co.

Requirements

1. Journalize the following transactions. (Moore uses a perpetual system, and all credit sales are n/30.) Omit explanations.

201X
Aug. 10　Purchased merchandise on account $2,500, n/30.
　　　11　Sold merchandise on account to Earl Miller for $90. Merchandise cost $40.
　　　13　Returned $200 of defective merchandise purchased August 10.
　　　14　Sold $200 of merchandise for cash. Merchandise cost $95.
　　　14　Allowed a return for credit of $40 from August 11. Merchandise cost $10.
　　　15　Received payment from Earl Miller for August 11 sale less return.

2. Calculate for Linch Co., which uses the periodic system, the cost of ending inventory by (a) FIFO, (b) LIFO, and (c) weighted average from the following information.

	Cable Boxes	Cost per Box
Beginning Inventory Jan. 1	31,000	$30
Purchases:		
Mar. 1	13,000	32
June 1	5,000	40
Sept. 1	3,000	46
Dec. 1	2,000	64

Assume 1,800 boxes were left in inventory.

Solutions

Requirement 1

Date		Accounts	Dr.	Cr.
201X				
Mar.	10	Merchandise Inventory	2,500	
		Accounts Payable		2,500
	11	Accounts Receivable, Earl Miller	90	
		Sales		90
	11	Cost of Goods Sold	40	
		Merchandise Inventory		40
	13	Accounts Payable	200	
		Merchandise Inventory		200
	14	Cash	200	
		Sales		200
	14	Cost of Goods Sold	95	
		Merchandise Inventory		95
	14	Sales Returns and Allowances	40	
		Accounts Receivable, Earl Miller		40
	14	Merchandise Inventory	10	
		Cost of Goods Sold		10
	15	Cash	50	
		Accounts Receivable, Earl Miller		50

Tips for Journalizing Perpetual Transactions

Purchases of merchandise are recorded in the Merchandise Inventory account. When merchandise is sold on account, the result is to increase Accounts Receivable and increase Sales. At the same time, the company must show that the Cost of Goods Sold has increased and the cost of Merchandise Inventory has decreased. In a return back to the seller, the Sales Returns and Allowances increases and the Accounts Receivable decreases. At the same time, the Merchandise Inventory account increases and the Cost of Goods Sold decreases. So to summarize, there are two journal entries to record the sale and two journal entries to reverse the sale.

Requirement 2

	Cable Boxes	Cost per Box	Total Cost
Beg. Inventory Jan. 1	31,000	$30	$930,000
Mar. 1	13,000	32	416,000
June 1	5,000	40	200,000
Sept. 1	3,000	46	138,000
Dec. 1	2,000	64	128,000
	54,000		$1,812,000

Ending Inventory:

Weighted average: 1,800 boxes $\times$ $33.56 per box = $60,408

FIFO: 1,800 boxes $\times$ $64 = $115,200

LIFO: 1,800 boxes $\times$ $30 = $54,000

Tips for Calculating Inventory Methods in a Periodic System

The first step is to calculate the total cost of goods available for sale. The $1,812,000 is the total cost of the goods available for sale. Note that in weighted average, you divide the total cost of goods available for sale by total units available for sale to get the average cost per unit. Keep in mind for FIFO that the old goods are sold first, leaving the new goods for ending inventory. LIFO, on the other hand, assumes new goods are sold first, leaving the old goods to make up the cost of ending inventory.

SUCCESS COACH

The following Success Tips are from Learning Units 15-1 to 15-4. Take the Do It Right Now Checkup and use the Check Your Score to see how you are doing. The Success Coach provides tips before each Checkup to help you avoid common accounting errors.

LU 15-1 Transactions for a Perpetual and Periodic Inventory System

Do It Right Tips: In the perpetual inventory system there are no accounts for freight-in, purchases, purchases discounts, or purchases returns and allowances. The information about these accounts is debited or credited to the Merchandise Inventory account. An important account in the perpetual inventory system is the Cost of Goods Sold account.

Do It Right Now Checkup: Answer true or false to the following statements.

1. The Cost of Goods Sold account is used in the periodic inventory system.
2. Freight costs in the perpetual inventory system result in a credit to Merchandise Inventory.
3. Merchandise inventory being returned in the perpetual inventory system results in a credit to Merchandise Inventory for the seller.
4. When merchandise is sold in the perpetual inventory system, Cost of Goods Sold is not used.
5. In the perpetual inventory system, sales returns and allowances may result in Accounts Receivable being reduced by the seller.

LU 15-2 Using a Subsidiary Ledger for Inventory; Calculating Cost of Ending Inventory Using a Perpetual System

Do It Right Tips: Subsidiary ledgers are only needed if there is a large variety of inventory. Each inventory record keeps a running balance of units purchased as well as sold. Each sale results in a decrease to Merchandise Inventory and an increase in Cost of Goods Sold. The Merchandise Inventory account balance in the general ledger should equal the balances of the subsidiary ledgers.

Do It Right Now Checkup: Answer true or false to the following statements.

1. A subsidiary ledger for inventory is the controlling account.
2. Cost of Goods Sold decreases in a sale.
3. Computers replace all subsidiary ledgers.
4. In FIFO, new goods are assumed to be sold first.
5. In LIFO, old or new goods are assumed to be sold first.

LU 15-3 Inventory Methods to Calculate Ending Inventory in a Periodic System

Do It Right Tips: Keep in mind when assigning a cost to inventory that the cost of goods may not follow the actual flow of goods. The specific method matches costs exactly with sales. FIFO assumes that old goods are sold first. LIFO assumes that new goods are sold first. Weighted-average falls between LIFO and FIFO because it uses an average unit cost.

Do It Right Now Checkup: Answer true or false to the following statements.

1. In the specific invoice method, the flow of goods and flow of costs are not the same.
2. A fish market would like to sell its merchandise using LIFO.
3. LIFO matches current cost with current selling price.
4. If merchandise is nonsalable it should be added to the cost of inventory.
5. Goods in transit may be included in the cost of inventory.

LU 15-4 Estimating Ending Inventory by the Retail and Gross Profit Methods

Do It Right Tips: In the periodic inventory system, taking inventory can be quite expensive. Ending inventory can be estimated using the retail or gross profit methods. Keep in mind that if the cost of ending inventory is miscalculated it will have an effect on cost of goods sold in one period as well as the next period. Remember that ending inventory of one period becomes the beginning inventory of the next period.

Do It Right Now Checkup: Answer true or false to the following statements.

1. The retail method requires the use of a cost ratio.
2. The retail method uses the net sales figure at cost.
3. The gross profit method requires net purchases to be calculated.
4. If ending inventory is overstated, profit is understated.
5. The retail method is used in the perpetual inventory system.

CHECK YOUR SCORE: Answers to the Do It Right Now Checkup

LU 15-1

1. False—Cost of Goods Sold is used in the perpetual inventory system.
2. False—Freight costs in the perpetual inventory system result in a debit to Merchandise Inventory.
3. False—When inventory is returned, we debit Merchandise Inventory and credit Cost of Goods Sold.
4. False—When merchandise is sold in the perpetual inventory system, Cost of Goods Sold is used.
5. True

LU 15-2

1. False—Merchandise Inventory is the controlling account.
2. False—Cost of Goods Sold increases in a sale.
3. False—Even with the widespread use of computers, subsidiary ledgers can still be used.
4. False—In FIFO, old goods are assumed to be sold first.
5. False—In LIFO, only new goods are assumed to be sold first.

LU 15-3

1. False—In the specific invoice method, the flow of goods and flow of costs are the same.
2. False—A fish market would like to sell its merchandise using FIFO.
3. True
4. False—If merchandise is nonsalable it should be subtracted from cost of inventory.
5. True

LU 15-4

1. True
2. False—The retail method uses the net sales figure at retail, not cost.
3. True
4. False—If ending inventory is overstated, profit is overstated.
5. False—The retail method is used in the periodic inventory system.

BLUEPRINT: METHODS OF DETERMINING THE VALUE OF INVENTORY

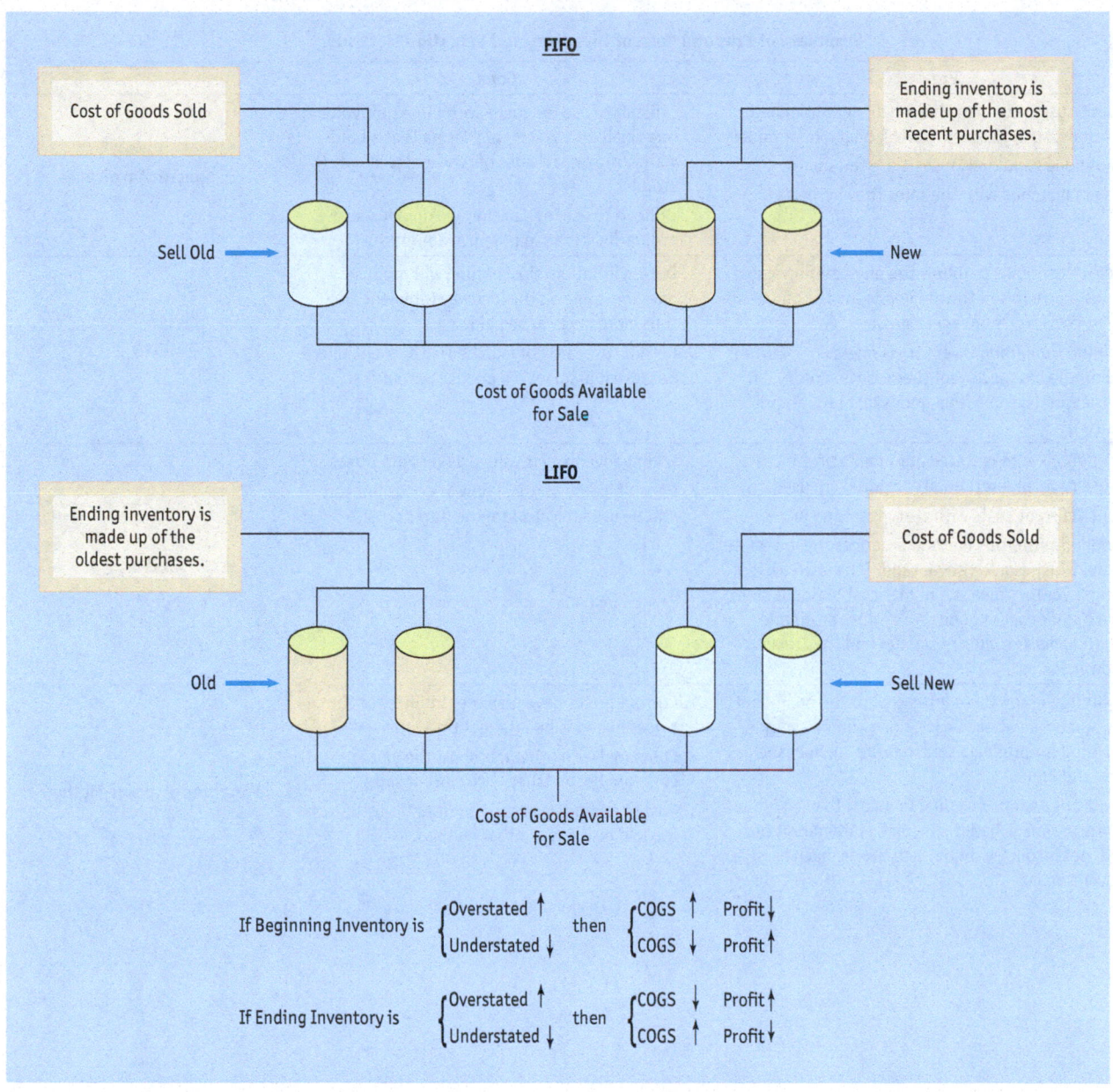

FIFO

Cost of Goods Sold

Ending inventory is made up of the most recent purchases.

Sell Old → ← New

Cost of Goods Available for Sale

LIFO

Ending inventory is made up of the oldest purchases.

Cost of Goods Sold

Old → ← Sell New

Cost of Goods Available for Sale

If Beginning Inventory is $\begin{cases} \text{Overstated} \uparrow \\ \text{Understated} \downarrow \end{cases}$ then $\begin{cases} \text{COGS} \uparrow \quad \text{Profit} \downarrow \\ \text{COGS} \downarrow \quad \text{Profit} \uparrow \end{cases}$

If Ending Inventory is $\begin{cases} \text{Overstated} \uparrow \\ \text{Understated} \downarrow \end{cases}$ then $\begin{cases} \text{COGS} \downarrow \quad \text{Profit} \uparrow \\ \text{COGS} \uparrow \quad \text{Profit} \downarrow \end{cases}$

BLUEPRINT: METHODS OF DETERMINING THE VALUE OF INVENTORY (*Continued*)

Summary of Pros and Cons of Inventory and Valuation Methods

Pros	Cons	
1. Simple to use if company has small amount of high-cost goods, such as autos, jewels, boats, or antiques. 2. Flow of goods and flow of costs are the same. 3. Costs are matched with the sales they helped to produce.	1. Difficult to use for goods with large unit volume and small unit prices, such as nails at a hardware store or packages of toothpaste at a drug store. 2. Difficult to use for decision-making purposes; ordinarily it is an impractical approach.	**Specific Invoice**
1. The cost flow tends to follow the physical flow; most businesses try to sell the old goods first (e.g., perishables such as fruits or vegetables). 2. The figure for ending inventory is made up of current costs on the balance sheet (because inventory left over is assumed to be from goods last brought into the store).	1. During inflation, this method will produce higher income on the income statement and thus more taxes to be paid. 2. Recent costs are not matched with recent sales because it assumes *old* goods are sold first.	**FIFO**
1. Cost of goods sold is stated at or near current costs because costs of *latest* goods acquired are used. 2. Matches current costs with current selling prices. 3. During inflation, this method produces the lowest net income, which is a tax advantage. (The lower cost of ending inventory means a higher cost of goods sold; with a higher cost of goods sold, gross profit and ultimately net income are smaller and thus taxes are lower.)	1. Ending inventory is valued at very old prices. 2. Doesn't match physical flow of goods but can still be used to calculate the flow of costs.	**LIFO**
1. Weighted-average takes into account the number of units purchased at each cost, not a simple average cost. Good for products sold in large volume, such as grains and fuels. 2. Accountant assigns an equal unit cost to each unit of inventory; thus, when the income statement is prepared, net income will not fluctuate as much as with other methods.	1. Current prices have no more significance than prices of goods bought months earlier. 2. Compared with other methods, the most recent costs are *not* matched with current sales. 3. Cost of ending inventory is not as up-to-date as it could be using another method.	**Weighted-Average Method**

Discussion Questions and Critical Thinking/Ethical Case

1. Why would a manager prefer the perpetual inventory system over the periodic system of inventory?

2. What are the two key accounts in the perpetual inventory system?

3. In the perpetual system, what account is debited to record the cost of merchandise purchased?

4. Why are there two entries required to record each sale in the perpetual inventory system?

5. Explain the relationship between the Merchandise Inventory account and the subsidiary inventory ledger.

6. Must the flow of cost in inventory match the physical movement of merchandise? Please explain.

7. What are the four methods of inventory valuation? Explain each.

8. During inflation, which inventory method will provide the lowest income on the income statement?

9. Which inventory method provides the most current valuation of inventory on the balance sheet? Please explain.

10. Explain why goods in transit (F.O.B. shipping point) to buyer and goods issued on consignment are added to inventory valuations.

11. When ending inventory is understated, what effect will it have on cost of goods sold and net income?

12. Why would a company use the retail method to determine the value of the ending inventory? Why would it use the gross profit method?

13. Lyon Co. has used a perpetual inventory system for 6 months. The president of the company issued a memo stating that the new computer system failed to deliver acceptable standards in servicing the customers and that too many goods are out of stock. Fran, Lyon's accountant, blames the computer department and tells the president to fire the head of that department. The president wants to return immediately to a periodic inventory system. You make the call. Write down your recommendations to the president.

Concept Checks

MyLabAccounting

Transaction Analysis

 **L01** *(5 min)*

1. What four titles along with their classification are involved in the sale of goods in a perpetual system?

Journal Entries
Use the perpetual inventory system.

L01 *(10 min)*

2. Journalize the following transaction in correct form:

201X		
Apr.	1	Sold merchandise on account, $1,230. The merchandise cost $680.

3. Journalize the following transaction in correct form:

L01 *(10 min)*

201X		
Mar.	15	A customer returned merchandise for a cash refund of $190. The item cost the seller $75.

4. Journalize the following transaction in correct form:

L01 *(10 min)*

201X		
Mar.	20	The business returned to the vendor a damaged inventory item that cost $350.

(30 min) **LO3** ▶

Estimating Inventory Value

5. From the following information, calculate the cost of ending inventory and cost of goods sold using the (a) FIFO, (b) LIFO, and (c) weighted-average methods.

		Units	Cost
January 1	Beginning Inventory	6	$4
March 6	Purchased	6	3
August 9	Purchased	10	6
December 10	Purchased	2	9

The ending inventory reveals nine items unsold.

Retail Inventory Method

(30 min) **LO4** ▶

6. Complete the following using the retail inventory method. (Round cost ratio to the nearest whole percent.)

	Cost	Retail
Goods Available for Sale		
Beginning Inventory	$61	$110
Net Purchases	26	64
Cost of Goods Available for Sale	A	B
Cost Ratio	C	
Net Sales at Retail		124
Ending Inventory at Retail		D
Ending Inventory at Cost	E	

(30 min) **LO4** ▶

Gross Profit Method

7. Complete the following using the gross profit method. Assume a normal gross profit rate of 24% of net sales.

Goods Available for Sale		
Inventory January 1, 201X		$67
Net Purchases		23
Cost of Goods Available for Sale		A
Less: Estimated Cost of Goods Sold:		
Net Sales at Retail	$50	
Cost Percentage	B	
Estimated Cost of Goods Sold		C
Estimated Inventory Jan. 31, 201X		D

MyLabAccounting

Exercises

Set A

(20 min) **LO1**

15A-1. The Brown Electric Company uses the perpetual inventory system. Record these transactions in a two-column journal.

201X		
Feb.	3	Purchased 45 model 77DX light fixtures on account from Nonstop Electric at total cost of $1,800; terms n/30.
	5	Sold 9 model U67 light fixtures for cash for $252 total. The cost of these 9 fixtures amounted to $162.
	6	Our customer returned 4 model U67 light fixtures. We gave the customer a $112 cash refund.
	10	We issued a debit memo for $120 to Nonstop Electric for 3 model 77DX light fixtures that came in damaged in the shipment of February 3.

15A-2. The MJM Company uses the perpetual inventory system with a subsidiary ledger for inventory. Enter the following information in the inventory balance for product U47. Be sure to keep the balance on hand up-to-date.

 **L01,2** *(20 min)*

201X		
Nov.	5	Purchased on account 11 units at a cost of $2 each. (Inventory on hand prior to this purchase was zero units.)
	6	Sold 1 unit for $16.30. (*Hint*: The inventory record only contains information about the cost of a product, not the selling price!) This is a cash sale.
	7	Sold 3 units for $15.50 each. This is a cash sale.
	10	Purchased on account 19 additional units at a cost of $2 each.

15A-3. Journalize and post the preceding transactions (for Exercise 15A-2) using a two-column journal and T accounts.

 **L01,2** *(20 min)*

15A-4. Mannon Sales uses the FIFO method with the perpetual inventory system. Enter the following information in the inventory record form for product 44BX. Be sure to keep the balance on hand up-to-date.

 **L03** *(20 min)*

201X		
Apr.	1	Balance on hand: 8 units at a cost of $20 each.
	2	Purchased 8 units at a cost of $23 each.
	5	Sold 3 units for $31 each. (Remember to use cost and not selling price in the inventory record.)
	6	Sold 11 units for $31 each.
	8	Purchased 9 units at a cost of $24 each.

15A-5. The Ballard Company uses the periodic inventory system. Calculate the cost of ending inventory and cost of goods sold using the (a) FIFO, (b) LIFO, and (c) weighted-average methods. Ballard sells only one product, called SM57.

L03 *(20 min)*

		Units	Cost per Unit
January 1	Beginning inventory	59	$ 8
March 18	Purchased	19	9
August 19	Purchased	43	11
November 8	Purchased	47	12

Ending inventory is 61 units.

15A-6. From the following facts, calculate the correct cost of inventory for Sam Company.

L03 *(20 min)*

- Cost of inventory on shelf, $4,200, which includes $280 of goods received on consignment.
- Goods in transit en route to Sam Company shipped F.O.B. shipping point, $22,000.
- Goods in transit en route to Sam shipped F.O.B. destination, $375.
- Sam Company has $625 worth of goods on consignment in Alice's Dress Shop.

15A-7. Goodman Company's April 1 inventory had a cost of $59,500 and a retail value of $73,200. During April, net purchases cost $255,600 with a retail value of $405,000. Net sales at retail for Goodman Company during April were $227,800. Calculate the ending inventory at cost using the retail inventory method. (Round the cost ratio to the nearest hundredth percent.)

 **L04** *(15 min)*

15A-8. Kelly Company on April 1, 201X, had inventory costing $33,000 and during April had net purchases of $68,000. Over the years, Kelly Company's gross profit averaged 40% on sales. Given that the company has net sales of $107,500, calculate an estimated cost of ending inventory using the gross profit method.

L04 *(15 min)*

Set B

(20 min) **LO1**

15B-1. The Black Electric Company uses the perpetual inventory system. Record these transactions in a two-column journal.

201X		
Feb.	3	Purchased 10 Model 77DX light fixture(s) on account from Flashing Electric at total cost of $400; terms n/30.
	5	Sold 8 model U67 light fixtures for cash for $224 total. The cost of these 8 fixtures amounted to $144.
	6	Our customer returned 5 model U67 light fixture(s). We gave the customer a $140 cash refund.
	10	We issued a debit memo for $80 to Flashing Electric for 2 model 77DX light fixture(s) that came in damaged in the shipment of February 3.

(20 min) **LO1,2**

15B-2. The JAB Company uses the perpetual inventory system with a subsidiary ledger for inventory. Enter the following information into the inventory balance for product U47. Be sure to keep the balance on hand up-to-date.

201X		
Nov.	5	Purchased on account 5 units at a cost of $8 each. (Inventory on hand prior to this purchase was zero units.)
	6	Sold 2 units for $16.40 each. (*Hint*: The inventory record only contains information about the cost of a product, not the selling price!) This is a cash sale.
	7	Sold 2 units for $15.40 each. This is a cash sale.
	10	Purchased on account 13 additional units at a cost of $8 each.

(20 min) **LO1,2**

15B-3. Journalize and post the preceding transactions (Exercise 15B-2) using a two-column journal and T accounts.

(20 min) **LO3**

15B-4. Mullen Sales uses the FIFO method with the perpetual inventory system. Enter the following information into the inventory record form for product 44BX. Be sure to keep the balance on hand up-to-date.

201X		
Jan.	1	Balance on hand: 7 units at a cost of $19.00 each.
	2	Purchased 14 units at a cost of $23.00 each.
	5	Sold 3 units for $31.25 each. (Remember to use cost and not selling price in the inventory record.)
	6	Sold 12 units for $31.25 each.
	8	Purchased 14 units at a cost of $22.00 each.

(20 min) **LO3**

15B-5. The Dandylion Company uses the periodic inventory system. Calculate the cost of ending inventory and cost of goods sold using the (a) FIFO, (b) LIFO, and (c) weighted-average methods. Dandylion sells only one product, called SM57.

		Units	Costs per Unit
January 1	Beginning inventory	50	$12
March 18	Purchased	15	13
August 19	Purchased	40	15
November 8	Purchased	45	16

Ending inventory is 60 units.

15B-6. From the following facts, calculate the correct cost of inventory for Bob Company.   **L03** *(20 min)*

- Cost of inventory on shelf, $4,300, which includes $310 of goods received on consignment.

- Goods in transit en route to Bob Company shipped F.O.B. shipping point, $22,200.

- Goods in transit en route to Bob shipped F.O.B. destination, $300.

- Bob Company has $700 worth of goods on consignment in Alice's Dress Shop.

15B-7. Miles Company's November 1 inventory had a cost of $59,800 and a retail value of $72,600. During November, net purchases cost $256,000 with a retail value of $405,200. Net sales at retail for Miles Company during November were $228,600. Calculate the ending inventory at cost using the retail inventory method. (Round the cost ratio to the nearest hundredth percent.)   **L04** *(15 min)*

15B-8. Amy Company on November 1, 201X, had inventory costing $32,000 and during November had net purchases of $67,100. Over the years, Amy Company's gross profit averaged 44% on sales. Given that the company has net sales of $110,500, calculate an estimated cost of ending inventory using the gross profit method.   **L04** *(15 min)*

Problems

Set A

15A-1. The Athol Company uses the perpetual inventory system. Record these transactions in a two-column journal. All credit sales are n/30.   **L01** *(20 min)*

201X		
July	5	Purchased merchandise on account totaling $2,000; terms n/30.
	6	Sold merchandise on account to Tommy Donaldson for $85. This merchandise cost $76.
	8	Returned $100 of defective merchandise purchased July 5.
	9	Sold $170 of merchandise for cash. This merchandise cost $93.
	9	Allowed a return for credit of $7 of merchandise sold on July 6. The cost of the returned merchandise was $6. (*Hint:* Don't forget to return the cost of the merchandise to the Merchandise Inventory account.)
	10	Purchased $500 of merchandise on account from JJ Supply; terms n/30.
	12	Received payment from Tommy Donaldson for the July 6 sale less the return.
	13	Sold $460 of merchandise for cash. The cost was $330.

Check Figure:
July13
Dr. Cost of Goods Sold $330
Cr. Merch. Inventory $330

15A-2. Sturebridge Electronics, an electronics supply company, uses the perpetual inventory system with a subsidiary inventory ledger to maintain control over an inventory of thousands of electronic parts. The quantities and costs for three of the parts in inventory follow: **L01,2** *(40 min)*

Part No.	Quantity on Hand	Cost per Unit
KT88	8	$20.00
EL34	19	17.00
12AX7	10	6.00

Check Figure:
KT88 Ending Balance $220.00

Your job is to do the following:

1. Enter the preceding beginning balances in the inventory record forms; beginning inventory is $543.

2. Journalize and post the following transactions.

201X

Nov.   10   Purchased the following on account:

Part No.	Quantity	Cost per Unit
KT88	21	$20.00
12AX7	35	6.00

(*Hint*: Be sure to update each inventory record.)

11   Sold 2 number KT88 units for cash at a selling price of $29.00 each.
(*Hint*: Remember to record both the revenue and the cost. The cost data will be found in the inventory record form for this part number. Don't forget to update the form.)

13   Sold the following for cash:

Part No.	Quantity	Sales Price per Unit
KT88	16	$29.00
EL34	8	21.00
12AX7	12	12.00

15   A customer brought back 5 of the KT88 units bought 2 days ago because they did not work.

16   Sturebridge Electronics sent back to the vendor the faulty KT88 units that the customer brought back.

(30 min) **LO1,2**

15A-3.   Ashley Company uses a perpetual inventory system. From the following information, prepare an inventory record form (a) assuming that the FIFO method is in use and (b) assuming that the LIFO method is in use. Assume on January 1, 201X, a beginning inventory of 806 units at a cost of $12 each.

Check Figure:
Ending balance (b) $10,558

Received			Sold	
Date	Quantity	Cost per Unit	Date	Quantity
Apr. 15	228	$ 5	Mar. 8	508
Nov. 12	800	9	Oct. 5	356
Dec. 31	700	7	Nov. 30	398

(30 min) **LO3**

S50 / **QB**

Check Figure:
(b) LIFO Cost of Goods Sold $79,540

15A-4.   Ashlyn Company, using the periodic inventory system, began the year with 280 units of product B in inventory with a unit cost of $35. The following additional purchases of the product were made:

Apr. 1	280 units @ $42 each
July 5	440 units @ 59 each
Aug. 15	520 units @ 69 each
Nov. 20	180 units @ 75 each

At end of year, Ashlyn Company had 460 units of its product unsold. Calculate the cost of ending inventory as well as cost of goods sold by the (a) FIFO, (b) LIFO, and (c) weighted-average methods. (Round the weighted average to the nearest cent.)

(20 min) **LO4**

15A-5.   Mosher Company uses the retail method to estimate the cost of ending inventory for its monthly interim reports. From the following facts, estimate Mosher's ending inventory at cost for the end of January. (Round the cost ratio to the nearest tenth percent.)

January 1 inventory at cost	$ 16,300
January 1 inventory at retail	32,400
Net purchases at cost	111,100
Net purchases at retail	195,100
Net sales at retail	186,000

Check Figure:
$23,240 Ending Inventory at cost

15A-6. Over the past 4 years, the gross profit rate for Setzer Company was 28%. Last week a fire destroyed all of Setzer's inventory. Luckily, all the records for Setzer were in a fireproof safe and indicated the following facts:

L04 *(20 min)*

Inventory (January 1, 201X)	$ 38,700
Sales	128,000
Sales Returns	3,300
Purchases	78,300
Purchases Returns and Allowances	2,600

Check Figure:
$24,616 Estimated inventory lost in fire

Estimate the cost of inventory that was lost in the fire.

Set B

15B-1. The Antrim Company uses the perpetual inventory system. Record the transactions in a two-column journal. All credit sales are n/30.

L01 *(20 min)*

201X			
July	5	Purchased merchandise on account totaling $2,000; terms n/30.	
	6	Sold merchandise on account to Tommy Donaghey for $70. This merchandise cost $52.	
	8	Returned $150 of defective merchandise purchased July 5.	
	9	Sold $140 of merchandise for cash. This merchandise cost $93.	
	9	Allowed a return for credit of $9 of merchandise sold on July 6. The cost of the returned merchandise was $8. (*Hint*: Don't forget to return the cost of the merchandise to the Merchandise Inventory account.)	
	10	Purchased $1,000 of merchandise on account from RJ Supply; terms n/30.	
	12	Received payment from Tommy Donaghey for the July 6 sale less the return.	
	13	Sold $360 of merchandise for cash. The cost was $350.	

Check Figure:
July 13
Dr. Cost of Goods Sold $ 350
Cr. Merch. Inventory $ 350

15B-2. Salem Electronics, an electronics supply company, uses the perpetual inventory system with a subsidiary inventory ledger to maintain control over an inventory of thousands of electronic parts. The quantities and costs for three of the parts in the inventory follow:

L01,2 *(40 min)*

Part No.	Quantity on Hand	Cost per Unit
KT88	7	$19.00
EL34	22	12.00
12AX7	5	5.00

Check Figure:
KT88 Ending Balance $266.00

Your job is to do the following:

1. Enter the beginning balances in the inventory record forms; beginning inventory is $422.

2. Journalize and post the following transactions.

201X

Nov. 10   Purchased the following on account:

Part No.	Quantity	Cost per Unit
KT88	28	$19.00
12AX7	34	5.00

(*Hint*: Be sure to update each inventory record.)

11   Sold 7 number KT88 units for cash at a selling price of $27.00 each.
(*Hint*: Remember to record both the revenue and the cost. The cost data will be found in the inventory record form for this part number. Don't forget to update the form.)

13   Sold the following for cash:

Part No.	Quantity	Sales Price per Unit
KT88	14	$27.00
EL34	11	24.00
12AX7	12	12.00

15   A customer brought back 4 of the KT88 units bought 2 days ago because they did not work.

16   Salem Electronics sent back to the vendor the faulty KT88 units that the customer brought back.

(30 min) **L01,2**

Check Figure:
Ending Balance (a) $13,198

15B-3.   Agree Company uses a perpetual inventory system. From the following information, prepare an inventory record form (a) assuming that the FIFO method is in use and (b) assuming that the LIFO method is in use. Assume on January 1, 201X, a beginning inventory of 804 units at a cost of $9 each.

Received			Sold	
Date	Quantity	Cost per Unit	Date	Quantity
Apr. 15	218	$ 12	Mar. 8	494
Nov. 12	798	13	Oct. 5	348
Dec. 31	704	8	Nov. 30	396

(30 min) **L03**

S50 / **QB**

Check Figure:
(b) LIFO $68,890 Cost of Goods Sold

15B-4.   Addison Company, using the periodic inventory system, began the year with 220 units of product B in inventory with a unit cost of $39. The following additional purchases of the product were made:

Apr. 1	320 units @ $41 each
July 5	410 units @ 56 each
Aug. 15	470 units @ 64 each
Nov. 20	160 units @ 76 each

At the end of year, Addison Company had 450 units of its product unsold. Calculate the cost of ending inventory as well as cost of goods sold by the (a) FIFO, (b) LIFO, and (c) weighted-average methods. (Round the weighted average to the nearest cent.)

(20 min) **L04**

15B-5.   Matthew Company uses the retail method to estimate the cost of ending inventory for its monthly interim reports. From the following facts, estimate

Matthew's ending inventory at cost for the end of January. (Round the cost ratio to the nearest tenth percent.)

January 1 inventory at cost	$ 16,500
January 1 inventory at retail	32,000
Net purchases at cost	110,900
Net purchases at retail	195,500
Net sales at retail	188,000

Check Figure:
$22,120.00 Ending Inventory

15B-6. Over the past 4 years the gross profit rate for Davidson Company was 26%. Last week a fire destroyed all of Davidson's inventory. Luckily, all the records for Davidson were in a fireproof safe and indicated the following facts:

L04 *(20 min)*

Inventory (January 1, 201X)	$ 39,100
Sales	128,500
Sales Returns	3,200
Purchases	77,900
Purchases Returns and Allowances	2,200

Check Figure:
$ 22,078 Estimated Inventory

Estimate the cost of inventory that was lost in the fire.

Financial Report Problem

Reading Amazon's Annual Report
Go to the 2016 annual report for Amazon at **https://tinyurl.com/slaterca14e**. Look on page 39 and find out the balance of inventory. Which method to calculate ending inventory was used by Amazon? (Please see page 45.)

L03 *(10 min)*

KEEPING IT REAL SUAREZ COMPUTER CENTER

MyLabAccounting

L03 *(45 min)*

Suarez Computer Center had 350 pieces of merchandise inventory as of June 30, 201X. The inventory was purchased with prices as follows:

Lot	Price Each Piece	Number of Pieces	Total Cost
First lot	$2.50	110	$275
Second lot	$3.00	110	$330
Third lot	$4.50	90	$405
Fourth lot	$4.10	110	$451
Fifth lot	$3.10	110	$341

Lot numbers represent oldest to newest.

Assignment
Using the FIFO, LIFO, and weighted-average methods, calculate the dollar value of Suarez Computer Center's ending inventory.

SAGE 50 SOFTWARE SIMULATION

Computerized Accounting Application for Chapter 15

Refresher on using Sage 50 Complete Accounting

Before starting this assignment, you may want to refresh your memory by reading the following PDF documents in the multimedia library of the MyAccountingLab website. Remember to choose the PDF document for your version of Sage 50.

1. An Introduction to Sage 50
2. Correcting Sage 50 Transactions
3. How to Repeat or Restart a Sage 50 Assignment
4. Backing Up and Restoring Your Work in Sage 50

You also should have completed the following workshops:

1. Simulation 1 Atlas Company from Chapter 3
2. Simulation 2 Zell Company from Chapter 4
3. Simulation 3 Sherman Realty from Chapter 5
4. Simulation 4 Pete's Market from Chapter 8
5. Simulation 5 Part A Mars Company from Chapter 10
6. Simulation 5 Part B Abby's Toy House from Chapter 10
7. Simulation 6 The Elegant Dress Shop from Chapter 12

Simulation 7:

Perpetual Inventory System

In this workshop, you focus on maintaining inventory for The Paint Place using Sage 50's perpetual inventory system. Tasks include creating inventory records, reviewing costing systems, and recording sales and purchases of inventory. You will also prepare inventory reports, aged receivables and aged payable reports, general journal and general ledger reports, a trial balance, and financial statements.

Instructions and the data file for completing this assignment are in the multimedia library of the MyAccountingLab website. Open the **Workshop 7 The Paint Place** PDF document for your version of Sage 50 and download **The Paint Place** data file for your version of Sage 50.

QUICKBOOKS SOFTWARE SIMULATION

Computerized Accounting Application for Chapter 15

Refresher on using QuickBooks Accountant

Before starting this assignment, you may want to refresh your memory by reading the following PDF documents in the multimedia library of the MyAccountingLab website. Remember to choose the PDF document for your version of QuickBooks.

1. An Introduction to QuickBooks
2. Correcting QuickBooks Transactions
3. How to Repeat or Restart a QuickBooks Assignment
4. Backing Up and Restoring Your Work in QuickBooks

You also should have completed the following workshops:

1. Simulation 1 Atlas Company from Chapter 3
2. Simulation 2 Zell Company from Chapter 4
3. Simulation 3 Sherman Realty from Chapter 5

4. Simulation 4 Pete's Market from Chapter 8
5. Simulation 5 Part A Mars Company from Chapter 10
6. Simulation 5 Part B Abby's Toy House from Chapter 10
7. Simulation 6 The Fantastic Dress Shop from Chapter 12

Simulation 7:

Perpetual Inventory System

In this simulation, you focus on maintaining inventory for The Paint Place using QuickBooks' perpetual inventory system. Tasks include creating inventory records, reviewing costing systems, and recording sales and purchases of inventory. You will also prepare inventory reports, aged receivables and aged payable reports, general journal and general ledger reports, a trial balance, and financial statements.

Instructions and the data file for completing this assignment are in the multimedia library of the MyAccountingLab website. Open the *Workshop 7 The Paint Place* PDF document for your version of QuickBooks and download *The Paint Place* data file for your version of QuickBooks.

Accounting for Property, Plant, Equipment, and Intangible Assets

16

CHAPTER PREVIEW: ACCOUNTING IN ACTION

Janet Kuro read in her local paper about the new renovations being done to the Pechanga Resort and Casino in her town. She decided to take her family out for dinner to check it out. The owners of the resort have been doing renovations and have built a new wing for the resort hotel. How do the owners of the resort handle the cost of building the new wing? Do they get any tax incentives through depreciation? Does this new wing extend the future life of the resort hotel? In this chapter, we look at the concept of calculating depreciation. We discuss how improving certain assets may decrease your tax liability.

Learning Objectives – Relating Accounting Theory By Unit

LO1   Calculate the Cost of Property, Plant, and Equipment

LO2   Explain and Calculate Depreciation Methods

LO3   Journalize Entries for Capital and Revenue Expenditures and Disposal of Plant Assets

LO4   Journalize Transactions for Natural Resources and Intangible Assets

When you visit a resort, do you ever think about how the equipment and building are depreciated? In Chapter 12 we classified assets as either current or plant and equipment. Current assets are used up in a company's operations or converted into cash within 1 year or one accounting cycle, whichever is longer. Long-term assets, such as plant and equipment, provide benefits to a company for more than 1 year or one accounting cycle. Types of long-term assets include property (such as land), plant (such as buildings), and equipment (such as trucks and tools). Another classification of assets is called intangible assets. These assets are rights owned by a business that do not involve a *physical* object. Examples are patents or franchises. Intangible assets are also considered long-term assets.

Intangible assets Assets having no physical substance (such as patents or franchises).

In this chapter, we look at how to calculate a long-term asset's overall cost and its depreciation (depreciation being the allocation of the cost of the asset over its lifetime). We also show how to record expenditures involved in improving or repairing an asset and how to account for the disposal of these assets.

LEARNING UNIT 16-1

LO1

Calculating the Cost of Property, Plant, and Equipment

The cost of property, plant, and equipment is not just the price one pays to buy it. One must also include the cost involved in getting it into position and in condition for use in the company. Thus, the cost of a machine includes freight, assembly, and all other costs that are needed to get the machine up and ready to run.

For example, Kimble ordered a machine with a list price of $20,000 with terms of 3/10, n/30 and paid within the discount period. A freight charge of $1,500 covered transportation to the railroad station. Kimble paid $250 to transport the machine from the railroad station to corporate headquarters. Total costs of assembly and installation amounted to $700. In addition, Kimble purchased a special concrete foundation for $900 to keep the machine from tilting when operational. The life of the machine is expected to be 15 years.

SUCCESS TIP

Note that cash discount is deducted in arriving at total cost of the machine. If sales tax were involved, it too would be added to the cost of the asset.

How Kimble Calculates Cost of the Machine	
List price	$20,000
Less: Cash discount (0.03 × $20,000)	600
Net purchase price	19,400
Freight	1,500
Transportation from railroad station	250
Assembly and installation	700
Special foundation	900
Total cost of machine	$22,750

Entries to record freight, assembly, installation, and so forth would be made as a debit to the Machinery account and as a credit to Cash.

The $22,750 cost of the asset will be spread over the years the machine helps Kimble produce revenue. This example is one of the matching principles. Notice, however, that all the additional costs were reasonable and necessary to get the machine *ready for use*. If the buyer causes negligence, illegal acts, or gross inefficiencies to occur, it will be charged to an expense and not to the cost of the asset.

Let's look now at how to record the cost of land.

Land and Land Improvements

When land (which has unlimited useful life) is purchased, many incidental costs are usually considered part of the cost of the land. These costs include surveying, commissions to attorneys and real estate brokers, title searches, and grading, draining, and clearing the property.

Any special one-time assessment made for paving a street or installing sewers should be charged to the cost of land because it adds "permanent value" to the land.

Now let's look at some items related to land that will not be added to the cost of land. Land Improvements is an asset account that records improvements to land that have a *limited* useful life. Some examples are driveways, fences, shrubbery, paving of parking lots, and sprinkler systems. These improvements are subject to depreciation, and thus we need an account that is kept separate from the Land account (which does *not* depreciate).

Buildings

The cost of buying a building would include the purchase price and the cost of repairs and other expenses to get the building *ready for use*. For construction of a new building, the cost would include all reasonable and necessary payments for labor, insurance, building permits, architect's fees, legal fees, and so on to get the building ready for use. Interest paid for financing during the time of construction is added, too.

If a building and land are purchased for one lump-sum payment, the cost must be separated (allocated) for each because land will not depreciate but buildings will.

Now let's check your progress.

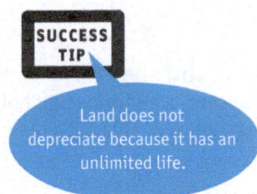

SUCCESS TIP

Land does not depreciate because it has an unlimited life.

Land Improvements Asset account that records improvements made to land; such improvements have a limited life and are subject to depreciation (examples are a driveway or fences).

 # TRY IT!   Learning Unit 16-1

Calculate the cost of the machine given the following:

List Price	$3,150
Cash Discount	2%
Freight	$ 63
Repair	$ 55 (buyer dropped machine at seller's store)
Assembly and installation	$ 180

TRY IT!   Solution Learning Unit 16-1

$3,150 − $63 discount + $63 freight + 180 assembly = $3,330

Depreciation Methods

Now that you know which long-term assets are depreciable, let's look at different methods for computing depreciation. If you want to check any of the concepts of depreciation we discussed in Chapter 4, take a moment to refer back to the chapter.

When a company calculates its periodic depreciation expense, different methods will produce significantly different results. Thus, the method of depreciation chosen will affect the net income for current as well as future periods and the book value (cost of asset less accumulated depreciation) of the asset on the balance sheet.

Let's assume that Prado Company purchased a truck on January 1, 201X, for $20,000, with a residual (salvage) value of $2,000 and an estimated life of 5 years. The following are the three common depreciation methods that Prado Company could use:

1. Straight-line method
2. Units-of-production method
3. Double declining-balance method

LEARNING UNIT 16-2

◀ **LO2**

Book value Cost of asset less accumulated depreciation.

Residual (salvage) value Amount of the asset's cost that will be recovered when the asset is sold, traded in, or scrapped.

SUCCESS TIP

Think
1. Determine cost.
2. Determine life (years, units).
3. Determine residual value.
4. Choose a method.

Straight-line method Method that allocates an equal amount of depreciation over an asset's period of usefulness.

Useful life At the time an asset is acquired, an estimate is made of its usefulness in terms of years, output, and so forth.

Straight-Line Method

The straight-line method is simple to use because it allocates the cost of the asset (less residual value) evenly over its estimated useful life. (At the time an asset is acquired, an estimate is made of its usefulness or useful life in terms of number of years it would last, amount of output expected, and so forth.) Let's look at how Prado Company calculates its depreciation expense for each of the estimated 5 years of usefulness using the straight-line method. Take a moment to read the key points in the parentheses in the accompanying table.

The formula is

$$\frac{\text{Cost} - \text{Residual Value}}{\text{Useful Life in Years}} = \frac{\$20{,}000 - \$2{,}000}{5} = \$3{,}600$$

End of Year	Cost of Delivery Truck	Yearly Depreciation Expense*	Accumulated Depreciation, End of Year	Book Value, End of Year (Cost – Accum. Dep.)
1	$20,000	$3,600	$ 3,600	$16,400
2	20,000	3,600	7,200	12,800
3	20,000	3,600	10,800	9,200
4	20,000	3,600	14,400	5,600
5	20,000	3,600	18,000	2,000
	↑	↑	↑	↑
	(Cost of the machine doesn't change.)	(Note that depreciation expense is the same each year.)	(Accumulated depreciation increases by $3,600 each year.)	(Book value each year is lowered by $3,600 until residual value of $2,000 is reached.)

*The depreciation rate is 100% ÷ 5 years = 20%. The 20% is then multiplied by the cost minus the residual value.

Units-of-Production Method

Units-of-production method Depreciation method that is based on usage and not on time. An example of units of production is the numbers of shoes a machine could produce in its expected useful life.

With the units-of-production method it is assumed that *passage of time* does not determine the amount of depreciation taken. Depreciation expense is based on *use*, be it total estimated miles, tons hauled, or estimated units of production (e.g., the number of shoes a machine could produce in its expected useful life). The accompanying table shows the calculations that Prado Company makes for its truck using the units-of-production method. (*Note:* For this example the truck is assumed to have an estimated life of 90,000 miles.)

The formula is

$$\frac{\text{Cost} - \text{Residual Value}}{\text{Estimated Units of Production}} = \frac{\$20{,}000 - \$2{,}000}{90{,}000 \text{ Miles}} = \$0.20 \text{ per Mile}$$

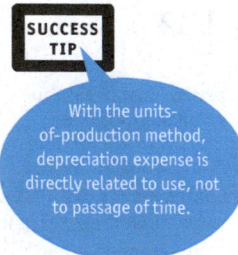

SUCCESS TIP

With the units-of-production method, depreciation expense is directly related to use, not to passage of time.

End of Year	Cost of Delivery Truck	Miles Driven in Year	Yearly Depreciation, Expense	Accumulated Depreciation, End of Year	Book Value, End of Year (Cost – Accum. Dep.)
1	$20,000	30,000	$6,000	$ 6,000	$14,000
2	20,000	21,000	4,200	10,200	9,800
3	20,000	15,000	3,000	13,200	6,800
4	20,000	5,000	1,000	14,200	5,800
5	20,000	19,000	3,800	18,000	2,000
		↑	↑		↑
		(After 5 years, truck has been driven 90,000 miles.)	(Depreciation expense is directly related to number of miles driven.)		(Residual value of $2,000 is reached.)

Double Declining-Balance Method

The double declining-balance method is an accelerated method in which a larger depreciation expense is taken in earlier years and smaller amounts in later years. For this reason it is called an accelerated depreciation method. This method uses twice the straight-line rate, which is why it is called the *double* declining-balance method.

The capturing of more depreciation in the early years of an asset's life can significantly benefit some companies. Think of a rental car company like Hertz. They are going to dispose of the asset, their rental car, after only a few years of use. Therefore, their ability to be able to write off more of the expense of the asset in the first few years of life is going to be of great benefit to them.

A key point in this method is that *residual*, or *salvage*, *value* is *not* deducted from cost in the calculations, and the asset cannot be depreciated below its residual value. For accelerated methods of depreciation, residual, or salvage value, comes into play at the end of the asset's life, unlike straight-line and the units-of-production method where we account for it in the beginning. To calculate depreciation, use the following steps:

1. Calculate the straight-line rate and double it:

$$\frac{100\%}{\text{Useful Life}} \times 2$$

2. At the *end of each year* multiply the rate by the book value of the asset at the beginning of the year.

Double declining-balance method Accelerated depreciation method that uses twice the straight-line rate multiplied by the book value of asset to calculate depreciation expense. Residual value is not subtracted from the cost of an asset in this calculation.

Accelerated depreciation method More depreciation taken in the early years of an asset's life, decreasing amounts in later years.

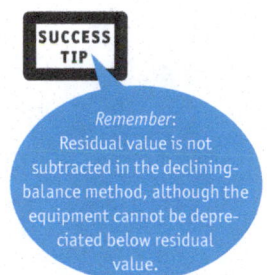

SUCCESS TIP

Remember: Residual value is not subtracted in the declining-balance method, although the equipment cannot be depreciated below residual value.

Let's look at how Prado Company calculates the depreciation on its truck using this method. Be sure to note the $592 in year 5 of depreciation expense. We could not take more than the $592 or we would have depreciated the asset below the residual value.

End of Year	Cost	Accumulated Depreciation, Beg. of Year	Book Value Beg. of Year (Cost – Acc. Dep.)	Dep. Exp. (Book Value Beg. of Year × Rate)	Accumulated Depreciation, End of Year	Book Value, End of Year (Cost – Acc. Dep.)
1	$20,000		$20,000	$8,000 ($20,000 × 0.40*)	$ 8,000	$12,000 (20,000 − 8,000)
2	20,000	$8,000	12,000	4,800 (12,000 × 0.40)	12,800 (8,000 + 4,800)	7,200
3	20,000	12,800	7,200	2,880 (7,200 × 0.40)	15,680	4,320
4	20,000	15,680	4,320	1,728 (4,320 × 0.40)	17,408	2,592
5	20,000	17,408	2,592	592	18,000	2,000
	↑ (Original cost remains the same.)			↑ (Depreciation is limited to $592 because the asset cannot depreciate below the residual value.)		↑ (The book value now equals the residual value.)

*Note that the rate of 0.40 is not changed ($20% × 2).

Depreciation for Partial Years

When depreciating for partial years, we assume that for any asset purchased before the 15th of the month, depreciation is calculated for a full month. After the 15th of the month, the depreciation is disregarded for the month.

Straight-Line Method. For Prado Company, if the truck was purchased on May 4, depreciation expense would be calculated as follows:

$$\frac{\$20,000 - \$2,000}{5 \text{ Years}} \times \frac{8}{12} = \$2,400$$

We use 8 because the truck was bought on May 4. Do not count the first 4 months of the year in the calculation of depreciation. The following year, the full yearly depreciation would be taken.

Units-of-Production Method. The units-of-production method would not be affected because depreciation is based on usage, not passage of time.

Double Declining-Balance Method. Because Prado has the benefit of the truck for 8 months, his depreciation on year 1 would be as follows:

$$(\$20,000 \times 0.40) \times \tfrac{8}{12} = \$5,333$$

In year 2 and in future years, the annual rate of 40% is multiplied by the *current* book value.

Depreciation for Tax Purposes: Modified Accelerated Cost Recovery System

General Motors and Home Depot keep two sets of depreciation records, one for financial records and one for tax reporting.

For the purposes of tax return preparation, the IRS requires the use of a special method of depreciation called the Modified Accelerated Cost Recovery System (MACRS). The previous methods we have discussed have been used for financial reporting, not for tax purposes. Current tax law requires a business to depreciate assets placed in service after December 31, 1986. Starting in 2010 under MACRS, taxpayers could choose the General Depreciation System (GDS) or an alternative system called the Alternative Depreciation System (ADS). We focus on the GDS system since it provides the opportunity to expense more in a shorter time, resulting in increased depreciation expense and lower business taxes. To do so, two factors must be known: recovery classification and MACRS depreciation rates.

Look for a moment at Figure 16.1. According to the tax law currently in effect, classes 3, 5, 7, and 10 use 200% declining balance, switching to straight line, whereas classes 15 and 20 use 150% declining balance, switching to straight line. Both residential and nonresidential real property must use straight line. Note that the recovery period is 27½ years for residential rental property and 39 years for nonresidential real property.

Let's use Table 16.1 to calculate depreciation on the purchase of a nonluxury car for $10,000 on March 19, 2017.

Modified Accelerated Cost Recovery System (MACRS) System for businesses to calculate depreciation for tax purposes based on current tax law; also known as the General Depreciation System (GDS). Check with IRS for new tax act regarding updates for depreciation effective 2018.

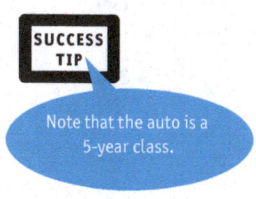

Note that the auto is a 5-year class.

Figure 16.1
Summary of Classes for the Tax Reform Act of 1986

The following classes use a 200% declining balance, switching to straight line:

- **3 year:** Race horses more than 2 years old or any horse other than a race horse that is more than 12 years old at time placed into service; special tools of certain industries
- **5 year:** Automobiles (not luxury); taxis; light general-purpose trucks; semiconductor manufacturing equipment; computer-based telephone central office switching equipment; qualified technological equipment; property used in connection with research and experimentation
- **7 year:** Railroad track; single-purpose agricultural (pigpens) or horticultural structure; fixtures, equipment, and furniture
- **10 year:** The 1986 law doesn't add any specific property under this class.

The following classes use a 150% declining balance, switching to straight line:

- **15 year:** Municipal wastewater treatment plants; telephone distribution plants and comparable equipment used for two-way exchange of voice and data communications
- **20 year:** Municipal sewers

The following classes use straight line:

- **27.5 year:** Only residential rental property
- **39 year:** Only nonresidential real property

TABLE 16.1 Annual Recovery (Percent of Original Depreciable Basis)

Recovery Year	3-Year Class (200% Depreciable Basis)	5-Year Class (200% Depreciable Basis)	7-Year Class (200% Depreciable Basis)	10-Year Class (200% Depreciable Basis)	15-Year Class (150% Depreciable Basis)	20-Year Class (150% Depreciable Basis)
1	33.00	20.00	14.28	10.00	5.00	3.75
2	45.00	32.00	24.49	18.00	9.50	7.22
3	15.00*	19.20	17.49	14.40	8.55	6.68
4	7.00	11.52*	12.49	11.52	7.69	6.18
5		11.52	8.93*	9.22	6.93	5.71
6		5.76	8.93	7.37	6.23	5.28
7			8.93	6.55*	5.90*	4.89
8			4.46	6.55	5.90	4.52
9				6.55	5.90	4.46*
10				6.55	5.90	4.46
11				3.29	5.90	4.46
12					5.90	4.46
13					5.90	4.46
14					5.90	4.46
15					5.90	4.46
16					3.00	4.46
17						

*Identifies when the switch is made to the straight-line method.

Year	Depreciation		
1	0.20 × 10,000 =	$2,000
2	0.32 × 10,000 =	$3,200
3	0.1920 × 10,000 =	$1,920
4	0.1152 × 10,000 =	$1,152
5	0.1152 × 10,000 =	$1,152
6	0.0576 × 10,000 =	$576

When we use Table 16.1, we do not have to decide which year we should switch from the declining-balance to the straight-line method.

Current IRS regulations have some specific rules regarding the depreciation of cellular phones and similar equipment under MACRS. Because cellular phones are subject to personal use, current tax law treats them as listed property. Thus, unless business use is greater than 50%, the straight-line method of depreciation is required.

Now let's check your progress.

▶ TRY IT!   Learning Unit 16-2

Calculate the first-year depreciation for Straight-Line, Double Declining-Balance, Units-of-Production, and MACRS (assume a 5-year class):

Cost of machine (5-year useful life)	$ 95,000
Trade-in value	10,000
Estimated units machine will produce	170,000
Units produced in year 1	40,000

Straight Line

$17,000 ($85,000/5 years) (Note residual value was subtracted from the $95,000.)

Double Declining Balance

95,000 × 0.4 = $38,000

Units of Production

$85,000/170,000 = $0.50 per unit

$0.50 × $40,000 = $20,000

MACRS $19,000 ($95,000 × $0.20)

LEARNING UNIT 16-3

L03

Capital expenditures Original cost of an asset as well as additions or enlargements, extraordinary repairs, and betterments.

Additions or enlargements Major changes or improvements that increase the value of an asset (such as adding a new wing to a school).

Extraordinary repairs Infrequent expenditures that extend an asset's life (such as a new engine in a car).

Betterments Improvements that increase the efficiency of an asset by adding accessories or replacing parts with more effective/powerful ones.

Journalizing Entries for Capital and Revenue Expenditures and Disposal of Plant Assets

Now that we have seen depreciation calculations, let's look at capital and revenue expenditures and the disposal of plant assets.

Capital Expenditures

Capital expenditures include the original cost of an asset as well as payments that improve on or enlarge existing assets. Capital expenditures may be broken down into three categories: additions or enlargements, extraordinary repairs, and betterments. The differences among these three categories are based on whether the change will add to the value of the asset, extend the life of the asset, or improve the asset's efficiency. For example, adding a new wing to a school building will increase the value of the asset, so it is categorized as an addition or enlargement. Overhauling an aircraft engine definitely extends the life of the asset, so it is categorized as an extraordinary repair. Adding solar panels to the roof of a school building improves the efficiency of the asset but does not extend its life, so it is categorized as a betterment. These three categories are shown in the chart in Figure 16.2.

Figure 16.2 Three Categories of Capital Expenditures

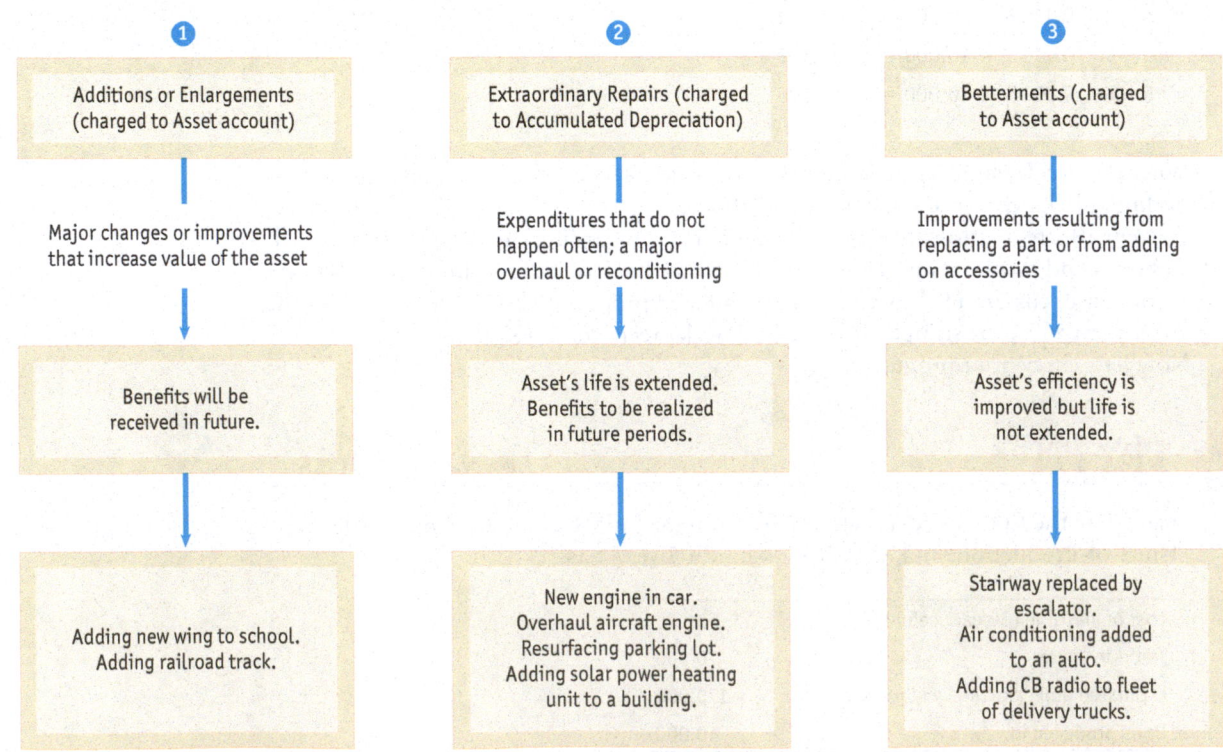

It may be a little difficult at first to see the difference between betterments and extraordinary repairs. Betterments do not extend the life of the asset; the cost of a betterment is debited to the asset account. Extraordinary repairs do extend the life of the asset. The result of the extraordinary repair is to cancel some of the accumulated past depreciation.

The following is an example of how to analyze and record an extraordinary repair to a machine that has a cost of $20,000, has no residual value, and has an estimated life of 10 years.

Machine			Accumulated Depreciation, Machine	
Dr.	Cr.		Dr.	Cr.
20,000				16,000 (after 8 years)

Note that after 8 years the book value of the machine is $4,000 ($20,000 − $16,000) On March 30, a major overhaul of the machine is completed for $3,000. It is believed that this overhaul will extend the machine's life by 3 years. Thus, the journal entry to record this extraordinary repair is as shown in Figure 16.3.

Mar.	30	Accumulated Depreciation, Machine	3 0 0 0 00		
		Cash		3 0 0 0 00	
		To record extraordinary repair			

Figure 16.3
Overhaul Extends Asset's Life

Because the machine's life is extended by 3 years, the owner can now take 5 years of depreciation. The new annual depreciation of $1,400 (instead of $2,000) is calculated as follows:

Book value before extraordinary repair	$4,000
Extraordinary repair	+3,000
New book value	$7,000 ÷ 5 years = $1,400 per year

If the machine had an estimated residual value, it would be subtracted from the new book value.

Revenue Expenditures

Another type of expenditure occurs after an asset has been acquired. Revenue expenditures are payments made for ordinary maintenance of an asset or unnecessary or unreasonable situations. These expenditures occur on a regular basis and are recorded as expenses. Examples include changing oil and greasing a car, replacing window panes, changing tires on a truck, repainting a car, and adding a sun roof. When an expenditure is treated as a revenue expenditure, it is recorded on the income statement as an expense and thus reduces net income in the period in which it occurred. Now let's turn our attention to the disposal of certain plant assets.

Revenue expenditures
Payments made for ordinary maintenance of an asset or unnecessary or unreasonable situations.

Disposal of Plant Assets

We now move on to the basic accounting procedures followed when disposing of plant assets in the following ways:

A. Discarding plant assets

B. Selling plant assets

C. Exchanging plant assets

We present a different example for each category (A, B, or C). It is important to remember that depreciation is recorded up until the date a plant asset is disposed of. Take time to compare journal entries to T accounts in each example.

A. Disposal by Discarding Plant Assets. A company discards a plant asset when it is no longer operational (e.g., machinery or a truck that no longer works). That also means that no other company is willing to pay or exchange something for the asset.

Situation 1: No Gain or Loss. Boulder Company is disposing of a $7,000 truck with no residual value that has been fully depreciated (remember that it is possible to keep using a fully depreciated asset, but in this case the asset—the truck—is no longer in working order). Because the asset has been fully depreciated, it is not necessary to bring any depreciation up-to-date before disposing of it.

The journal entry shown in Figure 16.4 is made after disposing of the truck.

Figure 16.4
Disposing the Fully Depreciated
Truck

Accumulated Depreciation, Truck	7 0 0 0 00	
Truck		7 0 0 0 00

Here is how the ledger for these accounts would look after posting:

Truck		Accumulated Depreciation, Truck	
Dr.	Cr.	Dr.	Cr.
7,000	7,000	7,000	7,000

Therefore, the truck and the accumulated depreciation associated with it are off the books. Note that no gain or loss occurs here.

Situation 2: Loss on Disposal. Moore Company disposed of a partially depreciated truck. The truck, costing $6,000, was considered worthless (depreciation of $5,000 to date). Because nothing is received for this asset that has a book value of $1,000, the difference between the cost of the truck and the accumulated depreciation is a loss. The Loss on Disposal account is categorized as Other Expense on the income statement. Let's look at the journal entry for this loss on disposal (Figure 16.5) and see how the ledger would look after posting.

Figure 16.5
Loss on Disposal of Truck

Loss on Disposal of Plant Asset	1 0 0 0 00	
Accumulated Depreciation, Truck	5 0 0 0 00	
Truck		6 0 0 0 00

Truck		Accumulated Depreciation, Truck		Loss on Disposal of Plant Asset	
Dr.	Cr.	Dr.	Cr.	Dr.	Cr.
6,000	6,000	5,000	5,000	1,000	

Situation 3: Loss from Fire. Missan Company received a check for $500 from an insurance company, settling a claim on a machine costing $1,500 that was damaged by fire before the end of its useful life. The balance in Accumulated Depreciation was $900. Figure 16.6 shows the journal entry Missan Company records when it receives the $500 check.

Cash		5 0 0 00	
Loss from Fire		1 0 0 00	
Accumulated Depreciation, Machinery		9 0 0 00	
Machinery			1 5 0 0 00

Figure 16.6
Loss from Fire

A loss from the fire amounts to $100; the book value of the machine was $600 ($1,500 − $900), and the amount received from the insurance company was $500. Here is how the partial ledger would look after posting:

Machinery		Accumulated Depreciation, Machinery		Loss from Fire	
Dr.	Cr.	Dr.	Cr.	Dr.	Cr.
1,500	1,500	900	900	100	

Now our attention turns to situations when assets could be sold rather than discarded.

B. Disposal by Selling Plant Assets

Situation 4: Gain on Sale. Mason Company sold a truck costing $7,000 for $1,500 cash. The balance in Accumulated Depreciation is $6,000.

To see whether this sale results in a gain or loss, Mason Company must calculate whether the amount of cash received is greater or less than the book value of the truck. If the amount received is greater than the book value, the company realizes a gain. A gain on the sale of a plant asset is categorized as Other Income on the income statement. While it is income, it does not go to the revenue account, as that is reserved for monies generated through the regular business activities of the business. Let's look at the calculation:

Cost of truck	$7,000	Amount received	$1,500
Less accumulated depreciation	6,000	Less book value	1,000
Book value	$1,000	Gain on sale	$ 500

Because the sale results in a gain, the journal entry in Figure 16.7 is made.

Cash		1 5 0 0 00	
Accumulated Depreciation, Truck		6 0 0 0 00	
Truck			7 0 0 0 00
Gain on Sale of Plant Asset			5 0 0 00

Figure 16.7
Gain on Sale of Truck

Here is what the partial ledger would look like after posting:

Truck		Accumulated Depreciation, Truck	
Dr.	Cr.	Dr.	Cr.
7,000	7,000	6,000	6,000

Gain on Sale of Plant Asset	
Dr.	Cr.
	500

Situation 5: Loss on Sale. Let's assume that in the previous situation Mason Company receives only $900 cash for the truck.

Now let's look at the calculation Mason Company does to see whether the sale results in a loss or gain:

Cost of truck	$ 7,000
Less accumulated depreciation	−6,000
Book value	1,000
Amount received	− 900
Loss on sale	$ 100

When price is less than book value, the company realizes a loss. Because Mason's truck has a book value of $1,000 and the cash received is $900, the end result is a loss of $100 on the sale of the plant asset. This entry is categorized as Other Expense on the income statement. Figure 16.8 shows the journal entry prepared by Mason to record this loss.

Figure 16.8
Loss on Sale of Truck

	Dr.	Cr.
Cash	900 00	
Accumulated Depreciation, Truck	6000 00	
Loss on Sale of Plant Asset	100 00	
Truck		7000 00

Here is what the partial ledger would look like after posting:

Truck		Accumulated Depreciation, Truck		Cash	
Dr.	Cr.	Dr.	Cr.	Dr.	Cr.
7,000	7,000	6,000	6,000	900	

Loss on Sale of Plant Asset	
Dr.	Cr.
100	

The final category of disposal is exchanging a plant asset rather than discarding or selling it.

C. Disposal by Exchanging Plant Assets. Accounting rules can change or be modified over time to reflect changes in the economy or to clarify the recording of a particular transaction. One change (FASB Statement No. 153) concerns the exchange of a plant asset for another plant asset.

We will focus on that part of the change in accounting treatment that focuses on exchanges that have commercial substance. Commercial substance has been defined as when the future cash flows of an entity are expected to change materially as a result of the exchange. If a company were to exchange an older copying machine for a newer one that is not only faster, but has other capabilities as well like scanning and emailing, then that increase in productivity will lead to increased revenues, thus increasing the cash flow of the business. This exchange of assets could also result in a loss which also must be recognized when dealing with a transaction that falls under the umbrella of having commercial substance.

In recording the exchange, the old asset will be taken off the books and the new asset will be recorded at its market value. When there is an additional cash exchange in the transaction, which is called "boot", the receipt or payment of that cash is also brought into the calculation of gain or loss on the exchange. Plant Asset exchanges that do not have commercial substance will not be covered here.

Calculating Gain or Loss on an Exchange of Assets with Commercial Substance. Let's explore this from the perspective of two companies, Alpha and Beta. Alpha is exchanging some smaller equipment for some larger equipment that Beta has. Alpha has equipment that originally cost them $10,000 several years ago. As of the exchange, the equipment has accumulated depreciation of $3,000 and has a fair market value of $8,500. The transaction has commercial substance to Alpha.

Beta's equipment originally cost $20,000 and has accumulated depreciation of $11,000. The fair market value of Beta's equipment is $7,800. In addition, Beta Company has agreed to pay Alpha Company an additional $700 in cash, or boot, to close the deal. In this scenario, Alpha is the receiver of boot and Beta is the payer of boot. The transaction has commercial substance to Beta.

Situation 6: Gain on the Exchange of Equipment. First, we look at the transaction from the perspective of Alpha Company:

Market Value of the equipment received	$7,800
Plus: Cash received (boot)	700
Minus: Book Value of the equipment exchanged	(7,000)
Gain on the exchange	$1,500

Then, this information is recorded in the accounting records. Figure 16.9 shows the journal entry prepared by Alpha Company.

	Debit	Credit
Equipment (new)	7 8 0 0 00	
Accumulated Depreciation, Equipment	3 0 0 0 00	
Cash	7 0 0 00	
Equipment (old)		10 0 0 0 00
Gain on Exchange		1 5 0 0 00

Figure 16.9
Exchange of Equipment

The entry puts on the books the cost of the new equipment as well as recording the receipt of boot and the gain on the exchange and the removal of the old machine and the related accumulated depreciation. Note that cash is increased by the receipt of boot.

Situation 7: Loss on the Exchange of Equipment. Now, we will look at the transaction from the perspective of Beta company:

Market Value of the equipment received	$8,500
Less: Cash paid (boot)	(700)
Less: Book Value of the equipment exchanged	(9,000)
Loss on the exchange	($1,200)

Then, this information is recorded in the accounting records. Figure 16.10 shows the journal entry prepared by Beta Company.

	Debit	Credit
Equipment (new)	8 5 0 0 00	
Accumulated Depreciation, Equipment	11 0 0 0 00	
Loss on Exchange	1 2 0 0 00	
Cash		7 0 0 00
Equipment (old)		20 0 0 0 00

Figure 16.10
Exchange of Equipment

The entry puts on the books the cost of the new equipment as well as recording the payment of boot and the loss on the exchange and the removal of the old machine and the related accumulated depreciation. Note that cash is decreased by the payment of boot.

 **TRY IT!**

Journalize the following transactions:

201X

July 5   Sold a truck for $1,800 that cost $6,500 and had accumulated depreciation of $4,900.

7   Exchange a machine costing $17,000 with $14,000 accumulated depreciation and cash of $15,000 for a new machine with a market value of $20,000. This was a transaction with commercial substance.

(Depreciation is up-to-date.)

TRY IT!   **Solution Learning Unit 16-3**

Date	Account	Dr.	Cr.
201X			
July 5	Cash	1,800	
	Accumulated Depreciation, Truck	4,900	
	Truck		6,500
	Gain on sale		200
($6,500 − $4,900 = $1,600 BV; $1,800 − $1,600 = $200 Gain)			

Date	Account	Dr.	Cr.
July 7	Equipment (new)	20,000	
	Accumulated Depreciation, Equipment (old)	14,000	
	Equipment (old)		17,000
	Cash		15,000
	Gain on Exchange		2,000
($20,000 MV − $15,000 Cash − $3,000 BV = $2,000 Gain)			

LEARNING UNIT 16-4

L04

Transactions for Natural Resources and Intangible Assets

Depletion Amount of natural resources that has been exhausted by mining, pumping, and so forth for a period of time.

Another type of long-term asset is natural resources. Natural resources consist of natural assets such as oil, coal, or timber. The acquisition of oil wells or timber is recorded at cost, and as the oil or timber is extracted from the earth, the allocation of that cost occurs through a process known as depletion. Depletion is similar to the units-of-production method of depreciation, discussed earlier in the chapter, and is listed as an operating expense on the income statement.

Let's take the example of a coal deposit. If a coal deposit has 200,000 tons available and was purchased for $200,000, the depletion per ton is $1. Thus, if 91,000 tons were removed from the deposit in 201X, the depletion charge that year would be recorded as shown in Figure 16.11.

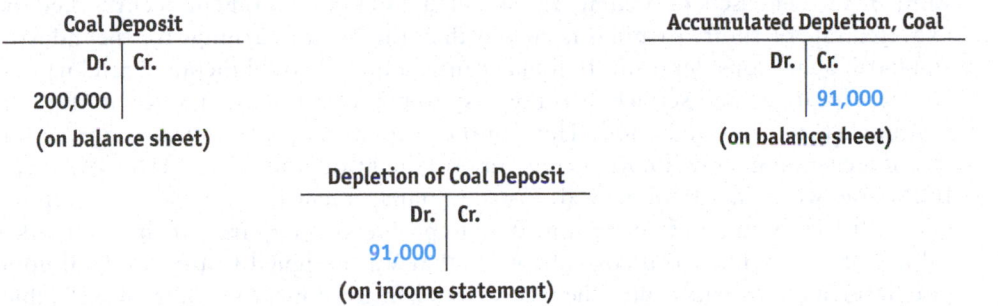

Figure 16.11

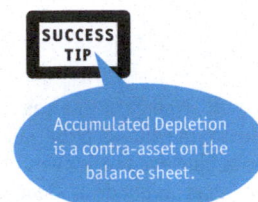

Accumulated Depletion is a contra-asset on the balance sheet.

Intangible Assets and the Concept of Impairment

Intangible assets are long-lived assets that have no physical existence but do represent valuable legal rights and monetary relationships that benefit a company. (In fact, Prepaid Insurance, Notes, and Accounts Receivable are intangible, but they are classified as *current* assets.) We are looking at intangible assets classified in the *long-term* asset section. Examples include patents, copyrights, franchises, and goodwill. Intangible assets are recorded at cost on the balance sheet and usually have no contra-accounts.

The process of allocating the cost of an intangible asset over all the periods it provides benefits is called *amortization*. The cost incurred in acquiring these assets is amortized; that means it is written off over a fixed number of years. Amortization Expense is an operating expense on the income statement.

Patents. A patent is an exclusive right to the owner to sell or produce his or her discovery or invention. Let's assume that on January 1, 201X, a patent costing $100,000 is amortized over 10 years. The adjusting entry shown in Figure 16.12 is made.

Amortize To charge a portion of an expenditure over a fixed number of years. Those assets with indefinite lives are not subject to amortization.

Amortization Expense Operating expense on the income statement relating to intangible assets.

Patent Exclusive right to sell or produce one's discovery or invention. A patent is good for 20 years.

Figure 16.12

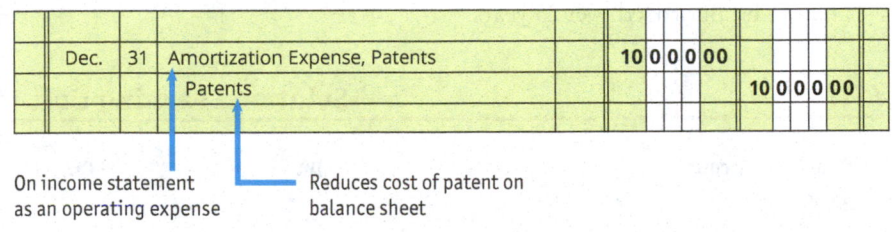

On income statement as an operating expense

Reduces cost of patent on balance sheet

Copyrights. Copyrights are exclusive rights granted to owners by the federal government to publish artistic, literary, or musical work. In the United States, a copyright is granted for the life of the creator and for 70 years thereafter. The cost of the copyright is recorded as an asset and amortized over its expected useful life in an account called Amortization Expense, Copyrights because the useful life of a copyright is short.

Copyright Exclusive right that is granted by the federal government to sell and reproduce literary, musical, or artistic works for a period of time.

Franchise Right granted by a business or government to produce or sell goods in a specific geographic region. Examples are Burger King and Holiday Inn.

Franchises. A franchise is the result of someone purchasing an exclusive privilege or right to sell a manufacturer's product or a service in a specifically defined geographical location. Holiday Inns, for example, are franchises. The useful life of many franchises are indefinite and thus not amortized.

Goodwill. When all or part of a business is purchased, the difference between the price paid and the fair value of the identifiable assets less liabilities (i.e., the fair value of the net assets of a company) is called goodwill. Goodwill occurs when the expected rate of future earnings is greater than the rate of earnings for the industry standard. Some considerations that may cause goodwill could include brand names, business location, and service. It is not easy to pinpoint the exact amount of goodwill in each accounting period. Thus, in the accounting profession it is agreed not to put a cost on goodwill until a company is bought or sold. Under U.S. GAAP and IFRS, goodwill is never amortized. Instead, management is responsible for valuing goodwill every year and to determine if an impairment is required. If the fair market value goes below historical cost (the value that was assigned to the goodwill upon purchase), an impairment must be recorded to bring it down to its fair market value. However, an increase in the fair market value would not be accounted for in the financial statements.

Goodwill When a business is purchased, the difference between the price paid and the fair value of the net assets is goodwill. Goodwill may depend on brand names, business location, service, or other elements; it is a valuable asset that plays an important part in the expected rate of future earnings of a business.

Impairment Value of an intangible asset that decreases and is written off.

Accounting for the Impairment of an Intangible Asset. Some intangible assets have indefinite lives and therefore are not subject to amortization, as shown above in regard to goodwill. If the intangible asset experiences some type of impairment, or loses value, you may write down the amount of the loss in value by a debit to Loss on Intangible Asset and a credit to the asset that suffered the impairment.

Now it's time to check your progress.

 **TRY IT!** _____ **Learning Unit 16-4**

Journalize the adjusting entry to amortize a patent from the following:

Cost of Patent purchased on January 1, $350,000

Patent to be amortized over 25 years

TRY IT! _____ **Solution Learning Unit 16-4**

Date	Account	Dr.	Cr.
201X			
Dec. 31	Amortization Expense, Patents	14,000	
	Patents		14,000

DEMONSTRATION SUMMARY PROBLEM

L01,2,3,4

Requirements

From the following information:

1. Calculate cost of new equipment.
2. Calculate depreciation for the first year for:
   a. Straight line
   b. Double declining balance
   c. Units of production

Facts:

Cost of machine $2,000
Freight $300
10% discount
$500 repair from dropping machine
Special base $400
Estimated life 5 years
Residual value $500
Output for life 4,000 units
300 units produced in the first year

3. Journalize the following exchange of equipment:

A piece of equipment costing $9,800 with $4,600 of accumulated depreciation was exchanged for a new piece of equipment having a market value of $8,000 and a cash payment of $3,000. This was a transaction with commercial substance.

Solutions

Requirement 1

$2,000 − 10%($2,000) = $1,800 + Freight $300 + Special Base $400 = $2,500

Cost of Equipment

Requirement 2

Straight line

$$\frac{\$2,500 - \$500}{5 \text{ years}} = \$400 \text{ year 1 depreciation}$$

Double declining balance

$100\%/5 = 20\% \times 2 = 40\%$

Year 1: $2,500 × 0.40 = $1,000

Units of production

$$\frac{\$2,500 - \$500}{4,000 \text{ units}} = \$0.50 \text{ per unit}$$

Year 1: 300 × $0.50 = $150

Requirement 3

Market value of equipment received		$8,000
Less:		
Book value of equipment exchanged	$5,200	
Cash paid	3,000	8,200
Loss in exchange		$ 200

Account	Dr.	Cr.
Equipment (new)	8,000	
Accum. Dep., Equip.	4,600	
Loss on Exchange	200	
Equipment (old)		9,800
Cash		3,000

Tips for Calculating Cost of Asset and Depreciation Methods

When figuring the cost of a piece of equipment, assembly, freight, discounts, and new base are added to the cost. Expenses caused by negligence are not added to the cost of the asset. When calculating depreciation for double declining balance, be sure *not* to subtract the residual value from the asset.

SUCCESS COACH

The following Success Tips are from Learning Units 16-1 to 16-4. Take the Do It Right Now Checkup and use the Check Your Score to see how you are doing. The Success Coach provides tips before each Checkup to help you avoid common accounting errors.

LU 16-1 Calculating the Cost of Property, Plant, and Equipment

Do It Right Tips: The cost of property, plant, and equipment is not just the price you pay to get it. Other costs like freight and assembly will be added to the asset. Keep in mind when doing improvements to land that some items will not be added to the cost of land. Remember that land is an asset that will not depreciate.

Do It Right Now Checkup: Answer true or false to the following statements.

1. Some land will depreciate.
2. Cost of freight will be subtracted from the cost of the asset.
3. Land improvements are a liability.
4. Addition of a new driveway is subject to depreciation.
5. The matching principle compares the cost of machines with the revenue they produce.

LU 16-2 Depreciation Methods

Do It Right Tips: The straight-line method does subtract residual value in its calculations. The units-of-production method subtracts residual value when calculating unit depreciation. The double declining-balance method does not subtract residual value in its calculations. The book value of a plant asset can never go below the residual value.

Do It Right Now Checkup: Answer true or false to the following statements.

1. The straight-line method has a different amount of depreciation each period.
2. The units-of-production method is based on the passage of time.
3. The straight-line method is an accelerated type of depreciation.
4. In the double declining-balance method, residual value is subtracted.
5. MACRS is never used for tax purposes.

LU 16-3 Journalizing Entries for Capital and Revenue Expenditures and Disposal of Plant Assets

Do It Right Tips: Capital expenditures can be broken down into three categories: additions or enlargements, extraordinary repairs, and betterments. For additions, benefits are received in the future; for extraordinary repairs, an asset's life is extended; and for betterments, an asset's life is not extended, but the asset's efficiency is improved.

Do It Right Now Checkup: Answer true or false to the following statements.

1. Adding a new school wing is a betterment.
2. Adding air conditioning is an extraordinary repair.
3. Replacing an engine in a car is an enlargement.
4. A gain on sale of plant asset could result from disposal by selling plant assets.
5. On an exchange of assets that has commercial substance, gains and losses are recognized in full.

LU 16-4 Transactions for Natural Resources and Intangible Assets

Do It Right Tips: Accumulated Depletion is a contra-asset on the balance sheet. Patents, copyrights, and franchises are examples of intangible assets. These intangible assets can be amortized as these intangibles are used up. Amortization expense is an operating expense on the income statement.

Do It Right Now Checkup: Answer true or false to the following statements.

1. Goodwill is the cost of an asset purchased plus the value of the assets identified.
2. A patent expires after 10 years.
3. Intangible assets are classified in the current liabilities section of the balance sheet.
4. A franchise's useful life is indefinite and thus is not amortized.
5. Intangible assets are really short-lived assets.

CHECK YOUR SCORE: Answers to the Do It Right Now Checkup

LU 16-1

1. False—Land does not depreciate.
2. False—Cost of freight will be added to the cost of the asset.
3. False—Land improvements are an asset.
4. True
5. True

LU 16-2

1. False—The straight-line method has the same amount of depreciation each period.
2. False—The units-of-production method is based on usage.
3. False—In the straight-line method, depreciation is the same amount each year and is not accelerated.
4. False—In the double declining-balance method, residual value is not subtracted from cost.
5. False—MACRS is used for tax purposes.

LU 16-3

1. False—Adding a new school wing is an addition.
2. False—Adding air conditioning is a betterment.
3. False—A new engine in a car is an extraordinary repair.
4. True
5. True

LU 16-4

1. False—Goodwill is the cost of a business purchased less the fair value of the net assets.
2. False—A patent expires after 20 years.
3. False—Intangible assets are classified in the Long-Term Assets section of the balance sheet.
4. False—A franchise can be amortized.
5. False—Intangible assets are really long-lived assets.

BLUEPRINT: KEY ACCOUNTS

Review of Key Accounts				
Account	Category*	↑	Normal Balance	Financial Statements Found on
Equipment	Plant Asset	Dr.	Dr.	Balance Sheet
Buildings	Plant Asset	Dr.	Dr.	Balance Sheet
Land	Plant Asset	Dr.	Dr.	Balance Sheet
Loss on Disposal of Plant Asset	Other Expense	Dr.	Dr.	Income Statement
Loss from Fire	Other Expense	Dr.	Dr.	Income Statement
Gain on Sale of Plant Asset	Other Income	Cr.	Cr.	Income Statement
Loss on Exchange of Machinery	Other Expense	Dr.	Dr.	Income Statement
Depletion of Natural Resource	Operating Expense	Dr.	Dr.	Income Statement
Accumulated Depletion	Contra-Asset	Cr.	Cr.	Balance Sheet
Coal Deposit	Natural Resource	Dr.	Dr.	Balance Sheet
Patents	Intangible Asset	Dr.	Dr.	Balance Sheet
Amortization Expense	Operating Expense	Dr.	Dr.	Income Statement
Copyrights, Franchises, or Goodwill	Intangible Assets	Dr.	Dr.	Balance Sheet
Loss of Goodwill	Other Expense	Dr.	Dr.	Income Statement

*We use Plant Assets to represent property, plant, and equipment.

Discussion Questions and Critical Thinking/Ethical Case

1. What types of costs are considered "reasonable and necessary" when determining the cost of an asset?

2. What is the purpose of the Land Improvements account?

3. What is the difference between revenue and capital expenditures?

4. What are three methods of calculating depreciation? Briefly explain the key points of each.

5. What is the purpose of the Modified Accelerated Cost Recovery System?

6. A betterment is a revenue expenditure. True or false? Please explain.

7. Which method of depreciation does *not* deduct residual value in its calculation?

8. When a plant asset is sold, a loss results if the cash received is greater than book value. Agree or disagree? Please explain.

9. A loss on an exchange of plant assets that has commercial substance must be recognized in the accounting records. True or false?

10. What is the purpose of the Accumulated Depletion account?

11. List and describe three intangible assets.

12. Pete went to an auto dealer to buy a new Jeep. The salesperson told Pete that cars really appreciate in value. He cited antique cars as a perfect example. The dealer went on to tell Pete that buying a car represents some great tax savings. He told Pete that leasing is getting less and less popular. Should Pete buy a new car? You make the call. Write down your recommendations to Pete.

Concept Checks

MyLabAccounting

Cost of Property, Plant, and Equipment

L01 *(5 min)*

1. Calculate the total cost of the machine given the following:

List price	$3,400
Cash discount	8%
Freight	$ 58
Assembly	350
Special foundation	63

Straight-Line Method

L02 *(10 min)*

2. Bob Rink depreciates his truck by the straight-line method. Calculate the yearly depreciation expense given the following:

Cost	$7,300
Residual value	$2,500
Service of useful life	4 years

Book Value

L02 *(10 min)*

3. If a machine had a cost of $6,400 with an accumulated depreciation of $630, what would be its book value?

(10 min) **LO2**

Units-of-Production Method

4. If Leo Stone depreciated his truck by the units-of-production method, calculate the first year's depreciation based on the following:

Cost	$ 4,840
Residual value	$ 1,600
Estimated mileage	54,000

The truck was driven 7,000 miles in year 1.

(10 min) **LO2**

Double Declining-Balance Method

5. If Mark Stone depreciated his truck by the double declining-balance method, calculate the depreciation expense for year 1.

Cost	$9,600
Residual value	$1,900
Service of useful life	4 years

(5 min) **LO3**

Capital and Revenue Expenditures

6. Identify each situation as a capital expenditure or revenue expenditure.

Situation	Capital Expenditure	Revenue Expenditure	Addition	Betterment/ Extraordinary Repair
a. New truck engine replaced				
b. New furnace filters				
c. Oil change on truck				
d. New addition on prep school				

(5 min) **LO3**

Loss and Gains

7. Complete the following:

Account	Category	Financial Statement Found on
a. Gain on Sale of Plant Assets		
b. Accumulated Depletion		
c. Loss on Disposal of Plant Assets		

(15 min) **LO3**

Exchange with Loss

8. In a transaction with commercial substance, April Co. exchanged an old machine costing $19,800 with Accumulated Depreciation of $10,400 for a new machine with a market value of $19,100 and a cash payment of $6,010.
   a. What is the book value of the old machine? What is the recognized gain on the exchange?
   b. Provide a journal entry to record the exchange.

(15 min) **LO3**

Exchange with Gain

9. Assume that in the scenario in Concept Check 8 the cash payment was $10,800.
   a. What is the loss on the exchange?
   b. Provide a journal entry to record the exchange.

Exercises

Set A

16A-1. Austin Company incurred the following expenditures to buy a new machine:
- Invoice, $31,000 less 13% cash discount.
- Freight charges, $480.
- Assembly charges, $1,400.
- Special base to support machine, $500.
- Machine dropped and repaired, $300.

What is the actual cost of the machine?

LO1 (15 min)

16A-2. From the following, prepare depreciation schedules for the first 2 years for (a) straight-line, (b) units-of-production, and (c) double declining-balance at twice the straight-line rate methods.
- Machine purchased on January 1, $1,480.
- Residual value, $300.
- Estimated useful life, 4 years.
- Total estimated output, 500 units.
- Output year 1, 100 units.
- Output year 2, 150 units.

LO2 (30 min)

16A-3. Falcon Co., whose accounting period ends on December 31, purchased a machine for $6,900 on January 1 with an estimated residual value of $760 and an estimated useful life of 5 years. Prepare depreciation schedules for the current as well as the following year using (a) straight-line and (b) double declining-balance at twice the straight-line rate methods.

LO2 (30 min)

16A-4. On May 1, 2018, Lincoln Company bought a patent at a cost of $6,120. It is estimated that the patent will give Lincoln a competitive advantage for 6 years. Record in general journal form amortization for 2018 and 2019. (Assume December 31 is the end of the accounting period for Lincoln.)

LO4 (10 min)

16A-5. Menard Company bought a light general-purpose truck for $8,500 on February 6, 2006. Calculate the yearly depreciation using the MACRS method.

LO2 (10 min)

Set B

16B-1. Ralph Company incurred the following expenditures to buy a new machine:
- Invoice, $35,000 less 8% cash discount
- Freight charges, $440.
- Assembly charges, $1,500.
- Special base to support machine, $502.
- Machine dropped and repaired, $390.

What is the actual cost of the machine?

LO1 (15 min)

16B-2. From the following, prepare depreciation schedules for the first 2 years for (a) straight-line, (b) units-of-production, and (c) double declining-balance at twice the straight-line rate methods.
- Machine purchased on January 1, $1,420.
- Residual value, $220.
- Estimated useful life, 4 years.
- Total estimated output, 600 units.
- Output year 1, 90 units.
- Output year 2, 190 units.

LO2 (30 min)

(30 min) **LO2**

16B-3. Lakeville Co., whose accounting period ends on December 31, purchased a machine for $6,920 on January 1 with an estimated residual value of $800 and an estimated useful life of 4 years. Prepare depreciation schedules for the current as well as the following year using (a) straight-line and (b) double declining-balance at twice the straight-line rate methods.

(10 min) **LO4**

16B-4. On May 1, 2018, April Company bought a patent at a cost of $5,940. It is estimated that the patent will give April a competitive advantage for 4 years. Record in general journal form amortization for 2018 and 2019. (Assume December 31 is the end of the accounting period for April.)

(10 min) **LO2**

16B-5. Harrison Company bought a light general-purpose truck for $9,000 on March 5, 2006. Calculate the yearly depreciation using the MACRS method.

MyLabAccounting

Problems

Set A

(30 min) **LO1,3**

S50 / **QB**

16A-1. Record the following transactions (all paid in cash except on March 24) in the general journal of Yellow Company:

Check Figure:
Feb. 18
Dr. Land Improvement $4,800
Cr. Cash $4,800

201X		
Feb.	5	Purchased land for $94,000. The $94,000 included attorney's fees of $5,700.
	18	Yellow Company decided to pave the parking lot for $4,800.
Mar.	24	Purchased a building for $94,000, putting down 32% and mortgaging the remainder.
	29	Bought equipment for $30,000. Freight and assembly were an additional $5,000.
May	10	Added a new wing for $180,000 to building that was purchased on March 24.
June	15	Performed ordinary repair work on equipment purchased March 29, $600, to maintain its normal operations.
July	1	Bought a truck for $15,000.
Oct.	15	Added a hydraulic loader to truck, $1,800.
Nov.	30	Truck purchased in July was brought in for grease and oil, $30.
Dec.	30	Overhauled truck's motor for $1,000, extending its life by more than 1 year.
Dec.	31	Changed tires on truck, $400.

(60 min) **LO2**

16A-2. On January 1, 2018, a machine was installed at Jillian Factory at a cost of $58,000. Its estimated residual value at the end of its estimated life of 4 years is $22,000. The machine is expected to produce 180,000 units with the following production schedule:

Check Figure:
(b) Book value end of year 2021
$22,000

- 2018: 37,000 units
- 2019: 35,000 units
- 2020: 41,000 units
- 2021: 67,000 units

Complete depreciation schedules for (a) straight-line, (b) units-of-production, and (c) double declining-balance at twice the straight-line rate methods.

(60 min) **LO2**

16A-3. On May 13, 2018, Cook Company bought equipment for $4,080. Its estimated life is 4 years with a residual value of $240. Prepare depreciation schedules for 2018, 2019, and 2020 for (a) straight-line and (b) double declining-balance at twice the straight-line rate methods.

Check Figure:
(b) Book value end of year 2020
$680

Set B

16B-1. Record the following transactions (all paid in cash except on March 24) in the general journal of Green Company:

201X		
Feb.	5	Purchased land for $89,000. The $89,000 included attorney's fees of $6,100.
	18	Green Company decided to pave the parking lot for $5,600.
Mar.	24	Purchased a building for $90,000, putting down 30% and mortgaging the remainder.
Mar.	29	Bought equipment for $32,000. Freight and assembly were an additional $5,000.
May	10	Added a new wing for $190,000 to building that was purchased on March 24.
June	15	Performed ordinary repair work on equipment purchased March 29, $1,000, to maintain its normal operations.
July	1	Bought a truck for $15,500.
Oct.	15	Added a hydraulic loader to truck, $2,200.
Nov.	30	Truck purchased in July was brought in for grease and oil, $38.
Dec.	30	Overhauled truck's motor for $1,400, extending its life by more than 1 year.
Dec.	31	Changed tires on truck, $500.

Check Figure:
Oct 15:
Dr. Truck $2,200
Cr. Cash $2,200

16B-2. On January 1, 2018, a machine was installed at Dunbar Factory at a cost of $53,000. Its estimated residual value at the end of its estimated life of 4 years is $20,000. The machine is expected to produce 66,000 units with the following production schedule:

- 2018: 8,000 units
- 2019: 25,000 units
- 2020: 18,000 units
- 2021: 15,000 units

Complete depreciation schedules for (a) straight-line, (b) units-of-production, and (c) double declining-balance at twice the straight-line rate methods.

Check Figure:
(b) Book value end of year 2021
$20,000

16B-3. On September 13, 2018, Cagnacci Company bought equipment for $6,000. Its estimated life is 4 years with a residual value of $288. Prepare depreciation schedules for 2018, 2019, and 2020 for (a) straight-line and (b) double declining-balance at twice the straight-line rate methods.

Check Figure:
(b) Book value end of year 2020 $1,250

Financial Report Problem

MyLabAccounting

Reading Amazon's Annual Report

Go to **https://tinyurl.com/slaterca14e** to access Amazon's 2016 Annual Report. Go to page 51 and find out balance in Accumulated Depreciation for 2016.

Partagernship

CHAPTER PREVIEW: ACCOUNTING IN ACTION

John Abboud has operated his law office as a sole proprietorship for the past 20 years. In the local media, including the business's Facebook page, he announced that he will be taking on a new partner and forming a new partnership for his law practice. A partnership is a common form of ownership for accountants, doctors, and lawyers. In this chapter, we look at the responsibilities of partners along with how cash is split when a partnership dissolves.

Learning Objectives–Relating Accounting Theory By Unit

LO1   Journalize Entries to Form a Partnership

LO2   Journalize Entries to Record Division of Net Income and Net Loss Among Partners

LO3   Journalize Entries to Record Admissions and Withdrawals of Partners

LO4   Journalize Entries to Record Liquidation of a Partnership

Partnership Association of two or more persons who act as co-owners of a business.

Uniform Partnership Act Laws enacted in most states that govern how a partnership is formed, operated, and liquidated.

Up to this point we have been using the sole proprietorship form of business organization in discussing the accounting process. We are now ready to look at another form of business organization, the partnership.

A partnership, as defined by the Uniform Partnership Act, is "an association of two or more persons to carry on as co-owners of a business for profit." Examples of partnerships include service businesses and professional practitioners, such as physicians, dentists, attorneys, and accountants. Many small wholesale as well as retail companies are formed as partnerships. Your local convenience store may be a partnership.

The recording of business transactions involving assets, liabilities, revenue, and expenses is handled the same for both a sole proprietorship and a partnership. The major difference in recording business transactions for these two forms of organizations lies in the equity account(s). A sole proprietorship has only one capital and withdrawals account, whereas in a partnership each partner has his or her own separate capital and withdrawals account. First, we look at the characteristics of a partnership and how it is formed.

LEARNING UNIT 17-1

L01

Journalizing Entries to Form a Partnership

It is quite easy to form a partnership. Partnership agreements can be found by searching the Internet. Many Internet sites, such as **legalzoom.com™**, list what to do and the forms needed to create a partnership. When two or more people agree orally or in writing to be partners, a contract results. Although the oral agreement is binding, it makes more sense to seek legal advice and have a formal written agreement prepared. Putting agreements in writing may minimize conflicts in the future. This written agreement, which formalizes the partners' relationship, is called the articles of partnership.

Articles of partnership Written contract that spells out the details of the agreement among the partners.

Some things that should be included in the written articles of partnership are:

1. Name and address of each partner, along with the date of agreement
2. Rights and responsibilities of each partner
3. Amount that each partner is investing
4. Specific manner in which partners' profits or losses will be shared
5. Provisions for one or more partners leaving the partnership
6. How new partners will be admitted
7. How assets will be distributed if the business is completely terminated
8. How accounting records will be maintained

Characteristics of Partnerships

Limited life Partnership is dissolved by admission, withdrawal, or death of a partner. Although the partnership is dissolved, the operations of the business can continue if a new partnership is formed.

Limited Life. A partnership has a limited life. An advantage is that it does have more flexibility than some other forms of ownership to react to the marketplace because legal restrictions are minimal. However, when a change takes place in the membership of a partnership—when someone new joins or when someone leaves—the partnership is dissolved. Dissolution can occur if a partner dies, becomes incapacitated, goes bankrupt, or withdraws. Admission of a new partner or expiration of the life of the partnership as stated in the articles of partnership could also result in the partnership being dissolved. If a partnership is dissolved, a new partnership can be formed and the business can continue to operate without any interruptions.

Mutual agency Act of a single partner is binding on all members of the partnership.

Mutual Agency. Mutual agency means that the actions of one partner are binding on all the other partners. For example, Jill Joy, who is a partner in a merchandise business, enters into a contract with Flynn Company to lease a building. This contract is binding on all Jill's partners because the transaction was within the scope of the business. If Jill, on the other hand, entered into a contract to provide *legal* work to another company, it would not be binding on the partners because legal work is not in the normal scope of a merchandise company.

Mutual agency allows each partner to act for the partnership as a whole because all the partners are agents for the business. Poor judgment on the part of one partner, however, could, through mutual agency, result in heavy losses to all partners. An advantage of a partnership is that a credit rating is usually higher because more than one partner is responsible for the company's debt. So the mutual agency characteristic of a partnership can be both an advantage and a disadvantage.

Unlimited Liability. Unlimited liability means that if a partnership is unable to pay its obligations, all general partners are individually liable to cover with their *personal* assets the obligations the partnership cannot meet. Think of a general partner as one who risks not only the personal investment in the partnership but also personal assets. If the personal assets of some of the partners are exhausted, the other partners have the responsibility for covering the debts outstanding. Note that a few exceptions apply to this rule. First, a partner just entering an existing partnership is not held liable for past obligations before joining the partnership. Second, in some states, some members of a partnership have liability only up to the amount they invested in the partnership. These people are called limited partners.

Co-ownership of Property. Co-ownership of property means that all partners share all the assets of the partnership. For example, if Bill Boyd invests cash and Joyce Regan invests a building in their partnership, the assets become the property of the partnership. Joyce no longer has a specific claim to the building. Ownership is now shared by Bill and Joyce.

Taxation. The partnership itself does not pay taxes, but the partners pay taxes on the share of net income that has been allocated to each of them. (Note that the tax is on the net income and not on the amount that a partner has withdrawn from the partnership.) Remember that in a sole proprietorship, like a partnership, owners are not paid salaries. They take withdrawals from the company. A partnership then is defined for tax purposes as a "flow-through entity" as the net result of revenues and expenses flows through to the individual partners for reporting on their individual tax returns.

Formation of a Partnership

Let's look now at the journal entries that are needed when a partnership is formed. The important point is that when partners invest in a business, the assets should be recorded at their current fair market value. This value is established by having the assets appraised. Partners have to agree on the amounts assigned to the noncash assets. These costs now represent the true acquisition cost to the partnership. Appraising of assets at their current fair market value avoids inequities in the balances of the capital accounts of the partners.

Let's look at the following situation: On June 1, 201X, Jane Reedy and Bill Burr enter into a partnership. Reedy invests from her old business $9,000 cash and store equipment worth $25,000 with accumulated depreciation of $5,000. The current appraised value of the equipment is $28,000. Also on the books is Accounts Receivable of $2,000 with an Allowance for Doubtful Accounts of $500. The partnership will take on the responsibility for a $6,000 note issued by Reedy. Burr invests $20,000 cash in the partnership. The journal entries in Figure 17.1 record this information.

Unlimited liability Partners may be personally liable for debts of the partnership.

General partner Partner who has unlimited liability.

Limited partner Partner's liability is limited to the amount of investment in the partnership.

Co-ownership of property Each partner owns a share of the assets.

201X June	1	Cash	9 0 0 0 00		
		Accounts Receivable	2 0 0 0 00		
		Store Equipment	28 0 0 0 00		
		Allowance for Doubtful Accounts		5 0 0 00
		Notes Payable		6 0 0 0 00
		J. Reedy, Capital		32 5 0 0 00
	1	Cash	20 0 0 0 00		
		B. Burr, Capital		20 0 0 0 00

Figure 17.1
Investing into a Partnership

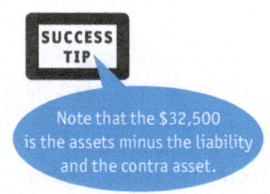

Note that the $32,500 is the assets minus the liability and the contra asset.

Note that the store equipment has no accumulated depreciation associated with it because the appraised value is now the new book value. If the old book value was used, Reedy's capital would be understated. Reedy should not be penalized because the value of her equipment has increased. Any additional investments made by the partners will result in a journal entry that debits Cash and credits the partners' capital accounts.

Now let's check your progress.

 **TRY IT!**   **Learning Unit 17-1**

Journalize the formation for the following partnership:

July 8, 201X, Phil Ackerman and Judy Spencer enter into a partnership. Ackerman invests $2,000 of his cash and computer equipment worth $9,400 with accumulated depreciation of $3,400. The current appraised value of the equipment is $11,900. The partnership will take the responsibility of a $3,200 note issued by Phil Ackerman. Judy Spencer will invest $6,500 cash into the partnership.

TRY IT!   **Solution Learning Unit 17-1**

Date		Account	Dr.	Cr.
201X				
July	8	Cash	2,000	
		Computer Equipment	11,900	
		Notes Payable		3,200
		P. Ackerman, Capital		10,700
	8	Cash	6,500	
		J. Spencer, Capital		6,500

LEARNING UNIT 17-2

L02

Journalizing Entries to Record Division of Net Income and Net Loss Among Partners

Partners work so as to gain a share of the net income of their partnership; they do not earn salaries as their employees do. As a matter of fact, they cannot legally hire themselves and pay themselves a salary. Net income and net loss can be divided among partners in several ways based on partners' differing talents and abilities, time spent working for the partnership, and amount of investment in the partnership.

We need to introduce two terms to help describe how net income is divided among partners. One way is through a salary allowance. A salary allowance is not the same thing as the Salary Expense involved in paying employees, and it is not in fact a salary at all; it is just a way to divide net income. It is usually used to account for unequal service contributions among partners, such as if one partner worked full time for the business and the other put in only 20 hours a week. In such a case, the partners might agree to pay $1,000 per week to the first partner and $500 per week to the other. This amount would come out of the net income earned by the partnership.

Another way to divide net income among partners is through interest allowance. This method is usually used when partners have put different amounts into the partnership as initial investment plus any additional investment. Let's say that one partner has invested $5,000 and the other one has invested $10,000. At the end of the accounting period, they

Salary allowance Mechanism for dividing earnings of a partnership based on personal services provided by the partners (not an expense).

Interest allowance Mechanism for dividing earnings of a partnership based on a percentage of capital balances of the partners (not an expense).

would each get 10% interest on their investment: The first would get $500 ($5,000 × 0.10) and the second would get $1,000 ($10,000 × 0.10). This method is used because it would be unfair to give half of net income to the first partner when that partner invested only one-third of the capital.

Now let's look at several different situations to see how a partnership might divide its net income or net loss. These situations will be based on the following facts. Dot Alexander, John Sullivan, and Sheldon Brown invested $8,000, $6,000, and $4,000, respectively, in a partnership. The partnership in the first year had a net income of $24,300.

Situation 1. Partners could not agree on how to share net income of $24,300. The law states that if an agreement is not reached on how partners share earnings, it will be divided equally.

$$24,300 ÷ 3 = 8,100 \text{ to each partner}$$

The journal entry at closing to allocate net income will look like the one in Figure 17.2. Note that the closing process now divides the net income into the *three* capital accounts. In a sole proprietorship, the net income was closed to the one capital account.

	201X								
	Dec.	31	Income Summary			24 3 0 0 00			
			Dot Alexander, Capital				8 1 0 0 00		
			John Sullivan, Capital				8 1 0 0 00		
			Sheldon Brown, Capital				8 1 0 0 00		

Figure 17.2
Share Net Income Equally

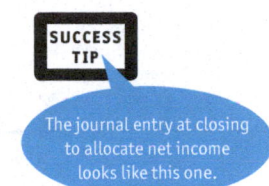

SUCCESS TIP

The journal entry at closing to allocate net income looks like this one.

If this situation involved net loss instead of net income, each capital account would be debited and the credit would be to Income Summary.

Situation 2. Partners share net income of $24,300 in the ratio of their beginning capital investments.

STEP 1: Find the total capital invested:

Alexander	$ 8,000
Sullivan	6,000
Brown	4,000
	$18,000

STEP 2: Set up a ratio (fraction) of each partner's investment to the total capital invested ($18,000):

Alexander	Sullivan	Brown
$ 8,000	$ 6,000	$ 4,000
$18,000	$18,000	$18,000

STEP 3: Multiply the ratio in step 2 by the amount of income to be distributed.

Alexander: $\dfrac{\$ 8,000}{\$18,000} \times \$24,300 = \$10,800$

Sullivan: $\dfrac{\$ 6,000}{\$18,000} \times \$24,300 = \$ 8,100$

Brown: $\dfrac{\$ 4,000}{\$18,000} \times \$24,300 = \$ 5,400$

The journal entry at closing to allocate net income will look like the one in Figure 17.3.

Figure 17.3
Share Net Income Based on Ratio of Investments

201X					
Dec.	31	Income Summary	24 3 0 0 00		
		Dot Alexander, Capital		10 8 0 0 00	
		John Sullivan, Capital		8 1 0 0 00	
		Sheldon Brown, Capital		5 4 0 0 00	

The ratio in step 2 may be used if the net income of the company is related only to the amount the partners have invested. Alexander has invested the most ($8,000) and thus receives the largest portion of the earnings ($10,800).

Alternative to Ratio Based on Investment Only. Some partnerships share net income according to an agreed-upon ratio. If a ratio is 3:2:1, it means that 3/6 of net income goes to one partner, 2/6 to the next, and 1/6 to the last. Such a fractional ratio could be based on service as well as capital investment. Such ratios are called profit-and-loss ratios.

Profit-and-loss ratio Agreed-upon ratio used to divide earnings or losses of a partnership.

Situation 3. Partners' services and capital contributions are unequal, but net income does cover salary and interest allowances. The salary allowance is used to compensate for the partners' unequal service contributions, and the interest allowance is used to compensate for their unequal investments. One way to share net income in this situation is as illustrated in the following example:

a. Annual salary allowance of $6,000 to Alexander, $6,000 to Sullivan, and $9,000 to Brown.

b. Ten percent interest on each partner's capital investment.

c. Remaining net income or net loss shared equally.

	Alexander		Sullivan		Brown		Total
a. Salary Allowance	$6,000	+	$6,000	+	$9,000	=	$21,000
b. Interest on Capital Investments							
0.10 × $8,000	800						
0.10 × $6,000		+	600				
0.10 × $4,000				+	400		
Total Interest Allowance						=	1,800
Total Salary and Interest Allowances	$6,800	+	$6,600	+	$9,400	=	$22,800
c. Net Income	$24,300						
Less: Salary and Interest Allowances	−22,800						
Income to Be Distributed Equally	$ 1,500	500		500		500	1,500
Share of Net Income to Partners		$7,300	+	$7,100	+	$9,900	=	$24,300

The journal entry at closing to allocate net income will look like Figure 17.4.

Figure 17.4
Net Income Left After Salary and Interest Allowances

201X					
Dec.	31	Income Summary	24 3 0 0 00		
		Dot Alexander, Capital		7 3 0 0 00	
		John Sullivan, Capital		7 1 0 0 00	
		Sheldon Brown, Capital		9 9 0 0 00	

Note that in this case, some net income remained after salary and interest allowances and was distributed equally. In the next situation we see that net income doesn't always cover all the salary and interest allowances.

Situation 4. Partners' services and capital contributions are unequal, but net income does not cover salary and interest allowances. Assume (1) net income is $20,700 and (2) salary and interest allowances are the same as in Situation 3.

Whether net income covers the salaries and interest makes *no difference* in calculating the salary or interest allowance. As shown in the accompanying calculation, the total of salaries and allowances is $22,800. Net income is only $20,700; thus, the partners must all share the difference by $700 each in a reduction of the profits allocated to them. Remember that items (a) and (b) are calculated first *before* we consider the difference between net income and the amount that is needed to cover salary and interest allowances. It is not necessary to think of the $700 deficit (negative reduction to each partner) as a loss; think of it as a reduction in the share of profits because not all the interest and salary allowances were covered.

Deficit Amount by which net income falls short of salary and interest allowances. Also an abnormal, or debit, balance in a partner's capital account.

		Alexander		Sullivan		Brown		Total
a. Salary Allowance		$6,000	+	$6,000	+	$9,000	=	$21,000
b. Interest on Capital Investments:								
0.10 × $8,000		800						
0.10 × $6,000			+	600				
0.10 × $4,000					+	400		
Total Interest Allowance							=	1,800
Total Salary and Interest Allowances		$6,800	+	$6,600	+	$9,400	=	$22,800
c. Net Income	$ 20,700							
Less: Salary and Interest Allowances	−22,800							
Deficit to Be Shared Equally	($ 2,100)	(700)		(700)		(700)		(2,100)
Share of Net Income to Partners		$6,100	+	$5,900	+	$8,700	=	$20,700

The journal entry at closing to allocate the deficit will look like Figure 17.5.

	201X							
	Dec.	31	Income Summary		20 7 0 0 00			
			Dot Alexander, Capital			6 1 0 0 00		
			John Sullivan, Capital			5 9 0 0 00		
			Sheldon Brown, Capital			8 7 0 0 00		

Figure 17.5
Deficit to Be Shared Equally by All Partners

Partnership Financial Statement

Just as we had a statement of owner's equity for a sole proprietorship, we can prepare a statement of partners' equity. The statement in Figure 17.6 was prepared from Situation 3.

Statement of partners' equity
Financial statement that reveals each partner's ownership percentage of the firm's capital. The ending figure for the firm's capital is then placed on the balance sheet.

Figure 17.6
Statement of Partners' Equity

ALEXANDER, SULLIVAN, AND BROWN STATEMENT OF PARTNERS' EQUITY FOR YEAR ENDED DECEMBER 31, 201X			
	Alexander	Sullivan	Brown
Capital Balances, January 1, 201X	$ 8 0 0 0 00	$ 6 0 0 0 00	$ 4 0 0 0 00
Add: Net Income for 201X	7 3 0 0 00	7 1 0 0 00	9 9 0 0 00
Subtotal	$ 15 3 0 0 00	$ 13 1 0 0 00	$ 13 9 0 0 00
Less: Withdrawals	4 0 0 0 00	5 0 0 0 00	8 0 0 0 00
Capital Balances, December 31, 201X	$ 11 3 0 0 00	$ 8 1 0 0 00	$ 5 9 0 0 00

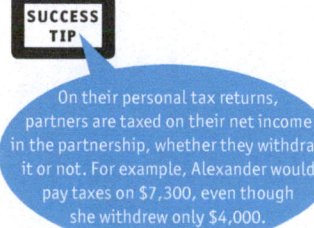

SUCCESS TIP

On their personal tax returns, partners are taxed on their net income in the partnership, whether they withdraw it or not. For example, Alexander would pay taxes on $7,300, even though she withdrew only $4,000.

The ending balances for each partner would then be reported on the balance sheet. Think of the statement of partners' equity as a supporting document to arrive at a new figure for each capital account on the balance sheet.

Now let's check your progress.

 **TRY IT!**   **Learning Unit 17-2**

From the following partnership, calculate the amount of deficit distribution that will affect Abigail Edelman and Megan Anderson after calculating Salary Allowance, Interest Allowance, and distribution of Net Income.

Salary Allowance	$58,000 Abigail Edelman
	49,000 Megan Anderson

Interest Allowance is 12% of their beginning balances (Edelman, $154,000; Anderson, $66,000).

Remainder of the net income is divided equally. Net income for the year was $130,600.

TRY IT!   **Solution Learning Unit 17-2**

	Edelman		Anderson	=	Total
Salary Allowance	$58,000	+	$49,000	=	$107,000
Interest on Capital Investment	18,480	+	7,920	=	26,400
Total Salary and Interest Allowances	$76,480	+	$56,920	=	$133,400
Net Income less Salary and Interest Allowances ($130,600 − $133,400 = $2,800)	(1,400)	+	(1,400)	=	(2,800)
Share of Net Income to Partners	$75,080	+	$55,520	=	$130,600

LEARNING UNIT 17-3

L03 ▶

Journalizing Entries to Record Admissions and Withdrawals of Partners

This unit looks at how the capital structure of a partnership may change due to (1) admission of a new partner or (2) withdrawal of a partner.

Admission of a New Partner

Joining a partnership can happen in two ways:

Purchase of an equity interest
Transfer of ownership between an existing partner and a new partner.

1. Purchase of an equity interest from one or more of the existing partners.
2. Make an investment in the business.

No matter what approach is taken, the admission of a new partner will technically dissolve the old partnership. Let's look at how Peter Mix bought into the partnership of Jones and Ryan.

Buying an Equity Interest from an Original Partner. The partners' balance sheet of Jones and Ryan looked as shown in Figure 17.7 before Peter Mix purchased an interest in the company (there are no liabilities).

JONES AND RYAN				
Assets		**Partners' Equity**		
Cash	$ 5 0 0 0 00	Jones, Capital	$ 6 0 0 0 00	
Other Assets	7 0 0 0 00	Ryan, Capital	6 0 0 0 00	
Total Assets	$ 12 0 0 0 00	Total Equities	$ 12 0 0 0 00	

Figure 17.7
Balances Before Mix Bought an
Equity Interest

On April 3 Ryan sold Peter Mix his equity in the company for $9,000. The entry is recorded on the books of the partnership as shown in Figure 17.8.

Apr.	3	Ryan, Capital	6 0 0 0 00	
		Mix, Capital		6 0 0 0 00

Figure 17.8
Sale of Equity to Peter Mix

The end result of this transaction is to transfer the $6,000 capital account of Ryan to Mix. Note that the difference in the selling price of $3,000 ($9,000 − $6,000) doesn't affect the books of the partnership because the cash is paid directly to Ryan and not to the business. Think of it as a side transaction. All this transaction does is transfer the equity amounts. Any personal profit the former partner makes is of a personal nature and is not reflected in the accounts of the business.

Keep in mind also that Jones must agree to the equity exchange by Ryan if Mix is to become a partner. If Jones agrees, a new partnership contract is formed along with new profit or loss ratios. If Jones doesn't accept Mix as a partner, Mix still has the right to share in Ryan's profits and losses, but he will have no voice in the running of the company until he is admitted as a partner.

Investing in an Existing Partnership. As an alternative to buying equity from an existing partner, one may simply invest assets in the partnership on one's own. For example, assume Roger Foss wants to invest cash in a business on July 8 so that he will have a one-third interest in the partnership. Before Roger makes his investment, the partners' equity is as follows:

Partners' Equity	
B. Blee, Capital	$3,000
A. Jarvis, Capital	1,000

Roger wants one-third interest, and the $4,000 ($3,000 + $1,000) represents two-thirds interest. One-third interest would be $2,000 and, therefore, Roger will have to contribute $2,000 to gain the one-third interest.

$4,000	Blee and Jarvis, Capital
+$2,000	Roger's Contribution
$6,000	Total Capital with Roger's Contribution

The entry to record the admission of Roger Foss would be as shown in Figure 17.9.

July	8	Cash	2 0 0 0 00	
		R. Foss, Capital		2 0 0 0 00

Figure 17.9
Admission of a New Partner

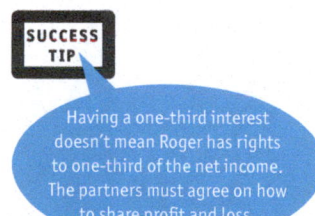

Having a one-third interest doesn't mean Roger has rights to one-third of the net income. The partners must agree on how to share profit and loss.

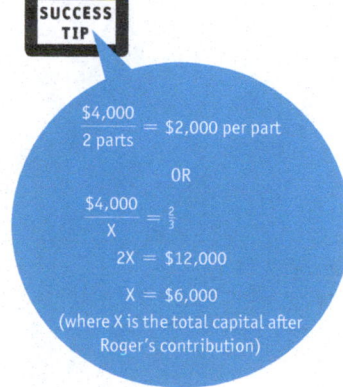

$$\frac{\$4,000}{2 \text{ parts}} = \$2,000 \text{ per part}$$

OR

$$\frac{\$4,000}{X} = \frac{2}{3}$$

$$2X = \$12,000$$

$$X = \$6,000$$

(where X is the total capital after Roger's contribution)

Recording a Bonus to the Old Partners When Admitting a New Partner. When the equity of a partnership in reality is worth more than the amounts recorded in its accounting records, the partners may require an incoming partner to pay an additional amount or **bonus** that will increase old partners' equity. This situation could result if a company had an outstanding earnings record with even higher expectations in the future compared with other companies in the industry. Let's see how it would work from the previous example of Roger Foss, assuming the partners Blee and Jarvis on July 8 require a payment of $3,500 (instead of $2,000) to give Foss a one-third interest.

Bonus When a new partner is admitted, he or she may pay more or less than equity interest. If the new partner pays more, the old partners share a bonus in the profit-and-loss ratio. Of course, the opposite could result, and the new partner could receive a bonus if he or she invests less than equity interest.

Blee and Jarvis, Capital	$4,000
Investment of Foss	+ 3,500
Capital of New Partnership	$7,500
$\frac{1}{3}$ Interest of Foss $\left(\frac{1}{3} \times \$7,500\right)$	$2,500

Foss only needed to invest $2,000 to gain a one-third interest, but the old partners required $3,500.

Note that the $1,000 ($3,500 − $2,500) difference represents the bonus the old partners will share. The old partners share all losses and gains equally. Thus, the journal entry to admit Foss is as shown in Figure 17.10.

Figure 17.10
Admission of a Partner Resulting in a Bonus to the Old Partners

July	8	Cash	3 5 0 0 00		
		B. Blee, Capital		5 0 0 00	
		A. Jarvis, Capital		5 0 0 00	
		R. Foss, Capital		2 5 0 0 00	

Recording a Bonus to a New Partner. A firm is often anxious to bring into the company a new partner who has special skills, business contacts, or abilities. The old partners then must accept a reduction in their capital balances to make up the difference in what the new partner invests compared with the new partner's capital balance. Let's play back the previous example by looking at how "anxious" Blee and Jarvis are to obtain the managerial talents of Roger Foss. Now the old partners have required Foss on July 8 to invest only $1,400 to have a one-third interest in the business.

Blee and Jarvis, Capital	$4,000
Investment of Foss	1,400
Capital of New Partnership	$5,400
$\frac{1}{3}$ Interest of Foss $\left(\frac{1}{3} \times \$5,400\right)$	$1,800

Note that Foss invested only $1,400, while in reality he needed to invest $1,800. Thus, the old partners are absorbing equally the bonus to Foss of $400 ($1,800 − $1,400) by reducing their capital balance. The journal entry to record the admitting of Foss to the partnership is as shown in Figure 17.11.

Figure 17.11
Journalizing Bonus to Partners

July	8	Cash	1 4 0 0 00		
		B. Blee, Capital	2 0 0 00		
		A. Jarvis, Capital	2 0 0 00		
		R. Foss, Capital		1 8 0 0 00	

Recording Permanent Withdrawal of a Partner

When a partnership contract is drawn up, it usually states the procedures to be followed when a partner withdraws. Often the procedures include an audit of the accounting records and the adjustment of the assets to their current fair market value. These steps are done so that the capital of the retiring partner does indeed reflect the current value of his or her equity. Let's look at (1) the balance sheet before revaluation of Ring, Rotter, and Freeze; (2) the entry made to record revaluation; (3) the new, revalued balance sheet; and (4) withdrawal of J. Freeze (assume no liabilities). Partners of Ring, Rotter, and Freeze have a profit-and-loss ratio of $\frac{1}{2}$, $\frac{1}{4}$, and $\frac{1}{4}$, respectively.

1. The balance sheet before revaluation is shown in Figure 17.12.

Figure 17.12 Balance Sheet Before Revaluation

RING, ROTTER, AND FREEZE					
Assets			Partners' Equity		
Cash		$2 2 0 0 00	A. Ring, Capital		$4 4 0 0 00
Merchandise Inventory		3 2 0 0 00	B. Rotter, Capital		2 0 0 0 00
Store Equipment	$4 0 0 0 00		J. Freeze, Capital		2 0 0 0 00
Less: Acc. Dep.	1 0 0 0 00	3 0 0 0 00			
Total Assets		$8 4 0 0 00	Total Equities		$8 4 0 0 00

2. When the accountant completes the audit, it is reported that inventory, owing to market conditions, is overvalued by $400. The journal entry to record the revaluation is shown in Figure 17.13.

Figure 17.13 Journal Entry to Record Revaluation

Nov.	30	A. Ring, Capital	2 0 0 00	
		B. Rotter, Capital	1 0 0 00	
		J. Freeze, Capital	1 0 0 00	
		Merchandise Inventory		4 0 0 00

SUCCESS TIP

Ring $= \frac{1}{2} \times \$400$
$= \$200$
Rotter $= \frac{1}{4} \times \$400$
$= \$100$
Freeze $= \frac{1}{4} \times \$400$
$= \$100$

3. Here is the new, revalued balance sheet (Figure 17.14).

Figure 17.14 New Revalued Balance Sheet

RING, ROTTER, AND FREEZE					
Assets			Partners' Equity		
Cash		$2 2 0 0 00	A. Ring, Capital		$4 2 0 0 00
Merchandise Inventory		2 8 0 0 00	B. Rotter, Capital		1 9 0 0 00
Store Equipment	$4 0 0 0 00		J. Freeze, Capital		1 9 0 0 00
Less Acc. Dep.	1 0 0 0 00	3 0 0 0 00			
Total Assets		$8 0 0 0 00	Total Equities		$8 0 0 0 00

4. The entry to record the withdrawal of Freeze from the partnership is shown in Figure 17.15.

Nov.	30	J. Freeze, Capital	1 9 0 0 00	
		Cash		1 9 0 0 00

Figure 17.15
Withdrawal of Partner

Recording Permanent Withdrawal When a Partner Takes Assets of Less Value Than Book Equity

In the last situation, Freeze received the revalued amount of his capital by taking out $1,900 in cash. Often, when a partner retires, the assets may not be revalued. In this case, the partners have to agree whether the assets are overvalued and whether the withdrawing partner should settle for less than the book value of his or her equity. For example, let's look at the balance sheet for Joll, Smoot, and Jangles (Figure 17.16) to see what will happen if Smoot settles for less than his book value on July 31 (assume a profit-and-loss ratio of 2:2:1).

Figure 17.16
Balance Sheet Before Settlement

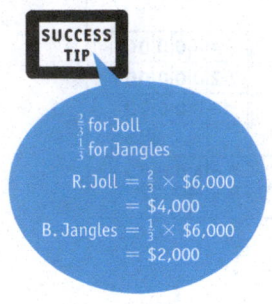

SUCCESS TIP

$\frac{2}{3}$ for Joll
$\frac{1}{3}$ for Jangles

R. Joll $= \frac{2}{3} \times \$6,000$
$= \$4,000$
B. Jangles $= \frac{1}{3} \times \$6,000$
$= \$2,000$

JOLL, SMOOT, AND JANGLES				
Assets		**Partners' Equity**		
Cash	$25 0 0 0 00	R. Joll, Capital	$28 0 0 0 00	
Merchandise Inventory	29 0 0 0 00	A. Smoot, Capital	18 0 0 0 00	
		B. Jangles, Capital	8 0 0 0 00	
Total Assets	$54 0 0 0 00	Total Equities	$54 0 0 0 00	

Smoot is extremely anxious to withdraw from the partnership and is willing to accept a cash settlement of $12,000. Joll and Jangles will share the $6,000 ($18,000 − $12,000) of capital that Smoot does not take with him in the ratio of 2:1. The journal entry to record the withdrawal of Smoot is shown in Figure 17.17.

Figure 17.17
Withdrawal of Smoot When Smoot Settles for Less Than His Book Equity

July	31	A. Smoot, Capital	18 0 0 0 00		
		Cash		12 0 0 0 00	
		R. Joll, Capital		4 0 0 0 00	
		B. Jangles, Capital		2 0 0 0 00	

Now let's look at what could happen if Smoot withdrew assets valued at *more* than his book equity.

Recording Permanent Withdrawal When a Partner Takes Assets of Greater Value Than Book Equity

Using the previous example, Smoot might withdraw assets valued at *more* than book equity if (1) partnership assets are undervalued and (2) Joll and Jangles are anxious to have him retire. Assume that the assets are undervalued by $12,000 and the owners want to leave them this way. Thus, Smoot's capital would be increased by $4,800 $\left(\frac{2}{5} \times \$12,000 \right)$, and the other partners' equity would be reduced to cover this $4,800 increase to Smoot's capital. The entries in Figure 17.18 would be recorded when Smoot leaves the partnership.

Figure 17.18
Smoot Settles for More Than His Book Equity

July	31	R. Joll, Capital	3 2 0 0 00		
		B. Jangles, Capital	1 6 0 0 00		
		A. Smoot, Capital		4 8 0 0 00	
		A. Smoot, Capital	22 8 0 0 00		
		Cash		22 8 0 0 00	

Note that Smoot receives in cash the $18,000 value of his capital plus the $4,800 to reflect the capital of $22,800 agreed upon by the other partners. Note also how the capital of Joll and Jangles was reduced according to their profit-and-loss ratio.

Remember that when a partner dies, the partnership ends and the estate is entitled to receive the proper value of the capital account of the deceased after an audit and revaluation of the assets. Journal entries for the death of a partner are similar to those for other situations when a partner leaves. To have enough cash to pay the full value of the deceased partner's capital account, partnerships often carry life insurance policies on partners.

Now let's check your progress.

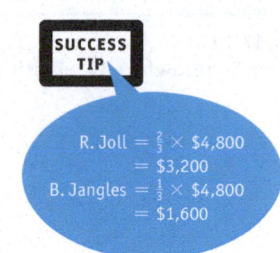

R. Joll = $\frac{2}{3} \times \$4,800$
= $3,200
B. Jangles = $\frac{1}{3} \times \$4,800$
= $1,600

 **TRY IT!**   **Learning Unit 17-3**

Write explanations for each journal entry:

Date		Account	Dr.	Cr.
Apr.	9	Logan, Capital	500	
		Fox, Capital		500
		A		
July	15	Cash	700	
		R. Lesser, Capital		700
		B		
Nov.	8	Fox, Capital	300	
		Lesser, Capital	300	
		Merchandise Inventory		600
		C		

TRY IT!   **Solution Learning Unit 17-3**

A. Transfer of only equity amounts; Fox purchased Logan's interest

B. Owner investment into partnership

C. Inventory overvalued by $600 and written down

Entries for the Liquidation of a Partnership

Up to this point we have looked at the admission and withdrawal of partners. Each time this happens, a new partnership is formed and any losses or gains are shared in an agreed-upon ratio. The operations of the business continue, of course, even when the new partnership is formed. In this unit, we look at three situations in which a partnership is liquidated.

Liquidation occurs when the business is completely ended by converting assets into cash and paying off obligations and the partners. The following steps complete a liquidation:

Liquidation Occurs when a business is terminated, the assets are sold, and liabilities and partners are paid off.

1. Assets are sold for cash with any loss or gain recognized.

2. Any loss or gain is divided among the partners based on their profit-and-loss ratio.

3. Creditors are paid off.

4. Remaining cash is distributed to the partners based on their capital balances.

We look at three different situations based on the following information. Peters, French, and Smith are liquidating their business on May 31, 201X. The partners have a profit-and-loss ratio of 3:2:1. Figure 17.19 shows the updated balance sheet at the end of May. Note that at this point we've closed out the temporary accounts.

Figure 17.19
Balance Sheet Before Liquidation

PETERS, FRENCH, AND SMITH
BALANCE SHEET
MAY 31, 201X

Assets		
Cash	$	7 0 0 0 00
Other Assets		138 0 0 0 00
Total Assets		$ 145 0 0 0 00
Liabilities and Partners' Equity		
Liabilities		$ 25 0 0 0 00
J. Peters, Capital		30 0 0 0 00
J. French, Capital		70 0 0 0 00
A. Smith, Capital		20 0 0 0 00
Total Liabilities and Partners' Equity		$ 145 0 0 0 00

Using this information, let's look at three different situations in which liquidation occurs.

Situation 1. Selling assets at a gain (assets sold for $144,000).

The Liquidation Process

Realization Conversion of noncash assets into cash in the liquidation process.

STEP 1: Record sale of assets along with any loss or gain from realization* (gain = $144,000 − $138,000) on June 7 (Figure 17.20).

Figure 17.20
Selling Assets at a Gain

June	7	Cash	144 0 0 0 00	
		Other Assets		138 0 0 0 00
		Loss or Gain from Realization		6 0 0 0 00

STEP 2: Loss or gain from realization is allocated to each partner in a ratio of 3:2:1 (Figure 17.21).

Figure 17.21
Allocation of Gain to Partners' Capital Accounts

June	7	Loss or Gain from Realization	6 0 0 0 00	
		J. Peters, Capital		3 0 0 0 00
		J. French, Capital		2 0 0 0 00
		A. Smith, Capital		1 0 0 0 00

Peters: ⅜ × $6,000
French: ⅖ × $6,000
Smith: ⅙ × $6,000

STEP 3: Pay claims of the creditors on June 15 (Figure 17.22).

Figure 17.22
Payment to Creditors

June	15	Liabilities	25 0 0 0 00	
		Cash		25 0 0 0 00

Realization means the conversion of noncash assets into cash as part of the liquidation process. It can result in either gain or loss. The account Loss or Gain from Realization is similar to the Cash Short and Over account discussed in Chapter 6. The account will be closed separately because closing entries take place before liquidation. In using this account think of loss as a debit and gain as a credit.

Recognition is when a realized gain or loss has a tax consequence. Realization and Recognition generally move together in that a realized gain will be recognized for tax purposes.

The Ledger Before Step 4

J. Peters, Capital	J. French, Capital	A. Smith, Capital	Cash
30,000	70,000	20,000	7,000 | 25,000
3,000	2,000	1,000	144,000 |
			Bal: 126,000 |

STEP 4: Distribute cash that is left to partners based on their capital balances (Figure 17.23). Profit-and-loss ratios are not used in this step.

June	30	J. Peters, Capital	33 0 0 0 00	
		J. French, Capital	72 0 0 0 00	
		A. Smith, Capital	21 0 0 0 00	
		Cash		126 0 0 0 00

Figure 17.23
Cash Paid to Partners

The accompanying statement of liquidation gives a comprehensive report of the liquidation process involved in Situation 1. Keep in mind that the liquidation process takes time to complete; it isn't done overnight.

Peters, French, and Smith
Statement of Liquidation for Month of June 201X

	Cash	+	Other Assets	=	Liabilities	+	Peters	+	French	+	Smith
Balances before realization	$ 7,000	+	$138,000	=	$25,000	+	$30,000	+	$70,000	+	$20,000
Recording gain from sales of assets	+$144,000	−	$138,000				+3,000		+2,000		+1,000
Balances updated	$151,000			=	$25,000	+	$33,000	+	$72,000	+	$21,000
Paying of liabilities	−$ 25,000				−$25,000						
Balances updated	$126,000			=			+$33,000	+	$72,000	+	$21,000
Distribution of cash to partners	−$126,000			=			−$33,000	−	$72,000	−	$21,000

Now let's look at what would happen if the assets were sold at a loss.

Situation 2. Selling assets at a loss (assets sold for $126,000).

The Liquidation Process

STEP 1: Record sale of assets with loss or gain from realization (loss = $138,000 − $126,000) on June 7 (Figure 17.24).

June	7	Cash	126 0 0 0 00	
		Loss or Gain from Realization	12 0 0 0 00	
		Other Assets		138 0 0 0 00

Figure 17.24
Selling Assets at a Loss

STEP 2: Loss or gain from realization is allocated to each partner in ratio of 3:2:1 (Figure 17.25).

June	7	J. Peters, Capital	6 0 0 0 00	
		J. French, Capital	4 0 0 0 00	
		A. Smith, Capital	2 0 0 0 00	
		Loss or Gain from Realization		12 0 0 0 00

Figure 17.25
Loss Allocated to Partners

STEP 3: Pay claims of creditors (Figure 17.26).

Figure 17.26
Payment to Creditors

June	15	Liabilities	25 0 0 0 00		
		Cash		25 0 0 0 00	

The Ledger Before Step 4

J. Peters, Capital	J. French, Capital	A. Smith, Capital	Cash
6,000 | 30,000	4,000 | 70,000	2,000 | 20,000	7,000 | 25,000
			126,000
			Bal: 108,000 |

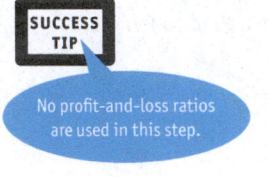

No profit-and-loss ratios
are used in this step.

STEP 4: Distribute cash that is left to partners based on their capital balances on June 30 (Figure 17.27).

Figure 17.27
Payments to Partners

June	30	J. Peters, Capital	24 0 0 0 00	
		J. French, Capital	66 0 0 0 00	
		A. Smith, Capital	18 0 0 0 00	
		Cash		108 0 0 0 00

The accompanying statement of liquidation provides a comprehensive report of this liquidation process.

Peters, French, and Smith
Statement of Liquidation for Month of June 201X

	Cash	+	Other Assets	=	Liabilities	+	Capital				
							Peters	+	French	+	Smith
Balances before realization	$ 7,000	+	$138,000	=	$25,000	+	$30,000	+	$70,000	+	$20,000
Recording loss from sales of assets	+$126,000	−	$138,000				−6,000		−4,000		−2,000
Balances updated	$133,000			=	$25,000	+	$24,000	+	$66,000	+	$18,000
Paying of liabilities	−$ 25,000				−$25,000						
Balances updated	$108,000			=			$24,000	+	$66,000	+	$18,000
Distribution of cash to partners	−$108,000			=			−$24,000	−	$66,000	−	$18,000

In the final situation, the partners are unable to cover a deficit from the sale of assets.

Situation 3. Selling assets at a loss, with some partners' capital not being enough to cover the deficit (assets sold for only $42,000).

The Liquidation Process

STEP 1: Record sale of assets along with any loss or gain from realization (loss of $96,000 = $138,000 − $42,000) on June 7 (Figure 17.28).

Figure 17.28
Loss from Realization

June	7	Cash	42 0 0 0 00	
		Loss or Gain from Realization	96 0 0 0 00	
		Other Assets		138 0 0 0 00

STEP 2: Loss or gain from realization is allocated to each partner in the ratio of 3:2:1 (Figure 17.29).

June	7	J. Peters, Capital	48 0 0 0 00			
		J. French, Capital	32 0 0 0 00			
		A. Smith, Capital	16 0 0 0 00			
		Loss or Gain from Realization			96 0 0 0 00	

Figure 17.29
Loss Allocated to Each Partner

When the loss exceeds the capital balance of a partner and the partner cannot make up the deficit, the other partners have unlimited liability to make up the deficit.

Peters, Capital		French, Capital		Smith, Capital	
48,000	30,000	32,000	70,000	16,000	20,000

Note that Peters has a deficit of $18,000 ($48,000 − $30,000). The other partners must share this deficit in their profit-and-loss ratio of 2:1 (Figure 17.30).

June	7	J. French, Capital	12 0 0 0 00			
		A. Smith, Capital	6 0 0 0 00			
		J. Peters, Capital			18 0 0 0 00	

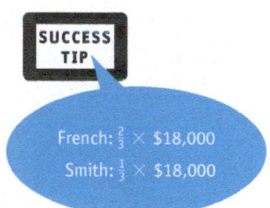

Figure 17.30
Sharing of Deficit by Partners

Peters, Capital		French, Capital		Smith, Capital	
48,000	30,000	32,000	70,000	16,000	20,000
18,000	18,000	12,000		6,000	

Note that now *Smith* has a $2,000 deficit. French is the only partner left with a capital balance and thus is liable for this deficit (Figure 17.31).

June	7	J. French, Capital	2 0 0 0 00			
		A. Smith, Capital			2 0 0 0 00	

Figure 17.31
French Only Partner Left with a Balance

STEP 3: Pay claims of creditors on June 15 (Figure 17.32).

June	15	Liabilities	25 0 0 0 00			
		Cash			25 0 0 0 00	

Figure 17.32
Pay Creditors

STEP 4: Distribute remaining cash on June 30 (Figure 17.33).

June	30	J. French, Capital	24 0 0 0 00			
		Cash			24 0 0 0 00	

Figure 17.33
Pay Cash to Partner

The accompanying statement of liquidation provides a comprehensive report of this liquidation process.

Peters, French, and Smith
Statement of Liquidation for Month of June 201X

	Cash	+	Other Assets	=	Liabilities	+	Peters	+	French	+	Smith
									Capital		
Balances before realization	$ 7,000	+	$138,000	=	$25,000	+	$30,000	+	$70,000	+	$20,000
Recording loss from sale of assets	+$42,000	–	$138,000	=		–	48,000	–	32,000	–	16,000
Balances updated	$49,000				$25,000	–	$18,000	+	$38,000	+	$ 4,000
Deficit of Peters covered by partners in a ratio of 2:1						+	$18,000	–	$12,000	–	6,000
Balances updated	$49,000			=	$25,000			+	$26,000	–	$ 2,000
Deficit of Smith covered by French								–	$ 2,000	+	$ 2,000
Balances updated	$49,000			=	$25,000			+	$24,000		
Paying of liabilities	–$25,000				–$25,000						
Balances updated	$24,000			=					$24,000		
Distribution of cash to French	–$24,000								–$24,000		

Now let's check your progress.

 TRY IT!   **Learning Unit 17-4**

Journalize the following liquidation entries:

July	8	Sold other assets of partnership that were valued at $154,000, recovering $98,000.
	9	The loss from July 8 is shared in the ratio of 6:1:3 (J. Sherwood; J. Lowell; G. Wagman).
	15	Paid claims of creditors $12,000.

TRY IT!   **Solution Learning Unit 17-4**

Date		Account	Dr.	Cr.
July	8	Cash	98,000	
		Loss or Gain from Realization	56,000	
		Other Assets		154,000
	9	J. Sherwood, Capital	33,600	
		J. Lowell, Capital	5,600	
		G. Wagman, Capital	16,800	
		Loss or Gain from Realization		56,000
	15	Liabilities	12,000	
		Cash		12,000

L01,2,3,4  ● **DEMONSTRATION SUMMARY PROBLEM**

Betsy Foss runs her own bookkeeping service. Today she is working on two projects. Project 1 involves the partnership of Ranch, Small, and Lesen. Project 2 involves the partnership of Jack, Ross, and Fey. Please journalize the entries for these two projects given the following (we show each project separately):

Project 1

On July 31, 201X, the balance sheet of Ranch, Small, and Lesen was as follows:

Cash	$ 9,000	Ranch, Capital	$ 8,000
Merchandise Inventory	5,000	Small, Capital	8,000
Other Assets	7,000	Lesen, Capital	5,000
Total Assets	$21,000	Total Capital	$21,000

Partners share all losses and gains in a 2:2:1 ratio. Lesen is withdrawing from the partnership. For each independent situation, journalize the withdrawal of Lesen.

Situation 1: Lesen sells his equity to Angel for $9,000. Partners agree to the admission of Angel.

Situation 2: On withdrawal of Lesen, inventory is determined to be overvalued by $1,500. Assets are revalued to current face value. (Revalue inventory as well as withdrawal of Lesen.)

Situation 3: Lesen is paid $4,000 out of the assets of the partners because assets were overvalued. The partners do not want to decrease asset values.

Solutions for Project 1

	Account	Dr.	Cr.
Situation 1	Lesen, Capital	5,000	
	Angel, Capital		5,000
Situation 2	Ranch, Capital	600	
	Small, Capital	600	
	Lesen, Capital	300	
	Merchandise Inventory		1,500
	Lesen, Capital	4,700	
	Cash		4,700
Situation 3	Lesen, Capital	5,000	
	Cash		4,000
	Ranch, Capital		500
	Small, Capital		500

Tips

In Situation 1, it does not matter what cash is transacted. The bookkeeper wipes out old value of capital and replaces same value to the new partner.

In Situation 2, merchandise inventory is overvalued, and the result is that the partners absorb the loss in merchandise value.

In Situation 3, Ranch and Small share in the difference between the cash and balance in the Lesen, Capital account.

Project 2

Given:

Cash	$20,000	Liabilities	$10,000
Other Assets	14,000	Jack, Capital	12,000
		Ross, Capital	8,000
		Fey, Capital	4,000
Total Assets	$34,000	Total Liabilities and Owner's Capital	$34,000

In the liquidation process, all gains and losses are shared in a ratio of 3:2:1. Journalize the following entries:

Apr.	8	Sold other assets	$20,000
	15	Paid off Liabilities	
	15	Distributed Cash to partners	

Solution for Project 2

Date		Account	Dr.	Cr.
Apr.	8	Cash	20,000	
		Other Assets		14,000
		Loss or Gain from Realization		6,000
	8	Loss or Gain from Realization	6,000	
		Jack, Capital		3,000
		Ross, Capital		2,000
		Fey, Capital		1,000
	15	Liabilities	10,000	
		Cash		10,000
	15	Jack, Capital	15,000	
		Ross, Capital	10,000	
		Fey, Capital	5,000	
		Cash		30,000

Tip

Because other assets sold for more than what was on the books, the partners share the $6,000 gain based on the profit-and-loss ratio.

SUCCESS COACH

The following Success Tips are from Learning Units 17-1 to 17-4. Take the Do It Right Now Checkup and use the Check Your Score to see how you are doing. The Success Coach provides tips before each Checkup to help you avoid common accounting errors.

LU 17-1 Journalizing Entries to Form a Partnership

Do It Right Tips: A partnership has a limited life. If the partnership is dissolved, a new partnership can be formed and business continues without any disruption. Other characteristics of a partnership include mutual agency, unlimited liability, and co-ownership of property. The partnership does not pay taxes; it is the owners who pay tax on net income received.

Do It Right Now Checkup: Answer true or false to the following statements.

1. "Mutual agency" means that actions of one partner are not binding on the other.
2. "Unlimited liability" means that partners have a limited liability.
3. Articles of partnership are never written.
4. A partnership itself does not pay taxes.
5. "Co-ownership" means that all partners share all assets of the partnership.

LU 17-2 Journalizing Entries to Record Division of Net Income and Net Loss Among Partners

Do It Right Tips: Salaries and interest allowances are not expenses but mechanisms used to divide net income or net loss among the partners. Whether net income covers the salaries and interest makes no difference in calculating the salary or interest allowance.

Do It Right Now Checkup: Answer true or false to the following statements.

1. A salary allowance is the same as a salary expense.
2. Net income can be divided among partners by an interest allowance.
3. A closing journal entry cannot allocate net income to partners.
4. A profit-and-loss ratio could be based on service as well as capital investment.
5. The ending balance of each partner is reported on the income statement.

LU 17-3 Journalizing Entries to Record Admissions and Withdrawals of Partners

Do It Right Tips: When a new partner buys equity interest from an existing partner, all that results is a change in the name on the capital account. The profit-and-loss ratio agreed upon by partners will decide how the partnership's earnings are shared. A partner may withdraw from a partnership for less or more than book equity.

Do It Right Now Checkup: Answer true or false to the following statements.

1. Purchasing an equity interest from a partner could result in admission of a new partner.
2. Bonuses never happen in a partnership.
3. A withdrawal from a partnership could mean a new profit-and-loss ratio.
4. If some partners are anxious for another partner to retire, this may result in assets valued at more than book equity.
5. When a partner dies the partnership does not end.

LU 17-4 Entries for the Liquidation of a Partnership

Do It Right Tips: When a partnership is liquidated, the following steps must happen:

a. Sell assets for cash.
b. Divide the loss or gain from realization among partners.
c. Pay the creditors.
d. Pay remaining cash to all partners based on their capital balances.

Do It Right Now Checkup: Answer true or false to the following statements.

1. Liquidation of a partnership begins when a partnership is formed.
2. A loss in the Loss or Gain from Realization account is a credit.
3. Ratios are used to allocate loss or gain from realization.
4. A deficit occurs when the loss is less than the capital balances of the partners.
5. Partners have a limited liability to make up deficits.

CHECK YOUR SCORE: Answers to the Do It Right Now Checkup

LU 17-1

1. False—"Mutual agency" means that actions of one partner are binding on the other.
2. False—"Unlimited liability" means that partners have an unlimited liability.
3. False—Articles of partnership are always written.
4. True
5. True

LU 17-2

1. False—A salary allowance is not the same as a salary expense.
2. True
3. False—A closing journal entry can allocate net income to partners.
4. True
5. False—The ending balance of each partner is reported on the balance sheet.

LU 17-3

1. True
2. False—Bonuses do happen in a partnership.
3. True
4. True
5. False—When a partner dies the partnership does end but business may continue.

LU 17-4

1. False—Liquidation of a partnership begins when a partnership is dissolved.
2. False—A loss in the Loss or Gain from Realization account is a debit.
3. True
4. False—A deficit occurs when the loss is more than the capital balances of the partners.
5. False—Partners have an unlimited liability to make up deficits.

BLUEPRINT: ADVANTAGES AND DISADVANTAGES OF A PARTNERSHIP

Advantages	Disadvantages
1. Ease of formation; legal status under Uniform Partnership Act.	1. Limited life expectancy; any changes in membership dissolve the partnership.
2. Ability to raise more capital than a sole proprietorship.	2. Mutual agency; action by one partner binds all other partners.
3. Pooled resource of talents.	3. Unlimited liability; each partner must cover partnership debts with personal assets.
4. Flexibility to react to the marketplace because legal restrictions are minimal.	4. Cannot admit a new partner without agreement of all other partners; a partner cannot withdraw without agreement of all other partners.
5. Credit rating usually higher because more than one partner is responsible for the company's debts.	

Discussion Questions and Critical Thinking/Ethical Case

1. How is the equity of a partnership different from that of a sole proprietorship?
2. List five characteristics of a partnership.
3. What is the function of the articles of partnership?
4. Explain how a company could operate even when being dissolved.
5. Mutual agency could create unlimited liability. Agree or disagree? Defend your position.
6. Explain why salary and interest allowances are not expenses for a partnership.
7. Give an example of a fractional ratio.
8. The statement of partners' capital is a required report. Agree or disagree? Defend your position.
9. What is meant by a "side transaction" when a new partner is admitted by an existing partner's selling the new partner equity?
10. What is meant by a "bonus" when a partner is admitted?
11. When a partner withdraws, why would a partnership revalue its assets?
12. Why would a partner who is withdrawing take more or less than book equity?
13. What are the four steps of the liquidation process?
14. Jee Jones is in a partnership with Alvin Scott and Morry Flynn. Jee signed a long-term contract with a supplier without telling either partner. When Alvin heard about it, he hit the roof. He told Jee the partnership could not afford this contract and he would have nothing to do with it. Do you think Alvin should be upset? You make the call. Write down your recommendations to Alvin.

Concept Checks

MyLabAccounting

Forming a Partnership

LO1 *(10 min)*

1. Bob Pillow and Ronald Slate enter into a partnership. On December 1, 201X, Bob invests $6,900 cash in the partnership. Ronald invests $4,300 cash and store equipment worth $6,400 with accumulated depreciation of $2,100. The equipment has a current appraised value of $9,400. Prepare a journal entry to record this transaction.

Division of Net Income

LO2 *(10 min)*

2. John Smith, Norman Stapleson, and Dakota Menard invested $12,000, $7,500, and $10,500, respectively. At the end of the first year, the company's net income was $90,000. Assuming no agreement was reached on how to share net income, prepare a journal entry at closing to allocate net income.

Division of Net Income Based on Beginning Capital Balances

LO2 *(10 min)*

3. If the partners in Concept Check 2 share net income based on their beginning capital investments, what would be the journal entry at closing to allocate net income?

Calculating Total Salary and Interest Allowances

LO2 *(15 min)*

4. If the partners in Concept Check 2 have the following agreement, please calculate the total salary and interest allowances:
   a. *Salary Allowance:* Smith, $8,600; Stapleson, $6,900; and Menard, $5,800.
   b. 6% interest on capital investments.

Share of Net Income to Partners; Deficit Sharing

LO2 *(15 min)*

5. Using your answer from Concept Check 4, how much more income is to be distributed to the partners (assume each shares equally) after the salary and interest allowances? If net income was $14,250, how much would the partners share in the deficit?

(10 min) **LO3**  **Admission of a New Partner**

6.   On August 8, Art O'Toole sold his equity in the partnership to Bill Morrison for $5,300. Art's capital account had a $4,000 balance. Record the journal entry.

(15 min) **LO3**  **Investing into an Existing Partnership**

7.   Phyllis Richardson wants to have a one-third interest in a law practice that has two partners with capital balances as follows:

Ronald Small, Capital	$5,600
Al Prior, Capital	2,000

How much must Phyllis invest into the partnership?

(15 min) **LO2**  **Calculating Profit-and-Loss Ratio**

8.   From the following capital balances, calculate the profit-and-loss ratio for each account:

Billy Bliss, Capital	$200
Antonio James, Capital	900
Teddy Pennington, Capital	800

(15 min) **LO4**  **Liquidation**

9.   From the following, journalize the (a) sale of assets and (b) loss or gain from liquidation realization. Given:

Cash	$ 3,300
Other Assets	18,500
Liabilities	4,400
Maxwell, Capital	5,200
Casey, Capital	7,400
Eaton, Capital	8,300

Partners agreed to share losses or gains in a 3:3:4 ratio and sold other assets for $22,500.

MyLab**Accounting**

Exercises

Set A

(20 min) **LO1**   **17A-1.**   Ethan Smith and Crystal Banks form a partnership on May 1, 201X. Smith contributes cash of $40,000. Banks contributes $28,000 cash and land costing $18,100 with a current fair value of $29,500. A $30,000 note payable due to Banks is assumed by the new partnership. Please prepare the journal entries to record Smith's and Banks's investment in the partnership.

(20 min) **LO2**   **17A-2.**   A. Langer and B. Semon have decided their partnership earnings will be shared as follows: (a) 14% interest allowance on capital balances at beginning of year, (b) remainder to be shared equally. Capital balances of Langer and Semon at the beginning of the year are $79,000 and $30,000, respectively. Net income is $17,000 for the year. Record the journal entry to update the capital balances of Langer and Semon on December 31.

(20 min) **LO3**   **17A-3.**   Judy Eagleson, Tina DiVito, and Amy Ellars are partners who share losses and gains in a ratio of 2:2:1. Their capital balances are $4,800, $7,200, and $4,300, respectively. The partners are anxious to have Tina retire and have paid her $12,900. Give the journal entry to record the payment to Tina along with the absorption of the amount over book equity by Judy and Amy on July 31, 201X.

(20 min) **LO3**   **17A-4.**   L. White, V. Sabin, and E. Rackhaus are partners with capital balances of $92,000, $81,000, and $69,000, respectively. Rackhaus sells his interest in the company for $90,000 to P. Solvay. White and Sabin have consented to the new partner. Record the journal entry for the admission of Solvay on April 8.

17A-5. Sabin, Roe, and Herber have capital balances before liquidation of $14,000, $22,000, and $31,000, respectively. Cash balance is $39,000, and the partners share losses and gains in a 3:2:1 ratio. All noncash assets with a book value of $28,000 are sold, for a gain on realization of $36,000. In your calculations assume that no liabilities are a factor. What will each partner receive in cash in the liquidation process?

 **LO4** *(20 min)*

Set B

17B-1. Ed Hobbs and Carrie Lewis form a partnership on May 1, 201X. Hobbs contributes $39,000. Lewis contributes $30,000 cash and land costing $18,500 with a current fair value of $30,500. A $32,000 note payable due to Lewis is assumed by the new partnership. Please prepare the journal entries to record Hobbs's and Lewis's investment in the partnership.

 **LO1** *(20 min)*

17B-2. A. Larsen and B. Samec have decided their partnership earnings will be shared as follows: (a) 13% interest allowance on capital balances at the beginning of the year, (b) remainder to be shared equally. Capital balances of Larsen and Samec at the beginning of the year are $77,000 and $26,000, respectively. Net income is $14,000 for the year. Record the journal entry to update the capital balances of Larsen and Samec on December 31.

 **LO2** *(20 min)*

17B-3. Jessica Eaglen, Tracey DaVeiga, and Allison Ellard are partners who share losses and gains in a ratio of 2:2:1. Their capital balances are $4,700, $5,100, and $4,200, respectively. The partners are anxious to have Tracey retire and have paid her $11,100. Give the journal entry to record the payment to Tracey along with the absorption of the amount over book equity by Jessica and Allison on July 31, 201X.

 **LO3** *(20 min)*

17B-4. L. Waddell, V. Sage, and E. Rabel are partners with capital balances of $91,000, $84,000, and $68,000, respectively. Rabel sells his interest in the company for $87,000 to P. Solvay. Waddell and Sage have consented to the new partner. Record the journal entry for the admission of Solvay on April 8.

 **LO3** *(20 min)*

17B-5. Sullivan, Ritchie, and Haas have capital balances before liquidation of $15,000, $26,000, and $36,000, respectively. Cash balance is $51,000, and the partners share losses and gains in a 3:2:1 ratio. All noncash assets with a book value of $26,000 are sold, for a gain on realization of $27,000. In your calculations, assume that no liabilities are a factor. What will each partner receive in cash in the liquidation process?

 **LO4** *(20 min)*

Problems

MyLabAccounting

Set A

17A-1. a. The partnership of Katie and Leo began with the partners investing $6,000 and $2,000, respectively. At the end of the first year, the partnership earned net income of $8,400. Under each of the following independent situations, calculate how much of the $8,400 each is entitled to:

LO2 *(30 min)*

Situation 1: No agreement on how income was to be shared.

Situation 2: Katie and Leo share income based on the beginning-of-year investment ratio.

Situation 3: Salary allowance of $2,800 to Katie and $2,420 to Leo. Ten percent interest on beginning year's investment. Remainder split equally.

b. In Situation 3, what would the earnings to each partner be if net income were $4,200?

Check Figure:
(b) Deficit to be shared equally $910

(30 min) **L03**

S50 / **QB**

Check Figure:
Sit. 3: $750 bonus to old partners

17A-2. Bob Miller and Whitney Allen are partners with capital balances of $1,750 and $350, respectively. They share all profits and losses equally. From the following independent situations, journalize the admission of the new partner, Jack Worth:

Situation 1: Worth purchased Allen's interest for $5,800, paying it personally to Allen.

Situation 2: Worth invested an amount exactly equal to one-third interest in the partnership.

Situation 3: Worth invested $3,300 for a one-third interest. Miller and Allen share the bonus.

Situation 4: Worth invested $750 for a one-third interest. Bonus is credited to Worth's account.

(30 min) **L03**

Check Figure:
Sit. 1:
Dr. Verlander, Capital $5,300
Cr. Jennings, Capital $5,300

17A-3. Lambert, Ray, and Verlander are partners. On July 30, 201X, the balance sheet was as follows:

Cash	$11,800	Lambert, Capital	$ 7,200
Merchandise Inventory	4,700	Ray, Capital	12,100
Other Assets	8,100	Verlander, Capital	5,300
Total Assets	$24,600	Total Liab. & Equity	$24,600

The partners agree to share all losses and gains in a 2:2:1 ratio. Verlander is withdrawing from the partnership. From the following independent situations, journalize the withdrawal of Verlander.

Situation 1: Verlander sells his equity to Jennings for $18,400. Partners agree to admission of Jennings.

Situation 2: On withdrawal of Verlander, inventory is determined to be overvalued by $1,000. (Before withdrawal, assets are revalued to current fair market value.) Be sure to record entry to revalue inventory as well as the withdrawal of Verlander.

Situation 3: Verlander is paid $3,800 out of the assets of the partnership. The partners do not want to change the recorded asset values.

Situation 4: Verlander is paid $9,000 out of the assets of the partnership. The partners do not want to change the recorded asset values.

(30 min) **L04**

Check Figure:
Sit. 2: Gain or loss from realization
$9,000 Dr.

17A-4. The partnership of Jackson, Rackley, and Sutter is being liquidated. All gains and losses are shared in a 3:2:1 ratio. Before liquidation, their balance sheet looks as follows:

Cash	$21,600	Liabilities	$ 5,700
Other Assets	15,600	A. Jackson, Capital	11,600
		C. Rackley, Capital	17,900
		J. Sutter, Capital	2,000
Total Assets	$37,200	Total Liab. & Equity	$37,200

Journalize the entries needed in the liquidation process under the following independent situations and assume a date of February 1, 201X, for sale of assets and a date of February 15 for paying off liabilities and distributing cash to partners:

Situation 1: Sold other assets for $33,000.

Situation 2: Sold other assets for $6,600.

Situation 3: Sold other assets for $1,800. Sutter cannot cover his deficit.

Set B

17B-1. **a.** The partnership of Susan and Randy began with the partners investing $6,600 and $2,200, respectively. At the end of the first year, the partnership earned net income of $8,600. Under each of the following independent situations, calculate how much of the $8,600 each is entitled to:

 **LO2** *(30 min)*

Situation 1: No agreement on how income was to be shared.

Situation 2: Susan and Randy share income based on the beginning-of-year investment ratio.

Situation 3: Salary allowance of $2,860 to Susan and $2,470 to Randy. Ten percent interest on beginning year's investment. Remainder split equally.

Check Figure:
(b) Deficit to be shared equally $1,105

b. In Situation 3 what would the earnings to each partner be if net income were $4,000?

17B-2. Bob Miller and Whitney Benson are partners with capital balances of $1,600 and $500, respectively. They share all profits and losses equally. From the following independent situations, journalize the admission of the new partner, Jack Tilton:

 **LO3** *(30 min)*

Situation 1: Tilton purchased Benson's interest for $5,900, paying it personally to Benson.

Situation 2: Tilton invested an amount exactly equal to one-third interest in the partnership.

Situation 3: Tilton invested $1,800 for a one-third interest. Miller and Benson share the bonus.

Check Figure:
Sit. 3: $250 bonus to old partners

Situation 4: Tilton invested $660 for a one-third interest. Bonus is credited to Tilton's account.

17B-3. Lane, Ramirez, and Valverde are partners. On July 30, 201X, the balance sheet was as follows:

LO3 *(30 min)*

Cash	$12,800	Lane, Capital	$ 7,800
Merchandise Inventory	4,900	Ramirez, Capital	12,600
Other Assets	8,100	Valverde, Capital	5,400
Total Assets	$25,800	Total Liab. & Equity	$25,800

The partners agree to share all losses and gains in a 2:2:1 ratio. Valverde is withdrawing from the partnership. From the following independent situations, journalize the withdrawal of Valverde:

Situation 1: Valverde sells his equity to Jimenez for $18,000. Partners agree to admission of Jimenez.

Situation 2: On withdrawal of Valverde, inventory is determined to be over-valued by $1,700. (Before withdrawal, assets are revalued to current fair market value.) Be sure to record the entry to revalue inventory as well as the withdrawal of Valverde.

Check Figure:
Sit. 1:
Dr. Valverde, Capital $5,400
Cr. Jimenez, Capital $5,400

Situation 3: Valverde is paid $3,900 out of the assets of the partnership. The partners do not want to change the recorded asset values.

Situation 4: Valverde is paid $8,900 out of the assets of the partnership. The partners do not want to change the recorded asset values.

(30 min) **LO4**

17B-4. The partnership of Jones, Rains, and Sussman is being liquidated. All gains and losses are shared in a 3:2:1 ratio. Before liquidation their balance sheet looks as follows:

Check Figure:
Sit. 2: Loss or gain from realization
$8,100 Dr.

Cash	$22,200	Liabilities	$ 6,050
Other Assets	14,700	A. Jones, Capital	11,100
		C. Rains, Capital	18,000
		J. Sussman, Capital	1,750
Total Assets	$36,900	Total Liab. & Equity	$36,900

Journalize the entries needed in the liquidation process under the following independent situations and assume a date of February 1, 201X, for sale of assets and a date of February 15 to pay off liabilities and distribute cash to partners:

Situation 1: Sold other assets for $33,300.

Situation 2: Sold other assets for $6,600.

Situation 3: Sold other assets for $2,100. Sussman cannot cover his deficit.

MyLabAccounting

Financial Report Problem

(15 min) **LO1**

Reading Amazon's Annual Report
Go to the 2016 annual report for Amazon at **https://tinyurl.com/slaterca14e** and explain the benefits of being a corporation rather than a partnership.

Corporations: Organizations and Stock

18

CHAPTER PREVIEW: ACCOUNTING IN ACTION

In 1971, Starbucks first started out as a small coffee shop in Seattle, selling a regular coffee for about 45 cents. Today, wherever you go, there is a Starbucks nearby. When Starbucks became a corporation, it was able to raise capital and expand its business by selling stock. This is why this type of business organization is so popular today. Here we look at the advantages and disadvantages of this form of ownership and how to record accounting transactions for a corporation.

Learning Objectives – Relating Accounting Theory By Unit

LO1 Explain the Advantages and Disadvantages of the Corporate Structure

LO2 Explain Retained Earnings and Stockholders' Equity

LO3 Journalize Capital Stock Transactions and Calculate Dividends

LO4 Journalize Entries to Record Capital Stock Transactions for a Subscription Plan

Corporation Business organization that is both a legal and accounting entity.

So far we've learned about sole proprietorships and partnerships; now we are going to learn about corporations. A corporation such as Starbucks is a separate legal entity. We first look at how a corporation is formed, along with its main characteristics.

The Advantages and Disadvantages of the Corporate Structure

Four steps are involved in forming a corporation.

Incorporators Persons responsible for getting the corporation formed.

Articles of incorporation Document submitted by incorporators when applying for a charter.

STEP 1: The incorporators, those wishing to form the corporation, apply to a state for a charter. They do so by submitting articles of incorporation drawn up by an attorney, together with a fee. The articles of incorporation consist of the following information:

1. Name of the corporation and incorporation date
2. Purpose of business
3. Organizational structure
4. Expected life (usually "forever")
5. Primary location of business
6. Types of stock to be offered (Stock is what owners purchase to gain ownership rights in the company. We look at stock in detail in a few moments.)

Charter Document issued to a corporation by the state that includes certificate of incorporation along with articles of incorporation.

Certificate of incorporation Document granted by the state authorizing the creation of a corporation.

Stockholders Owners of the stock of the corporation.

Directors Officers elected by stockholders to represent the company and establish policies for the company.

Minute book Book that records meetings of the board of directors or stockholders.

STEP 2: The Office of the Secretary of State reviews the application and, if deemed in order, a charter (often called a certificate of incorporation) is issued to the incorporators. Copies of the charter and the articles of incorporation are placed on file for public record.

STEP 3: The stock is issued by the corporation to the owners (called stockholders).

STEP 4: The stockholders meet to elect a board of directors and adopt the bylaws of the corporation. Often in a new corporation the stockholders become the directors. As the company grows, people are appointed to the board who are not stockholders. Records of meetings of the board of directors and stockholders are kept in a minute book, as directed by law. The board of directors appoints the officers to run the company; it is the board's job to oversee the overall management of the corporation, whereas the officers follow the policies set up by the board.

Advantages of the Corporate Form of Organization

Limited liability Freedom of stockholders from personal liability for the debts of the corporation.

1. **Limited Liability/Separate Legal Entity.** Stockholders have limited liability; they are not personally liable for the obligations of the corporation because a corporation is a separate and distinct legal entity. The corporation enters into contracts, buys or sells property, and sues or is sued in its own name. Thus, the only amount the stockholders can lose is the amount of their investment in the business. Of course, stockholders can still be held liable for any fraudulent or negligent actions they perform in connection with the corporation.

2. **Unlimited Life.** A corporation's life is perpetual (goes on forever) except in the case of bankruptcy, mergers, or vote of the stockholders.

Stock certificate Formal document issued to investors in a corporation that shows the number of shares purchased.

3. **Ease of Transferring Ownership Interest.** When an owner invests in a corporation, each share of ownership is represented by one or more formal documents called stock certificates. The stockholder can sell or transfer shares of some corporations through *brokerage firms*, companies that act as intermediaries in the trading of stock. This trading occurs at various marketplaces called *stock exchanges*. Today many of the transactions are done electronically. On the back of the certificate is a form that the seller endorses. A key point is that when the shares of stock are sold by the stockholder, the sale has *no* effect on the company's assets and liabilities. What happens is really a *shift* in the ownership.

4. **No Mutual Agency.** A corporation is not subject to mutual agency the way a partnership is. For example, if John Jones is a stockholder of Passon Corporation and enters into a contract with the City of Lynn, this action by John cannot bind the corporation to complete the contract with the City of Lynn.

5. **Ease of Raising Capital.** With no mutual agency, with limited liability, and with the ease of transferring ownership interest, the investment in a corporation becomes attractive to many people. As a result, the corporation can raise large amounts of capital by assembling investment groups of stockholders.

Disadvantages of the Corporate Structure

1. **Difficulties in Forming a Corporation/Government Regulations.** Because of the steps involved, a corporation is more difficult to form than a sole proprietorship or a partnership. Incorporators must complete the articles of incorporation and pay an incorporation fee. The complexity of forming a corporation also usually means hiring a lawyer to deal with legal aspects. When granted a certificate of incorporation, corporations are required to fulfill many state and federal regulations and to file various governmental reports.

2. **Corporate Taxation.** Because the corporation is a separate legal entity, its income is taxed by the federal government and may also be taxed at the state and local levels. At the same time, any income that is distributed to the stockholders is taxable to the stockholders. Thus, a corporation's earnings face double taxation.[1]

Now let's check your progress.

 # TRY IT! Learning Unit 18-1

Complete the following table by placing an X in the appropriate column:

	Advantage of a Corporation	Disadvantage of a Corporation
Corporate Taxation		
Ease of Raising Capital		
Government Regulations		
Unlimited Life		
Separate Legal Entity		
Ease of Transferring Ownership Interest		

TRY IT! Solution Learning Unit 18-1

	Advantage of a Corporation	Disadvantage of a Corporation
Corporate Taxation		X
Ease of Raising Capital	X	
Government Regulations		X
Unlimited Life	X	
Separate Legal Entity	X	
Ease of Transferring Ownership Interest	X	

---

[1] *Note:* S corporations have fewer than 100 stockholders, are not publicly traded, and are only taxed at the stockholder level, similar to a partnership. That is why they are called "flow-through entities." Not all companies have to be an S corporation.

Retained Earnings and Stockholders' Equity

The equity section of a balance sheet of a corporation differs from that of a sole proprietorship or a partnership. In the sole proprietorship, we have simply a Capital Account and a Withdrawals Account. In the partnership, separate Capital and Withdrawals Accounts are kept for each partner. With the corporation, the stockholders' equity section is broken down into two major parts:

Paid-In Capital Section of stockholders' equity representing what stockholders have invested into the corporation.

Retained Earnings Accumulated profits of a corporation that have been kept in the business and not paid out as dividends. Retained earnings is part of stockholders' equity.

1. **Paid-In Capital** is the amount that stockholders have invested in the business. It is equal to the values of the assets (usually cash) that have been contributed to the business in exchange for stocks.
2. **Retained Earnings** are accumulated profits that are retained or kept in the corporation. Retained earnings does not mean cash; cash is an *asset*, whereas retained earnings is part of stockholders' *equity*.

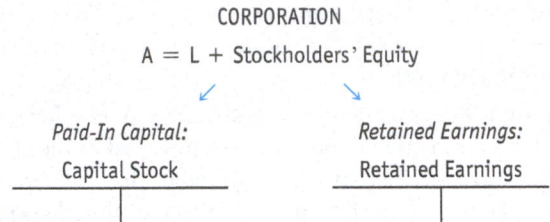

Let's look more closely at the term *capital stock*.

Capital Stock

Capital stock Classes of stock that represent the fractional elements of ownership of a corporation.

Authorized capital stock As stated in its charter, the number of shares of capital stock (common and preferred) that a corporation can sell.

Issued capital stock Stock that the corporation issues for assets or services contributed by the stockholders.

Outstanding capital stock Stock that is held and owned by stockholders.

Common stock Part of paid-in capital representing the basic ownership equity of the corporation. If the corporation has only one class of stock, it will be common stock.

Preemptive right The right of the stockholder to purchase additional shares of stock to maintain a proportionate interest when the corporation issues additional stock.

In return for their investment in the corporation, stockholders are issued shares of capital stock. Think of ownership of a corporation as being represented by shares of stock. The two classes of capital stock are common and preferred. The charter of the corporation indicates the maximum amount of shares of each class of capital stock that a company can legally issue, but the company does not have to issue all of it. Most companies will ask for a larger amount of stock to issue than they intend to sell right away. This allows them to plan for the future. Authorized capital stock is the amount listed in the charter, issued capital stock refers to the shares sold to the stockholders, and outstanding capital stock means shares sold and in the stockholders' possession. Let's look at the two classes of capital stock: common stock and preferred stock.

Characteristics of Common Stock

The most prevalent type of capital stock is called common stock. When a corporation has only one kind of capital stock, it will be common stock. When the stock is issued, the owners receive certain rights from the corporation. These rights include:

1. The right to vote at stockholders' meetings.
2. The right to share in profits by receiving dividends.
3. The right to dispose of or sell their stock.
4. The right to maintain their proportionate ownership interest in the company. This right is called a preemptive right. For example, if Jill Evans owns 15% of the common stock of the corporation, she would have the chance to also purchase 15% of any *additional* common stock that is issued, before it is offered to the public at large.
5. The right, when a company is liquidated, to share in assets after creditors and others with prior claims are paid off.

Characteristics of Preferred Stock

Another type of capital stock some corporations may issue is called preferred stock. This stock provides stockholders with prior claim to a corporation's profits and assets over holders of common stock. Corporations watch current market conditions and try to offer preferred stock that will be attractive to investors. Holders of preferred stock often give up some of the rights that go with common stock—such as voting rights, preemptive rights, or even some earnings potential—in return for their more stable earnings that come from preferred stock. In many ways preferred stock is a less risky investment than common stock.

Preferred stock Class of capital stock that has preference to a corporation's profits and assets.

Dividends on Common and Preferred Stock

Dividends are paid to stockholders as their share of the corporation's profits. A dividend must be voted by the board of directors, and if it has been a bad year for profits, the board may refuse to vote a dividend. Keep in mind that a company may decide against a dividend in a good year, feeling it may be wise to reinvest money in some aspect of the company's business, such as research and development. For many years Microsoft did not declare a dividend, choosing instead to keep those earnings within the corporation for future expansion.

Dividends Cash, other assets, or shares of stock that a corporation issues to the stockholders.

As mentioned, preferred stock gives its stockholders a prior claim to a corporation's profits over holders of common stock. This preferential treatment can happen in several ways:

1. If a stock is cumulative preferred stock, the holders have a right to a certain dividend every year. If in some years the board does not issue a dividend, the amount payable will accumulate until the earnings justify the payout. At this time the preferred stockholders will get dividends for all past years as well as the current year before the holders of noncumulative preferred stock and common stock get any dividend.

   For example, Moore Company has 3,000 shares of cumulative preferred stock that are entitled to a dividend of $3 per share. In 2018, based on financial difficulties, Moore Company decided to pay no dividend. Thus, the company has dividends in arrears of $9,000. No dividends can be paid to noncumulative preferred stockholders and common stockholders until the preferred dividends are paid off in full: the amount in arrears plus the current year's dividend. Because financial conditions improved in 2019, Moore paid the $9,000 of dividends in arrears (3,000 shares × $3) to holders of preferred stock plus the current year's dividend of $9,000.

2. If a stock is noncumulative preferred stock, holders have a right to the current year's dividend, but without any holdovers from past years in which dividends were not declared.

3. If a stock is nonparticipating preferred stock, each year the holders of preferred stock receive their promised dividend and the remainder goes to common stock. Thus, if a company declared a dividend of $50,000, the preferred stockholders would get their usual percentage, and the common stockholders would get all the rest, even if it was a greater percentage dividend than preferred stock.

4. If a stock is participating preferred stock, preferred stockholders get their yearly dividend and can get a percentage of what's left over, splitting it in various ways with common stockholders.

Cumulative preferred stock Stock that entitles its holders to any undeclared dividends that have accumulated before common stockholders receive their dividends.

Dividends in arrears Dividends owed to cumulative preferred stockholders that must be paid before common stockholders can receive their dividends.

Noncumulative preferred stock Preferred stock that does not entitle its holders to a dividend for any year in which a dividend is not declared.

Nonparticipating preferred stock Preferred stock that entitles its holders only to a certain percentage of dividend, the remainder going to holders of common stock.

Participating preferred stock Stock that entitles its holders not only to a fixed dividend but also to an opportunity to share in additional dividends with common stockholders.

Stock Value (for Capital Stock)

When a corporation is created, it issues a certain number of shares of stock, which are then sold to stockholders. At the time that the corporation receives its charter, the board of directors may assign a par value to the stock, something like $25 or $50 a share. This value is entirely arbitrary; no one can say that the stock is really worth that much. It is a way of dividing up ownership of the corporation into a number of units and putting a value on each unit.

Par value An arbitrary value that is placed on each share of stock. Par value represents legal capital and not market value.

Figure 18.1 Par, No-Par, and Stated Value

Stock Can Be Issued with:

①

Par Value

An arbitrary value placed on each share at the time of authorization.

↓

Printed on stock certificates and used in accounting entries to credit stock account.

↓

Par value of all outstanding stock becomes minimum legal capital, what is kept in the business to pay off creditors as stipulated by laws of the state.

↓

A change in par value must be approved by the state that issued the charter.

↓

In no way does par value represent the market value of the stock.

②

No-Par Value with No Stated Value

No-par value placed on stock certificate.

↓

The total proceeds from the stock that is issued become the minimum legal capital.

③

No-Par Value with Stated Value

↓

Directors assign a stated value that is like par value but is not printed on stock certificates.

↓

The total stated value of all outstanding shares becomes the minimum legal capital.

↓

Directors can change stated value without approval of the state.

↓

Stated value doesn't mean market value.

Legal capital Minimum amount of capital that a corporation must leave in the company (cannot be withdrawn by stockholders) for the protection of the creditors.

No-par stock Stock with no-par value. A stated value could be placed on it.

Stated value Arbitrary value placed by the board of directors on each share of no-par stock to fulfill legal capital requirements.

Many companies have par values of 5 or 10 cents per share. The key point about par value is that it is a value assigned arbitrarily. It is stated on the stock certificate. Figure 18.1 can be used as a summary as you read the rest of the chapter.

In most states the assigning of par value per share times the number of shares issued for a corporation represents the legal capital, an amount that a corporation must retain in the business for the protection of creditors. Because the concept of par value can be quite misleading, some corporations will issue no-par stock, stock with no-par value. Thus, the *entire* proceeds from selling this issue represent the legal capital (number of shares issued times amount investors paid for each share).

Most states permit (or some require) the directors of a company to set a stated value on the shares. This value is also arbitrary but can be changed by the board of directors. Stated value, which has the same purpose as par value, may be less confusing to investors because it is not printed on the stock certificates.

Whether a stock is issued at par value, no-par value with no stated value, or no-par value with stated value, the capital stock account can be recorded with entries that indicate whether investors paid more or less than par value or stated value. We look at specific examples of recording capital stock in the next unit.

Now let's check your progress.

 **TRY IT!**   **Learning Unit 18-2**

Complete the following table by placing an X in the appropriate column:

	No-Par Value with No Stated Value	No-Par Value with Stated Value	Par Value
1. Par Value does not replace Market Value			
2. Printed on Stock Certificates			
3. Directors can change Stated Value without state approval			
4. Stated Value not printed on Stock Certificates			
5. Director cannot change Par Value without approval of state that issued charter			
6. No-Par Value placed on Stock Certificate with no Stated Value			

TRY IT!   **Solution Learning Unit 18-2**

	No-Par Value with No Stated Value	No-Par Value with Stated Value	Par Value
1. Par Value does not replace Market Value			X
2. Printed on Stock Certificates			X
3. Directors can change Stated Value without state approval		X	
4. Stated Value not printed on Stock Certificates		X	
5. Director cannot change Par Value without approval of state that issued charter			X
6. No-Par Value placed on Stock Certificate with no Stated Value	X		

Capital Stock Transactions and Calculating Dividends

 L03

In this unit, we look at how to record the issuing of stock that has (1) par value, (2) no-par value, and (3) no-par value with stated value. We also see how to record transactions in which stock is exchanged for noncash assets. We then look at how to calculate dividends for preferred and common stock.

Recording the Sale of Stock That Has Par Value

Situation 1: Selling Common Stock at Par. Katya Company sells 200 shares of a $10 par value common stock at $10 per share on February 3, 201X.

Here is an analysis of the transaction:

Accounts Affected	Category	↑↓	Rules	
Cash	Asset	↑	Dr. $2,000	$ 10 par
Common Stock	SE	↑	Cr. $2,000	× 200 shares = $2,000

Common stock is recorded at number of shares times par value per share. That value represents the legal capital. The journal entry would be as shown in Figure 18.2.

Figure 18.2
Selling Stock at Par

| 201X Feb. | 3 | Cash | | | | 2 0 0 0 00 | | |
| | | Common Stock | | | | | 2 0 0 0 00 | |

Situation 2: Selling Preferred Stock at Par. Katya Co. sells 300 shares of $50 par value preferred stock at $50 on March 18, 201X.

Once again, here is an analysis of the transaction:

Accounts Affected	Category	↑↓	Rules	
Cash	Asset	↑	Dr. $15,000	} $ 300 shares
Preferred Stock	SE	↑	Cr. $15,000	× $ 50 par
				= $15,000

Preferred Stock is recorded at number of shares times par value per share. The journal entry would be as shown in Figure 18.3.

Figure 18.3
Selling Preferred Stock at Par

| 201X Mar. | 18 | Cash | | | | 15 0 0 0 00 | | |
| | | Preferred Stock | | | | | 15 0 0 0 00 | |

Situation 3: Selling Common Stock at a Premium (More Than Par Value). Katya Co. sells 50 shares of $10 par value common stock at $15 on June 8, 201X.

The Analysis. The common stock is recorded at par value. Because this stock is sold at a premium (more than par value), the excess of the par value will be recorded in a new account called Paid-In Capital in Excess of Par Value—Common. Note in the transactional analysis that follows that this account is part of stockholders' equity. On the balance sheet it will be listed below Common Stock in the Paid-In Capital section of stockholders' equity.

Premium A term that records the sale of stock at more than par value. In this book we use the account Paid-In Capital in Excess of Par Value to record the premium received.

Paid-in Capital in Excess of Par Value—Common Difference between what stockholders invest and par value. This amount is not credited to the Common Stock account.

Accounts Affected	Category	↑↓	Rules	
Cash	Asset	↑	Dr. $750	→ 50 shares × $15
Common Stock	SE	↑	Cr. $500	→ 50 shares × $10 par
Paid-In Capital in Excess of Par Value—Common	SE	↑	Cr. $250	→ 50 shares × $5 excess per share over par

The journal entry will be as shown in Figure 18.4.

Figure 18.4
Selling Common Stock at a Premium

201X June	8	Cash				7 5 0 00		
		Common Stock					5 0 0 00	
		Paid-In Capital in						
		Excess of Par Value—Common					2 5 0 00	

Situation 4: Selling Common Stock at a Discount (Below Par).[2] Katya Co. sells 100 shares of $10 par value common stock at $8 on July 3, 201X.

The Analysis. When a stock is sold below par, a discount on stock results. An account called Discount on Common Stock records the discount. It is a contra-stockholders' equity account that will reduce the Common Stock account it is related to. Some states do not allow stock to be sold at a discount.

Discount on stock The difference between the par value of the stock and an amount less than the par value that the stockholders have contributed. Discounts do not happen often.

---

[2] This situation does not occur often and it makes the purchaser liable for the discount amount in the future if there is a bankruptcy.

Accounts Affected	Category	↑↓	Rules	
Cash	Asset	↑	Dr. $ 800	→ 100 shares × $8
Discount on Common Stock	Contra-SE	↑	Dr. $ 200	→ 100 shares × $2 ($10 par − $8)
Common Stock	SE	↑	Cr. $1,000	→ 100 shares × $10 par

The journal entry will be as shown in Figure 18.5.

201X July	3	Cash		800 00			
		Discount on Common Stock		200 00			
		Common Stock			1 000 00		

Figure 18.5
Selling Common Stock at a Discount

Now let's look at how to record the sale of stock with no-par value, with or without stated value.

Recording Sale of Stock with No-Par Value and Stated Value

Situation 5: Selling No-Par Common Stock with No Stated Value. Moss Co. sells 300 shares of no-par common stock for $20 per share on July 19, 201X.

The transaction analysis chart shows the following:

Accounts Affected	Category	↑↓	Rules	
Cash	Asset	↑	Dr. $6,000	} 300 shares × $20
Common Stock	SE	↑	Cr. $6,000	

The journal entry will be as shown in Figure 18.6.

201X July	19	Cash		6 000 00	
		Common Stock			6 000 00

Figure 18.6
Selling No-Par Common Stock with No Stated Value

Situation 6: Selling No-Par Common Stock with a Stated Value. Reese Co. sells 200 shares of no-par common stock with a stated value of $40 for $50 per share on July 19, 201X.

The Analysis. An excess over the stated value will be recorded in a stockholders' equity account called Paid-In Capital in Excess of Stated Value—Common.

Accounts Affected	Category	↑↓	Rules	
Cash	Asset	↑	Dr. $10,000	→ 200 shares × $50
Common Stock	SE	↑	Cr. $ 8,000	→ 200 shares × $40
Paid-In Capital in Excess of Stated Value—Common	SE	↑	Cr. $ 2,000	→ 200 shares × $10 ($50 − $40)

The journal entry will be as shown in Figure 18.7.

201X July	19	Cash		10 000 00	
		Common Stock			8 000 00
		Paid-In Capital in Excess of			
		Stated Value—Common			2 000 00

SUCCESS TIP

Note: Corporations cannot legally sell stock at less than the stated value.

Paid-In Capital in Excess of Stated Value—Common
Difference between what stockholders invest and the stated value placed on stock by the board of directors. This amount is not credited to the Common Stock account.

Figure 18.7
Selling No-Par Common Stock with Stated Value

Recording Transactions in Which Stock Is Exchanged for Noncash Assets

Situation 7: Exchanging Stock for Noncash Assets. On July 8, Moss Corporation exchanged 3,000 shares of $10 par-value common stock for machinery, buildings, and land. The assets had fair market values of $5,000, $10,000, and $20,000, respectively.

The Analysis. Assets are recorded at fair market value; common stock is recorded at par value. If fair market value is not available for assets, one can try to find the market (not par) value of the stock. In this chapter, we assume that fair market value of assets is available. The difference between fair market value and par is recorded in the account Paid-In Capital in Excess of Par Value. Par value is never used to measure the fair market value of the assets.

Accounts Affected	Category	↑↓	Rules	
Machinery	Asset	↑	Dr. $ 5,000	⎫
Buildings	Asset	↑	Dr. $10,000	⎬ fair market value
Land	Asset	↑	Dr. $20,000	⎭
Common Stock	SE	↑	Cr. $30,000	→ 3,000 shares × $10 par
Paid-In Capital in Excess of Par Value—Common	SE	↑	Cr. $ 5,000	→ ($35,000 − $30,000)

The journal entry will be as shown in Figure 18.8.

Figure 18.8
Exchanging Stock for Noncash Assets

	201X								
	July	8	Machinery		5 0 0 0 00			
			Buildings		10 0 0 0 00			
			Land		20 0 0 0 00			
			Common Stock				30 0 0 0 00	
			Paid-In Capital in Excess of					
			Par Value—Common				5 0 0 0 00	

Situation 8:[3] Issuing Stock to Organizers of a Business for Services Performed. On June 8, Rose Corporation issued 2,000 shares of $10 par common stock to the organizers of the business for services performed. The fair market value of the services performed is $20,000.

Organization cost Intangible asset that records the initial cost of forming the corporation, such as legal and incorporating fees. Today, it is being expensed.

The Analysis. Organization cost in the formation of a corporation (legal fees, printing of stock certificates, etc.) is an intangible asset on the balance sheet. It is usually amortized over 5 years (can be up to 40 years) because that life is used for income tax returns.

Accounts Affected	Category	↑↓	Rules
Organization Cost	Asset*	↑	Dr. $20,000
Common Stock	SE	↑	Cr. $20,000

*Now being expensed.

The journal entry will be as shown in Figure 18.9.

Figure 18.9
Organization Costs

	201X								
	June	8	Organization Cost		20 0 0 0 00			
			Common Stock				20 0 0 0 00	

---

[3] For the purposes of GAAP, organization costs are generally expensed for financial presentation (by accounts, timing, etc.) rather than treated as an asset and amortized, unless they are of a significant amount. For our discussion, it is treated as an asset that will be amortized.

How to Calculate Dividends

Table 18.1 summarizes the process of calculating dividends, which is divided into four steps. For our calculation, we use these basic facts:

- $150,000 dividend declared.
- Preferred stock is 6% and fully participating.
- Preferred stock: 1,000 shares, $200 par.
- Common stock: 6,000 shares, $100 par.

TABLE 18.1   Four-Step Procedure for Calculating Dividends with Cumulative, Fully Participating Preferred Stock

The Formula	The Calculation	Preferred Stock	Common Stock	Total Dividends
Step 1: Dividend for preferred	1,000 shares × $200 × 0.06 = $12,000	$12,000		$ 12,000
Number of Preferred Shares × Par Value per Share × Rate of Dividend				
Step 2: Dividend for common	6,000 shares × $100 × 0.06 = $36,000		$ 36,000	36,000
Number of Common Shares × Par Value per Share × Rate of Dividend				
Step 3: Find total par value				
Number of Shares × Par Value per Share (Preferred)	1,000 shares × $200 = $200,000			
plus				
Number of Shares × Par Value per Share (Common)	6,000 shares × $100 = $600,000			
	Total par = $800,000			
Step 4: Allocate remainder of dividend based on par value				
Preferred = $\dfrac{\text{Par Value of Preferred}}{\text{Total Par Value}}$ × Remainder of Dividend	$\dfrac{\$200,000}{\$800,000}$ × $102,000* = $25,500	25,500		25,500
Common = $\dfrac{\text{Par Value of Common}}{\text{Total Par Value}}$ × Remainder of Dividend	$\dfrac{\$600,000}{\$800,000}$ × $102,000* = $76,500	$37,500	76,500 $112,500	76,500 $150,000

*$150,000 − $48,000 = $102,000.

STEP 1:   To calculate preferred dividends, you multiply the number of preferred shares (1,000) times the par value ($200) per share times the rate of dividend (6%). The result is a $12,000 dividend to preferred.

STEP 2:   To calculate the common stock dividend, you multiply the number of shares (6,000) times the par value per share ($100) times the same rate of dividend (6%). The result is a dividend of $36,000.

STEP 3:   At this point $48,000 of the $150,000 of dividends has been apportioned. Because the preferred is participating—which means it can share in additional dividends beyond the 6% dividend—the next step is to find the total par value and allocate the remainder of the dividend based on the total par.

Note in step 3 how the number of shares of preferred is multiplied by the $200 par and the number of common shares is multiplied by the $100 par. Thus, total par is $800,000.

STEP 4:   Because preferred is one-fourth of the total par, preferred is allocated $25,500 $\left(\frac{1}{4} \times \$102,000\right)$ and common is allocated three-fourths of the $102,000, or $76,500.

We can see that both stocks were paid the same percentage on par by the following calculations:

Preferred:

$$\frac{\text{Total Dividends}}{\text{Total Par Value of Preferred}} = \frac{\$ 37,500}{\$200,000} = 18.75\%$$

Common:

$$\frac{\text{Total Dividends}}{\text{Total Par Value of Common}} = \frac{\$112,500}{\$600,000} = 18.75\%$$

The end result is that the dividends were equally divided in terms of percentage because preferred was fully participating.

Now let's check your progress.

 **TRY IT!**   **Learning Unit 18-3**

1. Complete the following table:

Account	Category	Rules of Dr./Cr.	
		Increase	Decrease
Cash			
Preferred Stock			
Paid-In Capital in Excess of Par Value—Common			
Common Stock			
Discount on Common Stock			

2. From the following, calculate the dividend given to Preferred and Common stockholders (round to nearest dollar if necessary):

4% fully participating Preferred Stock; $350,000 Dividend declared; Preferred Stock has 2,700 shares with a $30 par value; Common Stock has 5,400 shares with a $60 par value

TRY IT!   **Solution Learning Unit 18-3**

1.

Account	Category	Increase	Decrease
Cash	Asset	Dr.	Cr.
Preferred Stock	SE	Cr.	Dr.
Paid-In Capital in Excess of Par Value—Common	SE	Cr.	Dr.
Common Stock	SE	Cr.	Dr.
Discount on Common Stock	Contra-SE	Dr.	Cr.

2. Dividend: Preferred 2,700 × $30 × 0.04 = $ 3,240
           Common 5,400 × $60 × 0.04 = $ 12,960
                                        $ 16,200

$350,000 − $16,200 = $333,800 left to distribute

Total Par = $81,000 + $324,000 = $405,000

Preferred: 2/10 × $333,800 = $66,760

Common: 8/10 × $333,800 = $267,040

Total to Preferred: $3,240 + $66,760 = $70,000

Total to Common: $12,960 + $267,040 = $280,000

Journalizing Entries to Record Capital Stock Transactions for a Subscription Plan

 **L04**

In the last unit, we assumed that stocks were immediately issued and full payment of cash or other assets was received. In this unit, we examine stock transactions under stock subscription plans. Under such plans, buyers pledge to buy certain stocks but pay in installments or in a later lump sum. In most cases, companies will not issue the actual stock certificates to these buyers until payment is complete.

Let's look at how Krump Corporation receives subscriptions for 1,000 shares of $100 par-value common stock at $160 per share on April 1, 201X. Two equal installments will be paid on August 1 and November 1 by the buyer.

April 1: Accepted Subscription for 1,000 Shares at $160 per Share. Because the stock certificates will not be issued until paid in full, Krump Corporation records the ownership at par value in a temporary stockholders' equity account called Common Stock Subscribed. This account is shown in the Paid-In Capital section below the issue of the Common Stock. The amount due is recorded in an account called Subscriptions Receivable—Common Stock. The difference between the par value and the issue price is accumulated in a permanent account called Paid-In Capital in Excess of Par Value—Common.

Here is an analysis of the transaction:

Stock subscription Contractual agreement to buy a certain number of shares of stock from a corporation at a specific price.

Common Stock Subscribed Temporary stockholders' equity account that records at par value stock that has been subscribed to but not fully paid for.

Subscriptions Receivable— Common Stock Current asset on balance sheet that represents amount due on stock subscriptions.

	Accounts Affected	Category	↑↓	Rules
Represents amount due on stock subscription. It is a current asset on the balance sheet.	Subscriptions Receivable—Common Stock*	Asset	↑	Dr. $160,000
Stock reserved but not fully paid (1,000 shares × $100 par).	Common Stock Subscribed	SE	↑	Cr. $100,000
	Paid-In Capital in Excess of Par Value—Common	SE	↑	Cr. $ 60,000

1,000 shares × $160

1,000 shares × $ 60 par

*The SEC requires Subscriptions Receivable to be reported as a contra-account to Stockholders' Equity. As a result, most companies report it there. Otherwise, paid-in capital is overstated. This book will report Subscriptions Receivable as a current asset, which is also an accepted treatment.

The journal entry will be as shown in Figure 18.10.

201X Apr.	1	Subscriptions Receivable—Common Stock	160 0 0 0 00	
		Common Stock Subscribed		100 0 0 0 00
		Paid-In Capital in Excess of Par Value—Common		60 0 0 0 00

Figure 18.10
Accepted Subscriptions in Excess of Par

August 1: Received First Installment on Common Stock Subscription

Accounts Affected	Category	↑↓	Rules
Cash	Asset	↑	Dr. $80,000
Subscriptions Receivable—Common Stock	Asset	↓	Cr. $80,000

The journal entry will be as shown in Figure 18.11.

Figure 18.11
Received Installment from Stock
Subscription

	201X Aug.	1	Cash		80 0 0 0 00			
			Subscriptions Receivable—					
			Common Stock				80 0 0 0 00	

November 1: Received Final Installment on Common Stock Subscription

Accounts Affected	Category	↑↓	Rules
Cash	Asset	↑	Dr. $80,000
Subscriptions Receivable—Common Stock	Asset	↓	Cr. $80,000

The journal entry will be as shown in Figure 18.12.

Figure 18.12
Received Final Installment
from Stock Subscription

	201X Nov.	1	Cash		80 0 0 0 00			
			Subscriptions Receivable—					
			Common Stock				80 0 0 0 00	

November 1: Issued 1,000 Shares of Fully Paid Common Stock

Accounts Affected	Category	↑↓	Rules
Common Stock Subscribed	SE	↓	Dr. $100,000
Common Stock	SE	↑	Cr. $100,000

The journal entry will be as shown in Figure 18.13.

Figure 18.13
Issued Fully Paid Common Stock

	201X Nov.	1	Common Stock Subscribed		100 0 0 0 00			
			Common Stock				100 0 0 0 00	

Remember that stock is recorded at par value. At this point the Common Stock Subscribed account in the ledger (when posted) is reduced to a zero balance, and the Common Stock account records the issued stock (which has been paid for).

The numbers in Figure 18.14 are not related to the previous situations. The goal here is to show you the structure of Paid-In Capital and Retained Earnings.

Figure 18.14
Stockholders' Equity Section of
Balance Sheet

Stockholders' Equity		
Paid-In Capital:		
Common Stock, $100 par value; authorized		
10,000 shares, 7,000 issued and outstanding	$ 700 0 0 0 00	
Common Stock Subscribed, 2,000 shares at par	200 0 0 0 00	
Paid-In Capital in Excess of Par Value—Common	300 0 0 0 00	
Total Paid-In Capital	$1,200 0 0 0 00	
Retained Earnings	400 0 0 0 00	
Total Stockholders' Equity	$1,600 0 0 0 00	

Stockholders' Equity

Before concluding this chapter, let's take a moment to set up a simplified stockholders' equity section of a balance sheet. In the Blueprint, the complete layout of stockholders' equity is illustrated by the source-of-capital approach, which lists classes of stockholders first. An alternative way, called the legal capital approach, lists all legal capital first and is illustrated in the next chapter. Both approaches are acceptable.

Now let's check your progress.

Source-of-capital approach Method of preparing Paid-In Capital by listing classes of stockholder sources of capital.

Legal capital approach Method of preparing Paid-In Capital by listing the legal section first. (See Blueprint at end of Chapter 19.)

 **TRY IT!** Learning Unit 18-4

From the following, journalize the entries to record the stock subscription for Jackson Co.:

Jackson Co. on November 1 received a subscription for 500 shares of $60 par-value common stock stated at $95 per share. The buyer pays two equal installments on January 31 and April 30.

TRY IT! Solution Learning Unit 18-4

Date		Account	Dr.	Cr.
201X				
Nov.	1	Subscriptions Receivable—Common Stock	47,500	
		Common Stock Subscribed		30,000
		Paid-In Capital in Excess of Par Value—Common Stock		17,500
Jan.	31	Cash	23,750	
		Subscriptions Receivable—Common Stock		23,750
Apr.	30	Cash	23,750	
		Subscriptions Receivable—Common Stock		23,750
	30	Common Stock Subscribed	30,000	
		Common Stock		30,000

DEMONSTRATION SUMMARY PROBLEM

Joan Ring owns Ring's Bookkeeping Service. Her agenda for the day is to complete four different projects. Based on the following, help Joan complete the projects (we will show each project and solution separately).

Project 1

Journalize the following independent entries for Besy Co. The company was authorized to have 40,000 shares of common stock. Besy issued 7,000 shares at $9 on June 30, 201X.

A. Common stock has a $5 par value.
B. Common stock has no par and no stated value.
C. Common stock is no par with a stated value of $5.

Solution for Project 1

A.

Date		Account	Dr.	Cr.
201X				
June	30	Cash	63,000	
		Common Stock		35,000
		Paid-In Capital in Excess of Par Value—Common		28,000

B.

Date	Account	Dr.	Cr.
201X			
June 30	Cash	63,000	
	Common Stock		63,000

C.

Date	Account	Dr.	Cr.
201X			
June 30	Cash	63,000	
	Common Stock		35,000
	Paid-In Capital in Excess of Stated Value—Common		28,000

Tips

A. Common Stock recorded at the number of shares issued times the par value (7,000 × $5 = $35,000).
B. Since there is no par or stated value, record common stock at full price (7,000 shares × $9 = $63,000).
C. Common Stock recorded at stated value times number of shares (7,000 × $5 = $35,000).

Project 2

Jenson Co. is paying dividends to common and preferred stock. The preferred stock is 4% fully participating. The board declared a $90,000 dividend. There are 2,000 preferred shares at $30 par and 4,000 common shares at $50 par. Calculate total dividends that are due to preferred and common stockholders.

Solution for Project 2

- Preferred: 2,000 × $30 × 0.04 = $ 2,400
- Common: 4,000 × $50 × 0.04 =   8,000
                                  $10,400

$90,000 − $10,400 = $ 79,600 left to distribute
         2,000 × $30 = $ 60,000
         4,000 × $50 = 200,000

                Total $260,000

60,000/260,000 = 3/13
3/13 × $79,600 = $18,369 + $2,400 = $20,769 to preferred
10/13 × $79,600 = $61,231 + $8,000 = $69,231 to common

Tips

Multiply the number of shares of preferred and common times the par value and dividend rate. The $10,400 of dividends went to preferred and common, leaving $79,600 left to be paid to preferred and common. To find out how much each class of stock gets, you first need to calculate the total par value (this is the $260,000). Then you take the total par value of preferred as a fraction of the total par of preferred and common stock, and then allocate three parts out of 13 go to preferred and 10 parts out of 13 to common.

Project 3

Record the appropriate journal entries to record the stock subscription for Lion Co.

On June 8, 201X, Lion Co. issued a stock subscription of 2,000 shares at $50 par value for common stock at $65 per share. On July 12, Lion recorded one-half of the installment. The remainder of the subscription was received on August 12.

Solution for Project 3

Date		Account	Dr.	Cr.
201X				
June	8	Subscriptions Receivable—Common Stock	130,000	
		Common Stock Subscribed		100,000
		Paid-In Capital in Excess of Par Value—Common		30,000
July	12	Cash	65,000	
		Subscriptions Receivable—Common Stock		65,000
Aug.	12	Cash	65,000	
		Subscriptions Receivable—Common Stock		65,000
Aug.	12	Common Stock Subscribed	100,000	
		Common Stock		100,000

Tips

Subscriptions Receivable—Common Stock represents the full amount of cash that Lion Co. will receive. Common Stock Subscribed is the par value of the stock times the number of shares. The Paid-In Capital account is the difference between the par value per share and what was received in cash per share. When the final payment is received, the Common Stock Subscribed is converted into Common Stock.

Project 4

Prepare a Stockholders' Equity section for Randy Co. on December 31, 201X.

Randy Co. began its business on January 1, 201X. It sold at $30 per share 5,000 shares of no-par common stock with a stated value of $18. Randy's charter indicates 25,000 shares were authorized. Retained Earnings were $33,000 on December 31.

Solution for Project 4

Randy Co.
Stockholders' Equity
December 31, 201X

Paid-In Capital	
Common Stock, No-Par Value, Stated Value $18 per share, authorized	
25,000 shares, 5,000 shares issued and outstanding	$ 90,000
Paid-In Capital in Excess of Stated Value—Common	60,000
Total Paid-In Capital	$150,000
Retained Earnings	33,000
Total Stockholders' Equity	$183,000

Tips

The Paid-In Capital in Excess of Stated Value—Common account accumulates the excess of the stated value of the stock that was issued ($30 − $18 = $12 excess per share). Retained Earnings is added to the Paid-In Capital to get Total Stockholders' Equity.

SUCCESS COACH

18

The following Do It Right Tips are from Learning Units 18-1 to 18-4. Take the Do It Right Now Checkup and use the Check Your Score to see how you are doing. The Success Coach provides tips before each Checkup to help you avoid common accounting errors.

LU 18-1 The Advantages and Disadvantages of the Corporate Structure

Do It Right Tips: The advantages of forming a corporation result in limited liability, unlimited life, ease of transferring ownership, no mutual agency, and ease of raising capital. Keep in mind that there could be some difficulties in forming a corporation, along with taxes levied on the corporation.

Do It Right Now Checkup: Answer true or false to the following statements.

1. A charter is issued by the corporation.
2. Bankruptcy could affect the unlimited life of a corporation.
3. Stock transfers represent a shift in ownership.
4. A corporation is not a separate legal entity.
5. A corporation is not subject to mutual agency.

LU 18-2 Retained Earnings and Stockholders' Equity

Do It Right Tips: Stocks can be issued with par value, no-par value with no stated value, or no-par value with stated value. Keep in mind that par value is an arbitrary value placed on each share. Par value does not represent the market value of the stock. Stated value does not mean market value.

Do It Right Now Checkup: Answer true or false to the following statements.

1. "Retained earnings" means cash.
2. Preemptive rights allow a stockholder to maintain his or her proportionate ownership in a company.
3. A cumulative dividend means that you have no right to past dividends.
4. Noncumulative stock means that you have rights to prior dividends.
5. Holders of common stock receive dividends before holders of preferred stock.

LU 18-3 Capital Stock Transactions and Calculating Dividends

Do It Right Tips: Common stock is part of stockholders' equity. The balance of the account is normally a credit.

Paid-In Capital in Excess of Par Value is part of stockholders' equity. This account increases with a credit. Discount on Common Stock is a contra-stockholders' equity account. It increases with a debit. When calculating dividends, the par value will be used.

Do It Right Now Checkup: Answer true or false to the following statements.

1. Selling common stock for cash will result in a debit to common stock.
2. If stock is sold for a value higher than par value, the Paid-In Capital in Excess of Par Value account will be credited.
3. In calculating dividends, the amount allocated to common and preferred would be based on total market value.
4. Common stock is an asset.
5. Discount on common stock is a contra-stockholders' equity account.

LU 18-4 Journalizing Entries to Record Capital Stock Transactions for a Subscription Plan

Do It Right Tips: Common Stock Subscribed is a stockholders' equity account that records the amount of stock reserved at par before it is fully paid. Any excess of par is recorded in the Paid-In Capital in Excess of Par Value account. When payment is received, the Subscriptions Receivable account is reduced and Common Stock Subscribed is moved into Common Stock.

Do It Right Now Checkup: Answer true or false to the following statements.

1. Subscriptions Receivable—Common Stock is an asset.
2. Common Stock Subscribed is recorded at market value.
3. Retained Earnings is an asset.
4. The source-of-capital approach is one way to set up stockholders' equity.
5. The Common Stock Subscribed account increases with a debit.

CHECK YOUR SCORE: Answers to the Do It Right Now Checkup

LU 18-1

1. False—A charter is received by the corporation.
2. True
3. True
4. False—A corporation is a separate legal entity.
5. True

LU 18-2

1. False—Retained earnings is part of stockholders' equity.
2. True
3. False—A cumulative dividend means that you have the right to past dividends.
4. False—Noncumulative stock means that you have no rights to prior dividends.
5. False—Holders of preferred stock receive dividends before holders of common stock.

LU 18-3

1. False—Selling common stock for cash will result in a credit to common stock.
2. True
3. False—In calculating dividends, the amount allocated to common and preferred would be based on par value.
4. False—Common Stock is part of stockholders' equity.
5. True

LU 18-4

1. True
2. False—Common Stock Subscribed is recorded at par value.
3. False—Retained Earnings is part of stockholders' equity.
4. True
5. False—Common Stock Subscribed increases with a credit.

BLUEPRINT: SOURCE-OF-CAPITAL APPROACH

VALLEY CO. PARTIAL BALANCE SHEET			
Assets			
Current Assets:			
Subscriptions Receivable, Common Stock	XXX		
Intangible Assets:			
Organization Cost		XXX	
Total Assets			XXX
Liabilities			

Note that preferred stock is listed before common stock.

Stockholders' Equity			
Paid-In Capital:			
Preferred 12% stock, $10 par value,			
authorized 20,000 shares, 8,000 shares			
issued and outstanding	XXX		
Paid-In Capital in Excess of Par			
Value—Preferred	XXX		
Total Paid-In Capital by preferred			
stockholders		XXX	
Common Stock, no-par value, stated			
value $10 per share, authorized			
100,000 shares, 30,000 shares issued and			
outstanding	XXX		
Common Stock Subscribed, 1,000 shares			
at stated value	XXX		
Paid-In Capital in Excess of Stated			
Value—Common	XXX		
Total Paid-In Capital by common			
stockholders		XXX	
Total Paid-In Capital		XXX	
Retained Earnings		XXX	
Total Stockholders' Equity			XXX

Discussion Questions and Critical Thinking/Ethical Case

1. What is the difference between the articles of incorporation and a charter?
2. Who elects the board of directors?
3. List the advantages of the corporate form of organization.
4. Explain the difference between Paid-In Capital and retained earnings.
5. What is the maximum number of shares a company may legally issue?
6. What does *preemptive right* mean?
7. Distinguish among legal capital, par value, no-par value, and no-par value with a stated value.
8. Preferred stock can never be cumulative *and* nonparticipating: true or false? Support your answer.
9. What is the normal balance and the category of the account Discount on Common Stock?
10. How does one calculate Paid-In Capital in Excess of Par Value or Stated Value?
11. Explain the account Paid-In Capital in Excess of Par Value as it relates to exchange of stock for noncash assets.
12. What is the purpose of the account Organization Costs?
13. In stock subscriptions, why does one credit Common Stock Subscribed?
14. Avan Corporation just published its financial statements. The president of Avan told the accountants not to include in the annual report any information about a pending lawsuit. The president thought it would only worry the stockholders. Do you think the president is correct in not including any information about the pending lawsuit in the annual report? You make the call. Write down your recommendations to the president.

Concept Checks

MyLabAccounting

Stockholders' Equity

 **L02** *(15 min)*

1. Lang Corporation has capital stock of $7,300. Its Retained Earnings account has a $14,700 balance. Cash has a balance of $9,800. What is the total of stockholders' equity for Lang Corporation?

Cumulative Preferred

 **L03** *(15 min)*

2. Prior to the current year, Jargon Co. owed $14,900 each year for 6 years to holders of cumulative preferred stock. This year Jargon pays out $190,000 in dividends to preferred and common. How much did each class of stock receive?

Journalizing Sales of Stock

 **L02,3** *(20 min)*

3. Journalize the following:

May.	7	Patches Co. sells 400 shares of $23 par-value common stock at $23.
Oct.	17	John Co. sells 500 shares of $13 par-value common stock at $17.
Nov.	25	Able Co. sells 500 shares of no-par common stock with a stated value of $16 for $25 per share.
Dec.	28	Lowe Co. issues 600 shares of $9 par-value common stock to organizers of the firm for services rendered costing $8,500.

Cumulative and Participating Preferred

 **L03** *(20 min)*

4. From the following, calculate the dividends for common and preferred stock:
   - 14% fully participating preferred stock.
   - The board declared a $220,000 dividend.
   - Preferred stock 3,200 shares, $90 par value; common stock 9,600 shares, $70 par.

(20 min) **LO4**   **Stock Subscriptions**

5. Journalize the entries to record the stock subscription plan for Gray Co. On July 1, Gray received subscriptions for 1,000 shares of $31 par-value common stock at $44 per share. The buyer will pay two equal installments on September 30 and December 31.

MyLabAccounting   ## Exercises

Set A

(20 min) **LO2,3**    **18A-1.**   Lucy Corporation was authorized to issue 29,000 shares of common stock. Record the journal entry for each of the following independent situations, assuming Lucy issues 6,300 shares at $13 on July 20, 201X:

a. Common stock has an $11 par value.
b. Common stock has no-par and no stated value.
c. Common stock is no-par stock with a stated value of $5.

(20 min) **LO3**    **18A-2.**   On July 10, 201X, Vixen Corporation issued 2,800 shares of common stock with a par value of $103 in exchange for equipment with a fair market value of $327,000. Journalize the appropriate entry.

(30 min) **LO3**    **18A-3.**   Quincy Corporation in its first 3 years of operation paid out the following dividends:

*   Year 1: $0
*   Year 2: $32,000
*   Year 3: $85,000

Given that Quincy has 3,100 shares of $97 par 12% cumulative, nonparticipating preferred stock and 14,600 shares of $27 par-value common stock, what would be the total dividends paid each year to holders of common and preferred stock?

(30 min) **LO4**   **18A-4.**   On January 1, 201X, Brown Corporation issued on a subscription basis 1,040 shares of $51 par-value common stock at $90 per share. Two equal installments were to be made on July 1 and December 31. Prepare the appropriate journal entries on January 1, July 1, and December 31 to record this stock subscription for Brown Corporation.

(30 min) **LO4**    **18A-5.**   Pearker Corporation began its business on January 1, 201X. It sold at $32 per share 6,400 shares of no-par common stock with a stated value of $19 per share. The charter of Pearker indicated that 37,000 shares were authorized. Retained earnings were $61,000 on December 31. Prepare the stockholders' equity section for Pearker on December 31, 201X.

Set B

(20 min) **LO2,3**   **18B-1.**   Larry Corporation was authorized to issue 30,000 shares of common stock. Record the journal entry for each of the following independent situations, assuming Larry issues 5,800 shares at $12 on July 20, 201X:

a. Common stock has an $11 par value.
b. Common stock has no par and no stated value.
c. Common stock is no-par stock with a stated value of $3.

(20 min) **LO3**   **18B-2.**   On July 10, 201X, Happy Corporation issued 3,100 shares of common stock with a par value of $99 in exchange for equipment with a fair market value of $321,000. Journalize the appropriate entry.

18B-3. Lakeshore Corporation in its first 3 years of operation paid out the following dividends:

L03 *(30 min)*

- Year 1: $0
- Year 2: $26,000
- Year 3: $95,000

Given that Lakeshore has 3,300 shares of $97 par 11% cumulative, nonparticipating preferred stock and 14,500 shares of $28 par-value common stock, what would be the total dividends paid each year to holders of common and preferred stock?

18B-4. On January 1, 201X, Lane Corporation issued on a subscription basis 1,010 shares of $48 par-value common stock at $86 per share. Two equal installments were to be made on July 1 and December 31. Prepare the appropriate journal entries on January 1, July 1, and December 31 to record this stock subscription for Lane Corporation.

L04 *(30 min)*

18B-5. Billings Corporation began its business on January 1, 201X. It sold at $28 per share 6,500 shares of no-par common stock with a stated value of $21 per share. The charter of Billings indicated 37,000 shares were authorized. Retained earnings were $59,000 on December 31. Prepare the stockholders' equity section for Billings on December 31, 201X.

L04 *(30 min)*

Problems

MyLabAccounting

Set A

18A-1. The following is the Paid-In Capital section of stockholders' equity for the Renzo Corporation on June 1, 201X:

L03,4 *(50 min)*

Paid-In Capital:	
Preferred Stock, $108 par, authorized 22,000 shares, 4,500 shares issued	$ 486,000
Paid-In Capital in Excess of Par Value—Preferred Stock	116,000
Common Stock, $21 par, authorized 54,000 shares, 22,000 shares issued	462,000
Paid-In Capital in Excess of Par Value—Common Stock	165,000
Total Paid-In Capital	$1,229,000

Check Figure:
(2) Total Paid-In Capital $2,870,000

The following transactions occurred in the months of June and July:

201X			
June	1	Issued 3,300 shares of preferred stock at $112 per share.	
	2	Issued 7,000 shares of common stock at $38 per share.	
	15	Issued 8,400 shares of common stock at $38 per share.	
July	2	Issued 5,100 shares of preferred stock at $112 per share.	
	18	Issued 1,700 shares of common stock in exchange for building and land with fair market value of $62,000 and $53,000, respectively.	

1. Journalize the preceding entries and update the stockholders' equity ledger.
2. Prepare a new Paid-In Capital section of stockholders' equity as of July 31, 201X.

18A-2. Kirk Corporation has 19,000 shares outstanding of $8 par value, 8% preferred stock, and 38,000 shares outstanding of $8 par-value common stock. In its first 5 years of operation, the company paid the following dividends: 2015, $0; 2016, $12,160; 2017, $36,480; 2018, $0; 2019, $68,440. Calculate the dividends paid to preferred and common stockholders under the following three independent situations:

L03 *(50 min)*

a. Preferred stock is noncumulative and nonparticipating.
b. Preferred stock is cumulative and nonparticipating.
c. Preferred stock is cumulative and fully participating.

Check Figure:
(b) Pref.
$12,160	2016
$24,320	2017
$24,320	2019

(40 min) **L04**

18A-3. From the following partial mixed list, select the appropriate titles and prepare a stockholders' equity section using the source-of-capital approach as shown in the Blueprint example for Neon Corporation on July 31, 201X:

Office Equipment	$ 75,000
Land	190,000
Paid-In Capital in Excess of Par Value—Preferred Stock	100,000
Building	90,000
Accounts Receivable	115,000
Notes Receivable	41,000
Organization Costs	14,000
Common Stock, $10 par value (57,000 shares issued and outstanding; 100,000 shares authorized)	570,000
Retained Earnings	208,000
Subscriptions Receivable—Common Stock	75,000
Patents	8,000
Preferred 12% Stock, $53 Par (5,700 shares issued; 10,000 shares authorized)	302,100
Common Stock Subscribed at Par	245,000
Paid-In Capital in Excess of Par Value—Common Stock	18,000

Check Figure:
Stockholders' Equity $1,443,100

(40 min) **L03,4**

18A-4. Lincoln Corporation was just issued a charter by the state of New York. This charter gives Lincoln the authority to issue 275,000 shares of $8 par-value common stock. From the following transactions:

1. Prepare journal entries to record the transactions of Lincoln Corp. for the month of August.
2. Prepare the Paid-In Capital section of Lincoln's balance sheet at the end of the month.

201X		
Aug.	10	Issued 2,250 shares of stock for land and building with fair market values of $17,500 and $19,000, respectively.
	15	Accepted subscriptions to 18,800 shares of stock for $250,000 to be paid in two equal installments.
	21	Collected first installment on 9,400 shares of the common stock subscribed on August 15.
	27	Sold 7,800 shares of stock for $98,000.
	29	Collected last installment on 9,400 shares of the common stock subscribed on August 15 and issued the shares.

Check Figure:
Total Paid-In Capital $384,500

Set B

(50 min) **L03,4**

18B-1. The following is the Paid-In Capital section of stockholders' equity for the Royce Corporation on June 1, 201X:

Paid-In Capital:	
Preferred Stock, $104 par, authorized 24,000 shares, 4,000 shares issued	$ 416,000
Paid-In Capital in Excess of Par Value—Preferred Stock	115,000
Common Stock, $23 par, authorized 50,000 shares, 21,000 shares issued	483,000
Paid-In Capital in Excess of Par Value—Common Stock	170,000
Total Paid-In Capital	$1,184,000

The following transactions occurred in the months of June and July:

201X		
June	1	Issued 2,700 shares of preferred stock at $108 per share.
	2	Issued 7,100 shares of common stock at $34 per share.
	15	Issued 7,800 shares of common stock at $48 per share.
July	2	Issued 5,400 shares of preferred stock at $110 per share.
	18	Issued 2,300 shares of common stock in exchange for building and land with fair market value of $65,000 and $49,000, respectively.

Check Figure:
Total Paid-In Capital $2,799,400

1. Journalize the entries and update the stockholders' equity ledger.
2. Prepare a new Paid-In Capital section of stockholders' equity as of July 31, 201X.

18B-2.   Dickens Corporation has 25,000 shares outstanding of $10 par value, 6% preferred stock, and 50,000 shares outstanding of $10 par-value common stock. In its first 5 years of operation, the company paid the following dividends: 2015, $0; 2016, $15,000; 2017, $45,000; 2018, $0; 2019, $77,400. Calculate the dividends paid to preferred and common stockholders under the following three independent situations:

 **L03** *(50 min)*

a. Preferred stock is noncumulative and nonparticipating.
b. Preferred stock is cumulative and nonparticipating.
c. Preferred stock is cumulative and fully participating.

Check Figure:
(b) Pref: 2016 $15,000
            2017 $30,000
            2019 $30,000

18B-3.   From the following partial mixed list, select the appropriate titles and prepare a stockholders' equity section using the source-of-capital approach as shown in the Blueprint example for Ration Corporation on July 31, 201X.

 **L04** *(40 min)*

Office Equipment	$90,000
Land	175,000
Paid-In Capital in Excess of Par Value—Preferred Stock	125,000
Building	105,000
Accounts Receivable	110,000
Notes Receivable	35,000
Organization Costs	9,000
Common Stock, $11 par value (65,000 shares issued and outstanding; 75,000 shares authorized)	715,000
Retained Earnings	203,000
Subscriptions Receivable—Common Stock	75,000
Patents	10,000
Preferred 10% Stock, $48 par value (6,600 shares issued; 10,500 shares authorized)	316,800
Common Stock Subscribed at Par	280,000
Paid-In Capital in Excess of Par Value—Common Stock	19,000

Check Figure:
Total Stockholders'
Equity $1,658,800

18B-4.   Rebal Corporation was just issued a charter by the state of New York. This charter gives Rebal the authority to issue 325,000 shares of $7 par-value common stock. Consider the following transactions:

 **L03,4** *(40 min)*

1. Prepare journal entries to record the transactions of Rebal Corp. for the month of September.

2. Prepare the Paid-In Capital section of Rebal Corporation's balance sheet at the end of the month.

201X		
Sept.	9	Issued 2,150 shares of stock for land and building with fair market values of $14,500 and $18,000, respectively.
	14	Accepted subscriptions to 18,400 shares of stock for $246,000 to be paid in two equal installments.
	20	Collected first installment on 9,200 shares of common stock subscribed on September 14.
	26	Sold 6,600 shares of stock for $96,000.
	28	Collected last installment on 9,200 shares of common stock subscribed on September 14 and issued the shares.

Financial Report Problem

(20 min) **LO1,2**

Reading Amazon's Annual Report

Go to https://tinyurl.com/slaterca14e to access Amazon's 2016 Annual Report. Go to page 39 and find the par value of Amazon stock.

Corporations: Stock Values, Dividends, Treasury Stocks, and Retained Earnings

19

CHAPTER PREVIEW: ACCOUNTING IN ACTION

In Jose Reyes's forensic accounting class, his professor talked about how Bernie Madoff defrauded investors out of $65 billion. Madoff was sent to prison for 150 years for bilking individuals and institutional investors out of billions of dollars. As a part of the fraudulent activities of his accounting firm on behalf of Madoff's company, David Friehling was convicted of signing off on fraudulent financial statements. As an investor, you need to be able to read corporate financial statements and have faith that the numbers are accurately and ethically representative of the business's performance. In this chapter, we learn about stock values, dividends, treasury stock, and retained earnings and how to account for them.

Learning Objectives – Relating Accounting Theory By Unit

LO1 Calculate Redemption, Market, and Book Value

LO2 Calculate and Journalize Dividends

LO3 Journalize Treasury Stock Transactions

LO4 Explain Appropriation of Retained Earnings and Statement of Retained Earnings

When making dividend decisions, Amazon must take many things into account, including how the company is performing, along with its responsibility to stockholders. In this chapter, we continue the study of aspects of corporate equity that we began in the last chapter. We discuss a number of topics, including stock values, how and why dividends are declared and paid, why a corporation buys back its own stock, and the restrictions on retained earnings.

LEARNING UNIT 19-1

Redemption, Market, and Book Value

L01

Redemption value Price per share a corporation pays to redeem or retire capital stock.

Redemption Value

When a corporation issues preferred stock, it often reserves the right to retire or redeem that stock for a specific price. At the time the stock is issued, this price per share, called redemption value, is determined, and people buy the stock knowing that the corporation can redeem it at this price.

Market Value

Market value Price that a buyer pays to purchase shares of capital stock in the open market. Of course, for every buyer there is a seller.

The price at which shares of capital stock are bought and sold in the open market is called the market value. Economic conditions, a company's earnings, and investors' expectations all play a factor in determining the market price.

Book Value per Share

Book value per share Amount of net assets that a stockholder would receive on a per share basis, assuming no gain or loss on the sale of the assets.

Book value per share is, in general, the total of stockholders' equity (assets minus liabilities) divided by the number of shares issued. Why is book value used? For several reasons:

1. When a company seeks a loan, banks may specify a minimum book value for a loan to be approved.

2. If a merger is being negotiated, book value may be used as a factor in setting an exchange ratio of stock. For example, based on book value, one share of Octon Co. stock could fairly be issued for three shares of Xeron Co. stock, if the book value of Octon stock is $30 and the book value of Xeron stock is $10.

3. Book value may be used when contracts are made. For example, an individual may receive in the future an option to buy or sell stock based on future book value. (That value is *not* market value, which is based on current prices.)

It is important to emphasize that book value doesn't represent what an owner might receive if the assets of a company were *liquidated*. At the time of liquidation the assets may be sold at prices quite different from the values on the books, which are based on cost and not current market prices.

Calculating Book Value with Only One Class of Stock

When a corporation has only common stock, book value per share is calculated using the following equation:

$$\text{Book Value Per Share} = \frac{\text{Total Stockholder' Equity}}{\text{Total Shares Outstanding}}$$

As an example, we use the stockholders' equity shown in Figure 19.1 for Jones Corporation and calculate book value per share of common stock.

The book value is $45 per share ($450,000/10,000 shares). Thus, for each share of stock owned, $45 would be received *if* the corporation were liquidated without any losses from disposing of assets. By the time assets are disposed of, the owner might get much less than book value.

JONES CORPORATION STOCKHOLDERS' EQUITY		
Paid-In Capital:		
Common Stock, $25 par value; 10,000 shares		
authorized, issued, and outstanding	$ 250 0 0 0 00	
Paid-In Capital in Excess of Par Value—Common	110 0 0 0 00	
Total Paid-In Capital	$ 360 0 0 0 00	
Retained Earnings	90 0 0 0 00	
Total Stockholders' Equity	$ 450 0 0 0 00	

Figure 19.1
Stockholders' Equity

Calculating Book Value with Both Preferred and Common Stock

When a company has two classes of stock, before book value can be calculated, the stockholders' equity must be allocated (divided up) for each class of stock. First, for preferred stock, a corporation assigns the redemption value (or par value if the stock has no redemption value) of the stock along with any dividends in arrears (any dividends that are owed to holders of preferred stock but have not yet been paid out). This total of redemption value plus dividends in arrears is divided by the number of preferred shares outstanding. The *remainder* of stockholders' equity is assigned to the common stockholders, and the book value of the common stock is calculated by that amount divided by the number of common stock shares outstanding. Book value per share can be shown in the following formulas:

$$\text{Book Value Per Share, Preferred} = \frac{\text{Redemption Value} + \text{Dividends in Arrears}}{\text{Number of Shares of Preferred Stock Outstanding}}$$

$$\text{Book Value Per Share, Common} = \frac{\text{Total Stockholders' Equity} - \text{Total Amount Assigned to Preferred}}{\text{Number of Shares of Common Stock Outstanding}}$$

Let's illustrate this situation by looking at the stockholders' equity of Ryan Corporation (Figure 19.2) and performing the necessary calculations.

Given: Redemption value of preferred is $103; there are $14,000 worth of dividends in arrears.

Thus,

$$\text{Book Value Per Share, Preferred} = \frac{\$206,000 + \$14,000}{2,000 \text{ Shares}}$$

$$= \frac{\$220,000}{2,000 \text{ Shares}} = \$110 \text{ per Share}$$

and

$$\text{Book Value Per Share, Common} = \frac{\$894,000 - \$220,000}{10,000 \text{ Shares}}$$

$$= \frac{\$674,000}{10,000 \text{ Shares}} = \$67.40 \text{ per Share}$$

Note: When preferred stock is redeemed, the paid-in capital in excess of par is *not* returned and thus is *not* included as part of the preferred equity in the book value calculation.

Figure 19.2
Calculating Book Value
from Stockholders' Equity

RYAN CORPORATION STOCKHOLDERS' EQUITY		
Paid-In Capital:		
Preferred 7% Stock, $100 per value, authorized		
3,000 shares cumulative and nonparticipating,		
2,000 shares issued and outstanding	$ 200 0 0 0 00	
Paid-In Capital in Excess of Par Value—Preferred	10 0 0 0 00	
Total Paid-In Capital by Preferred Stockholders		$ 210 0 0 0 00
Common Stock, $50 par value, authorized 12,000		
shares, 10,000 shares issued and outstanding	500 0 0 0 00	
Paid-In Capital in Excess of Par Value—Common	20 0 0 0 00	
Total Paid-In Capital by Common Stockholders		520 0 0 0 00
Total Paid-In Capital		$ 730 0 0 0 00
Retained Earnings		164 0 0 0 00
Total Stockholders' Equity		$ 894 0 0 0 00

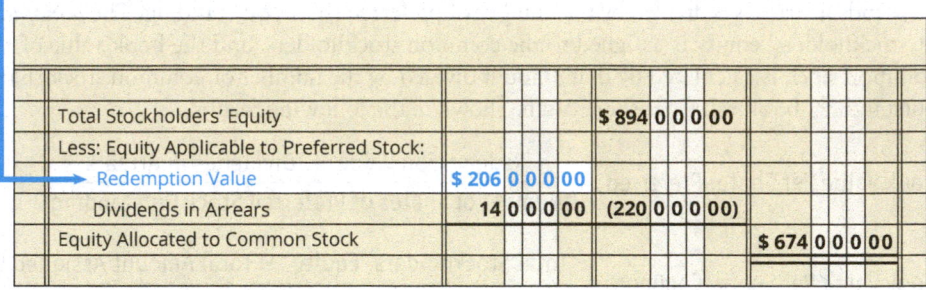

Redemption value
$103 × 2,000 shares

Total Stockholders' Equity		$ 894 0 0 0 00
Less: Equity Applicable to Preferred Stock:		
Redemption Value	$ 206 0 0 0 00	
Dividends in Arrears	14 0 0 0 00	(220 0 0 0 00)
Equity Allocated to Common Stock		$ 674 0 0 0 00

Now let's check your progress.

 ## TRY IT! Learning Unit 19-1

Calculate book value per share for (a) preferred and (b) common stock given the following:

> Redemption value of preferred stock is $107. There are $3,100 of preferred dividends in arrears. Preferred stock has 3,100 shares issued and outstanding while common stock has 8,900 shares issued and outstanding. Total Stockholders' Equity is $779,800.

TRY IT! Solution Learning Unit 19-1

BV Preferred = ($331,700 + $3,100)/3,100 shares = $108
Note the $331,700 was $107 × 3,100 shares
BV Common = ($779,800 − $334,800)/8,900 = $50.00

LEARNING UNIT 19-2

L02

Dividend Cash or other assets that a corporation distributes as earnings to stockholders.

Calculating and Journalizing Dividends

In this unit, we discuss the distribution of cash, stock, or other assets that the board of directors declares as dividends. Dividends, as we have seen, are the distribution of earnings of the corporation. It is important to realize that only the board of directors of a corporation has the authority to determine whether a dividend is to be paid, how much it will be, who receives it, and when and how it will be paid.

Three important dates are associated with the dividend process.

1. Date of declaration: The day the board of directors announces its decision to pay a dividend. This date creates a liability to the company called Dividend Payable.
2. Date of record: The date established by the board of directors that determines which stockholders will receive the dividend. These stockholders can be identified in the corporation's subsidiary stockholders' ledger at this date of record.
3. Date of payment: The date that the dividend is actually paid to stockholders of record.

Cash Dividends

The distribution of earnings of a corporation in the form of cash to its stockholders is called a cash dividend. For example, on March 8, 201X, the board of directors of Tell Corporation declares a $2 cash dividend per share on the 5,000 shares issued and outstanding. The dividend will be paid on April 16, 201X, to stockholders of record on March 25, 201X. Let's look at how to analyze as well as record this cash dividend.

Date of Declaration: March 8, 201X.   The following chart analyzes this transaction.

Declaration of dividends reduces Retained Earnings. A legally declared dividend is a current liability on the balance sheet.

Accounts Affected	Category	↑↓	Rules
Retained Earnings	SE	↓	Dr. $10,000
Dividends Payable	Liability	↑	Cr. $10,000

The journal entry will look like Figure 19.3.

Mar.	8	Retained Earnings	10 0 0 0 00	
		Dividends Payable		10 0 0 0 00
		Dividends declared of $2 to stockholders		
		of record Mar. 25, 201X: payable on		
		Apr. 16, 201X, as declared by board		
		of directors		

Date of Payment: April 16, 201X.   Here is an analysis of the dividend payment.

Accounts Affected	Category	↑↓	Rules
Dividends Payable	Liability	↓	Dr. $10,000
Cash	Asset	↓	Cr. $10,000

The journal entry will look like Figure 19.4.

Apr.	16	Dividends Payable	10 0 0 0 00	
		Cash		10 0 0 0 00
		Payment of dividend to stockholders of		
		record on Mar. 25, 201X		

Date of declaration   Date upon which the board of directors of a corporation formally declares a dividend.

Dividend Payable   Liability showing amount of cash dividend owed.

Date of record   Date of ownership that determines which stockholders will receive the dividend.

Date of payment   Date the dividend is paid.

Cash dividend   Dividend that is paid in cash.

Figure 19.3
Declaring a Cash Dividend

Note that no entry is made at the date of record.

Remember: Retained Earnings doesn't mean Cash. Cash is an asset, whereas Retained Earnings is part of stockholders' equity.

Figure 19.4
Payment of a Cash Dividend

The end result of these transactions is to reduce Cash and Retained Earnings. In effect, the company is distributing part of its accumulated income to stockholders.

The Stock Dividend

Stock dividend Stock that is distributed to stockholders instead of cash or other assets.

A stock dividend occurs when a corporation issues its own stock instead of a distribution of assets to its stockholders. A company may declare a stock dividend instead of a cash dividend for a number of reasons:

1. To satisfy stockholders' expectations. The corporation doesn't have enough cash to pay a cash dividend and offers the stock dividend instead. The stockholders make no new investment to receive this type of dividend.
2. To increase permanent capital in the business (because more stock is issued).
3. To reduce the market value of the stock because the price may be too high in the trading on the open market. When more stock is supplied with no additional demand for it, stock prices will go down.
4. Because stockholders postpone paying income tax until the stock received is sold.

Recording a Stock Dividend

A stock dividend will *not* reduce total stockholders' equity the way a cash dividend does. The end result of a stock dividend is to transfer an amount based on the market value of the stock from Retained Earnings to Paid-In Capital.[1] After a stock dividend, a stockholder will own a larger number of shares, but the *total* ownership equity stays the same. Let's look at Jesse Corporation to illustrate recording a stock dividend.

On December 27, 201X, Jesse Corporation declared a 10% stock dividend distributable January 27 to stockholders of record on January 13. Figure 19.5 shows the stockholders' equity of Jesse Corporation before the dividend was declared. The current fair market value of the stock is $30 per share.

Figure 19.5
Stockholders' Equity

Recording the Declaration of the Dividend. The following chart is an analysis of this transaction.

Accounts Affected	Category	↑↓	Rules
Retained Earnings	SE	↓	Dr. $30,000
Common Stock Dividend Distributable	SE	↑	Cr. $20,000
Paid-In Capital in Excess of Par Value—Stock Dividend	SE	↑	Cr. $10,000

---
[1] For larger stock dividends (over 25% of the outstanding stock), the amount is based on par.

Retained Earnings is decreased by $30,000. To arrive at that figure, we multiply the market value of the stock ($30) by the number of shares issued in the dividend (1,000). The number of shares issued in the dividend is the number of shares outstanding (10,000) times the percent of dividend declared (10%). The Common Stock Dividend Distributable is 1,000 shares times the par value of the common stock ($20).

The journal entry will look like Figure 19.6.

201X						
Dec.	27	Retained Earnings	30 0 0 0 00	
		Common Stock Dividend Distributable		20 0 0 0 00
		Paid-In Capital in Excess of Par		
		Value—Stock Dividend		10 0 0 0 00
		Records declaration of a 10% stock		
		dividend to stockholders of record		
		as of Jan. 13; distributable Jan. 27 as		
		declared by the board of directors		

Figure 19.6
Declaration of Stock Dividend

Note that the Common Stock Dividend Distributable account, which records the par value of the stock, is *not* a liability; it is not payable with assets. It is part of stockholders' equity. When the stock is issued, this account will be reduced and transferred into Common Stock.

Let's first see what the stockholders' equity would look like if it were prepared between the declaration and the payment date. Note that in Figure 19.7 the stocks are listed first, followed by all the additional paid-in capital. This type of layout is called the *legal capital approach*; earlier we showed the *source-of-capital* approach. Both ways are acceptable.

Common Stock Dividend Distributable Stockholders' equity account that accumulates a stock dividend that has been declared but not yet issued and distributed.

Figure 19.7
Legal Capital Approach

Stockholders' Equity		
Paid-In Capital:		
Common Stock, $20 par value,		
15,000 shares authorized, 10,000 shares issued		
and outstanding	$ 200 0 0 0 00	
Common Stock Dividend Distributable,		
1,000 shares	20 0 0 0 00	
Total Common Stock issued and		
to be issued		$ 220 0 0 0 00
Additional Paid-In Capital:		
Paid-In Capital in Excess of Par		
Value—Common	24 0 0 0 00	
Paid-In Capital in Excess of Par		
Value—Stock Dividend	10 0 0 0 00	
Total Additional Paid-In Capital		34 0 0 0 00
Total Paid-In Capital		$ 254 0 0 0 00
Retained Earnings		32 0 0 0 00
Total Stockholders' Equity		$ 286 0 0 0 00

Recording the Issuance of the Stock Dividend. Let us first analyze the legal capital approach.

Accounts Affected	Category	↑↓	Rules
Common Stock Dividend Distributable	SE	↓	Dr. $20,000
Common Stock	SE	↑	Cr. $20,000

Then the journal entry would look like Figure 19.8.

Figure 19.8
Issuance of Stock Dividend

Jan.	27	Common Stock Dividend Distributable	20 0 0 0 00	
		Common Stock		20 0 0 0 00
		Issuance of stock dividend declared		
		on Dec. 27 to stockholders of record		
		as of Jan. 13		

Stock split Issuing of additional shares of stock to stockholders; total par or stated value remains the same.

The Stock Split. A stock split is the issuance by a corporation of additional stock to cause a large drop in the market price of the outstanding stock; no assets are received in return. The corporation reduces the par value or stated value of the authorized stock with an increase in the number of shares issued and outstanding. The stock split, however, doesn't change the Retained Earnings account as a stock dividend did. To repeat, the stock split will do the following:

1. Increase the number of shares outstanding.
2. Reduce the par or stated value in proportion.

For example, a two-for-one split on 10,000 shares of $20 par stock would result in 20,000 shares with a $10 par value. The total equity remains the same. Because the stock split doesn't change the balance of any ledger account, only a *memorandum notation*[2] in the journal, as well as in the Common Stock account, would be needed to update the accounting record. The number of shares in this transaction doubled, but the corporation's total equity did not change; thus the market price of $80 per share drops to approximately $40. If stockholder Jay Owen owned 100 shares before the split, he would own 200 now, but his total market value would be the same.

Before	After
100 shares × $80 = $8,000	200 shares × $40 = $8,000

Jay will benefit from the stock split if the stock price rises on the market or dividends per share are increased.

Now let's check your progress.

 **TRY IT!**   **Learning Unit 19-2**

Journalize the appropriate entries from the following:

> On October 8, 201X, the directors of Deer Co. declared a 3% stock dividend to be issued on November 2 to stockholders of record on October 25. There are 10,000 shares outstanding. The stock has a par value of $8 and a current market value of $17.

---

[2] An example of such a notation is, "Called in the outstanding $20 par value 10,000 shares of common stock and issued 20,000 shares of $10 par value common stock for old shares previously outstanding."

Solution Learning Unit 19-2

Date	Account	Dr.	Cr.
201X			
Oct. 8	Retained Earnings	5,100	
	Common Stock Dividend Distributable		2,400
	Paid-In Capital in Excess of Par Value—Stock Dividend		2,700
	Note: The debit amount to Retained Earnings was 300 shares × $17.		
	The credit to Common Stock Dividend Distributable was 300 shares × $8.		
	The credit to Paid-In Capital in Excess of Par Value was 300 shares × $9.		
Nov. 2	Common Stock Dividend Distributable	2,400	
	Common Stock		2,400

Journalizing Treasury Stock Transactions

LEARNING UNIT 19-3

 L03

Previously issued preferred or common stock that has been reacquired by the corporation (or given as a gift to the corporation) is known as treasury stock. Why would a corporation reacquire previously issued stock? Some reasons include:

Treasury stock Stock that has been issued but has been bought back by the corporation or received as a gift.

1. A need to issue more stock for stock option plans or for use in acquiring other corporations.
2. A desire to reduce the number of shares of stock outstanding, which might be done to create a favorable market for the sale of the stock.
3. Anticipation of an opportunity at a later date to reissue stock at a higher price.

The following are some of the characteristics of treasury stock:

1. The purchase of treasury stock does not change the amount of issued stock.
2. The purchase of treasury stock does reduce outstanding stock. Remember that stock can be issued but not outstanding.
3. Treasury stock does not have dividends or voting rights (because it is not outstanding).
4. Treasury stock is a contra-stockholders' equity account.
5. When treasury stock is bought, it is recorded at the purchase price. This purchase of treasury stock does not reduce the balance in the Retained Earnings account.
6. Many state laws will restrict the amount of retained earnings available for dividends if treasury stock exists because the purchase of treasury stock reduces assets and stockholders' equity (like a cash dividend). This restriction is commonly shown in a footnote on the balance sheet.

Let's look now at how to record the purchase of treasury stock.

Purchase of Treasury Stock

On June 1, 201X, Ashley Corporation has 5,000 shares of $10 par value common stock and 2,000 shares of preferred stock outstanding. The corporation on June 1 purchases 1,000 shares of its own common stock at a price of $12 per share. The following is the analysis as well as journal entry to record the purchase:

	Accounts Affected	Category	↑↓	Rules
(1,000 shares × $12) ⟶	Treasury Stock—Common	Contra-SE	↑	Dr. $12,000
	Cash	Asset	↓	Cr. $12,000

Record treasury stock at the purchase price of $12 (Figure 19.9). Note that the par value of common is not affected. Think of an *increase* in treasury stock as a reduction to stockholders' equity.

Figure 19.9
Purchase of Treasury Stock

June	1	Treasury Stock—Common	12 0 0 0 00		
		Cash			12 0 0 0 00
		Purchase at $12 per share of			
		1,000 shares of previously			
		issued stock			

Sale of Treasury Stock

Treasury stock can be reissued at a price above or below the cost of reacquiring the stock. Let's look at how Ashley Company could on July 8 sell 100 shares at $15 per share of the treasury stock that had been reacquired on June 1 for $12 per share.

The following chart analyzes the transaction:

	Accounts Affected	Category	↑↓	Rules
(100 shares × $15) ⟶	Cash	Asset	↑	Dr. $1,500
(100 shares × $12) ⟶	Treasury Stock—Common	Contra-SE	↓	Cr. $1,200
(100 shares × $13) ⟶	Paid-In Capital from Treasury Stock	SE	↑	Cr. $ 300

Think of a *decrease* in treasury stock resulting in an increase to stockholders' equity.

The journal entry looks like Figure 19.10.

Figure 19.10
Sale of Treasury Stock

July	8	Cash	1 5 0 0 00		
		Treasury Stock—Common			1 2 0 0 00
		Paid-In Capital from Treasury Stock			3 0 0 00
		Sold 100 shares of Treasury Stock			
		purchased at $12			

Paid-In Capital from Treasury Stock Stockholders' equity account that records amounts more or less than par value of treasury stock sold. The balance of this account can never be negative.

The Treasury Stock account is decreased by the number of shares reissued times the *cost* when the stock was reacquired by the company. The credit to Paid-In Capital from Treasury Stock represents the amount over what was paid for acquiring the treasury stock.

If a corporation sells treasury stock for less than cost, the result is a decrease in stockholders' equity that is recorded in Paid-In Capital from Treasury Stock until the balance of the account is 0. Any further decrease in this account will directly reduce Retained Earnings because Paid-In Capital from Treasury Stock cannot have a negative balance.

Example of Stockholders' Equity with Treasury Stock

Now let's see what Ashley Co.'s stockholders' equity will look like with the accounts Treasury Stock and Paid-In Capital from Treasury Stock (Figure 19.11).

Paid-In Capital:						
Preferred 14% Stock, $100 par value,						
authorized 6,000 shares, 2,000 shares						
issued and outstanding				$ 200 0 0 0 00		
Common Stock $10 par, authorized 9,000						
shares, 5,000 shares issued and 4,100 shares						
outstanding, 900 shares in treasury				50 0 0 0 00*		
Additional Paid-In Capital:						
Paid-In Capital in Excess of Par						
Value—Preferred		10 0 0 0 00				
Paid-In Capital in Excess of Par						
Value—Common		30 0 0 0 00				
Paid-In Capital from Treasury Stock		3 0 0 00				
Total Additional Paid-In Capital				40 3 0 0 00		
Total Paid-In Capital				$ 290 3 0 0 00		
Retained Earnings				60 0 0 0 00		
				$ 350 3 0 0 00		
Deduct: Treasury Stock—Common						
(900 shares at cost)				10 8 0 0 00		
Total Stockholders' Equity				$ 339 5 0 0 00		

*$50,000 = shares issued (5,000) × par ($10)

Figure 19.11
Stockholders' Equity

SUCCESS TIP

The 900 shares of treasury stock don't reduce the number of shares issued; they reduce the number of shares outstanding.

Now it's time to check your progress.

 **TRY IT!** Learning Unit 19-3

Journalize the following transactions:

1. Maple Co. acquired 130 shares of its own $7 par common stock for $13.
2. Forty-four of the treasury shares were reissued for $18 per share.
3. Forty-four of the treasury shares were reissued for $8 per share.

TRY IT! Solution Learning Unit 19-3

1.

Account	Dr.	Cr.
Treasury Stock—Common (130 shares × $13)	1,690	
Cash		1,690

2.

Account	Dr.	Cr.
Cash (44 shares × $18)	792	
Paid-In Capital from Treasury Stock (44 shares × $5)		220
Treasury Stock—Common (44 shares × $13)		572

3.

Account	Dr.	Cr.
Cash (44 shares × $8)	352	
Paid-In Capital from Treasury Stock (44 shares × $5)	220	
Treasury Stock—Common (44 shares × $13)		572

L04

Appropriation of Retained Earnings and the Statement of Retained Earnings

In the first two units of this chapter, we saw that cash dividends as well as stock dividends reduce the amount of retained earnings. Now we look at how companies indicate to those reading their financial reports that some of the retained earnings are not available for declaration of dividends; they are appropriated (restricted) retained earnings.

Appropriated (restricted) retained earnings That portion of Retained Earnings that is not available for dividends.

This *appropriating* of retained earnings could be either voluntary or contractual. For example, the board of directors could voluntarily decide that a portion of earnings should be used for plant expansion instead of for dividends. If a company enters into a loan with a bank, the bank may require the company to keep a minimum balance in Retained Earnings to protect its rights until the loan is repaid. Companies in many states are required to keep a minimum in the Retained Earnings account at the level of legal capital.

In years past these special appropriations were recorded by transferring portions of the Retained Earnings account to accounts such as Retained Earnings Appropriated for Plant Expansion or Retained Earnings Appropriated for Contra Obligations. In reality, these appropriations didn't reduce total Retained Earnings; they just *shifted* a portion into an account that revealed its special purpose. For example, an entry to restrict $20,000 for plant expansion would be as shown in Figure 19.12.

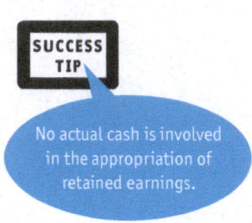

SUCCESS TIP

No actual cash is involved in the appropriation of retained earnings.

Figure 19.12
Plant Expansion Restriction

Retained Earnings	20 0 0 0 00	
Retained Earnings Appropriated for Plant Expansion		20 0 0 0 00

After the appropriation or restriction has passed (e.g., the loan has been paid off), the balance is transferred back to the Retained Earnings account. No cash is involved in the appropriation.

Today, to make things clear to investors, most companies report restrictions by using a footnote to the Retained Earnings account. Restrictions on retained earnings do not have to be updated in the ledger; thus the use of a footnote is a common practice. (It is good practice to write a memo in the Retained Earnings account to identify each appropriation.) A footnote to announce such restrictions would look like the following:

> *The loan agreement with Jones Bank contains a restriction on the payment of cash dividends. Approximately $600,000 of retained earnings was free of such a restriction as of June 30, 201X.*

Preparing the Statement of Retained Earnings

Statement of retained earnings Financial report that reveals the changes in retained earnings for a particular period of time.

In past chapters we discussed the income statement, balance sheet, statement of owner's equity, and statement of partners' equity. We now turn our attention to a statement of retained earnings that will reveal the changes in retained earnings over a period of time. The changes in retained earnings result from the following:

1. Net income or loss
2. Dividends declared
3. Effects of prior period adjustments

Prior period adjustment Correction made in the current year of a mistake made in previous years. The adjustment is updated on the statement of retained earnings.

Often an error in a financial report of a company from a prior period may not be discovered until a later period. If the error is considered *material*, a prior period adjustment should be made to the beginning balance of Retained Earnings. Let's look at a specific example.

Eight months after the closing of its accounting books, Ralston Company discovered in 2019 that depreciation was understated by $12,000 in 2018, which meant that in the old period Depreciation Expense was understated by $12,000 and Net Income was overstated by $12,000. If Net Income was overstated, Retained Earnings also was overstated because Net Income is closed into Retained Earnings. Thus, the entry shown in Figure 19.13 is recorded in the *new* year to adjust the prior period error (we ignore tax effect here).

Retained Earnings (Prior Period Adjustment)	12 00 00 0	
Accumulated Depreciation, Equipment		12 00 00 0

Figure 19.13
Adjustment of Prior Period Error

A statement of retained earnings for the Ralston Company would look like Figure 19.14.

RALSTON COMPANY
STATEMENT OF RETAINED EARNINGS
YEAR ENDED DECEMBER 31, 2019

Retained Earnings, Jan. 1, 2019	$ 350 00 0 00
Less: Prior Period Adjustment:	
Correction of 2018 error	12 00 0 00
Retained Earnings, Jan. 1, 2019, corrected	$ 338 00 0 00
Add: Net Income for 2019	40 00 0 00
Subtotal	$ 378 00 0 00
Deduct: Dividends declared in 2019	28 00 0 00
Retained Earnings, Dec. 31, 2019	$ 350 00 0 00

Figure 19.14
Statement of Retained Earnings

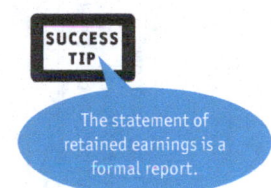

SUCCESS TIP

The statement of retained earnings is a formal report.

This ending figure of $350,000, as shown in the statement of retained earnings in Figure 19.14, will appear in the Stockholders' Equity section of the balance sheet.

Accounting Cycle for a Corporation

Before we conclude our discussion of corporations, Figure 19.15 provides a simplified sample of a worksheet for a corporation. This worksheet will give you a better idea of what titles such as Subscriptions Receivable, Common Stock, Paid-In Capital, and Retained Earnings look like when all are combined on one worksheet.

Figure 19.15 Worksheet for Jane Corporation

JANE CORPORATION
WORKSHEET
FOR YEAR ENDED DECEMBER 31, 201X

Account Name	Trial Balance Dr.	Trial Balance Cr.	Adjustments Dr.	Adjustments Cr.	Adjusted Trial Balance Dr.	Adjusted Trial Balance Cr.	Income Statement Dr.	Income Statement Cr.	Balance Sheet Dr.	Balance Sheet Cr.
Cash	X				X				X	
Accounts Receivable	X				X				X	
Notes Receivable	X				X				X	
Subscriptions Rec., Com. Stock	X				X				X	
Merchandise Inventory	X		O		O				O	
Prepaid Rent	X				X				X	
Office Equipment	X				X				X	
Acc. Dep., Office Equip.		X		X		X				X
Organization Costs	X				X				X	
Accounts Payable		X				X				X
Notes Payable		X				X				X
Dividends Payable, Com.		X				X				X
Common Stock		X				X				X
Common Stock Div. Dist.		X				X				X
Common Stock Subscribed		X				X				X
Paid-In Capital in Excess										
of Par Value—Common		X				X				X
Paid-In Capital										
from Treasury Stock		X				X				X
Retained Earnings		X				X				X
Sales (totals)		X				X		X		
Cost of Goods Sold	X				X		X			
Expenses (totals)	X				X		X			
Expenses (adjusted)			X		X		X			
Income Tax Expense	X		X		X		X			
Income Tax Payable				X		X				X

The cycle is then to prepare financial reports as well as journalize and post the adjusting and closing entries. We use Retained Earnings instead of Capital in the closing process. Also in the adjusting process we adjust the income tax owed. The Income Tax Expense account is closed to Income Summary. The steps are quite similar to those discussed for a merchandise company.

A key point is that the net income shown on the income statement could be substantially different from that reported for tax purposes; certain deductions on the tax return will differ from the expenses on the corporation's accounting books.

Now let's check your progress.

 **TRY IT!**   **Learning Unit 19-4**

Complete the following chart by placing an X in the appropriate column.

Account	Added to Statement of Retained Earnings	Subtracted from Statement of Retained Earnings
1. Net Income		
2. Error, Net Income Understated		
3. Dividends Declared		
4. Net Loss		
5. Beg. Retained Earnings		
6. Error, Net Income Overstated		

TRY IT!   **Solution Learning Unit 19-4**

Account	Added to Statement of Retained Earnings	Subtracted from Statement of Retained Earnings
1. Net Income	X	
2. Error, Net Income Understated	X	
3. Dividends Declared		X
4. Net Loss		X
5. Beg. Retained Earnings	X	
6. Error, Net Income Overstated		X

DEMONSTRATION SUMMARY PROBLEM

Cynthia Hartman's Bookkeeping Service has hired a new accounting intern from a local community college. The new intern has been assigned four projects to complete today. Please complete these projects (each project and its solution are presented separately).

Project 1

Determine book value per share for preferred and common given the following:

Redemption Value—Preferred $300,000

Dividend in Arrears—Preferred $16,000

Total Stockholders' Equity $750,000

10,000 shares Preferred Stock issued and outstanding

20,000 shares Common Stock issued and outstanding

Solution for Project 1

$$\text{Preferred: } \$300{,}000 + \$16{,}000 = \$316{,}000/10{,}000 = \$31.60$$
$$\text{Common: } \$750{,}000 - \$316{,}000 = \$434{,}000/20{,}000 = \$21.70$$

Tips

To calculate book value per share for preferred stock, take redemption value plus any dividends in arrears and divide by the number of preferred shares outstanding. To calculate book value per share for common stock, take the total of stockholders' equity less the amount given to preferred and divide by the number of common shares outstanding.

Project 2

Journalize the appropriate entries given the following:

Common Stock $10 par 7,000 shares issued and outstanding.

On August 10, 201X, the board of directors declared a 10% stock dividend to be issued on Sept. 30, 201X, to stockholders of record on Sept. 15, 201X. The market price of the stock was $22 per share.

Solution for Project 2

Date	Account	Dr.	Cr.
201X			
Aug. 10	Retained Earnings	15,400	
	Common Stock Dividend Distributable		7,000
	Paid-In Capital in Excess of Par Value—Stock Dividend		8,400
Sept. 30	Common Stock Dividend Distributable	7,000	
	Common Stock		7,000

Tips

The debit to Retained Earnings was 700 shares $\times$ $22. The 700 comes from 10% of the 7,000 shares. The credit to Common Stock Dividend Distributable was 700 shares $\times$ $10 par.

The credit to the Paid-In Capital in Excess of Par Value—Stock Dividend was $12 (which is the difference between the market value [$22] and the par value [$10]). Note on September 30, the Common Stock Dividend Distributable was moved into Common Stock.

Project 3

Journalize the appropriate entries given the following:

Common Stock has an $8 par value with 80,000 shares authorized and 50,000 shares issued.

201X		
May 8	Issued 4,000 shares at $10.	
12	Reacquired 200 shares at $6.	
15	Reissued 100 shares of Treasury Stock at $9.	
17	Reissued 50 shares of Treasury Stock at $4.	

Solution for Project 3

Date	Account	Dr.	Cr.
201X			
May 8	Cash	40,000	
	Common Stock		32,000
	Paid-In Capital in Excess of Par Value—Common		8,000
12	Treasury Stock—Common	1,200	
	Cash		1,200
15	Cash	900	
	Treasury Stock—Common		600
	Paid-In Capital from Treasury Stock		300
17	Cash	200	
	Paid-In Capital from Treasury Stock	100	
	Treasury Stock—Common		300

Tips

May 8	Cash of $40,000 is number of shares 4,000 × $10. The $32,000 to Common Stock is from 4,000 shares × $8 par. The Paid-In Capital account is $40,000 less $32,000 par value.
12	Remember Treasury Stock is a contra-stockholder equity category. It takes a debit to increase the balance.
15	The Cash is 100 shares × $9. The credit to the Treasury Stock is 100 shares × price paid when acquired ($6). The Paid-In Capital account is the difference ($3 × 100 shares).
17	Cash is debited for $200 (50 shares × $4). The debit to the Paid-In Capital account was 50 shares × $2 or $100. The credit to Treasury Stock is 50 shares × $6 (the price the stock was acquired for).

Project 4

Prepare a Statement of Retained Earnings for Hudson Co. for the year ended December 31, 2019, from the following:

Beginning Retained Earnings, January 2019, $60,000

Net Income, 2019, $90,000

Prior period adjustment, overstated expense, $6,000, for land in 2018 (disregard taxes)

Dividend declared in 2019, $14,000

Solution for Project 4

Hudson Co.
Statement of Retained Earnings
Year Ended December 31, 2019

Retained Earnings, January 1, 2019	$ 60,000
Add: Correction of 2018 error	6,000
Retained Earnings, January 1, 2019, with correction	66,000
Add: Net Income for 2019	90,000
Subtotal	156,000
Deduct: Dividend declared 2019	14,000
Retained Earnings, December 31, 2019	$142,000

Tips

The prior year error overstated expenses so Retained Earnings will now increase. Net income for 2019 increases Retained Earnings while the dividend reduces the Retained Earnings account.

SUCCESS COACH

The following Success Tips are from Learning Units 19-1 to 19-4. Take the Do It Right Now Checkup and use the Check Your Score to see how you are doing. The Success Coach provides tips before each Checkup to help you avoid common accounting errors.

LU 19-1 Redemption, Market, and Book Value

Do It Right Tips: Book value per share is total stockholders' equity divided by total shares outstanding. Book value can be used when seeking loans, when mergers are being negotiated, and when contracts are negotiated. When calculating book value per share for preferred stock, be sure that the numerator has redemption value plus dividend in arrears.

Do It Right Now Checkup: Answer true or false to the following statements.

1. Market value and book value are always the same.
2. Book value may be used when seeking a loan.
3. If a company is liquidated, book value represents what an owner might receive.
4. When calculating book value per share for preferred stock, par value may be used instead of redemption value.
5. The Paid-In Capital in Excess of Par Value account is included in the book value calculation of common stock.

LU 19-2 Calculating and Journalizing Dividends

Do It Right Tips: Declaring a cash dividend will reduce retained earnings and increase dividends payable. At the date of record no entry would be made. A stock dividend does not reduce cash or the total of stockholders' equity. Common Stock Dividend Distributable is part of stockholders' equity.

Do It Right Now Checkup: Answer true or false to the following statements.

1. Dividends Payable is an asset.
2. Dividends Payable is recorded at the date of record.
3. Retained Earnings is the same as cash.
4. Stock dividends will reduce stockholders' equity.
5. Common Stock Dividend Distributable uses par value in its calculation.

LU 19-3 Journalizing Treasury Stock Transactions

Do It Right Tips: Treasury stock is stock held by a corporation. It is recorded in a contra-account for stockholder's equity. Whenever you increase the number of shares held by a corporation, the Treasury Stock account will increase and Stockholder's Equity will decrease. Think of an *increase* to treasury stock as a *reduction* in stockholders' equity.

Do It Right Now Checkup: Answer true or false to the following statements.

1. Treasury stock is an asset.
2. Treasury stock can be reissued only at a price below the cost of reacquiring the stock.
3. Treasury stock is a contra-liability.
4. Cash is not involved in the purchase of treasury stock.
5. Paid-In Capital from Treasury Stock cannot be a negative balance.

LU 19-4 Appropriation of Retained Earnings and the Statement of Retained Earnings

Do It Right Tips: Some of the retained earnings not available for dividends are appropriated retained earnings. No cash is involved in the appropriation of retained earnings. Keep in mind that when a statement of retained earnings is prepared, it is a formal report that shows how the ending balance in retained earnings is calculated.

Do It Right Now Checkup: Answer true or false to the following statements.

1. A reduction in retained earnings is a debit.
2. When retained earnings is appropriated, cash is involved.
3. If net income is overstated, retained earnings will be understated.
4. Net income or loss can be seen on the statement of retained earnings.
5. Any dividends declared will be shown on the statement of retained earnings.

CHECK YOUR SCORE: Answers to the Do It Right Now Checkup

LU 19-1

1. False—Market value and book value are not always the same.
2. True
3. False—If a company is liquidated, book value does not represent what an owner might receive.
4. True
5. True

LU 19-2

1. False—Dividends Payable is a liability.
2. False—Dividends Payable is recorded at the date of declaration.
3. False—Retained Earnings is part of stockholders' equity.
4. False—Stock dividends will not affect stockholders' equity.
5. True

LU 19-3

1. False—Treasury stock is part of stockholders' equity.
2. False—Treasury stock can be reissued at a price below or above the cost of reacquiring the stock.

3. False—Treasury stock is a contra-stockholders' equity.
4. False—Cash is usually involved in the purchase of treasury stock.
5. True

LU 19-4

1. True
2. False—When retained earnings is appropriated, no cash is involved.
3. False—If net income is overstated, retained earnings will be overstated.
4. True
5. True

BLUEPRINT: LEGAL CAPITAL APPROACH

MOOSE COMPANY PARTIAL BALANCE SHEET			
Stockholders' Equity			
Paid-In Capital:			
Preferred 12% Stock, $10 par value, authorized 30,000 shares, 9,000 shares issued and outstanding		XX	
Common Stock, $10 par value, authorized 100,000 shares, 40,000 shares issued and 29,000 shares outstanding, 11,000 shares in treasury	XX		
Common Stock Dividend Distributable	XX	XX	
Additional Paid-In Capital:			
Paid-In Capital in Excess of Par Value—Preferred	XX		
Paid-In Capital in Excess of Par Value—Common	XX		
Paid-In Capital in Excess of Par Value—Stock Dividend	XX		
Paid-In Capital from Treasury Stock	XX		
Total Additional Paid-In Capital		XX	
Total Paid-In Capital		XX	
Retained Earnings		XX	
Deduct: Treasury Stock		XX	
Total Stockholders' Equity			XX

Note that legal capital is listed first. Both approaches are acceptable, and in the real world both are used.
See the Blueprint in Chapter 18 for an example of the source-of-capital approach.

Discussion Questions and Critical Thinking/Ethical Case

1. What is the difference between market value and book value?

2. List the three important dates that are associated with the dividend process.

3. Why is no journal entry needed at the date of record?

4. Explain some possible reasons a company may declare a stock dividend instead of a cash dividend.

5. Explain why stock dividends will not reduce total stockholders' equity.

6. Common Stock Dividend Distributable is a liability. Agree or disagree? Defend your position.

7. Explain the difference between a stock dividend and a stock split.

8. Treasury stock is really an asset. Defend or reject. Support your argument.

9. All treasury stock is recognized as issued and outstanding for dividends. True or false? Please explain.

10. Explain the purpose of the account Paid-In Capital from Treasury Stock.

11. Appropriation of retained earnings is always done for a contractual reason. Agree or disagree? Defend your position.

12. Restrictions on retained earnings have to be updated in the ledger. Agree or disagree? Why?

13. What elements make up the statement of retained earnings?

14. Alan Homes serves on the board of directors of Flynn Company. The president of Flynn told him that in 3 weeks the corporation would announce a 25% increase in dividends. Alan called his neighbor to tell him to buy some stock. The neighbor told his friend about the stock, and the friend told him that Alan was acting unethically. The neighbor called Alan back, and Alan told him that no one will know the difference, that in business this happens all the time, and that he shouldn't be left out. Do you think Alan's behavior is appropriate? You make the call. Write down your recommendation to Alan's neighbor.

MyLabAccounting

Concept Checks

(15 min) **L01**

Book Value per Share for Preferred and Common Stock

1. Given the following, prepare the book value per share for preferred and common stock:
   - Preferred Stock $97,000; 1,100 shares issued and outstanding.
   - Common Stock $164,000; 1,800 shares issued and outstanding.
   - Retained Earnings, $65,250.
   - Preferred Dividends in Arrears, $3,300.
   - Paid-in capital in excess of par: preferred, $7,400.
   - Paid-in capital in excess of par: common, $7,750.
   - Redemption value on preferred stock, $21.

(15 min) **L02**

Cash Dividend

2. On March 20, 201X, the board of directors of Dustin Corporation declared $3 cash dividend per share on the 8,000 shares issued and outstanding. The dividend will be paid on April 28, 201X, to stockholders of record on March 22, 201X. Record journal entries for date of declaration and date of payment.

Stock Dividend

3.   On July 24, 201X, Flowers Corporation declared a 9% stock dividend distributable August 18 to stockholders of record on August 8. Currently Flowers has 6,500
shares of common stock issued and outstanding. The stock has a par value of $18.
The current fair market value of the stock is $33. Journalize (a) the declaration of
the dividend and (b) the issuance of the stock dividend.

Treasury Stock

4.   Journalize the following transactions:

   a.   Jarrod Co. acquired 110 shares of its own $5 par value common stock at $16
per share.

   b.   Twenty-seven of the treasury shares are reissued at $21 per share.

   c.   Twenty of the treasury shares are reissued at $9 per share.

Prior Period Adjustment

5.   Seven months after its closing, Trees Co. discovered that depreciation was understated by $16,000. Provide the journal entry to adjust the prior period error (ignore
any tax effects).

Exercises

MyLabAccounting

Set A

19A-1.   From the following information, determine the book value per share for preferred and common stock assuming $14,000 of dividends are in arrears on the
preferred stock.

Stockholders' Equity	
Preferred 10% Stock cumulative and nonparticipating, $15 par value, $13 redemption value, 7,000 shares issued and outstanding	$105,000
Common Stock, $7 par value, 42,000 shares issued and outstanding	294,000
Retained Earnings	462,000
Total Stockholders' Equity	$861,000

19A-2.   Simpson Corporation has 300,000 shares of common stock issued and outstanding. On June 9, 201X, the board of directors declared a $0.52 per share
dividend, payable on July 16, 201X, to stockholders of record on June 29,
201X. Record the appropriate journal entries on June 9 and July 16.

19A-3.   On July 31, 201X, Lucky Corporation had the following stockholders' equity:

Common Stock, $13 par value, authorized 89,000 shares, 59,000 shares issued and outstanding	$767,000
Retained Earnings	240,000
Total Stockholders' Equity	$ 1,007,000

On August 5, 201X, the board of directors declared a 7% stock dividend to
be issued on September 6, 201X, to the stockholders of record on August 19,
201X. At time of declaration the market price was $25 per share. Prepare the
appropriate journal entries for this stock dividend.

(20 min) **LO3** ▶

19A-4.   Given the following stockholders' equity:

Common Stock, $7 par value, authorized 98,000 shares, 79,000 shares issued and outstanding	$ 553,000
Retained Earnings	520,000
Total Stockholders' Equity	$1,073,000

Journalize the following entries:

201X		
Apr.	3	Issued 4,700 shares at $12 per share.
	9	Reacquired 197 shares at $6 per share.
	15	Reissued 109 shares of treasury stock at $10 per share.
	17	Reissued 51 shares of treasury stock at $2 per share.

(20 min) **LO4** ▶

19A-5.   From the following, prepare in proper form a statement of retained earnings for Quincy Company for the year ended December 31, 2019.

Retained Earnings, January 1, 2019	$44,000	Prior period adjustment: overstated expense for Land in 2017 (disregard taxes)	$ 9,000
Net Income, 2019	$63,000	Dividends Declared, 2019	$24,000

Set B

(20 min) **LO1**

19B-1.   From the following information, determine the book value per share for preferred and common stock assuming $16,000 of dividends are in arrears on the preferred stock.

Stockholders' Equity	
Preferred 9% Stock cumulative and nonparticipating, $16 par value, $13 redemption value, 8,000 shares issued and outstanding	$128,000
Common Stock, $11 par value, 40,500 shares issued and outstanding	445,500
Retained Earnings	235,000
Total Stockholders' Equity	$808,500

(20 min) **LO2** ▶

19B-2.   Dixon Corporation has 320,000 shares of common stock issued and outstanding. On June 9, 201X, the board of directors declared a $0.45 per share dividend, payable on July 16, 201X, to stockholders of record on June 29, 201X. Record the appropriate journal entries on June 9 and July 16.

(20 min) **LO2** ▶

19B-3.   On July 31, 201X, Nicole Corporation had the following stockholders' equity:

Common Stock, $13 par value, authorized 85,000 shares, 54,000 shares issued and outstanding	$702,000
Retained Earnings	170,000
Total Stockholders' Equity	$872,000

On August 5, 201X, the board of directors declared a 8% stock dividend to be issued on September 6, 201X, to the stockholders of record on August 19, 201X. At time of declaration the market price was $22 per share. Prepare the appropriate journal entries for this stock dividend.

19B-4. Given the following stockholders' equity:

 **L03** *(20 min)*

Common Stock, $3 par value, authorized 99,000 shares, 81,000 shares issued and outstanding	$243,000
Retained Earnings	460,000
Total Stockholders' Equity	$703,000

Journalize the following entries:

201X		
Apr.	3	Issued 5,200 shares at $11 per share.
	9	Reacquired 196 shares at $5 per share.
	15	Reissued 102 shares of treasury stock at $9 per share.
	17	Reissued 54 shares of treasury stock at $3 per share.

19B-5. From the following, prepare in proper form a statement of retained earnings for Johnson Company for the year ended December 31, 2019.

L04 *(20 min)*

Retained Earnings, January 1, 2019	$35,000	Prior period adjustment: overstated expense for Land in 2017 (disregard taxes)	$18,000
Net Income, 2019	$58,000	Dividends Declared, 2019	$15,000

Problems

MyLabAccounting

Set A

19A-1. The stockholders' equity of Darwin Company is as follows:

L01 *(30 min)*

Stockholders' Equity		
Paid-In Capital:		
Preferred 10% Stock, $98 par value, authorized 48,000 shares, cumulative and nonparticipating, 4,400 shares issued and outstanding	$431,200	
Paid-In Capital in Excess of Par Value—Preferred	56,000	
Total Paid-In Capital by Preferred Stockholders		$487,200
Common Stock, $49 par value, authorized 11,000 shares, 5,600 shares issued and outstanding	$274,400	
Paid-In Capital in Excess of Par Value—Common	56,000	
Total Paid-In Capital by Common Stockholders		330,400
Total Paid-In Capital		$817,600
Retained Earnings		165,000
Total Stockholders' Equity		$982,600

Check Figure:
Book value preferred (a) $104

Given a redemption value of $104 per share for the preferred stock, calculate the book value per share of preferred and common stock, assuming the following:

a. No preferred dividends in arrears
b. Two years' preferred dividends in arrears

(30 min) **LO2**

19A-2. Racette Corporation has 400,000 shares of $4 par value common stock issued and outstanding. Record the following entries into the general journal for Racette:

201X		
July	2	Declared a cash dividend of $0.75 per share.
Aug.	1	Paid the $0.75 cash dividend to the stockholders.
	4	Declared a 7% stock dividend. The current market price is $12 per share.
Sept.	12	Issued the stock dividend declared on August 4.
Oct.	1	Declared a 10% stock dividend. The current market price is $15 per share.
Nov.	2	Issued the stock dividend on October 1.

Check Figure:
Aug. 4 Paid-In Capital in Excess of Par
Value—Stock Dividend $ 224,000 Cr.

(50 min) **LO2,3,4**

19A-3. At the beginning of January 201X, the stockholders' equity of Country View Corporation consisted of the following:

Paid-In Capital:		
Common Stock, $18 par value, authorized 55,000 shares, 13,900 shares issued and outstanding	$250,200	
Paid-In Capital in Excess of Par Value—Common	71,000	
Total Paid-In Capital by Common Stockholders	$321,200	
Retained Earnings	157,000	
Total Stockholders' Equity		$478,200

Check Figure:
Total Stockholders' Equity $535,280

1. Record the transactions in general journal form.
2. Prepare the stockholders' equity section at year-end using the Blueprint in this chapter as a guide.
3. Prepare a statement of retained earnings at December 31, 201X.

Accounts are provided in the working papers that accompany this text. Be sure to put in the beginning balances.

201X		
June	4	Country View Corporation purchased 980 shares of treasury stock at $22.
	21	The board of directors voted a $0.50 per share cash dividend payable on July 13 to stockholders of record on July 3.
July	13	Cash dividend declared on June 21 is paid.
Sept.	9	Sold 280 shares of the treasury stock at $30 per share.
	29	Sold 700 shares of the treasury stock at $21 per share.
Oct.	12	The board of directors declared a 10% stock dividend distributable on January 2 to stockholders of record on November 2. The market value of the stock is currently $30 per share.
Dec.	31	Closed the net income of $62,000 in the Income Summary account to Retained Earnings.

19A-4. The following is the stockholders' equity of Pierotti Corporation on October 1, 201X:

L02,3,4 *(60 min)*

S50 / QB

Paid-In Capital:			
Preferred Stock, $13 par value, authorized 5,700 shares, 3,500 shares issued and outstanding		$ 45,500	
Common Stock, $6 par value, authorized 19,000 shares, 7,000 shares issued and outstanding		42,000	
Additional Paid-In Capital:			
Paid-In Capital in Excess of Par Value—Preferred	$11,000		
Paid-In Capital in Excess of Par Value—Common	7,500		
Paid-In Capital in Excess of Par Value—Stock Dividend	2,000		
Total Additional Paid-In Capital		20,500	
Total Paid-In Capital		$108,000	
Retained Earnings		240,000	
Total Stockholders' Equity			$348,000

Check Figure:
Total Stockholders' Equity $425,760

1. Journalize the transactions in general journal form.

2. Prepare the stockholders' equity section of the balance sheet using the legal capital approach as of December 31, 201X.

The working papers that accompany this text have accounts to update ledger balances. Be sure to put in the beginning balances.

201X		
Oct.	3	Declared a $0.55 per share dividend on the common stock and a $1.60 per share dividend on the preferred. (The Dividends Payable account will record amounts for both common and preferred, although companies could set up Common Dividend Payable and Preferred Dividend Payable accounts.)
Nov.	15	Dividends were paid that were declared on October 3.
	18	Purchased 340 shares of its own common stock at $15 per share.
	25	Reissued 70 shares at $21 per share.
	26	Declared a 20% stock dividend on common. Market value of stock is $50 per share.
Dec.	29	Distributed stock dividend declared on November 26.
	30	Reissued 60 shares of treasury stock at $14 per share.
	31	Closed the Income Summary account, which had net income of $90,000, to Retained Earnings.

Set B

(30 min) **LO1**

19B-1. The stockholders' equity of Hadley Company is as follows:

Stockholders' Equity			
Paid-In Capital:			
Preferred 10% Stock, $99 par value, authorized 49,000 shares, cumulative and nonparticipating, 4,000 shares issued and outstanding	$396,000		
Paid-In Capital in Excess of Par Value—Preferred	49,000		
Total Paid-In Capital by Preferred Stockholders		$445,000	
Common Stock, $54 par value, authorized 11,800 shares, 5,500 shares issued and outstanding	$297,000		
Paid-In Capital in Excess of Par Value—Common	59,000		
Total Paid-In Capital by Common Stockholders		356,000	
Total Paid-In Capital		$801,000	
Retained Earnings		159,000	
Total Stockholders' Equity		$960,000	

Check Figure:
Book value preferred (b) $127.80

Given a redemption value of $108 per share for the preferred stock, calculate the book value per share of preferred and common stock, assuming the following:

a. No preferred dividends in arrears
b. Two years' preferred dividends in arrears

(30 min) **LO2**

19B-2. Rollin Corporation has 420,000 shares of $7 par value common stock issued and outstanding. Record the following entries into the general journal for Rollin:

201X		
July	2	Declared a cash dividend of $0.50 per share.
Aug.	1	Paid the $0.50 cash dividend to the stockholders.
	4	Declared a 7% stock dividend. The current market price is $10 per share.
Sept.	12	Issued the stock dividend declared on August 4.
Oct.	1	Declared a 5% stock dividend. The current market price is $15 per share.
Nov.	2	Issued the stock dividend on October 1.

Check Figure:
Aug. 4 Paid-In Capital in Excess of Par Value—Stock Dividend $88,200

(30 min) **LO2,3,4**

19B-3. At the beginning of January 201X, the stockholders' equity of Hillside Corporation consisted of the following:

Paid-In Capital:		
Common Stock, $26 par value, authorized 47,000 shares, 12,400 shares issued and outstanding	$322,400	
Paid-In Capital in Excess of Par Value—Common	69,000	
Total Paid-In Capital by Common Stockholders	391,400	
Retained Earnings	154,000	
Total Stockholders' Equity		$545,400

Check Figure:
Total Stockholders' Equity $594,768

1. Record the transactions in general journal form.
2. Prepare the stockholders' equity section at year-end, using the Blueprint in this chapter as a guide.
3. Prepare a statement of retained earnings at December 31, 201X.

Accounts are provided in the working papers that accompany this text. Be sure to put in the beginning balances.

201X		
June	4	Hillside Corporation purchased 1,080 shares of treasury stock at $30.
	21	The board of directors voted a $0.60 per share cash dividend payable on July 13 to stockholders of record on July 3.
July	13	Cash dividend declared on June 21 is paid.
Sept.	9	Sold 360 shares of treasury stock at $38 per share.
	29	Sold 720 shares of treasury stock at $29 per share.
Oct.	12	The board of directors declared a 6% stock dividend distributable on January 2 to stockholders of record on November 2. The market value of the stock is currently $38 per share.
Dec.	31	Closed the net income of $54,000 in the Income Summary account to Retained Earnings.

19B-4. The following is the stockholders' equity of Pierro Corporation on October 1, 201X:

L02,3,4 *(60 min)*

S50 / **QB**

Paid-In Capital:		
Preferred Stock, $10 par value, authorized 6,100 shares, 3,800 shares issued and outstanding		$ 38,000
Common Stock, $8 par value, authorized 20,000 shares, 11,000 shares issued and outstanding		88,000
Additional Paid-In Capital:		
Paid-In Capital in Excess of Par Value—Preferred	$8,000	
Paid-In Capital in Excess of Par Value—Common	4,500	
Paid-In Capital in Excess of Par Value—Stock Dividend	2,500	
Total Additional Paid-In Capital		15,000
Total Paid-In Capital		$141,000
Retained Earnings		220,000
Total Stockholders' Equity		$361,000

Check Figure:
Total Stockholders' Equity $440,270

1. Journalize the transactions in general journal form.
2. Prepare the stockholders' equity section of the balance sheet using the legal capital approach as of December 31, 201X.

The working papers that accompany this text have accounts to update ledger balances. Be sure to put in beginning balances.

201X		
Oct.	3	Declared a $0.50 per share dividend on the common stock and a $1.15 per share dividend on the preferred. (The Dividends Payable account will record amounts for both common and preferred, although companies could set up Common Dividend Payable and Preferred Dividend Payable accounts.)
Nov.	15	Dividends were paid that were declared on October 3.
	18	Purchased 360 shares of its own common stock at $13 per share.
	25	Reissued 60 shares at $21 per share.
	26	Declared a 12% stock dividend on common. Market value of stock is $38 per share.
Dec.	29	Distributed stock dividend declared on November 26.
	30	Reissued 130 shares of treasury stock at $12 per share.
	31	Closed the Income Summary account, which had net income of $91,000, to Retained Earnings.

MyLabAccounting

(10 min) **L03**

Financial Report Problem

Reading Amazon's Annual Report

Go to **https://tinyurl.com/slaterca14e** to access Amazon's 2016 Annual Report. Go to page 39 and find the cost of Treasury Stock in 2016.

Corporations and Bonds Payable

20

CHAPTER PREVIEW: ACCOUNTING IN ACTION

Julian Kraft works for a bank that offers businesses lines of credit. This type of loan is not for everyone. Companies have sometimes been denied certain lines of credit due to a cash crisis and have to decide on an alternative course of action. Today, companies can still go to banks for loans; however, there are two other options. The options include selling stock or selling bonds. Unlike stocks, bonds are loans to the company by investors. In return, the company pays back the loan in fixed amounts along with interest. In this chapter, we look at how to record bond transactions of a company along with interest paid to the bondholders.

Learning Objectives – Relating Accounting Theory By Unit

LO1   Journalize Issuance and Interest Payments of Bonds

LO2   Explain and Journalize Amortization of Bonds by the Straight-Line Method

LO3   Explain and Journalize Amortization of Bonds by the Interest Method

LO4   Journalize Bond Sinking Fund Transactions

Bond Interest-bearing note payable usually in $1,000 denominations issued by a corporation to a large group of lenders.

A corporation can raise funds by issuing stock or long-term notes payable. Notes or stock are good sources of funds when a company borrows from only one bank or other type of lending institution, but they may not provide the total amount of funds needed. In the last two chapters we saw how companies issue stock. Now our attention shifts to notes. After all, businesses such as Uber and Tesla may need to borrow millions of dollars. This chapter looks at how corporations can raise large amounts of money from groups of lenders by issuing a type of long-term interest-bearing note payable called a bond.

Journalizing Issuance and Interest Payments of Bonds

Bond certificate Piece of paper held by a bondholder showing evidence of a bond issued by a corporation to be payable on a specified date for a specific sum to the order of the person named in the bond certificate or to the bearer.

Face value Amount the corporation must repay to the bondholder at the maturity date.

Contract rate Rate of interest (based on face value) stated on bond certificate and bond indenture.

Each bond certificate, usually issued in denominations of $1,000, contains the following:

1. Face value (principal or par value) is the amount that the corporation must repay to the lender at the maturity date.
2. Contract rate (stated interest rate or coupon rate) is the annual interest rate, which is based on face value. Usually this interest is paid *semi*annually. The dates of interest payment are also printed on the certificate.

For example, if Trey Wynn owns a $1,000, 12%, 20-year bond with semiannual interest payments that is issued by Von Corporation, it means the following:

1. At the end of 20 years Trey will receive the $1,000.
2. Every 6 months Trey will receive an interest check for $60 ($1,000 $\times$ 0.12 $\times$ $\frac{6}{12}$).

Another way to calculate semiannual interest is as follows:

$$\frac{12\%}{2} = \text{Semiannual Rate of 6\%}$$

$$0.06 \times \$1,000 = \$60$$

Bond indenture Contract that spells out the provisions of the contract between the corporation and bondholder.

Trustee Organization (usually a bank) or person who monitors a bond indenture for the protection of bondholders.

The information on the bond certificate is written by the corporation into a more formal agreement called the bond indenture. This agreement is usually monitored by a trustee (often a bank), who represents the group of bondholders.

If, before the 20 years have passed, Trey wants to cash in the bond, he can sell it on the securities exchange (like the stock exchange, but dealing in the buying and selling of bonds rather than stock). Bonds are negotiable and generally transferable. Let's assume Trey calls his broker, who indicates that the current market price of the bond is quoted at 94, a percentage (94%) of the bond's face value. This price can be higher or lower than the face amount (100, or 100%), depending on current rates of interest as well as other market factors. If market interest rates are high compared with the current bond's interest rate, the percentage would be lower. Why? The reason is that the bond's interest is not as attractive as current rates. The 94 means that a buyer is willing to pay $940 (0.94 $\times$ $1,000) for the bond. If the quote were 104, then Trey could receive $1,040 (1.04 $\times$ $1,000) for the bond.

The following is a list of different types of bonds. Keep in mind that each bond issue may have special arrangements besides the customary repayment plans. Don't memorize this list; use it as a reference.

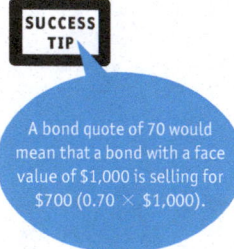

SUCCESS TIP

A bond quote of 70 would mean that a bond with a face value of $1,000 is selling for $700 (0.70 $\times$ $1,000).

Types of Bonds

Corporations can offer many types of bonds. The following are some examples.

Secured bond Bond issued by a corporation that pledges specific assets as security to meet the terms of the bond agreement.

Secured bonds: The corporation issuing the bonds pledges specific assets such as equipment or property as security for meeting the terms of the bond agreement.

Debenture bonds: The issuing corporation pledges no specific assets as collateral; therefore, the bonds are unsecured. Risk is higher than with secured bonds; these bonds will generally require a higher rate of interest to make them attractive to the investor.

Serial bonds: These bonds are made up of a series, each having its own maturity date. For example, a bond issue of $2,000,000 could be made up of a series of 20, $100,000 bonds, one series maturing at the end of each year for a period of 20 years.

Registered bonds: Owners of bonds are registered with the issuing company, and interest is mailed to the owners of record.

Callable bonds: These bonds have a provision stating that they can be called in by a corporation after a certain date. When a bond issue is called in, the corporation usually has to pay a price above the face value of the bond.

Convertible bonds: The bondholder may be allowed to convert bonds into shares of stock. For this right, bondholders give up fixed interest payments for what they hope will be higher dividends and/or stock prices.

Debenture bonds Bonds that are unsecured and are issued only on the general credit of a corporation.

Serial bonds Bonds issued in a series, each one of which has a different maturity date and thus comes due at a different time.

Registered bond Bondholders of record are registered with the corporation, and interest checks are sent directly to them.

Callable bond Bond with a provision that it can be called in by the issuing corporation after a certain date.

Convertible bond Bondholders have the option of converting bonds into stock at a specified exchange rate.

Stocks versus Bonds

Why would a corporation prefer to raise money by selling bonds rather than by issuing and selling stock? Let's look at an example. Should Sharpton Corporation obtain long-term funds by selling $500,000 worth of 12%, 10-year bonds, or issue 12% preferred stock for $500,000? Sharpton Corporation wants to make the most of its tax savings as well as earnings per share (EPS) of common stock:

$$\text{EPS} = \frac{\text{After-Tax Earnings} - \text{Dividends for Preferred}}{\text{Number of Shares of Common Stock Outstanding}}$$

We are assuming Sharpton Corporation has earnings of $700,000 and we assume a tax rate of 40%. Table 20.1 is a worked-out solution to this problem by the corporation's accountant.

TABLE 20.1 Stocks versus Bonds (Stock Dividends versus Bond Interest)

	$500,000 12% Preferred Stock Issued	$500,000 12% Bonds (10-Year) Issued
Earnings before Taxes or Finance Costs	$700,000	$700,000
Less: Bond Interest	—0—	60,000 (0.12 × $500,000)
Earnings Subject to Income Tax	$700,000	$640,000
Less: Income Tax (40%)	280,000	256,000
Net Income	420,000	384,000
Less: Preferred Dividend	60,000 (0.12 × $500,000)	—0—
Earnings Available to Common Stockholders	$360,000	$384,000
Number of Common Stock Shares Outstanding	80,000	80,000
Earnings per Share	$ 4.50 $\left(\dfrac{\$360,000}{80,000}\right)$	$ 4.80 $\left(\dfrac{\$384,000}{80,000}\right)$

Looking just at the numbers, Sharpton Corporation would be better off issuing *bonds* because the $60,000 of bond interest that the corporation would pay to bondholders would serve to reduce earnings on which the corporation would have to pay tax. On the other hand, *dividends* paid to stockholders do not reduce earnings on which the corporation would pay taxes (the dividend for preferred stock is not an expense, as bond interest is, but a distribution of net income *after* tax). With bonds, the common stockholders have an earnings per share of $4.80 versus $4.50.

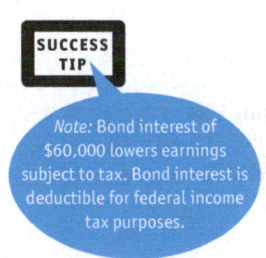

SUCCESS TIP

Note: Bond interest of $60,000 lowers earnings subject to tax. Bond interest is deductible for federal income tax purposes.

Other factors, however, should be considered when deciding whether to issue stocks or bonds to raise money, such as how interest rates are moving in the economy or whether the corporation can meet the bond interest payments each period for 10 years. If interest rates are high, it may be that the bond issue should be delayed to get more favorable interest rates.

For a comparison of stocks and bonds, see the Blueprint at the end of the chapter.

Before concluding this unit, let's see how Sharpton Corporation would record the sale and pay interest on the 12%, 10-year, $500,000 bonds.

On January 1, Sharpton Corporation issued its bonds (Figure 20.1).

Figure 20.1
Issuance of Bonds

Jan.	1	Cash		500 00 0 00	
		Bonds Payable			500 0 0 0 00
		Records issuance of bonds			

It then made semiannual interest payments to its bondholders (Figure 20.2).

Figure 20.2
Semiannual Interest Paid

Jun.	30	Bond Interest Expense		30 0 0 0 00	
		Cash			30 0 0 0 00
		Paid semiannual interest expense			

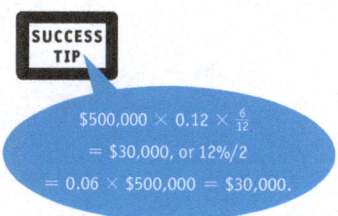

SUCCESS TIP

$500,000 \times 0.12 \times \frac{6}{12}$
$= \$30,000$, or 12%/2
$= 0.06 \times \$500,000 = \$30,000.$

This entry will be recorded twice a year for 10 years. At the end of 10 years, Sharpton will record the bond's maturity.

On the year of retirement, the journal entry would look like Figure 20.3.

Figure 20.3
Bonds Retired

Dec.	31	Bonds Payable		500 00 0 00	
		Cash			500 0 0 0 00
		Retired bonds			

The face value of the bond, $500,000, has been repaid on the maturity date.

Bonds Sold between Interest Dates

What would happen if Sharpton Corporation printed and dated the bonds on January 1 but did not actually sell them until March 1? Interest would be paid for all 6 months from January through June, even though the bonds weren't sold until March 1. How is that handled? And what happens if a person buys a bond that was issued in August, but the person buys it in November? As stated earlier, bond issuers only pay interest every 6 months. So when a buyer purchases a bond between the 6-month interest dates, the buyer pays the purchase price of the bond *plus* the interest that has built up since the last interest payment date. Keep in mind that interest is being paid only twice a year. Think of it as an adjustment as the interest accrues. On the next payment, the buyer will receive the full interest payment for the 6-month period. Let's show this situation by seeing how Sharpton Corporation records the sale of bonds on March 1 that were dated January 1 (Figure 20.4).

Figure 20.4
Bonds Issued with Accrued Interest

Mar.	1	Cash		510 0 0 0 00	
		Bonds Payable			500 0 0 0 00
		Bond Interest Payable			10 0 0 0 00
		Bond issue plus 2 months' accrued interest			

Note that the buyer pays $510,000 instead of $500,000 because $10,000 of the accrued interest has been accumulated. On June 30, the $10,000 is repaid along with interest earned for 4 months (Figure 20.5).

		Description			
Jun.	30	Bond Interest Payable	10 0 0 0 00		
		Bond Interest Expense	20 0 0 0 00		
		Cash		30 0 0 0 00	
		Record semiannual interest payment			

Figure 20.5
Semiannual Interest Paid

In the next unit, we look at how to record bond issues when the selling price is less or more than the face value.

Now let's check your progress.

 # TRY IT!   Learning Unit 20-1

Journalize the following entries:

1. On October 1, issued eight $22,000, 10% bonds that mature in 25 years at face value.
2. Paid semiannual interest on March 31.
3. Bonds retired at end of 25 years.

TRY IT!   Solution Learning Unit 20-1

	Accounts	Dr.	Cr.
1.	Cash	176,000	
	Bonds Payable		176,000
2.	Bond Interest Expense	8,800	
	Cash		8,800
	($176,000 × 0.10 × 6/12)		
3.	Bonds Payable	176,000	
	Cash		176,000

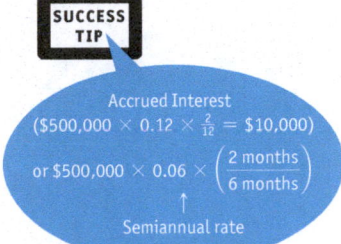

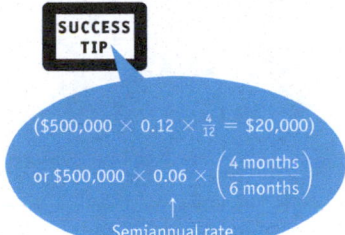

LEARNING UNIT 20-2

 L02

Journalizing Amortization of Bonds by the Straight-Line Method

When a corporation issues bonds, it must do the following:

1. Receive approval from the board of directors of the corporation as well as from a governmental regulatory agency, the Securities and Exchange Commission.
2. Print the bonds.
3. Advertise the bond issue.

The problem is that by the time these steps have been done, the rate of interest stated on the bond, the *contract* rate, may be lower or higher than the current *market* rate of interest. Investors may require higher rates of interest if the bond issue appears to be different from others offered by companies that may have had fewer financial difficulties.

For example, let's assume that Salas Corporation is attempting to sell its 12% bond issue. The current market rate is 13.2%. To make its bonds more attractive (investors are looking for the best return on their investment), Salas decides to sell the bonds for less than face value (91, or 91% of the face value of $1,000). The bondholder will still receive yearly interest of $120 per bond (0.12 × $1,000) but will only pay $910 (0.91 × $1,000) per bond. Thus, the investors' annual or effective rate of interest is 13.2% ($120/$910). The difference between the *issue price* ($910) and the face value ($1,000) is called the *discount*.

Conversely, if Salas Corporation sells the bond for *more* than the face value (if its contract rate is higher than the market rate), the difference between issue price and face value is called a *premium*.

Effective rate Real or actual rate of interest to the borrowing corporation.

Recording and Amortizing Bonds Issued at a Discount

To illustrate how to record a bond discount, let's look at the Horizon Corporation, which on January 1, 201X, issued 200, 12%, $1,000, 10-year bonds at 97 (97% of face value). The discount is used because the current market rate is 12.4%, and Horizon has to be competitive to make its bond attractive to investors. Bondholders will receive yearly bond interest of $120 with an effective rate of 12.4% ($120/$970). The accounts that will make up the journal entry include:

Cash	Asset	↑	Dr. $194,000	← 0.97 × $200,000
Discount on Bonds Payable	Contra-Liability	↑	Dr. $ 6,000	← ($200,000 − $194,000)
Bonds Payable	Liability	↑	Cr. $200,000	← Face value

The journal entry will look like Figure 20.6.

Figure 20.6
Bond Issued at a Discount

Jan.	1	Cash	194 0 0 0 00		
		Discount on Bonds Payable	6 0 0 0 00		
		Bonds Payable		200 0 0 0 00	
		Record bond issue			

Let's look at how the Discount on Bonds Payable would look on the balance sheet.

Long-Term Liabilities:		
12% Bonds Payable	$200,000	
Less: Discount on Bonds Payable	6,000	$194,000

Carrying value (book value) Face value of bond less bond discount or plus bond premium.

For bonds like Horizon Co.'s that were sold at a discount, the carrying value (also called book value) of $194,000 is the face value of $200,000 minus the Discount on Bonds Payable of $6,000. At maturity (after 10 years), the carrying value will be the same as face value ($200,000).

Discount on Bonds Payable Account used when bonds are issued below face value; indicates market rate of interest is higher than contract rate. This account is a contra-liability account.

When each interest payment is made, a portion of the Discount on Bonds Payable is transferred to increase Interest Expense. This portion is called amortization of discount on bonds payable. Bond discount causes the total interest expense to increase because the bond is sold for less than face value, resulting in higher costs of borrowing.

Amortization of discount on Bonds Payable, amortization of premium on Bonds Payable Writing off the bond premium or discount as a decrease or increase to interest expense for each interest period.

Before looking at how to amortize the discount, let's prove that the interest expense will be more than the contract amount of interest of $240,000 (0.12 × $200,000 × 10 years) for 10 years.

Total amount to be paid to bondholder	$440,000 ($200,000 bonds + $240,000 interest)
Total amount to be received from sale of bond	−$194,000
Interest to be paid over life of bond	$246,000
Average interest expense per year	$ 24,600 ($246,000 ÷ 10 years)
Semiannual interest expense	$ 12,300

If no discount has been made, the semiannual interest expense would be $12,000 ($200,000 $\times$ 0.12 $\times \frac{6}{12}$ or $200,000 $\times$ 0.06). Now the discount results in an additional $300 of interest expense for *each* semiannual payment ($6,000 ÷ 20 periods).

The journal entry for each semiannual payment and amortization of discount will be as shown in Figure 20.7.

Jun.	30	Bond Interest Expense	12 3 0 0 00		
		Discount on Bonds Payable		3 0 0 00	
		Cash		12 0 0 0 00	
		Semiannual interest payment and amortization			
		of discount			

Figure 20.7
Semiannual Payment and Amortization of Discount by Straight-Line Method

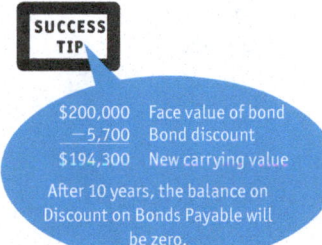

$200,000   Face value of bond
−5,700   Bond discount
$194,300   New carrying value
After 10 years, the balance on Discount on Bonds Payable will be zero.

After posting, the ledger would look as follows:

Discount on Bonds Payable			Bond Interest Expense	
6,000	300		12,300	
5,700				

After this amortization the carrying value (book value) of the bond increased from $194,000 to $194,300. By the end of 10 years the carrying value will have gone up to $200,000, or the amount due at maturity.

In this unit, we calculate amortization of the bond's discount by the straight-line method; in the next unit we use the *interest* method. The straight-line method transfers an equal amount of bond discount to interest expense over equal periods of time.

Table 20.2 shows the straight-line method of amortizing a bond discount over the life of the bond for each semiannual period. At the end of the life of the bond, the Discount on Bonds Payable shows a zero balance, with the original $6,000 transferred to Interest Expense. At this point, the book value or carrying value of a bond ($200,000) is the same amount as paid at maturity.

Straight-line method Method recognizing equal amounts of interest expense for each period when amortizing a bond discount or premium.

TABLE 20.2 Amortization Schedule for Bond Discount Using the Straight-Line Method for Each Semiannual Period

Period	Carrying Value, Beg. of Period	Total Interest Expense	Interest Paid to Bondholders (0.06 × Face Value)*	Amortized Discount Transferred to Increase Interest Expense	Carrying Value, End of Period
1	$194,000	$12,300	$12,000	$300	$194,300
	(200,000 − 6,000)		(200,000 × 0.06)	(6,000 ÷ 20 periods)	(194,000 + 300)
2	194,300	12,300	12,000	300	194,600
3	194,600	12,300	12,000	300	194,900
4	194,900	12,300	12,000	300	195,200
19	199,400	12,300	12,000	300	199,700
20	199,700	12,300	12,000	300	200,000

The balance in the Discount on Bonds Payable account will be equal to zero at the end of the 20 periods.
* Half of annual rate of 12% = 6% semiannual rate.

Year-End Adjusting Entry: Accrued Interest and Amortization of Discount on Bonds Payable. Let's consider what would happen if the semiannual interest payment were on April 1 and October 1. On December 31, $6,000, 3 months' interest, would be accrued ($12,000 $\times \frac{3}{6}$). The amount of discount to be amortized would be $150 ($300 $\times \frac{3}{6}$). The journal entry would be recorded as shown in Figure 20.8.

Figure 20.8
Discount to Be Amortized
by Straight-Line Method

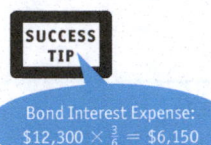

Bond Interest Expense:
$12,300 \times \frac{3}{6} = \$6,150$

Dec.	31	Bond Interest Expense	6 1 5 0 00		
		Discount on Bonds Payable		1 5 0 00	
		Bond Interest Payable		6 0 0 0 00	
		Accrued interest and amortization of discount			

Note that the Discount on Bonds Payable does indeed increase total bond interest expense from $6,000 to $6,150. This adjusting entry would then be reversed on January 1, as shown in Figure 20.9.

Figure 20.9
Reversing Entry

Jan.	1	Bond Interest Payable	6 0 0 0 00		
		Discount on Bonds Payable	1 5 0 00		
		Bond Interest Expense		6 1 5 0 00	
		Reversing entry			

The regular payment made on April 1 would look like Figure 20.10.

Figure 20.10
Paid Semiannual Interest
and Amortized Discount

Apr.	1	Bond Interest Expense	12 3 0 0 00		
		Discount on Bonds Payable		3 0 0 00	
		Cash		12 0 0 0 00	
		Semiannual interest payment and amortization			
		of discount			

Recording and Amortizing Bonds Issued at a Premium

To illustrate bonds issued at a premium, let's look at Horizon Corporation again, but assume that on January 1 it issued its 200, 12%, 10-year, $1,000 bonds at 102 (102% of face value). This premium occurred because the current market rate was 11.8%, and Horizon's bonds were thus attractive to investors. The bondholders would receive per bond the yearly interest payment of $120 (0.12 × $1,000 bond) with an effective rate of 11.8% ($120/$1,020). The accounts that will make up the journal entry include:

SUCCESS TIP

The Premium on Bonds Payable is added to the face value of the bond.

Cash	Asset	↑	Dr. $204,000 ◄——— 1.02 × $200,000
Premium on Bonds Payable	Liability	↑	Cr. $ 4,000 ◄——— ($204,000 − $200,000)
Bonds Payable	Liability	↑	Cr. $200,000 ◄——— Face value

The journal entry will look like Figure 20.11.

Figure 20.11
Bond Issued at a Premium

Jan.	1	Cash	204 0 0 0 00		
		Premium on Bonds Payable		4 0 0 0 00	
		Bonds Payable		200 0 0 0 00	
		Issued bond at premium			

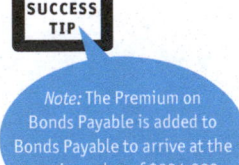

Note: The Premium on Bonds Payable is added to Bonds Payable to arrive at the carrying value of $204,000.

Let's see how the Premium on Bonds Payable would look on the balance sheet:

Long-Term Liabilities:		
12% Bonds Payable	$200,000	
Add: Premium on Bonds Payable	4,000	$204,000

When each interest payment is made, a portion of the Premium on Bonds Payable is transferred to *reduce* Interest Expense. This portion is called **amortization of premium on bonds payable**. Let's prove that the interest expense will be less than the contractual amount of $240,000 for 10 years.

Premium on Bonds Payable
Account used when bonds are issued above face value; it indicates that market interest rate is below contract rate. This account is a liability account.

Total amount to be paid to bondholders	$440,000 ($200,000 bonds + $240,000 interest)
Total amount to be received from sale of bonds	−204,000
Interest to be paid over life of bond	$236,000
Average interest expense per year	$ 23,600 ($236,000 ÷ 10 years)
Semiannual interest expense	$ 11,800

If no premium were paid, the semiannual interest expense would be $12,000 ($200,000 × 12% × $\frac{6}{12}$ or $200,000 × 0.06). Now the premium results in *reducing* the interest expense for each semiannual payment by $200 ($4,000 premium ÷ 20 periods).

The journal entry for the semiannual payment will look like Figure 20.12.

Jun.	30	Bond Interest Expense	11 80 0 00	
		Premium on Bonds Payable	2 0 0 00	
		Cash		12 00 0 00
		Semiannual payment and premium		
		amortization		

Figure 20.12
Paid Semiannual Payment and Amortized Premium

After posting, the ledger will look like the following:

Premium on Bonds Payable			Bond Interest Expense	
200	4,000		11,800	
	3,800			

We're using the straight-line method of amortizing the bond premium over the life of the bond for each semiannual period. This method is shown in Table 20.3. Note that at the end of the schedule, the carrying value is reduced to $200,000 and the balance in the Premium account is zero.

TABLE 20.3 Amortization Schedule for Bond Premium Using the Straight-Line Method for Each Semiannual Period

Period	Carrying Value, Beg. of Period	Total Interest Expense	Interest Paid to Bondholder (0.06 × Face Value)	Amortized Premium to Decrease Interest Expense	Carrying Value, End of Period
1	$204,000	$11,800	$12,000	$200	$203,800
	(200,000 + 4,000)		(0.06 × 200,000)		(204,000 − 200)
2	203,800	11,800	12,000	200	203,600
3	203,600	11,800	12,000	200	203,400
4	203,400	11,800	12,000	200	203,200
19	200,400	11,800	12,000	200	200,200
20	200,200	11,800	12,000	200	200,000

The balance in the Premium on Bonds Payable account should be equal to zero at the end of the 20 periods.

Now let's check your progress.

 **TRY IT!**   **Learning Unit 20-2**

Prepare a partial amortization schedule using the straight-line method for the first two semiannual periods based on the following facts (use same headings as in text):

50, 11%, 10-year bonds issued at 92. Each bond had a $4,000 face value.

Hint: Remember, this is semiannually so adjust the interest rate.

TRY IT!   **Solution Learning Unit 20-2**

Per.	Carry. Value (beg.)	Total Interest Expense	Interest Payment	Amort. Disc.	Carry. Val. (end.)
1	$184,000	$11,800	$11,000	$800	$184,800
2	184,800	11,800	11,000	$800	185,600

Interest = $200,000 × 0.11 × 1/2 = $11,000
Amort. Disc. $16,000/20 per. = $800

LEARNING UNIT 20-3

L03 ▶

Journalizing Amortization of Bonds by the Interest Method[1]

In the last unit, we amortized the discount or premium by the straight-line method. The problem with this method is that it recognizes an equal amount of interest expense each period, even though the bond's carrying value changes. Accountants think it is inconsistent for interest expense to stay the same while the amount owed changes. They think interest should be a *constant percentage of the carrying value.* For this reason, another method, called the *interest method*, is used in amortizing bond discounts and premiums. Generally the straight-line method may be used only if the results do not materially differ from those of the interest method.

Amortizing the Bond Discount by the Interest Method

Interest method of amortization This method amortizes the premium or discount to *record* interest expense, being equal to the carrying value of the bond times the market rate times the time period. The interest expense is a constant percentage of the carrying value. The discount or premium to be amortized is the difference between the interest to be recorded and the interest paid to bondholders.

The interest method of amortization makes interest expense a constant percentage of the bond carrying value.

The goal of the interest method is to calculate the interest expense to be recorded each year as a constant percentage of the carrying value of the bonds. The interest amount will thus not be the same each period. Two formulas provide the calculations necessary to reach this goal:

1. Carrying Value of Bonds at Beginning of Period × Market Interest Rate = Interest Expense to Be Recorded
2. Face Value × Contract Rate = Interest Payment to Bondholders

The discount to be amortized is the difference between (1) and (2).

To illustrate this method, let's assume Yang Corporation is issuing $200,000 of 12%, 10-year bonds on April 1. Interest is to be paid on October 1 and April 1. The selling price of the bonds is $178,808. The market rate is 14%.

Look at the amortization schedule shown in Table 20.4. Note that the discount amount to be amortized is not constant, as it is in the straight-line method. To prove that the interest expense is a constant percentage of the carrying value, let's look at semiannual periods 2 and 19.

$$\text{Period 2: } \frac{\$12,553}{\$179,325} = 0.07 \quad \text{Period 19: } \frac{\$13,746}{\$196,373} = 0.07$$

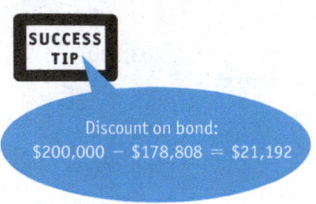
SUCCESS TIP
Discount on bond: $200,000 − $178,808 = $21,192

---

[1] Often referred to as effective interest method.

TABLE 20.4 Amortization Schedule for Bond Discount for Each Semiannual Period Using the Interest Method

Period	(1) Carrying Value, Beginning of Period	(2) Interest Paid to Bondholders (0.06 × Face Value)*	(3) Interest Expense Recorded (0.07 × Carrying Value)	(4) Discount to Be Amortized (2) – (3)	(5) Carrying Value, End of Period
1	$178,808	$12,000	$12,517	$ 517	$179,325
	(200,000 − 21,192)		(0.07 × 178,808)		(178,808 + 517)
2	179,325	12,000	12,553	553	179,878
3	179,878	12,000	12,591	591	180,469
19	196,373	12,000	13,746	1,746	198,119
20	198,119	12,000	13,881**	1,881	200,000

* Use 6% because 12% is for the whole year and the calculations are made semiannually.
** Adjusted for rounding.

On October 1, the date of the first semiannual interest payment, the entry in Figure 20.13 would occur.

Oct.	1	Bond Interest Expense		12 5 1 7 00	
		Discount on Bonds Payable			5 1 7 00
		Cash			12 0 0 0 00
		Semiannual payment and amortization			
		of discount			

Figure 20.13
Paid Semiannual Interest and Amortized Discount by Interest Method

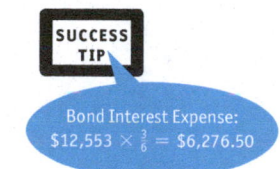

Bond Interest Expense: $12,553 × $\frac{2}{6}$ = $6,276.50

Year-End Adjustment

On December 31, 3 months' interest of $6,000 ($\frac{3}{6}$ × $12,000) has accrued, as well as $276.50 ($\frac{3}{6}$ of $553), half of the second-period discount shown on the amortization schedule. The adjusting year-end entry in Figure 20.14 is prepared.

Dec.	31	Bond Interest Expense		6 2 7 6 50	
		Discount on Bonds Payable			2 7 6 50
		Bond Interest Payable			6 0 0 0 00
		Year-end adjustment			

Figure 20.14
Year-End Adjustment

The reversing entry on January 1 and the entry to record payment of interest on April 1 would look like Figure 20.15.

Jan.	1	Bond Interest Payable		6 0 0 0 00	
		Discount on Bonds Payable		2 7 6 50	
		Bond Interest Expense			6 2 7 6 50
		Reversing entry			
Apr.	1	Bond Interest Expense		12 5 5 3 00	
		Discount on Bonds Payable			5 5 3 00
		Cash			12 0 0 0 00
		Semiannual interest payment and amortization			
		of discount			

Figure 20.15
Reversing Entry and Payment of Interest

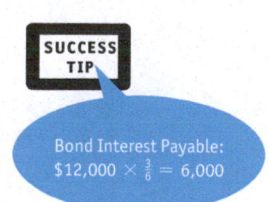

Bond Interest Payable: $12,000 × $\frac{3}{6}$ = 6,000

Amortizing the Bond Premium by the Interest Method

On April 1, Yang Corporation issues $200,000 of 12%, 10-year bonds with interest paid on October 1 and April 1. The selling price of the bonds is $224,926. The market interest rate is 10%. The amortization schedule is shown in Table 20.5. On October 1, the entry in Figure 20.16 records the semiannual payment.

TABLE 20.5 Amortization Schedule for Bond Premium for Each Semiannual Period Using the Interest Method

Period	(1) Carrying Value, Beg. of Period	(2) Interest Paid to Bondholder (0.06 × Face Value)	(3) Interest Expense Recorded (0.05 × Carrying Value)	(4) Premium to Be Amortized (2) – (3)	(5) Carrying Value, End of Period (1) – (4)
1	$224,926	$12,000	$11,246	$ 754	$224,172 ($224,926 − $754)
2	224,172	12,000	11,209	791	223,381
19	203,726	12,000	10,186	1,814	201,912
20	201,912	12,000	10,088*	1,912	200,000

* Adjusted for rounding.

Figure 20.16
Paid Interest and Amortized Premium Using the Interest Method

Oct.	1	Bond Interest Expense	11 2 4 6 00		
		Premium on Bonds Payable	7 5 4 00		
		Cash		12 0 0 0 00
		Semiannual interest payment and premium		
		amortization		

Year-End Adjustment

It should be noted that on December 31, 3 months' interest expense has accrued ($\frac{3}{6}$ × $11,209) as well as the need to amortize half the premium for the second period ($\frac{3}{6}$ of $791). The journal entry in Figure 20.17 records this year-end adjustment.

Figure 20.17
Year-End Adjustment

Dec.	31	Bond Interest Expense	5 6 0 4 50		
		Premium on Bonds Payable	3 9 5 50		
		Bond Interest Payable		6 0 0 0 00
		Year-end adjustment		

SUCCESS TIP

Bond Interest Expense:
$\frac{3}{6}$ × $11,209 = $5,604.50

Premium on Bonds Payable:
$\frac{3}{6}$ × $791 = $395.50

Bond Interest Payable:
$\frac{3}{6}$ × $12,000 = $6,000

The reversing entry on January 1 and the payment of interest in April would look like Figure 20.18.

Figure 20.18 Reversing Entry and Payment of Interest

Jan.	1	Bond Interest Payable	6 0 0 0 00		
		Premium on Bonds Payable		3 9 5 50
		Bond Interest Expense		5 6 0 4 50
		Reversing entry		
Apr.	1	Bond Interest Expense	11 2 0 9 00		
		Premium on Bonds Payable	7 9 1 00		
		Cash		12 0 0 0 00
		Semiannual interest payment and amortization		
		of premium		

Now let's check your progress.

TRY IT!   Learning Unit 20-3

Prepare a partial amortization table like in Learning Unit 20-3, using the interest method for the first two periods based on the following information:

180, 8%, 9-year $1,500 bonds issued at a selling price of $211,531. Assume a market rate of 12% and semiannual interest.

TRY IT!   **Solution Learning Unit 20-3**

Per.	Carrying Value (beg.)	Int. Payment	Total Interest Expense	Disc. to Be Amort.	Carrying Val. (end.)
1	$211,531	$10,800	$12,692	$1,892	$213,423
2	213,423	10,800	12,805	2,005	215,428

Period 1
(Beg. Carrying Value was $211,531)
$270,000 × .04 = $10,800
$211,531 × .06 = $12,692
Difference is $1,892

Period 2
$270,000 × .04 = $10,800
$213,423 × .06 = $12,805
Difference is $2,005

Note that the $12,805 was the result of multiplying the beginning carrying value of $213,423 by the market rate of 6%.

Journalizing Bond Sinking Fund Transactions   LEARNING UNIT 20-4

L04

In the first unit of this chapter, we mentioned callable bonds, which permit the corporation to reacquire bonds at a price based on a percentage of face value. Some corporations retire them and issue new bonds (called *bond refunding*) to take their place, paying a lower rate of interest. If this call provision doesn't exist, a company can repurchase its bonds in the open market and then retire them. By retiring bonds, companies can decrease the amount of debt they owe. If the stated interest rates of the bonds are high, the retirement of bonds could result in substantial cash savings, even if new bonds are issued at lower interest rates.

When the bonds are retired before they reach maturity, the following points must be recognized:

1. Any amortization of discount or premium must be brought up-to-date at the time of retirement.

2. The premium or discount as well as the bond liability account must be removed.

3. Any gain or loss is recognized on the retirement of the bonds as other income or other expense that will be shown on the income statement.

Let's use Samuel Corporation as an example. On June 30 the corporation retired a $500,000, 10% bond issue that had an unamortized premium of $19,000. The bonds were called in at 105 (105% of face value). All journal entries relating to interest payments and premium amortization were completed before the bonds' retirement. The entry to record the retirement of the bonds by Samuel Corporation would look like Figure 20.19.

Note that the difference between the bond carrying value of $519,000 ($500,000 + $19,000) and actual cash paid results in the loss of $6,000. Of course, if the carrying value were greater than the cash paid, a gain would be realized.

Figure 20.19
Retirement of Bond

Bonds Payable	500 0 0 0 00	
Premium on Bonds Payable	19 0 0 0 00	
Loss on Bond Retirement	6 0 0 0 00	
Cash		525 0 0 0 00
Retirement of bond		

The Bond Sinking Fund

Sinking fund Fund that accumulates cash to pay off bonds when they are retired.

Often a corporation will agree to establish a fund that will accumulate assets over the life of the bond so as to pay off the bondholders at maturity. In fact, such a fund is often a requirement stated in the bond indentures. This fund is called a sinking fund.

For example, Elliott Corporation issued 8%, 15-year bonds for $80,000, agreeing to deposit $2,946.36 at the end of each year during the lifetime of the bond so that by the end of the 15th year the fund would contain $80,000 to pay off bondholders. Sinking fund tables are available that make these periodic deposits easy to calculate. For example, Elliott's accountant would go to a sinking fund table and look up 8% for 15 periods and find a table factor of 0.0368295. By multiplying $80,000 × 0.0368295, one comes up with a yearly deposit of $2,946.36, which, invested at this rate of interest (8%) compounded annually, will at the end of 15 years bring a total of $80,000.

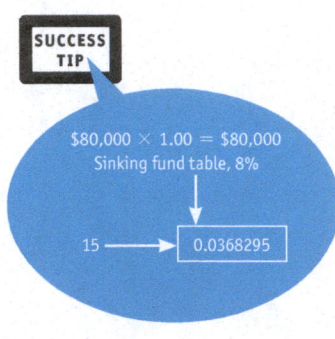

$80,000 × 1.00 = $80,000
Sinking fund table, 8%

15 ⟶ 0.0368295

Long-term investment ⟶	Bond Sinking Fund	Asset	↑	Dr.
	Cash	Asset	↓	Cr.

The annual journal entries for Elliott Corporation for establishing an annual continuation of the sinking fund appear in Figure 20.20.

Figure 20.20
Bond Sinking Fund Established

Bond Sinking Fund	2 9 4 6 36	
Cash		2 9 4 6 36
Establishing sinking fund		

Bond Sinking Fund Interest Earned Other revenue account used to record earnings on sinking fund balance.

When interest is earned on the balance in the sinking fund, the Bond Sinking Fund Interest Earned account is credited and the following entry results (Figure 20.21):

Bond Sinking Fund	Asset	↑	Dr.
Bond Sinking Fund Interest Earned	Other Revenue	↑	Cr.

Figure 20.21
Interest Earned on Bond Sinking Fund

Bond Sinking Fund	2 3 5 71	
Bond Sinking Fund Interest Earned		2 3 5 71
($2,946.36 × 0.08)		
Interest earned		

When the bonds are paid off, a little more or less cash than is needed may be in the sinking fund. The entry to record the payment of the bonds by Elliott is shown in Figure 20.22 (assume $50 extra in the sinking fund).

Keep in mind that the money in the sinking fund cannot be used to meet other current expenses or liabilities. Thus, the sinking fund is reported in the long-term investment section of the balance sheet. Any cash left over is returned to the Cash account.

		Dr.		Cr.	
Cash		5 0 00			
Bonds Payable		80 0 0 00			
Bond Sinking Fund				80 0 5 0 00	
Payment of bonds					

Figure 20.22
Payoff of Bonds

Now let's check your progress.

 **TRY IT!** Learning Unit 20-4

Journalize the following transactions:

a. Retired $170,000 of bonds that had an unamortized $11,000 premium at 105.
b. Set up a bond sinking fund with an initial deposit of $2,200.
c. Earned $150 interest on sinking fund balance.
d. Bond sinking fund of $52,000 was used to reduce bondholders' amount of $52,000 due at maturity.

TRY IT! Solution Learning Unit 20-4

	Accounts	Dr.	Cr.
a.	Bonds Payable	170,000	
	Premium on Bonds Payable	11,000	
	Cash		178,500
	Gain on Bond Retirement		2,500
b.	Bond Sinking Fund	2,200	
	Cash		2,200
c.	Bond Sinking Fund	150	
	Bond Sinking Fund Interest Earned		150
d.	Bonds Payable	52,000	
	Bond Sinking Fund		52,000

DEMONSTRATION SUMMARY PROBLEM

LO1,2,3,4

Marsha Rey, an accountant, is planning her workday around catching up on transactions relating to bonds for three different clients. Help her complete these three projects (each one is shown separately).

Project 1
Showy Corporation issued $200,000 of 4%, 20-year bonds at 95 on January 1, 201X, with semiannual interest payable on July 1 and December 31. Amortization of the discount is by using the straight-line method. Record the following entries:

a. Issuance of bond
b. Semiannual payment on July 1 and amortization of discount
c. Retirement of bonds at maturity
d. Redo a, b, and c assuming bonds sold at 103.

Solutions for Project 1

	Date	Accounts	Dr.	Cr.
a.	201X			
	Jan. 1	Cash	190,000	
		Discount on Bonds Payable	10,000	
		Bonds Payable		200,000
b.	July 1	Bond Interest Expense	4,250	
		Discount on Bonds Payable		250
		Cash		4,000
c.	Dec. 31	Bonds Payable	200,000	
		Cash		200,000
d. a.	201X			
	Jan. 1	Cash	206,000	
		Premium on Bonds Payable		6,000
		Bonds Payable		200,000
b.	July 1	Bond Interest Expense	3,850	
		Premium on Bonds Payable	150	
		Cash		4,000
c.	Dec. 31	Bonds Payable	200,000	
		Cash		200,000

Tip

The discount of $10,000 is amortized *equally* over the 40 periods or $250 per period. The discount will increase bond interest whereas a premium (d) will decrease bond interest. Note that the bond premium amortized was calculated by dividing $6,000 by 40 periods to equal $150.

Project 2

On July 1, Advent Co. issued a 4%, 10-year bond with a face value of $200,000 for $145,639 because the current market rate was 8%. Record the following entries, assuming the interest method is used to amortize the discount on the bond and semiannual interest. Round the discount to the nearest dollar:

a. Issuance of bond

b. Semiannual interest payment on December 31 and amortization of the discount

c. Semiannual interest payment on June 30 and amortization of the discount

Solution for Project 2

	Date	Accounts	Dr.	Cr.
a.	July 1	Cash	145,639	
		Discount on Bonds Payable	54,361	
		Bonds Payable		200,000

b.	Dec. 31	Bond Interest Expense	5,826	
		Discount on Bonds Payable		1,826
		Cash		4,000

c.	June 30	Bond Interest Expense	5,899	
		Discount on Bonds Payable		1,899
		Cash		4,000

Tips

$200,000 − $54,361 = $145,639 carrying value

Interest paid to bondholders	$200,000 × 2% = $4,000
Interest expense recorded	$145,639 × 4% = 5,826
Discount to be amortized	$1,826
New carrying value	$147,465
Interest expense	$200,000 × 2% = $4,000
Interest expense recorded	$147,465 × 4% = $5,899
Discount to be amortized	$1,899

Project 3

On January 1, Aster Co. sold $300,000 of 10-year sinking fund bonds. The corporation expects to earn 10% on the sinking fund balance and is required to deposit $21,000 at the end of each year with the trustee. From the following, record the journal entries for Aster:

a. The first deposit

b. Earning $2,850 at end of first period

c. Payment of bondholders at maturity with sinking funds that have a balance of $305,000

Solutions for Project 3

	Accounts	Dr.	Cr.
a.	Bond Sinking Fund	21,000	
	Cash		21,000
b.	Bond Sinking Fund	2,850	
	Bond Sinking Fund Interest Earned		2,850
c.	Cash	5,000	
	Bonds Payable	300,000	
	Bond Sinking Fund		305,000

Tips

Bond Sinking Fund	Asset	Balance Sheet
Bond Sinking Fund Interest Earned	Revenue	Income Statement
Bonds Payable	Liability	Balance Sheet
Cash	Asset	Balance Sheet

SUCCESS COACH

The following Success Tips are from Learning Units 20-1 to 20-4. Take the Do It Right Now Checkup and use the Check Your Score to see how you are doing. The Success Coach provides tips before each Checkup to help you avoid common accounting errors.

LU 20-1 Journalizing Issuance and Interest Payments of Bonds

Do It Right Tips: When deciding between stocks and bonds, a corporation must look at its bottom line. If bonds are issued, the company's earnings are reduced and it pays less in taxes. If stock is issued, dividends paid to stockholders will not reduce earnings and the corporation will pay more in taxes. Another factor that should be considered is the current interest rate. If the rate is too high bonds may not be the best way to go.

Do It Right Now Checkup: Answer true or false to the following statements.

1. The face value of a bond is the principal.
2. The stated rate on a bond is the contract rate.
3. Bonds can never be convertible.
4. Bond interest is not tax deductible.
5. Accrued interest is added to the issue price of a bond if it is purchased between interest dates.

LU 20-2 Journalizing Amortization of Bonds by the Straight-Line Method

Do It Right Tips: If a bond is sold for a discount (less than the bond's face value), an account called Discount on Bonds Payable results. It is a contra-liability located on the balance sheet. An increase in the discount is a debit. When it is amortized, the discount account will be credited and interest expense will be debited. If the bond is sold at a premium, the account Premium on Bonds Payable will result. This account has a credit balance and will reduce interest expense when amortized.

Do It Right Now Checkup: Answer true or false to the following statements.

1. When interest payment is made, Discount on Bonds Payable will decrease the interest expense.
2. The normal balance of Discount on Bonds Payable is a debit.
3. The straight-line method transfers unequal amounts of bond discount to interest expense.
4. The Premium on Bonds Payable is added to the face value of the bond.
5. The Premium on Bonds Payable will reduce interest expense.

LU 20-3 Journalizing Amortization of Bonds by the Interest Method

Do It Right Tips: The interest method of amortization makes interest expense a constant percentage of the bond carrying value. Keep in mind that the carrying value is determined by whether there is a discount or premium. A discount results in a lower carrying value than face value, while a premium has a higher carrying value than face value.

Do It Right Now Checkup: Answer true or false to the following statements.

1. Both the straight-line method and the interest method of amortizing bond discounts can be used if results materially differ.
2. Face value minus contract rate equals interest expense to bondholder.
3. A discount is subtracted from the original bond price.
4. The Discount on Bonds Payable account increases when a semiannual payment is made.
5. A reversing entry may be used for the accrual of bond interest expense.

LU 20-4 Journalizing Bond Sinking Fund Transactions

Do It Right Tips: If current interest rates are going down, it makes sense to retire some older bonds that are carrying a high rate of interest. The bond sinking fund is an asset that accumulates money to pay back the bondholders at a future date. When the bond comes due, cash is available to pay off the bonds. The Bond Sinking Fund is reported in the long-term investment section of the balance sheet.

Do It Right Now Checkup: Answer true or false to the following statements.

1. The sinking fund represents a liability.
2. Sinking funds cannot earn interest.
3. Any gain or loss from the retirement of a bond is shown on the balance sheet.
4. Sinking Fund Interest Earned is categorized as other revenue.
5. When a bond is retired, all premiums and/or discounts must be removed from the accounts.

CHECK YOUR SCORE: Answers to the Do It Right Now Checkup

LU 20-1

1. True
2. True
3. False—Bonds can be convertible.
4. False—Bond interest is tax deductible.
5. True

LU 20-2

1. False—When interest payment is made, Discount on Bonds Payable will increase the interest expense.
2. True
3. False—The straight-line method transfers equal amounts of bond discount.
4. True
5. True

LU 20-3

1. False—The straight-line method cannot be used if results are materially different from the effective interest method.
2. False—Face value times contract rate equals interest paid to bondholder.
3. False—A discount is subtracted from face value of bond.
4. False—A discount decreases when a semiannual payment is made.
5. True

LU 20-4

1. False—The sinking fund represents an asset.
2. False—Sinking funds are assumed to earn interest.
3. False—Any gain or loss from the retirement of a bond is shown on the income statement.
4. True
5. True

BLUEPRINT: STOCKS VERSUS BONDS

Stocks	Bonds
1. Stockholders are the owners of the corporation.	1. Bondholders are creditors to a corporation.
2. Stockholders are paid off in liquidation only after claims of creditors are satisfied.	2. Bondholders, in liquidation, have claims on assets (along with other creditors) before stockholders.
3. Dividends are paid only if earnings are sufficient; no fixed charge is associated with stocks as with bond interest. Preferred stock has a fixed dividend rate. Dividends are not an expense; they are a distribution of income.	3. Interest expense is a fixed charge. Failure to pay could result in creditors bringing bankruptcy proceedings against the corporation.
4. Stockholders have voting rights except with preferred stock.	4. Bondholders have no voting rights.
5. Dividends are deducted *after* tax on earnings.	5. Interest is deductible from earnings *before* tax.
6. Stockholders continue to receive dividends; they are not "paid off."	6. Bondholders are eventually repaid the principal.

Discussion Questions and Critical Thinking/Ethical Case

1. Explain the selling price of a bond quoted at 99.

2. What is the difference between a secured bond and a debenture bond?

3. Dividends reduce earnings before taxes. True or false? Explain.

4. Accrued interest results in the seller paying extra for bonds. True or false? Explain.

5. Explain why a bond may sell at a premium.

6. Why isn't Discount on Bonds Payable an immediate expense?

7. Premium on Bonds Payable will cause total interest expense to be reduced. True or false?

8. The straight-line method of amortizing a bond discount or premium will result in an uneven amount of discount or premium that increases or decreases expense each period. Agree or disagree? Why?

9. What is the carrying value of a bond?

10. Why does the interest method of amortizing a discount or premium use the market rate in calculating interest expense to be recorded?

11. Explain how a gain or loss on retirement of bonds before the maturity date is recorded.

12. What is the purpose of a bond sinking fund?

13. Alice wants to buy bonds, but her husband, Pete, thinks stocks would be a better deal. Pete was watching a finance show on TV that said stocks would be going up and that now is the time to buy stock. He called Alice over and said, "I told you so." Alice told her husband that it was no time to take a risk with their money. Do you think Pete is correct in his thinking? You make the call. Write down your recommendations to Alice and her husband.

MyLabAccounting

Concept Checks

(15 min) **LO1** ▶

Bond Journal Entries

1. Journalize the following transactions:
   a. Issued three $35,000, 8% bonds that mature in 12 years at face value on May 1.
   b. Paid semiannual interest on October 31.
   c. Bonds retired at end of 12 years.

(10 min) **LO1** ▶

Bond Issued at a Discount

2. On January 1, Borg Co. issued five $2,200, 4%, 20-year bonds at 92. Record the journal entry.

(10 min) **LO2** ▶

Interest and Amortization of Discount with Straight-Line Method

3. From Concept Check 2, record the June 30 semiannual payment and amortization of the discount. Use the straight-line method.

(15 min) **LO2** ▶

Bond Issued at Premium

4. Redo Concept Check 2 with the straight-line method, assuming that the bond sells for 112.

Interest and Amortization of Premium with Straight-Line Method

LO2 *(15 min)*

5. From Concept Check 4, record the June 30 semiannual payment and amortization of Premium on Bonds Payable.

Amortization of Bond Discount by Interest Method

LO3 *(20 min)*

6. *Facts:* Bond issue: $100,000, 7%, 10-year bonds; selling price of bonds $93,165; market rate 8%. Use the interest method. Calculate the following:

   a. Carrying value at beginning of period
   b. Interest paid to bondholders every 6 months
   c. Interest expense for the first semiannual period
   d. Discount to be amortized for the first semiannual period
   e. Carrying value at end of first semiannual period

Journalizing the Semiannual Payment of Amortization of Discount

LO3 *(10 min)*

7. From Concept Check 6, record a journal entry for the first semiannual interest payment on October 1.

Amortization of Bond Premium by Interest Method

LO3 *(20 min)*

8. *Facts:* Bond issue: $104,000, 11%, 25-year bonds; selling price of bonds $249,600; market rate 3%. Use the interest method. Calculate the following:

   a. Carrying value at beginning of period
   b. Interest paid to bondholders each 6 months
   c. Interest expense for the first semiannual period
   d. Premium to be amortized for the first semiannual period
   e. Carrying value at end of first semiannual period

Journalizing the Semiannual Payment and Amortization of Bond Premium

LO3 *(10 min)*

9. From Concept Check 8, record the journal entry for the first semiannual interest payment on October 1.

Sinking Fund

LO4 *(30 min)*

10. Journalize the following transactions:

    a. Set up a bond sinking fund with an initial deposit of $7,000.
    b. Earned $230 interest on sinking fund balance.
    c. Sinking fund of $25,000 was used to pay off bondholders in the amount of $25,000.

Exercises

MyLabAccounting

Set A

LO1 *(30 min)*

20A-1. Boice Corporation and Hamlin Corporation have both earned $180,000 before bond interest and taxes. The companies have the same number of outstanding shares but different capital structures. The bond and stocks have been outstanding all year. Calculate the earnings per share of common stock for both companies from the following:

	Boice	Hamlin
8% Bond Payable	180,000	— 0 —
8% Preferred stock	— 0 —	180,000
Common stock $17 par, 30,000 shares outstanding	510,000	510,000
Operating income before interest and taxes (assume a 25% tax rate)	180,000	180,000

(30 min) **L01** ▶ **20A-2.** On May 1, 201X, Maltby Corporation issued $925,000 of 12%, 25-year bonds to lenders at par (100). Interest is to be paid semiannually on November 1 and May 1. Journalize the following entries:

    a. Issued the bonds.
    b. Paid semiannual interest payment.
    c. Retirement of bonds, assuming interest expense is up-to-date.

(50 min) **L01,2** ▶ **20A-3.** Quick Corporation issued $275,000 of 4%, 10-year bonds at 96 on February 1, 201X, with semiannual interest payable on February 1 and August 1. Amortization of discount is by the straight-line method. Record the journal entries for the following:

    a. Issuance of bonds.
    b. Semiannual interest payment on August 1 and amortization of discount.
    c. Retirement of bonds at maturity.

(50 min) **L01,2** ▶ **20A-4.** Redo the journal entries for Exercise 20A-3, assuming that bonds sold at 106.

(50 min) **L01,3** ▶ **20A-5.** On July 1, Johnson Corporation issued 6%, 12-year bonds with a face value of $100,000 for $62,350 because the current market rate is 12%. Record the following entries, assuming that the *interest method* is used to amortize the discount on bonds. Round discount to the nearest dollar.

    a. Issuance of bonds.
    b. Semiannual interest payment on December 31 and amortization of discount.
    c. Semiannual interest payment on June 30 and amortization of discount.

(35 min) **L04** ▶ **20A-6.** On January 1 Rixon Corporation sold $360,000 of 10-year sinking fund bonds. The corporation expects to earn 9% on the sinking fund balance and is required to deposit $23,000 at the end of each year with the trustee. Record the following entries:

    a. The first deposit.
    b. Earnings of $2,070 at end of first period.
    c. Payment of bondholders at maturity with sinking fund having a balance of $360,425.

(30 min) **L02,4** ▶ **20A-7.** From the following, prepare the long-term liabilities section of a balance sheet:

    a. Bond sinking fund $375,000
    b. Premium on 5% bonds   5,000
    c. Discount on 9% bonds   15,000
    d. 5% Bonds Payable   470,000
    e. 9% Bonds Payable   275,000

Set B

(30 min) **L01** ▶ **20B-1.** Ryan Corporation and Hart Corporation have both earned $160,000 before bond interest and taxes. The companies have the same number of outstanding shares but different capital structures. The bond and stocks have been outstanding all year. Calculate the earnings per share of common stock for these companies from the following:

	Ryan	Hart
12% Bond Payable	200,000	— 0 —
12% Preferred stock	— 0 —	200,000
Common stock $11 par, 32,000 shares outstanding	352,000	352,000
Operating income before interest and taxes (assume a 20% tax rate)	160,000	160,000

20B-2. On November 1, 201X, Alpha Corporation issued $875,000 of 3%, 12-year bonds to lenders at par (100). Interest is to be paid semiannually on May 1 and November 1. Journalize the following entries:

L01 *(30 min)*

  a. Issued the bonds.
  b. Paid semiannual interest payment.
  c. Retirement of bonds, assuming interest expense is up-to-date.

20B-3. Morris Corporation issued $250,000 of 11%, 20-year bonds at 88 on March 1, 201X, with semiannual interest payable on March 1 and September 1. Amortization of discount is by the straight-line method. Record the journal entries for the following:

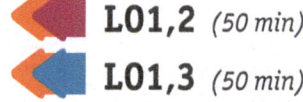
L01,2 *(50 min)*

  a. Issuance of bonds.
  b. Semiannual interest payment on September 1 and amortization of discount.
  c. Retirement of bonds at maturity.

20B-4. Redo the journal entries for Exercise 20B-3, assuming that bonds sold at 104.

L01,2 *(50 min)*

20B-5. On July 1, Colden Corporation issued 6%, 25-year bonds with a face value of $105,000 for $66,641 because the current market rate is 10%. Record the following entries, assuming the *interest method* is used to amortize the discount on bonds. Round discount to the nearest dollar.

L01,3 *(50 min)*

  a. Issuance of bonds.
  b. Semiannual interest payment on December 31 and amortization of discount.
  c. Semiannual interest payment on June 30 and amortization of discount.

20B-6. On January 1 Lincoln Corporation sold $400,000 of 10-year sinking fund bonds. The corporation expects to earn 10% on the sinking fund balance and is required to deposit $23,100 at the end of each year with the trustee. Record the following entries:

L04 *(35 min)*

  a. The first deposit.
  b. Earnings of $2,310 at the end of first period.
  c. Payment of bondholders at maturity with sinking fund having a balance of $400,475.

20B-7. From the following, prepare the long-term liabilities section of a balance sheet:

L02,4 *(30 min)*

  a. Bond sinking fund $450,000
  b. Premium on 9% bonds   3,000
  c. Discount on 11% bonds   13,000
  d. 9% Bonds Payable   580,000
  e. 11% Bonds Payable   200,000

Problems

MyLabAccounting

Set A

20A-1. On January 1, 201X, Lester Corporation sold $380,000 of 5%, 10-year bonds at 99. Interest is to be paid on June 30 and December 31. The straight-line method of amortizing the discount is used. Prepare (1) an amortization schedule for the first three semiannual periods and (2) journal entries to record the following:

L01,2 *(60 min)*

  a. Bond issue on January 1.
  b. Semiannual interest payments on June 30 and December 31 for interest and amortization of discount.
  c. If the bonds were issued on April 1 and interest was paid on October 1 and April 1, what would be the year-end adjusting entry on December 31 to record accrued interest and amortization of discount?

Check Figure:
Amortized discount each period $190

(60 min) **LO1,2**

20A-2. On May 1, 201X, Douglas Corporation issued $600,000 of 6%, 20-year bonds at 107. The interest is payable on November 1 and May 1. The premium is amortized by the straight-line method. Prepare an amortization schedule for the first three semiannual periods and journalize the following transactions:

Check Figure:
Amortized premium $1,050

201X		
May	1	Bonds issued.
Nov.	1	Paid semiannual interest and amortized premium.
Dec.	31	Accrued bond interest and amortized premium.

(70 min) **LO1,2,3**

20A-3. On January 1, 201X, Acorn Corporation issued $300,000 of 10%, 10-year bonds for $265,650, yielding a market rate of 12%. Interest is paid on July 1 and December 31. Acorn uses the interest method to amortize the discount.

1. Prepare an amortization schedule for the first three semiannual periods.
2. Prepare journal entries to record the following:
   a. Bond issue on January 1.
   b. Semiannual interest payments on July 1 and December 31 as well as amortization of discount.
3. If the bond were issued on March 1 and interest was paid on September 1 and March 1, what would be the year-end adjusting entry on December 31, 201X, to record accrued interest and amortization of discount?

Check Figure:
Discount to be amortized Period 1
$939.00

(70 min) **LO1,2,3**

20A-4. On June 1, 201X, Leffer Corporation issued $300,000 of 10%, 5-year bonds for $324,465, yielding a market rate of 8%. Interest is paid on December 1 and June 1. Leffer Corporation uses the interest method to amortize the premium.

1. Prepare an amortization schedule for the first three semiannual periods.
2. Prepare journal entries to record the following:
   a. Bond issue on June 1.
   b. Semiannual interest payment and amortization of premium on December 1.
   c. The year-end adjusting entry to record expense and premium amortization.

Check Figure:
Premium to be amortized Period 1
$2,021.40

Set B

(60 min) **LO1,2**

20B-1. On January 1, 201X, Lemming Corporation sold $480,000 of 6%, 10-year bonds at 96. Interest is to be paid on June 30 and December 31. The straight-line method of amortizing the discount is used. Prepare (1) an amortization schedule for the first three semiannual periods and (2) journal entries to record the following:

a. Bond issue on January 1.
b. Semiannual interest payments on June 30 and December 31 for interest and amortization of discount.
c. If the bonds were issued on June 1 and interest was paid on December 1 and June 1, what would be the year-end adjusting entry on December 31 to record accrued interest and amortization of discount?

Check Figure:
Amortized discount each period $960

(60 min) **LO1, 2**

20B-2. On May 1, 201X, Langston Corporation issued $400,000 of 12%, 20-year bonds at 109. The interest is payable on November 1 and May 1. The premium is amortized by the straight-line method. Prepare an amortization schedule for the first three semiannual periods and journalize the following transactions:

Check Figure:
Amortized premium $900

201X		
May	1	Bonds issued.
Nov.	1	Paid semiannual interest and amortized premium.
Dec.	31	Accrued bond interest and amortized premium.

20B-3. On January 1, 201X, Wilcox Corporation issued $300,300 of 10%, 10-year bonds for $265,916, yielding a market rate of 12%. Interest is paid on July 1 and December 31. Wilcox uses the interest method to amortize the discount.

1. Prepare an amortization schedule for the first three semiannual periods.
2. Prepare journal entries to record the following:
   a. Bond issue on January 1.
   b. Semiannual interest payments on July 1 and December 31 as well as amortization of discount.
3. If the bonds were issued on March 1 and interest was paid on September 1 and March 1, what would be the year-end adjusting entry on December 31, 201X, to record accrued interest and amortization of discount?

Check Figure:
Discount to be amortized period 1
$939.96

20B-4. On April 1, 201X, Leffer Corporation issued $160,000 of 11%, 5-year bonds for $179,537, yielding a market rate of 8%. Interest is paid on October 1 and April 1. Leffer Corporation uses the interest method to amortize the premium.

1. Prepare an amortization schedule for the first three semiannual periods.
2. Prepare journal entries to record the following:
   a. Bond issue on April 1.
   b. Semiannual interest payment and amortization of premium on October 1.
   c. The year-end adjusting entry to record interest expense and premium amortization.

Check Figure:
Premium to be amortized period 1
$1,618.52

Financial Report Problem

MyLabAccounting

Reading Amazon's Annual Report

Go to the annual 2016 report for Amazon at **https://tinyurl.com/slaterca14e** and find the amount of long-term debt in 2016. How much of that debt relates to Bonds?

Statement of Cash Flows

21

CHAPTER PREVIEW: ACCOUNTING IN ACTION

Jimmy Ray loves classic guitars. He regularly brings his instruments to his local luthier to get them repaired and restored. The owner tells Jimmy that he accepts only cash. "Jimmy, I almost went out of business last year because my flow of cash was always negative. I have to pay my suppliers within 30 days, I have bills to pay to run the shop, and I have to pay my employees. On paper I had good net income and good financial statements; however, I need a positive cash flow to survive." In this chapter, we look at the financial statement called the *statement of cash flows*. It will show the sources and uses of cash.

Learning Objectives – Relating Accounting Theory by Unit

LO1 Prepare a Statement of Cash Flows by the Indirect Method

LO2 Prepare a Statement of Cash Flows by the Direct Method

In preceding chapters we analyzed as well as prepared three financial statements. Let's quickly review the purposes of each statement.

- *Income statement:* Shows the results of the company's operations for a given period. The net income or loss results in an increase or decrease to retained earnings.
- *Statement of retained earnings:* Summarizes the changes in retained earnings of a company during a period of time.
- *Balance sheet:* Shows the end-of-period financial position of a company at a particular date.

In this chapter, we turn our attention to a fourth major financial statement that is used to better understand the operating, investing, and financing activities of a company such as PepsiCo. It is called the statement of cash flows, and it summarizes the sources and uses of cash by a company during an accounting period. It is easy to compute the change in cash balance by looking at the comparative balance sheet, but just the change in total cash tells us nothing about specific cash transactions. The statement of cash flows not only shows in detail the sources and uses of cash; it also gives readers of the financial statements a good basis for judging the possible future cash flows. Internal users of the financial statements (such as management) can also benefit by understanding how to read the statement of cash flows.

Statement of cash flows
Financial report that provides a detailed breakdown of the specific increases and decreases in cash during an accounting period. It helps readers of the statement evaluate past performance as well as predict future cash flows of the business.

Usefulness and Layout

Keep in mind that cash does not just refer to the amount of money a company has in the bank or on hand. Cash may include the following types of liquid assets that can be quickly turned into cash: money market accounts and investment in government securities.

Table 21.1 previews the parts of a cash flows statement that we will be looking at. In Learning Units 21-1 and 21-2, we look at specifics. Use this table as a road map as you progress through the chapter.

TABLE 21.1 Layout of a Cash Flows Statement (Direct Method)

1. Operating Activities (Day-to-Day Operations of a Business):
   Cash Inflows:
   - sales of goods and services
   - interest and dividends received
   Cash Outflows:
   - payments for supplies, inventory, taxes, interest, and other expenses

2. Investing Activities:
   Cash Inflows:
   - sales of plant, property, and equipment
   - collecting loans
   - selling bonds or stocks of other companies
   Cash Outflows:
   - buying plant, property, and equipment
   - making loans
   - buying bonds or stocks of other companies

3. Financing Activities:
   Cash Inflows:
   - issuing bonds and notes
   - issuing stock
   Cash Outflows:
   - paying dividends
   - buying back own stock (treasury stock)
   - repayment of long-term debt (principal)

Let's now look at the two different ways we calculate/determine the cash flow from operating activities. In Learning Unit 21-1 we look at the indirect method and in Learning Unit 21-2 we look at the direct method. Table 21.2 presents the big picture of both approaches.

TABLE 21.2 Indirect and Direct Methods

Indirect Method	Direct Method
Reconciles net income to net cash that is provided by operations	Will show all the cash receipts and payments from operating activities
Bottom line for both methods:	
Each method will give the same amount of net cash from operations.	
Neither of the two methods has any effect on investing or financing activities.	

Preparing a Statement of Cash Flows by the Indirect Method

We use as our example in this chapter the Zabel Company, which sells soccer equipment and supplies. To prepare a statement of cash flows, we need to obtain information from the other financial statements prepared for the company: the income statement, the statement of retained earnings, and the balance sheet. These statements are shown in Figures 21.1, 21.2, and 21.3. Note that the balance sheet shown in Figure 21.3 is slightly different from the ones we have shown previously. This one is a comparative balance sheet, which shows figures from two separate years side by side. We discuss this type of statement in more detail in Chapter 22.

LO1

Comparative balance sheet A balance sheet listing financial condition for 2 or more years in a side-by-side manner. This format allows the reader to make quick comparisons between the two balance sheet dates.

Figure 21.1
Financial Statement of Zabel—
Income Statement

ZABEL COMPANY INCOME STATEMENT FOR YEAR ENDED DECEMBER 31, 2019		
Sales		$ 190 0 0 0 00
Cost of Goods Sold		106 0 0 0 00
Gross Profit		$ 84 0 0 0 00
Operating Expenses:		
Salaries Expense	$ 51 0 4 0 00	
Insurance Expense	7 2 0 0 00	
Rent Expense	3 6 0 0 00	
Depreciation Expense	11 0 0 0 00	
Miscellaneous Expense	1 2 0 0 00	
Total Operating Expenses		74 0 4 0 00
Net Income		$ 9 9 6 0 00

Figure 21.2
Financial Statement of Zabel—
Statement of Retained Earnings

ZABEL COMPANY STATEMENT OF RETAINED EARNINGS FOR YEAR ENDED DECEMBER 31, 2019		
Retained Earnings, January 1, 2019		$ 38 1 4 0 00
Net Income for the Year	$ 9 9 6 0 00	
Less: Cash Dividends	8 0 0 0 00	
Increase in Retained Earnings		1 9 6 0 00
Retained Earnings, December 31, 2019		$ 40 1 0 0 00

Figure 21.3
Comparative Balance Sheet
for Zabel

ZABEL COMPANY
COMPARATIVE BALANCE SHEET
AS OF DECEMBER 31, 2018, AND DECEMBER 31, 2019

Assets	2019	2018	Increase (Decrease)
Current Assets:			
Cash	$ 2 900 00	$ 2 480 00	$ 420 00
Accounts Receivable	19 560 00	14 720 00	4 840 00
Merchandise Inventory	30 000 00	32 000 00	(2 000 00)
Prepaid Insurance	600 00	400 00	200 00
Total Current Assets	$ 53 060 00	$ 49 600 00	$ 3 460 00
Plant and Equipment:			
Office Equipment	$ 96 000 00	$ 66 000 00	$ 30 000 00
Accum. Dep., Office Equipment	(37 200 00)	(26 200 00)	(11 000 00)
Total Plant and Equipment	$ 58 800 00	$ 39 800 00	$ 19 000 00
Total Assets	$ 111 860 00	$ 89 400 00	$ 22 460 00
Liabilities			
Current Liabilities:			
Notes Payable—Short Term (used to purchase inventory)	$ 17 400 00	$ 14 800 00	$ 2 600 00
Accounts Payable	360 00	460 00	(100 00)
Total Current Liabilities	$ 17 760 00	$ 15 260 00	$ 2 500 00
Long-Term Liabilities:			
Long-Term Note Payable	$ 28 000 00	$ 20 000 00	$ 8 000 00
Total Liabilities	$ 45 760 00	$ 35 260 00	$ 10 500 00
Stockholders' Equity			
Common Stock, $10 par	$ 11 000 00	$ 10 000 00	$ 1 000 00
Paid-In Capital in Excess of Par	15 000 00	6 000 00	9 000 00
Retained Earnings	40 100 00	38 140 00	1 960 00
Total Stockholders' Equity	$ 66 100 00	54 140 00	$ 11 960 00
Total Liabilities and Stockholders' Equity	$ 111 860 00	$ 89 400 00	$ 22 460 00

Operating activities Those activities most closely related to conducting the business for which the enterprise was established. Activities such as selling merchandise and services to customers and paying salaries and other expenses needed to continue earning the operating revenue are classified as operating activities.

Cash inflow Any increase in cash is called a cash inflow or a source of cash. When listing the total for a major section of the statement of cash flows, if cash is increased, the figure is often described as "cash provided" by operating activities (or by investing activities or financing activities).

Cash outflow Decrease in cash is called a cash outflow or a use of cash. When listing a total for a major section of the statement of cash flows, if cash has decreased, the figure is often described as "cash used" in operating activities (or in investing activities or financing activities).

Investing activities Activities such as purchase and sale of plant and equipment and placing excess cash in stocks, bonds, and notes of other companies.

Financing activities Activities relating to raising money from investors and creditors such as the issuance of stocks, bonds, and long-term notes; also, repurchase of outstanding stock and retiring bonds and notes as well as paying dividends.

The statement of cash flows consists of three main sections: (1) cash flows from operating activities, (2) cash flows from investing activities, and (3) cash flows from financing activities. Some of the complexities of this statement are beyond the scope of this text, but the following paragraphs contain a few examples of transactions reported in each of the three sections.

Operating activities include selling products or services to customers. Cash inflows from operating activities include cash collected from customers. Cash outflows from operating activities include paying for merchandise inventory, salaries, rent, and other such expenses.

Investing activities include such things as purchase or sale of plant and equipment, buying stocks and bonds (of other companies), and making loans to other businesses or individuals.

Financing activities include raising money by issuing stocks and bonds, repurchasing of the company's stock, and paying cash dividends to the stockholders.

A fourth classification reported on the statement of cash flows is called noncash investing and financing activities, which includes such transactions as issuing shares of stock in exchange for assets such as land and buildings. Although cash is not involved, the event is reported because no other financial statement specifically discloses the transaction. If the stock was issued for cash (financing activity, a cash increase) and if we used the cash proceeds to purchase land and a building (investing activity, a cash decrease), the event would be disclosed on the statement of cash flows in two separate sections. Because our example is a noncash transaction, it can be reported on the statement of cash flows as a footnote or on a separate schedule listing such transactions.

Cash Flows from Operating Activities: Indirect Method

A business needs a positive cash flow to survive. A company's ability to raise money from financing activities (issuing stocks, bonds, or long-term notes) is often tied to its success in generating cash flow from its operations. The operating activities section of the statement of cash flows is therefore of great importance to potential investors and creditors.

This section introduces a procedure known as the indirect method of reporting cash flows from operating activities. Note that the distinction between the indirect method and the direct method (discussed in the next learning unit) only applies to the operating activities section of the statement of cash flows.

In the indirect method, we are converting the net income on the income statement from the accrual basis to the cash basis. As we have been learning throughout this text, businesses normally report their net income on the accrual basis, which places the primary emphasis on *when* the revenues are earned and *when* the expenses are incurred.

The indirect method's name comes from the way we view the income statement. We begin with the bottom line of the income statement and work backward until we have computed net cash flow from operating activities. We begin the operating activities section with the net income as reported on the income statement (see Figure 21.1) and convert it from the accrual basis to the cash basis. Figure 21.4 shows how the net cash flows from operating activities are computed for the Zabel Company using the indirect method.

Noncash investing and financing activities
Transactions such as the issuance of stock in exchange for land would be listed in a footnote or a separate schedule to the statement of cash flows because such transactions would not be reported separately on any other financial statement.

Indirect method One of two methods of preparing the net cash flow from the operating activities section of the statement of cash flows. Involves converting the accrual basis net income figure from the income statement to the net cash flows from operating activities.

ZABEL COMPANY STATEMENT OF CASH FLOWS (INDIRECT METHOD) FOR YEAR ENDED DECEMBER 31, 2019		
Cash Flows from Operating Activities:		
Net Income	$9 960 00	
Add (deduct) Items to Convert Net Income from		
Accrual Basis to Cash Basis:		
Depreciation Expense	11 000 00	
Increase in Accounts Receivable	(4 840 00)	
Decrease in Merchandise Inventory	2 000 00	
Increase in Prepaid Insurance	(200 00)	
Increase in Notes Payable (Short Term)	2 600 00	
Decrease in Accounts Payable	(100 00)	
Net Cash Provided by Operating Activities		$20 420 00

Figure 21.4
Statement of Cash Flows—
Indirect Method

In this example, the first item to be added to the net income is Depreciation Expense. The depreciation is *added back* to net income because it was subtracted out as an expense on the income statement to derive the $9,960 net income. You will recall that when depreciation is recorded, the entry involves a debit to Depreciation Expense and a credit to Accumulated Depreciation. Neither of these accounts involves cash. Because depreciation is therefore a "noncash" expense, it is added back to net income when using the indirect method. Next, each of the current assets and current liabilities is examined to determine its effect on cash flow.

The aid sheet shown in Figure 21.5 is useful for remembering whether to add or subtract a given item on the statement of cash flows. Alternatively, some instructors prefer the simple opposite effect/same effect approach. For current assets, cash flow has the *opposite effect*, whereas for current liabilities, the cash flow has the *same effect*. For example, the increase in Accounts Receivable (a current asset) must be subtracted, whereas the increase in Short-Term Notes Payable (a current liability) would be added.

Figure 21.5
Aid Sheet for Converting from Accrual Basis to Cash Basis

	Add to Net Income If This Account Has:	Deduct from Net Income If This Account Has:
Current Assets	DECREASED	INCREASED
Current Liabilities	INCREASED	DECREASED

After each of the items is listed with its proper sign, the entire list is combined with net income to compute the net cash provided by operating activities of $20,420. The term *net cash provided* by operating activities is commonly used if the result is positive, whereas *net cash used* in operating activities indicates that the result is negative. As you might imagine, the goal is to have a strong positive cash flow from operating activities. A negative operating cash flow cannot be tolerated for long. Investors and creditors would hesitate to provide funds to a firm that cannot generate a positive cash flow from its operating activities.

Cash Flows from Investing Activities

The cash flows from the investing activities section of the statement of cash flows includes (1) the purchase and sale of other companies' stocks and bonds, (2) the buying and disposal of plant assets, and (3) making loans to other parties. We analyze the noncurrent asset accounts to find these activities. For example, the following transactions would be reported in this section:

1. Sale or purchase of equipment
2. Sale or purchase of land
3. Cash spent to invest in other companies' stocks and bonds
4. Cash received from sales of stock or bond investments
5. Loaning cash to borrowers

On the balance sheet for Zabel Company, we see an increase in plant and equipment from 2018 to 2019 of $30,000. We are assuming this is a cash purchase. Thus, the cash outflow for equipment would be reported as shown in Figure 21.6.

Figure 21.6
Cash Outflow for Equipment

Cash Flows from Investing Activities		
Purchase of Plant Asset	$ (30 0 0 0 00)	
Net Cash Used by Investing Activities		$ (30 0 0 0 00)

Cash Flows from Financing Activities

The cash flows from the financing activities section of the statement of cash flows records transactions such as:

1. Issuance of long-term notes and bonds
2. Issuance of common stock
3. Purchasing and reissuing treasury stock
4. Payment of cash dividends
5. Retirement of bonds

From the comparative balance sheet for Zabel Company, we see that the Long-Term Notes Payable account increased by $8,000. This increase is shown as a source (increase) of cash because an increase in Long-Term Notes Payable means that more cash has been borrowed and therefore has been received by the business. Also, note that the issuance of $10,000 of common stock has *increased* the cash flows, whereas the payment of $8,000 in dividends results in a *decrease* in cash flows. The end result is that net cash provided by financing activities is $10,000, as shown in Figure 21.7.

Cash Flows from Financing Activities		
Issuance of Long-Term Note	$ 8 0 0 0 00	
Issuance of Common Stock	10 0 0 0 00	
Payment of Dividends	(8 0 0 0 00)	
Net Cash Provided by Financing Activities		$ 10 0 0 0 00

Figure 21.7
Net Cash Flows Provided
by Financing Activities

To arrive at the net change in cash for the overall statement, we perform the following calculation:

Net Cash Provided by Operating Activities	$ 20,420
− Cash Flow Used by Investing Activities	$(30,000)
+ Net Cash Provided by Financing Activities	10,000
= Net Increase in Cash	$ 420

Figure 21.8 shows all three sections together in the statement of cash flows.

ZABEL COMPANY
STATEMENT OF CASH FLOWS (INDIRECT METHOD)
FOR YEAR ENDED DECEMBER 31, 2019

Cash Flows from Operating Activities		
Net Income	$ 9 9 6 0 00	
Add (Deduct) Items to Convert Net Income		
from Accrual Basis to Cash Basis:		
Depreciation Expense	11 0 0 0 00	
Increase in Accounts Receivable	(4 8 4 0 00)	
Decrease in Merchandise Inventory	2 0 0 0 00	
Increase in Prepaid Insurance	(2 0 0 00)	
Increase in Short-Term Notes Payable	2 6 0 0 00	
Decrease in Accounts Payable	(1 0 0 00)	
Net Cash Provided by Operating Activities		$ 20 4 2 0 00
Cash Flows from Investing Activities		
Purchase of Plant Asset	$ (30 0 0 0 00)	
Net Cash Used by Investing Activities		(30 0 0 0 00)
Cash Flows from Financing Activities		
Issuance of Long-Term Note	$ 8 0 0 0 00	
Issuance of Common Stock	10 0 0 0 00	
Payment of Dividends	(8 0 0 0 00)	
Net Cash Provided by Financing Activities		10 0 0 0 00
Net Increase in Cash		$ 4 2 0 00
Beginning Balance of Cash		2 4 8 0 00
Ending Balance of Cash		$ 2 9 0 0 00

Figure 21.8
Statement of Cash Flows—
Indirect Method

Note that at the bottom of the statement of cash flows the cash has increased by $420 (just as is shown for cash on the comparative balance sheet), but this report gives us a complete breakdown of just what caused the cash to increase by $420.

The statement of cash flows is helpful in evaluating, comparing, and predicting future cash flows. By dividing this report into three sections, creditors as well as investors can judge how cash flows from operations compared with those from investing or financing activities. For example, in the case of Zabel Company, an investor or a creditor can see a substantial reduction in cash in one area (investing) that is offset by an increase in cash from the other areas (operating and financing).

A second approach, known as the direct method, gives a more useful presentation of cash flows from operating activities. Although this method gives more understandable data, many firms think it is much easier to use the indirect method to prepare the reports. Regardless of the method used, the net cash flows from operating activities will be the same. The direct method is illustrated in Learning Unit 21-2.

Now let's check your progress.

TRY IT!   Learning Unit 21-1

Complete the following chart by placing a + or − in the appropriate column. Use the indirect method. Assume the short-term notes payable are used in operations.

Title	Net Cash Flows from Operating	Net Cash Flows from Investing	Net Cash Flows Financing
Depreciation Expense			
Increase in Accounts Receivable			
Decrease in Merchandise Inventory			
Increase in Prepaid Insurance			
Increase in Short-Term Notes Payable			
Decrease in Accounts Payable			
Purchases of Plant Assets			
Issuance of Long-Term Note			
Issuance of Common Stock			
Payment of Dividends			

TRY IT!   Solution Learning Unit 21-1

Title	Net Cash Flows from Operating	Net Cash Flows from Investing	Net Cash Flows Financing
Depreciation Expense	+		
Increase in Accounts Receivable	−		
Decrease in Merchandise Inventory	+		
Increase in Prepaid Insurance	−		
Increase in Short-Term Notes Payable	+		
Decrease in Accounts Payable	−		
Purchase of Plant Assets		−	
Issuance of Long-Term Note			+
Issuance of Common Stock			+
Payment of Dividends			−

Preparing a Statement of Cash Flows by the Direct Method

 LO2

As indicated in Learning Unit 21-1, cash flows from operating activities include the cash effects of transactions such as selling goods or services to customers and paying for merchandise inventory and operating expenses. Many accountants prefer the direct method of reporting the cash flows from operating activities. This approach provides useful information and is easily understood by the users of the financial statements.

Direct method One of two methods of preparing the cash flow from operating activities section of the statement of cash flows. Each of the major areas of sources and uses of cash for operations is detailed separately.

The direct method requires listing major groups of operating cash receipts and cash payments. We first compute cash receipts from customers. Because most firms sell products or services on account as well as for cash, the sales figure on the income statement is not the same as total cash received. We analyze Accounts Receivable and combine its change (increase or decrease) with the sales figure from the income statement. An *increase* in Accounts Receivable results in a negative impact on cash, so the amount of the increase is *subtracted* from sales. A *decrease* in Accounts Receivable results in a positive effect on cash, so the amount of the decrease is *added* to sales. Thus, for computing cash received from customers, we can treat Accounts Receivable as we did in the indirect method by using the *opposite effect*.

The same reasoning applies to cash payments, except that because these payments are outflows of cash, any change with a *positive* cash effect is *subtracted* (because a positive effect means less cash to pay out). Any change with a *negative* cash effect is *added* (because a negative effect means more cash to pay out).

Our first example of an operating cash outflow is cash paid for merchandise inventory. We begin the computation with Cost of Goods Sold and then adjust by the change in the Merchandise Inventory account. A further adjustment is necessary to account for changes in Accounts Payable and Short-Term Notes Payable (if notes were used to pay for inventory, as in our example). Specifically, an *increase* in the balance of Merchandise Inventory means a *negative* cash effect that would be *added* in the computation of cash paid for merchandise. A *decrease* in Merchandise Inventory results in a *positive* cash effect that is *subtracted* to compute cash paid for merchandise. After adjusting for inventory changes, if Accounts Payable increased, the cash effect is positive and thus would be subtracted from the computation. If Accounts Payable decreased, the cash effect is negative and thus would be added to the calculation. The changes in Short-Term Notes Payable (assuming notes were used to pay for inventory) would be analyzed in the same way as Accounts Payable.

Cash paid for operating expenses is handled in much the same way as cash paid for merchandise inventory. Cash paid for salaries, for instance, is computed by combining the change in Salaries Payable with the amount of Salaries Expense from the income statement. If Salaries Payable increased (positive cash effect), the amount of the increase would be subtracted from Salaries Expense. If this account decreased (negative cash effect), the amount of the decrease would be added to the Salaries Expense.

For expenses involving a prepayment (such as Prepaid Insurance), the insurance expense balance would be combined with the change in Prepaid Insurance. If Prepaid Insurance increased (negative cash effect), the amount of the change would be added to insurance expense to compute cash paid for insurance. If Prepaid Insurance had decreased (positive cash effect), the amount of the change would be subtracted from insurance expense.

We now look at an example of the computation of net cash flow from operating activities. The Zabel Company computes cash received from customers by combining the sales figure from the income statement with the change in Accounts Receivable from the comparative balance sheet (see Figures 21.1 and 21.3). Sales is $190,000, and Accounts Receivable *increased* by $4,840. Because the increase in Accounts Receivable means a negative cash effect (more of our money is currently in the pockets of our customers!), it is *subtracted* from sales to arrive at the cash collected from customers figure of $185,160. This computation is illustrated in Figure 21.9.

A second computation in Figure 21.9 shows cash paid for inventory. The Cost of Goods Sold figure is adjusted for changes in Merchandise Inventory, Accounts Payable, and Short-Term Notes Payable (if such notes are used to finance inventory). In our example, Cost

To summarize, we can still use the "same effect/opposite effect" reasoning mentioned in the previous learning unit. Current asset cash effects are always the opposite effect, whereas current liability cash effects are always the same effect.

of Goods Sold of $106,000 is adjusted by subtracting the decrease in Inventory ($2,000), subtracting the increase in Short-Term Notes Payable ($2,600), and adding the decrease in Accounts Payable ($100) to arrive at the Cash Paid for Inventory figure of $101,500.

Cash Paid for Insurance is also illustrated in Figure 21.9 by adding the increase in Prepaid Insurance to the Insurance Expense to yield $7,400 for Cash Paid for Insurance.

Figure 21.9
Computations for Zabel Company's Net Cash Flows from Operating Activities

Cash Received
from Customers = Sales   {+ Decrease in Accounts Receivable
                          {− Increase in Accounts Receivable

= $190,000   − $4,840

= $185,160 Cash Inflows

Cash Paid for
Inventory = COGS   {+ Increase in Inventory   {+ Decrease in Accounts Payable, ST Notes Payable
                    {− Decrease in Inventory   {− Increase in Accounts Payable, ST Notes Payable

= $106,000   − $2,000   − $2,600   + $100

= $101,500 Cash Outflow

Cash Paid for
Insurance   Insurance   {+ Increase in Prepaid Insurance
          = Expense   {− Decrease in Prepaid Insurance

= $7,200   + $200

= $7,400 Cash Outflow

Note: The other items on Zabel's income statement do not require any adjustment, because no changes occurred in current assets or current liabilities for such items as salaries, rent, and miscellaneous expenses.

Figure 21.10 shows the complete statement of cash flows for the Zabel Company using the direct method. Note that the investing activities and financing activities sections are

Figure 21.10
Statement of Cash Flows—Direct Method

ZABEL COMPANY STATEMENT OF CASH FLOWS—DIRECT METHOD FOR YEAR ENDED DECEMBER 31, 2019		
Cash Flows from Operating Activities		
Cash Received from Customers		$ 185 160 00
Cash Paid for Merchandise Inventory	$ (101 500 00)	
Cash Paid for Salaries	(51 040 00)	
Cash Paid for Insurance	(7 400 00)	
Cash Paid for Rent	(3 600 00)	
Cash Paid for Miscellaneous Expenses	(1 200 00)	
Total Cash Paid for Operating Activities		(164 740 00)
Net Cash Provided by Operating Activities		$ 20 420 00
Cash Flows from Investing Activities		
Purchase of Plant Asset	$ (30 000 00)	
Net Cash Used by Investing Activities		(30 000 00)
Cash Flows from Financing Activities		
Issuance of Long-Term Note	$ 8 000 00	
Issuance of Common Stock	10 000 00	
Payment of Dividends	(8 000 00)	
Net Cash Provided by Financing Activities		10 000 00
Net Increase in Cash		$ 4 200 00
Beginning Balance of Cash		24 800 00
Ending Balance of Cash		$ 29 000 00

the same as in Figure 21.8 because the distinction between the indirect and direct methods only applies to the cash flows from the operating activities section.

Now let's check your progress.

 **TRY IT!** **Learning Unit 21-2**

Given the following, complete a net cash flow from operating activities. Use the direct method.

Sales, $8,700; Increase in Accounts Receivable, $470; Cost of Goods Sold, $1,300; Decrease in Inventory, $150; Increase in Accounts Payable, $425; Salaries Expense, $575; Decrease in Salaries Payable, $55; Advertising Expense, $170; Decrease in Prepaid Advertising, $145

TRY IT! **Solution Learning Unit 21-2**

Cash Flows from Operating Activities		
Cash Received from Customers		$8,230
Cash Paid for Merchandise Inventory	$(725)	
Cash Paid for Salaries	(630)	
Cash Paid for Advertising	(25)	
Total Cash Paid for Operating Activities		(1,380)
Net Cash Provided by Operating Activities		$6,850

How $8,230 was calculated:

$8,700 Sales less $470 increase in Accounts Receivable

How $(725) was calculated:

$1,300 Cost of Goods Sold less $150 decrease in Inventory less $425 increase in Accounts Payable

How $(630) was calculated:

Salaries Expense $575 plus a $55 decrease in Salaries Payable

How $(25) was calculated:

$170 Advertising Expense less $145 decrease in Prepaid Advertising

DEMONSTRATION SUMMARY PROBLEM

 **L01, 2**

Requirement

From the following Income Statement, Statement of Retained Earnings, and Comparative Balance Sheet, prepare (1) a statement of cash flows using the indirect method and (2) a statement of cash flows using the direct method. Assume office equipment is purchased with cash.

Jones Company
Income Statement
For Year Ended December 31, 2019

Sales		$57,000
Cost of Goods Sold		31,800
Gross Profit		$25,200
Operating Expenses		
Salaries Expense	$15,312	
Insurance Expense	2,160	
Rent Expense	1,080	
Depreciation Expense	3,300	
Miscellaneous Expense	360	
Total Operating Expenses		22,212
Net Income		$ 2,988

Jones Company
Statement of Retained Earnings
For Year Ended December 31, 2019

Retained Earnings, January 1, 2019		$11,442
Net Income for the Year	$2,988	
Less: Cash Dividends	−2,400	
Increase in Retained Earnings		588
Retained Earnings, December 31, 2019		$12,030

Jones Company
Comparative Balance Sheet
As of December 31, 2018, and December 2019

	2019	2018	Inc./Dec.
Assets			
Current Assets			
Cash	$ 870	$ 744	$ 126
Accounts Receivable	5,868	4,416	1,452
Merchandise Inventory	9,000	9,600	(600)
Prepaid Insurance	180	120	60
Total Current Assets	$15,918	$14,880	$ 1,038
Plant and Equipment			
Office Equipment	$28,800	$19,800	$ 9,000
Accum. Dep., Office Equip.	(11,160)	(7,860)	(3,300)
Total Plant and Equip.	$17,640	$11,940	$ 5,700
Total Assets	$33,558	$26,820	$ 6,738

	2019	2018	Inc./Dec.
Liabilities			
Current Liabilities			
Notes Payable (used to purchase inventory)	$ 5,220	$ 4,440	$ 780
Accounts Payable	108	138	(30)
Total Current Liabilities	$ 5,328	$ 4,578	$ 750
Long-Term Liabilities			
Long-Term Notes Payable	$ 8,400	$ 6,000	$ 2,400
Total Liabilities	$ 13,728	$10,578	$ 3,150
Stockholders' Equity			
Common Stock, $10 par	$ 3,300	$ 3,000	$ 300
Paid-In Capital in Excess of Par	4,500	1,800	2,700
Retained Earnings	12,030	11,442	588
Total Stockholders' Equity	$ 19,830	$16,242	$ 3,588
Total Liab. and Stock. Equity	$ 33,558	$26,820	$ 6,738

Solution for Indirect Method

Jones Company
Statement of Cash Flows (Indirect Method)
For Year Ended December 31, 2019

Net Cash Flows from Operating Activities		
Net Income	$ 2,988	
Add (Deduct) Items to Convert Net Income from Accrual Basis to Cash Basis		
Depreciation Expense	3,300	
Increase in Accounts Receivable	(1,452)	
Decrease in Merchandise Inventory	600	
Increase in Prepaid Insurance	(60)	
Increase in Short-Term Notes Payable	780	
Decrease in Accounts Payable	(30)	3,138
Net Cash Provided by Operating Activities		$6,126
Cash Flows from Investing Activities		
Purchase of Plant Asset	$(9,000)	
Net Cash Used by Investing Activities		(9,000)
Cash Flows from Financing Activities		
Issuance of Long-Term Note	$ 2,400	
Issuance of Common Stock	3,000	
Payment of Dividends	(2,400)	
Net Cash Provided by Financing Activities		3,000
Net Increase in Cash		126
Beginning Cash Balance		744
Ending Balance of Cash		$ 870

Tips for Indirect Method

The depreciation expense comes from the income statement. All other calculations come from the balance sheet. When we show the direct method in the next section, the $870 ending balance in cash will be the same.

Solution for Direct Method

Jones Company
Statement of Cash Flows—Direct Method
For Year Ended December 31, 2019

Net Cash Flows from Operating Activities		
Cash Received from Customers		$55,548
Cash Paid for Merchandise Inventory	$(30,450)	
Cash Paid for Salaries	(15,312)	
Cash Paid for Insurance	(2,220)	
Cash Paid for Rent	(1,080)	
Cash Paid for Miscellaneous Expenses	(360)	
Total Cash Paid for Operating Expenses		(49,422)
Net Cash Provided by Operating Activities		$ 6,126
Cash Flows from Investing Activities		
Purchase of Plant Asset	$ (9,000)	
Net Cash Used by Investing Activities		(9,000)
Cash Flows from Financing Activities		
Issuance of Long-Term Note	$ 2,400	
Issuance of Common Stock	3,000	
Payment of Dividends	(2,400)	
Net Cash Provided by Financing Activities		3,000
Net Increase in Cash		$ 126
Beginning Balance of Cash		744
Ending Balance of Cash		$ 870

Tips for Direct Method

How $55,548 was calculated:

> $57,000 from income statement
>
> −1,452 increase in Accounts Receivable from balance sheet

How $55,548 was calculated:

Cost of Goods Sold from income statement	$31,800
Less: Decrease in Merch. Inv. from balance sheet	(600)
Add: Decrease in Accounts Payable from balance sheet	30
Less: Increase in Notes Payable from balance sheet	(780)
	$30,450

How $2,220 was calculated:

Cash Paid for Insurance from income statement	$ 2,160
Add: Increase in Prepaid Insurance from balance sheet	60
	$ 2,220

SUCCESS COACH

The following Success Tips are from Learning Units 21-1 and 21-2. Take the Do It Right Now Checkup and use the Check Your Score at the bottom of the page to see how you are doing. The Success Coach provides tips before each Checkup to help you avoid common accounting errors.

LU 21-1 Preparing a Statement of Cash Flows by the Indirect Method

Do It Right Tips: The statement of cash flows summarizes the sources and uses of cash during an accounting period. The statement of cash flows consists of three main sections: net cash flows from operating activities, net cash flows from investing activities, and net cash flows from financing activities. The indirect method will reconcile net income to net cash that is provided by operations. In the indirect method, we convert the net income on the income statement from an accrual basis to a cash basis. Keep in mind that the (noncash) depreciation expense is added back to net income because it was shown as an expense on the income statement.

Do It Right Now Checkup: Answer true or false to the following statements.

1. Cash collected from customers is an investing activity.
2. Paying a cash dividend is an operating activity.
3. Transactions involving purchases of plant assets are investing activities.
4. The indirect method converts cash basis net income to accrual basis.
5. The retirement of bonds is a financing activity.

LU 21-2 Preparing a Statement of Cash Flows by the Direct Method

Do It Right Tips: The direct method reports the cash flow from operating activities differently than the indirect method. Both methods provide the same result for the ending figure of net cash flows from operating activities. The section cash flows from investing activities and the section cash flows from financing activities are the same for the direct and indirect methods.

Do It Right Now Checkup: Answer true or false to the following statements.

1. A current asset increase has a positive effect on cash.
2. A current asset decrease cannot happen in the direct method.
3. A current liability increase has a positive effect on cash.
4. Indirect and direct methods have different figures for net cash flows from operating activities.
5. The ending cash balance in the statement of cash flows should equal the ending cash balance on the balance sheet.

CHECK YOUR SCORE: Answers to the Do It Right Now Checkup

LU 21-1

1. False—Cash collected from customers is an operating activity.
2. False—Paying a cash dividend is a financing activity.
3. True
4. False—The indirect method converts accrual basis to cash basis.
5. True

LU 21-2

1. False—A current asset increase has a negative effect on cash.
2. False—A current asset decrease can happen in the direct method.
3. True
4. False—Indirect and direct methods have the same figures for net cash flows from operating activities.
5. True

BLUEPRINT: STATEMENT OF CASH FLOWS

Indirect Method

Cash Flows from Operating Activities		
Net Income		XXX
Add (Deduct) Items to Convert Net		
Income from Accrual Basis to Cash Basis:		
Depreciation Expense		XX
Increase in Accounts Receivable		(XX)
Decrease in Inventory		XX
Increase in Prepaid Expenses		(XX)
Increase in Accounts Payable		XX
Decrease in Salaries Payable		(XX)
Net Cash Flows Provided by Operating Activities		XXX
Cash Flows from Investing Activities		
Purchase of Investment Securities	(XXX)	
Purchase of Equipment	(XXX)	
Sale of Land	XXX	
Net Cash Used by Investing Activities		(XXX)
Cash Flows from Financing Activities		
Issuance of Common Stock	XX	
Payment of Dividends	(X)	
Net Cash Provided by Financing Activities		XX
Net Increase (Decrease) in Cash		XXX
Beginning Balance of Cash		XXX
Ending Balance of Cash		XXX

Direct Method

Cash Flows from Operating Activities		
Cash Received from Customers		XXX
Cash Paid for Inventory	(XXX)	
Cash Paid for Salaries	(XX)	
Cash Paid for Insurance	(X)	
Cash Paid for Rent	(X)	
Cash Paid for Other Expenses	(XX)	
Total Cash Paid for Operations		(XX)
Net Cash Provided by Operating Activities		XXX

Discussion Questions and Critical Thinking/Ethical Case

1. List the three main sections of the statement of cash flows.

2. Explain how net cash flows from operating activities is calculated using the indirect method.

3. Explain how net cash flows from operating activities is calculated using the direct method.

4. The issuance of stock is an investing activity. Agree or disagree? Why?

5. Explain how a creditor might analyze a statement of cash flows.

6. Explain what is meant by financing activities.

7. Explain why depreciation is *added* to net income when using the indirect method.

8. Risch Company prepares an income statement and balance sheet each year. Tom Martin, the controller, issued a memo to Debbie Kreiger, vice president, that the company should prepare a statement of cash flows. Debbie called the comptroller and told him that she would not let a cash flows statement be published, that this type of information is for internal purposes only, and that the public has no right to these data. She said that the competition would kill them if they got this information. Do you agree with Debbie's position or with Tom's? Write your recommendation to Dave Risch, the chief executive officer.

Concept Checks

Calculating Net Cash Flows from Operating Activities: Indirect Method

1. The following accounts showed an increase or a decrease from the comparative balance sheet. Explain which account will be added to net income and which will be subtracted in calculating net cash flows for operating activities using the indirect method.

   L01 *(15 min)*

   a. Accounts Receivable: Decrease
   b. Merchandise Inventory: Increase
   c. Mortgage Payable: Decrease
   d. Accounts Payable: Increase

2. From the following, calculate the net cash flow from operating activities using the indirect method:

   L01 *(20 min)*

	2018	2019
Accounts Receivable	$ 620	$ 850
Merchandise Inventory	2,500	4,400
Prepaid Insurance	750	290
Accounts Payable	1,000	780
Salaries Payable	610	840
For the year ended 2019:		
Net Income		$2,450
Depreciation Expense		630

(30 min) LO2

Calculating Net Cash Flows from Operating Activities: Direct Method

3. Using the data from Concept Check 2 plus the additional information in Figure 21.11, compute net cash flows from operating activities using the direct method.

Figure 21.11
Income Statement

Sales				$ 8 4 0 0 00
Cost of Goods Sold				2 2 9 0 00
Gross Profit				$ 6 1 1 0 00
Expenses:				
Depreciation Expense	$ 6 3 0 00			
Salaries Expense	2 2 5 0 00			
Insurance Expense	5 0 0 00			
Miscellaneous Expense	2 8 0 00			
Total Expenses			3 6 6 0 00	
Net Income			$ 2 4 5 0 00	

(15 min) LO1, 2

Calculating Cash Flows from Financing Activities

4. From the following, calculate net cash flows from financing activities:

Payments of dividends	$ 17,000
Issuance of common stock	4,000
Issuance of long-term note payable	16,075

(15 min) LO1, 2

Calculating Change in Cash

5. Given the following, calculate net change in cash:

Net cash provided by operating activities	$6,000
Net cash used by investing activities	(2,200)
Net cash provided by financing activities	1,300

MyLabAccounting

Exercises

Set A

(45 min) LO1

21A-1. Complete the following chart by placing an X in the appropriate column. Use the indirect method.

	Add to Cash Flow from Operations	Subtract from Cash Flow from Operations
Increase in Inventory		
Decrease in Accounts Payable		

(45 min) LO1

21A-2. From the following, calculate the net cash flows from operating activities (use the indirect method):

	2018	2019
Accounts Receivable	$ 4,900	$7,300
Prepaid Insurance	908	851
Accounts Payable	3,993	4,602
Salaries Payable	1,100	2,100
For the year ended 2019:		
Net Income	$18,000	
Depreciation Expense	3,800	

21A-3. From the following, calculate the net cash flows from operating activities (use the direct method):

 **L02** *(45 min)*

Sales	$9,700
Cost of Goods Sold	4,200
Salaries Expense	1,200
Insurance Expense	800
Other Expenses (all cash)	940
Changes in current assets and liabilities:	
Accounts Receivable increased by $560.	
Inventory increased by $480.	
Accounts Payable increased by $100.	
Salaries Payable decreased by $210.	
Prepaid Insurance decreased by $190.	

21A-4. For each of the following transactions, identify the appropriate section of the statement of cash flows (OA, Operating; IA, Investing; FA, Financing; and NC, Noncash). Use the direct method.

L02 *(10 min)*

____ **a.** Paid for merchandise from vendors.
____ **b.** Purchase of land.
____ **c.** Loaning cash to borrowers.
____ **d.** Issuance of common stock.
____ **e.** Paid rent.
____ **f.** Issue stock in exchange for equipment.

Set B

21B-1. Complete the following chart by placing an X in the appropriate column. Use the indirect method.

L01 *(45 min)*

	Add to Cash Flow from Operations	Subtract from Cash Flow from Operations
Increase in Accounts Receivable		
Increase in Prepaid Insurance		

21B-2. From the following, calculate the net cash flows from operating activities (use the indirect method):

L01 *(45 min)*

	2018	2019
Accounts Receivable	$ 5,200	$7,400
Prepaid Insurance	905	849
Accounts Payable	4,000	4,597
Salaries Payable	900	2,050
For the year ended 2019:		
Net Income	$17,900	
Depreciation Expense	3,900	

(45 min) **LO2**

21B-3. From the following, calculate the net cash flows from operating activities (use the direct method):

Sales	$9,300
Cost of Goods Sold	4,400
Salaries Expense	1,400
Insurance Expense	840
Other Expenses (all cash)	1,400

Changes in current assets and liabilities:

    Accounts Receivable increased by $570.

    Inventory increased by $500.

    Accounts Payable increased by $95.

    Salaries Payable decreased by $150.

    Prepaid Insurance decreased by $170.

(10 min) **LO2**

21B-4. For each of the following transactions, identify the appropriate section of the statement of cash flows (OA, Operating; IA, Investing; FA, Financing; and NC, Noncash). Use the direct method.

____ **a.** Receive payments on account from customers.
____ **b.** Sale of equipment.
____ **c.** Sale of stock or bond investments.
____ **d.** Purchase and reissuance of treasury stock.
____ **e.** Paid insurance expense.
____ **f.** Issue stock in exchange for equipment.

MyLabAccounting

Problems

Set A

(60 min) **LO1**

S50 / **QB**

Check Figure:
Net Cash Provided by Operating Activities $9,500 increase

21A-1. From the following income statement (Figure 21.12), balance sheet (Figure 21.13), and additional data for Salmon Company, prepare a statement of cash flows using the indirect method.

Additional Data

1. All Plant and Equipment were purchased with cash.
2. Sold additional 5,500 shares of stock for cash at par.
3. A $2,000 dividend was declared and paid.
4. Short-term notes used to finance inventory.

Figure 21.12
Income Statement for Salmon

SALMON COMPANY INCOME STATEMENT FOR THE YEAR ENDED DECEMBER 31, 2018		
Sales		$ 96 6 0 0 00
Cost of Goods Sold		68 9 0 0 00
Gross Profit		$ 27 7 0 0 00
Operating Expenses:		
Rent Expense	$ 7 7 0 0 00	
Depreciation Expense	7 3 0 0 00	
Salary Expense	6 8 0 0 00	
Miscellaneous Expense	3 3 5 0 00	
Total Operating Expenses		25 1 5 0 00
Net Income		$ 2 5 5 0 00

SALMON COMPANY BALANCE SHEET DECEMBER 31, 2018		
Assets	2018	2017
Current Assets:		
Cash	$ 3 3 0 0 00	$ 2 5 0 0 00
Accounts Receivable, Net	5 9 0 0 00	5 0 0 0 00
Merchandise Inventory	2 6 5 0 00	1 8 0 0 00
Prepaid Rent	8 5 0 00	1 3 5 0 00
Total Current Assets	$ 12 7 0 0 00	$ 10 6 5 0 00
Plant and Equipment:		
Store Equipment	$ 57 2 0 0 00	$ 50 5 0 0 00
Accum. Dep., Store Equipment	(12 3 0 0 00)	(5 0 0 0 00)
Total Plant and Equipment	$ 44 9 0 0 00	$ 45 5 0 0 00
Total Assets	$ 57 6 0 0 00	$ 56 1 5 0 00
Liabilities		
Current Liabilities:		
Notes Payable—Short Term	$ 6 9 0 0 00	$ 5 6 0 0 00
Accounts Payable	4 3 5 0 00	4 7 5 0 00
Total Current Liabilities	$ 11 2 5 0 00	$ 10 3 5 0 00
Long-Term Liabilities:		
Bonds Payable	$ 9 0 0 0 00	$ 20 0 0 0 00
Total Liabilities	$ 20 2 5 0 00	$ 30 3 5 0 00
Stockholders' Equity		
Common Stock, $1 par	$ 30 8 0 0 00	$ 19 8 0 0 00
Retained Earnings	6 5 5 0 00	6 0 0 0 00
Total Stockholders' Equity	$ 37 3 5 0 00	$ 25 8 0 0 00
Total Liabilities and Stockholders' Equity	$ 57 6 0 0 00	$ 56 1 5 0 00

Figure 21.13
Balance Sheet for Salmon

21A-2. From the financial statements and additional information provided in Problem 21A-1 for Salmon Company, prepare a statement of cash flows using the direct method.

L02 *(60 min)*

Check Figure:
Net Change in Cash $800 increase

Set B

21B-1. From the following income statement (Figure 21.14), balance sheet (Figure 21.15), and additional data for Webber Company, prepare a statement of cash flows using the indirect method.

L01 *(60 min)*
S50 / QB

Additional Data

1. All Plant and Equipment were purchased with cash.
2. Sold additional 2,500 shares of stock for cash at par.
3. A $1,500 dividend was declared and paid.
4. Short-term notes used to finance inventory.

Check Figure:
Net Cash Provided by Operating
Activities $8,400 increase

Figure 21.14
Income Statement for Webber

WEBBER COMPANY				
INCOME STATEMENT				
FOR THE YEAR ENDED DECEMBER 31, 2018				
Sales			$96 1 0 0 00	
Cost of Goods Sold			69 5 0 0 00	
Gross Profit			$26 6 0 0 00	
Operating Expenses:				
Rent Expense	$ 7 1 0 0 00			
Depreciation Expense	7 5 0 0 00			
Salary Expense	6 7 0 0 00			
Miscellaneous Expense	3 0 5 0 00			
Total Operating Expenses			24 3 5 0 00	
Net Income			$ 2 2 5 0 00	

Figure 21.15
Balance Sheet for Webber

WEBBER COMPANY			
BALANCE SHEET			
DECEMBER 31, 2018			
Assets		2018	2017
Current Assets:			
Cash		$ 3 3 5 0 00	$ 2 5 5 0 00
Accounts Receivable, Net		5 7 0 0 00	4 3 0 0 00
Merchandise Inventory		2 6 5 0 00	1 9 5 0 00
Prepaid Rent		9 5 0 00	1 4 0 0 00
Total Current Assets		$ 12 6 5 0 00	$ 10 2 0 0 00
Plant and Equipment:			
Store Equipment		$ 55 1 0 0 00	$ 49 0 0 0 00
Accum. Dep., Store Equipment		(13 0 0 0 00)	(5 5 0 0 00)
Total Plant and Equipment		$ 42 1 0 0 00	$ 43 5 0 0 00
Total Assets		$ 54 7 5 0 00	$ 53 7 0 0 00
Liabilities			
Current Liabilities:			
Notes Payable—Short Term		$ 6 5 0 0 00	$ 5 3 0 0 00
Accounts Payable		4 0 0 0 00	4 9 0 0 00
Total Current Liabilities		$ 10 5 0 0 00	$ 10 2 0 0 00
Long-Term Liabilities:			
Bonds Payable		$ 5 0 0 00	$ 18 0 0 0 00
Total Liabilities		$ 11 0 0 0 00	$ 28 2 0 0 00
Stockholders' Equity			
Common Stock, $7 par		$ 37 5 0 0 00	$ 20 0 0 0 00
Retained Earnings		6 2 5 0 00	5 5 0 0 00
Total Stockholders' Equity		$ 43 7 5 0 00	$ 25 5 0 0 00
Total Liabilities and Stockholders' Equity		$ 54 7 5 0 00	$ 53 7 0 0 00

21B-2. From the financial statements and additional information provided in Problem 21B-1 for Webber Company, prepare a statement of cash flows using the direct method.

 L02 *(60 min)*

Check Figure:
Net Cash Used by Financing Activities ($1,500)

Financial Report Problem

Reading Amazon's Annual Report

Go to the 2016 annual report for Amazon at **https://tinyurl.com/slaterca14e** on page 17 and find the net cash provided by operating activities in 2016.

 L01 *(20 min)*

Analyzing Financial Statements

22

CHAPTER PREVIEW: ACCOUNTING IN ACTION

Alexa just received her credit report. She is very happy with her credit rating of 775, which is very good. Businesses are no different and continually monitor their operations. Corporations send out annual reports for investors to read. This chapter teaches you how to analyze these reports. Similar to comparing your medical results to the "normal" range of the general population, you can then make your own decisions about how the company is performing compared to others in the industry.

Learning Objectives – Relating Accounting Theory By Unit

LO1   Prepare a Horizontal and Vertical Analyses of a Comparative Balance Sheet

LO2   Prepare a Horizontal and Vertical Analyses of an Income Statement

LO3   Calculate Financial Ratios

When you look at your Apple or Android phone, do you ever wonder how companies like Apple and Samsung keep track of all their financial data? Financial reports are used by investors, creditors, and management to assist in making business decisions. Typical business decisions might involve such questions as:

- *For investors:* How profitable is the company when compared with competing companies? Will dividends be paid? Can the company expand with adequate financing?
- *For creditors:* Does the company have enough cash to pay back periodic interest payments as well as the balance on maturity?
- *For management:* Is the company, like Apple or Samsung, operating as efficiently as possible? How can we do better?

The four financial statements that we have discussed in earlier chapters—the balance sheet, the income statement, the statement of retained earnings, and the statement of cash flows—help provide the answers to these questions. In this chapter, we discuss how to analyze the numbers that appear on these statements.

Numbers on a financial statement may not have meaning in and of themselves; they must be placed in a context. This context may be a comparison with last year's figures, a comparison with other companies in the same industry, or even a comparison with other figures on the same report.

In the following units, we look at what the numbers mean as well as how to apply that meaning toward making useful business decisions.

LEARNING UNIT 22-1

LO1

Comparative balance sheets
Current and past financial reports covering two or more successive periods that place data in single columns side by side.

Horizontal analysis Amounts of items compared on the same line of comparative financial reports. Horizontal analysis can also be in the form of a trend analysis.

Horizontal and Vertical Analyses of Comparative Balance Sheets

In the comparative balance sheet, a statement showing data from two or more periods side by side, shown in Figure 22.1, the accountant has placed the current year's balance sheet figures next to figures from the preceding year's balance sheet. The third column shows the amount of increase or decrease in the 2020 figures over the 2019 figures, and the last column shows the percentage of decrease or increase of 2020 over 2019. This type of analysis, in which each item on the report is compared with the same item in other periods, is called horizontal analysis.

Horizontal Analysis of the Balance Sheet

Let's perform a sample horizontal analysis on one of the items on Scrupper Supply Company's comparative balance sheet. Look at the entry for Cash in Figure 22.1. In 2020 it is $3,040 and in 2019 it was $4,080, for a decrease of $1,040. This decrease is placed in parentheses on the report to show that it is a decrease and not an increase. To figure the percentage that this decrease represents, you use the equation

$$\text{Percentage Change} = \frac{\text{Amount of Change(New Year)}}{\text{Base(Old Year)}}$$

In this case it would be

$$\frac{\$(1,040)}{\$4,080} = (25.5)\%$$

This type of analysis is called horizontal analysis because in each case you are comparing two figures across columns, from one period to another, rather than comparing figures within a column. Although cash decreased by 25.5%, Scrupper's retained earnings increased by 23.1%. You can see that the percentages in the last column in Figure 22.1 cannot be added down the column to total 100%; each figure relates only to the figures for the same item across the other columns. These percentages provide us with a quick way of monitoring specific accounts.

Figure 22.1
Comparative Balance Sheet

SCRUPPER SUPPLY COMPANY
COMPARATIVE BALANCE SHEET
AS OF DECEMBER 31, 2020, AND DECEMBER 31, 2019

Note: Most recent year is shown first.	December 31		Amount of Increase or Decrease During 2020	Percent Increase or Decrease During 2020
Assets	2020	2019		
Current Assets:				
Cash	$ 3 0 4 0 00	$ 4 0 8 0 00	$ (1 0 4 0 00)	(25.5)
Accounts Receivable, Net	20 0 0 0 00	16 0 0 0 00	4 0 0 0 00	25.0
Merchandise Inventory	24 1 6 0 00	26 1 2 0 00	(1 9 6 0 00)	(7.5)
Prepaid Expenses	8 0 0 00	6 0 0 00	2 0 0 00	33.3
Total Current Assets	$ 48 0 0 0 00	$ 46 8 0 0 00	$ 1 2 0 0 00	2.6
Plant and Equipment:				
Office Equipment, Net	$ 125 2 0 0 00	$ 116 8 0 0 00	$ 8 4 0 0 00	7.2
Total Assets	$ 173 2 0 0 00	$ 163 6 0 0 00	$ 9 6 0 0 00	5.9
Liabilities				
Current Liabilities:				
Notes Payable	$ 20 9 6 0 00	$ 17 3 2 0 00	$ 3 6 4 0 00	21.0
Accounts Payable	2 4 0 00	2 8 0 00	(4 0 00)	(14.3)
Total Current Liabilities	$ 21 2 0 0 00	$ 17 6 0 0 00	$ 3 6 0 0 00	20.5
Long-Term Liabilities:				
Mortgage Payable	60 0 0 0 00	60 0 0 0 00	– 0 –	–0–
Total Liabilities	$ 81 2 0 0 00	$ 77 6 0 0 00	$ 3 6 0 0 00	4.6
Stockholders' Equity				
Common Stock, $10 par value	$ 60 0 0 0 00	$ 60 0 0 0 00	– 0 –	–0–
Retained Earnings	32 0 0 0 00	26 0 0 0 00	6 0 0 0 00	23.1
Total Stockholders' Equity	$ 92 0 0 0 00	$ 86 0 0 0 00	$ 6 0 0 0 00	7.0
Total Liabilities and				
Stockholders' Equity	$ 173 2 0 0 00	$ 163 6 0 0 00	$ 9 6 0 0 00	5.9

Vertical Analysis of the Balance Sheet

In vertical analysis, each item on a report is shown as a percentage of a total base. For the balance sheet, the base will be total assets for the asset accounts and total liabilities and stockholders' equity for those related accounts, and it will be total sales on an income statement. Look at the comparative balance sheet in Figure 22.2. Each item is listed for 2020, and next to it is a percentage, which is that item's percentage of total assets or total liabilities and stockholders' equity. In the next column, each item is listed for the preceding year, 2019, and then the item is listed as a percentage of total assets or total liabilities and stockholders' equity.

Take the item Cash as an example again. In 2020, Cash is $3,040 and total assets are $173,200; thus, Cash represents 1.8% of total assets for this year. In 2019, Cash was $4,080 and total assets are $163,600; thus, Cash was 2.5% of total assets in that year.

Vertical analysis Comparing items in a financial report by expressing each item as a percentage of a certain base total.

Figure 22.2
Vertical Analysis of a Comparative
Balance Sheet

SCRUPPER SUPPLY COMPANY COMPARATIVE BALANCE SHEET DECEMBER 31, 2020, AND DECEMBER 31, 2019				
Assets	2020		2019	
Current Assets:				
Cash	$ 3 0 4 0 00	1.8%	$ 4 0 8 0 00	2.5%
Accounts Receivable, Net	20 0 0 0 00	11.5	16 0 0 0 00	9.8
Merchandise Inventory	24 1 6 0 00	13.9	26 1 2 0 00	16.0
Prepaid Expenses	8 0 0 00	0.5	6 0 0 00	0.4
Total Current Assets	$ 48 0 0 0 00	27.7%	$ 46 8 0 0 00	28.7%
Plant and Equipment:				
Office Equipment, Net	125 2 0 0 00	72.3%	116 8 0 0 00	71.4%
Total Assets	$ 173 2 0 0 00	100.0%	$ 163 6 0 0 00	100.0%*
Liabilities				
Current Liabilities:				
Notes Payable	$ 20 9 6 0 00	12.1%	$ 17 3 2 0 00	10.6%
Accounts Payable	2 4 0 00	0.1	2 8 0 00	0.2
Total Current Liabilities	$ 21 2 0 0 00	12.2%	$ 17 6 0 0 00	10.8%
Long-Term Liabilities:				
Mortgage Payable	60 0 0 0 00	34.6%	60 0 0 0 00	36.7%
Total Liabilities	$ 81 2 0 0 00	46.8%	$ 77 6 0 0 00	47.5%
Stockholders' Equity				
Common Stock, $10 par value	$ 60 0 0 0 00	34.6%	$ 60 0 0 0 00	36.7%
Retained Earnings	32 0 0 0 00	18.5	26 0 0 0 00	15.9
Total Stockholders' Equity	$ 92 0 0 0 00	53.1%	$ 86 0 0 0 00	52.6%
Total Liabilities and Stockholders' Equity	$ 173 2 0 0 00	100.0%*	$ 163 6 0 0 00	100.0%*

*Total will be rounded to 100%.

Note how in this type of analysis you do add down the columns to total 100%, unlike horizontal analysis. Keep in mind that vertical analysis provides us with *another* way of analyzing financial reports that contain data for two or more successive accounting periods.

A shorter version of this report in Figure 22.3 lists only the percentages of the two columns that have been analyzed. Such a report in general is called a common-size statement; this particular one is a common-size comparative balance sheet.

The common-size statement makes it easy to see, for example, that from 2019 to 2020 the level of inventory dropped (from 16% to 13.9% as a percentage of total assets) and accounts receivable increased (from 9.8% to 11.5%). In a comparison of companies of different sizes, common-size statements prevent the dollar amounts from getting in the way and make it easier to see each item as a percentage of the base in each company.

Common-size statements
Comparative reports in which each item is expressed as a percentage of a base amount without dollar amounts.

	December 31	
SCRUPPER SUPPLY COMPANY **COMMON-SIZE COMPARATIVE BALANCE SHEET** **DECEMBER 31, 2020, AND DECEMBER 31, 2019**		
Assets	2020	2019
Current Assets:		
Cash	1.8%	2.5%
Accounts Receivable, Net	11.5	9.8
Merchandise Inventory	13.9	16.0
Prepaid Expenses	0.5	0.4
Total Current Assets	27.7%	28.7%
Plant and Equipment:		
Office Equipment, Net	72.3%	71.4%
Total Assets	100.0%	100.0%*
Liabilities		
Current Liabilities:		
Notes Payable	12.1%	10.6%
Accounts Payable	0.1	0.2
Total Current Liabilities	12.2%	10.8%
Long-Term Liabilities:		
Mortgage Payable	34.6%	36.7%
Total Liabilities	46.8%	47.5%
Stockholders' Equity		
Common Stock, $10 par value	34.6%	36.7%
Retained Earnings	18.5	15.9
Total Stockholders' Equity	53.1%	52.6%
Total Liabilities and Stockholders' Equity	100.0%*	100.0%*

*Total will be rounded to 100%.

Figure 22.3
Common-Size Comparative
Balance Sheet

Now let's check your progress.

TRY IT!   Learning Unit 22-1

From the following, calculate (a) the amount of increase or decrease and (b) the percent increase or decrease.

	2020	2019
Cash	$45,600	$30,000
Accounts Receivable, Net	11,100	15,000
Merchandise Inventory	16,800	6,000

TRY IT!   Solution Learning Unit 22-1

	Increase/Decrease	Percentage Change
Cash	+$15,600	52% ($15,600/$30,000)
Accounts Receivable	−$3,900	−26% (−$3,900/$15,000)
Merchandise Inventory	+$10,800	180% ($10,800/$6,000)

LO2 ▶

Horizontal and Vertical Analyses of Income Statements

In the last unit, we showed how to perform a horizontal and a vertical analyses of the balance sheet for Scrupper Supply Company. We now show how to perform the same two types of analyses on the income statement for Scrupper Supply Company.

Horizontal Analysis of the Income Statement

Figure 22.4 shows a comparative income statement for Scrupper Supply Company using horizontal analysis. As in horizontal analysis for the balance sheet, each item on the income statement is compared with the same item for the preceding year; the amount of increase or decrease is recorded and then shown as a percentage. For net sales, the amount was $302,000 in 2019 compared with $317,600 in 2020; that is an increase of $15,600, which comes out to a 5.2% increase ($15,600/$302,000). The percent increase or decrease is the amount of increase or decrease divided by the figure for the base year of 2019.

Figure 22.4
Horizontal Analysis of a
Comparative Income Statement

SCRUPPER SUPPLY COMPANY COMPARATIVE INCOME STATEMENT FOR YEARS ENDED DECEMBER 31, 2020, AND 2019				
	December 31		Amount of Increase or Decrease During 2020	Percent of Increase or Decrease During 2020
	2020	2019		
Net Sales*	$ 317 600 00	$ 302 000 00	$ 15 600 00	5.2
Cost of Goods Sold	198 000 00	194 000 00	4 000 00	2.1
Gross Profit from Sales	$ 119 600 00	108 000 00	11 600 00	10.7
Operating Expenses:				
Selling	$ 63 600 00	$ 55 000 00	8 600 00	15.6
General and Administrative	20 000 00	26 000 00	(6 000 00)	(23.1)
Total Operating Expenses	$ 83 600 00	$ 81 000 00	$ 2 600 00	3.2
Operating Income	$ 36 000 00	$ 27 000 00	9 000 00	33.3
Less Interest Expense	4 200 00	4 300 00	(1 00 00)	(2.3)
Income Before Taxes	$ 31 800 00	$ 22 700 00	$ 9 100 00	40.1
Income Taxes	15 900 00	11 350 00	4 550 00	40.1
Net Income	$ 15 900 00	$ 11 350 00	$ 4 550 00	40.1

*Net sales is 100% or the base.

Vertical Analysis of the Income Statement

Figure 22.5 shows the vertical analysis of a comparative income statement for Scrupper Supply Company. In the case of an income statement, the base used is net sales. (On a balance sheet, it is total assets or total liabilities and stockholders' equity.) Thus, on the vertical analysis of an income statement, each item is calculated as a percentage of net sales.

From such an analysis of a comparative income statement, we can easily see that cost of goods sold decreased (from 64.2% to 62.3%) from 2019 to 2020, selling expenses increased (from 18.2% to 20.0%), and profit before tax was up (7.5% to 10.0%). If we had listed just the percentages (each item as percentage of net sales) and left out the dollar amounts, we would have produced a common-size comparative income statement.

SCRUPPER SUPPLY COMPANY
COMPARATIVE INCOME STATEMENT
FOR YEARS ENDED DECEMBER 31, 2020, AND DECEMBER 31, 2019

	2020		2019	
Net Sales*	$ 317 6 0 0 00	100%	$ 302 0 0 0 00	100%
Cost of Goods Sold	198 0 0 0 00	62.3	194 0 0 0 00	64.2
Gross Profit from Sales	$ 119 6 0 0 00	37.7%	108 0 0 0 00	35.8%
Operating Expenses:				
Selling	$ 63 6 0 0 00	20.0%	$ 55 0 0 0 00	18.2%
General and Administrative	20 0 0 0 00	6.3	26 0 0 0 00	8.6
Total Operating Expenses	$ 83 6 0 0 00	26.3%	$ 81 0 0 0 00	26.8%
Operating Income	$ 36 0 0 0 00	11.3%	27 0 0 0 00	8.9
Less Interest Expense	4 2 0 0 00	1.3	4 3 0 0 00	1.4
Income Before Taxes	$ 31 8 0 0 00	10.0%	$ 22 7 0 0 00	7.5%
Income Taxes	15 9 0 0 00	5.0%	11 3 5 0 00	3.76
Net Income	$ 15 9 0 0 00	5.0%	$ 11 3 5 0 00	3.76%

*Net sales is 100% or the base.
Tax rate is 50% of income before taxes.

Figure 22.5
Vertical Analysis of a Comparative Income Statement

Trend Analysis

A special type of horizontal analysis, called a trend analysis, deals with the percentage of changes in a certain item over several years. For example, if we want to understand why sales in 2022 are 118% of 2019 sales of Scrupper Supply Company, we have to look at figures for several years. The following figures list sales, cost of goods sold, and gross profit for 2019 to 2022:

Trend analysis Type of horizontal analysis that deals with percentage changes in items on the financial reports for several years; uses a base year to calculate the percentage change of each item.

	2022	2021	2020	2019
Sales	$317,600	$302,000	$290,000	$270,000
Cost of Goods Sold	198,000	194,000	184,000	142,000
Gross Profit	$119,600	$108,000	$106,000	$128,000

When the trend analysis is developed, a base year is chosen. We will choose 2019 (the base year is usually the earliest year listed). For each of the following years, each item is stated as a percentage of the amount of the base year. For example, sales in 2022 as a percentage of the base year equal 118%. The calculation is as follows:

$$\text{BASE} \longrightarrow \frac{\$317,600}{\$270,000} = 118\%$$

Thus, sales in 2022 have increased by 18% since 2019. Over a period of years, these percentages are analyzed in relation to a company's history as well as to industry averages that are supplied by companies such as Risk Management Association (formerly Robert Morris Associates) and Dun & Bradstreet.

The following is the trend analysis for Scrupper Supply Company for sales, cost of goods sold, and gross profit.

	2022	2021	2020	2019
Sales	118%	112%	107%	100%
Cost of Goods Sold	139	137	130	100
Gross Profit	93	84	83	100

Note that in 2020, sales increased 7% from 2019, but cost of goods sold was up 30%, resulting in gross profit being down 17%. Such analysis can reveal internal problems in Scrupper Supply

Company or industry-wide problems in a certain year. For example, Scrupper might want to investigate why/cost of goods sold rose 39% in the last 3 years.

Now let's check your progress.

 **TRY IT!**   **Learning Unit 22-2**

From the following partial income statement, prepare a vertical analysis. Assume that the net sales is 100% of the base:

	2020	2019
Net Sales	$11,000	10,000
Cost of Goods Sold	2,750	7,000
Gross Profit	8,250	3,000

TRY IT!   **Solution Learning Unit 22-2**

	2020	%	2019	%
Net Sales	$11,000	100%	$10,000	100%
Cost of Goods Sold	2,750	25	7,000	70
Gross Profit	8,250	75	3,000	30

Cost of Goods Sold $2,750/$11,000 = 25% (2020)
Cost of Goods Sold $7,000/$10,000 = 70% (2019)

LEARNING UNIT 22-3

Calculate Financial Ratios

L03

Ratio Relationship of two quantities or numbers, one divided by the other.

Ratio analysis Examination of the relationship between two numbers or sets of numbers on financial reports. Analyses of ratios, especially over time, can give a fairly clear picture of how well a company conducts its business.

Liquidity ratios Two ratios—current ratio and acid test ratio—that measure a company's ability to pay off short-term debts.

Asset management ratios Those ratios—accounts receivable turnover, average collection period, inventory turnover, and asset turnover—that measure how effectively a company uses its assets.

Debt management ratios Those ratios—debt to total assets, debt to stockholders' equity, and times interest earned—that measure a company's mix of debt and equity financing.

Profitability ratios Those ratios—gross profit rate, return on sales, return on total assets, and return on common stockholders' equity—that measure a company's ability to earn a profit.

Another method for understanding the numbers on the financial statements is the use of ratio analysis. A ratio is the relationship of two quantities or numbers, one divided by the other. Ratio analysis looks at the relationship of figures on the financial statements. For example, if Broome company has a net income of $10,000 and sales are $100,000, the ratio of net income to sales may be expressed as follows:

a. Net income is $\frac{1}{10}$ or 10% of sales ($10,000/$100,000 = 0.1 = $\frac{1}{10}$ = 10%).

b. Ratio of sales to net income is 10 to 1 or 10 times net income (10:1).

c. For every $10 of sales, Broome Company earns $1.00 of net income.

In this unit, we look at a number of different ratios that are used to analyze different aspects of a business. To be meaningful, ratios are often compared with other standards, such as past company ratios or industry-wide ratios. The ratios we discuss fall into four general categories:

- Liquidity ratios measure a company's ability to meet short-term obligations.
- Asset management ratios measure how effectively a company is using its assets.
- Debt management ratios measure how well a company is using debt versus its equity position.
- Profitability ratios measure a company's ability to earn profits.

Let's now do the calculations as well as provide an explanation of each ratio. All calculations for the ratios come from the financial reports for 2020 of Scrupper Supply Company presented in the last two units.

Liquidity Ratios

Current Ratio. The current ratio expresses the relationship of Scrupper's current assets to its current liabilities, as follows:

$$\text{Total Current Assets} = \$48,000$$
$$\text{Total Current Liabilities} = \$21,200$$

$$\text{Current Ratio} = \frac{\text{Current Assets}}{\text{Current Liabilities}} = \frac{\$48,000}{\$21,200} = 2.26{:}1$$

Thus, for each $1 of debt, Scrupper has $2.26 of current assets to meet its short-term debt obligations.

It is important to note that this ratio should be evaluated in terms of (1) the type of business Scrupper is in, (2) the composition of current assets, and (3) the type of credit terms Scrupper extends. Ratios can also be compared from year to year to spot trends in a company or in an industry. For example, in 2019 the current ratio for Scrupper Supply Company was 2.66 ($46,800/$17,600). This year's current ratio is 2.26, which means that Scrupper's ability to pay off short-term debts has decreased from last year to this year. The ratio is something creditors and investors, as well as the management of Scrupper, will be interested in.

Depending on the inventory or prepaid expenses, the current assets might not be worth what is shown on the balance sheet. For example, if Scrupper Supply Company has overstocked amounts of inventory, a high current ratio could occur. If Scrupper has a large amount of prepaid insurance or rent, it will not be possible to convert these assets into cash because they have already been paid for. Thus, the current ratio is not a very rigorous test of Scrupper's ability to pay its short-term debts. The next ratio we discuss shows that more clearly.

Acid Test Ratio (Quick Ratio). The acid test ratio divides those assets that are most easily converted into cash (called quick assets) by the current liabilities. To determine quick assets, we subtract Merchandise Inventory and Prepaid Expenses from current assets (which usually leaves Cash, Notes Receivable, and Accounts Receivable). Thus, the acid test ratio would look like this calculation:

$$\text{Acid Test Ratio} = \frac{\text{Current Assets} - \text{Merchandise Inventory} - \text{Prepaid Expenses}}{\text{Current Liabilities}}$$

$$= \frac{\$23,040}{\$21,200} = 1.09:1$$

Thus, for each $1 of short-term debt, Scrupper has $1.09 of current or quick assets to meet them. This ratio should be at least 1:1 to pass the acid test or be acceptable. If you compare this 1.09:1 ratio with the current ratio figure of 2.26:1, you will see what a difference the inclusion of Merchandise Inventory and Prepaid Expenses makes.

Asset Management Ratios

Accounts Receivable Turnover. The accounts receivable turnover ratio shows how many times in a year Scrupper is able to convert its accounts receivable into cash. Usually, the higher the turnover, the better, because a company does not want its money tied up in something that is not yielding any revenue. The turnover rate depends on the length of the credit period Scrupper gives its customers (for Scrupper, all sales are on credit).

$$\text{Accounts Receivable Turnover} = \frac{\text{Net Credit Sales}}{\text{Average Accounts Receivable}}$$

At the end of 2019, Accounts Receivable was $16,000; at the end of 2020, it was $20,000. We thus take $18,000 as a figure for *average* accounts receivable.

$$\text{Accounts Receivable Turnover} = \frac{\$317,600}{\$18,000} = 17.6$$

Thus, Scrupper is able to turn over its accounts receivable 17.6 times a year. Of course, this turnover rate has to be compared with industry standards and must be seen in the context of how aggressive Scrupper is in its attempts to collect the accounts receivable. The next ratio breaks these steps into the number of days per collection period for accounts receivable.

Average Collection Period. In 2020, Scrupper Supply Company turns its accounts receivable into cash every 20.7 days:

$$\text{Average Collection Period} = \frac{365 \text{ days}}{\text{Accounts Receivable Turnover}} = \frac{365}{17.6}$$

$$= 20.7$$

Current ratio Liquidity ratio; current assets are divided by current liabilities to indicate a company's ability to pay its short-term debt. This ratio does not provide as much certainty as the acid test ratio.

Acid test ratio Liquidity ratio; those assets that are most easily converted to cash are divided by current liabilities to indicate ability to pay off short-term debt; also called *quick ratio*.

Quick assets Those assets—mainly cash, accounts receivable, and notes receivable—that can be easily turned into cash.

Accounts receivable turnover ratio Ratio that indicates the number of times accounts receivable are converted to cash within a given period and the effectiveness of a company's credit policy.

Average collection period
Ratio that shows how quickly moneys owed are received from customers and thereby measures how effectively a company collects its accounts receivable.

Inventory turnover ratio Asset management ratio that indicates how quickly inventory moves off the shelf and therefore how well a company sells its product.

If Scrupper's average collection period increases, although its credit terms have not changed, it may necessitate a greater emphasis on collecting outstanding accounts receivable.

Inventory Turnover. The inventory turnover ratio calculates the number of times the *inventory* turns over in one period. Usually, a high inventory turnover means that the company has tied up less cash in inventory. Scrupper calculates its inventory turnover for 2020 as follows:

$$\text{Inventory Turnover} = \frac{\text{Cost of Goods Sold}}{\text{Average Inventory}}$$
$$= \frac{\$198,000}{\$25,140} = 7.9$$

$$\left(\frac{\$24,160 + \$26,120}{2}\right)$$

A high inventory turnover means less inventory obsolescence. If inventory turnover is slow, it could mean that Scrupper's sales are not keeping pace with the purchasing department.

Asset turnover ratio Ratio that indicates how efficiently a company uses its assets to generate sales and thus helps measure the overall efficiency of the company.

Asset Turnover. The asset turnover ratio shows whether Scrupper Supply Company is using its assets effectively to generate sales. Scrupper calculates this ratio as follows for 2020:

$$\text{Asset Turnover} = \frac{\text{Net Sales}}{\text{Total Assets}} = \frac{\$317,600}{\$173,200} = 1.8 \text{ Times}$$

(*Note:* Assets that are not used in producing sales, such as investments, are subtracted from total assets.) In general, the higher the asset turnover rate, the better. A low asset turnover rate compared with industry standards could mean that the company is not generating enough sales for its investment in its assets.

Debt Management Ratios

Debt to total assets ratio Ratio that shows how much of a company's assets are financed by creditors.

Debt to Total Assets. The debt to total assets ratio indicates the amount of assets that are financed by creditors. A low ratio would be favorable to creditors because in liquidation they would be more likely to be paid. On the other hand, stockholders like to see a higher ratio so as to attempt to maximize their return. The following is Scrupper's debt to total assets ratio for 2020:

$$\text{Debt to Total Assets} = \frac{\text{Total Liabilities}}{\text{Total Assets}} = \frac{\$81,200}{\$173,200} = 46.9\%$$

A low percentage (if that were the case for Scrupper) could possibly mean that more financing by bonds and so forth may be in order.

Debt to stockholders' equity ratio Ratio in which total liabilities are divided by the amount of stock that is owned to measure the risk creditors run in comparison with stockholders.

Debt to Stockholders' Equity. The debt to stockholders' equity ratio attempts to measure the risk of the creditors in relation to the risk taken by the stockholders. For example, for 2020 the ratio of debt to stockholders' equity for Scrupper Supply Company is as follows:

$$\text{Debt to Stockholders' Equity} = \frac{\text{Total Liabilities}}{\text{Stockholders' Equity}} = \frac{\$81,200}{\$92,000} = 88.3\%$$

If the industry norm is 60%, Scrupper's ratio could mean that the company has too much debt financing.

Times Interest Earned (Interest Coverage Ratio). The times interest earned ratio is of interest to creditors because it indicates the degree of risk to creditors from a company defaulting on interest payments. For example, for 2020 Scrupper Supply Company calculates its times interest earned ratio as follows:

$$\text{Times Interest Earned} = \frac{\text{Income Before Taxes and Interest Expense}}{\text{Interest Expense}}$$

$$= \frac{\$36,000}{\$4,200} = 8.6 \text{ Times}$$

The higher the times interest earned ratio is, the more likely it is that the interest payment will be made, even if earnings start to decline.

Now let's turn our attention to calculating ratios involving the profitability of the company.

Profitability Ratios

Gross Profit Rate. The gross profit rate reveals how much profit from each sales dollar is generated to cover administrative and selling expenses. For example, for Scrupper Supply Company in 2020, $0.38 of each $1 resulted in profit *before* selling and general administrative expenses. This ratio was calculated as follows:

$$\text{Gross Profit Rate} = \frac{\text{Gross Profit}}{\text{Net Sales}} = \frac{\$119,600}{\$317,600} = 37.7\%$$

Return on Sales. In 2020, Scrupper Supply Company earned 10 cents for each sales dollar. This return on sales ratio is calculated as follows:

$$\text{Return on Sales} = \frac{\text{Net Income Before Taxes}}{\text{Net Sales}} = \frac{\$31,800}{\$317,600} = 10\%$$

Stores that have a low inventory turnover (furniture, autos) will have a high return on sales because the goods are priced high. On the other hand, a store that has a high inventory turnover (like a grocery store) will usually price its goods lower, resulting in a lower return per dollar of sales. If the 10 percent is low compared with its competitors, Scrupper should try to lower its cost and expenses as a percentage of its total sales.

Rate of Return on Total Assets. Scrupper Supply Company wishes to measure the amount of profitability it has earned in 2020 on each dollar it has invested in assets. This figure can be calculated by the rate of return on total assets ratio, as follows:

$$\text{Rate of Return on Total Assets} = \frac{\text{Net Income Before Interest and Taxes}}{\text{Total Assets}}$$

$$= \frac{\$36,000}{\$173,200} = 20.8\%$$

If the 20.8% rate is lower than that of Scrupper's competitors, it could be the result of decreases in return on sales or asset turnover (or a combination of both), which can be seen from the following alternative calculation:[1]

$$\left(\begin{array}{c}\text{Return on}\\\text{Sales}\end{array}\right) \times \left(\begin{array}{c}\text{Total Asset}\\\text{Turnover}\end{array}\right) = \left(\begin{array}{c}\text{Rate of Return on}\\\text{Total Assets}\end{array}\right)$$

$$\frac{\$36,000^*}{\$317,600} \times \frac{\$317,600}{\$173,200} = 20.8\%$$

Times interest earned ratio Debt management ratio indicating the degree of risk to lenders that a company will default on its interest payments; also called *interest coverage ratio*.

Remember: Debt is not bad. It provides a company with flexible financing plans.

Gross profit rate Profitability ratio that indicates how well net sales cover administrative and selling expenses.

Return on sales ratio Profitability ratio that shows the relationship of net income before taxes to net sales and thereby the effectiveness of a company's pricing policy.

Return on total assets ratio Profitability ratio that measures how wisely a company has invested in and managed its assets. This ratio can be arrived at in two ways: (1) net income before interest and taxes divided by total assets and (2) return on sales multiplied by asset turnover.

[1] The $36,000 is before interest and taxes.

Return on common stockholders' equity ratio
Profitability ratio that indicates how well a company is managing debt financing to earn a profit for holders of common stock.

Rate of Return on Common Stockholders' Equity (Return on Equity). The return on common stockholders' equity ratio aids Scrupper in evaluating how well it is earning profit for its common stockholders. The rate of return on common stockholders' equity is calculated as follows:

$$\left(\begin{array}{c} \text{Rate of Return} \\ \text{on Common} \\ \text{Stockholders'} \\ \text{Equity} \end{array} \right) = \frac{\text{Net Income Before Taxes} - \text{Preferred Dividends}}{\text{Common Stockholders' Equity}}$$

$$= \frac{\$31,800 - 0}{\$92,000} = 34.6\%$$

Scrupper compares this return with its competitors' returns. If its rate is higher than the industry standards, Scrupper is using debt financing wisely.

Now let's check your progress.

TRY IT!   Learning Unit 22-3

From the following information, calculate the following ratios (round to nearest hundredth as needed). Assume there are no cash sales.

a. Current Ratio
b. Acid Test Ratio
c. Accounts Receivable Turnover
d. Inventory Turnover
e. Asset Turnover
f. Gross Profit Rate

Current Liabilities	$ 4,000
Current Assets	24,400
Merchandise Inventory	9,000
Prepaid Expenses	4,800
Net Credit Sales	25,000
Av. Acc. Receivable	1,000
Av. Inventory	2,100
Total Assets	50,000
Cost of Goods Sold	10,500

TRY IT!   **Solution Learning Unit 22-3**

a. 6.10 (Current Assets/Current Liabilities)
b. 2.65 (Current Assets − Merchandise Inventory − Prepaid Exp.)/Current Liabilities
c. 25.00 (Net Credit Sales/Average Accounts Receivable)
d. 5.00 (Cost of Goods Sold/Average Inventory)
e. 0.50 (Net Credit Sales/Total Assets)
f. 58.00% (Gross Profit/Net Credit Sales)

DEMONSTRATION SUMMARY PROBLEM

 LO1,2,3

Pete Aster is running an in-house training class for non-accountants. He will be handing out a set of five quizzes. Please do these quizzes for Pete (each quiz and solution is shown separately).

Quick Quiz 1

Calculate the amount of increase or decrease as well as percentage of increase or decrease from the following:

	2020	2019
a. Accounts Receivable	$1,200	$800
b. Accounts Payable	1,600	2,000

Solution for Quick Quiz 1

Increase/Decrease	Percentage Change
a. +$400	$400/$800 = 50%
b. −$400	−$400/$2,000 = −20%

Tip

The old year is the base, which is 2019.

Quick Quiz 2

Complete a vertical analysis of the following assets (round to the nearest tenth of a percent as needed).

a. Cash	$ 600
b. Accounts Receivable	900
c. Merchandise Inventory	1,400
d. Office Equipment	3,000
Total Assets	$5,900

Solution for Quick Quiz 2

a. $ 600/$5,900 = 10.2%
b. $ 900/$5,900 = 15.3%
c. $1,400/$5,900 = 23.7%
d. $3,000/$5,900 = 50.8%

Tip

Note the total assets of $5,900 is the base or the total.

Quick Quiz 3

Prepare a common-size income statement from the following (use net sales as 100%). Round to nearest whole percent as needed.

Net Sales	$3,000
Cost of Goods Sold	500
Gross Profit from Sales	2,500
Operating Expenses	600
Net Income	$1,900

Solution for Quick Quiz 3

Net Sales	100%
Cost of Goods Sold	17%
Gross Profit from Sales	83%
Operating Expenses	20%
Net Income	63%

Tip

Take each individual amount over the base of $3,000.

Quick Quiz 4

Complete a trend analysis from the following data for Hercher Corporation, using 2019 as the base year (round to the nearest percent).

	2022	2021	2020	2019
Sales	$1,200	$900	$700	$400
Gross Profit	300	200	150	100
Net Income	150	110	70	100

Solution for Quick Quiz 4

	2022	2021	2020	2019
Sales	300%	225%	175%	100%
Gross Profit	300	200	150	100
Net Income	150	110	70	100

Tip

For Sales, take each amount over $400. For Gross Profit and Net Income, take each amount over $100.

Quick Quiz 5

From the data given, calculate the following (round to the nearest hundredth or hundredth of a percent as needed).

a. Current Ratio
b. Acid Test Ratio
c. Asset Turnover Ratio
d. Gross Profit Rate

Net Sales	$250,000
Current Assets	52,000
Gross Profit	95,000
Current Liabilities	26,000
Total Assets	175,000
Merchandise Inventory	16,000
Prepaid Expenses	8,000

Solution for Quick Quiz 5

a. 2.00
b. 1.08
c. 1.43
d. 38%

Tips

For Current Ratio: Current Assets/Current Liabilities

For Acid Test:
(Current Assets − Merchandise Inv. − Prepaid Expenses)/Current Liabilities

For Asset Turnover: Net Sales/Total Assets

For Gross Profit Rate: Gross Profit/Net Sales

SUCCESS COACH

The following Success Tips are from Learning Units 22-1 to 22-3. Take the Do It Right Now Checkup and use the Check Your Score at the bottom of the page to see how you are doing. The Accounting Coach provides tips before each Checkup to help you avoid common accounting errors.

LU 22-1 Horizontal and Vertical Analyses of Comparative Balance Sheets

Do It Right Tips: The comparative balance sheet shows data from two or more periods side by side. For horizontal analysis, the percent for each line item is calculated by the amount of change over the base or old year. For vertical analysis, each item is shown as a percentage of the total base. Some reports only containing percentages are called common-size statements.

Do It Right Now Checkup: Answer true or false to the following statements.
1. Creditors usually do not look at financial statements.
2. The base in a calculation of the percentage change in a financial statement item is the new year.
3. A comparative report can only be for two periods.
4. Horizontal analysis compares numbers down a column.
5. Common-size reports use only percents.

LU 22-2 Horizontal and Vertical Analyses of Income Statements

Do It Right Tips: A trend analysis is a type of horizontal analysis in which each amount is divided by the base year chosen. In horizontal analysis, numbers are analyzed across, while in vertical analysis the numbers are compared downward.

Do It Right Now Checkup: Answer true or false to the following statements.
1. Income statements do not use vertical analysis.
2. A trend analysis is a type of vertical analysis.
3. Trend analysis answers all questions for investors.
4. Trend analysis requires the analysis of the income statement for five periods.
5. Cost of goods sold is not used in a trend analysis.

LU 22-3 Calculate Financial Ratios

Do It Right Tips: Ratios are basically divided into categories: liquidity, asset management, debt management, and profitability. The ratios are usually compared to industry standards so that the company can see how it is competing in the marketplace.

Do It Right Now Checkup: Answer true or false to the following statements.
1. The current ratio shows how much in long-term assets a company has to meet its short-term debt for each dollar of debt.
2. A quick ratio subtracts merchandise inventory and prepaid expenses from current assets.
3. A high asset turnover means that a company may not be generating enough sales for its investment in assets.
4. Ratios need to be compared to industry averages.
5. If the gross profit rate goes down it may mean that competitors are lowering prices.

CHECK YOUR SCORE: Answers to the Do It Right Now Checkup

LU 22-1
1. False—Creditors usually do look at financial statements.
2. False—The base in a calculation of the percentage change in a financial statement item is the old year.
3. False—A comparative report can be for two or more periods.
4. False—Horizontal analysis compares numbers across a row.
5. True

LU 22-2
1. False—Income statements use vertical analysis.
2. False—A trend analysis is a type of horizontal analysis.
3. False—Trend analysis answers some questions for investors.
4. False—Trend analysis requires two or more periods to be analyzed from the income statement.
5. False—Cost of goods sold is used in a trend analysis.

LU 22-3
1. False—The current ratio shows how much in current assets a company has to meet its short-term debt for each dollar of debt.
2. True
3. False—A low asset turnover means that a company may not be generating enough sales for its investment in assets.
4. True
5. True

BLUEPRINT: CALCULATING FINANCIAL RATIOS

Ratio	Formula	What Calculation Says	Key Points
1. Current ratio	$$\frac{\text{Current Assets}}{\text{Current Liabilities}}$$	For each $1 of current liabilities, how many dollars of current assets are available to meet the current debt.	The ratio should be evaluated based on the type of business credit terms, along with the composition of the current assets.
2 Acid test ratio	$$\frac{\text{Current Assets} - \text{Merchandise Inventory} - \text{Prepaid Expenses}}{\text{Current Liabilities}}$$	For each $1 of current liabilities, how many dollars of cash and near-cash assets are available to meet the current debt.	Because inventory and prepaid expenses may not be easily converted into cash, they are not used in the calculation.
3. Accounts receivable turnover	$$\frac{\text{Net Credit Sales}}{\text{Average Accounts Receivable}}$$	How many times accounts receivable are collected and turned into cash.	Cash sales are not included in the calculation. High turnover is often the best unless the credit terms cause a reduction in sales.
4. Average collection period	$$\frac{365 \text{ Days}}{\text{Accounts Receivable Turnover}}$$	The number of days that it takes a business to collect its accounts receivable.	If the average collection period goes up and the credit terms remain the same, increased collection attempts should be emphasized.
5. Inventory turnover	$$\frac{\text{Cost of Goods Sold}}{\text{Average Inventory}}$$	The number of times a company sells or turns over its average amount of inventory per year.	High turnover rates indicate that the company sold its average amount of inventory several times per year. Care should be taken to avoid running out of inventory and losing sales due to insufficient inventory on hand.
6. Asset turnover	$$\frac{\text{Net Sales}}{\text{Total Assets}}$$	How effectively the company is using its assets to generate sales (i.e., how much in sales the company generates per $1 dollar invested in assets).	A low turnover could mean excessive investment in assets or that the sales volume is too low.
7. Debt to total assets	$$\frac{\text{Total Liabilities}}{\text{Total Assets}}$$	Amount of assets financed by the creditors.	A low percentage reduces creditors' risk if liquidation occurs. The higher the percentage, the more debt financing a company is using.
8. Debt to stockholders' equity	$$\frac{\text{Total Liabilities}}{\text{Stockholders' Equity}}$$	Amount of debt in relation to total stockholders' equity.	The higher the percentage, the more interest cost results for stockholders.
9. Times interest earned	$$\frac{\text{Income Before Taxes and Interest Expense}}{\text{Interest Expense}}$$	Degree of risk to creditors if a company defaults on interest payments by indicating how many times a company could cover their interest obligations with their income before interest and taxes.	A high times interest earned means a company can have declines in earnings but have the ability to meet its annual interest obligations.
10. Gross profit rate	$$\frac{\text{Gross Profit}}{\text{Net Sales}}$$	Profit generated from each sales dollar that will be used to cover expenses (general, selling, etc.).	This rate could drop if stiff competition results in price cuts.
11. Return on sales	$$\frac{\text{Net Income Before Taxes}}{\text{Net Sales}}$$	How much net income a company earns on each sales dollar.	A company with a low inventory turnover rate usually prices goods for a high return on sales.
12. Rate of return on total assets	$$\frac{\text{Net Income Before Interest and Taxes}}{\text{Total Assets}}$$	Without looking at how assets are financed, this ratio measures how productively total assets have been used (i.e., how much net income is generated by each dollar invested in assets).	The rate of return can be increased by controlling costs and expenses as well as increasing asset turnover.
13. Rate of return on common stockholders' equity	$$\frac{\text{Net Income Before Taxes} - \text{Preferred Dividends}}{\text{Common Stockholders' Equity}}$$	Measures a company's ability to earn profits for the common stockholder by indicating how much net income is generated by each dollar of common SE.	If this rate is higher than return on total assets, the company is using financial leverage to its benefit.

Discussion Questions and Critical Thinking/Ethical Case

1. Compare and contrast the needs of investors, creditors, and management as they relate to financial statement analysis.

2. Horizontal analysis cannot be presented on comparative financial statements. Agree or disagree? Please explain.

3. What is meant by vertical analysis?

4. Common-size statements use horizontal analysis. Agree or disagree? Please explain.

5. Why is a base year chosen in trend analysis?

6. How can ratios be expressed?

7. Explain the following types of ratios:
    a. Liquidity
    b. Asset management
    c. Debt management
    d. Profitability

8. What current asset accounts are deleted in the calculation of the acid test ratio? Why?

9. What could a low accounts receivable turnover rate indicate?

10. Stockouts could easily result if inventory is higher than it should be. Agree or disagree? Please explain.

11. What does possible liquidation have to do with the ratio of debt to total assets?

12. Rate of return on assets is affected by return on sales and asset turnover. Agree or disagree?

13. Jill Land, president of Loon Co., is happy to report to the company's stockholders that the company increased its cash position by 20% from last year. Its average collection period decreased by 12 days. Jill knows some customers are unhappy about the new credit terms but believes that you cannot please everyone; that's part of business. Do you think Loon Co. is on the right track? One shareholder is quite upset to learn that the company is holding so much cash. Do you agree with the company's belief that increasing the cash position by 20% is sound? You make the call. Write down your recommendation to Jill.

Concept Checks

MyLabAccounting

Horizontal Analysis Balance Sheet

 **LO1** *(10 min)*

1. Calculate the amount of increase or decrease as well as the percentage of increase or decrease. (Round to the nearest tenth of a percent as needed.)

	2020	2019	Amount	%
a. Accounts Receivable	$650	$520		
b. Accounts Payable	520	650		

(15 min) **LO1**

Vertical Analysis Balance Sheet

2. Complete a vertical analysis of the assets. (Round to the nearest tenth of a percent as needed.)

a.	Cash	$ 784
b.	Accounts Receivable	952
c.	Merchandise Inventory	1,064
d.	Office Equipment	2,800
	Total Assets	$5,600

(15 min) **LO1, 2**

Common-Size Income Statement

3. Prepare a common-size income statement from the following (use net sales as 100%):

Net Sales	$1,100
Cost of Goods Sold	385
Gross Profit from Sales	715
Operating Expenses	275
Net Income	$440

(15 min) **LO2**

Trend Analysis

4. Complete a trend analysis from the following data of Carter Corporation using 2019 as the base year. (Round to the nearest percent.)

	2022	2021	2020	2019
Sales	$1,000	$650	$550	$400
Gross Profit	350	250	350	160
Net Income	220	88	55	55

(15 min) **LO3**

Ratios

5. From the data given calculate the following. (Round to the nearest hundredth or hundredth of a percent as needed.)

    a. Current ratio
    b. Acid test ratio
    c. Asset turnover ratio
    d. Gross profit rate

Net Sales	$240,000
Current Assets	51,300
Gross Profit	96,000
Current Liabilities	19,000
Total Assets	480,000
Merchandise Inventory	14,000
Prepaid Expenses	8,800

Exercises

Set A

LO2 *(30 min)*

22A-1. Prepare a horizontal analysis of the comparative income statement for Alvin Co. for the years ending December 31, 2019, and December 31, 2020. (Round to the nearest hundredth of a percent as needed.)

	2020	2019
Net Sales	$110,000	$60,000
Cost of Goods Sold	38,000	19,000
Operating Expenses	17,700	12,000
Interest Expense	4,700	4,000
Net Income (loss)	49,600	25,000

22A-2. From the following, prepare a common-size income statement for Tony Co. by converting the dollar amounts into percentages. (Round to the nearest hundredth of a percent.) Use net sales as 100%.

LO1, 2 *(30 min)*

	2020	2019
Net Sales	$ 750,000	$430,000
Cost of Goods Sold	540,000	352,600
Gross Profit from Sales	210,000	77,400
Operating Expenses	52,500	43,000
Net Income	$ 157,500	$ 34,400

22A-3. From the following comparative balance sheet of Howard Co., prepare a common-size comparative balance sheet. (Round all percentages to the nearest tenth of a percent.)

LO1 *(50 min)*

	2020	2019
Current Assets	$104,550	$ 74,700
Plant and Equipment	510,450	340,300
Total Assets	$615,000	$415,000
Current Liabilities	$ 67,650	$ 66,400
Long-Term Liabilities	61,500	83,000
Common Stock	258,300	228,250
Retained Earnings	227,550	37,350
Total Liabilities and Stockholders' Equity	$615,000	$415,000

22A-4. Complete a trend analysis from the following data of Hall Corporation using 2019 as the base year. (Round to the nearest percent.)

LO2 *(30 min)*

	2022	2021	2020	2019
Sales	$580,000	$490,000	$400,000	$310,000
Gross Profit	168,000	141,750	112,000	124,000
Net Income	48,800	40,800	21,800	39,000

(30 min) **LO3**

22A-5. From the given income statement and additional information of Connors Co., compute the following:

a. Asset turnover for 2020
b. Inventory turnover for 2020
c. Accounts receivable turnover for 2020

	2020	2019
Net Sales	$680,000	$750,000
Cost of Goods Sold	500,500	502,000
Gross Profit	$179,500	$248,000
Operating Expenses (includes taxes)	79,000	163,000
Net Income	$100,500	$ 85,000

	2020	2019
Year-End Accounts Receivable	$ 64,000	$ 4,000
Year-End Inventory	86,000	57,000
All sales were on credit		
Total Assets	170,000	150,000

Set B

(30 min) **LO2**

22B-1. Prepare a horizontal analysis of the comparative income statement for Abbie Co. for the years ending December 31, 2020, and December 31, 2019. (Round to the nearest hundredth of a percent as needed.)

	2020	2019
Net Sales	$70,000	$45,000
Cost of Goods Sold	36,000	20,000
Operating Expenses	17,900	11,600
Interest Expense	4,700	3,900
Net Income (loss)	$11,400	$ 9,500

(30 min) **LO1, 2**

22B-2. From the following, prepare a common-size income statement for Tom Co. by converting the dollar amounts into percentages. (Round to the nearest hundredth of a percent.) Use net sales as 100%.

	2020	2019
Net Sales	$700,000	$450,000
Cost of Goods Sold	504,000	346,500
Gross Profit from Sales	196,000	103,500
Operating Expenses	63,000	36,000
Net Income	$133,000	$ 67,500

22B-3. From the following comparative balance sheet of Holt Co., prepare a common-size comparative balance sheet. (Round all percentages to the nearest tenth of a percent.)

 **L01** *(50 min)*

	2020	2019
Current Assets	$123,900	$ 65,250
Plant and Equipment	466,100	369,750
Total Assets	$590,000	$435,000
Current Liabilities	$ 94,400	$ 78,300
Long-Term Liabilities	53,100	100,050
Common Stock	259,600	204,450
Retained Earnings	182,900	52,200
Total Liabilities and Stockholders' Equity	$590,000	$435,000

22B-4. Complete a trend analysis from the following data of Hail Corporation using 2019 as the base year. (Round to the nearest percent.)

 **L02** *(30 min)*

	2022	2021	2020	2019
Sales	$620,000	$530,000	$440,000	$350,000
Gross Profit	169,000	141,500	112,000	124,400
Net Income	48,400	40,000	23,200	38,400

22B-5. From the given income statement and additional information of Clark Co., compute the following:

 **L03** *(30 min)*

a. Asset turnover for 2020
b. Inventory turnover for 2020
c. Accounts receivable turnover for 2020

	2020	2019
Net Sales	$1,000,000	$750,000
Cost of Goods Sold	556,000	504,000
Gross Profit	$ 444,000	$246,000
Operating Expenses (includes taxes)	73,000	160,000
Net Income	$ 371,000	$ 86,000

	2020	2019
Year-End Accounts Receivable	$ 80,000	$ 45,000
Year-End Inventory	88,000	51,000
All sales were on credit		
Total Assets	200,000	155,000

MyLabAccounting   **Problems**

Set A

(60 min) **L01**

22A-1. From the comparative balance sheet of Dean Corporation in Figure 22.6: (a) prepare a horizontal analysis of each item for the amount of increase or decrease as well as the percent increase or decrease (to the nearest tenth of a percent); (b) vertically analyze the 2020 column of the balance sheet (to the nearest tenth of a percent).

Figure 22.6
Comparative Balance Sheet
of Dean Corporation

Check Figure:
(a) Cash increase 8.6%

DEAN CORPORATION COMPARATIVE BALANCE SHEET AS OF DECEMBER 31, 2020, AND DECEMBER 31, 2019		
	December 31	
Assets	2020	2019
Current Assets:		
Cash	$ 3 800 00	$ 3 500 00
Accounts Receivable, Net	28 000 00	16 300 00
Merchandise Inventory	52 000 00	19 000 00
Prepaid Expenses	1 580 00	1 230 00
Total Current Assets	$ 85 380 00	$ 40 030 00
Plant and Equipment:		
Office Equipment, Net	$ 124 000 00	$ 110 000 00
Total Assets	$ 209 380 00	$ 150 030 00
Liabilities		
Current Liabilities:		
Notes Payable	$ 21 000 00	$ 24 000 00
Accounts Payable	20 700 00	23 500 00
Total Current Liabilities	$ 41 700 00	$ 47 500 00
Long-Term Liabilities:		
Mortgage Payable	$ 51 500 00	$ 38 500 00
Total Liabilities	$ 93 200 00	$ 86 000 00
Stockholders' Equity		
Common Stock, $1 par	$ 51 000 00	$ 25 000 00
Retained Earnings	65 180 00	39 030 00
Total Stockholders' Equity	$ 116 180 00	$ 64 030 00
Total Liabilities and Stockholders' Equity	$ 209 380 00	$ 150 030 00

22A-2. From the comparative income statement of Wayda Company in Figure 22.7, do the following:

a. Prepare a horizontal analysis with the amount of increase or decrease during 2020 along with the percent increase or decrease during 2019 (to the nearest tenth of a percent).

b. Vertically analyze the 2020 column of the income statement (to the nearest tenth of a percent).

c. Prepare a common-size comparative income statement (to the nearest tenth of a percent) for 2019 and 2020.

LO1 *(60 min)*

Check Figure:
(a) Cost of goods sold increase 6.7%

Figure 22.7
Comparative Income Statement for Wayda Co.

WAYDA COMPANY COMPARATIVE INCOME STATEMENT FOR YEARS ENDED DECEMBER 31, 2020, AND DECEMBER 31, 2019	December 31	
	2020	2019
Net Sales	$ 290 000 00	$ 310 000 00
Cost of Goods Sold	175 000 00	164 000 00
Gross Profit from Sales	$ 115 000 00	$ 146 000 00
Operating Expenses:		
Selling	$ 20 000 00	$ 48 000 00
General and Administrative	17 000 00	33 000 00
Total Operating Expenses	$ 37 000 00	$ 81 000 00
Operating Income	$ 78 000 00	$ 65 000 00
Less Interest Expense	5 000 00	6 800 00
Income Before Taxes	73 000 00	58 200 00
Income Taxes	29 200 00	23 280 00
Net Income	$ 43 800 00	$ 34 920 00

22A-3. From the income statement (Figure 22.8) and balance sheet (Figure 22.9) of Augustus Company, compute the following for 2020: (a) current ratio, (b) acid test ratio, (c) accounts receivable turnover, (d) average collection period, (e) inventory turnover, (f) asset turnover, (g) debt to total assets, (h) debt to stockholders' equity, (i) times interest earned, (j) gross profit rate, (k) return on sales, (l) return on total assets, and (m) return on common stockholders' equity. Assume all sales are on credit.

LO3 *(60 min)*

Check Figure:
Current ratio 2.63

Figure 22.8
Comparative Income Statement for Augustus Co.

AUGUSTUS COMPANY COMPARATIVE INCOME STATEMENT FOR YEARS ENDED DECEMBER 31, 2020, AND 2019	December 31	
	2020	2019
Net Credit Sales	$ 440 000 00	$ 380 000 00
Cost of Goods Sold	231 000 00	223 000 00
Gross Profit from Sales	$ 209 000 00	$ 157 000 00
Operating Expenses:		
Selling	$ 119 400 00	$ 107 000 00
General and Administrative	22 600 00	18 400 00
Total Operating Expenses	$ 142 000 00	$ 125 400 00
Operating Income	$ 67 000 00	$ 31 600 00
Less Interest Expense	8 200 00	3 600 00
Income Before Taxes	$ 58 800 00	$ 28 000 00
Income Taxes	17 640 00	11 200 00
Net Income	$ 41 160 00	$ 16 800 00

Figure 22.9
Comparative Balance Sheet for
Augustus Co.

AUGUSTUS COMPANY COMPARATIVE BALANCE SHEET DECEMBER 31, 2020, AND DECEMBER 31, 2019		
	December 31	
Assets	2020	2019
Current Assets:		
Cash	$ 14 0 0 0 00	$ 26 4 0 0 00
Accounts Receivable, Net	44 6 0 0 00	35 4 0 0 00
Merchandise Inventory	63 2 0 0 00	60 4 0 0 00
Prepaid Expenses	6 6 0 0 00	7 2 0 0 00
Total Current Assets	$ 128 4 0 0 00	$ 129 4 0 0 00
Plant and Equipment:		
Office Equipment, Net	$ 67 6 0 0 00	$ 66 0 0 0 00
Total Assets	$ 196 0 0 0 00	$ 195 4 0 0 00
Liabilities		
Current Liabilities:		
Notes Payable	$ 36 8 0 0 00	$ 30 5 0 0 00
Accounts Payable	12 0 0 0 00	13 8 0 0 00
Total Current Liabilities	$ 48 8 0 0 00	$ 44 3 0 0 00
Long-Term Liabilities:		
Mortgage Payable	$ 36 6 0 0 00	$ 32 0 0 0 00
Total Liabilities	$ 85 4 0 0 00	$ 76 3 0 0 00
Stockholders' Equity		
Common Stock, $10 par value	$ 78 0 0 0 00	$ 58 9 0 0 00
Retained Earnings	32 6 0 0 00	60 2 0 0 00
Total Stockholders' Equity	$ 110 6 0 0 00	$ 119 1 0 0 00
Total Liabilities and Stockholders' Equity	$ 196 0 0 0 00	$ 195 4 0 0 00

(30 min) **L01,2,3**

22A-4. From the information about Valerius Corporation in Figures 22.10 and 22.11, do the following:

a. For each year calculate its current ratio and acid test ratio.
b. For each year prepare the income statement in common-size percentages. (Round to the nearest tenth of a percent.)
c. Prepare a trend analysis of the balance sheet using 2018 as the base year. (Round to the nearest percent.)

Check Figure:
(c) 2020 Current assets 72%

VALERIUS CORPORATION
COMPARATIVE INCOME STATEMENT
FOR YEARS ENDED DECEMBER 31, 2020, 2019, 2018

	2020	2019	2018
Net Sales	$ 45 0 0 0 00	$ 50 0 0 0 00	$ 25 0 0 0 00
Cost of Goods Sold	20 0 0 0 00	19 6 0 0 00	19 0 0 0 00
Gross Profit from Sales	$ 25 0 0 0 00	$ 30 4 0 0 00	$ 6 0 0 0 00
Operating Expenses:			
Selling	$ 3 5 0 0 00	$ 1 5 0 0 00	$ 3 0 0 0 00
General and Administrative	3 5 0 0 00	1 0 0 0 00	2 5 0 0 00
Total Operating Expenses	$ 7 0 0 0 00	$ 2 5 0 0 00	$ 5 5 0 0 00
Operating Income Before Taxes	$ 18 0 0 0 00	$ 27 9 0 0 00	$ 5 0 0 00
Income Taxes	7 0 0 00	2 0 0 00	3 0 0 00
Net Income	$ 17 3 0 0 00	$ 27 7 0 0 00	$ 2 0 0 00

Figure 22.10
Comparative Income Statement
for Valerius Corporation

VALERIUS CORPORATION
COMPARATIVE BALANCE SHEET
FOR YEARS ENDED DECEMBER 31, 2020, 2019, 2018

Assets	2020	2019	2018
Current Assets*	$ 2 3 0 0 00	$ 2 2 0 0 00	$ 3 2 0 0 00
Plant and Equipment	8 0 0 0 00	7 0 0 0 00	8 9 0 0 00
Total Assets	$ 10 3 0 0 00	$ 9 2 0 0 00	$ 12 1 0 0 00
Liabilities and Stockholders' Equity			
Current Liabilities	$ 1 3 0 0 00	$ 1 0 0 0 00	$ 1 2 0 0 00
Common Stock	6 3 0 0 00	5 8 0 0 00	5 9 0 0 00
Retained Earnings	2 7 0 0 00	2 4 0 0 00	5 0 0 0 00
Total Liabilities and Stockholders' Equity	$ 10 3 0 0 00	$ 9 2 0 0 00	$ 12 1 0 0 00

*2020 Inventory, $500; 2019, $310; 2018, $580.

Figure 22.11
Comparative Balance Sheet
for Valerius Corporation

Set B

22B-1. From the comparative balance sheet of Salmon Corporation in Figure 22.12, do the following: (a) Prepare a horizontal analysis of each item for the amount of increase or decrease as well as the percent increase or decrease (to the nearest tenth of a percent). (b) Vertically analyze the 2020 column of the balance sheet (to the nearest tenth of a percent).

 **L01** *(20 min)*

Check Figure:
(a) Cash increase 26.5%

Figure 22.12
Comparative Balance Sheet
for Salmon Corporation

SALMON CORPORATION COMPARATIVE BALANCE SHEET AS OF DECEMBER 31, 2020, AND DECEMBER 31, 2019		
	December 31	
Assets	**2020**	**2019**
Current Assets:		
Cash	$ 4 3 0 0 00	$ 3 4 0 0 00
Accounts Receivable, Net	30 0 0 0 00	15 9 0 0 00
Merchandise Inventory	50 0 0 0 00	12 0 0 0 00
Prepaid Expenses	1 5 6 0 00	1 2 4 0 00
Total Current Assets	$ 85 8 6 0 00	$ 32 5 4 0 00
Plant and Equipment:		
Office Equipment, Net	$ 119 0 0 0 00	$ 112 0 0 0 00
Total Assets	$ 204 8 6 0 00	$ 144 5 4 0 00
Liabilities		
Current Liabilities:		
Notes Payable	$ 19 9 0 0 00	$ 23 0 0 0 00
Accounts Payable	21 1 0 0 00	23 6 0 0 00
Total Current Liabilities	$ 41 0 0 0 00	$ 46 6 0 0 00
Long-Term Liabilities:		
Mortgage Payable	$ 49 0 0 0 00	$ 40 5 0 0 00
Total Liabilities	$ 90 0 0 0 00	$ 87 1 0 0 00
Stockholders' Equity		
Common Stock, $1 par	$ 47 5 0 0 00	$ 27 0 0 0 00
Retained Earnings	67 3 6 0 00	30 4 4 0 00
Total Stockholders' Equity	$ 114 8 6 0 00	$ 57 4 4 0 00
Total Liabilities and Stockholders' Equity	$ 204 8 6 0 00	$ 144 5 4 0 00

(60 min) **LO2**

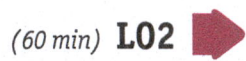

Check Figure:
(a) 2020 Net sales decrease 15.0%

22B-2.   From the comparative income statement of Miller Company in Figure 22.13, do the following:

   a.   Prepare a horizontal analysis with the amount of increase or decrease during 2020 along with the percent increase or decrease during 2019 (to the nearest tenth of a percent).

   b.   Vertically analyze the 2020 column of the income statement (to the nearest tenth of a percent).

   c.   Prepare a common-size comparative income statement (to the nearest tenth of a percent) for 2019 and 2020.

MILLER COMPANY COMPARATIVE INCOME STATEMENT FOR YEARS ENDED DECEMBER 31, 2020, AND DECEMBER 31, 2019	December 31	
	2020	2019
Net Sales	$ 260 0 0 0 00	$ 306 0 0 0 00
Cost of Goods Sold	185 0 0 0 00	150 0 0 0 00
Gross Profit from Sales	75 0 0 0 00	156 0 0 0 00
Operating Expenses:		
Selling	20 0 0 0 00	78 0 0 0 00
General and Administrative	24 0 0 0 00	33 0 0 0 00
Total Operating Expenses	44 0 0 0 00	111 0 0 0 00
Operating Income	31 0 0 0 00	45 0 0 0 00
Less Interest Expense	6 0 0 0 00	12 0 0 0 00
Income Before Taxes	25 0 0 0 00	33 0 0 0 00
Income Taxes	10 0 0 0 00	13 2 0 0 00
Net Income	$ 15 0 0 0 00	$ 19 8 0 0 00

Figure 22.13
Comparative Income Statement for Miller Co.

22B-3. From the income statement and balance sheet of Andrews Company (Figures 22.14 and 22.15), compute the following for 2020: (a) current ratio, (b) acid test ratio, (c) accounts receivable turnover, (d) average collection period, (e) inventory turnover, (f) asset turnover, (g) debt to total assets, (h) debt to stockholders' equity, (i) times interest earned, (j) gross profit rate, (k) return on sales, (l) return on total assets, and (m) return on stockholders' equity. Assume all sales are on credit.

 **L03** *(60 min)*

Check Figure:
Current ratio 2.55

ANDREWS COMPANY COMPARATIVE INCOME STATEMENT FOR YEARS ENDED DECEMBER 31, 2020, AND DECEMBER 31, 2019	December 31	
	2020	2019
Net Credit Sales	$ 420 0 0 0 00	$ 382 0 0 0 00
Cost of Goods Sold	236 0 0 0 00	217 0 0 0 00
Gross Profit from Sales	$ 184 0 0 0 00	$ 165 0 0 0 00
Operating Expenses:		
Selling	$ 124 4 0 0 00	$ 112 0 0 0 00
General and Administrative	19 6 0 0 00	24 4 0 0 00
Total Operating Expenses	$ 144 0 0 0 00	$ 136 4 0 0 00
Operating Income	$ 40 0 0 0 00	$ 28 6 0 0 00
Less Interest Expense	8 2 0 0 00	6 6 0 0 00
Income Before Taxes	$ 31 8 0 0 00	$ 22 0 0 0 00
Income Taxes	9 5 4 0 00	8 8 0 0 00
Net Income	$ 22 2 6 0 00	$ 13 2 0 0 00

Figure 22.14
Comparative Income Statement for Andrews Co.

Figure 22.15
Comparative Balance Sheet
for Andrews Co.

ANDREWS COMPANY
COMPARATIVE BALANCE SHEET
DECEMBER 31, 2020, AND DECEMBER 31, 2019

Assets	December 31 2020	December 31 2019
Current Assets:		
Cash	$ 15 0 0 0 00	$ 21 4 0 0 00
Accounts Receivable, Net	42 6 0 0 00	41 4 0 0 00
Merchandise Inventory	58 2 0 0 00	65 2 0 0 00
Prepaid Expenses	8 6 0 0 00	2 2 0 0 00
Total Current Assets	$ 124 4 0 0 00	$ 130 2 0 0 00
Plant and Equipment:		
Office Equipment, Net	$ 64 6 0 0 00	$ 62 0 0 0 00
Total Assets	$ 189 0 0 0 00	$ 192 2 0 0 00
Liabilities		
Current Liabilities:		
Notes Payable	$ 34 8 0 0 00	$ 30 5 0 0 00
Accounts Payable	14 0 0 0 00	10 8 0 0 00
Total Current Liabilities	$ 48 8 0 0 00	$ 41 3 0 0 00
Long-Term Liabilities:		
Mortgage Payable	$ 36 6 0 0 00	$ 29 0 0 0 00
Total Liabilities	$ 85 4 0 0 00	$ 70 3 0 0 00
Stockholders' Equity:		
Common Stock, $10 par value	$ 66 0 0 0 00	$ 63 7 0 0 00
Retained Earnings	37 6 0 0 00	58 2 0 0 00
Total Stockholders' Equity	$ 103 6 0 0 00	$ 121 9 0 0 00
Total Liabilities and Stockholders' Equity	$ 189 0 0 0 00	$ 192 2 0 0 00

(20 min) **LO1,2,3**

22B-4. From the information about Vargo Corporation in Figures 22.16 and 22.17, do the following:

  a. For each year calculate its current ratio and acid test ratio.
  b. For each year prepare the income statement in common-size percentages. (Round to the nearest tenth of a percent.)
  c. Prepare a trend analysis of the balance sheet using 2018 as the base year. (Round to the nearest percent.)

Check Figure:
(c) 2020 Current assets 63%

VARGO CORPORATION COMPARATIVE INCOME STATEMENT FOR YEARS ENDED DECEMBER 31, 2020, 2019, 2018	2020	2019	2018
Net Sales	$ 60 000 00	$ 40 000 00	$ 50 000 00
Cost of Goods Sold	18 000 00	19 600 00	20 000 00
Gross Profit from Sales	$ 42 000 00	$ 20 400 00	$ 30 000 00
Operating Expenses:			
Selling	$ 1 500 00	$ 2 500 00	$ 2 000 00
General and Administrative	4 500 00	1 000 00	2 000 00
Total Operating Expenses	$ 6 000 00	$ 3 500 00	$ 4 000 00
Operating Income Before Taxes	$ 36 000 00	$ 16 900 00	$ 26 000 00
Income Taxes	700 00	500 00	500 00
Net Income	$ 35 300 00	$ 16 400 00	$ 25 500 00

Figure 22.16
Comparative Income Statement for Vargo Corporation

VARGO CORPORATION COMPARATIVE BALANCE SHEET FOR YEARS ENDED DECEMBER 31, 2020, 2019, 2018			
Assets	2020	2019	2018
Current Assets*	$ 1 900 00	$ 1 600 00	$ 3 000 00
Plant and Equipment	12 000 00	8 500 00	7 900 00
Total Assets	$ 13 900 00	$ 10 100 00	$ 10 900 00
Liabilities and Stockholders' Equity			
Current Liabilities	$ 900 00	$ 700 00	$ 1 100 00
Common Stock	7 000 00	6 100 00	6 200 00
Retained Earnings	6 000 00	3 300 00	3 600 00
Total Liabilities and Stockholders' Equity	$ 13 900 00	$ 10 100 00	$ 10 900 00

*2020 Inventory: $520; 2019, $310; 2018, $540.

Figure 22.17
Comparative Balance Sheet for Vargo Corporation

Financial Report Problem

Reading Amazon's Annual Report

Go to the annual report for Amazon at **https://tinyurl.com/slaterca14e** and calculate the Current Ratio for 2016.

MyLabAccounting

L01,2,3 *(30 min)*

The Voucher System

23

CHAPTER PREVIEW: ACCOUNTING IN ACTION

Rashad Allen traveled to a seminar on managing big data 4 weeks ago. It has been 8 weeks, and his travel reimbursement has not yet been processed. In most businesses, employees seeking reimbursement need to get their reimbursement approved before the company can process payment. This voucher system used by a company makes certain that cash payments are properly authorized and validated before a check is issued. This chapter focuses on the voucher system and how reimbursements are authorized, validated, and recorded before issuance of a reimbursement check.

Learning Objectives – Relating Accounting Theory By Unit

LO1 Explain How to Handle Transactions in a Voucher System

LO2 Explain Purchases Returns and Allowances, Partial Payments, and Recording Purchases at Net or Gross in a Voucher System

In small companies, owners may be able to do or look at every step of their business themselves. However, as such companies grow larger and as the sheer number of business transactions multiplies, like at Home Depot, that individual control becomes impossible. How, then, do owners or managers keep control over the activities of a company? If they don't sign every check themselves or approve every purchase themselves, how do they know whether money is being spent in approved ways, or even where it's going? Some rules must be formulated for employees to impose order; such rules and procedures are referred to as *internal control*. One type of system used to implement this internal control is called a *voucher system*.

Today with accounting software packages such as QuickBooks, Sage 50, and enterprise resource planning (ERP) packages like Sage 100, more companies are using a computerized accounting system that holds all vendor information, pays bills, tracks payments, and even monitors when bills are due.

In Chapter 10, we discussed the steps taken when a company purchases goods. You might take a moment to look back at those pages because we use these steps in this chapter to explain how a voucher system works. The steps include the following:

1. Preparing a purchase requisition and getting it authorized.
2. Preparing a purchase order, which specifies details such as company, number of items, and so forth, and getting it authorized.
3. The vendor receiving the purchase order preparing a sales invoice specifying number and type of goods and price.
4. The company receiving the goods, inspecting the shipment, checking it against the purchase order and the sales invoice, and completing a receiving report.
5. Someone in the accounting department verifying the numbers (checking the purchase order, the invoice, and the receiving report to make sure the numbers are in agreement and no steps are left out). This person then issuing a voucher for payment, which is authorized.
6. Issuing payment in the form of a check (or electronic form).

These steps show internal control, in the form of a voucher system, at work. Other procedures discussed in other chapters of this text are also part of internal control, including banking procedures and petty cash and change funds.

What is a voucher? A voucher is a written authorization form that is used for every cash payment the company makes. It contains all the details of the transaction in question along with the signatures of appropriate employees as authorization. A voucher system, then, is a system in which no payment is made without an approved voucher.

Characteristics of a Voucher System

A number of principles of internal control are embedded in the voucher system. Perhaps the most important is the separation of duties. In a voucher system, no one person in a company is in control of all transactions or of everything to do with one transaction. The person who approves purchase and/or payment is different from the person who makes the accounting entries related to these functions, and that person is different from the person who signs and mails the checks. In this way no one can do anything without other people supplying approval.

A second important principle, perhaps the backbone of a voucher system, is the rule that no purchases are made without an approved voucher backed up by documentation. Several layers of documentation and authorization begin with a purchase requisition, move on to a purchase order, and end up with actual payment by a check. At every layer and step the appropriate documents are presented, checked, and approved before going further.

A lot of cross-referencing and cross-checking takes place in a voucher system. Every document is numbered; transactions are recorded in different places by different people and backed up by reference to numbers of other documents. In this way, it is always possible to trace one transaction all the way through the system. After a purchase is made and paid for, the documents and forms are kept on file for a certain period of time to allow such cross-checks to be made.

Voucher Written authorization form containing data about a transaction along with proper authorizations for payment, account distributions, and so forth.

Voucher system Internal control system designed to control a company's cash payments.

In the next two learning units, we show how a voucher system works in a specific company and then how certain transactions that don't fit into the voucher system are handled.

Handling Transactions in a Voucher System

Jones Supply Company is a medium-sized merchandise business that believes in strong internal control practices and procedures. It uses the voucher system to control all cash payments except payments out of the petty cash fund. Company rules state that all invoices must be compared with purchase requisitions, purchase orders, and receiving reports before payment and that all payments must, of course, be supported by appropriate documents and authorizations.

Jones Supply Company's voucher system is made up of the following elements:

1. Vouchers
2. Voucher register
3. Unpaid voucher file
4. Check register
5. Paid voucher file

To see this system in action, let's follow one transaction all the way through. To begin with, Jones Supply Company decides to buy $4,500 worth of merchandise from Beam Enterprises. The purchase order is shown in Figure 23.1. When the merchandise is received, along with an invoice (Figure 23.2), a special serially numbered form called a *voucher* is prepared (Figure 23.3).

The Voucher

In preparing the voucher, the accountant responsible for vouchers compares the invoice from Beam Enterprises with the purchase requisition, purchase order, and receiving report to be sure that it matches the specific requirements and prices of the order. For example, the information in Figure 23.1, the purchase order, does indeed match the information on the invoice shown in Figure 23.2.

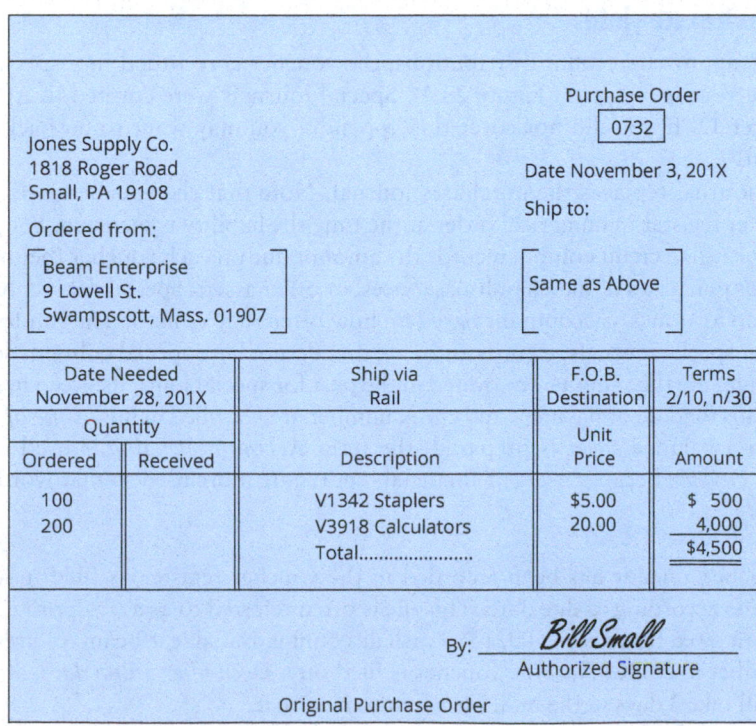

Figure 23.1
Purchase Order

Figure 23.2
Invoice

Original Invoice

The original supporting documents (purchase orders, etc.) are attached to the voucher (Figure 23.3), which contains information on its front and back sides. The front side indicates the voucher number, invoice number and date, purchase order number, to whom the amount will be paid, and verification steps. For Jones Supply Company, all supporting documents are attached to the front of the voucher and folded. The back side shows the account distribution along with space to complete the payment summary and final approvals as needed. Keep in mind that, today, with computerized systems, many of the steps in the manual system will automatically be processed electronically.

The Voucher Register

Voucher register Special journal replacing the purchases journal; it records prenumbered vouchers at the time the liabilities are incurred.

Using the approved account distributions, the voucher is recorded in a special journal called the voucher register (Figure 23.4). Special journals were covered in Appendix A of Chapter 12. If you did not cover this appendix you may want to go back and read through it.

Vouchers Payable Liability account in the general ledger that represents the controlling account for the sum of individual vouchers.

This journal replaces the purchases journal. Note that the vouchers are entered in the voucher register in numerical order at the time the liability is *incurred*. For Jones, the Vouchers Payable credit column records the amount due on each voucher (before any discounts) for purchases of merchandise, services, or other assets. Special debit columns have been set up for Jones's accountant based on how often they're used. The sundry column, as in other special journals, records amounts that do not have special columns set up. The posting rules are the same as we covered in the past for special journals. Keep in mind that the columns for date of payment and check number are *not* filled in until *time of payment*.

When a balance sheet is prepared, the term *Accounts Payable* is used instead of *Vouchers Payable* because users of financial reports are more used to that wording.

Unpaid Voucher File

Unpaid voucher file (tickler file) File containing unpaid vouchers arranged by due dates to take advantage of cash discounts.

Each voucher, once it has been recorded in the voucher register, is filed in an unpaid voucher file according to due date. This file is often referred to as a tickler file. Although the amount owed Beam is $4,500, a $90 cash discount is available if Beam receives payment by December 8, 201X. Thus the voucher is filed on a *December 5 due date*, anticipating that it will take 3 days in the mail for Beam to receive it.

Figure 23.3
Voucher

(front)

```
                          VOUCHER

Jones Supply Co.                  Voucher No. 23
1818 Roger Road
Small, PA 19108                   Date check needed:
                                  December 5, 201X
Invoice
Number and Date:                  Payable to:   Beam Enterprise
B20 November 28, 201X                           9 Lowell St.
                                                Swampscott, MA 01907
Purchase
Order Number: 0732                Invoice Amount      $4,500
                                  Less: Discount          90
                                  Net Amount Due      $4,410


Verification Steps:               Approved by:        Date

(1) Invoice compared with purchase
    requisition and purchase order      JS           12/1/1X
(2) Invoice compared with receiving
    report                               BM           12/1/1X
(3) Extensions and footings done         BJ           12/1/1X
(4) Approved for payment                 PS           12/3/1X
```

(back)

Account Distribution		Voucher No. 23
Debit	Amount	Date check needed: 12/5/1X
Purchases	$4,500	Payable to:
Supplies		
Salaries Expense		Beam Enterprise
Repair Expense		9 Lowell St.
Sundry		Swampscott, MA 01907
		Summary of Voucher
		Invoice Amount $4,500
		Less: Discount 90
		Net Amount Due $4,410
		Payment Summary of Voucher
		Date: 12/5/1X
		Amount: $4,410
		Check No.: 55
		Recorded in Voucher
Credit Vouchers		Register by: ___PM___
Payable for Total	$4,500	
Distribution approved by: ___JS___		
(Accounting Department)		

In the voucher system, the accounts payable ledger is not used; for Jones, the unpaid file is its subsidiary ledger for the controlling account Vouchers Payable in the general ledger. At the end of the month, Jones Supply Company will prepare a schedule of vouchers payable, just as we discussed in Chapter 10 for the schedule of accounts payable, with the total of all unpaid vouchers being equal to the ending balance in Vouchers Payable in the general ledger.

Figure 23.4 Voucher Register

VOUCHER REGISTER

Date		Voucher Number	Payable to	Date of Payment	Check Number	Vouchers Payable Cr.	Purchases Dr.	Supplies Dr.	Repair Expense Dr.	Sundry Accounts Account	Sundry Accounts PR	Sundry Accounts Dr.	Sundry Accounts Cr.
201X Dec.	2	22	Petty Cash	12/4	53	50.00				Petty Cash	114	50.00	
	3	23	Beam Enterprise	12/5	55	4,500.00	4,500.00						
	3	24	Ron Co.	12/4	54	425.00		425.00					
	7	25	Rose Co.	12/9	56	28.00			28.00				
	9	26	Blew Co.	12/30	67	1,000.00				Equip.	121	1,000.00	
	15	27	Security Bank	12/27	58	5,150.00				Note Payable	211	5,000.00	
										Int. Exp.	531	150.00	
	28	42	Internal Revenue Service	12/28	65	900.00				FICA Tax* Payable	212	250.00	
										FIT Tax Payable	216	650.00	
	29	43	Payroll	12/29	66	4,000.00				Salary and Wages Payable	210	4,000.00	
						20,665.00	7,950.00	600.00	1,015.00			11,100.00	
						(212)	(513)	(116)	(562)			(X)	

*Includes Medicare and Social Security.

Check Register

On December 5, Jones Company records the payment to Beam in a special journal called a check register. The check register replaces the cash payments journal in recording the payment of vouchers payable. Note in Figure 23.5 that the Vouchers Payable account is debited for $4,500, whereas Purchases Discount is credited for $90 and Cash in Bank is credited for $4,410. The date of payment, along with the check number, is updated in the voucher register. Posting of the check register follows the same rules as other special journals. (*Note:* Once the voucher has been paid, it should be marked "Paid" so as to avoid duplication of payments.)

Check register Special journal that replaces the cash payments journal in recording payments of vouchers.

Figure 23.5 Check Register

	Date	Check Number	Payable to	Voucher Number	Vouchers Payable Dr.	Purchases Discount Cr.	Cash in Bank Cr.	Bank Deposits	Bank Bal.
202X Dec.	1	49	Broom Co.	21	4 6 0 00		4 6 0 00		1 2 0 0 00
									7 4 0 00
	2	50	Moore Co.	22	6 0 0 00	1 2 00	5 8 8 00	4 0 0 00	5 5 2 00
	4	54	Ron Co.	24	4 2 5 00		4 2 5 00	1 0 0 0 00	1 1 2 7 00
	5	55	Beam Ent.	23	4 5 0 0 00	9 0 00	4 4 1 0 00	4 0 0 0 00	7 1 7 00
	28	65	Internal Revenue	42	9 0 0 00		9 0 0 00		8 2 0 0 00
	29	66	Payroll	43	4 0 0 0 00		4 0 0 0 00		4 2 0 0 00
					(212)	(514)	(111)		

Paid Voucher File

After Beam's voucher is paid, it is filed by Jones in a paid voucher file. The voucher is filed in sequential order according to the voucher numbers. Some companies will file the voucher alphabetically based on the creditor's name. Jones keeps all paid vouchers for 6 years. This amount of time will vary from company to company.

Now let's check your progress.

Paid voucher file Holds paid vouchers filed either in sequential order by voucher number or alphabetically by creditor's name.

TRY IT! Learning Unit 23-1

Journalize the following transactions in a periodic inventory system:

201X		
Dec.	4	Recorded a purchase on account of $800 from Curran Co. using voucher no. 20 in the voucher register.
	12	Paid from the check register amount owed Curran Co. less a 1% discount.

TRY IT! Solution Learning Unit 23-1

201X				
Dec.	4	Purchases	800	
		Vouchers Payable, Curran Co.		800
	12	Vouchers Payable, Curran Co.	800	
		Purchases Discount		80
		Cash		720

LO2

Purchases Returns and Allowances, Partial Payments, and Recording Purchases at Net or Gross in a Voucher System

Situation 1: Purchases Returns and Allowances after Voucher Has Been Recorded

On December 26, Jones Supply Company prepared voucher no. 32 for merchandise that was bought from Booth Company for $400. The accountant records the voucher in the voucher register as a debit to Purchases and a credit to Vouchers Payable for $400. On December 28, $100 of the merchandise is found to be defective and is returned to Booth Company. The procedure that Jones Supply Company uses is to cancel the original voucher and prepare a new voucher for $300. Figure 23.6 shows how Jones records the cancellation of voucher no. 32 and the recording of the revised voucher no. 39. The end result is a debit to Vouchers Payable of $400, a credit of $300 to Vouchers Payable, and a credit to Purchases Returns and Allowances of $100. Another way of handling this transaction is to modify the original voucher and make a *general journal* entry that debits Vouchers Payable $100 and credits Purchases Returns and Allowances $100.

Situation 2: Partial Payments Planned after Voucher Prepared for Full Amount

On January 18, voucher no. 64 was prepared by Jones Supply Company on the assumption it would pay Ron Company $15,000 for office equipment in one payment. The top section of Figure 23.7 shows a debit to Office Equipment and a credit to Vouchers Payable for $15,000.

Owing to a cash shortage, on January 29 it was decided by Jones Supply Company to pay Ron Company in three equal installments on February 8, 19, and 21. Thus, the original voucher on January 18 is canceled and a *new* voucher is prepared for each installment. Note in Figure 23.7 how the old voucher is canceled and the new vouchers are prepared. In the date of payment column, the January 18 line shows the cancellation along with the new date recording the new vouchers (1/29). The check number column indicates which new vouchers are replacing the canceled voucher. Note in the sundry column how Vouchers Payable is debited to cancel the original voucher.

Recording Purchases at Net Amount

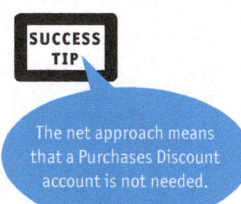

SUCCESS TIP

The net approach means that a Purchases Discount account is not needed.

In this chapter, Jones Supply Company recorded all invoices at the gross amount, although the check register did show a purchases discount column. Many companies, on the other hand, record purchases at net. When a discount is missed using the net approach, a title called Discount Lost is shown in a debit column of the check register. Let's look at journal entries showing the same purchase recorded at gross and at net.

(a) Mill Company buys merchandise on account from Ryan Company for $8,000. Terms are 2/10, n/30. Mill Company issues voucher no. 299.

Gross			Net		
(a) Purchases	8,000		(a) Purchases	7,840	
Vouchers Payable, Ryan Co.		8,000	Vouchers Payable, Ryan Co.		7,840
		Both would be recorded in the voucher register.			

Figure 23.6 Voucher Register with Purchases Returns and Allowances

VOUCHER REGISTER

Date	Voucher Number	Payable to	Date of Payment	Check Number	Vouchers Payable Cr.	Purchases Dr.	Account	Sundry Accounts PR	Sundry Accounts Dr.	Sundry Accounts Cr.
Dec. 26	32	Booth Co.	Canceled Voucher	See no. 39	400 00	400 00				
28	39	Booth Co.			300 00		Voucher Payable	212	400 00	
							Purchases Returns and Allowances	515		100 00

Figure 23.7 Voucher Register with Partial Payments

VOUCHER REGISTER

Date	Voucher Number	Payable to	Date of Payment	Check Number	Vouchers Payable Cr.	Account	Sundry Accounts PR	Sundry Accounts Dr.	Sundry Accounts Cr.
Jan. 18	64	Ron Co.	Canceled 1/29	V69-71	1 50 00 00	Office Equip.	121	1 50 00 00	
29	69	Ron Co.			50 00 00				
29	70	Ron Co.			50 00 00				
29	71	Ron Co.			50 00 00	Vouchers Payable	212	1 50 00 00	

If Discount Is Taken on Time. (b) Mill Company issues check no. 531 in payment of voucher no. 299 less the cash discount.

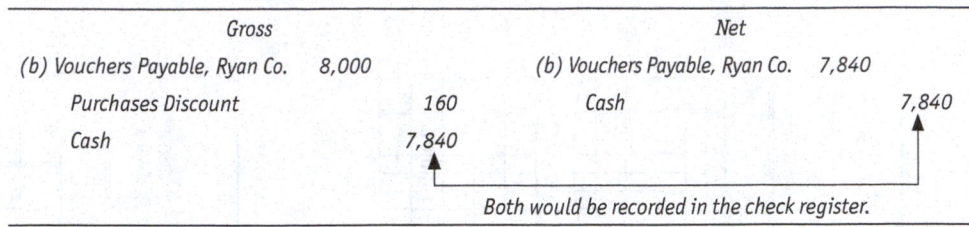

	Gross			Net	
(b) Vouchers Payable, Ryan Co.	8,000		(b) Vouchers Payable, Ryan Co.	7,840	
Purchases Discount		160	Cash		7,840
Cash		7,840			

Both would be recorded in the check register.

If Discount Is Missed. (c) Mill Company issues check no. 531 in payment of voucher no. 299. The discount date has passed.

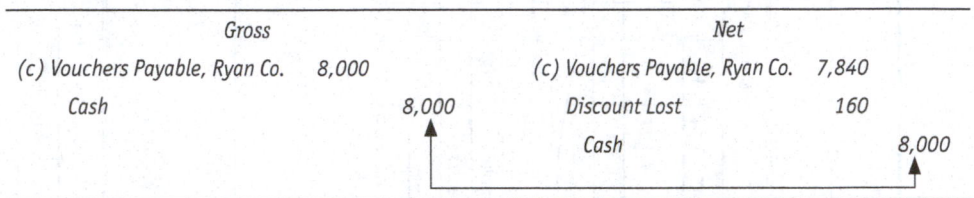

	Gross			Net	
(c) Vouchers Payable, Ryan Co.	8,000		(c) Vouchers Payable, Ryan Co.	7,840	
Cash		8,000	Discount Lost	160	
			Cash		8,000

Note that when the discount is missed in the net method, the Discount Lost account is used. (The end-of-chapter problems and exercises record all vouchers at gross unless otherwise stated.)

Now let's check your progress.

 **TRY IT!**   **Learning Unit 23-2**

Journalize the following transactions in a periodic inventory system at net:

Aug. 15, 201X
a. Lytle Co. buys merchandise inventory on account using voucher no. 41 from Evelyn Co. for $9,000; terms 3/10, n/30.

Sept. 15, 201X
b. Lytle pays off Evelyn Co. using check no. 55 in payment of voucher no. 41. The discount date has passed.

TRY IT!   **Solution Learning Unit 23-2**

Date	Accounts	Dr.	Cr.
201X			
Aug. 15	Purchases	8,730	
	Vouchers Payable, Evelyn Co.		8,730
Sept. 15	Vouchers Payable, Evelyn Co.	8,730	
	Discount Lost	270	
	Cash		9,000

DEMONSTRATION SUMMARY PROBLEM

Requirements

Pete Lowe works in the accounting office of Peirce Co., which is a medium-sized company using a voucher system and the periodic inventory method. From the following, record (1) the transactions at gross and (2) redo the entries assuming recording at net.

201X		
July	8	Voucher no. 60 was prepared for the purchase on account of $5,000 of merchandise from Sun Co.; terms 2/10, n/30.
	12	Voucher no. 61 was prepared for the purchase on account of $4,000 of merchandise from Logan Co.; terms 2/10, n/30.
	15	Check no. 62 was issued for payment of voucher no. 60.
	28	Check no. 63 was issued for payment of voucher no. 61.

Solutions

Requirement 1

At gross:

Date	Accounts	Dr.	Cr.
201X			
July 8	Purchases	5,000	
	Vouchers Payable, Sun Co.		5,000
12	Purchases	4,000	
	Vouchers Payable, Logan Co.		4,000
15	Vouchers Payable, Sun Co.	5,000	
	Purchases Discount		100
	Cash		4,900
28	Vouchers Payable, Logan Co.	4,000	
	Cash		4,000

Tips

When recording at gross, the purchases are recorded at full price. If a discount is met, the Purchases Discount account is used. If a discount is missed, no account is used to show the company missed the discount.

Requirement 2

At net:

Date	Accounts	Dr.	Cr.
201X			
July 8	Purchases	4,900	
	Vouchers Payable, Sun Co.		4,900
12	Purchases	3,920	
	Vouchers Payable, Logan Co.		3,920
15	Vouchers Payable, Sun Co.	4,900	
	Cash		4,900
28	Vouchers Payable, Logan Co.	3,920	
	Discount Lost	80	
	Cash		4,000

Tip

When recording at net, you assume the discount will be taken. On July 15, the discount was taken, but on July 28 the discount was missed. The result is a new account, called Discount Lost, which was debited to show the discount that was missed. This account will end up on the income statement.

SUCCESS COACH

The following Success Tips are from Learning Units 23-1 and 23-2. Take the Do It Right Now Checkup and use the Check Your Score at the bottom of the page to see how you are doing. The Success Coach provides tips before each Checkup to help you avoid common accounting errors.

LU 23-1 Handling Transactions in a Voucher System

Do It Right Tips: The voucher system is made up of these elements: the voucher, the voucher register, unpaid voucher file, check register, and paid voucher file. The voucher register records purchases. Payments are recorded in the check register.

Do It Right Now Checkup: Answer true or false to the following statements.

1. Vouchers Payable is an asset.
2. A voucher remains in the unpaid file until paid.
3. In a voucher system, the accounts payable subsidiary ledger is required.
4. Purchases Discount is a debit in the check register.
5. Vouchers Payable is a credit in the voucher register.

LU 23-2 Purchases Returns and Allowances, Partial Payments, and Recording Purchases at Net or Gross in a Voucher System

Do It Right Tips: Companies that record invoices at net would need to record any discounts missed. The account to record this would be Discount Lost, normally a debit balance.

Do It Right Now Checkup: Answer true or false to the following statements.

1. Vouchers can never be cancelled.
2. Purchases returns and allowances could be used in a voucher register.
3. Sundry means miscellaneous.
4. The net approach means a purchases discount account is needed.
5. Discount Lost has a normal balance of a debit.

CHECK YOUR SCORE: Answers to the Do It Right Now Checkup

LU 23-1

1. False—Vouchers Payable is a liability.
2. True
3. False—In a voucher system, the vouchers payable subsidiary ledger is required.
4. False—Purchases Discount is a credit in the check register.
5. True

LU 23-2

1. False—Vouchers can be cancelled.
2. True
3. True
4. False—The net approach means a Purchases Discount account is not needed.
5. True

BLUEPRINT: STEPS TO RECORD AND PAY A LIABILITY USING THE VOUCHER SYSTEM

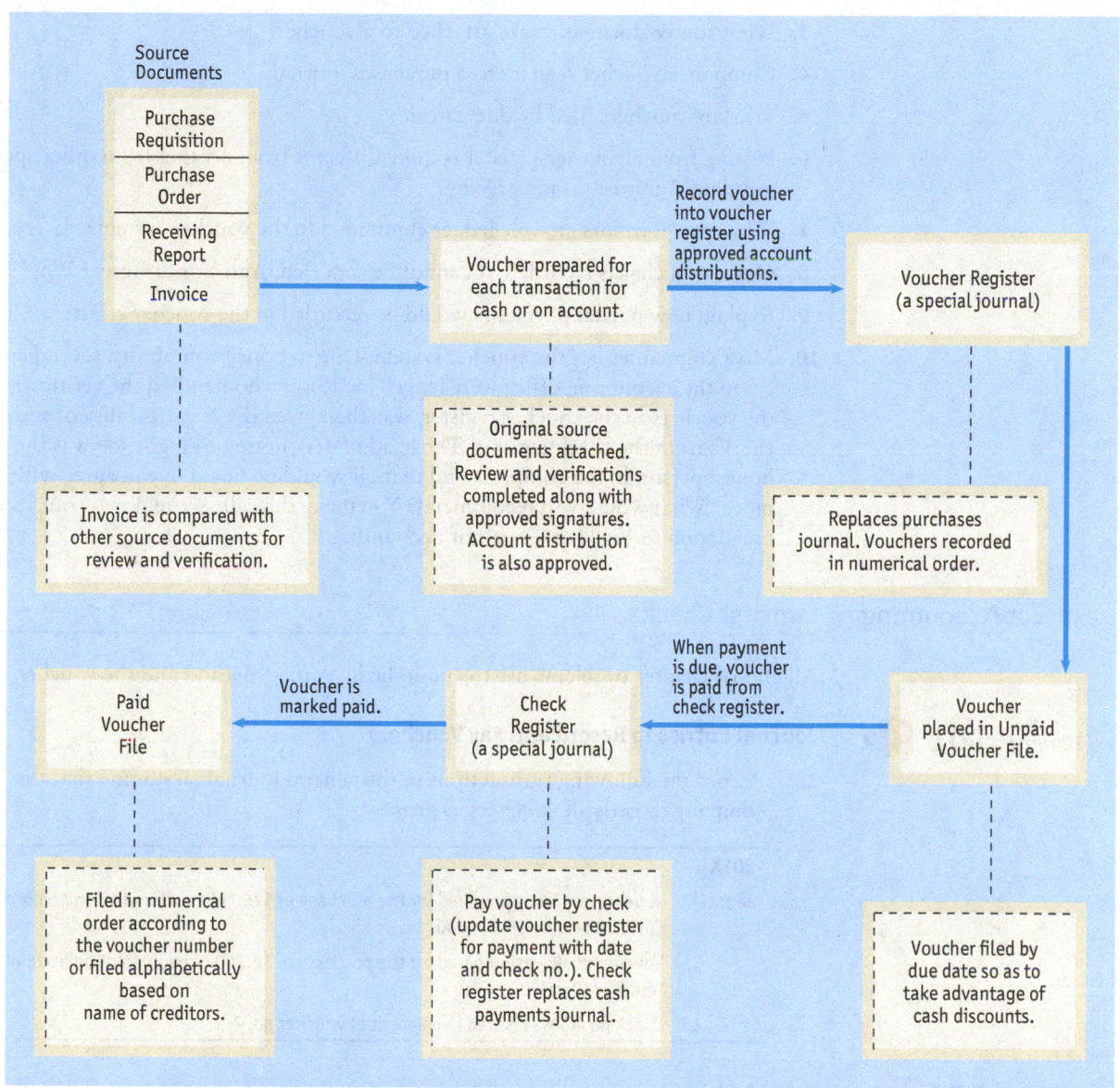

Source Documents

| Purchase Requisition |
| Purchase Order |
| Receiving Report |
| Invoice |

Voucher prepared for each transaction for cash or on account.

Record voucher into voucher register using approved account distributions.

Voucher Register (a special journal)

Invoice is compared with other source documents for review and verification.

Original source documents attached. Review and verifications completed along with approved signatures. Account distribution is also approved.

Replaces purchases journal. Vouchers recorded in numerical order.

Paid Voucher File

Voucher is marked paid.

Check Register (a special journal)

When payment is due, voucher is paid from check register.

Voucher placed in Unpaid Voucher File.

Filed in numerical order according to the voucher number or filed alphabetically based on name of creditors.

Pay voucher by check (update voucher register for payment with date and check no.). Check register replaces cash payments journal.

Voucher filed by due date so as to take advantage of cash discounts.

Discussion Questions and Critical Thinking/Ethical Case

1. What is the structure of a voucher?

2. List the five components of a voucher system.

3. What source documents are attached to a voucher?

4. Compare a voucher register to a purchases journal.

5. Why are vouchers filed by due dates?

6. Posting from a voucher register is quite different from posting from other special journals. Agree or disagree? Why?

7. Why is an accounts payable ledger eliminated in the voucher system?

8. Once a voucher is recorded, it cannot be canceled. Agree or disagree? Why?

9. Explain how partial payments would be recorded in the voucher register.

10. Most companies use the voucher system. Due to poor profitability, several employees in the accounting office were let go. Joe Rose, who handled the verification of the vouchers in the voucher register, was then given the responsibility of writing the checks from the check register. The head of accounting thought Joe was the most honest person in the company and that all would be fine. Do you agree with this move? What would you recommend? You make the call. Write down your recommendation to Jay Flynn, head of accounting.

MyLab Accounting

Concept Checks

All end-of-chapter problems use the periodic inventory method and the voucher system.

(10 min) **LO1**

Journal Entries to Record and Pay Vouchers

1. Record the following transactions in the general journal, assuming that the company records all vouchers as gross:

201X		
Jan.	7	Voucher no. 7 was prepared for the purchase of $700 of merchandise on account from Curik Co.; terms 4/10, n/30.
	11	Voucher no. 8 was prepared for the purchase of $2,200 of equipment on account; terms 4/10, n/30.
	14	Check no. 15 was issued in payment of voucher no. 7.

(10 min) **LO1**

Petty Cash

2 Record the following transactions into the general journal. The company uses a voucher system along with a petty cash fund.

201X		
Mar.	11	Voucher no. 12 was prepared to establish petty cash for $170.
	23	Voucher no. 36 was prepared to replenish the petty cash fund from the following receipts: supplies, $30; delivery, $37.

(10 min) **LO2**

Purchases Returns and Allowances

3 On November 15, Lesko Co. prepared a voucher for $750 for merchandise purchased on account from Rowe Co. On November 19, Lesko Co. decided to return merchandise valued at $100 due to poor workmanship. Record the general journal entries.

Equal Installments

LO2 (10 min)

4 On August 6, Lane Co. prepared voucher no. 14 to record purchases of equipment on account for $1,300. On August 11, Lane Co. decided to pay the $1,300 in two equal installments (voucher nos. 17 and 18). Record the general journal entries.

Gross versus Net

LO2 (10 min)

5 Record the following transactions at (a) gross and (b) net:

201X		
Sept.	3	Bought merchandise on account from Fisher Co.; terms 9/10, n/30, $8,000. Voucher no. 34 was prepared.
	18	Issued check no. 481 in payment of voucher no. 34.

Exercises

MyLabAccounting

Set A

23A-1. Becky Company, which is a medium-sized firm, uses a voucher system. Record each of the following entries in general journal form. Assume that Becky Company records all vouchers at gross.

LO1 (30 min)

201X		
May	3	Voucher no. 50 was prepared for the purchase of $6,700 of merchandise on account from Mark Company; terms 3/10, n/30.
	6	Voucher no. 51 was prepared for the purchase of $4,100 of equipment on account; terms 3/10, n/30.
	12	Check no. 55 was issued in payment of voucher no. 51.
	17	Check no. 56 was issued in payment of voucher no. 50.

23A-2. Elliott Company uses a voucher system along with a petty cash fund. Record each of the following entries in general journal form. Assume that Elliott Company records all vouchers at gross.

LO1 (35 min)

201X		
Aug	3	Purchased $450 of merchandise on account from Greely Company; voucher no. 151 was prepared; terms 2/10, n/30.
	5	Voucher no. 152 was prepared to establish petty cash for $105.
	7	Issued check no. 58 in payment of voucher no. 151.
	11	Check no. 59 was issued to pay voucher no. 152.
	27	Voucher no. 153 was prepared to replenish the petty cash fund from the following receipts: supplies, $25; delivery, $29.

23A-3. On November 10, 201X, a voucher for $1,000 for merchandise purchased on account from Beverly Company was prepared by Lake Corporation. On November 14, Lake decided to return merchandise due to poor workmanship. The price of the merchandise returned was $570. Record the entries in general journal form for November 10 and 14.

LO2 (20 min)

23A-4. On August 15, 201X, Quincy Company prepared voucher no. 90 to record the purchase of equipment on account for $930. On August 18, Quincy Company decided to pay $930 in two equal installments. (Voucher nos. 91 and 92 were prepared.) Prepare the appropriate journal entries in general journal form for August 15 and 18.

LO2 (20 min)

(20 min) **LO2**   **23A-5.** Lamy Company records invoices at gross in its voucher system. From the following transactions, (a) record in general journal form the appropriate entries at gross and (b) record the entries as if Lamy Company recorded invoices at net.

201X		
May	7	Bought merchandise on account from Hubley Corporation; terms 2/10, n/30, $9,000. Voucher no. 304 was prepared.
	19	Issued check no. 620 in payment of voucher no. 304.

Set B

(30 min) **LO1**  **23B-1.** Carney Company, which is a medium-sized firm, uses a voucher system. Record each of the following entries in general journal form. Assume that Carney Company records all vouchers at gross.

201X		
June	7	Voucher no. 50 was prepared for the purchase of $7,400 of merchandise on account from Nathan Company; terms 4/10, n/30.
	10	Voucher no. 51 was prepared for the purchase of $3,700 of equipment on account; terms 4/10, n/30.
	16	Check no. 55 was issued in payment of voucher no. 51.
	22	Check no. 56 was issued in payment of voucher no. 50.

(35 min) **LO1**   **23B-2.** Dome Company uses a voucher system along with a petty cash fund. Record each of the following entries in journal entry form. Assume that Dome Company records all vouchers at gross.

201X		
May	11	Purchased $900 0f merchandise on account from Green Company; voucher no. 147 was prepared; terms 2/10, n/30.
	14	Voucher no. 148 was prepared to establish petty cash for $70.
	16	Issued check no. 63 in payment of voucher no. 147.
	17	Check no. 64 was issued to pay voucher no. 148.
	27	Voucher no. 149 was prepared to replenish the petty cash fund from the following receipts: supplies, $18; delivery, $23.

(20 min) **LO2**  **23B-3.** On November 10, 201X, a voucher for $1,020 for merchandise purchased on account from Gardner Company was prepared by Nicole Corporation. On November 14, Nicole decided to return the merchandise due to poor workmanship. The price of the defective merchandise was $560. Record the entries in general journal form for November 10 and 14.

(20 min) **LO2**   **23B-4.** On June 15, 201X, Thompson Company prepared voucher no. 93 to record the purchase of equipment on account for $870. On June 18, Thompson Company decided to pay $870 in two equal installments. (Voucher nos. 94 and 95 were prepared.) Prepare the appropriate journal entries in general journal form for June 15 and 18.

(20 min) **LO2** ▶ **23B-5.** Morrow Company records invoices at gross in its voucher system. From the following transactions, (a) record in general journal form the appropriate entries at gross and (b) record the entries as if Morrow Company recorded invoices at net.

201X		
Aug.	12	Bought merchandise on account from Kable Corporation; terms 2/10, n/30, $9,500. Voucher no. 297 was prepared.
	26	Issued check no. 600 in payment of voucher no. 297.

Problems

Set A

23A-1. Farrah Corporation uses a voucher system. Record the following transactions in the voucher register:

 **L01** *(30 min)*

201X

June 8 Purchased office equipment on account from Takala Corporation, $1,400; voucher no. 300 was prepared.

    12 Established a petty cash fund of $90; voucher no. 301 was prepared.

    14 Purchased merchandise on account from Scott Corporation, $700; voucher no. 302 was prepared.

    15 Purchased office supplies on account from Lian Corporation, $900; voucher no. 303 was prepared.

    29 Voucher no. 304 was prepared to replenish the petty cash fund based on the following receipts: supplies, $14; postage, $16.

Check Figure:
June 12
Dr. Petty Cash (sundry) $90
Cr. Vouchers Payable $90

23A-2. Sabin Corporation uses a voucher system and records invoices at gross. Record the following transactions in the voucher register and/or check register as appropriate:

 **L01** *(30 min)*

201X

July 5 Purchased merchandise on account for $2,200 from Daisy Company; terms 5/10, n/30; voucher no. 280 was prepared authorizing payment on July 15.

    8 Purchased merchandise on account for $5,800 from Hank Company; terms 5/10, n/30; voucher no. 281 was prepared authorizing payment on July 18.

    15 Paid amount due Daisy Company from voucher no. 280; check no. 91.

    18 Paid amount due Hank Company from voucher no. 281; check no. 92.

    29 Voucher no. 282 was prepared for July rent to be paid to Lacy Realty, $2,600.

    30 Purchased office equipment on account for $3,300 from Lydie Company; voucher no. 283 was prepared.

    30 Paid amount due Lacy Realty from voucher no. 282; check no. 93.

Check Figure:
July 18
Dr. Vouchers Payable $5,800
Cr. Purchases Discount $290
Cr. Cash $5,510

23A-3. Jace Corporation has been using a voucher system for several years and records invoices at gross. Prepare entries in the voucher register and check register for the following transactions:

 **L01,2** *(45 min)*

201X

Sept. 1 Purchased merchandise inventory on account from Rocco Corporation for $6,400; terms 2/10, n/30; voucher no. 68 was prepared.

    5 Purchased merchandise inventory on account from Raine Corporation for $7,200; terms 2/10, n/30; voucher no. 69 was prepared.

    8 Issued check no. 75 to pay for voucher no. 69.

    10 Issued check no. 76 to pay for voucher no. 68.

    14 Purchased merchandise inventory on account from Lani Corporation for $9,000; terms 2/10, n/30; voucher no. 70 was prepared.

    17 Returned $3,400 of merchandise to Lani Corporation due to poor workmanship; voucher no. 71 was prepared to replace voucher no. 70.

    20 Issued check no. 77 to pay for voucher no. 71.

Check Figure:
Sept. 8
Dr. Vouchers Payable $7,200
Cr. Purchases Discount $144
Cr. Cash $7,056

23A-4. The Sikes Company uses a voucher system and records invoices at gross. Record the following transactions in the voucher register and/or check register as appropriate:

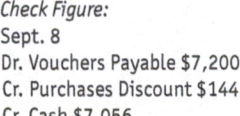 **L01,2** *(60 min)*

201X

Oct.	1	Voucher no. 500 was prepared for the purchase of $4,000 worth of merchandise inventory on account from Roland Company; terms 2/10, n/30.
	2	Voucher no. 501 was prepared for freight-in that was to be paid to Labaro Company, $290.
	3	Office supplies were purchased on account from Macaskill Company for $490; terms 2/10, n/30; voucher no. 502 was prepared.
	8	Check no. 630 was issued in payment of voucher no. 500.
	10	Purchased office equipment on account from Herm Company for $10,900; payment is to be in two equal installments. Vouchers nos. 503 and 504 were prepared to cover these payments.
	12	Check no. 631 was issued to pay voucher no. 503.
	12	Check no. 632 was issued to pay voucher no. 501.
	18	Purchased $6,200 of merchandise on account from Lou Corporation; terms 2/10, n/30; voucher no. 505 was prepared.
	20	Purchased $2,900 of merchandise on account from Karl Company; terms 2/10, n/30; voucher no. 506 was prepared.
	25	Check no. 633 was issued to pay voucher no. 505.
	27	Returned $1,250 of merchandise bought from Karl Company; voucher no. 506 was canceled and voucher no. 507 was prepared.
	29	Issued check no. 634 to pay voucher no. 507.

Check Figure:
Oct 25
Dr. Vouchers Payable $6,200
Cr. Purchases Discount $124
Cr. Cash $6,076

Set B

(30 min) **L01**

S50 / **QB**

23B-1. Fairwell Company uses a voucher system. Record the following transactions in the voucher register:

201X

June	8	Purchased office equipment on account from Taffy Corporation, $700; voucher no. 300 was prepared.
	12	Established a petty cash fund of $150; voucher no. 301 was prepared.
	14	Purchased merchandise on account from Seko Corporation, $800; voucher no. 302 was prepared.
	15	Purchased office supplies on account from Longview Corp., $1,100; voucher no. 303 was prepared.
	29	Voucher no. 304 was prepared to replenish the petty cash fund based on the following receipts: supplies, $84; postage, $52.

Check Figure:
June 12
Dr. Petty Cash (sundry) $150
Cr. Vouchers Payable $150

(30 min) **L01**

23B-2. Saidi Corporation uses a voucher system and records invoices at gross. Record the following transactions in the voucher register and/or check register as appropriate:

201X

July	5	Purchased merchandise on account for $1,600 from Dara Company; terms 7/10, n/30; voucher no. 280 was prepared authorizing payment on July 15.
	8	Purchased merchandise on account for $6,600 from Hart Company; terms 7/10, n/30; voucher no. 281 was prepared authorizing payment on July 18.
	15	Paid amount due Dara from voucher no. 280; check no. 91.
	18	Paid amount due Hart from voucher no. 281; check no. 92.
	29	Voucher no. 282 was prepared for July rent to be paid to Leah Realty, $2,000.
	30	Purchased office equipment on account for $3,600 from Lynna Company; voucher no. 283 was prepared.
	30	Paid amount due Leah Realty from voucher no. 282; check no. 93.

Check Figure:
July 18
Dr. Vouchers Payable $6,600
Cr. Purchases Discount $462
Cr. Cash $6,138

23B-3. Joie Corporation has been using a voucher system for several years and records invoices at gross. Prepare entries in the voucher register and check register for the following transactions:

 **LO1,2** *(45 min)*

201X

Sept. 1 Purchased merchandise inventory on account from River Corporation for $6,800; terms 3/10, n/30; voucher no. 68 was prepared.

5 Purchased merchandise inventory on account from Reed Corporation for $7,400; terms 3/10, n/30; voucher no. 69 was prepared.

8 Issued check no. 75 to pay for voucher no. 69.

10 Issued check no. 76 to pay for voucher no. 68.

14 Purchased merchandise inventory on account from Lucy Corporation for $9,100; terms 3/10, n/30; voucher no. 70 was prepared.

17 Returned $3,100 of the merchandise to Lucy Corporation due to poor workmanship; voucher no. 71 was prepared to replace voucher no. 70.

20 Issued check no. 77 to pay for voucher 71.

Check Figure:
Sept. 8
Dr. Vouchers Payable $7,400
Cr. Purchases Discount $222
Cr. Cash $7,178

23B-4. The Swellon Company uses a voucher system and records invoices at gross. Record the following transactions in the voucher register and/or check register as appropriate:

 **LO1,2** *(60 min)*

201X

Dec. 1 Voucher no. 250 was prepared for the purchase of $3,600 worth of merchandise inventory on account from Rodney Company; terms 2/10, n/30.

2 Voucher no. 251 was prepared for freight-in that was to be paid to Labatt Company, $330.

3 Office supplies were purchased on account from Marsha Company for $500; terms 2/10, n/30; voucher no. 252 was prepared.

8 Check no. 640 was issued in payment of voucher no. 250.

10 Purchased office equipment on account from Hanks Company for $9,800; payment is to be in two equal installments. Voucher nos. 253 and 254 were prepared to cover these payments.

12 Check no. 641 was issued to pay voucher no. 253.

12 Check no. 642 was issued to pay voucher no. 251.

18 Purchased $6,000 of merchandise on account from Lenny Corporation; terms 2/10, n/30; voucher no. 255 was prepared.

20 Purchased $2,800 of merchandise on account from Kull Company; terms 2/10, n/30; voucher no. 256 was prepared.

25 Check no. 643 was issued to pay voucher no. 255.

27 Returned $1,050 of merchandise bought from Kull Company; voucher no. 256 was canceled and voucher no. 257 was prepared.

29 Issued check no. 644 to pay voucher no. 257.

Check Figure:
Dec. 25
Dr. Vouchers Payable $6,000
Cr. Purchases Discount $120
Cr. Cash $ 5,880

Financial Report Problem

MyLabAccounting

Reading Amazon's Annual Report

Go to **https://tinyurl.com/slaterca14e** to access Amazon's 2016 Annual Report. Do you think Amazon uses a voucher system?

 **LO1** *(20 min)*

Departmental Accounting

24

CHAPTER PREVIEW: ACCOUNTING IN ACTION

Sonia Reyes went to her local Barnes & Noble bookstore and noticed how much space was being devoted to toys and electronics. Why the change? Toys and electronics are more profitable than some categories of books. Thus, Barnes & Noble consolidated some of its book offerings to make space for new lines of products, related to technology and other items like children's toys. In this chapter, we focus on departmental accounting to see which departments warrant expansion and which need to be consolidated or even closed based on financial performance. Businesses are always looking to maximize the performance of their business units as this directly affects their profitability.

Learning Objectives – Relating Accounting Theory By Unit

LO1   Explain the Income Statement Focused on Gross Profit by Departments

LO2   Explain How Operating Expenses Are Broken Down by Departments

LO3   Explain Contribution Margin on the Income Statement: Calculate Contribution Margin

Many large companies like Barnes & Noble find it necessary to keep separate accounting records for their various departments so that management can see how efficient each department is and how each contributes to overall performance. This chapter focuses on various accounting and reporting aids that allow management to do so.

We use as our example Diamond's Department Store, which sells mainly clothing. The manager of the adult clothing department at the store is quite concerned about the department's performance; upper management is discussing the possibility of reducing the space of the adult department in favor of expanding the children's department.

LEARNING UNIT 24-1

LO1

Profit center Unit or department that incurs costs and generates revenues.

Cost center Unit or department that incurs costs but does not generate revenues.

Figure 24.1
Income Statement for Diamond's Department Store

The Income Statement Focused on Gross Profit by Departments

Each department of Diamond's Department Store is a unit in which the manager has the responsibility for controlling and incurring certain costs as well as generating revenue. Each unit, or department, is known as a profit center. If a manager had the responsibility for controlling costs, but not for directly generating revenue, the unit would be called a cost center (an example is the office maintenance department at Diamond's).

Figure 24.1 shows the income statement for Diamond's Department Store. As you can see from this figure, the total gross profit of the company is $373,800 ($841,300 − $467,500), and the operating expenses are $170,000.

DIAMOND'S DEPARTMENT STORE INCOME STATEMENT FOR YEAR ENDED DECEMBER 31, 201X			
Revenue from Sales:			
Sales		$ 870 0 0 0 00	
Less: Sales Returns and Allowances	$ 14 7 0 0 00		
Sales Discount	14 0 0 0 00	28 7 0 0 00	
Net Sales			$ 841 3 0 0 00
Cost of Goods Sold			$ 467 5 0 0 00
Gross Profit on Sales			373 8 0 0 00
Operating Expenses			170 0 0 0 00
Income Before Taxes			203 8 0 0 00
Income Tax Expense			89 5 2 0 00
Net Income			$ 114 2 8 0 00

To break down the gross profit figure by department, a company must gather information about each department. It does so by setting up separate accounting records for each department, with separate accounts for Sales, Sales Returns and Allowances, Sales Discount, and Cost of Goods Sold. Once this information is separated by department, we can calculate the gross profit for each department. Today, computers make it possible to record and gather information for many departments easily and quickly.

Let's look at an example. Figure 24.2 on the following page shows how the sales journal of Diamond's Department Store includes a Sales account for the children's department and one for the adult department. In the Chapter 12 Appendix, sales journals were introduced. The sales journal represents where sales on account transactions are recorded.

DIAMOND'S DEPARTMENT STORE SALES JOURNAL								
Date		Account Debited	Invoice Number	Post. Ref.	Accounts Receivable Dr.	Children's Sales Cr.	Adult Sales Cr.
Nov. 3		Marsie Rose	325	✔	1 9 0 00	1 0 0 00	9 0 00
8		Bill Stone	326	✔	1 8 5 00	1 7 5 00	1 0 00
					(1 1 5)	(4 1 1)	(4 1 2)

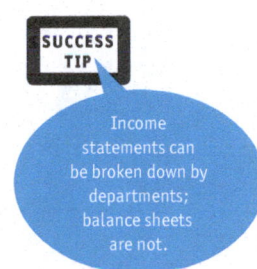

Figure 24.2
Sales Journal of Diamond's
Department Store

The income statement in Figure 24.3 on the following page shows the gross profit for each department and the combined totals. You would not see a balance sheet prepared in this way, broken down by department; only an income statement is prepared this way. Keep in mind that an income statement indicates how well a business or department is performing.

Now let's check your progress.

SUCCESS TIP

Income statements can be broken down by departments; balance sheets are not.

 ## TRY IT!   Learning Unit 24-1

Rearrange the following accounts as you would see them on an income statement from top to bottom:

Sales Discount; Sales Returns and Allowances; Operating Expenses; Sales; Cost of Goods Sold; Gross Profit; Net Sales; Net Income or Loss

TRY IT!   Solution Learning Unit 24-1

Sales; Sales Returns and Allowances; Sales Discounts; Net Sales; Cost of Goods Sold; Gross Profit; Operating Expenses; Net Income or Loss

How Operating Expenses are Broken Down by Departments

LEARNING UNIT 24-2

 L02

Departmental Income from Operations

So far we have looked at the way gross profit is accumulated by department. In this unit we look at how the $170,000 of operating expenses can be allocated by department if we want to extend departmental reporting beyond gross profit.

The operating expenses of Diamond's Department Store that can be traced and identified directly to separate departments are called direct expenses. An example is the salaries of the salespeople who work only for the children's department at Diamond's. The operating expenses that cannot be identified with a specific department but are incurred on behalf of the company are called indirect expenses. An example is the expense incurred in the upkeep of the building in which Diamond's is located. Since indirect costs cannot be directly traced to a department, they must be allocated using a factor like square footage or percent of sales.

Direct expenses Expenses that can be traced directly to a specific department.

Indirect expenses Expenses that cannot be traced directly to one department.

Figure 24.3 Income Statement with Gross Profit Broken Down by Department

DIAMOND'S DEPARTMENT STORE
INCOME STATEMENT SHOWING DEPARTMENTAL GROSS PROFIT
FOR YEAR ENDED DECEMBER 31, 201X

	Children's		Adult		Total	
Revenue from Sales:						
Sales	$580 000 00		$290 000 00		$870 000 00	
Less: Sales Returns and Allowances	$6 500 00		$8 200 00			
Sales Discounts	8 000 00	14 500 00	6 000 00	14 200 00	28 700 00	
Net Sales		$565 500 00		$275 800 00		$841 300 00
Cost of Goods Sold		$269 900 00		$197 600 00		$467 500 00
Gross Profit on Sales		$295 600 00		$78 200 00		$373 800 00
Operating Expenses						170 000 00
Income Before Taxes						203 800 00
Income Tax Expense						89 520 00
Net Income						$114 280 00

In Figure 24.4, we can see a sample of operating expenses that can now be apportioned to the children's and adult departments.

Figure 24.4
Operating Expenses Apportioned
by Department

DIAMOND'S DEPARTMENT STORE INCOME STATEMENT SHOWING DEPARTMENTAL INCOME BEFORE TAX FOR YEAR ENDED DECEMBER 31, 201X			
	Children's	Adult	Totals
Net Sales	$565 500 00	$275 800 00	$841 300 00
Cost of Goods Sold	269 900 00	197 600 00	467 500 00
Gross Profit on Sales	$295 600 00	$ 78 200 00	$373 800 00
Operating Expenses:			
Sales Salaries	$ 25 000 00	$ 15 000 00	$ 40 000 00
Building Expense	12 000 00	4 000 00	16 000 00
Delivery Expense	6 000 00	4 000 00	10 000 00
Advertising Expense	9 000 00	5 000 00	14 000 00
Depreciation Expense	22 500 00	7 500 00	30 000 00
Administrative Expense	40 000 00	20 000 00	60 000 00
Total Operating Expenses	$114 500 00	$ 55 500 00	$170 000 00
Income Before Taxes	$181 100 00	$ 22 700 00	$203 800 00
Income Tax Expense			89 520 00
Net Income			$114 280 00

Note that the total is still $170,000. Now let's see how these figures for operating expenses were calculated. Figure 24.5 is a summary of how the expenses were apportioned. Following that is a detailed explanation. Use Figure 24.5 as a reference as you read the explanation.

Figure 24.5 Direct and Indirect Operating Expenses by Department

	Children's		Adult		Total Operating Expenses	
	Direct	Indirect	Direct	Indirect	Direct	Indirect
(1) Sales Salaries	$25,000.00		$15,000.00		$40,000.00	
(2) Building Expense		$12,000.00		$ 4,000.00		$ 16,000.00
(3) Delivery Expense	6,000.00		4,000.00		10,000.00	
(4) Advertising Expense	7,000.00	2,000.00	4,000.00	1,000.00	11,000.00	3,000.00
(5) Depreciation Expense		22,500.00		7,500.00		30,000.00
(6) Administrative Expense		40,000.00		20,000.00		60,000.00
	$38,000.00	$76,500.00	$23,000.00	$32,500.00	$61,000.00	$109,000.00
					$170,000	

1. **Sales Salaries** The payroll records of Diamond's show that salespeople in the children's department were paid $25,000 and salespeople in the adult department were paid $15,000. These expenses can be identified with specific departments, so they are considered direct expenses.

2. **Building Expense** The costs relating to the occupancy of the Diamond's building are lumped into an account called Building Expense. Building Expense is an indirect expense, apportioned on the basis of square footage. Diamond's allocates the total cost of Building Expense of $16,000 on the basis of the number of square feet

that each department occupies. Diamond's total space is 40,000 square feet, with the children's department occupying 30,000 square feet and the adult department occupying 10,000 square feet. Building Expense is allocated to each department as follows:

Children's	Adult
$\dfrac{30{,}000\ \text{ft}^2}{40{,}000\ \text{ft}^2} = 0.75 = 75\%$	$\dfrac{10{,}000\ \text{ft}^2}{40{,}000\ \text{ft}^2} = 0.25 = 25\%$
$0.75 \times \$16{,}000 = \$12{,}000$	$0.25 \times \$16{,}000 = \$4{,}000$

Thus, of the $16,000 in Building Expense, the children's department is allocated $12,000 and the adult department $4,000.

3. **Delivery Expense** The children's department shipped 60% of all merchandise, and the adult department shipped 40%. The total cost of Delivery Expense is $10,000. Because the exact amount of Delivery Expense is traceable to each department, it is considered a direct expense. If the cost of delivery is *not* specifically traceable to each department, it is considered an indirect expense and can be charged to departments based on past delivery records. Delivery Expense is calculated as follows:

Children's	Adult
$0.60 \times \$10{,}000 = \$6{,}000$	$0.40 \times \$10{,}000 = \$4{,}000$

4. **Advertising Expense** Advertising Expense for Diamond's totaled $14,000. Of that total, $4,000 was spent on advertising adult clothes and $7,000 on advertising children's clothes. The remaining $3,000 ($14,000 − $11,000) was spent on advertising the store's image in general. Thus, this $3,000 is an indirect expense. How would you divide this expense by department? One common way is to apportion it based on gross sales of each department, as follows:

Gross Sales:	$580,000	Children's
	290,000	Adult
	$870,000	Total Gross Sales

Children's	Adult
$\dfrac{\$580{,}000}{\$870{,}000} \times \$3{,}000$	$\dfrac{\$290{,}000}{\$870{,}000} \times \$3{,}000$
$= \tfrac{2}{3} \times \$3{,}000 = \$2{,}000$	$= \tfrac{1}{3} \times \$3{,}000 = \$1{,}000$

Thus, of the $3,000 of indirect expenses, $2,000 is charged to the children's department and $1,000 to the adult department.

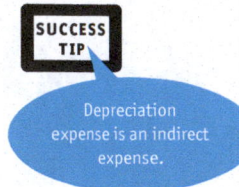

SUCCESS TIP

Depreciation expense is an indirect expense.

5. **Depreciation Expense** Diamond's Department Store apportions depreciation on its building based on the square footage each department occupies. (Some companies apportion depreciation based on the average cost of the equipment in each department.) Diamond's has 40,000 square feet, of which the children's department takes up 30,000 (3/4) and the adult department takes up 10,000 (1/4). The amount of Depreciation Expense charged to each department is calculated as follows:

Children's	Adult
$\tfrac{3}{4} \times \$30{,}000 = \$22{,}500$	$\tfrac{1}{4} \times \$30{,}000 = \$7{,}500$

6. **Administrative Expense** Administrative expenses are incurred for the company as a whole and are not broken down by department; they are thus indirect expenses. In the case of Diamond's, it was decided that the Administrative Expense of $60,000 would be divided on the basis of each department's gross sales. We saw this method of allocation used for Advertising Expense. The calculation for indirect expenses charged to each department is as follows:

$580,000	Children's
290,000	Adult
$870,000	Total Gross Sales

Children's	Adult
$\dfrac{\$580,000}{\$870,000} = \dfrac{2}{3}$	$\dfrac{\$290,000}{\$870,000} = \dfrac{1}{3}$
$\dfrac{2}{3} \times \$60,000 = \$40,000$	$\dfrac{1}{3} \times \$60,000 = \$20,000$

Take a moment to review Figures 24.4 and 24.5 to make sure you understand how we arrived at the total operating expenses of $170,000.

Now let's check your progress.

 **TRY IT!** **Learning Unit 24-2**

Given the following, apportion the rent expense on the basis of floor space:

	Dept. A	Dept. B	Total
Floor space	247,500	202,500	450,000
Rent expense			$130,000

TRY IT! **Solution Learning Unit 24-2**

Dept. A: $247,500 / $450,000 × $130,000 = $71,500
Dept. B: $202,500 / $450,000 × $130,000 = $58,500

Contribution Margin on the Income Statement

 LEARNING UNIT 24-3

L03

As shown in Figure 24.4 in Learning Unit 24-2, income before taxes for the children's department equaled $181,100 and the adult department equaled $22,700. Some accountants think these figures are misleading because the indirect expenses in Figure 24.5 were apportioned to the total operating expenses of each department. An alternative to this approach to indirect expense allocation is shown in Figure 24.6, which lists direct departmental expenses and the contribution each department makes to cover indirect expenses. This breakdown is called the contribution margin, which can also be defined as the gross profit of a department minus its direct expenses. This approach charges to a department only those expenses that are directly traceable to it. Note in Figure 24.6 that the children's department contributes $257,600 to cover indirect expenses and net income. This figure is quite different from the $181,100 listed in Figure 24.4.

Contribution margin Department's net profit, used to cover indirect expenses.

Supporters of this approach think indirect expenses are not controlled by the department manager and thus should not be used in evaluating departmental performance. Some accountants contend that even if a department is eliminated, the indirect expenses would not be decreased. For example, Diamond's spends $3,000 in advertising that is basically aimed at advertising the store's overall image, and that expense would still remain if the adult department or the children's department were eliminated.

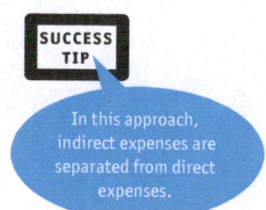
SUCCESS TIP

In this approach, indirect expenses are separated from direct expenses.

Figure 24.6
Income Statement Showing
Departmental Contribution
Margin

DIAMOND'S DEPARTMENT STORE INCOME STATEMENT SHOWING DEPARTMENTAL CONTRIBUTION MARGIN FOR YEAR ENDED DECEMBER 31, 201X			
	Children's	Adult	Totals
Net Sales	$ 565 500 00	$ 275 800 00	$ 841 300 00
Cost of Goods Sold	269 900 00	197 600 00	467 500 00
Gross Profit on Sales	$ 295 600 00	$ 78 200 00	373 800 00
Direct Departmental Expenses			
Sales Salaries	$ 25 000 00	$ 15 000 00	$ 40 000 00
Advertising Expense	7 000 00	4 000 00	11 000 00
Delivery Expense	6 000 00	4 000 00	10 000 00
Total Direct Departmental Expenses	$ 38 000 00	$ 23 000 00	$ 61 000 00
Contribution Margin	$ 257 600 00	$ 55 200 00	$ 312 800 00
Indirect Departmental Expenses			
Building Expense			$ 16 000 00
Advertising Expense			3 000 00
Depreciation Expense			30 000 00
Administrative Expense			60 000 00
Total Indirect Expenses			$ 109 000 00
Income Before Taxes			$ 203 800 00
Income Tax Expense			89 520 00
Net Income			$ 114 280 00

Determining whether certain departments at Diamond's should be expanded or reduced would involve investigation of the financial reports presented in the chapter along with topics such as:

1. The effect that dropping a department would have in terms of loss of its contribution margin. For example, would closing a jewelry department in a clothing store reduce the store's total administrative expenses?

2. The effect one department has in drawing customers to other departments. Do customers who come into the store to look at jewelry go on to look at dresses in another department?

3. Trends in the industry. Even though a certain department is not doing well, all the competing stores have such a department; the answer may be to cut down the size of the department rather than eliminate it.

4. Ability of suppliers to meet increasing demand for items. For example, it would not be a good idea to open a pastry shop in Diamond's until one had lined up a number of good, reliable suppliers.

We conclude this unit with an example that shows how eliminating a department that has a net loss but a positive contribution margin may in fact cause an even greater loss in the overall net income for the company. The situation is as follows:

	Depts. A, B, C	Dept. D Only	Totals for Depts. A–D	Totals if Dept. D Is Eliminated
Sales	$1,469,000	$130,000	$1,599,000	$1,469,000
Cost of Goods Sold	869,000	82,000	951,000	869,000
Gross Profit	$ 600,000	$ 48,000	$ 648,000	$ 600,000
Direct Expenses	340,000	31,000	371,000	340,000
Contribution Margin	$ 260,000	$ 17,000	$ 277,000	$ 260,000
Indirect Expenses	130,000	26,000	156,000	156,000
Net Income (Loss)	$ 130,000	$ (9,000)	$ 121,000	$ 104,000

Note that if Department D is eliminated, net income of the other departments is reduced by $17,000, from $121,000 to $104,000. This change is the result of losing the contribution margin of $17,000 from Department D.

Now let's check your progress.

 **TRY IT!**   **Learning Unit 24-3**

Given the following, calculate the contribution margin for each of these two departments:

	Dept. A	Dept. B
Net Sales	$67,000	$76,000
Cost of Goods Sold	43,000	36,000
Direct Departmental Expenses		
Sales Salaries	4,000	13,000
Advertising	12,000	6,000

TRY IT!   **Solution Learning Unit 24-3**

Dept. A: $67,000 − $43,000 = $24,000 GP − $16,000 (total direct) = $8,000 contribution margin

Dept. B: $76,000 − $36,000 = $40,000 GP − $19,000 (total direct) = $21,000 contribution margin

DEMONSTRATION SUMMARY PROBLEM

Dick Jones, accountant for Better Buy Co., is holding a workshop for employees so that they will better understand the importance of accounting in analyzing each department. He has set up three problems to present. Please work them out for Dick. We show each problem (requirement) and solution separately.

Requirement 1

The cost of rent of $3,000 for Better Buy Co. is appropriated to each department based on its sales. Given the following information, assign the cost of rent to each department:

	Jewelry	Hardware	Automotive
Sales	$30,000	$50,000	$20,000

Solution for Requirement 1

$30,000/$100,000 × $3,000 = $900 Jewelry

$50,000/$100,000 × $3,000 = $1,500 Hardware

$20,000/$100,000 × $3,000 = $600 Automotive

Tip

Take each department sales over the total of $100,000.

Requirement 2

From the following information, calculate departmental income before tax and final net income. Assume a tax rate of 36%.

	Bakery	Deli
Net Sales	$180,000	$220,000
Cost of Goods Sold	95,000	105,000
Delivery Expense	18,000	30,000
Advertising Expense	21,000	20,500
Depreciation Expense	19,000	20,000

Solution for Requirement 2

	Bakery	Deli	Total
Net Sales	$180,000	$220,000	$400,000
Cost of Goods Sold	95,000	105,000	200,000
Gross Profit on Sales	$ 85,000	$115,000	$200,000
Operating Expenses			
Advertising Expense	21,000	20,500	41,500
Delivery Expense	18,000	30,000	48,000
Depreciation Expense	19,000	20,000	39,000
Total Operating Expenses	$ 58,000	$ 70,500	$128,500
Income Before Taxes	$ 27,000	$ 44,500	$ 71,500
Income Tax Expense			25,740
Net Income			$ 45,760

SUCCESS TIP

Net Sales − Cost of Goods Sold = Gross Profit − Operating Expenses = Net Income

Requirement 3

Calculate the contribution margin for each department and net loss for both departments based on the following information:

	Sporting Goods 11,000 sq. feet	Cosmetics 19,000 sq. feet
Net Sales	$60,000	$82,000
Cost of Goods Sold	26,000	60,000

Sales Salaries $9,000 (50% directly related to Sporting Goods and 50% directly related to Cosmetics)

Rent Expense $8,000

Advertising Expense $40,000 ($2,000 directly related to Sporting Goods and $8,000 directly related to Cosmetics)

Solution for Requirement 3

	Sporting Goods	Cosmetics	Total
Net Sales	$60,000	$82,000	$142,000
Cost of Goods Sold	26,000	60,000	86,000
Gross Profit on Sales	$34,000	$22,000	$ 56,000
Direct Dept. Expenses			
Sales Salaries	4,500	4,500	9,000
Advertising Expense	2,000	8,000	10,000
Total Direct Dept. Expenses	$ 6,500	$12,500	$ 19,000
Contribution Margin	$27,500	$ 9,500	$ 37,000
Indirect Departmental Expenses			
Rent Expense			8,000
Advertising Expense			30,000
Total Indirect Expenses			$ 38,000
Net Loss			($ 1,000)

SUCCESS TIP

Advertising is both a Direct and Indirect Expense; $10,000 is directly related to the departments, and the other $30,000 is the Indirect Expense.

SUCCESS COACH

The following Success Tips are from Learning Units 24-1 to 24-3. Take the Do It Right Now Checkup and use the Check Your Score at the bottom of the page to see how you are doing. The Success Coach provides tips before each Checkup to help you avoid common accounting errors.

LU 24-1 The Income Statement Focused on Gross Profit by Departments

Do It Right Tips: The profit center is a unit or department in which the manager has responsibility for controlling costs and generating revenue. In a cost center, the manager only controls costs and not revenue.

Do It Right Now Checkup: Answer true or false to the following statements.

1. The balance sheet can be broken down by departments.
2. Cost centers control revenues.
3. Sales Returns and Allowances are not used in departmental accounting.
4. Gross profit is the same as net income.
5. Departmental sales could be broken down in a sales journal.

LU 24-2 How Operating Expenses Are Broken Down by Departments

Do It Right Tips: If an expense can be directly related to a specific department, it is called a direct expense. Those expenses not directly related to a specific department are called indirect expenses.

Do It Right Now Checkup: Answer true or false to the following statements.

1. Depreciation is a direct expense.
2. Sales salaries are indirect expenses.
3. Administrative expenses are direct expenses.
4. Advertising expense could be both an indirect and a direct expense.
5. A building expense would be an indirect expense.

LU 24-3 Contribution Margin on the Income Statement

Do It Right Tips: The indirect expenses are not combined with direct expenses when income statements are prepared showing the contribution margin. Remember that the contribution margin is gross profit less direct departmental expenses.

Do It Right Now Checkup: Answer true or false to the following statements.

1. The contribution margin is gross profit plus departmental expenses.
2. In contribution margin calculations, indirect expenses are not separated from direct expenses.
3. Eliminating a department with a positive contribution margin could cause a company even higher losses.
4. Net income and the contribution margin are the same.
5. Depreciation expense is used in calculating the contribution margin.

CHECK YOUR SCORE: Answers to the Do It Right Now Checkup

LU 24-1

1. False—The income statement can be broken down by departments.
2. False—Cost centers only control costs.
3. False—Sales Returns and Allowances are used in departmental accounting.
4. False—Gross profit is not the same as net income.
5. True

LU 24-2

1. False—Depreciation is an indirect expense.
2. False—Sales salaries are direct expenses.
3. False—Administrative expenses are indirect expenses.
4. True
5. True

LU 24-3

1. False—The contribution margin is gross profit minus departmental expenses.
2. False—In contribution margin calculations, indirect expenses are separated from direct expenses.
3. True
4. False—Net income is the bottom line, while contribution margin shows gross profit on sales minus direct departmental expenses.
5. False—Depreciation expense is not used in calculating the contribution margin.

BLUEPRINT: DEPARTMENTAL ACCOUNTING

		Dept. A	Dept. B	Total*
Situation 1: Income statement showing departmental gross profit	Net Sales	1	2	3 (1 + 2)
	− Cost of Goods Sold	4	5	6 (4 + 5)
	= Gross Profit on Sales	7 (1 − 4)	8 (2 − 5)	9 (3 − 6)
	− Operating Expenses			10
	= Income Before Taxes			11 (9 − 10)
	− Income Tax Expense			12
	= Net Income			13 (11 − 12)

		Dept. A	Dept. B	Total
Situation 2: Income statement showing departmental income before tax	Net Sales	1	2	3 (1 + 2)
	Cost of Goods Sold	4	5	6 (4 + 5)
	Gross Profit on Sales	7 (1 − 4)	8 (2 − 5)	9 (3 − 6)
	Operating Expenses			
Direct and indirect expenses allocated	Salaries Expense	10	11	12 (10 + 11)
	Delivery Expense	13	14	15 (13 + 14)
	Depreciation Expense	16	17	18 (16 + 17)
	Administrative Expense	19	20	21 (19 + 20)
	Total Operating Expenses	22 (10 + 13 + 16 + 19)	23 (11 + 14 + 17 + 20)	24 (12 + 15 + 18 + 21)
	Income Before Taxes	25 (7 − 22)	26 (8 − 23)	27 (9 − 24)
	Income Tax Expense			28
	Net Income			29 (27 − 28)

		Dept. A	Dept. B	Total
Situation 3: Income statement showing departmental contributions to indirect expenses	Net Sales	1	2	3 (1 + 2)
	Cost of Goods Sold	4	5	6 (4 + 5)
	Gross Profit on Sales	7 (1 − 4)	8 (2 − 5)	9 (3 − 6)
	Direct Departmental Expenses			
	Sales Salaries	10	11	12 (10 + 11)
	Advertising Expense	13	14	15 (13 + 14)
	Delivery Expense	16	17	18 (16 + 17)
	Total Direct Expenses	19 (10 + 13 + 16)	20 (11 + 14 + 17)	21 (12 + 15 + 18)
	Contribution to Indirect Expenses	22 (7 − 19)	23 (8 − 20)	24 (9 − 21)
	Indirect Departmental Expenses			
	Building Expense			25
	Advertising Expense			26
	Depreciation Expense			27
	Total Indirect Expenses			28 (25 + 26 + 27)
	Income Before Taxes			29 (24 − 28)
	Income Tax Expense			30
	Net Income			31 (29 − 30)

* These numbers do not show calculations but show order of operations.

Discussion Questions and Critical Thinking/Ethical Case

1. What is the difference between a cost center and a profit center?

2. Explain how gross profit is calculated.

3. Special journals are not used in departmental accounting. Agree or disagree? Please explain.

4. Compare and contrast indirect expenses and direct expenses.

5. Explain how advertising expense could be both a direct cost and an indirect cost for a company.

6. Square footage is often used to allocate indirect costs to various departments within a company. Agree or disagree?

7. An income statement showing departmental income before tax does not list individual operating expenses for each department. Agree or disagree? Please explain.

8. Explain why a company might prepare an income statement showing each department's contribution margin.

9. Hernando Favor had been working in the bakery department of Long Company for 4 years when he was promoted to the accounting department. Since his promotion, sales in the bakery department have slipped, and management is considering cutting the department in half. Hal Moore, who works in the bakery, will be laid off. Hernando thought about shifting some of the sales figures in his accounting records to the bakery department from other departments in order to save his friend Hal from losing his job. Hernando thinks no one will find out in the long run because he knows the bakery can increase sales. Do you feel Hernando has clear justification for his actions? You make the call. Write down your recommendation to Hernando.

MyLabAccounting

Concept Checks

Appropriating Rent to Departments Based on Sales

(10 min) **L02**

1. The cost of rent of $25,000 for Kable Co. is appropriated to each department based on its sales. Given the following, assign the cost of rent to each department:

Rent	Toys Sales	Clothing Sales
$25,000	$15,200	$60,800

Appropriating Fire Insurance Based on Square Footage

(10 min) **L02**

2. Calculate the assignment of fire insurance of $30,000 to each department based on square footage.

Indirect Expense	Basis of Assignment	Bakery	Grocery
Fire Insurance	5,800 square feet total	1,160 square feet	4,640 square feet

Calculating Net Income from Total Operating Expenses

(15 min) **L02**

3. Given the following, calculate net income:

	Dept. 1	Dept. 2	
Net Sales	$38,000	$46,000	
Cost of Goods Sold	18,000	36,000	
Operating Expenses			$21,150
Income Tax Expense, 40% rate			

Calculating Departmental Net Income

LO2 *(20 min)*

4. From the following, calculate departmental income before tax. Assume a tax rate of 20%.

	Dept. A	Dept. B
Net Sales	$4,000	$6,000
Cost of Goods Sold	2,000	2,200
Delivery Expense	640	830
Advertising Expense	490	630
Depreciation Expense	270	370

Calculating Contribution Margin

LO3 *(30 min)*

5. Calculate the contribution margin for each department and income before taxes, based on the following:

	Dept. A 1,500 square feet	Dept. B 3,600 square feet
Net Sales	$5,500	$11,200
Cost of Goods Sold	2,100	5,600
Sales Salaries	$ 550 (20% directly related to Dept. A and 80% related to Dept. B)	
Rent Expense	$ 950 for both departments combined	
Advertising Expense	$1,100 ($900 directly related to Dept. A and $200 related to Dept. B)	

Exercises

MyLabAccounting

Set A

24A-1. The cost of rent of $9,000 for Wilberg Company is appropriated to each department based on its sales. Given the following, assign the cost of rent to each department:

LO2 *(20 min)*

	Jewelry	Hardware	Automotive
Sales	$24,000	$41,280	$30,720

24A-2. Complete the assignment of fire insurance expense to each department.

LO2 *(20 min)*

Indirect Expense	Amount	Basis of Assignment	Candy Sales	Ice Cream Sales	Pizza Sales
Fire Insurance	$115,000	33,000 sq. ft.	a. 15,510 sq. ft.	b. 9,240 sq. ft.	c. 8,250 sq. ft.

24A-3. Given the following, calculate net income:

LO2 *(20 min)*

	Dept. 1	Dept. 2
Net Sales	$39,000	$43,000
Cost of Goods Sold	24,000	30,000
Operating Expenses		$16,400
Income Tax Expense, 30% rate		

(20 min) **LO2** **24A-4.** From the following, calculate departmental income before tax. Assume a tax rate of 30%.

	Dept. A	Dept. B
Net Sales	$210,000	$280,000
Cost of Goods Sold	108,000	129,000
Delivery Expense	24,800	28,200
Advertising Expense	23,400	22,050
Depreciation Expense	24,000	22,500

(30 min) **LO3** **24A-5.** Calculate the contribution margin for each department and income before taxes, based on the following:

	Dept. A 12,000 square feet	Dept. B 18,000 square feet
Net Sales	$51,000	$87,000
Cost of Goods Sold	21,000	38,000
Sales Salaries	$6,500 (40% directly related to Dept. A and 60% to Dept. B)	
Rent Expense	$6,000	
Advertising Expense	$27,000 ($1,500 directly related to Dept. A and $7,800 to Dept. B)	

Set B

(20 min) **LO2** **24B-1.** The cost of rent of $8,200 for Lee Company is appropriated to each department based on its sales. Given the following, assign the cost of rent to each department:

	Jewelry	Hardware	Automotive
Sales	$26,320	$47,000	$20,680

(20 min) **LO2** **24B-2.** Complete the assignment of fire insurance expense to each department.

Indirect Expense	Amount	Basis of Assignment	Candy Sales	Ice Cream Sales	Pizza Sales
Fire Insurance	$118,000	31,200 sq. ft.	a. 13,728 sq. ft.	b. 9,048 sq. ft.	c. 8,424 sq. ft.

(20 min) **LO2** **24B-3.** Given the following, calculate net income:

	Dept. 1	Dept. 2
Net Sales	$36,000	$42,000
Cost of Goods Sold	21,000	33,000
Operating Expenses		$16,500
Income Tax Expense, 30% rate		

(20 min) **LO2** **24B-4.** From the following, calculate departmental income before tax. Assume a tax rate of 30%.

	Dept. A	Dept. B
Net Sales	$220,000	$350,000
Cost of Goods Sold	104,000	127,000
Delivery Expense	24,500	28,600
Advertising Expense	23,300	22,300
Depreciation Expense	20,000	23,000

24B-5. Calculate the contribution margin for each department and income before taxes, based on the following:

L03 *(30 min)*

	Dept. A 7,000 square feet	Dept. B 17,000 square feet
Net Sales	$66,000	$81,000
Cost of Goods Sold	24,000	48,000
Sales Salaries	$7,500 (48% directly related to Dept. A and 52% to Dept. B)	
Rent Expense	$5,000	
Advertising Expense	$33,000 ($3,600 directly related to Dept. A and $9,600 to Dept. B)	

Problems

MyLabAccounting

Set A

24A-1. From the following data, prepare in proper form an income statement showing departmental gross profit (assume a 20% tax rate) for Instant Stop for the year ended December 31, 201X.

L02 *(60 min)*

S50 / QB

Cash	$13,000
Accounts Receivable	8,000
Allowance for Doubtful Accounts	1,600
Equipment	16,000
Accumulated Depreciation, Equipment	8,700
Accounts Payable	10,200
B. Smith, Capital	11,000
B. Smith, Withdrawals	3,100
Sales, Grocery	20,000
Sales, Pizza	16,000
Sales Returns and Allowances, Grocery	2,100
Sales Returns and Allowances, Pizza	3,000
COGS, Grocery	8,000
COGS, Pizza	10,100
Total Operating Expenses	4,000

Check Figure:
Total Net Income $7,040

24A-2. Given the following information about the clothing and hardware departments of Herrings Company, prepare a departmental expense allocation sheet showing expenses by department.

L02 *(60 min)*

		Direct Expenses	
Account	Indirect Expenses	Clothing	Hardware
Rent Expense	$13,000		
Insurance Expense	6,600	$1,400	$2,100
Depreciation Expense		350	670
Advertising Expense	2,300		
Supplies Expense	3,250		
Salaries Expense	6,400		

Check Figure:
Total Indirect Expenses $31,550

Additional Facts		
	Clothing	Hardware
Net Sales	$75,000	$38,000
Cost of Goods Sold	57,000	21,000
Floor Space	220 square feet	550 square feet

Allocation Basis	
Rent and Insurance:	Floor space
Advertising and Supplies:	Net sales
Salaries:	Gross Profit of Clothing and Hardware Departments

(50 min) **LO2**

24A-3. From the following partial data, prepare an income statement showing departmental income before tax along with net income for Jay's Corporation for the year ended December 31, 201X.

Net Sales, TVs	$120,000
Net Sales, Washers	24,000
Cost of Goods Sold, TVs	37,000
Cost of Goods Sold, Washers	20,000
Income tax Expense, 35% rate	
TV Dept., 4,400 square feet	
Washers, 4,400 square feet	

Check Figure:
Net Income $48,425

		Basis of Allocation
Sales Salary Expense	$3,900	Net Sales
Building Expense	5,200	Square Footage
Delivery Expense	3,000	Net Sales
Depreciation Expense	400	Square Footage

(60 min) **LO2,3**

24A-4. Sabatini Company has requested that you (1) assign indirect expenses to its jewelry and shoes departments as appropriate and (2) prepare an income statement for August 201X showing departmental contribution margins along with net income. Assume a 25% tax rate.

Check Figure:
Total Indirect Expenses $77,000

	Jewelry (32,000 square feet)	Shoes (12,000 square feet)	Indirect Cost
Net Sales	$277,000	$218,000	
Cost of Goods Sold	203,000	115,000	
Salaries Expense	2,800	1,750	$ 9,900
Depreciation Expense	23,800	21,200	
Advertising Expense	850	2,250	22,000
Administrative Expense			32,600
Rent Expense			12,500

Salaries are based on net sales. All other indirect expenses are based on square footage.

Set B

24B-1. From the following data, prepare in proper form an income statement showing departmental gross profit (assume a 18% tax rate) for Prompt Stop for the year ended December 31, 201X.

◀ **L02**   *(60 min)*

S50 / **QB**

Cash	$13,500
Accounts Receivable	8,000
Allowance for Doubtful Accounts	1,700
Equipment	15,500
Accumulated Depreciation, Equipment	8,900
Accounts Payable	9,900
B. Smades, Capital	12,500
B. Smades, Withdrawals	2,600
Sales, Grocery	20,000
Sales, Pizza	22,000
Sales Returns and Allowances, Grocery	1,700
Sales Returns and Allowances, Pizza	2,800
COGS, Grocery	7,200
COGS, Pizza	10,600
Total Operating Expenses	5,000

Check Figure:
Net Income $12,054

24B-2. Given the following information about the clothing and hardware departments of Nickolas Company, prepare a departmental expense allocation sheet showing expenses by department.

◀ **L02**   *(60 min)*

		Direct Expenses	
Account	**Indirect Expenses**	**Clothing**	**Hardware**
Rent Expense	$16,500		
Insurance Expense	6,200	$1,450	$3,000
Depreciation Expense		320	660
Advertising Expense	1,800		
Supplies Expense	3,250		
Salaries Expense	6,800		

Check Figure:
Total Indirect Expenses $34,550

Additional Facts		
	Clothing	**Hardware**
Net Sales	$72,000	$35,000
Cost of Goods Sold	56,000	19,000
Floor Space	340 square feet	490 square feet

Allocation Basis	
Rent and Insurance:	Floor Space
Advertising and Supplies:	Net Sales
Salaries:	Gross Profit of Clothing and Hardware Departments

(50 min) **LO2**

24B-3.   From the following partial data, prepare an income statement showing departmental income before tax along with net income for Jack's Corporation for the year ended December 31, 201X.

Check Figure:
Net Income $23,100

Net Sales, TVs	$66,000
Net Sales, Washers	33,000
Cost of Goods Sold, TVs	38,000
Cost of Goods Sold, Washers	15,000
Income tax rate, 30%	
TV Dept., 6,000 square feet	
Washers, 2,000 square feet	

		Basis of Allocation
Sales Salary Expense	$5,100	Net Sales
Building Expense	4,200	Square Footage
Delivery Expense	2,100	Net Sales
Depreciation Expense	1,600	Square Footage

(60 min) **LO2,3**

24B-4.   Park Company requested that you (1) assign indirect expenses to its jewelry and shoes departments as appropriate and (2) prepare an income statement for September 201X showing departmental contribution margins along with net income. Assume a 25% tax rate.

Check Figure:
Total Indirect Expenses $73,800

	Jewelry (30,000 square feet)	Shoes (10,000 square feet)	Indirect Cost
Net Sales	$278,000	$222,000	
Cost of Goods Sold	119,500	20,196	
Salaries Expense	3,300	2,000	$ 9,000
Depreciation Expense	24,800	21,200	
Advertising Expense	940	2,200	19,500
Administrative Expense			33,500
Rent Expense			11,800

Salaries are based on net sales. All other indirect expenses are based on square footage.

MyLabAccounting   **Financial Report Problem**

(10 min) **LO1**

Reading Amazon's Annual Report
Go to the 2016 annual report for Amazon at **https://tinyurl.com/slaterca14e**. Go to page 15 and find the amount for leased square footage for North America and International for 2016.

Manufacturing Accounting

CHAPTER PREVIEW: ACCOUNTING IN ACTION

The Josh Samson family visited the Taylor Guitars factory in Southern California last summer. The Taylor Guitars factory is very high tech. Manufacturing accounting helps Taylor prepare a statement of cost of goods manufactured, manufacturing schedules, and worksheets, as well as record transactions involving raw materials, work in process, and finished goods inventories. After reading this chapter, you will have a better appreciation of the manufacturing process and how you record the costs associated with manufacturing. In manufacturing, two key concepts are at play— cost and quality—and they are directly related.

Learning Objectives – Relating Accounting Theory By Unit

LO1   Calculate Statement of Cost of Goods Manufactured

LO2   Journalize Entries to Record Flow of Manufacturing Costs

LO3   Prepare a Worksheet for a Manufacturing Company

Manufacturing accounting refers to the specialized accounting concepts and techniques that are required to record, report, and control the operations of a manufacturing company, like Hershey, properly. The financial accounting procedures discussed in the previous merchandising chapters are all still valid in a manufacturing firm, but they are supplemented by the manufacturing accounting to be presented in this chapter, including some new terms and techniques that were not considered or required in the accounting for merchandising operations.

LEARNING UNIT 25-1

L01 ▶

Cost of Goods Manufactured and the Income Statement

In a manufacturing company, it is necessary to separate the manufacturing costs from all other selling and administrative expenses because product costs, inventory costs, and even gross profit come from the manufacturing process. One way of thinking about it is to imagine manufacturing costs being incurred in one building and the other costs in another building, as shown in Figure 25.1.

Figure 25.1
Manufacturing Costs

MANUFACTURING	ADMINISTRATIVE
Raw Material	Selling
Direct Labor	Administrative
Overhead	

All the costs incurred in the manufacturing building are manufacturing costs, including the managers' salaries, maintenance, all the labor, all materials and supplies, electricity, rent, and the depreciation of manufacturing property and machinery.

The administrative building would house top management, sales personnel, and other administrative personnel and their supplies and expenses.

Elements of Manufacturing Cost

Once we determine which costs are administrative and which are manufacturing, we can break the manufacturing costs into three elements: raw material, direct labor, and manufacturing overhead.

Raw material (or direct material) consists of all the items of material that will become a part of the product or will change the quality or characteristics of the product. For example, for a furniture manufacturer, the raw material includes lumber, metal parts, fabric, epoxy, finishing material, and even nuts and bolts. In a company that manufactures aluminum products, raw material includes the pure aluminum and the additives that are inserted to make the aluminum shiny or dull or rigid or flexible.

Direct labor includes the wages of those *personnel* whose efforts directly change the quality or characteristics of the products. In a furniture manufacturing company, the direct labor includes the person who saws the tabletop, the person who paints the furniture, the person who attaches the handles to the drawers, and so on. In that same company, however, the supervisor, the maintenance person, and the forklift driver are *not* direct labor.

Manufacturing overhead consists of all other manufacturing costs not included in raw material or direct labor. Manufacturing overhead includes many diverse items such as indirect labor, maintenance, engineering, manufacturing supervision, and supplies. Some of the most common items of manufacturing overhead are:

- Maintenance wages and supplies
- Production supervision and expenses
- Depreciation expense of manufacturing assets
- Rent expense for buildings or machinery

Raw material Material that is to be processed into a finished product or that changes the quality or characteristics of the product.

Direct labor Wages of those persons whose efforts directly affect the quality or other characteristics of the products manufactured.

Manufacturing overhead All the manufacturing costs except raw material and direct labor.

- Electricity for manufacturing
- Insurance expense for manufacturing
- Indirect labor: material handlers
- Manufacturing clerical wages

Manufacturing Inventories

In a merchandise firm, one inventory is made up of goods for sale. A manufacturing firm tracks *three* major inventories: raw material, work-in-process, and finished goods. (In addition, other minor inventories are used for such things as maintenance supplies and operating supplies.)

The *raw material inventory* consists only of the cost of the items of raw material being held for production plus the freight cost to bring the material in.

The *work-in-process inventory* represents the cost of the products being processed (the step before becoming finished goods) and includes the raw material, direct labor, and the manufacturing overhead costs incurred at the time of production.

The *finished goods inventory* consists of the manufacturing cost of the products that have been completed and are awaiting shipment to customers.

Cost of Goods Sold

To prepare an income statement for a manufacturing company, we first must figure the cost of goods sold. This section of the income statement for a manufacturing company is somewhat different from that of a merchandise company. The following diagram shows how cost of goods sold is calculated for a merchandise firm and for a manufacturing company.

Layout to Calculate Cost of Goods Sold

Merchandising Company	Manufacturing Company
Beginning Merchandise Inventory	Beginning Finished Goods Inventory
+ Net Purchases	+ Cost of Goods Manufactured
= Cost of Goods Available for Sale	= Cost of Goods Available for Sale
− Ending Merchandise Inventory	− Ending Finished Goods Inventory
= Cost of Goods Sold	= Cost of Goods Sold

As you can see in the diagram, the cost of goods manufactured replaces the purchases of the merchandise company statement. The purpose of the cost of goods sold section is to properly match the manufacturing costs with the sales, and for this reason it is necessary to include the beginning and ending finished goods inventories so as to calculate the cost. For example, the sales may have been for 500 units of product, whereas the company manufactured only 400 units this month. In this case there would be a 100-unit reduction in inventory. Thus, by adding the cost of goods manufactured to the beginning inventory and subtracting the ending inventory, the result will be the cost of 500 units of product. Similar reasoning is applied if the units manufactured for the month exceed the units sold.

The cost of goods manufactured is figured on a separate form or schedule. This statement is shown in Figure 25.2. It is helpful to remember a few key points when preparing this figure:

1. Cost of raw materials placed into production equals beginning raw materials inventory plus purchases of raw materials inventory, less ending inventory of raw materials.

2. Total manufacturing costs incurred equal the following:

   Cost of Raw Material Used
   + Direct Labor
   + Factory Overhead

Figure 25.2
Statement of Cost of Goods
Manufactured

DUKE MANUFACTURING COMPANY STATEMENT OF COST OF GOODS MANUFACTURED FOR MONTH ENDED 6/30/201X			
Direct Materials:			
Raw Material Inventory, 6/1/201X		$ 5 000 00	
Plus: Net Purchases	55 000 00		
Less: Raw Material Inventory, 6/30/201X	8 000 00	47 000 00	
Raw Material Used			$ 52 000 00
Direct Labor			90 000 00
Manufacturing Overhead:			
Factory Supervision	$ 37 000 00		
Maintenance Labor	15 000 00		
Electricity	6 000 00		
Maintenance Supplies	5 000 00		
Operating Supplies	3 000 00		
Depreciation of Machinery	4 000 00		
Total Overhead			70 000 00
Total Manufacturing Costs			212 000 00
+ Work-in-Process Inventory, 6/1/201X			7 000 00
− Work-in-Process Inventory, 6/30/201X			9 000 00
Total Cost of Goods Manufactured			$ 210 000 00

3. Cost of goods manufactured equals the following:
   Total Manufacturing Costs
   + Beginning Work-in-Process
   − Ending Work-in-Process

The first step in preparing the cost of goods manufactured is the calculation of the raw material cost for the month. If the accounting department has its records on a computer, the cost of raw material used may be readily available. If it is not, the cost must be calculated as shown by adding raw material purchases to the beginning raw material inventory and then subtracting the ending inventory. The direct labor cost is usually a single figure found on the payroll or the labor distribution report. The manufacturing overhead costs are then totaled and added to the raw material and direct labor to arrive at the total costs for the month. *The final step is to add the beginning work-in-process inventory and subtract the ending work-in-process inventory.* Keep in mind that we subtract ending inventory because it is not part of the cost of goods manufactured (yet).

Let's see how this figure is then used in preparing the income statement, shown in Figure 25.3.

Figure 25.3
Income Statement for a
Manufacturing Firm

DUKE MANUFACTURING COMPANY INCOME STATEMENT FOR MONTH ENDED 6/30/201X			
Sales			$ 400 000 00
Cost of Goods Sold:			
Finished Goods Inventory 6/1/201X	$ 25 000 00		
Plus: Cost of Goods Manufactured	210 000 00		
Cost of Goods Available for Sale	235 000 00		
Less: Finished Goods Inventory 6/30/201X	15 000 00		
Cost of Goods Sold		220 000 00	
Gross Profit		180 000 00	
Operating Expenses:			
Selling Expenses	$ 55 000 00		
Administrative Expense	65 000 00	120 000 00	
Net Income (before taxes)		$ 60 000 00	

Now let's check your progress.

 **TRY IT!** Learning Unit 25-1

From the following account balances, calculate gross profit for Wang Manufacturing Co.

Finished Goods Inventory 7/1/201X	40,000
Finished Goods Inventory, 7/31/201X	25,000
Cost of Goods Manufactured	300,000
Sales	430,000

TRY IT! **Solution Learning Unit 25-1**

The Cost of Goods Sold number was calculated as: $40,000 + $300,000 − $25,000 = $315,000.

Journalizing the Flow of Costs for a Manufacturing Company

LEARNING UNIT 25-2

 **L02**

The Accumulation of Manufacturing Costs

As the raw material, direct labor, and overhead are used in the manufacturing process, they must be recorded. The issuance of material from the warehouse, the assignment of labor to departments, and the movement of the products through the process must be reported to the cost accountants as the basis for journal entries.

Source Documents. The required data are submitted to the cost accountants through various source documents. The timely receipt of legible documents is often a problem in some companies, and employees must be made aware of their importance.

Receiving reports are prepared by the receiving department to acknowledge receipt of all material and supplies from vendors. A typical receiving report is shown in Figure 25.4. The accounting copy becomes a part of the vendor payment voucher, along with the purchase order and the vendor invoice.

Receiving report Document prepared by the receiving department to evidence the receipt of material or supplies that have been ordered.

Figure 25.4
Receiving Report

RECEIVING REPORT			
Received from: Adams Company		Receiving Report No. 1031 Date: 6/20/201X	
Quantity	Description	Unit Price	Total Price
50 Gals.	Paint	$6.50/Gal.	$325.00
	Revilo Manufacturing Co. Inspected By MS Received By BJ		

Material requisitions are the documents initiated by the manufacturing personnel, or other users, to request material from the inventory warehouse. The requisition (Figure 25.5) is presented to the storekeeper as the materials are issued. Copies of the requisitions are kept in accounting as a basis for charging material to production.

Material requisition Document used to order material or supplies from the storeroom that provides the basis for charging material into production.

Figure 25.5
Material Requisition

MATERIAL REQUISITION			
Department Finishing		Requisition No. __3648__ Date: 6/20/201X	
Quantity	Description	Unit Price	Total Price
8 Gals.	White Paint	$6.50	$52.00
	Revilo Manufacturing Co. Inspected By __CY__ Received By __FU__		

Clock card Card used by employees when clocking in and out of a factory; becomes the basis for the payroll.

A clock card is a card used by each hourly employee to clock in and out of the factory each day. A typical clock card is shown in Figure 25.6. The cards are collected each week by the payroll department and become a basis for the payroll check and for charging labor to production. Keep in mind that the clock card is being replaced with new automated systems.

Figure 25.6
Clock Card

CLOCK CARD

Name: David Ross
Social Sec. No. 420-80-5178
Department: Cutting
Clock No. 1432

Day	In	Out	In	Out	Hours
Mon	7:58			4:03	8
Tue	7:57			4:01	8
Wed	8:00			4:02	8
Thu	7:59			5:02	9
Fri	7:57			4:03	8
Sat					
Sun					
				Total Hours	41

Lot ticket Document prepared to show the movement of materials or products between departments; also called *move ticket*

Lot tickets, or *move tickets*, are documents that are written by departmental managers to reflect the movement of products, or parts of products, from one department to another. The department receiving the products must verify the quantity and quality of the products. These tickets become the basis for transferring costs between departments and to finished goods inventory. An example of a lot ticket is shown in Figure 25.7. Keep in mind that with today's technology, new systems are replacing the manual system.

Figure 25.7
Lot Ticket

LOT TICKET	
Date Transferred from: Assembling	Transferred to: Finishing
Quantity	Description
20 Tables 20 Tables	36" Oak 36" Pine
	Received By __MB__

A labor distribution report is a by-product of the payroll that has been allocated to the categories of direct labor, maintenance labor, and so forth. Based on this report, the cost accountants charge labor to the appropriate departments. An example of a typical labor distribution report is shown in Figure 25.8.

Labor distribution report Report issued by the payroll department to categorize all the types of labor incurred during the week.

LABOR DISTRIBUTION REPORT WEEK ENDING 9/10/201X				
Employee	Department	Hours	Rate	Total
Direct Labor:				
James Amos	Cutting	42	$6.20	$260.40
Andrew Brown	Cutting	39	6.00	234.00
—				
Indirect Labor:				
Don Able	Cutting	40	7.20	288.00
Carl Baker	Cutting	40	7.50	300.00

Figure 25.8
Labor Distribution Report

Bills of lading are documents that show the shipment of products to customers. The cost accounting copies of the bills become the basis for recording the transfer of the cost of the products from the finished goods inventory to the cost of goods sold. A typical bill of lading is shown in Figure 25.9.

Bill of lading Formal document issued to the carrier of the finished product; basis for charging the cost of goods sold.

BILL OF LADING			
Shipper's No.			7/15/201X
Name of Customer A.R. Owens			
Consigned to Same			
Destination Chicago	State IL		
Route _____			

No. of Packages	Description	Weight	Class
60	Tables	3600	2

B.P. Smith Co.
Atlanta, Georgia ____A.R.____ Agent

Figure 25.9
Bill of Lading

The Flow of Manufacturing Costs

To record and control manufacturing costs as the products move through the manufacturing process properly, it is necessary to establish the pattern of the flow of the costs. To do so, we use a flowchart.

The Flowchart. Figure 25.10 illustrates the movement of the material, labor, and overhead through the operation. Each step of the flow, from (a) to (h), is illustrated and is followed by an example of the journal entries and the source documents for each step. *Note that the journal entries reflect a debit to the destination and a credit to the source.*

This process may seem overwhelming, so take the time to match each step in Figure 25.10 with its corresponding journal entry in Figure 25.11. Remember that the debit is to the destination and the credit is to the source. See the Blueprint at the end of the chapter for samples involving T accounts.

Overhead Application. As shown in the flow of cost journal entries (c), (d), and (e), the debit is to an account called Manufacturing Overhead—Control and in (f) the credit is to the account Manufacturing Overhead—Applied. It is desirable to maintain both these overhead accounts to avoid errors and confusion. Manufacturing Overhead—Control is

Figure 25.10
Flow of Costs

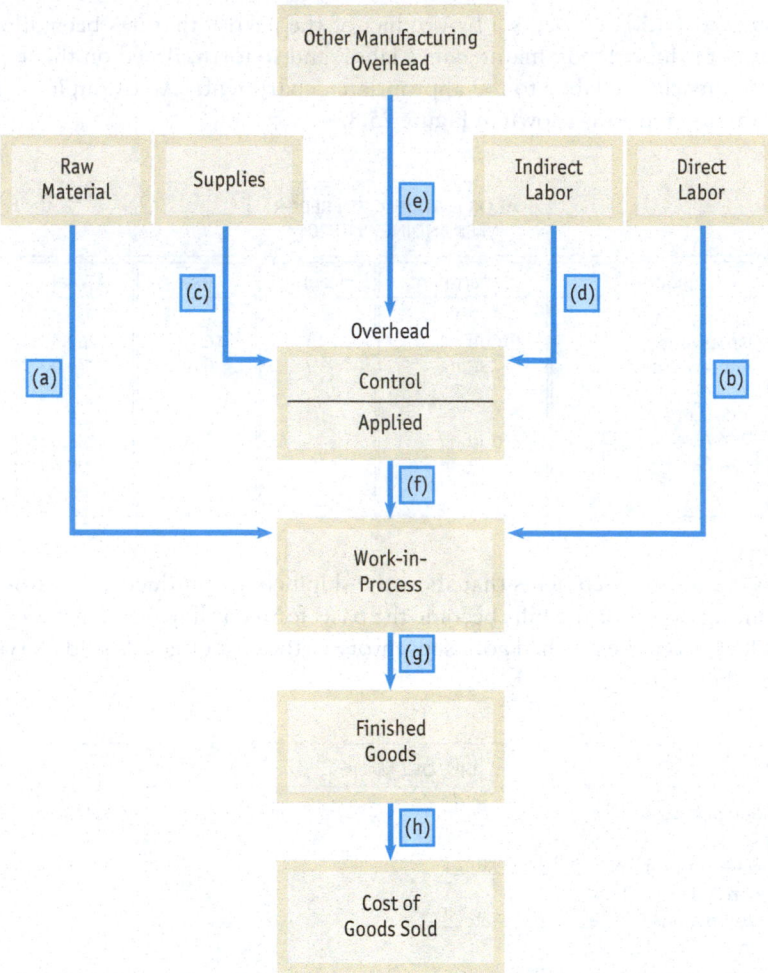

used for the accumulation of all actual overhead costs as debits, and the Manufacturing Overhead—Applied is credited for the application of overhead to production.

It is necessary to apply overhead each week to determine the total costs for that week. Some overhead accounts, however, such as electricity, supervision, and depreciation, are not known until the end of the month. For this reason, an overhead rate must be established as a basis for applying the overhead. Several methods help to determine a rate, depending on the type of operation of the company.

The most common and practical methods are based on direct labor or machine hours. A rate can be developed from the annual budget of the overhead costs and the *direct labor dollars* (wages of those persons whose efforts *directly* affect the characteristics of the products manufactured) as follows:

$$\text{Annual Manufacturing Overhead} \div \text{Annual Direct Labor Dollars}$$
$$\$500,000 \div \$1,000,000 = 50\%$$

Based on this calculation, overhead can be applied to production each week or month at a rate of 50% of the direct labor cost charged to production. For example, if the direct labor this month is $20,000, overhead would be applied at $10,000, as shown in Figure 25.12.

Another much-used rate is based on *direct labor hours*:

$$\text{Annual Overhead} \div \text{Annual Direct Labor Hours}$$
$$\$500,000 \div 200,000 \text{ Hours} = \$2.50/\text{Hour}$$

In this case, the rate of $2.50 per direct labor hour would be applied as overhead. If direct labor hours this month were 2,000 hours, the applied overhead would be $5,000, as shown in Figure 25.13.

Figure 25.11 Journal Entries

SOURCE DOCUMENTS				Dr.	Cr.
Material requisitions	(a)	Work-in-Process Inventory		20 000 00	
		Raw Material Inventory			20 000 00
Labor distribution report	(b)	Work-in-Process Inventory		50 000 00	
		Payroll Payable			50 000 00
Indirect material requisitions	(c)	Manufacturing Overhead—Control		4 000 00	
		Supplies Inventory			4 000 00
Indirect labor distribution report	(d)	Manufacturing Overhead—Control		10 000 00	
		Payroll Payable			10 000 00
Various	(e)	Manufacturing Overhead—Control		10 000 00	
		Supervision Salaries Expense			6 000 00
		Rent Expense			1 000 00
		Depreciation Expense			2 000 00
		Electricity Expense			1 000 00
None	(f)	Work-in-Process Inventory		25 000 00	
		Manufacturing Overhead—Applied			25 000 00
Lot tickets	(g)	Finished Goods Inventory		22 000 00	
		Work-in-Process Inventory			22 000 00
Bills of lading	(h)	Cost of Goods Sold		24 000 00	
		Finished Goods Inventory			24 000 00
		Accounts Receivable		40 000 00	
		Sales			40 000 00

		Dr.	Cr.
Work-in-Process Inventory		10 000 00	
Manufacturing Overhead—Applied			10 000 00

Figure 25.12
Applying Overhead

		Dr.	Cr.
Work-in-Process Inventory		5 000 00	
Manufacturing Overhead—Applied			5 000 00

Figure 25.13
Applying Overhead by Direct
Labor Hours

Still another method that is convenient in some companies is based on *machine hours*, as follows:

Annual Overhead ÷ Annual Machine Hours
$500,000 ÷ 100,000$ Machine Hours $= \$5.00$/Hour

Using the $5.00 per machine hour rate, if the machine ran 3,000 hours, the overhead applied would be $15,000.

To further illustrate the journal entries and overhead application, consider the following transactions and the resulting journal entries (Figure 25.14) for the month of August:

a. Issued raw material from the storeroom costing $69,000.
b. Charged direct labor to production, $60,000.
c. Issued supplies from the storeroom costing $6,000.
d. Incurred indirect labor costs of $15,000.
e. Charged the following expenses to overhead: rent, $3,000; supervision, $12,000; depreciation, $4,000; electricity, $6,000.
f. Applied overhead at 85% of direct labor dollars.
g. Transferred completed products costing $200,000 to finished goods.
h. Sold products on account costing $208,000. The selling price was $500,000. The perpetual inventory system is used.

Figure 25.14
Manufacturing Transactions

Journal Entries

(a)	Work-in-Process Inventory	69 000 00	
	Raw Material Inventory		69 000 00
(b)	Work-in-Process Inventory	60 000 00	
	Payroll Payable		60 000 00
(c)	Manufacturing Overhead—Control	6 000 00	
	Supplies Inventory		6 000 00
(d)	Manufacturing Overhead—Control	15 000 00	
	Payroll Payable		15 000 00
(e)	Manufacturing Overhead—Control	25 000 00	
	Rent Expense		3 000 00
	Supervision Expense		12 000 00
	Depreciation Expense		4 000 00
	Electricity Expense		6 000 00
(f)	Work-in-Process Inventory	51 000 00	
	Manufacturing Overhead—Applied		51 000 00
(g)	Finished Goods Inventory	200 000 00	
	Work-in-Process Inventory		200 000 00
(h)	Cost of Goods Sold	208 000 00	
	Finished Goods Inventory		208 000 00
	Accounts Receivable	500 000 00	
	Sales		500 000 00

Now let's check your progress.

TRY IT!   Learning Unit 25-2

Journalize the following entries:

a. Charged raw materials to production, $8,500.
b. Charged direct labor to production, $4,200.
c. Issued operating supplies, $1,400.
d. Charged indirect labor to production, $5,800.
e. Incurred the following overhead: Supervisory, $4,200; Rent, $1,000; Depreciation, $1,500; Electrical, $440; Maintenance, $1,700.

f. Applied overhead production at 140% of direct labor dollars.

g. Transferred products to finished goods, $4,800.

h. Sold products on account costing $13,000. The selling price was $15,500. The perpetual inventory system was used.

TRY IT!   **Solution Learning Unit 25-2**

Accounts	Dr.	Cr.
a. Work-in-Process Inventory	8,500	
Raw Materials Inventory		8,500
b. Work-in-Process Inventory	4,200	
Payroll Payable		4,200
c. Manufacturing Overhead—Control	1,400	
Supplies Inventory		1,400
d. Manufacturing Overhead—Control	5,800	
Payroll Payable		5,800
e. Manufacturing Overhead—Control	8,840	
Supervision Expense		4,200
Rent Expense		1,000
Depreciation Expense		1,500
Electricity Expense		440
Maintenance Expense		1,700
f. Work-in-Process Inventory	5,880	
Manufacturing Overhead—Applied		5,880
g. Finished Goods Inventory	4,800	
Work-in-Process Inventory		4,800
h. Cost of Goods Sold	13,000	
Finished Goods Inventory		13,000
Accounts Receivable	15,500	
Sales		15,500

LEARNING UNIT 25-3

Preparing a Worksheet for a Manufacturing Company

 LO3

In past chapters we viewed worksheets for a service company as well as a merchandise company. We now examine and explain the preparation of a worksheet for a manufacturing company. Figure 25.15 shows a worksheet for Roe Corporation. We changed companies to provide you with more insight into other account titles used by different companies. The theory is the same. We then see how reports are prepared from the worksheet. Let's first look at some key points to remember when a worksheet is prepared. Keep in mind that the steps of the accounting cycle for a manufacturing company are the same as those used for a merchandise company.

Key Points to Look at on the Worksheet

Key points on the worksheet as denoted on the worksheet by number include:

1. New set of columns for statement of cost of goods manufactured.

2. Beginning balances of raw materials inventory, $570, and work-in-process, $1,230, are listed in the debit column of the statement of cost of goods manufactured. Ending balances of $960 and $1,590 are entered in the credit column.

3. Finished goods inventory is not listed on the statement of cost of goods manufactured. The beginning figure of finished goods, $750, is listed in the debit column of the income statement, whereas the ending balance of finished goods, $540, is listed in the credit column of the income statement and debit column of the balance sheet.

4. These expenses are not part of the cost of manufacturing and thus are not listed on the statement of cost of goods manufactured.

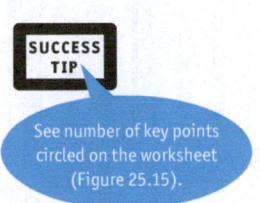

SUCCESS TIP

See number of key points circled on the worksheet (Figure 25.15).

Figure 25.15 Worksheet for a Manufacturing Company

Account Titles	Trial Balance Dr.	Trial Balance Cr.	Adjustments Dr.	Adjustments Cr.	Statement of Cost of Goods Manufactured Dr.	Statement of Cost of Goods Manufactured Cr.	Income Statement Dr.	Income Statement Cr.	Balance Sheet Dr.	Balance Sheet Cr.
Cash	135000								135000	
Accounts Receivable	153000								153000	
Allowance for Doubtful Accounts		48000		66000						114000
Raw Materials Inventory	57000				② 57000	② 96000			② 96000	
Work-in-Process Inventory	123000				② 123000	② 159000			② 159000	
Finished Goods Inventory	75000						③ 75000	54000	54000	
Factory Supplies	99000			78000					21000	
Prepaid Factory Insurance	105000			75000					30000	
Factory Machinery	648000								648000	
Accumulated Dep., Factory Mach.		120000		84000						204000
Note Payable (due within 30 days)		225000								225000
Common Stock $10		225000								225000
Retained Earnings		180000								180000
Sales (Net)		2430000						2430000		
Raw Material Purchases (Net)	540000				540000					
Direct Labor	330000		132000		462000					
Indirect Labor	102000		48000		150000					
Heat, Light, and Power	174000				174000					
Machinery Repairs	45000				45000					
Rent Expense—Factory	180000				180000					
Selling Expense—Control	261000						④ 261000			
Administrative Expenses (Control)	201000		33000				234000			
Totals	3228000	3228000								
Factory Supplies Expense			78000		78000					
Bad Debts Expense			66000				66000			
Dep. Expense—Factory Mach.			84000		84000					
Factory Insurance Expense			75000		75000					
Accrued Payroll Payable				213000						213000
Totals			516000	516000	1968000	255000	2349000	2484000	1296000	1161000
Cost of Goods Manufactured						1713000	1713000			
Net Income							135000			135000
Totals					1968000	1968000	2484000	2484000	1296000	1296000

① Statement of Cost of Goods Manufactured

Reports Prepared from the Worksheet

The following reports can be prepared from the worksheet (see Figure 25.15). Let's look at Figure 25.16, which shows the Statement of Cost of Goods Manufactured.

Statement of Cost of Goods Manufactured

ROE CORPORATION STATEMENT OF COST OF GOODS MANUFACTURED FOR YEAR ENDED DECEMBER 31, 201X		
Direct Materials:		
Raw Materials Inventory (Beg.)	$ 5 7 0 00	
Raw Materials Purchases (Net)	5 4 0 0 00	
Cost of Available Raw Materials	5 9 7 0 00	
Less: Raw Materials Inventory (End.)	9 6 0 00	
Cost of Raw Materials Used		$ 5 0 1 0 00
Direct Labor		4 6 2 0 00
Factory Overhead:		
Indirect Labor	$ 1 5 0 0 00	
Heat, Light, and Power	1 7 4 0 00	
Rent Expense	1 8 0 0 00	
Machinery Repairs	4 5 0 00	
Factory Supplies Expense	7 8 0 00	
Depreciation Expense, Factory Machinery	8 4 0 00	
Factory Insurance Expense	7 5 0 00	
Total Factory Overhead		$ 7 8 6 0 00
Total Manufacturing Cost Incurred		1 7 4 9 0 00
Plus: Work-in-Process (Beg.)		1 2 3 0 00
Less: Work-in-Process (End.)		1 5 9 0 00
Cost of Goods Manufactured*		$ 1 7 1 3 0 00

*This amount will go on the cost of goods sold section of the income statement, as shown in Figure 25.17.

Figure 25.16
Statement of Cost of Goods Manufactured

The Income Statement. Figure 25.17 is the income statement for Roe Corporation. Note how the $17,130 from the statement of cost of goods manufactured is listed below the beginning finished goods inventory. Note that the operating expenses, which were

ROE CORPORATION INCOME STATEMENT FOR YEAR ENDED DECEMBER 31, 201X		
Net Sales		$ 2 4 3 0 0 00
Cost of Goods Sold:		
Finished Goods Inventory (Beg.)	$ 7 5 0 00	
Cost of Goods Manufactured	1 7 1 3 0 00	
Cost of Goods Available for Sale	$ 1 7 8 8 0 00	
Less: Finished Goods Inventory (End.)	5 4 0 00	
Cost of Goods Sold		$ 1 7 3 4 0 00
Gross Profit on Sales		$ 6 9 6 0 00
Operating Expenses:		
Selling Expense*	$ 3 2 7 0 00	
Administrative Expense	2 3 4 0 00	
Total Operating Expenses		$ 5 6 1 0 00
Net Income (before taxes)		$ 1 3 5 0 00

*Includes the $660 of bad debt expense.

Figure 25.17
Income Statement

not part of the cost of the goods sold, are listed below gross profit. For example, Bad Debts Expense, a selling expense, had no part in the production of bean bag chairs for Roe. Remember that the cost of goods manufactured is not the same as the cost of goods sold.

The Balance Sheet. Figure 25.18 below is the completed balance sheet of Roe Corporation. The net income of $1,350 in Figure 25.17 helps update retained earnings in Figure 25.18. Note how under current assets the manufacturing company lists its raw materials and work-in-process as well as finished goods.

Figure 25.18
Balance Sheet

ROE CORPORATION BALANCE SHEET DECEMBER 31, 201X				
Assets				
Current Assets:				
Cash				$1 3 5 0 00
Accounts Receivable		$1 5 3 0 00		
Less: Allowance for Doubtful Accounts		1 1 4 0 00		$ 3 9 0 00
Inventories				
Raw Materials		$ 9 6 0 00		
Work-in-Process		1 5 9 0 00		
Finished Goods		5 4 0 00		$3 0 9 0 00
Prepaid Expenses:				
Factory Supplies		$ 2 1 0 00		
Prepaid Factory Insurance		3 0 0 00		$ 5 1 0 00
Total Current Assets				$5 3 4 0 00
Plant and Equipment:				
Factory Machinery		$6 4 8 0 00		
Less: Accum. Depreciation, Factory Machinery		2 0 4 0 00		$4 4 4 0 00
Total Assets				$9 7 8 0 00
Liabilities and Stockholders' Equity				
Current Liabilities:				
Notes Payable		$2 2 5 0 00		
Accrued Payroll Payable		2 1 3 0 00		$4 3 8 0 00
Stockholders' Equity				
Common Stock, $10 par 225 shares		$2 2 5 0 00		
Retained Earnings*		3 1 5 0 00		$5 4 0 0 00
Total Liabilities and Stockholders' Equity				$9 7 8 0 00

*Beginning Retained Earnings ($1,800) + Net Income ($1,350) = Retained Earnings

Now let's check your progress.

 TRY IT! Learning Unit 25-3

Complete the following chart by placing an X in the appropriate column(s).

	Statement of Cost of Goods Manuf.	Income Statement	Balance Sheet
Sales			
Cost of Goods Manufactured			
Beg. Finished Goods Inventory			
End. Finished Goods Inventory			
Allow. for Doubtful Accounts			
Work-in-Process Inventory (Beg.)			
Work-in-Process Inventory (End.)			
Factory Overhead			
Retained Earnings			
Raw Materials Inventory (End.)			

TRY IT! Solution Learning Unit 25-3

	Statement of Cost of Goods Manuf.	Income Statement	Balance Sheet
Sales		X	
Cost of Goods Manufactured	X	X	
Beg. Finished Goods Inventory		X	
End. Finished Goods Inventory		X	X
Allow. for Doubtful Accounts			X
Work-in-Process Inventory (Beg.)	X		
Work-in-Process Inventory (End.)	X		X
Factory Overhead	X		
Retained Earnings			X
Raw Materials Inventory (End.)	X		X

DEMONSTRATION SUMMARY PROBLEM

 LO1,2,3

John Swift is studying for his manufacturing accounting exam. Help John solve the following three requirements that he is having trouble with. Each requirement and solution is shown separately.

Requirement 1

From the following information, calculate total manufacturing costs:

Direct Labor	$ 68,000
Raw Materials Inventory, June 30	8,000
Raw Materials Purchases	59,000
Raw Materials Inventory, June 1	9,000
Overhead	60,000
Finished Goods Inventory	110,000

Solution for Requirement 1

Raw Materials Inventory, June 1	$ 9,000
+ Raw Materials Purchases	59,000
Raw Materials Available for Use	68,000
− Raw Materials Inventory, June 30	8,000
Cost of Raw Materials Used	60,000
+ Direct Labor	68,000
+ Overhead	60,000
Total Manufacturing Cost	$188,000

Be sure to subtract ending raw materials inventory and add cost of raw material purchases plus direct labor and overhead.

Requirement 2

From the following transactions, prepare the appropriate general journal entries for the month of June:

a. Raw materials costing $66,000 were issued from the storeroom.

b. Direct labor of $90,000 was charged to production.

c. Supplies costing $5,800 were issued from the storeroom.

d. Indirect labor of $15,800 was incurred.

e. Rent of $2,000 and depreciation of $1,500 were charged to overhead.

f. Overhead was applied at 80% of direct labor dollars.

g. Completed products costing $60,000 were transferred to finished goods.

h. Sold products costing $40,000 on account. Selling price is $100,000. The perpetual inventory system is used.

Solution for Requirement 2

a.	Work-In-Process Inventory	66,000	
	Raw Materials Inventory		66,000
b.	Work-In-Process Inventory	90,000	
	Payroll Payable		90,000
c.	Manufacturing Overhead—Control	5,800	
	Supplies Inventory		5,800
d.	Manufacturing Overhead—Control	15,800	
	Payroll Payable		15,800
e.	Manufacturing Overhead—Control	3,500	
	Rent Expense		2,000
	Depreciation Expense		1,500
f.	Work-in-Process Inventory	72,000	
	Manufacturing Overhead—Applied		72,000
g.	Finished Goods Inventory	60,000	
	Work-in-Process Inventory		60,000
h.	Cost of Goods Sold	40,000	
	Finished Goods Inventory		40,000
	Accounts Receivable	100,000	
	Sales		100,000

Requirement 3

a. In which columns of the worksheet would the following additional data be placed?

	Year-End Figures	Column
Raw Materials Inventory	$30,000	
Work-in-Process Inventory	20,000	
Finished Goods Inventory	40,000	

b. In which columns would the beginning-of-the-year inventory figures be placed?

Solution for Requirement 3

a.

	Debit Column	Credit Column
Raw Materials Inventory	BS	Statement of Cost of Goods Manufactured
Work-in-Process Inventory	BS	Statement of Cost of Goods Manufactured
Finished Goods Inventory	BS	Income Statement

b.

	Debit Columns
Raw Materials Inventory	Statement of Cost of Goods Manufactured & Trial Balance
Work-in-Process Inventory	Statement of Cost of Goods Manufactured & Trial Balance
Finished Goods Inventory	Income Statement & Trial Balance

SUCCESS TIP

When you record materials, labor, and overhead, remember the debit represents the destination and the credit represents the source.

SUCCESS TIP

The cost of goods manufactured is recorded on the worksheet. The ending balance is then used to update the income statement. Keep in mind that corporations use common stock and retained earnings, not capital.

SUCCESS COACH

The following Success Tips are from Learning Units 25-1 to 25-3. Take the Do It Right Now Checkup and use the Check Your Score at the bottom of the page to see how you are doing. The Success Coach provides tips before each Checkup to help you avoid common accounting errors.

LU 25-1 Cost of Goods Manufactured and the Income Statement

Do It Right Tips: The three main elements of manufacturing costs include raw materials, direct labor, and manufacturing overhead. The inventories are broken down into raw materials, work-in-process and finished goods. When the income statement is prepared, cost of goods sold includes beginning finished goods inventory plus cost of goods manufactured less ending finished goods inventory.

Do It Right Now Checkup: Answer true or false to the following statements.

1. The buying of raw materials is recorded in the Sales account.
2. Depreciation expense is part of direct labor.
3. Work-in-Process Inventory is part of the statement of cost of goods manufactured.
4. Finished goods inventory is part of cost of goods manufactured.
5. Freight costs are subtracted from the cost of raw materials.

LU 25-2 Journalizing the Flow of Costs for a Manufacturing Company

Do It Right Tips: When you record journal entries to record materials, labor, and overhead, remember that the debit is the destination and each credit is the source. Keep in mind that overhead is usually applied based on direct labor hours, labor dollars, or machine hours.

Do It Right Now Checkup: Answer true or false to the following statements.

1. Lot tickets reflect the movement of products.
2. Material requisitions would debit Raw Materials Inventory and credit Work-in-Process Inventory.
3. Payroll is not a by-product of a labor distribution report.
4. A bill of lading ends with the cost of goods sold decreasing.
5. Receiving reports are prepared by the payroll department.

LU 25-3 Preparing a Worksheet for a Manufacturing Company

Do It Right Tips: The worksheet for a manufacturing company has columns to record the cost of goods manufactured. This ending balance is then used to update the income statement. Remember, corporations use common stock and retained earnings, not capital.

Do It Right Now Checkup: Answer true or false to the following statements.

1. Finished Goods Inventory is a credit balance on the trial balance.
2. Direct labor will go on the statement of cost of goods manufactured.
3. Indirect labor cannot be adjusted on the worksheet.
4. Ending finished goods inventory will only appear on the income statement.
5. Direct labor can be adjusted on the worksheet.

CHECK YOUR SCORE: Answers to the Do It Right Now Checkup

LU 25-1

1. False—The buying of raw materials is recorded in the Purchases account.
2. False—Depreciation expense is part of manufacturing overhead.
3. True
4. False—Ending Finished Goods Inventory is not part of cost of goods manufactured.
5. False—Freight costs are added on to the cost of raw materials.

LU 25-2

1. True
2. False—Material requisitions trigger a debit to Work-in-Process Inventory and credit to Raw Materials Inventory.

3. True
4. False—A bill of lading ends with the cost of goods sold increasing.
5. False—Receiving reports are prepared by the receiving department to acknowledge receipt of all material and supplies from vendors.

LU 25-3

1. False—Finished Goods Inventory is a debit balance on the trial balance.
2. True
3. False—Indirect labor can be adjusted.
4. False—Ending Finished Goods Inventory will appear on the income statement and on the balance sheet.
5. True

BLUEPRINT: MANUFACTURING ELEMENTS

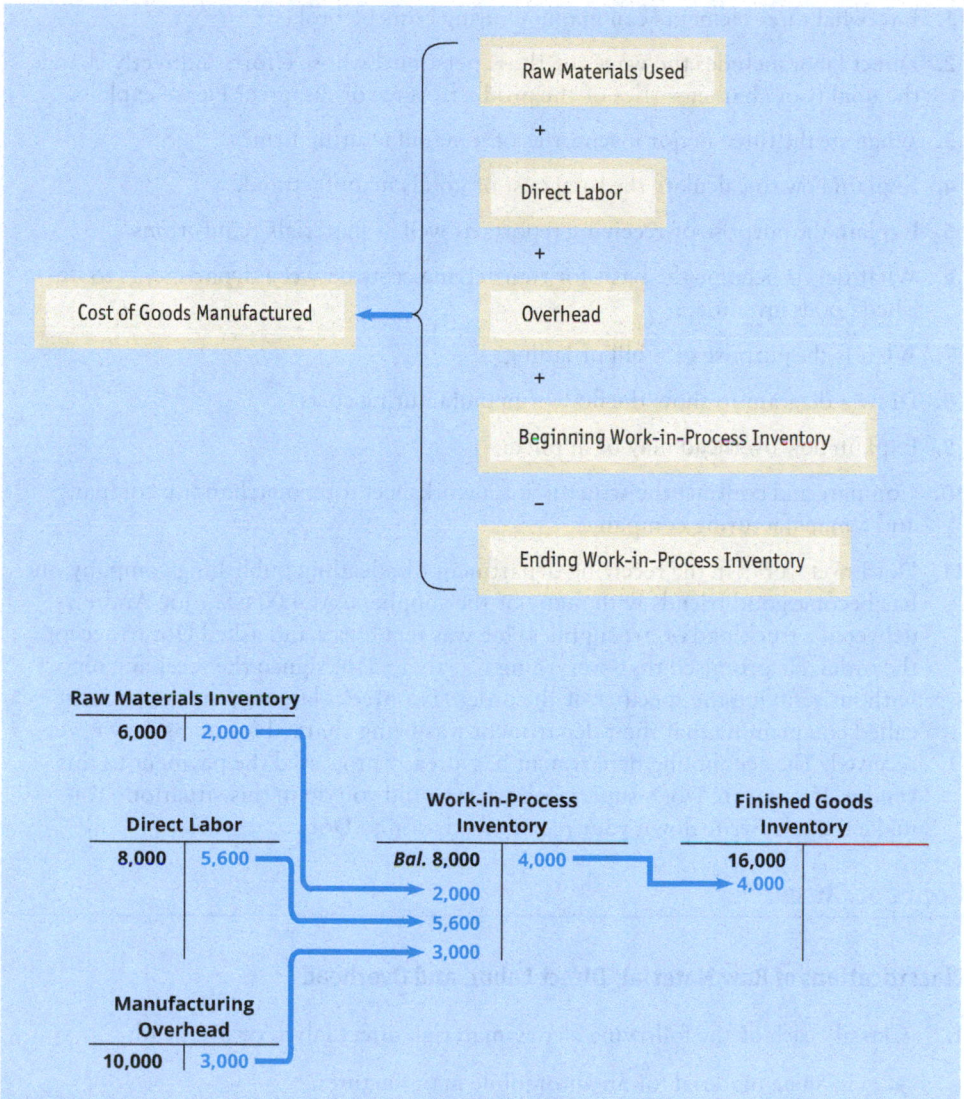

Discussion Questions and Critical Thinking/Ethical Case

1. Into what three elements can manufacturing costs be broken?

2. Direct labor includes the wages of those personnel whose efforts indirectly change the quality or characteristics of the product. Agree or disagree? Please explain.

3. What are the three major inventories of a manufacturing firm?

4. Explain how to calculate the total cost of goods manufactured.

5. Explain the purpose of receiving reports as well as materials requisitions.

6. What tickets become the basis for transferring costs between departments to finished goods inventory?

7. What is the purpose of a bill of lading?

8. Draw a diagram to show the flow of manufacturing costs.

9. Explain how overhead may be applied.

10. Compare and contrast the structure of a worksheet for a merchandise company and a manufacturing company.

11. Dot Lovet works in the receiving department of a leading publishing company. She has become good friends with many of the suppliers. At 4:00 P.M., Joe Andrews delivered a truckload of art supplies. Joe was in a hurry and asked Dot to accept the order. He promised that everything was there. Dot signed the receiving report without verifying the specifics of the order. Two weeks later the art department called complaining that their department was being charged for items they never received. The accounting department has already processed the payment to this vendor. If you were Dot's supervisor, what would you do in this situation? You make the call. Write down your recommendation to Dot.

MyLab**Accounting**

Concept Checks

Classifications of Raw Material, Direct Labor, and Overhead

(10 min) **LO1**

1. Classify each of the following as raw material, direct labor, or overhead:

   a. Finishing material for an automobile manufacturer
   b. Labor of a person who paints automobiles for an automobile manufacturer
   c. Depreciation expense of manufacturing assets
   d. Pure steel in a company that manufactures steel products

Calculating Cost of Raw Materials

(10 min) **LO1**

2. From the following, calculate the cost of raw materials used:

Raw Materials Inventory, January 1	$ 6,100
Raw Materials Inventory, December 31	13,300
Purchases of Raw Materials	70,000

Calculating Total Manufacturing Costs

3.   From the following, calculate total manufacturing costs:

L01 *(15 min)*

Direct Labor	$ 8,200
Raw Materials Inventory, June 30	5,400
Raw Materials Purchases	17,400
Raw Materials Inventory, June 1	4,600
Overhead	6,800
Finished Goods Inventory	9,600

Journal Entries to Record Manufacturing Costs

4.   Journalize the following transactions:

L02 *(15 min)*

   a. Storeroom issued raw materials costing $5,000.
   b. Direct labor of $4,300 was charged to production.
   c. Supplies costing $3,000 were issued by the storeroom.
   d. Indirect labor cost of $4,800 was incurred.
   e. Rent of $1,300 and depreciation of $450 were charged to overhead.

Prepare Worksheet for a Manufacturing Company

5.   Identify where each title is placed on the worksheet.

L03 *(10 min)*

   a. Direct labor
   b. Ending finished goods inventory
   c. Beginning finished goods inventory
   d. Ending raw materials inventory

Exercises

Set A

25A-1.   Classify each of the following as raw material, direct labor, or overhead:

L01 *(10 min)*

   a. The steel in making automobiles
   b. The rent for a factory
   c. The wages of a line employee
   d. A manufacturing foreman's salary

25A-2.   From the following balances, calculate the cost of raw material used:

L01 *(10 min)*

Raw Materials Inventory, January 1	$ 68,000
Raw Materials Inventory, December 31	92,000
Purchases of Raw Materials	840,000

25A-3.   From the following, calculate total manufacturing costs:

L01 *(20 min)*

Direct Labor	$ 74,000
Raw Materials Inventory, May 31	8,600
Raw Materials Purchases	76,000
Raw Materials Inventory, May 1	9,600
Overhead	79,000
Finished Goods Inventory	125,000

(25 min) **LO2**

25A-4. From the following transactions, prepare the appropriate general journal entries for the month of May:

  a. Raw materials costing $77,000 were issued from the storeroom.
  b. Direct labor of $50,000 was charged to production.
  c. Supplies costing $7,200 were issued from the storeroom.
  d. Indirect labor costs of $17,500 were incurred.
  e. Rent of $3,400 and depreciation of $500 were charged to overhead.
  f. Overhead was applied at 80% of direct labor dollars.
  g. Completed products costing $60,000 were transferred to finished goods.
  h. Products costing $37,000 were sold on account for $68,000.

(30 min) **LO2**

25A-5. **a.** In which columns of the worksheet would the following additional data be placed?

Inventories	Year-End Figures	Column
Raw Materials	$30,000	
Work-in-Process	15,500	
Finished Goods	22,000	

  b. In which columns would the beginning-of-year figures be placed?

Set B

(10 min) **LO1**

25B-1. Classify each of the following as raw material, direct labor, or overhead:

  a. The flour in making muffins
  b. The utilities for a factory
  c. The wages of a baker
  d. A factory foreman's salary

(10 min) **LO1**

25B-2. From the following balances, calculate the cost of raw material used:

Raw Materials Inventory, January 1	$ 64,000
Raw Materials Inventory, December 31	99,000
Purchase of Raw Materials	880,000

(20 min) **LO1**

25B-3. From the following, calculate total manufacturing costs:

Direct Labor	$ 88,000
Raw Materials Inventory, May 31	10,000
Raw Materials Purchases	68,000
Raw Materials Inventory, May 1	8,800
Overhead	77,000
Finished Goods Inventory	135,000

(25 min) **LO2**

25B-4. From the following transactions, prepare the appropriate general journal entries for the month of May:

  a. Raw materials costing $72,000 were issued from the storeroom.
  b. Direct labor of $60,000 was charged to production.
  c. Supplies costing $7,400 were issued from the storeroom.
  d. Indirect labor costs of $18,500 were incurred.
  e. Rent of $3,400 and depreciation of $800 were charged to overhead.

    f. Overhead was applied at 30% of direct labor dollars.

    g. Completed products costing $66,000 were transferred to finished goods.

    h. Products costing $39,000 were sold on account for $64,000.

25B-5. **a.** In which columns of the worksheet would the following additional data be placed?

 **LO3** *(30 min)*

Inventories	Year-End Figures	Column
Raw Materials	$40,000	
Work-in-Process	21,000	
Finished Goods	35,000	

    b. In which columns would the beginning-of-year figures be placed?

Problems

MyLab**Accounting**

Set A

25A-1. An analysis of the accounts of Walden Manufacturing reveals the following data for the month ended April 30, 201X:

LO1 *(30 min)*

Inventories	Beginning	Ending
Raw Materials	$19,000	$21,000
Work-in-Process	12,000	17,500
Finished Goods	16,000	14,900

Check Figure:
Total Cost of Goods Manufactured
$318,200

    Costs Incurred: Raw materials purchased, $140,000; direct labor, $132,000; manufacturing overhead, $53,700. These specific overheads included indirect labor, $19,500; factory insurance, $8,800; depreciation on machinery, $11,700; machinery repairs, $4,900; factory utilities, $6,400; and miscellaneous factory costs, $2,400.

    Instructions: Prepare a cost of goods manufactured statement.

25A-2. As the bookkeeper of Ace Manufacturing, you are to record the following transactions in the general journal for the month of November:

LO2 *(50 min)*

    a. Raw materials of $84,000 were issued from the storeroom.

    b. Charged $65,000 of direct labor to production.

    c. Supplies costing $7,900 were issued from the storeroom.

    d. Incurred indirect labor costs of $19,000.

    e. The following expenses were charged to overhead: rent, $3,200; supervision, $7,400; depreciation, $4,200; electricity, $6,000.

    f. Overhead was applied at 60% of direct labor dollars.

    g. Transferred completed products costing $150,000 to finished goods.

    h. Products costing $200,000 were sold on account for $220,000.

Check Figure:
(d) Dr. Manufacturing Overhead-Control
$19,000
Cr. Payroll Payable $19,000

25A-3. From the trial balance in Figure 25.19 and the provided year-end information, prepare a worksheet for Forest Corporation (assume no adjustments).

LO3 *(60 min)*

Year-End Figures	
Raw Materials Inventory	$11,550
Work-in-Process Inventory	8,260
Finished Goods Inventory	10,100

Check Figure:
Raw Materials Inventory Balance Sheet
$11,550

Figure 25.19 Trial Balance of Forest Corporation

	TRIAL BALANCE	
	Dr.	Cr.
Cash	6 1 5 0 00	
Raw Materials Inventory	8 7 0 0 00	
Work-in-Process Inventory	7 5 2 0 00	
Finished Goods Inventory	10 5 5 0 00	
Factory Supplies	3 2 4 0 00	
Prepaid Factory Insurance	3 8 0 00	
Desks	9 7 0 00	
Machinery	57 2 4 0 00	
Accumulated Depreciation, Machinery		8 0 5 0 00
Accounts Payable		3 1 5 0 00
Common Stock $10 Par		60 0 0 0 00
Retained Earnings		8 1 2 0 00
Sales		115 1 8 0 00
Raw Material Purchases	36 9 0 0 00	
Direct Labor	23 3 8 0 00	
Indirect Labor	9 7 0 0 00	
Machinery Repairs	6 8 0 00	
Selling Expenses	14 6 5 0 00	
Administrative Expense	10 0 8 0 00	
Factory Supplies Expense	1 2 2 0 00	
Depreciation Expense, Machinery	3 1 4 0 00	
Totals	194 5 0 0 00	194 5 0 0 00

Set B

(30 min) **L01** ▶

25B-1.   An analysis of the accounts of Manning Manufacturing reveals the following data for the month ended February 28, 201X:

Inventories	Beginning	Ending
Raw Materials	$17,000	$26,000
Work-in-Process	16,000	21,000
Finished Goods	14,000	12,200

Check Figure:
Total Cost of Goods Manufactured
$299,400

Costs Incurred: Raw materials purchased, $134,000; direct labor, $126,000; manufacturing overhead, $53,400. These specific overheads included indirect labor, $19,200; factory insurance, $9,600; depreciation on machinery, $10,500; machinery repairs, $4,200; factory utilities, $6,500; and miscellaneous factory costs, $3,400.

Instructions: Prepare a cost of goods manufactured statement.

(50 min) **L02** ▶

25B-2.   As the bookkeeper of Bishop Manufacturing, you are to record the following transactions in the general journal for the month of November:

Check Figure:
(d) Dr. Manufacturing Overhead-Control
$19,000
Cr. Payroll Payable $19,000

a.   Raw materials of $72,000 were issued from the storeroom.
b.   Charged $52,000 of direct labor to production.
c.   Supplies costing $7,600 were issued from the storeroom.
d.   Incurred indirect labor costs of $19,000.
e.   The following expenses were charged to overhead: rent, $2,600; supervision, $8,600; depreciation, $4,000; electricity, $6,000.

f. Overhead was applied at 50% of direct labor dollars.

g. Transferred completed products costing $180,000 to finished goods.

h. Products costing $192,000 were sold on account for $213,000.

25B-3. From the trial balance in Figure 25.20 and the provided year-end information, prepare a worksheet for Forest Corporation (assume no adjustments).

 **L03** *(60 min)*

Check Figure:
Raw Materials Inventory Balance Sheet
$11,590

Year-End Figures	
Raw Materials Inventory	$11,590
Work-in-Process Inventory	8,340
Finished Goods Inventory	10,200

Figure 25.20
Trial Balance of Forest Corporation

	TRIAL BALANCE	
	Dr.	Cr.
Cash	6 2 5 0 00	
Raw Materials Inventory	9 0 0 0 00	
Work-in-Process Inventory	7 4 8 0 00	
Finished Goods Inventory	9 8 9 0 00	
Factory Supplies	3 1 5 0 00	
Prepaid Factory Insurance	3 7 0 00	
Desks	9 2 0 00	
Machinery	62 5 0 0 00	
Accumulated Depreciation, Machinery		8 3 0 0 00
Accounts Payable		3 1 9 0 00
Common Stock $10 Par		58 0 0 0 00
Retained Earnings		7 9 6 0 00
Sales		123 0 7 0 00
Raw Material Purchases	39 4 0 0 00	
Direct Labor	21 3 8 0 00	
Indirect Labor	10 1 0 0 00	
Machinery Repairs	7 5 0 00	
Selling Expenses	14 7 6 0 00	
Administrative Expense	10 0 8 0 00	
Factory Supplies Expense	1 7 2 0 00	
Depreciation Expense, Machinery	2 7 7 0 00	
Totals	200 5 2 0 00	200 5 2 0 00

Financial Report Problem

 MyLabAccounting

Reading Amazon's Annual Report

Go to the annual report for Amazon at **https://tinyurl.com/slaterca14e** and see if Amazon has a work-in-process inventory account.

L01 *(10 min)*

Index

NOTES

NOTES

NOTES

NOTES

NOTES

NOTES

NOTES

NOTES

Photo Credits

Chapter 1, Page 1: Neil Fraser/Alamy Stock Photo

Chapter 2, Page 31: P.D Amedzro/Alamy Stock Photo

Chapter 3, Page 65: Kristoffer Tripplaar/Alamy Stock Photo

Chapter 4, Page 103: highbrow/StockimoNews/Alamy Stock Photo

Chapter 5, Page 143: stephen searle/Alamy Stock Photo

Chapter 6, Page 197: Scanrail1/Shutterstock

Chapter 7, Page 233: dpa picture alliance/Alamy Stock Photo

Chapter 8, Page 263: VIEW Pictures Ltd/Alamy Stock Photo

Chapter 9, Page 299: Ian Dagnall/Alamy

Chapter 10, Page 339: Chih-Chung Johnny Chang/Alamy Stock Photo

Chapter 11, Page 367: Ian Dagnall/Alamy Stock Photo

Chapter 12, Page 393: Jill Morgan/Alamy Stock Photo

Chapter 13, Page 471: Chuck Place/Alamy Stock Photo

Chapter 14, Page 493: John Crowe/Alamy Stock Photo

Chapter 15, Page 523: IanDagnall Computing/Alamy Stock Photo

Chapter 16, Page 557: Paul Vidler/Alamy Stock Photo

Chapter 17, Page 583: Gary A Nelson/Dembinsky Photo Associates/Alamy Stock Photo

Chapter 18, Page 611: PjrTravel/Alamy Stock Photo

Chapter 19, Page 637: WENN Ltd/Alamy Stock Photo

Chapter 20, Page 665: Elena Elisseeva/Shutterstock

Chapter 21, Page 691: Robert Kneschke/Shutterstock

Chapter 22, Page 715: garagestock/Shutterstock

Chapter 23, Page 745: Alexander Image/Shutterstock

Chapter 24, Page 765: SG cityscapes/Alamy Stock Photo

Chapter 25, Page 785: Jim West/Alamy Stock Photo

ALL: ESB Professional/Shutterstock

ALL: michaeljung/Shutterstock

ALL: ESB Professional/Shutterstock

ALL: Wavebreak Media Ltd/123RF

ALL: Vadim Guzhva/123RF

Cover: LueratSatichob/Getty Images

Text Credits

Chapter 1, MULTI: Pearson Education, Inc.

Chapter 2, MULTI: Pearson Education, Inc.

Chapter 3, MULTI: Pearson Education

Chapter 4, MULTI: Pearson Education, Inc.

Chapter 4, Page 105: U.S. Department of Labor Bureau of Labor Statistics

Chapter 5, MULTI: Pearson Education, Inc.

Chapter 6, MULTI: Pearson Education, Inc.

Chapter 7, MULTI: Pearson Education, Inc.

Chapter 8, MULTI: Pearson Education, Inc.

Chapter 9, MULTI: Pearson Education, Inc.

Chapter 10, MULTI: Pearson Education

Chapter 11, MULTI: Pearson Education Inc.

Chapter 12, MULTI: Pearson Education, Inc.